American Casebook Series
Hornbook Series and Basic Legal Texts
Nutshell Series

of

WEST PUBLISHING COMPANY
P.O. Box 64526
St. Paul, Minnesota 55164–0526

ACCOUNTING

Faris' Accounting and Law in a Nutshell, 377 pages, 1984 (Text)

Fiflis, Kripke and Foster's Teaching Materials on Accounting for Business Lawyers, 3rd Ed., 838 pages, 1984 (Casebook)

Siegel and Siegel's Accounting and Financial Disclosure: A Guide to Basic Concepts, 259 pages, 1983 (Text)

ADMINISTRATIVE LAW

Davis' Cases, Text and Problems on Administrative Law, 6th Ed., 683 pages, 1977 (Casebook)

Gellhorn and Boyer's Administrative Law and Process in a Nutshell, 2nd Ed., 445 pages, 1981 (Text)

Mashaw and Merrill's Cases and Materials on Administrative Law–The American Public Law System, 2nd Ed., 976 pages, 1985 (Casebook)

Robinson, Gellhorn and Bruff's The Administrative Process, 3rd Ed., 978 pages, 1986 (Casebook)

ADMIRALTY

Healy and Sharpe's Cases and Materials on Admiralty, 2nd Ed., 876 pages, 1986 (Casebook)

Maraist's Admiralty in a Nutshell, 390 pages, 1983 (Text)

Schoenbaum's Hornbook on Admiralty and Maritime Law, Student Ed., about 675 pages, 1987 (Text)

Sohn and Gustafson's Law of the Sea in a Nutshell, 264 pages, 1984 (Text)

AGENCY—PARTNERSHIP

Fessler's Alternatives to Incorporation for Persons in Quest of Profit, 2nd Ed., 326 pages, 1986 (Casebook)

AGENCY—PARTNERSHIP—Cont'd

Henn's Cases and Materials on Agency, Partnership and Other Unincorporated Business Enterprises, 2nd Ed., 733 pages, 1985 (Casebook)

Reuschlein and Gregory's Hornbook on the Law of Agency and Partnership, 625 pages, 1979, with 1981 pocket part (Text)

Selected Corporation and Partnership Statutes and Forms, about 550 pages, 1987

Steffen and Kerr's Cases and Materials on Agency-Partnership, 4th Ed., 859 pages, 1980 (Casebook)

Steffen's Agency-Partnership in a Nutshell, 364 pages, 1977 (Text)

AGRICULTURAL LAW

Meyer, Pedersen, Thorson and Davidson's Agricultural Law: Cases and Materials, 931 pages, 1985 (Casebook)

ALTERNATIVE DISPUTE RESOLUTION

Kanowitz' Cases and Materials on Alternative Dispute Resolution, 1024 pages, 1986 (Casebook)

Riskin and Westbrook's Dispute Resolution and Lawyers, about 525 pages, 1987 (Coursebook)

Teple and Moberly's Arbitration and Conflict Resolution, (The Labor Law Group), 614 pages, 1979 (Casebook)

AMERICAN INDIAN LAW

Canby's American Indian Law in a Nutshell, 288 pages, 1981 (Text)

Getches and Wilkinson's Cases on Federal Indian Law, 2nd Ed., 880 pages, 1986 (Casebook)

ANTITRUST LAW

Gellhorn's Antitrust Law and Economics in a Nutshell, 3rd Ed., 472 pages, 1986 (Text)

List current as of June, 1987

T7202—1g

I

LAW SCHOOL PUBLICATIONS—Continued

ANTITRUST LAW—Cont'd

Gifford and Raskind's Cases and Materials on Antitrust, 694 pages, 1983 with 1985 Supplement (Casebook)

Hovenkamp's Hornbook on Economics and Federal Antitrust Law, Student Ed., 414 pages, 1985 (Text)

Oppenheim, Weston and McCarthy's Cases and Comments on Federal Antitrust Laws, 4th Ed., 1168 pages, 1981 with 1985 Supplement (Casebook)

Posner and Easterbrook's Cases and Economic Notes on Antitrust, 2nd Ed., 1077 pages, 1981, with 1984–85 Supplement (Casebook)

Sullivan's Hornbook of the Law of Antitrust, 886 pages, 1977 (Text)

See also Regulated Industries, Trade Regulation

ART LAW

DuBoff's Art Law in a Nutshell, 335 pages, 1984 (Text)

BANKING LAW

Lovett's Banking and Financial Institutions in a Nutshell, 409 pages, 1984 (Text)

Symons and White's Teaching Materials on Banking Law, 2nd Ed., 993 pages, 1984, with 1987 Supplement (Casebook)

BUSINESS PLANNING

Painter's Problems and Materials in Business Planning, 2nd Ed., 1008 pages, 1984 with 1987 Supplement (Casebook)

Selected Securities and Business Planning Statutes, Rules and Forms, about 475 pages, 1987

CIVIL PROCEDURE

Casad's Res Judicata in a Nutshell, 310 pages, 1976 (text)

Cound, Friedenthal, Miller and Sexton's Cases and Materials on Civil Procedure, 4th Ed., 1202 pages, 1985 with 1987 Supplement (Casebook)

Ehrenzweig, Louisell and Hazard's Jurisdiction in a Nutshell, 4th Ed., 232 pages, 1980 (Text)

Federal Rules of Civil-Appellate Procedure—West Law School Edition, about 600 pages, 1987

Friedenthal, Kane and Miller's Hornbook on Civil Procedure, 876 pages, 1985 (Text)

Kane's Civil Procedure in a Nutshell, 2nd Ed., 306 pages, 1986 (Text)

Koffler and Reppy's Hornbook on Common Law Pleading, 663 pages, 1969 (Text)

Marcus and Sherman's Complex Litigation—Cases and Materials on Advanced Civil Procedure, 846 pages, 1985 (Casebook)

Park's Computer-Aided Exercises on Civil Procedure, 2nd Ed., 167 pages, 1983 (Coursebook)

CIVIL PROCEDURE—Cont'd

Siegel's Hornbook on New York Practice, 1011 pages, 1978 with 1987 Pocket Part (Text)

See also Federal Jurisdiction and Procedure

CIVIL RIGHTS

Abernathy's Cases and Materials on Civil Rights, 660 pages, 1980 (Casebook)

Cohen's Cases on the Law of Deprivation of Liberty: A Study in Social Control, 755 pages, 1980 (Casebook)

Lockhart, Kamisar, Choper and Shiffrin's Cases on Constitutional Rights and Liberties, 6th Ed., 1266 pages, 1986 with 1987 Supplement (Casebook)—reprint from Lockhart, et al. Cases on Constitutional Law, 6th Ed., 1986

Vieira's Civil Rights in a Nutshell, 279 pages, 1978 (Text)

COMMERCIAL LAW

Bailey's Secured Transactions in a Nutshell, 2nd Ed., 391 pages, 1981 (Text)

Epstein and Martin's Basic Uniform Commercial Code Teaching Materials, 2nd Ed., 667 pages, 1983 (Casebook)

Henson's Hornbook on Secured Transactions Under the U.C.C., 2nd Ed., 504 pages, 1979 with 1979 P.P. (Text)

Murray's Commercial Law, Problems and Materials, 366 pages, 1975 (Coursebook)

Nickles, Matheson and Dolan's Materials for Understanding Credit and Payment Systems, 923 pages, 1987 (Casebook)

Nordstrom and Clovis' Problems and Materials on Commercial Paper, 458 pages, 1972 (Casebook)

Nordstrom, Murray and Clovis' Problems and Materials on Sales, 515 pages, 1982 (Casebook)

Nordstrom, Murray and Clovis' Problems and Materials on Secured Transactions, 594 pages, 1987 (Casebook)

Selected Commercial Statutes, about 1500 pages, 1987

Speidel, Summers and White's Teaching Materials on Commercial Law, 4th Ed., about 1400 pages, 1987 (Casebook)

Speidel, Summers and White's Commercial Paper: Teaching Materials, 4th Ed., about 565 pages, 1987 (Casebook)—reprint from Speidel, et al. Commercial Law, 4th Ed.

Speidel, Summers and White's Sales: Teaching Materials, 4th Ed., about 756 pages, 1987 (Casebook)—reprint from Speidel, et al. Commercial Law, 4th Ed.

Speidel, Summers and White's Secured Transactions—Teaching Materials, 4th Ed., about 463 pages, 1987 (Casebook)—reprint from Speidel, et al. Commercial Law, 4th Ed.

LAW SCHOOL PUBLICATIONS—Continued

COMMERCIAL LAW—Cont'd

Stockton's Sales in a Nutshell, 2nd Ed., 370 pages, 1981 (Text)

Stone's Uniform Commercial Code in a Nutshell, 2nd Ed., 516 pages, 1984 (Text)

Uniform Commercial Code, Official Text with Comments, 994 pages, 1978

UCC Article 9, Reprint from 1962 Code, 128 pages, 1976

UCC Article 9, 1972 Amendments, 304 pages, 1978

Weber and Speidel's Commercial Paper in a Nutshell, 3rd Ed., 404 pages, 1982 (Text)

White and Summers' Hornbook on the Uniform Commercial Code, 2nd Ed., 1250 pages, 1980 (Text)

COMMUNITY PROPERTY

Mennell's Community Property in a Nutshell, 447 pages, 1982 (Text)

Verrall and Bird's Cases and Materials on California Community Property, 4th Ed., 549 pages, 1983 (Casebook)

COMPARATIVE LAW

Barton, Gibbs, Li and Merryman's Law in Radically Different Cultures, 960 pages, 1983 (Casebook)

Glendon, Gordon and Osakive's Comparative Legal Traditions: Text, Materials and Cases on the Civil Law, Common Law, and Socialist Law Traditions, 1091 pages, 1985 (Casebook)

Glendon, Gordon, and Osakwe's Comparative Legal Traditions in a Nutshell, 402 pages, 1982 (Text)

Langbein's Comparative Criminal Procedure: Germany, 172 pages, 1977 (Casebook)

COMPUTERS AND LAW

Maggs and Sprowl's Computer Applications in the Law, 316 pages, 1987 (Coursebook)

Mason's An Introduction to the Use of Computers in Law, 223 pages, 1984 (Text)

CONFLICT OF LAWS

Cramton, Currie and Kay's Cases-Comments-Questions on Conflict of Laws, 4th Ed., about 925 pages, 1987 (Casebook)

Scoles and Hay's Hornbook on Conflict of Laws, Student Ed., 1085 pages, 1982 with 1986 P.P. (Text)

Scoles and Weintraub's Cases and Materials on Conflict of Laws, 2nd Ed., 966 pages, 1972, with 1978 Supplement (Casebook)

Siegel's Conflicts in a Nutshell, 469 pages, 1982 (Text)

CONSTITUTIONAL LAW

Barron and Dienes' Constitutional Law in a Nutshell, 389 pages, 1986 (Text)

CONSTITUTIONAL LAW—Cont'd

Engdahl's Constitutional Federalism in a Nutshell, 2nd Ed., 411 pages, 1987 (Text)

Lockhart, Kamisar, Choper and Shiffrin's Cases-Comments-Questions on Constitutional Law, 6th Ed., 1601 pages, 1986 with 1987 Supplement (Casebook)

Lockhart, Kamisar, Choper and Shiffrin's Cases-Comments-Questions on the American Constitution, 6th Ed., 1260 pages, 1986 with 1987 Supplement (Casebook)—abridgment of Lockhart, et al. Cases on Constitutional Law, 6th Ed., 1986

Manning's The Law of Church-State Relations in a Nutshell, 305 pages, 1981 (Text)

Miller's Presidential Power in a Nutshell, 328 pages, 1977 (Text)

Nowak, Rotunda and Young's Hornbook on Constitutional Law, 3rd Ed., Student Ed., 1191 pages, 1986 (Text)

Rotunda's Modern Constitutional Law: Cases and Notes, 2nd Ed., 1004 pages, 1985, with 1987 Supplement (Casebook)

Williams' Constitutional Analysis in a Nutshell, 388 pages, 1979 (Text)

See also Civil Rights

CONSUMER LAW

Epstein and Nickles' Consumer Law in a Nutshell, 2nd Ed., 418 pages, 1981 (Text)

Selected Commercial Statutes, about 1500 pages, 1987

Spanogle and Rohner's Cases and Materials on Consumer Law, 693 pages, 1979, with 1982 Supplement (Casebook)

See also Commercial Law

CONTRACTS

Calamari & Perillo's Cases and Problems on Contracts, 1061 pages, 1978 (Casebook)

Calamari and Perillo's Hornbook on Contracts, 3rd Ed., 904 pages, 1987 (Text)

Corbin's Text on Contracts, One Volume Student Edition, 1224 pages, 1952 (Text)

Fessler and Loiseaux's Cases and Materials on Contracts, 837 pages, 1982 (Casebook)

Friedman's Contract Remedies in a Nutshell, 323 pages, 1981 (Text)

Fuller and Eisenberg's Cases on Basic Contract Law, 4th Ed., 1203 pages, 1981 (Casebook)

Hamilton, Rau and Weintraub's Cases and Materials on Contracts, 830 pages, 1984 (Casebook)

Jackson and Bollinger's Cases on Contract Law in Modern Society, 2nd Ed., 1329 pages, 1980 (Casebook)

Keyes' Government Contracts in a Nutshell, 423 pages, 1979 (Text)

Schaber and Rohwer's Contracts in a Nutshell, 2nd Ed., 425 pages, 1984 (Text)

LAW SCHOOL PUBLICATIONS—Continued

CONTRACTS—Cont'd

Summers and Hillman's Contract and Related Obligation: Theory, Doctrine and Practice, 1074 pages, 1987 (Casebook)

COPYRIGHT

See Patent and Copyright Law

CORPORATIONS

Hamilton's Cases on Corporations—Including Partnerships and Limited Partnerships, 3rd Ed., 1213 pages, 1986 with 1986 Statutory Supplement (Casebook)

Hamilton's Law of Corporations in a Nutshell, 2nd Ed., 515 pages, 1987 (Text)

Henn's Teaching Materials on Corporations, 2nd Ed., 1204 pages, 1986 (Casebook)

Henn and Alexander's Hornbook on Corporations, 3rd Ed., Student Ed., 1371 pages, 1983 with 1986 P.P. (Text)

Jennings and Buxbaum's Cases and Materials on Corporations, 5th Ed., 1180 pages, 1979 (Casebook)

Selected Corporation and Partnership Statutes, Regulations and Forms, about 550 pages, 1987

Solomon, Stevenson and Schwartz' Materials and Problems on Corporations: Law and Policy, 1172 pages, 1982 with 1986 Supplement (Casebook)

CORPORATE FINANCE

Hamilton's Cases and Materials on Corporate Finance, 895 pages, 1984 with 1986 Supplement (Casebook)

CORRECTIONS

Krantz's Cases and Materials on the Law of Corrections and Prisoners' Rights, 3rd Ed., 855 pages, 1986 (Casebook)

Krantz's Law of Corrections and Prisoners' Rights in a Nutshell, 2nd Ed., 386 pages, 1983 (Text)

Popper's Post-Conviction Remedies in a Nutshell, 360 pages, 1978 (Text)

Robbins' Cases and Materials on Post Conviction Remedies, 506 pages, 1982 (Casebook)

CREDITOR'S RIGHTS

Bankruptcy Code, Rules and Forms, Law School Ed., about 835 pages, 1988

Epstein's Debtor-Creditor Law in a Nutshell, 3rd Ed., 383 pages, 1986 (Text)

Epstein, Landers and Nickles' Debtors and Creditors: Cases and Materials, 3rd Ed., about 1175 pages, 1987 (Casebook)

LoPucki's Player's Manual for the Debtor-Creditor Game, 123 pages, 1985 (Coursebook)

Riesenfeld's Cases and Materials on Creditors' Remedies and Debtors' Protection, 4th Ed., 914 pages, 1987 (Casebook)

CREDITOR'S RIGHTS—Cont'd

White's Bankruptcy and Creditor's Rights: Cases and Materials, 812 pages, 1985, with 1987 Supplement (Casebook)

CRIMINAL LAW AND CRIMINAL PROCEDURE

Abrams', Federal Criminal Law and its Enforcement, 882 pages, 1986 (Casebook)

Carlson's Adjudication of Criminal Justice, Problems and References, 130 pages, 1986 (Casebook)

Dix and Sharlot's Cases and Materials on Criminal Law, 3rd Ed., 846 pages, 1987 (Casebook)

Federal Rules of Criminal Procedure—West Law School Edition, about 475 pages, 1987

Grano's Problems in Criminal Procedure, 2nd Ed., 176 pages, 1981 (Problem book)

Israel and LaFave's Criminal Procedure in a Nutshell, 3rd Ed., 438 pages, 1980 (Text)

Johnson's Cases, Materials and Text on Criminal Law, 3rd Ed., 783 pages, 1985 (Casebook)

Johnson's Cases on Criminal Procedure, about 790 pages, 1987 (Casebook)

Kamisar, LaFave and Israel's Cases, Comments and Questions on Modern Criminal Procedure, 6th Ed., 1558 pages, 1986 with 1987 Supplement (Casebook)

Kamisar, LaFave and Israel's Cases, Comments and Questions on Basic Criminal Procedure, 6th Ed., 860 pages, 1986 with 1987 Supplement (Casebook)—reprint from Kamisar, et al. Modern Criminal Procedure, 6th ed., 1986

LaFave's Modern Criminal Law: Cases, Comments and Questions, 789 pages, 1978 (Casebook)

LaFave and Israel's Hornbook on Criminal Procedure, Student Ed., 1142 pages, 1985 with 1986 P.P. (Text)

LaFave and Scott's Hornbook on Criminal Law, 2nd Ed., Student Ed., 918 pages, 1986 (Text)

Langbein's Comparative Criminal Procedure: Germany, 172 pages, 1977 (Casebook)

Loewy's Criminal Law in a Nutshell, 2nd Ed., about 350 pages, 1987 (Text)

Saltzburg's American Criminal Procedure, Cases and Commentary, 2nd Ed., 1193 pages, 1985 with 1987 Supplement (Casebook)

Uviller's The Processes of Criminal Justice: Investigation and Adjudication, 2nd Ed., 1384 pages, 1979 with 1979 Statutory Supplement and 1986 Update (Casebook)

LAW SCHOOL PUBLICATIONS—Continued

CRIMINAL LAW AND CRIMINAL PROCEDURE—Cont'd

Uviller's The Processes of Criminal Justice: Adjudication, 2nd Ed., 730 pages, 1979. Soft-cover reprint from Uviller's The Processes of Criminal Justice: Investigation and Adjudication, 2nd Ed. (Casebook)

Uviller's The Processes of Criminal Justice: Investigation, 2nd Ed., 655 pages, 1979. Soft-cover reprint from Uviller's The Processes of Criminal Justice: Investigation and Adjudication, 2nd Ed. (Casebook)

Vorenberg's Cases on Criminal Law and Procedure, 2nd Ed., 1088 pages, 1981 with 1985 Supplement (Casebook)

See also Corrections, Juvenile Justice

DECEDENTS ESTATES

See Trusts and Estates

DOMESTIC RELATIONS

Clark's Cases and Problems on Domestic Relations, 3rd Ed., 1153 pages, 1980 (Casebook)

Clark's Hornbook on Domestic Relations, 754 pages, 1968 (Text)

Krause's Cases and Materials on Family Law, 2nd Ed., 1221 pages, 1983 with 1986 Supplement (Casebook)

Krause's Family Law in a Nutshell, 2nd Ed., 444 pages, 1986 (Text)

Krauskopf's Cases on Property Division at Marriage Dissolution, 250 pages, 1984 (Casebook)

ECONOMICS, LAW AND

Goetz' Cases and Materials on Law and Economics, 547 pages, 1984 (Casebook)

See also Antitrust, Regulated Industries

EDUCATION LAW

Alexander and Alexander's The Law of Schools, Students and Teachers in a Nutshell, 409 pages, 1984 (Text)

Morris' The Constitution and American Education, 2nd Ed., 992 pages, 1980 (Casebook)

EMPLOYMENT DISCRIMINATION

Jones, Murphy and Belton's Cases on Discrimination in Employment, 1116 pages, 1987 (Casebook)

Player's Cases and Materials on Employment Discrimination Law, 2nd Ed., 782 pages, 1984 (Casebook)

Player's Federal Law of Employment Discrimination in a Nutshell, 2nd Ed., 402 pages, 1981 (Text)

Player's Hornbook on the Law of Employment Discrimination, about 575 pages, 1987 (Text)

See also Women and the Law

ENERGY AND NATURAL RESOURCES LAW

Laitos' Cases and Materials on Natural Resources Law, 938 pages, 1985 (Casebook)

Rodgers' Cases and Materials on Energy and Natural Resources Law, 2nd Ed., 877 pages, 1983 (Casebook)

Selected Environmental Law Statutes, about 800 pages, 1987

Tomain's Energy Law in a Nutshell, 338 pages, 1981 (Text)

See also Environmental Law, Oil and Gas, Water Law

ENVIRONMENTAL LAW

Bonine and McGarity's Cases and Materials on the Law of Environment and Pollution, 1076 pages, 1984 (Casebook)

Findley and Farber's Cases and Materials on Environmental Law, 2nd Ed., 813 pages, 1985 (Casebook)

Findley and Farber's Environmental Law in a Nutshell, 343 pages, 1983 (Text)

Rodgers' Hornbook on Environmental Law, 956 pages, 1977 with 1984 pocket part (Text)

Selected Environmental Law Statutes, about 800 pages, 1987

See also Energy Law, Natural Resources Law, Water Law

EQUITY

See Remedies

ESTATES

See Trusts and Estates

ESTATE PLANNING

Kurtz' Cases, Materials and Problems on Family Estate Planning, 853 pages, 1983 (Casebook)

Lynn's Introduction to Estate Planning, in a Nutshell, 3rd Ed., 370 pages, 1983 (Text)

See also Taxation

EVIDENCE

Broun and Meisenholder's Problems in Evidence, 2nd Ed., 304 pages, 1981 (Problem book)

Cleary and Strong's Cases, Materials and Problems on Evidence, 3rd Ed., 1143 pages, 1981 (Casebook)

Federal Rules of Evidence for United States Courts and Magistrates, about 330 pages, 1987

Graham's Federal Rules of Evidence in a Nutshell, 2nd Ed., 473 pages, 1987 (Text)

Kimball's Programmed Materials on Problems in Evidence, 380 pages, 1978 (Problem book)

LAW SCHOOL PUBLICATIONS—Continued

EVIDENCE—Cont'd

Lempert and Saltzburg's A Modern Approach to Evidence: Text, Problems, Transcripts and Cases, 2nd Ed., 1232 pages, 1983 (Casebook)

Lilly's Introduction to the Law of Evidence, 2nd Ed., about 600 pages, 1987 (Text)

McCormick, Sutton and Wellborn's Cases and Materials on Evidence, 6th Ed., 1067 pages, 1987 (Casebook)

McCormick's Hornbook on Evidence, 3rd Ed., Student Ed., 1156 pages, 1984 with 1987 P.P. (Text)

Rothstein's Evidence, State and Federal Rules in a Nutshell, 2nd Ed., 514 pages, 1981 (Text)

Saltzburg's Evidence Supplement: Rules, Statutes, Commentary, 245 pages, 1980 (Casebook Supplement)

FEDERAL JURISDICTION AND PROCEDURE

Currie's Cases and Materials on Federal Courts, 3rd Ed., 1042 pages, 1982 with 1985 Supplement (Casebook)

Currie's Federal Jurisdiction in a Nutshell, 2nd Ed., 258 pages, 1981 (Text)

Federal Rules of Civil-Appellate Procedure—West Law School Edition, about 600 pages, 1987

Forrester and Moye's Cases and Materials on Federal Jurisdiction and Procedure, 3rd Ed., 917 pages, 1977 with 1985 Supplement (Casebook)

Redish's Cases, Comments and Questions on Federal Courts, 878 pages, 1983 with 1986 Supplement (Casebook)

Vetri and Merrill's Federal Courts, Problems and Materials, 2nd Ed., 232 pages, 1984 (Problem Book)

Wright's Hornbook on Federal Courts, 4th Ed., Student Ed., 870 pages, 1983 (Text)

FUTURE INTERESTS

See Trusts and Estates

HEALTH LAW

See Medicine, Law and

IMMIGRATION LAW

Aleinikoff and Martin's Immigration Process and Policy, 1042 pages, 1985, with 1987 Supplement (Casebook)

Weissbrodt's Immigration Law and Procedure in a Nutshell, 345 pages, 1984 (Text)

INDIAN LAW

See American Indian Law

INSURANCE

Dobbyn's Insurance Law in a Nutshell, 281 pages, 1981 (Text)

INSURANCE—Cont'd

Keeton's Cases on Basic Insurance Law, 2nd Ed., 1086 pages, 1977

Keeton's Basic Text on Insurance Law, 712 pages, 1971 (Text)

Keeton's Case Supplement to Keeton's Basic Text on Insurance Law, 334 pages, 1978 (Casebook)

York and Whelan's Cases, Materials and Problems on Insurance Law, 715 pages, 1982, with 1985 Supplement (Casebook)

INTERNATIONAL LAW

Buergenthal and Maier's Public International Law in a Nutshell, 262 pages, 1985 (Text)

Folsom, Gordon and Spanogle's International Business Transactions – a Problem-Oriented Coursebook, 1160 pages, 1986, with Documents Supplement (Casebook)

Frank and Glennon's United States Foreign Relations Law: Cases, Materials and Simulations, about 875 pages, 1987 (Casebook)

Henkin, Pugh, Schachter and Smit's Cases and Materials on International Law, 2nd Ed., 1517 pages, 1987 with Documents Supplement (Casebook)

Jackson and Davey's Legal Problems of International Economic Relations, 2nd Ed., 1269 pages, 1986, with Documents Supplement (Casebook)

Kirgis' International Organizations in Their Legal Setting, 1016 pages, 1977, with 1981 Supplement (Casebook)

Weston, Falk and D'Amato's International Law and World Order—A Problem Oriented Coursebook, 1195 pages, 1980, with Documents Supplement (Casebook)

Wilson's International Business Transactions in a Nutshell, 2nd Ed., 476 pages, 1984 (Text)

INTERVIEWING AND COUNSELING

Binder and Price's Interviewing and Counseling, 232 pages, 1977 (Text)

Shaffer and Elkins' Interviewing and Counseling in a Nutshell, 2nd Ed., 487 pages, 1987 (Text)

INTRODUCTION TO LAW STUDY

Dobbyn's So You Want to go to Law School, Revised First Edition, 206 pages, 1976 (Text)

Hegland's Introduction to the Study and Practice of Law in a Nutshell, 418 pages, 1983 (Text)

Kinyon's Introduction to Law Study and Law Examinations in a Nutshell, 389 pages, 1971 (Text)

See also Legal Method and Legal System

LAW SCHOOL PUBLICATIONS—Continued

JUDICIAL ADMINISTRATION

Nelson's Cases and Materials on Judicial Administration and the Administration of Justice, 1032 pages, 1974 (Casebook)

JURISPRUDENCE

Christie's Text and Readings on Jurisprudence—The Philosophy of Law, 1056 pages, 1973 (Casebook)

JUVENILE JUSTICE

Fox's Cases and Materials on Modern Juvenile Justice, 2nd Ed., 960 pages, 1981 (Casebook)

Fox's Juvenile Courts in a Nutshell, 3rd Ed., 291 pages, 1984 (Text)

LABOR LAW

Atleson, Rabin, Schatzki, Sherman and Silverstein's Collective Bargaining in Private Employment, 2nd Ed., (The Labor Law Group), 856 pages, 1984 (Casebook)

Gorman's Basic Text on Labor Law—Unionization and Collective Bargaining, 914 pages, 1976 (Text)

Grodin, Wollett and Alleyne's Collective Bargaining in Public Employment, 3rd Ed., (the Labor Law Group), 430 pages, 1979 (Casebook)

Leslie's Labor Law in a Nutshell, 2nd Ed., 397 pages, 1986 (Text)

Nolan's Labor Arbitration Law and Practice in a Nutshell, 358 pages, 1979 (Text)

Oberer, Hanslowe, Andersen and Heinsz' Cases and Materials on Labor Law—Collective Bargaining in a Free Society, 3rd Ed., 1163 pages, 1986 with Statutory Supplement (Casebook)

See also Employment Discrimination, Social Legislation

LAND FINANCE

See Real Estate Transactions

LAND USE

Callies and Freilich's Cases and Materials on Land Use, 1233 pages, 1986 (Casebook)

Hagman's Cases on Public Planning and Control of Urban and Land Development, 2nd Ed., 1301 pages, 1980 (Casebook)

Hagman and Juergensmeyer's Hornbook on Urban Planning and Land Development Control Law, 2nd Ed., Student Edition, 680 pages, 1986 (Text)

Wright and Gitelman's Cases and Materials on Land Use, 3rd Ed., 1300 pages, 1982, with 1987 Supplement (Casebook)

Wright and Wright's Land Use in a Nutshell, 2nd Ed., 356 pages, 1985 (Text)

LEGAL HISTORY

Presser and Zainaldin's Cases on Law and American History, 855 pages, 1980 (Casebook)

See also Legal Method and Legal System

LEGAL METHOD AND LEGAL SYSTEM

Aldisert's Readings, Materials and Cases in the Judicial Process, 948 pages, 1976 (Casebook)

Berch and Berch's Introduction to Legal Method and Process, 550 pages, 1985 (Casebook)

Bodenheimer, Oakley and Love's Readings and Cases on an Introduction to the Anglo-American Legal System, 161 pages, 1980 (Casebook)

Davies and Lawry's Institutions and Methods of the Law—Introductory Teaching Materials, 547 pages, 1982 (Casebook)

Dvorkin, Himmelstein and Lesnick's Becoming a Lawyer: A Humanistic Perspective on Legal Education and Professionalism, 211 pages, 1981 (Text)

Greenberg's Judicial Process and Social Change, 666 pages, 1977 (Casebook)

Kelso and Kelso's Studying Law: An Introduction, 587 pages, 1984 (Coursebook)

Kempin's Historical Introduction to Anglo-American Law in a Nutshell, 2nd Ed., 280 pages, 1973 (Text)

Kimball's Historical Introduction to the Legal System, 610 pages, 1966 (Casebook)

Murphy's Cases and Materials on Introduction to Law—Legal Process and Procedure, 772 pages, 1977 (Casebook)

Reynolds' Judicial Process in a Nutshell, 292 pages, 1980 (Text)

See also Legal Research and Writing

LEGAL PROFESSION

Aronson, Devine and Fisch's Problems, Cases and Materials on Professional Responsibility, 745 pages, 1985 (Casebook)

Aronson and Weckstein's Professional Responsibility in a Nutshell, 399 pages, 1980 (Text)

Mellinkoff's The Conscience of a Lawyer, 304 pages, 1973 (Text)

Mellinkoff's Lawyers and the System of Justice, 983 pages, 1976 (Casebook)

Pirsig and Kirwin's Cases and Materials on Professional Responsibility, 4th Ed., 603 pages, 1984 (Casebook)

Schwartz and Wydick's Problems in Legal Ethics, 285 pages, 1983 (Casebook)

Selected Statutes, Rules and Standards on the Legal Profession, about 300 pages, 1987

Smith's Preventing Legal Malpractice, 142 pages, 1981 (Text)

Wolfram's Hornbook on Modern Legal Ethics, Student Edition, 1120 pages, 1986 (Text)

LAW SCHOOL PUBLICATIONS—Continued

LEGAL RESEARCH AND WRITING

Cohen's Legal Research in a Nutshell, 4th Ed., 450 pages, 1985 (Text)

Cohen and Berring's How to Find the Law, 8th Ed., 790 pages, 1983. Problem book by Foster, Johnson and Kelly available (Casebook)

Cohen and Berring's Finding the Law, 8th Ed., Abridged Ed., 556 pages, 1984 (Casebook)

Dickerson's Materials on Legal Drafting, 425 pages, 1981 (Casebook)

Felsenfeld and Siegel's Writing Contracts in Plain English, 290 pages, 1981 (Text)

Gopen's Writing From a Legal Perspective, 225 pages, 1981 (Text)

Mellinkoff's Legal Writing—Sense and Nonsense, 242 pages, 1982 (Text)

Ray and Ramsfield's Legal Writing: Getting It Right and Getting It Written, 250 pages, 1987 (Text)

Rombauer's Legal Problem Solving—Analysis, Research and Writing, 4th Ed., 424 pages, 1983 (Coursebook)

Squires and Rombauer's Legal Writing in a Nutshell, 294 pages, 1982 (Text)

Statsky's Legal Research and Writing, 3rd Ed., 257 pages, 1986 (Coursebook)

Statsky and Wernet's Case Analysis and Fundamentals of Legal Writing, 2nd Ed., 441 pages, 1984 (Text)

Teply's Programmed Materials on Legal Research and Citation, 2nd Ed., 358 pages, 1986. Student Library Exercises available (Coursebook)

Weihofen's Legal Writing Style, 2nd Ed., 332 pages, 1980 (Text)

LEGISLATION

Davies' Legislative Law and Process in a Nutshell, 2nd Ed., 346 pages, 1986 (Text)

Eskridge and Frickey's Cases on Legislation, about 930 pages, 1987 (Casebook)

Nutting and Dickerson's Cases and Materials on Legislation, 5th Ed., 744 pages, 1978 (Casebook)

Statsky's Legislative Analysis and Drafting, 2nd Ed., 217 pages, 1984 (Text)

LOCAL GOVERNMENT

McCarthy's Local Government Law in a Nutshell, 2nd Ed., 404 pages, 1983 (Text)

Reynolds' Hornbook on Local Government Law, 860 pages, 1982, with 1987 pocket part (Text)

Valente's Cases and Materials on Local Government Law, 3rd Ed., 1010 pages, 1987 (Casebook)

MASS COMMUNICATION LAW

Gillmor and Barron's Cases and Comment on Mass Communication Law, 4th Ed., 1076 pages, 1984 (Casebook)

MASS COMMUNICATION LAW—Cont'd

Ginsburg's Regulation of Broadcasting: Law and Policy Towards Radio, Television and Cable Communications, 741 pages, 1979, with 1983 Supplement (Casebook)

Zuckman and Gayne's Mass Communications Law in a Nutshell, 2nd Ed., 473 pages, 1983 (Text)

MEDICINE, LAW AND

Furrow, Johnson, Jost and Schwartz' Health Law: Cases, Materials and Problems, 1005 pages, 1987 (Casebook)

King's The Law of Medical Malpractice in a Nutshell, 2nd Ed., 342 pages, 1986 (Text)

Shapiro and Spece's Problems, Cases and Materials on Bioethics and Law, 892 pages, 1981 (Casebook)

Sharpe, Fiscina and Head's Cases on Law and Medicine, 882 pages, 1978 (Casebook)

MILITARY LAW

Shanor and Terrell's Military Law in a Nutshell, 378 pages, 1980 (Text)

MORTGAGES

See Real Estate Transactions

NATURAL RESOURCES LAW

See Energy and Natural Resources Law

NEGOTIATION

Edwards and White's Problems, Readings and Materials on the Lawyer as a Negotiator, 484 pages, 1977 (Casebook)

Peck's Cases and Materials on Negotiation, 2nd Ed., (The Labor Law Group), 280 pages, 1980 (Casebook)

Williams' Legal Negotiation and Settlement, 207 pages, 1983 (Coursebook)

OFFICE PRACTICE

Hegland's Trial and Practice Skills in a Nutshell, 346 pages, 1978 (Text)

Strong and Clark's Law Office Management, 424 pages, 1974 (Casebook)

See also Computers and Law, Interviewing and Counseling, Negotiation

OIL AND GAS

Hemingway's Hornbook on Oil and Gas, 2nd Ed., Student Ed., 543 pages, 1983 with 1986 P.P. (Text)

Kuntz, Lowe, Anderson and Smith's Cases and Materials on Oil and Gas Law, 857 pages, 1986, with Forms Manual (Casebook)

Lowe's Oil and Gas Law in a Nutshell, 443 pages, 1983 (Text)

See also Energy and Natural Resources Law

PARTNERSHIP

See Agency—Partnership

LAW SCHOOL PUBLICATIONS—Continued

PATENT AND COPYRIGHT LAW

Choate, Francis and Collins' Cases and Materials on Patent Law, 3rd Ed., about 1050 pages, 1987 (Casebook)

Miller and Davis' Intellectual Property—Patents, Trademarks and Copyright in a Nutshell, 428 pages, 1983 (Text)

Nimmer's Cases on Copyright and Other Aspects of Entertainment Litigation, 3rd Ed., 1025 pages, 1985 (Casebook)

PRODUCTS LIABILITY

Noel and Phillips' Cases on Products Liability, 2nd Ed., 821 pages, 1982 (Casebook)

Noel and Phillips' Products Liability in a Nutshell, 2nd Ed., 341 pages, 1981 (Text)

PROPERTY

Bernhardt's Real Property in a Nutshell, 2nd Ed., 448 pages, 1981 (Text)

Boyer's Survey of the Law of Property, 766 pages, 1981 (Text)

Browder, Cunningham and Smith's Cases on Basic Property Law, 4th Ed., 1431 pages, 1984 (Casebook)

Bruce, Ely and Bostick's Cases and Materials on Modern Property Law, 1004 pages, 1984 (Casebook)

Burke's Personal Property in a Nutshell, 322 pages, 1983 (Text)

Cunningham, Stoebuck and Whitman's Hornbook on the Law of Property, Student Ed., 916 pages, 1984, with 1987 P.P. (Text)

Donahue, Kauper and Martin's Cases on Property, 2nd Ed., 1362 pages, 1983 (Casebook)

Hill's Landlord and Tenant Law in a Nutshell, 2nd Ed., 311 pages, 1986 (Text)

Kurtz and Hovenkamp's Cases and Materials on American Property Law, 1296 pages, 1987 (Casebook)

Moynihan's Introduction to Real Property, 2n Ed., about 250 pages, 1987 (Text)

Uniform Land Transactions Act, Uniform Simplification of Land Transfers Act, Uniform Condominium Act, 1977 Official Text with Comments, 462 pages, 1978

See also Real Estate Transactions, Land Use

PSYCHIATRY, LAW AND

Reisner's Law and the Mental Health System, Civil and Criminal Aspects, 696 pages, 1985, with 1987 Supplement (Casebooks)

REAL ESTATE TRANSACTIONS

Bruce's Real Estate Finance in a Nutshell, 2nd Ed., 262 pages, 1985 (Text)

Maxwell, Riesenfeld, Hetland and Warren's Cases on California Security Transactions in Land, 3rd Ed., 728 pages, 1984 (Casebook)

REAL ESTATE TRANSACTIONS—Cont'd

Nelson and Whitman's Cases on Real Estate Transfer, Finance and Development, 3rd Ed., about 1184 pages, 1987 (Casebook)

Nelson and Whitman's Hornbook on Real Estate Finance Law, 2nd Ed., Student Ed., 941 pages, 1985 (Text)

Osborne's Cases and Materials on Secured Transactions, 559 pages, 1967 (Casebook)

REGULATED INDUSTRIES

Gellhorn and Pierce's Regulated Industries in a Nutshell, 2nd Ed., 389 pages, 1987 (Text)

Morgan, Harrison and Verkuil's Cases and Materials on Economic Regulation of Business, 2nd Ed., 666 pages, 1985 (Casebook)

See also Mass Communication Law, Banking Law

REMEDIES

Dobbs' Hornbook on Remedies, 1067 pages, 1973 (Text)

Dobbs' Problems in Remedies, 137 pages, 1974 (Problem book)

Dobbyn's Injunctions in a Nutshell, 264 pages, 1974 (Text)

Friedman's Contract Remedies in a Nutshell, 323 pages, 1981 (Text)

Leavell, Love and Nelson's Cases and Materials on Equitable Remedies and Restitution, 4th Ed., 1111 pages, 1986 (Casebook)

McCormick's Hornbook on Damages, 811 pages, 1935 (Text)

O'Connell's Remedies in a Nutshell, 2nd Ed., 320 pages, 1985 (Text)

York, Bauman and Rendleman's Cases and Materials on Remedies, 4th Ed., 1029 pages, 1985 (Casebook)

REVIEW MATERIALS

Ballantine's Problems

Black Letter Series

Smith's Review Series

West's Review Covering Multistate Subjects

SECURITIES REGULATION

Hazen's Hornbook on The Law of Securities Regulation, Student Ed., 739 pages, 1985, with 1987 P.P. (Text)

Ratner's Securities Regulation: Materials for a Basic Course, 3rd Ed., 1000 pages, 1986 (Casebook)

Ratner's Securities Regulation in a Nutshell, 2nd Ed., 322 pages, 1982 (Text)

Selected Securities and Business Planning Statutes, Rules and Forms, about 470 pages, 1987

LAW SCHOOL PUBLICATIONS—Continued

SOCIAL LEGISLATION

Hood and Hardy's Workers' Compensation and Employee Protection Laws in a Nutshell, 274 pages, 1984 (Text)

LaFrance's Welfare Law: Structure and Entitlement in a Nutshell, 455 pages, 1979 (Text)

Malone, Plant and Little's Cases on Workers' Compensation and Employment Rights, 2nd Ed., 951 pages, 1980 (Casebook)

SPORTS LAW

Schubert, Smith and Trentadue's Sports Law, 395 pages, 1986 (Text)

TAXATION

Dodge's Cases and Materials on Federal Income Taxation, 820 pages, 1985 (Casebook)

Dodge's Federal Taxation of Estates, Trusts and Gifts: Principles and Planning, 771 pages, 1981 with 1982 Supplement (Casebook)

Garbis, Struntz and Rubin's Cases and Materials on Tax Procedure and Tax Fraud, 2nd Ed., 687 pages, 1987 (Casebook)

Gelfand and Salsich's State and Local Taxation and Finance in a Nutshell, 309 pages, 1986 (Text)

Gunn's Cases and Materials on Federal Income Taxation of Individuals, 785 pages, 1981 with 1985 Supplement (Casebook)

Hellerstein and Hellerstein's Cases on State and Local Taxation, 4th Ed., 1041 pages, 1978 with 1982 Supplement (Casebook)

Kahn and Gann's Corporate Taxation and Taxation of Partnerships and Partners, 2nd Ed., 1204 pages, 1985 (Casebook)

Kragen and McNulty's Cases and Materials on Federal Income Taxation: Individuals, Corporations, Partnerships, 4th Ed., 1287 pages, 1985 (Casebook)

McNulty's Federal Estate and Gift Taxation in a Nutshell, 3rd Ed., 509 pages, 1983 (Text)

McNulty's Federal Income Taxation of Individuals in a Nutshell, 3rd Ed., 487 pages, 1983 (Text)

Pennell's Cases and Materials on Income Taxation of Trusts, Estates, Grantors and Beneficiaries, about 400 pages, 1987 (Casebook)

Posin's Hornbook on Federal Income Taxation of Individuals, Student Ed., 491 pages, 1983 with 1987 pocket part (Text)

Selected Federal Taxation Statutes and Regulations, 1576 pages, 1987

Solomon and Hesch's Cases on Federal Income Taxation of Individuals, 1068 pages, 1987 (Casebook)

TAXATION—Cont'd

Sobeloff and Weidenbruch's Federal Income Taxation of Corporations and Stockholders in a Nutshell, 362 pages, 1981 (Text)

TORTS

Christie's Cases and Materials on the Law of Torts, 1264 pages, 1983 (Casebook)

Dobbs' Torts and Compensation—Personal Accountability and Social Responsibility for Injury, 955 pages, 1985 (Casebook)

Green, Pedrick, Rahl, Thode, Hawkins, Smith, and Treece's Advanced Torts: Injuries to Business, Political and Family Interests, 2nd Ed., 544 pages, 1977 (Casebook)

Keeton, Keeton, Sargentich and Steiner's Cases and Materials on Torts, and Accident Law, 1360 pages, 1983 (Casebook)

Kionka's Torts in a Nutshell: Injuries to Persons and Property, 434 pages, 1977 (Text)

Malone's Torts in a Nutshell: Injuries to Family, Social and Trade Relations, 358 pages, 1979 (Text)

Prosser and Keeton's Hornbook on Torts, 5th Ed., Student Ed., 1286 pages, 1984, with 1987 pocket part (Text)

See also Products Liability

TRADE REGULATION

McManis' Unfair Trade Practices in a Nutshell, 444 pages, 1982 (Text)

Oppenheim, Weston, Maggs and Schechter's Cases and Materials on Unfair Trade Practices and Consumer Protection, 4th Ed., 1038 pages, 1983 with 1986 Supplement (Casebook)

See also Antitrust, Regulated Industries

TRIAL AND APPELLATE ADVOCACY

Appellate Advocacy, Handbook of, 2nd Ed., 182 pages, 1986 (Text)

Bergman's Trial Advocacy in a Nutshell, 402 pages, 1979 (Text)

Binder and Bergman's Fact Investigation: From Hypothesis to Proof, 354 pages, 1984 (Coursebook)

Goldberg's The First Trial (Where Do I Sit?, What Do I Say?) in a Nutshell, 396 pages, 1982 (Text)

Haydock, Herr and Stempel's, Fundamentals of Pre-Trial Litigation, 768 pages, 1985 (Casebook)

Hegland's Trial and Practice Skills in a Nutshell, 346 pages, 1978 (Text)

Hornstein's Appellate Advocacy in a Nutshell, 325 pages, 1984 (Text)

Jeans' Handbook on Trial Advocacy, Student Ed., 473 pages, 1975 (Text)

Martineau's Cases and Materials on Appellate Practice and Procedure, about 550 pages, 1987 (Casebook)

LAW SCHOOL PUBLICATIONS—Continued

TRIAL AND APPELLATE ADVOCACY—Cont'd

McElhaney's Effective Litigation, 457 pages, 1974 (Casebook)

Nolan's Cases and Materials on Trial Practice, 518 pages, 1981 (Casebook)

Parnell and Shellhaas' Cases, Exercises and Problems for Trial Advocacy, 171 pages, 1982 (Coursebook)

Sonsteng, Haydock and Boyd's The Trialbook: A Total System for Preparation and Presentation of a Case, Student Ed., 404 pages, 1984 (Coursebook)

TRUSTS AND ESTATES

Atkinson's Hornbook on Wills, 2nd Ed., 975 pages, 1953 (Text)

Averill's Uniform Probate Code in a Nutshell, 2nd Ed., 454 pages, 1987 (Text)

Bogert's Hornbook on Trusts, 6th Ed., Student Ed., about 800 pages, 1987 (Text)

Clark, Lusky and Murphy's Cases and Materials on Gratuitous Transfers, 3rd Ed., 970 pages, 1985 (Casebook)

Gulliver's Cases and Materials on Future Interests, 624 pages, 1959 (Casebook)

Gulliver's Introduction to the Law of Future Interests, 87 pages, 1959 (Casebook)—reprint from Gulliver's Cases and Materials on Future Interests, 1959

McGovern's Cases and Materials on Wills, Trusts and Future Interests: An Introduction to Estate Planning, 750 pages, 1983 (Casebook)

Mennell's Wills and Trusts in a Nutshell, 392 pages, 1979 (Text)

Simes' Hornbook on Future Interests, 2nd Ed., 355 pages, 1966 (Text)

TRUSTS AND ESTATES—Cont'd

Turano and Radigan's Hornbook on New York Estate Administration, 676 pages, 1986 (Text)

Uniform Probate Code, 5th Ed., Official Text With Comments, 384 pages, 1977

Waggoner's Future Interests in a Nutshell, 361 pages, 1981 (Text)

Waterbury's Materials on Trusts and Estates, 1039 pages, 1986 (Casebook)

WATER LAW

Getches' Water Law in a Nutshell, 439 pages, 1984 (Text)

Sax and Abram's Cases and Materials on Legal Control of Water Resources in the United States, 941 pages, 1986 (Casebook)

Trelease and Gould's Cases and Materials on Water Law, 4th Ed., 816 pages, 1986 (Casebook)

See also Energy and Natural Resources Law, Environmental Law

WILLS

See Trusts and Estates

WOMEN AND THE LAW

Kay's Text, Cases and Materials on Sex-Based Discrimination, 2nd Ed., 1045 pages, 1981, with 1986 Supplement (Casebook)

Thomas' Sex Discrimination in a Nutshell, 399 pages, 1982 (Text)

See also Employment Discrimination

WORKERS' COMPENSATION

See Social Legislation

SALES
TEACHING MATERIALS

By

Richard E. Speidel
Professor of Law
Northwestern University School of Law

Robert S. Summers
McRoberts Research Professor of Law
Cornell University School of Law

James J. White
Robert A. Sullivan Professor of Law
University of Michigan School of Law

This book is an abridgement of Speidel, Summers and White's
"Commercial Law: Teaching Materials, Fourth Edition".

AMERICAN CASEBOOK SERIES

WEST PUBLISHING CO.
ST. PAUL, MINN., 1987

This is an abridgement of Speidel, Summers and White's
"*Commercial Law: Teaching Materials, Fourth Edition*",
West Publishing Co. 1987
COPYRIGHT © 1987 By WEST PUBLISHING CO.
                50 West Kellogg Boulevard
                P.O. Box 64526
                St. Paul, Minnesota 55164–0526

Library of Congress Cataloging-in-Publication Data

Speidel, Richard E.
  Sales: teaching materials.

  (American casebook series)
  Includes index.
  1. Sales—United States—Cases. I. White, James J.,
1934–   . II. Summers, Robert S. III. Title. IV. Series.
KF914.S64 1987   346.73'072   87–19009
                        347.30672

ISBN 0–314–61283–1

  (S., S. & W.) Sales ACB

Preface

The materials contained in this volume are reprinted from R. Speidel, R. Summers, and J. White, COMMERCIAL LAW: TEACHING MATERIALS, Fourth Edition (West, 1987), a comprehensive Commercial Law casebook which includes materials on Sales, Secured Transactions, and Commercial Paper. In its fourth edition, COMMERCIAL LAW: TEACHING MATERIALS has been completely updated and, rather than a mere revision, is largely a new work.

RES
RSS
JJW

June, 1987

*

Summary of Contents

Table of Contents

___

PART FIVE. THE RECEIPT–INSPECTION STAGE

PART SIX. DISPUTES AMONG CREDITORS OVER POSSESSION OF GOODS SOLD

Table of Cases

The principal cases are in bold type. Cases cited or discussed in the text are roman type. References are to pages. Cases cited in principal cases and within other quoted materials are not included.

xxxi

*

Table of Statutes

SALES

TEACHING MATERIALS

*

Chapter One

THE NATURE AND SOURCES OF COMMERCIAL LAW

SECTION 1. A BRIEF CURRICULAR NOTE TO THE STUDENT

The student must not think of Security, Sales, and Commercial Paper as three wholly separate subjects. They are closely related, functionally, analytically, and historically. Instructors differ, however, on modes of integration and we have arranged the materials to facilitate varied approaches.

The materials have this in common, too: They may be viewed, in part, as a kind of advanced course in contracts. Contract necessarily undergirds nearly the whole of the law school curriculum; we do not apologize for its reappearance here. Indeed, our own classroom experience tells us that a great many students would profit from an exact repetition of their first year contracts course! (And two of us teach first year contracts regularly.) But the materials we offer here will duplicate few of your first year experiences. These materials will treat a few contracts topics to which you were exposed in your first year, but generally in greater depth or from a quite different angle. Further, we will take you into new and distinctive areas of advanced contracts including security, credit, documents of title, and commercial paper. In addition, here you will encounter far more regulatory law than is true in first year contracts courses. As we shall see, in some branches of our subject, freedom of contract is dramatically waning and regulatory law is rapidly supplanting it. Finally, and perhaps most important of all, the materials that follow afford students opportunities to develop skills in working with complex statutory schemes far beyond anything possible in the first year contracts course. We are now in the Age of the Statute.

SECTION 2. ORIGINS OF NEEDS FOR COMMERCIAL LAW

Millions of "deals" occur each day in the United States. Many are between businessmen and many are between businessmen and consumers. These deals and their performance are the stuff of commercial and consumer life to which these materials will be addressed.

1

The deals involved vary greatly. Many involve sales of goods or intangibles, and the like. Many consist of leasing arrangements. Many involve loans or extensions of credit, with or without "security interests" (interests that give a creditor priority rights in a specific asset of the debtor). Many involve the rendition of services by insurers, carriers, storers and the like. Many involve the use of notes, checks and other "negotiable instruments." The overwhelming majority of these deals go through without incident. But when something does go wrong, there may be occasion to resort to law and to legal processes. What kinds of law? What kinds of processes? The answers to these questions turn on the nature of the real world problems which generate the needs for laws and legal processes in the first place.

Suppose, for example, that one party to an alleged deal simply denies that a deal was ever made. He, in effect, says that under the law no binding relationship came into being. To determine whether he is correct, resort to what might be called *rules of validation* is required. These rules specify the requisites of a valid contract of sale, or of a valid security interest, and so on. The legal need is for *such rules,* and for them to be clear, definite, accessible, and ascertainable, in advance of deals. Rules specifying *how* to "make it legal" are fundamental. Without them, private ordering under law could not exist. One of the primary functions of bodies of commercial and consumer law is to facilitate and sanction private ordering and private autonomy. In our system there is, we think, positive value in affording individuals extensive power to give their deals the force of law. *How* they must do this is the province of rules of validation.

Parties to a transaction may have sought, in writing, to specify their wants and expectations in Durer-like detail, only to find, at a later point, that they disagree over the interpretation or construction of some part of their agreement. Here the specific legal need is for rational and just *rules of interpretation and construction.* Such rules guide courts; they facilitate counseling; they may also lead parties to settle their differences without resort to courts.

Assume the parties have not planned out their deal in detail. At some later stage, something goes wrong or some question arises on which their written agreement or their general understanding, as the case may be, is wholly silent. For example, goods contracted for are destroyed by fire while in transit. Or a pledgee of goods pledged to secure a loan decides he would like to repledge these same goods to a third party. Or a borrower wants to know if he has the right to pay back a loan without penalty. Here the legal need is for substantive *suppletive rules,* rules which presuppose and supplement the incomplete private transaction with specific "terms." To be generally fair and just, such rules should be based upon the likely commercial or consumer understanding of such matters. For, insofar as there is a standard understanding, it is not unreasonable to feed it into the skeletal deal.

A variation on the immediately preceding problem is this: The reality of many deals is that parties typically do not specify their expected performances in detail. Here the legal need is for rationally conceived suppletive rules which specify the substance of the deal. In modern law, "implied warranties" are perhaps the best example. In many simple sales nothing is ever said at the time of the deal about the standard to which the goods must conform. Such warranty or warranties are left to be supplied by law. The very existence of such suppletive law gives rise to a further distinctive kind of legal need: the need for *rules of disclaimer,* rules which specify *how* the parties can modify or exclude altogether what the suppletive law would otherwise supply. That such rules should generally be clear, definite, and ascertainable in advance requires no argument.

People being what they are, and society being what it is, some parties will try to take advantage of others and some sometimes will not know what is in their own best interest. For example, a consumer may enter an entirely lopsided and unfair deal. The "real" world thus generates the problem of whether or not the terms of such deals are to be enforced. And the law must then face another specific kind of legal need—a need for what might be called *regulatory policing rules.* It has been suggested that the "core task" of commercial and consumer law is "to determine the relatively few rules which are not subject to change by agreement, the rules which are designed to stake out the necessary minimum area of protection for parties whose bargaining power is inferior." See Schlesinger, *The Uniform Commercial Code in the Light of Comparative Law,* 1 Inter-Am.L.Rev. 11, 33 (1959). Extensive needs for policing rules to regulate exchanges have only recently been recognized in our system. Such rules plainly invade the province of private autonomy and limit freedom of contract. That, so far as possible, parties should know in advance what they cannot enforceably agree to seems obvious.

Akin to regulatory policing rules are rules which may be designated as *third party protection rules.* Many consumer and commercial transactions, occurrences, and events impinge directly or indirectly on the interests of third parties not privy to the transaction at hand. Some occur fraudulently, as where a seller of goods in his possession sells these same goods successively to two different parties and then absconds. But other such transactions are not necessarily dishonest, as where a creditor establishes a preferred position *vis a vis* other creditors of the same debtor. Here the specific legal need is for rules which protect, as far as possible, the interests of all concerned. For example, in the creditor situation, the law might require that any creditor seeking such a preferred position must in some way give public notice of this fact so that interested third parties may act accordingly. Like policing rules, third party protection rules limit freedom of contract, for to be effective they must not be subject to variation by agreement of the parties.

Within the world of commerce, the activities of selling and buying and of lending and borrowing are ubiquitous. And they are often intertwined. Buyer-debtors are actually more common than general debtors. Seldom is a debtor a debtor of only one person. Moreover, in a typical year, a significant minority of debtors fall into financial difficulty. Assuming that such a debtor does not have enough assets to pay all of his debts, which creditors are to receive what? The specific legal need generated by such problems is for *rules of priority,* rules which, in circumstances of scarcity, determine who gets what. Prospective lenders, as well as sellers selling on credit, would often want to know in advance the bearing such rules could have on their situations.

Failure to pay a debt when due is but one kind and perhaps the simplest kind of failure of promised performance known to the law. Among others are non-delivery or nonconforming delivery of, goods; failure of a carrier or a bank to obey agreed instructions from the seller or the buyer; misconduct of a warehouseman, and so forth. Here, the specific legal need is for *suppletive remedial rules and procedures.* Of course, the parties themselves might agree in advance on remedies and on the steps to be taken to perfect rights to such remedies. But in most transactions, remedies and remedial procedures are left to be supplied by the law. "Remedies" is used here in an appropriately broad sense to include all of the permissible responses to breach of a deal: abandonment, specific relief, and damages. "Procedures" is used here to include the various hoops to be jumped through in order to perfect rights to particular remedies. Thus the law might, with reason, require a disgruntled buyer to notify his seller immediately of any specific defects in goods he wishes to reject for nonconformity. Similarly, the law might specify a whole series of steps that a creditor should take in order to walk off with some asset of a debtor against the protests of other similarly unpaid creditors. The law must provide remedial rules and procedures if "making a deal legal" is to have any meaning at all in that vast majority of transactions in which the parties, assuming business will go forward as usual, say nothing of such matters in their agreement. To be fair, and in order to further one of the fundamental purposes of our law, such rules and procedures must, over the mine-run of conflict situations, provide remedies that protect the general expectations of parties similarly situated in deals of that kind. What such expectations are is a fact to be approximated, if not ascertained, and then embodied in the relevant legal doctrines.

Rules of validation, rules of interpretation and construction, substantive suppletive rules, rules of disclaimer, policing rules, third party protection rules, priority rules, and remedial suppletive rules and procedures: these, and others, are the kinds of rules that a legal system must introduce, through code law or case law, to meet legal needs arising out of commercial and consumer activities. One or more of these kinds of rules, in turn, furthers one or more of the varied general aims of such law, whether it be statutory or judge-made: to minimize the occasions for disputes in the course of commercial and consumer dealings; to facilitate *private* ordering of human relations; to protect justified expectations; to protect individuals from various forms of over-reaching and from their own improvidence; to safeguard the interests of third parties; and more.

There is one further type of legal need that the stuff of consumer and commercial life generates, one which cuts across most of the others identified here. This is the need for rules, principles, and processes capable of accommodating and governing the *ever changing varieties* of transaction patterns that occur in the real world of commerce and business. Change and variety are now, have been, and certainly will continue to be distinctively dominant themes in this field.

SECTION 3. THE UNIFORM COMMERCIAL CODE AND ITS ANTECEDENTS—CODIFICATION OF COM-MERCIAL LAW

The foremost champion of codification in the entire history of the Common Law was the 19th Century British jurist Jeremy Bentham. His pupil, John Austin, favored codification, but was cautious about it.

AUSTIN, 2 LECTURES ON JURISPRUDENCE 132–133 (Campbell ed. 1869).

"Whoever has considered the difficulty of making a good statute, will not think lightly of the difficulty of making a code. To conceive distinctly the general purpose of a statute, and the subordinate provisions through which that must be accomplished, and to express both in adequate and unambiguous language, is a task of extreme delicacy and difficulty. It is far easier to conceive justly what would be useful law, than so to construct that same law that it may accomplish the design of the lawgiver. Accordingly, statutes made with great deliberation, and by learned and judicious lawyers, have been expressed so obscurely, or constructed so unaptly, that decisions interpreting or supplementing their provisions, have been of necessity heaped upon them by the Courts of Justice. Such is notably the case with the celebrated Statute of Frauds.

"It follows that the question of Codification is a question of time and place. Speaking in abstract, or without reference to the circumstances of a given community, there can be no doubt that a complete code is better than a body of judiciary law; or is better than a body of law partly consisting of judiciary law, and partly of statute law stuck patchwise on a body of judiciary.

"But taking the question in concrete, or with a view to the expediency of codification in this or that community, a doubt may arise. For here we must contrast the existing law—not with the beau idéal of possible codes, but—with that particular code which an attempt to codify would then and there engender. And that particular and practical question, as Herr von Savigny has rightly judged, will turn mainly on the answer that must be given to another: namely, Are there men, then and there, competent to the difficult task of successful codification? of producing a code, which, on the whole, would more than compensate the evil that must necessarily attend the change?

"The vast difficulty of successful codification, no rational advocate of codification will deny or doubt. Its impossibility none of its rational opponents will venture to affirm."

Bentham, had he heard them, might have been offended by these remarks, for he considered himself competent to codify any law, anywhere, any time. Bentham died in 1832 without having much impact on the codification of English law during his lifetime. But partly as a result of his posthumous influence, a codification movement in England and in America began within fifty years of his death. Interestingly enough, some of these early efforts at codification were in fields of commercial law. The British Bills of Exchange Act of 1882 was the first successful attempt to codify a major branch of English commercial law. This Act was followed in 1893 by the British Sale of Goods Act. M.D. Chalmers, the principal draftsman of these two Codes, was invited to address the convention of the American Bar Association in 1902 on the desirability of codifying commercial law. He closed his speech with these remarks:

CHALMERS, CODIFICATION OF MERCANTILE LAW, 19 L.Q. Rev. 10, 17–18 (1903).

"In the United States, the case for codifying mercantile law is stronger than in England. I am told that an American lawyer who wishes to keep abreast of the current of judicial decision has to take in some fifty-eight volumes of Law Reports every year. In America, there is no choice between common law on the one hand and statute law on the other. Each state is independent in matters of legislation and judicature. The American lawyer, therefore, has to deal not with one but with forty streams of common law, each of which is liable to be disturbed by the action of an independent Legislature. But Commerce knows nothing of State boundaries, and it seems intolerable that if a man in Chicago makes a contract with a man in New York, his rights and duties cannot be determined without an elaborate investigation into the conflict of laws. The only possible remedy that I can see for this state of affairs is codification."

At the time Chalmers spoke, the movement to codify particular branches of commercial law in the United States was already underway. In the 1890's the National Conference of Commissioners on Uniform State Laws had been formed, with representatives from each state many of whom were dedicated to the cause of uniform codification. In 1896, the Conference promulgated the Negotiable Instruments Law, a Code governing the rights and liabilities of parties to checks, promissory notes, and other kinds of commercial paper. Ultimately, the "NIL" was adopted by all state legislatures. In 1906, the Conference presented the Uniform Sales Act for adoption and more than two-thirds of the states enacted it. With this Act, American law professors entered the codification arena, and have been central figures there ever since. Professor Samuel Williston of the Harvard Law School drafted the Uniform Sales Act on behalf of the Conference, and also the Uniform Warehouse Receipts Act, promulgated in 1906, and the Uniform Bills of Lading Act promulgated in 1909 both of which became law in all states. Later, Professor Karl Llewellyn of the Columbia Law School drafted the Uniform Trust Receipts Act, which the Conference promulgated in 1933. Thirty-two states adopted it. Another uniform commercial act, dealing with "conditional" sales, was drafted by Professor Bogert, but it met with success in only ten state legislatures.

In 1940, the idea of a single comprehensive commercial code covering all the foregoing branches of commercial law was conceived and proposed to the Conference of Commissioners on Uniform State Laws. The foregoing uniform acts had become outdated in two ways: changes had occurred in the patterns of commercial activity extant when these laws were enacted, and wholly new patterns had emerged giving rise to new kinds of legal needs. Moreover, even with the Uniform Acts most widely enacted, uniformity no longer existed, for the various state legislatures and judiciaries had added their own distinctive amendments and glosses.

The American Law Institute joined with the National Conference of Commissioners to co-sponsor the "Uniform Commercial Code" project. Professor Karl Llewellyn, then still at Columbia Law School, became chief architect, and his wife, Ms. Soia Mentschikoff, his principal assistant (designated, respectively, "Chief Reporter" and "Associate Chief Reporter"). Ms. Mentschikoff described the drafting process, in Mentschikoff, *The Uniform Commercial Code: An Experiment in Democracy in Drafting,* 36 A.B.A.J. 419 (1950). The drafting process is also discussed extensively in a recent symposium to which five drafters contributed. See *Symposium, Origins and Evolution: Drafters Reflect Upon the Uniform Commercial Code,* 43 Ohio St.L.J. 537–642 (1982).

In 1951, the sponsors promulgated the Uniform Commercial Code, and, with minor revisions, it was enacted in Pennsylvania in 1953, effective July 1, 1954. Between 1953 and 1955, the New York Law Revision Commission dropped all other work and made a thorough study of the Code, recommending many changes in the official text. During the hearings there were, from time to time, rather sharp conflicts between academicians defending the Code and practitioners attacking it.

In 1956, the Editorial Board of the Code made recommendations for revision of the 1952 Official Text, many of which were based on criticisms made at the New York Law Revision Commission Hearings. In 1957 a revised Official Text was promulgated incorporating recommended changes. Further Official Texts, with minor changes, were promulgated in 1958 and 1962.

By 1968, the Uniform Commercial Code had been enacted by all but one state in the United States. A "Permanent Editorial Board" was established by the sponsoring organizations primarily to consider the wisdom of proposed amendments to the Code. (The idea for such a Board was set forth in Schlesinger, *The Uniform Commercial Code in the Light of Comparative Law,* 1 N.Y.Law Revision Commission 87 (1955). This Board has made various reports.

The Code's sponsors and its Permanent Editorial Board have not left it alone. In 1972, the new "1972" Official Text of the Code was promulgated. That Text left nearly all of the 1962 Official Text intact except in the field of personal property security governed by Article 9. Article 9 was given a good overhaul in the 1972 Official Text, though its basic theory, structure, and scope remains the same. As of 1987, the 1972 text of Article Nine was in force in forty five states. There is now also a new "1978" Official Text, which in 1987 had been adopted by 19 states. This version includes changes in Article Eight, Investment Securities.

The Code is divided into nine substantive articles. The first is a general article bearing on various aspects of the entire Code. The remaining eight articles are broken down first into "Parts" and the "Parts" are in turn subdivided into sections. Some brief remarks on each article are in order:

Article 2: Sales

Article 2 applies to "transactions in goods" and supersedes the Uniform Sales Act. Major innovations in Article 2 include de-emphasis of the title concept in settling sales controversies, several novel provisions governing formation of the sales contract, and different standards of conduct applicable to merchants and to nonmerchants in discharging their contract obligations.

Article 3: Commercial Paper

Article 3 is a revision of the Uniform Negotiable Instruments Law. It includes fewer innovations than any other major Article of the Code. Unlike the Uniform Negotiable Instruments Law, Article 3 does not apply to bank deposits and collections, letters of credit, or corporate securities. Articles 4, 5, and 8, respectively, deal with these subjects.

Consolidation was a chief aim of the draftsmen of Article 3. While the Uniform Negotiable Instruments Law had 198 provisions, Article 3 has only 80. The most dramatic instance of consolidation in the entire Code appears in Article 3: The Code takes only 11 sections to deal with presentment, notice of dishonor, and protest, while the Uniform Negotiable Instruments Law took 67 sections to deal with these subjects.

Article 4: Bank Deposits and Collections

Article 4 replaces statutes governing bank deposits and collections. There was no prior uniform act in this field. Article 4 therefore fills an important void. Article 4 includes basic provisions settling such old questions as: When does a depository bank buy an item rather than take it for collection only? UCC 4–201, 4–213. And, as of what point in time does a bank pay an item? UCC 4–213. Among the novel provisions of Article 4 are those requiring depositors to exercise due care in discovering forgeries, UCC 4–406(1), and a provision granting bank and depositor full freedom to govern their relations by contract, "except that no agreement can disclaim a bank's responsibility for its own lack of good faith or failure to exercise ordinary care * * *." UCC 4–103(1).

Article 5: Letters of Credit

Article 5 governs a subject that in most states has been governed almost entirely by case law. In the typical letter of credit transaction, a bank, at the buyer's request, issues a "letter" to the seller, providing that the bank will, under certain conditions, honor drafts drawn by the seller on the buyer for payment of the purchase price of goods.

Article 6: Bulk Transfers

Article 6 deals with bulk transfers and, as such, emphasizes protection of the transferor's creditors.

Article 7: Documents of Title

Article 7 applies both to warehouse receipts and to bills of lading, two types of documents of title formerly governed separately by the Uniform Warehouse Receipts Act and the Uniform Bills of Lading Act.

Article 8: Investment Securities

Article 8 replaces the Uniform Stock Transfer Act and related statutes, including several provisions of the Uniform Negotiable Instruments Law. Article 8 is often called a "negotiable instruments" law for investment securities. It endows certain bonds, stocks, and other securities with attributes of negotiability and defines the rights and liabilities of issuers, transferors, and transferees. Article 8 does not supersede regulatory laws governing issuance of securities.

Article 9: Secured Transactions

Article 9 is the most novel division in the Code. It is designed to provide a simple and unified structure within which the immense variety of present-day secured financing transactions can be effected with less cost and greater certainty. The most radical innovation in Article 9 is its substitution of a unitary security device for the plethora of security devices previously in use. Terms such as "mortgagee," "pledgee," "conditional sale," and "trust receipt" do not appear in Article 9. Instead, its unitary security device is formulated in terms of four basic concepts: "secured party," "debtor," "collateral," and "security interest."

The foregoing, then, represents the general structure of the Code and demonstrates that its scope is broad. Chronologically, the Code applies to transactions "entered into" after its effective date. See UCC

10–102(2). In terms of territorial application, it applies to transactions "bearing an appropriate relation" to the enacting state. In terms of subject-matter, it applies to a wide-range of transactions. There is not, in the Code, a single "scope" provision which defines the *subject-matter* to which the *entire* Code applies. Instead, the Code is divided into ten "articles," eight of which purport to govern aspects of basic types of commercial transactions. The precise scope of each such article must usually be determined by examining not merely a specific "scope" provision within the article (if there be one) but other provisions as well, some of which are definitional in nature. The student should, at this point, become familiar with the basic "scope" provisions of Articles 9, 2, and 3.

There is no general "de-minimus" limitation on the Code's application. Thus, for example, Article 2 could apply to the sale of a fifteen-cent hamburger. See UCC 2–314.

While many of the articles of the Code can, in relation to some kinds of transactions, apply separately and alone, frequently provisions from more than one article will be applicable to the transaction at hand.

The Code recognizes the possibilities of conflict between Articles, and includes provisions governing such possibilities. See, e.g., UCC 2–102, 9–113, 3–103, 4–102(1), 8–102(1)(c), and 9–102.

SECTION 4. WHAT KIND OF A CODE IS THE UNIFORM COMMERCIAL CODE?

One of the Code drafters had this to say:

GILMORE, ARTICLE 9: WHAT IT DOES FOR THE PAST, 26 La. L.Rev. 285, 286 (1966).

"Surely the principal function of a Code is to abolish the past. At least a common lawyer assumes that that was the theory on which the great civil law codes were based. From the date of the Code's enactment, the pre-Code law is no longer available as a source of law. The gaps, the ambiguities, the unforeseen situations cannot be referred for decision to the accumulated wisdom of the past. There is a fresh start, a new universe of legal discourse, in which the only permissible way of solving a problem is to find (or pretend to find) the answer in the undefiled, the unconstrued, the uncontaminated text of the Code itself. How well the theory worked in practice, or whether it worked at all, you, as civilians, are much better equipped to say than I.

"The Uniform Commercial Code, so-called, is not that sort of Code—even in theory. It derives from the common law, not the civil law, tradition. We shall do better to think of it as a big statute—or a collection of statutes bound together in the same book—which goes as far as it goes and no further. It assumes the continuing existence of a large body of pre-Code and non-Code law on which it rests for support, which it displaces to the least possible extent, and without which it could not survive. The solid stuff of pre-Code law will furnish the rationale of decision quite as often as the Code's own gossamer substance."

A useful general discussion of the jurisprudence of the Uniform Commercial Code, primarily Article 2, appears in Danzig, *A Comment on the Jurisprudence of the Uniform Commercial Code,* 27 Stan.L.Rev. 621 (1975).

SECTION 5. THE SPECIAL PITFALLS IN USING THE UNIFORM COMMERCIAL CODE (AND SIMILAR CODES)

These pitfalls are numerous. First, the Code includes more than the usual quota of definitions. Consider, for example, the first *line* of UCC 2–205. How many of the fourteen words in that line are defined in other provisions of the Code? Where is "offer" defined? How is the researcher to know what words are defined and what ones are not? Are the "Definitional Cross References" in the Comments always exhaustive? They purport to be, but, as will be seen, they are not.

Once all defined terms have been looked up, it is still not possible to be sure that the Code answer has been found. It is essential that the researcher also check the bearing of any related provisions in the Code. The Code is an "integrated" and "interrelated" body of law. This poses a special pitfall, for it means that it often compels research beyond what seems on the surface to be the controlling provision. Check, for example, the bearing of UCC 2–508 and 2–609 on 2–601. How is one to know of such related provisions? There are "Cross References" in the Comments, but it should not be assumed that they are exhaustive.

The "legislative history" relevant to interpreting the Code is of several kinds, each posing its own special problems. The four types of such history are: (1) Official Comments, (2) Prior versions of the Code, (3) Legislative hearings and reports made prior to enactment in specific states, and (4) Books and articles by Code draftsmen. See generally, Braucher, *Legislative History of the Uniform Commercial Code,* 58 Colum.L.Rev. 798 (1958). An extensive treatment of the major research sources on the Uniform Commercial Code is Kavass, *Uniform Commercial Code Research: A Brief Guide to the Sources,* 88 Commercial L.J. 547 (1983). See also, Kelly, *Uniform Commercial Code Drafts* (1984), Vols. I & II.

As promulgated by the American Law Institute and the Conference of Commissioners on Uniform State Laws, the Official Text of the Code appears with comments on each section. As enacted by state legislators, however, only the Official Text (with whatever amendments were made) appears on the statute books. In many states the Code with comments (and local annotations) is available to the bar through private publishing houses. A lawyer must, however, bear in mind that the Official Comments are not authoritative and further that they do not cover a state's changes in the Official Text.

The Comment to each section usually contains five parts. In the first, entitled "Prior Uniform Statutory Provisions," there appears a list of references to provisions of prior Uniform Acts displaced by the section. In the second part, designated "Changes," the difference, if any, between the superseded law and the Official Text are indicated in a general way. In the third part of the Comments, called "Purposes of Changes" or "Purposes of Changes and New Matter," the purposes of the particular Official Text Code section are explained, and, in some instances, illustrated. In the fourth part, "Cross References," there is a list of related Code provisions. In the last part there appears a list of definitional cross references.

It should not be assumed that for purposes of interpretation and construction, the Official Comments stand in the same relation to the Official Text as true legislative history typically stands to the language of ordinary statutes. The Comments, or some of them, differ from such history in several ways. They were not always laid before the enacting legislators at the time of Code adoption. Some of the present Comments were not even in existence when the sections commented on were enacted into law in some states. Some of the existing Comments appear to have been addressed to earlier drafts of sections of the Code different from the later sections enacted into law. In some important parts of the Code, the draftsman of the Comments was not the draftsman of the section commented on. See generally Skilton, *Some Comments on the Comments to the Uniform Commercial Code,* 1966 Wis.L. Rev. 597.

Still, the Comments have influenced many judicial decisions and will certainly continue to do so. That they are not entitled to exactly the same weight as true legislative history may, therefore, be unimportant. But it is important to appreciate the special hazards and pitfalls in the use of the Comments. A detailed appreciation of these must await immersion in the processes of problem solving that lie ahead in this book. For now, a general survey of the most common hazards and pitfalls must do.

Perhaps the principal hazard in using the Comments (apart from the inexhaustiveness of their cross references) is that they not uncommonly add to or vary the Code language. Some insight into why this is so is revealed in the following passage from a speech made by the chief draftsman of the Code, Karl N. Llewellyn:

LLEWELLYN, WHY A COMMERCIAL CODE? 22 Tenn.L.Rev. 779, 784, 794, 782 (1953).

"I am ashamed of it in some ways; there are so many places that I could make a little better, there are so many beautiful ideas I tried to get in that would have been good for the law, but I was voted down * * * when we weren't allowed to put in where we wanted to go * * *, we at least got the thing set up so that we are allowed to state in accompanying comments where the particular sections are trying to go."

The Comments are both expansive and restrictive in nature. Their expansiveness frequently takes the form of explicit rejection of negative implications from the text of the section. In view of such Comments, the maxim *expressio unius exclusio alterius est* (the expression of one thing is the exclusion of the other) loses some of its force. (See, for an example, the Comments to UCC 2–318.) On the restrictiveness of Comments, it has been remarked that, "it would not be difficult to cite examples where the draftsman has wisely left a breathing space, so to say, in the text to allow a free case-law development and then come back to the comment to nail the coffin lid down tightly." Gilmore, *On the Difficulties of Codifying Commercial Law,* 57 Yale L.J. 1341, 1355 (1948). Of course, if the Comments are not *law* then perhaps the lid is not so tight as all that.

It has been said that the definitional and sectional "cross references" in the Comments cannot be relied on as exhaustive. As an example, note that the definitional cross references to UCC 2–316 fail to mention the crucial fact that "conspicuous" is defined in UCC 1–201(10). And there are still other sources of frustration. Comments often blithely assume that the reader is familiar with the details of prior law. Some Comments deal with sections other than the one they are addressed to. (See, e.g., Comment 2 to UCC 2–312 dealing with UCC 2–607). Comments vary greatly in quality. Some are overly long, others not long enough. Some offer insight. Some confuse.

We turn, now, to earlier versions of the Code as a distinctive source of guidance and misguidance in resolving problems of interpretation and construction. The lawyer should know of the existence of such earlier drafts. The main prior drafts are:

1945   Drafts and Redrafts of Parts of the Proposed Code (Unpublished).

1949   Proposed Draft with Comments.

1950   Proposed Final Draft with Comments.

1951   Final Text with Comments.

       Amendments in May, 1951.

       Amendments in September, 1951.

1952   Official Text with Comments.

1953   Changes Recommended by a Meeting of the Enlarged Editorial Board. Part A, Part B.

1956   Recommendations of the Editorial Board.

1957   Official Text with Comments.

       Supplement to the 1957 Official Edition of the Code.

1958   Official Text with Comments.

1962   Amendments to the Uniform Commercial Code, Permanent Editorial Board for the U.C.C., Report 1.

1962   Official Text with Comments.

1965   Report No. 2 of the Permanent Editorial Board for the Uniform Commercial Code.

1966   Report No. 3 of the Permanent Editorial Board for the Uniform Commercial Code.

1971   Review Committee for Article Nine, Final Report.

1972   Official Text with Comments.

1978   Official Text with Comments.

Inferences based on changes in the language of successive revisions of Code sections are inherently unreliable. They are all the more unreliable because "frequently matters have been omitted as being implicit without statement and language has been changed or added solely for clarity." This quote comes from the comment to a section in the 1952 text of the Code which read: "Prior drafts of text and comments may not be used to ascertain legislative intent." This section itself was eventually deleted from the Official Text of the Code. It should have been left in. It will have to be left to the Supreme Court of the United States to rule out the use of prior versions of sections and comments as an unconstitutional form of cruel and inhuman punishment of fellow lawyers. Or perhaps the decisive argument will be that because of their scarcity (only a few libraries have them) their use denies equal protection of the laws.

Another basic type of material that is of relevance in resolving problems of Code interpretation and construction consists of legislative hearings and official reports made by agencies of enacting states. These form the more immediate background of Code enactment. Their status is somewhat uncertain in regard to the Code, for it includes its own "legislative" history in the form of comments. In the face of conflict, which is to control? And there are other problems.

A further type of material that has figured in Code interpretation and construction consists of books and articles and memoranda written by persons who participated in the drafting of the Code. The outstanding instance to appear to date is a two volume treatise: Gilmore, Security Interests in Personal Property (1965). In a footnote at p. 289 of the first volume of this treatise, Professor Gilmore confesses that he had a large hand in the drafting of Article 9 of the Code. And his treatise has been justly acclaimed in reviews.

John Locke might have said that Professor Gilmore's treatise has a natural and inalienable right to be quoted and cited on any and all Article 9 problems. Actually such is not without parallel. After the Uniform Sales Act, promulgated in 1906, was widely enacted, its draftsman, Professor Samuel Williston, published a treatise, *Williston on Sales*, which explained what the Act was all about. It would startle no one to find that Williston's treatise influenced the law. Similarly, Gilmore's has influenced the law.

An exceptionally fine article on methods of interpreting the Uniform Commercial Code is: McDonnell, *Purposive Interpretation of the*

Uniform Commercial Code: Some Implications for Jurisprudence, 126 U.Pa.L.Rev. 795 (1978). Modesty forbids two of us from calling attention to another book that lawyers and judges regularly resort to: J. White and R. Summers, The Uniform Commercial Code (2d ed. 1980). In moments of levity we will refer to it as the "Crutch." Otherwise, it is known as "White and Summers."

SECTION 6. COMMERCIAL LAW NOT IN THE UNIFORM COMMERCIAL CODE

Despite its seemingly wide sweep, the Code is far from comprehensive. There are some transactions it does not govern at all, and there are many aspects of many transactions to which its provisions might apply but will not, for various reasons.

First and at the fore, the parties can generally make their own "law." As one authority has put it, "We are within that area of law where—to use an old-fashioned, pre-positivistic phrase—businessmen are free to make their own law. They do so expressly through contract, implicitly through a course of dealing, collectively through custom and resultant business understanding." By their own agreement, then, the parties to a commercial deal can vary most of the provisions of the Code.

Second, the Code itself, by its own terms, does not purport to control many important types of transactions that can fairly be called commercial. For example, it does not apply to sales of commercial realty nor to security interests therein. It does not apply to the formation, performance, and enforcement of insurance contracts. It does not apply to suretyship transactions (except where a surety is a party to a negotiable instrument). It does not encompass the law of bankruptcy. It does not govern legal tender.

Third, the Code does not even purport to govern exhaustively all aspects of all transactions to which its provisions do apply. Many of its provisions obviously can come into play only by virtue of some key event, e.g., "default," which may be defined by the terms of the agreement between the parties. See, e.g., UCC 9–501(1). Furthermore, resort to supplemental principles of law outside the Code will often be necessary. See generally, UCC 1–103. Consider the following three examples. To apply the provisions on authorized and unauthorized signatures in Article 3 (UCC 3–403 and 3–404), local agency principles must be considered. To determine what title a "transferor" has under UCC 2–403, it is essential to refer to non-Code law. The "grounds" of impossibility and frustration as a defense to the breach of a contract of sale are not exhaustively stated in the Code. See UCC 2–613, 2–614, and 2–615. Presumably additional grounds recognized in "general contract law" can be invoked. In addition, the Code has its own "gaps"—situations arising within the framework of the Code on specific aspects of which the Code is altogether silent.

Fourth, there are state statutes, most of which are regulatory in nature, which either supplement or supersede Code provisions altogether. See, e.g., UCC 2–102, 9–201, and 9–203(4) for references to the possible existence of such statutes. Usury laws and so-called "Retail Installment Sales Acts" are outstanding examples. It is appropriate at this point to emphasize that the Code does *not*, in terms, concern itself with the general problems of the *consumer* as consumer.

Fifth, the Uniform Commercial Code is *state* law. This means that any valid and conflicting federal commercial law supersedes it. Thus, for example, there are the Federal Consumer Protection Act and the Magnuson-Moss Warranty Act. The Federal Bills of Lading Act (sometimes called the Pomerene Act) 49 U.S.C.A. §§ 81–124 (1982), rather than Article 7 of the Code, applies to all interstate bills of lading transactions.

Sixth, there is a growing body of federal regulatory law that supplements commercial law at many points. For example, the federal Food and Drug Act imposes controls on the quality of goods sold and on the ways they are marketed. The Robinson-Patman Act operates to regulate the price of some goods. Federal statutes govern the creation of security interests in some types of collateral. See, e.g., the Ship Mortgage Act, 1920, referred to in UCC 9–104 Comment 1.

Seventh, this survey of non-Code sources of commercial law would not be complete without some reference to procedural law. Generally, commercial claims are litigated in accordance with the procedures applicable in any ordinary case. There are, however, a few procedural doctrines that have a distinctively commercial flavor. Some of these are incorporated in the Code, although it generally does not purport to cover procedural law. See, e.g., the "vouching in" provisions of UCC 2–607(5).

Finally, there are practices and attitudes of legal officials and of men of commerce which cannot really be captured in the language of any Code but which, nonetheless, have an inevitable impact on legal evolution. Professor Edwin W. Patterson has said of these that they seem "to be a part of the societal matrix, a kind of semantic and narrative substratum of law and other articulate forms of social control." 1 N.Y. Law Revision Commission Report 56 (1955) (footnote omitted).

Part One

INTRODUCTORY MATERIALS

Chapter Two

NATURE AND SCOPE OF ARTICLE 2 ON SALES

SECTION 1. WHY DO SALES AND CONTRACTS FOR SALE TAKE PLACE?

Sales law evolved in response to disputes between private parties over agreements to transfer the ownership of personal property, usually goods, for a price. As in all areas of private law, the transaction, whether a sale or a contract to sell, came first and the law of sales followed. Indeed, it is probable that the various bodies of specialized commercial law, such as negotiable instruments, developed in response to the particular needs of the parties before the need for a general law of contracts occurred to anyone. See G. Gilmore, The Death of Contract 11–12 (1974).

If not compelled by law, why do sales occur? One answer is that in an exchange economy sales have to take place. To put this abstractly, a productive unit in a modern economy specializes in making one or but a few types of goods. Such a unit does not make enough of everything to satisfy all its own needs. It is not self sufficient and must engage in exchanges with other productive units.

But why such specialization in the first place? First, since men and organizations have different capacities and abilities, it becomes economical to match capacities and abilities with productive tasks for which they are best suited. Second, since different regions differ in natural resources and climate it becomes economical to put regions to work on productive activities for which they are best suited. Third, even if capacities, abilities, resources and climates were undifferentiated, it would still be advantageous to have specialization and therefore to have an exchange economy, whether the advantage comes from a greater quantity of production, time saved or improved quality through concentration of effort. See A. Smith, The Wealth of Nations 7–9 (Mod. Lib.Ed.1937).

A variety of factors, then, begets specialization and specialization begets exchanges—sales. According to Ian Macneil, four conditions should exist for an economy based upon exchange to flourish: (1) Specialization of labor and exchange; (2) A sense by individuals of their capacity for choice and the consequences of its exercise; (3) An awareness of the continuum between past, present, and future; and (4) A social matrix which reinforces the exercise of choices made with an eye to the future. Macneil, *The Many Futures of Contracts,* 47 S.Cal.L.Rev. 691, 696–712 (1974).

But the sale, a completed exchange, is one thing and a contract to sell in the future quite another. One might imagine a very simple society in which sales of goods took place but never pursuant to prior contracts to sell. In a complex industrialized society such as ours, however, contracts to sell and to buy goods are essential to planned economic activity. A manufacturer, for example, must have raw materials, and he must be able to rely on receiving them at designated times and places if he is to operate efficiently. For such reason he will make agreements to purchase raw materials, and recognition of these agreements, frequently of long duration, will make it more certain that his business will function as planned.

Another factor is required for a market directed economy to flourish: The legal system must permit and facilitate the acquisition, use and transfer of private property. Article 2 of the UCC is, with a minimum of regulation, devoted to this support function.

SECTION 2. A ROADMAP TO THE SALES ARTICLE OF THE UCC

As part of his essential background, the user of Article Two needs a basic roadmap to the 104 provisions involved. The presentation here will be in terms of stages of the modern mercantile sales deal, which is typically for future delivery of goods on credit, and therefore a deal that progresses from initial agreement through performance to discharge. The discrete stages along the way are typically these: agreement; post-agreement—pre-shipment; the stage of getting the goods (or documents therefor) to the buyer; receipt and inspection, and payment. The overwhelming majority of deals progress all the way through to payment without incident. But a significant proportion do not, and these break down at different stages, in different ways, and for different reasons. Thus, what follows here will be "pathologically oriented" in the respect that, at each stage, the focus will be on the *kinds* of things that can go wrong.

One caveat: Because the discussion in this section is by way of prelude, it is necessarily general and to some extent oversimplified.

Also, it is not comprehensive. In each of these respects, so, too, a roadmap.

A. The Agreement Stage

Perhaps the most drastic of all things that can go wrong is for the parties to assume that they have made a binding contract only to find that in law they have not. This is much less of a risk, however, under Article 2 than it is in general contract law. This is so for two reasons. First, Article 2 makes contract formation easier than it is in the general law. Formalities are delimited. See, UCC 2–201 and 2–203. The consideration doctrine is modified with a bias toward contract formation. See UCC 2–205, and 2–209(1). The requirement that an acceptance must be precisely within the terms of an offer to constitute an acceptance is abolished. See UCC 2–207, and 2–206(1)(a). A non-conforming shipment of goods in response to a unilateral offer is, under certain circumstances, nonetheless an acceptance. UCC 2–206(1)(b). Contracts can be formed by mere conduct alone, even though the precise moment of making is undetermined. UCC 2–204(1) and (2).

Second, Article 2 includes a general provision to the effect that a contract for sale does not fail for indefiniteness if the parties have intended to make a contract and there is a reasonably certain basis for giving an appropriate remedy. UCC 2–204(3). Further to this, the Article includes many "gap-filler" provisions which come into play to fill gaps in agreements that might otherwise fail under general contract law for indefiniteness. See UCC 2–204(3), 2–305, 2–306, 2–307, 2–308, 2–309, 2–310, 2–311, 2–503, 2–504, 2–507, and 2–511.

In addition to failures of contract formation, disputes may arise over (1) whether a term is or is not a part of the contract and (2) whether a given term is to be interpreted in one way rather than another. These kinds of disputes can arise at any stage, but it is appropriate to allude to them here. On whether a term is or is not a part of the contract, the parol evidence rule of UCC 2–202 governs. Under Article 2, lawyers and judges will resolve problems of interpretation and construction in part by reference to UCC 1–102 on rules of construction, UCC 1–205 on course of dealing and usage of trade, and UCC 2–208 and 2–207(3) on course of performance or practical construction.

The alert, careful lawyer should, through draftsmanship and advice, be able to reduce if not eliminate altogether any risks that the parties will fail to make a binding contract or even that significant disputes over interpretation will arise.

B. The Post-Agreement—Pre-Shipment Stage

A seller will either have the goods on hand, or have to manufacture them or acquire them elsewhere. In any of these events, there is often a time lapse between the date when the contract is made and the time when the goods are sent to the buyer. During this period, the buyer may repudiate, or the seller may repudiate, or it may become clear that one of the parties will not later be able to perform.

UCC 2–610 and 2–611 deal with repudiation. Assume it is the buyer who repudiates. The seller can call off the deal. See UCC 2–610(b) and 2–703(f). Or he can also seek damages under UCC 2–706 or 2–708 as appropriate. Can he choose to go forward with the transaction and force the goods on the buyer? Yes, under limited circumstances. See UCC 2–704(1)(a) and 2–709(1)(b).

UCC 2–704(2) gives the *manufacturing* seller flexibility in the event of repudiation.

Now let us assume that the seller repudiates at this stage. What are the buyer's rights? Again, the buyer, too, may call off the deal, UCC 2–610(b), 2–711(1), or he may also have damages. UCC 2–711(1), 2–712, 2–713. Can he choose to go forward with the transaction and force the goods out of the seller? See UCC 2–610(b) and 2–711(2)(a) and (b). As with most "goods oriented" remedies, this alternative may put the buyer in conflict with creditors of and purchasers from the seller. If the buyer has a prior perfected Article 9 security interest, he would prevail over most such third parties. Otherwise, the buyer must rely on his right, if any, to specific performance or replevin as specified in UCC 2–716, and this right is generally subject to third party interests.

A closer look at the parties' damages remedy is in order. Can it be combined with other remedies? Yes. The Code does not favor "election" doctrines. (Even cancellation does not extinguish a right to damages. See UCC 2–720). Are there any significant parallels between the seller's damages remedy and that of the buyer? Yes. Both can go into the market and "fix" damages against the other party, so to speak. See UCC 2–706(1) and 2–712(1) and (2). Yet neither is *required* to do this. Both can simply sue for damages for repudiation and get the full market-contract-price differential rather than the differential between contract or market and a substitute transaction consummated by the "reselling" seller or "covering" buyer. See UCC 2–708(1) and 2–713. Can the parties get consequential damages? It is clear that the buyer can. See UCC 2–715.

The rights of a party to call off the deal, to get damages, or to go forward with the deal, are the basic remedial options. They are carefully analyzed in detail in Peters, *Remedies for Breach of Contracts Relating to the Sale of Goods Under the Uniform Commercial Code: A Roadmap for Article Two,* 73 Yale L.J. 199 (1963).

After the agreement and prior to shipment, other things can go wrong besides repudiation. It may emerge that one of the parties will not, later, at the appointed time, be *able* to perform. In such circumstances, UCC 2–609 allows the aggrieved party to demand adequate assurances of performance. Failure to provide such assurances within a reasonable time is classed as a "repudiation." Prospective inability to perform will, when it exists, entitle the aggrieved party to pursue the same general remedial options as may be available upon repudiation.

Insolvency should be mentioned as a special form of prospective inability to perform which inherently introduces third parties. When opposing third party interests are in the picture, "going forward" with the deal becomes less desirable to the seller where the buyer is insolvent, and less freely available to the buyer where the seller is insolvent. Compare UCC 2–702(1) and 2–502(1).

Casualty to goods identified to the contract is another kind of event that can occur after contract and prior to shipment. In some circumstances, it will excuse the seller. See UCC 2–613. The topic of casualty and attendant risk of loss problems will be considered in the next section.

C. *The Stage of Getting the Goods or Documents Therefor to the Buyer*

Many commercial contracts call for the seller to deliver the goods to the buyer at the buyer's town or place of business. For the time, manner and place of delivery, *absent* such contractual stipulation, see UCC 2–309, 2–307, 2–308, 2–503 and 2–507.

Here the primary focus is on seller's performance. Several basic things can go wrong with it at this stage. The seller may deliver late, or at the wrong place, or in improper manner.

Also, the seller who is required or authorized to send the goods to the buyer must, unless otherwise agreed, make a "proper contract" of carriage and notify the buyer of shipment. See UCC 2–504. The seller may simply fail to do this, thereby incurring liability to the buyer. Of course, the rights of the buyer upon default at this stage vary with the nature of the default. Can the buyer always call the deal off? No. See e.g., the last paragraph of UCC 2–504, 2–612, 2–614, and 2–615. But he will generally be entitled to damages. See UCC 2–711.

The carrier may fail to perform *its* obligations. The duties of such a carrier will be specified in the contract of carriage (bill of lading) and in Article 7 of the Code, where the deal is intrastate. If interstate, the Federal Bill of Lading Act governs. The carrier will be liable for damages caused by improper loading for which it is responsible. See UCC 7–301(4). The carrier may negligently cause damage to the goods for which liability lies under UCC 7–309. Or the carrier may simply fail to follow instructions thereby causing loss. For example, the seller may have a right to stop the goods in transit under UCC 2–705 and the carrier may fail to honor stoppage instructions. Here, though, the seller rather than the buyer would be the aggrieved party.

The goods in transit may be lost or damaged (with or without the carrier's fault). The carrier's insurance will often cover most of the loss. But "risk of loss" problems can arise. Generally, risk passes upon tender at destination when the contract calls for delivery at the buyer's city. See UCC 2–509(1)(b). Hence, as between seller and buyer, seller would be responsible for loss occurring during carriage in such a deal. It should be noted that UCC 2–510 says, among other things, that a seller cannot pass the risk of loss *re* non-conforming goods.

If, before risk passes to the buyer, the goods "suffer" total casualty, without fault of either party, then under UCC 2–613 the seller will be excused from the contract if the contract was one which required for its performance goods identified when the contract was made.

The foregoing discussion has centered on deals for goods only. What if the contract calls for delivery of a document of title to the buyer in exchange for the buyer's cash payment on the spot or his signature to a time draft? See UCC 2–503(5). Most of the main kinds of things that can go wrong in procuring and transmitting documents can be readily inventoried. As procured, the document may fail to describe the goods properly. See UCC 7–301. Or it may not be in correct form. See UCC 2–503(5)(a). The document may be lost or stolen. See UCC 7–601. Or it may get into the wrong hands, and, if negotiable, and the transferee takes by due negotiation, then the transferee will generally get title to the document and to the goods. See UCC 7–501 and UCC 7–502. But see UCC 7–503. Or the document may be altered. See UCC 7–306.

D. The Receipt-Inspection Stage

This, in commercial deals, is, to seller and buyer alike, the crucial stage. Here the seller will typically lose any control he has over the goods. Here the buyer will, usually for the first time, inspect and decide whether to accept or reject. Naturally, the buyer will generally prefer to inspect before paying. Blind payment puts him at a disadvantage: when the goods turn out not to be conforming, he finds himself a potential plaintiff, whereas, if there is to be litigation at all, it is generally better to be a potential defendant who has first inspected and then rejected the goods for nonconformity. The blindly paying buyer is also at a disadvantage in the respect that he, as plaintiff, must assume the risk of the seller's insolvency in regard to satisfaction of any judgment he gets against a defaulting seller. Further, the buyer who pays blindly may find that he has assumed control over and therefore responsibility for the goods. See generally, Honnold, *The Buyer's Right of Rejection,* 97 U.Pa.L.Rev. 457 (1949).

Contracts often specifically provide for a right of the buyer to inspect before payment or acceptance. But what if the contract is silent? UCC 2–513 says that the buyer has a right to inspect before payment or acceptance unless he has contracted it away. One way the buyer can give up this right is by agreeing to pay "against documents" covering the goods. UCC 2–513(3)(b), 2–512, 2–310.

What are the ways a seller can fail to perform at this stage (other than "failures of delivery" already considered)? In the main, the seller may fail to tender goods to which he has title, or fail to tender goods that are of the right quantity or of the right quality. These latter two kinds of breaches are not uncommon, as breaches go. And they both may take a variety of forms, depending on the nature of the goods. Similarly, the seller may tender non-conforming *documents* covering goods.

What is the general standard of performance to which the seller is held? The contract is the first touchstone. But, in general contract law, it is familiar that under the doctrine of substantial performance, some departures from the contract are permitted with the result that the non-performing party can still recover "on the contract." Is it the same under the Code? Generally, no. UCC 2–601 seemingly requires "perfect tender." As to quality, the warranty provisions of Article 2 (UCC 2–312—2–315) determine the relevant standard of performance as to quality to the extent the contract is silent. The perfect tender doctrine is, however, modified by UCC 2–508, 2–612, and other provisions.

Assuming the seller has failed to make perfect tender, and that he cannot rely on the doctrine of substantial performance, what are the buyer's rights? His basic damages remedy has already been outlined. See UCC 2–712 and 2–713. The emphasis here should be on the buyer's "goods-oriented" options. If the buyer wishes, he may reject. UCC 2–601. To do so, he has to jump through the right hoops. UCC 2–602, 2–605. If he is a merchant, he may have duties in regard to care and disposition of the goods. UCC 2–603, 2–604. The buyer may, however, want the seller to perform—to send goods that do conform. He *may* be entitled to specific performance or replevin under UCC 2–716.

What if the buyer has accepted the goods (UCC 2–606) and has later discovered a defect, or has accepted the goods with seller's assurances that non-conformities would be corrected, but such has not occurred? Has the buyer forever lost his right to throw the goods back at the seller? No. See UCC 2–608. But the buyer, again, must jump through the right hoops. See UCC 2–608(2) and 2–607(3)(a).

Such revocation of acceptance, along with rejection, leaves the buyer free, too, to pursue damages. See UCC 2–608(3), 2–711(1), and 2–714.

Finally, the buyer may choose to retain non-conforming goods and recover damages. See UCC 2–714(1) and (2). But, if he is to take this avenue, he must give notice of the breach under UCC 2–714(1). In commercial cases, this avenue is more common than in consumer cases where the defect in the goods often makes them of no value at all, and the buyer's main concern is to get damages for breach of warranty, often consequential damages of a personal injury or property damage character. See 2–715(2)(b). Most of Article 2 litigation is warranty of quality litigation, consumer and non-consumer. The Code's basic warranty provisions, to be treated intensively later, are UCC 2–313, 2–314, 2–315, 2–316, 2–317, and 2–318.

To turn, now, to non-performance by the *buyer* at the receipt-inspection stage. He may fail to provide proper facilities for presentation of the goods for inspection. See UCC 2–503(1). He may make a wrongful demand for inspection. See UCC 2–513(3)(b). He may fail to follow contractual or statutorily prescribed procedures for inspection. See UCC 2–513(1). He may "impose" unagreed upon standards of conformity. He may deny the seller's right to cure. UCC 2–508. He may deny any right of the seller to supply less than perfectly conforming goods. UCC 2–612(2). He may mistakenly think the goods do not conform. He may fail to jump through prescribed rejection hoops. UCC 2–602. He may fail to take over the goods and care for or dispose of them as required under UCC 2–603 and UCC 2–604. Perhaps most significant in the usual run of cases, he may refuse, for some reason, to pay at this time as agreed or as required in the absence of agreement. See UCC 2–507(1).

The appropriate maneuver for the seller will vary with the nature of the buyer's breach and the course of action the buyer takes. Often the seller will want and will be entitled to damages, a general remedy already outlined at the post-agreement stage. See UCC 2–703. Here the focus will be on (1) the seller's "goods oriented" remedies assuming the buyer is retaining the goods, and (2) the seller's right to the price, whether or not the buyer retains the goods.

Generally, if the buyer is refusing payment, and payment is due at this stage, the seller will be entitled to replevy the goods from the buyer under UCC 2–507(2) and 2–511. As with most goods-oriented remedies, third parties may enter the picture and defeat the aggrieved party. As against creditors, UCC 2–702 controls. As against buyers from the buyer, UCC 2–403 must be consulted. And, of course, as in all situations, any relevant cases. But the seller could retain a security interest in the goods of high priority entitling him to defeat almost all third parties except "buyers in ordinary course of business." See UCC 9–107, 9–201, 9–307(1).

And when is the seller entitled to the price against a buyer in breach at this stage? If the buyer has accepted the goods (UCC 2–606) and has not properly rejected them or justifiably revoked his acceptance of them, then the seller may have the price. UCC 2–709. The seller may also get the price in two other, more restricted, situations under UCC 2–709(1).

E. The Payment Stage

[handwritten marginalia: Not Real Important to us — Covered in More detail in upper class courses on UCC §3+4]

The overwhelming majority of transactions pass on through the payment stage without incident. But some hang up at this stage, too. Payment due on delivery has already been treated. But in the overwhelming majority of commercial deals, and in a substantial proportion of consumer deals, payment is strung out over some period *after* the buyer comes into possession of the goods. Breakdowns in the payment process in deals of this nature will now be considered.

If the deal is silent on payment, then payment is due on tender of delivery. UCC 2–507. C.O.D. deals and transactions calling for payment of a draft upon presentation of documents may be thought of as assimilations of cash deals.

Credit must be agreed upon. Terms vary. Extension of credit may be *secured* under Article 9. Also, a buyer may be required to sign a time draft, thus giving the seller or his transferee the advantages of having a signed negotiable instrument to sue on. See UCC 3–305.

A buyer may fail to pay because of insolvency. In this situation, the seller will, again, be interested in goods-oriented remedies. His right to recover the goods from the buyer under Article 2 is quite limited. UCC 2–702(2). What is more, this right is itself "subject to" the claims of certain parties under UCC 2–702(3).

The buyer may undertake to pay by drawing a check to seller's order. A check is a negotiable instrument if in proper form (UCC 3–104). A check orders the drawer's bank to pay the payee or to the payee's order or to bearer. The buyer-drawer's bank may refuse to honor the check, for any one of a variety of reasons but most commonly because the check over-draws the buyer's account.

Assume the check is dishonored. What action could the seller take? He could sue the buyer on the underlying obligation. See UCC 3–802(1)(b). But he could not recover from the bank, for a check is not an assignment (UCC 3–409) and a party is not liable on an instrument unless his signature appears thereon. UCC 3–401. Nor is the seller recognized as a third party beneficiary of the contract of deposit between buyer's bank and buyer. It is possible, on the right facts, that bank would be liable to seller on a tort theory. See UCC 3–419.

If the buyer was not the drawer of the check, but simply was indorsing over a check made to him to seller, seller might be a holder in due course under UCC 3–302 and, in an action against the drawer, immune from most ordinary defenses (e.g., failure of consideration, fraud) that a drawer might have against someone suing him on the instrument. See UCC 3–413 and 3–305. Similarly, the seller might be a holder in due course against an indorser and immune from such defenses. See UCC 3–414 and 3–305. To hold such a drawer or indorser liable, though, the seller would have to give notice of dishonor etc. as required by UCC 3–413(2), 3–414, and Part 5 of Article 3. There is the further possibility that the seller will be entitled to recover from a transferor of the instrument on a "warranty" theory. See UCC 3–417(2).

To recapitulate: Upon dishonor of a check given in payment for goods, the seller might have recovery against the buyer on the underlying obligation, or against the buyer and possibly other parties "on the instrument," or possibly against a transferor on a "warranty" theory.

So much for how things might go upon dishonor. What if the buyer's bank does not dishonor the check, but rather, fails to pay the proper party, i.e., the seller, or fails to pay the proper amount? Such events can occur in a variety of ways. We shall at this juncture consider only two situations. Assume the buyer draws a check to seller, but is interrupted and does not sign it as drawer. A thief steals the check, forges buyer's signature, and then takes the check to X who cashes it, giving thief the money. X presents the check to buyer's bank and buyer's bank honors it. Later, the forgery is discovered. Buyer's bank is not entitled to charge drawer's account. UCC 4-401. But drawer-buyer is not, of course, discharged from liability to seller and still must pay. Can the bank retrieve its loss from X? See UCC 3-418.

The seller may be a wrongdoer. What if the seller alters the amount of the check upward and the bank pays? Again, drawer-buyer's account is not chargeable as to the excess unless he negligently contributed to the alteration. UCC 4-401, 3-406. The seller, if he can be found, can be prosecuted. And the bank can recover against seller.

So much for a *sample* of the kinds of things that can go wrong in the payment process where a check is used.

An intermediary bank or carrier may fail to perform its obligations in the payment process. The carrier in a C.O.D. deal may fail to pick up the cash. The bank in a documentary deal may (a) fail to secure proper payment from the buyer upon tender of the documents, or (b) fail to procure buyer's signature to a time draft as agreed. See UCC 4-501, 4-502, and 4-503. The moral for the seller is dual: utilize reliable intermediaries and deal with sound buyers.

What is the plight of a buyer who puts a check in the process of payment or signs a draft or pays cash on a sight draft and thereafter immediately discovers that the goods fail to conform? Is there anything he can do, through prompt action, to "undo" what he has done? These questions will be treated in the context of specific cases.

Conclusion

This concludes what is intended only to be a *general outline* of the main stages of the unfolding sale transaction, of the *kinds* of things that can go wrong at each stage, and of the generally relevant law bearing thereon. The remaining chapters of Book Two on Sales are generally presented according to the foregoing "stage" scheme of organization. Every problem and principle considered in this chapter will be treated again, usually in depth. What the student should now have is: (1) a general overview of the modern commercial sales transaction on credit as it progresses from the agreement stage thrugh performance and aymmeent, (2) some sense of the nature of the things that can go wrong at each stage, (3) a *functionally* useful roadmap through the structure of Article 2, and (4) some idea of how Articles 3, 4, 7, and 9 may bear on sales transactions. Obviously, this section of this chapter should be studied and reviewed. Properly digested, it can equip the student to appreciate more fully what lies ahead. The ultra-conscientious student who wishes to sample other versions of the "big picture" of Article 2 might consult Peters, *Remedies for Breach of Contracts Relating to the Sale of Goods under the Uniform Commercial Code: A*

Roadmap for Article Two, 73 Yale L.J. 199 (1963); Braucher, *Sale of Goods in the Uniform Commercial Code,* 26 La.L.Rev. 192 (1966); and Corman, *The Law of Sales under the Uniform Commercial Code,* 17 Rutgers L.Rev. 14 (1962).

SECTION 3.   THE SCOPE OF ARTICLE 2

To what disputes does Article 2 apply, either directly or by analogy? Section 2–102 provides that "unless the context otherwise requires, this Article applies to transactions in goods * * *."   Article 2, however, "does not apply to any transaction which although in the form of an unconditional contract to sell or present sale is intended to operate only as a security transaction * * *."   See UCC 2–102.

Section 2–102 raises more questions than its text answers.

What, for example, are goods?   Under UCC 2–105(1) and 2–107 goods are defined as "things * * * which are movable at the time of identification to the contract for sale" and excludes "money in which the price is to be paid, investment securities * * * and things in action."   Thus, in a contract for sale, a stereo is goods but an account receivable is not.   Compare UCC 9–102(1)(b) & 9–105(1)(h).

When are goods identified to the contract?   The question is answered in UCC 2–501.   What difference does it make whether goods are identified?   Goods must be "existing and identified before any interest in them" can pass to a buyer, UCC 2–105(2), whether that interest be title, UCC 2–401, or a "special" property interest, UCC 2–501(1).   The importance of these property interests will be explored later.   Note that an attempt to sell "future" goods, i.e., goods that are neither existing nor identified, operates as a "contract to sell."

What is a "transaction" in goods?   Section 2–106(1) provides that "In this Article unless the context otherwise requires 'contract' and 'agreement' are limited to those relating to the present or future sale of goods."   Thus, where those words are used in Article 2, the transaction is a sale or a contract to sell goods.   But the word "transaction" is not clearly defined.   Could it include a lease or a bailment?   What about a gift?

When does the context "otherwise" require?   For example, if the "transaction" is other than a contract for sale, should the context be invoked to broaden or narrow the scope of Article 2?   If the use of context broadens scope, should all or part of Article 2 be applied?

Finally, if Article 2 does not directly apply, can it be extended by analogy to the dispute before the court?   The comments if not the text of the UCC support this extension, see Comment 1, UCC 1–102, but the question remains when it is proper for a court to apply legislation to a dispute concededly beyond the scope intended by the legislature.   See, generally, D. Murray, *Under the Spreading Analogy of Article 2 of the Uniform Commercial Code,* 39 Fordham L.Rev. 447 (1971).

In approaching these questions, remember that there are two kinds of Code limitations on the seemingly unlimited scope of the word "transactions." First, there are other Articles, e.g., Article 7, on bailments for storage or carriage, which may supercede the specific provisions of Article 2. Secondly, many of the specific provisions of Article 2 are themselves cast in terms of "seller" and "buyer" or limited to "contracts for sale." It would thus appear that some provisions of Article 2 might apply to a non-sales situation, e.g., UCC 2–202, 2–206, 2–207, 2–210, 2–302, & 2–316, while other provisions are, seemingly, limited to sales, e.g., UCC 2–205, 2–312, 2–313, 2–314 & 2–315.

Here are some problems and cases. As you study them, ask "What difference does it make whether Article 2 applies?"

Problem 2–1

(1) F orally agreed to sell B his wheat crop yet to be planted for $3 a bushel. Bad weather sharpened the demand for wheat. Before the crop was planted, F repudiated the agreement with B and sold the crop to C for $4 a bushel. B sued F for damages. F defended, invoking the statute of frauds. UCC 2–201. B argued that UCC 2–201 does not apply. What result? See UCC 2–102, 2–105 and 2–201.

(2) S agreed to sell B timber standing on S's land to be severed by S. S severed half of the timber but before B could haul it away, all timber, standing or severed, that B agreed to buy was destroyed by fire. B argued that the Code's risk of loss provisions applied. See UCC 2–102, 2–107(1) and 2–509. Is B correct? What change did the 1972 Official Text make in UCC 2–107?

(3) S owned a building which he contracted to sell to B who was to remove it from its concrete foundation, put it on skids, and drag it away. Before removal, S repudiated. Does Article 2 govern B's remedial rights? See UCC 2–107(1), 2–711 and 2–713. (In Foster v. Colorado Radio Corporation, 381 F.2d 222 (10th Cir.1967), the court applied the Code's remedial provisions only to the goods involved in a combined real estate and personal property sale.)

BARCO AUTO LEASING CORP. v. PSI COSMETICS, INC.

Civil Court of the City of New York, 1984.
125 Misc.2d 68, 478 N.Y.S.2d 505.

EDWARD H. LEHNER, JUDGE.

The issue in this case is whether a lessor's disclaimer of all warranties in an automobile lease is enforceable where a vehicle to be used for business purposes failed to operate properly within a short period after delivery.

This action is against the corporate lessee and the individual grantors (officers of the corporate defendant) for breach of an automobile lease, seeking to recover the accelerated unpaid rental for the remainder of the lease term plus attorneys' fees. Defendants' answer sets forth a general denial and a counterclaim for loss of business resulting from an inability to attend certain business meetings due to the defective nature of the vehicle. Before the court is plaintiff's motion for summary judgment.

On September 27, 1982 defendant PSI Cosmetics, Inc. entered into an automobile lease agreement with plaintiff for the rental of a 1982 Renault. Defendants assert in their papers that: on November 28, 1982 the engine began to smoke and the car was towed to a nearby authorized Renault dealership where it took over three months to repair what was said to be a burned out motor; during this period defendants continued to make all rental payments despite being deprived of the use of the vehicle; upon picking up the vehicle from the repair shop Mr. Golumbia was informed that after driving the vehicle an additional 300 to 600 miles, he should have it retorqued; three days after this work was done the engine again began to burn, and the automobile was rendered inoperative and towed to plaintiff's lot. As a result of this experience Golumbia allegedly missed an important business meeting, resulting in the cancellation of a $40,000 contract, thereby providing the basis for the counterclaim.

The agreement, printed on plaintiff's standardized form without any typed or handwritten riders, contains myriad procedural safeguards by which the lessor seeks to insulate itself. The lease provides that the lessor retains title and a security interest in the vehicle. There is no option to purchase granted to the lessee, who waives "counterclaim, set off, reduction, abatement, deferment or any other kind of defense because of * * * unsatisfactory performance of the vehicle or for any reason whatever. * * *" Repairs and replacement of parts are made the responsibility of the lessee. Further insulation is provided for the lessor by a disclaimer of any warranties, except for the manufacturer's standard warranty. The implied warranties of merchantability and of fitness for a particular use are conspicuously disclaimed (UCC §§ 2–316(2); 1–201(10)).

Although not raised in their answer, defendants contend in their papers that both the warranty disclaimer and the waiver of counterclaims are unconscionable and that, as to the action for the unpaid balance, plaintiff has failed to mitigate its damages in that it failed to sell the automobile.

* * *

The first issue that must be decided is whether Article 2 of the Uniform Commercial Code and the implied warranties which it provides apply to the automobile lease herein. If so, what remains to be resolved is whether the warranty disclaimer is unconscionable.

Several cases in this jurisdiction have applied UCC Article 2 to the leasing of chattels * * *.

Judicial approaches to the applicability of Article 2 to leases has been "placed along a spectrum measuring willingness to depart from the sale construct." Note, Disengaging Sale Law from the Sale Construct: A Proposal to Extend the Scope of Article 2 of the UCC, 96 Harv.L.Rev. 470, 475 (1982).

The "exclusionary" view requires strict adherence to the premise that Article 2 applies only to paradigmatic sales, thereby excluding lease transactions as well as hybrid sales-plus-services contracts from coverage.

The "analogy" approach advocates that Article 2 be applied to transactions held not to be paradigmatic sales, but only when the transactions closely resemble such sales. Murray, Under the Spreading Analogy of Article 2 of the Uniform Commercial Code, 39 Ford.L.Rev. 447, 451 (1971). This has been the approach of the courts in this state. See: *Uniflex, Inc. v. Olivetti Corp. of America*, 86 A.D.2d 538, 445 N.Y.S.2d 993 (1st Dept.1982) (leases); *Aguiar v. Harper & Row Publishers Inc.*, 114 Misc.2d 828, 832, 452 N.Y.S.2d 519 (Civ.Ct.N.Y.Co.1982) (sales-plus-services). Thus, Article 2 is said to be "attended by a penumbra or umbrella of influence in areas of contract law not specifically within the literal definition of sales under section 2–102", Lupiano, J., dissenting in *Leasco Data Processing Equipment Corp. v. Starline Overseas Corp.*, 74 Misc.2d 898, 903, 346 N.Y.S.2d 288 (App.T. 1st Dept. 1973), aff'd 45 A.D.2d 992, 360 N.Y.S.2d 199, mot. for lv. to appeal dismissed, 35 N.Y.2d 963, 365 N.Y.S.2d 179, 324 N.E.2d 557 (1974). See also Restatement, Contracts Second, § 208 (1981), Comment *a*.

Related to the analogy approach is the "policy" approach which further departs from a rigid adherence to the sales model by the selective application of particular provisions of Article 2 whenever the policies underlying such provisions are appropriate to the transaction in issue. Note, The Uniform Commercial Code as a Premise for Judicial Reasoning, 65 Colum.L.Rev. 880 (1965). See, e.g. *Dillman and Associates Inc. v. Capitol Leasing Co.*, 110 Ill.App.3d 335, 66 Ill.Dec. 39, 442 N.E.2d 311, 316 (1982); *Walter E. Heller & Co. v. Convalescent Home of the First Church of Deliverance*, 49 Ill.App.3d 213, 8 Ill.Dec. 823, 365 N.E.2d 1285 (1977).

The most inclusive approach is a more complete departure from the sales construct, focusing on the Article 2 scope provision in § 2–102 ("transactions in goods"). Although the article is replete with terms such as "sale", "seller", and "buyer" [See: Lousin, Leases, Sales and the Scope of Article 2 of the U.C.C. in Illinois, 67 Ill.B.J. 468, 470 n. 20 (1979)], such language is nowhere to be found in § 2–102. An argument for such approach, as applied to lease transactions, is that it recognizes the modern economic realities of less-than-full-title property interests, rejecting the use of location of title as a basis for resolving issues. In eschewing the prevailing analysis of the analogy approach, it is said to avoid ad hoc determinations and the intellectually questionable pigeonholing of facts so that the transaction will more closely resemble a sale. Note, 96 Harv.L.Rev. 470; Murray, supra. Thus, unlike the analogy approach, it does not perpetuate the use of the "covert tools" in decision-making which the draftspersons of the UCC had hoped to avoid. See: UCC § 2–302, Official Comment 1; Llewelyn, The Common Law Tradition 365 (1960); Ackerman, Reconstructing American Law 22 (1984).

Though eloquently advocated, Note, 96 Harv.L.Rev. 470; Murray, supra, the inclusive approach has not been accepted. While it has been noted that "transactions in goods" encompasses a far wider area of activity than a "sale", e.g. *Hertz Commercial Leasing Corp. v. Transportation Credit Clearing House,* supra, 59 Misc.2d 226, at 230, 298 N.Y.S.2d 392, this has been more in the way of judicial lip service. The cases in New York have not specifically relied on the language of the Article 2 scope provision alone, most preferring instead to analyze the underlying facts of the transaction in issue in order to determine whether it sufficiently approximates a sale. See: Annotation, What Constitutes a Transaction, a Contract for Sale, or a Sale Within the Scope of UCC Article 2, 4 A.L.R. 4th 85, 109–118 (1981).

Therefore, much as this court might prefer to indulge in the flexible and inclusive approach in determining whether the lease transaction herein is subject to the provisions of Article 2, the inquiry will be limited to an analysis of the transaction in order to determine whether or not it is analogous to a sale.

The agreement provides for rental payments over a four year period totalling $9153.12. No information has been submitted as to the fair market value of the car at the time that the lease was entered into, nor as to what portion of the price represents finance charges. The lessee is responsible for insurance coverage, repairs and replacement of parts; it bears the risk of damage or loss of the vehicle; and it agrees to indemnify the lessor for any claims. Lessor retains title to the vehicle and a security interest. The agreement is denominated "an agreement of lease only." Finally, there is no option to purchase although the agreement states that such option may be provided by a purchase rider.

In determining the answer to the similar problem of whether a lease of personal property is intended to be a security interest the UCC has adopted a simple test: "Whether a lease is intended as security is to be determined by the facts of each case; however * * * an agreement that upon compliance with the terms of the lease the lessee shall become or has the option to become the owner of the property for no additional consideration or for a nominal consideration does make the lease one intended for security." (UCC § 1–201(37)). The absence of a purchase option does not foreclose the inquiry as to whether a particular transaction is a lease or a security interest; the court merely goes on to consider any other relevant factors in order to make its determination.

The same reasoning applies in determining whether a particular lease transaction is governed by Article 2. Thus, in *Uniflex, Inc. v. Olivetti Corp. of America,* supra, where there was no option to purchase, no provision for a renewal term at a nominal rental, and lessee was required to return the equipment at the end of the initial term, the

First Department held that an issue of fact existed as to the nature of the lease since the price for the rental was far in excess of the cost of the equipment. Defendant's affirmative defense based on the four year statute of limitations for the sale of goods (UCC § 2–725) rather than the six year period for contracts (CPLR § 213 subd. 2) was therefore reinstated.

Although the court lacks information as to the value of the car, the relationship of consideration to actual value, while an important factor, is not the only one. While the lessor retains title and a security interest, the fact that the lessee is saddled with both the risks and headaches of ownership suggests that there is no significant economic difference between full title ownership and the instant lease. Therefore the court concludes that the transaction at bar is governed by the provisions of Article 2 of the UCC, and that the lease is subject to the implied warranties of merchantability and of fitness for a particular purpose (UCC §§ 2–314, 2–315) unless they have been effectively disclaimed.

The form of the disclaimer of warranties herein complies with the requirements of UCC § 2–316(2). The question remains as to whether or not such disclaimer is unconscionable, since it is nonetheless subject to judicial scrutiny under UCC § 2–302. * * * See: White and Summers, Uniform Commercial Code 475–481 (2d ed. 1980).

* * *

Since it cannot be determined whether or not this agreement is enforceable without affording both sides the "opportunity to present evidence as to its commercial setting, purpose and effect" (UCC § 2–302 subd. 2), plaintiff's motion for summary judgment on the issue of liability under the agreement is denied.

UCC § 2–302 gives the court the power to refuse to enforce an unconscionable agreement. It does not, however, provide damages to a party who enters into such agreement. *Pearson v. National Budgeting Systems Inc.*, 31 A.D.2d 792, 297 N.Y.S.2d 59 (1st Dept.1969); *Vom Lehn v. Astor Art Galleries Ltd.*, 86 Misc.2d 1, 11, 380 N.Y.S.2d 532 (Sup.Ct. Suffolk Co.1976). Accordingly, defendants' counterclaim for damages is dismissed.

Note: Leases and Article 2

Because of tax advantages, among other things, many manufacturers prefer to lease rather than to sell goods to prospective purchasers. In a variation called leveraged leasing, the manufacturer sells the goods to a bank or other enterprise who will then lease them to the prospective purchaser. There is reason to believe that leasing is the dominant transaction where equipment for use in commercial activity is involved. Thus, an article in the New York Times estimated that the amount of new leases for 1985 would approach $88 billion and concluded that "lease financing has expanded to the point where it is the most important single source of funds to support business expenditures for capital equipment." "The Boom in Lease Financing," New York Times, Business Page, March 13, 1985.

Under a "true" lease, the lessor retains title, the lessee has a possessory interest defined by the lease and the lessor has a "reversionary" interest in the goods at the conclusion of the lease. In theory, at least, the lessor under a "true" lease does not retain a security interest subject to Article 9. A leading case is In re Marhoefer Packing Co., 674 F.2d 1139 (7th Cir.1982), reprinted in Chapter 7, Section 1. Furthermore, disputes over whether the lessor makes warranties and the effect of disclaimers and remedy limitations appear to be outside of the scope of Article 2. The warranty provisions are limited to sellers and buyers in contracts for sale, see UCC 2–313, 2–314 and 2–315, although the controls upon disclaimers and agreed remedies are more open ended. See UCC 2–302, 2–316 and 2–719.

The line between a "true" lease and an installment contract for the sale of goods is frequently difficult to draw. The cases are legion. Note, however, that the line may be more important in defining the scope of Article 9 rather than the scope of Article 2. As BARCO indicates, whether the transaction is a "true" lease or a sale, most courts will find some way to apply Article 2 to resolve disputes over warranties, disclaimers and agreed remedies. Another example is Briscoe's Foodland, Inc. v. Capital Associates, Inc., 42 UCC Rep.Serv. 1234 (Miss.1986). In this limited area, at least, there is no substantial difference in outcome, whether Article 2 applies or not.

The question under Article 9, however, is whether the transaction was "intended to create a security interest" in the goods leased. UCC 9–102(1). If so, retention of "title" is, in effect, the retention of a security interest, UCC 1–201(37), which must be perfected by filing to prevail over the trustee in bankruptcy. If not, the transaction is beyond the scope of Article 9, although a lessor under a "true" lease may file a financing statement to hedge its bets. UCC 9–408.

Given the uncertainty in determining whether a "true" lease was created, this precaution is justified. As you may recall from Chapter 7, some of the relevant questions include: (1) If the "lease" contains an option to purchase the goods, is the option price nominal in relation to the market value of the goods when exercised; (2) Does the total "rent" charged exceed the original cash price of the goods; (3) Does the "lessee" bear most or all of the responsibilities of ownership; and (4) Does the "lessee" have an equity in the goods before the option is exercised? If the answer to all four questions is yes, the essence of the transaction is, in all probability, an installment sale on credit rather than a "true" lease and Article 9 applies. See UCC 1–201(37); In re Rowe, 43 B.R. 157 (E.D.Mo.1984); In re Mitchell, 44 B.R. 485 (N.D.Ala.1984).

The tax advantages, i.e., investment tax credits, accelerated depreciation and, in leveraged leasing, the deduction of interest, suggest that a careful lessor will both structure the transaction to avoid Article 9 and make the optional filing under UCC 9–408 just in case. To what extent, then, should Article 2 be extended to govern disputes arising under the "true" lease? Should the distinction between a sale and a lease be maintained and, if so, why? The issues and solutions, whether they involve a separate "uniform" personal property leasing act, currently being prepared as a proposed Article 2A to the UCC, or an amendment of Article 2 to specifically include leases are complex and beyond the scope of this book. For an excellent, preliminary analysis, see Boss, *Panacea or Nightmare?* *Leases in Article 2,* 64 B.U.L.Rev. 39 (1984).

COAKLEY & WILLIAMS, INC. v. SHATTERPROOF GLASS CORP.

United States Court of Appeals, Fourth Circuit, 1983.
706 F.2d 456.

MURNAGHAN, CIRCUIT JUDGE:

The strategy of experienced trial lawyers is to avoid, in all but the clearest case, a defense on the basis of a Federal Rules of Civil Procedure 12(b)(6) motion contending that there has been a "failure to state a claim upon which relief can be granted." At so early a stage, all factual inferences must be made in favor of the plaintiff; the facts must be viewed as the plaintiff most strongly can plead them.

Hence, the issues presented to the district court, the foundation underlying much of the law which may govern at subsequent stages of the case, will be addressed in circumstances which may well prove unduly favorable to the plaintiff. With little or no chance of prevailing, the defendant, in filing a 12(b)(6) motion, risks educating the plaintiff to aspects of the case which might otherwise be overlooked or at least not arise in circumstances so predispositive to the plaintiff's side of things.

The present case illustrates the proposition. On an appeal from a dismissal under 12(b)(6) the accepted rule is "that a complaint should not be dismissed for failure to state a claim unless it appears beyond doubt that the plaintiff can prove no set of facts in support of his claim which would entitle him to relief." *Conley v. Gibson,* 355 U.S. 41, 45–46, 78 S.Ct. 99, 101–102, 2 L.Ed.2d 80 (1957). Liberal construction in favor of the plaintiff is mandated. *Jenkins v. McKeithen,* 395 U.S. 411, 421, 89 S.Ct. 1843, 1848, 23 L.Ed.2d 404 (1969). We state as "facts" the allegations and inferences most favorable to the plaintiff.

Washington Plate Glass Company had a contract "to furnish and install aluminum and glass curtain wall and store front work"[3] on a building located in Lanham, Maryland being built by Coakley & Williams, Inc., the plaintiff. To accomplish its contractual undertaking, Washington purchased the glass spandrel required from the defendant, Shatterproof Glass Corp. Still other materials needed for the project, predominantly aluminum, it appears were acquired in part at least elsewhere.

---

3. The contract referred to "Spandrel glass to be ¼" gold reflective glass with 1" rigid insulation fastened to curtain wall members approximately 1-½" behind glass spandrel." In addition the agreement called on Washington to provide, *inter alia*: a Texas Aluminum 400 series wall system, vision glass, aluminum objects of several kinds, steel anchor clips, field fasteners, and porcelain enamel panels.

The contract price under the Coakley and Washington agreement amounted to $262,500, subsequently increased by amendment to $271,350.[4] The glass purchased by Washington from Shatterproof cost $87,715.00,[5] with the proviso that units were "to be properly marked for field installation."

The work progressed and the contract for the aluminum and glass curtain wall and storefront work was completed in March of 1974. Discoloration of the glass ensued, and Coakley complained. To remedy the situation, Washington agreed to replace the glass at no cost to Coakley, and did in fact replace a substantial portion of the glass. Shatterproof supplied the replacement glass and reimbursed Washington for the cost of re-installation, accomplished in April of 1977.

By December of 1977, the glass had again discolored, and complaints began to flow from Coakley to Washington and Shatterproof in or about December 1978. Shatterproof declined to replace a second time. On January 14, 1981, Coakley filed suit against Shatterproof in the Circuit Court for Montgomery County, Maryland alleging breach of implied warranties of merchantability and fitness for a particular purpose. Reliance was placed on certain provisions of the Maryland Uniform Commercial Code, Annotated Code of Maryland, § 1–101 et seq. Removal to the United States District Court for the District of Maryland followed, and Shatterproof sought dismissal under Fed.R.Civ. P. 12(b)(6).

A hearing on the 12(b)(6) motion followed at which Shatterproof contended (1) that the U.C.C. was inapplicable, (2) that lack of privity was fatal to the claim, and (3) that the statute of limitations had run prior to commencement of the action. We now have the case before us on appeal from an order granting the 12(b)(6) motion and dismissing the case solely on the grounds that the U.C.C. was not applicable.

Whether the U.C.C. applies turns on a question as to whether the contract between Washington and Coakley involved principally a sale of goods, on the one hand, or a provision of services, on the other. U.C.C. § 2–314 creates an implied warranty "that the *goods* shall be merchantable" to be "implied in a contract for their sale." Section 2–315 establishes an implied warranty "that the *goods* shall be fit" for a

---

4. Of that increase of $8,850, the bulk ($8,000) reflected specification of ASG Reflectoview Tru-Therm, 1 lite coated with 20 GI Gold and temperal monolithic spandrel ¼″ 20 GI Gold to match. The remaining $850 increase was due to a change in the corner configuration from aluminum panel to ¼″ Gold Reflectiveview glass.

5. The complaint is silent as to dollar amounts assignable to the additional materials. Obviously, the more they cost, the less the amount of the contract price attributable to services. We are not in-

clined to rely on statements of counsel at the time of argument in lieu of well-pleaded allegations. Counsel for Coakley asserted that the evidence would show that the cost of materials was substantially in excess of the cost of installation, *i.e.* more than $130,000. Even without counsel's arguments as a basis, it is still appropriate to recognize that such a possibility is in no way foreclosed by the allegations in the complaint. The plaintiff, at the early 12(b) (6) stage, is entitled to the benefit of the doubt.

particular purpose, "[w]here the seller at the time of contracting has reason to know [the] particular purpose." (Emphasis added.)

Consequently, unless there has been a buyer of goods, the U.C.C. warranties of merchantability and of fitness for a particular use do not apply. Furthermore, unless there has been a buyer of goods,[9] the elimination of a requirement of privity would not have been achieved.[10] Accordingly, both questions (1) as to the availability of the warranties and (2) as to the amenability of Shatterproof, who was not in privity with Coakley, to suit by Coakley, come down to whether the transactions between Washington and Coakley was a sale of goods or the provision of services.

To resolve that question, we must address ourselves to a welter of cases reaching varying results depending on the considerations deemed to predominate in each particular case.[11] It should not pass unnoticed

9. Under U.C.C. § 2–103(1)(a), the term "buyer" is defined, in unexceptional terms, as "a person who buys or contracts to buy goods."

10. *See* U.C.C. § 2–314(1)(b): "Any previous requirement of privity is abolished as between the *buyer* and the seller in any action brought by the *buyer*." (Emphasis added.) Absent compliance with § 2–314(1)(b), the lack of privity would have been fatal to Coakley's maintenance of the cause of action. *E.g., Vaccarino v. Cozzubo,* 181 Md. 614, 31 A.2d 316 (1943).

If the transaction was one for goods, Coakley was self-evidently the buyer. Shatterproof was the seller of goods in a transaction in which the intermediary, Washington, not Coakley, was the buyer. However, Washington's purpose in buying was to apply the items purchased to uses benefitting Coakley.

11. *E.g., Bonebrake v. Cox,* 499 F.2d 951, 960 (8th Cir.1974) (The appeal was from an adjudication on the merits, following a full trial, and reached the conclusion that a contract to supply and install bowling equipment dealt predominantly with goods, even though the amount of services involved was substantial. "The test for inclusion or exclusion [in or from the provisions of the U.C.C.] is not whether they are mixed, but, granting that they are mixed, whether their predominant factor, their thrust, their purpose, reasonably stated, is the rendition of service, with goods incidentally involved (*e.g.*, contract with artist for painting) or is a transaction of sale, with labor incidentally involved (*e.g.*, installation of a water heater in a bathroom). The contract before us, construed in accordance with the applicable standards of the Code, is not excluded therefrom because it is 'mixed,' * * * "); *Burton v. Artery Co., Inc.,* 279 Md. 94, 96, 114–15, 367 A.2d 935, 936, 946 (1977) (In a case where entry of summary judgment was reversed, a standard form construction contract covering "all the work and services" to complete landscaping and sodding was, bearing in mind the canon of construction opposing narrow quibbling or falsely technical construction, held to be predominantly a transaction in goods rather than services); *Ranger Construction Co. v. Dixie Floor Co.,* 433 F.Supp. 442, 444–45 (D.S.C.1977) (On summary judgment, without any contention that pertinent facts were in dispute, the court characterized the agreement for furnishing all labor and materials necessary to install resilient flooring as predominantly a service contract, made by a service corporation in customary construction contract language); *United States v. Akron Mechanical Contractors, Inc.,* 308 F.Supp. 496 (D.Md.1970) (Here the case proceeded to the summary judgment stage. The facts were stipulated, eliminating any possibility of elaboration or resolution of conflicts of fact. The case concerned a building subcontract for plumbing, heating, ventilating and air conditioning work. It was agreed by the parties that the contract covered installation of complete systems and not merely the sale of the constituent materials. The furnishing of materials being incidental to the construction activities, the then applicable Uniform Sales Act was deemed not to apply to the transactions. The real point in the case was whether title was retained or passed, and title was found to have passed. Such a conclusion would be consistent with a contract either for goods or for services, so the decision is not relevant to the problem we confront); *Snyder v. Herbert Greenbaum and Associates, Inc.,* 38 Md.App. 144, 147–48, 380 A.2d 618, 621 (1977) (Here the appeal followed a full trial on the merits. The contract was to supply and install carpeting and the underlying carpet pad in a large group of apartments. The court held:

that all were decided at summary judgment or beyond. No case involving the issue appears to have been disposed of at the Rule 12(b)(6) or demurrer stage. They emphasize, in particular, three aspects which may, or may not, constitute indicia of the nature of the contract: (1) the language of the contract,[12] (2) the nature of the business of the supplier,[13] and (3) the intrinsic worth of the materials involved.[14]

"Despite this difference in the facts which tend to favor the service purpose of the contract, application of the *Bonebrake* test leads us to conclude that the primary thrust of this contract is the *sale*, rather than the installation, of the carpet. Therefore, the Sales Title [of the Uniform Commercial Code] applies to this contract." (emphasis in original)); *Pittsburgh-Des Moines Steel Co. v. Brookhaven Manor Water Co.*, 532 F.2d 572, 580 (7th Cir.1976) (A designer, fabricator and engineer undertook to construct a one-million gallon water tank. In holding the transaction to be a sale of goods, not services, the court had this to say: "We find ample support in the cases arising under the UCC itself that the scope of coverage of 'goods' is not to be given a narrow construction but instead should be viewed as being broad in scope so as to carry out the underlying purpose of the Code of achieving uniformity in commercial transactions. * * * In the words of the UCC this was a 'movable' 'thing' 'specially manufactured.' That which PDM agreed to sell and Brookhaven agreed to buy was not services but goods as defined in the UCC." The decision came following a full trial, and affirmed an award of a judgment n.o.v.); *Van Sistine v. Tollard*, 95 Wisc.2d 678, 681–85, 291 N.W.2d 636, 638–39 (1980) (After a full exploration, in a trial, of pertinent facts, the contract was deemed to be predominantly for supply of services, not goods, relying on the supplier's self-description as a contractor, the fact that over half of the monetary value was attributable to labor, with some materials furnished by the buyer. The decision was influenced by the court's disenchantment with a U.C.C. provision making a check in payment marked "paid in full" insufficient to its stated purpose where the payee cashed the instrument with an "under protest and without prejudice" endorsement); *Meyers v. Henderson Construction Co.*, 147 N.J.Super. 77, 82–83, 370 A.2d 547, 550 (1977) (A contract to furnish labor, materials (including glass purchased and mounted), tools and equipment for installation of overhead doors was, following a hearing on summary judgment, found to be predominantly for goods, not services, and so covered by the U.C.C.); *Air Heaters, Inc. v. Johnson Electric, Inc.*, 258 N.W.2d 649, 652 (N.D.1977) (On the basis of facts established in a full scale

trial on the merits, a contract to design, manufacture, and install a complete electrical distribution system was scrutinized to determine whether it was predominantly for goods or predominantly for services. The court concluded that the plaintiff, the party on whom the burden lay to establish that the agreement was predominantly for a sale of goods simply failed to meet the burden at trial. "In this case we are not able to determine from the record whether the predominant factor and thrust of this contract is the rendition of services, or a transaction of sale. The record does not include enough factual data concerning this particular contract for us to make that determination." The import of the decision was largely eradicated by a conclusion that, even outside the U.C.C., North Dakota law afforded a right to recover for breach of an implied warranty of fitness. Hence the outcome of the case was unaffected by the "goods or services" discussion); *Cork Plumbing Co., Inc. v. Martin Bloom Associates, Inc.*, 573 S.W.2d 947, 950, 958 (Mo.App.1978) (A judgment in the trial court, entered following a full-scale trial, was affirmed. Contracts were held to be predominantly for services which called for (a) completion of plumbing and sewer work in 176 apartment units and (b) plumbing work to be done on a clubhouse in the apartment complex. The character of the agreements as "construction contracts" appears to have influenced the decision.)

12. *Bonebrake v. Cox, supra*, 499 F.2d at 958 ("The language thus employed is that peculiar to goods, not services. It speaks of 'equipment,' and of lanes free from 'defects in workmanship and materials.' The rendition of services does not comport with such terminology."); *Ranger Construction Co. v. Dixie Floor Co., supra*, 433 F.Supp. at 445 ("It is interesting to note that throughout the contract the defendant, Dixie Floor Co., Inc., is not referred to as a materialman but rather as a subcontractor.").

13. *Ranger Construction Co. v. Dixie Floor Co., supra*, 433 F.Supp. at 445 ("The defendant's responses to interrogatories indicated that the defendant was essentially a service corporation engaged in the installation and construction of flooring.").

14. *Snyder v. Herbert Greenbaum & Associates, Inc., supra*, 38 Md.App. at 156–59,

A distillation of the cases outlined in the foregoing notes 11–14 produces an inescapable conclusion that, on the facts in their present pro-plaintiff posture,[15] a reasonable viewing of them would permit a factfinder to conclude that the contract between Washington and Coakley predominantly concerned a sale of goods, and consequently was governed by the U.C.C. A Rule 12(b)(6) motion simply cannot serve to dispose of the case.

As to the first of the emphasized aspects, the contract between Washington and Coakley speaks in terms of furnishing and installing a wall and performing storefront work. Clearly, at the very outset of performance Washington had the responsibility to bring to the affected premises the materials which ultimately would form the glass curtain wall and store front. The U.C.C. in § 2–105 defines "goods" as "*all* things (including specially manufactured goods) which are movable at the time of identification to the contract for sale other than the money in which the price is to be paid, investment securities (Title 8) and things in action." (Emphasis added.) That at least creates an uncertainty to be resolved only by a full factual presentation to determine whether the nature of the Washington business was predominantly the provision of goods or the furnishing of services. The fact that Coakley was a building contractor specializing in construction is not sufficient to provide a completely definitive answer. While often, and perhaps customarily, a contractor is engaged in the provision of services, the scope of a contractor's work is not necessarily monolithic and, in the present circumstances, it becomes a question of unresolved fact whether Coakley, for the purposes of the single relationship to which we are restricted, was a buyer of goods.

In this connection, it is not irrelevant that Coakley has alleged that the purchases by Washington from Shatterproof included anchor clips and field fasteners. At the early stage at which we find ourselves, the allegation requires us to indulge the inference urged by counsel for Coakley that putting the glass in place was a simple snap-on process requiring little expenditure of time or labor. One can readily imagine, without the advantage of specificity deriving from a full trial on the merits, that the contract largely contemplated the provision of precast panels as goods, without the installation being nearly so extensive or significant as the supplying of the glass itself.

The fact that the contract does not follow a standard, routine or regularized form, coupled with the plaintiff's contention that standard form contracts are virtually universal for construction (i.e., generally, service) contracts, operates to leave open the possibility of a finding

380 A.2d at 626–27 (The case recognizes that the U.C.C. contemplated as a seller of goods one who obtains the component parts for special assembly, yet who, upon breach of the other party, is restricted to realization of junk value. It reached its decision that a sale of goods, not a provision of services, was involved though neither party "in any sense proved the amount of the resale proceeds of the carpet.").

15. We, of course, have no way of knowing what will actually be developed when the parties are put to their respective proofs.

that the contract is more one for goods than would be the customary construction contract.

Turning to the second point, the nature of Washington's business, the fact that Washington was a dealer and not a manufacturer does not have any particularly dispositive significance. Many retailers of goods function in the role of middleman. Shatterproof sold Washington materials in a transaction which unquestionably, on the sparse record before us at the preliminary stage at which we find ourselves, was a sale of goods, and the question comes down essentially to whether those materials or the services which Washington also provided under its contract with Coakley predominated. Without full consideration of as yet unascertained facts that question is simply not ripe for resolution. It is one of fact, not law; at least it is at this early stage.

Third, the complaint affords no realistic, and certainly no dispositive, information as to the value of the spandrels et al. in case of breakup into the component parts of the glass curtain wall and store front work. That can only be determined by further development of the record, and is, in all events, but one of several factors which must be evaluated in conjunction with all the others in resolving the ultimate factual issue: did Washington and Coakley deal primarily with goods or services?

Accordingly, Coakley has alleged enough to survive a motion to dismiss under Fed.R.Civ.P. 12(b)(6). Nor, at the other extreme, has it alleged too much, permitting sure ascertainment that services, not goods, were the gravamen of the transaction. Coakley should, therefore, be permitted to show, unless the statute of limitations bars recovery, that it was a buyer of goods and, therefore, entitled to proceed under the U.C.C. provisions.[17]

* * *

[The court held that the claim was not barred under the statute of limitations, UCC 2–725.]

Accordingly, the judgment is reversed and the case remanded for further proceedings not inconsistent with this opinion.

17. Following argument on January 13, 1983 of the instant case, the Maryland Court of Appeals, on January 25, 1983, handed down its decision in *Anthony Pools, a Division of Anthony Industries, Inc. v. Sheehan,* 295 Md. 285, 455 A.2d 434 (1983). That case involves the somewhat different, although related, question of whether, in the case of a hybrid goods and services transaction, a disclaimer of an implied warranty of merchantability was unenforceable, as to the goods component of a contract predominantly for services, because such disclaimers are not legally permitted where there is a sale of consumer goods. U.C.C. § 2–316.1. The disclaimer was held unenforceable on the grounds that consumer goods retained their status as goods despite the fact that the contract was predominantly for services. The all or nothing contention that, the contract being predominantly one for services, none of the items covered by it should be treated as goods was rejected.

The Maryland Court of Appeals expressly reserved judgment as to whether U.C.C. § 2–316.1's ban on implied warranty disclaimers would also extend to consumer goods used up in the course of rendering the consumer service. At the very least, the result in *Anthony Pools* does nothing to question the soundness of the conclusion we have reached.

Reversed and remanded.

[Some footnotes omitted.]

Notes

1. Suppose, after trial, that the court determined that services rather than goods predominated in the transaction. Suppose, also, that the glass supplied by the defendant was unmerchantable, i.e., unfit for the "ordinary purposes for which such goods are used." UCC 2–314(2)(c). Should the plaintiff be entitled to claim breach of the implied warranty of merchantability imposed by UCC 2–314? Or is the plaintiff relegated to the law of service contracts outside of the UCC, where negligence rather than breach of warranty is the exclusive theory of liability?

2. The either-or effect of the "predominate purpose" test was rejected in Anthony Pools v. Sheehan, 295 Md. 285, 455 A.2d 434 (1983), cited by the principal case in footnote 17. Where services predominate, if the goods supplied (a diving board) were unmerchantable and caused loss (personal injuries), Article 2 could be applied both to impose an implied warranty of merchantability and to determine whether a clause purporting to disclaim the implied warranty of merchantability was enforceable. The court stressed that the goods had to be supplied under a commercial transaction, rather than a contract for professional services, and must "retain their character * * * after completion of the performance promised * * *" Note, however, that the goods were supplied to a consumer who suffered personal injuries. Should that make a difference in the analysis?

3. Is a contract to supply a computer software system a contract for the sale of goods or a contract for services? In RRX Industries, Inc. v. Lab-Con, Inc., 772 F.2d 543 (9th Cir.1985), Lab-Con agreed to supply RRX with a software system for use in its medical laboratories and to correct any malfunctions or "bugs" that arose in the system. "Bugs" appeared soon after installation and Lab-Con, even after upgrading the system, was unable to remove them. RRX claimed consequential damages under the UCC and Lab-Con argued that because the contract was for services the UCC did not apply. The court disagreed:

> In determining whether a contract is one of sale or to provide services we look to the essence of the agreement. * * * When a sale predominates, incidental services provided do not alter the basic transaction. * * * Because software packages vary depending on the needs of the individual consumer, we apply a case-by-case analysis.
>
> * * *
>
> Here, the sales aspect of the transaction predominates. The employee training, repair services, and system upgrading were incidental to sale of the software package and did not defeat characterization of the system as a good. 772 F.2d at 546.

Problem 2–2

A Law Reform Commission, considering possible amendments to Article 2 of the UCC, has proposed the following revision in the scope of Article 2. What do you think about it at this early stage of the course? See Note,

Disengaging Sales Law From the Sale Construct: A Proposal to Extend the Scope of Article 2 of the UCC, 96 Harv.L.Rev. 470 (1982) (title passage is an inadequate tool for resolving sales disputes).

Section 2–102. Scope; Certain Security and Other Transactions Excluded From This Article; Extension by Analogy.

1. This Act applies to every contract for the sale of goods.

2. This Act does not apply to any transaction that is intended to operate only as a secured transaction, whether or not it is in the form of an unconditional contract for sale.

3. Whether or not a contract in the form of a lease of goods, bailment, consignment or otherwise is a contract for sale depends on the intention of the parties, the substantial effect of the contract and all the other surrounding circumstances.

4. Any of the provisions of this Act, if relevant in principle and appropriate in the circumstances, may be applied by analogy to a transaction respecting goods other than a contract of sale, such as a lease of goods or a contract for the supply of labor and materials.

SECTION 4. SOME BASIC CONCEPTS IN ARTICLE 2

A. *Introduction*

The present form of Article 2, Sales, emerged from a careful and critical review of the 1952 Official Text by the New York Law Revision Commission in 1953–54, and was promulgated in the 1958 Official Text of the Uniform Commercial Code. The principal draftsperson in the early drafts of Article 2 and its predecessor (the Revised Uniform Sales Act), and its most effective champion until his death in 1962, was Professor Karl N. Llewellyn. (The drafts of Llewellyn's efforts from 1940–44 to revise the Uniform Sales Act are reproduced in E. Kelly, Uniform Commercial Code Drafts (1984), Vols. I and II. Work under the joint auspices of the National Conference of Commissioners on Uniform State Laws and the American Law Institute began on January 1, 1945. See Schnader, *A Short History of the Preparation and Enactment of the Uniform Commercial Code,* 22 U.Miami L.Rev. 1, 5 (1967).) In a real sense, Article 2 is "Karl's Kode:" His ideas and approach to commercial law, even though imperfectly achieved, tended to dominate the final product. For useful discussion, see W. Twining, Karl Llewellyn and the Realist Movement (1973). See also Wiseman, *The Limits of Vision: Karl Llewellyn and the Merchant Rules,* 100 Harv.L.Rev. 465 (1987). Compare Casebeer, *Escape from Liberalism: Fact and Value in Karl Llewellyn,* 1977 Duke L.J. 671 with Danzig, *A Comment on the Jurisprudence of the Uniform Commercial Code,* 27 Stan.L.Rev. 621 (1975). See also, Williams, *Book Review,* 97 Harv.L.Rev. 1495 (1984).

According to Richard Danzig, Llewellyn did not regard law as a "body of deduced rules, or as an instrument chosen by social planners from among a universe of alternatives." Rather, he "saw law as an articulation and regularization * * * of a generally recognized and almost indisputably right rule . . . inherent in, but very possibly obscured by, existing patterns of relationships." For him, law was "immanent" or "imbedded" in any situation and it was the task of the law authority, usually a judge, to discover it. Under this view, the task of the legislature is to prescribe standards, such as commercial reasonableness, on how to find the law and leave the task of particularization, i.e., finding the "situation sense," to the court. In the rejection of rules and the search for standards which responded to the behavior patterns of the disputants in context, Llewellyn was clearly in step with Arthur L. Corbin and other so-called "Realists." See Speidel, *Restatement Second: Omitted Terms and Contract Method,* 67 Cornell L.Rev. 785, 786–92 (1982).

Article 2 was also influenced by the nature of the problems and actors with which it deals. According to Danzig: "Commercial law is at the margin of public law. It deals with a subcommunity ('merchants'), whose members occupy a status position distinct from society at large, whose disputes are often resolved by informal negotiation or in private forums, whose relationships tend to continue over time rather than ending with the culmination of single transactions, and whose primary rules derive from a sense of fairness wide-spread—if imprecisely defined—within the commercial community.

B. Agreement, Not Promise, as the Foundation Stone

Students of commercial law have already learned a great deal about the concept of promise in the first year course in contracts. The Restatement (Second) of Contracts even defines a contract as "a promise or a set of promises for the breach of which the law provides a remedy, or the performance of which the law in some way recognizes as a duty." It is true that the analysis of commercial arrangements in terms of the concept of promise fits the facts of many contracts, including many involving the sale of goods. But the analysis fails to fit many other contracts, very felicitously, including some for the sale of goods, thus suggesting that there must be a more fundamental concept. That concept, as we will see, is the concept of agreement, and it is this that is the true foundation stone of Article Two.

Here we will offer some illustrative examples of features of consensual arrangements for the sale of goods that are more felicitously analyzable in terms of agreement rather than the exchange of promises as such. First, in the law of sales many express warranties arise by virtue of the seller's "affirmations of fact," not promises as such. UCC 2–312 expressly so states. Second, many other obligations in the law of sales arise in particular cases by virtue of tacit assumptions, custom, trade usage, course of dealing and course of performance. In such instances, there is rarely anything resembling an express promise, and the concept of an implied in fact promise seldom fits the facts more than fictionally. Third, many sale of goods transactions are not discrete, "one-shot," affairs but occur over time within longer term relationships. Many features of these relationships are not the subject of express promises (or even implied ones) yet they generate important obligations, obligations themselves shored up by the code doctrine of good faith and fair dealing to which we will soon turn. The broad structures of such relationships often pre-exist so that when the parties enter into a particular relation general obligations attendant upon such a relation attach. Finally, countless discrete, "one-shot," exchanges take place each day in which no promises are made on either side yet the law imposes obligations on both parties. "Over the counter" sales and supermarket sales are only the most familiar of these. In all of the foregoing examples, the most fundamental concept at work is that of agreement, not promise (and even agreement does not account for everything). The Code itself recognizes the primacy of agreement. In Article One, agreement and contract are defined in these terms:

1-201   General Definitions

(3) "Agreement" means the bargain of the parties in fact as found in their language or by implication from other circumstances including course of dealing or usage of trade or course of performance as provided in this Act (Sections 1-205 and 2-208). Whether an agreement has legal consequences is determined by the provisions of this Act, if applicable; otherwise by the law of contracts (Section 1-103). (Compare "Contract").

(11) "Contract" means the total legal obligation which results from the parties' agreement as affected by this Act and any other applicable rules of law. (Compare "Agreement.")

K is the whole-arising from Agreements

C. The Article Two "Merchant" Concept

Article Two includes fourteen provisions in which the term "merchant" appears. UCC 2-104(1) defines merchant to mean:

A person who deals in goods of the kind or otherwise by his occupation holds himself out as having knowledge or skill peculiar to the practices or goods involved in the transaction or to whom such knowledge or skill may be attributed by his employment of an agent or broker or other intermediary who by his occupation holds himself out as having such knowledge or skill.

The fourteen sections which employ the term "Merchant" are: 2-103(1)(b) (good faith); 2-201(2) (statute of frauds); 2-205 (firm offer); 2-207 ("battle of the forms"); 2-209(2) (modification, rescission and waiver); 2-312(3) (warranty of title); 2-314(1) (implied warranty of merchantability); 2-327(1)(c) (sale on approval); 2-402(2) (rights of creditors of sellers); 2-403(2) (entrusting); 2-509(3) (risk of loss); 2-603(1) (rightful rejection); 2-605(1)(b) (waiver of buyer's objections); and 2-609(2) (adequate assurance of performance).

Section 2-314 imposing an implied warranty of merchantability on merchants, and section 2-201 on the statute of frauds seem to have generated the most litigation over who qualifies as a merchant.

LOEB & COMPANY, INC. v. SCHREINER
Supreme Court of Alabama, 1975.
294 Ala. 722, 321 So.2d 199.

ALMON, JUSTICE.

This is an appeal from a judgment of the Circuit Court of Lowndes County. The court decreed that the plaintiff and the defendant entered into an oral contract for the purchase and sale of one hundred fifty bales of cotton but that the contract was unenforceable under the Alabama Uniform Commercial Code because the defendant was not a "merchant" as that term is used and defined.

Court says Δ was not a merchant

The plaintiff-appellant, Loeb and Company, Inc., is engaged in the marketing of raw cotton. James L. Loeb of Montgomery is President of the company and has bought cotton from the defendant-appellee, Charles Schreiner, for the past four or five years. Charles Schreiner is a cotton farmer and has been engaged in the farming of cotton and other crops since 1963.

Δ

Following a conversation on the 18th or 20th of April, 1973, with regard to the price paid by appellant company to Marlowe Reese, a neighbor of appellee, appellee telephoned appellant on April 23 and asked if the price paid Reese was available to him. He received from the president of appellant company a statement that he would pay appellee the same price. Appellant maintained at trial that appellee orally contracted with him during the telephone conversation to sell appellant company one hundred fifty bales of cotton. Appellee admitted that there were negotiations but maintained that he never agreed to sell the one hundred fifty bales.

π wants to enforce oral agreement for sale of cotton

π

Schreiner asked Co. if he could get same price as his neighbor. Pres. of Co. said yes.

The date, parties, terms and conditions of the alleged contract to sell were confirmed in the records of appellant company on April 23, 1973, and two copies of a confirming statement were mailed to appellee. Appellee received the confirming statement but neither signed it nor returned it, nor in any manner took exception to it until four months later when appellant telephoned him inquiring the whereabouts of the statement. In the meanwhile the price of raw cotton had risen from the price in the alleged contract of 37¼ cents to the middle 80 cents.

When appellant company telephoned appellee and inquired about the confirming statement, appellee said that he did not intend to sign and return it and told appellant to discuss the matter with his attorney.

The trial court found that there was an oral contract but that the contract was unenforceable under the Alabama Uniform Commercial Code because the appellee was not a merchant as that term is used in Tit. 7A, §§ 2–104 and 2–201, Code of Alabama, 1940, Recompiled 1958.

Court found there was a K, but it was not enforceable as Δ was not a "merchant"

Tit. 7A, § 2–201 is the section which sets out the statute of frauds for Article 2 of the Uniform Commercial Code. It governs all contracts for the sale of "goods." Cotton is included within the definition of "goods" as defined by the Code. *Cox v. Cox,* 292 Ala. 106, 289 So.2d 609 (1974). § 2–201 provides in pertinent part as follows:

> "Except as otherwise provided in this section a contract for the sale of goods for the price of $500 or more is not enforceable by way of action or defense unless there is some writing sufficient to indicate that a contract for sale has been made between the parties and signed by the party against whom enforcement is sought or by his authorized agent or broker. A writing is not insufficient because it omits or incorrectly states a term agreed upon but the contract is not enforceable under this paragraph beyond the quantity of goods shown in such writing.

> "(2) *Between merchants* if within a reasonable time a writing in confirmation of the contract and sufficient against the sender is received and the party receiving it has reason to know its contents, it satisfies the requirements of subsection (1) against such party unless written notice of objection to its contents is given within ten days after it is received." (Emphasis added).

Appellant contends that the trial court erred in finding that the appellee cotton farmer was not a merchant and that § 2–201(2) was not applicable. If appellee is not a "merchant," § 2–201 would act as a bar to the enforcement of the contract in question. However, if appellee is a "merchant," he would be liable on the contract because he did not within ten days give notice of objection to appellant's confirming statement. Tit. 7A, § 2–104(1) defines "merchant" as follows:

> "(1) 'Merchant' means a person who deals in goods of the kind or otherwise by his occupation holds himself out as having knowledge or skill peculiar to the practices or goods involved in the transaction or to whom such knowledge or skill may be attributed by his employment of an agent or broker or other intermediary who by his occupation holds himself out as having such knowledge or skill."

Only a few courts have considered the question of whether a farmer is a "merchant." In *Cook Grains v. Fallis,* 239 Ark. 962, 395 S.W.2d 555 (1965), the Arkansas Supreme Court held that a soybean farmer was not a merchant when he was merely trying to sell the commodities he had raised. The court stated that there was not

> "* * * a scintilla of evidence in the record, or proffered as evidence, that appellee is a dealer in goods of the kind or by his occupation holds himself out as having knowledge or a skill peculiar to the practices of goods involved in the transaction, and no such knowledge or skill can be attributed to him." 239 Ark. at 964, 395 S.W.2d at 556.

In *Oloffson v. Coomer,* 11 Ill.App.3d 918, 296 N.E.2d 871 (1973), the Third Division of the Appellate Court of Illinois stated in dictum that a farmer in the business of growing grain was not a "merchant" with respect to the merchandising of grain. However, in *Campbell v. Yokel,*

20 Ill.App.3d 702, 313 N.E.2d 628 (1974), the Fifth District of the Appellate Court of Illinois dealt with a case that involved an action against some soybean farmers on an alleged breach of an oral contract for the sale of soybeans. The court held that the soybean farmers, who had grown and sold soybeans for several years were "merchants" when selling crops and were therefore barred by § 2–201(2) from asserting the statute of frauds as a defense.

One court has suggested that whether or not a farmer is a "merchant" within the meaning of § 2–104 should turn upon whether or not he has engaged in a particular type of sale in the past. In *Fear Ranches, Inc. v. Berry,* 470 F.2d 905 (10th Cir.1972), a breach of warranty case, the court held that where the defendant cattle farmers made a sale to a non-meatpacker for resale when they had previously sold all of their cattle to meatpackers, they were not "merchants" with respect to the sale to the non-meatpacker. The court felt that the sale of cattle for resale was a sale of a different type of goods and made up a different type of business than the sale of cattle to meat-packers.

We hold that in the instant case the appellee was not a "merchant" within the meaning of § 2–104. We do not think the framers of the Uniform Commercial Code contemplated that a farmer should be included among those considered to be "merchants."

In order for a farmer to be included within the § 2–104 definition of "merchants," he must do one of the following:

1. deal in goods of the kind;

2. *by his occupation* hold himself out as having knowledge or skill peculiar to the practices or goods involved in the transaction; or

3. employ an agent or broker or other intermediary who by his occupation holds himself out as having such knowledge or skill.

Since the farmer in the instant case did not qualify as a merchant under 3 above, he would have to qualify under 1 or 2. It is not sufficient under 2 that one hold himself out as having knowledge or skill peculiar to the practices or goods involved, he must *by his occupation* so hold himself out. Accordingly, a person cannot be considered a "merchant" simply because he is a braggart or has a high opinion of his knowledge in a particular area. We conclude that a farmer does not solely *by his occupation* hold himself out as being a professional cotton merchant.

The remaining thing which a farmer might do to be considered a merchant is to become a dealer in goods. Although there was evidence which indicated that the appellee here had a good deal of knowledge, this is not the test. There is not one shred of evidence that appellee ever sold anyone's cotton but his own. He was nothing more than an astute farmer selling his own product. We do not think this was sufficient to make him a dealer in goods.

The official comment to § 2–104 states in part as follows:

"This Article assumes that transactions between *professionals* in a given field require special and clear rules which may not apply to a *casual or inexperienced seller or buyer*. It thus adopts a policy of expressly stating rules applicable 'between merchants' and 'as against a merchant', wherever they are needed instead of making them depend upon the circumstances of each case as in the statutes cited above. This section lays the foundation of this policy by defining those who are to be regarded as professionals or 'merchants' and by stating when a transaction is deemed to be 'between merchants'." (Emphasis added).

Although a farmer might sell his cotton every year, we do not think that this should take him out of the category of a "casual seller" and place him in the category with "professionals."

[handwritten margin note: If otherwise how many years would it take?!]

If indeed the statute of frauds has, as claimed, permitted an injustice, it is a matter which addresses itself to the legislature.

The judgment is due to be and is hereby

Affirmed.

HEFLIN, C.J., and MERRILL, MADDOX, FAULKNER, JONES, SHORES and EMBRY, JJ., concur.

HILLINGER, THE ARTICLE TWO MERCHANT RULES: KARL LLEWELLYN'S ATTEMPT TO ACHIEVE THE GOOD, THE TRUE, THE BEAUTIFUL IN COMMERCIAL LAW 73 Geo.L.J. 1141, 1146–1148, 1174, 1175, 1176–1180 (1985).

We are experiencing a merchant muddle that stems from a fundamental misunderstanding about the nature and purpose of the Article 2 merchant rules. They are not what we thought they were. Their intended purpose and function suggest a different approach both to the merchant rules themselves and to their application to nonmerchants.

This article demonstrates that the Article 2 merchant rules were never intended to codify merchant custom and trade usage. Llewellyn, the principal draftsman of Article 2, invented the merchant rules. The necessity that mothered his invention was his passionate desire to make "commercial law and practice clear, sane, *and safe*." The merchant rules are statutory expressions of Llewellyn's drafting creed that "[s]impler, clearer, and better adjusted rules, built to make sense and to protect good faith, make for more foreseeable and more satisfactory results both in court and out." Llewellyn sculpted the merchant rules to bring "the beautiful" to commercial law and commercial practice.[28] To Llewellyn's eye, legal beauty lay in functional rules—rules that could guide businessmen in conducting their business affairs, rules that could assist them in their "trouble shooting, trouble evasion and forward planning." Llewellyn drafted the merchant rules to apprise businessmen, attorneys, and courts of the peculiar obligations of businessmen. Their clarity, rationality and certainty in application would protect decent businessmen and promote sound, reasonable, and decent business practices.

The idea of separate merchant rules for businessmen sprang from Llewellyn's pragmatism. Llewellyn believed businessmen needed rules on which they could rely, rules that would produce predictable results. The existence of predictable rules would make commercial activity more rational and would thereby encourage its expansion. Moreover, Llewellyn believed the policies and considerations involved in a mercantile situation differed from those in a nonmercantile situation, and that a unitary approach to sales rules would inevitably muddle policies and rationales. This result would jeopardize the predictability he so wanted to create for businessmen. Under a single rule, governing both businessmen and nonbusinessmen, a court trying to protect Aunt Tilly might manipulate, distort, or misconstrue the rule, making uncertain its later interpretation or application to Tilly, Inc. Rules fashioned specifically for a commercial setting, and insulated from nonmercantile considerations, would thus protect the rules' predictability for businessmen. One set of sales rules for businessmen and another for Aunt Tilly would eliminate the possibility of undermining the commercial rule to do justice to Aunt Tilly.

Yet Llewellyn did not intend to preclude judicial application of the merchant rules to nonmerchants in every instance. If application to a nonmerchant would not jeopardize the rule's certainty and predictability, Llewellyn wanted the courts to apply the merchant rule to nonmerchants. Indeed, a provision in the 1949 draft expressly so provided.

How would we know? There would surely be ambiguity!!

* * *

In concluding that good commercial law and practice required special commercial rules, Llewellyn was not concluding that the commercial rules could have no application to a noncommercial context. Section 1–102(3) of the 1949 draft makes that clear: "A provision of this Act which is stated to be applicable 'between merchants' or otherwise to be of limited application need not be so limited when the circumstances and underlying reasons justify extending its application."

Later omitted

* * *

Had the 1949 provision authorizing liberal application of the merchant rules to nonmerchants survived and been enacted, the question of merchant status would not have assumed its current importance. Courts could have sidestepped many status questions by concluding that merchant status was ultimately irrelevant, and the reasons underlying the merchant rule—reasonableness, soundness, and decency—would justify its application to the nonmerchant. Unfortunately, the drafters finally bowed to merchant critics and eliminated section 1–102(3), apparently as a political concession to save the embattled Article 2 merchant distinction itself.

* * *

The farmer cases involving statute of frauds defenses all involve a similar plot. Farmer periodically calls Grain Elevator Company to check on current grain prices. During one call Farmer likes what he hears and the parties conclude a contract on the phone, the grain to be delivered some months later. Shortly after the oral deal, Grain Elevator Company prepares and sends a written confirmation of the phone deal to farmer. Farmer does not respond. Grain Elevator Company then contracts to sell Farmer's grain to a third party. At the time scheduled for delivery, the price of grain has skyrocketed, and not surprisingly, Farmer no longer likes the contract price. He sells his grain to someone else at the higher market price. Farmer's breach forces Grain Elevator Company to cover at the current market price to meet its contractual obligations. It ultimately sues Farmer to recover its loss.

Farmer appears in court outfitted in bib overalls and cowboy boots that cast off a faint perfume of manure. Farmer inevitably makes two responses to Grain Elevator Company's contract action: (1) "We never made a contract" and, (2) "Even if we did, I am a farmer, not a merchant, and therefore, the contract is unenforceable because I never signed anything." Grain Elevator Company always responds that Farmer is a merchant and the statute is therefore satisfied because Farmer never responded to its confirmation letter. As Article 2 is presently understood, the result of the litigation turns on the issue of the farmer's status.

In treating this question, some courts have concluded that the terms "farmer" and "merchant" are mutually exclusive: farmers are "tillers of the soil," while merchants are "traders in goods." The evidence indicates Llewellyn did not consider most farmers to be merchants for purposes of the statute of frauds. In a comment to an early draft, Llewellyn discussed the apple farmer who marketed three to six hundred bushels a year. Although such a farmer would give the implied warranty of merchantability (because he would qualify as a "goods" merchant), he would not be subject to section 2–207's rule that additional minor terms stated in a confirmation became part of the parties' contract (a "practices" merchant provision), because invocation of section 2–207(2)

> depends upon the established practice of regular merchants to attend and reply promptly to correspondence. No such practice exists among small farmers * * * his occupation does not hold him out as familiar with any practice "of the kind involved" or as having the general knowledge or skill in that aspect of a person in trade.

In defending the inapplicability of the statute of frauds to transactions under five hundred dollars, Llewellyn discussed farmers and merchants separately, noting that

> in regard to such transactions, a merchant is protected by his normal procedure of reducing transactions to written sales slip or

confirmation; a farmer is protected by his standing in the community.

In some of his articles, Llewellyn distinguished the horse and haystack from "wares-in-commerce," arguing the commercial sales rules that had evolved from horse and haystack deals were unsuited for the new world of modern commerce. One may surmise that Llewellyn intended to leave farmers with their haystack law and to give businessmen new "wares-in-commerce" law. This theory would explain why Llewellyn repeatedly distinguished merchants from farmers and housewives in his testimony before the New York Law Revision hearings.

Although Llewellyn probably would have agreed that a farmer is not an Article 2 "practices" merchant, he would have been upset with the consequences that flow from this conclusion. Courts that have held the farmer not to be a merchant have applied section 2–201(1) (the nonmerchant rule) and refused to enforce the contract. Llewellyn would have wanted the courts to apply section 2–201(2)'s confirmation letter exception despite the farmer's nonmerchant status, because the purpose and policies behind the merchant exception would justify such application. Llewellyn designed section 2–201(2) to accommodate oral deals that the decent businessman confirmed promptly in accordance with sound business practice. He intended section 2–201(2) to serve as a bulwark against one party's indecent speculation at the expense of the other. Here, Farmer's questionable conduct as contrasted with Grain Elevator Company's sound and good business practice of sending out a confirmation letter would justify the application of section 2–201(2). No harm could come to the merchant rule by invoking it in that situation and its application would produce a just and satisfactory result.

Other courts, confronted with the farmer situation, have concluded the farmer is a merchant; one court emphasized that the statutory definition, rather than common sense, controlled. Although these courts have interpreted the merchant definition to include those whom Llewellyn probably did not intend to include, their "misconstruction" enabled them to achieve the result Llewellyn would have wanted, through application of the merchant rule. In short, had 1–102(3) been enacted, courts could have dismissed many "Who is a merchant?" questions with a glib "Who cares?" If the policy fits, the merchant rule should govern. Given the merchant rules' inherent reasonableness, the policy would fit more often than not.

The loss of section 1–102(3) and a basic misunderstanding about the underlying purpose of the Article 2 merchant rules have created a flaw in Article 2's bifurcated system. Courts assume the existence of an Article 2 barrier, which precludes application of the merchant rules to situations involving only one merchant or only nonmerchants. Courts either respect the barrier, often reaching poor results, or surmount it by various means to reach the proper results. Those who are unquestionably nonmerchants suffer most. They can never find refuge in the

Article 2 merchant rules. This situation is especially ridiculous because there does not appear to be anything intrinsically commercial about most of the Article 2 merchant rules. The merchant rules for firm offers, the statute of frauds, risk of loss, and so on, are edicts issuing forth from the temple of reason, not the marketplace. The merchant rules embody good sense, not just good commercial sense.

Compared with the nonmerchant rules, the merchant rules seem enlightened. The merchant rules impose only the mildest, most modest of responsibilities, such as the duty to open one's mail and respond to it promptly. The merchant's failure to abide by these duties often results in equally innocuous consequences. For example, the businessman who fails to reply to a confirmation letter simply loses his statute of frauds defense against contract enforcement. The businessman who fails to read or respond to the offeree's letter of acceptance is bound by *minor* additional contract terms contained in the acceptance. These are rules which, in most instances, could apply to the common man with little fear of judicial distortion or doctrinal confusion. In fact, it may be said that what's good for businessmen in Article 2 is good for the rest of us. Reprinted from Volume 73 of the Georgetown Law Journal by permission of Professor Ingrid M. Hillinger, © 1985.

D. *Power to Contract Out of Article Two*

It is one thing for a lawyer and his client to find themselves properly within Article Two of the Code. It is quite another for the relevant Code provisions therein to be controlling in the face of contrary agreement of the parties. For many are not. Article Two, like prior law, grants broad freedom of contract. Scope for the lawyer's role as planner is therefore very great. And, as Llewellyn once stressed:

> "[I]n the normal modern case the first measure of the parties' rights is * * * the contract * * *, only an analysis which stresses the contract first and hammers on the necessity of keeping it in mind as the framework of all that follows, is adequate to teaching * * * only by emphasis, from the beginning, on the contract, can one bring to due honor the problem of draftsmanship * * *." Llewellyn, Cases and Materials on Sales xiv–xv (1931).

It should be noted that the "contract" to which Llewellyn refers may be one of three basic kinds. First, it may be fully negotiated between the parties and its terms reduced to writing. This is the least common form. Second, the contract may take the form of a signed standardized printed agreement. This is a very common form. Third, because the parties agree only on the barest essentials of goods and price, the contract may consist largely of "terms" supplied by statute. This is the most common form. Much of Article Two can be viewed as a statutorily standardized contract which comes into play to the extent the agreement of the parties is silent.

Regardless of the form of the contract, the lawyer will need to know his freedom of contract: that is, what Article Two allows, does not allow, and supplies absent contrary agreement. And the good commercial lawyer who is in a position to structure things in advance for his client will be especially alert to the kinds of things that might go wrong with his client's deal as it progresses from stage to stage.

To the lawyer, perhaps the most fundamental distinction here is that between planning and drafting the affirmative business content of a deal, and planning and drafting, *prophylactically* as it were, for things that can go wrong. With regard to the former, the businessman is dominant, though the lawyer contributes as draftsman. *Re* the latter, the lawyer is at the fore. The businessman supplies "business" specifications, e.g., nature, quality and quantity of goods, payment terms and the like, and the lawyer drafts in these, but his most distinctive contributions are frequently not here; rather, they are to try to envision the unfolding transaction as it progresses from stage to stage, to identify the kinds of things that can go wrong at each stage, and then to bring his preventive and remedial sophistication to bear on these possible eventualities *in advance at the agreement stage.*

But while the *contract is,* by virtue of the broad freedom granted in UCC 1–102(3), *primary,* and Article Two secondary, it does not, of course, follow that just any clause the lawyer drafts will stand up under Article Two, (and even if it will stand up under Article Two, other, non-Code law, may sometimes be invoked to strike it down). So far as *Code* limitations on freedom of contract are concerned, it is useful to differentiate four kinds applicable within Article 2. First, there is the type of *specific* Article Two provision that is itself not variable by agreement. Second, Article 2, in UCC 2–302, generally invalidates unconscionable contracts and unconscionable contract clauses. Third, UCC 1–203 imposes an "obligation of good faith" in the performance or enforcement of every contract or duty within the Act. Fourth, UCC 1–103 provides that certain equitable principles shall be controlling. The first kind of limitation will be considered in a general way in the present section, the second, third, and fourth in subsequent sections of this chapter.

The provisions of Article Two fall into three categories: (1) those which themselves explicitly state that they can be varied by agreement, (2) those which themselves *explicitly* state that they can not be varied by agreement, and (3) those which are not thus flagged one way or the other at all. The first kind poses no problems for the draftsman of a sales contract. The second kind he must identify and keep in mind. See, e.g., UCC 2–616(3), 2–718(1), 2–209(3), 2–318, 2–725(1), and 1–204(1). But provisions of the third type (unflagged either way) pose a real problem, for it is *clear* that some of these provisions cannot be varied by agreement, despite the general green light in UCC 1–102(3). Examples are UCC 2–201 on the Statute of Frauds, UCC 2–719(3) protecting "underdogs", and such third party protection provisions as UCC 2–702, 2–502, and 2–403. Yet within this same broad category of unflagged provisions are some that clearly can be varied by agreement. See, for example, the Code provisions on recoverable damages for breach, UCC 2–713, 2–714 and 2–718. The problem, then, is this: If, as is plainly the case, our third category of unflagged provisions includes some which can be varied by agreement and some which cannot, by what criteria are we to determine which is which?

Problem 2–3

Consider the validity of the following clauses which purport to vary the effect of the sections cited. *All three ↓ would be highly suspect*

(1) "Pursuant to this basic agreement, the parties shall make subsequent agreements for the purchase and sale of lumber, each such subsequent agreement to constitute a binding contract only when and if the parties have fully agreed to all material terms." See UCC 2–204(2), (3), and various gap-filler provisions in Part 3 of Article 2.

(2) "In the event that buyer discovers a nonconformity upon delivery of said goods, buyer shall not be required to notify seller thereof, provided that buyer commences any legal proceedings therefor against seller within two years of discovery of said breach." See UCC 2–607(3)(a) and 1–102(3).

(3) "In the event buyer defaults hereunder, seller shall be entitled to recover the agreed price for said goods whether or not Article Two of the Uniform Commercial Code so provides." See UCC 2–709.

E. Legal Controls on Article Two Contractual Behavior: Unconscionability and Good Faith

Below we discuss and consider UCC 2–302, providing that unconscionable contract clauses are invalid, and UCC 1–203, imposing a general obligation of good faith. You have already met both of those sections in your first year course in contracts. It is sometimes said that the unconscionability limitation on freedom of contract applies at the formation stage whereas the good faith limitation applies only to the performance or enforcement stage. Yet that good faith may have some bearing on issues normally resolved at the formation stage is quite evident, as with section 2–305(2) which provides that "A price to be fixed by the seller or by the buyer means a price for him to fix in good faith." Indeed, good faith may even have a bearing on liability for acts or omissions of one party as early as the negotiation stage. Of course, this would have to be via UCC 1–103 on supplemental general principles, for UCC 1–203 itself only imposes an obligation of good faith in the "performance" and "enforcement" of the contract. Similarly, the student will do well to entertain the possibility that unconscionability may have a bearing at *post* formation stages:

ZAPATHA v. DAIRY MART, INC.

Supreme Judicial Court of Massachusetts.
381 Mass. 284, 408 N.E.2d 1370 (1980).

WILKINS, JUSTICE.

We are concerned here with the question whether Dairy Mart, Inc. (Dairy Mart), lawfully undertook to terminate a franchise agreement under which the Zapathas operated a Dairy Mart store on Wilbraham Road in Springfield. The Zapathas brought this action seeking to

Trial Ct ruled:

1. Δ did not act in "good faith"

2. Termination provision was unconscionable

3. Termination without cause was an unfair + deceptive act.

Appellate Ct reverses!

enjoin the termination of the agreement, alleging that the contract provision purporting to authorize the termination of the franchise agreement without cause was unconscionable and that Dairy Mart's conduct was an unfair and deceptive act or practice in violation of G.L. c. 93A. The judge ruled that Dairy Mart did not act in good faith, that the termination provision was unconscionable, and that Dairy Mart's termination of the agreement without cause was an unfair and deceptive act. We granted Dairy Mart's application for direct appellate review of a judgment that stated that Dairy Mart could terminate the agreement only for good cause and that the attempted termination was null and void. We reverse the judgments.

Mr. Zapatha is a high school graduate who had attended college for one year and had also taken college evening courses in business administration and business law. From 1952 to May, 1973, he was employed by a company engaged in the business of electroplating. He rose through the ranks to foreman and then to the position of operations manager, at one time being in charge of all metal finishing in the plant with 150 people working under him. In May, 1973, he was discharged and began looking for other opportunities, in particular a business of his own. Several months later he met with a representative of Dairy Mart. Dairy Mart operates a chain of franchised "convenience" stores. The Dairy Mart representative told Mr. Zapatha that working for Dairy Mart was being in business for one's self and that such a business was very stable and secure. Mr. Zapatha signed an application to be considered for a franchise. In addition, he was presented with a brochure entitled "Here's a Chance," which made certain representations concerning the status of a franchise holder.[1]

Dairy Mart approved Mr. Zapatha's application and offered him a store in Agawam. On November 8, 1973, a representative of Dairy Mart showed him a form of franchise agreement, entitled Limited Franchise and License Agreement, asked him to read it, and explained that his wife would have to sign the agreement as well.

Under the terms of the agreement, Dairy Mart would license the Zapathas to operate a Dairy Mart store, using the Dairy Mart trademark and associated insignia, and utilizing Dairy Mart's "confidential" merchandising methods. Dairy Mart would furnish the store and the equipment and would pay rent and gas and electric bills as well as certain other costs of doing business. In return Dairy Mart would receive a franchise fee, computed as a percentage of the store's gross sales. The Zapathas would have to pay for the starting inventory, and maintain a minimum stock of saleable merchandise thereafter. They

---

1. It included the following statements: "* * * you'll have the opportunity to own and run your own business * * *"; "We want to be sure we're hooking up with the right person. A person who sees the opportunity in owning his own business * * * who requires the security that a multi-million dollar parent company can offer him * * * who has the good judgment and business sense to take advantage of the unique independence that Dairy Mart offers its franchisees * * * We're looking for a partner * * * who can take the tools we offer and build a life of security and comfort * * *"

were also responsible for wages of employees, related taxes, and any sales taxes. The termination provision, which is set forth in full in the margin,[2] allowed either party, after twelve months, to terminate the agreement without cause on ninety days' written notice. In the event of termination initiated by it without cause, Dairy Mart agreed to repurchase the saleable merchandise inventory at retail prices, less 20%.

The Dairy Mart representative read and explained the termination provision to Mr. Zapatha. Mr. Zapatha later testified that, while he understood every word in the provision, he had interpreted it to mean that Dairy Mart could terminate the agreement only for cause. The Dairy Mart representative advised Mr. Zapatha to take the agreement to an attorney and said "I would prefer that you did." However, he also told Mr. Zapatha that the terms of the contract were not negotiable. *This is my offer!* The Zapathas signed the agreement without consulting an attorney. When the Zapathas took charge of the Agawam store, a representative of Dairy Mart worked with them to train them in Dairy Mart's methods of operation.

In 1974, another store became available on Wilbraham Road in Springfield, and the Zapathas elected to surrender the Agawam store. They executed a new franchise agreement, on an identical printed form, relating to the new location.

In November, 1977, Dairy Mart presented a new and more detailed form of "Independent Operator's Agreement" to the Zapathas for execution. Some of the terms were less favorable to the store operator than those of the earlier form of agreement.[3] Mr. Zapatha told representatives of Dairy Mart that he was content with the existing contract and had decided not to sign the new agreement. On January 20, 1978, Dairy Mart gave written notice to the Zapathas that their contract was being terminated effective in ninety days. The termination notice stated that Dairy Mart "remains available to enter into discussions with you with respect to entering into a new Independent Operator's

2. "(9) The term of this Limited Franchise and License Agreement shall be for a period of Twelve (12) months from date hereof, and shall continue uninterrupted thereafter. If DEALER desires to terminate after 12 months from date hereof, he shall do so by giving COMPANY a ninety (90) day written notice by Registered Mail of his intention to terminate. If COMPANY desires to terminate, it likewise shall give a ninety (90) day notice, except for the following reasons which shall not require any written notice and shall terminate the Franchise immediately:

Both parties have an "out"!

"(a) Failure to pay bills to suppliers for inventory or other products when due.

"(b) Failure to pay Franchise Fees to COMPANY.

"(c) Failure to pay city, state or federal taxes as said taxes shall become due and payable.

"(d) Breach of any condition of this Agreement."

3. In his testimony, Mr. Zapatha said that he objected to a new provision under which Dairy Mart reserved the option to relocate an operator to a new location and to a requirement that the store be open from 7 A.M. to 11 P.M. every day. Previously the Zapathas' store had been open from 8 A.M. to 10 P.M.

There were other provisions, such as an obligation to pay future increases in the cost of heat and electricity, that were more burdensome to a franchisee. A few changes may have been to the advantage of the franchisee.

Agreement; however, there is no assurance that Dairy Mart will enter into a new Agreement with you, or even if entered into, what terms such Agreement will contain." The notice also indicated that Dairy Mart was prepared to purchase the Zapathas' saleable inventory.

The judge found that Dairy Mart terminated the agreement solely because the Zapathas refused to sign the new agreement. He further found that, but for this one act, Dairy Mart did not behave in an unconscionable manner, in bad faith, or in disregard of its representations. There is no evidence that the Zapathas undertook to discuss a compromise of the differences that led to the notice of termination.

Trial Judge ruled that Article 2 applies – "and even if it doesn't, the Unconscionability clause should by analogy!

On these basic facts, the judge ruled that the franchise agreement was subject to the sales article of the Uniform Commercial Code (G.L. c. 106, art. 2) and, even if it were not, the principles of unconscionability and good faith expressed in that article applied to the franchise agreement by analogy. He further ruled that (1) the termination provision of the agreement was unconscionable because it authorized termination without cause, (2) the termination without cause violated Dairy Mart's obligation of good faith, and (3) the termination constituted "an unfair method of competition and unfair and deceptive act within the meaning of G.L. c. 93A, § 2."

Appellate Court first decided that UCC Article 2 does indeed apply

1. We consider first the question whether the franchise agreement involves a "transaction in goods" within the meaning of those words in article two of the Uniform Commercial Code (G.L. c. 106, § 2–103, as appearing in St.1957, c. 765, § 1), and that consequently the provisions of the sales articles of the Uniform Commercial Code govern the relationship between the parties. The Zapathas point specifically to the authority of a court to refuse to enforce "any clause of the contract" that the court finds "to have been unconscionable at the time it was made." G.L. c. 106, § 2–302, as appearing in St.1957, c. 765, § 1.[4] They point additionally to the obligation of good faith in the performance and enforcement of a contract imposed by G.L. c. 106, § 1–203, and to the specialized definition of "good faith" in the sales article as meaning "in the case of a merchant * * * honesty in fact and the observance of reasonable commercial standards of fair dealing in the trade." G.L. c. 106, § 2–103(1)(b), as appearing in St.1957, c. 765, § 1.[5]

4. General Laws c. 106, § 2–302, as appearing in St.1957, c. 765, § 1, reads as follows:

"**§ 2–302. Unconscionable Contract or Clause**

"(1) If the court as a matter of law finds the contract or any clause of the contract to have been unconscionable at the time it was made the court may refuse to enforce the contract, or it may enforce the remainder of the contract without the unconscionable clause, or it may so limit the application of any unconscionable clause as to avoid any unconscionable result.

"(2) When it is claimed or appears to the court that the contract or any clause thereof may be unconscionable the parties shall be afforded a reasonable opportunity to present evidence as to its commercial setting, purpose, and effect to aid the court in making the determination."

5. Generally throughout the Uniform Commercial Code, "good faith" is defined to mean "honesty in fact in the conduct or transaction concerned." G.L. c. 106, § 1–201(19). The definition of "good faith" in the sales article includes a higher standard of conduct by adding a requirement that

We need not pause long over the question whether the franchise agreement and the relationship of the parties involved a transaction in goods. Certainly, the agreement required the plaintiffs to purchase goods from Dairy Mart. "Goods" for the purpose of the sales article means generally "all things * * * which are movable." G.L. c. 106, § 2–105(1), as appearing in St.1957, c. 765, § 1. However, the franchise agreement dealt with many subjects unrelated to the sale of goods by Dairy Mart. About 70% of the goods the plaintiffs sold were not purchased from Dairy Mart. Dairy Mart's profit was intended to come from the franchise fee and not from the sale of items to its franchisees. Thus, the sale of goods by Dairy Mart to the Zapathas was, in a commercial sense, a minor aspect of the entire relationship. We would be disinclined to import automatically all the provisions of the sales article into a relationship involving a variety of subjects other than the sale of goods, merely because the contract dealt in part with the sale of goods. Similarly, we would not be inclined to apply the sales article only to aspects of the agreement that concerned goods. Different principles of law might then govern separate portions of the same agreement with possibly inconsistent and unsatisfactory consequences.

We view the legislative statements of policy concerning good faith and unconscionability as fairly applicable to all aspects of the franchise agreement, not by subjecting the franchise relationship to the provisions of the sales article but rather by applying the stated principles by analogy. * * * This basic common law approach, applied to statutory statements of policy, permits a selective application of those principles expressed in a statute that reasonably should govern situations to which the statute does not apply explicitly. See Note, Article Two of the Uniform Commercial Code and Franchise Distribution Agreements, 1969 Duke L.J. 959, 980–985.

2. We consider first the plaintiffs' argument that the termination clause of the franchise agreement, authorizing Dairy Mart to terminate the agreement without cause, on ninety days' notice, was unconscionable by the standards expressed in G.L. c. 106, § 2–302.[6] The same standards are set forth in Restatement (Second) of Contracts § 234 (Tent.Drafts Nos. 1–7, 1973). The issue is one of law for the court, and the test is to be made as of the time the contract was made. G.L. c. 106, § 2–302(1), and comment 3 of the Official Comments. See *W.L. May, Co. v. Philco-Ford Corp.*, 273 Or. 701, 707, 543 P.2d 283 (1975). In measuring the unconscionability of the termination provision, the fact that the law imposes an obligation of good faith on Dairy Mart in its performance under the agreement should be weighed. See *W.L. May, Co. v. Philco-Ford Corp.*, 543 P.2d 283.

"merchants" observe "reasonable commercial standards of fair dealing in the trade." G.L. c. 106, § 2–103(1)(b). There is no doubt that Dairy Mart is a "merchant" as defined under the sales article. See G.L. c. 106, § 2–104.

6. The agreement permitted immediate termination on the occurrence of certain conditions which are not involved in this case.

[margin note: Official Comments]

The official comment to § 2–302 states that "[t]he basic test is whether, in the light of the general commercial background and the commercial needs of the particular trade or case, the clauses involved are so one-sided as to be unconscionable under the circumstances existing at the time of the making of the contract. * * * The principle is one of prevention of oppression and unfair surprise * * * and not of disturbance of allocation of risks because of superior bargaining power." Official Comment 1 to U.C.C. § 2–302.[7] Unconscionability is not defined in the Code, nor do the views expressed in the official comment provide a precise definition. The annotation prepared by the Massachusetts Advisory Committee on the Code states that "[t]he section appears to be intended to carry equity practice into the sales field." See 1 R. Anderson, Uniform Commercial Code § 2–302:7 (1970) to the same effect. This court has not had occasion to consider in any detail the meaning of the word "unconscionable" in § 2–302. Because there is no clear, all-purpose definition of "unconscionable," nor could there be, unconscionability must be determined on a case by case basis (see *Commonwealth v. Gustafsson*, 370 Mass. 181, 187, 346 N.E.2d 706 [1976]), giving particular attention to whether, at the time of the execution of the agreement, the contract provision could result in unfair surprise and was oppressive to the allegedly disadvantaged party.

[margin note: No clear cut definition]
[margin note: Therefore,]
[margin note: Case by case determination]

[margin note: Termination without cause is not by definition unconscionable]

We start with a recognition that the Uniform Commercial Code itself implies that a contract provision allowing termination without cause is not per se unconscionable. See *Corenswet, Inc. v. Amana Refrigeration, Inc.*, 594 F.2d 129, 138 (5th Cir.1979) ("We seriously doubt, however, that public policy frowns on any and all contract clauses permitting termination without cause."); *Division of Triple T Serv., Inc. v. Mobil Oil Corp.*, 60 Misc.2d 720, 730, 304 N.Y.S.2d 191 (1969), aff'd 34 A.D.2d 618, 311 N.Y.S.2d 961 (N.Y.1970). Section 2–309(3) provides that "[t]ermination of a contract by one party except on the happening of an agreed event requires that reasonable notification be received by the other party and an agreement dispensing with notification is invalid if its operation would be unconscionable." G.L. c. 106, § 2–309, as appearing in St.1957, c. 765, § 1. This language implies that termination of a sales contract without agreed "cause" is authorized by the Code, provided reasonable notice is given. * * * There is no suggestion that the ninety days' notice provided in the Dairy Mart franchise agreement was unreasonable.

[margin note: 2-309(3) deals with clauses of this nature]
[margin note: Here 90 days who given]
[margin note: No suggestion this was unreasonable]

We find no potential for unfair surprise to the Zapathas in the provision allowing termination without cause. We view the question of unfair surprise as focused on the circumstances under which the

---

7. The comment has been criticized as useless and at best ambiguous (J. White & R. Summers, The Uniform Commercial Code, 116 [1972]), and § 2–302 has been characterized as devoid of any specific content. Leff, Unconscionability and the Code—(The Emperor's New Clause, 115 U.Pa.L.Rev. 485, 487–489 [1967]). On the other hand, it has been said that the strength of the unconscionability concept is its abstraction, permitting judicial creativity. See Ellinghaus, In Defense of Unconscionability, 78 Yale L.J. 757 (1969).

agreement was entered into.[8] The termination provision was neither *Not buried or hidden* obscurely worded, nor buried in fine print in the contract. Contrast Williams v. Walker-Thomas Furniture Co., 350 F.2d 445, 449 (D.C.Cir. 1965). The provision was specifically pointed out to Mr. Zapatha before it was signed; Mr. Zapatha testified that he thought the provision was "straightforward," and he declined the opportunity to take the agreement to a lawyer for advice. The Zapathas had ample opportunity to consider the agreement before they signed it. Significantly, the subject of loss of employment was paramount in Mr. Zapatha's mind. He testified that he had held responsible jobs in one company from 1952 to 1973, that he had lost his employment, and that he "was looking for something that had a certain amount of security; something that was stable and something I could call my own." We conclude that a person *No element of unfair surprise* of Mr. Zapatha's business experience and education should not have been surprised by the termination provision and, if in fact he was, there was no element of unfairness in the inclusion of that provision in the agreement. * * *

We further conclude that there was no oppression in the inclusion *No oppression by including the clause* of a termination clause in the franchise agreement. We view the question of oppression as directed to the substantive fairness to the parties of permitting the termination provisions to operate as written. The Zapathas took over a going business on premises provided by Dairy Mart, using equipment furnished by Dairy Mart. As an investment, the Zapathas had only to purchase the inventory of goods to be sold but, as Dairy Mart concedes, on termination by it without cause Dairy Mart was obliged to repurchase all the Zapathas' saleable merchandise inventory, including items not purchased from Dairy Mart, at 80% of its retail value. There was no potential for forfeiture or loss of investment. There is no question here of a need for a reasonable time to recoup the franchisees' initial investment. See * * * Gellhorn, Limitations on Contract Termination Rights—Franchise Cancellations, 1967 Duke L.J. 465, 479–481. The Zapathas were entitled to their net profits through the entire term of the agreement. They failed to sustain their burden of showing that the agreement allocated the risks and benefits connected with termination in an unreasonably disproportionate way and that the termination provision was not reasonably related to legitimate commercial needs of Dairy Mart. * * * To find the termination clause oppressive merely because it did not require cause for termination would be to establish an unwarranted barrier to the use of termination at will clauses in contracts in this Common-

---

8. As we shall note subsequently, the concept of oppression deals with the substantive unfairness of the contract term. This two-part test for unconscionability involves determining whether there was "an absence of meaningful choice on the part of one of the parties, together with contract terms which are unreasonably favorable to the other party." *Williams v. Walker-* *Thomas Furniture Co.,* 350 F.2d 445, 449 (D.C.Cir.1965). See *Corenswet, Inc. v. Amana Refrigeration, Inc.,* 594 F.2d 129, 139 (5th Cir.1979). The inquiry involves a search for components of "procedural" and "substantive" unconscionability. See generally Leff, Unconscionability and the Code—The Emperor's New Clause, 115 Pa. L.Rev. 485 (1967). * * *

wealth, where each party received the anticipated and bargained for consideration during the full term of the agreement.

3. We see no basis on the record for concluding that Dairy Mart did not act in good faith, as that term is defined in the sales article ("honesty in fact and the observance of reasonable commercial standards of fair dealing in the trade") G.L. c. 106, § 2–103(1)(b). There was no evidence that Dairy Mart failed to observe reasonable commercial standards of fair dealing in the trade in terminating the agreement. If there were such standards, there was no evidence of what they were.

The question then is whether there was evidence warranting a finding that Dairy Mart was not honest "in fact." The judge concluded that the absence of any commercial purpose for the termination other than the Zapathas' refusal to sign a new franchise agreement violated Dairy Mart's obligation of good faith. Dairy Mart's right to terminate was clear, and it exercised that right for a reason it openly disclosed. The sole test of "honesty in fact" is whether the person was honest. * * * We think that, whether or not termination according to the terms of the franchise agreement may have been arbitrary, it was not dishonest.[9]

The judge concluded that bad faith was also manifested by Dairy Mart's introductory brochure, which made representations of "security, comfort, and independence." Although this brochure and Mr. Zapatha's mistaken understanding that Dairy Mart could terminate the agreement only for cause could not be relied on to vary the clear terms of the agreement, the introductory brochure is relevant to the question of good faith. However, although the brochure misstated a franchisee's status as the owner of his own business, it shows no lack of honesty in fact relating to the right of Dairy Mart to terminate the agreement. Furthermore, by the time the Zapathas executed the second agreement, and even the first agreement, they knew that they would operate the franchise, but that they would not own the assets used in the business (except the goods to be sold); that the franchise agreement could be terminated by them and, at least in some circumstances, by Dairy Mart; and that in fact the major investment of funds would be made by Dairy Mart. We conclude that the use of the brochure did not warrant a finding of an absence of "honesty in fact." See *Corenswet, Inc. v. Amana Refrigeration, Inc.*, 594 F.2d 129, 138 (5th Cir.1979); *Mason v. Farmers Ins. Cos.*, 281 N.W.2d 344, 347 (Minn.1979).[10]

9. Under G.L. c. 106, § 1–203, "[e]very contract * * * imposes an obligation of good faith *in its performance or enforcement*" (emphasis supplied). We shall assume that an act of termination falls within the "performance" of the agreement. See *Baker v. Ratzlaff*, 1 Kan.App.2d 285, 288, 564 P.2d 153 (1977). But see Summers, "Good Faith" in General Contract Law and the Sales Provisions of the Uniform Commercial Code, 54 Va.L.Rev. 195, 252 (1968).

10. It has been suggested that, despite the limited definition of good faith in the Code, in some contexts the general obligation of good faith in § 1–203 can be used to import an objective standard of "decency, fairness or reasonableness in performance or enforcement" into a contract to which it applies. Farnsworth, Good Faith Perform-

4. Although what we have said disposes of arguments based on application by analogy of provisions of the sales article of the Uniform Commercial Code, there remains the question whether the judge's conclusions may be supported by some general principle of law. The provisions of the Uniform Commercial Code with which we have dealt by analogy in this opinion may not have sufficient breadth to provide protection from conduct that has produced an unfair and burdensome result, contrary to the spirit of the bargain, against which the law reasonably should provide protection. See Restatement (Second) of Contracts § 231 (Tent.Drafts Nos. 1–7 1973); Corbin, Contracts § 654A (C.K. Kaufman 1980 Supp.).[11]

The law of the Commonwealth recognizes that under some circumstances a party to a contract is not free to terminate it according to its terms. In *Fortune v. National Cash Register Co.*, 373 Mass. 96, 104–105, 364 N.E.2d 1251 (1977), we held that where an employer terminated an at will employment contract in order to deprive its employee of a portion of a commission due to him, the employer acted in bad faith. There, the employer correctly argued that termination of the employee was expressly permitted by the contract, and that all amounts payable under the terms of the contract at the time of termination had been paid. We concluded, however, that the law imposed an obligation of good faith on the employer and that the employer violated that obligation in terminating the relationship in order to avoid the payment of amounts earned, but not yet payable. The Legislature has limited the right of certain franchisors to terminate franchise agreements without cause.[12] On the other hand, the Legislature has not adopted limitations

---

ance and Commercial Reasonableness Under the Uniform Commercial Code, 30 U.Chi.L.Rev. 666, 668 (1963). Good faith in this sense can be regarded as an "excluder," barring varied forms of unreasonable conduct in different circumstances. See Summers, "Good Faith" in General Contract Law and the Sales Provisions of the Uniform Commercial Code, 54 Va.L.Rev. 195, 196 (1968). Rather than stretch the Code definition of good faith beyond the plain meaning of the words used to define good faith, we prefer, as we are about to do, to analyze the question of fairness and reasonableness independently of the Code.

11. The unconscionability provision of G.L. c. 106, § 2–302, concerns circumstances determined at the time of the making of the agreement and relates only to the unconscionability of a term or terms of the contract. The "good faith" obligation of G.L. c. 106, § 1–203, deals with "honesty in fact," a question of the state of mind of the merchant or of his adherence to whatever reasonable commercial standards there may be in his trade. A merchant's conduct might not be dishonest and might adhere to reasonable standards, if any, in

his trade and thus might be in good faith under § 1–203, and yet be unfair and unreasonably burdensome.

12. See G.L. c. 93B, § 4(3)(e), (4) concerning the cancellation or nonrenewal of a motor vehicle dealer's franchise and requiring good cause for manufacturer's or distributor's action; G.L. c. 93E, §§ 5, 5A, requiring cause for a supplier's termination or nonrenewal of a gasoline station dealer's agreement and imposing an obligation on the supplier to repurchase merchantable products sold to the dealer.

New Jersey has a Franchise Practices Act of general applicability that "prohibits a franchisor from terminating, cancelling or failing to renew a franchise without good cause which is defined as the failure by the franchisee to substantially comply with the requirements imposed on him by the franchise. N.J.S.A. 56:10–5." *Shell Oil Co. v. Marinello*, 63 N.J. 402, 409, 307 A.2d 598, 602 (1973), cert. denied, 415 U.S. 920, 94 S.Ct. 1421, 39 L.Ed.2d 475 (1974). Although the act applied only prospectively (N.J.S.A. 56:10–8), in the *Marinello* case the New Jersey Supreme Court applied the

on the right to terminate all franchise agreements in general, and its failure to do so is understandable because of the varied nature of franchise arrangements, where such varying factors exist as the relative bargaining power of the parties, the extent of investment by franchisees, and the degree to which the franchisee's goodwill, as opposed to that of the franchisor, is involved in the business operation. Further, in recognition of a general duty of good faith and fair dealing in business transactions under the law of the Commonwealth, c. 93A of the General Laws imposes on any person who engages in the conduct of any trade or commerce an obligation not to use any "unfair or deceptive acts or practices," as defined in G.L. c. 93A, § 2(a), as appearing in St.1967, c. 813, § 1, in dealing with another person who engages in any trade or commerce. G.L. c. 93A, § 11, as amended through St.1979, c. 72, § 2.

We thus analyze the case before us in terms of whether in terminating the agreement Dairy Mart failed to act in good faith in a broader sense than the term is used in G.L. c. 106, § 1–203, or dealt unfairly with the Zapathas, and whether Dairy Mart engaged in any unfair or deceptive act or practice. Much of what we said in discussing unconscionability and bad faith in terms of the Uniform Commercial Code applies here and need not be repeated. There is no showing that Dairy Mart usurped funds to which the Zapathas were reasonably entitled. Certainly Dairy Mart did not deprive the Zapathas of income that they had fairly earned, as the employer attempted to do in the *Fortune* case. We know nothing of any goodwill that the Zapathas had developed in their own name. There was no showing that, by their special efforts, the Zapathas built up the business at the Springfield store. As far as the record shows, they would lose no financial investment on termination and would not be left with unsaleable inventory or special purpose supplies and equipment. * * *

We are most concerned, as was the judge below, with the introductory circular that Dairy Mart furnished Mr. Zapatha. The judge ruled that the introductory circular contained misleading information concerning the Zapathas' status as franchisees. However, we cannot find in that document any deception or unfairness that has a bearing on the right of Dairy Mart to terminate the agreement as it did. A representative read the termination clause to Mr. Zapatha before the Zapathas signed the agreement. Mr. Zapatha declined an invitation to take the agreement to a lawyer. He understood individually every word of the termination clause. Moreover, when Dairy Mart terminated the agree-

expressed public policy to bar termination of a service station operator's franchise in the absence of good cause, as so defined.

The special status of service station operators has prompted some courts to adopt common law rules requiring good cause for termination in spite of contract language that seemed to allow termination without cause. See *Arnott v. American Oil Co.,* 609 F.2d 873, 880–884 (8th Cir.1979), cert. denied, ___ U.S. ___, 100 S.Ct. 1852, 64 L.Ed. 2d 272; *Atlantic Richfield Co. v. Razumic,* 480 Pa. 366, 390 A.2d 736 (1978); *Ashland Oil, Inc. v. Donahue,* 223 S.E.2d 433 (W.Va. 1976).

ment, it offered to negotiate further, and the Zapathas did not take the opportunity to do so.

Unless we were to take the position that termination without cause of a franchise agreement of the character involved here is prohibited invariably by the law of the Commonwealth, a position we decline to adopt * * *, Dairy Mart lawfully terminated the agreement because there was no showing that in terminating it Dairy Mart engaged in any unfair, deceptive, or bad faith conduct.

Judgments reversed.

[Some footnotes omitted. Those retained have been renumbered. Eds.]

SUMMERS, "GOOD FAITH" IN GENERAL CONTRACT LAW AND THE SALES PROVISIONS OF THE UNIFORM COMMERCIAL CODE, 54 Va.L.Rev. 195, 199–202 (1968).

What is the best way to determine a judge's meaning when he uses the phrase "good faith"? In the case law taken as a whole, does the term have a single general meaning of its own, or perhaps several such meanings? (The answers to these questions are closely linked.) Sometimes what a judge means by good faith will be instantly obvious, but frequently it will not be. When not, it may be that he is using the phrase loosely. But even if he is using it with care, there may still be unclarity. He might indicate only that, in a given context, parties are to act in good faith or that a party did or did not act in good faith, without elaborating at all. Or he might elaborate without communicating in any specific way—for example, by laying down some very general definition of good faith, such as acting "honestly" or "being faithful to one's duty or obligation." The analyst of such an opinion is likely to inquire: What is the meaning of good faith itself? He seems to assume that the phrase has some general meaning or meanings, one of which the judge presumably intends.

One of the principal theses of this Article is that in cases of doubt, a lawyer will determine more accurately what the judge means by using the phrase "good faith" if he does not ask what good faith itself means, but rather asks: What, in the actual or hypothetical situation, does the judge intend to rule out by his use of this phrase? Once the relevant form of bad faith is thus identified, the lawyer can, if he wishes, assign a specific meaning to good faith by formulating an "opposite" for the species of bad faith being ruled out. For example, a judge may say: "A public authority must act in good faith in letting bids." And from the facts or the language of the opinion it may appear that the judge is, in effect, saying: "The defendant acted in bad faith because he let bids only as a pretense to conceal his purpose to award the contract to a favored bidder." It can then be said that "acting in good faith" here simply means: letting bids without a preconceived design to award the contract to a favored bidder.

If good faith had a general meaning or meanings of its own—that is, if it were either univocal or ambiguous—there would seldom be occasion to derive a meaning for it from an opposite; its specific uses would almost always be readily and immediately understood. But good faith is not that kind of doctrine. In contract law, taken as a whole, good faith is an "excluder." It is a phrase without general meaning (or meanings) of its own and serves to exclude a wide range of heterogeneous forms of bad faith. In a particular context the phrase takes on specific meaning, but usually this is only by way of contrast with the specific form of bad faith actually or hypothetically ruled out. Aristotle was one of the first to recognize that the function of some words and phrases is not to convey general, "extractable" meanings of their own, but rather is to exclude one or more of a variety of things. He thought "voluntary" was such a word. And the late Professor J.L. Austin of Oxford made much of "excluders."

Note: Good Faith in the Uniform Commercial Code

As we have seen, Uniform Commercial Code section 1–203 generally provides that "[e]very contract or duty within this Act imposes an obligation of good faith in its performance or enforcement." Thirteen sections of Article Two of the Code (on the sale of goods) explicitly require good faith. Nineteen sections of Article Two include comments which also use the phrase. In Article One ("General Provisions") good faith is defined in section 1–201(19) to mean (unless the context otherwise requires) "honesty in fact in the conduct or transaction concerned." However, in Article Two on sales of goods, section 2–103(1)(b) states that "unless the context otherwise requires * * * good faith, in the case of a merchant means honesty in fact and the observance of reasonable commercial standards of fair dealing in the trade."

Problem 2–4

(1) Frank is a book wholesaler in New York City, John a book retailer in a University town where a great law school exists. John has a lot of used copies of a great commercial law casebook about to be superseded by a fourth edition, a fact known to John but not to Frank. John sells a large number of the books to Frank without disclosing the foregoing fact. Later, Frank discovers the fact and seeks to rescind. What result? Assume John's non-disclosure does not constitute "fraud" under tort law. Assume, too, that John has broken no warranty. See UCC 1–203 and 1–201(19). Does UCC 1–203 apply? Is this the only relevant provision? Among other things, what of UCC 1–103? To make effective use of UCC 1–103, what kind of extra-Code case law would you hope to find?

(2) For three years, Ice, Inc., a small ice manufacturer, has been selling roughly 25 tons of ice a month to the Sam McGee Storage, Co., pursuant to a contract one clause of which empowers McGee to order "such ice as it requires." On January 20, McGee, having decided to expand its operations, ordered three hundred tons of ice from Ice, Inc. for February. Ice, Inc., of course, could not supply this amount, and so notified McGee. McGee then

declared itself "free to buy all our needs from Prime, Inc., a manufacturer more our size." Ice, Inc. has come to you for advice. What would you advise? Among other things, see UCC 1–203, 1–201(19), 2–306, 2–103(1)(b) and 2–311(1).

(3) Rowan brokered custom-made (new and old) cars, a very special market. Martin, his best customer, wanted a special car for which he was willing to pay dearly $15,000 provided he could get it in time to drive it in the Grand Nationale. Tucker, an always-do-well "consumer" known to Rowan, had such a car which he agreed to sell Rowan for $13,000. Later and just before the Grand Nationale, Tucker, having learned of Rowan's resale price to Martin, insisted that Rowan pay $14,500 "or the deal is off." Rowan finally agreed, got the car, resold it to Martin for $15,000 and then came to you for advice. Does he have any recourse against Tucker? Among other things, see UCC 2–209(1) and relevant comments, 1–203, 1–201(19).

(4) Milk-O-Wheat, Inc. wanted to buy some grain. It had never dealt with seller before, but nonetheless placed a binding order with seller for 100 tons of wheat "delivery no later than August 2, our terminal." One hundred tons of good wheat arrived but not until August 4, due to an unexpected railway disaster. The delay did not slow up Milk-O-Wheat's operations any, but it rejected anyway, since the market had fallen and it was possible to get such wheat much more cheaply elsewhere. You are to assume that in the trade, prompt deliveries are expected, for usually the buyer is relying on such for the efficient conduct of his operations. Seller comes to you for advice. What would you advise? Among other things, see UCC 2–601, 2–508, 2–504, 1–203, 1–201(19), and 2–103(1)(b).

SECTION 5. SUPPLEMENTAL GENERAL PRINCIPLES

Section 1–103 of the Uniform Commercial Code provides:

Unless displaced by the particular provisions of this Act, the principles of law and equity, including the law merchant and the law relative to capacity to contract, principal and agent, estoppel, fraud, misrepresentation, duress, coercion, mistake, bankruptcy, or other validating or invalidating cause shall supplement its provisions.

Equitable principles (not displaced) generally remain intact under the foregoing provision, *even in the face of contrary contractual provisions.* Thus, the parties cannot contract out of the bearing of most equitable notions having to do with estoppel, fraud, misrepresentation, duress, coercion, mistake and the like. See, generally, Summers, *General Equitable Principles Under Section 1–103 of the Uniform Commercial Code,* 72 Nw.U.L.Rev. 906 (1978).

Problem 2–5

(1) Section 2–509(3) of Article Two provides: "In any case not within subsection (1) or (2), the risk of loss passes to the buyer on his receipt of the goods if the seller is a merchant, otherwise the risk passes to the buyer on tender of delivery". Assume the buyer hires the seller to build a boat

mast. After the mast is under way, it occurs to the seller that the work should be insured. The buyer represents that insurance he already has covers the work, and, relying on this the seller does not insure. After completion but before delivery, the mast is destroyed by fire and the buyer discovers that his policy does not cover the mast. The seller sues the buyer for the price under section 2–709. The buyer defends by citing section 2–509(3) under which the risk of loss was on the seller, and denies liability. What result? Assume the preamble to the contract between buyer and seller recites that their agreement is the sole controlling law governing the rights of the parties. Would this affect the result? Cf. Mercanti v. Persson, 160 Conn. 468, 280 A.2d 137 (1971).

(2) Seller was in the business of selling lumber to various parties, including Buyer. Buyer knew Seller was operating "close to the margin". Buyer stopped payment of checks issued to pay for the lumber sold and delivered to Buyer and offered to pay only a sum $2000 less than that due under the contract "in full settlement." Seller told Buyer that if Seller failed to get the money, "he would be ruined financially." Buyer told Seller that he, Buyer, had "taken steps to stop payment of money due Seller from other parties too". Seller then agreed to the settlement at $2000 less. Is the settlement valid? Would it make any difference if the settlement recited that the agreement was in all respects a valid and binding contract? Cf. Vyne v. Glenn, 41 Mich. 112, 1 N.W. 997 (undated).

Part Two
THE AGREEMENT STAGE

Chapter Three
CONTRACT FORMATION

SECTION 1. INTRODUCTION

A classic function of courts and contract law is to determine when
parties negotiating for an agreed exchange have concluded an enforceable bargain. At what point have they crossed the line beyond which
neither party can withdraw without liability for breach?

[handwritten margin note: At what point do negotiations become enforceable bargains?]

Under the Restatement, Second, of Contracts, the answer depends
upon concepts with which you should now be familiar. First, contract
is defined as a "promise or a set of promises for the breach of which the
law gives a remedy. * * *" Section 1. Not all promises, however,
are contracts. In bargain transactions, defined in Section 3 of the
Restatement, Second as an agreed exchange of promises or performances, there must be a "bargain in which there is a manifestation of
mutual assent to the exchange and a consideration." Section 17(1).
According to Section 22(1), the manifestation of mutual assent to an
exchange "ordinarily takes the form of an offer or proposal by one
party followed by an acceptance by the other party or parties. * * *"
(An offer is defined as a "manifestation of willingness to enter into a
bargain, so made as to justify another person in understanding that his
assent to that bargain is invited and will conclude it." Section 24. An
acceptance of an offer is defined as a "manifestation of assent to the
terms thereof made by the offeree in a manner invited or required by
the offer." Section 50(1).)

To constitute consideration, "a performance or a return promise
must be bargained for," Section 71(1), i.e., "sought by the promisor in
exchange for his promise and * * * given by the promisee in exchange for that promise." Section 71(2).

How does Article 2 conform to the Restatement, Second formula, "Offer plus acceptance plus consideration = contract?"

UCC Definitions

First, contract "means the total legal obligation which results from the parties' agreement as affected by this Act and any other applicable rules of law." UCC 1–201(11). In contract formation disputes, the relevant provisions of "this Act" are found in Article 2, Part 2, as supplemented by UCC 1–103.

Second, agreement means the "bargain of the parties in fact as found in their language or by implication from other circumstances including course of dealing or usage of trade or course of performance as provided in this Act (Sections 1–205 and 2–208)." Note that the definition of "bargain * * * in fact" does not include a requirement that there be a promise. Further, although the concept of bargain is consistent with an agreed exchange, there is no explicit requirement that the exchange be bargained for. In short, although the agreement may contain promises and the exchange may be bargained for, there is no explicit requirement of either a promise or consideration to satisfy the definition. See Murray, *The Article 2 Prism: The Underlying Philosophy of the Uniform Commercial Code*, 21 Washburn L.J. 1 (1981).

Third, UCC 2–204 is the key formation section in Article 2, Part 2. Read it, please. Note that UCC 2–204(1) and (2) sweep away technical rules on how and when the contract is made: Important evidence will be "conduct by both parties which recognizes the existence of such a contract." Further, UCC 2–204(3) provides a standard to deal with disputes where one party withdraws before all of the material terms have been agreed: "Even though one or more terms are left open a contract for sale does not fail for indefiniteness if the parties have intended to make a contract and there is a reasonably certain basis for giving an appropriate remedy." Thus, there are no rules specifying the quantity of agreement that must be reached before a contract can be formed. Rather, the issue turns on what the parties have "intended" and whether the court can fill the "gaps" with reasonable certainty when giving an appropriate remedy. By "intended," UCC 2–204(3) presumably means an intention to conclude the bargain without further agreement, rather than an intention that the bargain be legally binding. Compare Restatement, Second 21 ("neither real nor apparent intention that a promise be legally binding is essential to the formation of a contract. * * *").

Read Article 2, Part 2, including the Comments and then work through the following materials.

SECTION 2.   OFFER AND ACCEPTANCE—UCC 2–204, 2–205 AND 2–206

In the following problems, first formulate the statutory issues posed and then resolve them as best you can from the Code.

Problem 3–1

S, a retailer, sold personal computers manufactured by M. After
preliminary negotiations, B, a corporation, mailed to S a printed form
prepared by B inviting S to make an "offer" to sell 10 described personal
computers for $25,000. The form contained five paragraphs of printed
matter, inserted on a single page between blank lines to be filled in at the
top and a signature line at the bottom. The third paragraph above the
signature line provided: THIS OFFER WILL BE HELD OPEN FOR 30
DAYS AFTER RECEIPT BY THE OFFEREE. S filled in the blanks as
requested by B, signed the form, dating it May 30, 1987, and returned it to
B, who received it on June 3, 1987. On June 15, 1987, S notified B by
telegram that the offer was revoked: A better deal had been worked out
with C for the personal computers. On June 16, 1987, B telegraphed to S
an acceptance of the offer, which was received the same day. B insists that
there was a contract. Is B correct? Start with UCC 2–205.

[handwritten margin notes: Note – This is the buyer's form; to buyer sell; Conspicuous language]

Problem 3–2

S, a manufacturer, had a quantity of used computer hardware which it
was willing to sell with a limited warranty for $50,000. On June 1, B, a
retailer, examined the equipment and discussed terms. An oral agreement
was reached on all terms except price. On June 5, B mailed S a signed
offer to purchase the equipment for $40,000 and enclosed a $4,000 check as
a down payment. S received the offer and check on June 7 and, on June 8,
deposited the check in its business account. S did not communicate with B.
On June 10, S received an offer from C to purchase the equipment for
$50,000 cash. The offer was accepted the same day. On June 11, S
informed B that its offer had been rejected and mailed to B a cashier's
check for $4,000.

B claims that a contract was formed on June 8 when S deposited the
check. B supports his claim with the following arguments: (1) The offer
should be construed as inviting an acceptance "in any manner and by any
medium reasonable in the circumstances," and depositing the check was a
reasonable manner of acceptance, UCC 2–206(1)(a); (2) Depositing the check
was a "reasonable mode of acceptance" under UCC 2–206(2); and (3) The
sending by B and the deposit by S of the check was "conduct by both
parties which recognizes the existence of a contract," UCC 2–204(1), or
demonstrated that the "parties have intended to make a contract" under
UCC 2–204(3).

Which, if any, of these arguments should the court accept?

Problem 3–3

S, a manufacturer of fertilizer, and B, a farmer, had done business for
10 years. When fertilizer was needed, B would order by telegram a specific
quantity and quality and S would fill the order at S's current wholesale
price, shipping the goods to B by carrier FOB point of shipment. Frequently, S would ship less or more than what B ordered, but the deviation would
never exceed 15%. B invariably accepted and paid for what was actually

shipped without objection. On July 10, 1987, a time of price instability in the fertilizer market, B telegraphed to S an order for 500 bags of a specified fertilizer "for prompt shipment." The wholesale price on that date was $18 per bag. On July 12, 1987, S shipped 400 bags of fertilizer to B and mailed an invoice for the wholesale price on that date, $20.00. On July 15, 1987, while the goods were still in transit and the wholesale price was $25.00 per bag, S notified B that the offer had been rejected and diverted the shipment to C, who agreed to pay $26 per bag.

§ 2-206(1)(b) applies to orders for prompt shipment

B claimed that there was a contract for the sale of 500 bags of fertilizer on July 12, 1987 at $20.00. B relied upon UCC 2–206(1)(b), asserting that this was precisely the case contemplated in Comment 4. Is B correct?

MID–SOUTH PACKERS v. SHONEY'S, INC.

United States Court of Appeals, Fifth Circuit, 1985.
761 F.2d 1117.

Before WILLIAMS, JOLLY, and HILL, CIRCUIT JUDGES.

PER CURIAM:

This diversity action on a Mississippi contract is before us following the district court's entry of summary judgment in favor of plaintiff Mid-South Packers, Inc., (Mid-South) and against defendant Shoney's, Inc., (Shoney's). We affirm.

I.

Facts

The facts, as viewed in the light most favorable to Shoney's, are as follows. In the spring of 1982, Mid-South and Shoney's engaged in negotiations for the sale by Mid-South to Shoney's of various pork products including bacon and ham. A business meeting was held between representatives of the two companies on April 17, 1982, at the offices of Mid-South in Tupelo, Mississippi. The discussion concerned prices and terms at which Mid-South could supply bacon and ham to Shoney's. At this meeting, Mid-South submitted a letter styled "Proposal" that set forth prices and terms at which Mid-South would supply Shoney's with various types of meat. The letter also provided that Shoney's would be informed forty-five days prior to any adjustment in price. The letter contained neither quantity nor durational terms. Shoney's expressed neither assent to nor rejection of the prices outlined in the letter. Shoney's estimated its needs from Mid-South at 80,000 pounds of meat per week. The legal effect of the letter proposal is the center of the controversy.

In July 1982, Shoney's began purchasing goods from Mid-South. The transactions were initiated by Shoney's, either through purchase orders or through telephone calls. On the day following each shipment, Mid-South sent invoices to Shoney's containing additional provisions for payment of both fifteen percent per annum interest on accounts not paid within seven days and reasonable collection costs, including attorney's fees. Shoney's bought vast quantities of bacon from Mid-South until August 12, 1982. On that date, Mid-South informed Shoney's at a meeting of their representatives that the price for future orders of bacon would be raised by $0.10 per pound, due to a previous error in computation by Mid-South. Shoney's objected to the price modification, apparently in reliance on the forty-five day notice provision contained in the disputed letter proposal. After negotiations, Mid-South agreed to increase the price by only $0.07 per pound. Shoney's neither agreed nor refused to purchase at the new price. Mid-South's new proposal was never reduced to writing.

On the first Shoney's purchase order sent after the August 12 meeting, Shoney's requested shipment at the old lower price. When Mid-South received the purchase order its representative, Morris Ates, called Shoney's representative, Ray Harmon, and advised Harmon that Mid-South would only deliver at the new higher price. The uncontradicted testimony of Ates is that Harmon told Ates to ship the bacon and to note the higher price on Shoney's purchase order. The bacon was shipped, and an invoice at the new price followed as did Shoney's payment, also at the new price.

From August 18 until October 5, 1982, Shoney's placed numerous orders for goods, including bacon, with Mid-South. Some if not all of these orders involved telephone conversations between representatives of the two companies, at which time Mid-South again quoted its increased selling price. The telephone conversations were followed by written purchase orders from Shoney's which quoted both the new price from Mid-South and a price computed at the original amount of $0.07 less per pound. In all cases, the orders were filled by Mid-South and invoiced at the new price. These invoices also included the additional terms providing for interest on delinquent accounts and reasonable collection costs. Shoney's paid Mid-South's quoted prices in all instances except the final order. On the final order before Shoney's began purchasing from another supplier, Shoney's offset the amount due on the invoice by $26,208, the amount allegedly overcharged on prior orders as a result of the $0.07 price increase.

Mid-South then brought this action to recover the amount offset plus interest and reasonable collection costs, including attorney's fees, as provided in the invoices. Shoney's admits that it owes $8,064.00 of the offset to Mid-South, inasmuch as this amount is attributable to orders placed after the expiration of the forty-five day notice period which, Shoney's contends, commenced on August 12 when Mid-South asked for the price increase.

II.

Shoney's contends that it accepted the proposal of Mid-South to supply it meat by placing orders with Mid-South, thereby forming a binding contract between the parties. Shoney's characterizes the contract as a "requirements contract" and asserts that the quantity term under the contract was that amount it reasonably and in good faith required. Accordingly, Shoney's argues that the notice provision contained in the letter proposal contractually bound Mid-South to notify Shoney's forty-five days before increasing its prices.

Mid-South asserts that the proposal was at most a "firm offer." Mid-South argues that under Miss.Code Ann. § 75–2–205 (1972), Uniform Commercial Code § 2–205, (hereinafter referred to as U.C.C. or the Code), a firm offer is irrevocable despite a lack of consideration "during the time stated or if no time is stated for a reasonable time; but in no event may such period of irrevocability exceed three (3) months." Thus, Mid-South contends that under any construction of the document, the offer must have expired three months after April 17, 1982, the date of the letter proposal, or on approximately July 17, 1982; therefore, it asserts the right on August 12, 1982, to increase the selling price without notice.

The district court, on consideration of cross summary judgment motions, adopted Mid-South's theory, holding that no long-term requirements contract was created and that each purchase order constituted a separate contract for the amount stated at the price required by Mid-South.

Requirements contracts are recognized in Mississippi and are not void for indefiniteness. Miss.Code Ann. § 75–2–306(1). However, an essential element of a requirements contract is the promise of the buyer to purchase exclusively from the seller either the buyer's entire requirements or up to a specified amount. * * * Absent such a commitment, the requirements contract fails for want of consideration. * * *

Ray Harmon, Shoney's agent in the transaction, maintained that Shoney's at all times had the right to purchase goods from suppliers other than Mid-South, that Shoney's continued to purchase from Mid-South because it was satisfied with its service and the quality of its goods, and that the purchase orders sent by Shoney's to Mid-South beginning in July 1982 "would have been the only commitment (Shoney's) would have made." Mid-South agrees that Shoney's had the right to change suppliers. Thus, by Shoney's own admission, no requirements contract could have arisen from the April 17 letter proposal and the meeting at which it was discussed.

Under the Code, the letter proposal and surrounding negotiations constituted, at most, a "firm offer" which was irrevocable, without consideration, only for a period of three months commencing on April 17 and ending on July 17, 1982. Miss.Code Ann. § 75–2–205.[2] Thus, Mid-South had the right, after July 17, to raise its offered price as it did and the district court was correct in so holding.

2. Section 75–2–205 provides, in part:

An offer by a merchant to buy or sell goods in a signed writing which by its terms gives assurance that it will be held open is not revocable, for lack of consideration, during the time stated or if no time is stated for a reasonable time, but in no event may such period of irrevocability exceed three (3) months.

The district court was also correct in holding that each purchase order stood on its own as a contract between Shoney's and Mid-South. More specifically, Mid-South's letter proposal was its offer in the sense that it was a promise to sell at the listed prices, justifying Shoney's in understanding that its assent, *i.e.,* its purchase orders or telephone calls, would close the bargain. *Boese-Hilburn Co. v. Dean Machinery Co.,* 616 S.W.2d 520 (Mo.App.1981); *Propane Industrial, Inc.,* 429 F.Supp. at 219; 1 A. Corbin, Contracts § 11 at 25 (1963); 1 S. Williston, Contracts § 24A (3d ed.1957); Restatement (Second) of Contracts § 24 (1981) (offer as promise). Thus, each time Shoney's manifested its assent, in telephone calls or purchase orders to Mid-South, a new and independent contract between the parties was created. *See Coastal Chemical Corporation v. Filtrol Corporation,* 374 F.2d 108, 109 (5th Cir. 1967) (Mississippi law); 1A A. Corbin, Contracts § 157 at 40–46 (where the theory here espoused is discussed at length).

Mid-South's offer, held open in its discretion at least after July 17, was properly revoked and replaced by the offer of a seven-cent price increase at the August 12 meeting. *Cf.* 1A A. Corbin § 157 at 46. Shoney's accepted this new offer for the first time on August 18 when Harmon, having been informed by Ates that Mid-South would not sell except at the new price, ordered shipment. Thereafter, Shoney's created separate contracts and obligated itself to pay the new price each time it mailed purchase orders with that price noted on them.[3] Shoney's practice of also noting the old price on the purchase orders had no contractual significance since Harmon admitted that the practice was "a tracking procedure" used by Shoney's internally in order to determine the difference between the old price and the new. Ates' testimony is uncontradicted that Harmon also told him this.

In addition, Harmon admitted that Shoney's ordered at and paid the new price with the intention of causing Mid-South to believe that Shoney's had accepted the new price so that the shipments would continue; and Mid-South attached precisely that significance to Shoney's conduct. Shoney's secretly harbored intent to later deduct the difference between the old and new price could not bind Mid-South. *See, e.g., Hotchkiss v. National City Bank,* 200 Fed. 287, 293 (S.D.N.Y. 1911) (Hand, J.), *aff'd* 231 U.S. 50, 34 S.Ct. 20, 58 L.Ed. 115 (1913) (only manifested assent is binding); Restatement (Second) of Contracts §§ 20(2)(a), 201(2)(a) (1981) (same). Conduct may bind a party to a contract if it "show[s] agreement." Miss.Code Ann. § 75–2–204(1); § 75–2–207(3). "Agreement" of the parties must be manifested either in language or conduct in the circumstances. Miss.Code Ann. § 75–1–201(3). The only manifestations Shoney's made were those consistent with assent to Mid-South's new offer. Finally, the parties' "course of performance" is consistent only with Mid-South's expressed offer and

---

3. The purchase orders also contained a column entitled "amount" which showed the total purchase price arrived at by multiplying the per unit price by the quantity ordered. On most of the post-August 12 purchase orders, Shoney's used the new higher price in computing the amount total.

Shoney's expressed acceptance of the new price. Miss.Code Ann. § 75–1–205(3)–(4); *Cf.* Miss.Code Ann. § 75–2–202(a).

What they could have done

Shoney's remedy under the circumstances was either to reserve whatever right it might have had to the old price by sending its purchase orders with an "explicit reservation," Miss.Code Ann. § 75–1–207, or to find a supplier who would sell at an acceptable price. No rational theory of the law of contracts could permit Shoney's to manifest acceptance of Mid-South's new offer, thus inducing performance, and then revoke that acceptance and demand compliance with the terms of the prior, withdrawn offer. *See* Miss.Code Ann. § 75–2–606(1)(b); § 75–2–607(1). Hence, the entire $26,208 offset by Shoney's is due and owing Mid-South and the district court's judgment, to this extent, was proper.

* * *

[The Court held that Mid-South's invoices containing additional provisions for payment and attorney fees were "confirmations" under UCC 2–207(1) and that the "additional" terms became part of the agreement under UCC 2–207(2).]

Affirmed. [Some footnotes omitted.]

Note: Conduct and Mutual Intent to Contract

When does conduct by both parties support a mutual intent to contract, even though material terms have not been agreed? The issue was raised with disputed results in a complex litigation between Bethlehem Steel Corporation and Litton Industries. After extensive negotiations, Litton agreed to construct a newly designed ore vessel for Bethlehem at a fixed price. Thereafter, the parties agreed in writing that Bethlehem should have an option, for a stated period of time, to have Litton construct up to five additional ore vessels of the same design at a stated base price of $20.4 million. If Bethlehem exercised an option, the base price was subject to escalation to be agreed by the parties for both labor and material costs under stated indices, with the escalation computed to the date a contract was executed. Despite Litton's initial requests, Bethlehem refused to exercise the option or to negotiate over price. After Litton closed its shipyard, however, Bethlehem sought to exercise the option for three additional vessels. Both parties negotiated over the escalated price but, despite apparent good faith efforts, were unable to agree. Bethlehem then sued Litton for $95,000,000 in damages, claiming that despite the failure to agree on price, the parties intended to contract for the three vessels, see UCC 2–204(3), and that the court should supply a reasonable, escalated price, see UCC 2–305(1).

The trial court treated the intention issue as a question of fact and concluded that, given the importance of the escalation clause to the contract, the complexity of the determinations involved, and the rapid inflation underway, the parties did not intend to contract unless an agreement could be reached on price. This decision was reversed, on appeal, by a three judge panel, Bethlehem Steel Corp. v. Litton Industries, Inc., 35 UCC Rep.Serv. 1091 (Pa.Super.1982). On rehearing, a panel of seven judges reversed the decision of the three judge panel and reinstated the decision of the trial court to the effect that there was no contract. 468 A.2d 748 (Pa.Super.1983). The "panel of seven's" decision was affirmed by an equally divided Supreme Court in Bethlehem Steel Corp. v. Litton Industries, Inc., 507 Pa. 88, 488 A.2d 581 (1985).

The supreme court justices voting to affirm the decision of the trial court stressed: (1) the writings of the parties were ambiguous and many terms were left open; (2) there was competent evidence to support the conclusion that the conduct of the parties was inconsistent with an intent to be bound; (3) there was no reasonably certain basis for giving an appropriate remedy; and (4) the "option" was not supported by consideration.

Justice Zappala, speaking for the justices voting to find a contract concluded, on the other hand, that Litton had acted in bad faith in negotiating over the escalation provision. Despite Bethlehem's willingness to consider a number of price indices, Litton, according to Justice Zappala, "did not intend to develop any language regarding a proposed ship construction contract" and "prevented execution of a ship construction contract by failing to bargain in good faith on the open terms." 488 A.2d at 600. On his view, this was a breach for which Bethlehem was entitled to damages.

SECTION 3. OFFER AND ACCEPTANCE—THE BATTLE OF THE FORMS AND UCC 2–207

Every student knows of the "mirror-image" rule of general contract law: An "acceptance" which varies the terms of an offer is not an acceptance at all, but a counter-offer. This is an old rule, and it makes some sense. But consider its application to the following hypothetical case: Seller sends a written offer to Buyer offering to sell processed rubber at a stated price. Buyer replies by ordering a quantity of rubber from Seller within the terms of Seller's offer, except that Buyer's order form states at the bottom in conspicuous type: "The acceptance of this order you must in any event promptly acknowledge." Seller fails promptly to acknowledge, but ships the rubber. When the rubber arrives, Buyer refuses it, having preferred to buy elsewhere, say because the price has fallen. Seller sues Buyer for breach of contract. Buyer defends claiming that because of his "acknowledgment clause" in his order form, this form was not an acceptance, but was a counter-offer which was never accepted since Seller did not acknowledge promptly. Held: for Buyer, citing the mirror-image rule. Cf. Poel v. Brunswick-Balke-Collender Co., 216 N.Y. 310, 110 N.E. 619 (1915).

There have been such decisions. And they can be traced to the influence of the mirror-image rule. If such decisions are objectionable, then they are peculiarly objectionable in the commercial field, for the scope for such decisions there is great. This is so because of the widespread and long-standing practice whereby many sellers and buyers of goods use their own standard forms in doing business: Seller sends an offer on a form containing printed terms: Buyer "accepts" using his own form with printed terms, or vice versa. Any reasonably close correspondence between the two sets of terms is, in many lines of business, sheerest coincidence. Yet, the parties nonetheless go forward with their transactions. When something goes wrong, in the unusual case, then is there a contract? If so, on what terms—Seller's? Buyer's? Courts applying the mirror-image rule, willy-nilly, might say there is no contract at all, and not even reach the second of these questions. Objections to this solution have been several, as some students once noted:

NOTE, 111 U.Pa.L.Rev. 132, 133 (1962).

"At common law and under the Uniform Sales Act, a purported acceptance which modifies the terms of the offer is a rejection and a counter-offer. Although this rule is supposed to promote certainty in the terms of the agreement, businessmen frequently undertake performance in reliance on the mistaken assumption that such an "acceptance" has created a contract. Moreover, in the context of modern business practice of using standard forms to transmit and acknowledge orders, the rule encourages a "battle of forms"—a constant effort by businessmen to gain an advantage in their transactions by qualifying their obligations by means of forms containing unilaterally beneficial conditions. In addition, the rule provides a loophole for parties wishing to extricate themselves from unfavorable deals which in commercial understanding have been closed." [Footnotes omitted.]

The Official Text of section 2–207 went through still more changes, (including the one reflected in the Roto-Lith case at p. 77 infra), until it took its present form in the 1962 Official Text, which continues to be the form set forth below. (Revisions in the Official Comments were made in 1966.)

§ 2–207. Additional Terms in Acceptance or Confirmation

(1) A definite and seasonable expression of acceptance or a written confirmation which is sent within a reasonable time operates as an acceptance even though it states terms additional to or different from those offered or agreed upon, unless acceptance is expressly made conditional on assent to the additional or different terms.

(2) The additional terms are to be construed as proposals for addition to the contract. Between merchants such terms become part of the contract unless:

(a) the offer expressly limits acceptance to the terms of the offer;

(b) they materially alter it; or

(c) notification of objection to them has already been given or is given within a reasonable time after notice of them is received.

(3) Conduct by both parties which recognizes the existence of a contract is sufficient to establish a contract for sale although the writings of the parties do not otherwise establish a contract. In such case the terms of the particular contract consist of those terms on

which the writings of the parties agree, together with any supplementary terms incorporated under any other provisions of this Act.

Problem 3–4

Review the final version of UCC 2–207. It contemplates contract formation by at least three routes. Route A consists of that part of subsection (1) up to the comma. Route B is that which appears after the comma in subsection (1). Route C is found in UCC 2–207(3). Before going farther in this Chapter, answer the following questions.

 1. May a contract be formed *via* Route B by conduct? If so, does Route B overlap with Route C?

 2. To which of these routes does UCC 2–207(2) relate?

 3. Which route is intended to change the "mirror image" rule?

 4. Does any route purport, under some circumstances, to preserve the "mirror image" rule? What circumstances?

 5. How would you state the general goals of UCC 2–207?

———

Today, there is a vast body of case law under 2–207. Indeed, almost any law firm with a substantial commercial practice will have at least one "2–207 case" in its office at any given time. One of your co-editors knows of a firm that had five such cases at one time. The section is not only of great practical significance, it tends also to be neglected (or at least not given its due) in most first year courses in contracts. Hence, we provide an opportunity here to plumb some of its depths. We offer only three cases, however. The first, *Roto-Lith, Ltd. v. F.P. Bartlett & Co.,* a 1962 case decided by the Court of Appeals for the first circuit was the first major case under 2–207 and continues to be the one most discussed. It also provides some exceptional object lessons on how 2–207 ought *not* to be interpreted. The second case, *Dorton v. Collins & Aikman Corp.,* decided in 1972, poses a sharp contrast in 2–207 methodology. The court seeks to work hard with the purposes and language of 2–207 (the final official text) and addresses several of the issues in a creditable fashion. It also explores the relationships between the various subsections of 2–207 more satisfactorily than Roto-Lith. The third case, *Daitom, Inc. v. Pennwalt Corp.* is surely one of the most important of the many relatively recent cases on 2–207. It also addresses frontally the question of what happens to "different" terms under 2–207.

Controversial Case – first to apply §2–207!

ROTO–LITH, LTD. v. F.P. BARTLETT & CO.

One Commentator called decision "Clearly Counter-majoritarian"

United States Court of Appeals, First Circuit, 1962.
297 F.2d 497.

ALDRICH, CIRCUIT JUDGE.

Plaintiff-appellant Roto-Lith, Ltd., is a New York corporation engaged *inter alia* in manufacturing, or "converting," cellophane bags for packaging vegetables. Defendant-appellee is a Massachusetts corporation which makes emulsion for use as a cellophane adhesive. This is a field of some difficulty, and various emulsions are employed, depending upon the intended purpose of the bags. In May and October 1959 plaintiff purchased emulsion from the defendant. Subsequently bags produced with this emulsion failed to adhere, and this action was instituted in the district court for the District of Massachusetts. At the conclusion of the evidence the court directed a verdict for the defendant.[1] This appeal followed.

Δ claims that its sales contract expressly negatived any warranties

Defendant asks us to review the October transaction first because of certain special considerations applicable to the May order. The defense in each instance, however, is primarily the same, namely, defendant contends that the sales contract expressly negatived any warranties.[2] We will deal first with the October order.

π wanted emulsion for wet pack bags, Δ sent dry pack (yet this was never a question!)

On October 23, 1959, plaintiff, in New York, mailed a written order to defendant in Massachusetts for a drum of "N–132–C" emulsion, stating "End use: wet pack spinach bags." Defendant on October 26 prepared simultaneously an acknowledgment and an invoice. The printed forms were exactly the same, except that one was headed "Acknowledgment" and the other "Invoice," and the former contemplated insertion of the proposed, and the latter of the actual, shipment date. Defendant testified that in accordance with its regular practice the acknowledgment was prepared and mailed the same day. The plaintiff's principal liability witness testified that he did not know whether this acknowledgment "was received, or what happened to it." On this state of the evidence there is an unrebutted presumption of receipt. Johnston v. Cassidy, 1932, 279 Mass. 593, 181 N.E. 748; cf. Tobin v. Taintor, 1918, 229 Mass. 174, 118 N.E. 247. The goods were shipped to New York on October 27. On the evidence it must be found that the acknowledgment was received at least no later than the goods. The invoice was received presumably a day or two after the goods.

The acknowledgment and the invoice bore in conspicuous type on their face the following legend, "All goods sold without warranties, express or implied, and subject to the terms on reverse side." In somewhat smaller, but still conspicuous, type there were printed on the back certain terms of sale, of which the following are relevant:

> "1. Due to the variable conditions under which these goods may be transported, stored, handled, or used, Seller hereby expressly excludes any and all warranties, guaranties, or representations whatsoever. Buyer assumes risk for results obtained from use of these goods, whether used alone or in combination with other products. Seller's liability hereunder shall be limited to the replacement of any goods that materially differ from the Seller's

1. Also involved was a counter-claim, but this requires no separate discussion.

2. The defendant also contends that the warranties, if any there might have been, were not broken. This is a question of fact with which we are not concerned.

sample order on the basis of which the order for such goods was made.

"7. This acknowledgment contains all of the terms of this purchase and sale. No one except a duly authorized officer of Seller may execute or modify contracts. Payment may be made only at the offices of the Seller. *If these terms are not acceptable, Buyer must so notify Seller at once.*" (Ital. suppl.)

It is conceded that plaintiff did not protest defendant's attempt so to limit its liability, and in due course paid for the emulsion and used it. It is also conceded that adequate notice was given of breach of warranty, if there were warranties. The only issue which we will consider is whether all warranties were excluded by defendant's acknowledgment.[3]

The first question is what law the Massachusetts court would look to in order to determine the terms of the contract. Under Massachusetts law this is the place where the last material act occurs. Autographic Register Co. v. Philip Hano Co., 1 Cir., 1952, 198 F.2d 208; Milliken v. Pratt, 1878, 125 Mass. 374. Under the Uniform Commercial Code, Mass.Gen.Laws Ann. (1958) ch. 106, § 2–206, mailing the acknowledgment would clearly have completed the contract in Massachusetts by acceptance had the acknowledgment not sought to introduce new terms. Section 2–207 provides:

"(1) A definite and seasonable expression of acceptance or a written confirmation which is sent within a reasonable time operates as an acceptance even though it states terms additional to or different from those offered or agreed upon, unless acceptance is expressly made conditional on assent to the additional or different terms.

"(2) The additional terms are to be construed as proposals for addition to the contract. Between merchants such terms become part of the contract unless:

"(a) the offer expressly limits acceptance to the terms of the offer;

"(b) they materially alter it; or

"(c) notification of objection to them has already been given or is given within a reasonable time after notice of them is received."

Plaintiff exaggerates the freedom which this section affords an offeror to ignore a reply from an offeree that does not in terms coincide with the original offer. According to plaintiff defendant's condition that there should be no warranties constituted a proposal which "materially altered" the agreement. As to this we concur. See Uniform Commercial Code comment to this section, Mass.Gen.Laws annotation, supra, paragraph 4. Plaintiff goes on to say that by virtue of the

---

3. Defendant also relies upon the terms of the invoice in view of the fact that it was admittedly received before plaintiff *used* the goods. Whether an invoice not received until after the goods can modify the contract raises some possible matters which we do not reach.

Court at least is aware that there many be problems, but we will look at those when problems arise.

statute the acknowledgment effected a completed agreement without this condition, and that as a further proposal the condition never became part of the agreement because plaintiff did not express assent. We agree that section 2–207 changed the existing law, but not to this extent. Its purpose was to modify the strict principle that a response not precisely in accordance with the offer was a rejection and a counteroffer. Kehlor Flour Mills Co. v. Linden, 1918, 230 Mass. 119, 123, 119 N.E. 698; Saco-Lowell Shops v. Clinton Mills Co., 1 Cir., 1921, 277 F. 349. Now, within stated limits, a response that does not in all respects correspond with the offer constitutes an acceptance of the offer, and a counteroffer only as to the differences. If plaintiff's contention is correct that a reply to an offer stating additional conditions unilaterally burdensome upon the offeror is a binding acceptance of the original offer plus simply a proposal for the additional conditions, the statute would lead to an absurdity. Obviously no offeror will subsequently assent to such conditions.

The statute is not too happily drafted. Perhaps it would be wiser in all cases for an offeree to say in so many words, "I will not accept your offer until you assent to the following: * * *" But businessmen cannot be expected to act by rubric. It would be unrealistic to suppose that when an offeree replies setting out conditions that would be burdensome only to the offeror he intended to make an unconditional acceptance of the original offer, leaving it simply to the offeror's good nature whether he would assume the additional restrictions. To give the statute a practical construction we must hold that a response which states a condition materially altering the obligation solely to the disadvantage of the offeror is an "acceptance * * * expressly * * * conditional on assent to the additional * * * terms."

Plaintiff accepted the goods with knowledge of the conditions specified in the acknowledgment. It became bound.[4] Garst v. Harris, 1900, 177 Mass. 72, 58 N.E. 174; Doerr v. Woolsey, 1889, 5 N.Y.S. 447 (Com.Pl.Gen.Term); cf. Joseph v. Atlantic Basin Iron Works, Inc., Sup., 1954, 132 N.Y.S.2d 671, aff'd Sup., 143 N.Y.S.2d 601 (App.Div.). Whether the contract was made in Massachusetts or New York, there has been no suggestion that either jurisdiction will not give effect to an appropriate disclaimer of warranties. See Mass.Gen.Laws Ann. c. 106, § 2–316; New York Personal Property Law, McKinney's Consol. Laws, c. 41, § 152. This disposes of the October order.

With respect to the May order a different situation obtains. Here plaintiff ordered a quantity of "N–136–F," which was defendant's code number for a dry-bag emulsion. The order stated as the end use a wet bag. Accordingly, defendant knew, by its own announced standards, that the emulsion ordered was of necessity unfit for the disclosed purpose. In this bald situation plaintiff urges that the defendant

4. It does not follow that if the acknowledgment had miscarried plaintiff's receipt of the goods would have completed a contract which did not include the terms of the acknowledgment. We are not faced with the question of how the statute may affect the common law under such circumstances.

cannot be permitted to specify that it made no implied warranty of fitness.

We do not reach this question. In the court below, when plainly asked to state its opposition to the direction of a verdict, plaintiff did not advance the arguments it now makes, and in no way called the court's attention to any distinction between the May and the October orders. An appellant is not normally permitted to have the benefit of a new theory on appeal. It is true that this is not an absolute prohibition. The court in its discretion may relax the rule in exceptional cases in order to prevent a clear miscarriage of justice. Hormel v. Helvering, 1941, 312 U.S. 552, 61 S.Ct. 719, 85 L.Ed. 1037; Bergeron v. Mansour, 1 Cir., 1945, 152 F.2d 27, 32; Palo Blanco Fruit Co. v. Palo Alto Orchards Co., 1 Cir., 1952, 195 F.2d 90. Plaintiff's point, however, is by no means clear-cut. Financially the consequences are not large. Plaintiff was represented by competent counsel, and has had an eight-day trial. We do not think the case one for making an exception to the salutary rule that a party is normally entitled to but one "day" in court.

No question remains as to the counterclaim.

Judgment will be entered affirming the judgment of the District Court.

DORTON v. COLLINS & AIKMAN CORP.

United States Court of Appeals, Sixth Circuit, 1972.
453 F.2d 1161.

Before CELEBREZZE, BROOKS and MILLER, CIRCUIT JUDGES.

CELEBREZZE, CIRCUIT JUDGE.

This is an appeal from the District Court's denial of Defendant-Appellant's motion for a stay pending arbitration, pursuant to Section 3 of the United States Arbitration Act of 1925, 9 U.S.C. § 3. The suit arose after a series of over 55 transactions during 1968, 1969, and 1970 in which Plaintiffs-Appellees [hereinafter The Carpet Mart], carpet retailers in Kingsport, Tennessee, purchased carpets from Defendant-Appellant [hereinafter Collins & Aikman], incorporated under the laws of the State of Delaware, with its principal place of business in New York, New York, and owner of a carpet manufacturing plant [formerly the Painter Carpet Mills, Inc.] located in Dalton, Georgia. The Carpet Mart originally brought this action in a Tennessee state trial court, seeking compensatory and punitive damages in the amount of $450,000 from Collins & Aikman for the latter's alleged fraud, deceit, and misrepresentation in the sale of what were supposedly carpets manufactured from 100% Kodel polyester fiber. The Carpet Mart maintains that in May, 1970, in response to a customer complaint, it learned that not all of the carpets were manufactured from 100% Kodel polyester fiber but rather some were composed of a cheaper and inferior carpet fiber. After the cause was removed to the District Court on the basis of diversity of citizenship, Collins & Aikman moved for a stay pending arbitration, asserting that The Carpet Mart was bound to an arbitration agreement which appeared on the reverse side of Collins & Aikman's printed sales acknowledgment forms. Holding that there existed no binding arbitration agreement between the parties, the District Court denied the stay. For the reasons set forth below, we remand the case to the District Court for further findings.

I

We initially note that the denial of a motion to stay pending arbitration, although interlocutory in nature, is appealable to this Court * * *.

We also find that there is no conflicts of law problem in the present case, the Uniform Commercial Code having been enacted in both Georgia and Tennessee at the time of the disputed transactions. * * *

II

The primary question before us on appeal is whether the District Court, in denying Collins & Aikman's motion for a stay pending arbitration, erred in holding that The Carpet Mart was not bound by the arbitration agreement appearing on the back of Collins & Aikman's acknowledgment forms. In reviewing the District Court's determination, we must look closely at the procedures which were followed in the sales transactions which gave rise to the present dispute over the arbitration agreement.

In each of the more than 55 transactions, one of the partners in The Carpet Mart, or, on some occasions, Collins & Aikman's visiting salesman, telephoned Collins & Aikman's order department in Dalton, Georgia, and ordered certain quantities of carpets listed in Collins & Aikman's catalogue. There is some dispute as to what, if any, agreements were reached through the telephone calls and through the visits by Collins & Aikman's salesman. After each oral order was placed, the price, if any, quoted by the buyer was checked against Collins & Aikman's price list, and the credit department was consulted to determine if The Carpet Mart had paid for all previous shipments. After it was found that everything was in order, Collins & Aikman's order department typed the information concerning the particular order on one of its printed acknowledgment forms. Each acknowledgment form bore one of three legends: "Acknowledgment," "Customer Acknowledgment," or "Sales Contract." The following provision was printed on the face of the forms bearing the "Acknowledgment" legend:

"The acceptance of your order is subject to all of the terms and conditions on the face and reverse side hereof, including arbitration, all of which are accepted by buyer; it supersedes buyer's order form, if any. It shall become a contract either (a) when signed and delivered by buyer to seller and accepted in writing by seller, or (b) at *Seller's* option, when buyer shall have given to seller specification of assortments, delivery dates, shipping instructions, or instructions to bill and hold as to all or any part of the merchandise herein described, or when buyer has received delivery of the whole or any part thereof, or when buyer has otherwise assented to the terms and conditions hereof."

Similarly, on the face of the forms bearing the "Customer Acknowledgment" or "Sales Contract" legends the following provision appeared:

"This order is given subject to all of the terms and conditions on the face and reverse side hereof, including the provisions for arbitration and the exclusion of warranties, all of which are accepted by Buyer, supersede Buyer's order form, if any, and constitute the entire contract between Buyer and Seller. This order shall become a contract as to the entire quantity specified either (a) when signed and delivered by Buyer to Seller and accepted in writing by Seller or (b) when Buyer has received and retained this order for ten days without objection, or (c) when Buyer has accepted delivery of any part of the merchandise specified herein or has furnished to Seller specifications or assortments, delivery dates, shipping instructions, or instructions to bill and hold, or when Buyer has otherwise indicated acceptance of the terms hereof."

The small print on the reverse side of the forms provided, among other things, that all claims arising out of the contract would be submitted to arbitration in New York City. Each acknowledgment form was signed by an employee of Collins & Aikman's order department and mailed to The Carpet Mart on the day the telephone order was received or, at the latest, on the following day.[1] The carpets were thereafter shipped to The Carpet Mart, with the interval between the mailing of the acknowledgment form and shipment of the carpets varying from a brief interval to a period of several weeks or months. Absent a delay in the mails, however, The Carpet Mart always received the acknowledgment forms prior to receiving the carpets. In all cases The Carpet Mart took delivery of and paid for the carpets without objecting to any terms contained in the acknowledgment form.

In holding that no binding arbitration agreement was created between the parties through the transactions above, the District Court relied on T.C.A. § 47–2–207 [UCC § 2–207], which provides: [the Court quoted UCC 2–207.]

*   *   **

The District Court found that Subsection 2–207(3) controlled the instant case, quoting the following passage from 1 W. Hawkland, A Transac-

---

    1. The District Court found that "[Collins & Aikman] has not established to this point that the aforementioned acknowledgment forms were received in each instance." The affidavit of J.A. Castle, a partner in The Carpet Mart, however, states that " * * * I would receive a yellow sheet of paper which I believed to be an acknowledgment that my order was being processed and was being sent to me."

And at oral arguments before this Court, counsel for The Carpet Mart did not attempt to overcome the presumption that the acknowledgments, having been mailed in each instance according to William T. Hester's affidavit, were received. *See* W.E. Richmond & Co. v. Security National Bank, 16 Tenn.App. 414, 64 S.W.2d 863 (1933); Roto-Lith, Ltd. v. F.P. Bartlett & Co., 297 F.2d 497, 498 (1st Cir.1962).

Looks at an interpretation tional Guide to the Uniform Commercial Code § 1.090303, at 19–20 (1964):

> "If the seller * * * ships the goods and the buyer accepts them, a contract is formed under subsection (3). The terms of this contract are those on which the purchase order and acknowledgment agree, and the additional terms needed for a contract are to be found throughout the U.C.C. * * * [T]he U.C.C. does not impose an arbitration term on the parties where their contract is silent on the matter. Hence, a conflict between an arbitration and a no-arbitration clause would result in the no-arbitration clause becoming effective."

Court held No arbitration clause Under this authority alone the District Court concluded that the arbitration clause on the back of Collins & Aikman's sales acknowledgment had not become a binding term in the 50–odd transactions with The Carpet Mart.

In reviewing this determination by the District Court, we are aware of the problems which courts have had in interpreting Section 2–207. This section of the UCC has been described as a "murky bit of prose," Southwest Engineering Co. v. Martin Tractor Co., 205 Kan. 684, 694, 473 P.2d 18, 25 (1970), as "not too happily drafted," Roto-Lith Ltd. v. F.P. Bartlett & Co., 297 F.2d 497, 500 (1st Cir.1962), and as "one of the most important, subtle, and difficult in the entire Code, and well it may be said that the product as it finally reads is not altogether satisfactory." Duesenberg & King, Sales and Bulk Transfers under the Uniform Commercial Code, (Vol. 3, Bender's Uniform Commercial Code Service) § 3.03, at 3–12 (1969). Despite the lack of clarity in its language, Section 2–207 manifests definite objectives which are significant in the present case.

As Official Comment No. 1 indicates, UCC § 2–207 was intended to apply to two situations:

> "The one is where an agreement has been reached either orally or by informal correspondence between the parties and is followed by one or both of the parties sending formal acknowledgments or memoranda embodying the terms so far as agreed upon and adding terms not discussed. The other situation is one in which a wire or letter expressed and intended as the closing or confirmation of an agreement adds further minor suggestions or proposals such as 'ship by Tuesday,' 'rush,' 'ship draft against bill of lading inspection allowed,' or the like." T.C.A. § 47–2–207 [UCC § 2–207], Official Comment 1.

Although Comment No. 1 is itself somewhat ambiguous, it is clear that Section 2–207, and specifically Subsection 2–207(1), was intended to alter the "ribbon matching" or *mirror* rule of common law, under which the terms of an acceptance or confirmation were required to be identical to the terms of the offer or oral agreement, respectively. 1 W. Hawkland, *supra,* at 16; R. Nordstrom, Handbook of the Law of Sales, Sec. 37, at 99–100 (1970). Under the common law, an acceptance or a confirmation which contained terms additional to or different from those of the offer or oral agreement constituted a rejection of the offer or agreement and thus became a counter-offer. The terms of the counter-offer were said to have been accepted by the original offeror when he proceeded to perform under the contract without objecting to the counter-offer. Thus, a buyer was deemed to have accepted the seller's counter-offer if he took receipt of the goods and paid for them without objection.

Under Section 2–207 the result is different. This section of the Code recognizes that in current commercial transactions, the terms of the offer and those of the acceptance will seldom be identical. Rather, under the current "battle of the forms," each party typically has a printed form drafted by his attorney and containing as many terms as could be envisioned to favor that party in his sales transactions. Whereas under common law the disparity between the fine-print terms in the parties' forms would have prevented the consummation of a contract when these forms are exchanged, Section 2–207 recognizes that in many, but not all, cases the parties do not impart such significance to the terms on the printed forms. *See* 1 W. Hawkland, *supra;* § 1.0903, at 14, § 1.090301, at 16. Subsection 2–207(1) therefore provides that "[a] definite and seasonable expression of acceptance or a written confirmation * * * operates as an acceptance even though it states terms additional to or different from those offered or agreed upon, unless acceptance is expressly made conditional on assent to the additional or different terms." Thus, under Subsection (1), a contract is recognized notwithstanding the fact that an acceptance or confirmation contains terms additional to or different from those of the offer or prior agreement, provided that the offeree's intent to accept the offer is definitely expressed, *see* Sections 2–204 and 2–206, and provided that the offeree's acceptance is not expressly conditioned on the offeror's assent to the additional or different terms. When a contract is recognized under Subsection (1), the additional terms are treated as "proposals for addition to the contract" under Subsection (2), which contains special provisions under which such additional terms are deemed to have been accepted when the transaction is between merchants. Conversely, when no contract is recognized under Subsection 2–207(1)— either because no definite expression of acceptance exists or, more specifically, because the offeree's acceptance is expressly conditioned on the offeror's assent to the additional or different terms—the entire transaction aborts at this point. If, however, the subsequent conduct of the parties—particularly, performance by both parties under what they apparently believe to be a contract—recognizes the existence of a contract, under Subsection 2–207(3) such conduct by both parties is sufficient to establish a contract, notwithstanding the fact that no contract would have been recognized on the basis of their writings alone. Subsection 2–207(3) further provides how the terms of contracts recognized thereunder shall be determined.

[Handwritten marginal notes:] When K under (1) add'l terms are "proposals for addition to K"

When no K under (1) — entire transaction aborts ↓ But if conduct Under (3) suggests a K, then it is!

With the above analysis and purposes of Section 2–207 in mind, we turn to their application in the present case. We initially observe that the affidavits and the acknowledgment forms themselves raise the question of whether Collins & Aikman's forms constituted acceptances or confirmations under Section 2–207. The language of some of the acknowledgment forms ("The acceptance of your order is subject to * * *") and the affidavit of Mr. William T. Hester, Collins & Aikman's marketing operations manager, suggest that the forms were the only acceptances issued in response to The Carpet Mart's oral offers. However, in his affidavit Mr. J.A. Castle, a partner in The Carpet Mart, asserted that when he personally called Collins & Aikman to order carpets, someone from the latter's order department would agree to sell the requested carpets, or, alternatively, when Collins & Aikman's visiting salesman took the order, he would agree to the sale, on some occasions after he had used The Carpet Mart's telephone to call Collins & Aikman's order department. Absent the District Court's determination of whether Collins & Aikman's acknowledgment forms were acceptances or, alternatively, confirmations of prior oral agreements, we will consider the application of section 2–207 to both situations for the guidance of the District Court on remand.

Viewing Collins & Aikman's acknowledgment forms as acceptances under Subsection 2–207(1), we are initially faced with the question of whether the arbitration provision in Collins & Aikman's acknowledgment forms were in fact "additional to or different from" the terms of The Carpet Mart's oral offers. In the typical case under Section 2–207, there exist both a written purchase order and a written acknowledgment, and this determination can be readily made by comparing the two forms. In the present case, where the only written forms were Collins & Aikman's sales acknowledgments, we believe that such a comparison must be made between the oral offers and the written acceptances.[2] Although the District Court apparently assumed that The Carpet Mart's oral orders did not include in their terms the arbitration provision which appeared in Collins & Aikman's acknowledgment forms, we believe that a specific finding on this point will be required on remand.[3]

Assuming, for purposes of analysis, that the arbitration provision was an addition to the terms of The Carpet Mart's oral offers, we must next determine whether or not Collins & Aikman's acceptances were "expressly made conditional on assent to the additional * * * terms"

---

2. In describing the second (offer-acceptance) situation to which Section 2–207 was intended to apply, Official Comment No. 1 describes the acceptance as a "wire or letter" but makes no such reference to a written offer. As in the situation where there is but one written confirmation sent subsequent to an oral agreement—which is expressly referred to in Comment No. 1—we believe the drafters anticipated cases, such as the present one, where a written acceptance would be sent in response to an oral offer.

3. It is not inconceivable that a buyer might request that all claims be submitted to arbitration, see Universal Oil Products v. S.C.M. Corp., 313 F.Supp. 905 (D.Conn. 1970), or that a buyer might orally submit to the seller's known policy of arbitration in order to facilitate acceptance of the offer.

therein, within the proviso of Subsection 2–207(1). As set forth in full above, the provision appearing on the face of Collins & Aikman's acknowledgment forms stated that the acceptances (or orders) were "subject to all of the terms and conditions on the face and reverse side hereof, including arbitration, all of which are accepted by buyer." The provision on the "Acknowledgment" forms further stated that Collins & Aikman's terms would become the basis of the contract between the parties

> "either (a) when signed and delivered by buyer to seller and accepted in writing by seller, or (b) at Seller's option, when buyer shall have given to seller specification of assortments, delivery dates, shipping instructions, or instructions to bill and hold as to all or any part of the merchandise herein described, or when buyer has received delivery of the whole or any part thereof, or when buyer has otherwise assented to the terms and conditions hereof."

Similarly, the provision on the "Customer Acknowledgment" and "Sales Contract" forms stated that the terms therein would become the basis of the contract

> "either (a) when signed and delivered by Buyer to Seller and accepted in writing by Seller or (b) when Buyer has received and retained this order for ten days without objection, or (c) when Buyer has accepted delivery of any part of the merchandise specified herein or has furnished to Seller specifications or assortments, delivery dates, shipping instructions to bill and hold, or when Buyer has otherwise indicated acceptance of the terms hereof."

Although Collins & Aikman's use of the words "subject to" suggests that the acceptances were conditional to some extent, we do not believe the acceptances were "expressly made conditional on [the buyer's] assent to the additional or different terms," as specifically required under the Subsection 2–207(1) proviso. In order to fall within this proviso, it is not enough that an acceptance is expressly conditional on additional or different terms; rather, an acceptance must be *expressly* conditional on the offeror's *assent* to those terms. Viewing the Subsection (1) proviso within the context of the rest of that Subsection and within the policies of Section 2–207 itself, we believe that it was intended to apply only to an acceptance which clearly reveals that the offeree is unwilling to proceed with the transaction unless he is assured of the offeror's assent to the additional or different terms therein. See 1 W. Hawkland, *supra,* § 1.090303, at 21. That the acceptance is predicated on the offeror's assent must be "directly and distinctly stated or expressed rather than implied or left to inference." Webster's Third International Dictionary (defining "express").

Although the UCC does not provide a definition of "assent," it is significant that Collins & Aikman's printed acknowledgment forms specified at least seven types of action or inaction on the part of the buyer which—sometimes at Collins & Aikman's option—would be deemed to bind the buyer to the terms therein. These ranged from the buyer's signing and delivering the acknowledgment to the seller—which indeed could have been recognized as the buyer's assent to Collins & Aikman's terms—to the buyer's retention of the acknowledgment for ten days without objection—which could never have been recognized as the buyer's assent to the additional or different terms where acceptance is expressly conditional on that assent.[4]

To recognize Collins & Aikman's acceptances as "expressly conditional on [the buyer's] assent to the additional * * * terms" therein, within the proviso of Subsection 2–207(1), would thus require us to ignore the specific language of that provision.[5] Such an interpretation is not justified in view of the fact that Subsection 2–207(1) is clearly designed to give legal recognition to many contracts where the variance between the offer and acceptance would have precluded such recognition at common law.

Because Collins & Aikman's acceptances were not expressly conditional on the buyer's assent to the additional terms within the proviso of Subsection 2–207(1), a contract is recognized under Subsection (1), and the additional terms are treated as "proposals" for addition to the contract under Subsection 2–207(2).[6] Since both Collins & Aikman and The Carpet Mart are clearly "merchants" as that term is defined in Subsection 2–104(1), the arbitration provision will be deemed to have been accepted by The Carpet Mart under Subsection 2–207(2) unless it materially altered the terms of The Carpet Mart's oral offers. T.C.A.

4. The common law has never recognized silence or inaction as a mode of acceptance. *See* 1 W. Hawkland, *supra,* § 1.090301, at 17. Under the counter-offer approach which Section 2–207 was designed to modify, the offeror had to take receipt of and pay for the goods without objection before he was deemed to have accepted the terms of the counter-offer. And although Subsection 2–207(2)(c) provides that certain additional terms can be accepted by the offeror's failure to object, nothing in the Code suggests that silence or inaction can be recognized as an offeror's assent in the present context.

5. We are aware that at least two Courts of Appeals have not chosen to read the Subsection 2–207(1) proviso as strictly as we do here. *See* Roto-Lith, Ltd. v. F.P. Bartlett & Co., 297 F.2d 497, 499–500 (1st Cir.1962); Construction Aggregates Corp. v. Hewitt-Robins, Inc., 404 F.2d 505, 509 (5th Cir.1969) (dictum). But see Matter of Doughboy Industries, Inc., and Pantasote Co., 17 A.D.2d 216, 233 N.Y.S.2d 488 (1962). We believe, however, that the approach adopted here is dictated by both the language of the proviso and the purpose of Subsection 2–207(1).

6. Apparently believing that Collins & Aikman's acknowledgments were acceptances "expressly * * * conditional on assent to the additional or different terms" under the Subsection 2–207(1) proviso, the District Court recognized contracts between the parties under Subsection 2–207(3) since the subsequent performance by both parties clearly recognized the existence of a contract. Absent our conclusion that Collins & Aikman's acknowledgments do not fall within the Subsection 2–207(1) proviso, we believe that the District Court correctly applied Subsection 2–207(3) to Collins & Aikman's "acceptances" notwithstanding the fact that some of the language of that Subsection appears to refer to the typical situation under Section 2–207 where there exist both a written offer and a written acceptance. Although we recognize the value that writings by both parties serve in sales transactions, where Subsection 2–207(3) is otherwise applicable we do not believe the purposes of that Subsection should be abandoned simply because the offeror chose to rely on his oral offer. In such a case, we believe that the District Court's comparison of the terms of the oral offer and the written acceptance under Subsection (3) would have been correct.

§ 47–2–207(2)(b) [UCC § 2–207(2)(b)].[7] We believe that the question of whether the arbitration provision materially altered the oral offer under Subsection 2–207(2)(b) is one which can be resolved only by the District Court on further findings of fact in the present case.[8] If the arbitration provision did in fact materially alter The Carpet Mart's offer, it could not become a part of the contract "unless expressly agreed to" by The Carpet Mart. T.C.A. § 47–2–207 [UCC § 2–207], Official Comment No. 3.

We therefore conclude that if on remand the District Court finds that Collins & Aikman's acknowledgments were in fact acceptances and that the arbitration provision was additional to the terms of The Carpet Mart's oral orders, contracts will be recognized under Subsection 2–207(1). The arbitration clause will then be viewed as a "proposal" under Subsection 2–207(2) which will be deemed to have been accepted by The Carpet Mart unless it materially altered the oral offers.

If the District Court finds that Collins & Aikman's acknowledgment forms were not acceptances but rather were confirmations of prior oral agreements between the parties, an application of Section 2–207 similar to that above will be required. Subsection 2–207(1) will require an initial determination of whether the arbitration provision in the confirmations was "additional to or different from" the terms orally agreed upon. Assuming that the District Court finds that the arbitration provision was not a term of the oral agreements between the parties, the arbitration clause will be treated as a "proposal" for addition to the contract under Subsection 2–207(2), as was the case when Collins & Aikman's acknowledgments were viewed as acceptances above. The provision for arbitration will be deemed to have been accepted by The Carpet Mart unless the District Court finds that it materially altered the prior oral agreements, in which case The Carpet Mart could not become bound thereby absent an express agreement to that effect.

As a result of the above application of Section 2–207 to the limited facts before us in the present case, we find it necessary to remand the case to the District Court for the following findings: (1) whether oral

7. The parties do not dispute the fact that The Carpet Mart made no objections to the terms embodied in Collins & Aikman's acknowledgments. Therefore, Subsection 2–207(2)(c) is not relevant in the present case. And although it is not inconceivable that an oral offer could "expressly [limit] acceptance to the terms of the offer" under Subsection 2–207(2)(a), The Carpet Mart has never asserted that this was the nature of its offers to Collins & Aikman. We are therefore concerned with only Subsection 2–207(2)(b).

8. While T.C.A. § 47–2–207 [UCC § 2–207]. Official Comment Nos. 4 and 5 provide examples of terms which would and would not materially alter a contract, an arbitration clause is listed under neither. Although we recognize the rule "that the agreement to arbitrate must be direct and the intention made clear, without implication, inveiglement or subtlety," Matter of Doughboy Industries, Inc., and Pantasote Co., 17 A.D.2d 216, 218, 233 N.Y.S.2d 488, 492 (1962) (indicating in dictum that an arbitration clause would materially alter a contract under 2–207(2)(b), we believe the question of material alteration necessarily rests on the facts of each case. See American Parts Co. v. American Arbitration Ass'n, 8 Mich.App. 156, 171, 154 N.W.2d 5, 14 (1967).

agreements were reached between the parties prior to the sending of Collins & Aikman's acknowledgment forms; if there were no such oral agreements, (2) whether the arbitration provision appearing in Collins & Aikman's "acceptances" was additional to the terms of The Carpet Mart's oral offers; and, if so, (3) whether the arbitration provision materially altered the terms of The Carpet Mart's oral offers. Alternatively, if the District Court does find that oral agreements were reached between the parties before Collins & Aikman's acknowledgment forms were sent in each instance, it will be necessary for the District Court to make the following findings: (1) whether the prior oral agreements embodied the arbitration provision appearing in Collins & Aikman's "confirmations"; and, if not, (2) whether the arbitration provision materially altered the prior oral agreements. Regardless of whether the District Court finds Collins & Aikman's acknowledgment forms to have been acceptances or confirmations, if the arbitration provision was additional to, and a material alteration of, the offers or prior oral agreements, The Carpet Mart will not be bound to that provision absent a finding that it expressly agreed to be bound thereby.

III

If, on remand, the District Court finds that the arbitration provision exists as a term of the contracts recognized under this application of Section 2–207, Collins & Aikman's motion for a stay pending arbitration must be granted despite the fact that this is an action in fraud. In Prima Paint Corp. v. Flood & Conklin Mfg. Co., 388 U.S. 395, 87 S.Ct. 1801, 18 L.Ed.2d 1270 (1967), the Supreme Court held that in passing upon a motion for a stay pending arbitration under 9 U.S.C. § 3, a federal court may not consider claims of fraud in the inducement of the overall contract when the arbitration clause is sufficiently broad to encompass claims of fraud. Rather, in such cases a federal court may consider only claims which relate to the "making" of the arbitration agreement itself. 388 U.S. at 402–404, 87 S.Ct. 1801. In the present case, the language of Collins & Aikman's arbitration clause is virtually identical to that of the arbitration agreement in the Prima Paint case.[9] Moreover, although The Carpet Mart challenges the legibility of the fine-print arbitration provision on the reverse side of Collins & Aikman's forms (which was specifically called to the buyer's attention on the face of those forms), The Carpet Mart's claim of fraud relates only to the substitutions for Kodel polyester fibers under the overall contract and not to the arbitration clause itself. Therefore, upon a finding by the District Court that the arbitration clause was a term of the contracts recognized under T.C.A. § 47–2–207 (UCC § 2–207), Collins & Aikman's motion for a stay pending arbitration must be granted.

9. Collins & Aikman's clause reads in pertinent part: "Any controversy arising out of or relating to this contract shall be settled by arbitration. * * *" In comparison, the arbitration agreement in the Prima Paint case read in pertinent part: "Any controversy or claim arising out of or relating to this Agreement, or the breach thereof, shall be settled by arbitration. * * *" 388 U.S. at 398, 87 S.Ct. at 1803.

For the reasons set forth above, the case is remanded to the District Court for further findings consistent with this opinion. [Some footnotes omitted.]

J. WHITE AND R. SUMMERS, HANDBOOK OF THE LAW UNDER THE UNIFORM COMMERCIAL CODE 27–31 (2d ed. 1980).

Assume that buyer sends a purchase order which provides that any dispute will be governed by arbitration. Seller responds with an acknowledgement which provides that any dispute will not be resolved by arbitration. If the *bargained* terms on the purchase order and acknowledgement agree, we would find that the seller's document is a definite and seasonable expression of acceptance under 2–207 and that a contract has been formed by the exchange of the documents. We would thus bind the welsher who seeks to get out of the contract before either performs.

Assume that the seller then ships the goods, the buyer receives and pays for them, and the parties fall into dispute about their quality. Does the contract call for arbitration or does it not? ?* * *

* * * [T]he seller can argue that his acceptance is only an acceptance of the terms on which the two documents agree, and they did not agree on arbitration, nor do Code gap fillers provide for arbitration. This argument finds no explicit support in 2–207, but one of us (White) thinks it finds some support in part of Comment 6.
* * *

In the end, how would our hypothetical case come out under the Code? One of us (White) would turn to [Official Comment 6] and find that the two terms cancel one another. On this view the seller's form was only an acceptance of terms in the offer which did not conflict with any terms in the acceptance. Thus the ultimate deal would not include an arbitration clause unless the course of performance (2–208), course of dealing (1–205), or usage of trade (1–205) supplies one. The Code does not expressly authorize this result, but it does not bar it either.

The other of us (Summers) believes that Comment 6 is not applicable. In his view it applies only to variant terms on *confirming* forms, not to variant terms on forms one of which is an offer and the other an acceptance under 2–207(1) (a distinction itself drawn in Comment 1). Thus the buyer's arbitration clause controls, for the seller's no-arbitration clause, as a *different* term embodied in the accepting form, simply falls out; 2–207(2) cannot rescue it since that provision applies only to *additional* terms. White answers that, among other things, this reading gives the sender of the first form (the buyer here) an unearned advantage. Summers does not agree that the "advantage" is entirely unearned. The recipient of the first form at least had an opportunity to object to its contents. Moreover, Summers believes that White's approach is relatively more unfair to the offeror than Summers's approach is to the offeree. According to Summers, the offeror has more (even if only a little more) reason to expect that his clause will control than the offeree has to expect that his will. After all, when the offeree sends his form he will have already received a form from the offeror, and offerees know full well that forms of different parties rarely coincide. But even if the offeror's advantage is to some extent unearned, the text of 2–207, according to Summers, appears more or less plainly to authorize it, and if the drafters intended the White approach, they could have easily drafted the section accordingly.

What if the "different" term comes into being partly by operation of a Code gap filler provision * * * rather than by virtue of a conflict of terms specified in the two forms (as in our hypothetical case)? For example, in Air Products & Chemicals, Inc. v. Fairbanks Morse, Inc.,[12] the seller's accepting form limited consequential damages. The buyer's offering form was silent on this subject but the buyer appears to have urged that the relevant Code gap filler (2–714(3)) "impliedly" provided for full consequential damages, that the seller's term was therefore a "different" term under 2–207(1), and that *it* alone thus fell out, thereby preserving the buyer's Code-provided right to full consequential damages. The Court ultimately reached this result (though not on precisely this reasoning). In light of the text, Summers concurs, though he is concerned that this reading may give the sender of the offering form too much of an overall advantage. (Summers would redraft the statute.)

Consider this further variation. Assume for example that the form offer contains an otherwise valid disclaimer of warranties and that the acceptance contains a conflicting *express* warranty. According to White, neither become part of the contract under 2–207(1) despite the fact that the contract is formed. Likewise neither enters the contract through 2–207(2) because the term in the acceptance is a different, not an additional term. Moreover by its terms 2–207(3) does not apply to this case but applies only to the case where "the writings of the parties do not otherwise establish a contract." Is it possible, nonetheless, that an *implied* warranty enters the contract directly as a gap filler without reference to 2–207(3)? White believes that it does and that indeed most of the gap fillers do not depend upon 2–207 to enter the contract. He says there are many contracts adequately formed by an offer and an acceptance which a gap filler dealing with price or warranty or terms of delivery would enter without any reference to 2–207. On White's view, that seems the proper result in this case. He thinks that the court in Bosway Tube & Steel Corp. v. McKay Machine Co. reached just this result by applying both 2–207(1) and 2–207(3). It seems to him that the court's result is correct (but that it is technically incorrect in finding that 2–207(3) can apply to a case in which the court has already found a 2–207(1) contract).

12. 58 Wis.2d 193, 206 N.W.2d 414, 12 UCC 794 (1973).

On White's analysis the foregoing outcome favors neither party. But if the buyer-offeror's argument be accepted, the offeror will almost always get his own terms. If, on the other hand, the *Roto-Lith* decision be followed, and the second document is not an acceptance or is expressly conditional and therefore cannot "operate" as an acceptance, the second party will almost always get his own terms because the second document will constitute a counteroffer accepted by performance. White believes that neither of these results is sound, and would not give either party a term when their documents conflict as to that term. The Code may then provide a term substantially identical to one of those rejected. So be it. At least a term so supplied has the merit of being a term that the draftsmen considered fair.

Summers does not read the cases as does White. More important, Summers believes White misreads 2–207, both in text and in spirit. Summers would, in the foregoing further hypothetical case, uphold the otherwise valid disclaimer as to both express and implied warranties. [Some footnotes omitted.]

Vermont Law School

South Royalton, Vermont 05068

Telephone: 302/763–8303

September 10, 1980

Professor Robert S. Summers
Cornell University Law School
Ithaca, NY 14853

Dear Professor Summers:

I have meant for a long time to write you and your collaborator, Professor White, to express my admiration for your handbook on the Code. I often consult it and always with profit.

I have most recently been reading your admirable discussion of § 2–207. Let me say at the outset that I thoroughly approve of your decision to let the disagreement between you and White on the proper construction of that abominable section hang out instead of papering it over.

I do think that insufficient attention has been paid to the tangled drafting history of § 2–207. (I am not about to reveal any ''secret history''; I had nothing to do with the drafting of § 2–207 at any stage and I cannot remember ever having discussed it with Karl Llewellyn.) The point is that as late as the 1952 draft of the Code, § 2–207 consisted only of what are now subsections (1) and (2). <u>Subsection (3) was added in response to criticisms of the New York Law Revision Commission (which were probably based on suggestions by John Honnold, who acted as a consultant on Article 2 for the Commission)</u>. The

1952 version of § 2-207 was bad enough (particularly in the (2)(b) reference to ''material alteration'') but the addition of subsection (3), without the slightest explanation of how it was supposed to mesh with (1) and (2), turned the section into a complete disaster. To make matters worse, the 1952 Comment (which had presumably been drafted at a much earlier point by Llewellyn) was never adequately revised to take the new subsection (3) into account. (Beginning in 1949 or 1950, Llewellyn refused to have anything to do with the Article 2 Comments, which were thereafter periodically updated by an anonymous hack in the Philadelphia office of the American Law Institute. It might be interesting to check back through earlier drafts of the Code to see how the text and Comment of § 2-207 evolved through 1952.) The later (1966) revisions of the Comment, which you attribute to Braucher, were band-aid jobs.

My principal quarrel with your discussion of § 2-207— and all the other discussions I have read—is that you treat the section much too respectfully—as if it had sprung, all of a piece, like Minerva from the brow of Jove. The truth is that it was a miserable, bungled, patched-up job—both text and Comment—to which various hands—Llewellyn, Honnold, Braucher and my anonymous hack—contributed at various points, each acting independently of the others (like the blind men and the elephant). It strikes me as ludicrous to pretend that the section can, or should, be construed as an integrated whole in the light of what ''the draftsman'' ''intended.'' (I might note that, when subsection (3) was added, Llewellyn had ceased to have anything to do with the Code project.) One of the chores which we hire courts (and commentators) to perform is to clean up the messes which statutory draftsmen leave behind them. The proper approach to § 2-207, which is arguably the greatest statutory mess of all time, is to take it light-heartedly (or, as Professor Corbin used to say, cheerfully).

Which brings me to the ''infamous'' Rotolith case * * *. On the facts of the case with respect to the October shipment as Judge Aldrich stated them, I think it would have been outrageous to have saddled the seller with warranties which (as the buyer knew) he had expressly (and quite reasonably) disclaimed. I grant you that the opinion does considerable violence to the statutory language, even in the 1952 version * * *. Even so, I find it hard to conceive of a situation in which the commission of statutory mayhem was more justifiable or more necessary. Surely, when the legislature goes mad, the courts can (and should) restore us to sanity.

In the 1950's I used to go around the country peddling the Code. On one occasion I had to explain Article 2 to a group of ''corporate counsel'' in California—they rep-

resented airplane manufacturers and similar great enterprises. When I finished with § 2-207, they were, so
far as I could tell, appalled. They were not so much
concerned with the obvious drafting ambiguities as they
were with the (equally obvious) intent to bind contracts
at the earliest possible point. They evidently preferred not to be bound (whether their clients were selling or buying) until all the formalities had been accomplished, the last i dotted, the last t crossed. Perhaps,
as Stuart Macaulay has suggested, businessmen don't really want binding contracts. Perhaps there was something to be said for the common law rules of offer and
acceptance. At all events: Down with § 2-207.

Yours,

Grant Gilmore Says

Grant Gilmore
Professor of Law

Don't take §2-207 too seriously!

jlm

DAITOM, INC. v. PENNWALT CORP.

United States Court of Appeals, Tenth Circuit, 1984.
741 F.2d 1569.

Before BARRETT, DOYLE and LOGAN, CIRCUIT JUDGES.

WILLIAM E. DOYLE, CIRCUIT JUDGE.

I. STATEMENT OF THE CASE

This is an appeal from the grant of summary judgment against
Daitom, Inc. (Daitom), the plaintiff below. The result was dismissal by
the United States District Court for the District of Kansas of all three
counts of Daitom's complaint.

Daitom had brought this diversity action in federal court on March
7, 1980 against Pennwalt Corporation and its Stokes Vacuum Equipment Division (Pennwalt). Counts I and II of Daitom's complaint *I + II Remanded*
alleged breach of various express and implied warranties and Count III
alleged negligent design and manufacture by Pennwalt of certain
rotary vacuum drying machines sold to and used commercially by
Daitom in the production of a vitamin known properly as dextro
calcium pantothenate and commonly as Vitamin B-5.

Daitom is a Delaware chartered corporation having its principal
place of business in Kansas. It was formed to implement a joint
venture between Thompson-Hayward Chemical Company, Inc. of Kansas City, Kansas and Daiichi-Seiyakii Co., Ltd., of Tokyo, Japan.
Pennwalt is a Pennsylvania chartered corporation with its principal
place of business in Pennsylvania.

Daitom requests a reversal of the district court's grant of summary judgment against Daitom on all counts of its complaint and seeks a remand for a trial on the merits.

We have concluded that there should be a reversal with respect to Counts I and II, together with a remand to the district court for a trial on the merits of those claims. On the other hand, we have concluded that there should be an affirmance of the summary judgment against Daitom on Count III of its complaint.

II. FACTS

The essential facts so far as they pertain to the issues presented in this appeal are as follows.

For the purpose of implementing its joint venture, Daitom planned to construct and operate a manufacturing plant to commercially produce dextro calcium pantothenate. The design of the plant was undertaken and handled on behalf of Daitom by Kintech Services, Inc. (which company will be referred to as Kintech), an engineering design firm located in Cincinnati, Ohio. Kintech had the responsibility not only for designing the plant; it also was responsible for investigating various means of drying the product during the production process, and for negotiating the purchase of certain equipment to be used in the plant. Included in the equipment was automated drying equipment to be used in removing methonol and water from the processed vitamin as part of the purification process.

There were numerous tests made and conducted at Kintech's request by equipment manufacturers. Kintech formulated specifications for the automated drying equipment. (This is referred to as Kintech Specification 342, Record, Volume I, at 59–65). On behalf of Daitom, Kintech invited various vendors to bid on the needed equipment.

Pennwalt, on September 7, 1976, submitted a proposal for the sale of two rotary vacuum dryers with dust filters and heating systems to dry dextro calcium pantothenate. The typewritten proposal specified the equipment to be sold, the f.o.b. price, and delivery and payment terms. A pre-printed conditions of sale form was also attached to the proposal and explicitly made an integral part of the proposal by the typewritten sheet.

Kintech recommended to Daitom that Pennwalt's proposal be accepted and on October 5, 1976, well within the thirty-day acceptance period specified in the proposal, Daitom issued a purchase order for the Pennwalt equipment. The purchase order consisted of a pre-printed form with the identification of the specific equipment and associated prices typewritten in the appropriate blank spaces on the front together with seventeen lengthy "boilerplate" or "standard" terms and conditions of sale on the back. In addition, on the front of the purchase order in the column marked for a description of the items purchased, Daitom typed the following:

Rotary vacuum dryers in accordance with Kintech Services, Inc. specification 342 dated August 20, 1976, and in accordance with Stokes proposal dated September 7, 1976.

The two rotary vacuum dryers and the equipment that went along with them were manufactured by Pennwalt and delivered to Daitom's plant in early May 1977. For the reason that there had been no construction of Daitom's plant, the crated equipment was not immediately installed. Instead, it was stored outside in crates. On June 15, 1978, the dryers were finally installed and first operated by Daitom. Daitom notified Pennwalt of serious problems with the operation of the dryers on June 17, 1978.

Daitom's contention was that the dryers suffered from two severe defects: 1) they were delivered with misaligned agitator blades causing a scraping and damaging of the dryer interiors and an uneven distribution of the products being dried; and 2) they were undersized necessitating an overloading of the dryers and a "lumping up" of the product rendering it unsuitable for further use. Pennwalt's repair personnel visited the Daitom plant to investigate the alleged operating difficulties, but Daitom contends the dryers were not repaired and have never performed as required under the specifications and as represented by Pennwalt. This was the basis for the lawsuit.

This suit was brought in federal court on March 7, 1980, after Pennwalt's alleged failure to correct the difficulties with the dryers. On Pennwalt's motion, the district court granted summary judgment against Daitom on all three counts of its complaint. The court dismissed Counts I and II after applying section 2–207 of the Uniform Commercial Code (U.C.C.) and finding that Daitom's breach of warranties claims were barred by the one-year period of limitations specified in Pennwalt's proposal. The court further concluded that alleged damages in Count III for the negligent design and manufacture of the dryers were not available in tort; the sole remedy being in an action for breach of warranties which here was barred by the period of limitations. Consequently, summary judgment was granted against Daitom. Daitom's subsequent motion for reconsideration was denied by the district court on June 3, 1982, and following that, this appeal took place.

III. DISCUSSION

A. The Issues

It is to be noted that the district court granted summary judgment against Daitom on Counts I and II of the complaint, finding the breach of warranties claim barred by the one-year period of limitations which was set forth in Pennwalt's proposal. In ruling against Daitom the court followed a three step analysis. First, it concluded that pursuant to U.C.C. § 2–207(1), a written contract for the sale of the rotary dryers was formed by Pennwalt's September 7, 1976 proposal and Daitom's October 5, 1976 purchase order accepting that proposal. Second, the

[handwritten margin note: District Ct found Breach of Warranties Claim Was barred by 1-yr limit per Δ's proposal]

court found that the one year period of limitations specified in Pennwalt's proposal and shortening the typical four-year period of limitations available under the U.C.C. became part of the contract of sale and governed the claims for breach of warranties. Thus, the court accepted the proposal that was contained in the documents that had been submitted by the defendant-appellee. Third, the court concluded that the one-year period of limitations was not tolled by any conduct of Pennwalt's, so that consequently, Daitom's claims were barred because they were brought after the expiration of the one year limitations period. The view we have of the submission and response is that the approval was initial and general and contemplated further discussion and improvement.

The circumstances surrounding the delivery of this equipment and what occurred thereafter is of high importance. The equipment was delivered in crates and boxes, and at that time Daitom had no plant. Instead of seeking to protect the equipment in some way, Pennwalt simply delivered the boxes and left. The documents which were part of the delivery provided for this one-year period of limitations specified in the Pennwalt proposal. Seemingly, this conduct on the part of Pennwalt in making a quick delivery and quick departure took hold in connection with the motion for summary judgment, the court ruling that more than one year had passed before they were able to try out the machinery and discover the defects. The suggestion is made as to how this machinery could have been utilized or contested because of the conditions that were present. Why, then should the one-year limitations period, created by Pennwalt, be allowed to take effect?

Daitom has challenged the district court's findings as to the terms which became a part of the contract. Daitom argues that its October 5, 1976 purchase order did not constitute an acceptance of Pennwalt's September 7, 1976 proposal. Instead, Daitom claims that its purchase order explicitly made acceptance conditional on Pennwalt's assent to the additional or different terms in the purchase order. As a consequence, Daitom argues, pursuant to U.C.C. § 2–207(1),[1] the exchanged writings of the parties did *not* form a contract, because Pennwalt failed to assent to the additional or different terms in the purchase order. The most relevant additional or different terms Daitom alleges were in *its* purchase order were the terms reserving all warranties and remedies available in law, despite Pennwalt's limitation of warranties and remedies in its proposal. In a sense Pennwalt argues it enjoyed an exclusive right to set the conditions.

---

1. The parties, throughout this litigation and through their briefs, agree that the law of Pennsylvania governs their warranty claims. The parties further agree that Pennsylvania has adopted the provisions of the Uniform Commercial Code and that for the purpose of this action the Pennsylvania statute does not modify the U.C.C. provisions. See 13 Pa.C.S.A. § 2207 (Purdon's 1984). Therefore, throughout this memorandum the relevant code sections will be referred to only by the U.C.C. numeral designation.

Daitom argues that on their face the writings failed to create a contract, and, instead, that a contract was to be formed by *the conduct* of both parties, pursuant to § 2–207(3), and the resulting contract consisted of the terms on which the writings agreed, together with "any supplementary terms incorporated under any other provision of [the UCC]." Therefore, Daitom concludes, the resulting contract governing the sale of the rotary dryers incorporated the U.C.C. provisions for express warranties (§ 2–313), implied warranties (§§ 2–314, 2–315), and a four year period of limitations.

As an alternative argument, Daitom contends that even if its October 5, 1976 purchase order did constitute an acceptance of Pennwalt's September 7, 1976 proposal and did form a contract, all conflicting terms between the two writings were "knocked out" and did not become part of the resulting contract, because of their being at odds one with the other. Therefore, Daitom concludes once again that the resulting contract consisted of only those terms in which the writings agreed and any supplementary or "gap-filler" terms incorporated under the provisions of the U.C.C.; specifically §§ 2–313, 2–314, 2–315, 2–725.

Daitom makes a further argument which has some appeal and that is that even if the one-year period of limitations specified in Pennwalt's proposal became a part of the sales contract, it was tolled by Pennwalt's wrongful conduct, which included fraudulent concealment of the equipment's defects and failure of the essential purpose of the limited remedies. Since this court's decision does not rely on the question of the tolling of the limitations period, we will not devote detailed argument to this.

*   *   *

B. *The Applicable Law*

The district court found the dispute between Daitom and Pennwalt involved a "transaction in goods," between persons who are "merchants" and, therefore, was governed by Article 2 of the U.C.C. U.C.C. §§ 2–102, 2–104. The district court also stated that the dispute is a classic example of the "battle of the forms."

As previously noted, there has been agreement that the law of Pennsylvania governs these claims for breach of warranty and Pennsylvania has adopted the provisions of the U.C.C. Section 2–207 of the U.C.C. was specifically drafted to deal with the battle of the forms and related problems. U.C.C. § 2–207, Comment 1.

Section 2–207 has been commented on in one case as a "murky bit of prose," (*Southwest Engineering Co., Inc. v. Martin Tractor Co., Inc.*, 205 Kan. 684, 473 P.2d 18, 25 (1970)), and as "one of the most important, subtle, and difficult in the entire code, and well it may be said that the product as it finally reads is not altogether satisfactory." (Duesenberg & King, 3 *Sales and Bulk Transfer Under the Uniform Commercial Code,* § 3.03 at 3–12 (1984)). The Pennsylvania Supreme

Court has not addressed the issues presented by this case. In the absence, therefore, of an authoritative pronouncement from the state's highest court, our task is to regard ourselves as sitting in diversity and predicting how the state's highest court would rule. * * * This court must also follow any intermediate state court decision unless other authority convinces us that the state supreme court would decide otherwise. * * * Also, the policies underlying the applicable legal doctrines, the doctrinal trends indicated by these policies, and the decisions of other courts may also inform this court's analysis * * *. With these standards in mind, we proceed to consider and analyze the case.

C. The Writings and the Contract

The trial court concluded that the parties' exchanged writings formed a contract. Thus, there was not a formal single document. Pennwalt's September 7, 1976 proposal constituted the offer and Daitom's October 5, 1976 purchase order constituted the acceptance.

It is essentially uncontested that Pennwalt's proposal constituted an offer. The proposal set forth in some detail the equipment to be sold to Daitom, the price, the terms of shipment, and specifically stated that the attached terms and conditions were an integral part of the proposal. One of those attached terms and conditions of sale limited the warranties to repair and replacement of defective parts and limited the period of one year from the date of delivery for any action for breach of warranty.[3]

The proposal was sent to Kintech and forwarded to Daitom with a recommendation to accept the proposal. Daitom sent the October 5, 1976 purchase order to Pennwalt. This purchase order constituted an acceptance of Pennwalt's offer and formed a binding contract for the

---

3. Paragraph 5 of the terms and conditions of sale stated in full (emphasis added):

6. WARRANTIES:

a. Seller warrants that at the time of delivery of the property to the carrier, it will be, unless otherwise specified, new, free and clear of all lawful liens and security interests or other encumbrances unknown to Buyer. If, within a period of one year from the date of *such delivery* any parts of the property (except property specified to be used property or normal wear parts) fail because of material or workmanship which was defective at the time of such delivery, Seller will repair such parts, or furnish parts to replace them f.o.b. Seller's or its supplier's plant, provided such failure is due solely to such defective material or workmanship and is not contributed to by any other cause, such as improper care or unreasonable use, and provided such de-

fects are brought to Seller's attention for verification when first discovered, and the parts alleged to be so defective are returned, if requested, to Seller's or its supplier's plant. *No action for breach of warranty shall be brought more than one year after the cause of action has accrued*

SELLER MAKES NO OTHER WARRANTY OF ANY KIND, EXPRESS OR IMPLIED, INCLUDING ANY WARRANTY OF FITNESS OF THE PROPERTY FOR ANY PARTICULAR PURPOSE EVEN IF THAT PURPOSE IS KNOWN TO SELLER.

In no event shall Seller be liable for consequential damage.

b. Because of varied interpretations of standards at the local level, Seller cannot warrant that the property meets the requirements of the Occupational Safety and Health Act.

sale only pursuant to 2–207(1), despite the statement of terms additional to or different from those in the offer.[4] But these terms were not without meaning or consequence. However, the acceptance was not expressly conditioned on Pennwalt accepting these additional or different terms.

There is a provision which Daitom contends made the acceptance expressly conditional on Pennwalt's accepting the additional or different terms which appeared in the pre-printed, standard "boilerplate" provisions on the back of the purchase order. It stated:

> **Acceptance.** Immediate acceptance is required unless otherwise provided herein. It is understood and agreed that the written acceptance by Seller of this purchase order or the commencement of any work performance of any services hereunder by the Seller, (including the commencement of any work or the performance of any service with respect to samples), shall constitute acceptance by Seller of this purchase order and of all the terms and conditions of such acceptance is *expressly limited to such terms and conditions, unless each deviation is mutually recognized therefore in writing.* (Emphasis added.)

[margin note: Does this meet test of expressly conditional to A's assent? Court says NO]

This language does not preclude the formation of a contract by the exchanged writings pursuant to § 2–207(1). Nor does it dictate the adoption of a conclusion holding that as a result the acceptance provided the applicable terms of the resulting contract. First, it is well established that a contract for the sale of goods may be made in any manner to show agreement, requiring merely that there be some objective manifestation of mutual assent, but that there must be. There is not a contract until it takes place. See U.C.C. § 2–204; *Ore & Chemical Corporation v. Howard Butcher Trading Corp.*, 455 F.Supp. 1150, 1152 (E.D.Pa.1978). Here there is such an objective manifestation of agreement on essential terms of equipment specifications, price, and the terms of shipment and payment, all of which took place before the machinery was put to any test. The purchase order explicitly referred to and incorporated on its front Kintech's equipment specifications and Pennwalt's proposal. But we are unwilling to hold such a typewritten reference and incorporation by Daitom brings the matter to a close. The acceptance and warranty terms as provided for by the above excerpted acceptance clause, does manifest a willingness on all essential terms to accept the offer and form a contract. *Cf., Daitom v. Henry Vogt Machine Co.*, No. 80–2081 (D.Kan., unpublished 2/22/82) (In that

[margin note: This language doesn't preclude formation of K.]

[margin note: Court says this clause is contained in a purchase order inviting acceptance, how then can it mean they would not proceed without it]

[margin note: Court says this detracts from P's argument]

---

4. The principal additional or different terms referred to the reservation of warranties. Specifically:

(8) WARRANTY. The Seller warrants that the supplies covered by this purchase order will conform to the specifications, drawings, samples, or other descriptions furnished or specified by buyer, and will be fit and sufficient for the purpose intended, merchantable, of good material and workmanship, and free from defect. The warranties and remedies provided for in this paragraph * * * shall be in addition to those implied by or available at law and shall exist not withstanding [sic] the acceptance by Buyer of all or a part of this applies with respect to which such warranties and remedies are applicable.

case the court held that under identical factual circumstances and involving the identical purchase order form language, such typewritten reference and incorporation of the offer constituted a written modification of the purchase order's boilerplate acceptance terms to conform to those in the offer.) This was, of course, before an attempt was made to use the equipment.

Second, the boilerplate provision does not directly address the instant case. The purchase order is drafted principally as an *offer* inviting acceptance. Although this court recognizes that the form may serve a dual condition depending on the circumstances, the imprecision of language that permits such service detracts from Daitom's argument of conditional acceptance.

Third, the courts are split on the application of § 2–207(1) and the meaning of "expressly made conditional on assent to the additional or different terms." *See Boese-Hilburn Co. v. Dean Machinery*, 616 S.W.2d 520 (Mo.App.1981). *Roto-Lith Ltd. v. F.P. Bartlett & Co., Inc.*, 297 F.2d 497 (1st Cir.1962) represents one extreme of the spectrum, that the offeree's response stating a term materially altering the contractual obligations solely to the disadvantage of the offeror constitutes a conditional acceptance. The other extreme of the spectrum is represented by *Dorton v. Collins & Aikman Corporation*, 453 F.2d 1161 (6th Cir.1972), in which case the court held that the conditional nature of the acceptance should be so clearly expressed in a manner sufficient to notify the offeror that the offeree is unwilling to proceed with the transaction unless the additional or different terms are included in the contract. The middle of the spectrum providing that a response merely "predicating" acceptance on clarification, addition or modification is a conditional acceptance is represented by *Construction Aggregates Corp. v. Hewitt-Robins, Inc.*, 404 F.2d 505 (7th Cir.1968), *cert. denied*, 395 U.S. 921, 89 S.Ct. 1774, 23 L.Ed.2d 238 (1969).

The facts of this case, Daitom asserts, are not of a character that would suggest that there had been an unequivocal acceptance. The defendant-appellee was aware that the machinery had not even been tried. Once it was tried, it broke down in a very short time. It is hard to see a justifiable acceptance, Daitom asserts, when the buyer does not even know whether it works, and, in fact, learns after the fact, that it does not work. This fact alone renders the "contract" to be questionable.

The better view as to the meaning and application of "conditional acceptance," and the view most likely to be adopted by Pennsylvania, is the view in *Dorton* that the offeree must explicitly communicate his or her unwillingness to proceed with the transaction unless the additional or different terms in its response are accepted by the offeror. * * *

Having found an offer and an acceptance which was not made expressly conditional on assent to additional or different terms, we must now decide the effect of those additional or different terms on the resulting contract and what terms became part of it. The district court simply resolved this dispute by focusing solely on the period of limitations specified in Pennwalt's offer of September 7, 1976. Thus, the court held that while the offer explicitly specified a one-year period of limitations in accordance with § 2–725(1) allowing such a reduction, Daitom's acceptance of October 5, 1976 was silent as to the limitations period. Consequently, the court held that § 2–207(2) was inapplicable and the one-year limitations period controlled, effectively barring Daitom's action for breach of warranties.

While the district court's analysis undertook to resolve the issue without considering the question of the application of § 2–207(2) to additional or different terms, we cannot accept its approach or its conclusion. We are unable to ignore the plain implication of Daitom's reservation in its boilerplate warranties provision of all its rights and remedies available at law. Such an explicit reservation impliedly reserves the statutory period of limitations; without such a reservation, all other reservations of actions and remedies are without effect.

The statutory period of limitations under the U.C.C. is four years after the cause of action has accrued. U.C.C. § 2–725(1). Were we to determine that this four-year period became a part of the contract rather than the shorter one-year period, Daitom's actions on breach of warranties were timely brought and summary judgment against Daitom was error.[5]

We realize that our conclusion requires an inference to be drawn from a construction of Daitom's terms; however, such an inference and construction are consistent with the judicial reluctance to grant summary judgment where there is some reasonable doubt over the existence of a genuine material fact. *See Williams v. Borden, Inc.,* 637 F.2d 731, 738 (10th Cir.1980). When taking into account the circumstances surrounding the application of the one-year limitations period, we have little hesitation in adopting the U.C.C.'s four-year limitations reservation, the application of which permits a trial on the merits. Thus, this court must recognize that certain terms in Daitom's acceptance differed from terms in Pennwalt's offer and decide which become part of the contract. The district court certainly erred in refusing to recognize such a conflict.[6]

The difficulty in determining the effect of different terms in the acceptance is the imprecision of drafting evident in § 2–207. The

---

5. Daitom filed its complaint on March 7, 1980. While the parties dispute when the cause of action accrued and the period of limitations began to run, resolution of the dispute is unnecessary if this court concludes the four-year limitations period controls. Even if it is found the action accrued in May 1977 on delivery of the dryers to Daitom's plant, the four-year period of limitations had not expired on March 7, 1980 when the complaint was filed.

6. There is some indication in its memorandum and order that had the district court considered the effect of the conflicting terms, it would have applied § 2–207(2)(b) and concluded that the terms in Pennwalt's offer controlled because Daitom's conflicting terms would have materially altered the content. Memorandum and Order at 11. Because we hold, *infra,* that conflicting terms should not be analyzed pursuant to § 2–207(2), this conclusion of the district court is also in error.

language of the provision is silent on how different terms in the acceptance are to be treated once a contract is formed pursuant to § 2–207(1). That section provides that a contract may be formed by exchanged writings despite the existence of additional or different terms in the acceptance. Therefore, an offeree's response is treated as an acceptance while it may differ substantially from the offer. This section of the provision, then, reformed the mirror-image rule; that common law legal formality that prohibited the formation of a contract if the exchanged writings of offer and acceptance differed in any term.

Once a contract is recognized pursuant to § 2–207(1), § 2–207(2) provides the standard for determining if the additional terms stated in the acceptance become a part of the contract. Between merchants, such *additional* terms become part of the resulting contract *unless* 1) the offer expressly limited acceptance to its terms, 2) the additional terms materially alter the contract obligations, or 3) the offeror gives notice of his or her objection to the additional terms within a reasonable time. Should any one of these three possibilities occur, the *additional* terms are treated merely as proposals for incorporation in the contract and absent assent by the offeror the terms of the offer control. In any event, the existence of the additional terms does not prevent a contract from being formed.

Section 2–207(2) is silent on the treatment of terms stated in the acceptance that are *different,* rather than merely additional, from those stated in the offer. It is unclear whether "different" terms in the acceptance are intended to be included under the aegis of "additional" terms in § 2–207(2) and, therefore, fail to become part of the agreement if they materially alter the contract. Comment 3 suggests just such an inclusion.[7] However, Comment 6 suggests that different terms in exchanged writings must be assumed to constitute mutual objections by each party to the other's conflicting terms and result in a mutual "knockout" of both parties' conflicting terms; the missing terms to be supplied by the U.C.C.'s "gap-filler" provisions.[8] At least one commentator, in support of this view, has suggested that the drafting history of the provision indicates that the word "different" was intentionally deleted from the final draft of § 2–207(2) to preclude its treatment

---

7. Comment 3 states (emphasis added):

Whether or not *additional or different* terms will become part of the agreement depends upon the provision of subsection (2).

It must be remembered that even official comments to enacted statutory text do not have the force of law and are only guidance in the interpretation of that text. *In re Bristol Associates, Inc.,* 505 F.2d 1056 (3rd Cir.1974) (while the comments to the Pennsylvania U.C.C. are not binding, the Pennsylvania Supreme Court gives sub-

stantial weight to the comments as evidencing application of the Code).

8. Comment 6 states, in part:

Where clauses on confirming forms sent by both parties conflict each party must be assumed to object to a clause of the other conflicting with one on the confirmation sent by himself * * *. The contract then consists of the terms expressly agreed to, terms on which the confirmations agree, and terms supplied by the Act, including subsection (2).

under that subsection.[9] The plain language, comments, and drafting history of the provision, therefore, provide little helpful guidance in resolving the disagreement over the treatment of different terms pursuant to § 2–207.

Despite all this, the cases and commentators have suggested three possible approaches. The first of these is to treat "different" terms as included under the aegis of "additional" terms in § 2–207(2). Consequently, different terms in the acceptance would never become part of the contract, because, by definition, they would materially alter the contract (i.e., the offeror's terms). Several courts have adopted this approach. *E.g., Mead Corporation v. McNally-Pittsburg Manufacturing Corporation*, 654 F.2d 1197 (6th Cir.1981) (applying Ohio law); *Steiner v. Mobil Oil Corporation*, 20 Cal.3d 90, 141 Cal.Rptr. 157, 569 P.2d 751 (1977); *Lockheed Electronics Company, Inc. v. Keronix, Inc.*, 114 Cal. App.3d 304, 170 Cal.Rptr. 591 (1981).

The second approach, which leads to the same result as the first, is that the offeror's terms control because the offeree's different terms merely fall out; § 2–207(2) cannot rescue the different terms since that subsection applies only to *additional* terms. Under this approach, Comment 6 (apparently supporting a mutual rather than a single term knockout) is not applicable because it refers only to conflicting terms in confirmation forms following *oral* agreement, not conflicting terms in the *writings* that form the agreement. This approach is supported by Professor Summers. J.J. White & R.S. Summers, *Uniform Commercial Code*, § 1–2, at 29 (2d ed. 1980).

The third, and preferable approach, which is commonly called the "knock-out" rule, is that the conflicting terms cancel one another. Under this view the offeree's form is treated only as an acceptance of the terms in the offeror's form which did not conflict. The ultimate contract, then, includes those non-conflicting terms and any other terms supplied by the U.C.C., including terms incorporated by course of performance (§ 2–208), course of dealing (§ 1–205), usage of trade (§ 1–205), and other "gap fillers" or "off-the-rack" terms (e.g., implied warranty of fitness for particular purpose, § 2–315). As stated previously, this approach finds some support in Comment 6. Professor White supports this approach as the most fair and consistent with the purposes of § 2–207. *White & Summers, supra*, at 29. Further, several courts have adopted or recognized the approach. *E.g., Idaho Power Company v. Westinghouse Electric Corporation*, 596 F.2d 924 (9th Cir. 1979) (applying Idaho law, although incorrectly, applying § 2–207(3) after finding a contract under § 2–207(1)); *Owens-Corning Fiberglass Corporation v. Sonic Development Corporation*, 546 F.Supp. 533 (D.Kan. 1982) (Judge Saffels applying Kansas law); *Lea Tai Textile Co., Ltd. v. Manning Fabrics, Inc.*, 411 F.Supp. 1404 (S.D.N.Y.1975); *Hartwig Farms, Inc. v. Pacific Gamble Robinson Company*, 28 Wash.App. 539,

---

9. See D.G. Baird & R. Weisberg, *Rules, Standards, and the Battle of the Forms: A* *Reassessment of § 2–207*, 68 Va.L.R. 1217, 1240, n. 61.

625 P.2d 171 (1981); *S.C. Gray, Inc. v. Ford Motor Company,* 92 Mich. App. 789, 286 N.W.2d 34 (1979).

We are of the opinion that this is the more reasonable approach, particularly when dealing with a case such as this where from the beginning the offeror's specified period of limitations would expire before the equipment was even installed. The approaches other than the "knock-out" approach would be inequitable and unjust because they invited the very kind of treatment which the defendant attempted to provide.

Thus, we are of the conclusion that if faced with this issue the Pennsylvania Supreme Court would adopt the "knock-out" rule and hold here that the conflicting terms in Pennwalt's offer and Daitom's acceptance regarding the period of limitations and applicable warranties cancel one another out. Consequently, the other provisions of the U.C.C. must be used to provide the missing terms.

This particular approach and result are supported persuasively by the underlying rationale and purpose behind the adoption of § 2–207. As stated previously, that provision was drafted to reform the infamous common law mirror-image rule and associated last-shot doctrine that enshrined the fortuitous positions of senders of forms and accorded undue advantages based on such fortuitous positions. *White & Summers, supra* at 25. To refuse to adopt the "knock-out" rule and instead adopt one of the remaining two approaches would serve to re-enshrine the undue advantages derived solely from the fortuitous positions of when a party sent a form. Cf., 3 Duesenberg & King at 93 (1983 Supp.). This is because either approach other than the knock-out rule for different terms results in the offeror and his or her terms always prevailing solely because he or she sent the first form. Professor Summers argues that this advantage is not wholly unearned, because the offeree has an opportunity to review the offer, identify the conflicting terms and make his or her acceptance conditional. But this joinder misses the fundamental purpose of the U.C.C. in general and § 2–207 in particular, which is to preserve a contract and fill in any gaps if the parties intended to make a contract and there is a reasonable basis for giving an appropriate remedy. U.C.C. § 2–204(3); § 2–207(1); § 2–207(3). Thus, this approach gives the offeree some protection. While it is laudible for business persons to read the fine print and boilerplate provisions in exchanged forms, there is nothing in § 2–207 mandating such careful consideration. The provision seems drafted with a recognition of the reality that merchants seldom review exchanged forms with the scrutiny of lawyers. The "knock-out" rule is therefore the best approach. Even if a term eliminated by operation of the "knock-out" rule is reintroduced by operation of the U.C.C.'s gap-filler provisions, such a result does not indicate a weakness of the approach. On the contrary, at least the reintroduced term has the merit of being a term that the U.C.C. draftpersons regarded as fair.

We now address the question of reverse and remand regarding Counts I and II. The result of this court's holding is that the district court erred in granting summary judgment against Daitom on Counts I and II of its complaint. Operation of the "knock-out" rule to conflicting terms results in the instant case in the conflicting terms in the offer and acceptance regarding the period of limitations and applicable warranties cancelling. In the absence of any evidence of course of performance, course of dealing, or usage of trade providing the missing terms, §§ 2–725(1), 2–313, 2–314, 2–315 may operate to supply a four-year period of limitations, an express warranty,[10] an implied warranty of merchantability, and an implied warranty of fitness for a particular purpose, respectively. The ruling of the district court on Counts I and II does not invite this kind of a broad inquiry, and thus, we must recognize the superiority in terms of justice of the "knock-out" rule. Consequently, the ruling of the district court on Counts I and II must be reversed and the matter remanded for trial consistent with this court's ruling.

* * *

[The court held that there was no Cause of Action in tort where an allegedly defective product caused only economic loss.]

Accordingly, the district court correctly concluded that Daitom's requested damages are not recoverable in tort. The court's summary judgment ruling against Daitom on Count III, therefore, should be affirmed. As explained above, we reverse the trial court with respect to Counts I and II. The cause is remanded for further proceedings consistent with this opinion.

BARRETT, CIRCUIT JUDGE, dissenting:

I respectfully dissent. Insofar as the issue of contract formation is concerned in this case, we are confronted with a "battle of the forms" case involving the interpretation and application of U.C.C. § 2–207. I would affirm.

Pennwalt's proposal of September 7, 1976, was an "offer." It was submitted to Daitom in response to solicitations initiated by Daitom and it contained specific terms relating to price, delivery dates, etc., and its terms were held "open" for Daitom's acceptance within 30 days. In my view, Daitom accepted the offer with its purchase order. That order repeated the quantity, model number, and price for the items as those terms appeared in the Pennwalt proposal and, by reference, it incorporated four pages of specifications attached to Pennwalt's proposal or "offer." The purchase order did contain some different and additional language from that contained in Pennwalt's proposal. However, the Code has rejected the old mirror image rule. Thus, I agree with the district court's finding/ruling that a contract was formed in the circumstances described.

---

10. Daitom alleges that several letters from Pennwalt expressly warrantied the performance of the rotary dryers. *E.g.,* Pretrial Order, Record Volume II at 59, para. 12, 13, 14, 15.

I also agree with the district court's conclusion that the terms of Pennwalt's proposal constituted the "terms of the contract." I do not agree, as Daitom argues, that its "acceptance" was made "conditional" upon Pennwalt's assent to the additional/different terms set forth in Daitom's purchase order. The court correctly found no such *express* condition in Daitom's acceptance.

The "knock-out" rule should not, in my view, be reached in this case. It can be applied only if, as Daitom argues and the majority agrees, the "conflicting terms" cancel each other out. The "knock-out" rule does have substantial support in the law, but I do not believe it is relevant in this case because the *only* conflicting terms relate to the *scope* of the warranty. In this case, it is not an important consideration because, pursuant to the express time limitations contained in Pennwalt's "offer," Daitom lost its right to assert any warranty claim. There was no term in Daitom's purchase order in conflict with the express one-year limitation within which to bring warranty actions. I agree with the district court's reasoning in rejecting Daitom's contentions that the one-year limitation period should not apply because (1) the term failed of "its essential purpose" of providing Daitom with a limited remedy under U.C.C. § 2–719(2) and (2) the time-limit was tolled due to Pennwalt's alleged fraudulent concealment of the defect. I concur with the trial court's finding that Daitom made no showing that the one-year limitation period was unreasonable because of some act of Pennwalt. As to the fraudulent concealment allegation, the court properly observed that Daitom did not plead this claim with the particularity required and, further, that the alleged fraudulent acts were not independent of the alleged breaches proper.

[Some footnotes omitted.]

Note: Should UCC 2–207 Be Repealed?

The three preceding cases give you a taste of the issues raised in litigation under UCC 2–207. They are but tips of the iceberg of cases and scholarly comment on this legislative attempt to relax the supposed unfairness of the common law "mirror-image" rule.

Let us work with a simple case, based upon the *Bethlehem Steel* litigation, discussed supra. Suppose, after negotiations and agreement on all terms but price, Bethlehem sent Litton a written offer to pay $20.5M for construction of the ship according to the specifications. Litton promptly responded by letter as follows: "We accept your offer to pay $20.5M for construction of the vessel, as specified, plus price escalation to be determined by the attached clause." Bethlehem, claiming that the response was a counteroffer, rejected it and withdrew from the deal. Was there a contract?

At common law the answer was no: The reply was a counteroffer. Under UCC 2–207(1) and Section 59 of the Restatement, Second, of Contracts, however, the answer is yes if Litton's "definite * * * expression of acceptance" was not "expressly made conditional on assent to the additional or different terms." (Section 59 states that a "reply to an offer which purports to accept it but is conditional on the offeror's assent to terms additional or different from those offered is not an acceptance but is a counter-offer.")

But, as the *Diatom* case indicates, a different or additional term which materially alters the bargain does not, alone, constitute an "express" condition: Additional, unequivocal language of condition is required. Thus, Bethlehem, a commercial party, is bound to a contract for $20.5M under UCC 2–207(1) even though Litton wants price escalation and there has been no conduct by both parties which recognizes the existence of a contract. See UCC 2–204(1). Furthermore, Bethlehem is forced to deal with the complex issues in UCC 2–207(2): Is the term automatically part of the bargain or not and, if not, what must Bethlehem do to avoid incorporation? Similarly, suppose Litton's definite acceptance was for a fixed price of $25 million. Should Bethlehem bear the risk that there was a contract under UCC 2–207(1), that the materially different terms cancel each other out and that the price is a "reasonable price at the time for delivery?" UCC 2–305(1).

Between commercial parties where no standard forms are involved, and, therefore, little risk of unfair surprise, the answer to these questions should be no. Whatever the reasons for reversing the presumption of the "mirror image" rule, they make little sense where there is no conduct by both parties supporting an intention to contract and no other evidence of usage or prior dealing to support a conclusion that, in commercial understanding, the deal had been closed. See UCC 2–207, Comment 2. In short, despite Litton's purported acceptance without an express condition, Bethlehem should have the option either to continue negotiations or withdraw on the assumption that no contract has been formed. Surely, the same factors that influenced the Pennsylvania Supreme Court to find no contract where there was a failure to agree on price under UCC 2–204 are relevant to the UCC 2–207 issue. Compare Dataserv Equipment, Inc. v. Technology Finance Leasing Corp., 364 N.W.2d 838 (Minn.1985) (rejection of counteroffer terminates negotiations).

Taking the next step, suppose that Litton responded with a different or additional price term and there was either no "definite ∗ ∗ ∗ acceptance" or there was an express condition. In short, there was no contract under UCC 2–207(1): Litton made a counteroffer which Bethlehem was free to accept, reject or to attempt to negotiate. Suppose, however, that without further explicit agreement on price, there was conduct by both parties which recognized the existence of some contract. What should the price term be if the writings involved do not agree on a price? See UCC 2–207(3).

Again, the choices are similar to those in *Daitom* where there was a contract under UCC 2–207(1) but there were different terms: (1) Bethlehem's price controls; (2) Litton's price controls; or (3) A reasonable price at the time of delivery controls. Assuming that UCC 2–207(3) applies to this dispute, most courts have concluded that unless Bethlehem's conduct was with express awareness of Litton's price term, the "reasonable" price option should be invoked. But, again, how can a commercial party without standard forms not be aware of Litton's price term? If aware (no risk of unfair surprise), then the choice to engage in mutual conduct consistent with the existence of some contract should be sufficient to incorporate Litton's price term into the agreement. There is no reason to protect Bethlehem, who has made an informed choice, from Litton's last proposed price.

The answer, then, to the question posed, "Should UCC 2–207 be Repealed?," is no. But it should be revised to differentiate between transactions where standard forms, and thus the risk of unfair surprise, are included and those where they are not involved. Without the risk of unfair surprise, there is no obvious justification for imposing a contract on Bethlehem, even on its own terms, unless Bethlehem makes an informed choice either to continue negotiations or assent to Litton's terms.

SECTION 4. THE STATUTE OF FRAUDS

A. History and Purposes

A statute of frauds imposes additional conditions upon the enforceability of agreements which otherwise qualify as contracts. In general, there must be a writing consistent with the existence of a contract, specifying some if not all of the terms, and signed or authenticated by the party to be charged. The UCC has several such statutes of frauds, see, e.g., UCC 1–206, 8–319 (contract for sale of securities), 9–203(1) (creation of enforceable security interest), including UCC 2–201, which governs contracts for the "sale of goods for the price of $500 or more." UCC 2–201(1).

At least three justifications for the statute of frauds have been asserted. First, the statute avoids fraudulent or perjured claims that some contract was in fact made. Second, the statute avoids fraudulent or perjured claims regarding the terms of a contract admittedly made. Third, the statute serves a useful purpose in so far as it contributes to the business habit of making a writing. See Vold, *The Application of the Statute of Frauds Under the Uniform Sales Act,* 15 Minn.L.Rev. 391, 393–94 (1931).

The first two justifications have long been criticised as anachronistic. The conditions existing in 17th Century England—uncontrolled jury discretion, restrictions upon the competency of witnesses and immature contract doctrine—no longer obtain. See Willis, *The Statute of Frauds—A Legal Anachronism,* 3 Ind.L.J. 427, 429–31 (1928). Attacks of this sort, plus the opportunity provided by the statute for "technical unmeritorious defenses" induced Parliament, in 1954, to repeal the statute of frauds provision in the British Sale of Goods Act. See Grunfield, *Law Reform (Enforcement of Contracts) Act,* 1954, 17 Mod.L.Rev. 451 (1954).

The third justification is more difficult to undercut. According to Professor Vold, the "cases that justify the statute are * * * the thousands of uncontested current transactions where misunderstanding and controversy are avoided by the presence of a writing which the statute at least indirectly aided to procure. * * *" *Vold,* supra. But see Comment, *The Statute of Frauds and the Business Community: A Re-Appraisal in Light of Prevailing Practices,* 66 Yale L.J. 1038 (1957) (reliance on an oral order rather than the practice of employing writings is prevalent practice). Karl Llewellyn agreed with Vold's assessment, see Llewellyn, *What Price Contract? An Essay in Perspective,* 40 Yale L.J. 704, 746–48 (1931), and his views were influential in the drafting of UCC 2–201.

What justifications exist for UCC 2–201? Should the statute of frauds in Article 2 be repealed? Keep these questions in mind as you work through the following simple problems.

B. Illustrative Problems and Cases

The following problems and cases illustrate some of the issues that have arisen over the scope and application of UCC 2–201.

Problem 3-5 *For 1/27*

On February 1, S, a farmer, entered into an oral contract with B, a grain dealer, to plant his fields in corn and to harvest and deliver the output for $2.30 per bushel by October 1. B immediately resold the corn to C, a cereal producer, for $2.60 per bushel. On April 1, before the fields had been planted, S informed B that he had entered into a written contract with D, another dealer, to sell his output of corn for $3.00 per bushel. B claimed a breach of contract, but S's lawyer stated that the alleged contract was not enforceable because of the statute of frauds. As B's lawyer, identify and assess all arguments that the transaction was not within the scope of UCC 2–201(1).

Problem 3-6 *For 1/27*

Suppose that on April 1, S had written and signed the following note to B: "The rising corn futures prices makes it necessary for me to cancel our deal. Sorry. Perhaps we can do business again next year." B's lawyer argues that if the oral transaction was within the scope of UCC 2–201(1), that statute satisfied by the note. B is also prepared to prove that the parties had done business for 10 years and that S had always sold B the output from his land. As S's lawyer, identify and assess all of the arguments to the contrary.

Problem 3-7 *For 1/28 → 2/2*

Suppose that on February 1, B had written S a signed letter asking whether S would be willing to sell his output of corn "again this year." In response, S had hand written but not signed the following note, which was delivered by a family member: "George. Output is fine, but no deal until *← Still negotiating stage* we agree on a fair price." On February 5, B (George) visited S on the farm and an oral agreement to sell the output of corn at $2.30 per bushel was reached. On February 7, B mailed the following letter to S, which was received by S on February 9: "Dear Silas. This is to confirm our agreement for the sale of corn at $2.30 per bushel, delivery by October 1. George." S did not respond to the letter. On April 1, S wrote the following signed note to B: "Dear George: We never had a deal. I have sold my *last letter does not give "evidence" of an oral agreement* output to D. (s) Silas." B's lawyer makes two arguments: (1) The statute of frauds was satisfied by application of UCC 2–201(2); (2) When all of the writings are considered, the statute of frauds has been satisfied. How would you rule?

111-121 for 4/28

THOMSON PRINTING MACHINERY CO. v. B.F. GOODRICH CO.

United States Court of Appeals, Seventh Circuit, 1983.
714 F.2d 744.

Before WOOD and CUDAHY, CIRCUIT JUDGES, and GRANT, SENIOR DISTRICT JUDGE.

CUDAHY, CIRCUIT JUDGE.

Appellant Thomson Printing Company ("Thomson Printing") won a jury verdict in its suit for breach of contract against appellee B.F. Goodrich Company ("Goodrich"). The district court concluded, however, that as a matter of law the contract could not be enforced against Goodrich because it was an oral contract, the Statute of Frauds applied and the Statute was not satisfied. Because we conclude that the contract was enforceable on the basis of the "merchants" exception to the Statute of Frauds, we reverse.

District Ct ruled K not enforceable under Statute of Frauds

Appellate Court reverses! Statute of Frauds applies between Merchants

INTRODUCTION

Thomson Printing buys and sells used printing machinery. On Tuesday, April 10, 1979, the president of Thomson Printing, James Thomson, went to Goodrich's surplus machinery department in Akron, Ohio to look at some used printing machinery which was for sale. James Thomson discussed the sale terms, including a price of $9,000, with Goodrich's surplus equipment manager, Ingram Meyers. Four days later, on Saturday, April 14, 1979, James Thomson sent to Goodrich in Akron a purchase order for the equipment and a check for $1,000 in part payment.

Thomson Printing sued Goodrich when Goodrich refused to perform. Goodrich asserted by way of defense that no contract had been formed and that in any event the alleged oral contract was unenforceable due to the Statute of Frauds. Thomson Printing argued that a contract had been made and that the "merchants" and "partial performance" exceptions to the Statute of Frauds were applicable and satisfied. The jury found for Thomson Printing, but the district court entered judgment for Goodrich on the grounds that the Statute of Frauds barred enforcement of the contract in Thomson's favor.

Δ argues:
1. No K
2. Even if, it was oral + thus not enforceable

Π argues:
1. There was a K
2. "Merchants" or "partial perf" can invoke S.g frauds

HISTORICAL BACKGROUND

In 1671, in Old Marston, Oxfordshire, England, defendant Egbert was sued by plaintiff John over an alleged oral promise by Egbert to sell to John a fighting cock named Fiste. John's friend, Harold, claimed he overheard the "deal" and by that dubious means John won, though in fact there apparently was no deal. In 1676 courts did not allow parties to a lawsuit to testify so Egbert could not testify to rebut Harold's story. Compounding the problem was the fact that courts then could not throw out jury verdicts manifestly contrary to the evidence. So, in response to the plight of the Egberts of this world and to the recurring mischief of the Johns, as well as to combat possible "fraude and perjurie" by the Harolds, Parliament passed in 1677 a "statute of frauds" which required that certain contracts for the sale of goods be in writing to be enforceable.[1]

THE "MERCHANTS" EXCEPTION

A modern exception[2] to the usual writing requirement is the "merchants" exception of the Uniform Commercial Code, OHIO REV. CODE ANN. § 1302.04(B) (Page 1979) (U.C.C. § 2–201(2)), which provides:

> Between merchants if within a reasonable time a writing in confirmation of the contract and sufficient against the sender is received and the party receiving it has reason to know its contents, it satisfies the [writing requirement] against such party unless written notice of objection to its contents is given within 10 days after it is received.

[margin handwritten: §2-201(2)]

We must emphasize that the only effect of this exception is to take away from a merchant who receives a writing in confirmation of a contract the Statute of Frauds defense if the merchant does not object. The sender must still persuade the trier of fact that a contract was in fact made orally, to which the written confirmation applies.

[margin handwritten: Only effect is to take away the defense if merchant received written confirmation of K & does not object!]

[left margin handwritten: Oral K must still be proved.]

In the instant case, James Thomson sent a "writing in confirmation" to Goodrich four days after his meeting with Ingram Meyers, a Goodrich employee and agent. The purchase order contained Thomson Printing's name, address, telephone number and certain information about the machinery purchase.[3] The check James Thomson sent to

---

1. This historical background is based on J. White & R. Summers, Handbook of the Law Under the Uniform Commercial Code 50 (2d ed. 1980) (footnotes omitted). *See generally* E.A. Farnsworth, CONTRACTS ch. 6 (1982).

2. An exception of longstanding, which was also argued here, is the "partial performance" exception. We express no opinion on the application of this exception.

[margin handwritten: Court will express no opinion on it's argument that partial performance applies here.]

3. Complete Erection Service   Miehle Factory Trained Erectors   Sales and Service   N⁰ 8756

THOMSON PRINTING MACHINERY CO.

MAINTENANCE • REPAIRING • REBUILDING

1936 to 1940 Augusta Boulevard • Chicago, Illinois 60622 • Phone 227-8600

BF GOODRICH COMPANY
500 S. MAIN STREET
AKRON, OHIO 44318

Date___4-14-79___

Order No._____

PURCHASE ORDER

1   # 70 MIEHLE C&C WITH BERRY LIFT

1   # 3/0 MIEHLE TWO COLOR PRINTING PRESS

1   STAUDE MASTER GLUER & ASSORTED PARTS

PACKAGE PRICE $ 9000.00

                       DEPOSIT $ 1000.00

              BALANCE UPON REMOVAL $ 8000.00

CERTIFICATE OF INSURANCE BEING MAILED
BY CRITCHELL-MILLER AGENCY

Goodrich with the purchase order also had on it Thomson Printing's name and address, and the check carried notations that connected the check with the purchase order.[4]

Goodrich argues, however, that Thomson's writing in confirmation cannot qualify for the 2–201(2) exception because it was not received by anyone at Goodrich who had reason to know its contents.[5] Goodrich claims that Thomson erred in not specifically designating on the envelope, check or purchase order that the items were intended for Ingram Meyers or the surplus equipment department. Consequently, Goodrich contends, it was unable to "find a home" for the check [6] and purchase order despite attempts to do so, in accordance with its regular procedures, by sending copies of the documents to several of its various divisions. Ingram Meyers testified that he never learned of the purchase order until weeks later when James Thomson called to arrange for removal of the machines. By then, however, the machines had long been sold to someone else.

We think Goodrich misreads the requirements of 2–201(2). First, the literal requirements of 2–201(2), as they apply here, are that a writing "is received" and that Goodrich "has reason to know its contents." There is no dispute that the purchase order and check were received by Goodrich, and there is at least no specific or express requirement that the "receipt" referred to in 2–201(2) be by any Goodrich agent in particular.

> These issues are not resolved by [2–201(2)], but it is probably a reasonable projection that a delivery at either the recipient's principal place of business, a place of business from which negotiations were conducted, or to which the sender may have transmitted previous communications, will be an adequate receipt.

3 R. Duesenberg & L. King, Bender's UCC Service § 2–204[2] at 2–70 (1982).

As for the "reason to know its contents" requirement, this element "is best understood to mean that the confirmation was an instrument which should have been anticipated and therefore should have received the attention of appropriate parties." *Perdue Farms, Inc. v. Motts, Inc.*, 459 F.Supp. 7, 20 (N.D.Miss.1978) (quoting from Bender's UCC Service, *supra*, § 2–204[2] at 2–69). "The receipt of a spurious document would not burden the recipient with a risk of losing the [Statute of Frauds] defense * * *." *Id.* In the case before us there is no doubt that the confirmatory writings were based on actual negotiations (although the

---

4. The notations in the upper left hand corner of the check were "1 70 C & C, 1 3/0 T.C. and 1 Staude Master Gluer." See PX 1. Compare these notations with the Purchase Order the check accompanied, *supra*, note 3.

5. The district court found that both parties were merchants for the purpose of 2–201(2). We agree. "For purposes of [2–201(2)] almost every person in business would, therefore, be deemed to be a 'merchant' * * * since the practices involved in the transaction are non-specialized business practices such as answering mail." U.C.C. § 2–104, Comment 2.

6. The check itself was deposited pending clarification in a Goodrich "liability" account.

[Handwritten marginalia:]
Δ argues this exception can't apply because writing was not received by a merchant! Court says in ⑤ almost everyone who works there is a merchant

Δ claims error in not directing order + check to Mr. Meyers

But writing was received

§2-207 doesn't provide requirements for delivery

§2-204 (2) helps

And Δ should have had reason to know its contents ✓

Check was deposited into a liability acct.

legal effect of the negotiations was disputed), and therefore the documents were not "spurious" but could have been anticipated and appropriately handled.

[margin note: Given oral negotiation document could have been anticipated]

Even if we go beyond the literal requirements of 2–201(2) and read into the "receipt" requirement the "receipt of notice" rule of 1–201(27), we still think Thomson Printing satisfied the "merchants" exception. Section 1–201, the definitional section of the U.C.C., provides that notice received by an organization

[margin note: Even if we go further and read into it § 1–201(27) it is still satisfied]

> is effective for a particular transaction * * * from the time when it would have been brought to [the attention of the individual conducting that transaction] if the organization had executed *due diligence.*

U.C.C. § 1–201(27) (emphasis supplied). The Official Comment states:

> reason to know, knowledge, or a notification, although "received" for instance by a clerk in Department A of an organization, is effective for a transaction conducted in Department B only from the time when it was *or should have been* communicated to the individual conducting that transaction.

U.C.C. § 1–201(27), Official Comment (emphasis supplied).

Thus, the question comes down to whether Goodrich's mailroom, given the information it had, should have notified the surplus equipment manager, Ingram Meyers, of Thomson's confirmatory writing. At whatever point Meyers should have been so notified, then at that point Thomson's writing was effective even though Meyers did not see it. *See* 2 A. Squillante & J. Fonseca, WILLISTON ON SALES § 14–8 at 284 (4th ed. 1974) ("the time of receipt will be measured as if the organization involved had used due diligence in getting the document to the appropriate person").

[margin note left: Whatever point Meyers should have been notified is the point Its writing is effective regardless of actual notification]

[margin note right: Court Rules]

[margin note right: Due Dilligence is assumed]

The definitional section of the U.C.C. also sets the general standard for what mailrooms "should do":

> An organization exercises due diligence if it maintains reasonable routines for communicating significant information to the person conducting the transaction and there is reasonable compliance with the routines.

[margin note: Due Dilligence = Reasonable Compliance with reasonable rules]

U.C.C. § 1–201(27). One cannot say that Goodrich's mailroom procedures were reasonable as a matter of law: if Goodrich had exercised due diligence in handling Thomson Printing's purchase order and check, these items would have reasonably promptly come to Ingram Meyers' attention. First, the purchase order on its face should have alerted the mailroom that the documents referred to a purchase of used printing equipment. Since Goodrich had only one surplus machinery department, the documents' "home" should not have been difficult to find. Second, even if the mailroom would have had difficulty in immediately identifying the kind of transaction involved, the purchase order had Thomson Printing's phone number printed on it and we think a "reasonable routine" in these particular circumstances would

[margin note: If Goodrich had exercised due dilligence Meyers probably would have been notified.]

[margin note: 1. Purchase Order indicated Used Equipment — Had only one Surplus dept]

[margin note: 2. If in doubt could have called T.]

have involved at some point in the process a simple phone call to Thomson Printing. Thus, we think Goodrich's mailroom mishandled the confirmatory writings. This failure should not permit Goodrich to escape liability by pleading non-receipt. *See* WILLISTON ON SALES, *supra*, § 14–8 at 284–85.

[margin note: A's failure should not work for them]

We note that the jury verdict for Thomson Printing indicates that the jury found as a fact that the contract had in fact been made and that the Statute of Frauds had been satisfied. Also, Goodrich acknowledges those facts about the handling of the purchase order which we regard as determinative of the "merchants" exception question. We think that there is ample evidence to support the jury findings both of the existence of the contract and of the satisfaction of the Statute.

[margin note: Appellate Court agrees with jury verdict over-rules District Ct]

The district court, in holding as a matter of law that the circumstances failed to satisfy the Statute of Frauds, was impressed by James Thomson's dereliction in failing to specifically direct the purchase order and check to the attention of Ingram Meyers or the surplus equipment department. We agree that Thomson erred in this respect, but, for the reasons we have suggested, Goodrich was at least equally derelict in failing to find a "home" for the well-identified documents. Goodrich argues that in the "vast majority" of cases it can identify checks within a week without contacting an outside party; in the instant case, therefore, if Goodrich correctly states its experience under its procedures, it should presumably have checked with Thomson Printing promptly after the time it normally identified checks by other means— in this case, by its own calculation, a week at most. Under the particular circumstances of this case, we therefore think it inappropriate to set aside a jury verdict on Statute of Frauds grounds.

[margin note: Even though T erred in not directing it to Meyer, Δ erred also.]

The district court's order granting judgment for Goodrich is reversed and the cause is remanded for further proceedings consistent with this opinion.

Reversed and remanded.

[margin note: Exception to Statute of Frauds applies   Oral K enforceable!]

QUANEY v. TOBYNE

Supreme Court of Kansas, 1984.
236 Kan. 201, 689 P.2d 844.

PRAGER, JUSTICE:

[margin note: Facts]

This is an action brought by the sellers against the buyer to recover damages for breach of an oral contract for the sale and purchase of 285 steers. The plaintiffs are J. Martin Quaney and his sons, William E. Quaney, and James Daniel Quaney, farmers and cattlemen residing in Osage County. The defendant, Lowell Tobyne, is a farmer-rancher and feed lot operator who resides in Washington County, Kansas. In this action, plaintiffs sought to recover the difference between the price which defendant agreed to pay for the cattle and the price received for the cattle when sold by plaintiffs after defendant Tobyne refused to take delivery of the cattle on the agreed delivery date.

[margin note: Remedy Sought]

* * *

The defendant filed a motion for summary judgment based upon the defense that the statute of frauds (K.S.A. 84–2–201) barred enforcement of the oral agreement, and, furthermore, that the doctrine of promissory estoppel was not applicable in the case. Defendant's motion for summary judgment was denied by the trial court. The case was then tried by a jury which found in its special verdicts that the plaintiffs and defendant had entered into an oral contract for the purchase and sale of the cattle and that the terms of the contract were for the sale of 285 head of cattle (steers) at 65¢ per pound, with no allowance for shrinkage, with an $8,000 down payment and a written contract to be provided by defendant. The cattle were to be picked up on or before October 1, 1982, and the balance was due upon possession of the cattle. The jury also found that the doctrine of promissory estoppel, as explained in the instructions, should be used to enforce the oral agreement of the parties, and that the total amount of damages sustained by the plaintiffs was $16,826.45. Defendant's motion for a new trial was thereafter denied, and he appealed.

The sole point presented in the defendant's brief is stated as follows: Whether the trial court erred in not applying the statute of frauds to bar the claim of the plaintiffs against the defendant where the evidence of the plaintiffs when viewed in a light most favorable to the plaintiffs does not allow the plaintiffs to avail themselves of the exception of promissory estoppel to the bar created by the statute of frauds. As we see it, there are two basic issues of law to be determined on the appeal:

(1) Does the statute of frauds (K.S.A. 84–2–201) bar the plaintiffs from recovery on the oral contract in this case or is the exception set forth in subsection (3)(b) applicable to remove the bar of the statute?

(2) If the exception is not applicable, does the doctrine of promissory estoppel apply so as to enable the plaintiffs to avoid the defense of the statute of frauds?

We first consider the issue whether plaintiffs' action on the oral sales contract is barred by the statute of frauds (K.S.A. 84–2–201) which provides as follows:

* * *

"(3) A contract which does not satisfy the requirements of subsection (1) but which is valid in other respects is enforceable

"(a) if the goods are to be specially manufactured for the buyer and are not suitable for sale to others in the ordinary course of the seller's business and the seller, before notice of repudiation is received and under circumstances which reasonably indicate that the goods are for the buyer, has made either a substantial beginning of their manufacture or commitments for their procurement; or

"(b) if the party against whom enforcement is sought admits in his pleading, testimony or otherwise in court that a contract for sale

*was made, but the contract is not enforceable under this provision
beyond the quantity of goods admitted;* or

"(c) with respect to goods for which payment has been made
and accepted or which have been received and accepted (section 84–
2–606)." (Emphasis supplied.)

Under subsection (1) of the statute an oral contract for the sale of
goods for the price of $500 or more is not enforceable unless one of the
exceptions under subsection (3) is satisfied. It is agreed that the
exceptions contained in subsection (3)(a) and (c) are not applicable, and
that plaintiffs must rely solely on section (3)(b) in order to avoid the
application of the statute. The issue of law presented is whether, on
the record before us, the defendant as the party against whom enforcement of the oral contract is sought, admitted in his pleadings, testimony, or otherwise in court that an oral contract for sale was made. This
exception was held applicable in *Wendling v. Puls,* 227 Kan. 780, 610
P.2d 580 (1980), which like this case also involved an action for the
breach of an oral contract for the purchase and sale of cattle. In
Wendling, K.S.A. 84–2–201 was discussed and it was noted that all of
the parties had frankly and openly admitted the existence of the
contract during their oral testimony, with complete agreement on price,
quantity of purchase, and date of delivery. In addition, the seller had
served a written notice on the buyers containing the provisions of the
contract to which the buyers offered neither written nor oral objections.
In the case now before us, the plaintiffs/sellers did not serve such a
notice on the defendant buyer. So it is necessary that the record
establish that the defendant/buyer made the admissions required under
K.S.A. 84–2–201(3)(b). It also should be noted that K.S.A. 84–2–201 was
set up as a defense to an oral contract in *Miller v. Sirloin Stockade,* 224
Kan. 32, 578 P.2d 247 (1978), which held that the exception provided for
in subsection (3)(b) is applicable only if the admission is made by a
party to the litigation or by an authorized agent of a party before the
termination of his authority. A former employee of a corporation was
held to be without authority to bind the corporation by "admissions"
made during the course of taking the former employee's deposition.

In the case now before us, we are required to consider the "admissions" made by the defendant, Lowell Tobyne, in the course of the
litigation. This requires us to consider any admissions made in his
pleadings, testimony, or otherwise in court to the effect that a contract
for sale was made. In this case, the only admissions made by defendant
were either in his deposition or in his testimony taken at the time of
trial. Before taking up defendant's admissions, we should first consider
the principles of law involved in the construction and application of
K.S.A. 84–2–201. There is an annotation on this subject in 88 A.L.R.3d
416, where cases from various jurisdictions are set forth discussing the
purposes of the statute and the question as to what constitutes an
admission that the contract for sale was made within the meaning of
the statute. In its summary, the annotation indicates that the courts

have found three reasons for the adoption of the statutory provision contained in K.S.A. 84–2–201(3)(b) excepting from the operation of the statute of frauds contracts whose existence has been admitted by the party against whom enforcement is sought. It has been stated by the courts that the purposes of the statute are (1) to provide that a party cannot admit the existence of an oral contract for the sale of goods and simultaneously claim the benefit of the statute of frauds, (2) to prevent the statute of frauds from becoming an aid to fraud, and (3) to expand the exceptions to the nonenforceability of oral contracts under the statute of frauds.

Purpose of (3)(b)

In order to come within the terms of the exceptions stated in 84–2–201(3)(b), a statement must in fact constitute an admission, and the courts in several cases have expressly considered what constitutes an admission that a contract for sale was made within the meaning of the statutory exception. A problem has arisen in this regard where a party *admits* the essential terms of the oral contract but denies that a final agreement or meeting of the minds was ever actually consummated. In several cases it has been held that the testimony of the party against whom enforcement of an oral contract for the sale of goods is sought, which, while denying the existence of the oral contract, admits facts which as a matter of law establish the existence of the contract, constitutes an admission within the meaning of the statute.

* * *

We have considered all of these various authorities and the principles of law established thereby and have concluded that the exception to the statute of frauds contained in K.S.A. 84–2–201(3)(b) is satisfied when the party who has denied the existence of an oral contract in reliance on the statute takes the stand and, without admitting explicitly that a contract was made, testifies as to his statements or his actions which establish the terms of the oral contract claimed by the opposing party. It is not necessary that there be an express declaration in which the party admits the making of the oral contract. It is sufficient if his words or admitted conduct reasonably lead to that conclusion.

An absolute declaration of an oral K is not required. Words & conduct reasonably suggesting that conclusion are sufficient

Turning to the testimony of the buyer, Lowell Tobyne, in the record now before us, the question to be determined is whether there are sufficient admissions as to the existence and terms of the oral contract to satisfy the statutory exception in K.S.A. 84–2–201(3)(b). As noted above, the defendant in one portion of his testimony denied that there had been a final meeting of the minds and further testified that there was to be no binding contract until the contract was reduced to writing. On cross-examination, however, the defendant testified that he telephoned plaintiff Martin Quaney and asked him if he had any cattle for sale, and Quaney replied that he did. He was told that all of the cattle were steers and that Quaney was asking a price of 65¢ per pound. At Quaney's suggestion, he met Quaney at the pasture on August 15, 1982, and drove around and looked at the cattle in the large pasture. He stated that he was satisfied with the quality and type of those cattle. He was told that Quaney had cattle in another pasture and Quaney offered to take him down to the other pasture. He admitted that he did not need to see the other cattle if they were similar to the cattle he had just looked at. He was told by Quaney that they were the same type of cattle that he had just seen. Defendant stated that he *agreed* on a 65¢ per pound price for the cattle on that day. He *agreed* with Quaney that he would load the cattle out around October 1, 1982. He *agreed* that the cattle would be weighed at either St. Marys or Manhattan, Kansas. It was discussed that Mr. Hess would round up the cattle and deliver the same to the defendant for loading. A down payment of $8,000 was agreeable with both parties. He mentioned to Quaney that he was going to put together a written agreement and bring it down to Quaney. From this testimony, it seems clear to us that the defendant admitted in his testimony all of the terms of the agreement for sale and purchase of the cattle as claimed by the plaintiffs. To summarize, in his testimony the defendant testified as to the following terms of the contract:

(1) He was satisfied with the quality and type of cattle—285 steers were to be purchased.

(2) He agreed on a price of 65¢ per pound.

(3) He agreed that the cattle would be weighed at St. Marys or Manhattan to establish their weight.

(4) A loading date for the cattle around October 1, 1982, was agreed upon.

(5) He agreed on a down payment of $8,000.

In addition to this, the defendant testified as to *conduct* which gave recognition to the finality and binding effect of the agreement. After Martin Quaney was injured in the automobile accident on August 19, 1982, the defendant had several telephone conversations with William E. Quaney and James Daniel Quaney. He admitted that in none of these conversations did he state that he was not buying the cattle or indicate that an agreement had not been consummated. As late as September 23, and September 30, 1982, the defendant discussed with Oliver Hess, the manager of the pasture leased to plaintiffs where the cattle were kept, arrangements for the defendant to pick up the cattle. It was agreed that October 2, 1982, was to be the date for the loading of the cattle. On October 1, 1982, the defendant called Martin Quaney and told him that he would not be able to purchase the cattle.

From our analysis of this testimony, we have concluded that, although the defendant did not openly and frankly admit to an oral agreement, his testimony sufficiently establishes that an oral agreement existed. The defendant acknowledged all the principal terms of the agreement. The parties had agreed on a price per pound, type and quality of the cattle, place of loading, place of weighing, and the down payment. Although the defendant never paid the down payment or drew up a written contract as he volunteered to do, we hold that his testimony contained admissions of his statements and actions sufficient to satisfy the requirements of K.S.A. 84–2–201(3)(b).

Since the defendant raised several defenses to the contract, the issues were submitted to the jury and the jury found that the plaintiff and defendant had entered into an oral contract for the purchase and sale of the cattle. There was substantial competent evidence to support that finding. In view of the admissions which the defendant made in his testimony at the trial, the defense of the statute of frauds was removed from the case in accordance with K.S.A. 84–2–201(3)(b).

In view of our holding on this issue, the question as to the applicability of the doctrine of promissory estoppel as a defense to the bar created by the statute of frauds becomes moot. We note, however, the holding of this court in *Decatur Cooperative Association v. Urban*, 219 Kan. 171, 547 P.2d 323. That case involved an action for breach of an oral contract for the sale and purchase of wheat. In that case promissory estoppel was successfully asserted to preclude the statute of frauds as a defense to an oral contract for the sale of goods.

On the basis of the record before us, we find that the issues were properly formulated by court and counsel and submitted to the jury which resolved all issues in favor of the plaintiffs in accordance with established legal principles.

The judgment of the district court is affirmed.

\#

✓ Problem 3–8 *Omit* ✓

IBM and Epprecht entered an oral agreement allegedly for the production by Epprecht of 50,000 print-head assemblies for computers. The assemblies were to conform to particular specifications prepared and furnished by IBM. IBM issued purchase orders for 7,000 assemblies, 4,000 of which were accepted and 3,000 of which were rejected by IBM. IBM paid the price of the assemblies accepted but, claiming quality problems, refused to pay anything for the rejected assemblies and cancelled the agreement. Epprecht, alleging the facts stated above, sued for damages caused by IBM's "wrongful" rejection of 3,000 units. IBM moved for a summary judgment on the basis of UCC 2–201. Epprecht argued that the summary judgment should be denied: Although there was no writing, the statute of frauds was satisfied under UCC 2–201(3)(a) & (c). Epprecht cited Impossible Electronic Techniques, Inc. v. Wackenhut Protective Systems, Inc., 669 F.2d 1026, 1036–37 (5th Cir.1982), where the court stated that the "statute exempts contracts involving 'specially manufactured' goods from the writing requirement because in these cases the very nature of the goods serves as a reliable indication that a contract was indeed formed." Further: "Where the seller has commenced or completed the manufacture of goods that conform to the special needs of a particular buyer and thereby are not suitable for sale to others, not only is the likelihood of a perjured claim of a contract diminished, but denying enforcement to such a contract would impose substantial hardship on the aggrieved party. ＊ ＊ ＊ The unfairness is especially acute where ＊ ＊ ＊ the seller has incurred substantial, unrecoverable expense in reliance on the oral promise of the buyer.

* * * The crucial inquiry is whether the manufacturer could sell the goods in the ordinary course of his business to someone other than the original buyer. If with slight alterations the goods could be so sold, then they are not specially manufactured; if, however, essential changes are necessary to render the goods marketable by the seller to others, then the exception does apply." How should the court rule?

LIGE DICKSON CO. v. UNION OIL CO. OF CAL.

Supreme Court of Washington, 1981.
96 Wash.2d 291, 635 P.2d 103.

DORE, JUSTICE.

The Ninth Circuit Court of Appeals certified the following question to us:

Under the law of the State of Washington, may an oral promise otherwise within the statute of frauds, Wash.Rev.Code § 62A.2–201, nevertheless be enforceable on the basis of promissory estoppel? *See* Restatement (Second) of Contracts § 217A. *See generally Klinke v. Famous Recipe Fried Chicken, Inc.,* 94 Wash.2d 255, 616 P.2d 644 (1980).

Our answer to this question is "no". Analysis and elaboration follow.

The business relationship between plaintiff Lige Dickson Company (or its predecessor partnership) and defendant Union Oil Company of California is long standing, dating from 1937. Plaintiff was a general contractor and purchased its oil-based products from defendant. In 1964, defendant encouraged and aided plaintiff in entering the asphalt paving business. From 1964 through 1973, with one exception, plaintiff purchased all its liquid asphalt from defendant. In the ordinary course of business, plaintiff telephoned orders to defendant, plaintiff was invoiced, and all bills were paid. Plaintiff and defendant never executed a written contract providing for the sale and purchase of liquid asphalt.

From 1964 until late 1970, the defendant's price for liquid asphalt remained constant. In December 1970, all of the suppliers of liquid asphalt in the Tacoma area raised their prices. Responding to this in May or June of 1971, plaintiff requested, and defendant provided, an oral guarantee against further increases insofar as would affect those contracts which committed the plaintiff to manufacture and sell asphalt paving at fixed, agreed sums. A list was made of the plaintiff's contracts and the parties computed the amount of liquid asphalt needed to fulfill them. At the same time, defendant promised plaintiff that any upward change in price would be applicable only to contracts which plaintiff entered into after the price increase.

At trial, an official of defendant conceded that by November 1973 there was an unwritten custom in the liquid asphalt business in the Tacoma area, well known and acted upon by suppliers, and users, that any increase in price of liquid asphalt would not be applicable to

[handwritten margin note: Is this enough of an admission to satisfy (3)(b)?]

manufacturers' then-existing contracts. From mid–1971 until November 1973, defendant's sales representatives visited plaintiff and ascertained tonnage of liquid asphalt needed for plaintiff to fulfill existing paving contracts and also promised plaintiff that the price for that liquid tonnage would be protected.

Nevertheless, in November 1973 defendant wrote to plaintiff that the price of liquid asphalt was rising by $3 per ton and plaintiff was informed on December 6 and 13, 1973 of further increases. The new prices were to be applicable to all purchases made after December 31, 1973. This was plaintiff's first notification that defendant was abandoning the parties' price protection agreement. In addition, the new prices were on a "verbal, indefinite basis * * * subject to change" with or without notice.

[handwritten margin note: don't know from day to day — Anything could happen.]

Without a firm supplier, plaintiff was unable to seek new paving contracts during the first part of 1974. What liquid asphalt was available was used by plaintiff to complete existing contracts. Plaintiff incurred a total increased out-of-pocket cost of $39,006.50 in acquiring liquid asphalt to perform existing contracts.

Plaintiff brought suit against defendant in the United States District Court for Western Washington for breach of contract. The trial court found that there was an oral contract between the parties, but the statute of frauds, RCW 62A.2–201 rendered the contract unenforceable. The cause was appealed to the Ninth Circuit which certified the question quoted above to this court.

[handwritten margin note: Trial Ct found an oral K but statute of frauds made it unenforceable]

The facts as outlined above are contained in the District Court's Findings of Facts which were made part of the record before this court. In the Ninth Circuit appeal, defendant has assigned errors to certain of these findings. These contentions, however, are not before us. We do not need certainty in the facts to answer the pure question of law presented for our determination. The Ninth Circuit has retained jurisdiction over all matters but the narrow question of law certified here.

The Restatement (Second) of Contracts § 217A (Tent.Drafts Nos. 1–7, 1973)[3] (hereinafter § 217A) authorizes enforcement of a promise

3. The Restatement (Second) of Contracts § 217A (Tent.Drafts Nos. 1–7, 1973) reads:

"Enforcement by Virtue of Action in Reliance

"(1) A promise which the promisor should reasonably expect to induce action or forbearance on the part of the promisee or a third person and which does induce the action or forbearance is enforceable notwithstanding the Statute of Frauds if injustice can be avoided only by enforcement of the promise. The remedy granted for breach is to be limited as justice requires.

"(2) In determining whether injustice can be avoided only by enforcement of the promise, the following circumstances are significant:

"(a) the availability and adequacy of other remedies, particularly cancellation and restitution;

"(b) the definite and substantial character of the action or forbearance in relation to the remedy sought;

"(c) the extent to which the action or forbearance corroborates evidence of the making and terms of the promise, or the making and terms are otherwise established by clear and convincing evidence;

which induced action or forbearance by a promisee notwithstanding the statute of frauds. Adoption of § 217A was before this court in *Klinke v. Famous Recipe Fried Chicken, Inc.,* 94 Wash.2d 255, 616 P.2d 644 (1980).

In *Klinke,* the plaintiff had been induced by defendant to leave his employ in Alaska and to move to Washington to establish a food franchise. Defendant had promised plaintiff that defendant would qualify and register in Washington as a dealer in franchises. After plaintiff's move, defendant failed to secure the proper dealer registration and later abandoned its efforts to do so. The plaintiff claimed $200,000 in lost time and wages and other damages. On summary judgment, the trial court dismissed the case because RCW 19.36.010(1) [4] voids unwritten contracts which cannot be performed in one year. The Court of Appeals reversed the trial court based on two theories. *Klinke v. Famous Recipe Fried Chicken, Inc.,* 24 Wash.App. 202, 600 P.2d 1034 (1979). First, defendant's failure to reduce the agreement with plaintiff to a writing, and plaintiff's reliance on such promise, estopped defendant from asserting the statute of frauds as a defense. Restatement of Contracts, §§ 90, 178, comment f (1932). Second, the Court of Appeals adopted § 217A. On review of that decision, we refused to adopt § 217A but affirmed the court's reversal on its first theory. We stated:

> The unforseen application of section 217A to areas of law outside the scope of the facts of this case convinces us that it would be unwise to adopt that section now unless necessary to effectuate justice. That is not mandated by the facts of this case.

Klinke v. Famous Recipe Fried Chicken, Inc., 94 Wash.2d 255, 262, 616 P.2d 644 (1980).

Plaintiff in the subject case urges us to now adopt § 217A as being "necessary to effectuate justice". Plaintiff focuses on the parties' longstanding relationship and defendant's responsibility "in great part" for introducing plaintiff into the asphalt paving business. Plaintiff also asserts that defendant's price protection agreement and assurances encouraged (i.e., induced?) plaintiff to make bids and enter into contracts.

Defendant asks this court to distinguish the statute of frauds at issue in *Klinke* from the statute of frauds contained within the Uniform Commercial Code (U.C.C.) at issue here.[5] Such distinction has been recognized.

"(d) the reasonableness of the action or forbearance:

"(e) the extent to which the action or forbearance was foreseeable by the promisor."

[§ 139 in final version. Ed.]

4. RCW 19.36.010 states, in part:

"In the following cases, specified in this section, any agreement, contract and promise shall be void, unless such agreement, contract or promise, or some note or memorandum thereof, be in writing, and signed by the party to be charged therewith, or by some person thereunto by him lawfully authorized, that is to say: (1) Every agreement that by its terms is not to be performed in one year from the making thereof * * *"

5. The Uniform Commercial Code as adopted in Washington is found at RCW Title 62A. Reference to U.C.C. § 2-201

The statute of frauds requirements may vary as to the nature of the agreements involved, and a close examination of the subject matter of the oral promise in question is therefore warranted. For example, if the oral promise in question concerned the sale of goods, the attorney would want to be aware of the requirements set out in UCC § 2–201(3) which states the circumstances under which a contract for the sale of goods may be enforceable notwithstanding the statute of frauds * * * It should be pointed out that where there exists, in statute or in case law, clearly established means under which a contract dealing with a particular subject matter may be rendered enforceable notwithstanding the statute of frauds, the courts may be hesitant to apply promissory estoppel in such a manner as to enlarge upon those means of avoiding the statute.

Annotation Comment Note.—Promissory Estoppel as Basis for Avoidance of Statute of Frauds, 56 A.L.R.3d 1037, 1045 (1932). (Footnotes omitted.) The Ninth Circuit Court of Appeals has held, in interpreting and applying California law, that U.C.C. § 2–201 cannot be overcome through the application of the doctrine of promissory estoppel. *C.R. Fedrick, Inc. v. Borg-Warner Corp.,* 552 F.2d 852 (9th Cir.1977). The Kentucky Supreme Court reached the same conclusion based upon the U.C.C.'s internal method of avoiding § 2–201's hardship. *C.G. Campbell & Son, Inc. v. Comdeq. Corp.,* 586 S.W.2d 40 (Ky.App.1979). It reasoned that the statutory avoidance of § 2–201 found in § 2–201(3) was as far as the legislature was willing to go and

> any attempt by the courts to judicially amend this statute which is plain on its face would contravene the separation of powers mandated by the Constitution.

Campbell at page 41.

On the other hand, the Iowa Supreme Court reached the opposite result in *Warder & Lee Elevator, Inc. v. Britten,* 274 N.W.2d 339 (Iowa 1979). That court found that U.C.C. § 1–103 [6] provided the authority for the use of promissory estoppel to defeat the statute of frauds. That section provides, *inter alia,* that "unless displaced by the particular provision of this chapter" estoppel and other validating or invalidating doctrines shall supplement the U.C.C. The court reasoned that the exceptions to the statute of frauds found at § 2–201(3)(a)–(c) are "definitional" and were not meant to displace equitable and legal principles otherwise applicable to contract actions.

> If [2–201] were construed as displacing principles otherwise preserved in [1–103], it would mean that an oral contract coming

and § 1–103 in this opinion are intended to refer to Washington's corresponding sections.

6. Washington's version of § 1–103, found at RCW 62A.1–103, reads:

"Unless displaced by the particular provisions of this Title, the principles of law

and equity, including the law merchant and the law relative to capacity to contract, principal and agent, estoppel, fraud, misrepresentation, duress, coercion, mistake, bankruptcy, or other validating or invalidating cause shall supplement its provisions."

within its terms would be unenforceable despite fraud, deceit, misrepresentation, dishonesty or any other form of unconscionable conduct by the party relying upon the statute. No court has taken such an extreme position. Nor would we be justified in doing so. Despite differences relating to the availability of an estoppel defense, courts uniformly hold "that the Statute of Frauds, having been enacted for the purpose of preventing fraud, shall not be made the instrument of shielding[,] protecting, or aiding the party who relies upon it in the perpetration of a fraud or in the consummation of a fraudulent scheme." 3 Williston on Contracts § 553A at 796 (Third Ed. Jaeger, 1960).

Warder & Lee Elevator, Inc. v. Britten, supra at page 342.

Defendant asks us to adopt the view of the dissent in *Warder & Lee Elevator, Inc. v. Britten, supra.* The thrust of the dissent is that § 1-103 allows estoppel to supplement the U.C.C. "unless displaced by the particular provisions of this chapter"; and § 2-201 contains its own limiting language in that the statute of frauds applies "except as otherwise provided *in this section.*" (Italics ours.) Further, the dissent noted that a party to an oral contract who has been defrauded has available the equitable remedy of restitution. In such a case, the recovery is based on the wrong, not on a contract.

From the limited record before us in the subject case, it appears that equitable estoppel is not available to the plaintiff. There seems to be neither allegation nor proof of fraud or deceit. Plaintiff's only remedy may be based upon breach of the oral contract. *Nonetheless,* we must hold that promissory estoppel cannot be used to overcome the statute of frauds in a case which involves the sale of goods.

The Uniform Commercial Code was adopted to regulate commercial dealings. Uniformity among different jurisdictions in decisions concerning commerce was a major motivation behind development of the U.C.C. By so doing, it was hoped that this area of the law would become clearer and disputes would be more readily resolved. These policies are enunciated in the U.C.C., in part, as follows:

62A.1-102 Purposes; rules of construction; variation by agreement * * *

(2) Underlying purposes and policies of this Title are

(a) to simplify, clarify and modernize the law governing commercial transactions;

* * *

(c) to make uniform the law among the various jurisdictions.

It was hoped that commercial transactions could take place across state boundaries without the stultifying effect caused by differences in states' laws.

The Uniform Commercial Code, hammered out by lawyers, judges and law teachers dedicated to clarity and good business sense in commercial law, has brought together into one coherent statement the best laws and practices prevalent in the United States.

American Bar Association, *Uniform Commercial Code Handbook,* "The Uniform Commercial Code," at 1 (1964).

> Because of the federal system, the American lawyer, probably more than any other, has been conscious of the disadvantages of differing laws. Internally he has tried to do something about it.

American Bar Association, *Uniform Commercial Code Handbook,* "The Uniform Commercial Code," at 19 (1964).

If we were to adopt § 217A as applicable in the context of the sale of goods, we would allow parties to circumvent the U.C.C. *See Warder & Lee Elevator, Inc. v. Britten, supra,* (Reynoldson, C.J., dissenting). For example, to prove justifiable reliance (an element of promissory estoppel), the promisee may offer evidence of course of dealing between the parties, as plaintiff did in this case. The Official Comments to RCWA 62A.1–205(4) state that the statute of frauds

> restrict[s] the actions of the parties, and * * * cannot be abrogated by agreement, or by a *usage of trade* * * *

RCWA 62A.1–205 at 71. (Italics ours.)

Notwithstanding our appreciation of plaintiff's dilemma, we cannot help but foresee increased litigation and confusion as being the necessary result of the eroding of the U.C.C. if § 217A is adopted in this case. We join the other courts which limit the doctrine of promissory estoppel from overcoming a valid defense based on the statute of frauds contained within the Uniform Commercial Code. By so doing, we make no comment on the applicability of § 217A to defeat the raising of the statute of frauds as a defense under RCW 19.36.010.

BRACHTENBACH, C.J., and DOLLIVER, WILLIAMS, STAFFORD, DIMMICK and UTTER, JJ., concur.

ROSELLINI, JUSTICE (concurring specially).

I agree with the majority that, in order to preserve the integrity of the Uniform Commercial Code, the question submitted by the Ninth Circuit Court of Appeals must be answered in the negative. It is evident that the legislature gave careful thought to the circumstances which would justify exceptions to the requirement of a written contract, and those exceptions are set forth in the act itself. They do not include circumstances which in other areas of law might invoke the doctrine of promissory estoppel.

While the code makes no provision for relief under the theory of promissory estoppel, it does provide an exception to the requirement of a writing

> if the party against whom enforcement is sought admits in his pleading, testimony or otherwise in court that a contract for sale

Concurring judge: Suggests possibly Δ made admission of K at trial? Code provides its own remedy in §2-201 (3) (b)

was made, but the contract is not enforceable under this provision beyond the quantity of goods admitted; * * *

RCW 62A.2–201(3)(b).

There is in the district court's findings some suggestion that there may have been such an admission here. If that were the case, the code itself would provide a remedy.

HICKS, J., concurs.

[Some footnotes omitted.]

Chapter Four

THE POTENTIALLY ADVERSE BEARING OF "PRE-CONTRACT" FACTS AND EVENTS UPON THE AGREEMENT

SECTION 1. INTRODUCTION

Suppose the seller and buyer have concluded a bargain which is enforceable as a contract under Article 2, Part 2. The bargain is reduced to writing and signed by both parties. After performance commences, a dispute erupts over the obligations under the contract. The dispute may involve either the scope of the agreement in fact or the meaning of terms clearly within the scope of agreement. In either case, there is an honest disagreement.

How does Article 2 deal with disputes of this sort? For example, one party, to support his argument about the scope or meaning of the agreement, will undoubtedly seek to introduce evidence beyond the "four corners" of the writing. Can the other party exclude this evidence and, if so, under what circumstances?

The starting place is the definition of agreement in UCC 1–201(3): Agreement means "the bargain of the parties in fact as found in their language or by implication from other circumstances including course of dealing or usage of trade or course of performance as provided in this Act (Sections 1–205 and 2–208.)" Under this expansive definition, agreement may not be limited to the terms in the writing: It may include terms derived from trade usage, a prior course of dealing between the parties or the negotiations leading up to the particular bargain at stake. Thus, as the *Columbia Nitrogen* case, infra at page 130, reveals, one party may seek to supplement a price term contained in the writing by a usage or practice of the trade. See UCC 1–205(2).

If the statutory conditions for admissibility are satisfied, the next question is whether the parties, by agreement, have attempted to limit the scope of their bargain. Have they, for example, attempted to "contract out" of relevant trade usage or the expectations created by a prior course of dealing? If so, should that attempt be recognized by the

[handwritten marginal note: Under UCC Agreement means]

129

court? See UCC 1–205(4), where an ordering principle is stated. Similarly, did both parties intend that their writing be a partial or total integration of their agreement, i.e., did they intend to exclude from the writing terms that were in fact agreed prior to or contemporaneously with its adoption? If so, the stage is set for application of the infamous parol evidence rule, UCC 2–202.

Finally, if the scope of agreement is determined, how are disputes over the meaning of terms to which the parties agreed to be resolved? What does the UCC say with regard to contract interpretation disputes and the evidence which is relevant to their resolution?

These questions will occupy our attention in this Chapter.

SECTION 2. PRE–CONTRACT FACTS OR EVENTS WHICH VARY, SUPPLEMENT OR GIVE MEANING TO THE AGREEMENT

COLUMBIA NITROGEN CORP. v. ROYSTER CO.

United States Court of Appeals, Fourth Circuit, 1971.
451 F.2d 3.

BUTZNER, CIRCUIT JUDGE.

Columbia Nitrogen Corp. appeals a judgment in the amount of $750,000 in favor of F.S. Royster Guano Co. for breach of a contract for the sale of phosphate to Columbia by Royster. Columbia defended on the grounds that the contract, construed in light of the usage of the trade and course of dealing, imposed no duty to accept at the quoted prices the minimum quantities stated in the contract. It also asserted an antitrust defense and counterclaim based on Royster's alleged reciprocal trade practices. The district court excluded the evidence about course of dealing and usage of the trade. It submitted the antitrust issues based on coercive reciprocity to the jury, but refused to submit the alternative theory of non-coercive reciprocity. The jury found for Royster on both the contract claim and the anti-trust counterclaim. We hold that Columbia's proffered evidence was improperly excluded and Columbia is entitled to a new trial on the contractual issues. With respect to the antitrust issues, we affirm.

I.

Royster manufactures and markets mixed fertilizers, the principal components of which are nitrogen, phosphate and potash. Columbia is primarily a producer of nitrogen, although it manufactures some mixed fertilizer. For several years Royster had been a major purchaser of Columbia's products, but Columbia had never been a significant customer of Royster. In the fall of 1966, Royster constructed a facility which enabled it to produce more phosphate than it needed in its own operations. After extensive negotiations, the companies executed a contract for Royster's sale of a minimum of 31,000 tons of phosphate each year for three years to Columbia, with an option to extend the term. The contract stated the price per ton, subject to an escalation clause dependent on production costs.

Phosphate prices soon plunged precipitously. Unable to resell the phosphate at a competitive price, Columbia ordered only part of the scheduled tonnage. At Columbia's request, Royster lowered its price for diammonium phosphate on shipments for three months in 1967, but specified that subsequent shipments would be at the original contract price. Even with this concession, Royster's price was still substantially above the market. As a result, Columbia ordered less than a tenth of the phosphate Royster was to ship in the first contract year. When pressed by Royster, Columbia offered to take the phosphate at the current market price and resell it without brokerage fee. Royster, however, insisted on the contract price. When Columbia refused delivery, Royster sold the unaccepted phosphate for Columbia's account at a price substantially below the contract price.

II.

Columbia assigns error to the pretrial ruling of the district court excluding all evidence on usage of the trade and course of dealing between the parties. It offered the testimony of witnesses with long experience in the trade that because of uncertain crop and weather conditions, farming practices, and government agricultural programs, express price and quantity terms in contracts for materials in the mixed fertilizer industry are mere projections to be adjusted according to market forces.*

* One witness testified, in part, as follows:

"The contracts generally entered into between buyer and seller of materials has always been, in my opinion, construed to be the buyer's best estimate of his anticipated requirements for a given period of time. It is well known in our industry that weather conditions, farming practices, government farm control programs, change requirements from time to time. And therefore allowances were always made to meet these circumstances as they arose."

"Tonnage requirements fluctuate greatly, and that is one reason that the contracts are not considered as binding as most contracts are, because the buyer normally would buy on historical basis, but his normal average use would be per annum of any given material. Now that can be affected very decidedly by adverse weather conditions such as a drought, or a flood, or maybe governmental programs which we have been faced with for many, many years, seed grain programs. They pay the farmer not to plant. If he doesn't plant, he doesn't use the fertilizer. When the con-

tracts are made, we do not know of all these contingencies and what they are going to be. So the contract is made for what is considered a fair estimate of his requirements. And, the contract is considered binding to the extent, on him morally, that if he uses the tonnage that he will execute the contract in good faith as the buyer. * * * "

"I have never heard of a contract of this type being enforced legally. * * * Well, it undoubtedly sounds ridiculous to people from other industries, but there is a very definite, several very definite reasons why the fertilizer business is always operated under what we call gentlemen's agreements. * * * "

"The custom in the fertilizer industry is that the seller either meets the competitive situation or releases the buyer from it upon proof that he can buy it at that price * * *. [T]hey will either have the option of meeting it or releasing him from taking additional tonnage or holding him to that price. * * * "

And this custom exists "regardless of the contractual provisions."

Columbia also offered proof of its business dealings with Royster over the six-year period preceding the phosphate contract. Since Columbia had not been a significant purchaser of Royster's products, these dealings were almost exclusively nitrogen sales to Royster or exchanges of stock carried in inventory. The pattern which emerges, Columbia claimed, is one of repeated and substantial deviation from the stated amount or price, including four instances where Royster took none of the goods for which it had contracted. Columbia offered proof that the total variance amounted to more than $500,000 in reduced sales. This experience, a Columbia officer offered to testify, formed the basis of an understanding on which he depended in conducting negotiations with Royster.

The district court held that the evidence should be excluded. It ruled that "custom and usage or course of dealing are not admissible to contradict the express, plain, unambiguous language of a valid written contract, which by virtue of its detail negates the proposition that the contract is open to variances in its terms. * * *"

A number of Virginia cases have held that extrinsic evidence may not be received to explain or supplement a written contract unless the court finds the writing is ambiguous. E.g., Mathieson Alkali Works v. Virginia Banner Coal Corp., 147 Va. 125, 136 S.E. 673 (1927). This rule, however, has been changed by the Uniform Commercial Code which Virginia has adopted. The Code expressly states that it "shall be liberally construed and applied to promote its underlying purposes and policies," which include "the expansion of commercial practices through custom, usage and agreement of the parties. * * *" Va. Code Ann. § 8.1–102 (1965). The importance of usage of trade and course of dealing between the parties is shown by § 8.2–202, which authorizes their use to explain or supplement a contract. The official comment states this section rejects the old rule that evidence of course of dealing or usage of trade can be introduced only when the contract is ambiguous. And the Virginia commentators, noting that "[t]his section reflects a more liberal approach to the introduction of parol evidence * * * than has been followed in Virginia," express the opinion that Mathieson, supra, and similar Virginia cases no longer should be followed. Va.Code Ann. § 8.2–202, Va.Comment. See also Portsmouth Gas Co. v. Shebar, 209 Va. 250, 253 n. 1, 163 S.E.2d 205, 208 n. 1 (1968) (dictum). We hold, therefore, that a finding of ambiguity is not necessary for the admission of extrinsic evidence about the usage of the trade and the parties' course of dealing.

We turn next to Royster's claim that Columbia's evidence was properly excluded because it was inconsistent with the express terms of their agreement. There can be no doubt that the Uniform Commercial Code restates the well established rule that evidence of usage of trade

"[T]he custom was that [these contracts] were not worth the cost of the paper they were printed on." [451 F.2d at 7, n. 3]

and course of dealing should be excluded whenever it cannot be reasonably construed as consistent with the terms of the contract. Division of Triple T Service, Inc. v. Mobil Oil Corp., 60 Misc.2d 720, 304 N.Y.S.2d 191, 203 (1969), aff'd mem., 311 N.Y.S.2d 961 (1970). Royster argues that the evidence should be excluded as inconsistent because the contract contains detailed provisions regarding the base price, escalation, minimum tonnage, and delivery schedules. The argument is based on the premise that because a contract appears on its face to be complete, evidence of course of dealing and usage of trade should be excluded. We believe, however, that neither the language nor the policy of the Code supports such a broad exclusionary rule. Section 8.2–202 expressly allows evidence of course of dealing or usage of trade to explain or supplement terms intended by the parties as a final expression of their agreement. When this section is read in light of Va. Code Ann. § 8.1–205(4), it is clear that the test of admissibility is not whether the contract appears on its face to be complete in every detail, but whether the proffered evidence of course of dealing and trade usage reasonably can be construed as consistent with the express terms of the agreement.

The proffered testimony sought to establish that because of changing weather conditions, farming practices, and government agricultural programs, dealers adjusted prices, quantities, and delivery schedules to reflect declining market conditions. For the following reasons it is reasonable to construe this evidence as consistent with the express terms of the contract:

(1) The contract does not expressly state that course of dealing and usage of trade cannot be used to explain or supplement the written contract.

(2) The contract is silent about adjusting prices and quantities to reflect a declining market. It neither permits nor prohibits adjustment, and this neutrality provides a fitting occasion for recourse to usage of trade and prior dealing to supplement the contract and explain its terms.

(3) Minimum tonnages and additional quantities are expressed in terms of "Products Supplied Under Contract." Significantly, they are not expressed as just "Products" or as "Products Purchased Under Contract." The description used by the parties is consistent with the proffered testimony.

(4) Finally, the default clause of the contract refers only to the failure of the buyer to pay for delivered phosphate. During the contract negotiations, Columbia rejected a Royster proposal for liquidated damages of $10 for each ton Columbia declined to accept. On the other hand, Royster rejected a Columbia proposal for a clause that tied the price to the market by obligating Royster to conform its price to offers Columbia received from other phosphate producers. The parties, having rejected both proposals, failed to state any consequences of Columbia's refusal to take delivery—the kind of default Royster alleges in this

case. Royster insists that we span this hiatus by applying the general law of contracts permitting recovery of damages upon the buyer's refusal to take delivery according to the written provisions of the contract. This solution is not what the Uniform Commercial Code prescribes. Before allowing damages, a court must first determine whether the buyer has in fact defaulted. It must do this by supplementing and explaining the agreement with evidence of trade usage and course of dealing that is consistent with the contract's express terms. Va.Code Ann. §§ 8.1–205(4), 8.2–202. Faithful adherence to this mandate reflects the reality of the marketplace and avoids the overly legalistic interpretations which the Code seeks to abolish.

Royster also contends that Columbia's proffered testimony was properly rejected because it dealt with mutual willingness of buyer and seller to adjust contract terms to the market. Columbia, Royster protests, seeks unilateral adjustment. This argument misses the point. What Columbia seeks to show is a practice of mutual adjustments so prevalent in the industry and in prior dealings between the parties that it formed a part of the agreement governing this transaction. It is not insisting on a unilateral right to modify the contract.

Nor can we accept Royster's contention that the testimony should be excluded under the contract clause:

> "No verbal understanding will be recognized by either party hereto; this contract expresses all the terms and conditions of the agreement, shall be signed in duplicate, and shall not become operative until approved in writing by the Seller."

Course of dealing and trade usage are not synonymous with verbal understandings, terms and conditions. Section 8.2–202 draws a distinction between supplementing a written contract by consistent additional terms and supplementing it by course of dealing or usage of trade. Evidence of additional terms must be excluded when "the court finds the writing to have been intended also as a complete and exclusive statement of the terms of the agreement." Significantly, no similar limitation is placed on the introduction of evidence of course of dealing or usage of trade. Indeed the official comment notes that course of dealing and usage of trade, unless carefully negated, are admissible to supplement the terms of any writing, and that contracts are to be read on the assumption that these elements were taken for granted when the document was phrased. Since the Code assigns course of dealing and trade usage unique and important roles, they should not be conclusively rejected by reading them into stereotyped language that makes no specific reference to them. Cf. Provident Tradesmen's Bank & Trust Co. v. Pemberton, 196 Pa.Super. 180, 173 A.2d 780. Indeed, the Code's official commentators urge that overly simplistic and overly legalistic interpretation of a contract should be shunned.

We conclude therefore that Columbia's evidence about course of dealing and usage of trade should have been admitted. Its exclusion requires that the judgment against Columbia must be set aside and the case retried. *Columbia's evidence of trade usages, etc. should have been allowed!* * * *

[After affirming the district court's charges to the jury on modification and damage issues and judgment on the anti-trust issue, the court remanded the case for a new trial.]

[Footnotes omitted.]

Notes

1. To achieve the outcome in Columbia Nitrogen, the moving party *Columbia had to prove:* was required: (1) to prove the existence and scope of the trade usage "as *1. Trade Usage as Fact* facts", UCC 1–205(2); (2) to prove that both parties were in the trade or, if not, that they were or "should be" aware of the usage, 1–205(3); (3) to *2. Both were in the trade* persuade the court to admit the usage for a proper purpose, i.e., to "give *3. Proper purpose* particular meaning to and supplement or qualify" the terms of the agreement, UCC 1–205(3); (4) to survive a possible claim that the established *4. Usage is not unreasonable* usage was unreasonable, UCC 1–205, Comment 6; and (5) to persuade the court that the usage can be "construed wherever reasonable as consistent" *5. should be construed when reasonable & consistent* with any express terms purporting to "contract out" of the usage. UCC 1–205(4). The outcome in the *Columbia Nitrogen* case has been criticized:

(Criticism of the Outcome)

> The court's attempt to demonstrate a possible consistent interpretation is a strained exercise in semantic quibbling that * * * boggles the reasonable mind. The opinion reads so poorly because the court did not address the correct issue * * * the inquiry should have examined the relationship of the usage of trade to the facts of the case. That 'contracts' have been treated as 'fair estimates' is not enough: additional facts must be known about the types of contracts so regarded. * * * The * * * opinion, however, did not discuss relevance and only stated some of the facts about the usage of trade. The facts that are detailed in the opinion require further inquiry because they indicate that the disputed contract was unlike the contracts treated as estimates in the trade. Kirst, *Usage of Trade and Course of Dealing: Subversion of the UCC Theory,* 1977 U.Ill.L.F. 811, 844–45 (footnotes omitted).

Do you agree?

2. Shell Oil entered long-term contracts for the supply of Nanakuli's asphalt requirements on the Island of Oahu, Hawaii. Under the 1969 contract, the price was to be Shell's posted price at the time of delivery. In January, 1974, Shell raised the price from $44 to $76 per ton. Nanakuli, however, had previously committed 7,200 tons of asphalt to paving contractors at prices calculated at the $44 per ton price. When Shell charged $76 per ton for the asphalt, Nanakuli refused to pay this price and claimed that it was entitled to "price protection" under a usage of the asphalt paving trade in Hawaii and that this usage was incorporated into the contract. Price protection required that Shell hold the price on all tonnage committed in reliance upon the $44 per ton price prior to the price increase. The jury returned a verdict of $220,000 for Nanakuli on the ground that Shell had breached the contract by failing to protect the $44 price. The federal district judge set aside the verdict and granted Shell's motion for judgment

n.o.v. The Ninth Circuit Court of Appeals vacated the district court's decision and reinstated the jury verdict.

In a long, complex opinion, which was clearly sympathetic to the UCC's emphasis on context, the Court held, inter alia, that: (1) the trial judge did not abuse his discretion in defining the applicable trade as the asphalt paving trade, rather than the purchase and sale of asphalt alone; (2) the "price protection" usage in that trade was established and Shell was or should have been aware of it; (3) the usage was reinforced by the conduct of Shell in the performance of the contract with Nanakuli; and (4) the jury could have reasonably construed the price protection usage as consistent with the express price term in the contract and a clause purporting to exclude all prior "oral" agreements from the writing.

The court stated that the agreement must be examined in "light of the close, symbiotic relations between Shell and Nanakuli on the island of Oahu, whereby the expansion of Shell on the island was intimately connected with the business growth of Nanakuli." In addition, the UCC "looks to the actual performance of a contract as the best indication of what the parties intended those terms to mean." Finally, the court concluded that "price protection" was consistent with the express price term "as long as it does not totally negate it." The usage "only came into play at times of price increases and only for work committed prior to those increases on non-escalation contracts." It was, therefore an "exception to, rather than a total negation of, the express price term" which was known to Shell and constituted an "intended part of the agreement, as that term is broadly defined by the Code. * * *" Nanakuli Paving & Rock Co. v. Shell Oil Co., Inc., 664 F.2d 772 (9th Cir.1980). The Nanakuli court cited and discussed Columbia Nitrogen as a "leading case" in a group of federal decisions that "usually have been lenient in not ruling out consistent additional terms or trade usage for apparent inconsistency with express terms." The court, however, noted Professor Kirst's criticism of *Columbia Nitrogen* for failing to examine the relationship of the trade usage to the facts of the case, but concluded that this objection had been met in *Nanakuli.*

3. It is clear that particular parties can "contract out" of a general usage of trade which otherwise would be part of the agreement. UCC 1–205(4). Draft a one sentence clause which, in your judgment, would be effective to exclude the usages involved in the *Columbia Nitrogen* and *Shell Oil* cases.

ALASKAN NORTHERN DEVELOPMENT, INC. v. ALYESKA PIPELINE SERVICE CO.

Supreme Court of Alaska, 1983.
666 P.2d 33.

James J. White,* Ann Arbor, Mich., * * * for appellant.

Before BURKE, C.J., and RABINOWITZ, MATTHEWS and COMPTON, JJ.

* Could this person be one of the editors of this casebook?

OPINION

COMPTON, JUSTICE.

Alaska Northern Development, Inc. ("AND") appeals a judgment in favor of Alyeska Pipeline Service Co. ("Alyeska") in a dispute involving contract formation and interpretation. For the reasons stated below, we affirm.

I. FACTUAL AND PROCEDURAL BACKGROUND

In late October or early November 1976, David Reed, a shareholder and corporate president of AND, initiated discussion with Alyeska personnel in Fairbanks regarding the purchase of surplus parts. The Alyeska employees with whom Reed dealt were Juel Tyson, Clarence Terwilleger and Donald Bruce.

After a series of discussions, Terwilleger indicated that Reed's proposal should be put in writing so it could be submitted to management. With the assistance of AND's legal counsel, Reed prepared a letter of intent dated December 10, 1976. In this letter, AND proposed to purchase "the entire Alyeska inventory of Caterpillar parts." The place for the purchase price was left blank.

Alyeska responded with its own letter of intent dated December 11, 1976. The letter was drafted by Bruce and Tyson in consultation with William Rickett, Alyeska's manager of Contracts and Material Management. Again, the price term was absent. The letter contained the following language, which is the focus of this lawsuit: "Please consider this as said letter of intent, *subject to the final approval of the owner committee*." (Emphasis added.)

Reed was given an unsigned draft of the December 11 letter, which was reviewed by AND's legal counsel. Reed then met with Rickett, and they agreed on sixty-five percent of Alyeska's price as the price term to be filled in the blank on the December 11 letter. Rickett filled in the blank as agreed and signed the letter. In March 1977, the owner committee rejected the proposal embodied in the December 11 letter of intent.

AND contends that the parties understood the subject to approval language to mean that the Alyeska owner committee [1] would review the proposed agreement only to determine whether the price was fair and reasonable. Alyeska contends that Reed was never advised of any such limitation on the authority of the owner committee. In April 1977, AND filed a complaint alleging that there was a contract between AND and Alyeska, which Alyeska breached. The complaint was later amended to include counts for reformation and punitive damages.

Alyeska moved for summary judgment on the punitive damages and breach of contract counts. The superior court granted summary judgment in favor of Alyeska on the punitive damages count. The

---

1. The owner committee is composed of the owner oil companies of Alyeska, a joint venture.

court initially denied Alyeska's motion for summary judgment on the breach of contract claim; however, based on a review of the case after discovery had closed, the court announced at a hearing on September 26, 1980, that it would reverse its earlier ruling and grant Alyeska's motion. The court confirmed this ruling at a hearing on November 5, 1980, after consideration of AND's Motion for Clarification.

The superior court explained its rationale for granting summary judgment against AND on the breach of contract claim as follows. The court recognized that AND predicated its breach of contract claim on the theory that Reed's letter of December 10th was an offer and that Rickett's letter of December 11th was an acceptance of that offer. Viewed in that light, the court addressed "four theoretical possibilities in analyzing the interplay between the December 11th letter and the December 10th letter." First, the writings could be construed as an offer with a responding promise to pass the offer on to the owner committee, which was responsible for making such determinations. Second, the letters could be construed as an offer and a counter-offer that AND rejected. Third, the letters could be considered as an offer with a responding counter-offer containing, among other things, the unlimited right of the owner committee to review and approve. The court ruled that if the letters were ultimately found to fall into one of these three categories, AND would not prevail, either because the offer embodied in the December 10 letter was never accepted, or because the owner committee never approved the proposal.

The only way in which AND might prevail was on the fourth possibility, i.e., the letters could be construed as an offer followed by a counter-offer limiting the authority of the owner committee to review only the contract price. The court ruled that AND could not establish a breach of contract claim under the fourth construction of the letters because the parol evidence rule barred the admission of extrinsic evidence that might limit the scope of the owner committee's approval power.[2] The only recourse for AND, therefore, was to seek reformation of the December 11 letter that limited the owner committee approval clause.

The case proceeded to trial on the reformation claim. After a six-week trial, the superior court concluded that AND had failed to establish that a specific agreement was not properly reduced to writing and therefore rejected its request to reform the December 11 letter. Attorney's fees were awarded to Alyeska.

On appeal, AND does not challenge the superior court's denial of reformation. Instead, it contends that the superior court erred in granting summary judgment on the breach of contract and punitive damages counts, erred in denying a trial by jury on the reformation

---

2. AND also predicated its breach of contract claim on the existence of a prior oral agreement. The superior court im- plicitly rejected this theory in its analysis of the parol evidence rule.

count, erred in not permitting cross-examination for purposes of impeachment, and erred in awarding attorney's fees to Alyeska.

II. APPLICATION OF THE PAROL EVIDENCE RULE

The superior court held that the parol evidence rule of the Uniform Commercial Code, section 2–202, codified as AS 45.02–202,[3] applied to the December 11 letter and therefore no extrinsic evidence could be presented to a jury which limited the owner committee's right of approval. AND contends that the court erred in applying the parol evidence rule. We disagree.

In order to exclude parol evidence concerning the inclusion of additional terms to a writing, a court must make the following determinations. First, the court must determine whether the writing under scrutiny was integrated, i.e., intended by the parties as a final expression of their agreement with respect to some or all of the terms included in the writing. Second, the court must determine whether evidence of a prior or contemporaneous agreement contradicts or is inconsistent with the integrated portion. If the evidence is contradictory or inconsistent, it is inadmissible. If it is consistent, it may nevertheless be excluded if the court concludes that the consistent term would necessarily have been included in the writing by the parties if they had intended it to be part of their agreement. AS 45.02.202; *Braund, Inc. v. White*, 486 P.2d 50, 56 (Alaska 1971); U.C.C. § 2–202 comment 3 (1977).

A. Was the December 11 Letter a Partial Integration?

An integrated writing exists where the parties intend that the writing be a final expression of one or more terms of their agreement. *Kupka v. Morey*, 541 P.2d 740, 747 n. 8 (Alaska 1975); Restatement (Second) of Contracts § 209(a) (1979). Whether a writing is integrated is a question of fact to be determined by the court in accordance with all relevant evidence. Restatement (Second) of Contracts § 209 comment c (1979).

In granting summary judgment on the breach of contract claim, the superior court stated that it had carefully considered all relevant evidence, including oral and written records of all facets of the business deal in question, to arrive at its finding that the agreement was

---

3. AS 45.02.202 provides:

Final written expression; parol or extrinsic evidence. Terms with respect to which the confirmatory memoranda of the parties agree, or which are otherwise set out in a writing intended by the parties as a final expression of their agreement with respect to the terms included in the writing, may not be contradicted by evidence of a prior agreement or of a contemporaneous oral agreement, but may be explained or supplemented

(1) by course of dealing or usage of trade (AS 45.01.205) or by course of performance (AS 45.02.208); and

(2) by evidence of consistent additional terms unless the court finds the writing was intended also as a complete and exclusive statement of the terms of the agreement.

partially integrated.[4] After the six-week trial on the reformation issue, the superior court reaffirmed this finding:

35. The plaintiff initially contends that the letter of December 11, 1976 (the letter) was not integrated or partially integrated and therefore the court was in error in granting summary judgment in favor of defendant on the contract counts of the plaintiff's complaint on September 26, 1980.

36. After considering the evidence submitted at trial, the court reaffirms its prior conclusion that the letter was integrated as to the Owners Committee's approval clause.

37. The parties intended to write down their discussions in a comprehensive form which allowed Reed to seek financing and allow the primary actors (Tyson, Bruce, Terwilleger, Rickett) to submit the concept embodied by the letter to higher management * * *.

38. There are three subjects upon which plaintiff seeks reformation. * * * As to the first, [limiting the Owner Committee to a consideration of price] which has been plaintiff's primary focus, the court finds that such reference was integrated such that the parole [sic] evidence rule would bar any inconsistent testimony. Testimony that the owners were limited to "price" in their review is inconsistent.

* * *

41. With respect to the Owners Committee's approval clause, according to the plaintiff's contention the owners were entitled to review the transaction, on whatever basis, only one time. This was testified to by both Mr. Reed and argued by plaintiff in closing. * * * It was also conceded in closing that the review by the owners, on whatever standard, would occur prior to any formal contract being negotiated and executed. * * * This is also consistent with the testimony of each of the participants.

42. In addition, Mr. Reed, in consultation with Ed Merdes and Henry Camarot, his attorneys, tendered the letter of March 4, 1977, as a document which could serve as "the contract". * * * The March 4 letter contains no further reference to the Owners Committee's approval function * * *. Therefore, I find that as to the Owners Committee's approval * * * the letter of December 11 constitutes an integration or partial integration * * *. This

---

4. At the hearing on AND's Motion for Clarification, the superior court stated:

[I]t seems to me absolutely conclusive on this evidence, and I'm making this as a finding of fact, that this agreement is partially integrated, and I'm not making it by reference only to the four corners of the—of the writings but reference to all the extrinsic evidence that has been proffered to me, read everybody's deposition, considered in detail all the process-es of negotiations, everything that was said and done by everybody as related by them up till the time that Rickett included the language in the letter and turned it over to Reed. So we're not here talking about the for [sic] corners or ambiguity or anything like that. We're talking about all the extrinsic evidence, meaning on balance to a conclusion more probable than not that this is a partially integrated agreement.

having been established, the analysis outlined by the court on September 26, 1980, when granting defendant's motion for summary judgment on the contract claims is applicable. [Citations omitted.]

After reviewing the record, we cannot say that this finding of a partial integration was clearly erroneous.

AND contends that the "clearly erroneous" standard used for reviewing findings of fact issued after a trial does not apply because the breach of contract claim was dismissed by summary judgment. Under the circumstances of this case, we believe that the clearly erroneous standard applies rather than the standard of review used in summary judgment cases because the summary judgment ruling was not a final judgment for purposes of appeal.

Rule 54(b) of the Alaska Rules of Civil Procedure provides in relevant part:

When more than one claim for relief is presented in an action * * * the court may direct the entry of a final judgment as to one * * * of the claims * * * upon an express determination that there is no just reason for delay and upon an express direction for the entry of judgment. In the absence of such determination and direction * * * the order or other form of decision is subject to revision at any time before the entry of judgment adjudicating all the claims and the rights and liabilities of all the parties.

In the pre-trial conference, the superior court indicated that it would make a Rule 54(b) determination if the parties so desired. The parties did not request a Rule 54(b) determination and none was made. During this conference, the court also made it clear that it was willing at the reformation trial to hear all evidence bearing on contract formation, including the negotiations leading up to the letters of intent and the meaning the parties placed on these negotiations and letters. The court emphasized that it was "not cutting out anybody on presenting extrinsic evidence * * * [and] that under Rule 54 the court can, until the end of the case * * * change any decision it's previously reached."

AND contends that the superior court's determination that the only issue at trial concerned reformation "necessarily foreclosed a variety of factual and legal issues on contract formation and interpretation," but does not indicate what evidence it was foreclosed from presenting on these issues. Our review of the record indicates that the integration issue was fully explored by AND during the trial.

After six weeks of testimony, during which time the court had the opportunity to view the demeanor and to judge the credibility of the witnesses, the superior court entered written findings of fact and conclusions of law. As shown in the portion quoted above, these findings reviewed and reaffirmed the findings made in the court's prior summary judgment ruling. Accordingly, the appropriate standard of review is the same as for any other finding of fact, i.e., that the superior court's findings of fact must be upheld unless "clearly erroneous." Alaska R.Civ.P. 52(a). As stated above, the finding of partial integration was not clearly erroneous; therefore, we find no merit in AND's contentions to the contrary.

B. Does the Excluded Evidence Contradict the Integrated Terms?

Having found a partial integration, the next determination is whether the excluded evidence contradicts the integrated portion of the writing. Comment b to section 215 of the Restatement (Second) of Contracts is helpful in resolving this issue.[5] Comment b states:

> An earlier agreement may help the interpretation of a later one, but it may not contradict a binding later integrated agreement. Whether there is a contradiction depends * * * on whether the two are consistent or inconsistent. This is a question which often cannot be determined from the face of the writing; the writing must first be applied to its subject matter and placed in context. The question is then decided by the court as part of a question of interpretation. Where reasonable people could differ as to the credibility of the evidence offered and the evidence if believed could lead a reasonable person to interpret the writing as claimed by the proponent of the evidence, the question of credibility and the choice among reasonable inferences should be treated as questions of fact. But the asserted meaning must be one to which the language of the writing, read in context, is reasonably susceptible. If no other meaning is reasonable, the court should rule as a matter of law that the meaning is established.

According to comment b, therefore, a question of interpretation may arise before the contradiction issue can be resolved. If the evidence conflicts, the choice between competing inferences is for the trier of fact to resolve. *Alyeska Pipeline Service Co. v. O'Kelley,* 645 P.2d 767, 771 n. 2 (Alaska 1982). The meaning is determined as a matter of law, however, if "the asserted meaning [is not] one to which the language of the writing, read in context, is reasonably susceptible." Restatement (Second) of Contracts § 215 comment b (1979). See also J. Calamari & J. Perillo, The Law of Contracts §§ 3–12, 3–13 (2d ed. 1977).

AND contends that the superior court erred in granting summary judgment because the evidence conflicted as to the meaning of the owner committee approval clause. It concludes that under *Alyeska* it was entitled to a jury trial on the interpretation issue. Alyeska contends, and the superior court ruled, that a jury trial was inappropriate because, as a matter of law, AND's asserted meaning of the clause

---

5. Restatement (Second) of Contracts § 215, which parallels the rule stated in U.C.C. § 2–202, reads: "Except as stated in the preceding Section, where there is a binding agreement, either completely or partially integrated, evidence of prior or contemporaneous agreements or negotiations is not admissible in evidence to contradict a term of the writing."

at issue was not reasonably susceptible to the language of the writing. The superior court stated:

> The Court is making the * * * ruling that the offer of evidence to show that Rickett's letter really meant to limit owner committee approval to the price term alone * * * is not reasonably susceptible—or the writing is not reasonably susceptible to that purpose. And therefore, that extrinsic evidence operates to contradict the writing, not specific words in the writing, but the words in the context of the totality of the writing and the totality of the extrinsic evidence.

We agree that the words used in the December 11 letter are not reasonably susceptible to the interpretation advanced by AND. Therefore, we find no merit to AND's contention that it was entitled to a jury trial on the interpretation issue.

After rejecting the extrinsic evidence for purposes of interpretation, the superior court found AND's offered testimony, that the owner committee's approval power was limited to approval of the price, to be inconsistent with and contradictory to the language used by the negotiators in the December 11 letter. AND contends that the offered testimony did not contradict, but rather explained or supplemented the writing with consistent additional terms. For this contention, AND relies on the standard articulated in *Hunt Foods & Industries, Inc. v. Doliner*, 26 A.D.2d 41, 270 N.Y.S.2d 937 (N.Y.App.1966). In *Hunt Foods*, the defendant signed an option agreement under which he agreed to sell stock to Hunt Foods at a given price per share. When Hunt Foods attempted to exercise the option, the defendant contended that the option could only be exercised if the defendant had received offers from a third party. The court held that section 2–202 did not bar this evidence from being admitted because it held that the proposed oral condition to the option agreement was not "inconsistent" within the meaning of section 2–202; to be inconsistent, "the term must contradict or negate a term of the writing. A term or condition which has a lesser effect is provable." *Id.* 270 N.Y.S.2d at 940.

The narrow view of consistency expressed in *Hunt Foods* has been criticized. In *Snyder v. Herbert Greenbaum & Associates, Inc.*, 38 Md. App. 144, 380 A.2d 618 (Md.App.1977), the court held that the parol evidence of a contractual right to unilateral rescission was inconsistent with a written agreement for the sale and installation of carpeting. The court defined "inconsistency" as used in section 2–202(b) as "the absence of reasonable harmony in terms of the language *and* respective obligations of the parties." *Id.* 380 A.2d at 623 (emphasis in original) (citing U.C.C. § 1–205(4)). *Accord: Luria Brothers & Co. v. Pielet Brothers Scrap Iron & Metal, Inc.*, 600 F.2d 103, 111 (7th Cir.1979); *Southern Concrete Services, Inc. v. Mableton Contractors, Inc.*, 407 F.Supp. 581 (N.D.Ga.1975), *aff'd mem.*, 569 F.2d 1154 (5th Cir.1978).

We agree with this view of inconsistency and reject the view expressed in *Hunt Foods*.[6] Under this definition of inconsistency, it is clear that the proffered parol evidence limiting the owner committee's right of final approval to price is inconsistent with the integrated term that unconditionally gives the committee the right to approval. Therefore, the superior court was correct in refusing to admit parol evidence on this issue.[7]

* * *

[The court also held that the trial court was correct to deny a jury trial on the reformation issue and to grant a summary judgment against AND on the punitive damage issue.]

Notes

1. In the absence of a "merger" clause, how does the court determine whether the writing was "intended by the parties as a final expression of their agreement" as to some or all of the terms? UCC 2–202. Put differently, how does one evaluate the decision in the *Alaska Northern* case that the writing was intended to be a partial integration with regard to the "approval" clauses? The question is important, for in the absence of any integration, the term limiting the power to reject would be part of the agreement, whether included in the writing or not.

UCC 2–202 and the comments are silent on this question. It may be useful to indulge a presumption, see UCC 1–201(31), that a writing which "reasonably appears to be a complete agreement" is "an integrated agreement unless it is established by other evidence that the writing did not constitute a final expression." Restatement, Second, Contracts 209(3). Since there was no "other" persuasive evidence in the *Alaska Northern* case, the determination that the parties intended a partial integration at least seems sound. What constitutes "other" evidence? According to Comment (c) to Restatement § 209, incompleteness of the writing may be shown by "any relevant evidence, oral or written, that an apparently complete writing never became fully effective, or that it was modified after initial adoption."

2. If the writing is integrated in whole or in part, terms in that writing "may not be contradicted by evidence of any prior agreement or of a contemporaneous oral agreement. * * *" UCC 2–202. Accord: Restatement, Second, Contracts § 215. But if there is a partial integration, as in *Alaska Northern*, the writing may be supplemented "by evidence of consistent additional terms." UCC 2–202(b). Section 216(2) of the Restate-

---

6. *Hunt Foods* was implicitly rejected in *Johnson v. Curran*, 633 P.2d 994, 996–97 (Alaska 1981) (parol evidence concerning an early termination right based on nightclub owner's dissatisfaction with the band's performance was inconsistent with parties' written contract specifying definite time without mention of any right of early termination and thus inadmissible).

7. Our affirmance of the superior court's holding that the proposed version is inconsistent with the integrated clause obviates discussion of whether the addition, if consistent, would have been included in the December 11 letter. Furthermore, we decline to reach AND's contentions regarding the applicability of U.C.C. § 2–207 because AND never raised the § 2–207 argument at the superior court level. *See, e.g., Jeffries v. Glacier State Telephone Co.*, 604 P.2d 4, 11 (Alaska 1979).

ment, Second, Contracts puts the matter more affirmatively: "An agreement is not completely integrated if the writing omits a consistent additional term. * * *" We now return to a question that has dominated the trade usage cases: What is a consistent additional term? Is the "absence of reasonable harmony" test applied in *Alaska Northern* the same as the test expressed in Comment 3 to UCC 2–202, i.e., that the term, if agreed upon, "would certainly have been included in the document * * *?" Or, must the "consistent additional agreed term" be one "as in the circumstances might naturally be omitted from the writing?" Section 216(2)(b). For still another application of the "absence of reasonable harmony" test, See ARB. Inc. v. E–Systems, Inc., 663 F.2d 189 (D.C.Cir.1980) (after review of extrinsic evidence, "merger" clause held to express genuine intention of parties).

3. What is the effect of a "merger" clause providing that the writing is the "final and complete agreement of the parties" and that there are "no understandings, agreements, or obligations unless specifically set forth in the writing?" Assuming that the clause is not unconscionable, Seibel v. Layne & Bowler, Inc., 56 Or.App. 387, 641 P.2d 668 (1982) (ordinary consumer unfairly surprised by fine-print merger clause in standard form contract), and assuming that the clause or the contract was not induced by fraud, see UCC 1–103 and Franklin v. Lovitt Equipment Co., 420 So.2d 1370 (Miss.1982), and assuming that there was no other evidence establishing a contrary intention, the UCC answer seems clear: The writing may neither be contradicted by evidence of "any prior agreement or of a contemporaneous agreement" nor "supplemented * * * by evidence of consistent additional terms." UCC 2–202.

May, however, the total integration be "explained or supplemented * * * by course of dealing or usage of trade * * * or by course of performance?" Despite some ambiguity in UCC 2–202, the answer appears to be yes, subject to the limitations imposed by UCC 1–205(4). Thus, evidence of a prior course of dealing has been admitted to explain or supplement the terms of an integrated writing, see e.g., Ralph's Distributing Co. v. AMF, Inc., 667 F.2d 670 (8th Cir.1981), and evidence of trade usage and a prior course of dealing that was thought to "contradict" terms in the writing has been excluded. See, e.g., General Plumbing & Heating, Inc. v. American Air Filter, 696 F.2d 375 (5th Cir.1983). We return, then, full circle to the test of consistency raised in the trade usage cases.

Problem 4–1

Fiber Industries sold fiber to carpet manufacturers for use in the making of carpets. Salem Carpet bought trademark fiber from Fiber Industries on an order-by-order basis. There was no written agreement other than the individual purchase orders. Both Salem's purchase order form and Fiber Industries acknowledgment form contained "merger" clauses, which provided that the form "contains all the terms and conditions of the purchase agreement and shall constitute the complete and exclusive agreement between Seller and Purchaser." In August, 1980 Fiber Industries announced that it was withdrawing from the carpet industry, but that it would supply all customers in an "orderly fashion" until the phase-out was complete. Salem accepted a final order of fiber at a contract price of $407,128.40, but refused to pay the full amount because of losses suffered as a result of Fiber Industries' withdrawal from the market. Salem claimed that there was a "customary practice" in the carpet industry obligating Fiber Industries to fill all orders made by Salem during the projected market life of any carpet style which utilized fiber manufactured by Fiber Industries. Salem was prepared to establish a usage that the "carpet manufacturer will continue to make its branded fiber available for the useful life of the carpet style or for sufficient time to allow the carpet manufacturer to produce and sell sufficient carpet to recoup the large start-up expenses incurred in introducing and marketing a new line of branded carpet."

Assume that both contract forms were silent on the issue. Assume, further, that the usage could be established. Under UCC 1–205(4) and 2–202, should the court admit evidence of the usage as part of the agreement?

FRIGALIMENT IMPORTING CO. v. B.N.S. INTERNATIONAL SALES CORP.

United States District Court, Southern District of New York, 1960.
190 F.Supp. 116.

FRIENDLY, CIRCUIT JUDGE.

The issue is, what is chicken? Plaintiff says "chicken" means a young chicken, suitable for broiling and frying. Defendant says "chicken" means any bird of that genus that meets contract specifications on weight and quality, including what it calls "stewing chicken" and plaintiff pejoratively terms "fowl". Dictionaries give both meanings, as well as some others not relevant here. To support it, plaintiff sends a number of volleys over the net: defendant essays to return them and adds a few serves of its own. Assuming that both parties were acting in good faith, the case nicely illustrates Holmes' remark "that the making of a contract depends not on the agreement of two minds in one intention, but on the agreement of two sets of external signs—not on the parties' having *meant* the same thing but on their having *said* the same thing." The Path of the Law, in Collected Legal Papers, p. 178. I have concluded that plaintiff has not sustained its burden of persuasion that the contract used "chicken" in the narrower sense.

The action is for breach of the warranty that goods sold shall correspond to the description, New York Personal Property Law, McKinney's Consol.Laws, c. 41, § 95. Two contracts are in suit. In the first, dated May 2, 1957, defendant, a New York sales corporation, confirmed the sale to plaintiff, a Swiss corporation, of

"U S Fresh Frozen Chicken, Grade A, Government Inspected, Eviscerated

2½–3 lbs. and 1½–2 lbs. each

all chicken individually wrapped in cryovac, packed in secured fiber cartons or wooden boxes, suitable for export

75,000 lbs. 2½–3 lbs. . . . . at $33.00

25,000 lbs. 1½–2 lbs. .... at $36.50

per 100 lbs. FAS New York

scheduled May 10, 1957 pursuant to instructions from Penson & Co., New York."

The second contract, also dated May 2, 1957, was identical save that only 50,000 lbs. of heavier "chicken" were called for, the price of the smaller birds was $37 per 100 lbs., and shipment was scheduled for May 30. The initial shipment under the first contract was short but the balance was shipped on May 17. When the initial shipment arrived in Switzerland, plaintiff found, on May 28, that the 2½–3 lbs. birds were not young chicken suitable for broiling and frying but stewing chicken or "fowl"; indeed, many of the cartons and bags plainly so indicated. Protests ensued. Nevertheless, shipment under the second contract was made on May 29, the 2½–3 lbs. birds again being stewing chicken. Defendant stopped the transportation of these at Rotterdam.

This action followed. Plaintiff says that, notwithstanding that its acceptance was in Switzerland, New York law controls under the principle of Rubin v. Irving Trust Co., 1953, 305 N.Y. 288, 305, 113 N.E. 2d 424, 431; defendant does not dispute this, and relies on New York decisions. I shall follow the apparent agreement of the parties as to the applicable law.

[The court first determined that the contract language offered no assistance in determining the meaning of the word, "chicken", which standing alone was ambiguous.]

Plaintiff's next contention is that there was a definite trade usage that "chicken" meant "young chicken." Defendant showed that it was only beginning in the poultry trade in 1957, thereby bringing itself within the principle that "when one of the parties is not a member of the trade or other circle, his acceptance of the standard must be made to appear" by proving either that he had actual knowledge of the usage or that the usage is "so generally known in the community that his actual individual knowledge of it may be inferred." 9 Wigmore, Evidence (3d ed. 1940) § 2464. Here there was no proof of actual knowledge of the alleged usage; indeed, it is quite plain that defendant's belief was to the contrary. In order to meet the alternative requirement, the law of New York demands a showing that "the usage is of so long continuance, so well established, so notorious, so universal and so reasonable in itself, as that the presumption is violent that the parties contracted with reference to it and made it a part of their agreement." Walls v. Bailey, 1872, 49 N.Y. 464, 472–473.

Plaintiff endeavored to establish such a usage by the testimony of three witnesses and certain other evidence. Strasser, resident buyer in New York for a large chain of Swiss cooperatives, testified that "on chicken I would definitely understand a broiler." However, the force of this testimony was considerably weakened by the fact that in his own transactions the witness, a careful businessman, protected himself by using "broiler" when that was what he wanted and "fowl" when he wished older birds. Indeed, there are some indications, dating back to a remark of Lord Mansfield, Edie v. East India Co., 2 Burr. 1216, 1222 (1761), that no credit should be given "witnesses to usage, who could not adduce instances in verification." 7 Wigmore, Evidence (3d ed. 1940), § 1954; see McDonald v. Acker, Merrall & Condit Co., 2d Dept. 1920, 192 App.Div. 123, 126, 182 N.Y.S. 607. While Wigmore thinks this goes too far, a witness' consistent failure to rely on the alleged usage deprives his opinion testimony of much of its effect. Niesielowski, an officer of one of the companies that had furnished the stewing chicken to defendant, testified that "chicken" meant "the male species of the poultry industry. That could be a broiler, a fryer or a roaster", but not a stewing chicken; however, he also testified that upon receiving defendant's inquiry for "chickens", he asked whether the desire was for "fowl or frying chickens" and, in fact, supplied fowl, although taking the precaution of asking defendant, a day or two after plaintiff's acceptance of the contracts in suit, to change its confirmation of its order from "chickens," as defendant had originally prepared it, to "stewing chickens." Dates, an employee of Urner-Barry Company, which publishes a daily market report on the poultry trade, gave it as his view that the trade meaning of "chicken" was "broilers and fryers." In addition to this opinion testimony, plaintiff relied on the fact that the Urner-Barry service, the Journal of Commerce, and Weinberg Bros. & Co. of Chicago, a large supplier of poultry, published quotations in a manner which, in one way or another, distinguish between "chicken," comprising broilers, fryers and certain other categories, and "fowl," which, Bauer acknowledged, included stewing chickens. This material would be impressive if there were nothing to the contrary. However, there was, as will now be seen.

Defendant's witness Weininger, who operates a chicken eviscerating plant in New Jersey, testified "Chicken is everything except a goose, a duck, and a turkey. Everything is a chicken, but then you have to say, you have to specify which category you want or that you are talking about." Its witness Fox said that in the trade "chicken" would encompass all the various classifications. Sadina, who conducts a food inspection service, testified that he would consider any bird coming within the classes of "chicken" in the Department of Agriculture's regulations to be a chicken. The specifications approved by the General Services Administration include fowl as well as broilers and fryers under the classification "chickens." Statistics of the Institute of American Poultry Industries use the phrases "Young chickens" and "Mature chickens," under the general heading "Total chickens," and the Department of Agriculture's daily and weekly price reports avoid use of the word "chicken" without specification.

* * *

[The court next reviewed arguments that the defendant's meaning of the word "chicken" was supported by definitions in Department of Agriculture regulations, by its inability to obtain young chickens at the agreed contract price and by plaintiff's conduct after the first shipment was received.]

When all the evidence is reviewed, it is clear that defendant believed it could comply with the contracts by delivering stewing chicken in the 2½–3 lbs. size. Defendant's subjective intent would not be significant if this did not coincide with an objective meaning of "chicken." Here it did coincide with one of the dictionary meanings, with the definition in the Department of Agriculture Regulations to which the contract made at least oblique reference, with at least some usage in the trade, with the realities of the market, and with what plaintiff's spokesman had said. Plaintiff asserts it to be equally plain that plaintiff's own subjective intent was to obtain broilers and fryers; the only evidence against this is the material as to market prices and this may not have been sufficiently brought home. In any event it is unnecessary to determine that issue. For plaintiff has the burden of showing that "chicken" was used in the narrower rather than in the broader sense, and this it has not sustained.

This opinion constitutes the Court's findings of fact and conclusions of law. Judgment shall be entered dismissing the complaint with costs. [Footnotes omitted.]

Notes

1. Why, you ask, did we include this "old saw?" Here are a few reasons.

First, the case demonstrates that the UCC parol evidence rule has little to do with issues of interpretation. Rather, extrinsic evidence is admissible to assist the trier of fact in determining the meaning of a term which is part of the agreement. See Farnsworth, *Meaning in the Law of Contracts,* 76 Yale L.J. 939 (1967); Corbin, *The Interpretation of Words and the Parol Evidence Rule,* 50 Cornell L.Rev. 161 (1965).

Second, the case supports the attack by the "realists" on the belief that words have a "plain meaning" that can be determined from the four corners of a writing. As Chief Justice Traynor put it, the " * * * test of admissibility of extrinsic evidence to explain the meaning of a written instrument is not whether it appears to the court to be plain and unambiguous on its face, but whether the offered evidence is relevant to prove a meaning to which the language of the instrument is reasonably susceptible." Pacific Gas and Elec. Co. v. G.W. Thomas Drayage & Rigging Co., 69 Cal.2d 33, 69 Cal.Rptr. 561, 442 P.2d 641, 644 (1968). See UCC 2–202, Comment 1(b).

Third, the case illustrates the wide range of facts, including trade usage, that may be relevant to interpretation disputes. It is consistent with the UCC's position that the "meaning of the agreement of the parties is to be determined by the language used by them and by their action, read and interpreted in the light of commercial practices and other circumstances." UCC 1–205, Comment 1. It also illustrates that even with access to evidence from the commercial context, the plaintiff failed to establish that his meaning of "chicken" should prevail. According to the Restatement, in order for the plaintiff to prevail, he would have to establish that either (a) he did not know the different meaning attached by the defendant to "chicken" and the defendant knew the meaning attached by the plaintiff, or (b) the plaintiff had no reason to know of the different meaning attached by the defendant and the defendant had reason to know the meaning attached by the plaintiff. Section 201, Restatement, Second, Contracts. See also, 202–203, 219–223. Does the Restatement test square with the outcome in the "chicken" case? Does the UCC provide any guidance on what the plaintiff must establish to prevail? (We think that the answer is no.)

Fourth, (and finally), the case shows that even though the purpose of the claimed trade usage was proper—to give meaning to the term "chicken"—the plaintiff failed to prove the usage. Review the facts and Judge Friendly's opinion to determine why the proof failed and consider the following note.

Note: Proof of Trade Usage and Other Context Evidence

Trade usage and other context evidence are facts to be established by the moving party, i.e., the party seeking to persuade the court that his interpretation of the scope or meaning of the agreement should prevail. UCC 1–205(2). Since these facts are normally not presumed to exist, see UCC 1–201(31), the plaintiff has the "burden of establishing" them, i.e., he must persuade the "triers of fact that the existence of the fact is more probable than its non-existence." UCC 1–201(8). The moving party, therefore, has both the burden of production and the burden of persuasion. These burdens are normally satisfied, if at all, through expert witnesses and documents, see UCC 1–205(2), in an atmosphere where objections to the expert's qualifications, the authenticity of documents and hearsay and relevance are routine. See, e.g., C. McCormick, Evidence 13 (2d ed. 1972); McElhaney, *Expert Witnesses and the Federal Rules of Evidence,* 28 Mercer L.Rev. 463 (1977). The pitfalls in this process are illustrated by the "Chicken" case.

But there are more problems for the moving party. According to Professors Allen and Hillman, a "comprehensive set of proof rules would establish who must bear the burden of pleading, of persuasion, and of producing evidence, and would define the appropriate contours of judicial comment on the evidence." Allen & Hillman, *Evidentiary Problems In— And Solutions For—the Uniform Commercial Code,* 1984 Duke L.J. 92, 98. They suggest that if the Drafters had stopped with the burden of persuasion rule in UCC 1–201(8) and the burden of production rule in UCC 1–201(31), the "Code's approach to proof problems, if liberally construed, would have been nearly adequate." The Code "could have been interpreted to place on plaintiffs and moving parties the burdens of production and persuasion on all issues—the normal rule—unless it specifically allocated one or the other burden by using the terminology of either section 1–201(8) or 1–201(32)." Further, trial judges "could then have determined pleading requirements and the scope of their authority to comment on the evidence by referring to their jurisdiction's procedural law." Id.

The questions in particular cases, such as proof of trade usage, are (1) whether other Code provisions are inconsistent with these general principles of production and persuasion and, if so, (2) whether the Code contains rules of proof that describe how the burdens should be allocated and provide guidance on pleading or the conditions under which a judge may comment on the evidence. In areas other than proof of trade usage, Professors Allen and Hillman answer the two questions "yes" and "no" and conclude that these failures, as manifested in judicial opinions, have interferred with a basic purpose of the Code to promote clarity and consistency in commercial dealings. Id. at 98–105.

The potential for trouble exists in the trade usage areas as well. Suppose, for example, that a buyer of steel seeks to establish a trade usage that a written contract for goods described as "36 inch steel" is satisfied by steel with a width between 36″ and 37″. (For such a case, see Decker Steel Co. v. Exchange Nat'l Bank of Chicago, 330 F.2d 82 (7th Cir.1964) and Problem 11–2, infra.) Here are some trouble spots for which the Code has no answers.

(1) At what point in the plaintiff's case does the burden of production shift to the defendant and what proof must the defendant adduce to satisfy that intermediate burden?

(2) Suppose the defendant, by way of affirmative defense, attacks the established usage as unreasonable or unconscionable. Comment 6 to UCC 1–205 states that the "very fact of commercial acceptance makes out a prima facie case that the usage is reasonable, and the burden is no longer on the usage to establish itself as being reasonable." What does this mean for the burdens of production and persuasion?

(3) Finally, suppose the defendant raises express written language purporting to totally integrate the writing, UCC 2–202, or to exclude the usage. Is there a presumption that the writing expresses the intention of both parties? If so, do both the burden of production and the burden of persuasion shift to the plaintiff? How are those burdens satisfied?

In order to clarify the rules governing the proof of facts in a trial under the Code, Professors Allen and Hillman propose the following addition:

"Section 1–210.   Rules Governing the Proof of Facts at Trial

(1) Definitions

(a) A burden of production is a requirement that a party produce sufficient evidence on an issue to avoid a directed verdict on that issue. The phrases "to presume" or "prima facie case," and any derivations thereof, shall be interpreted to refer to a burden of production, unless expressly provided otherwise.

(b) A burden of persuasion is a requirement that a party convince the finder of fact to a previously specified level of certainty of the truth of an issue. The phrases "to establish" or "to show" and any derivations thereof shall be interpreted to refer to a burden of persuasion, unless expressly provided otherwise.

(2) General Provisions

(a) Pleading. Unless expressly provided otherwise, all pleading matters shall be governed by the Rule (or Code) of Civil Procedure.

(b) Burden of Production and Persuasion. Unless expressly provided otherwise or unless the interests of justice clearly require otherwise, plaintiffs and moving parties shall bear the burden of production and persuasion on all contested issues. The justification for any judicial exception must be specifically provided by the trial court and is subject to review on appeal. A question of fact upon which allocation of a burden of production or persuasion is conditoned shall be decided by the court for the purpose of allocating the burden of production or persuasion.

(c) Standard of Persuasion. Unless expressly provided otherwise or unless the interests of justice clearly require otherwise, a burden of persuasion is satisfied if the party, bearing it convinces the fact finder that the existence of the fact is more probable than its non-existence, and a burden of production is satisfied if the court determines that a reasonable person could so find. The justification for any judicial exception must be specifically provided by the trial court and is subject to review on appeal.

(d) Peremptory Instruction or Ruling. The trial court may remove an issue from the consideration of the jury if reasonable persons with an understanding of the commercial practices involved would not disagree about the matter.

(e) Order of Proof. The trial court may require the presentation of evidence in the order that it determines would best facilitate the trial process.

(f) Judicial Comment on the Evidence. After the close of the evidence and arguments of counsel, the court may fairly and impartially sum up the evidence or examine the implication of the evidence, or both, for the benefit of the jury. Notice of intended comment shall be provided to counsel, and an opportunity to respond with evidence or argument shall be permitted."

Id. at 105–06.

Problem 4–2

The following excerpt is from the trial transcript in the case of Decker Steel Co. v. Exchange Nat'l Bank of Chicago, 330 F.2d 82 (7th Cir.1964). In that case, Decker Steel, a disappointed buyer, sued its seller and the bank which had issued a letter of credit to its seller. One of the issues was whether the delivered steel had in fact conformed to the contract specifications which called for "prime Thomas quality 36″ X coiled hot rolled steel." Plaintiff alleged that the steel did not conform to the contract because it was 37 inches wide and was not the proper thickness. In the following testimony, the defendant attempted to prove that trade usage accepted 37″ steel under a contract calling for 36″ steel. As you read the transcript, try to visualize how thorny the path to established trade usage can be. What road blocks did the opposing counsel put in the way of proof? Can you think of additional arguments which might have been made for or against the submission of the offered testimony? Would UCC 1–205 help with the problems of proof?

Proceedings Before Hon. Richard B. Austin, June 25, 1963:

Sydney Borenstein, called as a witness on behalf of the defendants, having been first duly sworn, was examined and testified as follows:

Direct Examination

By Mr. Joseph:

Q. Would you state your name and address, please?

A. Sydney Borenstein, 2710 Marl Oak Drive, Highland Park, Illinois.

Q. What is your occupation, Mr. Borenstein?

A. I buy and sell steel and am a warehouser and distributor of steel.

Q. What is the name of your organization?

A. Superior Steel Service.

Q. What is your position with that organization?

A. President.

Q. How many years have you been in the steel business, Mr. Borenstein?

A. About thirteen years.

Q. Among the steel you deal with there, would prime Thomas quality hot rolled steel coils be included?

A. Yes, sir.

Q. And you are acquainted with that kind of steel?

A. Yes, I am.

Q. Mr. Borenstein, are you acquainted with the market conditions for steel at the end of 1959 and the beginning of 1960?

A. Yes, sir.

* * *

Q. Mr. Borenstein, are you acquainted with permissible tolerances in connection with the buying and selling of prime Thomas quality hot rolled steel in coils?

Mr. Marshall: I object, if your Honor please. The documents in the case recite whatever tolerances relate to this transaction.

The Court: The only tolerances that I am aware of in regard to a purchase order is the spread that is permitted in regard to the gauge, and I saw nothing in there in regard to any spreads in regard to the width.

Mr. Joseph: Well, I am prepared to prove, your Honor, that when nothing is said, something else is understood.

* * *

The Court: The objection of this question is overruled. You are each pursuing your own theory of the case.

By Mr. Joseph:

Q. Are you acquainted with permissible tolerances, Mr. Borenstein, in connection with prime Thomas quality hot rolled steel coils?

A. Well, normally in the trade there are references that are made to specifications and when a—

Q. Can you answer the question yes or no? Are you familiar with tolerances?

A. I am familiar with the tolerances and the books from which the specifications can be read.

* * *

Q. Are you acquainted with the American Society for Testing Materials?

A. I am acquainted with that book, and I am also acquainted with the AISI, a copy of which I have with me.

The Court: Which means what, AISI?

The Witness: Well, can I get the book? It is American Iron and Steel Institute.

The Court: This document is what kind of a document of that institute?

The Witness: It is a reference book telling the tolerances, the type tolerances that are permissible and used by the mills in the production of carbon steel sheets.

The Court: And is Thomas steel in that category of prime steel?

The Witness: Yes, sir.

By Mr. Joseph:

Q. Now, can you find in that book—

Mr. Joseph: Let's mark the book as an exhibit—well, let's find the page first.

By Mr. Joseph:

Q. Can you find in this book, Mr. Borenstein, a page which contains a reference to steel of this nature showing the tolerances as to width?

A. I think so.

* * *

Q. What page is it?

A. Page 52.

Q. Is there any part of that page 52 which you have specific reference to?

A. Table 9. Can I read it?

* * *

Q. Is there an item in that column which refers to 36–inch steel?

The Court: Yes or no.

By The Witness:

A. Yes.

By Mr. Joseph:

Q. What is the tolerance indicated for 36–inch steel?

Mr. Marshall: I object, if your Honor please.

The Court: I think maybe the document itself is the best evidence.

Mr. Joseph: All right.

Mr. Marshall: I think that the document, in addition, your Honor, is hearsay.

I have had no opportunity at all to cross examine the author of that document.

I submit to your Honor—It hasn't been marked for identification yet and that is why I have been waiting.

The Court: I think that that page should be at this time, counsel.

Mr. Marshall: But I do object to any reference to the book, and anticipating to some extent that it will be offered in evidence, I will object to it at that time. I think that the book is hearsay.

The Court: I am not aware as to what the American Iron and Steel Institute is. It may be a neighborhood pool hall or a tavern, as far as I know from the evidence.

Mr. Joseph: All right.

Will the reporter please mark this Defendant Exchange National Bank's Exhibit No. 7 for identification.

(Said document marked Defendant's Exhibit 7 for identification.)

By Mr. Joseph:

Q. Mr. Borenstein, what relationship does—what use does this book of which Defendant's Exhibit 7 is a page have in the steel community?

A. Well, the specifications and tolerances as defined by the AISI are the specifications and tolerances used by the mills in the production of their material.

Mr. Marshall: I object. This witness does not know, if your Honor pleases, of his own knowledge what the mills use, and I object to his answer and move to strike it. It must be hearsay.

The Witness: I beg your pardon.

Mr. Joseph: The witness has testified as to what he knows about the document.

The Court: Well, he hasn't testified as to what he knows about what the mills use. I don't know whether he has ever bought any steel in a mill in his life. There is nothing in the record to so indicate it.

By Mr. Joseph:

Q. Mr. Borenstein, what is your business?

A. I buy and sell steel.

Q. From whom do you buy and to whom do you sell?

A. I buy steel from mills. I have imported steel. I buy steel from warehouses. I buy surplus steel.

Q. To whom do you sell?

A. We sell to end users essentially.

Q. What is an end user?

A. A person who takes a piece of raw steel and converts it to a useful purpose.

Q. All right. Are you acquainted with the buying and selling practices of mills and of steel brokers?

A. Yes, I am.

Q. Do you know whether or not the specifications in Defendant's Exhibit 7 for identification are used by the buyers and sellers of steel?

Mr. Marshall: If your Honor please, now the vice of this, and I submit to your Honor that it is immaterial and irrelevant. We have agreements here between these parties. There is no reference in any of the papers to the AISI tolerances book, manual or anything else. The parties to this transaction are available. Mr. Decker is available. He testified in respect to those documents on direct and Mr. Joseph had the opportunity to cross examine him in respect to those documents. The other parties to the transaction, Associated Steel, are available. All of the persons who have signed any of these papers are subject to the processes of this court, and I submit to your Honor that it is not proper by this method to attempt to incorporate these tolerances into some contract between Decker and Associated or some letter of credit between Exchange and Decker and Associated and The First National Bank. There is nothing in the documents if your Honor please, that makes any reference to these tolerances. These parties, when they wanted a tolerance, specified a tolerance and this is true, I might say, not only of the Decker-Associated transaction, but it is also true of the Associated-Brown-Strauss transaction. They specified tolerances as well.

The Court: Which were, as far as I understand it, unknown to either bank other than the 36–inch width, is that right?

Mr. Joseph: That is right.

The Court: There is nothing in either letter of credit that has to do with the gauge.

Mr. Joseph: That is correct, your Honor.

The Court: So we are just talking about width, and I assume that based on the witness' testimony that the stamp of AISI may have the same standing in the trade as AMA does in regard to a medical product or ADS does in regard to Crest toothpaste, and they are an outstanding collection of members of a profession or business who must have some standard to go by so that they can do business with each other, and I am assuming that based upon what has been said here that this is some kind of an understanding that has been drawn up and signed and put down and is the basis for buying and selling of steel.

Mr. Marshall: If your Honor please, there is no reference in the contract, any of the agreements among the various parties to this litigation that makes any reference to this type of tolerance table.

Mr. Joseph: I am not aware, for example, your Honor, that in court that we have mentioned rules of evidence but we live by them just the same because lawyers in court understand, and it is just a matter of our way of proceeding.

Now, sometimes you can have disputes about such things but we all understand that when we have a trial, without saying it, that that is the procedure that we are operating under. If it is the custom and usage in the steel industry to allow for certain tolerances, that is part of the contract because that is the way one steel man talks to another.

Mr. Marshall: That may be true in a general situation, your Honor, but it cannot be true where the parties themselves have specified tolerances. It cannot be.

The Court: Let me see the letter of credit, both letters of credit.

Mr. Joseph: Here is the first—

Mr. Marshall: You have the first one, Judge.

The Court: I have the first here, yes.

Mr. Marshall: I haven't a copy of it.

The Court: No, there is the first one.

Mr. Marshall: I say that I have not got a copy of the Exchange.

The Court: Do you have a copy of the Exchange?

Mr. Joseph: Here, your Honor.

Mr. Marshall: I might also say in respect to the Exchange letter of credit that Mr. Joseph has attempted to lay the foundation to show that other rules in regard to that transaction were all incorporated by reference, a lengthy set of rules. There is nothing in those rules in regard to these tolerances.

I really submit to your Honor that Mr. Joseph by this testimony is seeking to alter the agreements of the parties here.

Mr. Joseph: I am intending to explain the agreements of the parties.

Mr. Marshall: They don't need any explanation. They are not ambiguous on their face. There is no ambiguity on the face of the documents at all and none has been raised by the testimony.

The Court: I know this, I know nothing about the steel business. I don't know whether the First National or Exchange knows anything about it. I am just assuming, because we haven't even got in the evidence what is in Table 9 yet, but had the First—or the Exchange called in recognized authorities in the steel business, and maybe those who belong to the American Iron and Steel Institute all were recognized authorities and had shown them these coils as an additional precaution, which they are not under legal obligation to do, and asked them, "Is this 36–inch steel?"

I assume that these gentlemen would have said that it is 36–inch steel regardless of the fact that it may have been wider than 36 inches as long as it was within the tolerances that have been adopted by those in the trade.

Mr. Joseph: Precisely, your Honor.

Mr. Marshall: If your Honor pleases, though, when the seller of the goods, as is true in the case at bar, Associated Steel Corporation states as it did in the telegram to Mr. Decker that the goods are not 36 inches wide, that is the interpretation that that seller has placed upon the contract and we look to the contract itself to see whether it is ambiguous.

The Court: What do we do in the circumstances—and I am staying with the evidence at this time—where a superior to Mr. Archer in the Associated Corporation assures Exchange National Bank that this should be disregarded, that it is 36–inch steel? Must they accept a telegram from an underling or the verbal assurance of the president of the corporation?

Mr. Marshall: Well, if your Honor pleases, there was one additional fact in regard to the episode of which your Honor refers as Mr. Decker testified: Mr. Fox stated that he didn't know the width of the steel. He didn't know whether it was 36 or 37 inches wide.

Mr. Joseph: That was at the time of the telephone conversation, not at the time—

Mr. Marshall: That was at the time, if your Honor pleases, that the conversations occurred at the bank and Mr. Fox told Mr. Decker to disregard the telegram. Mr. Fox said, "I don't know what the dimensions are," and then Mr. Decker took from him the invoice reciting that it was 36 inches wide. That is a part of my case.

The Court: I understand that.

Let's proceed.

* * *

(The question was read.)

The Court: The objection to that question is overruled.

* * *

By Mr. Joseph:

Q. Is there an item in that table referring to steel of 36 inches— excuse me, strike that and I will start over.

Is there an item in the table which refers to 36–inch steel of the kind that we have been talking about?

A. Yes, there is.

Q. What is the tolerance shown for such steel?

Mr. Marshall: I object, your Honor. The document speaks for itself and I renew my objections.

The Court: Are you offering this page in evidence?

Mr. Joseph: Yes, I am offering this page.

The Court: All right, it may be received and now that it is in evidence he may read from it and you may renew your objection, and if you want to state something for the record, you can; otherwise, it is overruled.

* * *

By Mr. Joseph:

Q. Mr. Borenstein, what is the tolerance shown for steel of 36–inch width in that table?

A. In this table, 36–inch width has a tolerance over and none under of an inch and a quarter.

Q. By that it is meant what?

A. It is meant that the steel, when it comes off the mill, can be wider than 36 inches by 1¼ inches.

The Court: By not more than 1¼ inches.

The Witness: But not more than.

By Mr. Joseph:

Q. And can it be under anything?

A. No, no tolerance under.

* * *

Q. Does it ever occur, Mr. Borenstein, that a buyer of steel would want steel which is precisely 36 inches with no tolerance?

A. Well, there are instances where people want to limit their tolerances. There is no instance where steel is produced exactly to the thousandths. There is a permissible tolerance under all circumstances.

However, if you are interested in getting material as close to 36 as it is possible to get, then you call for coils that are slit, specifically slit to that width so that the specifications that prevail under those terms will apply to the steel.

Q. Would that cost more?

A. Yes.

Q. Mr. Borenstein, do steel brokers ever sell steel one to the other?

A. Yes, they do.

Q. Does it ever happen that you buy steel from one broker and sell it to another broker?

A. Yes, I do.

Q. In connection with purchasing steel from one broker and selling it to another, do you ever arrange to have the bills of lading on which the steel is shipped to you exchanged for other bills of lading from you to your customer?

A. It is a standard procedure in the reshipment of goods when you change title, so to speak, you get new bills issued by surrendering original bills.

Q. What is the purpose of so doing?

* * *

A. Well, in most instances it is a normal transfer of title that occurs. If one broker was buying and selling to another person, in shipping that material he would automatically name the person to whom it was being shipped. That is one of the reasons.

Another reason is that frequently the people who are doing the selling do not wish to divulge their source of steel, so consequently they change—

* * *

A. (Continuing) So it is the practice with such a situation to exchange bills of lading in order to conceal this source.

* * *

Q. Mr. Borenstein, is the width on the outside of a coil necessarily the same as the width on the inside of a coil?

A. If we are talking about inside and outside diameters, they can vary.

The Court: And in 36–inch steel would the variance be more than a quarter of an inch, or if it did, would it take it out of the 36–inch steel category?

The Witness: I will answer the first part. It could vary more than a quarter of an inch.

The Court: I mean an inch and a quarter, let me put it that way.

The Witness: It is possible that it might, your Honor.

The Court: And that portion that measured more than the inch and a quarter above 36 inches would then no longer be 36–inch steel, is that right?

The Witness: Yes, your Honor.

* * *

By Mr. Marshall:

Q. Now, Defendant's Exhibit No. 7, Mr. Borenstein, the page in the American Iron and Steel Institute, this is an American association, is it not?

A. Yes, it is.

Q. And it relates to American production, does it not?

A. It relates to mill practices.

Q. American mill practices?

A. I don't know that it specifically limits it to American mill practices, because for your information a large number of foreign mills are of American manufacture.

Q. Well, does this manual relate to American mills or foreign mills, or both?

A. I would say—

Q. Or do you know, sir?

A. I would say that in the purchase of steel you would use that as the Bible whether you purchased it for domestic or foreign.

Q. Now, I don't think you have answered my question.

* * *

Q. Does the book relate to American specifications or foreign specifications or both?

* * *

The Witness: I don't know.

* * *

Q. Who are members of the American Iron and Steel Institute, Mr. Borenstein?

A. In general? May I—are you asking this in general?

Q. Yes. Do you know what the membership consists of generally?

A. Yes. I would say all the steel mills, all steel producing mills and testing laboratories, people who are especially interested in the resolution of specifications.

Q. And by that you mean the American mills and American testing institutes and so forth, correct?

A. In addition to others, I am sure.

Q. And isn't it a fact, Mr. Borenstein, that the information contained in the book consists of information that has been reported to the American Iron and Steel Institute by its members?

A. Does it say that in there?

Q. Well, I am asking you if you know if that is a fact, sir.

A. I presume that is where they get their information.

* * *

Chapter Five

THE EFFECT OF OPEN TERMS
AND RESERVED DISCRETION

SECTION 1. INTRODUCTION: THE UCC AS A SOURCE OF SUPPLETIVE TERMS

In the bargain envisioned by the drafters of the First Restatement of Contracts, promulgated in 1931, the transaction was a relatively discrete exchange and the parties were expected to agree on all of the material terms before a contract was formed. Thus, if material terms, such as quantity or price, were left open or to be agreed, the odds were strong that a court would hold that no enforceable contract was created until there was agreement. Examples of this approach include Transamerica Equip. Leasing Corp. v. Union Bank, 426 F.2d 273 (9th Cir. 1970); Walker v. Keith, 382 S.W.2d 198 (Ky.1964); Wilhelm Lubrication Co. v. Brattrud, 197 Minn. 626, 268 N.W. 634 (1936).

In the bargain envisioned by the drafters of Article 2, prepared in the years after World War II, the transaction is not limited to a discrete exchange where promises are made. As we have seen, the definition of agreement, UCC 1–201(3), employs a broader theory of relevant behavior: the bargain can be derived from the particular parties' past, present and future conduct, as well as the practices and usages of others engaging in exchange in the same trade or market. In short, Article 2 allows for relational as well as discrete exchange. See Macneil, *Relational Contract: What We Do and Do Not Know*, 1985 Wis.L.Rev. 483, 485–91. Thus, the parties may, by choice or because of complexity, intend to conclude a bargain without agreeing on every material term. Even in a discrete exchange, they may leave an important term, such as the price, open, or to be agreed, or to be fixed by one of the parties. In exchanges of longer duration or where circumstances are expected to change in unanticipated ways, this technique is especially salutary. It obviates the need for complete risk allocation at the time of contracting and puts a premium on negotiation and adjustment in the light of change.

Section 2–204(3) does not require complete agreement on material terms. Rather, it incorporates standards that permit the parties to conclude a contract "even though one or more terms are left open" if they have "intended to make a contract" and there is a "reasonably certain basis for giving an appropriate remedy."

The first question, then, is to decide whether the parties intended to conclude the bargain and, thus, to "make" a contract, when a material term is left open or to be agreed. What factors are relevant to this determination of intent? If the parties did so intend, the second question is whether there is a "reasonably certain basis for giving an appropriate remedy?" Article 2, Part 3, itself, provides many terms to fill "gaps" in the agreement. Study these "off the rack" gap fillers now, for in many cases they will furnish the basis for certainty of remedy.

Another permitted technique is to leave discretion for fixing or defining the terms of performance to one of the parties. Thus, the agreement may provide that the price is to be the price fixed by the seller at the time of delivery, or that the quantity ordered is to be the buyer's requirements. Similarly, the buyer may agree to use "best efforts" to market a product or to purchase described goods "if satisfied" or both parties may agreed to negotiate over an open term in the future. What effect will reserved discretion by one party have on the enforceability of the agreement? Will the illusory character of the deal mean that there was not consideration? If not, what controls should be imposed upon the exercise of that discretion? See UCC 1–203 (good faith duty in performance and enforcement of the contract). For now, work these simple problems, using the provisions of Article 2, Part 3.

Problem 5–1

A. Seller, a dealer in Delaware Cobbler Potatoes, sells existing goods from cold storage. On February 1, Seller agreed, in a writing signed by both parties, to sell Buyer "1,000 sacks of Delaware Cobbler Potatoes." The writing contained no other terms except the following clause: "The parties to this agreement intend to make a contract and consider themselves bound to this writing." On March 15, Seller, without justification and before any potatoes were identified, repudiated the agreement. Buyer promptly "covered," i.e., purchased 1,000 sacks of Delaware Cobblers for $10 a sack on the open market, in full compliance with UCC 2–712. The market price had been $7 per sack on February 1. What damages, if any, can Buyer recover under UCC 2–712?

B. Suppose, in A above, the writing stated that Seller agreed to sell Buyer "Delaware Cobbler Potatoes for $7 per sack with delivery no later than March 15." Seller failed to deliver. On March 15 the market price for Delaware Cobblers was $10 per sack. What damages, if any, can Buyer recover under UCC 2–713?

C. One last problem. Suppose, in A above, that the writing stated that Seller agreed to sell 1,000 sacks of Delaware Cobbler potatoes, delivery by March 15, at a price "to be fixed by the seller." The market price on February 1 was $7 per sack. On March 15, Seller tendered delivery of the goods and fixed a price of $20 per sack. The current market price was $12 and rising. Buyer rejected the tender and "covered" under UCC 2–712 for $13 per sack. Both parties claim that the other breached the contract. Who should prevail?

Note: The Methodology of "Gap" Filling

Article 2 imposes three controls on the power of a court to fill "gaps" in the agreement and, thus, to make a contract for the parties.

First, the issue must arise outside of the scope of the parties' agreement, which includes all express and implicit terms, as fairly interpreted. UCC 1–201(3). Although trade usage may be introduced to supplement terms of the contract, it is not, strictly speaking, a "gap" filler. Rather, it, too, is part of the agreement of the parties.

Second, the parties must intend to conclude the bargain even though some terms have not been agreed. As the Bethlehem Steel litigation, p. 74, indicates, the more important and complex the term, the less likely it is that the requisite intention is present.

Third, even if the parties so intended, the terms to be supplied by the court are defined by the statutory provisions in Article 2, Part 3, which, in turn, are rooted in standards of reasonableness. According to Judge Richard Posner, the judicial power to fill "gaps" reduces the "cost of contract negotiation by supplying contract terms that the parties would probably have adopted explicitly had they negotiated over them." Posner and Rosenfield, *Impossibility and Related Doctrines in Contract Law*, 6 J.Leg.Studies 83, 88–89 (1977).

What are these standards of reasonableness and how should they be elaborated from the surrounding circumstances? Keep these questions in mind as we examine problems dealing, primarily, with quantity and price. Has the UCC gone too far in substituting standards for rules, and in expecting the parties and the court to search for law that is "immanent" in the commercial context? Dean Murray, whose viewpoint follows, would say no. One of your co-authors, however, is more skeptical. He fears that the Code standards have led the courts to the waters of commercial context without instructing them on how to drink. Speidel, *Restatement, Second: Omitted Terms and Contract Method*, 67 Cornell L.Rev. 785 (1982).

SECTION 2. DISPUTES OVER QUANTITY AND PRICE

A. Introduction

A problem for the attorney asked to plan a long-term contract for the sale of goods is to draft an agreement which is legally enforceable and preserves flexibility in the areas thought by the client to be the most troublesome or uncertain during performance. The seasoned practitioner may say that the real challenge is to achieve realistic flexibility and risk allocation rather than legal enforceability. This is discussed further in Macneil, *Contracts: Adjustment of Long-term Eco-*

nomic Relations Under Classical, Neoclassical and Relational Contract Law, 72 Nw.U.L.Rev. 854 (1978) (difficulties in planning long-term supply contract).

The lawyer must understand the client's business needs and risks, assess the probability of changed circumstances, draft appropriate clauses and, in negotiating with the other side, be capable of achieving a mutually satisfactory agreement. This challenge is strikingly posed when problems of quantity and price are involved. Goldberg, *Price Adjustments in Long-Term Contracts,* 1985 Wisconsin L.Rev. 527; Note, *Requirements Contracts: Problems of Drafting and Construction,* 78 Harv.L.Rev. 1212 (1965).

Remember, the statute of frauds, UCC 2–201(1), states that a "contract is not enforceable * * * beyond the quantity of goods shown * * *" in the writing "signed by the party against whom enforcement is sought. * * *" A commitment to supply output or to buy requirements, however, is a quantity term which, because it can be interpreted and limited under UCC 2–306, satisfies the statute of frauds. For effective criticism of the statute of fraud's quantity policy, see Bruckel, *The Weed and the Web: Section 2–201's Corruption of the Code's Substantive Provisions—The Quantity Problem,* 1983 U.Ill.L.F. 811.

B. Quantity

Our primary concern in this subsection is with "output" and "requirements" contracts. Here is a "warm-up" problem on the interpretation of UCC 2–306.

Problem 5–2 ✓

Seller, a wholesale dealer in plywood, and Buyer, a producer of pine veneer, entered into a five year contract under which Buyer agreed to purchase 50,000 square feet of plywood per year at $1.00 per square foot. Terms on the time and method of shipment and payment were also agreed. The written contract was dated July 1, 1984.

A. On July 1, 1987, the market price of plywood had climbed to $4.00 per square foot. The increase was due, primarily, to sharpened demand for forest products. Buyer was operating at full capacity and Seller could resell all of the plywood obtained from the manufacturers. Seller, however, was unhappy with its arrangement with Buyer. Buyer, no softy, said: "Tough. You assumed the risk!" Is Buyer correct?

B. Assume the same facts except that Buyer agreed to purchase its annual "requirements" of plywood from Seller at $1.00 per square foot. The contract did not explicitly say "all of our requirements exclusively from Seller." Furthermore, the contract did not provide for estimates of quantity or maximum-minimum quantities which Buyer could not exceed. Buyer's annual requirements for the first three years were 25,000, 32,500 and 35,000 square feet. During the fourth year, with the market price at $4.50 per square foot, Buyer requested a total of 60,000 square feet, the capacity of its production facility. Seller objected and Buyer, still no softy, said: "Tough. You assumed the risk!" Seller's lawyer responded by quoting to buyer's lawyer during negotiations from Billings Cottonseed, Inc. v. Albany Oil Mill, Inc., 173 Ga.App. 825, 328 S.E.2d 426, 429, 430 (1985):

> Appellant's argument that a valid requirements contract was established by partial performance on its part is also without merit. Ordinarily, partial performance renders enforceable a contract unenforceable for lack of consideration and mutuality by supplying the lack of mutuality. * * * There can be no partial performance in the context of a requirements contract, however, for it is the promise of exclusivity that provides the consideration to the seller. * * * The promise to buy alone is not sufficient performance, for without exclusivity the purchaser's promise is merely to buy when he wants and the promise of the seller becomes merely an invitation for orders. * * * Thus, the requisite mutuality is not supplied." (Citations omitted.)

What arguments should Buyer make at this point? Should they prevail? See, particularly, Bruckel, *Consideration in Exclusive and Nonexclusive Open Quantity Contracts Under the U.C.C.: A Proposal for a New System of Validation,* 68 Minn.L.Rev. 117 (1983), who rejects the exclusivity requirement.

C. In light of hindsight, what is the best contractual arrangement for an enterprise selling plywood to a producer with a finite capacity, in a period where prices are expected to rise due primarily to increased demand for the product:

(1) Fixed-price plus "requirements," with an upper limit on quantity;

(2) Fixed-price plus an agreement to sell all or a specified part of the seller's "output" of plywood exclusively to the buyer;

(3) An "open" or market price plus either a requirements or an output agreement;

(4) Either separate contracts or short term, i.e., one year, arrangements with fixed prices and fixed quantities;

(5) Other?

ORANGE & ROCKLAND, etc. v. AMERADA HESS CORP.

Supreme Court of New York, Appellate Division, 1977.
59 A.D. 110, 397 N.Y.S.2d 814.

MARGETT, JUSTICE.

This action, for damages as a result of an alleged breach of a requirements contract, raises related but distinctly separate issues as to whether the plaintiff buyer's requirements occurred in good faith and whether those requirements were unreasonably disproportionate to the estimates stated in the contract.

In a fuel oil supply contract executed in early December, 1969, defendant Amerada Hess Corporation (Hess) agreed to supply the requirements of plaintiff Orange and Rockland Utilities, Inc. (O & R) at plaintiff's Lovett generating plant in Tompkins Cove, New York. A fixed price of $2.14 per barrel for No. 6 fuel oil, with a sulphur content of 1% or less, was to continue at least through September 30, 1974, with the price subject to renegotiation at that time. Estimates of the amounts required by plaintiff were included in the contract clause entitled "Quantity". Insofar as those estimates are relevant to the instant controversy, they were as follows:

1970—1,750,000 barrels

1971—1,380,000 barrels

1972—1,500,000 barrels

1973—1,500,000 barrels

The estimates had been prepared by plaintiff on December 30, 1968, as part of a five-year budget projection. The estimates anticipated that gas would be the primary fuel used for generation during the period in question.[1] This was a result of the lower cost of gas and of the fact that gas became readily available for power generation during the warmer months of the year as a result of decreased use by gas customers. Plaintiff expressly reserved its right to burn as much gas as it chose by the inclusion, in the "Quantity" provision of the requirements contract, of a clause to the effect that "[n]othing herein shall preclude the use by Buyer of * * * natural gas in such quantities as may be or become available".

Within five months of the execution of the requirements contract, the price of fuel oil began to ascend rapidly. On April 24, 1970 the market price of the oil supplied to plaintiff stood at between $2.65 and $2.73 per barrel. On May 1, 1970 the price was in excess of $3 per barrel. The rise continued and was in excess of $3.50 per barrel by mid-August, and more than $4 per barrel by the end of October, 1970. By March, 1971 the lowest market price was $4.30 per barrel—more than double the price set forth in the subject contract.

Coincident with the earliest of these increases in the cost of oil, O & R proceeded to notify Hess, on four separate dates, of increases in the fuel oil requirements estimates for the year. By letter dated April 16, 1970, O & R notified Hess that it was expected that over 1,460,000 barrels of oil would be consumed over the period April–December, 1970. Since well over 600,000 barrels of oil had been consumed during the first three months of the year, the total increase anticipated at that time was well in excess of 300,000 barrels over the estimate given in the contract.

Eight days later, by letter dated April 24, 1970, O & R furnished Hess with a revised estimate for the period May through December, 1970. The figure given was nearly 1,580,000 barrels which, when

---

1. For example, it was projected that in 1970 gas would generate 14,047,545,000,000 BTU while oil would be used to generate 10,810,740,000,000 BTU. The comparable ratios for the following years are: 1971—15/8; 1972—16/9; 1973—9/5.

combined with quantities which had already been delivered or were in the process of delivery during the month of April, exceeded the contract estimate by over 700,000 barrels—a 40% increase.

The following month the estimates were again increased—this time to nearly one million barrels above the contract estimate. Hess was so notified by letter dated May 22, 1970. Finally, a letter dated June 19, 1970 indicates a revised estimate of more than one million barrels in excess of the 1,750,000 barrels mentioned in the contract; an increase of about 63%.

On May 22, 1970, the date of the third of the revised estimates, representatives of the two companies met to discuss the increased demands. At that meeting O & R's president allegedly attributed the increased need for oil to the fact that O & R could make more money *selling* gas than burning it for power generation. Hess refused to meet the revised requirements, but offered to supply the amount of the contract estimate for the year 1970, plus an additional 10 percent.

The June 19, 1970, letter referred to above recited that the Hess position was "wholly unacceptable" to O & R. It attributed the vastly increased estimates to (a) an inability to burn as much natural gas as had been planned and (b) the fact that O & R had been "required" to meet higher electrical demands on its "own system" and to furnish "more electricity to interconnected systems" than had been anticipated.

Thereafter, for the remainder of 1970, Hess continued to supply the amount of the contract estimates plus 10 percent. A proposal by Hess, in October, 1970, to modify the existing contract by setting minimum and maximum quantities, and by setting a price keyed to market prices, was ignored by O & R. Although the proposed modification set a price 65 cents lower than the market price, it was more advantageous for O & R to insist on delivery of the estimated amounts in the December, 1969 contract (at $2.14 per barrel) and to purchase additional amounts required at the full market price.

During the remainder of the contract period Hess continued to deliver quantities approximately equal to the estimates stated in the subject contract. O & R purchased additional oil for its Lovett plant from other suppliers. The contract between Hess and O & R terminated one year prematurely by reason of an environmental regulation which took effect on October 1, 1973 and which necessarily curtailed the use of No. 6 fuel oil with a sulphur content as high as 1%. During the period 1971 through September, 1973 O & R consistently used more than double its contract estimates of oil at Lovett.[2]

---

2. The Hess contract estimated 1971 usage at 1,380,000 barrels. In fact, 1,301,045 barrels were supplied that year by Hess and 1,844,947 barrels were supplied by other companies, for a total of 3,145,993 barrels. The contract estimate for 1972 was 1,500,000 barrels; a total of 3,325,037 barrels was purchased by O & R. The contract estimate for the first nine months of 1973 was 1,125,000 barrels (75% of the 1,500,000 listed in the contract as an estimate for all of 1973); 2,401,979 barrels were received by O & R during that nine-month period.

This action was commenced in mid–1972. O & R's complaint seeks damages consisting of the difference between its costs for fuel oil during the period in question and the cost it would have incurred had Hess delivered the total amount used by O & R at the fixed contract price of $2.14 per barrel. The trial was conducted in September, 1975 before Mr. Justice Donohoe, sitting without a jury. In an opinion dated March 8, 1976, Trial Term held that plaintiff should be denied any recovery on the ground that its requirements were not incurred in good faith. Specifically, Trial Term found that plaintiff's greatly increased oil consumption was due primarily to (a) increases in sales of electricity to other utilities and (b) a net shift from other fuels, primarily gas, to oil. The former factor was condemned on the premise that "[i]ndirectly, O & R called upon Hess to supply the demands for electricity to the members of the [New York Power] Pool. O & R then shared the savings in the cost of fuel with the other members of the Pool". The latter factor was not elaborated on to any great degree. Trial Term did, however, infer that O & R seized "the opportunity to release its reserve commitment of gas" and thereby reaped very substantial profits.

Although Trial Term stated in its opinion that one of the questions before it was whether plaintiff's demands were unreasonably disproportionate to the estimates set forth in the contract, it failed to reach this question in the light of its conclusion that plaintiff had failed to act in good faith. Plaintiff contends on this appeal (1) that Trial Term's finding of an absence of good faith is unsupported by the record and (2) that since its requirements for the entire term of the contract were less than twice total contract estimates, its demands were not "unreasonably disproportionate" as a matter of law. We reject both contentions upon the facts of this case and affirm Trial Term's dismissal of the complaint.

It is noted at the outset that the parties agreed, pursuant to their contract, that New Jersey law should apply. The governing statute is section 2–306 (subd. [1]) of the Uniform Commercial Code (UCC), which provides, in relevant part:

> "A term which measures the quantity [to be supplied by a seller to a purchaser of goods] by the * * * requirements of the buyer means such actual * * * requirements as may occur in good faith, except that no quantity unreasonably disproportionate to any stated estimate or in the absence of a stated estimate to any normal or otherwise comparable prior * * * requirements may be * * * demanded" (N.J.Stat.Ann., 12A:2–306, subd. [1], [matter in brackets added]).

There is, as Trial Term observed, a good deal of pre-Code case law on the requirement of "good faith". It is well settled that a buyer in a rising market cannot use a fixed price in a requirements contract for speculation. * * * Nor can a buyer arbitrarily and unilaterally change certain conditions prevailing at the time of the contract so as to take advantage of market conditions at the seller's expense * * *.

There is no judicial precedent with respect to the meaning of the term "unreasonably disproportionate" which appears in subdivision (1) of section 2–306 of the UCC. Obviously this language is not the equivalent of "lack of good faith"—it is an elementary rule of construction that effect must be given, if possible, to every word, clause and sentence of a statute. * * * The phrase is keyed to stated estimates or, if there be none, to "normal or otherwise comparable prior" requirements. While "reasonable elasticity" is contemplated by the section (see Official Comment, par. 2 to UCC § 2–306), an agreed estimate shows a clear limit on the intended elasticity, similar to that found in a contract containing minimum and maximum requirements (see Official Comment, par. 2 to UCC § 2–306). The estimate "is to be regarded as a center around which the parties intend the variation to occur" (supra).

The limitation imposed by the term "unreasonably disproportionate" represents a departure from prior case law, wherein estimates were generally treated as having been made simply for the convenience of the parties and of no operative significance (Note, Requirements Contracts under the Uniform Commercial Code, 102 U.Pa.L.Rev. 654, 660–661; Note, Requirements Contracts: Problems of Drafting and Construction, 78 Harv.L.Rev. 1212, 1218; cf. Shader Contr. v. United States, 276 F.2d 1, 149 Ct.Cl. 535). It is salutary in that it insures that the expectations of the parties will be more fully realized in spite of unexpected and fortuitous market conditions (see Note, Requirements Contracts under the Uniform Commercial Code, 102 U.Pa.L.Rev. 654, 666–667, supra). Thus, even where one party acts with complete good faith, the section limits the other party's risk in accordance with the reasonable expectations of the parties.

It would be unwise to attempt to define the phrase "unreasonably disproportionate" in terms of rigid quantities. In order that the limitation contemplated by the section take effect, it is not enough that a demand for requirements be disproportionate to the stated estimate; it must be *unreasonably* so in view of the expectation of the parties. A number of factors should be taken into account in the event a buyer's requirements greatly exceed the contract estimate. These include the following: (1) the amount by which the requirements exceed the contract estimate; (2) whether the seller had any reasonable basis on which to forecast or anticipate the requested increase * * *; (3) the amount, if any, by which the market price of the goods in question exceeded the contract price; (4) whether such an increase in market price was itself fortuitous; and (5) the reason for the increase in requirements.

Turning once again to the facts of the instant case, we conclude that, at least as to the year in which this controversy first arose, there was ample evidence to justify a finding of lack of good faith on plaintiff's part. Even through the thicket of divergent and contrasting figures entered into exhibit at trial, the following picture emerges: non-firm sales [3] from plaintiff's Lovett plant, presumably in large part to the New York Power Pool, increased nearly sixfold from 67,867 mega-watt hours in 1969 to 390,017 megawatt hours in 1970. The significance of that increase in *non-firm* sales lies in the fact that such sales did not enter into the budget calculations which formed the basis of the estimates included in the contract. Even assuming that a prudent seller of oil could anticipate some additional requirements generated by non-firm sales, an increase of the magnitude which occurred in 1970 is unforeseeable. That increase, of 322,150 megawatt hours, translates into the equivalent of over 500,000 barrels of oil.[4] The conclusion is inescapable that this dramatic change in plaintiff's relationship with the New York Power Pool came about as a result of the subject requirements contract, which insured it a steady flow of cheap oil despite swiftly rising prices.[5] O & R's use of the subject contract to suddenly and dramatically propel itself into the position of a large seller of power to other utilities evidences a lack of good faith dealing.[6]

In addition to this massive increase in sales of power to other utilities, the evidence indicates that at about the time O & R was demanding roughly one million barrels of oil in excess of the 1970 contract estimate, there was an internal O & R proposal to release gas to a supplier which represented the equivalent of 542,000 barrels of oil. An internal O & R memorandum dated May 26, 1970 (four days after the meeting at which Hess refused to supply the one million additional barrels demanded) recommended that in view of the Hess position, the proposed release be cancelled. Significantly, O & R never did burn as much oil as had been demanded in May and June, 1970. Its total usage for the year was 2,294,845 barrels—471,155 barrels less than its maximum demand. This was explained, by O & R officials, in part, on the ground that their "gas department" had made a "pessimistic estimate" which did not turn out to be quite true.

Thus it appears that in May, 1970 Hess refused an O & R demand of roughly one million barrels in excess of the contract estimate, which demand was occasioned by greatly increased sales to other utilities and

3. Non-firm sales are to be contrasted with "firm" sales, which are synonymous with predictable sales. Firm sales include predictable sales to O & R's own customers and sales pursuant to contract with other utilities.

4. A figure of 515,400 barrels of oil is arrived at by multiplying the increase in sales of non-firm megawatt hours (322,150) by a very conservative conversion factor of 1.6.

5. Notwithstanding the fact that Hess failed to supply all that was demanded by O & R, it is apparent that even with a mix of Hess and non-Hess oil, plaintiff's costs of producing electricity with oil would have been lower than those of any companies

purchasing oil on the open market or with "floating" contracts. This observation is underscored by the fact that O & R found it more advantageous to purchase the balance of its "requirements" on the open market (over and above the contract estimates which Hess was supplying) rather than to renegotiate the contract at a price 65 cents lower than posted market prices.

6. "[A] sudden expansion of the plant by which requirements are to be measured would not be included within the scope of the contract as made but normal expansion undertaken in good faith would be within the scope of this section." (Official Comment, par. 2 to UCC § 2–306.)

a proposed release of gas which might otherwise normally have been burned for power generation.[7] The former factor is tantamount to making the other utilities in the State silent partners to the contract * * *, while the latter factor amounts to a unilateral and arbitrary change in the conditions prevailing at the time of the contract so as to take advantage of market conditions at the seller's expense. Hess was therefore justified in 1970 in refusing to meet plaintiff's demands, by reason of the fact that plaintiff's "requirements" were not incurred in good faith.

With respect to subsequent years however, the record is ambiguous as to the cause of plaintiff's drastically increased requirements. Non-firm sales from Lovett actually declined slightly in 1971 and 1972 although they were still greatly in excess of 1969 sales.[8] If one takes 1969 as a base year, increased non-firm sales from Lovett in 1971 amounted to the equivalent of about one-half million barrels of oil[9], while in 1972 they amounted to the equivalent of just over 300,000 barrels.[10] Comparable figures for 1973 are impossible to arrive at with any degree of confidence because sales figures in the record are for the

7. While there was testimony by O & R officials to the effect that this gas, supplied by the Home Gas Company, could not be burned at the Lovett plant because that gas was only transmitted to another geographical sector of O & R's territory, it strains credulity to believe that the interstate pipeline system is so parochial that releases in one sector would not affect operations in another sector. Home Gas Company was, in fact, a subsidiary of the Columbia Gas Transmission Company at the time, and Columbia Gas was burned at the Lovett plant. Furthermore, plaintiff's contention is belied by (a) the May 26, 1970 memo which linked the proposed release to oil deliveries at Lovett and (b) a revised calculation from O & R's gas department, dated May 19, 1970, which allocated Home gas between O & R's two geographical divisions for the purpose of showing gas availability for electrical generation.

8. In 1971 total sales from Lovett amounted to 387,874 MWH; firm sales were 17,294 MWH. Assuming these firm sales were all generated at Lovett, total non-firm sales would have been 370,580 MWH—down slightly from the 390,017 MWH sold on a non-firm basis in 1970. In 1972 total sales from Bowline (a new generating plant), from Lovett, and from gas turbines amounted to 722,329 MWH. Firm sales for the year were 423,734, of which 374,327 MWH were generated at Bowline. Assuming that the remaining 49,407 MWH in firm sales were generated at Lovett (and not by the gas turbines), that plant's non-firm sales for the year would have amounted to 256,320 MWH.

We have focused on non-firm sales in our analysis because the record does not reveal whether firm sales during this period were taken into account in the preparation of the December 30, 1968 budget projection which formed the basis of the contract estimates. If they were, they would be meaningless in attempting to explain the tremendous increase in plaintiff's oil requirements.

While there was evidence that electrical power is "fungible" and that allocation of sales to various plants is an "accounting function", the testimony at trial did establish that the allocation is performed in a sufficiently rational manner. We therefore decline to attribute all O & R sales to the Lovett plant.

9. We choose the increase over 1969 rather than the absolute figure for sales because a certain amount of power pool sales, based on O & R's past experience, would be reasonably foreseeable. In 1971, non-firm sales from Lovett amounted to 370,580 MWH (see n. 8), an increase of 303,007 MWH over the 67,867 MWH sold on a non-firm basis in 1969. If we multiply this increase by the very conservative conversion factor of 1.6, we arrive at a barrel equivalent of 484,811.

10. This calculation is made in exactly the same manner as the one for 1971. The increase in sales of non-firm power amounts to 188,453 MWH (256,320 MWH less 67,867 MWH) and application of the conversion factor results in a barrel equivalent of 301,525.

full year, while defendant's obligation to supply oil extended through only three-quarters of the year. In any event, it is apparent that O & R's tremendously expanded use of oil during the period subsequent to 1970 cannot be explained solely by reference to increased sales to other utilities. In 1971 oil use exceeded the contract estimate by over 1,750,000 barrels; the 1972 figure was in excess of 1,825,000 barrels; and for the first nine months of 1973 the increase was more than 1,275,000 barrels.[11]

It appears that a large portion of the difference between actual use and contract estimates during this period can be attributed to a rather large decline in plaintiff's "actual take" of gas as opposed to the estimates of gas availability which were made in 1968 (and which were used in the computation of the December 30, 1968 budget). This decline, with the equivalent figure in barrels of oil,[12] was as follows:

Estimate (Mcf)	Actual Take (Mcf)	Decrease	Equiv. Barrels of Oil
1971—40,615,000	34,518,000	6,097,000	1,016,167
1972—43,661,000	36,274,000	7,387,000	1,231,167
1973			
(9 mos)			
34,034,700	25,783,000	8,251,700	1,375,283

Even allowing for the fact that O & R's actual system requirements were slightly lower during this period than the estimated system requirements (thus theoretically leaving more gas available for electric generation), it is clear that the decline from the estimates in gas received by O & R was a very major factor in plaintiff's increased use of oil during this period.

The record is unclear as to why this decline came about. Plaintiff introduced into evidence a Public Service Commission memorandum which indicates that gas supplies available to interstate transmission companies had become extremely tight. However plaintiff failed to call one witness who was expert in its gas operations and who could testify as to the link, if any, between this general shortage and plaintiff's operations. While an unfavorable inference may be drawn when a party fails to produce evidence which is within his control and which he is naturally expected to produce, we decline to speculate as to causes of the decline in gas received by plaintiff. In any event, such speculation is not necessary for resolution of this appeal.

We hold that under the circumstances of this case, any demand [13] by plaintiff for more than double its contract estimates, was, as a

---

11. This figure is arrived at by subtracting three-quarters of the contract estimate from total oil deliveries during the first nine months of 1973.

12. One barrel of oil is equivalent in heating value to 6 Mcf of gas.

13. There is no indication in the record that O & R continued to supply Hess with up-dated "requirements" demands after June 19, 1970. In fact, it can be inferred from a fair reading of the record that O & R entered into a contract with another supplier to furnish amounts required in

matter of law, "unreasonably disproportionate" (UCC, § 2–306, subd. [1]) to those estimates. We do not adopt the factor of more than double the contract estimates as any sort of an inflexible yardstick.[14] Rather, we apply those standards set forth earlier in this opinion, which are calculated to limit a party's risk in accordance with the reasonable expectations of the parties.

Here, as noted, plaintiff's requirements during the period 1971 through September, 1973, were more than double the contract estimates. Defendant had no reasonable basis on which to forecast or anticipate an increase of this magnitude. Indeed the contract suggests the parties contemplated that any variations from the estimate would be on the downside—else why did plaintiff expressly reserve for itself the right to burn as much as it chose? The market price of the grade of oil supplied had more than doubled by March, 1971. It stayed at or above $4.00 per barrel for the rest of the applicable period and had reached nearly $5.00 per barrel by the end of September, 1973. The record is silent as to whether defendant had any reason to anticipate this enormous increase in oil prices. Finally, the increase in requirements was due in part to plaintiff's increased sales to other utilities and also due to a significant decline in anticipated deliveries of gas, the cause of which was inadequately explained by plaintiff. The quantities of oil utilized by plaintiff during the period subsequent to 1970 were not within the reasonable expectations of the parties when the contract was executed, and accordingly we hold that those "requirements" were unreasonably disproportionate to the contract estimates (see UCC, § 2–306, subd. [1]).

Judgment of the Supreme Court, Rockland County, entered June 4, 1976, affirmed, with costs.

Notes

1. Since 1977, there has been little litigation of significance on the issues decided in Orange & Rockland. See Homestake Mining Co. v. Washington Public Power Supply, 476 F.Supp. 1162, 1167–69 (N.D.Cal.1979) (bad faith for buyer under requirements contract to insist on goods not needed for the particular business activity referred to in contract). For commentary, see White & Summers, Section 3–8; Note, *Requirements Contracts, "More or Less," Under the Uniform Commercial Code,* 33 Rutgers L.Rev. 105 (1980). For discussions of the good faith issue in flexible quantity contracts, see Burton, *Breach of Contract and the Common Law Duty to Perform in Good Faith,* 94 Harv.L.Rev. 369, 381–84, 395–97 (1980);

excess of the amounts Hess was willing to supply. Nevertheless, we assume for the sake of argument that there was a continuing "demand" by plaintiff for its total requirements.

14. Interestingly, plaintiff would have us hold as a matter of law that where an actual requirement varies "only by a factor of two from a stated estimate", it is not unreasonably disproportionate to such estimate.

Muris, *Opportunistic Behavior and the Law of Contracts*, 65 Minn.L.Rev. 521, 556–65 (1981).

2. The court in Orange & Rockland used factors existing and events foreseeable at the time of contracting to determine whether the buyer's orders were "unreasonably disproportionate" to the stated estimates. Where the estimates did not apply, however, the court used motives and factors existing at the time the requirements were ordered to determine whether the buyer's conduct was in bad faith. The buyer lost on both counts. Suppose, however, that the amounts ordered were unreasonably disproportionate to the stated estimates but the buyer's actual requirements were in good faith. Which limitation upon the exercise of discretion should prevail under UCC 2–306(1)?

3. Going Out of Business. Suppose the buyer claims that its actual requirements for the goods described in the contract were non-existent or drastically reduced from prior years. Such a decision appears to be justified if made in good faith. UCC 2–306(1). As one court put it, the "seller assumes the risk of all good faith variations in the buyer's requirements even to the extent of a determination to liquidate or discontinue the business." It might be said that the buyer's duty to buy is conditioned upon the existence of actual requirements. Further: "The rule is based on a reliance on the self-interest of the buyer, who ordinarily will seek to have the largest possible requirements. Protection against abuse is afforded by penetrating through any device by which the requirement is siphoned off in some other form to the detriment of the seller. The requirement of good faith is the means by which this is enforced and self-interest in its undistorted form is maintained as the standard." HML Corporation v. General Foods Corporation, 365 F.2d 77 (3d Cir.1966) (burden on seller to prove bad faith).

What, then, is bad faith in this setting? What if the decision is not to curtail losses but simply to make more profits on an alternative line of production? Inferences of bad faith abound when the seller has some demand for its output or the buyer still has some requirements and the decision is "merely to curtail losses." UCC 2–306, Comment 2. A leading case is Feld v. Henry S. Levy & Sons, Inc., 37 N.Y.2d 466, 373 N.Y.S.2d 102, 106, 335 N.E.2d 320, 323 (1975), where the court concluded that an "output" seller was justified in a good faith cessation of a single operation rather than entire business "only if its losses from continuance would be more than trivial". A cessation "merely to curtail losses" would be improper. Should the amount of loss from continued performance be the major issue? How much is too much? One of your co-authors believes that the standards derived from the Comments to UCC 2–306 are impossible to apply.

Problem 5–3

A five year "requirements" contract contained an estimate that Buyer would need 20,000 units per year. For the first two years, Buyer ordered 18,750 and 20,500 units. In the third year, Buyer ordered 10,000 units and, shortly thereafter, discontinued that line of its business. It is stipulated that at all times Buyer acted in good faith. Seller, however, argued that

Buyer was obligated, despite good faith, to approximate the stated estimates for five years, and that the third year reduction and the discontinuance, because they were unreasonably disproportionate, were breaches of contract. Seller relies on the text of UCC 2–306(1): Actual requirements in good faith is limited by the "except" clause. Buyer points to Comment 2 to UCC 2–306 as permitting "good faith variations from prior requirements * * * even when the variation may be such as to result in discontinuance." R.A. Weaver & Assoc., Inc. v. Asphalt Const., Inc., 587 F.2d 1315, 1321–22 (D.C.Cir.1978) (good faith reduction, though drastic, is permitted even though unreasonably disproportionate). How should this dispute be resolved?

Note: Best Efforts in Exclusive Dealing Relationships

UCC 2–306(2) provides that a "lawful agreement by either the seller or the buyer for exclusive dealing in the kind of goods concerned imposes unless otherwise agreed an obligation by the seller to use best efforts to supply the goods and by the buyer to use best efforts to promote their sale."

An exclusive dealing relationship is a continuing, highly interdependent agency, franchise or contract for distribution. It facilitates the manufacturer's effort to market the goods. It is common for the distributor to agree to order requirements as generated by "best efforts" from and to deal exclusively in some defined territory with the manufacturer. When the agreement to use "best efforts" is coupled with exclusive dealing, there is consideration. Hunt Foods, Inc. v. Phillips, 248 F.2d 23 (9th Cir.1957). There is some risk, however, that the arrangement, because of its restriction upon competition, will run afoul of the antitrust laws. See L. Sullivan, Anti-Trust 163–66 (1977). In any event, the arrangement must be lawful under state and federal law and an agreement by the distributor to make best efforts must exist. See Gerard v. Almouli, 746 F.2d 936 (2d Cir.1984) (no best efforts agreement where condition precedent fails). UCC 2–306(2) presumes that the "best efforts" agreement exists unless the parties have otherwise agreed.

What are "best efforts" when the duty is part of the agreement? Beyond the requirement that the distributor make an honest effort in the particular setting, there is disagreement among the courts. For a leading case and some helpful analysis, see Bloor v. Falstaff Brewing Corp., 601 F.2d 609 (2d Cir.1979) and Goetz & Scott, *Principles of Relational Contracts*, 67 Va.L.Rev. 1089 (1981).

C. The Price Term

In a market directed economy, the sale price is the result of seller costs, buyer demand, information available to and negotiations between the parties and the quality of competition in the relevant market area. Since price is a material term in any sale, the determination of what price was agreed, as well as the method for ascertainment, is important when disputes arise.

Sections 2–204(3) and 2–305 are the key UCC sections. Review them and work through the following materials.

Problem 5–4

During the latter part of 1981, Irving Molever began to entertain the idea of opening a discount house retail business in Wheeling, West Virginia. At that time he came in contact with Ernest Berez, a long-time friend and Vice-President of the Associated Hardware Supply Company, a Pennsylvania corporation and wholesaler of hardware, household goods and other merchandise. Molever incorporated his business in West Virginia under the name of The Big Wheel Distributing Company, and as its representative attempted to negotiate a contract with Associated. Several meetings between the representatives of both corporations were held in the early months of 1982. The primary topic of discussion at these meetings was the method of pricing to be used. Big Wheel insisted that the prices be computed on a cost plus ten percent basis for shipments from Associated's warehouse and cost plus five percent for direct factory shipments. Associated maintained that it could not price goods on this basis because its IBM billing system was geared to discount pricing. Big Wheel alleges that at this time it was told by Associated that the dealer-catalogue less 11% method was equal to the cost plus method it desired. These discussions culminated in an exchange of letters between the parties; the letter from Associated on February 9, 1982, confirmed an offer made at one of these meetings; the reply from Big Wheel on February 24 impliedly agreed to some of the confirmation but explicitly rejected the method of pricing contained therein. (These letters are set out below.)

February 9, 1982

Mr. Irving Molever
400 Carlton House
Pittsburgh, Pa.

Dear Mr. Molever:

We wish to confirm the special offer that we have made to you for the purpose of supplying your new promotional department store, ''The Big Wheel,'' in Wheeling, W.Va.

Specifically, we have agreed to do the following:

We will make available to you on a maximum 48 hour shipment schedule all merchandise from our Pittsburgh warehouse at the same low price that appears in our dealer catalogue. In addition, you will receive 11% beyond these prices as cash discount. Further, we shall make available to you the merchandising services of our organization as they are presently available to all regular dealer accounts. There will be no additional rebates on purchases beyond these discounts. This offer is subject to your purchasing an average of approximately $5,000 per week in carton lot quantities to be delivered at one time from our Pittsburgh warehouse. All merchandise is sold FOB Pittsburgh.

Factory shipments which we make at your direction, are available to you on the basis of our normal dealer cost plus the additional 11% cash discount. Should we be willing to sell an additional operation of this type, this same offer and schedule prices would be available to them providing they meet all other requirements. In return you have agreed to do the following: The initial order of merchandise which we ship at your direction is to be paid less the preferential 11% discount as noted above upon receipt of the merchandise. You have agreed that all invoices from the first through the twenty-fourth of the month will be paid by the 5th of the following month. Invoices from the twenty-fifth through the thirty-first of the month are to be considered as having been shipped as of the next month.

Since we have asked for no financial information on this new corporation, you have agreed to be personally responsible for all credit regardless of amounts that we extend to this corporation.

We further ask that you do not make public the arithmetic of this special offer.

We would appreciate your acknowledging these conditions, and returning a copy for our files.

Very Sincerely Yours,

ASSOCIATED HARDWARE
SUPPLY CO.

Agreed: IRVING MOLEVER   /s/ ERNEST S. BEREZ
                           Ernest S. Berez
                           Vice President

ESB/o

February 24, 1982

Mr. Ernest S. Berez
Associated Hardware Supply Co.
1020 Saw Mill Run Blvd.
Pittsburgh 26, Pa.

Dear Ernie:

In reply to your letter of February 19 [sic], I cannot possibly sign this and return it.

In the first place, I have talked to some of my other suppliers and, quite frankly, I am still at a loss to understand why you can't set up your bookkeeping and administrative procedures similarly to theirs.

I have discussed this matter thoroughly with Fred, and he is very much concerned that with the inexperienced help we have in your departments much confusion and loss of time will be the results if you bill us at catalogue prices, less an 11% credit memo. You can certainly appreciate his problems. Therefore, if your invoices would come in, similar to Stem Distributing Co., simply at cost, plus 10% it would certainly simplify our pricing procedure at floor level and expedite our getting the merchandise on the floor priced for sale.

Ernie, I can appreciate your problem of the retails already set up on your I.B.M. cards for your dealer accounts—however, it is incomprehensible to me as a C.P.A. to believe that merely handbilling our invoices would result in the necessity of hiring another assistant—especially when you must consider the time consumed in preparing the 11% credit memos on the method you have suggested.

Fred is still so concerned about the confusion which will result in our pricing the goods on the floor that I should like to repeat my statement of the other day; that is, go ahead and bill us on a simple cost plus basis, and if you find it necessary to hire a full-time assistant we will either absorb a pro rated share of her salary, or make some alteration of invoicing to ease your situation.

I might add that Fred is also concerned in view of the Robinson-Pactman [sic] Act that we would not be able to sign your letter without consulting legal counsel.

Since I promised to personally guarantee credit until our current financial statement is finished if you will please send a corrected request I will execute it and return.

IMM:bg

However, either sometime prior to or shortly after sending its letter of February 24, Big Wheel placed an order with Associated for a large quantity of goods which was included in the store's inventory when it opened on March 5. The price paid for the original shipment and for every shipment received thereafter for the next two years was computed on a dealer catalogue less eleven percent basis.

Sales made during this period were not without complaint. As early as August, 1982, Big Wheel began to doubt that the prices it was paying were the equivalent of cost plus 10% on warehouse shipments and cost plus 5% on direct factory shipments. By the following March, at least one of Big Wheel's officers was certain that the prices charged by Associated were considerably higher than cost plus ten percent. These objections were communicated to Associated, which allegedly assured Big Wheel that the prices paid would average out to cost plus 10%.

In spite of its objections to the pricing method, Big Wheel continued to order, receive and pay for merchandise on a dealer catalogue less eleven percent basis until March of 1984. From March through June of 1984, Big Wheel placed orders and received the goods but refused to pay for the merchandise received. Big Wheel, while not denying liability for the goods received, argues that the amount due under the agreement was no more than cost plus 10% and since more than that had been paid on goods previously ordered, it was entitled to an appropriate offset on the goods in dispute.

Is Big Wheel's contention correct under the UCC? Please support your answer with appropriate references to the Code.

IN RE GLOVER CONSTRUCTION CO., INC.
United States Bankruptcy Court, Western District of Kentucky, 1985.
49 B.R. 581.

MERRITT S. DIETZ, BANKRUPTCY JUDGE. Simple contract elements— the offer, acceptance and "meeting of the minds" that bind bargaining parties to their promises—rarely play a part in today's complex bankruptcy litigation. But the outcome of the case at hand depends exactly on the basic question of whether the parties, in the extensive course of their dealings, ever really had an enforceable agreement between them.

In the fall of 1981, the debtors, Glover Construction Company, Inc. and Glover Contracting Company, Inc. (Glover), and the plaintiff, Fleetwash Systems, Inc. (Fleetwash), began negotiating for a contract whereby Fleetwash would furnish Glover with vehicle washing equipment for installation on a construction project at Fort Knox, Kentucky. In February of 1982 the parties executed a "contract" [1] for the purchase of the equipment. The terms of this "purchase order" called for a total price of $370,000 and payments by Glover of "net 30th of month following month in which material is delivered". The purchase order also contained the following language concerning the equipment's price:

Terms: (Options)   10% Down Payment upon approval by owner $37,000.00. 2% Discount on 370,000.00 = $7,400.00 off Final Payment.

25% Down Payment upon approval by Owner $92,500.00. 5% Discount on 370,000.00 = 18,500.00 off Final Payment. 60% Annual Interest Rate.

Immediately after the signing of the purchase order, Glover and Fleetwash began quarreling as to the exact meaning of the above quoted terms. Fleetwash has constantly maintained that the contract called for Glover to make *either* a 10% or 25% down payment before they were to ship the contract materials. Glover, however, has consistently argued that the contract merely granted Glover the *option to earn a discount by making either a 10% or 25% down payment* and that the only mandatory payment terms were those calling for "Net 30th of month following month in which material is delivered". The conduct

---

1. Although the parties stipulated that they entered into a contract, the facts indicate that a valid contractual relationship never existed. See note 3 infra and accompanying text.

of the parties following the signing of the purchase order as well as their testimony at the trial showed that neither party intended to be bound by the terms of the purchase order unless the other party agreed to their interpretation of the price/payment provisions.

In September of 1982, Glover offered to make a 25% down payment on the vehicle washing equipment if Fleetwash would provide Glover with releases of liens on the equipment from both Fleetwash and its suppliers. Fleetwash could only provide Glover with a release of its own against the equipment, and Glover did not make the down payment.

On November 10, 1982 Glover filed a petition for reorganization under Chapter 11 of the Bankruptcy Code. Robert C. Glover was appointed debtor in possession and Glover continued work on the Fort Knox project. A trustee was appointed by this court for the limited purpose of collecting and disbursing Glover's progress payments.

In February of 1983, one year after the signing of the original purchase order, Fleetwash offered to deliver a portion of Glover's order if Glover would "walk the invoice through [the U.S. Army Corps of Engineers' billing procedures]". The total invoice price of this shipment was $144,200. At the time Fleetwash made this partial shipment, the two parties still had not agreed on the price and payment terms. Glover received the equipment and submitted to the U.S. Army Corps of Engineers a pay request covering the Fleetwash invoice. The Army approved the pay request and issued a check in the net amount of $129,780 [2] to the trustee who still holds these funds. Glover objected to the disbursement of these funds to Fleetwash on a number of grounds, and the present action ensued.

* * *

The initial issue we must address is whether the parties had a valid contract for the sale of the vehicle washing equipment. Although the parties stipulated that they entered into a contract with the signing of the purchase order on February 15, 1982, it is an ancient and unchallenged principle of contract law that for there to be a valid contract there must first be agreement as to the essential terms of that contract.[3] This rule has been modified to some extent by the Uniform Commercial Code (UCC) and its "gap-filler provisions". The provision of Kentucky's [4] version of the UCC which deals with open price terms, KRS 355.2–305, provides that:

2. All payment by the Army Corps of Engineers were subject to a 10% retainage.

3. Smith v. Hilliard, 408 S.W.2d 440 (Ky.1966); Vidt v. Burgess, 136 S.W.2d 1080 (Ky.1940); Dean v. Meter, 8 Ky.Opin. 746 (Ky.1874).

4. As a general rule of law the place of performance of the contract governs the rights of the parties absent a clear showing of contrary intent. Smith v. Stone, 202 F.Supp. 11 (E.D.Ky.1962). In this case the parties intended to have the purchase order "governed and construed according to the laws of the state of Kentucky" since that language was included as a choice of law provision in the order form.

"(1) The parties, if they so intend can conclude a contract for sale *even though the price is not settled.* In such a case the price is a *reasonable price* at the time for delivery if

* * *

"(b) the price is left to be agreed by the parties and they fail to agree

* * *

"(4) *Where, however the parties intend not to be bound unless the price be fixed or agreed and it is not fixed or agreed there is no contract.* In such case the buyer must return any goods already received or if unable so to do must pay their *reasonable value* at the time of delivery"
* * * [emphasis added]

In the present case the parties entered into the purchase order without having agreed on the contract's price and payment terms. Kentucky's version of the UCC would ordinarily supply the price terms of the contract, except that the parties to this action clearly intended not to be bound to the terms of the purchase order unless their interpretation of the price terms was accepted by the opposing party. Both KRS 355.2–305(4) and pre-UCC case law [5] state that in such a case *there is no contract between the parties.* Due to this finding [6] we need not consider the parties' lengthy, if misplaced, arguments on the issues of breach and damages.[7] Our ruling that no contract existed between Glover and Fleetwash does not preclude payment to Fleetwash for goods delivered to Glover. KRS 355.2–305(4) provides that where there is no contract "the buyer must return any goods already received or if unable so to do must pay their reasonable value at the time of delivery [to the seller]". We therefore must determine the reasonable value of the goods.

Although neither the UCC, applicable case law nor White & Summers define what constitutes "reasonable value", in our opinion the term "reasonable value" as used in this context is merely a codification of the doctrine of restitution [8] as the basis of recovery in cases involving a quasi-contract, or contract implied in law.[9] The term "reasonable value" is not to be considered synonymous with the term "reasonable

5. Herman v. Jackson, 405 S.W.2d 9 (Ky.1966); Thompson v. Hunters Ex'r et al., 269 S.W. 266 (Ky.1954); Marshall's Adm'r v. Webster, 155 S.W.2d 13 (Ky.1941).

6. "Whether an agreement has been concluded, in most cases, is a question to be determined by the trier of fact." KRS 355.2–305, Kentucky Commentary (1983). In this case our determination on this issue is clearly factual and is subject to the "clearly erroneous" standard of review. See In re Calhoun, 715 F.2d 1103, 1110 (6th Cir.1983).

7. See White & Summers, Uniform Commercial Code § 3–7, p. 117 (2d ed. 1980).

8. Black's Law Dictionary, (5th ed. 1979) defines restitution as:

"act of restoring; * * * the act of making good or giving equivalent for any loss, damage or injury; * * * restoration of status quo and is amount which would put plaintiff in as good a position as he would have been if *no contract had been made* and restores to plaintiff [the] value of what he parted with in performing [the] contract * * * a person who has been unjustly enriched at the expense of another is required to make restitution to the other. [emphasis added]

9. A contract implied in law or quasi contract indicates a duty imposed by law, "without mutual assent, for the purpose of affording a remedy or right of recovery where money or property or services were received under such circumstances that in

price", although it is possible—and certainly a commercial ideal—that an item's reasonable value and reasonable price might coincide.

At trial both parties offered extensive evidence as to the value of the equipment. Fleetwash, arguing that the parties intended to contract but merely left open the price and payment terms, placed the reasonable price of the equipment at approximately $137,000. Glover, on the other hand, produced three estimates of value ranging from $32,000 to $34,000.

After carefully reviewing all estimates of the value of the vehicle washing equipment delivered to Glover by Fleetwash, and considering the credibility and reliability of all witnesses as well as the circumstances surrounding their estimates, it is our opinion that the reasonable value of the equipment in question is $43,000. Our basis for this particular figure comes from a letter written by Melvin Wiegand, Vice President of Fleetwash, to the attorney who was representing them in the Chapter 11 reorganization of their predecessor brother-sister corporation, Wiegand Engineering, before a bankruptcy court in Texas. In that letter Fleetwash told its attorney that it would invoice Glover in the net amount of $123,000 for the equipment it sent to be installed at the Fort Knox construction site. The letter went on to say that "This transaction will result in an income of approximately $80,000. * * *" It is our opinion that this letter which indicates the reasonable value to be $43,000 is entitled to more weight by this court than either of the self-serving estimates prepared by interested parties in anticipation of litigation *before this court*,[10] or the hopelessly confused estimate presented by the Army Corps of Engineers.[11] This award of $43,000 covers both the 2–wheeled vehicle washing systems as well as the miscellaneous hose station equipment, since from a review of the limited cost data provided by Fleetwash, it is clear that an award of $43,000 for the vehicle washing systems alone would be over-generous. In fact, in making this award we are being extremely generous to Fleetwash by accepting the value estimate contained in their letter to their Texas bankruptcy counsel, instead of placing the reasonable value of the equipment at the figure urged by Glover. This award is in line with the restitutional nature of the "reasonable value" language of KRS 355.2–305(4) since, by Fleetwash's own

---

equity and good conscience the recipient [must] pay for them." Thompson v. Hunter's Ex'r, 269 S.W.2d at 269.

10. We arrived at a reasonable value of the equipment from this letter by subtracting the expected income from the net invoice amount. For a full text of the letter and the pro forma invoice on the 2 wheeled vehicle wash systems see Appendix A [omitted].

11. The Army Corps of Engineers estimate of the value of the equipment Fleet-

wash sold Glover, would generally be given much weight by this court. However due to the confused manner in which their evaluation was prepared, the third-hand nature of their representative's testimony at trial and the fact that the Army Corps of Engineers had to "clarify", by unsworn letter, the testimony another representative gave at a deposition on this matter led this court to attach very little weight to their estimate.

admission, this amount should place them in as good a position as they would have occupied if they had never made the shipment to Glover.

Therefore it is the opinion of this court that the parties to the purchase order in controversy, Fleetwash and Glover, never agreed as to the meaning of the price and payment terms of the order and did not intend to be bound by the terms of the order unless the other party acquiesced to their interpretation of the price and payment terms. Further the court finds that, in light of the fact that no contract existed between the parties, Fleetwash is entitled to the reasonable value of the goods they delivered to Glover, which we set at $43,000.

An appropriate order reflecting these findings of fact and conclusions of law will be entered by the court.

Notes

1. Consider three questions: (1) What method did the parties adopt to determine the price, see UCC 2–305(1)(b); (2) When that method failed, what evidence persuaded the court that the parties did not intend to be bound unless the price was agreed; and (3) What difference, if any, exists between the price if the parties had intended to be bound, UCC 2–305(1), and the restitution remedy invoked because they did not so intend, UCC 2–305(4)? Review the discussion of the Bethlehem Steel-Litton litigation, supra at 74. See also, Flowers Baking Co. of Lynchburg, Inc., v. R–P Packaging, Inc., 229 Va. 370, 329 S.E.2d 462, 465 (1985), where the court, in concluding that there was no intention to contract, stated: "While it is true that the UCC has greatly modified the rigors of the common-law rules governing the formation of contracts, it remains a prerequisite that the parties' words and conduct must manifest an intention to be bound. Although they may make a contract which deliberately leaves material terms open for future determination, no contract results where their words and conduct demonstrate a lack of intention to contract. * * * Such a lack is not remedied by evidence of custom and usage in the trade * * * or by a written memorandum purporting to confirm oral discussion which did not in themselves amount to an agreement * * *."

2. Under UCC 2–305(1), the same questions are posed if "nothing is said as to price" or the "price is to be fixed in terms of some agreed market or other standard as set or recorded by a third person or agency and it is not so set or recorded:" (1) Did the parties intend to "conclude a contract even though the price is not settled;" (2) If not, what remedies are available under UCC 2–305(4); and (3) If so, what is a "reasonable price at the time for delivery?" The pre-Code law is reviewed in Prosser, *Open Price in Contracts For the Sale of Goods*, 16 Minn.L.Rev. 733 (1932); Comment, *UCC Section 2–305(1)(c): Open Price Terms and the Intention of the Parties in Sales Contracts*, 1 Valpo.L.Rev. 381 (1967).

TCP INDUSTRIES, INC. v. UNIROYAL, INC.

United States Court of Appeals, Sixth Circuit, 1981.
661 F.2d 542.

Before ENGEL, KEITH and KENNEDY, CIRCUIT JUDGES.

CORNELIA G. KENNEDY, CIRCUIT JUDGE.

TCP Industries, Inc. (TCP) filed this breach of contract action against Uniroyal, Inc. (Uniroyal) to recover profits lost when Uniroyal refused to purchase butadiene pursuant to an April 1, 1974 contract. Uniroyal counterclaimed seeking damages from TCP and Donald C. Fresne (Fresne), its president and principal shareholder, for fraud, breach of an earlier 1970 contract, and breach of the 1974 contract. The jury returned a verdict for TCP in the amount of $1,045,650 and judgments of no cause of action on Uniroyal's three counterclaims. Uniroyal appeals. The parties agree that the Uniform Commercial Code applies. They did not object to the District Court's application of Michigan law, the law of the forum.

Butadiene is a petrochemical product extracted from gas and oil and principally used in the production of synthetic rubber. TCP does not produce butadiene but has since 1966 acted as a middleman in arranging sales of the product from El Paso Products Company (El Paso), a Texas refinery, to Uniroyal. TCP sold to Uniroyal at the same price it purchased butadiene from El Paso. Historically, its sole profit was limited to a commission or a reseller's discount of two-tenths (²/₁₀) of a cent per pound which El Paso paid TCP out of El Paso's price.

On November 3, 1970, TCP and Uniroyal entered into the 1970 contract. That contract covered the period of April 1, 1971 through March 31, 1974 and provided for the annual sale of 50 million pounds of butadiene at 8.00 to 8.25 cents per pound, depending on place of delivery. The contract restricted any price increase to the third year of the contract and then only to passing on those escalations in El Paso's production costs specifically related to increased labor or natural or butane gas costs which El Paso passed on to TCP. The contract also included a meet or release clause which provided that if Uniroyal received a bona fide offer from another producer to sell it at least 10,000,000 pounds of butadiene at a lower price, then TCP would have to meet that price within 30 days or release Uniroyal from its obligation to purchase such amount under the contract.

El Paso continued to sell butadiene to TCP which resold it to Uniroyal under these conditions until September 1973, six months before the expiration of TCP's contract with Uniroyal, when, unknown to Uniroyal, TCP's three year contract with El Paso expired. El Paso thereupon advised TCP that it would continue to sell it butadiene but that its reseller's discount would be discontinued and TCP should look for its profits solely from its markup to Uniroyal.

In October 1973, TCP increased its price to Uniroyal by .00247 per pound. In February 1973, El Paso increased its price to TCP by 3.5 cents to 11.75 cents per pound. TCP passed this price increase on to Uniroyal along with an additional increase of almost three cents. On March 1, 1974, TCP initiated another one cent per pound increase.[1] Uniroyal continued to accept and pay for butadiene at the increased prices. The parties agree and it is undisputed that except for El Paso's 3.5 cent increase passed along by TCP in February, the remaining increases were contrary to the express provisions of the written contract, and resulted in an overcharge to Uniroyal of $301,679.

During the same period that TCP was raising the price of butadiene under the 1970 contract, the parties were negotiating the terms of the 1974 contract. These negotiations were conducted in an atmosphere described by those in the industry as nothing less than chaotic. Price controls for butadiene expired in early 1974. Because of the shortage of crude oil due to the Arab oil embargo, a greater proportion of the supply of oil was being used to produce fuel oil rather than petrochemicals such as butadiene. Butadiene sellers were refusing to take on new customers. Since Uniroyal could not make synthetic rubber without butadiene, TCP's 50 million pound annual supply was extremely valuable and Uniroyal adopted measures to ensure itself of this dependable supply of butadiene. After several months of bargaining, Uniroyal and TCP entered into a new contract which represented a dramatic departure in form and substance from their previous agreements. This contract did not have a price escalation clause but instead contained the following pricing provision:

> The price for butadiene purchased hereunder shall be $0.1347 per pound F.O.B. point of origin. The price for butadiene is subject to change providing Texas Chemical gives no less than fifteen days notice.

The 1974 contract did not contain a meet or release clause for the first two years of its four year term.

Soon after signing, TCP informed Uniroyal that the price would increase from 13.7 cents on April 1, 1974, to 20.75 cents on July 1, and to 22.55 cents on October 1. By November 1974, the shortage of butadiene had eased and producers were ready to take on new customers. That month Uniroyal took only 489,000 pounds of butadiene as opposed to an average of 3,642,000 pounds in each of the previous seven months. Uniroyal took no butadiene from December 1974 through February 1975, first saying that it needed no butadiene and then explaining that the price was too high. Uniroyal again started to purchase in March 1975 at about 19.0 cents per pound. The parties agreed to reserve their rights against each other under the contract.

* * *

1. These figures have been taken from the pretrial order. Although there are discrepancies between these figures and those found in the briefs, exhibits and transcripts of the proceedings, the parties do not dispute that the total amount in controversy is $301,679.

[The court affirmed the jury verdict denying Uniroyal's counterclaim for an alleged breach of the 1970 contract.]

THE 1974 CONTRACT

Uniroyal also argues that the evidence was insufficient to support the jury's finding that TCP was entitled to the price it set under the 1974 contract. The contract contained the following pricing provision:

> The price for butadiene purchased hereunder shall be $0.1347 per pound F.O.B. point origin. The price for butadiene is subject to change providing Texas Chemical gives no less than fifteen days notice.

The District Court held this language ambiguous and permitted parol evidence. Uniroyal claims that TCP was limited by the parties' prior course of dealing to passing on to Uniroyal changes in the prices charged to TCP by El Paso. Uniroyal contends that if TCP was not limited to passing through El Paso's price, then it failed to set a reasonable price in accordance with M.C.L.A. § 440.2305.

In the usual case, the question of the parties' intentions when a price term is left open is a question for the trier of fact. Official Comment 2, M.C.L.A. § 440.2305. The jury was presented with considerable evidence that the parties vigorously negotiated the 1974 contract. Fresne testified that he told Wills that he wanted the right to unilaterally set the price at the high end of the market. He explained that this was a major reason for the six month negotiation period. TCP negotiated the deletion of the standard meet or release clause during the first two years of the four year contract and refused to include Uniroyal's suggested right to cancel clause if the price charged for butadiene was unacceptable. Also persuasive that the prior course of dealing as to pricing did not govern the 1974 contract was that the pricing language of the 1970 contract was not carried over to, and in fact was changed dramatically in the 1974 contract. The parties intentionally deleted the explicit and elaborate formula for pricing (the escalation clause) found in the 1970 contract and in its place required that TCP give Uniroyal 15 days notice prior to implementing a price increase. If the parties had intended to continue the explicit pricing terms of the 1970 contract, or had intended that only El Paso's increases to TCP would be passed along to Uniroyal, such language could have again been utilized. In fact, that specific language was deleted. The jury was presented with sufficient evidence that the "subject to change" provision of the 1974 contract did not limit TCP's price increases to passing through El Paso's increased costs.

Nor do we accept Uniroyal's alternative argument. M.C.L.A. § 440.2305 governs the open price term of the 1974 contract. The pertinent provisions provide:

> (1) The parties if they so intend can conclude a contract for sale even though the price is not settled. In such a case the price is a reasonable price at the time for delivery if

(a) nothing is said as to price; or

(b) the price is left to be agreed by the parties and they fail to agree; or

(c) the price is to be fixed in terms of some agreed market or other standard as set or recorded by a third person or agency and it is not so set or recorded.

(2) A price to be fixed by the seller or by the buyer means a price for him to fix in good faith.

Official Comment 3, referring to subsection (2), states:

[D]ealing with the situation where the price is to be fixed by one party rejects the uncommercial idea that an agreement that the seller may fix the price means that he may fix any price he may wish by the express qualification that the price so fixed must be fixed in good faith. Good faith includes observance of reasonable commercial standards of fair dealing in the trade if the party is a merchant. (Section 2–103).

M.C.L.A. § 440.2103(1)(b) defines "good faith" in the case of a merchant as "honesty in fact and the observance of reasonable commercial standards of fair dealing in the trade."

Neither the Code nor the Official Comments to the Code require that a merchant-seller price at fair market value under a contract with an open price term, but specify that prices must be "reasonable" and set pursuant to "reasonable commercial standards of fair dealing in the trade."

When there is a gap as to price, 2–305 directs the court to determine 'a reasonable price,' provided the parties intended a contract. Note that the section says 'a reasonable price' and not 'fair market value of the goods.' In many instances these two would not be identical. For example, evidence of a prior course of dealing between the parties might show a price below or above market. Without more, a court could justifiably hold in these circumstances that the course of dealing price is the 'reasonable price.'

J. White & R. Summers, *Uniform Commercial Code,* § 3–7, 17 (2d ed. 1980).

Similarly, the price might be reasonable although not set pursuant to "reasonable commercial standards of fair dealing." An example would be where the party sets the open price at a reasonable retail price although reasonable commercial standards of fair dealing would require that the price be set at a reasonable wholesale rate. In the instant case the price was set within the wholesale range. The only issue is whether a spot market price within that range was reasonable vis-a-vis the existence of a long term contract price and whether that is a question of fact or of law.

At all times under the 1974 contract TCP sold or offered to sell butadiene to Uniroyal at prices within the range of those reported in the *Chemical Marketing Reporter,* a domestic publication specifically providing information on the butadiene market. The parties stipulated that the following price ranges appeared in the *Chemical Marketing Reporter* for the period April 1, 1974 to March 31, 1976.

April, 1974—June, 1974	12–17 cents
July, 1974—September, 1974	16–25 cents
October, 1974—January, 1975	17½–25 cents
February, 1975—March, 1976	18–22 cents

TCP's prices of 20.75 cents on July 1, 1974, and 22.25 cents on October 1, 1974, while tending toward the high end, were always well within the above range. Although Jesse Owens of El Paso initially testified that 22.25 cents per pound was not a "fair" price for the period of November 1974 through March 1975, he later explained that this conclusion was based on El Paso's long term contracts all of which contained a meet or release clause, the effect of which is to keep prices competitive to within ½ cent per pound. TCP, however, had negotiated with Uniroyal to omit such a clause during the first two years of the contract and include it for the final two years. On the other hand, Ralph Ericsson, president of a company which produces an annual survey of the world-wide butadiene industry, testified that during the last six months of 1974 butadiene prices were rising as high as 28.5 on a straight pass through basis. In his opinion, TCP's price was commercially reasonable under all the circumstances. Thus, there was evidence from which the jury could have reasonably found that TCP's price for butadiene under the 1974 contract was commercially reasonable and set in good faith. Uniroyal too narrowly defines good faith and commercial reasonableness when it contends that as a matter of law TCP met neither because it set its price in accord with total market prices including the spot market rate [rather] than pricing solely on long term contract prices.

While taking testimony on the market price of butadiene the District Court allowed Ralph Ericsson, qualified as an expert in the production and pricing of butadiene, to testify as to the meaning of the pricing clause contained in the 1974 contract. Over objection, Ericsson testified that he had never seen a price clause exactly like that one and that "the way I read this contract, the seller had the right to set the price and the buyer was obligated to accept that price." Following admission of this evidence, the District Court instructed the jury that the testimony was admitted for such value as the jury might wish to give it. Subsequently, Uniroyal's timely motion for new trial on this basis was denied.

Absent any need to clarify or define terms of art, science, or trade, expert opinion testimony to interpret contract language is inadmissible. * * * Here the witness was not testifying about a technical term which needed explaining. Since the witness had never seen a contract without a meet and release clause or cancellation clause where there was an open pricing provision the witness could not testify to the meaning given under such a contract by the trade. The question of what the contract clause meant was a factual one for the jury to determine from the testimony presented. *Loeb v. Hammond,* 407 F.2d 779, 781 (7th Cir.1969).

While we find that the District Court erred in admitting this testimony we note that no error in the admission or exclusion of evidence is ground for reversal or granting a new trial unless refusal to take such action appears to the court to be inconsistent with substantial justice. * * * Considering the entire record we do not find that the District Court's denial of Uniroyal's motion for new trial on the grounds of Ericsson's improper testimony was inconsistent with substantial justice.

* * *

The judgment of the District Court is affirmed.

Note

UCC 2–305(2) provides that a "price to be fixed by the seller or the buyer means a price for him to fix in good faith." In Au Rustproofing Center, Inc. v. Gulf Oil Corp., 755 F.2d 1231 (6th Cir.1985), Au contracted with Gulf to be a Gulf dealer for a period of ten years. Gulf agreed to pay Au a special allowance of two cents per gallon on all gasoline purchased at a "tankwagon" price to be set without contractual restriction by Gulf. After the 1973 oil crisis ruptured the market, Gulf suspended the special discount and charged Au a "tankwagon" price that was not competitive with other suppliers in the relevant market area. As a result, Au's gross margins substantially declined. In the ensuing litigation, the court held, inter alia, that Gulf had no duty to fix competitive gasoline prices for its dealers: " * * * (A)lthough Gulf assumed the implied duty of a party controlling the price to set a reasonable price * * * the record does not establish that the high price Gulf charged to Au was so unreasonable that it negated Gulf's substantial performance of the implied duty. * * * Gulf is required to fix a price in good faith. * * * Good faith includes observance of reasonable commercial standards of fair dealing in the trade or the general range of market prices. * * * Au contends that because its competitors sold gasoline for less than Au could buy it from Gulf, Gulf's prices were unreasonable. * * * In our view, this contention is insufficient to establish that prices set by Gulf contravened reasonable commercial standards in the gasoline market or otherwise constituted bad faith or commercially unreasonable behavior." But see Nanakuli Paving & Rock Co. v. Shell Oil Co., Inc., 664 F.2d 772 (9th Cir.1981) (Seller with discretion to fix price acted in bad faith in failing to follow "price protection" usage and to give reasonable notice of price increase).

Problem 5–5

B manufactures precious metal products and provides refining services. On July 1, 1979, S delivered 1,600 ounces of sterling silver to B under a contract for sale. B was to process the metal to determine its silver content and fix the price by multiplying the amount of silver by the market price on that day. S understood that B's normal processing time was four to six weeks. Due to B's negligence, however, the silver was misplaced and not found and processed until November 1. During this period, the per ounce price of silver was on the rise: On July 1 it was $17.25, on August 1 it was $18.50, on August 15 it was $20 and on November 1 it was $28. S, citing UCC 2–305(3), claims that it can cancel the contract and recover the silver and sell it on the open market. B argues that the case is governed by UCC 2–305(2): Thus, there was an enforceable contract even if B acted in bad faith and the price should be a reasonable price at the time when B should have completed the processing and fixed the price.

How should the court rule?

_____

V. GOLDBERG, PRICE ADJUSTMENT IN LONG–TERM CON-TRACTS, 1985 Wis.L.Rev. 527, 531–34.

* * *

II. THE ECONOMICS OF PRICE ADJUSTMENT

A. The Benefits of Price Adjustment

Business firms have ample incentives to include some form of price adjustment mechanism in their contracts even if both parties are risk neutral. Firms do not generally enter into multi-year contracts be-cause of their concern for the future course of prices. Rather, they enter into the agreements to achieve the benefits of cooperation. Hav-ing entered into such an agreement, the parties have to make some decision regarding the course of prices during the life of the agreement. That is, price adjustment will probably be ancillary to the main purposes of the agreement.

Price adjustment can be difficult and costly. Why then bother? Why not simply establish a price or a schedule of prices for the duration of the agreement? I will suggest four reasons that might lead business firms to consider using some form of price adjustment. First, if the contract concerns a complex product that will be continuously redefined during the life of the contract, a price adjustment mechanism can price the "amendments" to the original agreement. Examples include cost-plus pricing of sophisticated defense hardware and complex construction projects. Second, to properly coordinate their behavior, the parties want correct price signals. If the price of an input were below the market price (and if the buyer could not resell at a price greater than the contract price) the buyer would have an incentive to use "too much" of the input. Since this should be anticipated at the formation stage, the costs of poor coordination are borne by both parties. This is a pure "moral hazard" problem akin to an insured person consuming too much health care because the post-insurance price is too low.

Two other reasons are, analytically at least, more interesting: reduction of pre-contract search and post-agreement jockeying. In both these explanations, the success of price adjustment depends upon its ability to reduce the variance of outcomes. The reduced variance is not, however, valued directly. Rather, it enables the parties to curtail mutually harmful behavior, thereby increasing the value of the agreement to both parties.

A contract establishes gains to be divided between the parties; a fixed-price contract determines the distribution of these gains. The parties could attempt to increase their share of the gains before signing the contract by improving their information on the future course of costs and prices. The more they each spend on this search, the smaller the pie. *Ceteris paribus,* the larger the variance of the outcomes, the more resources would be devoted to this effort. The parties, therefore, have an incentive to incorporate into the initial agreement a device that would discourage this wasteful searching. Price adjustment mechanisms can do precisely that by reducing the value of the special information. This argument applies even for standardized commodities sold in thick markets.

If after the firms enter into a long-term agreement the contract price fails to track changing market conditions, the loser will be reluctant to continue performance. It could breach and suffer the legal and reputational consequences, but other, less severe, alternatives to willing compliance exist. A buyer could, for example, insist upon strict compliance with quality standards. The aggrieved party could read the contract literally—"working to the rules" as in labor disputes or in centrally planned economies. This is a variation on the pure moral hazard story. The incorrect price induces the aggrieved party to expend resources in attempting to renegotiate the terms of the agreement. The costs can arise directly from the effort to renegotiate or indirectly through strategic bargaining. That is, the loser might threaten to engage in acts which impose costs upon the other party but do not constitute a legal breach. These costs are a result of the failure to coordinate behavior in the face of changed circumstances. These costs would be unimportant if the parties had easy access to market alternatives; *ceteris paribus,* the more isolated from alternatives the contracting parties are, the more significant are the potential losses from poor coordination. Again, to the extent that the parties can anticipate these problems at the formation stage, the value of the exchange is reduced. If the probability of wasteful behavior increases as the divergence between contract price and the opportunity cost of the aggrieved party widens, price-adjustment rules which narrow the gap become increasingly attractive.

B. The Mechanics of Price Adjustment

The easiest way to adjust the price is to index. But what should the parties be indexing? The overall price level? Input costs? Market price? Ideally the parties would index the market price. The payoff from indexing, after all, is from the reduction in the divergence between the contract price and the market price. However, practical exigencies usually lead parties to index other prices as proxies. Indeed, in a long-term contract there often is no unique external market price. The implications of this fact will become clearer in the discussion of *Alcoa v. Essex* below.

Cost changes will be a reasonably good proxy for changes in the market price if demand does not fluctuate too much or if industry supply is very elastic. However, changes in input prices are not necessarily the same as changes in input costs. If the relative prices of inputs change, the firm has an incentive to alter factor proportions to take advantage of the new price relationships. Also, if factor productivity changes, the connection between input prices and costs deteriorates. Nevertheless, indexing to input prices is common.

While indexing would be the easiest price adjustment mechanism to implement, it has the obvious disadvantage of tracking changing conditions imperfectly. The poorer the correlation between the index and what it is supposed to be tracking, the less attractive it will be. Another relatively simple mechanical rule is permitting one party to solicit outside offers with the other party having the right of first refusal. This allows better tracking of that party's opportunity cost, but it discourages making relation-specific investments. That is, the direct costs of price adjustment would be low, but the indirect costs of discouraging entering into a long-term relationship in the first place might be quite high. Cost-plus pricing tracks cost changes more closely, but is more subject to manipulation; it also gives the seller poorer incentives to control costs, and requires that the parties devote more resources to monitoring performance.

Negotiation is, of course, always an option. Even if the contract explicitly utilizes one of the methods mentioned in the previous paragraph or unambiguously states that the contract is a fixed price agreement, one party could propose that the price be renegotiated. The contract price, the clarity of the legal rule, and the costs of invoking the legal rule provide the background against which the renegotiation might take place.

Renegotiation allows use of accurate, current information in revising the contract; but reopening the contract could result in cost-generating strategic behavior, especially if one of the parties is vulnerable to the threat of nonrenewal. Renegotiation is not a zero-sum affair with one side's gains offset by the other's loss. In exchange for an increased price, for example, a seller could offer a contract extension and the prospect of not working to the letter of the contract. (A threat, after all, is just a promise with the sign reversed.)

The contract could explicitly establish the conditions under which renegotiation is to take place. It could require renegotiation at fixed intervals or have it triggered by specific events (for example, a rise in a price index of more than 20%). Gross inequity clauses call for renegotiation if the contract price is too far out of line, but typically do not spell out the criteria for determining when a gross inequity exists. The parties could agree to renegotiate in good faith and determine what would happen if the negotiations break down. The failure to negotiate a new price could result in continued performance at the current price, termination, mediation or arbitration, and so forth.

There are, in sum, a lot of mechanisms available for adjusting price within a long-term contract. All are imperfect. Their relative costs and benefits will determine which, if any, the parties should choose.

* * *

[Footnotes omitted.]

Chapter Six

EXCUSE FROM OR ADJUSTMENT OF THE CONTRACT FOR CHANGED CIRCUMSTANCES

SECTION 1. INTRODUCTION

The question, "Who bears what risks arising from changed circumstances in a contract for sale?" is intriguing and eternal. If the "risk events" have been identified in the bargaining process and explicitly allocated in the agreement, the answer is clear: if the agreement is otherwise enforceable, i.e. not unconscionable or avoidable for fraud, and the language, reasonably interpreted, supports a particular risk allocation, then that allocation should prevail. Thus, an agreed fixed price in a contract for sale is thought to allocate the risk for both parties that, during performance, the market price for similar goods will go up or down.

But suppose there is neither an agreed nor a "tacit" risk allocation, yet the person seeking relief has made an unconditional promise. The seller agrees to deliver the goods by December 1 and the agreement says nothing about the risk that a strike may close the seller's major source of supply. When, if ever, should a court grant some relief from changed circumstances? What form should that relief take? The UCC provides a starting point for answers in Sections 2–613 through 2–616. Or, suppose that the parties, in response to changed circumstances, agree to modify or adjust the contract. When should a court enforce an agreed adjustment? The starting point here is UCC 2–209.

These problems have arisen with distressing frequency in the topsy-turvey economy of the last 20 years. We will take a brief look at some of them here. Since many of the cases involve changed circumstances which affect a price mechanism agreed to by the parties, there will be some necessary overlap with the price issues covered in Chapter Five. But the excuse issue is distinct and two of us, at least, believe that it deserves separate treatment.

195

SECTION 2. RELIEF FROM CHANGED CIRCUMSTANCES

Problem 6–1

S, an art dealer, owned a etching by Picasso. B, a collector, examined it at S's gallery and, after negotiations, S agreed to sell it to B for $75,000. Under the written contract for sale, B was to return with a cashier's check the next day and pick up the etching. B returned check in hand but, alas, the Picasso had been destroyed by fire during the night. What are the rights and duties of the parties? See UCC 2–613 and 2–509. Is this a case of changed circumstances?

WICKLIFFE FARMS, INC. v. OWENSBORO GRAIN CO.

Court of Appeals of Kentucky, 1984.
684 S.W.2d 17.

DUNN, JUDGE.

This is an appeal from a summary judgment in favor of appellee, Owensboro Grain Company, entered in the Daviess Circuit Court September 9, 1982, as amended September 29, 1982. The action arises out of a contract to sell No. 2 white corn and the defense of impossibility of performance resulting from a drought.

The appellant, Wickliffe Farms, Inc., in business since 1971, farms several contiguous farms in Muhlenberg County. Of the approximate 1980 acres it farms, the corporation owns about 250 acres, Reynolds Wickliffe, its president and principal shareholder, owns about 1000 acres, and Reynolds' father's estate, the J.W. Wickliffe Estate, owns 730 acres.

The Corporation had done business with the appellee, Owensboro Grain, since 1975, primarily thru Reynolds Wickliffe, representing the corporation, and Julian G. "Sonny" Hayden, employed by Owensboro Grain as a grain merchandiser.

In February, 1980, Wickliffe contacted Hayden by telephone and they orally agreed that the corporation would deliver 35,000 bushels of No. 2 white corn at $3.70 per bushel to Owensboro Grain between December 15, 1980, and January 31, 1981. The agreement was confirmed in a writing executed by Owensboro Grain and signed by Wickliffe on behalf of the corporation. The agreement, prepared by Owensboro Grain, was on its standard "fill in the blanks" form as to quantity, the grain commodity, the price, the routing, and shipment date. It was dated February 29, 1980, and identified the corporation as the accepting party. It contained no additional language of any significance other than the following part of a small print "force majeure" clause unilaterally favoring Owensboro Grain:

> All agreements, undertakings, obligations or liabilities hereunder, made or to be kept and performed by Owensboro Grain Company, are made and shall be kept and performed subject to and contin-

gent upon strikes, embargoes, fires, accidents, war restrictions, acts of God, or other conditions over which Owensboro Grain Company has no control and any inability on its part to keep, perform or satisfy the agreements, undertakings, obligations or liabilities hereunder caused or brought about by reason of any of the foregoing conditions shall, at the option of Owensboro Grain Company, render this contract null and void and the parties hereto shall have no further rights or obligations hereunder *   *   *

Owensboro Grain's principal business is dealing in the Chicago Board of Trade market area by purchasing grain for future delivery and by arranging an immediate sale of it to consumers or exporters at a margin of profit the market will competitively allow. In reference to his employer's business generally and to the instant transaction specifically, Hayden testified: " *   *   * my orders from the stockholders are to buy it, sell it, or hedge it. In this case you have to sell it because you can't hedge it."

In keeping with this practice, immediately after the contract was executed for Wickliffe to deliver the No. 2 white corn in the future, Owensboro Grain sold the 35,000 bushels, along with white corn similarly purchased from other farmers, to C.B. Fox, an exporter, at a price that guaranteed a 20 to 25 cent profit.

Unfortunately, in the summer of 1980, Muhlenburg County, together with the rest of western Kentucky, suffered a severe drought. Wickliffe's No. 2 white corn crop was severely damaged as were the crops of the other farmers in the area. Consequently, Wickliffe was unable to produce sufficient No. 2 white corn to fulfill its contract. In January, 1981, it delivered its entire crop, 18,718.57 bushels, to Owensboro Grain and was paid the agreed amount of $3.70 per bushel.

As a result of the short delivery, Owensboro Grain was required to purchase the amount of the shortage at $5.54 per bushel, the then market price, to satisfy its obligation to C.B. Fox entered into as a result of its futures contract with Wickliffe. The total amount spent to make up the bushels' deficit was $29,306.57. This amount was not withheld as a "set off" when it paid Wickliffe for the corn it managed to deliver, but $19,157.07 was withheld from amounts owed Wickliffe for purchase of corn and soybeans in January and February, 1982, by Owensboro Grain.

Wickliffe sued Owensboro Grain in the Daviess Circuit Court for the amount of the sale of the corn and soybeans. Owensboro Grain counterclaimed for its loss resulting from the partial non-delivery of No. 2 white corn in 1981. The trial court entered summary judgment in favor of Owensboro Grain on its counterclaim, later amended to include interest.

On appeal, as well as in the trial court, Wickliffe primarily relies on the defense of impossibility of performance caused by the severe drought, a "force majeure." We agree with the trial court that this defense is not applicable since the contract did not specify the land on which the corn was to be grown. Hence, we affirm.

There is no disagreement that the provisions of § 2–615 of the Uniform Commercial Code (U.C.C.) (1978), adopted as KRS 355.2–615, address the issue before us; also, there is no disagreement that there is no Kentucky law interpreting KRS 355.2–615, particularly with reference to U.C.C. § 2–615 comment 9 (1978), which in pertinent part is as follows:

> The case of a farmer who has contracted to sell crops *to be grown on designated land* may be regarded as falling within * * * this section, and he may be excused, when there is a failure of the specific crop. * * *

We have carefully considered Wickliffe's argument that the contract was one-sided or unconscionable because it contained no specific "force majeure" clause in its favor as it did in favor of Owensboro Grain and conclude the argument is without merit. We reach a like conclusion on Wickliffe's position that an "adhesion contract" resulted from the "fill in the blanks" form of the contract.

Wickliffe's principal argument is that the defense of impossibility provided by KRS 355.2–615 should be available to it due to the fact that it was contemplated by both parties that the No. 2 white corn was to be grown on its 2000 contiguous acres in Muhlenburg County and, that the adverse weather of the 1980 summer was a condition that was unforeseen and unforeseeable by the parties, and which rendered Wickliffe's performance impossible, and, pursuant to the statute, thereby excused his obligation to fully perform.

Nowhere in the contract, however, is there any reference to any specific acreage upon which the crop was to be grown. Wickliffe urges that KRS 355.2–202 permits contradiction of the written terms of the parties' intention by admission of proof of a contemporaneous oral agreement. This statute provides:

> Terms with respect to which the confirmatory memoranda of the parties agree or which are otherwise set forth in a writing intended by the parties as a final expression of their agreement with respect to such terms as are included therein may not be contradicted by evidence of any prior agreement or of a contemporaneous oral agreement but may be explained or supplemented
>
> (a) by course of dealing or usage of trade (KRS 355.1–205) or by course of performance (KRS 355.2–208); and
>
> (b) by evidence of consistent additional terms unless the court finds the writing to have been intended also as a complete and exclusive statement of the terms of the agreement.

This argument ignores the fact that to be admissible, the proof must come within the provisions of subparagraph (b) of the statute that requires the parol evidence be of additional terms consistent with the written contract. Here there is no consistency between Wickliffe's claim that the corn was to be produced off a particular part of a 2000 acre farm and a contract providing for nothing other than buying and selling 35,000 bushels of No. 2 white corn. There was no proof before the trial court, parol or otherwise, offered or proffered by Wickliffe, to establish that both parties contemplated and agreed upon a contract to sell the corn from any particularly designated acreage.

The undisputed admissible material facts before the trial court prove the ordinary "futures contract" of an agreement to buy and sell a quantity of grain at a given price per bushel, to be delivered at a future date, the purchaser thereafter arranging a "back to back" sale of the commodity. The sellers in such a transaction gamble the market price will not be greater at the time of delivery and the buyers gamble that it will not be lower. All Owensboro Grain was interested in was buying 35,000 bushels of No. 2 white corn from Wickliffe at $3.70 per bushel and nothing more. Its business was not to speculate either in the weather, crop yield or fluctuation of market price. It guaranteed its profit by selling immediately. Wickliffe's only interest was to sell it. It chose to contract to deliver the corn at a given price at a given future date and failed to do so.

Since there exists no issue of material fact and Owensboro Grain is entitled to judgment as a matter of law, the trial court committed no error in granting summary judgment on Owensboro Grain's counterclaims. *Shah v. American Synthetic Rubber Corp.*, Ky., 655 S.W.2d 489 (1983).

The Daviess Circuit Court summary judgment and amended summary judgment are affirmed.

All concur.

Notes

1. Suppose the corn had been planted on the seller's 2,000 acres at the time the contract was signed. Should the result be the same under UCC 2-613? See Bunge Corp. v. Recker, 519 F.2d 449 (8th Cir.1975) (no reference in contract to soybeans planted on particular land). Under either UCC 2-613 or 2-615(a), why must the seller establish an agreement to sell the corn from particularly designated acres?

2. If excuse is granted under UCC 2-613, the contract is avoided if the "loss is total." UCC 2-613(b). If the loss is partial or the goods no longer conform to the contract, the buyer is given a statutory option either to avoid the contract or to accept the goods with a price adjustment. UCC 2-613(b).

Under UCC 2-615, the adjustment process is more complicated. If delay or non-delivery of the entire performance is excused under UCC 2-615(a), the seller must give the buyer seasonable notification, UCC 2-615(c). The buyer then has the options set forth in UCC 2-616(1), including the right to "terminate and thereby discharge any unexecuted portion of the contract."

In excused cases of delay or non-delivery in "part," however, the seller "must allocate production and deliveries among his customers but may at his option include regular customers not then under contract as well as his own requirements for further manufacture" and this may be done in "any manner which is fair and reasonable." UCC 2–615(b). Note that the seller must now notify the buyer of the delay and the "estimated quota * * * made available for the buyer," UCC 2–615(c).

The buyer's option under UCC 2–616(1) with regard to an allocation "justified" under UCC 2–615(b) is either to terminate the contract or to "modify the contract by agreeing to take his available quota in substitution." But see UCC 2–616(2), imposing a duty on the buyer to act "within a reasonable time not exceeding thirty days." A seller who fails to allocate deliveries in a fair and reasonable manner cannot assert the defense of commercial impracticability under UCC 2–615. Roth Steel Products v. Sharon Steel Corp., 705 F.2d 134 (6th Cir.1983). A buyer who fails to exercise the statutory options within a reasonable time loses the opportunity to preserve an adjusted contract for future performance. See UCC 2–616(2); Federal Pants, Inc. v. Stocking, 762 F.2d 561 (7th Cir.1985) (contract lapses with respect to any deliveries affected).

#

Note: Failure of Seller's Source of Supply—Herein of the Force Majeure Clause

Section 261 of the Restatement, Second of Contracts provides a test for "discharge" that parallels UCC 2–615(a): "Where, after a contract is made, a party's performance is made impracticable without his fault by the occurrence of an event the non-occurrence of which was a basic assumption on which the contract was made, his duty to render that performance is discharged, unless the language or the circumstances indicate the contrary." This test is particularized for certain distinctive events. Thus, Sections 262 and 263 provide that the death or incapacity of a person whose existence or capacity is required for performance, or the destruction or deterioration of a thing necessary for performance, "makes performance impracticable" and, thus, are events "the non-occurrence of which was a basic assumption on which the contract was made." Compare UCC 2–613.

But what happens when a source of supply deemed necessary by the seller for performance of the seller's contract with the buyer fails? Under the Restatement, this is swept up under the general principle in Section 261 with a corollary that "a party generally assumes the risk of his own inability to perform his duty." Thus: "Even if a party contracts to render a performance that depends on some act by a third party, he is not ordinarily discharged because of a failure by that party because this is also a risk that is commonly understood to be on the obligor." See Section 261, Comment (e); Illustration 13.

An exception to this has been established in cases interpreting UCC 2–615(a). Thus, where a particular supplier is specified in the contract, assumed by the parties to be the exclusive source of supply, and fails to perform, the seller is excused, provided that it: (1) employed all "due measures" to assure that the agreed supplier would perform, and (2) turned over to the buyer any rights against the supplier corresponding to the seller's claim of excuse. UCC 2–615, Comment 5. In Zidell Explorations, Inc. v. Conval International, Ltd., 719 F.2d 1465 (9th Cir.1983), the court held that a failure to tender rights against the seller did not constitute a per se violation of the duty of good faith: Rather, the jury must determine in all the facts and circumstances whether the seller had satisfied its responsibility under Comment 5.

Frequently, a seller will attempt to protect itself against failures in a contemplated source of supply, whether agreed to be exclusive or not, by a force majeure clause. Such clauses vary in scope and content from industry to industry. A common form may look like this:

> "Neither party shall be liable for * * * loss, damage, claims or demands of any nature whatsoever due to delays or defaults in performance caused by impairment in any manner of seller's source of supply by (list causes or events) or by any other event, whether or not similar to the causes specified above * * *, which shall not be reasonably within the control of the party against whom the claim would otherwise be made."

When a force majeure clause is invoked, the following questions must be answered:

(1) Are the events specified and the relief sought within the scope of the clause;

(2) If so, was the event within the control or due to the fault or negligence of the party seeking relief;

(3) If not, did the party seeking relief exercise reasonable efforts after the event occurred to secure performance as agreed from some source, see Nissho-Iwai Co., Ltd. v. Occidental Crude Sales, Inc., 729 F.2d 1530 (5th Cir. 1984); and

(4) Is relief under a force majeure clause restricted in any way by UCC 2–615(a)? Put differently, if the parties clearly agree to expand the scope of excuse available under UCC 2–615(a), should the agreement be enforced? In InterPetrol Bermuda Ltd. v. Kaiser Aluminum International Corp., 719 F.2d 992 (9th Cir.1983), the answer was yes, subject to the requirement of conscionability and the good faith duty to seek an alternative source of performance. In addition, the court held that where excuse was based upon the force majeure clause rather than UCC 2–615, there was no requirement that the seller assign its rights against the defaulting source of supply to the buyer:

* * *

> We agree with the district court that comment 5 does not control in this case. Kaiser was not excused under § 2–615 and could not have been. Section 2–615 applies only when the events that made the performance of the contract impracticable were unforeseen at the time the contract was executed. See Taylor-Edwards Warehouse Co. v. Burlington Northern, Inc., 715 F.2d 1330, 1336 (9th Cir.1983). The extensive negotiations over the force majeure clause, discussed above, indicate that the parties not only foresaw the risk that Oxy Crude would default but also bargained over which party would bear the loss in that event. Accordingly, it would violate fundamental principles of

contract law, to use § 2–615 of the UCC to rewrite the contract to which the parties agreed. UCC § 2–615, comment 8 (§ 2–615 inapplicable if "contingency in question is * * * included among the business risks which are fairly to be regarded as part of the dickered terms. * * *").

Although there has been some doubt expressed as to whether the Code permits parties to bargain for exemptions broader than those available under § 2–615,[7] at least one circuit has concluded they may. See Eastern Airlines, Inc. v. McDonnell Douglas Corp., 532 F.2d 957, 990 (5th Cir.1976). See also Olson v. Spitzer, 257 N.W.2d 459 (S.D.1977) (exculpatory clause valid for defining events which excuse seller's performance). We agree with the Fifth Circuit. Comment 8 to § 2–615 plainly indicates that parties may "enlarge upon or supplant" § 2–615.[8] While exculpatory clauses phrased in general language should not be construed to expand excuses not provided for by the Code, circumstances surrounding a particular agreement may indicate that the parties intended to accord the seller an exemption broader than is available under the UCC.[9] Eastern Airlines, 532 F.2d at 990–91. We have already decided that the force majeure clause agreed to by Kaiser and InterPetrol was intended to excuse Kaiser prior to shipment of the crude from the Persian Gulf if Kaiser's supplier failed to deliver for any reason. We now hold that it was permissible for them to make such an agreement. Thus, if InterPetrol is to prevail on its claim that it succeeds to Kaiser's rights, it must do so on grounds apart from the Code.

California courts have read into force majeure clauses an implied covenant of good faith. Terry v. Atlantic Richfield Co., 72 Cal.App.3d 962, 964, 140 Cal.Rptr. 510, 511 (1977); see Milton v. Hudson Sales Corp., 152 Cal.App.2d 418, 427, 431, 313 P.2d 936, 942 (1957). This common law covenant of good faith is applicable to force majeure clauses such as the one agreed to by Kaiser and InterPetrol. If the common law requirement of good faith implies a requirement that a seller turn over to its buyer the seller's rights against a defaulting

7. See Hawkland, The Energy Crisis and Section 2–615 of the Uniform Commercial Code, 79 Com.L.J. 75 (1974).

8. Comment 8 to § 2–615 provides that:

"The provisions of this section are made subject to assumption of greater liability by agreement and such agreement is to be found not only in the expressed terms of the contract but in the circumstances surrounding the contracting, in trade usage and the like. Thus the exemptions of this section do not apply when the contingency in question is sufficiently foreshadowed at the time of contracting to be included among the business risks which are fairly to be regarded as part of the dickered terms, either consciously or as a matter of reasonable, commercial interpretation from the circumstances * * *. The exemption otherwise present through usage of trade under the present section may also be expressly negated by the language of the agreement. Generally express agreements as to exemptions designed to enlarge upon or supplant the provisions of this section are to be read in the light of mercantile sense and reason, for this section itself sets up the commercial standard for normal and reasonable interpretation and provides a minimum beyond which agreement may not go."

9. Force majeure clauses are, of course, limited by those sections of the Code prohibiting agreements which are manifestly unreasonable, in bad faith or unconscionable. See §§ 1–102(c), 1–203 and 2–302. See also Eastern Airlines, 532 F.2d at 991 n. 96; Transatlantic Financing Corp. v. United States, 363 F.2d 312, 315 n. 3 (D.C.Cir.1966).

supplier, then the district court erred in granting Kaiser's motion to dismiss.

InterPetrol failed to cite any instance under the common law, under circumstances similar to those of this case, where a buyer succeeded to the rights of the seller against a defaulting supplier.[10] The common law has not provided to a disappointed buyer the rights called for by InterPetrol.

We see no reason to now create a right which has not been recognized by the common law. There is a certain amount of economic wisdom in permitting a seller, consistent with the limiting provisions of the Code,[11] to contract out of liability. In a relatively free and fluid wholesale market, a seller should be entitled to utilize the power of his position to contract to his best advantage. That might include, as here, the extraction of a force majeure clause from a buyer. If the seller's supplier is not able because of market forces to require a similar provision in the agreement between seller and supplier, the result is that the seller is excused but the supplier is not. Yet we see no reason to award the windfall of recovery against the supplier to the buyer, who agreed to excuse the seller, instead of the seller, who was able to insist on better protections. When a trader is able to bargain for such favorable conditions, the natural trend will be for traders in the less favorable positions of buyer and supplier to move into the less competitive and therefore more contractually secure part of the market.

We find no reason to transfer the benefit of Kaiser's superior negotiating position to InterPetrol by giving InterPetrol Kaiser's rights against Trako and Oxy Crude. We do find that it serves the forces of natural market adjustments not to transfer Kaiser's rights. We therefore affirm the decision of the district court.[12]

* * *

[719 F.2d at 999–1001]

Note: *The ALCOA Case*

In Aluminum Company of America v. Essex Group, Inc., 499 F.Supp. 53 (W.D.Pa.1980), the facts of which are elaborated in the extract from *Goldberg,* infra at 205, the parties entered in 1967 into a 17 year contract under which ALCOA was to process alumina supplied by Essex into molten aluminum to be used by Essex in the manufacture of aluminum wire products. The long-term contract, called a "toll conversion service contract," was to be performed at a plant owned by ALCOA in Indiana. As part of the pricing mechanism, the parties agreed upon an escalation clause, developed by the noted economist Alan Greenspan, which varied with actual production costs at the plant. The clause was developed on the

10. InterPetrol did not rely on third-party beneficiary concepts at trial and did not attempt to raise the theory on appeal.

11. See supra note 9.

12. Our holding is based in part on the fact that Kaiser and InterPetrol were in relatively similar positions in the petroleum market. We have not considered circumstances involving traders from different levels in the hierarchy of the petroleum distribution network. We note too that InterPetrol was not obligated to other buyers to deliver oil it expected to get from Kaiser.

basis of past cost patterns and reflected projected cost variations that would give ALCOA a target profit of $.04 per pound.

In 1973, during the energy crisis, electricity costs at the Indiana plant began to escalate well beyond the projections in the price escalation clause. Even though the contract was profitable up to this time, it was estimated that ALCOA would lose $60 million over the balance of the contract due to a 500% variation between indexed and actual costs. At the same time, Essex was enjoying an apparent windfall gain by reselling converted aluminum for which it paid ALCOA $.364 per pound on the open market for $.733 per pound. When efforts by ALCOA to obtain an agreed price adjustment from Essex failed, ALCOA sued to obtain relief from the escalation clause and a reformation of the contract so that Essex must pay the actual costs incurred at the plant. Essex counterclaimed for breach damages and the issues were joined.

In an unprecedented decision, the court concluded that ALCOA was entitled to "some relief" from the changed circumstances and that the relief should be an equitable reformation of, rather than discharge from, the contract. The court, without the agreement of the parties, devised its own adjustment formula to fill the gap in the agreement. Essex appealed but the parties settled the dispute by agreement before the case could be heard.

Since the contract between ALCOA and Essex was characterized as for services rather than the sale of goods, UCC 2–615 was not directly applicable. The court, however, blended the doctrine of mutual mistake, commercial impracticability and frustration of purpose to achieve a result that, in part, could have been reached under UCC 2–615. The court's analysis was consistent with the four steps required to deal with UCC 2–615's "basic assumption" test:

First, did the seller assume by agreement a greater obligation than the degree of excuse normally available under UCC 2–615? If so, excuse should be denied. ALCOA's answer was no.

Second, if a greater obligation was not assumed, was the event that materialized a "contingency the non-occurrence of which was a basic assumption on which the contract was made?" If not, excuse should be denied. ALCOA's answer was yes: Both parties assumed at the time of contracting that the escalation clause was reasonable and the changed circumstances were not foreseen as likely to occur.

Third, if so, did the contingency make "performance as agreed ＊ ＊ ＊ impracticable?" If the answer is yes, then the seller is entitled to "some relief." ALCOA's answer was yes: A $60 million loss over the balance of a commercial contract made continued performance "commercially senseless and unjust," particularly where Essex was realizing "windfall" profits.

Fourth, if the seller is entitled to "some relief," what form should that relief take, discharge of the executory contract or preservation of the contract under a court-imposed price adjustment? The Code's answer is not clear. ALCOA's answer was to delete the existing price escalation clause, which had failed its intended purpose, and to impose in the gap a new price term which was thought to respond to the changed circumstances. For more discussion, see Speidel, *Court-Imposed Price Adjustments Under Long-Term Supply Contracts,* 76 Nw.U.L.Rev. 369 (1981).

ALCOA, to date, stands as the high (or low) water mark in disputes under UCC 2–615. Under circumstances comparable to ALCOA, i.e., rising costs of performance or sharply higher prices, other courts have denied any relief to the seller under UCC 2–615(a). See, Iowa Elec. Light and Power Co. v. Atlas Corp., 467 F.Supp. 129, 134 (N.D.Iowa 1978), rev'd on other grounds 603 F.2d 1301 (8th Cir.1979); Louisiana Power & Light v. Allegheny Ludlum Industries, 517 F.Supp. 1319 (E.D.La.1981); Mo. Public Serv. Co. v. Peabody Coal Co., 583 S.W.2d 721 (Mo.App.1979), cert. denied 444 U.S. 865, 100 S.Ct. 135, 62 L.Ed.2d 88 (1979). Under the opposite circumstances, i.e., a sharply reduced demand and, thus, lower prices for the product, buyers have fared no better than sellers. Although the courts, citing Comment 9, concede that UCC 2–615(a) protects buyers, little mercy has been shown to the buyer who, in the light of changed circumstances, has agreed to take goods at a quantity in excess of current needs and pay a price substantially in excess of market. See Northern Illinois Gas Co. v. Energy Cooperative, Inc., 122 Ill.App.3d 940, 78 Ill.Dec. 215, 225, 461 N.E.2d 1049, 1059 (1984), where the court said: " * * * (A)s any trader knows, the only certainty of the market is that prices will change. Changing and shifting markets and prices from multitudinous causes is endemic to the economy in which we live. Market forecasts by supposed experts are sometimes right, often wrong, and usually mixed. If changed prices, standing alone, constitute a frustrating event sufficient to excuse performance of a contract, then the law binding contractual parties to their agreements is no more." Accord: Northern Indiana Public Service Co. v. Carbon County Coal Company, 799 F.2d 265 (7th Cir.1986), where the court, speaking through Judge Posner, stated:

> Since impossibility and related doctrines are devices for shifting risk in accordance with the parties presumed intentions, which are to minimize the costs of contract performance, one of which is the disutility created by risk, they have no place when the contract explicitly assigns a particular risk to one party or the other. As we have already noted, a fixed-price contract is an explicit assignment of the risk of market price increases to the seller and the risk of market price decreases to the buyer, and the assignment of the latter risk to the buyer is even clearer where, as in this case, the contract places a floor under price but allows for escalation. If, as is also the case here, the buyer forecasts the market incorrectly and therefore finds himself locked into a disadvantageous contract, he has only himself to blame and so cannot shift the risk back to the buyer by invoking impossibility or related doctrines. * * * Since 'the very purpose of a fixed price agreement is to place the risk of increased costs on the promisor (and the risk of decreased costs on the promisee),' the fact that costs decrease steeply * * * cannot allow the buyer to walk away from the contract."

V. GOLDBERG, PRICE ADJUSTMENT IN LONG–TERM CONTRACTS, 1985 Wis.L.Rev. 527, 534–42.

* * *

III. ALCOA V. ESSEX *

A. *The Facts*

In 1967, Alcoa and Essex entered into a twenty year agreement in which Alcoa agreed to convert Essex's alumina into molten aluminum at Alcoa's Warrick, Indiana plant. Essex purchased its alumina from an Alcoa subsidiary under a second long-term contract. The trial judge insisted that the two contracts were separate and that by design Alcoa's left hand did not know what the right hand was doing. After conversion the molten aluminum would be loaded into crucibles owned by Essex and taken by truck to Essex's nearby fabricating plant built specifically to receive it. The contract was for 50 million pounds per year and included options for three additional blocks of 25 million pounds each. (By 1973, the parties had deleted the last two blocks.) Hence, the contract quantity at the time the litigation arose was 75 million pounds per year.

The initial contract price was 15 cents per pound, composed of a "demand charge" of five cents per pound,[22] and a "production charge". The latter included a fixed component of four cents per pound (which was the "profit" on the plant constructed to fulfill this contract) and three cents each for non-labor (primarily fuel) and labor costs. The former was indexed by the Industrial Component of the Wholesale Price Index and the latter by Alcoa's average hourly labor cost at the Warrick plant. The contract included a ceiling price of 65% of the price of a specified type of aluminum as reported in a trade journal; however, it did not specify a minimum price.

The demand charge was to be paid regardless of whether Essex took any aluminum. In effect, Essex "rented" a portion of Alcoa's Warrick plant at a fixed rate of $7.09 million per year ($4.09 million for the demand charge and $3 million for the fixed charge) and paid a service fee of six cents per pound that was indexed.

Problems arose following the large increase in fuel prices in 1973. In the ensuing years the market price of aluminum and the cost of producing it in Warrick increased far more rapidly than did the contract price. By 1979, Essex received aluminum from Alcoa under the contract at 36 cents per pound and resold some of it in the open market at 73 cents. Non-labor production costs rose from 5.8 cents to 22.7 cents in 1973–78, while the wholesale price index less than doubled. Alcoa attempted to renegotiate the price as early as 1975. In 1978, the dispute went to trial.

The trial court ruled in Alcoa's favor. Indexing non-labor production costs to the Wholesale Price Index was deemed a "mutual mistake"

---

* Aluminum Co. of America v. Essex Group, Inc., 499 F.Supp. 53 (W.D.Pa.1980).

22. Actually, this price was to be adjusted to cover increased construction costs at the Warrick plant when new blocks of aluminum capacity were ordered. The price of the first block (50 million pounds) was 5.27 cents per pound and the price for the second block was 5.82 cents per pound. These prices would remain constant for the life of the contract.

because it tracked those costs so badly. The court also accepted Alcoa's alternative theories of impracticability and frustration. The court reformed the contract, since rescission would result in a windfall for Alcoa and deprive Essex of the benefits of its long-term supply contract. The court rewrote the price term of the contract to include a minimum price assuring Alcoa a one cent per pound "profit".

The disputed contract represented only a small part of the business of Alcoa and Essex. Alcoa's sales and total assets in 1979 were each almost $5 billion.[23] By the time of trial, Essex had been acquired by United Technologies, another multi-billion dollar firm. Despite its losses on this contract, Alcoa's overall profits in 1979 were around $500 million; its rate of return on equity in 1978 exceeded 14 percent for the first time in 22 years.[24] This is not, clearly, a case in which a bad contract jeopardized the survival of a firm, as in *Westinghouse*. Rather, it is more instructive to view this contract as a poor performer in the firm's much larger portfolio of contracts, a portfolio which was performing very well overall.

B. The $75 Million Misunderstanding

The court placed considerable emphasis on the fact that projected losses from 1977 to 1987 were in the range of $75 million. This is one of those funny numbers that means nothing, but could end up as a fundamental part of the *Alcoa* doctrine, were one to emerge. Alcoa was excused because they stood to lose $75 million; we won't excuse X because it cannot prove that it will lose such a large amount. (As I will note below, the *Alcoa* judge distinguished another case on precisely this ground.) It is, therefore, useful to look at how the court determined the magnitude of the loss.

The "profits" are the revenue minus the actual production costs minus the demand charge (the 5 + cents per pound). The court assumed something (the decision does not make it quite clear what) about future costs and prices for the remaining life of the contract and then added them up. There are three obvious problems with this. First, the future profits are undiscounted. A dollar lost in 1984 is just as important as a dollar lost in 1979. Second, the estimates are based on guesses about the future course of prices; there is nothing wrong with guesses, but time has a way of transforming guesses into facts.[25] But these are quibbles. The most important point is that the estimate, even if done right, is irrelevant.

What does Alcoa lose if it must fulfill the contract? It loses the chance to sell the aluminum to someone else. That is the true measure of the loss, and in this case it is considerably greater than the figure cited by the judge. In the year the suit was brought the loss was over thirty cents per pound, over $20 million. The original cost of construc-

23. *The Fortune Directory,* Fortune, May 5, 1980, pp. 274, 276.

24. *Aluminum's Bosses Are Beaming,* Forbes, Nov. 27, 1978, at 40.

25. In fact, aluminum prices fell sharply in the early 1980's. That price decline undoubtedly facilitated settlement of the dispute.

tion of the plant is a red herring equivalent to "par value" for a stock, a vestige of the past with no economic content.

The error is important. In an earlier case,[26] the court refused to allow Gulf Oil to escape its obligation to deliver jet fuel under a five-year contract despite the fact that the price index utilized had inadequately tracked the course of oil prices. The court held that the cost data presented were insufficient to ascertain how much it cost Gulf to produce a gallon of jet fuel, and, therefore, Gulf had failed to prove that it had suffered losses on the contract. The *Alcoa* judge applied the "negative accounting profit" test in distinguishing this decision from *Alcoa.*

When faced with a claim of changed circumstances, courts or arbitrators should not look to accounting cost data to determine the merits of the claim. The relevant question is whether the difference between the contract price and the aggrieved party's next best option is large enough to warrant relief. An accounting cost or profit standard is an invitation to produce a lot of information with a low expected value.

C. Alcoa's Mistake

In retrospect, of course, Alcoa made a big mistake. However, the mistake singled out by the court to justify reformation of the contract was not the most important one. The failure of the price index to accurately measure the change in fuel prices accounted for only about ten to twelve cents of the difference between the contract price and the market price for aluminum in 1979 (that difference being over 30 cents). The main problem was that the contract did not track changing demand conditions and the demand for aluminum was soaring in the late 1970's.

Moreover, the contract was not designed to adjust to large changes in the overall price level. Sixty percent of the initial contract price (the demand charge plus the fixed "profit") was unadjusted for the life of the contract. A very simple example gives an indication of the type of problem this could cause. Suppose that the price level rises about 7% per year (doubling roughly every ten years); assume that the factors of production remain equally productive and that they continue to be used in the same proportions. The indexed production costs would then rise from six cents per pound to 24 cents per pound in the twentieth year. However, the remaining costs are unindexed, so the final contract price would rise only to $(24 + 9 =)$ 33 cents. To keep the real price of aluminum constant the contract price would have had to increase to 60 cents.

The relevant question is not whether Alcoa made what turned out to be a bad decision. They did. But was it a bad decision at the time they made it? The answer to that is less certain. When I began this

---

26. Eastern Air Lines v. Gulf Oil Corp., 415 F.Supp. 429 (S.D.Fla.1975).

project it seemed clear that Alcoa could have, and should have, done better. At a minimum, I thought, they should have indexed the remaining 60% of the costs. However, a more careful look leads me to believe that it is a much closer question.[30]

This long-term contract is in many respects similar to a lease or sale of part of Alcoa's Warrick production capacity to Essex. A fixed rental for long-term leases is not uncommon. Moreover, if one firm sells a durable asset to another, it is the rule rather than the exception, that the price is not to be readjusted after the sale has taken place. It can be argued, then, by analogy, that this component of the long-term contract that looks so much like a lease should also be at a fixed price.

If the contract price of a long-lived asset were to be readjusted to better track the market price, the parties would expend less resources today in pursuit of special information. If this benefit were great; we would expect the parties to incorporate price adjustment arrangements in their sales and leases of assets. However, the benefits will often be very small. Information regarding the future price level, for example, is already incorporated in the term structure of interest rates. It is not necessarily *accurate* information, ex post; however, the key question is whether it is *improvable* information, ex ante. Incorporating a general price index, therefore, need not result in reduced information costs.

The lease/sale analogy, however, has difficulties. A pure lease or sale is similar to a contract for a standardized commodity because further coordination between the two parties is unnecessary; the only issue is whether price adjustment reduces the initial price search. However, the more the outcomes depend upon future coordination by the parties, the less likely they will use a fixed price contract.[31] For example, shopping center leases in which the lessor engages in activities which generate business for the tenants will base at least part of the compensation on a percentage of the gross (which automatically provides for some price adjustment). If Alcoa were leasing the plant to Essex and allowing Essex to operate it, the fixed price arrangement would be routine. The fact that operation of the plant was in Alcoa's hands reduced the likelihood that a fixed price would be successful. The increased divergence between the contract price and Alcoa's best alternative would induce Alcoa to engage in strategic behavior, thereby reducing the value of the contract to both parties.

However, it is unlikely that indexing capital costs would result in a more accurate contract price. I would speculate that the pre-1973 experience would confirm that indexing this cost component to the

---

30. The question of whether Alcoa had made a mistake is unrelated to the court's finding of mutual mistake. I am only trying to determine whether the price adjustment mechanism in this contract was a reasonable one under the circumstances.

31. This discussion is highly speculative since I am only dimly aware of the adjustment mechanisms actually used in long-term leases. I should note that a common device is to use short-term agreements with fixed prices so that the price can be renegotiated on a regular basis. Such arrangements might also include an expectation, legal or otherwise, of renewal on reasonable terms.

general price level, construction costs, or any other conceivable cost-based measure would have resulted in a poorer fit between the market and contract price.[32]

Instead of using a cost-based price adjustment, the parties could have attempted to track market conditions by, for example, indexing to a particular aluminum price.[33] Using output prices to index is not without problems. First, other goods with published prices that are sufficiently close to the output that we are attempting to index might not exist. Second, the observable external prices are typically list prices, not transaction prices. If these diverge, the index suffers. It is plausible that the two would diverge in a concentrated industry like aluminum since list prices typically change more slowly in such industries.[34] Further, if the contract price were linked to the list price of a type of Alcoa's aluminum, then Alcoa would have an incentive, however modest, to set the list price in excess of the transaction price.

Even if list prices were accurate measures of transaction prices, a more fundamental difficulty remains. The parties do not necessarily confront the same external price. That is, the relevant price to each party is its opportunity cost—the net price it could get from the next best trading partner. In a market for a standardized commodity, the list price and these two opportunity costs would be roughly the same. However, in a long-term contract in which the parties deliberately isolate themselves from the external market, these three prices are more likely to diverge. Generally, the more isolated the contracting parties are from market alternatives, the poorer the relationship between these three prices is likely to be. Thus, while the parties might desire to index their agreement to a published market price, the very nature of a long-term contract makes it likely that the index price would not perform its function adequately. It is, therefore, not at all obvious that indexing the contract to changes in the published price of a particular type of output would be in the interest of the two parties.

In the instant case, Alcoa's opportunity cost is the net price it could receive by using the Warrick capacity to produce ingot for export to

32. Note that this is a different argument than the one accepted by the court. It emphasized how closely the wholesale price index had tracked one component of costs in the pre-contract period. I am claiming that there did not exist an index that would have closely tracked another, and larger, component of costs.

33. Note that in the previous paragraph I treated the capital cost as a historical cost. Alternatively, we could adjust to reflect the value of the fixed plant as it changes during the life of the structure. Thus, the cost of using the plant to fill this contract must include the opportunity cost of using the plant for other purposes (namely supplying aluminum to someone else). If the capital had a wide variety of other uses (for example, retail space or small vans), such an adjustment might be sensible. If, however, the capital was highly idiosyncratic, as in this case, its value would closely track changing market conditions. If these could be indexed accurately it would almost surely be unproductive to index the market value of capital either instead of or in addition to the market price of the output.

34. For example, in 1979 Business Week reported list prices for ingot of 66 cents per pound while the spot price was 75 cents. This is a bit misleading, however, because of the existence of price controls at the time. *Aluminum Wastes No Time Raising Prices*, BUS.WK., Oct. 15, 1979, at 36.

other customers. Essex's opportunity cost is the price of delivered aluminum ingot. There is no a priori reason to believe that these will be close to each other. However, for an index to work it is not necessary that the prices be close, only that they move together over time. Whether these two opportunity costs (and the market price for aluminum ingot) move together over time is an empirical question which I intend to explore in a later paper.

Essex chose to incorporate the output price information in the form of a maximum price. Alcoa, however, was not willing to pay (by agreeing to a lower initial contract price) for a price minimum. The failure to do so might well have been a mistake ex ante, but it is at least plausible that a ceiling indexed to published prices would be more valuable to Essex than a similarly indexed floor would have been to Alcoa. Alcoa's superior knowledge of the aluminum industry might make Essex suspicious of the manner in which costs were indexed. A bias in favor of Alcoa, because of Alcoa's superior knowledge, would make a bound on the index relatively more valuable to Essex.

Conceivably, therefore, Alcoa's failure to index plant costs or include a minimum price was not an error ex ante. Looking at the new contract may provide some insight on this issue. We know that the parties rejected the judicially imposed minimum price based on ex ante accounting costs. But we do not know whether that was a reason for rejection and we do not know what replaced it. I would speculate that the new contract includes a minimum and that the minimum depends upon output prices. If so, that would suggest that Alcoa had erred initially.

IV. RESOLUTION OF PRICE ADJUSTMENT DISPUTES

Suppose that contracting parties assign the task of resolving price adjustment disputes to an outsider (a court or an arbitrator). The outsider can be asked to resolve two very different questions: (a) have conditions changed sufficiently to justify relief; and (b) what form should relief take—what will the new price (or price formula) be? Since the parties bear the costs of producing the evidence, they must reckon the expected costs of producing evidence on production costs, accounting profits, market prices, opportunity costs, and so forth, and weigh these against the expected benefits (in terms of reducing the costs arising from the divergence of contract price from market price). These evidentiary costs provide the backdrop for subsequent renegotiation. Thus, for example, if a standard required that one party spend a lot to produce evidence to forestall price revision, its opposite party could use those potential costs as a bargaining chip in renegotiation.

For determining whether relief is justified, accounting cost data of the sort relied upon by the Alcoa judge are largely beside the point. The relevant question is whether the difference between the contract price and the aggrieved party's next best option is large enough to warrant relief. The requisite price differential would vary across contracts. There is no "magic number": if price goes up by at least

$X\%$ or losses total at least $\$Y$, adjust the price. A large divergence between the market and contract price for a standardized commodity, for example, would have little adverse effect on the expected value of a contract; it would, therefore, be unlikely that the parties would benefit from revision. Conversely, if a modest price divergence would generate considerable joint costs, revision could be effective. The problem is complicated by the fact that making relief easy to obtain generates additional joint costs as well. Rational parties might easily find that the potential benefits from price revision come at too high a cost.

This is especially true if there is no obvious standard for determining a new contract price. My initial presumption was that if a reasonable measure of the output price were available, the parties would want the arbitrator to use this to guide his decision. Further consideration has led me to conclude that this might not be very helpful. A simple example illustrates the problem. Suppose that when the contract was written Alcoa would have received 10 cents a pound for its aluminum on the open market, Essex would have paid 20 cents per pound, and the contract price was fifteen cents. When the case is litigated, Alcoa could sell at 50 cents and Essex buy at 70, and the contract price is 35 cents. What should the contract price be? Even if this information were costlessly produced and absolutely accurate, are the parties better off putting the decision in the hands of an arbitrator? What decision rule would they want him to apply? When the opportunity costs of the buyer and seller diverge, it is not at all clear what should guide the arbitrator in setting a new price. Thus, the possible divergence not only impairs the value of a published price as an index, but makes it more difficult for the parties to rely upon outsiders (arbitrators and judges) to revise the price. [Some footnotes omitted.]

* * *

INTERNATIONAL MINERALS & CHEMICAL CORP. v. LLANO, INC.

United States Court of Appeals, Tenth Circuit, 1985.
770 F.2d 879.

* * *

[International (IMC) agreed to purchase natural gas from Llano under a ten year contract, scheduled to terminate on June 30, 1982. IMC sought a declaratory judgment that it was excused from its obligation to "take and pay" for an agreed minimum quantity of natural gas during the last eighteen months of the contract, due to more stringent regulation by the New Mexico Environmental Improvement Board of particle emissions from existing combustion evaporators in IMC's plant. Under EIB Regulation 508, IMC was ultimately required to shut down the combustion evaporators, which had consumed approximately 60% of its natural gas requirements. Llano counterclaimed for $3,564,617.12, the amount that it claimed was due under the contract for gas for which IMC should have paid.

The trial court held: (1) UCC 2–615 was not applicable to buyers unless the contract was "conditioned on a definite and specific venture or assumption. * * *"; and (2) The "force majeure" and "adjustment of minimum bill" clauses in the contract, Paragraphs 15 and 16 set out below, did not excuse performance unless it became absolutely impossible or illegal to purchase the minimum amount of gas. On the facts, the trial court denied relief to IMC and concluded that IMC was liable for the contract price for gas it should have taken, even though Llano had been able to sell the gas elsewhere for a higher price.

IMC appealed and the court limited its consideration to whether IMC was excused under either UCC 2–615 or Paragraphs 15 and 16 of the contract.]

BARRETT, CIRCUIT JUDGE. *This court considers whether IMC was excused under either UCC § 2-615 or ¶'s 15+16 of K.*

* * *

The pertinent portions of the contract are as follows:

Now, therefore, in consideration of the premises and of the mutual covenants and agreements hereinafter set forth, the parties do hereby bargain, contract and agree as follows:

1. *SUPPLY OF NATURAL GAS:* Subject to the terms and conditions of this Contract, Seller will sell and deliver to Buyer and Buyer will take, purchase and pay for the entire fuel requirements of Buyer's Plant, provided that Buyer may at its option procure and maintain a supply of standby fuel to be used only to such extent as may be necessary when the gas supply from Seller may be interrupted or curtailed, as hereinafter provided, and in such other amounts as may be necessary from time to time to test such standby facilities and fuel.

* * *

6. *DELIVERY REQUIREMENTS:* During the term of this Contract, unless Seller agrees in writing to the contrary, the minimum daily deliveries that Seller shall make to Buyer and Buyer shall take from Seller shall be 4800 million BTU's per day except as hereafter provided. The maximum daily deliveries that Seller shall be required to make to Buyer shall be 133% of the average daily requirements of Buyer's Plant for the preceding 365 days provided, however, Seller shall at no time be required to deliver in excess of 6400 million BTU's per day unless Seller agrees in writing to the contrary.

Limits on how much Seller is required to deliver

Buyer does not contemplate reducing its operations, but on the contrary contemplates the increase thereof from the present daily requirements. In order to meet unanticipated contingencies, it is agreed that in the event Buyer during the term of this Contract reduces its operation by closing a portion of its plant, it shall have the right upon six months notice in writing to reduce the minimum requirements to a figure equal to 70% of the stated minimum of 4800 million BTU's per day. In the event of such reduction in minimum requirements, Seller's price to Buyer then in effect under

Buyer, upon 6 mos written notice can reduce min. delivery to 70%

but price goes up! (but not in excess of market)

the terms hereof shall be increased by ½¢ per million BTU's, but not in excess of the highest price for a like quantity of gas then being paid by any potash company in the area.

7. *MINIMUM ANNUAL PURCHASE:* During the term of this Contract, commencing with the first year, Buyer agrees to take from Seller a volume of gas having a BTU content of not less than 355 times the minimum daily deliveries specified in Section 6 hereof. Buyer agrees to pay Seller for such minimum volume of gas at the price set forth in Section 5 hereof provided that if Buyer fails during any calendar year to take such minimum volume of gas, then the deficiency between the volume actually taken and Buyer's minimum purchase obligation shall be paid at the price in effect during the calendar year in which such deficiency occurs.

Billing for any payment due by reason of a deficiency in Buyer's takings of gas hereunder during a particular calendar year shall be included on the bill rendered to Buyer for gas delivered to Buyer during the month of December in the calendar year in which such deficiency occurred and payment therefore shall be made in the manner provided for monthly bills in Section 11 hereof. Failure on the part of Seller to so bill Buyer for any such deficiency payment shall not constitute a waiver hereof by Seller.

* * *

15. *FORCE MAJEURE:* Either party shall be excused for delay or failure to perform its agreements and undertakings, in whole or in part, when and to the extent that such failure or delay is occasioned by fire, flood, wind, lightning, or other acts of the elements, explosion, act of God, act of the public enemy, or interference of civil and/or military authorities, mobs, labor difficulties, vandalism, sabotage, malicious mischief, usurpation of power, depletion of wells, freezing or accidents to wells, pipelines, permanent closing of Buyer's operations at its Eddy County mine and refinery, after not less than six (6) months notice thereof to Seller, or other casualty or cause beyond the reasonable control of the parties, respectively, which delays or prevents such performance in whole or in part, as the case may be; provided, however, that the party whose performance hereunder is so affected shall immediately notify the other party of all pertinent facts and take all reasonable steps promptly and diligently to prevent such causes if feasible to do so, or to minimize or eliminate the effect without delay. It is understood and agreed that settlement of strikes or other labor disputes shall be at the sole discretion of the party encountering the strike or dispute.

[handwritten: Reasonable Notice required]

Nothing contained herein, however, shall be construed as preventing the Buyer from discontinuing the operation of the plant for such periods of time as may be required by Buyer to perform necessary overhaul operations on plant properties or to accomplish preventative maintenance operations on such plant properties, which the Buyer may determine as necessary to safeguard its investment in the plant.

16. *ADJUSTMENT OF MINIMUM BILL:* In the event that Seller is unable to deliver or Buyer is unable to receive gas as provided in this Contract for any reason beyond the reasonable control of the parties, or in the event of force majeure as provided in Section 15 hereof, an appropriate adjustment in the minimum purchase requirements specified in Section 7 shall be made.

(Pl.Exh. 3, Def.Exh. C8b).

The contract may be characterized as a requirements contract, with an important limitation: Pursuant to paragraph 6, the buyer (IMC) is obligated to take, at a minimum, a daily average of 4800 million BTU's of gas. Pursuant to paragraph 7, if the buyer does not take this minimum amount, the buyer is obligated to pay for the minimum amount of gas anyway. These provisions are known in the industry as "take or pay" provisions, the purpose of which is to compensate the seller for being ready at all times to deliver the maximum amount of gas to the buyer and to eliminate the risk that the seller would face in a pure requirements contract were the buyer's requirements to drop too low. *See, e.g., Utah International, Inc. v. Colorado—Ute Electric Association,* 425 F.Supp. 1093 (D.Colo.1976) ("take or pay" coal purchase contract); *Mobile Oil Corporation v. Tennessee Valley Authority,* 387 F.Supp. 498 (N.D.Ala.1974) ("take or pay" electricity contract). The harshness of the "take or pay" provisions in this contract are to some extent ameliorated by the "force majeure" provision of paragraph 15 and the "adjustment of minimum bill" provision of paragraph 16; paragraphs 15 and 16 are discussed below.

* * *

On a fundamental level, this case is one of contract construction. Our primary objective, as always, in the construction or interpretation of a contract is to ascertain the intention of the parties. *Schultz & Lindsay Construction Co. v. State,* 93 N.M. 534, 494 P.2d 612, 613 (1972); *Yankee Atomic Electric Company v. New Mexico and Arizona Land Company,* 632 F.2d 855, 858 (10th Cir.1980) (interpreting New Mexico law.) We assume that the parties intended a reasonable interpretation of the language. *Smith v. Tinley,* 100 N.M. 663, 674 P.2d 1123, 1125 (1984). Accordingly, the legal context in which the contract was made will be relevant. As mentioned above, paragraphs 15 and 16 ameliorate the harshness of the "take or pay" provisions in that either party's duty of performance may be excused upon the occurrence of certain contingencies. As we examine the language of paragraphs 15 and 16, an appropriate area to look for guidance is the common law doctrine of impossibility/impracticability, codified at Section 2–615 of New Mexico's Uniform Commercial Code (N.M.Stat.Ann. § 55–2–615 (1978)), which was the law in New Mexico at the time the parties contracted and which remains the law today. While it is a basic premise of both

[handwritten margin notes: "This is a Requirements K but a minimum is required"; "'Take or Pay' Provisions"; "Primary objective is always to ascertain the intention of parties"; "legal context is relevant"; "§2–615 is a helpful guide in looking at paragraphs 15 & 16"]

Section 2–615 and the Uniform Commercial Code in general that the parties may allocate risks and penalties between themselves in any manner they choose, N.M.Stat.Ann. §§ 55–1–102 and 55–2–615 (1978), the Code and the common law upon which it is based remain a significant backdrop.

We first consider the effect of paragraph 15, the "force majeure" provision, on IMC's duty of performance under the circumstances of this case. Specifically, Paragraph 15 provides that either party is excused from performance if failure or delay in performance is "occasioned" by such events as fire, flood, act of God, interference of civil and/or military authorities, etc. The party seeking to be excused from performance must provide the other party with immediate notice of all pertinent facts and take all reasonable steps to prevent the occurrence. It also appears that the seller is entitled to six months notice before the buyer can be excused. We agree with the trial court that paragraph 15 does not operate to excuse IMC, although our conclusion is based on a somewhat different rationale. First, IMC's notice to Llano was inadequate in that no reasons were given as to why gas consumption would be decreased. Adequate notice was required to trigger the protections of the provision. Second, even if we assume *arguendo* that Rule 508 prevented IMC from taking the gas, Rule 508 would still pose no obstacle to IMC's ability to pay. Since this is a "take or pay" contract, the buyer can perform in either of two ways. It can either (1) take the minimum purchase obligation of natural gas (and pay) or (2) pay the minimum bill. It is settled law that when a promisor can perform a contract in either of two alternative ways, the impracticability of one alternative does not excuse the promisor if performance by means of the other alternative is still practicable. *Ashland Oil And Refining Co. v. Cities Service Gas Co.*, 462 F.2d 204, 211 (10th Cir.1972); *Glidden Company v. Hellenic Lines, Limited*, 275 F.2d 253, 257 (2d Cir.1960); Restatement (Second) of Contracts § 261, comment f (1981). Paragraph 15 does not compel a different result; it would at most excuse IMC from its duty to "take," not from its duty to "pay."

Paragraph 16, the "minimum bill" provision, however, affords the buyer additional protection. It provides that, in the event the buyer is "*unable to receive gas as provided in the Contract for any reason beyond the reasonable control* of the parties * * *" (emphasis added), then "an appropriate adjustment in the minimum purchase requirements specified in Section [paragraph] 7 shall be made." Paragraph 7, in turn, provides for a minimum bill based on the difference between the buyer's minimum purchase obligation and the gas actually taken. It follows that an adjustment of the buyer's minimum purchase requirements made pursuant to paragraph 16 would have the effect of lowering the buyer's minimum bill under paragraph 7. Llano's contention that paragraph 16 provides for a reduction in IMC's minimum purchase obligation but not its minimum bill obligation (Appellee's Brief at 4) is thus quickly disposed of.

The determinative question, then, is: Did the promulgation of Rule 508 constitute an event beyond the reasonable control of IMC that rendered IMC "unable" to receive its minimum amount of gas under the contract?

A simplistic, literal interpretation of the word "unable" would, in our view, be inappropriate and lead to absurd results: IMC could never be "unable" to take Llano's gas; IMC could always take the gas and vent it into the air, even if its facilities were completely destroyed. The word "unable" appears here as a term in a contract, prepared by businessmen and attorneys; thus, it is appropriate to construe the term in light of the common law as it existed in New Mexico when the contract was entered into. For our purposes, then, "unable" is synonymous with "impracticable," as that term is used in the common law and in Section 2–615.

The term "impracticable" has, over the years, acquired a fairly specific meaning. Although earlier cases required that performance be physically impossible before the promisor would be excused, strict impossibility is no longer required. *See* Restatement of Contracts (Second) § 261, comment d (1981). The New Mexico Supreme Court has described the doctrine of impracticability as follows:

> Regarding the meaning of "impossibility" as used in the rules that excuse the non-performance of contracts, it is stated:
>
> > "As pointed out in the Restatement of Contracts, the essence of the modern defense of impossibility is that the promised performance was at the making of the contract, or thereafter became, impracticable owing to some extreme or unreasonable difficulty, expense, injury, or loss involved, rather than that it is scientifically impossible. * * * The important question is whether an unanticipated circumstance has made performance of the promise vitally different from what should reasonably have been within the contemplation of both parties when they entered into the contract. If so, the risk should not fairly be thrown upon the promisor." *Wood v. Bartolino,* 48 N.M. 175, 146 P.2d 883, 886, (1944), *quoting* 6 Williston on Contracts, § 1931.

Cf. Gulf Oil Corporation v. Federal Power Commission, 563 F.2d 588, 599 (3d. Cir.1977), *cert. denied* 434 U.S. 1062, 98 S.Ct. 1235, 55 L.Ed.2d 762 (1978) ("The crucial question in applying that doctrine to any given situation is whether the cost of performance has in fact become so excessive and unreasonable that the failure to excuse performance would result in grave injustice. * * * "); *Mineral Park Land Co. v. Howard,* 172 Cal. 289, 156 P. 458, 460 (1916) ("a thing is impracticable when it can only be done at an excessive and unreasonable cost").

Performance will be excused when made impracticable by having to comply with a supervening governmental regulation. N.M.Stat.Ann. § 55–2–615 (1978); Restatement of Contracts (Second) § 264 (1981). Thus, for example, in the case of *Kansas City, Missouri v. Kansas City, Kansas,* 393 F.Supp. 1 (W.D.Mo.1975), the court held that the defendant city's obligation to accept the plaintiff city's sewage was excused by the enactment of the Federal Water Pollution Control Act Amendments of 1972. The federal act imposed new requirements with regard to the treatment of sewage that was discharged into the Missouri River; the court found that the added expense of such treatment would impose a significant, unreasonable burden on the defendant. *Accord City of Vernon v. City of Los Angeles,* 45 Cal.2d 710, 290 P.2d 841 (1955).

Inasmuch as there was no technically suitable way for IMC to comply with the EIB's Regulation 508 without shutting down the Ozarks and changing to the SOP, with the concomitant decrease in natural gas consumption, we hold that the adjustment provision of paragraph 16 of the contract was triggered. IMC was unable, for reasons beyond its reasonable control, to receive its minimum purchase obligation of natural gas between January 1, 1981 and June 30, 1982; thus, the minimum bill should have been adjusted appropriately. IMC should not be required to pay for any natural gas it did not take under the contract.

Llano contends that there was no supervening legal impracticability in this case because IMC was not required to be in final compliance until December 31, 1984, and that IMC cooperated with the EIB and came into compliance too early. The argument here is that, notwithstanding the interim standards contained in the schedules of compliance, IMC should have stalled in its negotiations with the state regulatory agency, which would have resulted in the pollution of air until the last minute. We must reject this contention on two grounds: First, as a matter of policy, individuals and corporations who cooperate with local regulatory agencies and comply with the letter and spirit of legally proper regulations, environmental or otherwise, are to be encouraged. Stalling tactics are not regarded favorably. Second, as a matter of law, government policy need not be explicitly mandatory to cause impracticability. Thus, for example, in *Eastern Air Lines, Inc. v. McDonnell Douglas Corporation,* 532 F.2d 957 (5th Cir.1976), an aircraft manufacturer was excused from its contractual obligation to deliver commercial jet airliners on certain scheduled dates because it had voluntarily complied with government requests to expedite production of military equipment needed for the war in Vietnam. Similarly, in the maritime context, shipowners have been excused from contractual obligations because they have anticipated governmental intrusion. *The Kronprinzessin Cecilie,* 244 U.S. 12, 37 S.Ct. 490, 61 L.Ed. 960 (1917) (German ship was justified in returning to New York rather than completing a voyage to Great Britain and France on the eve of the outbreak of hostilities in World War I); *The Clavaresk,* 264 F. 276 (2d Cir.1920) (shipowner may anticipate and need not resist government requisition of his ship for wartime service in order to be excused from performance of a charter agreement). There is, we recognize, a limit to the extent to which an individual can seek refuge in the context of a case such as this by cooperating with the government: "any action by the party claiming excuse which causes or colludes in inducing the governmental action preventing his performance would be in breach of good faith and would destroy his exemption." Official Comment 10, N.M.Stat.Ann. § 55–2–615 (1978). Here, Regulation 508 was promulgated by the EIB as part of New Mexico's State Implementation Plan mandated by the Clean Air Act. Regulation 508's existence and its enforcement mechanism is designed to eliminate pollution of the environment, thus serving the public health and welfare. IMC's recognition of the public benefit goal and its willingness to cooperate in eliminating pollution can hardly be termed improper collusion.

Compliance was Not improper Collusion!

For the reasons described above, the judgment of the trial court in favor of Llano is reversed. The case is remanded with direction that the court enter a declaratory judgment in accordance with this opinion.

Judgment for Llano is reversed

Problem 6–2

Softstuff, a coal producer, manufactures coke for steel production. Coke is made by subjecting coal to extreme heat in specially constructed ovens or batteries. Bitum is a steel maker. In May, 1978, the parties began to negotiate over a 10 year coke supply contract. It was agreed that Bitum was to take and pay for 20,000 tons of coke per month. This was, in effect, Softstuff's output from its coke batteries. In addition to agreements on quality, the parties agreed that Bitum was to pay a base price of $42 per ton, subject to escalation based upon externally compiled cost indices. These indices reflected the average costs incurred by coke producers rather than the actual costs of Softstuff's operation.

At the time of negotiation, the demand for coke was strong and the market price per ton was $41. The parties discussed the question of price stability over a ten year period. Softstuff "hoped" that strong demand would continue but Bitum was more pessimistic. Bitum proposed and Softstuff rejected a clause giving Bitum the option to terminate the contract at the end of any year wherein the market price of coke was 30% lower than the adjusted contract price for three or more months. There was no trade usage on price adjustment and the parties had not done business with each other before.

After further negotiations, the parties concluded a contract which, among other things, contained the following clause:

EXCUSE FOR BUYER

1. If because of Buyer's reduced blast furnace production, Buyer's requirements for coke cease or are reduced to a point where it is not practical for Buyer to purchase coke pursuant to this agreement, Buyer shall be released from its future obligations hereunder for the period of such cessation or reduction without any liability whatsoever upon Buyer giving Seller 90 days advance written notice.

2. Buyer's failure to comply or delay in compliance with the terms and conditions of this agreement shall be excused if due to any of the following which render performance commercially impracticable: act of God, fire, flood, strike, work stoppage, labor dispute, accident or mill interruption, complete or partial blast furnace relining, temporary

failure of supply of iron ore, pellets or flux, any action by governmental authority, including ecological authorities, or any other cause beyond Buyer's reasonable control.

On January 15, 1979, Softstuff shipped and Bitum accepted and paid for the first 20,000 ton installment of coke at the base contract price. This pattern of performance continued under January 15, 1983, when Bitum notified Softstuff in writing that due to a "collapse in the market for coke and steel products" the contract is "hereby terminated in 90 days." At that time, the escalated contract price for coke was $50 per ton. The market price for comparable coke, however, had dropped to $25 per ton and the demand for Bitum's steel products had dropped 60% since the time of contracting. After an unsuccessful effort to negotiate a modification, Bitum reaffirmed that, after the 90 days period had expired, it would not accept any more coke under the contract.

In August, 1983, Softstuff sued Bitum for breach of contract. The sole question for you is whether Bitum is excused from performance under either paragraph of the EXCUSE FOR BUYER clause.

SECTION 3. ENFORCEABILITY OF AGREED ADJUSTMENTS

The parties to a dispute over contract performance frequently settle the matter by agreement. In one type of settlement, claims are adjusted, payments are made and the contract is discharged. These settlements are sometimes described as an accord and satisfaction. In another type of settlement, contract duties are adjusted in a bargain under which performance is to continue. These settlements are called contract modifications. In both, the enforceability of the settlement may be subsequently attacked on the grounds of fraud, lack of consideration or duress. You have encountered both types in the course on contracts.

In this Section we will focus upon agreed modifications made in response to changed circumstances. The key provision is UCC 2–209.

Problem 6–3

A. Suppose, in Problem 6–2 supra, that before Bitum attempted to terminate the contract under the Excuse clause, Bitum explained the changing market situation and its impact on Bitum to Softstuff and requested Softstuff to consider and to negotiate over a proposed modification of the contract. Bitum suggested that the contract be adjusted in either of two ways for the remaining six years: (1) Keep the pricing structure but permit Bitum to order "requirements;" or (2) Keep the quantity term but permit Bitum to pay the market price of coke at the time of delivery. Bitum argued that S had, at a minimum, a duty to negotiate in good faith over the proposed adjustment, citing UCC 2–209, 1–203, 2–103(1)(b), and Comments 6 & 7 to 2–615. Softstuff declined, contending that unless the contract required it (and it did not), there was no duty to negotiate PERIOD. S cited Missouri Public Serv. Co. v. Peabody Coal Co., 583 S.W.2d 721 (Mo.App.1979), cert. denied 444 U.S. 865, 100 S.Ct. 135, 62 L.Ed.2d 88 (1979), where the court concluded: "Where an enforceable, untainted contract exists, refusing modification of price and seeking specific performance of valid covenants does not constitute bad faith or breach of contract * * *."

How should B respond?

B. Suppose, after negotiations, Softstuff agreed to substitute "market price" for escalated price for the duration of the contract. Thereafter, Softstuff determined that market price would not cover its production costs and claimed that the modification was not enforceable, citing UCC 2–209(1). What result? See the next case.

ROTH STEEL PRODUCTS v. SHARON STEEL CORP.

United States Court of Appeals, Sixth Circuit, 1983.
705 F.2d 134.

[In November, 1972, Roth contracted to purchase 200 tons of "hot rolled" steel per month from Sharon through December, 1973. The price was $148 per ton. Sharon also "indicated" that it could sell "hot rolled" steel on an "open schedule" basis for $140 and discussed the "probability" that Sharon could sell 500 tons of "cold rolled" steel at prices varying with the type ordered. At that time, the steel industry was operating at 70% of capacity, steel prices were "highly competitive" and Sharon's quoted prices to Roth were "substantially lower" than Sharon's book price for steel. In early 1973, market conditions changed dramatically due to the development of an attractive export market and an increased domestic demand for steel. During 1973 and 1974, the steel industry operated at full capacity, steel prices rose and nearly every producer experienced substantial delays in filling orders. In March, 1973, Sharon notified all purchasers, including Roth, that it was discontinuing price concessions given in 1972. After negotiations, the parties agreed that Roth would pay the agreed price until June 30, 1973 and a price somewhere between the agreed price and Sharon's published prices for the balance of 1973. Roth was initially reluctant to agree to this modification, but ultimately agreed "primarily because they were unable to purchase sufficient steel elsewhere to meet their production requirements." Sharon was supplying one-third of Roth's requirements and all other possible suppliers were "operating at full capacity and * * * were fully booked." The parties proceeded under this modification during the balance of 1973, although Sharon experienced difficulties in filling orders on time. During 1974, the parties did business on an entirely different basis. Roth would order steel, Sharon would accept the order at the price "prevailing at the time of shipment." During 1974 and 1975, Sharon's deliveries were chronically late, thereby increasing the price to Roth in a rising market. Roth, however, acquiesced in this pattern because it believed Sharon's assurances that late deliveries resulted from shortages of raw materials and the need for equitable allocation among customers and because there was "no practical alternative source of supply." This acquiescence was jolted in May, 1974 when Roth learned that Sharon was allocating substantial quantities of rolled steel to a subsidiary for sale at premium prices. After several more months of desultory performance on both sides, Roth sued Sharon for breach of contract, with special emphasis upon the modified contract for 1973. Sharon raised several defenses, including impracticability and, in the alternative, the agreed modification. The district court, after a long trial, held, *inter alia*, that Sharon was not excused from the 1973 contract on the grounds of impracticability and that the modification was unenforceable. A judgment for $555,968.46 was entered for Roth.

On appeal, the court of appeals affirmed the district court's decision on the impracticability, modification and other issues, but remanded the case for factual findings on whether Roth gave Sharon timely notice of breach. On the impracticability defense under UCC 2–615(a), the court held that "Sharon's inability to perform was a result of its policy accepting far more orders than it was capable of fulfilling, rather than a result of the existing shortage of raw materials." In refusing to enforce the modification of the 1973 contract, the court had this to say.]

CELEBREZZE, SENIOR CIRCUIT JUDGE.

* * *

C. In March, 1973, Sharon notified its customers that it intended to charge the maximum permissible price for all of its products; accordingly, all price concessions, including those made to the plaintiffs, were to be rescinded effective April 1, 1973. On March 23, 1973, Guerin [Roth's vice pres.] indicated to Metzger [Sharon's sales manager] that the plaintiffs considered the proposed price increase to be a breach of the November, 1972 contract. In an effort to resolve the dispute, Guerin met with representatives of Sharon on March 28, 1973 and asked Sharon to postpone any price increases until June or July, 1973. Several days later, Richard Mecaskey, Guerin's replacement, sent a letter to Sharon which indicated that the plaintiffs believed that the November, 1972 agreement was enforceable and that the plaintiffs were willing to negotiate a price modification if Sharon's cost increases warranted such an action. As a result of this letter, another meeting was held between Sharon and the plaintiffs. At this meeting, Walter Gregg, Sharon's vice-president and chairman of the board, agreed to continue charging the November, 1972 prices until June 30, 1973 and offered, for the remainder of 1973, to charge prices that were lower than Sharon's published prices but higher than the 1972 prices. Although the plaintiffs initially rejected the terms offered by Sharon for the second half of 1973, Mecaskey reluctantly agreed to Sharon's terms on June 29, 1973.

Before the district court, Sharon asserted that it properly increased prices because the parties had modified the November, 1973 contract to reflect changed market conditions. The district court, however, made several findings which, it believed, indicated that Sharon did not seek a modification to avoid a loss on the contract. The district court also found that the plaintiffs' inventories of rolled steel were "alarmingly deficient" at the time modification was sought and that Sharon had threatened to cease selling steel to the plaintiffs in the second-half of 1973 unless the plaintiffs agreed to the modification. Because Sharon had used its position as the plaintiffs' chief supplier to extract the price modification, the district court concluded that Sharon had acted in bad faith by seeking to modify the contract. In the alternative, the court concluded that the modification agreement was voidable because it was extracted by means of economic duress; the tight steel market prevented the plaintiffs from obtaining steel elsewhere at an affordable price and, consequently, the plaintiffs were forced to agree to the modification in order to assure a continued supply of steel. See e.g. Oskey Gasoline & Oil Co. v. Continental Oil Co., 534 F.2d 1281 (8th Cir.1976). Sharon challenges these conclusions on appeal.

The ability of a party to modify a contract which is subject to Article Two of the Uniform Commercial Code is broader than common law, primarily because the modification needs no consideration to be binding. ORC § 1302.12 (UCC § 2–209(1)). A party's ability to modify an agreement is limited only by Article Two's general obligation of good faith. * * * In determining whether a particular modification was obtained in good faith, a court must make two distinct inquiries: whether the party's conduct is consistent with "reasonable commercial standards of fair dealing in the trade," * * * and whether the parties were in fact motivated to seek modification by an honest desire to compensate for commercial exigencies; * * * ORC § 1302.01(2) (UCC § 2–103). The first inquiry is relatively straightforward; the party asserting the modification must demonstrate that his decision to seek modification was the result of a factor, such as increased costs, which would cause an ordinary merchant to seek a modification of the contract. See Official Comment 2, ORC § 1302.12 (UCC § 2–209) (reasonable commercial standards may require objective reason); J. White & R. Summers, Handbook of Law under the UCC at 41. The second inquiry, regarding the subjective honesty of the parties, is less clearly defined. Essentially, this inquiry requires the party asserting the modification to demonstrate that he was, in fact, motivated by a legitimate commercial reason and that such a reason is not offered merely as a pretext. * * * Moreover, the trier of fact must determine whether the means used to obtain the modification are an impermissible attempt to obtain a modification by extortion or over-reaching. * * *

Sharon argues that its decision to seek a modification was consistent with reasonable commercial standards of fair dealing because market exigencies made further performance entail a substantial loss. The district court, however, made three findings which caused it to conclude that economic circumstances were not the reason that Sharon sought a modification: it found that Sharon was partially insulated from raw material price increases, that Sharon bargained for a contract with a slim profit margin and thus implicitly assumed the risk that performance might come to involve a loss, and that Sharon's overall profit in 1973 and its profit on the contract in the first quarter of 1973 were inconsistent with Sharon's position that the modification was sought to avoid a loss. Although all of these findings are marginally related to the question whether Sharon's conduct was consistent with reasonable commercial standards of fair dealing, we do not believe that they are sufficient to support a finding that Sharon did not observe reasonable commercial standards by seeking a modification. In our view, these findings do not support a conclusion that a reasonable merchant, in light of the circumstances, would not have sought a modification in order to avoid a loss. For example, the district court's finding that Sharon's steel slab contract [26] insulated it from industry wide cost increases is correct, so far as it goes. Although Sharon was able to purchase steel slabs at pre–1973 prices, the district court's findings also indicate that it was not able to purchase, at those prices, a sufficient tonnage of steel slabs to meet its production requirements.[27] The district court also found that Sharon experienced substantial cost increases for other raw materials, ranging from 4% to nearly 20%. In light of these facts, the finding regarding the fixed-price contract for slab steel, without more, cannot support an inference that Sharon was unaffected by the market shifts that occurred in 1973. Similarly, the district court's finding that Sharon entered a contract in November, 1972 which would yield only a slim profit does not support a conclusion that Sharon was willing to risk a loss on the contract. Absent a finding that the market shifts and the raw material price increases were foreseeable at the time the contract was formed—a finding which was not made—Sharon's willingness to absorb a loss cannot be inferred from the fact that it contracted for a smaller profit than usual. Finally, the findings regarding Sharon's profits are not sufficient, by themselves, to warrant a conclusion that Sharon was not justified in seeking a modification. Clearly, Sharon's initial profit on the contract [28] is an important consideration; the district court's findings indicate, however, that at the time modification was sought substantial

26. Sharon was a party to a contract with United States Steel which allowed it to make monthly purchases of slab steel ranging from a minimum of 25,000 tons per month to a maximum of 45,000 tons per month. It was also a party to a contract with Wierton Steel which allowed it to purchase slab steel in amounts varying between 10,000 to 20,000 tons per month. Both of these contracts were entered prior to 1973, at a very attractive price. When the market strengthened in 1973, however, Sharon was unable to obtain the maximum monthly tonnages permitted under these contracts; U.S. Steel delivered only 30,000 tons per month and Wierton 10,000 tons per month.

27. The district court found that Sharon suffered a continuing shortage of slab steel. It found that in 1972 (when Sharon was operating at substantially less than full capacity) it received 602,277 tons of slab steel; that in 1973, it received 506,596 tons of slab steel; and that in 1974 it received 373,898 tons. Thus, the record is clear that Sharon was in a difficult position. As demand for steel increased, and as Sharon's mills began to work at a higher capacity, its supply of slab steel steadily diminished.

28. The district court noted that in the first three months of 1973, Sharon made $3,089.00 on sales to Roth and lost $263.00 on steel sold to Toledo. Although Sharon lost significant sums of money on its contract with the plaintiffs, Sharon enjoyed overall profits in 1973, with net earnings of $11,566,000 on net sales of $338,205,000.

future losses were foreseeable.[29]　A party who has not actually suffered a loss on the contract may still seek a modification if a future loss on the agreement was reasonably foreseeable.　Similarly, the overall profit earned by the party seeking modification is an important factor; this finding, however, does not support a conclusion that the decision to seek a modification was unwarranted.　The more relevant inquiry is into the profit obtained through sales of the product line in question. This conclusion is reinforced by the fact that only a few product lines may be affected by market exigencies; [30] the opportunity to seek modification of a contract for the sale of goods of a product line should not be limited solely because some other product line produced a substantial profit.

In the final analysis, the single most important consideration in determining whether the decision to seek a modification is justified in this context is whether, because of changes in the market or other unforeseeable conditions, performance of the contract has come to involve a loss.　In this case, the district court found that Sharon suffered substantial losses by performing the contract *as modified.*　See note 29, supra.　We are convinced that unforeseen economic exigencies existed which would prompt an ordinary merchant to seek a modification to avoid a loss on the contract; thus, we believe that the district court's findings to the contrary are clearly erroneous.　＊　＊　＊

The second part of the analysis, honesty in fact, is pivotal.　The district court found that Sharon "threatened not to sell Roth and Toledo any steel if they refused to pay increased prices after July 1, 1973" and, consequently, that Sharon acted wrongfully.　Sharon does not dispute the finding that it threatened to stop selling steel to the plaintiffs.　Instead, it asserts that such a finding is merely evidence of bad faith and that it has rebutted any inference of bad faith based on that finding.　We agree with this analysis; although coercive conduct is evidence that a modification of a contract is sought in bad faith, that prima facie showing may be effectively rebutted by the party seeking to enforce the modification.　＊　＊　＊　Although we agree with Sharon's statement of principles, we do not agree that Sharon has rebutted the inference of bad faith that rises from its coercive conduct.　Sharon asserts that its decision to unilaterally raise prices was based on language in the November 17, 1972 letter which allowed it to raise prices to the extent of any general industry-wide price increase.　Because prices in the steel industry had increased, Sharon concludes that it was justified in raising its prices.　Because it was justified in raising the contract price, the plaintiffs were bound by the terms of the contract to pay the increased prices.　Consequently, any refusal by the

29. The evidence indicates, and the district court found, that with the exception of hot rolled sheets Sharon absorbed a loss on every rolled steel product which it sold to the defendants in 1973, even though the modified prices were in effect during the third and the fourth quarters.

30. Apparently, Sharon's record overall profit was the result of other operations. It obtained a pre-tax profit of less than one percent on its total sales of rolled steel.

plaintiffs to pay the price increase sought by Sharon must be viewed as a material breach of the November, 1972 contract which would excuse Sharon from any further performance. Thus, Sharon reasons that its refusal to perform absent a price increase was justified under the contract and consistent with good faith.

This argument fails in two respects. First, the contractual language on which Sharon relies only permits, at most, a price increase for cold rolled steel; thus, even if Sharon's position were supported by the evidence, Sharon would not have been justified in refusing to sell the plaintiff's hot rolled steel because of the plaintiffs' refusal to pay higher prices for the product. More importantly, however, the evidence does not indicate that Sharon ever offered this theory as a justification until this matter was tried. Sharon's representatives, in their testimony, did not attempt to justify Sharon's refusal to ship steel at 1972 prices in this fashion. Furthermore, none of the contemporaneous communications contain this justification for Sharon's action. In short, we can find no evidence in the record which indicates that Sharon offered this theory as a justification at the time the modification was sought. Consequently, we believe that the district court's conclusion that Sharon acted in bad faith by using coercive conduct to extract the price modification is not clearly erroneous. Therefore, we hold that Sharon's attempt to modify the November, 1972 contract, in order to compensate for increased costs which made performance come to involve a loss, is ineffective because Sharon did not act in a manner consistent with Article Two's requirement of honesty in fact when it refused to perform its remaining obligations under the contract at 1972 prices.[31]

* * *

Notes

1. Section 89 of the Restatement, Second, of Contracts provides: "A promise modifying a duty under a contract not fully performed on either side is binding (a) if the modification is fair and equitable in view of circumstances not anticipated by the parties when the contract was made; or (b) to the extent provided by statute; or (c) to the extent that justice requires enforcement in view of material change of position in reliance on the promise." Is Roth consistent with the Restatement?

2. Following the logic of UCC 2–209(1) and the comments, Roth invalidated the modification because of Sharon's bad faith rather than because of economic duress. In fact, the court, in note 31, suggested that

31. The district court also found, as an alternative ground, that the modification was voidable because the plaintiffs agreed to the modification due to economic duress. See, e.g., Oskey Gasoline & Oil Co. v. Continental Oil, 534 F.2d 1281 (8th Cir.1976). Because we conclude that the modification was ineffective as a result of Sharon's bad faith, we do not reach the issue whether the contract modification was also voidable because of economic duress. We note, however, that proof that coercive means were used is necessary to establish that a contract is voidable because of economic duress. Normally, it cannot be used to void a contract modification which has been sought in good faith; if a contract modification has been found to be in good faith, then presumably no wrongful coercive means have been used to extract the modification.

proof of coercive means will not necessarily invalidate a modification made in good faith. Exactly what is bad faith in the Sixth Circuit?

3. Economic duress may be invoked to invalidate a modification where one party has made a "wrongful" threat to withhold delivery of needed goods, the threatened party can not obtain substitute goods from another source and the ordinary remedy of an action for breach of contract is not adequate. See Austin Instrument, Inc. v. Loral Corp., 29 N.Y.2d 124, 324 N.Y.S.2d 22, 272 N.E.2d 533 (1971). Professor Hillman, for one, favors this approach. See Hillman, *Contract Modification Under the Restatement (Second) of Contracts,* 67 Cornell L.Rev. 680 (1982). Could the modification in Roth be invalidated for economic duress?

Note: Modifications and the Statute of Frauds

Assume that S and B enter an oral contract to sell 10 units of goods for $400. The statute of frauds does not apply because the price is less than $500. UCC 2–201(1). Suppose that the parties, before any performance has occurred, modify the contract by adding 10 more units of goods for $400. This agreement modifying the contract is clearly enforceable under UCC 2–209(1). But now UCC 2–209(3) comes into play: "The requirements of the statute of frauds ∗ ∗ ∗ (Section 2–201) must be satisfied if the contract as modified is within its provisions." Without question, the "contract as modified" is within UCC 2–201(1), even though neither the original contract nor the modification were for a price of "$500 or more." Thus, it would appear that the modification must meet the requirement of a writing in UCC 2–201(1) or satisfy the exceptions listed in UCC 2–201(3). In addition, the modification should be in writing if it falls within UCC 2–201(1) on its own or if it changes the quantity term of an original contract that fell within UCC 2–201. A literal reading of this somewhat murky provision does not, however, support the conclusion that if the original contract was within UCC 2–201, any modification must also be in writing. See White & Summers 44–45.

The murkiness is not abated as one reads further. UCC 2–209(4) provides: "Although an attempt at modification or rescission does not satisfy the requirements of subsection ∗ ∗ ∗ (3) it can operate as a waiver." A waiver of what, the requirement of UCC 2–201(1) itself? Not likely. And what "operates" as a waiver? Article 2 does not say.

At common law, the concept of waiver was frequently invoked to excuse conditions precedent to a contractual duty to perform. Suppose, for example, that the contract provided that before the buyer had a duty to pay for goods delivered, they must be inspected and certified by a designated third party. In theory, the buyer has no duty to pay until the condition is satisfied. But if, with knowledge that no certificate had been issued, the buyer elected to accept and pay for the goods, the condition was waived. This was waiver by "election." Similarly, if B, before delivery, represented to S that the certificate would not be required and B relied upon that representation, the condition would be excused. This was waiver by estoppel. The former waived conditions which had already failed and the latter waived conditions which had not. See Restatement, Contracts (Second) 84. Although both types of waiver modified or discharged conditions in the contract, they did not affect the right of the waiving party to damages for defective performance:

Only a modification supported by consideration or other valid reasons for enforcement could do that. See National Utility Service, Inc. v. Whirlpool Corp., 325 F.2d 779 (2d Cir.1963).

With this sketchy background, look again at UCC 2–209(2), (4), and (5) and resolve the following problem. (Taken from Wisconsin Knife Works v. National Metal Crafters, 781 F.2d 1280 (7th Cir.1986)).

Problem 6–4

After negotiations, B mailed to S a written order for the purchase of 281,000 "spade bit blanks," for use in the manufacture of spade bits. The goods were to be delivered in installments by the dates stipulated in the purchase order. In addition, the purchase order contained, inter alia, the following "condition" of purchase: "No modification of this contract shall be binding upon Buyer unless made in writing and signed by Buyer's authorized representative. Buyer shall have the right to make changes in the Order by a notice, in writing, to seller." Seller accepted the purchase order in a written acknowledgment and commenced to manufacture the bits.

S was consistently late in tendering delivery. B, however, accepted the late deliveries without declaring a breach or invoking the written modification condition. After accepting 144,000 blanks, however, B, invoking the delivery schedule in the purchase order, cancelled the contract for breach and sued S for damages. (There was some evidence that B cancelled because of a dispute with a sub-purchaser of the completed spade bit rather than S's delays.)

You are clerk to the trial judge. She asks you for a memo on the following questions:

(1) Was the "no modification" condition in the purchase order enforceable against Seller, see UCC 2–209(2);

(2) If so, did B's conduct of accepting S's late deliveries "operate as a waiver" of either the contract delivery schedule or the "no modification" condition, see UCC 2–209(4);

(3) If the conduct did operate as a waiver, how is UCC 2–209(5) relevant to the dispute?

Note: Arbitration of Disputes Arising Under Long-Term Supply Contracts

Arbitration is an informal method of dispute resolution which occurs, in most cases, outside of the judicial process. It depends upon an enforceable agreement between the parties to submit existing or future disputes to arbitration.

The scope of the arbitrator's power to decide is determined by that agreement: It may include "all" disputes between the parties of any kind whatever or be limited to particular disputes, such as the failure to agree upon an adjustment or the excusability of one or both parties due to commercial impracticability.

Arbitration clauses are frequently found in long-term supply contracts, where the incentive of the parties to preserve the relationship while disputes over performance are being resolved is high. Whether an arbitration clause is part of the agreement, however, is frequently disputed in litigation involving the "battle of the forms." See Chapter Three, Section 3, supra.

Assume that the contract includes a "reopener" clause, which envisions three steps: (1) If changed circumstances not foreseeable as likely to occur substantially affect performance, either party may request the other to agree to an adjustment in the contract; (2) The parties shall negotiate over the requested adjustment in good faith; (3) If the parties fail to agree, the dispute shall be submitted to arbitration where the arbitrator shall determine whether changed circumstances justifying the requested adjustment existed and, if so, what the adjustment should be.

Suppose that the buyer invoked the clause and, after negotiations with the seller, no agreed modification was reached. The buyer then filed a demand for arbitration and the seller refused. In fact, when the buyer refused to pay for goods under the contract until the dispute was resolved, the seller cancelled and sued for breach of contract in a *state court*. What should the buyer do?

In this all too familiar situation, the steps are likely to look like this.

1. The buyer must determine whether state or federal law governs the dispute over arbitration. The issue is less important on matters of substance, i.e. the enforceability of agreements to arbitrate future disputes, since most commercial states have modern, comprehensive arbitration statutes, such as the Uniform Arbitration Act. Uniform Arbitration Act §§ 1–25 (1955) 7 U.L.A. 4 (1978). But the question is crucial in deciding where to sue to compel arbitration and determining what procedures will govern. Let us assume that the dispute is subject to the United States Arbitration Act, 9 U.S.C.A. §§ 1–14 (1982), and that any litigation will be commenced in the United States District Court and be subject to the Federal Rules of Civil Procedure.

2. The buyer should sue in the federal district court to stay the seller's suit for breach of contract and to compel arbitration under the contract. This is the critical early point in the arbitration, for the court must decide such questions as whether the arbitration clause is enforceable and, if so, whether the parties have agreed to arbitrate the dispute in question. If the answer to either question is no, then the suit to stay and compel is dismissed. If the answer to both questions is yes, then the federal court will issue a preemptive order to the state court to stay the law suit and issue an order to the seller to commence arbitration. The order to compel arbitration is, in effect, a decree of specific performance. See, e.g., Sharon Steel Corporation v. Jewell Coal & Coke Co., 735 F.2d 775 (3d Cir. 1984).

3. If the parties have been ordered to arbitrate, the next steps are to select the arbitrators, schedule hearings on the issues to be resolved and

conduct the arbitration. Frequently, the American Association of Arbitration (the AAA) will provide material assistance in this process through furnishing lists of potential arbitrators, providing rules and procedures to be followed during the arbitration and facilitating the process from beginning to end. See G. Goldberg, A Lawyer's Guide to Commercial Arbitration, 35–59 (2d ed. 1983).

4. Under American law, an arbitrator's decision on questions of fact and law is binding on the parties, unless judicial review is sought and one of the narrow grounds for overturning an award is satisfied. These grounds go to the honesty of the arbitrators and the integrity of the process rather than to the merits of the dispute. Thus, if the parties agree to arbitrate a clearly defined dispute subject to the rules and procedures of the AAA and one party, thereafter, refuses to arbitrate, the courts will compel arbitration, subject to limited attacks at the threshold upon the arbitrability of the dispute and, thereafter, confirm and enforce the award, subject to attacks upon the honesty of the arbitrators and the integrity of the process.

A standard reference is M. Domke, Domke on Commercial Arbitration (rev. ed by Wilner, 1984).

Part Three

THE POST-AGREEMENT—
PRE-SHIPMENT STAGE

Chapter Seven

BUYER'S BREACH—A SURVEY
OF SELLER'S REMEDIES

Chapter 7 deals with Buyer's breach & Seller's remedy

SECTION ONE.   A GENERAL INTRODUCTION TO CODE REMEDIES

Before the time for the seller's performance has arrived, the buyer might repudiate, commit a "total" breach of an installment contract, fail to make an advance payment when due, or the like.   In such circumstances, the seller will want to know (1) whether his own performance is excused and (2) to what remedies he may resort.

In this Chapter, after a preliminary consideration of the nature and significance of the buyer's wrongful conduct, we will survey the various remedies open to the seller.   In Chapter Eight, we will reverse the position of the parties, and consider the various remedies open to the buyer when the seller repudiates or commits a total breach of an installment contract.   These two chapters have been structured to afford the student maximum opportunity to compare seller's remedies and buyer's remedies in comparable situations.   Article 2 invites this kind of analysis, for it grants seller and buyer alike a wide range of parallel remedies.   Thus, the seller's action for the price (UCC 2–709) is parallel to the buyer's action for specific performance (UCC 2–716).   So, too: the respective rights of seller and buyer to damages based on contract-market price differentials (UCC 2–708 and 2–713) and the respective rights of seller and buyer to enter into substitute transactions and measure their losses accordingly (UCC 2–706 and 2–712).   A comprehensive analysis appears in Sebert, *Remedies Under Article Two of the Uniform Commercial Code: An Agenda for Review,* 130 U.Pa.L. Rev. 360 (1981).   The seminal article is Peters, *Remedies for Breach of*

Contracts Relating to the Sale of Goods Under the U.C.C.: A Roadmap for Article Two, 73 Yale L.J. 199 (1963).

Before going further, we should note and respond to the budding heresy (believed by White) that contract and sales remedies are without practical significance. See, generally, White, *Contract Law in Modern Commercial Transactions, An Artifact of Twentieth Century Business Life?,* 22 Washburn L.J. 1 (1982). According to White, the student who knew of the infrequency of suit (businessmen want to preserve relations), the modesty of sums recovered (*Hadley v. Baxendale* and all that) and the increasing resort to alternative forms of dispute resolution (arbitration) might be tempted to include contract and sales remedies among those things one has to study to get through law school but which have little relevance thereafter. In support of this thesis, the studies of Professor Stewart Macaulay might be cited, e.g., *Non-Contractual Relations in Business: A Preliminary Study,* 28 Am.Sociol.Rev. 55 (1963), which suggest that commercial parties themselves iron out most contract and sales disputes on their own on the basis of common sense and economics.

Even so, Speidel and Summers believe that it hardly follows that the student can ignore the remedial side of the coin. In the first place, not all contract recoveries are inconsequential or piddling. If the contract is a large one which has a long term, even a modest contract-market differential can produce a whopping sum of money. Moreover, a modest relaxation of *Hadley v. Baxendale* and a willingness of the courts to compensate sellers for lost profits and lost volumes could cause an important change in the picture.

More important, however, is the fact that the impact of contract remedy doctrine cannot properly be measured by the frequency of litigation. For surely, the predicted damage and specific performance awards that courts would grant play an important role in the negotiation of every contract dispute which is handled by lawyers. In such cases we bargain at least in part on the basis of the lawyer's judgment about what damages will be awarded at trial. Thus both the lawyer who is going to negotiate a settlement on behalf of an aggrieved client and the lawyer who is going to advise his client how best to extricate himself from a situation in which he or the opposing party has broken a contract need to know the variety of available remedies and the merits and demerits of each.

SECTION 2.   IMPAIRING SELLER'S EXPECTATION OF FULL PERFORMANCE: PROSPECTIVE INABILITY; REPUDIATION, AND INSTALLMENT CONTRACTS

A.   Insolvency and Prospective Inability—UCC 2–609

UCC 2–609(1) provides that a contract for sale "imposes an obligation on each party that the other's expectation of receiving due performance will not be impaired." This obligation is breached when one party gives the other "reasonable grounds for insecurity" with regard to the promised performance. At this point, the aggrieved party "may in writing demand adequate assurance of due performance and until he receives such assurance may if commercially reasonable suspend any performance for which he has not already received the agreed return." Comment 2 to UCC 2–609 stresses that the right to suspend performance includes "any preparation therefor." If the other party, upon receipt of a "justified" demand, fails "to provide within a reasonable time not exceeding thirty days such assurance of due performance as is adequate under the circumstances of the particular case," he has repudiated the contract and the aggrieved party may take appropriate remedial action, including cancellation. Between merchants, the reasonableness of grounds for insecurity and adequacy of any assurance offered "shall be determined according to commercial standards." UCC 2–609(2). Thus, an aggrieved party may suspend his performance even though the other party's conduct is short of breach or repudiation but the aggrieved party cannot cancel the contract until the mandatory communication procedure fails to produce "adequate assurance." In this process, a high incidence of consensual adjustment and continued performance is likely, particularly when the generality of the standards in UCC 2–609 is taken into account. On the other hand, if adjustment does not occur and one party has suspended his performance or cancelled the contract, the other may claim that such action was not justified. Within this framework, courts and lawyers will have to give some content to the phrases "reasonable grounds for insecurity" and "adequate assurance of due performance." For good background discussion, see Wardrop, *Prospective Inability in the Law of Contracts,* 20 Minn.L.Rev. 380 (1936); 6 Corbin, Contracts §§ 1259–1261 (1962); Note, *A Right to Adequate Assurance of Performance in All Transactions; UCC 2–609 Beyond Sales of Goods,* 48 S.Cal.L.Rev. 1358 (1975).

Suppose that under a written contract for the sale of goods the seller is to deliver in a single lot on March 1 and the buyer is to pay the full contract price on April 1. The buyer's basic obligation here is to accept and pay for the goods in accordance with the contract, UCC 2–301, and it is in this regard that grounds for insecurity may arise. Except insofar as the seller has rights under UCC 2–702(2), however, once the buyer has accepted the seller's tender of delivery, the seller can reduce any insecurity he feels about subsequent payment of the price only by exercising rights he may have under an Article 9 security interest—rights he may not have. As a practical matter, UCC 2–609 itself affords little protection to a seller who has fully performed his obligation before the alleged ground for insecurity arises.

Before delivery, however, UCC 2–609 is available and in some cases this availability is spelled out with precision for both seller and buyer alike. See UCC 2–210(5) and UCC 2–611(2). From the seller's point of view, two situations are described which justify protective action. When, in an installment contract, the buyer's default in past due payments is not sufficient to justify a cancellation, the seller may withhold delivery of goods then due until payment for past deliveries is received. UCC 2–612(3), Comment 7. When the seller, in a credit transaction, discovers the buyer to be insolvent (as defined in UCC 1–201(23)), he may "refuse delivery except for cash including payment for all goods theretofore delivered under the contract, and stop delivery" under UCC 2–705. This latter remedy finds firm support in §§ 53(1)(a) and 54(1) of the Uniform Sales Act and in prior case law. See, e.g., Leopold v. Rock-Ola Corporation, 109 F.2d 611 (5th Cir.1940). However, it has been held that insolvency alone does not justify cancellation of the contract. Koppelon v. Ritter Flooring Corp., 97 N.J.L. 200, 116 A. 491 (1922).

Short of the situations noted above, exactly what constitutes either reasonable grounds for insecurity or adequate assurance of due performance is less clear. Resolve the following problem, giving careful attention to the comments to UCC 2–609.

Problem 7–1

S agreed to manufacture special equipment for B. Delivery was to be in installments, with payment for each installment within 15 days of delivery. S commenced performance but, before any deliveries were made, S began to hear unfavorable comments about B's credit. After a quick check, the following facts emerged: (1) Dun & Bradstreet had recently reduced B's credit rating; (2) B's working capital was fully stretched out and some suppliers were experiencing delays in payment; (3) B had recently changed banks, and the "word" was out that B's financial condition was "extended" and that care should be exercised before extending credit; and (4) B's overall financial condition had worsened since the date of the contract.

A. You represent S. On the day before the first delivery was due, S called you for a conference. With the credit information on the table, S stated that unless you could persuade him otherwise, he would refuse to deliver the goods unless B paid cash. What would you recommend? See UCC 1–201(23), 2–702(1), 2–609.

B. Assume that you persuade S to exercise caution and talk to B before taking action. S, therefore, gives B a written demand for "adequate assurance" and temporarily suspends the first delivery. UCC 2–609(1). B, in response, establishes solvency and claims that the current situation is "temporary." B, however, states that long-term viability depends upon getting prompt delivery of the equipment, which is needed in the business, on credit. If there are delays, no assurances can be given.

Does this constitute "adequate assurance" of due performance? What else could S reasonably demand? On this last point, consider the following opinion by Cummings, Circuit Judge, concurring in Pittsburgh-Des Moines Co. v. Brookhaven Manor Water Co., 532 F.2d 572, 583–84 (7th Cir.1976):

"Although I agree with the result reached in the majority opinion, I differ with the reasoning. Reasonable men could certainly conclude that PDM had legitimate grounds to question Brookhaven's ability to pay for the water tank. When the contract was signed, the parties understood that

Brookhaven would obtain a loan to help pay for the project. When the loan failed to materialize, a prudent businessman would have 'reasonable grounds for insecurity.' I disagree that there must be a fundamental change in the financial position of the buyer before the seller can invoke the protection of UCC § 2–609. Rather, I believe that the Section was designed to cover instances where an underlying condition of the contract, even if not expressly incorporated into the written document, fails to occur. See Comment 3 to UCC § 2–609. Whether, in a specific case, the breach of the condition gives a party 'reasonable grounds for insecurity' is a question of fact for the jury.

"UCC § 2–609, however, does not give the alarmed party a right to redraft the contract. Whether the party invoking that provision is merely requesting an assurance that performance will be forthcoming or whether he is attempting to alter the contract is a mixed question of law and fact, depending in part upon the court's interpretation of the obligations imposed on the parties. In this case, PDM would have been assured only if significant changes in the contract were made, either by receiving Betke's personal guarantee, by attaining escrow financing or by purchasing an interest in Brookhaven. The district court could probably conclude as a matter of law that these requests by PDM demanded more than a commercially 'adequate assurance of due performance.' "

Note: Scope of Seller's Reclamation Rights

The Code protects a credit seller against specified events within the control of the buyer that occur before delivery. If the buyer commits a breach of contract, the seller may, at a minimum, withhold delivery of the goods involved, UCC 2–703(a), or, in a proper case, stop delivery by a carrier or other bailee to the buyer, UCC 2–705(1). If the buyer becomes insolvent, the seller may "refuse delivery except for cash" under UCC 2–702(1) or "stop delivery" under UCC 2–705(1). Where the buyer gives reasonable grounds for insecurity short of a breach or insolvency, the seller may, if commercially reasonable, "suspend any performance for which he has not already received the agreed return." UCC 2–609(2). The first two cases, at least, illustrate what the common law called a seller's possessory lien and what the Code calls a possessory security interest arising under Article 2. See UCC 1–201(37) & 9–113. So long as the seller retains actual or constructive possession of the goods after default by the credit buyer, it can enforce the security interest in the goods under Article 2, free from, or with priority over, the claims of the buyer's other creditors.

If the goods have been delivered to the buyer, however, the matter becomes more complicated. For now, note the following principles, to which we will return in Chapter Fifteen, Section 4(c).

(1) If the seller retains "title" until payment, the effect is to create a non-possessory security interest, which is within the scope of Article 9. See UCC 1–201(37), 2–401(1), & UCC 9–102(1). Although the security interest is enforceable against the buyer, i.e., the seller could repossess the goods from the buyer, see UCC 9–203(1), 9–501(1) & 9–503, it will be subject to the claims of lien and secured creditors of the buyer unless "perfected" by

filing a financing statement and otherwise entitled to priority. See UCC 9–201, 9–301(1), 9–302(1) & 9–312(5).

(2) If the seller does not retain title but the buyer was insolvent at the time of delivery, the seller has a limited claim to reclamation under UCC 2–702(2) & (3). Note that even if all the conditions of subsection (2) are met, the rights of a "buyer in ordinary course or other good faith purchaser" may have intervened.

(3) If the seller did not retain title and the buyer was not insolvent at the time of delivery, the seller has no interest in or claim to the goods upon default by the buyer. The seller has, in effect, only an unsecured claim for the price. UCC 2–709(1).

Problem 7–2

Suppose, in Problem 7–1, above, that on July 1, S shipped a carload of equipment to B by public carrier "FOB the place of shipment." (For what this means, see UCC 2–319(1)(a), 2–503(2) & 2–504). The carrier issued a non-negotiable bill of lading, naming B as "consignee," i.e., the person entitled to the goods under the document. On July 2, while the goods were still in transit, B resold the goods for cash to C, a good faith purchaser for value. On July 3, before receipt of the goods by B, S learned from reliable sources that B was insolvent. The goods were scheduled to arrive by 10 PM on July 3, but could not be picked up until July 5.

A. Can S on July 3 stop delivery of the goods under UCC 2–705?

B. If S can stop delivery against B, under what circumstances, if any, will C, a good faith purchaser for value, nevertheless take free of S's security interest in the goods? See UCC 2–401, 2–403 & 9–307. Is it clear that if S properly stops delivery under UCC 2–705 as against B and before C obtains possession of the goods, C will take subject to S's security interest?

B. Buyer's Repudiation

In the first year course in contracts, considerable attention is usually given to the cognate problems of determining whether a contracting party has repudiated or materially broken an installment contract. Accordingly, our treatment here will be an abbreviated one, emphasizing the relevant Code provisions and the role of the lawyer called upon to advise the seller on what to do in the face of the buyer's conduct. The consequences of an erroneous decision by the lawyer can be catastrophic. The seller's lawyer may advise that the buyer has repudiated or materially broken an installment contract, and that seller is free to cease his own performance and seek damages. If this advice proves incorrect, the seller will turn out to be the wrongdoer, and, accordingly, liable in damages. For such a case, see Teeman v. Jurek, 251 N.W.2d 698 (Minn.1977). In such a case he may just choose another lawyer to defend him. It should be added that the lawyer who renders advice in this context does not always have weeks to do research in the library. His client, the seller, may, be manufacturing the goods, and may want to know *now* what course of action he is free to take in the face of buyer's conduct.

What constitutes a "repudiation"? Although UCC 2–610 uses this word, the Code nowhere defines it. And in real life, it is a lucky and unusual lawyer whose client reports that the other contracting party has repudiated by such unequivocal language as "I repudiate" or "kiss my foot." A more common circumstance finds the other party slowly slipping down that incline into bankruptcy while believing and fully expecting that he will "have the money in just a few days," or that he will "have the goods in just a week." Another common cause for the same lawyer's headache is the chisler—the fellow who asks for more than the contract clearly entitles him to, but not enough more to make his request outrageous. But see Toppert v. Bunge Corp., 60 Ill.App.3d 607, 18 Ill.Dec. 171, 377 N.E.2d 324 (1978) (semi-outrageous conduct).

As we have seen, the client's situation (and therefore his lawyer's) in such a case is greatly eased by UCC 2–609 which gives him the right to demand assurance of performance from the other party and causes failure of assurances to be forthcoming to become a repudiation after "a reasonable time not exceeding thirty days." In some cases clients will be unwilling to twiddle their thumbs for 30 days and the lawyer will be called upon to determine whether a communication from the other party constitutes a repudiation.

The comments to UCC 2–610 give some guidance. Comment 1 reads in part as follows: " * * * anticipatory repudiation centers upon an overt communication of intention or an action which renders performance impossible or demonstrates a clear determination not to continue with performance." Comment 2 continues:

> It is not necessary for repudiation that performance be made literally and utterly impossible. Repudiation can result from action which reasonably indicates a rejection of the continuing obligation. And, a repudiation automatically results under the preceding section on insecurity when a party fails to provide adequate assurance of due future performance within thirty days after a justifiable demand therefor has been made. Under the language of this section, a demand by one or both parties for more than the contract calls for in the way of counter-performance is not in itself a repudiation nor does it invalidate a plain expression of desire for future performance. However, when under a fair reading it amounts to a statement of intention not to perform except on conditions which go beyond the contract, it becomes a repudiation.

Obviously, courts and lawyers will resort to extra-Code case law for guidance in deciding whether or not a given buyer has repudiated. See Restatement, Second, Contracts § 251.

Problem 7–3 (A)

In the Spring of 1986, Seller, a lumberyard, contracted to sell a quantity of specially selected hardwood to Buyer, a furniture manufacturer, at a fixed price. The lumber was to be shipped "fob Seller's lumberyard" within 10 days of demand by Buyer. No time for the demand was specified in the agreement. In May, 1986, Seller inquired when the demand would be made and was informed by Buyer "within the next few weeks." At the end of June, Seller, pressed for cash and storage space, requested by letter that Buyer "help us out" by placing the order quickly. When there was no response, Seller telegraphed that "much as we hate to we must ask for some relief" and requested a conference to "straighten the matter out." Buyer replied that it would be glad to have a conference but "if it is in regard to taking any lumber, we would say that we are not in a position, and do not intend to take any lumber this year and probably not until next Fall." Seller telegraphed that the response was "totally unacceptable" and demanded that Buyer take immediate delivery. Two weeks passed without a response. At this time the market price for the hardwoods was over 20% below the contract price.

Your client is furious and wants to cancel the contract, resell the hardwood and "sue those * * * for damages." And he wants action "right now."

A. Has the Buyer repudiated the contract? If you have doubts, what quick steps should be taken to minimize the risk? (Don't overlook the possibility that the Buyer is in breach because a reasonable time for making the demand has expired. See UCC 2–309(1) & 1–204.)

Omit B. If Buyer has repudiated, what remedial options are available? See UCC 2–610, 2–611 & 2–703.

Omit C. Suppose that the date for delivery had been set for December 1 and that the Buyer repudiated on July 3. If the seller cancelled the contract and immediately sued for damages, what would be the measure of damages? See UCC 2–708 & 2–723.

C. Buyer's Substantial Impairment of the Value to the Seller of His Installment Contract With the Buyer

What is an installment contract and what difference does it make to the seller and buyer?

UCC defines "installment Contract"

Under UCC 2–612(1), an installment contract "requires or authorizes the delivery of goods in separate lots to be separately accepted, even though the contract contains a clause 'each delivery is a separate contract' or its equivalent." Compare UCC 2–307; Stinnes Interoil, Inc. v. Apex Oil Co., 604 F.Supp. 978 (S.D.N.Y.1985) (whether parties intended installment deliveries or delivery in a single lot is question of fact).

Under an installment contract, payment is due "at the time and place at which the buyer is to receive the goods" unless "otherwise agreed." UCC 2–310(a). Suppose that the buyer fails to pay for an installment when due or repudiates the duty to pay for a single installment? What are the seller's remedies? Can, for example, the seller cancel the contract under UCC 2–703(f), and sue for damages?

Consider, first, a failure to pay a single installment when due. Under UCC 2–703, where the buyer "wrongfully * * * fails to make a payment due on or before delivery * * * then with respect to any goods directly affected and, if the breach is of the whole contract (Section 2–612), then also with respect to the whole undelivered balance, the aggrieved seller may * * * (f) cancel." UCC 2–612(3) provides that there is a "breach of the whole" whenever a "default with respect to one or more installments substantially impairs the value of the whole contract * * *" Thus, the answer is clear: No cancellation unless there is a breach of the "whole" under the substantial impairment standard set in UCC 2–612(3).

Suppose that the buyer fails to pay an installment due after delivery? UCC 2–703 appears to limit the remedy of cancellation to the failure to make payments due "on or before delivery." UCC 2–709(1)(a), however, provides the usual remedy: When the "buyer fails to pay the price as it becomes due the seller may recover * * * the price (a) of goods accepted. * * *" Thus, when the buyer has accepted the goods (and taken possession) and the price then becomes due, the seller is expected to enforce the contract by suing for the price rather than to cancel. Furthermore, UCC 2–709(1) appears to foreclose acceleration of a contract to pay in installments: An action to recover the price is proper when the buyer "fails to pay the price as it becomes due." Thus, if the seller had delivered all the goods in exchange for a promise to pay the price in installments and the buyer failed to pay one or more, the seller's remedy appears to be limited to an action for the price on each installment as the breach occurs.

What about a repudiation by the buyer of an installment not yet due? UCC 2–612(3) is limited to a "default with respect to one or more installments * * *" In common parlance, a repudiation is not a default. Does this mean that the seller can cancel the entire contract? The answer is no. Do you see why? Read UCC 2–610 and 2–703. Unless the repudiation "with respect to a performance not yet due" substantially impairs the value of the contract to the other, the aggrieved party, here the seller, may not resort to the remedies for breach in UCC 2–703.

Here, now, is one of the "great" cases on "material" breach in installment contracts.

PLOTNICK v. PENNSYLVANIA SMELTING & REFINING CO.

United States Court of Appeals, Third Circuit, 1952.
194 F.2d 859.

HASTIE, CIRCUIT JUDGE.

This litigation arises out of an installment contract for the sale of quantities of battery lead by a Canadian seller to a Pennsylvania buyer. The seller sued for the price of a carload of lead delivered but not paid for. The buyer counterclaimed for damages caused by the seller's failure to deliver the remaining installments covered by the contract. The district court sitting without a jury allowed recovery on both claim and counterclaim. This is an appeal by the seller from the judgment against him on the counterclaim. The ultimate question is whether the buyer had committed such a breach of contract as constituted a repudiation justifying rescission by the seller.

Suit was brought in the District Court for the Eastern District of Pennsylvania. Federal jurisdiction is based on diversity of citizenship. Consequently, the conflict of laws rules of the forum, Pennsylvania, are invoked to solve the choice of law problem. Klaxon Co. v. Stentor Electric Mfg. Co., 1941, 313 U.S. 487, 61 S.Ct. 1020, 85 L.Ed. 1477. This involves no difficulty since familiar conflict of laws doctrine accepted generally and in Pennsylvania tells us that legal excuse for the non-performance or avoidance of a contract is to be determined in accordance with the law of the place of performance. Restatement, Conflict of Laws, Pa.Annot. § 358 (1936). Beyond this, the parties agree, and correctly so, that Pennsylvania is the place of performance in this case. Therefore, we apply the substantive law of Pennsylvania, particularly the Uniform Sales Act, to determine the legal consequences of the operative facts.

Court will not apply UCC because UCC was not created yet. Will apply Uniform Sales Act

Uncontested findings of fact show that the contract in question was the last of a series of agreements, several of them installment contracts, entered into by the parties between June and October, 1947. Under these contracts, numerous shipments of lead were made by the seller in Canada to the buyer in Philadelphia. The seller frequently complained, and with justification, that payments were too long delayed. On the other hand, several shipments were not made at the times required by the contracts. However, by the end of March 1948, all contracts other than the one in suit had been fully performed by both parties. In this connection, it was the unchallenged finding of the district court that both parties waived the delays which preceded the buyer's breach involved in this suit. The earlier delays are relevant only insofar as they may reasonably have influenced either party in its interpretation of subsequent conduct of the other party.

The contract in suit was executed October 23, 1947 and called for deliveries aggregating 200 tons of battery lead to be completed not later than December 25, 1947. The agreed price was 8.1 cents per pound, or better if quality warranted. The court found that it was the understanding of the parties that at least 63 percent of the price should be paid shortly after each shipment was delivered and the balance within four weeks after that delivery. This finding is not contested.

Under this contract a first carload was delivered November 7, 1947. About 75 percent of the price was paid six days later. A second carload was received January 8, and about 75 percent of the price was paid 10 days later. Final adjustments and payments of small balances due on these two carloads were completed March 30, and these shipments are not now in dispute. The earliest shipment immediately involved in this litigation, the third under the contract, was a carload of lead received by the buyer on March 23, 1948. This delivery followed a March 12 conference of the parties. They disagree on what transpired at that conference. However, about 290,000 pounds of lead were then still to be delivered under the contract which stated December 25, 1947 as the agreed time for the completion of performance. And shortly after the conference, one carload of 43,000 pounds was delivered. No part of the price of this third carload has been paid. It is not disputed that plaintiff is entitled to the price of this shipment and his recovery on his claim in this suit vindicates that right.

On April 7, the buyer, who had been prodding the seller for more lead for some time, notified the seller that unless the balance of the lead should be delivered within thirty days he would buy in the open market and charge the seller any cost in excess of 8.1 cents per pound. On April 10, the seller replied refusing to ship unless the recently delivered third carload should be paid for. On May 12, buyer's attorney threatened suit unless the undelivered lead should be shipped promptly and at the same time promised to pay on delivery 75 percent of the price of this prospective shipment together with the full price of the third installment already received. Seller's solicitor replied on May 22 that seller regarded the contract as "cancelled" as a result of buyer's failure to pay for lead already delivered. At the same time the letter stated the seller's willingness to deliver at the originally agreed price if the overdue payment should be made by return mail and a letter of credit established to cover the price of the lead not yet shipped. Buyer's attorney replied on May 25 that buyer had withheld the price of the third carload "only as a set-off by reason of the failure of your client to deliver" and that buyer would place the overdue payment in escrow and would accept the remaining lead if shipped to Philadelphia "sight draft attached for the full invoice price of each car". On May 27, seller's solicitors reiterated the position stated in their March 22 letter and on June 2 seller notified buyer that the Canadian government had imposed export control on lead. The district court found, and it is here admitted, that between October 1947 and May 1948 the market price of battery lead increased from 8.1 cents to 11½ cents per pound.

The court concluded that the failure of defendant to make a down payment of at least 63 percent of the price of the third carload constituted a breach of contract but "not such a material breach of the contract as to justify plaintiff in refusing to ship the balance due under the contract within the meaning of section 45 of The Sales Act". This was the decisive conclusion of law which the seller has challenged.

Section 45 of the Sales Act as in force in Pennsylvania provides in relevant part as follows: "Where there is a contract to sell goods to be delivered by stated instalments, which are to be separately paid for, and * * * the buyer neglects or refuses to * * * pay for one or more instalments, it depends in each case on the terms of the contract, and the circumstances of the case, whether the breach of contract is so material as to justify the injured party in refusing to proceed further * * * or whether the breach is severable, giving rise to a claim for

compensation, but not to a right to treat the whole contract as broken."
Pa.Stat.Ann. Tit. 69, § 255 (Purdon, 1931).

Statute makes the circumstances determinable

We are dealing, therefore, with a situation in which the controlling
statute explicitly makes the circumstances of the particular case determine whether failure to pay the price of one shipment delivered under
an installment contract justifies the seller in treating his own obligation with reference to future installments as ended. Our problem is
how to determine the legal effect of non-payment in a particular case.

The Commercial sense of the statute yields two guidelines

1. nonpaym't may make it financially imps. for seller to make more deliveries

2. buyer's breach may cause pers. apprehension

We think the key is to be found in the rational basis of the statute
itself. The flexibility of the statute reflects the impossibility of general-
ization about the consequences of failure to pay promptly for installments as delivered. Yet, the commercial sense of the statute yields two
guiding considerations. First, nonpayment for a delivered shipment
may make it impossible or unreasonably burdensome from a financial
point of view for the seller to supply future installments as promised.
Second, buyer's breach of his promise to pay for one installment may
create such reasonable apprehension in the seller's mind concerning
payment for future installments that the seller should not be required
to take the risk involved in continuing deliveries. If any such consequence is proved, the seller may rescind. Moreover, the Pennsylvania
decisions indicate that these embarrassments and apprehensions are
normal consequences of non-payment; but the cases also make it clear
that they are not necessary consequences. American Tube & Stamping
Co. v. Erie Iron & Steel Co., 1924, 281 Pa. 10, 125 A. 304; G.B. Hurt,
Inc., v. Fuller Canneries Co., 1920, 269 Pa. 85, 112 A. 148; Cf., Helgar
Corp. v. Warner's Features, Inc., 1918, 222 N.Y. 449, 119 N.E. 113.

If any such consequence is proved, seller may Rescind!

① above↑ does not apply so not excuse if any must lie in ②

In this case there is no evidence that the delay in payment for one
carload made it difficult to provide additional lead. To the contrary,
seller admits that throughout the period in controversy he had sufficient lead on hand for the full performance of this contract. He could
have delivered had he chosen to do so. His excuse, if any, must be
found in reasonable apprehension as to the future of the contract
engendered by buyer's behavior.

District Ct did not find #2

The district court's finding number 16, with which seller takes
issue, is a direct negation of the claim of reasonable apprehension upon
which seller seeks to establish under Section 45 of the Sales Act his
asserted "right to treat the whole contract as broken." It reads as
follows: Plaintiff's claim of fear that the defendant would not pay for
the balance of battery lead due under Contract No. 5794 at the contract
price was without foundation and unreasonable."

In considering the propriety of this finding, it is to be borne in
mind that the point here is not the absence of legal justification for the
withholding of an overdue payment but rather whether, under the
circumstances, that withholding gave the seller reason to believe that
there was likelihood of continuing or additional default when and after
he should deliver the rest of the lead in accordance with his promise.
The substantiality of this alleged apprehension must be judged in the

W

light of the uncontroverted finding that no impairment of buyer's credit had been shown.   Moreover, the market was rising and all of the evidence indicates that buyer needed and urgently requested the undelivered lead.   Indeed, as early as March 1, before the delivery of the carload for which payment was withheld, the buyer had complained quite urgently of the non-delivery of the entire balance of some 290,000 pounds overdue since December.   Thereafter, when the seller shipped 43,000 pounds, about one-seventh of what was due, the buyer insisted that he was withholding payment because of the delay in delivery of the overdue balance.   The court's finding that buyer had waived any claim for damages for delay up to that time does not alter this factual picture or its rational implications.   In these circumstances, the trial court was justified in concluding that buyer's explanation of his conduct merited belief and that seller had no valid reason to be fearful that payment would not be forthcoming upon full delivery.

The clincher here is provided by the additional evidence concerning *Clincher* the possibility of delivery with sight draft attached.   While there is no specific finding on the point, the evidence, including testimony tendered on behalf of seller, shows without dispute that at the beginning of this series of contracts, the seller had the privilege of shipping on sight draft but elected not to do so.   And just before the collapse of the efforts of the parties to work out their difficulties amicably, the buyer specifically proposed that the seller assure himself of prompt payment by the use of sight drafts accompanying shipments.   It is again important that at this time the market was substantially higher than the contract price and that seller was advised of buyer's urgent need for lead to meet his own commitments.   In such circumstances it is incredible that the buyer would refuse to honor sight drafts for the contract price.   These facts considered together leave no basis for reasonable apprehension concerning payment.

There is one other relevant and important fact.   Throughout the controversial period the seller, with a stock of lead on hand adequate for the full performance of this contract, was using this lead in a rising market for sales to other purchasers at prices higher than agreed in the present contract.   The inference was not only allowable but almost *Who seller* inescapable that desire to avoid a bad bargain rather than apprehen- *acting in* sion that the buyer would not carry out that bargain caused the seller *Good faith?* to renounce the agreement and charge the buyer with repudiation. Recission for such cause is not permissible.   See Truitt v. Guenther Lumber Co., 1920, 73 Pa.Super. 445, 450.

It follows that the seller has failed to establish justification for recission under Section 45 of the Sales Act and that judgment for the buyer on the counterclaim was proper.

The judgment will be affirmed.   *Δ may recover on counterclaim*

Notes *Seller was not justified.*

1.   How should Plotnick be analyzed and decided under the UCC?

2. As a law professor, Ellen A. Peters was highly critical of UCC 2–612, especially as it applied to the buyer's remedies upon breach by an installment seller. She called it a "law professor's delight" in that it required "wandering through a maze of inconsistent statutory standards and elliptical cross references." Peters, *Remedies for Breach of Contracts Relating to the Sale of Goods Under the Uniform Commercial Code: A Roadmap for Article Two,* 73 Yale L.J. 199, 223–27 (1963). As a Justice on the Supreme Court of Connecticut, she had an opportunity to apply UCC 2–612(3) to a default by the buyer in payment.

In Cherwell-Ralli, Inc. v. Rytman Grain Co., Inc., 180 Conn. 714, 433 A.2d 984 (1980), the buyer fell behind in payment for nineteen accepted shipments under an oral installment contract with the seller. Nevertheless, the buyer demanded adequate assurance of due performance, based upon a concern that the seller would close its plant due to product shortages. The seller gave adequate assurances, stating that deliveries would continue if the buyer paid his account. The buyer issued a check for some of the arrearage but then, because of renewed but unfounded concerns about the seller's capacity to perform, stopped payment. The parties reached an impasse in discussions over payment and performance and, ultimately, the seller closed its plant because it could not deliver the goods and cancelled the contract. The seller sued for the price of goods accepted and the buyer counterclaimed for damages caused by the seller's failure to deliver the balance of the installments.

The Supreme Court affirmed the trial court's decision that the buyer, not the seller, had breached the contract. The court, speaking through Justice Peters, reached the following conclusions: (1) On the facts, the improper order to stop payment of the check coupled with the substantial arrearages in payment was a breach which impaired the value of the "whole" contract under UCC 2–612(3); (2) If the breach is of the "whole," the seller may cancel the contract without invoking the adequate assurance provisions of UCC 2–609; (3) The seller did not reinstate the contract by bringing suit to recover the price of past installments: UCC 2–612(3) does not apply where the seller has cancelled and sued for past installments due; (4) The trial court was correct in concluding that the buyer had no "reasonable grounds for insecurity," either before or after the check was issued; and (5) Implicitly, the seller could cancel the contract even though the breach related to payments due after delivery and the buyer did not repudiate its obligation to make future payments.

Note: Cancellation as a Remedy for Breach

As you have seen, the Code gives the seller a number of useful, if not risky, "self-help" remedies. Under UCC 2–609, the seller, if he satisfies the requisite conditions and procedures, may "suspend any performance for which he has not already received the agreed exchange." If the buyer is discovered to be insolvent, the seller may "refuse delivery except for cash * * * and stop delivery under this Article * * *." UCC 2–702(1). Similarly, the seller, under UCC 2–703, may withhold delivery or stop delivery by any bailee of goods "directly affected" by the buyer's breach. These remedies protect the unperformed balance of the seller's obligation but are not inconsistent with the ultimate completion by both parties of the exchange. The disruption may be adjusted and the contract performed.

The remedy of cancellation, however, is more drastic. UCC 2–703(f). Cancellation occurs "when either party puts an end to the contract for breach by the other." UCC 2–106(4). Cf. UCC 2–309 and 2–106(3) (termination occurs when either party "pursuant to a power created by agreement or law puts an end to the contract otherwise than for its breach"). How does an aggrieved party "cancel" a contract? The Code prescribes no procedure and requires no notice to the other party. Thus, if the seller determines that the buyer has breached, decides to cancel rather than to suspend performance or negotiate and takes action inconsistent with continued performance, e.g., resells identified goods, the cancellation is effective. See Mott Equity Elevator v. Svihovec, 236 N.W.2d 900 (N.D.1975). The effect of a cancellation is that the seller "retains any remedy for breach of the whole contract or any unperformed balance." UCC 2–106(4). But see UCC 1–107, where "any claim or right arising out of an alleged breach can be discharged in whole or in part without consideration by a written waiver or renunciation signed and delivered by the aggrieved party." Presumably, a written cancellation without more would not be a renunciation under UCC 1–107. See Goldstein v. Stainless Processing Co., 465 F.2d 392 (7th Cir.1972).

Even if the cancellation is effective, such drastic action must be justified under UCC 2–703. UCC 2–612 imposes one important limitation in installment contracts. And even if the buyer has repudiated, it must be with respect to "a performance not yet due the loss of which will substantially impair the value of the contract to the other. * * *" UCC 2–610. This question figures prominently in the cases. See, e.g., Pillsbury Co. v. Ward, 250 N.W.2d 35 (Iowa 1977) (buyer's unilateral extension of delivery date in rising soybean market substantially impaired the value of the contract to the seller).

Efficient though it may be, there are some limitations upon the remedy of "self help." In Kelly v. Miller, 575 P.2d 1221 (Alaska 1978), the seller, after the buyer had failed to pay the price due on goods delivered, moved in and "repossessed" them. The court, in a dispassionate opinion, found that "in repossessing the tractor without judicial process * * *" the seller had "fashioned his own remedy." Frontier ingenuity notwithstanding, no security interest had been retained under Article 9, there was no right to reclamation under UCC 2–702 and the seller was not entitled to replevin. The consequences? The seller's "failure to seek the remedy provided him under [UCC 2–709] combined with his resort to a remedy not recognized, so far as we have discovered, at either law or equity, precludes him from recovering damages for any loss he may have suffered as a result of [the] breach of contract."

Yet the seller still has the goods! What recourse, if any, is available to the buyer? Cf. UCC 9–507(2).

SECTION 3. SELLER'S ACTION FOR THE PRICE

Read UCC 2–709. Note that when the buyer "fails to pay the price as it becomes due the seller may recover * * * the price (a) of goods accepted. * * * " When goods are accepted is determined under UCC 2–606. See, e.g., Swift & Co. v. Rexton, Inc., 187 Conn. 540, 447 A.2d 9 (1982) (acceptance inferred from buyer's conduct). This is a neat, clean and efficient remedy. The seller gets cash for the goods without the loss of any business volume and the buyer assumes the burden of taking over and disposing of the goods. It is, loosely speaking, like specific performance, although the seller must ultimately proceed in rem, i.e., against the buyer's property. See Schumann v. Levi, 728 F.2d 1141 (8th Cir.1984) (equitable remedy of specific performance and Code's action for the price are "virtually identical").

If, however, the buyer has breached before accepting the goods or incurring the risk of loss, the seller is entitled to recover the price only "if the seller is unable after reasonable effort to resell them at a reasonable price or the circumstances reasonably indicate that such an effort will be unavailing." UCC 2–709(1)(b). Why should the seller have the burdens of possession and dispostion? According to Professor Llewellyn:

> * * * But then decently admeasured damages are all a seller needs, and are just what a seller needs, when the mercantile buyer repudiates. It is, indeed, social wisdom * * * (to require the seller) in most cases which have not involved shipment to a distant point, to dispose of whatever goods may have come into existence or into his warehouse; that is its business, and the buyer's prospective inability has already been evidenced. To force such goods on the buyer, where they are reasonably marketable by the seller, is social waste. * * *

Llewellyn, Through Title to Contract and A Bit Beyond, 25 N.Y. U.L.Q.Rev. 158, 176–177 (1938).

Problem 7–4
Simpka v. Volta: _A Continuing Drama_

[handwritten: A number of problems will deal with these facts]

BASIC FACTS:

Simpka manufactured office equipment and has its principal place of business in Ohio. Simpka sells in a 10–state market in the Northeast. The market is competitive and favors low cost and durability rather than style. Volta, a stock broker in New York City, is building a new building to house its expanding operations. It will require a wide assortment of office equipment, both standard and specially manufactured. After defining its needs, Volta negotiated with a number of office equipment firms, including Simpka. Volta decided in favor of Simpka and, on May 1, contracted for the following:

> The order is for for two lots: (1) Standard items; 200 desks, 200 chairs, 400 regular chairs, for $120,000, and (2) Custom furniture made to Volta's specifications; 20 desks, 20 desk chairs, 20 tables and 20 easy chairs, for $80,000. (1) Standard goods are to be shipped "fob Ohio" in four equal installments on June 1, July 1, September 1 and October 1.

②Custom goods are to be shipped in one installment not later than November 1. Payment is due for each installment within 30 days of delivery to the carrier.

Simpka v. Volta Scene 1

Assume it is now December 1. Volta has accepted all four shipments *Should have* of standard furniture and has paid for two. Volta has refused to purchase *pd for all 4* the custom furniture, which Simpka had already manufactured and identi- *Volta refuses* fied to the contract. Simpka informs you that it could resell the custom *custom furn.* furniture in the 10 state market for $40,000 and that it was at least possible that a higher price, not more than $50,000, could be obtained farther West. Simpka, angry at Volta, would like to hold the completed furniture and recover the $80,000 price. Simpka, however, will not pursue this remedy unless you give him an opinion that the odds are at least even that he will win the law suit. A Summer Associate has given you the extract, below, from Foxco Indus., Ltd. v. Fabric World, Inc., 595 F.2d 976, 983–84 (5th Cir.1979). Will you give Simpka such an opinion?

"UCC § 2–709(1)(b), that portion of § 2–709 which would apply here, provides that an action for the price of goods may be maintained "if the seller is unable after *reasonable* effort to resell them at a *reasonable* price or the circumstances *reasonably* indicate that such *Is 40 or 50 K* effort will be unavailing." Ala.Code tit. 7, § 2–709(1)(b) (1977) (empha- *reasonable?* sis added). The Official Comment to § 2–709 states, in pertinent part, that:

"2. The action for the price is now generally limited to those cases where resale of the goods is impracticable * * *

"3. This section substitutes an objective test by action for the former 'not readily resalable' standard. An action for the price under subsection (1)(b) can be sustained only after a 'reasonable effort to resell' the goods 'at reasonable price' has actually been made or where the circumstances 'reasonably indicate' that such an effort will be unavailing."

Ala.Code tit. 7, § 7–2–709, Official Comment (1977). As was recognized in Multi-Line Manufacturing, Inc. v. Greenwood Mills, Inc., 123 Ga. App. 372, 180 S.E.2d 917 (1971), a case involving the cancellation of a contract to purchase fabric, the language of § 2–709(1)(b) "clearly evinces legislative intent that these matters ordinarily should be subject to determination by a jury * * *" Id. at 373, 180 S.E.2d at 918. Thus, we will reverse only if, as a matter of law, there was no way in which the jury could find that Foxco was unable, after reasonable effort, to resell the fabric at a reasonable price or that it was reasonably clear that an effort to resell would have been fruitless.

"The evidence at trial clearly established that all of Foxco's goods were specially manufactured for the customer who ordered them and that it was difficult for Foxco to resell fabric manufactured for one purchaser to another buyer. Further, it was normally very difficult to sell Foxco's spring fabric after the spring buying season had ended; the precipitous decline of the knitted fabric market presented an additional barrier to resale. It was not until the next spring buying season returned that Foxco, in September 1975, finally sold a portion of the goods identified to Fabric World's October 1974 order.

"Fabric World argues that Foxco made no effort whatsoever to resell the goods during the months that intervened (between the contract breach and Foxco's eventual disposition of the fabric in September 1975) despite the presence of some market for the goods in that interim period. Thus Fabric World concludes, the requisites of § 2–709(1)(b) were not satisfied. Under § 2–709(1)(b), however, Foxco was required only to use *reasonable* efforts to resell its goods at a *reasonable* price. From the time of Fabric World's breach to September 1975 there was a 50% decline in the market price of this material. We cannot say that the jury was precluded from finding that Foxco acted reasonably under the circumstances or that there was no reasonable price at which Foxco could sell these goods. Fabric World breached its contract with Foxco, and the jury was entitled to a charge which gave Foxco the full benefit of its original bargain. * * *"

Simpka v. Volta: Scene 2

Suppose that on June 1 Simpka had tendered and Volta had accepted all of the standard items. Volta paid $30,000 on July 1. If Volta fails to pay on August 1, what is Simpka's remedy? Suppose Volta failed to pay and repudiated the contract on September 1. Could Simpka cancel the contract, accelerate the obligation and sue for the price of all goods accepted? See UCC 2–610(b) and 2–709(1).

SECTION 4. SELLER'S RIGHT TO "CONTRACT–MARKET" DAMAGES

If the seller is not entitled to the price under UCC 2–709, what other remedies are available?

One option is to resell the goods under UCC 2–706, whether they were identified to the contract before or after the buyer's breach. See UCC 2–703(c) & 2–704. When the conditions established in UCC 2–706 are satisfied, the seller may recover the "difference between the resale price and the contract price together with any incidental damages * * * but less expenses saved in consequence of the buyer's breach." UCC 2–706(1).

Another option, whether the goods have been resold or not, is to seek damages for "non-acceptance or repudiation" under UCC 2–708. See UCC 2–703. But the measures of damages under UCC 2–708 are strikingly different: Subsection (1), an objective standard, measures loss by the difference between the market price and the contract price while Subsection (2), a subjective standard, allows recovery of the "profit (including reasonable overhead) which the seller would have made from full performance by the buyer. * * *" on the particular contract in dispute.

These options pose two important questions: (1) What limitations, if any, are imposed upon a seller's decision to pursue a particular remedy; and (2) Once a proper remedy has been selected, how are damages to be measured?

Consider, first, UCC 2–708(1). The contract price-market price measure can be fraught with inappropriateness and difficulty. Further, it may either over-or under-compensate the seller. Should it be repealed?

Problem 7–5

Simpka v. Volta: Scene 3

Back to Simpka-Volta. Assume that the contract was for only the standard items and the deal was signed on March 1. The price and delivery schedule are unchanged. Volta repudiated on April 3.

A. On April 5, Simpka accepted Volta's repudiation, cancelled the contract and sued for damages under UCC 2–708(1). See UCC 2–610(b). The case came to trial in the next year and the following evidence was introduced: (1) The aggregate market price on April 5 in Ohio of the four lots was $110,000; (2) Also in Ohio, the market value of the June 1 installment was $24,000, the July 1 installment was $27,000, the September installment was $30,000 and the October installment was $24,000; (3) In New York, the prices are the same except for the October lot, which was $24,000. *Assume 30,000*

typo →

Assuming that Simpka has not resold the goods, to what damages is Simpka entitled under UCC 2–708(1)? On the time and place for tender, see UCC 2–503.

B. Assume that, on April 3, Simpka decided to wait to see whether Volta would retract the repudiation. UCC 2–611. Simpka waits until July 15, then cancels the contract and sues for damages under UCC 2–708(1). If Simpka does not resell, will its damages be the same as in A, above?

C. What if Simpka had resold on April 5 for $100,00? Is Simpka bound by this decision? See UCC 2–706. If the UCC 2–708(1) measure was more than $20,000, could Simpka pursue that remedy? See the next case. ✓

TRANS WORLD METALS, INC. v. SOUTHWIRE CO.

United States Court of Appeals, Second Circuit, 1985.
769 F.2d 902.

[In April, 1981 the parties entered into a contract for the sale of 12,000 metric tons of primary aluminum, to be delivered in monthly installments of 1,000 metric tons from January through December, 1982. The contract price was $.77 per pound, or a total price of $20.4 million. Seller shipped 750 metric tons in January, 1982 and the balance of the first installment in early February. Between April, 1981 and March, 1982, the market price of aluminum dropped "dramatically." On March 4, 1982, Buyer, without discussing the late first installment or issuing additional delivery instructions, cancelled the contract because of Seller's default. In Seller's suit for damages, the jury concluded that Buyer had accepted all deliveries and even if late, there was no substantial impairment of the value of either the first installment or the whole contract. Thus, buyer had repudiated the contract. This conclusion was affirmed on appeal.

Court concluded it was Buyer who breached

The jury awarded Seller damages of $7,122,141.84, consisting of $6,702,529 for Buyer's repudiation of the balance of the contract and $419,232.84 for the installment accepted. The district court added prejudgment interest of $1,304,804.88 and entered a judgment for $8,426,946.72. The propriety of this damage award under the UCC was attacked on appeal.]

Award of Damages

attacked on appeal

NEWMAN, J.

* * *

II.

Southwire complains that the damage award, calculated by the difference between contract and market prices, gave Trans World an unwarranted windfall. Southwire favors an alternative measure of damages based on the rate of profit earned by Trans World on the first month's completed shipments projected over the twelve-month life of the contract. Such a measure, Southwire argues, would better estimate the amount Trans World would have made had the contract been completed. We reject this alternative as contrary to the Uniform Commercial Code.

Seller's damages for repudiation are governed by section 2–708 of the Uniform Commercial Code. Subsection 1 of this section sets forth the general rule that damages are to be calculated by the difference between the contract and market prices:

UCC § 2-708(1) applies

K – MKT?

(1) Subject to subsection (2) and to the provisions of this Article with respect to proof of market price (Section 2–723), the measure of damages for non-acceptance or repudiation by the buyer is the difference between the market price at the time and place for tender and the unpaid contract price together with any incidental damages provided in this Article (Section 2–710), but less expenses saved in consequence of the buyer's breach.

Could this be read MKT – K?

N.Y.U.C.C. Law § 2–708(1). The drafters of the Uniform Commercial Code recognized that this measure would not adequately compensate certain types of sellers, generally referred to as "lost volume sellers." *See* J. White & R. Summers, Uniform Commercial Code § 7–9, at 274–76 (2d ed. 1980) ("White & Summers"). Therefore, an alternative measure of damages was provided for those sellers who would be *inadequately* compensated by the standard contract/market price differential:

Does (2) apply only to "lost volume sellers" or all sellers?

(2) If the measure of damages provided in subsection (1) is inadequate to put the seller in as good a position as performance would have done then the measure of damages is the profit (including reasonable overhead) which the seller would have made from

full performance by the buyer, together with any incidental damages provided in this Article (Section 2–710), due allowance for costs reasonably incurred and due credit for payments or proceeds of resale.

N.Y.U.C.C. Law § 2–708(2). This measure of damages is often preferred by sellers who have not acquired the goods to be sold prior to the buyer's repudiation because such sellers often would be undercompensated by the contract/market price measure of damages.[3] *Jobbers & Footnote ③*

Southwire argues that the "lost profits" measure should also apply when the seller would be *overcompensated* by section 2–708(1). We disagree. We do not doubt that the contract/market price differential "will seldom be the same as the seller's actual economic loss from breach." White & Summers § 7–7, at 269; *see* Peters, *Remedies for Breach of Contracts Relating to the Sale of Goods Under the Uniform Commercial Code: A Roadmap for Article Two*, 73 Yale L.J. 199, 259 (1963). However, nothing in the language or history of section 2–708(2) suggests that it was intended to apply to cases in which section 2–708(1) might overcompensate the seller. *See* White & Summers § 7–12, at 283. Nor has Southwire cited any New York case that interprets section 2–708(2) as Southwire urges us to interpret it. As a federal court sitting in diversity, we will not extend the application of this state law.

Nor are we convinced that Trans World has been overcompensated. No measure other than the contract/market price differential will award Trans World the "benefit of its bargain," that is, the "amount necessary to put [it] in as good a position as [it] would have been if the defendant had abided by the contract." *Western Geophysical Co. of America, Inc. v. Bolt Associates, Inc.*, 584 F.2d 1164, 1172 (2d Cir.1978) (quoting *Perma Research & Development Co. v. Singer Co.*, 402 F.Supp. 881, 898 (S.D.N.Y.1975), *aff'd*, 542 F.2d 111 (2d Cir.), *cert. denied*, 429 U.S. 987, 97 S.Ct. 507, 50 L.Ed.2d 598 (1976)). The contract at issue in this case is an aluminum supply contract entered into eight months prior to the initial deliveries called for by its terms. The last of the anticipated deliveries of aluminum would not have been completed until a full twenty months after the negotiations took place. It simply could not have escaped these parties that they were betting on which way aluminum prices would move. Trans World took the risk that the

3. Professors White and Summers refer to such sellers as "jobbers."

By "jobber" we refer to a seller who satisfies two conditions. First, he is a seller who never acquires the contract goods. Second, his decision not to acquire those goods after learning of the breach is commercially reasonable under 2–704. * * * Since he has no goods on hand to resell, he cannot even resell on the market at the time of tender and so recoup the amount necessary to make him whole by adding such proceeds to his 2–708(1) recovery. Thus the only recovery which grossly approximates the "jobber's" economic loss is a recovery based on lost profits.

White & Summers § 7–10, at 278. In a case involving a commodity like aluminum that fluctuates rapidly in price—as compared to standard-priced goods like cars, *see* 67 Am.Jur.2d *Sales* § 1129—the lost profits of a selling jobber may well be adequately reflected by the contract/market price differential.

[Handwritten margin annotations:]
△ argues that the "lost profit" measure should also apply when the seller would be overcompensated by § 2-708(1)
Court disagrees!
Nothing in the language or history of it suggest this! Also no cases do.
Court isn't even convinced that TT is over-compensated
Since both parties had a risk. This is an installment sale. No telling what mkt price would be at later deliveries — only speculation. Risk

[handwritten margin note: Both parties had assumed risk market price would change]

price would rise; Southwire took the risk that the price would fall. Under these circumstances, Trans World should not be denied the benefit of its bargain, as reflected by the contract/market price differential.[4] *Cf. Apex Oil Co. v. Vanguard Oil & Service Co.,* 760 F.2d 417 (2d Cir.1985) (defaulting seller obliged to pay damages based on contract/market price differential).

The decision primarily relied upon by Southwire is distinguishable from this case. *Nobs Chemical, U.S.A., Inc. v. Koppers Co., Inc.,* 616 F.2d 212 (5th Cir.1980), involved a seller acting as a middleman. The seller in Nobs had entered into a second fixed-price contract with its own supplier for purchase of the goods to be sold under the contract sued upon; its "market price" thus had been fixed in advance by contract. Because the seller had contractually protected itself against market price fluctuation, the Fifth Circuit concluded that it would have *[handwritten margin note: Not so here]* been unfair to permit the seller to reap a riskless benefit. As that Court noted, "the difference between the fallen market price and the contract price is [not] necessary to compensate the plaintiffs for the breach. Had the transaction been completed, their 'benefit of the bargain' would not have been affected by the fall in the market price. * * *" *Id.* at 215. Whether or not we would have reached the same result in *Nobs,* here the benefit of the bargain under a completed contract would have been affected by the fall in aluminum prices.[5] Because Trans World accepted the risk that prices would rise, it is entitled to benefit from their fall. *[handwritten: DIFFERENCE HERE]*

III.

[handwritten margin notes: Other points on appeal: ① What is proper mkt price? Δ argues mkt price should be March 4 price as date of repudiation. Court disagrees. Says damage is mkt price at time & place for tender]

Southwire raises a number of further points on appeal. The first involves the proper determination of the market price for purposes of calculating the contract/market price differential. The jury relied upon Trans World's damage calculations, which were based on the market price as reflected by bids received on April 26 (and projections discussed below). Southwire argues that because the contract was repudiated on March 4, the market price figure used to calculate damages should be the March 4 price. We do not agree. The measure of damages set forth in section 2–708(1) is "the difference between the market price *at the time and place for tender* and the unpaid contract price." N.Y.U.C.C. Law § 2–708(1) (emphasis added); *cf. id.* § 2–713(1) (*buyer's* damages for repudiation by *seller* measured by contract/market price differential "at the time when the buyer learned of the breach").

4. Southwire presented no evidence and made no claim concerning any expenses saved by Trans World as a result of Southwire's breach. Such expenses, if established, would have reduced the recoverable damages. N.Y.U.C.C. Law § 2–708(1); *see Katz Communications, Inc. v. The Evening News Association,* 705 F.2d 20, 26–27 (2d Cir.1983).

5. Although Trans World had available to it about 78,000 tons of aluminum at the time of the breach, Trans World had corresponding obligations to deliver about 76,000 tons of aluminum to buyers other than Southwire. Absent any indication that Trans World had "identified" any of this metal to the Southwire contract, *see* N.Y.U.C.C. Law § 2–501(b), we cannot say, as could the court in *Nobs,* that a change in the market price would not affect the seller's "benefit of the bargain."

Thus, the pertinent market price date is not the date of repudiation but the date for tender.

We would accept Southwire's argument that the date Trans World learned of the repudiation would be the correct date on which to calculate the market price had this action been tried *before* the time for full performance under the contract. *See* N.Y.U.C.C. § 2–723(1) (market price at time aggrieved party learned of repudiation used to calculate damages in action for anticipatory repudiation that "comes to trial before time for performance with respect to some or all of the goods"). However, where damages are awarded *after* the time for full performance, as in this case, the calculation of damages under section 2–708(1) should reflect the actual market price at each successive date when tender was to have been made under the repudiated installment contract. This was the rule prior to enactment of the Uniform Commercial Code. *United States v. Burton Coal Co.,* 273 U.S. 337, 340, 47 S.Ct. 351, 352, 71 L.Ed. 670 (1927) (following repudiation of supply contract, "seller may recover the difference between the contract price and the market value at the times when and the places where deliveries should have been made"); *L.W. Foster Sportswear Co. v. Goldblatt Brothers, Inc.,* 356 F.2d 906, 910 & n. 6 (7th Cir.1966) (recognizing same standard under pre-U.C.C. law and U.C.C. § 2–708); *see* 67A Am.Jur.2d *Sales* § 1115, at 505 n. 19 (2d ed. 1985); *id.* § 1118, at 510 n. 50. New York did not intend to deviate from this measure of damages upon adoption of the Uniform Commercial Code: The Official Comment to section 2–708 indicates that the "prior uniform statutory provision is followed generally in setting the current market price at the time and place for tender as the standard by which damages for non-acceptance are to be determined." N.Y.U.C.C. Law § 2–708 Official Comment 1. The "prior uniform statutory provision" indicated that where " 'there is an available market for the goods * * * [damages should be measured by] the difference between the contract price and the market or current price * * * when the goods ought to have been accepted, or, if no time was fixed for acceptance, then at the time of the refusal to accept.' " *Id.* § 2–708 Practice Commentary (quoting Sales Act § 64 (McKinney's Personal Property Law § 145)).

We therefore conclude that when calculating damages for a buyer's repudiation of an installment contract by the contract/market price differential, "time * * * for tender" under section 2–708(1) is the date for each successive tender of an installment, as specified in the contract. *See* 67A Am.Jur.2d *Sales* § 1118, at 510 ("[W]here the breach is of an installment contract, damages should be measured by the market price at the time of each delivery." (footnote omitted)). In this case the successive dates for tender were the last day of each month in 1982, at which time Trans World was authorized to invoice that month's shipments even if such shipments had not been "released" by Southwire's delivery instructions. A contract/market price differential should have been calculated for each month during 1982.

[Margin note: Measure of damages was inappropriate but lucky for D. Actual would have been worse!]

We recognize that the jury relied upon a damage calculation prepared for Trans World that did not use actual market prices for each month of scheduled tenders. Instead, Trans World's expert took the actual price for April 1982 and projected forward from that date "anticipated" increases of $15 per metric ton for each month thereafter. Though the use of such an estimate was inappropriate because the actual market price for each successive month was known by the date of the trial, Southwire has no basis for complaint. Trans World's projected monthly market prices were closer to the contract price than were the actual market prices. Trans World therefore received less in damages using its expert's projection than it would have received using the correct measure. Furthermore, Southwire did not preserve at trial the factual issue as to the correct market price on each successive date of tender. Southwire did not object to Trans World's use or the accuracy of projected prices nor otherwise raise the issue with the jury, relying instead on its unsuccessful effort to convince the jurors that the contract/market price differential was not an appropriate method for calculating damages. Having failed to preserve the point for appeal, Southwire may not now raise the issue for the first time. *See, e.g., Schmidt v. Polish People's Republic,* 742 F.2d 67, 70 (2d Cir.1984).

* * *

We have considered Southwire's remaining claims and find them to lack merit. The judgment of the District Court is affirmed.

Notes

1. Given the remedial objectives of UCC 1–106(1) and the general duty of good faith in the "enforcement" of the contract, UCC 1–203, was the seller overcompensated under UCC 2–708(1)? Retrace the statutory steps to the seller's victory: UCC 2–610(b), 2–703(e), 2–708(2) (rejected by the court), and 2–708(1). Relying on *Nobs Chemical,* which was distinguished in the principal case, the court in Union Carbide Corporation v. Consumers Power Co., 636 F.Supp. 1498 (E.D.Mich.1986), held that a seller who was a middleman and who did not, under the pricing arrangement, bear the risk of fluctuations in the market price, could not use UCC 2–708(1) when that measure resulted in overcompensation. The court interpreted the word "inadequate" in UCC 2–708(2) to mean "incapable or inadequate to accomplish the stated purpose of the UCC remedies of compensating the aggrieved person but not overcompensating that person or specifically punishing the other person." In short, where the measure of damages in UCC 2–708(1) fails fairly to measure the damages suffered by the plaintiff, that formula is "inadequate" and, to avoid a penalty, UCC 2–708(2) should be applied.

[Margin note: Court interprets "inadequate" under (2)]

2. Is there any support for the proposition that when the buyer repudiates, the seller's damages should be limited to the difference between the contract price for the entire undelivered balance and the market price determined at a commercially reasonable time after the repudiation? See UCC 2–610(a). Should this be the law when the seller, under the pricing

arrangement, has assumed the risk of movements up or down in market prices?

SECTION 5.   SELLER'S RIGHT TO RESELL AND "FIX" DAMAGES

In the *Trans World Metals* case, the seller did not have aluminum conforming or identified to the contract on hand at the time of the breach.   Suppose, however, that conforming aluminum in sufficient quantities was within the seller's possession or control.   See UCC 2–704(1).   If an action for the price is not possible, UCC 2–709(1)(b), the seller should consider the remedy of resale under UCC 2–706, a provision which permits the seller to resell and authoritatively fix his damages based upon the difference between the contract price and what is realized from the resale contract.   Lost volume problems aside, this recovery normally places the seller in the position he would have occupied if the buyer had fully performed.

Read UCC 2–706 carefully and work the next problem.

Problem 7–6   *Thurs 2/18*

Simpka v. Volta: Scene Four

In June, Simpka made the first shipment of standard furniture and received a $30,000 payment from Volta.   Volta, however, was dissatisfied with the shipment and a dispute over quality simmered over the summer, with Simpka withholding delivery.   On September 14, Volta repudiated the entire contract, including the custom furniture.   Assume that Volta's repudiation was a total breach of contract.   Simpka has three installments of standard furniture, for which Volta agreed to pay $90,000, and the custom furniture, for which Volta agreed to pay $80,000, on hand and identified to the contract.   Simpka would like to resell all of that furniture, either in Ohio or New York, and obtain the maximum damages under UCC 2–706.   It is now October 1 and you have the following facts before you:

1.   The cost of shipping each installment of standard furniture from Ohio to New York is $6,000.   The cost of shipping the custom furniture is $10,000.

2.   The market price of the custom furniture in Ohio on September 14 was $75,000.   It is expected to remain constant for the balance of the year. The market price of the custom furniture in New York on September 14 was $70,000.   It is uncertain how that market will perform in the future.

3.   The market price of an installment of standard furniture on September 14 was $30,000 in Ohio and $33,000 in New York.   On October 1, the respective prices were $27,000 in Ohio and $30,000 in New York.   It is estimated that on November 1, the respective prices will be $22,500 in Ohio and $27,000 in New York and that on December 1 the respective prices will be $18,000 in Ohio and $27,000 in New York.

A.   Develop a plan to resell all of the furniture that has the best chance to maximize damages and satisfy UCC 2–706.   *Re Still act commercially reasonably in good faith.*

B. What remedy, if any, is available if the conditions of UCC 2–706 are not satisfied? See Comment 2, UCC 2–706. How should you plan for this contingency? Remember, some courts have held that a seller who acts in bad faith is limited to the damages that should have been recovered under UCC 2–706 if all the conditions had been met. See Note: Seller's Remedial Choices, infra at p. 606.

C. If, upon resale, you satisfy the conditions of UCC 2–706, are you foreclosed from using UCC 2–708(1)? Have you made an election of remedies? See Comment 1, UCC 2–703.

AFRAM EXPORT CORP. v. METALLURGIKI HALYPS, S.A.

United States Court of Appeals, Seventh Circuit, 1985.
772 F.2d 1358.

POSNER, CIRCUIT JUDGE.

The appeal and cross-appeal in this diversity breach of contract suit raise a variety of interesting issues, in particular of personal jurisdiction and contract damages.

Afram Export Corporation, the plaintiff, is a Wisconsin corporation that exports scrap metal. Metallurgiki Halyps, S.A., the defendant, is a Greek corporation that makes steel. In 1979, after a series of trans-Atlantic telephone and telex communications, the parties made a contract through an exchange of telex messages for the purchase by Metallurgiki of 15,000 tons of clean shredded scrap, at $135 per ton, F.O.B. Milwaukee, delivery to be made by the end of April. Metallurgiki apparently intended to use the scrap to make steel for shipment to Egypt, pursuant to a contract with an Egyptian buyer. Afram agreed to pay the expenses of an agent of Metallurgiki—Shields—to inspect the scrap for cleanliness before it was shipped.

The scrap for the contract was prepared, in Milwaukee, by Afram Metal Processing Company. Both Afram Metal Processing and the plaintiff Afram Export are wholly owned subsidiaries of Afram Brothers. All three are Wisconsin corporations, and have the same officers and directors. Unless otherwise indicated, when we say "Afram" we mean "Afram Export."

Shields arrived to inspect the scrap on April 12. He told Afram that the scrap was clean but that Metallurgiki would not accept it, because the price of scrap had fallen. Sure enough, Metallurgiki refused to accept it. Afram brought this suit after selling the scrap to other buyers. Metallurgiki unsuccessfully challenged the court's jurisdiction over it, then filed a counterclaim alleging that Afram had broken the contract and had thereby made it impossible for Metallurgiki to fulfill its contract with the Egyptian purchaser.

After a bench trial, the district judge gave judgment for Afram for $425,149 and dismissed the counterclaim. 592 F.Supp. 446 (D.Wis. 1984). Metallurgiki has appealed from the judgment for Afram, and

Afram has cross-appealed, contending that the judge should have given it the full damages it sought based on the difference between the contract price and the cover price—$483,750—plus incidental damages of $40,665, prejudgment interest, the costs of a so-called public sale, and attorney's fees for defending against the counterclaim.

* * *

* * * Afram claims that it sold all of the scrap rejected by Metallurgiki at a public sale on June 15, 1979, and that its damages should therefore be based on the price of that sale, which was $102.75 per ton. The district judge disagreed. He found that two-thirds of the scrap had been sold at a substantially higher price to Luria Brothers on June 4 ($118—actually somewhat less, because Afram defrayed some freight costs) and the other third to International Traders on September 15 at a price of $103. Afram points out that the sale on June 4 actually was made by its affiliate, Afram Metal Processing Company, and further argues that since all Afram scrap is sold from the same pile in Milwaukee it is arbitrary to treat the first sale after the breach of contract as the cover transaction, rather than the sale that Afram designated as that transaction.

We agree with the district judge that the sale on June 4 was a cover transaction, even though the nominal seller was a different corporation from the plaintiff. Not only are both corporations wholly owned subsidiaries of another corporation, not only do all three corporations have the same officers and directors, but the record indicates substantial commingling of assets and operation of the three corporations as a single entity. Shortly after Metallurgiki's rejection, Zeke Afram, an officer of both Afram Export (the party to the contract with Metallurgiki) and Afram Metal Processing (the nominal owner of the scrap sold on June 4), called Luria Brothers and explained that he had extra scrap for sale because of a buyer's breach; apparently he did not bother to indicate which Afram corporation he was calling on behalf of. The June 4 sale followed shortly. The conversation and the timing of the sale are powerful evidence that the breach enabled the sale—that it would not have occurred but for the breach—and hence that the revenue from the sale must be subtracted from the contract price to determine Afram's loss. Cf. *Servbest Foods, Inc. v. Emessee Industries, Inc.*, 82 Ill.App.3d 662, 668–72, 37 Ill.Dec. 945, 951–53, 403 N.E.2d 1, 7–9 (1980).

But this does not dispose completely of the issue of the cover price. If the sale on June 15 was "made in good faith and in a commercially reasonable manner," it fixed Afram's damages on the remaining one-third of the scrap. UCC § 2–706(1), Wis.Stat. § 402.706(1). The question may seem less than earthshaking since the June 15 sale price and the September sale price which the district court used as the cover price for the remaining third were only 25¢ per ton apart. But the bona fides of the June 15 sale casts additional light on the intercorporate relations of the Afram group and hence on the proper interpretation of the sale to Luria Brothers. In any event, the district judge was entitled to find that neither condition in section 2–706(1) was satisfied. Cf. *Coast Trading Co. v. Cudahy Co.*, 592 F.2d 1074, 1080–81 (9th Cir. 1979). The June 15 "sale" was about as pure a bookkeeping transaction—as empty of economic significance—as can be imagined. Cf. *Milbrew v. Commissioner of Internal Revenue*, 710 F.2d 1302, 1305 (7th Cir.1983). It consisted of a transfer of the scrap on the books of one affiliated corporation to the books of another. The transferor and transferee were not only under common ownership but were operated as if they were limbs of a single organism. The scrap itself was not moved; it remained on the scrap heap till sold later on. No invoice or check for the sale was produced at trial. The inference that the sale was designed simply to maximize the enterprise's damages, leaving it free to resell the scrap at higher prices later on, is overpowering. The sale of the scrap three months later to International Traders at a (slightly) higher price provided better evidence of what the enterprise actually lost, so far as the scrap not sold to Luria Brothers is concerned, by Metallurgiki's breach of contract.

The next issue relates to incidental damages, which the Uniform Commercial Code allows a seller who is the victim of a breach of contract to recover in addition to the difference between sale price and cover price. UCC § 2–706(1), Wis.Stat. § 402.706(1). Incidental damages are "any commercially reasonable charges, expenses or commissions incurred in stopping delivery, in the transportation, care and custody of goods after buyer's breach, in connection with return or resale of the goods or otherwise resulting from the breach." UCC § 2–710, Wis.Stat. § 402.710. Afram says it borrowed $2.5 million from a bank of which $2.025 million was to finance the purchase of the junked cars that it shredded in order to produce scrap in the form called for by the contract with Metallurgiki. It has calculated the interest (some $40,000) that it paid between the date of breach and the date of cover on the amount of the loan used to finance the cars. But it can recover this interest, if at all, only as incidental damages, and not as consequential damages, for under the Uniform Commercial Code consequential damages are a buyer's not a seller's remedy. See UCC § 2–715, Wis. Stat. § 402.715; *Nobs Chemical, U.S.A., Inc. v. Koppers Co.*, 616 F.2d 212, 216 (5th Cir.1980).

The line between incidental and consequential damages is rather unclear. It may help in locating it to notice that in many cases of consequential damages, a buyer who is the victim of a seller's breach of contract is seeking damages for consequences that he could have avoided or minimized at lower cost than the contract breaker. *EVRA Corp. v. Swiss Bank Corp.*, 673 F.2d 951, 957 (7th Cir.1982). In the case that established the common law's position that consequential damages are not recoverable without special notice to the seller, *Hadley v. Baxendale*, 9 Ex. 341, 156 Eng.Rep. 145 (1854), the defendant, a carrier, broke a contract with the plaintiff to deliver the plaintiff's mill shaft to the manufacturer of the shaft for repair. Because the plaintiff had no spare shaft, it was forced to shut down the mill; and it sought the profits that it lost during the period of shut-down caused by the defendant's delay in delivering the shaft. The court refused to award these damages. They could easily have been avoided by the plaintiff's having a spare shaft, which prudence dictated that a mill owner have anyway. This omission could not fairly be charged to the seller. It was not—as the prerequisite for obtaining consequential damages in a contract case has come to be called, see, e.g., Farnsworth, Contracts § 12.14, at p. 876 (1982)—"foreseeable" by him, because a seller is not charged with foreseeing the buyer's imprudence.

This would be the same case, only in the unusual setting of a seller's seeking consequential damages, if Metallurgiki's breach of contract had precipitated Afram into bankruptcy because Afram was paying back-breaking interest on the loan that it had taken out to enable it to fulfill its obligations under the contract. Afram would be responsible for arranging its affairs in such a way as not to be abnormally vulnerable to a breach of contract; excessive leverage would be the counterpart to Hadley's failure to keep a spare shaft on hand. At the other end of the spectrum, reasonable expenses incurred by Afram in putting the scrap in a form where it would be salable to a substitute buyer would be recoverable as incidental damages; virtually by definition, such expenses could not be avoided by greater prudence on the seller's part.

The actual case is somewhere in the middle, but if we had to decide exactly where, we probably would disagree with the district judge, who regarded this as a case of consequential rather than incidental damages. Although knowledge of the details of the seller's financial arrangements is not chargeable to the buyer, it is obvious to the buyer and unavoidable by the seller that the seller will incur an interest cost (explicit or implicit, as we shall see) in the interval between the breach of the contract and the cover sale; and the party who is better able to avoid this expense and who therefore should bear the risk of its occurrence is the contract-breaking buyer, not the seller. The cases therefore allow the seller to recover the additional interest expense as incidental damages. See, e.g., *Bulk Oil (U.S.A.), Inc. v. Sun Oil Trading Co.,* 697 F.2d 481, 482–84 (2d Cir.1983); *Hofmann v. Stoller,* 320 N.W.2d 786, 792–93 (N.D.1982); *Gray v. West,* 608 S.W.2d 771, 781 (Tex.Civ.App. 1980).

The district judge also suggested that there was no damage, incidental or consequential: "presumably the interest costs for the money to purchase the junk cars would be recovered when the scrap which they had become was sold to some purchaser," so that Afram would be made "whole as to this cost of raw materials through the award of the difference between the contract price and the resale price." But this implies that the price charged to the substitute buyers, Luria Brothers and International Traders, would be calculated on a cost-plus basis, and thus include the additional interest expense that Afram incurred because of Metallurgiki's breach of contract.   Prices in competitive markets are not determined on that basis, however; and so far as the record shows the market for steel scrap is competitive.   The prices that Luria Brothers and International Traders were willing to pay for Afram's steel scrap depended on how much these buyers would have had to pay for the product from competing sellers, not on how much extra interest Afram had to pay because of the delay in selling its scrap.

Nevertheless we agree with the district court's conclusion that Metallurgiki is not liable for the interest that Afram seeks.   All the record contains is the computation of interest.   There is no evidence that Afram would have repaid the loan, or $2.025 million of it, on payment of the contract price by Metallurgiki, had that happy event occurred.   The loan agreement was not placed in evidence, and since the loan is for more than the amount used to buy the junked cars, there is no presumption that it would have been paid back as soon as the contract for which the junked cars had been bought was fulfilled. Indeed, we do not even know whether the loan was repaid when Afram resold the scrap to Luria Brothers and International Traders.   For purposes of computing prejudgment interest, a separate item of damages is discussed next.   Afram kept on calculating interest, at the same rate (prime plus .5 percent) as the interest rate on the loan, right up to the date of trial; this is consistent with Afram's not having repaid the loan when it resold the scrap.

So far as the proof shows, then, Afram is not really complaining about an extra interest expense; it is complaining about losing the use of part of the money it borrowed from the bank, the part that was tied up in the junked cars longer than it would have been had Metallurgiki not broken the contract.   This of course is a genuine loss; it is what economists call an "opportunity cost," and courts now understand that an opportunity cost is a real cost.   See, e.g., *Simmons v. United States,* 698 F.2d 888, 898 (7th Cir.1983).   In this case it would be measured by the interest or profit that Afram could have obtained from investing, or using elsewhere in its business, the money that it would have gotten from Metallurgiki by the end of April if Metallurgiki had not broken the contract, but that as a result of the breach it did not get till June and September.

But a forgone profit from exploiting a valuable opportunity that the breach of contract denied to the victim of the breach fits more comfortably under the heading of consequential damages than of incidental damages.   The profits that Afram might have made from using that $2.025 million elsewhere in its business are like the milling profits that Hadley might have made if the carrier had not delayed in delivering the mill shaft for repair.   Afram has not tried to establish its lost profits from the temporary loss of the use of the $2.025 million; all it is seeking is the extra interest it had to pay.   But its theory is one of opportunity cost, as it makes clear in its brief by stating that it would be entitled to interest as incidental damages even if it had not used borrowed money to pay for the junked cars. Afram is correct that it would incur an opportunity cost whether it used its own money or used money that it had borrowed; in either event it would lose the use of money that it could deploy elsewhere at a profit. But we do not think the law has evolved to the point where every time a buyer breaks a contract, the seller is entitled to the time value of the money tied up in the contract, as incidental damages. All the seller is entitled to is an out-of-pocket interest expense that would not have been incurred but for the breach. We have found no case where (so far as we are able to determine from the statement of facts in the case) the seller was able to recover interest on a general business loan not tied to the subject matter of the sale, but we have found two cases that imply he may not. See *Schiavi Mobile Homes, Inc. v. Gironda,* 463 A.2d 722, 727 (Me.1983); *S.C. Gray, Inc. v. Ford Motor Co.,* 92 Mich.App. 789, 811–12, 286 N.W.2d 34, 43–44 (1979).

*   *   *

Thus we affirm the judgment of the district court except with respect to the denial of prejudgment interest to Afram, as to which we remand the case for a determination of the amount of prejudgment interest to which Afram is entitled at the statutory rate of five percent. Wis.Stat. § 138.04; *Kilgust Heating Div. v. Kemp,* 70 Wis.2d 544, 550, 235 N.W.2d 292, 295–96 (1975). No costs in this court.

Affirmed in part, reversed in part, and remanded.

Notes

1. Why was the public resale on June 15 at $102.75 per ton improper? Should the September resale price of $103 per ton be used to measure damages under UCC 2–706(1)? UCC 2–708(1)?

2. According to the court, Afram was not a "lost volume" seller—but for the breach, Afram could not have resold the scrap. How, then, are the proceeds from the resale to be treated under UCC 2–706(1)?

3. Exactly how did Judge Posner classify and treat the interest payments made by Afram after the breach on an obligation incurred much earlier? If they are neither incidental nor consequential damages, what are they—fixed or "overhead" costs? In Ernst Steel Corp. v. Horn Construction Division, Halliburton Co., 104 A.D.2d 55, 481 N.Y.S.2d 833 (1984), the court stated: "In an appropriate case a seller is entitled to recover commercially reasonable finance and interest charges incurred as a result of a buyer's breach as a proper item of incidental damages *   *   * For the most part, however, interest expenses have only been awarded to sellers for indebtedness specifically identified to goods intended for resale to the breaching party and who, as a result of the breaching, cannot repay the loans."

4. Article 2 does not explicitly provide that the seller may recover consequential damages caused by a buyer's breach. Compare UCC 2–715(2). But does it foreclose such a recovery? Suppose that the buyer had

promised to pay $100,000 on August 1 for scrap delivered on July 1 and knew that the seller needed prompt payment to renew an advantageous contract with another supplier. Despite assurances that payment would be made, the buyer did not pay and the contract was not renewed. The seller, although making reasonable efforts, was unable to obtain alternative financing. It is clear, is it not, that this is a proper case for a consequential damage claim under general contract law? See UCC 1–103; Restatement, Second, Contracts § 351, Comment (e).

Note: Seller's Remedial Choices—Cumulation or Election?

Comment 1 to UCC 2–703 states that the section "rejects any doctrine of election of remedies as a fundamental policy" and stresses that the "index" is "essentially cumulative in nature" and includes "all of the available remedies for breach." Whether the choice or pursuit of one remedy "bars another depends entirely on the facts of the individual case." Thus, UCC 2–709(3) provides that a seller who pursues an action for the price and is "held not entitled" to it "shall nevertheless be awarded damages for non-acceptance under * * *" UCC 2–708. Similarly, Comment 2 to UCC 2–706 states that a failure to act properly under this section deprives the seller "of damages here provided and relegates him to that provided in Section 2–708." The primary risk of pursuing a particular remedy and failing is, apparently, one of evidence: will the record support a claim for damages under UCC 2–708? A case in point is B & R Textile Corp. v. Paul Rothman Indus., 101 Misc.2d 98, 420 N.Y.S.2d 609, aff'd, 420 N.Y.S.2d 609, 27 UCC Rep.Serv. 994 (N.Y.Sup.Ct.1979), where the buyer argued that the seller's reliance upon the price received in a resale where the required notice was not given constituted an election of remedies. This argument was rejected by a court, which held that the seller's prompt resale generated a price which, when supported by evidence of other sales contemporaneously made by the seller, established the "market price" under UCC 2–708(1). See also, Cole v. Melvin, 441 F.Supp. 193 (D.S.D.1977), where a defective resale left a thin but adequate record from which to establish the market price. The point for the litigator is clear: develop, if possible, the "fall back" evidence necessary to satisfy UCC 2–708(1).

Some policy questions lurk on the fringes. Suppose the seller pursues the resale remedy and complies fully with UCC 2–706. If, thereafter, he sues for higher damages under UCC 2–708(1) will he be limited by UCC 2–706(1)? Or, suppose the seller arguably should have resold under UCC 2–706 but failed to do so. Will a recovery under UCC 2–708(1) be reduced by what he could have obtained on a resale? The answers to these questions may become clearer after we have considered the so-called "lost volume" problem and the application of UCC 2–708(2) in the next section. At least one court, however, has held that if the seller is *not* a "lost volume" seller and has conducted a commercially unreasonable resale under UCC 2–706(1), the recovery under UCC 2–708(1) will be limited by what the seller *should* have received in damages if the resale had been proper. The seller's apparent bad faith in the resale limited the recovery to "actual losses" and precluded any windfall gains permitted under the formula in

UCC 2–708(1). See Coast Trading Co. v. Cudahy Co., 592 F.2d 1074 (9th Cir. 1978).

SECTION 6. SELLER'S RIGHT TO "PERSONALIZED" DAMAGES—UCC 2–708(2)

In the scheme of things, UCC 2–708(2) appears to be the seller's remedy of last resort. An assumption is that if conforming goods can be identified before or after the breach, the seller will prefer either an action for the price under UCC 2–709 or damages based upon a resale under UCC 2–706. If those remedies fail, the seller can resort to damages under UCC 2–708. But which part of 2–708, subsection (1) with its contract-market price formula, or subsection (2) which awards the "profit (including reasonable overhead) which the seller would have made from full performance by the buyer * * *?"

[handwritten margin note: This assumes the seller will prefer either an action for the price under §2-709 or damages based upon a resale §2-706.]

The Code answer is that UCC 2–708(1) should be applied unless the measure of damages is "inadequate to put the seller in as good a position as performance would have done. * * *" As we have seen, however, if subsection (1) puts the seller in a better position than subsection (2), and does not, when the policy of UCC 1–106(1) is considered, overcompensate, then the buyer cannot limit the seller to the profits that would have been made on their particular contract. This analysis, with its emphasis upon an objective measure of damages, reinforces the residual character of UCC 2–708(2), with its emphasis upon a particularized measure.

Accepting this analysis for the moment, the critical questions for the lawyer and judge are: (1) When should UCC 2–708(2) be used to measure the seller's damages; and (2) When applicable, how should those damages be measured? These questions have generated a continuing flow of law review commentary, much of which attempts to apply rather complex if not sophisticated economic analysis. For a recent example, see Note, *Lost-Profits Damage Awards Under Uniform Commercial Code Section 2–708(2)*, 37 Stan.L.Rev. 1109 (1985). For a clear and sensible analysis, see Sebert, *Remedies Under Article Two of the Uniform Commercial Code: An Agenda for Review*, 130 U.Pa.L.Rev. 360, 383–407 (1981).

Problem 7–7

Simpka v. Volta—Scene Five *!*

On July 1, Volta contracted to purchase office furniture, to be manufactured by Simpka, from Dolt, a distributor. The price was $90,000. Dolt then placed an order for the furniture with Simpka for $80,000, with delivery to Volta no later than October 1. On August 15, Volta, without justification, repudiated the contract with Dolt. Dolt promptly cancelled the order with Simpka, who had not started to work on the goods, for a customary cancellation charge of $1,000.

S comes to you for advice. The market price of the furniture at the "time and place for tender", October 1, under UCC 2–708(1) was estimated

[handwritten margin note: S = Seller M = Manufacturer B = Buyer]

to be $90,000. S had incurred $2,000 in expenses between July 1 and August 15. S would have paid M $80,000 for the furniture and spent another $1,500 to prepare the goods for delivery if B had not repudiated. These expenditures, however, were not made.

A. Which section should be used to measure S's damages? Why?

B. If UCC 2–708(2) is applicable, how should Dolt's damages be measured?

NATIONAL CONTROLS, INC. v. COMMODORE BUSINESS MACHINES, INC.

Court of Appeal of California, First District, 1985.
163 Cal.App.3d 688, 209 Cal.Rptr. 636.

SCOTT, ASSOCIATE JUSTICE.

Respondent National Controls, Inc. (NCI) brought an action for breach of contract against appellant Commodore Business Machines, Inc. (Commodore). After a court trial, judgment was entered awarding NCI over $280,000 in damages, and Commodore has appealed. *Judgment Affirmed*

I

Facts

NCI manufactures electronic weighing and measuring devices. Among its products is the model 3221 electronic microprocessor technology load cell scale (the 3221), which is designed to interface with a cash register for use at check-out stands. NCI sells the 3221 to cash register manufacturers, also termed original equipment manufacturers, or O.E.M.s. NCI does not maintain an inventory stock of the scales, but builds them to specific order by an O.E.M. The 3221 is a standard unit, which is modified by NCI to meet the specifications of each O.E.M. with respect to cash register compatability, paint, and logo.

In November 1980, Commodore had initial discussions with NCI about the possibility of Commodore becoming an O.E.M. customer. By telephone, Commodore purchased one 3221, which was sent by NCI to Commodore's Texas facility, along with NCI's standard specifications for the 3221 and its standard price schedule. In December 1980, Commodore ordered and paid for four more scales. Again, the orders were made by telephone. NCI did not receive a purchase order from Commodore; instead, Commodore merely gave NCI a Commodore purchase order number over the phone; that number was written on the sales order prepared by NCI and sent to Commodore.

In March 1981, Terry Rogers of Commodore ordered an additional 30 scales. The order was placed by telephone, and once again Commodore did not send NCI a purchase order. Instead, Rogers gave Wiggins of NCI a purchase order number by telephone; that number was entered by Wiggins on NCI's sales order.

On March 31, 1981, in a phone conversation with Wiggins, Rogers placed a firm order for 900 scales: 50 to be delivered in May, 150 in June, 300 in July, and 400 in August. Wiggins and Rogers agreed on quantity, price, and delivery schedule. As in the previous transactions,

Rogers gave Wiggins a purchase order number over the telephone, Wiggins then prepared an NCI sales order, entered on it the Commodore purchase order number, and mailed a copy of that sales order to Commodore. NCI also sent a copy of its sales order to its Florida manufacturing facility, which began manufacture of the units.

In a departure from its previous practice, Commodore also mailed its purchase order to NCI. Paragraph 19 of the reverse side of that order contained a provision limiting the damages for which Commodore would be responsible in the event of a breach; in particular, the provision disclaimed liability for any incidental or consequential damages.

Wiggins of NCI testified that he does not recall ever seeing the Commodore purchase order. Both he and Rogers testified that during their phone conversations, there was no discussion of any terms and conditions on that purchase order other than price, quantity, and delivery schedule. According to Commodore's Rogers, the primary purpose of its purchase order was to confirm what had been discussed by telephone and to provide a written copy of the delivery schedule.

Delivery was made to Commodore of the first 200 units, and 300 units were ready to ship in June of 1981. As of that date, the remaining 400 units of the order were nearly complete. However, Commodore accepted only the first 50 scales, and did not accept or pay for the remaining 850 units. Thereafter, all of the 850 units were resold to National Semiconductor, an existing O.E.M. customer. NCI's vice president and general manager in charge of its Florida manufacturing facility testified that in 1980 and 1981, the plant had the production capacity to more than double its output of 3221's.

Commodore took delivery of only first 50 scales

850 scales were re-sold by NCI

Among its findings and conclusions, the trial court concluded that the terms of the parties' contract were those established during their telephone discussions prior to and on March 31, 1981, and in the November 1980 letter from NCI to Commodore enclosing a price schedule, as well as "the terms" of NCI's prior sales orders. It then concluded that the provision on limitation of damages in Commodore's purchase order was a proposal for an additional term which did not become part of the contract because it was a material alteration thereof. The court also found that NCI was a "lost volume seller" who was entitled to recover the loss of profit it would have made on the sale of the 850 units to Commodore, notwithstanding its subsequent resale of those units to another customer.

TRIAL COURT FOUND:
1. Terms of K were those agreed to by phone + on 11/80 NCI letter
2. Commodore's ¶19 was an add'l term & not part of K.
3. NCI is a "lost volume" seller

* * *

[The court affirmed the trial court's ruling that Commodore's limitation of damage clause did not become part of the contract.]

III

Commodore also contends that the trial court erred when it relied on section 2708, subdivision (2), to award NCI damages by way of lost profits. In a related argument, Commodore contends that if lost profits

Commodore says Court erred in applying 2-708(2) for lost profits.

[handwritten margin note: And if lost profits are the measure Δ claims they are entitled to a credit for re-sale anove]

were the proper measure of damages, it was entitled under the plain language of section 2708 to credit for the proceeds of NCI's resale of the contract goods to National Semiconductor.

[handwritten margin note: Generally §2-706 Will apply.]

Damages caused by a buyer's breach or repudiation of a sales contract are usually measured by the difference between the resale price of the goods and the contract price, as provided by Uniform Commercial Code section 2–706. When it is not appropriate to use this difference to measure the seller's loss (as when the goods have not been resold in a commercially reasonable manner), the seller's measure of damages is the difference between the market and the contract prices as provided in Uniform Commercial Code section 2–708, subdivision (1).

[handwritten margin note: Then §2-708(1) if inadequate, (as here), then (2)]

Ordinarily, this measure will result in recovery equal to the value of the seller's bargain. However, under certain circumstances this formula is also not an adequate means to ascertain that value, and the seller may recover his loss of expected profits on the contract under subdivision (2) of Uniform Commercial Code section 2–708. (3 Hawkland, Uniform Commercial Code Series (1982–1984) §§ 2–708—2–708:04.)

Section 2708 provides [the court quoted the statute.]

[handwritten margin note: Lost Volume Seller]

When buyers have repudiated a fixed price contract to purchase goods, several courts elsewhere have construed subdivision (2) of Uniform Commercial Code section 2–708 or its state counterpart to permit the award of lost profits under the contract to the seller who establishes that he is a "lost volume seller," i.e., one who proves that even though he resold the contract goods, that sale to the third party would have been made regardless of the buyer's breach.[3] (*Neri v. Retail Marine Corporation* (1972) 30 N.Y.2d 393, 334 N.Y.S.2d 165, 168, 285 N.E.2d 311, 314; *Snyder v. Herbert Greenbaum & Assoc., Inc.* (1977) 38 Md.App. 144, 380 A.2d 618, 624–625; *Teradyne, Inc. v. Teledyne Industries, Inc.* (1st Cir.1982) 676 F.2d 865, 866–868; *Nederlandse, etc. v. Grand Pre-Stressed Corp.* (E.D.N.Y.1979) 466 F.Supp. 846, affd. (2nd Cir.) 614 F.2d 1289.) The lost volume seller must establish that had the breaching buyer performed, the seller would have realized profits from two sales. (See Goetz & Scott, *Measuring Sellers' Damages: The Lost-Profits Puzzle* (1979) 31 Stan.L.Rev. 323, 326.)

In *Neri v. Retail Marine Corporation, supra,* 285 N.E.2d 311, seller contracted to sell a new boat, which it ordered and received from its supplier. The buyer then repudiated the contract. Later, seller sold the boat to another buyer, for the same price. The court relied on Uniform Commercial Code section 2–708, subdivision (2), to award the seller its lost profits under the contract, reasoning that the record established that market damages would be inadequate to put the seller in as good a position as performance would have done. The court drew an analogy to an auto dealer with an inexhaustible supply of cars. A

3. One California court has applied subdivision (2) of section 2708 to hold that a "middleman" is entitled to lost profits. (*Distribu-Dor, Inc. v. Karadanis* (1970) 11 Cal.App.3d 463, 470, 90 Cal.Rptr. 231.) That case is not dispositive here, as it does not involve a lost volume seller.

breach of an agreement to buy a car at a standard price would cost that dealer a sale even though he was able to resell the car at the same price. In other words, had the breaching buyer performed, seller would have made two sales instead of one. (*Id.*, at pp. 312–315.)

While the seller in *Neri* was a retailer, the lost volume seller rule is also applicable to manufacturers. (*Nederlandse, etc. v. Grand Pre-Stressed Corp., supra,* 466 F.Supp. 846.) In *Nederlandse,* seller, a manufacturer of steel strand, brought an action against buyer for breach of an agreement to purchase approximately 1,180 metric tons of strand. Defendant had accepted only about 221 tons, and repudiated the remaining 958 tons, of which 317 tons had been already produced by seller. Seller resold the 317 tons to various third party purchasers. (*Id.*, at p. 849.)

The court held that seller was entitled to lost profits under Uniform Commercial Code section 2–708, subdivision (2), and that no set-off would be allowed for profits earned through the sales to third parties. The evidence established that seller had sufficient production capacity to supply not only the 1,180 tons required by the contract, but also the 317 tons sold to third parties. The fact that seller was a manufacturer rather than a retailer, and that he produced only to order rather than maintaining an inventory, was of no significance in determining the applicability of Uniform Commercial Code section 2–708. (*Id.*, at pp. 853–854.)

Commodore accurately points out that the lost volume seller rule has been criticized by some commentators as overly simplistic. (Goetz & Scott, *supra,* 31 Stan.L.Rev. 323, 330–354.) Nevertheless, those courts considering the question have held that Uniform Commercial Code section 2–708 does allow lost profits to a "lost volume seller" and that criticism has not resulted in any revision of the section.

Commodore also contends that if NCI was entitled to lost profits under the contract, Commodore should have received credit for the proceeds of the resale.

The literal language of section 2708, subdivision (2), does provide some support for that contention: "If the measure of damages provided in subdivision (1) is inadequate to put the seller in as good a position as performance would have done then the measure of damages is the profit (including reasonable overhead) which the seller would have made from full performance by the buyer, *together with * * * due credit for payments or proceeds of resale.*" (Emphasis added.) However, courts elsewhere have uniformly held that the underscored language does not apply to a lost volume seller. (See *Neri v. Retail Marine Corporation, supra,* 285 N.E.2d at p. 314, fn. 2; *Famous Knitwear Corporation v. Drug Fair, Inc.* (4th Cir.1974) 493 F.2d 251, 254, fn. 7; *Snyder v. Herbert Greenbaum & Assoc., Inc., supra,* 380 A.2d at pp. 625–626; *Teradyne, Inc. v. Teledyne Industries, Inc., supra,* 676 F.2d 865, 868.)

[margin handwritten note: Applying a credit to Δ for the re-sale of the goods is inconsistent with purpose of providing π lost profits. π could have rec'd both!]

As the court in *Snyder v. Herbert Greenbaum & Assoc., Inc., supra,* 380 A.2d 618 explained, "Logically, lost volume status, which entitles the seller to the § 2–708(2) formula rather than the formula found in § 2–708(1), is inconsistent with a credit for the proceeds of resale. The whole concept of lost volume status is that the sale of the goods to the resale purchaser could have been made with other goods had there been no breach. In essence, the original sale and the second sale are independent events, becoming related only after breach, as the original sale goods are applied to the second sale. To require a credit for the proceeds of resale is to deny the essential element that entitles the lost volume seller to § 2–708(2) in the first place—the mutual independence of the contract and the resale.

[margin handwritten note: If credit were applied, π's recovery would be no different than (1)]

"Practically, if the 'due credit' clause is applied to the lost volume seller, his measure of damages is no different from his recovery under § 2–708(1). Under § 2–708(1) he recovers the contract/market differential and the profit he makes on resale. If the 'due credit' provision is applied, the seller recovers only the profit he makes on resale plus the difference between the resale price and the contract price, an almost identical measure to § 2–708(1). If the 'due credit' clause is applied to the lost volume seller, the damage measure of 'lost profits' is rendered nugatory, and he is not put in as good a position as if there had been performance." (*Id.,* at p. 625.)

In this case, the evidence was undisputed that in 1980 and 1981, NCI's manufacturing plant was operating at approximately 40 percent capacity. The production of the 900 units did not tax that capacity, and the plant could have more than doubled its output of 3221's and still have stayed within its capacity. That evidence was sufficient to support the court's findings that NCI had the capacity to supply both Commodore and National Semiconductor, and that had there been no breach by Commodore, NCI would have had the benefit of both the original contract and the resale contract. Accordingly, the trial court correctly determined that NCI was a lost volume seller, that the usual "contract price minus market price" rule set forth in subdivision (1) of section 2708 was inadequate to put NCI in as good a position as performance would have done, and that NCI was therefore entitled to its lost profits on the contract with Commodore, without any set-off for profits on the resale to National Semiconductor.

[margin handwritten note: NCI could have supplied both Commodore and Nat'l Semiconductor.]

Judgment is affirmed.

WHITE, P.J., and BARRY-DEAL, J., concur.

Notes

1. Return to Problem 7–7. Does *Commodore* support a conclusion that Dolt can use UCC 2–708(2) because it was a "lost volume" seller? Professor Sebert concludes that a "jobber" or distributor, i.e., a "middleman whose only role is to procure finished goods and resell them," who decides not to procure the goods after the buyer's repudiation should be able to use UCC 2–708(2). Because the "jobber" does not have finished goods on hand,

"UCC 2–708(2) is the only Code damage provision that produces sensible results for such a seller; all of the other damage provisions contemplate the existence of finished goods." Sebert, 130 U.Pa.L.Rev. at 385. Accord: Blair International, Ltd. v. LaBarge, Inc., 675 F.2d 954 (8th Cir.1982) (UCC 2–708(1) not adequate where seller can't resell or does not have goods); Comeq, Inc. v. Mitternight Boiler Works, Inc., 456 So.2d 264 (Ala.1984).

2. The seller, in *Commodore,* was the manufacturer rather than a middleman and actually resold the goods intended for the buyer. What test does the court use to determine whether the plaintiff was a lost volume seller? In measuring damages under UCC 2–708(2), how does the court treat the proceeds of the resale? Does the court do damage to the language of UCC 2–708(2)? Recall in *Afram,* supra, that Judge Posner concluded, correctly we believe, that if the resale could not be made "but for" the breach, the buyer was entitled to credit for the proceeds of resale.

Problem 7–8

Simpka v. Volta—Scene Six

On March 1, Simpka contracted to manufacture custom furniture for Volta for $80,000, delivery f.o.b. Ohio no later than November 1. On May 1, Volta repudiated without justification. Simpka had commenced to manufacture the furniture but no item was completed. The market price of the furniture in Ohio was $60,000. The market price in New York was $55,000. The economy was in a mild recession, and the respective market prices in November were expected to be $40,000 in Ohio and $35,000 in New York.

A. A summer associate has given you the following memo: "It is clear that Simpka could complete the manufacture, UCC 2–704(2), and attempt to resell the custom furniture. See UCC 2–706(2), stating that it is 'not necessary that the goods be in existence or that any or all of them have been identified to the contract before the breach.' If a resale can be made, damages can be recovered under UCC 2–706(1), or, if there is lost volume, under UCC 2–708(2). If a resale cannot be made, Simpka can recover the price from Volta. UCC 2–709(1)(b). I recommend that we advise Simpka to complete the manufacturing process." Do you agree?

B. Suppose, in the exercise of reasonable commercial judgment, Simpka stopped the manufacturing process. UCC 2–704(2). (1) Simpka had components on hand purchased for the contract which cost $20,000. These components were scrapped for $15,000. (2) Simpka had incurred other performance costs ("variable" costs) of $15,000 which could not be salvaged. (3) Because of the breach, Simpka did not have to incur other performance of "variable" costs, estimated to be $25,000. What damages should Simpka recover under UCC 2–708(2)? Who has the burden of establishing that "overhead" is or is not reasonable?

Note: Who Is a Lost Volume Seller?

The assumption underlying the "lost volume" problem is simple to state: If a seller had the capacity to and probably would have made a second sale regardless of the buyer's breach, the goal of UCC 1–106(1) will be frustrated if the profit the seller would have made on the first sale is offset by the proceeds of the second sale. Embracing this assumption, *Commodore* and the authorities cited therein have used UCC 2–708(2) to protect the profit on the first sale without regard to the proceeds of any resale.

In so doing, the courts have adopted a simple test for determining lost volume: If, in the relevant time period, the seller had the capacity to make a second sale and, after the breach, in fact made a resale, the requirement is satisfied. Rejected is the view, advocated by some commentators, that lost volume exists when the seller satisfies three conditions: (1) The buyer who purchased the resold entity would have been solicited by the seller had there been no breach; (2) The solicitation would have been successful; and (3) The seller could have performed the additional contract. Harris, *A Radical Restatement of the Laws of Seller's Damages: Sales Act and Commercial Code Results Compared,* 18 Stan.L.Rev. 66, 80–83 (1965). In refusing to "require proof of a complex economic relationship," one court was satisfied by proof that the seller "would have made the sale to the resale purchaser even if" the buyer had performed, that the seller "resold the parts, and that it had an existing inventory of these parts." Islamic Republic of Iran v. Boeing Co., 771 F.2d 1279, (9th Cir.1985) (Washington law).

In addition, the courts have ignored (if not rejected) the claim by some that even if a second sale could have been made, it would not, in all probability, have been profitable. See Goetz & Scott, *Measuring Seller's Damages: The Lost-Profits Puzzle,* 31 Stan.L.Rev. 323 (1979). Why? The argument is summarized by Professor Sebert:

> One foundation of the Geotz and Scott argument is the accepted proposition that economically efficient entities, whether they be manufacturers or retailers, attempt to operate at a level of output where marginal cost equals marginal revenue. Economic theory also posits that these efficient sellers are likely to be producing at a level where marginal costs are rising as additional units are produced or sold, and that marginal revenue is likely to be falling, or at best remaining constant, because the increased supply caused by additional production or sales will cause the market price to fall. Based upon these traditional economic concepts, Goetz and Scott argue that, even if the seller had the capacity to do so, a seller operating at the level where marginal cost equals marginal revenue would not have produced the additional goods to sell to buyer 2 if buyer 1 had not breached. In a world of rising marginal costs and static or declining marginal revenue, it would not have been efficient for the seller to produce or obtain additional goods to sell to buyer 2 because the marginal cost of those goods would exceed the marginal revenue received from their sale and the seller would have lost money. Thus, Goetz and Scott suggest that the sale to buyer 2 is a sale that the efficient seller normally would not have made, and therefore the seller is not a lost volume seller.

Sebert at 389–90 *

* Another argument by Goetz and Scott, summarized by Sebert, is that a seller normally will not have lost volume because the buyer's breach will cause an increase

Professor Sebert rejects Goetz and Scott's presumption that the seller is not a lost volume seller, "even though a seller has the capacity to make an additional sale and even though the resale buyer probably would have bought from the seller had the original buyer not breached" without rejecting the possibility that the resale merely replaces the original sale because of the assumed rising marginal costs. He proposes the following approach: " *   *   * (O)nce the seller shows that he had the capacity to make an additional sale and that the resale buyer probably would have bought from him anyway, I would place the burden of proof on the breaching buyer to show that the seller would not have made an additional sale because of rising marginal costs." Sebert at 391.

in demand for the seller's product, offsetting any losses suffered because of the buyer's breach. The assumptions are that the breach indicates that the buyer did not want the goods, and that a sale by the buyer would likely be to someone who otherwise would have bought from the seller. "Because the buyer who breaches can no longer resell the goods, that breach will permit the seller to make an additional sale to a customer who otherwise would have bought from the breaching buyer." Sebert at 392. This argument has been criticized as misrepresenting the problem when the seller is a retailer. Goldberg, *An Economic Analysis of the Lost-Volume Seller,* 57 S.Cal.L.Rev. 283, 288–90 (1984).

Chapter Eight

SELLER'S REPUDIATION AND THE LIKE—A SURVEY OF BUYER'S REMEDIES

SECTION 1. INTRODUCTION *Buyer's Remedies*

There are three "garden" varieties of breach by a seller; repudiation, failure to deliver and a tender of delivery which does not conform to the contract. This chapter will feature the buyer's remedies which are responsive to the first two varieties, namely, permissible action when the expectation of receiving due performance is impaired, UCC 2–609, claims to goods in the possession of the seller, UCC 2–716 and 2–502, and damages, either after "cover" under UCC 2–712 or under the formula in UCC 2–713. Note that where the seller makes a non-conforming tender and the buyer "rightfully rejects or justifiably revokes acceptance," the buyer may claim damages under UCC 2–712 or 2–713. UCC 2–711(1). The special problems involved in the buyer's remedies of rejection, UCC 2–601, and revocation of acceptance, UCC 2–608, however, prompt us to defer their consideration to Chapter Eighteen. Similarly, we have deferred for more extensive treatment the non-conformity called breach of warranty and the remedies available to a buyer who has accepted defective goods and, for one reason or another, does not revoke acceptance under UCC 2–608. These important remedies include "direct," UCC 2–714(2), "incidental," UCC 2–715(1), and "consequential," UCC 2–715(2) damages. At the same time, we will examine the extent to which a seller can disclaim warranties, UCC 2–316, and the parties can alter by agreement code remedies normally available. UCC 2–719.

It is useful to identify the functional parallels between seller's and buyer's remedies. Compare UCC 2–703 and 2–711. And see UCC 2–702 and 2–502, 2–709 and 2–716, 2–706 and 2–712, 2–708 and 2–713, and 2–710 and 2–715(1). The parallelism is conscious, but there is one important difference from the buyer's perspective. Although the buyer, like the seller, is in business to make a profit (and, undoubtedly, most buyers are also sellers), the purchase contract is designed to

272

obtain goods which will be used in the overall business enterprise. The better the price, the quicker the delivery, and the higher the quality, then the more likely that the overall business will be profitable. Consequently, unless the buyer's plans have changed, an immediate concern upon breach by the seller will be replacement of the goods or inducing the seller to perform. Higher costs and delays in this replacement process both deprive the buyer of the benefit of his bargain and affect overall profitability. Thus, if the goods have not been tendered, the most important remedies will be specific performance, 2–716, or cover, 2–712, and, if delay is involved, recovery of consequential damages under UCC 2–715(2). The "formula" in UCC 2–713(1) is a residual remedy which is used when specific performance is not available and relief for "cover" in UCC 2–712(1) is, for whatever reason, not pursued. Some have urged that UCC 2–713 be repealed. See Childres, *Buyer's Remedies: The Danger of Section 2–713,* 72 Nw.U.L.Rev. 837 (1978). Whatever the value of this "residual" remedy, one thing is clear: since the buyer's contract, unlike the seller's, is not complicated by "lost volume" problems, there is, perhaps, a sounder basis for concluding that a buyer who did cover or should have covered is foreclosed from using UCC 2–713(1) when that would provide a higher recovery. Even if this option is preserved, the buyer cannot recover consequential damages caused by the breach which could have been "reasonably * * * prevented by cover or otherwise." UCC 2–715(2)(a). We will consider these possibilities in the balance of this chapter.

[handwritten margin note: 2–713 is a "residual remedy"]

SECTION 2. WHEN HAS SELLER REPUDIATED? COMMITTED A MATERIAL BREACH OF AN INSTALLMENT CONTRACT?

Just as the Code does not define what constitutes a repudiation by a buyer so it does not define what constitutes a repudiation by a seller. The same open-endedness permeates the "adequate assurance" provisions of UCC 2–609, and the impact of breach upon installment contracts, UCC 2–612. In many situations, relevant criteria will be similar for seller and buyer alike. Thus, if either party threatens to cease performance unless the other agrees to a performance not fairly within the scope of the original agreement, a repudiation may have occurred. For illustrations, compare Louis Dreyfus Corp. v. Brown, 709 F.2d 898 (5th Cir.1983), where the court held that a farmer repudiated a contract to deliver grain, with Bill's Coal Co., Inc. v. Board of Public Utilities of Springfield, Mo., 682 F.2d 883 (10th Cir.1982), where the court held that a supplier's bad faith interpretation of the price term was not a repudiation and the buyer's cancellation, therefore, was a breach.

In the *Plotnick* case, supra at 239, the court assessed the significance of the buyer's late payment partly in terms of whether it impaired the seller's capacity to continue performance. A court might ask similar questions about a seller's late delivery. See UCC 2–612(2). But such symmetry will not be found in all cases and there will be borderline situations. For a helpful discussion, see Jackson, *"Anticipa-*

tory Repudiation" and the Temporal Element of Contract Law: An Economic Inquiry into Contract Damages in Cases of Prospective Non-Performance, 31 Stan.L.Rev. 69, 75–101 (1978).

Problem 8–1

The Tivoli Manufacturing Co., a manufacturer of air compressors, contracted with the Ace Supply Co. to furnish at a fixed price a large quantity of specially tooled valves for use in the compressors. Ace agreed to deliver the valves in 6 equal installments at 3 month intervals. Tivoli stated that the installments were geared to a long range production schedule and a projected increase in demand for the compressors. Tivoli furnished design drawings to assist Ace in "tooling up," gave Ace 6 months of lead time, and advanced 25% of the contract price. Two weeks before the first installment was due, Tivoli appeared in your office with the following letter from Ace:

> Gentlemen:
>
> As suggested in our telephone conversation of last week, our engineers misread the design drawings which you furnished us.
>
> We must, therefore, retool our original model value at considerable extra expense and some delay. We regret that we will be unable to meet the first installment, scheduled for delivery in two weeks. We will make every effort to meet the second installment three months hence and to deliver the quantity promised in the first installment before the contract delivery schedule is completed.
>
> Yours sincerely,
> Ace Supply Co.

Tivoli states that it would like to cancel the contract and get back the 25% advance. Upon close questioning, you discover: 1) the delay in delivery will "wreak havoc" with Tivoli's production schedule and existing contractual commitments; 2) if the contract were cancelled, Tivoli would purchase 50% of the valves ordered from Ace from another manufacturer who guaranteed full performance in 4 months; 3) Tivoli's estimated demand for the compressors was about 50% too high; 4) in Tivoli's judgment, Ace would "probably" meet the next installment and make up the late deliveries. What is your advice?

SECTION 3. BUYER'S RIGHT TO GET THE GOODS—SPECIFIC PERFORMANCE AND REPLEVIN

Suppose, in Problem 8–1, that Ace repudiated the entire contract with Tivoli because it received an offer to purchase all of the compressor valves on hand and its output of similar valves during the next 12 months at a price that was "too good to refuse." Also, Ace estimated a 35–50% increase in the cost of production over the next year. At the time of repudiation, Ace had on hand 25% of the total quantity ordered by Tivoli. The valves were conforming and identified to the contract.

Tivoli needs the valves "yesterday" to meet production orders and estimates that it will take four months and 30% more money to establish a reliable source of supply. In short, Tivoli wants both the valves Ace has on hand and the future output of conforming valves at the agreed price until the quantity ordered has been satisfied.

Problem 8–2 _Omit_

You represent Tivoli in this matter and your client wants results. Which of the following alternatives is best suited to your client's interest and most likely to be successful?

1. Suspend performance and wait under UCC 2–610 and try to negotiate the matter with Ace. Offer more money and couple that with appropriate "non-legal" pressures.

2. Replevin of the valves under UCC 2–716(3). See Tatum v. Richter, 280 Md. 332, 373 A.2d 923 (1977) (replevin of used Ferrari).

3. Seek specific performance of the contract and an order restraining Ace from selling the existing goods and future output to third parties. See UCC 2–716(1); Kaiser Trading Co. v. Associated Metals & Minerals Corp., 321 F.Supp. 923 (N.D.Cal.1970), appeal dismissed 443 F.2d 1364 (9th Cir. 1971).

4. Recover the goods under UCC 2–502.

LACLEDE GAS CO. v. AMOCO OIL CO.

United States Court of Appeals, Eighth Circuit, 1975.
522 F.2d 33.

Ross, C.J.

The Laclede Gas Company (Laclede), a Missouri corporation, brought this diversity action alleging breach of contract against the Amoco Oil Company (Amoco), a Delaware corporation. It sought relief in the form of a mandatory injunction prohibiting the continuing breach or, in the alternative, damages. The district court held a bench trial on the issues of whether there was a valid, binding contract between the parties and whether, if there was such a contract, Amoco should be enjoined from breaching it. It then ruled that the "contract is invalid due to lack of mutuality" and denied the prayer for injunctive relief. The court made no decision regarding the requested damages. Laclede Gas Co. v. Amoco Oil Co., 385 F.Supp. 1332, 1336 (E.D.Mo.1974). This appeal followed, and we reverse the district court's judgment.

On September 21, 1970, Midwest Missouri Gas Company (now Laclede), and American Oil Company (now Amoco), the predecessors of the parties to this litigation, entered into a written agreement which was designed to provide central propane gas distribution systems to various residential developments in Jefferson County, Missouri, until such time as natural gas mains were extended into these areas. The agreement contemplated that as individual developments were planned the owners or developers would apply to Laclede for central propane gas systems. If Laclede determined that such a system was appropriate in any given development, it could request Amoco to supply the propane to that specific development. This request was made in the form of a supplemental form letter, as provided in the September 21 agreement; and if Amoco decided to supply the propane, it bound itself to do so by signing this supplemental form.

Once this supplemental form was signed the agreement placed certain duties on both Laclede and Amoco. Basically, Amoco was to "[i]nstall, own, maintain and operate * * * storage and vaporization facilities and any other facilities necessary to provide [it] with the capability of delivering to [Laclede] commercial propane gas suitable * * * for delivery by [Laclede] to its customers' facilities." Amoco's facilities were to be "adequate to provide a continuous supply of commerical propane gas at such times and in such volumes commensurate with [Laclede's] requirements for meeting the demands reasonably to be anticipated in each Development while this Agreement is in force." Amoco was deemed to be "the supplier," while Laclede was "the distributing utility."

For its part Laclede agreed to "[i]nstall, own, maintain and operate all distribution facilities" from a "point of delivery" which was defined to be "the outlet of [Amoco] header piping." Laclede also promised to pay Amoco "the Wood River Area Posted Price for propane plus four cents per gallon for all amounts of commercial propane gas delivered" to it under the agreement.

Since it was contemplated that the individual propane systems would eventually be converted to natural gas, one paragraph of the agreement provided that Laclede should give Amoco 30 days written notice of this event, after which the agreement would no longer be binding for the converted development.

Another paragraph gave Laclede the right to cancel the agreement. However, this right was expressed in the following language:

> "This Agreement shall remain in effect for one (1) year following the first delivery of gas by [Amoco] to [Laclede] hereunder. Subject to termination as provided in Paragraph 11 hereof [dealing with conversions to natural gas], this Agreement shall automatically continue in effect for additional periods of one (1) year each unless [Laclede] shall, not less than 30 days prior to the expiration of the initial one (1) year period or any subsequent one (1) year period, give [Amoco] written notice of termination."

Provision allowing T to cancel

There was no provision under which Amoco could cancel the agreement.

No such prov. for A

For a time the parties operated satisfactorily under this agreement, and some 17 residential subdivisions were brought within it by supplemental letters. However, for various reasons, including conversion to natural gas, the number of developments under the agreement had shrunk to eight by the time of trial. These were all mobile home parks.

During the winter of 1972–73 Amoco experienced a shortage of propane and voluntarily placed all of its customers, including Laclede, on an 80% allocation basis, meaning that Laclede would receive only up to 80% of its previous requirements. Laclede objected to this and pushed Amoco to give it 100% of what the developments needed. Some conflict arose over this before the temporary shortage was alleviated.

Then, on April 3, 1973, Amoco notified Laclede that its Wood River Area Posted Price of propane had been increased by three cents per gallon. Laclede objected to this increase also and demanded a full explanation. None was forthcoming. Instead Amoco merely sent a letter dated May 14, 1973, informing Laclede that it was "terminating" the September 21, 1970, agreement effective May 31, 1973. It claimed it had the right to do this because "the Agreement lacks 'mutuality.'" [1]

The district court felt that the entire controversy turned on whether or not Laclede's right to "arbitrarily cancel the Agreement" without Amoco having a similar right rendered the contract void "for lack of mutuality" and it resolved this question in the affirmative. We disagree with this conclusion and hold that settled principles of contract law require a reversal.

I.

* * *

We conclude that there is mutuality of consideration within the terms of the agreement and hold that there is a valid, binding contract between the parties as to each of the developments for which supplemental letter agreements have been signed.

II.

Since he found that there was no binding contract, the district judge did not have to deal with the question of whether or not to grant the injunction prayed for by Laclede. He simply denied this relief because there was no contract. Laclede Gas Co. v. Amoco Oil Co., supra, 385 F.Supp. at 1336.

Generally the determination of whether or not to order specific performance of a contract lies within the sound discretion of the trial court. Landau v. St. Louis Public Service Co., 364 Mo. 1134, 273 S.W.2d 255, 259 (1954). However, this discretion is, in fact, quite limited; and it is said that when certain equitable rules have been met and the contract is fair and plain "specific performance goes as a matter of right." Miller v. Coffeen, 365 Mo. 204, 280 S.W.2d 100, 102 (1955), quoting, Berberet v. Myers, 240 Mo. 58, 77, 144 S.W. 824, 830 (1912). (Emphasis omitted.)

a. While Amoco sought to repudiate the agreement, it resumed supplying propane to the subdivisions on February 1, 1974, under the mandatory allocation guidelines promulgated by the Federal Energy Administration under the Federal Mandatory Allocation Program for propane. It is agreed that this is now being done under the contract.

With this in mind we have carefully reviewed the very complete record on appeal and conclude that the trial court should grant the injunctive relief prayed. We are satisfied that this case falls within that category in which specific performance should be ordered as a matter of right. See Miller v. Coffeen, supra, 280 S.W.2d at 102.

Amoco contends that four of the requirements for specific performance have not been met. Its claims are: (1) there is no mutuality of remedy in the contract; (2) the remedy of specific performance would be difficult for the court to administer without constant and long-continued supervision; (3) the contract is indefinite and uncertain; and (4) the remedy at law available to Laclede is adequate. The first three contentions have little or no merit and do not detain us for long.

* * *

1. [The court, after stressing that the agreement was for the buyer's requirements and was supported by consideration, rejected summarily the notion that "both parties be mutually entitled to * * * specific performance in order that one of them be given that remedy by the court." The defendant's right to performance can be protected by a conditional decree. 2. The argument that specific performance would require excessive supervision was rejected on the ground that the rule invoked was "discretionary" and frequently ignored where the public interest, here providing propane to retail customers, was manifest. 3. Finally, the court concluded that the court could determine the terms of performance with "reasonable certainty." The "requirements" feature offered no problem to enforcement. Nor did the fact that the contract stated no "definite time of duration:" the evidence established that the last subdivision should be converted to natural gas in 10 to 15 years and this set "a reasonable time limit on performance."]

It is axiomatic that specific performance will not be ordered when the party claiming breach of contract has an adequate remedy at law. Jamison Coal & Coke Co. v. Goltra, 143 F.2d 889, 894 (8th Cir.), cert. denied, 323 U.S. 769, 65 S.Ct. 122, 89 L.Ed. 615 (1944). This is especially true when the contract involves personal property as distinguished from real estate.

However, in Missouri, as elsewhere, specific performance may be ordered even though personalty is involved in the "proper circumstances." Mo.Rev.Stat. § 400.2–716(1); Restatement of Contracts, supra, § 361. And a remedy at law adequate to defeat the grant of specific performance "must be as certain, prompt, complete, and efficient to attain the ends of justice as a decree of specific performance." National Marking Mach. Co. v. Triumph Mfg. Co., 13 F.2d 6, 9 (8th Cir. 1926). Accord, Snip v. City of Lamar, 239 Mo.App. 824, 201 S.W.2d 790, 798 (1947).

One of the leading Missouri cases allowing specific performance of a contract relating to personalty because the remedy at law was inadequate is Boeving v. Vandover, 240 Mo.App. 117, 218 S.W.2d 175, 178 (1949). In that case the plaintiff sought specific performance of a contract in which the defendant had promised to sell him an automobile. At that time (near the end of and shortly after World War II) new cars were hard to come by, and the court held that specific performance was a proper remedy since a new car "could not be obtained elsewhere except at considerable expense, trouble or loss, which cannot be estimated in advance."

We are satisfied that Laclede has brought itself within this practical approach taken by the Missouri courts. As Amoco points out, Laclede has propane immediately available to it under other contracts with other suppliers. And the evidence indicates that at the present time propane is readily available on the open market. However, this analysis ignores the fact that the contract involved in this lawsuit is for a long-term supply of propane to these subdivisions. The other two contracts under which Laclede obtains the gas will remain in force only until March 31, 1977, and April 1, 1981, respectively; and there is no assurance that Laclede will be able to receive any propane under them after that time. Also it is unclear as to whether or not Laclede can use the propane obtained under these contracts to supply the Jefferson County subdivisions, since they were originally entered into to provide Laclede with propane with which to "shave" its natural gas supply during peak demand periods. Additionally, there was uncontradicted expert testimony that Laclede probably could not find another supplier of propane willing to enter into a long-term contract such as the Amoco agreement, given the uncertain future of worldwide energy supplies. And, even if Laclede could obtain supplies of propane for the affected developments through its present contracts or newly negotiated ones, it would still face considerable expense and trouble which cannot be estimated in advance in making arrangements for its distribution to the subdivisions.

Specific performance is the proper remedy in this situation, and it should be granted by the district court.

CONCLUSION

For the foregoing reasons the judgment of the district court is reversed and the cause is remanded for the fashioning of appropriate injunctive relief in the form of a decree of specific performance as to those developments for which a supplemental agreement form has been signed by the parties. [Some footnotes omitted.]

Notes

1. Laclede Gas is one of the few cases under UCC 2–716(1) which both grants specific performance of a contract to sell goods and attempts to justify the decision on grounds of "other proper circumstances." More recently, specific performance with ancillary injunctive relief in long-term contracts for the supply of natural resources for energy has been granted without discussion. Iowa Elec. Light and Power Co. v. Atlas Corp., 467 F.Supp. 129, 138 (N.D.Iowa 1978), reversed on other grounds 603 F.2d 1301 (8th Cir.1979) (uranium oxide); Missouri Public Serv. Co. v. Peabody Coal

Co., 583 S.W.2d 721 (Mo.App.1979), cert. denied 444 U.S. 865, 100 S.Ct. 135, 62 L.Ed.2d 88 (1979) (bituminous coal). A useful history of UCC 2–716 and a comparison with the Restatement, Second of Contracts, is Greenberg, *Specific Performance Under Section 2–716 of the Uniform Commercial Code: "A More Liberal Attitude" in the "Grand Style,"* 17 N.Eng.L.Rev. 321, 344–53 (1982).

2. Should specific performance rather than damages be the preferred remedy in all cases of breach of contract? Put differently, if it were clear that specific performance (1) best protected the promisee's subjective value in the contract; (2) minimized if not avoided consequential damages; and (3) decreased the overall costs of judicial administration or the parties' post-breach negotiations, what are the arguments for the current rule, i.e., damages are preferred unless they are inadequate? An argument for specific performance "on demand" is made in Ulen, *The Efficiency of Specific Performance: Toward A Unified Theory of Contract Remedies,* 83 Mich.L.Rev. 341 (1984).

Problem 8–3 Omit

Suppose, in *Laclede Gas,* supra, that because of unanticipated events, the supplier's cost of production rose dramatically during performance of the contract. The supplier, in good faith, proposed a reasonable prospective modification, which the buyer, without negotiation, rejected. Upon repudiation by the supplier, the buyer sought specific performance plus injunctive relief. In response, the supplier made the following argument:

"May it please the court. We concede that at law our client would not be excused from performance under UCC 2–615 and that the buyer has stated a case for specific performance under UCC 2–716(1). We also concede that the law of this jurisdiction is that the buyer had no duty to negotiate over or agree to our proposed modification, no matter how reasonable. These are harsh outcomes 'at law.'

"Specific performance, however, is an equitable remedy to be granted in the discretion of the court. UCC 2–716(2) provides that a decree of specific performance 'may include such terms and conditions as to payment of the price, damages, or other relief as the court may deem just.' Comment 7 to UCC 2–615, although not directly on point, suggests that good faith may 'justify and even * * * require' a 'good faith inquiry seeking a readjustment of the contract terms to meet the new conditions.' Our proposed modification was fair and equitable in light of the changed circumstances. If the buyer had accepted it, the result would clearly be enforceable under UCC 2–209(1). Thus, your honor, we contend that it would be unjust to grant specific performance in this case without a price adjustment for the balance of the contract. We, therefore, urge the court to condition any decree for specific performance upon the buyer's consent to the reasonable modification which we have proposed."

How should the court rule?

SECTION 4. BUYER'S RIGHT TO "MARKET-CONTRACT" DAMAGES

Note first that UCC 2-713 instructs the court to use the market price "at the time when the buyer learned of the breach," and except in cases of rejection or revocation of acceptance indicates that the place for tender is the place to measure damages. The cognate provision for the seller's damages, UCC 2-708(1), directs the use of the "time and place for tender."

The meaning of the words "when the buyer learned of the breach" is likely to cause trouble only in the anticipatory repudiation situation, as we will see below, Professor Patterson suggested in the New York Law Revision Commission Reports that it was no more than a codification of the New York common law:

PATTERSON, 1 N.Y.LAW REV.COMM.REP. 697–699 (1955) "*Case law on Section UCC 2–713.*

"Since the 'ordinary' measure of damages for non-delivery by the seller (as defined in § 2-711(1)(b)) is the contract price less the market value of the goods, under the Uniform Sales Act enacted in New York in 1911, and even long before that year, we need not multiply New York citations to support that formula. The chief differences between Section 2-713 and the present statute are those relating to the *time when* and the *place where* market value is to be determined. * * *

"*Time when market value determined.*

"The present New York statute (P.P.L., § 148(3)) fixes the market value as of the time when the goods 'ought to have been delivered' or, if no time was fixed for delivery, 'at the time of refusal to deliver.' The proposed statute would make 'the time when the buyer learned of the breach' determine the market price. This is *apparently* a change in New York law; but actually it probably is not a change in the law as applied by New York courts. In at least two New York cases it was held that the market value was to be measured as of the time when the buyer knew of the default.* However, the Court of Appeals' language included 'should have known,' which would be different from the time when the buyer 'learned' of the breach. These cases do not purport to depart from the ordinary rule except where 'special circumstances' justify allowing the buyer a longer time to cover by a second buying in the market. Yet in one case an instruction that damages be measured by the price paid for similar goods bought by the buyer 'within a reasonable time after breach' (to allow him a reasonable time to cover),

---

* Professor Patterson describes the two New York cases as follows:

Perkins v. Minford, 235 N.Y. 301, 139 N.E. 276 (1923) (action by buyer for breach by seller in shipping at Cuban port (F.O.B.) a quantity of sugar 200,000 lbs. less than seller contracted to ship; buyer did not know of breach until much later, and this is a "special circum-stance" under § 148 calling for variation from ordinary damage rule, time of breach); Boyd v. Quinn, 8 Misc. 169, 41 N.Y.Supp. 391 (1896) (contract to ship goods by rail from Peoria, Ill., to New York; buyer didn't know, until he inquired of seller and received seller's refusal, that seller had defaulted).

was held reversible error. In this case it seems that the buyer learned of the breach at once. Ordinarily, it is believed, no significant lag would occur. The purpose of Section 2–713(1), which applies (§ 2–711) only as an alternative to cover (§ 2–712) is presumably to prevent the buyer's getting any more damages by waiting for the market to go down ("speculating at the seller's expense," some courts would say) after he learns of the breach; if the market goes up further, the buyer will have to pay more and yet will recover only the difference (market minus contract price) when he first learns of the breach. The buyer is thus encouraged to 'cover' promptly. However, under Section 2–712 the buyer may cover 'without unreasonable delay' after the *breach* (*not* "learning of the breach"), which means that the buyer could *delay* after (learning of) the breach and *then* fix damages. Then could not a buyer, after learning of the breach on May 1, wait until May 15, when he purchases a larger quantity of the same goods, and then have his option to fix damages on May 1, asserting his purchase on May 15 at a lower price was *not* a 'cover'; or, if the price goes up, to claim that his purchase on May 15 was a 'cover' not unreasonably delayed (§ 2–712) and fix damages at the higher price then prevailing? Should the alternative statement in Section 2–711(1) be tightened to avoid this?"

Problem 8–4

Volta v. Simpka Revisited

Review the facts of *Simpka v. Volta*, Problem 7–4. Suppose that Simpka was to ship the custom furniture in two installments on October 1 and October 15. The first installment, consisting of 60% of the goods, was shipped f.o.b. Ohio on October 1, arrived in New York on October 12 and was rejected by Volta for manufacturing defects on October 15. The second installment was never shipped by Simpka. At trial, the court found that Volta "learned of the breach" on the first installment on October 15 and "learned" of the breach on the second installment on October 20. Assume that the contract price on the first shipment was $48,000 and was $32,000 on the second. Neither side claims that UCC 2–712 governs the case.

The market price for goods comparable to the first installment on October 15 was $60,000 in New York and $50,000 in Ohio. The market price for comparable goods to the second installment on October 20 was $28,000 in Ohio and $40,000 in New York. You may assume that the total cost of shipment from Ohio to New York would have been $4,000, but since the first installment was shipped "for buyer's account," no payment has as yet been made.

How much in damages, if any, should the court award to Volta?

Problem 8–5

More Simpka v. Volta

In June, 1986 the *Simpka-Volta* contract was modified to provide that all of the furniture, both standard and custom, was to be shipped in one lot on March 1, 1987. The contract price was increased to $220,000. On July

1, 1986, however, Simpka repudiated the contract in unequivocal terms and no shipments were ever made under the contract. When the case came to trial in February, 1988, Volta made the following argument: "Our damages should be measured on either July 1, 1986, when we learned of the repudiation, or May 1, 1987, when we purchased furniture in substitution (covered) on the open market." The evidence revealed the relevant market prices for comparable goods during this time frame as follows:

July 1–31, 1986	$260,000 *Date Volta learned of breach*
August 1–December 31, 1986	200,000
March 1, 1987	220,000 *Date of full performance*
May 1, 1987	280,000 *Date Volta covered*

Simpka would like the damages to be measured as of March 1, 1987, the date the goods were to be delivered. You represent Simpka. Develop the strongest arguments you can to support Simpka's position. Then read the next case.

COSDEN OIL v. KARL O. HELM AKTIENGESELLSCHAFT

United States Court of Appeals, Fifth Circuit, 1984.
736 F.2d 1064.

REAVLEY, CIRCUIT JUDGE.

* * *

II. TIME FOR MEASURING BUYER'S DAMAGES

Here,
Both parties find fault with the time at which the district court *Seller argues that* measured Helm's damages for Cosden's anticipatory repudiation of *damages should be* orders 05, 06, and 07. Cosden argues that damages should be measured *measured when* when Helm learned of the repudiation. Helm contends that market *buyer learned of* price as of the last day for delivery—or the time of performance— *the breach.* should be used to compute its damages under the contract-market *Buyer contends that* differential. (We) reject both views, and hold that the district court *market price used* correctly measured damages at a commercially reasonable point after *should be the time* Cosden informed Helm that it was cancelling the three orders. *for performance.*

Court rejects both
Article 2 of the Code has generally been hailed as a success for its *and measures damages* comprehensiveness, its deference to mercantile reality, and its clarity. *at a commercially* Nevertheless, certain aspects of the Code's overall scheme have proved *reasonable point* troublesome in application. The interplay among sections 2.610, 2.711, *in between!* 2.712, 2.713, and 2.723, Tex.Bus. & Com.Code Ann. (Vernon 1968), represents one of those areas, and has been described as "an impossible legal thicket." J. White & R. Summers, *Uniform Commercial Code* § 6–7 at 242 (2d ed. 1980). The aggrieved buyer seeking damages for seller's anticipatory repudiation presents the most difficult interpretive problem.[6] Section 2.713 describes the buyer's damages remedy:

6. The only area of unanimous agreement among those that have studied the Code provisions relevant to this problem is that they are not consistent, present problems in interpretation, and invite amendment.

Buyer's Damages for Non-Delivery or Repudiation

(a) Subject to the provisions of this chapter with respect to proof of market price (Section 2.723), the measure of damages for non-delivery or repudiation by the seller is the difference between the market price *at the time when the buyer learned of the breach* and the contract price together with any incidental and consequential damages provided in this chapter (Section 2.715), but less expenses saved in consequence of the seller's breach.

(emphasis added).

Courts and commentators have identified three possible interpretations of the phrase "learned of the breach." If seller anticipatorily repudiates, buyer learns of the breach:

(1) When he learns of the repudiation;

(2) When he learns of the repudiation plus a commercially reasonable time; or

(3) When performance is due under the contract.

See, e.g., First National Bank of Chicago v. Jefferson Mortgage Co., 576 F.2d 479 (3d Cir.1978); *Cargill, Inc. v. Stafford,* 553 F.2d 1222 (10th Cir. 1977); J. White & R. Summers § 6–7 at 240–52; Note, *U.C.C. § 2–713: Anticipatory Repudiation and the Measurement of an Aggrieved Buyer's Damages,* 19 Wm. & Mary L.Rev. 253 (1977).

We would not be free to decide the question if there were a Texas case on point, bound as we are by *Erie* to follow state law in diversity cases. We find, however, that no Texas case has addressed the Code question of buyer's damages in an anticipatory repudiation context. Texas, alone in this circuit, does not allow us to certify questions of state law for resolution by its courts. *See United Services Life Insurance Co. v. Delaney,* 396 S.W.2d 855 (Tex.1965).

We do not doubt, and Texas law is clear, that market price at the time buyer learns of the breach is the appropriate measure of section 2.713 damages in cases where buyer learns of the breach at or after the time for performance. This will be the common case, for which section 2.713 was designed. *See* Peters, *Remedies for Breach of Contracts Relating to the Sale of Goods Under the Uniform Commercial Code: A Roadmap for Article Two,* 73 Yale L.J. 199, 264 (1963). In the relatively rare case where seller anticipatorily repudiates and buyer does not cover, * * * the specific provision for anticipatory repudiation cases, section 2.610, authorizes the aggrieved party to await performance for a commercially reasonable time before resorting to his remedies of cover or damages.

In the anticipatory repudiation context, the buyer's specific right to wait for a commercially reasonable time before choosing his remedy must be read together with the general damages provision of section 2.713 to extend the time for measurement beyond when buyer learns of the breach. Comment 1 to section 2.610 states that if an aggrieved party "awaits performance beyond a commercially reasonable time he cannot recover resulting damages which he should have avoided." This suggests that an aggrieved buyer can recover damages where the market rises during the commercially reasonable time he awaits performance. To interpret 2.713's "learned of the breach" language to mean the time at which seller first communicates his anticipatory repudiation would undercut the time that 2.610 gives the aggrieved buyer to await performance.

The buyer's option to wait a commercially reasonable time also interacts with section 2.611, which allows the seller an opportunity to retract his repudiation. Thus, an aggrieved buyer "learns of the breach" a commercially reasonable time after he learns of the seller's anticipatory repudiation. The weight of scholarly commentary supports this interpretation. *See* J. Calamari & J. Perillo, *Contracts* § 14–20 (2d ed. 1977); Sebert, *Remedies Under Article Two of the Uniform Commercial Code: An Agenda for Review*, 130 U.Pa.L.Rev. 360, 372–80 (1981); Wallach, *Anticipatory Repudiation and the UCC*, 13 U.C.C.L.J. 48 (1980); Peters, *supra*, at 263–68.

[margin note:] Seller still has opportunity to retract the repudiation (§2-611) if a reasonable time is allowed after breach.

Typically, our question will arise where parties to an executory contract are in the midst of a rising market. To the extent that market decisions are influenced by a damages rule, measuring market price at the time of seller's repudiation gives seller the ability to fix buyer's damages and may induce seller to repudiate, rather than abide by the contract. By contrast, measuring buyer's damages at the time of performance will tend to dissuade the buyer from covering, in hopes that market price will continue upward until performance time.

Allowing the aggrieved buyer a commercially reasonable time, however, provides him with an opportunity to investigate his cover possibilities in a rising market without fear that, if he is unsuccessful in obtaining cover, he will be relegated to a market-contract damage remedy measured at the time of repudiation. The Code supports this view. While cover is the preferred remedy, the Code clearly provides the option to seek damages. *See* § 2.712(c) & comment 3. If "[t]he buyer is always free to choose between cover and damages for non-delivery," and if 2.712 "is not intended to limit the time necessary for [buyer] to look around and decide as to how he may best effect cover," it would be anomalous, if the buyer chooses to seek damages, to fix his damages at a time before he investigated cover possibilities and before he elected his remedy. *(See id.* comment 2 & 3; *Dura-Wood Treating Co. v. Century Forest Industries, Inc.,* 675 F.2d 745, 754 (5th Cir.), *cert. denied,* 459 U.S. 865, 103 S.Ct. 144, 74 L.Ed.2d 122 (1982) ("buyer has some time in which to evaluate the situation").) Moreover, comment 1 to section 2.713 states, "The general baseline adopted in this section uses as a yardstick the market in which the buyer would have obtained cover had he sought that relief." *See* § 2.610 comment 1. When a buyer chooses not to cover, but to seek damages, the market is measured at the time he could have covered—a reasonable time after repudiation. *See* §§ 2.711 & 2.713.

[margin note:] Code encourages cover, but provides alternatives.

[margin note:] Although cover is preferred, buyer may seek damages!

[margin note:] See Dura-Wood!

[margin note:] When buyer chooses not to cover, damages are measured at the time he could have covered—

Persuasive arguments exist for interpreting "learned of the breach" to mean "time of performance," consistent with the pre-Code rule. *See* J. White & R. Summers, *supra.* § 6–7; Anderson, *supra.* If this was the intention of the Code's drafters, however, phrases in section 2.610 and 2.712 lose their meaning. If buyer is entitled to market-contract damages measured at the time of performance, it is difficult to explain why the anticipatory repudiation section limits him to a commercially reasonable time to await performance. *See* § 2.610 comment 1. Similarly, in a rising market, no reason would exist for requiring the buyer to act "without unreasonable delay" when he seeks to cover following an anticipatory repudiation. *See* § 2.712(a).

The interplay among the relevant Code sections does not permit, in this context, an interpretation that harmonizes all and leaves no loose ends. We therefore acknowledge that our interpretation fails to explain the language of section 2.723(a) insofar as it relates to aggrieved buyers. We note, however, that the section has limited applicability— cases that come to trial before the time of performance will be rare. Moreover, the comment to section 2.723 states that the "section is not intended to exclude the use of any other reasonable method of determining market price or of measuring damages. ∗ ∗ ∗" In light of the Code's persistent theme of commercial reasonableness, the prominence of cover as a remedy, and the time given an aggrieved buyer to await performance and to investigate cover before selecting his remedy, we agree with the district court that "learned of the breach" incorporates section 2.610's commercially reasonable time.[11]

∗ ∗ ∗

[Some footnotes omitted.]

11. We note that two circuits arrived at a similar conclusion by different routes. In *Cargill, Inc. v. Stafford,* 553 F.2d 1222 (10th Cir.1977), the court began its discussion of damages by embracing the "time of performance" interpretation urged by Professors White and Summers. *Id.* at 1226. Indeed, the court stated that "damages normally should be measured from the time when performance is due and not from the time when the buyer learns of repudiation." *Id.* Nevertheless, the court

conclude[d] that under § 4–2–713 a buyer may urge continued performance for a reasonable time. At the end of a reasonable period he should cover if substitute goods are readily available. If substitution is readily available and buyer does not cover within a reasonable time, damages should be based on the price at the end of that reasonable time rather than on the price when performance is due.

Id. at 1227. The *Cargill* court would employ the time of performance measure only if buyer had a valid reason for not covering.

In *First Nat'l Bank of Chicago v. Jefferson Mortgage Co.,* 576 F.2d 479 (3d Cir. 1978), the court initially quoted with approval legislative history that supports a literal or "plain meaning" interpretation of New Jersey's section 2–713. Nevertheless, the court hedged by interpreting that section "to measure damages within a commercially reasonable time after learning of the repudiation." *Id.* at 492. In light of the unequivocal repudiation and because cover was "easily and immediately ∗ ∗ ∗ available ∗ ∗ ∗ in the well-organized and easily accessible market," *id.* at 493 (quoting *Oloffson v. Coomer,* 11 Ill.App.3d 918, 296 N.E.2d 871 (1973)), a commercially reasonable time did not extend beyond the date of repudiation.

We agree with the *First National* court that "the circumstances of the particular market involved should determine the duration of a 'commercially reasonable time.'" 576 F.2d at 492; *see* Tex.Bus. & Com.Code § 1.204(b). In this case, however, there was no showing that cover was easily and immediately available in an or-

ALLIED CANNERS & PACKERS, INC. v. VICTOR PACKING CO.

Court of Appeal of California, First District, 1984.
162 Cal.App.3d 905, 209 Cal.Rptr. 60.

[In early September, 1976, Victor agreed to sell Allied 375,000 pounds of raisins for October, 1976 delivery at 29.75 cents per pound. Victor knew that Allied had contracted to resell the raisins to foreign purchasers. Allied expected to gain a profit of $4,462.50 on the resale transaction. On September 9, 1976, heavy rains severely damaged the region's raisin crop, including that of Victor. When Victor was unable to obtain raisins from other sources, it repudiated the contract with Allied on September 15, 1976. The regulated market for raisins did not reopen until October 18, 1976, at which time the price was 87 cents per pound. In the meantime, Allied's resale buyers had either agreed to rescind their contracts without liability or failed to assert claims for damages by the time of trial.

Allied sued Victor for damages under UCC 2–713(1), measured by the difference between the contract price, 29.75 cents per pound, and the market price at the time and place for delivery, 87 cents per pound. The trial court concluded that Allied was an exporter rather than a buyer for its own account. Accordingly, Allied could not use UCC 2–713 and was limited to its actual loss on the transaction, $4,462.50. The Court of Appeal, however, held that Allied was a buyer with forward resale contracts and that the buyer's remedies in the Code applied.

The court first reviewed Sections 2–712 through 2–715.

*   *   *

ROUSE, ASSOCIATE JUSTICE

Sections 2–712 and 2–713 of the Uniform Code are sometimes referred to as "cover" and "hypothetical cover," since the former involves an actual entry into the market by the buyer while the latter does not. (See Childres, *Buyer's Remedies: The Danger of Section 2–713* (1978) 72 Nw. U.L.Rev. 837, 841 [applying those terms] (hereafter cited as *Buyer's Remedies*); Peters, *Remedies for Breach of Contracts Relating to the Sale of Goods Under the Uniform Commercial Code: A Roadmap For Article Two* (1963) 73 Yale L.J. 199, 259 [market under section 2–713 is "purely theoretical"] (hereafter cited as *Remedies for Breach of Contracts*).) It has been recognized that the use of the market price-contract price formula

ganized and accessible market and that a commercially reasonable time expired on the day of Cosden's cancellation. We recognize that § 2.610's "commercially reasonable time" and § 2.712's "without unreasonable delay" are distinct concepts. Often, however, the two time periods will overlap, since the buyer can investigate cover possibilities while he awaits performance. *See* Sebert, *supra,* at 376–77 & n. 80.

Although the jury in the present case did not fix the exact duration of a commercially reasonable time, we assume that the jury determined market price at a time commercially reasonable under all the circumstances, in light of the absence of objection to the form of the special issue.

under section 2–713 does not, absent pure accident, result in a damage award reflecting the buyer's actual loss. (*Buyer's Remedies, supra,* at pp. 841–842; *Remedies for Breach of Contracts, supra,* at p. 259; *Market Damages, supra,* 92 Harv.L.Rev. 1395 et seq.; * White & Summers, Uniform Commercial Code, *supra,* at p. 224.)

For example, in this case it is agreed that Allied's actual lost profit on the transaction was $4,462.50, while application of the market-contract price formula would yield damages of approximately $150,000. In *Market Damages, supra,* Simon and Novack describe the courts as divided on the issue of whether market damages, even though in excess of the plaintiff's loss, are appropriate for a supplier's breach of his delivery obligations and observe: "Strangely enough, each view has generally tended to disregard the arguments, and even the existence, of the opposing view. These two rival bodies of law, imposing in appearance, have passed each other like silent ships in the night." (92 Harv. L.Rev. 1395, 1397.) In *Buyer's Remedies, supra,* Professor Childres similarly points out that the courts have generally not undertaken any real analysis of the competing considerations involved in determining the correct measure of damages in such circumstances. (72 Nw.U.L. Rev. 837, 844 et seq.) We will undertake such an analysis.

Professors White and Summers, after noting their belief that "the Code drafters did not by [section 2–713] intend to put the buyer in the same position as performance would have" (White & Summers, Uniform Commercial Code, *supra,* at p. 224), advance two possible explanations for the section. First, they suggest that it is simply a historical anomaly: "Since cover was not a recognized remedy under pre-Code law, it made sense under that law to say that the contract-market formula put buyer in the same position as performance would have *on the assumption that the buyer would purchase substitute goods.* If things worked right, the market price would approximate the cost of the substitute goods and buyer would be put 'in the same position. * * *' But under the Code, 2–712 does this job with greater precision, and 2–713 reigns over only those cases in which the buyer does not purchase a substitute. Perhaps the drafters retained 2–713 not out of a belief in its appropriateness, but out of fear that they would be dismissed as iconoclasts had they proposed that the court in noncover cases simply award the buyer any economic loss proximately caused by seller's breach." (*Ibid.*)

They conclude, however, that probably the best explanation for section 2–713 "is that it is a statutory liquidated damage clause, a breach inhibitor the payout of which need bear no close relation to plaintiff's actual loss." (White & Summers, Uniform Commercial Code, *supra,* at p. 225.) They then observe that this explanation conflicts with the policy set forth in section 1–106, which provides in subdivision (1): "The remedies provided by this code shall be liberally administered

---

* Simon & Novack, *Limiting the Buyer's Market Damages to Lost Profits: A Challenge*   *to the Enforceability of Market Contracts,* 92 Harv.L.Rev. 1395 (1979).

to the end that the aggrieved party may be put in as good a position as if the other party had fully performed but neither consequential or special nor penal damages may be had except as specifically provided in this code or by other rule of law." (Emphasis added.) They find section 2–713 consistent, however, with a belief that plaintiffs recover too little and too infrequently for the law of contracts to be effective, and offer no suggestion for resolution of the conflict. (*Ibid.*)

In her article *Remedies for Breach of Contracts, supra,* then-Professor Peters states: "Perhaps it is misleading to think of the market-contract formula as a device for the measurement of damages. * * * An alternative way of looking at market-contract is to view this differential as a statutory liquidated damages clause, rather than as an effort to calculate actual losses. If it is useful in every case to hold the party in breach to some baseline liability, in order to encourage faithful adherence to contractual obligations, perhaps market fluctuations furnish as good a standard as any." (73 Yale L.J. 199, 259.) She does not discuss the conflict between the market-contract formula and the "only as good a position as performance" policy embodied in section 1–106.

Simon and Novack state: "While it is generally recognized that the automatic invocation of market damages may sometimes overcompensate the plaintiff, a variety of arguments have been employed by commentators and courts to justify this result: the desirability of maintaining a uniform rule and of facilitating settlements; the public interest in encouraging contract performance and the proper functioning of the market; the prevention of defendant's unjust enrichment; the restoration of the very 'value' promised to plaintiff; and the inherent difficulty and complexity of proving actual economic losses not encompassed within the contract terms." (Fns. omitted; *Market Damages supra,* 92 Harv.L.Rev. 1395, 1403.) That a defendant not be unjustly enriched by a bad faith breach is a concern widely shared by commentators and courts. (*Id.,* at p. 1406, fn. 51, and cases there cited.)

Viewing section 2–713 as, in effect, a statutory provision for liquidated damages, it is necessary for us to determine whether a damage award to a buyer who has not covered is ever appropriately limited to the buyer's actual economic loss which is below the damages produced by the market-contract formula, and, if so, whether the present case presents a situation in which the damages should be so limited.

One view is that section 2–713 of the Uniform Code, or a substantively similar statutory provision, establishes the principle that a buyer's resale contract and damage claims made thereunder are irrelevant to an award of damages, and that damages therefore cannot be limited to a plaintiff's actual economic loss. (See 11 Williston, Contracts (3d ed. 1968) § 1388 [Uniform Code]; *Coombs and Company of Ogden v. Reed* (1956) 5 Utah 2d 419, 303 P.2d 1097 [Uniform Sales Act]; *Brightwater Paper Co. v. Monadnock Paper Mills* (1st Cir.1947) 161 F.2d 869 [Massachusetts Sales Act then in effect]; *Goldfarb v. Campe Corporation* (1917) 99 Misc. 475, 164 N.Y.S. 583 [New York Sales Act then in effect].)

Simon and Novack, while favoring that view, concede that it can be argued that the provision of section 1–106 that an aggrieved party be put " 'in as good a position as if the other party had fully performed' " calls for an opposite conclusion. (*Market Damages, supra,* 92 Harv.L. Rev. 1395, 1412–1413, fn. 71.)

Although we find no cases discussing the interaction of section 1–106 and section 2–713, we note that some pre-Uniform Code cases held that a limitation to actual losses should be placed upon the market price-contract price measure of damages under general contract principles. (See, e.g., *Foss v. Heineman* (1910) 144 Wis. 146 [128 N.W. 881]; *Isaacson v. Crean* (1917) 165 N.Y.S. 218; *Texas Co. v. Pensacola Maritime Corporation* (5th Cir.1922) 279 Fed. 19.) One author on the subject has apparently concluded that such a limitation is appropriate under the Uniform Code when the plaintiff-buyer has a resale contract and the existence of the resale contract is known to the defendant-seller: "It may be supposed ＊ ＊ ＊ that the buyer was bound by a contract made before the breach to deliver to a third person the very goods which the buyer expected to obtain from the seller, and the price under the resale contract may be less than the market price at the time of the breach. If the reason generally given for the rule permitting the recovery of additional damage because of an advantageous resale contract existing and known to the defendant when he contracted be applied, namely, that such consequential damages are allowed because the parties supposedly contract for them, it would follow that in every case the damage that the defendant might normally expect to follow from breach of his contract should be recovered even though the plaintiff actually suffered less damage than the difference between the contract price and the market price." (4 Anderson, Uniform Commercial Code (3d ed. 1983) § 2–711:15, pp. 430–431.)

The only California case directly applying section 2713 is *Gerwin v. Southeastern Cal. Assn. of Seventh Day Adventists* (1971) 14 Cal.App.3d 209, 92 Cal.Rptr. 111. There the plaintiff had contracted to purchase bar and restaurant equipment which he planned to use in a hotel he had recently acquired. The seller failed to deliver the equipment, and plaintiff, who had not covered, was awarded damages of $15,000 as the difference between the contract price and the market price of the equipment. The plaintiff had not covered because substitute items were not available at prices within his financial ability. (*Id.,* at pp. 218–219, 92 Cal.Rptr. 111.) Presumably, after recovering his damage award, the plaintiff in *Gerwin* paid it out to purchase other equipment. That case is inapposite to the present case because the plaintiff there had no resale contract which limited his liability and defined the actual profit he expected to make through the acquisition of the items covered by the sales contract.

We conclude that in the circumstances of this case—in which the seller knew that the buyer had a resale contract (necessarily so because raisins would not be released by RAC unless Allied provided it with the name of the buyer in its forward contract), the buyer has not been able to show that it will be liable in damages to the buyer on its forward contract, and there has been no finding of bad faith on the part of the seller—the policy of section 1106, subdivision (1), that the aggrieved party be put in as good a position as if the other party had performed requires that the award of damages to the buyer be limited to its actual loss, the amount it expected to make on the transaction. We note that in the context of a cover case under section 2712, a Court of Appeal has recently approved the use of section 1106 to limit damages to the amount that would put the plaintiff in as good a position as if the defendant had performed. (*Sun Maid Raisin Growers v. Victor Packing Co.* (1983) 146 Cal.App.3d 787, 792, 194 Cal.Rptr. 612.)

We need not determine in this case what degree of bad faith on the part of a breaching seller might warrant the award of market-contract price damages without limitation, in circumstances otherwise similar to those involved here, in order to prevent unjust enrichment to a seller who deliberately breaches in order to take advantage of a rising market. Although Allied implies that Victor was guilty of bad faith here because after its breach it allowed another packer to acquire reserve raisins to which it was entitled at 36.25 cents per pound, rather than acquiring the raisins and delivering them to Allied, the record is simply not clear on Victor's situation following the rains. It does appear clear, however, that, as the trial court found, the rains caused a severe problem, and Victor made substantial efforts to persuade RAC to release reserve raisins to it in spite of its failure to get its check to RAC before 8:30 a.m. on September 10, 1976. We do not deem this record one to support an inference that windfall damages must be awarded the buyer to prevent unjust enrichment to a deliberately breaching seller. (Compare *Sun Maid Raisin Growers v. Victor Packing Co., supra,* 146 Cal.App.3d 787, 194 Cal.Rptr. 612 [where, in a case coincidentally involving Victor, Victor was expressly found by the trial court to have engaged in bad faith by gambling on the market price of raisins in deciding whether to perform its contracts to sell raisins to Sun Maid].)

The judgment is affirmed. Each party is to bear its own costs on appeal.

KLINE, P.J., and SMITH, J., concur.

Notes

1. Accord: H–W–H Cattle Co., Inc. v. Schroeder, 767 F.2d 437 (8th Cir. 1985). But see Apex Oil Co. v. Vanguard Oil & Service Co., Inc., 760 F.2d 417, 424 (2d Cir.1985), where the court rejected the seller's contention that the buyer, a broker who intended to resell the oil to another customer, could not use the formula in UCC 2–713(1). The court, speaking through Judge Newman, offered the following reasons:

> The formula makes sense when an end user sues the breaching seller because, even if the end user elects not to go into the market and cover, thus demonstrating its out-of-pocket loss, it still has lost the value of

having the product. However, in this case, Apex was not an end user, but rather a broker who planned to resell the product to another customer. In the absence of proof that Apex had a customer willing to purchase the oil, it seems fictional to hold that Apex has "lost" the difference between the market price and contract price. However, Vanguard's arguments fail to consider the UCC formula from the perspective of the breaching seller, who always has the option of going into the market and buying products to satisfy its obligation to the buyer. Since Vanguard elected not to cover and thus fix its loss, it saved an amount equal to the difference between the market price and the contract price. The UCC formula reflects a policy judgment that it makes more sense to award the amount of that saving to the buyer than to permit the non-performing and non-covering seller to retain it. Whether that policy decision should be legislatively limited to buyers who demonstrate some prospect of foregone opportunity for profitable resale is not for us to say.

2. A "middleman" or "jobber," other than a consignee, is both a buyer and a seller. Review the treatment of this functionary when seeking damages as a seller. See supra Chapter Seven. What conclusions can you draw as to the availability of the standard damages formulas in UCC 2–708(1) and UCC 2–713(1) to the "jobber?"

SECTION 5. BUYER'S RIGHT TO COVER AND "FIX" DAMAGES

Cover, like resale (UCC 2–706), is an important Code innovation. It is an intelligent legal response to the legitimate needs of the ordinary buyer who, when faced with the seller's breach, must look elsewhere for the goods. Under the standard contract-market differential formula, an aggrieved buyer who repurchased to fulfill his needs was taking real pot luck. If, as was likely to be the case, the court measured the market at a time or place other than those at which he purchased, the contract-market paid too much or too little. UCC 2–712 will change all that.

Professor Honnold in the New York Law Revision Commission Reports has described the relation of the cover provision to the prior law in New York as follows:

HONNOLD—1 N.Y.LAW REV.COMM.REP. 569, 570 (1955)

(2) *Effect of "cover" in determining damages under Uniform Sales Act*

Under Section 67(1) and (3) of the Uniform Sales Act (P.P.L., § 148(1)(3)) the basic test for the measurement of damages recoverable by buyer is "the difference between the contract price and the *market or current* price of the goods at the time or times when they ought to have been delivered * * *". The Uniform Sales Act says nothing about "cover," and has no provision which gives binding effect to the price paid by buyer in buying substitute goods.

However, in one situation, at least, some decisions have given controlling effect to buyer's repurchase. If buyer purchases substitute goods for *less* than market price, this repurchase price may be the maximum amount on which damages can be measured. The Code would give a different result, since under Section 2–711(1), buyer is afforded a choice between damages based on "cover" (§ 2–712) and damages based on market price (§ 2–713).

The amount paid by buyer has been held an insufficient basis for proof of his damages if there was a current market for the goods; market price must be proved as the basis for computing damages. This rule has been criticized as unduly harsh to the wronged party, and it has at least one qualification: where the goods in question *are not* readily marketable, the price paid by buyer to secure the goods from another seller will be controlling. Under the Code, as we have seen, a buyer who "covers" need not prove the market price.

The conditions which one must meet to comply with UCC 2–712 are like those of UCC 2–706: at least superficially simple and unspecific.

One must purchase: 1) reasonably and in good faith;
                    2) without unreasonable delay; and
                    3) in substitution.

On reflection a few problems appear. The first is the recurring problem: what is the reasonable time and what is a commercially reasonable purchase? If the buyer routinely purchases separate lots of goods and now seeks to allocate one of those routinely purchased lots to this contract's cover, what result? A third problem is the question whether cover, if made, is the exclusive measure of damages. A fourth is, how does one adjust for the difference between cover items and those contracted for—what if the contract calls for AM radios but AM–FM radios are procured as cover?

Possible problems with "cover"

Problem 8–6

Return again to *Simpka-Volta.* Assume that Simpka missed the first delivery of standard furniture and, on June 15, mailed an unequivocal repudiation of the entire contract. On November 15, Volta replaced, from a supplier in Ann Arbor, the standard furniture for $150,000 and the custom furniture for $100,000. The shipment was f.o.b. New York. Volta claims $50,000 damages under UCC 2–712. Simpka's lawyer has responded with the following arguments:

initial breach on 6/1 — learned of breach?

1. UCC 2–712 is not available, since there was an unreasonable delay in the repurchase. The time starts running from the date of repudiation, not from the date upon which the contract would have been performed.

2. Even so, the $50,000 damages should be reduced by the $5,000 transportation cost which the second seller paid from Ann Arbor. Volta would have had to pay those costs under the repudiated f.o.b. point of shipment contract.

3. In fact, the market for the standard furniture was lower than the contract price. The goods which Volta purchased in New York were Grade

A and the contract called for Grade B furniture, merchandise of lesser quality.

What damages?

Assume that Simpka fails to perform the contract; a series of negotiations considering possible alternatives are conducted between Volta and Simpka, and these eventually break down in January. At that time Volta purchases nearly identical replacement furniture in the New York market for $188,000. Volta now sues Simpka under UCC 2–713 for the contract-market differential at the time of performance. Assume that the court has ruled in this particular case that the "time when the buyer learned of the breach" was the times of the respective deliveries to be made by Simpka and has further found that the contract market differential at those times is a total of $20,000.

Simpka's counsel has argued that the January purchase constituted a cover and that such cover is the exclusive measure of damages. In support of his argument Simpka's counsel cites comment 5 to UCC 2–713 which reads as follows:

> The present section provides a remedy which is completely alternative to cover under the preceding section and applies only when and to the extent that the buyer has not covered.

Volta has hired Professor (now Justice) Ellen Peters as its counsel, and she makes the following argument in response to the contention that UCC 2–712 is the exclusive remedy.

PETERS, REMEDIES FOR BREACH OF CONTRACTS RELATING TO THE SALE OF GOODS UNDER THE UNIFORM COMMERCIAL CODE: A ROADMAP FOR ARTICLE TWO, 73 Yale L.J. 199, 260–61 (1963).

"Comment 5 is clear enough; but nothing supporting this position can be found in the text of 2–713. However, 2–711, which lists the buyer's rights upon rightful rejection, states its alternatives in a sequence consistent with Comment 5: 'the buyer may * * * "cover" and have damages under the next section [which contains the cover-contract formula] * * *; or * * * recover damages for non-delivery [the market-contract formula].' Section 2–711 is clear that a buyer need not cover unless he so chooses, but seemingly requires damages to be measured by cover if cover has been effectuated. In the case of a seller suing for non-acceptance, there is no parallel limitation, either in comment or text. The only possible explanation for such a difference in the treatment of buyers and sellers would have to be derived from inequalities in the statements of the other half of the option, the market-contract formulae. Perhaps the seller needs a freer hand when he resells than the buyer who covers because the seller's market-contract formula is so erratic a measure of damages.

"But the history of the development of these remedies over the various drafts of the Uniform Commercial Code suggests a quite different explanation. Until the 1957 version, 2–713 on seller's remedies prefaced his right to recover damages for non-acceptance with 'so far as any goods have not been resold.' At that point then, the market-contract formula was equally conditional for both buyers and sellers, the buyer's rights then being identical in text and comment to their present 1962 statement. The 1957 amendment, deleting this language, was promulgated, according to the Report of the 1956 Recommendations of the Editorial Board, at the suggestion of the New York Law Revision Commission 'to make it clear that the aggrieved seller was not required to elect between damages under Section 2–706 and damages under Section 2–708.' This comment is instructive on two counts: it indicates a purpose to safeguard alternative remedies, and, more important, it characterizes the amendment as a clarification rather than as a change. The latter point might be dismissed as mere face-saving on the part of the revision committee but for the fact that changes are called changes in other comments. If the committee's characterization is correct, the reference to resale, even in the old 2–703 on seller's remedies, was addressed not to the existence of a resale but to whether the resale was being relied upon to measure damages. But if this is an accurate reading of the old 2–703, it is equally appropriate to a free choice among the buyer's remedies under 2–711.

"A non-restrictive reading of the various remedies sections to preserve full options to use or to ignore substitute transactions as a measure of damages makes more sense than Comment 5 for a number of reasons. It preserves a parity of remedy for buyers and sellers. It is consistent with a number of other Code sections which frown on premature election of remedies. It is a good deal easier to administer, since it would be most difficult to ferret out from a reluctant complainant information about transactions sufficiently related to the contract in breach to qualify as cover or resale. Finally, preservation of the option encourages recourse to actual market substitutes, since it guarantees to the injured party that he will not lose a remedy in the event of an unusually favorable substitute contract. It is thus consistent with the Code's overall interest in keeping goods moving in commerce as rapidly as possible."

What should Volta receive? For cases permitting recovery under UCC 2–713(1) despite evidence that the buyer had covered, see *Ralston Purina Co. v. McFarland*, 550 F.2d 967 (4th Cir.1977); *Interior Elevator Co. v. Limmeroth*, 278 Or. 589, 565 P.2d 1074 (1977).

DURA–WOOD TREATING CO. v. CENTURY FOREST INDUSTRIES, INC.

United States Court of Appeals, Fifth Circuit, 1982.
675 F.2d 745.

[After oral negotiations, Dura-Wood mailed a written order to purchase 20,000 creosote treated hardwood cross-ties from Century Forest at $8.60 each. Both parties were in the business of treating *Merchants* cross-ties. Dura-Wood's order was in partial fulfillment of a preexisting contract to supply ties to a third party, Smith. Century refused to deliver the ties, claiming that no oral agreement existed and, if it did, it was unenforceable under the statute of frauds. After obtaining price *"Cover" from with it?* quotations from other suppliers, Dura-Wood decided that it could produce the ties "internally at a lower price than it could purchase substitute ties from other manufacturers." Accordingly, Dura-Wood produced the ties, delivered them to Smith and sued Century Forest for damages based upon the difference between the cost to cover and the contract price. The trial court held that the parties had entered an enforceable contract and awarded Dura-Wood damages of $100,000. On appeal, the court of appeals first affirmed that there was an enforceable contract and then turned to the question of damages.]

* * *

JOHNSON, CIRCUIT JUDGE

III. DAMAGES

The district court's damage award will be addressed in three parts. First, there is a question regarding actual damages as they relate to Dura-Wood's "cover." The second part addresses the so-called "potential profits" allegedly lost as a result of Dura-Wood's method of covering. Finally, there is a question regarding profits that Dura-Wood would have received as a result of its contract with Smith Company, but lost because of Century Forest's breach of contract.

A. Cover

When a seller breaches a contract, the buyer "may 'cover' by making in good faith and without unreasonable delay any reasonable purchase of or contract to purchase goods in substitution for those due from the seller." Tex.Bus. & Com.Code Ann. § 2.712(a). "Covering" is an optional remedy for the buyer faced with securing a damage award. See Tex.Bus. & Com.Code § 2.711; Tex.Bus. & Com.Code § 2.712; Comment 3, Tex.Bus. & Com.Code § 2.712. If he chooses to cover, "The buyer may recover from the seller as damages the difference between the cost of cover and the contract price together with any incidental or consequential damages." Tex.Bus. & Com.Code § 2.712(b).

In the case sub judice, Dura-Wood claims—and the district court found—it engaged in a valid method of cover by manufacturing the necessary ties itself. Century Forest argues this is an invalid mechanism for cover. The basis of Century Forest's argument is that the Tex. Bus. & Com.Code does not contemplate a buyer's covering by purchasing from itself. Century Forest argues the purchase of or contract to purchase goods in substitution of those due from the seller must be made "on the market."

This Court recognizes the language of section 2.712, read literally, appears to contemplate the purchase of cover goods should be from an outside source. However, the Code is to be "liberally construed and applied to promote its underlying purposes and policies." Tex.Bus. & Com.Code § 1.102(a). The Code "is drawn to provide flexibility." Comment 1, Tex.Bus. & Com.Code § 1.102. Consequently, a buyer should be able to cover by manufacturing goods in substitution of those due from the seller, if such a cover otherwise satisfies and promotes the purposes and policies of the Tex.Bus. & Com.Code.

Comment one to section 2.712 states the "section provides the buyer with a remedy aimed at enabling him to obtain the goods he needs thus meeting his essential need." This statement essentially describes two purposes that may be fulfilled by an appropriate cover. First, it puts an aggrieved buyer in the same economic position in which it would have been had the seller actually performed. Second, it allows the buyer to achieve its prime objective, which is acquiring the needed goods. See, White, J. & Summers, R., *Handbook of the Law Under the Uniform Commercial Code* 222 (West 1980).

This Court acknowledges there is some language indicating the purchase of substitute goods should be "on the market." *See Kiser v. Lemco,* 536 S.W.2d 585 (Tex.Civ.App.—Amarillo 1976, no writ). However, this language is explained by the Texas courts' interpretations of section 2.712. As Century Forest itself points out, the Texas courts have noted that one policy behind section 2.712 is a presumption "that the cost of cover will approximate the market price of the undelivered goods." *Jon-T Farms, Inc. v. Good Pasture, Inc.,* 554 S.W.2d 743, 749 (Tex.Civ.App.—Amarillo 1977, writ ref'd n.r.e.). Indeed, an appropriate cover has the effect of setting the market price so that an aggrieved buyer does not have to prove damages through more onerous means. However, actually purchasing the cover goods from another source is not the exclusive means of satisfying the presumption of section 2.712. In an appropriate situation, internally producing the substitute or cover goods can satisfy the recognized underlying presumptions of section 2.712.

Regarding the case *sub judice,* this Court finds no error in the district court's actual damage award based upon Dura-Wood's cover. This Court determines that a buyer, at least in the case *sub judice,* may cover by manufacturing goods internally. The purposes and presumptions of the Tex.Bus. & Com.Code can be, and are, fulfilled in those instances—such as in the instant case—when the buyer is already in the marketplace and can produce the goods at a price approximating or lower than the market price. It would defy reason and the Tex.Bus. & Com.Code's purposes of flexibility and adaptation to reasonable commercial practice to require a buyer to increase losses by covering through the purchase of goods from another seller, if it could produce the goods itself at a lower price. This is particularly true when it is recognized that such a determination would remove the other advantages that section 2.712 contemplates from cover.

As a factual matter, cover by internal manufacturing must be in "good faith." The Tex.Bus. & Com.Code provides workable definitions of good faith in at least two pertinent places. Section 1.201(19) defines good faith as "honesty in fact in the conduct or transaction concerned." Section 2.103(a)(2) expands this basic definition in order to make it specifically applicable to merchants. " 'Good faith' in the case of a merchant means honesty in fact and the observance of reasonable commercial standards of fair dealing in the trade." Tex.Bus. & Com. Code § 2.103(a)(2).

Another factual matter concerns the necessity for the aggrieved buyer to cover without "unreasonable delay" and to make a "reasonable purchase." The Tex.Bus. & Com.Code provides only limited aid for the court attempting to determine whether a cover purchase is reasonable in the appropriate respects. However, there is some aid. Initially, section 1.204(b) provides guidelines for what a reasonable time within which to cover may be. The section states, "What is a reasonable time for taking any action depends on the nature, purpose and circumstances of such action." Additionally, Comment two to section 2.712 dictates, "The test of proper cover is whether at the time and place the buyer acted in good faith and in a reasonable manner, and it is immaterial that hindsight may later prove that the method of cover used was not the cheapest or most effective." At a minimum this "test" suggests a buyer has some time in which to evaluate the situation and attempt to determine what may be the best or most appropriate means to cover. *See* Comment 2, Tex.Bus. & Com.Code § 2.712.

Finally, there is the factual requirement that the goods be "in substitution for those due from the seller." Comment two to section 2.712 points out that "[t]he definition of 'cover' * * * envisages * * * goods not identical with those involved but commercially usable as reasonable substitutes under the circumstances of the particular case."

The record demonstrates good faith on the part of Dura-Wood in choosing to cover by manufacturing the cross-ties internally. Dura-Wood took price quotations and ultimately determined it could produce the ties at a lower price. The district court's finding that Dura-Wood acted in good faith—which is implicit in its determination regarding actual damages—is not clearly erroneous.

Additionally, the district court's finding that Dura-Wood covered within a reasonable time and provided a reasonable substitute was not clearly erroneous. The record reveals Dura-Wood waited to cover in order to evaluate the market for cross-ties. There is evidence demonstrating the cross-tie market is volatile and subject to fluctuations. The price of cross-ties was high during the time Dura-Wood was evaluating the market. Consequently, Dura-Wood's waiting to determine whether a decrease in market price might occur was not unreasonable. In addition, Dura-Wood continued to urge performance, as contemplated by section 2.610 of the Tex.Bus. & Com.Code. The record also demonstrates the internally produced cover goods were commercially usable as reasonable substitutes for those due from Century Forest.

B. Potential Profits

The district court awarded Dura-Wood $42,000 as "potential profits" that it lost "by using its own facilities to produce cross-ties to replace those which the defendant refused to provide." In other words, the district court found that, when Dura-Wood covered by internally manufacturing the cross-ties, it could have been producing cross-ties and selling them to new or different customers instead of producing them in substitution for goods due from Century Forest.

As a general proposition, lost profits are consequential damages as contemplated by Tex.Bus. & Com.Code § 2.715(b). *See General Supply & Equipment Co., Inc. v. Phillips,* 490 S.W.2d 913 (Tex.Civ.App.—Tyler 1973, writ ref'd n.r.e.). Section 2.715 establishes that consequential damages include "any loss resulting from general or particular requirements and needs of which the seller at the time of contracting had reason to know and which could not reasonably be prevented by cover or otherwise." Of course, section 2.712 allows a plaintiff to obtain consequential damages. Tex.Bus. & Com.Code § 2.712.

However, the district court's damage award for "potential profits" does not fall within the contemplation of section 2.715. It is true Dura-Wood, by manufacturing its own cross-ties, covered for less money than if it had purchased ties from some other source. It is also true that while Dura-Wood was producing its cross-ties, its facilities were tied up and Dura-Wood was unable to manufacture goods for new or different contracts. However, Dura-Wood could have minimized its overall losses. The cost of producing the ties plus the cost of lost profits resulting from Dura-Wood's inability to enter into new or different contracts was greater than the cost of simply purchasing the cover goods from another source. If Dura-Wood had purchased ties from someone else, its facilities would not have been tied up and Dura-Wood would have been able to enter new or different contracts. As a result, Dura-Wood would have had lower overall costs. Century Forest should not be obligated to pay for Dura-Wood's poor choice.

The so-called loss of potential profits could have reasonably been prevented by a different form of cover or otherwise. In the absence of such preventative measures, the district court's award of consequential damages, as it relates to the loss of potential profits, is not authorized by section 2.715.

C. Lost Profits on the Dura-Wood/Smith Contract

The district court also awarded Dura-Wood $13,000 for "lost profits on its contract with the third party [Smith Company]." This amount was computed by determining the amount of profit per tie Dura-Wood would have received from Smith Company had Century Forest performed, and was awarded as consequential damages. However, the award was erroneous since it allows Dura-Wood a double recovery as to the $13,000.

Dura-Wood received an actual damage award that considered the difference between the cost of cover and the contract price. Since Dura-Wood was able to provide Smith Company with cross-ties and received payment, there is no room for the $13,000 award. Stated another way, Dura-Wood already had been compensated for the fact that producing its own cross-ties was more expensive than buying them from Century Forest.

* * *

[Handwritten margin notes:]

Generally, lost profits are consequential damages under § 2-715

But the trial ct's award for potential profits does not fall here!

π could have covered elsewhere and still produced for itself.

The so-called loss of potential profits could have been avoided.

What about Comment 2 to 2-712?

But this would allow double recovery!

π was clearly compensated for the fact that its cover was more expensive than buying from Δ.

[Bottom handwritten notes:]

This would be double recovery.

IF K with Δ had been 10 but sold to Smith for 20 = $10 profit

If cover was 15 but sold for $20 → $5 profit + $5 for cover damage = $10

V. CONCLUSION

This Court affirms the district court's determination that Dura-Wood and Century Forest entered a legally enforceable contract. In addition, it affirms the district court's award of actual damages as expressed in the court's Finding of Fact No. 10. This Court, however, reverses the district court's award of lost profits as expressed in the court's Findings of Fact Nos. 11 and 12.

This case is remanded to the district court for entry of a judgment consistent with this opinion.

Affirmed in part, reversed in part, and remanded.

[Footnotes omitted.]

Notes

1. Accord: Cives Corp. v. Callier Steel Pipe & Tube, Inc., 482 A.2d 852, 858 (Me.1984), where the court, citing *Dura-Wood Treating,* supra, noted that the buyer did not "resort to in-house cover until after conducting a thorough search for an alternate supplier." The buyer "knew its own capabilities and correctly determined that it could with some extra effort and expense, produce the require steel tubes." Under these circumstances, "resort to in-house cover is a legitimate business decision." See also, Milwaukee Valve Co., Inc. v. Mishawaka Brass Manufacturing, Inc., 107 Wis.2d 164, 319 N.W.2d 885 (App.1982) (diverting existing orders to fill gap caused by seller's breach is a reasonable cover).

2. "Cover" by the buyer through internal production rather than by purchase from a third party raises a series of questions for which there are no easy answers. First, how can the courts get around the language of UCC 2–712(1) which appears to define cover in terms of a "purchase of or contract to purchase goods in substitution for those due from the seller?" Second, by what standard should the seller challenge the buyer's decision to make rather than to buy? Must that decision be "in good faith and without unreasonable delay?" UCC 2–712(1). Third, how does the seller challenge the buyer's claimed "cost of cover" through internal production? For example, must those costs be reasonable? Can the buyer use current market prices rather than historical cost to measure the cost of materials? Fourth, what are "incidental damages" in this setting? See UCC 2–715(1). In *Cives Corp.,* supra, the buyer claimed as incidental damages certain general overhead expenses allocated to the making of the cover over and above the direct cost of production. The exclusion by the trial court of some of these expenses was upheld on appeal. The court stated: "In order to recover overhead expenses in effecting cover Cives had to establish not only that a portion of its resources was unavailable for other projects for the time when it was effecting cover, but also that it had to forego the performance of other available construction projects. Recoverable proportionate overhead expenses must represent not only an expense, but a loss, i.e., it must be shown that other jobs would have been obtained to absorb such overhead, but had to be given up because of the cover undertaking." 482 A.2d at 860. Fifth, what are "consequential damages" in this setting,

see UCC 2–715(2)? Sixth, what are "expenses saved in consequence of the seller's breach?"

SECTION 6. CONSEQUENTIAL DAMAGES FOR BREACH BY DELAY OR NONDELIVERY

A commercial buyer may have different objectives in contracting to buy goods: (1) As a jobber or distributor, to resell goods in the same condition as delivered by the seller; (2) As a manufacturer, to use the goods as part of a product to be manufactured and resold; and (3) As a manufacturer, to use the goods as equipment to maintain or expand its capacity to produce goods for resale. Thus, a jobber would purchase, say, a completed woodstove for resale to consumers while a manufacturer would purchase either steel to be incorporated into a stove to be manufactured or equipment with which to manufacture the stove.

In each case, an unexcused delay or a failure to deliver by the seller results in two potential sources of damages, "direct" damages measured by the contract price and either the market price, UCC 2–713, or the cost to cover, UCC 2–712, and "consequential" damages, measured by the buyer's loss from being unable to use the goods. UCC 2–715(2)(a). Frequently, the buyer claims as consequential damages the net profits that would have been made if the goods had been delivered on time.

There are four traditional limitations upon the recovery of consequential damages. Three limitations are explicit in UCC 2–715(2)(a): (1) The loss must result from or be caused by the breach; (2) The loss must result from "general or particular requirements and needs" of the buyer "of which the seller at the time of contracting had reason to know * * *: and (3) The loss must be one "which could not reasonably be prevented by cover or otherwise." A fourth limitation, applicable to all claims for damages, is that the loss must be proved by the plaintiff with reasonable certainty. To prevail in a claim for consequential damages, the plaintiff must satisfy all four limitations.

For now, consider the following problem and case. We will return to the consequential damages problem in connection with the buyer's claim for damages with regard to accepted goods, infra at Chapter Fourteen, Section 3.

Problem 8–8

On May 1, F, a farmer, sold B, a dealer, 2,000 bushels of # 1 yellow corn, just planted in F's fields, for $3.00 a bushel. Delivery was promised no later than October 15. On May 15, B resold the corn to C, a cereal manufacturer, for $4.00 a bushel. Due to a drought in other parts of the country, the market price for # 1 yellow at the time of delivery was $5.00 per bushel. F failed to deliver and C demanded delivery from B of 1,000 bushels at $4.00 per bushel.

1. What should B do to maximize damages against F?

2. Suppose, after negotiations, C agreed to release B from the contract upon payment of $500. B paid the $500.

3. Suppose on May 15, B had been able to resell the corn to C for $6.00 a bushel even though the prevailing market price for futures was $4.00. What damages?

HYDRAFORM PRODUCTS CORP. v. AMERICAN STEEL & ALUMINUM CORP.

Supreme Court of New Hampshire, 1985.
127 N.H. 187, 498 A.2d 339.

SOUTER, JUSTICE.

The defendant, American Steel & Aluminum Corporation, appeals from the judgment entered on a jury verdict against it. The plaintiff, Hydraform Products Corporation, brought this action for direct and consequential damages based on claims of negligent misrepresentation and breach of a contract to supply steel to be used in manufacturing woodstoves. American claims that prior to trial, the Superior Court (Nadeau, J.) erroneously held that a limitation of damages clause was ineffective to bar the claim for consequential damages. American further claims, inter alia, that the Trial Court (Dalianis, J.) erred (a) in allowing the jury to calculate lost profits on the basis of a volume of business in excess of what the contract disclosed and for a period beyond the year in which the steel was to be supplied; (b) in allowing the jury to award damages for the diminished value of the woodstove division of Hydraform's business; (c) in failing to direct a verdict for the defendant on the misrepresentation claim; and (d) in allowing Hydraform's president to testify as an expert witness. We hold that the trial court properly refused to enforce the limitation of damages clause, but we sustain the other claims of error and reverse the judgment.

Hydraform was incorporated in 1975 and began manufacturing and selling woodstoves in 1976. During the sales season of 1977–78 it sold 640 stoves. It purchased steel from a number of suppliers until July 1978, when it entered into a "trial run" contract with American for enough steel to manufacture 40 stoves. Upon delivery of the steel, certain of Hydraform's agents and employees signed a delivery receipt prepared by American, containing the following language:

> "Seller will replace or refund the purchase price for any goods which at the time of delivery to buyer were damaged, defective or not in conformance with the buyer's written purchase order, provided that the buyer gives seller written notice by mail of such damage, defect or deviation within 10 days following its receipt of the goods. *In no event shall seller be liable for labor costs expended on such goods or other consequential damages.*"

(Emphasis added.)

When some of the deliveries under this contract were late, Hydraform's president, J.R. Choate, explained to an agent of American that late deliveries of steel during the peak season for manufacturing and selling stoves could ruin Hydraform's business for a year. In response, American's agent stated that if Hydraform placed a further order, American would sheer and stockpile in advance, at its own plant, enough steel for 400 stoves, and would supply further steel on demand. Thereafter Hydraform did submit a purchase order for steel sufficient to manufacture 400 stoves, to be delivered in four equal installments on the first days of September, October, November and December of 1978.

American's acceptance of this offer took the form of deliveries accompanied by receipt forms. The forms included the same language limiting American's liability for damages that had appeared on the receipts used during the trial run agreement. Hydraform's employees signed these receipts as the steel was delivered from time to time, and no one representing Hydraform ever objected to that language.

Other aspects of American's performance under the trial run contract reoccurred as well. Deliveries were late, some of the steel delivered was defective, and replacements of defective steel were tardy. Throughout the fall of 1978 Mr. Choate protested the slow and defective shipments, while American's agent continually reassured him that the deficient performance would be corrected. Late in the fall, Mr. Choate finally concluded that American would never perform as agreed, and attempted to obtain steel from other suppliers. He found, however, that none could supply the steel he required in time to manufacture stoves for the 1978–79 sales season. In the meantime, the delays in manufacturing had led to cancelled orders, and by the end of the season Hydraform had manufactured and sold only 250 stoves. In September, 1979, Hydraform sold its woodstove manufacturing division for $150,000 plus royalties.

In December, 1979, Hydraform brought an action for breach of contract, which provoked a countersuit by American. In January, 1983, American moved to dismiss Hydraform's claims for consequential damages to compensate for lost profits and for loss on the sale of the business. American based the motion on the limitation of damages clause and upon its defense that Hydraform had failed to mitigate its damages by cover or otherwise. In February, 1983, Hydraform's pretrial statement filed under Superior Court Rule 62 disclosed that it claimed $100,000 as damages for lost profits generally and $220,000 as a loss on the sale of the business. Later in February, 1983, the superior court permitted Hydraform to amend its writ by adding further counts, which included claims for fraudulent and negligent misrepresentation. Hydraform did not, however, proceed to trial on the claim of fraud.

In April, 1983, *Nadeau*, J., denied American's motion to dismiss the claims for consequential damages. He relied on the Uniform Commercial Code as adopted in New Hampshire, RSA chapter 382–A, in ruling that the limitation of damages clause was unenforceable on the alternative grounds that the clause would have been a material alteration of the contract, *see* RSA 382–A:2–207(2)(b), or was unconscionable or was a term that had failed of its essential purpose, *see* RSA 382–A:2–719(2) and (3). He further concluded that, under the circumstances of the case, the failure to cover, if proven, would not bar consequential damages.

The case was tried to a jury before *Dalianis, J.* American's exceptions at trial are discussed in detail below. At the close of the evidence, American objected to the use of a verdict form with provision for special findings, and the case was submitted for a general verdict, which the jury returned for Hydraform in the amount of $80,245.12.

* * *

Since the clause was not enforceable, the trial court allowed the jury to consider Hydraform's claims for lost profits in the year of the contract, 1978, and for the two years thereafter, as well as its claim for loss in the value of the stove manufacturing business resulting in a lower sales price for the business in 1979. American argues that the court erred in submitting such claims to the jury, and rests its position on three requirements governing the recovery of consequential damages.

First, under RSA 382–A:2–715(2)(a) consequential damages are limited to compensation for "loss resulting from general or particular requirements and needs of which the seller at the time of contracting had reason to know * * *" This reflection of *Hadley v. Baxendale,* 156 Eng.Rep. 145 (1854) thus limits damages to those reasonably foreseeable at the time of the contract. *See Gerwin v. Southeastern Cal. Ass'n of Seventh Day Adventists,* 14 Cal.App.3d 209, 220, 92 Cal.Rptr. 111, 118 (1971); *Petrie-Clemons v. Butterfield,* 122 N.H. 120, 124, 441 A.2d 1167, 1170 (1982). To satisfy the foreseeability requirement, the injury for which damages are sought "must follow the breach in the natural course of events, or the evidence must specifically show that the breaching party had reason to foresee the injury." *Salem Engineering & Const. Corp. v. Londonderry School Dist.,* 122 N.H. 379, 384, 445 A.2d 1091, 1094 (1982). Thus, peculiar circumstances and particular needs must be made known to the seller if they are to be considered in determining the foreseeability of damages. *Lewis v. Mobil Oil Corporation,* 438 F.2d 500, 510 (8th Cir.1971).

Second, the damages sought must be limited to recompense for the reasonably ascertainable consequences of the breach. *See* RSA 382–A:2–715, comment 4. While proof of damages to the degree of mathematical certainty is not necessary, *Smith v. State,* 125 N.H. 799, 805, 486 A.2d 289, 294 (1984), a claim for lost profits must rest on evidence demonstrating that the profits claimed were "reasonably certain" in the absence of the breach. *Whitehouse v. Rytman,* 122 N.H. 777, 780, 451 A.2d 370, 372 (1982). Speculative losses are not recoverable.

Third, consequential damages such as lost profits are recoverable only if the loss "could not reasonably be prevented by cover or otherwise." § 2–715(2)(a). *See* § 2–712(1) (*i.e.,* by purchase or contract to purchase goods in substitution for those due from seller). In summary, consequential damages must be reasonably foreseeable, ascertainable and unavoidable.

Applying these standards, we look first at the claim for lost profits for the manufacturing season beginning in September, 1978. There is no serious question that loss of profit on sales was foreseeable up to the number of 400 stoves referred to in the contract, and there is a clear evidentiary basis for a finding that Hydraform would have sold at least that number. There was also an evidentiary basis for the trial court's ruling that Hydraform acted reasonably even though it did not attempt to cover until the season was underway and it turned out to be too late. American had led Hydraform on by repeatedly promising to take steps to remedy its failures, and the court could find that Hydraform's reliance on these promises was reasonable up to the time when it finally and unsuccessfully tried to cover.

Lost profits on sales beyond the 400 stoves presents a foreseeability issue, however. Although American's agent had stated that American would supply steel beyond the 400 stove level on demand, there is no evidence that Hydraform indicated that it would be likely to make such a demand to the extent of any reasonably foreseeable amount. Rather, the evidence was that Mr. Choate had told American's agent that the business was seasonal with a busy period of about four months. The contract referred to delivery dates on the first of four separate months and spoke of only 400 stoves. Thus, there appears to be no basis on which American should have foreseen a volume in excess of 400 for the season beginning in 1978. Lost profits for sales beyond that amount therefore were not recoverable, and it was error to allow the jury to consider them.

Nor should the claims for profits lost on sales projected for the two subsequent years have been submitted to the jury. The impediment to recovery of these profits was not total unforeseeability that the breach could have effects in a subsequent year or years, but the inability to calculate any such loss with reasonable certainty. In arguing that a reasonably certain calculation was possible, Hydraform relies heavily on *Van Hooijdonk v. Langley,* 111 N.H. 32, 274 A.2d 798 (1971), a case that arose from a landlord's cancellation of a business lease. The court held that the jury could award damages for profits that a seasonal restaurant anticipated for the three years that lease should have run. It reasoned that the experience of one two-month season provided sufficient data for a reasonably certain opinion about the extent of future profits. The court thus found sufficient certainty where damages were estimated on the basis of one year of operation and profit, as compared with no operation and hence no profit in the later years.

Hydraform's situation, however, presents a variable that distinguishes it from *Van Hooijdonk.* In our case the evidence did not indicate that American's breach had forced Hydraform's stove manufacturing enterprise out of business, and therefore the jury could not assume that there would be no profits in later years. Without that assumption the jury could not come to any reasonably certain conclusion about the anticipated level of sales absent a breach by American. The jury could predict that Hydraform would obtain steel from another source and would be able to manufacture stoves; but it did not have the evidence from which to infer the future volume of manufacturing and sales. Thus, it could not calculate anticipated lost profits with a reasonable degree of certainty.

There is, moreover, a further reason to deny recovery for profits said to have been lost in the later years. Although Hydraform's pretrial statement disclosed that Hydraform claimed $100,000 in lost profits, it did not indicate that the claim related to the seasons beginning in 1979 and 1980. Since the pretrial statement also listed a claim for loss of the value of the business at the time of its sale in 1979, we believe that the statement could reasonably be read as claiming lost profit only for the one year before the business was sold. Therefore the claim for profits in 1979 and 1980 should have been disallowed for failure to disclose the claim as required by Superior Court Rule 62.

We consider next the claim for loss in the value of the business as realized at the time of its sale in 1979. As a general rule, loss in the value of a business as a going concern, or loss in the value of its good will, may be recovered as an element of consequential damages. *See Salem Engineering & Const. Corp. v. Londonderry School Dist.*, 122 N.H. at 384, 445 A.2d at 1094; *Salinger v. Salinger*, 69 N.H. 589, 591–92, 45 A. 558, 559–60 (1899); *see also J. Story, Partnership* § 99, at 169–70 (6th ed.1868).

In this case, however, it was error to submit the claim for diminished value to the jury, for three reasons. First, to the extent that diminished value was thought to reflect anticipated loss of profits in future years, as a capitalization of the loss, it could not be calculated with reasonable certainty for the reasons we have just discussed. Second, even if such profits could have been calculated in this case, allowing the jury to consider both a claim for diminished value resting on lost profits and a claim for the lost profits themselves would have allowed a double recovery. *See Westric Battery Co. v. Standard Electric Co., Inc.*, 522 F.2d 986, 989 (10th Cir.1975). Third, to the extent that diminished value was thought to rest on any other theory, there was no evidence on which it could have been calculated. There was nothing more than Mr. Choate's testimony that he had sold the business in September of 1979 for $150,000 plus minimum royalties, together with his opinion that the sales price was less than the business was worth. This testimony provided the jury with no basis for determining what the business was worth or for calculating the claimed loss, and any award on this theory rested on sheer speculation.

In summary, we hold that the jury should not have been allowed to consider any contract claim for consequential damages for lost profits beyond those lost on the sale of 150 stoves, the difference between the 400 mentioned in the contract and the 250 actually sold. Nor should the trial court have allowed the jury to consider the claim for loss in the value of the business.

*   *   *

Reversed.

Note: *Punitive Damages for Seller's Breach by Repudiation or Non-delivery*

Under what circumstances, if any, could Hydraform recover punitive damages for American Steel's breach of contract?

UCC 1–106(1) provides that "penal damages" may not be recovered "except as specifically provided in this Act or by other rule of law." There is nothing in the UCC which "specifically" authorizes punitive damages for any breach of a contract for sale. What about "other" rules of law? Compare UCC 1–103.

In the absence of legislation preempting the UCC, an accepted starting place is Section 355 of the Restatement, Second, of Contracts: "Punitive damages are not recoverable for a breach of contract unless the conduct constituting the breach is also a tort for which punitive damages are recoverable." Thus, if the breach is not "also" a tort, punitives are not recoverable. Even so, the breach which is a tort must, in the view of some courts, be "wilful" and "accompanied by fraud, malice, wantoness or oppression." McIntosh v. Magna Systems, Inc., 539 F.Supp. 1185, 1190 (N.D.Ill.1982). In most cases, this exacting test will not capture a breach that is simply negligent or a breach that is wilful where the objective is to recapture a gain that was foregone in the bargaining at the time of contracting. Moreover, the duty of good faith imposed by general contract law, see Section 205 of the Restatement, Second, Contracts, is classified as a term of the contract. Thus, bad faith in the performance or enforcement of the contract, however defined, is a breach of the bargain for which contract remedies are available. See Sections 5(2), 235(2) and Comment (b). See also, Speidel, *The Borderland of Contract,* 10 N.Ky.L.Rev. 163, 180–81, 188– 93 (1983).

A court could, however, decide that a "bad faith" breach was a tort which, if egregious, would support an award of punitive damages. California courts have done so in the context of insurance, and this result has been accepted in many states. Insurance contracts, however, contain elements not normally present in a commercial contract for sale between professional sellers and buyers. See Louderbach & Jurika, *Standards for Limiting the Tort of Bad Faith Breach of Contract,* 16 U.S.F.L.Rev. 187 (1982), who note the existence of a "special" relationship, with elements of unequal capacity, dependence and trust, between the individual insured and a corporate insurer. The absence of these special dimensions in commercial transactions has lead most courts to conclude that tort damages, including punitives, are not appropriate, regardless of the nature or purpose of the breach.

A possible portent of things to come is Seaman's Direct Buying Service, Inc. v. Standard Oil Co., 36 Cal.3d 752, 206 Cal.Rptr. 354, 686 P.2d 1158 (1984), where the Supreme Court of California, in a dispute between commercial parties, stated without clearly holding that a "party to a contract may incur tort remedies when, in addition to breaching the contract, it seeks to shield itself from liability by denying, in bad faith and without probable cause, that the contract exists." 686 P.2d at 1167. *Seaman's*, with its potential for converting all bad faith breaches into torts, has received much critical comment. See, e.g., Comment, *Extending the Bad Faith Tort Doctrine to General Commercial Contracts*, 65 B.U.L.Rev. 355 (1985). Although its future is uncertain, the nose of the punitive damage camel is clearly under the contract tent.

Part Four

THE STAGE OF GETTING THE GOODS OR DOCUMENTS TO THE BUYER

Chapter Nine

RISK OF LOSS

SECTION 1. THE BASIC GROUND RULES

There are many slips between the cup and the lip. One is that goods which have been identified to the contract for sale are destroyed or damaged before delivery without the fault or negligence of either party. Which party, seller or buyer, bears the risk of this loss?

The question is important. If the risk of loss has passed, the buyer must, unless insured, absorb the loss and pay the contract price. See UCC 2–709(1)(a). If the buyer has insured them, the insurance company will indemnify the buyer to the extent obligated under the policy and, through equitable or contractual subrogation, assert any claims that the buyer might have against third parties who caused the loss.

If the risk of loss has not passed, the seller, unless insured, must absorb the loss and, unless excused from performance, tender delivery of substitute goods. Again, if the goods are insured, the insurance company will indemnify the seller and, in all probability, assert any claims the seller may have against third parties through subrogation. When is the seller with the risk excused from performance because the goods were lost or damaged? The answer in most cases will be found in UCC 2–613 and 2–615, which you should review at this time.

When does the risk of loss pass? Section 22 of the Uniform Sales Act, which was enacted in 37 states, provided that the goods remained at the seller's risk until the "property" was transferred to the buyer. Thereafter, the risk was on the buyer "whether delivery had been made or not * * *." Section 18, however, provided that the property in "specific or ascertained goods" passed from the seller when the contract intended it to be transferred and Section 19 stated a series of five rules for ascertaining such intention when it was not otherwise made clear.

As the following excerpt reveals, the "property" or "title" approach to risk of loss was thought both to promote confusion and to ignore commercial realities.

LLEWELLYN, 1 HEARINGS BEFORE THE NEW YORK LAW REVISION COMMISSION ON THE UNIFORM COMMERCIAL CODE 96–97, [160–61] (1954).

Title should be abolished as means of establishing risk of loss

"May I say one other thing in that connection, and say it without any hesitancy at all for the record? The number of lawyers who have an accurate knowledge of sales law is extremely small in these United States. My brother Bacon has taught sales law for 28 years. When he says it isn't too difficult to determine where the court will decide the title is or isn't or is going to be or should be, he is speaking a truth within limits for people who have taught sales law for 28 years. I submit to you, sir, that there are not many of them.

"The ordinary lawyer, except for odds and ends of people who have specialized in this field, finds sales law as uncertain and as confused as you yourselves found it, if you are lawyers, when you finished the course in sales and wondered what the deuce you were going to do about an examination in confusion, dealing apparently with confused material and perhaps a confused professor.

"It is a body of law in which we just do not know our way around, and the thing that has been criticized, the elimination of the passing of title or the place where it is to pass, as the vital, focal factor for the courts to think about, is one of the great clarifications that has been offered to the law of these United States over many years.

"The way in which one comes to see that is not by praising the Code. The way in which one comes to see that is to turn to the only body of truly commercial sales law which operates almost entirely without use of the concept of title. There you have a body of sales law which is clean, clear, guidesome, which it is almost impossible to misconstrue, and which practically pays no attention to title at all. That is the law of the C.I.F. contract, and the inspiration of the law of the C.I.F. contract is the inspiration at least to try to bring it home to ordinary sales law, that just doesn't happen to be overseas and confined to a few people; that is what has led to the plan of the Code, working in terms of the facts, what the parties really thought about, and what the issues really are.

"So that, far from giving any excuse on behalf of the drafting staff or the supporting organizations for the elimination of the title concept as the center of the sales chapter, we bring it before you as what we conceive to be a true contribution and a true opportunity to bring a difficult, useful and troubled body of law within the compass of anybody, anytime, anyhow.

"Speaking to you, sir, as one law teacher to another, I suggest that this is going to be a great contribution to the law students of the United States. I think they can really learn their sales, and learn it fast, if you will give them Article 2."

The Code rejected title as the test for determining when the risk of loss has passed: "Each provision of this Article with regard to the rights, obligations and remedies of the seller, the buyer, purchasers or other third parties applies irrespective of title to the goods except where the provision refers to such title." UCC 2–401.

The primary provisions dealing with risk of loss are UCC 2–509 and 2–510. Note that the test is flexible rather than rigid and is keyed to the agreement of the parties and the stage of performance thereunder. More particularly, the risk is tied, in most cases at least, to which party has possession of or control over the goods. Two assumptions appear to underlie this approach: (1) The party in possession or in control is in the "best" position, cost considered, to minimize or avoid loss; and (2) The party in possession or in control is more likely to have insurance against losses that could not be avoided. In short, parties in control of goods are thought to be what economists call the "least cost loss avoiders" and the best insurers against risk. See Note, *Risk of Loss in Commercial Transactions: Efficiency Thrown Into the Breach*, 65 Va.L. Rev. 559 (1979). Thus, the Code sought to minimize the cases where the risk passed to the buyer before the goods changed hands—cases where the risk of loss was not on the party with possession and control and where the one with the risk would often not be insured for the loss. A useful discussion is Howard, *Allocation of Risk of Loss Under the UCC: A Transactional Evaluation of Sections 2–509 and 2–510*, 15 U.C. C.L.J. 334 (1983).

SECTION 2. RISK OF LOSS UNDER THE CODE IN THE ABSENCE OF BREACH

A. Seller Has No Obligation to Ship Goods; Goods in Possession of Bailee

Unless otherwise agreed, the seller has no obligation to ship the goods to the buyer. The place of delivery is the "seller's place of business or if he has none his residence." UCC 2–308(a). What the seller must do to tender delivery to the buyer is spelled out in UCC 2–503(1). If at the time of contracting, identified goods are in the possession "of a bailee and are to be delivered without being moved," what the seller must do to tender delivery is spelled out in UCC 2–503(4). See UCC 2–308(b). For the importance of this, read UCC 2–509(2) & (3) and work through the following materials.

Problem 9–1

Sam purchased a new VCR for $500 in June, 1987. In November, 1987, Sam, pressed for cash, advertised the VCR for sale. On Friday, Bob visited Sam's condo, inspected the unit and, after some negotiations, agreed to buy it for $300, with $150 down and the balance on delivery. Bob asked when he could take the VCR. Sam said he wanted it over the weekend to tape the Bear's game and that he would call Bob at work on Monday to set up a time "after work on Monday." Bob agreed. On Sunday evening, a self-appointed neighborhood "resource reallocator" forcibly entered Sam's condo and "removed" the VCR. When informed, Bob stopped payment on the $150 check. Sam argued that the VCR was Bob's and that he still owed Sam the entire $300. Neither party was insured. Who should prevail?

Problem 9–2

After negotiations and inspection, B agreed in writing to purchase identified, new factory equipment for $15,000. The agreement provided, in part, that the price was due "when goods received by the purchaser" and that delivery was to be to "purchaser's truck within 4 weeks of contract date, seller to give purchaser 7 days notice of delivery." Two weeks later, S notified B in writing that the goods were "in a deliverable state and at your disposal." The notice was received on a Friday. Over the weekend and before B took possession, vandals broke into S's plant and seriously damaged the machinery. B refused to take delivery, claiming that the risk of loss was on S. Neither party was insured. Who prevails?

SILVER v. WYCOMBE, MEYER & CO., INC.

Civil Court of the City of New York, 1984.
124 Misc.2d 717, 477 N.Y.S.2d 288.

DAVID B. SAXE, JUDGE.

This action by an insurance company, as subrogee, to recover proceeds paid to its insured, Martin Silver, was tried before the court on stipulated facts.

Plaintiff, through his agent, Elsie Simpson, an interior decorator, ordered custom furniture from defendant Wycombe, Meyer & Co., Inc. (Wycombe). The furniture was manufactured by codefendant Jackson-Allen Upholstery Corp. (Jackson-Allen), a subsidiary of defendant Wycombe, at its factory in Catasauqua, Pennsylvania. On or about February 23, 1982, Wycombe sent invoices to plaintiff advising that the furniture was ready for shipment. Plaintiff thereupon tendered payment in full and directed Wycombe to ship one room of furniture but to hold the other until instructed further. Accordingly, one room of furniture was shipped to plaintiff. But before any instructions were received as to the second room of furniture, it was destroyed in a fire which was not due to any negligence on the part of defendants. Fireman's Fund Insurance Co. paid plaintiff for the loss and seeks to recover the proceeds from defendants on the theory that the risk of loss never passed to the buyer, its insured.

In the absence of contrary agreement by the parties, risk of loss under the Uniform Commercial Code is determined by the manner in which delivery is to be made (U.C.C. 2–509). The original order, documented by defendant Wycombe's order form, indicates a price of

$7053 "+ del'y," and all invoices provide for shipment to plaintiff's home "Truck prepaid." It is clear that the provisions of U.C.C. 2–509 Subdiv. (1) govern the issue of when risk of loss passes to the buyer "where the contract requires or authorizes the seller to ship the goods by carrier * * *." Where the contract requires the seller to deliver the merchandise at a particular location, risk of loss passes upon tender of the goods at that location (U.C.C. 2–509(1)(b)) and where the contract does not require the seller to deliver the goods to a particular destination, it passes upon their delivery to the carrier (par. (a)). Where the contract provides for delivery at the seller's place of business or at the situs of the goods, risk of loss passes upon actual receipt by the buyer, if seller is a merchant, and otherwise upon tender of delivery (U.C.C. 2–509(3)).

Under the facts of the case at bar, the terms of the contract as it regards delivery are not stated. It is apparent, however, that regardless of the particular agreement between buyer and seller, defendants have set forth no facts sufficient to place the risk of loss upon plaintiff under any of the cited U.C.C. provisions. Indeed, the Official Comment 3 to U.C.C. 2–509 makes it clear that "a merchant seller cannot transfer risk of loss and it remains upon him until actual receipt by the buyer, even though full payment has been made and the buyer has been notified that the goods are at his disposal" (Note 3).

Defendants, however, advance the novel theory that, because of plaintiff's request that they hold the furniture subject to further instruction, they became mere bailees of the goods and that the provisions of U.C.C. 2–509(2) should govern this case. They argue that the invoices informing plaintiff that the furniture was ready for shipment constitute acknowledgment of the buyer's right to possession, transferring the risk of loss pursuant to U.C.C. 2–509(2)(b) to the buyer.

This position is entirely without merit. The provisions of U.C.C. 2–509(2) contemplate a situation in which goods are in the physical possession of a third party who will continue to hold them after consummation of the sale. Therefore, this is not a provision appropriately applied to the circumstances at bar which anticipate the passing of title *and* physical possession more or less simultaneously. Furthermore, bailment requires *delivery* of the goods to the bailee (see Black's Law Dictionary, 4th ed., p. 179, 1968). Having concluded that defendants failed to establish delivery of the furniture to plaintiff, by no stretch of the imagination may plaintiff be said to have redelivered it to defendants for safe-keeping.

Defendants cannot transform what is clearly a sale of goods into a bailment simply because they acceded to the buyer's request to postpone delivery. The agreement between buyer and seller clearly contemplates delivery at the buyer's home and, under the Uniform Commercial Code, risk of loss remains upon a merchant seller until he completes his performance with reference to the physical delivery of the goods (U.C.C. 2–401(2); U.C.C. 2–509(3) and Note 3 to U.C.C. 2–509;

Ramos v. Wheel Sports Center, 96 Misc.2d 646, 409 N.Y.S.2d 505, Civ. Ct., Bx.) It may be that defendant Jackson-Allen is a bailee for defendant Wycombe, but this Court is not required to rule on and makes no determination of this question.

Accordingly, judgment for plaintiff in the amount demanded in the complaint together with costs, disbursements and interest from April 13, 1982.

Notes

1. Under what circumstances, if any, can a merchant seller become a "bailee" for purposes of UCC 2–509(2)?

2. Note that the buyer's insurance company had indemnified the buyer for loss of the goods and sued the seller as a subrogee. Why did the insurer argue that risk of loss had not passed to the buyer? If the risk had passed, upon what theory could the insurer recover from the seller?

JASON'S FOODS, INC. v. PETER ECKRICH & SONS, INC.

United States Court of Appeals, Seventh Circuit, 1985.
774 F.2d 214.

POSNER, CIRCUIT JUDGE.

The jurisdictional question that led us to order a limited remand in *Jason's Foods, Inc. v. Peter Eckrich & Sons, Inc.,* 768 F.2d 189 (7th Cir. 1985), has been answered by the district judge: the defendant's principal place of business is Indiana, so there is diversity jurisdiction, and we can proceed to the merits of the appeal. Section 2–509(2) of the Uniform Commercial Code as adopted in Illinois (whose law, the parties agree, governs this diversity suit) provides that where "goods are held by a bailee to be delivered without being moved, the risk of loss passes to the buyer * * * (b) on acknowledgment by the bailee of the buyer's right to possession of the goods." Ill.Rev.Stat. ch. 26, ¶ 2–509(2). We must decide whether acknowledgment to the *seller* complies with the statute. There are no reported cases on the question, either in Illinois or elsewhere. Three commentators have opined that acknowledgment must be to the buyer, but without discussion. See Nordstrom, Handbook of the Law of Sales 404–05 (1970); Howard, *Allocation of Risk of Loss Under the UCC: A Transactional Evaluation of Sections 2–509 and 2–510,* 15 UCC L.J. 334, 347 n. 42 (1983); Comment, *Risk of Loss Under Section 2509 of the California Uniform Commercial Code,* 20 UCLA L.Rev. 1352, 1358 n. 30 (1973). There is a hint of the same position, again without explanation, in Latty, *Sales and Title and the Proposed Code,* 16 Law & Contemp.Prob. 3, 14 (1951); Note, *Risk of Loss Under the Uniform Commercial Code,* 7 Ind.L.Rev. 711, 726 (1974), and Note, *Commercial Transactions: Risk of Loss: What Does the Code Mean by Bailee?,* 21 Okla.L.Rev. 310 (1968). The defendant submitted in the district court an affidavit from a professor of commercial law at Ohio State University (Professor Clovis), who also concluded, also without elaboration, that acknowledgment must be to the buyer. The plaintiff did not question the admissibility of expert testimony on a pure issue of domestic law—though well it might have. See, e.g., *Marx & Co. v. Diners' Club, Inc.*, 550 F.2d 505, 510–11 (2d Cir.1977); *Loeb v. Hammond*, 407 F.2d 779, 781 (7th Cir.1969); *United States v. Zipkin*, 729 F.2d 384, 387 (6th Cir.1984). An alternative procedure would have been for the district judge to invite a disinterested expert on commercial law to submit a brief as *amicus curiae*. See Code of Judicial Conduct for United States Judges, Canon 3(A)(4) and commentary thereto.

On or about December 30, 1982, Jason's Foods contracted to sell 38,000 pounds of "St. Louis style" pork ribs to Peter Eckrich & Sons, delivery to be effected by a transfer of the ribs from Jason's' account in an independent warehouse to Eckrich's account in the same warehouse—which is to say, without the ribs actually being moved. In its confirmation of the deal, Jason's notified Eckrich that the transfer in storage would be made between January 10 and January 14. On January 13 Jason's phoned the warehouse and requested that the ribs be transferred to Eckrich's account. A clerk at the warehouse noted the transfer on its books immediately but did not mail a warehouse receipt until January 17 or January 18, and it was not till Eckrich received the receipt on January 24 that it knew the transfer had taken place. But on January 17 the ribs had been destroyed by a fire at the warehouse. Jason's sued Eckrich for the price. If the risk of loss passed on January 13 when the ribs were transferred to Eckrich's account, or at least before the fire, Jason's is entitled to recover the contract price; otherwise not. The district judge ruled that the risk of loss did not pass by then and therefore granted summary judgment for Eckrich.

Jason's argues that when the warehouse transferred the ribs to Eckrich's account, Jason's lost all rights over the ribs, and it should not bear the risk of loss of goods it did not own or have any right to control. Eckrich owned them and Eckrich's insurance covered any ribs that it owned; Jason's had no insurance and anyway, Jason's argues, it could not insure what it no longer owned. (The warehouse would be liable for the fire damage only if negligent. Cf. *Refrigeration Sales Co. v. Mitchell-Jackson, Inc.*, 770 F.2d 98 (7th Cir.1985).) Finally, Jason's points out that the draftsmen of the Uniform Commercial Code were careful and deliberate. Both subsections (a) and (c) of section 2-509(2)—the subsections that surround the "acknowledgment" provision at issue in this case—provide that the risk of loss passes to the buyer on or after "his receipt" of a document of title (negotiable in (a), nonnegotiable in (c)). If the draftsmen had meant that the acknowledgment of the buyer's right to possession of the goods—the acknowledgment that is subsection (b)'s substitute for a document of title—must be to the buyer, they would have said so.

Eckrich argues with great vigor that it cannot be made to bear the loss of goods that it does not know it owns. But that is not so *outré* a circumstance as it may sound. If you obtain property by inheritance, you are quite likely to own it before you know you own it. And Eckrich's position involves a comparable paradox: that Jason's continued to bear the risk of loss of goods that it knew it no longer owned. So the case cannot be decided by reference to what the parties knew or did not know; and neither can it be decided, despite Jason's' urgings, on the basis of which party could have insured against the loss. Both could have. Jason's had sufficient interest in the ribs until the risk of loss shifted to Eckrich to insure the ribs until then. You do not have to own goods to insure them; it is enough that you will suffer a loss if they are lost or damaged, *Hawkeye-Security Ins. Co. v. Reeg,* 128 Ill.App.3d 352, 83 Ill.Dec. 683, 470 N.E.2d 1103 (1984); *Prince v. Royal Indemnity Co.,* 541 F.2d 646, 649 (7th Cir.1976), as of course Jason's would if the risk of loss remained on it after it parted with title. See generally Stockton, *An Analysis of Insurable Interest Under Article Two of the Uniform Commercial Code,* 17 Vand.L.Rev. 815, 816–21 (1964). Section 2–509(2) separates title from risk of loss. Title to the ribs passed to Eckrich when the warehouse made the transfer on its books from Jason's' account to Eckrich's, but the risk of loss did not pass until the transfer was "acknowledged."

Title v. Risk of Loss

Thus, as is usually the case, insurability cannot be used to guide the assignment of liability. (The costs of insurance might sometimes be usable for this purpose, as we shall see, but not in this case.) Since whoever will be liable for the loss can insure against it, the court must determine who is liable before knowing who can insure, rather than vice versa. If acknowledgment to the seller is enough to place the risk of loss on the buyer, then Eckrich should have bought insurance against any losses that occurred afterward. If acknowledgment to the buyer is necessary (we need not decide whether acknowledgment to a third party may ever suffice), Jason's should have bought insurance against any losses occurring until then.

The suggestion that the acknowledgment contemplated by subsection (b) can be to the seller seems very strange. What purpose would it serve? When Jason's called up the warehouse and directed that the transfer be made, it did not add: and by the way, acknowledge to me when you make the transfer. Jason's assumed, correctly, that the transfer was being made forthwith; and in fact there is no suggestion that the warehouse clerk ever "acknowledged" the transfer to Jason's. If the draftsmen of subsection (b) had meant the risk of loss to pass when the transfer was made, one would think they would have said so, and not complicated life by requiring "acknowledgment."

A related section of the Uniform Commercial Code, section 2–503(4)(a), makes acknowledgment by the bailee (the warehouse here) a method of tendering goods that are sold without being physically moved; but, like section 2–509(2)(b), it does not indicate to whom acknowledgment must be made. The official comments on this section, however, indicate that it was not intended to change the corresponding

section of the Uniform Sales Act, section 43(3). See UCC comment 6 to *Rules on Tender*
§ 2-503. And section 43(3) had expressly required acknowledgment to
the buyer. See, e.g., *Peelle Co. v. Industrial Plant Corp.*, 120 N.J.L. 480,
200 A. 1007 (1938). Rules on tender have, it is true, a different
function from rules on risk of loss; they determine at what point the
seller has completed the performance of his side of the bargain. He
may have completed performance, but if the goods are still in transit
the risk of loss does not shift until the buyer receives them, if the seller
is a merchant. See UCC § 2-509(3) and UCC comment 3 to section 2-
509. In the case of warehouse transfers, however, the draftsmen
apparently wanted risk of loss to conform to the rules for tender. For
comment 4 to section 2-509 states that "where the agreement provides *Rules on Tender*
for delivery of the goods as between the buyer and seller without *apply to transfer*
removal from the physical possession of a bailee, the provisions on *of risk.*
manner of tender of delivery apply on the point of transfer of risk."
And those provisions as we have said apparently require (in the case *Require acknowl.*
where no document of title passes) acknowledgment to the buyer. The *to buyer.*
acknowledgment need not, by the way, be in writing, so far as we are
aware. Jason's could have instructed the warehouse to call Eckrich
when the transfer was complete on the warehouse's books. See *Whate-
ly v. Tetrault*, 29 Mass.App.Dec. 112, 5 UCC Rep.Serv. (Callaghan) 838
(1964). That is why Jason's case is not utterly demolished by the fact
that the document of title—that is, the warehouse receipt—was not
received by Eckrich till after the fire. Acknowledgment in a less *Written*
formal manner is authorized; indeed, section 509(2)(b) would have no *acknowledgement*
function if the only authorized form of acknowledgment were by docu- *was not required*
ment of title, whether negotiable or nonnegotiable.

The second sentence of comment 4 to section 509 is also suggestive:
"Due delivery of a negotiable document of title covering the goods or
acknowledgment by the bailee that he holds for the buyer completes
the 'delivery' and passes the risk." The reference to a document of title
is to subsections (a) and (c); and in both of those cases, of course, the
tender involves notice to the buyer. It would be surprising if the
alternative of acknowledgment did not.

All this may seem a rather dry textual analysis, remote from the *Policy Analysis*
purposes of the Uniform Commercial Code, so let us shift now to the
plane of policy. The Code sought to create a set of standard contract *1. Std terms*
terms that would reflect in the generality of cases the preferences of *(assignments of*
contracting parties at the time of contract. One such preference is for *liability, etc)*
assignments of liability—or, what amounts to the same thing, assignments of the risk of loss—that create incentives to minimize the *← to minimize*
adverse consequences of untoward events such as (in this case) a *Adverse consequences.*
warehouse fire. There are two ways of minimizing such consequences.
One is to make them less painful by insuring against them. Insurance *1. Know when to*
does not prevent a loss—it merely spreads it—but in doing so it reduces *insure*
(for those who are risk averse) the disutility of the loss. So if one of the
contracting parties can insure at lower cost than the other, this is an *2. Loss*
argument for placing the risk of loss on him, to give him an incentive to *prevention*

do so. But that as we have seen is not a factor in this case; either party could have insured (or have paid the warehouse to assume strict liability for loss or destruction of the goods, in which event the warehouse would have insured them), and so far as the record shows at equal cost.

The other method of minimizing the consequences of an unanticipated loss is through prevention of the loss. If one party is in a better position than the other to prevent it, this is a reason for placing the risk of loss on him, to give him an incentive to prevent it. It would be a reason for placing liability on a seller who still had possession of the goods, even though title had passed. But between the moment of transfer of title by Jason's and the moment of receipt of the warehouse receipt by Eckrich, neither party to the sale had effective control over the ribs. They were in a kind of limbo, until (to continue the Dantesque image) abruptly propelled into a hotter region. With Jason's having relinquished title and Eckrich not yet aware that it had acquired it, neither party had an effective power of control.

But this is not an argument for holding that the risk of loss shifted at the moment of transfer; it is just an argument for regarding the parties' positions as symmetrical from the standpoint of ability either to prevent or to shift losses. In such a case we have little to assist us besides the language of subsection (b) and its surrounding subsections and the UCC comments; but these materials do point pretty clearly to the conclusion that the risk of loss did not pass at the moment of transfer.

When did it pass? Does "acknowledgment" mean receipt, as in the surrounding subsections of 2–509(2), or mailing? Since the evidence was in conflict over whether the acknowledgment was mailed on January 17 (and at what hour), which was the day of the fire, or on January 18, this could be an important question—but in another case. Jason's waived it. The only theory it tendered to the district court, or briefed and argued in this court, was that the risk of loss passed either on January 13, when the transfer of title was made on the books of the warehouse, or at the latest on January 14, because Eckrich knew the ribs would be transferred at the warehouse sometime between January 10 and 14. We have discussed the immateriality of the passage of title on January 13; we add that the alternative argument, that Eckrich knew by January 14 that it owned the ribs, exaggerates what Eckrich knew. By the close of business on January 14 Eckrich had a well-founded expectation that the ribs had been transferred to its account; but considering the many slips that are possible between cup and lips, we do not think that this expectation should fix the point at which the risk shifts. If you were told by an automobile dealer from whom you bought a car that the car would be delivered on January 14, you would not take out insurance effective that day, without waiting for the actual delivery.

Finally, Jason's' argument from trade custom or usage is unavail- *T's argument*
ing. The method of transfer that the parties used was indeed custom- *on trade usage*
ary but there was no custom or usage on when the risk of loss passed to *offers them no help*
the buyer.

Affirmed. *Judgment for Δ (Buyer)*

Notes

1. At common law, if the goods were identified and in the possession
of a bailee, title and, thus, risk of loss, passed at the time of sale even
though the buyer was not entitled to take possession. See Tarling v.
Baxter, 6 B. & C. 360, 108 Eng.Rep. 484 (KB 1827). Compare UCC 2–401(3).
In *Jason's Foods,* the court held that even though title had passed, the risk
of loss did not pass until the bailee acknowledged to the buyer the buyer's
right to take possession. Do you agree? Compare UCC 2–705(2)(b).

2. The "bailee" in *Jason's Foods* was a warehouseman, i.e., a "person
who by a warehouse receipt * * * acknowledges possession of goods and
contracts to deliver them." UCC 7–102(1)(a). A warehouse receipt, UCC 1–
201(45), is a document of title which "in the regular course of business
* * * is treated as adequately evidencing that the person in possession of
it is entitled to receive, hold and dispose of the document and the goods it
covers." UCC 1–201(15). In *Jason's Foods,* the warehouse receipt issued
but not received by the buyer before the fire was not negotiable. See UCC
7–104(1). See UCC 2–509(2)(c) & 2–503(4)(b). Note that the buyer must
actually receive the written delivery order and, under UCC 2–503(4)(b), risk
of loss remains on the seller "until the buyer has had a reasonable time to
present the document or direction * * *." These sections further rein-
force Judge Posner's analysis, do they not? Does UCC 2–509(2)(b) even
apply to the case where a warehouseman regularly acknowledges a buyer's
right to possession by a non-negotiable document of title?

3. The warehouseman's duty of care is stated in UCC 7–204(1).

Problem 9–3

Red Feather, a fine yearling, won her first race. A pleased Owner
(much pleased) shipped her back to the stable by common carrier, taking a
non-negotiable bill of lading naming O as the consignee. While the horse
was in transit, O sold her to B for $10,000. Owner accepted a check for
$10,000, handed B the non-negotiable bill of lading and stated "she's all
yours." Two hours later, Red Feather was killed in an accident while still
in the carrier's possession.

A. B stopped payment on the check and insisted that the risk of loss
remained on S. Is B correct?

B. Suppose that, unknown to either party, Red Feather was dead at
the time of the contract. What result? See UCC 2–613.

B. Shipment Contracts

Probably the most common transaction in which risk of loss disputes will arise involves contracts that require or authorize the seller to

ship the goods to the buyer by carrier. It is also likely that the agreement will use certain delivery terms, such as "FOB seller's plant," FAS or CIF. See UCC 2–319 & 2–320. The Code drafters were aware of the common business understanding of these terms and consciously adapted the risk of loss provisions to them. Compare UCC 2–319(1) and 2–509(1). For what the seller must do under these terms to tender delivery, see UCC 2–503 & 2–504.

In most cases, the meaning and consequences of these delivery terms is clear. In an FOB point of origin or shipment contract, the buyer pays the cost of transportation and bears the risk of loss while the goods are in transit. UCC 2–319(1)(a) and 2–509(1)(a). In an FOB point of destination contract, the seller pays the cost of transportation and bears the risk while the goods are in transit. UCC 2–319(1)(b) and 2–509(1)(b). But occasionally there is some confusion.

RAYLO LUMBER COMPANY v. OREGON PACIFIC LUMBER COMPANY

Supreme Court of Oregon, 1960.
222 Or. 257, 352 P.2d 749.

HOLMAN, JUSTICE pro tem.

Plaintiff Raylo Lumber Company brought this action against defendant, Oregon Pacific Lumber Company, for the recovery of the price of a carload of lumber. For the purpose of clarity, this opinion will hereafter refer to the plaintiff, Raylo Lumber Company, as Seller and the defendant, Oregon Pacific Lumber Company, as Buyer.

At its mill in Fortuna, California, Seller received from Buyer a written order for lumber sent from Buyer's place of business in Portland, Oregon. The pertinent parts of the written order were as follows:

"To Raylo Lbr. Co. Box 575 Fortunia [sic], Calif. Ship to Oregon-Pacific Lumber Co. Council Bluffs, Iowa Rate 1.20 (Show on Bill of Lading) Routing SP UP (via Colby, Kansas) Shipment One week Terms: Regular 2% ADF 10 days Please Show Oregon-Pacific Lumber Co. As Shipper * * * Thoroughly Air Dried White Fir— WCLA Rules No. 15 Constr. & Btr., Allow. 25% standard ALS S4S EE DET—Clean Bright Stock Three (3) Carloads—Approx. 28/30M each. 2 × 4 R/L 70% 16' 60.00 24.00 84.00".

Seller successfully shipped two carloads about which there is no controversy. The loading of the third car on the siding at Seller's place of business was completed before noon on a particular day and the car was sealed. In the afternoon Seller prepared an invoice to Buyer for the lumber in the car, billing Buyer as follows:

"Shipped to Oregon—Pacific Lumber Company Council Bluffs, Iowa * * * F.O.B. Delivered $1.20 Rate. * * * 31,152' White Fir, A.D. 2 × 4 STD. & BTR. S4S, [at] $84.00 Per M—$2,616,77".

Seller also prepared a straight bill of lading naming Buyer both consignor and consignee as instructed, and around 5 o'clock in the afternoon presented it to the railroad at its nearest station at Alton, California, which was some distance from Seller's place of business. The railroad agent signed the bill of lading and Seller immediately deposited both it and the invoice in the mail to Buyer. Before Buyer received the bill of lading and before the carrier took the car from Seller's siding, fire broke out and the lumber was damaged. The fire was not shown to have been the fault of either party. The damaged lumber was sold with the consent of the parties without prejudice to their rights and the proceeds applied toward the purchase price. This action was brought for the balance, the trial judge tried the case without a jury, and entered findings of fact to the effect that Seller sold and delivered the lumber to Buyer and that the damage to the lumber occurred after the delivery of the lumber to Buyer in accordance with the terms of the agreement. Judgment was rendered for Seller and Buyer appeals.

The rules governing who should sustain the loss in a situation such as this are, of course, those set forth in the Uniform Sales Act which has been adopted by this state. Unless otherwise agreed, risk of loss follows the title to the property in question as the result of ORS 75.220 (Uniform Sales Act § 22), which is as follows:

> "Unless otherwise agreed, the goods remain at the seller's risk until the property therein is transferred to the buyer, the goods are at the buyer's risk whether delivery has been made or not, * * *."

Unless a contrary intention appears, the rules for ascertaining the intention of the parties as to the time title passes are set out in ORS 75.190 (Uniform Sales Act § 19). The pertinent parts of this section are as follows:

> "Unless a different intention appears, the following are rules for ascertaining the intention of the parties as to the time at which the property in the goods is to pass to the buyer:
>
> * * *
>
> "Rule 4. (1) Where there is a contract to sell unascertained or future goods by description, and goods of that description and in a deliverable state are unconditionally appropriated to the contract, * * * the property in the goods thereupon passes to the buyer.
>
> * * *
>
> "(2) Where, in pursuance of a contract to sell, the seller delivers the goods to * * * a carrier * * * for the purpose of transmission to * * * the buyer, he is presumed to have unconditionally appropriated the goods to the contract, except in the cases provided for in the next rule. * * *
>
> "Rule 5. If the contract to sell requires the seller to deliver the goods to the buyer, or at a particular place, or to pay the freight or cost of transportation to the buyer, or to a particular

place, the property does not pass until the goods have been delivered to the buyer or have reached the place agreed upon."

From the above, it is apparent that where there is a contract to sell unascertained or future goods by description, as was the case here, title passes when the goods are put in a deliverable state and unconditionally appropriated to the contract (Rule 4(1)). Where the Seller delivers the goods to a carrier for delivery to the Buyer, they are presumed to have been unconditionally appropriated to the contract (Rule 4(2)), except that if the contract requires delivery by the Seller to a particular place or to pay the cost of transportation, title does not pass until the goods have reached the place agreed upon. (Rule 5)

Seller claims that the rules set forth under ORS 75.190 do not apply, as by its provisions they are only applicable where no different intention appears; that this is a law case and the trial judge sitting as a jury, by making a finding that there was a sale and a delivery, found that a different intention did appear; that there is sufficient evidence in the record to support the findings and, therefore, they cannot be disturbed.

The question of intention is one of fact. However, if the whole contract of the parties is reduced to writing, or if the facts are so clear as to justify but one conclusion, and generally, if the facts are undisputed from which intention can be determined, the question is determined by the court. See 2 Williston, Sales (Rev.Ed.), p. 10, § 262. In this case, everything was in writing and there are no disputes as to the circumstances involved. This was a determination for the court as such and not one made by the court sitting as a jury.

The findings of the trial court that the lumber was sold, which imputes passage of title, and that there was a delivery is made in the face of Seller's invoice to Buyer which specifies the price as being "F.O.B. Delivered." This required Buyer to pay $84 per thousand for lumber delivered by Seller in Council Bluffs, Iowa. It imputes the passage of title at Council Bluffs and that Seller will pay the freight to that point. The term "F.O.B." has become recognized as having certain definite commercial and legal significance. A text written by Thomas G. Bugan entitled "When Does Title Pass From Shipper to Consignee And Who Has Risk of Loss or Damage in Transportation" (1951) has this to say about the term "F.O.B.": "This term has a certain legal significance of which the courts take judicial notice." After an examination of various judicial and text writers' definitions of the meaning of the term, he states as follows:

> The implication from the above definitions is, that the phrase F.O.B. will ordinarily determine the place where delivery is required and where the title will pass. Likewise, it will usually determine whether the seller or the buyer is to pay the transportation charges.

While recognizing that it may be varied by the other terms of the contract, the Oregon court has recognized the usual significance given the usage of the designation "F.O.B." in the case of Wade v. Johnson, 111 Or. 468, 477, 227 P. 466.

In his chapter entitled "F.O.B. Destination," which we take to be synonymous with the term "F.O.B. Delivered," Mr. Bugan discusses the intention of the parties regarding transfer of title as it affects the usage of the term "F.O.B." and comes to the following conclusion:

> The intent of the parties is the controlling element fixing the time and place of passage of title and risk.

> However, in the absence of a definite agreement as to time and place of passage of title, the Uniform Sales Act (or the principles of the common law where the Act does not apply) will prevail to determine the intent. If the words "f.o.b." are employed, they are especially important in solving the intent of the parties, for they have a definite commercial and legal significance of which the courts will take judicial notice.

The meaning of the use of the term has become so well ingrained in commercial and legal parlance that a contrary intention to its usual meaning must be demonstrated with a high degree of probability. The evidence here does not demonstrate such a probability and, therefore, there is no basis upon which to rest the trial court's findings of a sale and delivery.

Seller particularly contends that Buyer's instructions to Seller to ship the lumber showing Buyer as the shipper, shows a sufficient contrary intent. This is overcome, in our opinion, when coupled with an agreement for goods "F.O.B. Delivered." It could also just as logically be claimed that the instruction was for the purpose of not disclosing the identity of Buyer's supplier and customer to each other so they might deal directly without the necessity of a middle man.

The evidence not being sufficient to show a different intent as to the time of the passage of title, Rule 5 of ORS 75.190 is applicable. The Seller having undertaken to deliver the goods to Council Bluffs, Iowa, at the flat price of $84 per thousand and to pay the freight to that point, the property in the lumber had not passed at the time of the fire and risk of loss by virtue of ORS 75.220 was on the Seller.

The judgment of the lower court is reversed.

Notes

1. How would *Raylo* be decided under the Code? See UCC 2–319(1), 2–509(1), 2–503, Comment 5. See also, Pestana v. Karinol Corp., 367 So.2d 1096 (Fla.App.1979); Ninth St. East, Ltd. v. Harrison, 5 Conn.Cir. 597, 259 A.2d 772 (1968) (presumption of shipment rather than a destination contract).

2. In shipment contracts, the risk of loss passes at the time the seller completes or "duly" tenders delivery at the point to which the goods are to be delivered. UCC 2–509(1). In FOB point of shipment contracts, UCC 2–319(1)(a), the critical tender section is UCC 2–504. Although the seller

must do a number of things to tender delivery, obtaining insurance for the buyer's account is not one of them. Compare UCC 2–320 (C.I.F. term). For a case holding that the goods were not "duly" tendered where the seller failed to provide prompt notice of shipment in an FOB point of shipment contract, see Rheinberg-Kellerei GMBH v. Vineyard Wine Co., Inc., 53 N.C. App. 560, 281 S.E.2d 425 (1981). Does this position seem sound?

Note: Liability of Overland Carrier for Goods Lost or Damaged in Shipment

As we have seen, in an FOB place of shipment contract, risk of loss passes to the buyer when the seller "duly" tenders the goods to a carrier, whether that carrier be a truck, airplane, railroad or vessel. In addition, under the documents issued by the carrier, the buyer is the person "entitled" to the goods. See UCC 7–102(1)(b) & 7–403(4). Thus, if the goods are lost or damaged in transit, the buyer or its insurance company as subrogee has both the standing and the incentive * to bring suit against the carrier. Kumar Corp. v. Nopal Lines, LTD., 462 So.2d 1178 (Fla.App.1985), holds that plaintiffs with standing to sue the carrier include the party with the risk of loss or his agent and an insurance subrogee.

The common law liability of the overland carrier has been described as follows:

DOBIE, BAILMENTS AND CARRIERS 325 (1914)

"By the common law, the common carrier is, with certain exceptions, an insurer of the goods intrusted to him. According to the very early cases, the only exceptions to the common carrier's liability as an insurer of the safe delivery of the goods were: 1) the act of God; and 2) the public enemy. To these, however, our native justice and the genius of our jurisprudence have added: 3) the act of the shipper; 4) public authority; and 5) the inherent nature of the goods."

The common-law liability of common carriers, however, was subject to contractual limitations and exclusions inserted by carriers in the relevant documents.

The current status of carrier liability is determined under federal and state legislation and international treaties that, in turn, depend upon the type of carrier and the scope of its operation. Thus, the liability of international air carriers is determined by the Warsaw Convention, ratified by the United States in 1934, 49 Stat. 3000 (1934), T.S. No. 876, and the liability of vessels engaged in "foreign trade" is regulated by the Carriage of Goods by Sea Act, enacted by Congress in 1936. 49 Stat. 1207 (1936), 46 U.S.C.A. §§ 1300–15. A general survey appears in Sorkin, *Changing Concepts of Liability,* 17 Forum 710 (1981).

* Several things make the carrier an appealing defendant. First, it is likely that it causes or has the potential for causing more loss, destruction and damage than any other party associated with a typical sales transaction. Second, the carrier is almost always solvent. Third, it is easy to prove a case against a carrier. Finally, the carrier, as a public service enterprise, is obliged to deal with all persons and cannot readily use economic pressure of withholding services to forestall a suit. Ed.

The liability of domestic overland carriers in interstate commerce, i.e., railroads and truckers, is regulated by the 1906 Carmack amendments to the Interstate Commerce Commission Act of 1887, as reenacted in 1980 without substantial change. 49 U.S.C.A. § 11707. The statute is, essentially, a codification of the carrier's insurer liability at common law with the important benefit to the shipper that efforts to exclude or modify the scope of statutory liability by agreement are void. As the statute has been interpreted by the courts, the person entitled under the document states a *prima facie* case against the carrier by showing that the goods were delivered in good condition and arrived in a damaged condition and the amount of damages. To escape liability, the carrier has what is described as a "substantial double burden:" It must show both that it was free from negligence and that the damage to the cargo was due to one of the excepted causes relieving the carrier of liability at common law, i.e., act of God, public enemy, act of shipper himself, act of public authority or an inherent vice in the goods. See Martin Imports v. Courier Newsom Exp., Inc., 580 F.2d 240, 242 (7th Cir.1978), cert. denied 439 U.S. 983, 99 S.Ct. 574, 58 L.Ed. 2d 655 (1978). The seminal case in this line is Missouri P.R. Co. v. Elmore & Stahl, 377 U.S. 134, 84 S.Ct. 1142, 12 L.Ed.2d 194 (1964).

The liability of domestic overland carriers in intrastate commerce is determined by Article 7 of the UCC, more particularly, UCC 7-309. See UCC 7-103; Starmakers Pub. Corp. v. Acme Fast Freight, Inc., 615 F.Supp. 787 (S.D.N.Y.1985) (Carmack Act preempts UCC where interstate shipments are concerned). Subsection 7-309(1), which is poorly drafted, starts by imposing a duty of ordinary care on the carrier, but then states that the subsection "does not repeal or change any law or rule of law which imposes liability upon a common carrier for damages not caused by its negligence." Thus, in the many states where the common law liability of a carrier as insurer was recognized, the carrier could be liable even though exercising reasonable care. Subsection 7-309(2) gives limited effect to provisions in the bill of lading limiting liability: The carrier can limit liability to the value of the goods stated in the document but "no such limitation is effective with respect to the carrier's liability for conversion to its own use."

As one might expect, there has been no litigation of significance involving UCC 7-309.

SECTION 3. EFFECT OF BREACH ON RISK OF LOSS—2-510

UCC 2-510 modifies the risk of loss principles established by UCC 2-509 in certain circumstances where one of the parties is in breach. The consequences of this modification are twofold.

First, in some cases the breaching party will have to absorb the loss of or pay for lost, stolen or destroyed goods where, but for the breach, the risk of loss would have been on the other party. Thus, UCC 2-510 reallocates the risk of loss because one party breached the contract and negates the assumptions made ex ante about who was in the best position to insure. This reallocation has been questioned on policy grounds in McCoid, *Allocation of Loss and Property Insurance,* 39 Ind. L.J. 647 (1964).

Second, UCC 2–510 operates, in some circumstances, as an anti-subrogation clause. It places the risk on the non-breaching party's insurance company in circumstances where but for the insurance contract the risk of loss would be on the breaching party. Thus, under UCC 2–510(2), a buyer who, because of the seller's breach, rightfully revokes acceptance may treat the risk of loss as having rested on the seller "to the extent of any deficiency in his effective insurance coverage." Because of the statute, the insurance company must pay if there is no deficiency and, apparently, is precluded from any recovery as a subrogee against the seller. See Comment 3, which states: "This section merely distributes the risk of loss as stated and is not intended to be disturbed by any subrogation of an insurer."

What is the point of all this? One commentator has suggested that UCC 2–510 is of "dubious origin," has little practical impact on the way that insurance companies do business and "serves no practical purpose save the harassment of the legal mind." King, *UCC Section 2–510—A Rule Without Reason*, 77 Com.L.J. 272 (1972). Nothing has emerged since 1972 to cast serious doubt on this conclusion. Professor Howard, in *Allocation of Risk of Loss Under the UCC: A Transactional Evaluation of Sections 2–509 and 2–510*, 15 U.C.C.L.J. 334, 355–68 (1983), questions whether a commercial breach in the absence of bad faith is important enough to undercut the importance of insurance.

Here are some simple problems.

Problem 9–4

On June 1, S contracted to sell B 10 units of described goods for $10,000. S agreed to ship the goods "FOB point of shipment" by June 15 and B agreed to pay in full within 30 days of receipt. S had insurance on the goods until they were delivered to the carrier. B had insurance on the goods when "title" passed to him, i.e., at the "time and place of shipment."√ UCC 2–401(2)(a). S's insurance covered the current market value of the described goods. B's insurance covered 50% of the current market value of the goods.

A. S delivered the goods to the carrier on June 16 (they were shipped on June 17) and failed to give B any notice of the shipment. Review UCC 2–504. The goods were totally destroyed in transit on June 19. B, citing UCC 2–510, argues that the risk of loss was on S. Consequently, B had no liability for the price. Is B correct? See UCC 2–601 (right of rejection), 2–608 (cure) and 2–606 (acceptance).

B. Suppose, in (A) above, that the goods were not destroyed in transit. Rather, they were tendered by the carrier and accepted by B and taken to its plant. See UCC 2–606. The next day, the goods were destroyed without B's fault or negligence. Who has the risk of loss?

C. Continuing this exercise, suppose in (B) above, that after B accepted the goods, inspection at the plant revealed a latent, substantial defect which justified revocation of acceptance under UCC 2–608(1). B promptly notified S of the revocation. UCC 2–608(2). The next day, before S could send instructions, the goods were destroyed without the fault or negligence of B. Assuming that B, at the time of loss, had no liability for the price, see UCC 2–608(3), who has the risk of loss?

D. In light of these problems, what recommendations would you make for revision of UCC 2–510(1) & (2)? What problems, if any, do you see in the operation of UCC 2–510(3)?

SECTION 4. RISK OF LOSS AND INSURANCE

A. *Some General Principles*

As previously noted, the risk of loss rules in UCC 2–509 were designed, in part, to conform to assumptions about which party, seller or buyer, was in the best position, cost considered, either to prevent or to insure against loss of or damage to the goods. As Judge Posner put it in JASON'S FOODS, supra:

"The Code sought to create a set of standard contract terms that would reflect in the generality of cases the preferences of contracting parties at the time of contract. One such preference is for assignments of liability—or, what amounts to the same thing, assignments of the risk of loss—that create incentives to minimize the adverse consequences of untoward events such as * * * a warehouse fire. There are two ways of minimizing such consequences. One is to make them less painful by insuring against them. Insurance does not prevent a loss—it merely spreads it—but in doing so it reduces (for those who are risk averse) the disutility of the loss. So if one of the contracting parties can insure at lower cost than the other, this is an argument for placing the risk of loss on him, to give him an incentive to do so. * * * The other method of minimizing the consequences of an unanticipated loss is through prevention of the loss. If one party is in a better position than the other to prevent it, this is a reason for placing the risk of loss on him, to give him an incentive to prevent it. It would be a reason for placing liability on a seller who still had possession of the goods, even though title had passed. * * *" 774 F.2d at 218.

The Code, however, has very little to say about insurance. UCC 2–501 states some but not all the circumstances where the seller and buyer will have an insurable interest in the goods. Thus, the "buyer obtains a special property interest and an insurable interest in goods by identification of existing goods as goods to which the contract refers even though the goods so identified are non-conforming and he has an option to return or reject them * * *," UCC 2–501(1), and the "seller retains an insurable interest in the goods so long as title to or any security interest in the goods remains in him. * * *," UCC 2–501(2). But UCC 2–501(3) provides that "Nothing in this section impairs any insurable interest recognized under any other statute or rule of law." Thus, UCC 2–501 is a one-way ratchet provision: it can expand, but not contract the scope of insurable interest. For the scope of insurable interest in property insurance cases, one may consult Stockton, *An*

Analysis of Insurable Interest Under Article Two of the Uniform Commercial Code, 17 Vand.L.Rev. 815 (1964). See also, R. Keeton, Insurance Law 94–119 (1971); Pinzur, *Insurable Interest: A Search for Consistency,* 46 Ins.Counsel J. 109 (1979). Beyond insurable interest and the anti-subrogation rule of UCC 2–510, however, one must look elsewhere when disputes over insurance arise.

To sharpen the issues, read the following fact situation and puzzle over a few questions.

Problem 9–5

Repuenzel contracted to sell 1,000 pistons to Cicero for $10,000, $2,000 of which was paid upon contracting and the balance of which is due 30 days after delivery. Repuenzel created and perfected a security interest in the goods under Article 9 and shipped the goods "FOB place of Shipment," taking a non-negotiable bill of lading naming Cicero as consignee. During transit the goods were totally destroyed by fire. The contract for sale said nothing about risk of loss or insurance.

1. Which party has the risk of loss?

2. Which, if any, party has an insurable interest in the goods while in transit?

3. Standard fire insurance policies, with riders, have limited applicability to goods to be shipped to the buyer under a contract for sale. For the seller, personal property is likely to be defined as "property sold but not removed" from the building. For a buyer, coverage begins for "personal property * * * in cars on tracks when such cars are on the premises or within 100 feet of buildings described; in the open or in vehicles on the premises; on sidewalks, streets, alleys, or detached platforms when within 50 feet of buildings described."

Given these limitations, additional protection must be purchased by sellers and buyers with insurable interests while the goods are in transit. Read through the excerpts from the two types of policies which follow. Is Repuenzel's security interest covered by the Manufacturer's Output Policy? Is Buyer's ownership interest protection under the Transportation—All Risks Form?

MANUFACTURER'S OUTPUT POLICY

1. *Interest and Property Insured:* Except as hereinafter excluded, this policy insures:

   (a) The interest of the Insured in all personal property owned by the Insured;

   (b) The interest of the Insured in improvements and betterments to buildings not owned by the Insured;

   (c) The interest of the Insured in, and legal liability for personal property of others in the actual or constructive custody of the Insured;

   (d) Personal property of others

(1) Sold by the Insured which the Insured has agreed prior to loss to insure for the account of the purchaser during course of delivery;

(2) In the custody of the Insured which the Insured has agreed prior to loss to insurer;

(3) Sold by the Insured under an installation agreement whereby the Insured's responsibility continues until the installation is accepted by the purchaser.

2. *Interest and Property Excluded:* This policy does not insure:

(a) Currency, money, notes, securities, growing crops or standing timber;

(b) Property while covered under import or export ocean marine policies;

(c) Animals, aircraft or watercraft;

(d) Property sold by the Insured under conditional sale, trust agreement, installment payment, or other deferred payment plan;

(e) Loss resulting from interruption of business or other consequential loss extending beyond the direct physical loss of or damage to the insured property.

3. *Perils Insured:* This policy insures against all risks of direct physical loss of or damage to the insured property from any external cause (including general coverage and salvage charges on shipments covered while waterborne) except as hereinafter excluded.

*   *   *

9. *Specific Insurance:* Other insurance in name of and for the benefit of the Insured may be permitted or may be required to be effected applying specifically to any location covered by this policy. Such other insurance is hereinafter referred to as specific insurance. Where specific insurance has been required by the Company, the Insured agrees to effect and keep in force specific insurance in the specified amount until otherwise agreed to in writing by the Company, and in failure thereof this Company shall not be liable for that part of any loss which would have been recoverable or due thereunder had such specific insurance been in force, whether valid or not and whether collectible or not. With respect to any specific insurance, this policy shall be considered as excess insurance and shall not apply or contribute to the payment of any loss until the amount due from all such specific insurance whether collectible or not shall have been exhausted. Under the policy the Insured is to be reimbursed to the extent of the difference between the amount recoverable or due from any specific insurance whether collectible or not and the amount of loss otherwise recoverable hereunder, not exceeding however, the difference between the limit of liability under this policy at any specified location and the amount of specific insurance at such specified location for loss or damage arising out of the perils insured against by such specific insurance.

10. *Other Insurance:* Except as to specific insurance as defined in Section 9 of this policy, this policy shall not cover to the extent of any other insurance whether prior or subsequent hereto in date, and by whomsoever effected, directly or indirectly covering the same property, and this Company shall be liable for loss or damage only for the excess value beyond the amount due from such other insurance.

The Company agrees to advance to the Insured as a loan the amount which would have been collectible under this policy except for the provisions of this Section, such loan to be repayable only to the extent of and at the time of the Insured's collection from such other insurance.

* * *

15. *Assistance and Cooperation of the Insured:* The Insured shall cooperate with the Company and, upon the Company's request, shall attend hearings and trials and shall assist in effecting settlements, securing and giving evidence, obtaining the attendance of witnesses and in the conduct of suits. Other than as provided in Section 16 of this policy, the Insured shall not, except at his own cost voluntarily make any payment, assume any obligation or incur any expense.

* * *

19. *Carriers or Bailees:* This insurance shall not inure directly or indirectly to the benefit of any carrier, nor without the affirmative consent of the Insured, to the benefit of any other bailee. The Insured may accept without prejudice to this insurance the ordinary bills-of-lading used by common carriers, including released or partially released value bills-of-lading, and the Insured may waive subrogation against railroads under Side Track Agreements, and except as otherwise provided, the Insured shall not enter into any special agreement with carriers otherwise releasing them from their common law or statutory liability. The Company shall not be liable for any loss or damage which, without its consent, has been settled or compromised by the Insured.

20. *Company's Right of Recovery:* In the event of any payment under this policy, the Insured shall execute and deliver instruments and papers and do whatever else is necessary to secure the subrogation rights of the Company. The Insured shall do nothing after loss to prejudice such rights. However, the Company specifically waives its rights of subrogation against all the subsidiary and affiliated companies of the Insured. Any release from liability, other than as provided in Section 19, entered into prior to loss hereunder by the Insured shall not affect this policy or the right of the Insured to recover hereunder. At the option of the Company, the Insured will execute a loan agreement, to the extent of any loss collectible under this policy. Said loan will bear no interest and will be repayable only in the event and to the extent of the net recovery effected from any party believed to be liable for said loss. Upon payment of any loss or advancement or loan of moneys concerning the loss, the Insured will at the Company's request and expense make claim upon and institute legal proceedings against any party which the Company believes to be liable for such loss, and

will use all proper and reasonable means to recover the same, under the exclusive direction and control of the Company.

21. *Company's Options:* In the event of loss hereunder it shall be the option of the Company to take all, or any part, of the property at the agreed or appraised value, and also to repair, rebuild or replace the property destroyed or damaged, with other of like kind and quality, within a reasonable time, on giving notice of its intention so to do within thirty days after the receipt of the Proof of Loss herein required. There can be no abandonment to the Company of any property.

If branded or labeled merchandise covered by this policy is damaged and the Company elects to take all or any part of the property at the agreed or appraised value, the Insured may at his own expense stamp "salvage" on the merchandise or its containers or may remove the brands or labels, if such stamp or removal will not physically damage the merchandise.

TRANSPORTATION—ALL RISKS FORM

ASSURED CICERO CORP.

Loss, if any, payable to assured or order.

On goods and merchandise, including packages, consisting principally of PISTONS shipped by or to the assured at assured's risk within the limits of the Continental United States and Canada (excluding Alaska).

VALUATION: The said goods and merchandise shall be valued at actual invoice cost, including prepaid or advanced freight, if any, together with such costs and charges (including the commission of the assured as selling agent, but excluding duty), as may have accrued and become legally due thereon. In the event of there being no invoice, the valuation of the merchandise insured hereunder shall be the actual cash market value of the property insured at point of destination on the date of disaster.

This policy insures shipments consisting of the property insured for the following amounts in any one loss:

$15,000.　　while in the custody of any Truckman or Trucking Company,

$15,000.　　while in the custody of any Railroad or the Railway Express Agency (including while on ferries and/or railroad cars on transfers or lighters),

$1,000.=　　while in the custody of Air Carriers or Air Express Companies,

$15,000.　　during transportation to and from conveyances or premises of the above described carriers, in motor trucks or trailers operated by the Assured, (excluding theft, embezzlement, conversion or any wrongful act on the part of the assured, his servants or employees).

In no event shall this Company be liable for more than $30,000. in any one casualty, either in case of partial or total loss, or salvage charges, or any other charges, or expenses, or all combined.

Insurance hereunder attaches when the goods leave factory, store or warehouse at initial point of shipment, and covers continuously thereafter, including while on docks, wharves, piers, bulkheads, in depots, stations and/or on platforms of common carriers, all while in due course of transportation, until same are delivered at factory, store or warehouse at destination.

THIS POLICY INSURES AGAINST

All Risks of loss or damage to the insured property from any external cause (including General Average and/or salvage charges and expenses), except as herein excluded.

THIS POLICY DOES NOT INSURE

(a) Accounts, bills, deeds, evidences of debt, currency, money, coins, bullion, notes, securities, stamps, jewelry, precious stones or fine arts;

(b) Against loss or damage resulting from inadequate packing or improper preparation for shipment or from insecure stowage when not stowed by the carrier;

(c) Against loss or damage by vermin or against loss or damage by leakage, evaporation, shrinkage, breakage, marring, scratching, heat or cold, or by being scented, moulded, rusted, soured, or changed in flavor unless caused by fire, lightning, windstorm, flood, explosion or collision, derailment or overturning of vehicle while on land, or collision or crashing of aircraft while in flight, or by the vessel, craft or lighter being stranded, sunk, burned or in collision while waterborne.

(d) Against loss or damage resulting from delay or loss of market, howsoever caused;

(e) Against loss or damage caused by strikes, locked-out workmen, or persons taking part in labor disturbances, or arising from riot, or civil commotion;

Against loss or damage caused by or resulting from:

(f) (1) hostile or warlike action in time of peace or war, including action in hindering, combating or defending against an actual impending or expected attack, (a) by any government or sovereign power (de jure or de facto), or by any authority maintaining or using military, naval or air forces; or (b) by military, naval or air forces; or (c) by an agent of any such government, power, authority or forces;

(2) any weapon of war employing atomic fission or radioactive force whether in time of peace or war;

(3) insurrection, rebellion, revolution, civil war, usurped power, or action taken by governmental authority in hindering, com-

bating or defending against such an occurrence, seizure or destruction under quarantine or customs regulations, confiscation by order of any government or public authority, or risks of contraband or illegal transportation or trade.

(g) Export shipments laden on board export conveyance or under the protection of marine insurance, whichever first occurs;

(h) Import shipments until fully discharged from import conveyance and then only after marine insurance has ceased to cover;

(i) Shipments by parcel post and/or mail.

Premium Readjustment and Report of Shipments. The premium charged under this policy is based on an estimate of $300,000. value of shipments made during the period insured, and the Assured warrants to report to this Company at the end of _____

(Policy

_____the actual value of all shipments (in

year, unless otherwise specified)

accordance with the valuation clause contained in this policy) covered hereunder during the period for which such report is required, and upon the total of all reported shipments exceeding in the aggregate the said estimate of $300,000., the Assured agrees to pay this Company additional premium at the rate of .05 per $100, such additional premium to become due and payable to this Company immediately upon the furnishing of the aforesaid report or reports; but in the event of the actual shipments falling short of the said estimate of $_____ then this Company will return premium at the same rate on the deficiency, but no return premium shall become due or payable until the expiration of this policy; it being understood that by the acceptance of this readjustment clause, the reinstatement clause in the body of this policy is waived.

* * *

Claim Against Carrier. In the event of any loss or damage to the goods and/or merchandise insured hereunder the assured shall immediately make claim in writing against the carrier or carriers involved.

Insurer's Right to Institute Legal Proceedings in Name of Insured. It is expressly agreed that upon payment of any loss or advancement or loan of moneys concerning the same, that the Assured will at the request and expense of the Company, and through such counsel as the Company may designate, make claim upon and institute legal proceedings against any carrier, bailee, or other parties believed to be liable for such loss, and will use all proper and reasonable means to recover the same.

Impairment of Carrier's Liability. Any act or agreement by the Assured, prior or subsequent hereto, whereby any right of the Assured, in the event of loss or damage, to recover the full value of, or amount of damage to, any property insured hereunder, against any carrier, bailee or other party liable therefor, is released, impaired or lost, shall render this policy null and void, but the Insurer's right to retain or recover the premium shall not be affected. It shall, however, be permissible for the Assured, without prejudice to this insurance, to release any carrier to the extent of not less than Fifty Dollars ($50.) per package where the weight of the package does not exceed 100 pounds, or fifty cents per pound, actual weight, where the weight of the shipment exceeds 100 pounds. This Company is not liable for any loss or damage, which without its consent, has been settled or compromised by the Assured.

4. Reread the two insurance policies, reprinted above. To what extent do they confer subrogation rights to "collateral" sources, i.e., contract rights that the seller or buyer may have against each other?

Remember, if a loss occurs within the scope of the policy and all conditions precedent are satisfied, the insurer's liability is for the amount of the actual loss and no more. This principle of indemnification is designed, primarily, to control the insurer's incentive to realize a net gain from the receipt of insurance proceeds. See Keeton, Insurance Law § 3.1(b) (1971). Subrogation often supports the principle of indemnity, since the insurance company, upon paying the insured, steps into the insured's shoes and tries to assert claims of that insured against some other person (the carrier, the other party to the contract, some third party, etc.) for the loss for which it has paid. In theory, at least, subrogation rights and the return from enforcement ought to figure into the calculation by the insurer of the premiums to be charged.

According to conventional doctrine, there are two kinds of subrogation, legal or equitable and contractual. The former arises by operation of law and the latter is created by contract between the insurer and the insured. See Jorski Mill & Elevator Co. v. Farmer's Elevator Mut. Ins. Co., 404 F.2d 143, 147 (10th Cir.1968). The source of subrogation determines the scope of the right. Thus, if B with the risk of loss is insured and the goods are damaged by the negligence of a third party, the insurer, upon paying B, is subrogated by operation of law to any tort claims that B may have against the third party. See, e.g., Home Ins. Co. v. Bishop, 140 Me. 72, 34 A.2d 22 (1943). But what about contract rights that either seller or buyer may have against the other? Here's the rub, for some courts have labeled contract rights as "collateral" sources for subrogation and have required a contract clause specifically granting the right. Put another way, subrogation imposed by operation of law is sometimes held not to reach these collateral rights.

The difficulty * * * lies in the fact that the problem is basically one of allocation of the burden of loss as between an insurer and an innocent third party. And in the case of "equitable" or "legal" subrogation the equities in favor of the insurer are simply not so decisive as they are when the third party is a tort-feasor.

United States Fidelity & Guar. Co. v. Slifkin, 200 F.Supp. 563, 569 (N.D. Ala.1961).

5. Suppose that Cicero, with the risk of loss, is insured but Repuenzel, with a security interest and an insurable interest, is not insured. If the goods are destroyed without Cicero's fault or negligence and the insurer pays, does Repuenzel have any enforceable claim to the insurance pro-

ceeds? Or is the seller now unsecured with a claim only for the unpaid price?

The answers are no and yes, unless (1) The contract for sale required Cicero to obtain insurance for the benefit of Repuenzel and Cicero had complied, or (2) Repuenzel's claim is enforceable under UCC 9–306(1).

In the absence of a contractual obligation to insure, see Royal Zenith Corp. v. Citizens Publications, Inc., 179 N.W.2d 340 (Iowa 1970), casualty insurance is invariably treated as personal to the insured—it is intended to indemnify Cicero's loss (a matter of contract between Cicero and his insurer) not Repuenzel's. See Quigley v. Caron, 247 A.2d 94 (Me.1968). As a matter of planning, therefore, Repuenzel should insist that either Cicero obtain insurance for its benefit or Repuenzel should obtain a policy covering goods sold on a conditional sales contract to the extent of unpaid balances.

What about UCC 9–306(1)? The 1972 Official Text of UCC 9–306(1) provides that "Insurance payable by reason of loss or damage to the collateral is proceeds, except to the extent that it is payable to a person other than a party to the security agreement." This provision overruled decisions under the 1962 Official Text to the contrary, see *Note,* 65 Mich.L. Rev. 1514 (1966), but has some definite limitations: If the proceeds are payable to someone other than Repuenzel or, as cash proceeds, fall into the many pitfalls of maintaining a perfected security in proceeds under UCC 9– 306, the security will dissipate.

(6) Suppose Repuenzel, with an insurable interest, is insured to the full value of the goods and Cicero, with the risk of loss, has no insurance. If the goods are destroyed and Repuenzel is paid in full, can Cicero have the benefit of that insurance? Put differently, can Cicero have a credit for the insurance against any price still owed to Repuenzel? If the answer is yes, then Repuenzel's insurer would be denied any right to subrogation to collateral sources granted by contract.

Most courts, after balancing the equities, have answered the question in the negative. See McCoid, *Allocation of Loss and Property Insurance,* 39 Ind.L.J. 647, 669 (1964), who defends the outcome. For a contrary and definitely minority view, see In re Future Mfg. Corp., 165 F.Supp. 111 (N.D. Cal.1958). There have been no recent decisions of significance.

B. Carrier Liable to Insured Party with Risk of Loss: Conflicts Between Insurance Companies

Suppose that Cicero, insured and with the risk of loss, obtains a judgment against the carrier under the Carmack Act, supra, for the value of the goods destroyed. Cicero's insurer, who has paid Cicero, has participated in the litigation as subrogee. What additional problems are posed because the contest is, in essence, between two insurance companies, that of Cicero and that of the carrier?

SORKIN, ALLOCATION OF THE RISK OF LOSS IN THE TRANSPORTATION OF FREIGHT—THE FUNCTION OF INSUR-ANCE, 40 Fordham L.Rev. 67, 85–87 (1971).

*   *   *

IV. THE ROLE OF INSURANCE IN ALLOCATION OF THE
RISK OF LOSS

Although common carriers subject to the Carmack Amendment of
the Interstate Commerce Act are held to a high standard of liability,
there are some exceptions and limitations to a carrier's liability. Furthermore, the amount of damages sustained is always a potential issue.
If the loss or damage is substantial, the carrier will contest the claim,
provided it can find a legal basis upon which to do so. Consequently,
most commercial shippers are insured against loss or damage to their
property during the course of its transportation.

"The shipper's insurance company may be considered as a potential
third-party upon whom the ultimate economic burden of the risk of loss
or damage should be placed, since the insurance company receives its
compensation specifically for assuming the risk of loss or damage,
whereas the carrier's compensation is based primarily on the cost of
transportation. However, equity and economic burden have usually
not been determining factors in allocating the risk of loss between the
shipper's insurer and the carrier. The judicial resolution of the problem has historically been based upon the law of contracts and the
interpretation of the Interstate Commerce Act.

A. Benefit of Insurance Clauses in Bills of Lading

For over a century the standard form of carrier bill of lading has
provided, in effect, that if a shipper of merchandise has purchased
insurance against loss or damage to the shipper's goods during the
course of their transportation, and if the shipper's goods are lost or
damaged, the carrier shall receive the benefit of such insurance. The
intended result of such a clause is that the carrier will not be liable for
the loss or damage to the extent that the shipper or owner is compensated by his insurance carrier. Judicial recognition of the validity of
such benefit of insurance clauses has been established.

An insurer who pays the loss of a shipper is ordinarily subrogated
to the shipper's rights. However, if the insured has contracted with the
carrier giving the carrier the benefit of any insurance available to the
shipper in case of loss or damage, then it has long been held that the
insurer loses its right of subrogation. The shipper who insures his
goods against loss or damage during their transportation is involved in
at least two separate contracts—the contract between the shipper and
the common carrier (the bill of lading), and the contract between the
shipper and the insurance company (the policy). To counterbalance the
benefit of insurance clause in the bill of lading, the insurance companies changed their policies and added a provision which stated that if
an insured shipper entered into an agreement giving a carrier the
benefit of the shipper's insurance, then the insurance policy issued to
the shipper would be void.

The courts, when faced with both the bill of lading provision giving
the carrier the benefit of the shipper's insurance and the insurance

policy declaring the policy void upon the shipper's acceptance of such a bill of lading provision, concluded that both agreements were effective, i.e., the shipper could agree with the carrier to give the carrier the benefit of the shipper's insurance, but since the insurance was void the carrier received nothing and the shipper could not receive the insurance proceeds. This, of course, was harmful to the shipper and of no benefit to the carrier. The legal draftsmen of the insurance companies were victorious in their word war with the carriers' scriveners.

The bill of lading was then amended to provide that the carrier was to have the benefit of the insurance effected by the shipper 'so far as this shall not avoid the policies or contracts of insurance.' Thus, if the insurance policy stated that the policy would be void if the carrier could get the benefit of insurance, the bill of lading provision stated that in such event the carrier would not get the benefit of the shipper's insurance. The draftsmen for both sides had created a state of equilibrium, except in those cases where an insurance company neglected to provide that the policy would be void if the carrier received the benefit of the shipper's insurance. Thus the determination whether the ultimate burden of loss should be borne by the carrier or the shipper's insurer was made on the basis of interpretation of conflicting contracts without consideration of the economic justification of placing the burden either on the carrier or the insurer and without consideration of its effect upon interstate commerce." [Footnotes omitted]

TOWMOTOR CO. v. FRANK CROSS TRUCKING CO.

Superior Court of Pennsylvania, 1965.
205 Pa.Super. 448, 211 A.2d 38.

[Shipper sued common carrier Towmotor for damages to a vehicle which had been injured while in the possession of the carrier. Defendant responded that plaintiff had been fully insured, had recovered its loss from its insurance company, and under the terms of the bill of lading it was entitled "to the benefit of plaintiff's insurance." The court went on as follows, quoting first from the clause in the bill of lading.]

JACOBS, J.

*   *   *

"Any carrier or party liable on account of loss or damage to any of said property shall have the full benefit of any insurance that may have been effected upon or on account of said property so far as this shall not avoid the policies or contracts of insurance: Provided that the carrier reimburse the claimant for the premium paid thereon."

The plaintiff in its reply admits that the above quoted clause was included in the bill of lading. It further admits that the vehicle was insured by Aetna and that Aetna paid it the sum of $3,190.33 but avers that payment was made in the form of a loan rather than in payment of the loss, and asserts in its defense the following quoted condition of the Aetna policy:

"1. Carrier-Bailee. This insurance shall in no wise inure directly or indirectly to the benefit of any carrier or other bailee, and the Assured agrees that in case any agreement be made or accepted with any carrier or bailee by which it is stipulated that such or any carrier or bailee shall have, in case of any loss for which said carrier or bailee may be liable, the benefit of this insurance or exemption in any manner from responsibility grounded in the fact of this insurance, then and in that event this Company shall be discharged of any liability for such loss hereunder, but this policy in these and all cases of loss or damage by perils insured against shall be liable and owe actual payment for (only) what cannot be collected from carrier or bailee."

Aetna's policy as well as the release given to Aetna by plaintiff, provide that Aetna shall be subrogated to the rights of the plaintiff to recover for such loss from the persons, firms or corporations who have caused the loss.

If it were not for the benefit of insurance clause in the bill of lading this case would be easily decided. In general a common carrier of goods is regarded as an insurer against all losses. Arabian American Oil Company v. Kirby & Kirby, Inc., 171 Pa.Super. 23, 90 A.2d 410. No exception to the general rule has been averred by the defendant and unless the benefit of insurance clause is sufficient to save it, it is liable for the loss. The benefit of insurance clause in the bill of lading and the clauses referring to such benefit in the insurance policy are the result of the efforts of the insurance companies to shift the common law liability of the carriers on one hand and, on the other hand, to protect against such shifting of liability. We will endeavor to interpret the result of such legal maneuvering.

A benefit of insurance clause such as the one contained in the bill of lading in this case is valid because the carrier itself might have insured against the loss, even though occasioned by its own negligence. Luckenbach v. W.J. McCahan Sugar Refining Co., 248 U.S. 139, 39 S.Ct. 53, 63 L.Ed. 170. The important words in the benefit of insurance clause above quoted are "so far as this shall not avoid the policies or contracts of insurance." Absent those words, should the insurer pay the loss it would lose the benefit of the claim against the carrier to which it would otherwise be subrogated and the carrier would go free. However, when we read the above quoted words in connection with the provisions of the insurance policy we come to another conclusion.

* * *

The benefit of insurance clause not being available to the defendant, it is liable for the loss. Although the plaintiff is the shipper and has been paid for the loss, judgment may properly be entered in its favor. Both the insurance policy and the release given by plaintiff specifically provide that the insurer shall be subrogated to the rights of plaintiff and may sue in plaintiff's name. Any recovery will inure to the benefit of the insurance company.

Judgment affirmed.

FLOOD, J., absent.

Notes

1. In Salon Serv., Inc. v. Pacific & Atlantic Shippers, 24 N.Y.2d 15, 298 N.Y.S.2d 700, 246 N.E.2d 509 (1969), a conflict identical to that in *Towmotor* was manifest in the shipper's bill of lading from the carrier and the insurance policy from its insurer. In affirming the decision of the appellate division, the Court of Appeals, speaking through Judge Burke, held that the "benefit of insurance" clause in the bill of lading was invalid under Section 2 of the Interstate Commerce Act. Enforcing the clause would result in a prohibited rate discrimination because the carrier would, indirectly, receive greater compensation from a shipper who had effected insurance than from one who had not. The court quoted from National Garment Co. v. New York, C. & St.L.R. Co., 173 F.2d 32, 38 (8th Cir.1949):

> "Insurance for the benefit of a carrier is of value to the carrier from the beginning of the transportation and, in the event of transportation without loss, which we assume is the usual case, the carrier has received the compensation forbidden by the Interstate Commerce Act at the expense of the shipper. In the event of loss the carrier, if it so elects, returns to the shipper the cost of the compensation which it was forbidden by the Act to receive in the first place, avoids its liability as a carrier, and deprives the insurer of its rights under a valid contract." 246 N.E.2d at 511.

Problem 9–6

Seller ships lumber by rail under an FOB destination contract. In the course of shipment the lumber is destroyed by fire. The fire is not caused by an act of God, and the carrier is liable to the seller for the loss. The seller also has insurance which covers this loss. His insurance contract contains the following clauses:

19. *Carrier or Bailees:* "This insurance shall not inure directly or indirectly to the benefit of any carrier, nor without the affirmative consent of the insured, to the benefit of any other bailee. Insured may accept without prejudice to this insurance the ordinary bills of lading used by common carriers, including released or partially released value bills of lading, and the insured may waive subrogation against railroads under sidetrack agreement, and except as otherwise provided, the insured shall not enter into any special agreement with carriers otherwise releasing them from their common law or statutory liability. The companies shall not be liable for any loss or damage which without its consent has been settled or compromised by the insured.

20. *Company's Right of Recovery:* In the event of any payment under this policy, the Insured shall execute and deliver instruments and papers and do whatever else is necessary to secure the subrogation rights of the Company. The Insured shall do nothing after loss to

prejudice such rights. However, the Company specifically waives its rights of subrogation against all the subsidiary and affiliated companies of the Insured. Any release from liability, other than as provided in Section 19, entered into prior to loss hereunder by the Insured shall not affect this policy or the right of the Insured to recover hereunder. At the option of the Company, the Insured will execute a loan agreement, to the extent of any loss collectible under this policy. Said loan will bear no interest and will be repayable only in the event and to the extent of the net recovery effected from any party believed to be liable for said loss. Upon payment of any loss or advancement or loan of moneys concerning the loss, the Insured will at the Company's request and expense make claim upon and institute legal proceedings against any party which the Company believes to be liable for such loss, and will use all proper and reasonable means to recover the same, under the exclusive direction and control of the Company."

The bill of lading under which the seller shipped contained the following provision:

Any carrier or party liable on account of loss of or damage to any of said property shall have the full benefit of any insurance that may have been effected upon or on account of said property, so far as this shall not avoid the policies or contracts of insurance: provided, that the carrier reimburse the claimant for the premium paid thereon.

You are counsel for the insurance company. It would like to pay the seller and be subrogated to his rights against the railroad. Will the insurance company recover from the railroad? What precautions might you suggest to them?

Chapter Ten

"DOCUMENTARY" AND OTHER SALES INVOLVING DOCUMENTS OF TITLE: POSSIBLE BREAKDOWNS

SECTION 1. INTRODUCTION—DOCUMENTS OF TITLE

When buyers and sellers deal with each other, the goods will often be either (1) as yet unmanufactured, (2) located at the seller's place of business, (3) located at the place of business of the seller's supplier, (4) located in an independent warehouse, or (5) located somewhere else away from the buyer's place of business. Most sellers do not have their own trucking, rail, or waterway facilities. They must, therefore, turn to independent carriers to deliver the goods they sell. When goods are sold while in warehouses, (as is often true in deals made on the commodity exchanges) sellers must also rely on the services of independent warehousemen to make delivery (physically or through "attornment"). These independent third parties—carriers and warehousemen—typically issue "bills of lading" and "warehouse receipts," respectively, covering goods received from shippers and storers. In so doing, these bailees assume certain special obligations both under the terms of such documents and under applicable statutes, as we will see.

In the parlance of commercial lawyers, bills of lading and warehouse receipts (see the forms at pages 343–44) are called "documents of title." UCC 1–201(15) defines document of title as follows:

(15) "Document of title" includes bill of lading, dock warrant, dock receipt, warehouse receipt or order for the delivery of goods, and also any other document which in the regular course of business or financing is treated as adequately evidencing that the person in possession of it is entitled to receive, hold and dispose of the document and the goods it covers. To be a document of title a document must purport to be issued by or addressed to a bailee and purport to cover goods in the bailee's possession which are either identified or are fungible portions of an identified mass.

341

As we will see (Section 4 below), documents of title may be "negotiable" or "non-negotiable." It is now pertinent to list the main functions of these pieces of paper issued by carriers and warehousemen. A bill of lading or warehouse receipt serves:

1. As a receipt for the goods received by the bailee from the shipper or storer.

2. As a contract between the bailor and bailee for the transportation and/or storage of the goods.

3. As a kind of legal substitute for the goods themselves when the document is negotiable—the law says that *generally:* "title to the goods moves with title to the negotiable document."

4. As a means whereby the seller may either (a) himself retain a security interest in the goods until they are paid for or (b) readily create a security interest in the goods in favor of his own bank or other lender.

All of these functions of bills of lading and warehouse receipts are quite important. The importance of the function depends on the nature of the transaction involved—on how documents of title are utilized in the transaction. In the next section, one basic transaction pattern will be described.

The "front side" of a typical negotiable bill of lading looks like this:

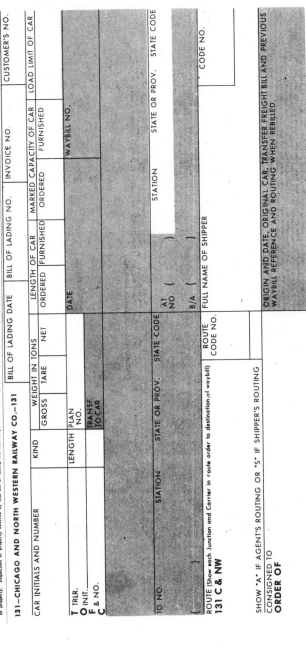

NOTIFY

AT

STATE OF   COUNTY OF

DESTINATION

SHIPPER'S SPECIAL INSTRUCTIONS

NO. PKGS.	DESCRIPTION OF ARTICLES, SPECIAL MARKS AND EXCEPTIONS	COMMODITY CODE NO.	★ WEIGHT (Subject to Correction)	RATE	FREIGHT	CHARGES ADVANCED	PREPAID

Received $____ to apply in prepayment of the charges on the property described hereon.

_____
Agent or Cashier.

Per _____
(The signature here acknowledges only the amount prepaid.)

WEIGHED

AT _____

GROSS _____

TARE _____

ALLOWANCE _____

NET _____

IF CHARGES ARE TO BE PREPAID, WRITE OR STAMP HERE "TO BE PREPAID".

WHEN SHIPPER IN THE UNITED STATES EXECUTES THE NO-RECOURSE CLAUSE OF SECTION 7 OF THE BILL OF LADING, INSERT "YES".

"If the shipment moves between two ports by a carrier by water, the law requires that the bill of lading shall state whether it is "carrier's or shipper's weight".

★ Indicate by symbol in Column provided how weights were obtained for L.C.L. Shipments only. R – Railroad Scale. S – Shipper's Tested Weights. E – Estimated – Weigh and Correct. T – Tariff Classification or Minimum.

DO NOT USE THIS SPACE

Subject to Section 7 of Conditions, if this shipment is to be delivered to the consignee without recourse on the consignor, the consignor shall sign the following statement: The carrier shall not make delivery of this shipment without payment of freight and all other lawful charges.

_____ PER _____
Signature of Consignor

Note—Where the rate is dependent upon value, shippers are required to state specifically in writing the agreed or declared value of the property. The agreed or declared value of the property is hereby specifically stated by the shipper to be not exceeding

SHIPPER _____ PER _____

AGENT _____ PER _____

DATE _____

The reverse side of both the negotiable and nonnegotiable bill of lading form contains about two acres of fine print called "contract terms and conditions." With the aid of a magnifying glass, these terms can be examined in R. Braucher & R. Riegert, Documents of Title 162–64 (3d ed. 1978).

SECTION 2. "DOCUMENTARY SALES"—THE STANDARD PATTERN

Documents of title may be used in a variety of ways in a sales transaction. In *one* type of transaction called the "documentary sale," the buyer agrees to pay cash in exchange for documents. Besides documents of title (usually bills of lading) this transaction also involves the use of what is called a "sight draft." A sight draft is a draft (see UCC 3–104) drawn up by a seller which orders the buyer to pay so much in cash "at sight" to the party presenting the draft. Below is an illustrative sight draft:

$ 1,000.00 August 7 (1978)	

At Sight _____ Pay to

the order of _____ Repeunzel Auto Parts

One thousand and no/100------------- Dollars

Value received and charge the same to account of

TO   Cicero's Automotive, Inc.
)   Repeunzel   /for

No.   28601   ) Repeunzel Auto Parts, Inc.

[C3044]

Now, how might the above piece of paper, and a document of title such as a bill of lading actually be put to functional use together in real life transactions? Professor Farnsworth has offered this account of the standard transaction pattern in the so-called "documentary sale":

—————

FARNSWORTH, DOCUMENTARY DRAFTS UNDER THE UNIFORM COMMERCIAL CODE, 22 Bus.Law. 479–487 (1967).

"*Introduction.* The Uniform Commercial Code has as a premise 'that "commercial transactions" is a single subject of the law, notwithstanding its many facets.' * * *

"No better transaction could be chosen to illustrate this recognition than the use of the documentary draft, since it involves the sale of goods, which is dealt with in Article 2 (Sales), a draft, which is dealt with in Article 3 (Commercial Paper), its collection, which is dealt with in Article 4 (Bank Deposits and Collection), and a bill of lading, which is dealt with in Article 7 (Warehouse Receipts, Bills of Lading and Other Documents of Title), in addition to being subject to Article 1 (General Provisions). If a letter of credit were involved, it would also be subject to Article 5 (Letters of Credit) and if the buyer were to finance his purchase by a trust receipt it would also be subject to Article 9 (Secured

Transactions: Sales of Accounts, Contract Rights and Chattel Paper). This discussion will not, however, be concerned with either letters of credit or secured transactions.

"Because the documentary draft has long been a feature of both domestic and international sales transactions, the terminology and the rules relating to documentary drafts are relatively well established. * * * This article will be in two parts: first, a description of a typical sales transaction involving a documentary draft with an analysis of the relevant provisions of the code; and second, a discussion of some variations from this standard pattern in the light of the provisions of the Code. Before either, however, a brief discussion of terminology is appropriate.

"*Terminology.* The term 'draft,' used by the Code to replace the older term 'bill of exchange,' in this discussion refers to the order drawn by the seller on the buyer of the goods (UCC 3–104(1)(b), (2)(a)). The term 'documentary draft' is used for a draft, whether negotiable or non-negotiable, with accompanying documents or other papers to be delivered when the draft is honored (UCC 4–104(1)(f)). By 'document' is meant a 'document of title' (UCC 7–102(1)(e)), including a 'bill of lading, dock warrant, dock receipt, warehouse receipt or order for the delivery of goods, and also any other document which in the regular course of business or financing is treated as adequately evidencing that the person in possession of it is entitled to receive, hold and dispose of the document and the goods it covers' (UCC 1–201(15)). The most significant of these for present purposes is the 'bill of lading,' which is defined as 'a document evidencing the receipt of goods for shipment issued by a person engaged in the business of transporting or forwarding goods, and includes an airbill' (UCC 1–201(6)). It may be a negotiable bill if by its terms the goods are to be delivered to bearer or to order or, where recognized in overseas trade, if it runs to a named person or assigns; otherwise it is a non-negotiable bill, the term used by the Code in preference to the traditional synonym 'straight' bill (UCC 7–104). These, then are the essential terms; now to the transaction.

Part I. The Basic Transaction

"*Purpose of the Transaction.* Many domestic and some foreign sales of goods are made on open credit, with payment to be made in 30, 60 or 90 days. But credit must be bargained for and a seller lacking faith in the buyer's credit may refuse to agree to a credit term. In the absence of such an agreement, the Code provides that the buyer must pay when he receives the goods (UCC 2–310(a)). In the simplest case, where the seller and the buyer carry out the exchange face to face, five consequences follow. First, the seller is assured of payment when he gives up control of the goods. Second, the buyer is assured of control of the goods when he pays. Third, the seller finances the transaction only until the goods leave his hands. Fourth, the buyer finances the transaction only after the goods reach his hands. And fifth, the buyer can inspect the goods before he pays (UCC 2–513(1)).

"When the parties are at a distance the situation changes and some means must be found to give each party a measure of the advantages which he enjoys in the simple face-to-face exchange. The traditional method is the documentary exchange, calling for payment by the buyer against a draft with a bill of lading attached. The immediate purpose of this discussion is to inquire into how the Uniform Commercial Code affects such a transaction.

"*The Agreement.* If the buyer's obligation, in the absence of a contrary agreement, is to pay against the delivery of goods, what contract terms suffice to vary this obligation and to oblige him to pay against documents? Since the Code provides no general words of art for this purpose, such conventional formulae as 'sight draft against bill of lading' will continue to suffice. Furthermore, where the goods are sold 'C.I.F.' (cost, insurance and freight), 'C. & F.' (cost and freight), 'F.O.B. vessel' (free on board vessel) or 'F.A.S.' (free along side), 'unless otherwise agreed the buyer must make payment against tender of the required documents and the seller may not tender nor the buyer demand delivery of the goods in substitution for the documents' (UCC 2–319(4), 2–320(4)). The reason is that these terms contemplate shipment to a distant port where the documents will arrive well ahead of the goods, and so a documentary exchange is presumed unless negated by the agreement. The rule does not apply to ordinary 'F.O.B.' (free on board) contracts which do not have these characteristics.

"*Shipment of the Goods.* When the parties have agreed to a documentary exchange, the seller will ordinarily place the goods in the hands of a carrier, obtaining a negotiable bill of lading to his own order. According to the Code, the effect of this 'shipment under reservation' is to reserve in him 'a security interest in the goods' (UCC 2–505(1)(a)). Beyond this, the bill of lading must satisfy the requirements of the sales article, Article 2, of the Code (UCC 7–509). For one example, where the contract contemplates overseas shipment and unless otherwise agreed, under an 'F.O.B. vessel' term, the seller must procure an 'on board' bill of lading, one stating that the goods have actually been loaded, whereas under a 'C.I.F.' or 'C. & F.' term a 'received for shipment' bill of lading, which falls short of stating that the goods have been loaded, is enough (UCC 2–323). For another example, unless otherwise agreed, under an 'F.O.B. point of shipment' contract, the seller must make such a contract for the transportation of the goods as is reasonable in the light of their nature and the other circumstances (UCC 2–504(a)). Although duplicate bills of lading, clearly marked as such, are regularly issued in this country, bills are not issued in sets of multiple originals for domestic trade. The Code expressly prohibits their issuance in sets except where customary in overseas transactions (UCC 7–304(1); see also UCC 7–402).

"The seller, having obtained the negotiable bill of lading to his own order, then attaches it, together with an invoice and any other documents required by the contract, to a sight, or demand, draft for the amount due him drawn by him as drawer upon the buyer as drawee to the seller's own order. The Code allows drafts to be drawn in sets, although their use is in practice confined to foreign trade, where an original may be drawn to go with each of the multiple originals of a bill of lading which has been issued in a set (UCC 3–801). The seller then indorses the draft and bill of lading and takes them to his bank. For the moment, it will be assumed that the bank takes the documentary draft for collection; the situation when it discounts will be discussed presently.

"*Collection of the Draft.* The bank, known as a 'collecting bank' (UCC 4–105(d)) and more specifically as the 'depositary bank' (UCC 4–105(a)), is required to 'present or send the draft and accompanying documents for presentment' (UCC 4–501), which it will normally do by forwarding them through 'customary banking channels' (UCC 2–308(c), 2–503(5)(b)). Most important, it will treat the draft as a 'collection' item rather than a 'cash' item. Checks, the most common items handled by banks, are dealt with in bulk as 'cash' items on the assumption that they will be honored in the overwhelming majority of cases; provisional credits are entered immediately for a check at all stages of the collection process and automatically become final without further action upon payment by the drawee bank (UCC 4–213(2)). Documentary drafts, on the other hand, are handled as 'collection' items and dealt with individually, rather than in bulk, and since no assumption is made that they will be honored, no credits, not even provisional credits, are given until the item has been paid by the buyer. Ultimately the draft will reach the 'presenting' bank (UCC 4–105(e)), which will undertake to present the documentary draft to the buyer.

"The presenting bank will know the identity and location of the buyer, who will be indicated on the bill of lading as the person to be notified of the arrival of the goods (cf. UCC 7–501(6)) as well as on the draft as the drawee. Unless otherwise instructed, the bank may make presentment to the buyer by sending him a written notice that it holds the item (UCC 4–210(1); see also UCC 2–503(1), (5) and Comment 3 to UCC 2–308). In the event that the buyer does not honor the draft before the close of business on the third banking day after the notice was sent, the bank may treat it as dishonored (UCC 4–210(2)). The buyer may, however, within this time require exhibition of the draft and documents by the bank so that he can determine whether it is properly payable (UCC 4–210, 3–505(1)(a), 3–506(2)). If direct presentment is made to the buyer, instead of presentment by notice, it must be made at the place specified in the draft, or if there be none at his place of business or residence (UCC 3–504(2)(c)), and he then has until the close of business on that day to pay (UCC 3–506(2)). Absent contrary instructions, a collecting bank may have an additional day 'in a good faith effort to secure payment'; it may also be excused for delay caused by circumstances beyond its control (UCC 4–108).

"As already pointed out, under the face-to-face transaction, which the documentary exchange is designed to supplant, the buyer had the right to inspect the goods before paying for them (UCC 2–513(1)). Since the goods will normally travel much more slowly than the documents, they will not ordinarily be available for inspection at the time that the buyer is required to pay under the rules just discussed. Therefore, absent agreement to the contrary, the buyer has no right to inspect the goods before he pays when the contract provides for payment against documents of title, except in the case, to be discussed later, where payment is due only after the goods are to become available for inspection (UCC 2–513(3)(b); see also UCC 2–310(b)). Indeed, the negotiable railway bill of lading typically bears the legend: 'Inspection of property covered by this bill of lading will not be permitted unless provided by law or unless permission is indorsed on this original bill of lading or given in writing by the shipper.' The Code goes on to provide that where, as in the transaction under discussion, the contract calls for payment before inspection, even the nonconformity of the goods does not, with rare exceptions, excuse the buyer from paying (UCC 2–512(1)). But it makes it clear that such payment does not amount to an acceptance of the goods by the buyer and that the buyer retains his right to inspect the goods upon delivery and all of his remedies against the seller for breach of contract (UCC 2–512(2)). He merely loses the opportunity of inspection before payment, an opportunity that gave him advantage of refusing to pay, rather than the disadvantage of having to sue to recover his payment, in the event of a non-conformity.

"Since the draft under discussion is a sight draft, the buyer is called upon to pay, rather than to accept it, before he gets the documents. Only when the draft is payable more than three days after presentment may the presenting bank release the documents against the buyer's acceptance rather than his payment (UCC 2–514, 4–503(a)). Payment may be easily effected if the buyer offers cash or if the presenting bank happens to be one in which the buyer has an account. Short of this, the Code permits the presenting bank to take a cashier's check (a check drawn by a bank on itself), a certified check (a check accepted by the bank on which it has been drawn), or other bank check or obligation [UCC 4–211(1)(d)]. Should the buyer tender his personal check on another bank, the presenting bank may hold the documents while it gets the check certified. Should it release the documents against his personal check, it will be liable to the seller for any loss caused by the dishonor of the check. The proceeds received from the buyer are then remitted by the presenting bank through banking channels.

"When the buyer honors the draft, he receives the bill of lading. When the goods arrive, he is notified by the carrier and surrenders the bill of lading in return for the goods. At this point the buyer will be able to inspect the goods. Should he find them to be defective, his only recourse will ordinarily be to journey to the seller's jurisdiction and there litigate the issues of breach and damages. Other possible remedies will be discussed presently.

"If the buyer does not pay the draft as outlined earlier, the presenting bank must treat it as dishonored. In this event the presenting bank 'must use diligence and good faith to ascertain the reason for dishonor, must notify its transferor of the dishonor and of the results of its effort to ascertain the reasons therefor and must request instructions' (UCC 4–503(b)). It need not, however, return the draft and documents unless so instructed (UCC 4–202(1)(b)). When the notice gets back to the depositary bank, which first took the draft for collection, it must 'seasonably notify its customer' of the dishonor (UCC 4–501). [The presenting bank] 'is under no obligation with respect to goods represented by the documents except to follow any reasonable instructions seasonably received; it has a right to reimbursement for any expense incurred in following instructions and to payment of or indemnity for such expenses' (UCC 4–503). If it has seasonably requested instructions after dishonor but has not received them in a reasonable time, it may 'store, sell or otherwise deal with the goods in any reasonable manner' (UCC 4–504(1)), and has a lien * * * on the goods or their proceeds for reasonable expenses incurred in doing so (UCC 4–504(2)). If, for example, it was commercially reasonable to put the goods in storage pending receipt of requested instructions, the presenting bank would be protected if it did so even though the requested instructions were later received (Comment to UCC 4–504). The Code seems, however, to make a request for instructions and a failure to receive them within a reasonable time prerequisites to the exercise of initiative by the presenting bank in dealing with the goods.

"In addition to the requirement that notice be given of the dishonor, there may be in some cases the additional requirement of protest. Protest, a formal statement of dishonor executed by a public functionary, such as a notary, is generally required in Continental countries in the case of any dishonor of a negotiable instrument. * * * [See UCC 3–501(3), 3–509 and 4–202(1)(d).]

"This, then, is the standard pattern followed in the documentary exchange where payment is to be made against a sight draft with bill of lading attached. How adequate a substitute for the face-to-face transaction has been achieved can be seen by a comparison with the five consequences noted earlier. First, the seller is still assured of payment when he gives up control of the goods, through surrender of the bill of lading. Second, the buyer is assured of control of the goods when he pays, through possession of the bill of lading. Third, the seller must now finance the transaction *after* the goods leave his hands and until the documentary draft has been paid and the proceeds remitted. Fourth, the buyer must now finance the transaction *before* the goods reach his hands, from the time that he pays the documentary draft until they have arrived. And fifth, the buyer can *not* inspect the goods before he pays. Thus while the first two consequences are unchanged, the third, fourth and fifth are different.

Part II. Some Variations

"*Discount of the Draft.* As to the third consequence, the seller must now finance the transaction for an additional period of time between his delivery of the goods to the carrier and the remission to him of the proceeds after the buyer has paid the draft. The seller may shift this burden of financing to his bank by having that bank discount the draft rather than merely take it for collection. The seller can then receive the face value of the draft, less a discount to cover interest charges, before collection, as soon as he has obtained the bill of lading, and the bank will finance the sale from that point until it receives payment. The bank that does this has a 'security interest' in the draft and in the accompanying documents, and this holds true even if the credit which it gives the seller is not withdrawn, as long as he has the right to withdraw it (UCC 4–208). The bank, however, has the same obligations to the seller with respect to presentment and notification on dishonor as if it were an ordinary collecting bank (UCC 4–501). In case of dishonor of course, the bank can hold the seller ultimately liable on the draft even though it has been discounted. By purchasing the draft it acquires not only its own rights under the draft and bill of lading, but also 'any rights of the seller in the goods including the right to stop delivery and the shipper's right to have the draft honored by the buyer' (UCC 2–506(1), 2–707). The right to stop delivery is a right to order the carrier not to deliver to the buyer goods in the possession of the carrier when the buyer has been discovered to be insolvent (UCC 2–705). If the goods are carload, truckload, planeload or larger shipments, delivery may be stopped in the event of buyer's breach regardless of his solvency. Since the bill of lading is a negotiable document of title, however, the carrier is not obliged to obey a notification to stop until surrender of the document (UCC 2–705(3)(c)).

"Where the depositary bank discounts the draft for the seller, it succeeds to his rights under the sales contract as would an assignee. This suggests the possibility that the discounting bank might also assume the obligations of the seller under the sales contract, and more particularly that it might be liable under the seller's warranties of quality in the event that the goods are defective. The Code makes it clear that this is not the case and that a collecting bank 'known to be entrusted with documents on behalf of another or with collection of a draft or other claim against delivery of documents warrants by such delivery of documents only its own good faith and authority,' and this is true 'even though the intermediary has purchased or made advances against the claim or draft to be collected' (UCC 7–508; compare UCC 7–507).

"This sets the stage for an analysis of the position of the buyer in the rare but not impossible event that he has discovered a breach by the seller after he has paid the draft but before the collecting bank has remitted the proceeds. In the event of the seller's breach, it may be possible for the buyer to get personal jurisdiction over the seller in the buyer's own state. The chances of this have increased with the enactment of 'long arm' statutes. But where personal jurisdiction over the seller cannot be had in the buyer's state, he will ordinarily have to journey to the seller's state and there litigate the issues of breach and damages. He would, of course, prefer to bring his action at home—and may be able to do so if he can attach the proceeds as the basis of jurisdiction in his action. Usually the proceeds will have been remitted well before the arrival of the goods. But in the unusual case where this is not so, the buyer may attach the proceeds as the basis of quasi in rem jurisdiction in an action against the seller, and if successful in the action, have judgment in an amount up to the amount of the proceeds. This, however, assumes that the proceeds are indeed the *seller's* proceeds. Should the draft have been discounted by the depositary bank, then it and not the seller would be entitled to the proceeds, and attachment of the proceeds would not give jurisdiction in an action against the seller. Since the depositary bank, even though it discounts the draft, makes no warranties, there is no possibility of using the proceeds as the jurisdictional basis of an action against the bank. In sum, the buyer's advantage through attachment of the proceeds is not only limited to the rare case where the breach is discovered before the proceeds are remitted, but even then is available only when the draft has not been discounted."   [Footnotes omitted.]

Notes

1. What factors motivate some sellers to use the device called the "documentary sale?"

2. What are the functions of the bill of lading and the sight draft in this transaction?

3. The so-called "documentary sale" for cash is not the only type of transaction in which documents of title and/or drafts figure. See White and Summers, pp. 717, 798–809.

SECTION 3. POSSIBLE BREAKDOWNS IN DEALS INVOLVING THE USE OF DOCUMENTS; APPLICABLE LAW

Here we will provide an inventory of the basic ways documentary and similar sales in which bailees hold the goods can break down, and we will identify the relevant sources of law governing these breakdowns. In subsequent sections of this chapter, we will focus on several of these types of breakdowns in more detail.

Below is a list of most of the important types of breakdowns:

(1) The goods may be lost, destroyed or damaged while in the hands of the issuer of the document of title. We have already treated this breakdown earlier in Chapter Nine.

(2) The carrier or other bailee may misdeliver the goods to a party other than a party authorized in the document of title. We will take up this breakdown in section 4 below.

(3) Third parties may intervene and claim goods and/or the documents. This will be treated in section 5 below.

(4) One of the parties to the underlying sales transaction may repudiate or become insolvent while the goods are en route. This will be the subject of section 6 below.

(5) The carrier or other bailee may fail, because of non-receipt, misdescription or the like, to deliver what the documents call for. See section 7 below.

(6) The carrier or other bailee may make late delivery. See Chapter Nine supra.

(7) The goods on arrival may fail to conform to warranties and either be rejectable or afford a basis for a breach of warranty action. Breakdowns of this nature will be treated in Chapters Twelve to Fifteen.

In the event of breakdowns such as the above, what law governs? As the Farnsworth extract indicates, most of the strictly sales aspects and commercial paper aspects are governed by Articles 2, 3 and 4 of the Uniform Commercial Code. But what of the rights and liabilities arising specifically from use of bills of lading and warehouse receipts as such?

A. Law Governing Bills of Lading

Of course, the language of the bill of lading itself will have important bearing. Otherwise, the rights and liabilities of parties to bills of lading (and related documents) are found principally in three places: Article Seven of the Uniform Commercial Code, the Federal Bills of Lading Act—also called the "Pomerene Act" (Federal Bills of Lading Act of 1916, ch. 415, §§ 1–44, 39 Stat. 538, 49 U.S.C.A. §§ 81–124 (1970)), and the Carmack Amendment to the Interstate Commerce Act (Interstate Commerce Act of 1887, ch. 104, Part I, § 20, 24 Stat. 386, as added, June 29, 1906, ch. 3591, § 7, 34 Stat. 593, as amended, 49 U.S.C.A. § 20(11), (1970)). Article Seven of the Code displaced, in relevant part, the Uniform Bills of Lading Act which had been law in all states. Article Seven also applies to warehouse receipts.

In 1916, Congress enacted the Federal Bills of Lading Act (FBLA) which is substantially identical to the old Uniform Bills of Lading Act. The FBLA includes 44 sections. (We will refer to it as the "FBLA" and will cite it by reference to its United States Code section numbers (49 U.S.C.A. §§ 81–124)). Courts have decided hundreds of cases under the

FBLA. Its presence and the presence of the Carmack Amendment on the federal statute books, and the vast case law under both, greatly diminish the significance of Article Seven's provisions on bills of lading. Whenever the FBLA is applicable, it rather than Article Seven controls. The FBLA is applicable to:

> Bills of lading issued by any common carrier for the transportation of goods in any Territory of the United States, or the District of Columbia, or from a place in a State to a place in a foreign country, or from a place in one State to a place in another State, or from a place in one State to a place in the same State through another State or foreign country * * *.

49 U.S.C.A. § 81.

Given the broad scope of the FBLA, what is left for Article Seven to govern? That Article applies mainly to (1) bills of lading issued for the transportation of goods from a place within one state to another place in the same state, provided the goods are not to pass through another state or foreign country *en route,* and (2) bills of lading issued for the transportation of goods from a foreign country into the United States. (A useful general discussion of the latter role of Article Seven is McCune, *Delivery of Cargo Carried Under Straight Bills of Lading,* 17 U.C.C.L.J. 344 (1985)). Even then the scope of Article Seven is cut down to the extent that other federal statutes besides the FBLA apply. Of other federal statutory law in this field the "Carmack Amendment" to the Interstate Commerce Act, 49 U.S.C.A. § 20(11) & (12), is of greatest importance. That amendment codifies the common law liability of interstate carriers for loss, destruction, or damage to goods, imposes this liability on the first of two or more connecting carriers for loss, destruction, or damage caused by any carrier in the chain of carriers transporting an interstate shipment, and proscribes carriers from using certain contract clauses limiting their liability. The Amendment applies to interstate shipments and to export shipments to adjoining countries. The Carmack Amendment covers two full pages in the statute book. The courts have interpreted and applied it in hundreds of cases. There are also various special federal statutes more limited in scope. In 1938, for instance, Congress enacted the Perishable Agricultural Commodities Act. 7 U.S.C.A. §§ 499a–499r. In 1893 and 1936, Congress passed the Harter Act, 46 U.S.C.A. §§ 190–196, and the Carriage of Goods by Sea Act, 46 U.S.C.A. §§ 1300–1315, respectively; both apply to ocean bills of lading.

Besides federal statutes, Article Seven, and relevant case law, the lawyer must often consult regulations and rulings of regulatory bodies, including those of the Interstate Commerce Commission. The I.C.C. has prescribed mandatory forms for bills of lading and has prescribed that "order" bills, which are negotiable because they state "deliver to order or bearer," must be printed on yellow paper and "straight" bills, which are nonnegotiable, on white paper. The I.C.C. has also promulgated numerous rules and regulations that affect the liabilities of interstate carriers.

B. Law Governing Warehouse Receipts

Again, the language of the receipt itself will have important bearing. Generally, Article Seven of the Code will govern, but even though a given state's version of Article Seven applies under relevant conflict of laws principles, some other law may control in the end. This law might be local non-Code state law, or it might be federal law, depending on the facts. Many states have enacted essentially regulatory statutes applicable to the dealings of warehousemen. As to these, UCC 7–103 is quite explicit: "To the extent that any * * * regulatory statute of this state or tariff, classification, or regulation filed or issued pursuant thereto is applicable, the provisions of this article are subject thereto." An illustrative example of a *state* regulatory provision is this California law:

> No warehousemen shall begin to operate any business of a warehouseman, as defined in subdivisions (b) or (c) of Section 239, without first having obtained from the commission a certificate declaring that public convenience and necessity require or will require the transaction of business by such warehouseman.

In addition to state regulatory law, federal law (statute, treaty, judicial decision) may also supersede or supplement Article Seven. The effect of federal law on warehouse receipts is confined mainly to the impact of the United States Warehouse Act, which applies to receipts covering agricultural products stored for interstate or foreign commerce. Most sections of this Act are regulatory, but those sections that specify the content of warehouse receipts and define delivery obligations override Article Seven.

The Code draftsmen intended originally to consolidate the old Uniform Warehouse Receipts Act and Uniform Bills of Lading Act into one unified statute, but the plan could not be fully executed. The result is that the lawyer must usually look in two places. He must look first in the relevant "special provisions" on warehouse receipts and second in the more general provisions covering *both* warehouse receipts and bills of lading. Sometimes the lawyer must search outside of Article Seven in other Articles of the Code, such as Article Nine, which applies to pledges of warehouse receipts.

SECTION 4. MISDELIVERY BY CARRIER OR OTHER BAILEE

As the cases in this section will indicate, "misdelivery" can take a variety of forms. In a misdelivery case, the lawyer must first determine the nature of the transaction involved. Was it a true documentary sale? Or what? Then the lawyer must determine how the case should be decided under *applicable law*. This law is to be found (1) in the terms of the document issued by the carrier or other bailee and (2) in relevant statutory and case law. Be sure to review the terms of any bill of lading. Also, review not only relevant Code provisions (especially UCC 7–403) but also sections 88 and 89 of the Federal Bill of Lading Act below:

§ 88. Duty to deliver goods on Demand; Refusal

A carrier, in the absence of some lawful excuse, is bound to deliver goods upon a demand made either by the consignee named in the bill for the goods or, if the bill is an order bill, by the holder thereof, if such a demand is accompanied by—

(a) An offer in good faith to satisfy the carrier's lawful lien upon the goods;

(b) Possession of the bill of lading and an offer in good faith to surrender, properly indorsed, the bill which was issued for the goods, if the bill is an order bill; and

(c) A readiness and willingness to sign, when the goods are delivered, an acknowledgment that they have been delivered, if such signature is requested by the carrier.

In case the carrier refuses or fails to deliver the goods, in compliance with a demand by the consignee or holder so accompanied, the burden shall be upon the carrier to establish the existence of a lawful excuse for such refusal or failure.

§ 89. Delivery; When Justified

A carrier is justified, subject to the provisions of sections 90–92 of this title, in delivering goods to one who is—

(a) A person lawfully entitled to the possession of the goods, or

(b) The consignee named in a straight bill for the goods, or

(c) A person in possession of an order bill for the goods, by the terms of which the goods are deliverable to his order; or which has been indorsed to him, or in blank by the consignee, or by the mediate or immediate indorsee of the consignee.

REFRIGERATED TRANSPORT CO. v. HERNANDO PACKING CO.

Supreme Court of Tennessee, 1976.
544 S.W.2d 613.

HENRY, JUSTICE.

This controversy between a consignor and a common carrier of property involves the carrier's liability for misdelivery of cargo transported under a straight bill of lading. The trial court found the issues against the carrier and we conclude that he reached the correct conclusion.

I.

On January 3, 1975, Hernando Packing Company, Inc., of Memphis, shipped via Refrigerated Transport Company, Inc., a truck load of frozen meat consigned as follows:

[T]o BROWARD COLD STORAGE (acct. of J & A Trading Co.) 3220 S.W. 2nd Avenue * * * Fort Lauderdale, Florida.

Broward is a public warehouse.

Prior to making this shipment Hernando had received a call from an individual who identified himself as *Al Hark* and held himself out to be a representative of J & A Trading Company. In point of fact he had no connection with J & A Trading Company and that company had gone out of business. Hernando had never done business with Al Hark, but on one prior occasion, had shipped to J & A Trading Company pursuant to a transaction with *Joseph Hark,* its then representative and owner, and father of Al Hark.

It is fairly inferable from the record that this unfamiliarity with Al Hark prompted the precaution of making the shipment to Broward, a public warehouse, for the account of J & A. However, the record is not specific in this regard and the shipment may have been made thusly as a matter of custom in the business or trade.

On January 6, 1975, upon the arrival of Refrigerated's truck in Fort Lauderdale, it was met *across the street from Broward* by Al Hark, but within sight of Broward's manager. Without the knowledge of Hernando or reconsignment or assent of Broward, and after representing himself to Refrigerated's driver as being a representative of J & A, Al Hark caused 84 boxes, or 5,040 pounds of boneless beef to be delivered to another address. Refrigerated's driver did not contact Broward and, insofar as the record shows, delivery was made solely on the basis of the verbal representations of Al Hark.

The next morning Refrigerated's truck came to Broward's dock and was again met by Al Hark. In the sight and presence of the Broward manager, Hark directed that a part of the remaining meat be reloaded on another truck and that the balance be stored with Broward to the account of J & A. Al Hark again represented himself to be a representative of J & A. The record does not show when, to whom, or if the driver surrendered the bill of lading.

By these maneuvers, Al Hark acquired possession of 246 boxes, or 9,520 pounds of meat ranging from ribeyes to oxtails and having a stipulated value of $5,880.86.

On January 7, 1976, Joseph Hark was informed of the arrival of the meat, whereupon he called Hernando and advised that J & A was out of business; that it had placed no order; and that this was not the first time his son, Al Hark, had placed such orders in the name of J & A. Hernando called Broward to direct that the meat not be delivered to Al Hark but was informed that delivery had already been made and without any reconsignment from Broward.

The trial judge, on this set of facts found and decreed:

That the consignee on the Straight Bill of Lading herein was Broward Cold Storage at 3220 S.W. Second Avenue, Ft. Lauderdale, Florida, and that the Defendant had an absolute duty to deliver the frozen meat involved herein to said consignee and to no other.

II.

This controversy pivots upon the precise provisions of the bill of lading, viz: the consignment to "Broward Cold Storage (account of J & A Trading Co.)." Refrigerated earnestly insists that this, in effect, was a consignment to "J & A Trading Co., care of Broward Cold Storage." While this position is plausible, when consideration is given to the nature and purpose of bills of lading, the duties and obligations arising thereunder, and to the plain terms of the consignment, we cannot embrace this theory of the case.

At the very outset we point out that we are dealing with a "straight" bill of lading which is "[a] bill in which it is stated that the goods are consigned or destined to a specified person", 49 U.S.C. Sec. 82, which is not negotiable and must be so marked (it was in this case), 49 U.S.C. Sec. 86, as opposed to an "order" bill, 49 U.S.C. Sec. 83.[1]

Delivery under a straight bill of lading may only be made to "[a] person lawfully entitled to the possession of the goods, or (b) the consignee named" therein. 49 U.S.C. Sec. 89.

While there are various areas of potential disagreement inherent in this controversy they all boil down to a single question: Who was the consignee under the bill of lading?

In our view, there is no ambiguity. The consignment was to Broward. The parenthetical matter inserted simply advised the warehouse as to the identity of the ultimate receiver of the goods upon Broward's reconsignment. The only address inserted was that of Broward. Al Hark's name does not appear on the bill. It is fairly inferable that the consignment was to Broward as a precautionary measure against an unknown purchaser. Such would have been reasonable and prudent. But we need not speculate since the language was clear. There is no way that this delivery could have been properly made except to Broward and at Broward's address. Most assuredly a street corner delivery to a stranger not named in the bill and not shown by the record to have presented any credentials or authority cannot constitute valid delivery. All the driver ever had to do was to present his bill of lading to an authorized representative of Broward. The failure to do so was a breach of the contract of carriage.

To constitute a valid delivery, absent special circumstances, it is imperative that delivery be made to the right person, at the proper

---

1. "Bills of lading issued by any common carrier for the transportation of goods. * * * from a place in one State to a place in another State", among others, are governed by the Federal Bills of Lading Act 49 U.S.C. Sections 81–124.

time and place and in a proper manner. This is implicit in the Contract of Carriage.[2]

It is stated in Volume 13, American Jurisprudence, 2nd, Carriers § 416 that "a carrier who delivers to an alleged agent of the consignee does so at its own peril with respect to his status as such." Cited in support of this assertion is our own case of *Dean v. Vaccaro & Co.*, 39 Tenn. 488 (1859), which is fully supportive.

Pertinent to the issue is the North Carolina case of *Griggs v. Stoker Service Co.*, 229 N.C. 572, 50 S.E.2d 914 (1948), wherein the Court said:

> The duty of a common carrier is not merely to carry safely the goods entrusted to him, but also to deliver them to the party designated by the terms of the shipment, or to his order, at the place of destination. 50 S.E.2d at 919.

Another case involving misdelivery of cargo, is *Dickman v. Daniels Motor Freight*, 185 Pa.Super. 374, 138 A.2d 165 (1958), wherein the delivery was made to a business establishment having a similar name and under circumstances suggestive of fraudulent conduct by a "swindler" who placed the order. The bill of lading was directed to a definite company at a definite address. The Court said:

> A common carrier is under an absolute duty to deliver goods to the person designated in the instructions of the shipper. If it fails to follow the express instructions of the shipper in making delivery, it acts at its peril and assumes the risk of wrong delivery. 138 A.2d at 167.

In *Richardson v. Railway Express Agency, Inc.*, 258 Or. 170, 482 P.2d 176 (1971), the Court held that a carrier making a delivery to one other than the named consignee "has the burden of proof to establish the ownership and right of possession of the goods at the time of such delivery." 482 P.2d at 178. The Court indicated the settled rule to be that carriers

> * * * are held strictly to the performance of their duty to make delivery of goods at the place of destination to the person designated to receive them if he presents himself or can be found with reasonable diligence. 482 P.2d at 179.

Refrigerated makes the urgent insistence that delivery to an imposter will discharge the common carrier "if it is to the imposter that the consignor actually intends to ship." We do not fault this as a general rule of law; but, as already pointed out, the shipment, for reasons we think self-evident, was to Broward.

Refrigerated relies upon *Chicago, M., St. P. & P.R. Co. v. Flanders*, 56 F.2d 114 (8th Cir.1932); however, there the imposter held all documentary indicia of ownership and the cattle were consigned to him.

---

2. See Vol. 13 Am.Jur.2d, Carriers, Sec. 405 et seq., and particularly Sections 405, 406, 411 and 415.

Also relied upon is *Malvern Cold Storage Co. v. American Ry. Exp. Co.*, 206 Iowa 292, 220 N.W. 322 (1938); however, according to Refrigerated's brief filed in this Court, "[t]he circumstances were such that the consignor's actual *intention* was to deliver to [the imposter]." (Emphasis supplied).

Next we are cited to *Fulton Bag & Cotton Mills v. Hudson Navigation Co.*, 157 F. 987 (S.D.N.Y.1907). There no public warehouse was involved; identity of names was involved; due inquiry was made by the carrier prior to delivery; and proper notification was given pursuant to the bill of lading.

Other cases cited by appellee are also distinguishable.

In 54 A.L.R. at 1330, in an annotation relating to delivery to an imposter, it is stated that "the general rule places liability on a carrier for a misdelivery to an imposter of goods placed in the hands of the carrier for shipment". Among the cases cited in support of this proposition is our case of *Sword v. Young*, 89 Tenn. 126, 14 S.W. 481 (1890).

Sword is analogous to the instant case. One Gillenwaters ordered a brick machine under the assumed name of Magrauder, representing Magrauder to be a firm name. Upon arrival of the machine in Knoxville, Gillenwaters presented the bill of lading made in the name of Charles G. Magrauder, paid the freight and took possession of the machine.

The Court recognized the "well settled general rule that the carrier must deliver to the consignee at the place appointed", and thereafter stated:

> It can make no difference that the defendant carrier thought, because Gillenwaters had the bill of lading, that he was Charles G. Magrauder. If he was a stranger, as the proof shows him to be, it was the duty of the carrier to have required him to identify himself as the consignee or his rightfully constituted agent.
>
> * * *
>
> The consignment was to Charles G. Magrauder. That name was fixed on the machine, and it was a duty to deliver to him only, or, if he could not be discovered, to notify the consignor.
>
> There is no difference between this case and one in which a consignment has been made to an actual person, and the goods delivered by accident, mistake, or carelessless to a cheat who represents himself as the real consignee. It is necessary in both to have proof of identity or authority to receive. 89 Tenn. at 128–29, 14 S.W. at 481.

We hold that Refrigerated breached its duty to deliver the cargo to Broward, the party designated in the bill of lading; that delivery to Al Hark was at Refrigerated's peril; that the burden of validating this delivery by establishing Al Hark's ownership and right to possession was upon Refrigerated and that it failed to carry that burden.

While we make this holding within the context of our view that Broward was the consignee, had we adopted Refrigerated's view that J & A Trading Company was the consignee, with the goods being shipped "in care of" Broward, the result would be the same. This necessarily follows from the facts that J & A was not in existence; that Al Hark had no connection with J & A; and that delivery was made to him without proper inquiry and without notice to Broward, or J & A. Had such inquiry been made and such notice given the driver would have discovered that he was dealing with an imposter.

III.

Refrigerated counter-claimed for the unpaid freight bill in the sum of $675.00 together with interest thereon. The trial court dismissed the counter-claim, without assigning any reason therefor.

We note that the bill of lading contains the entry "FREIGHT TO BE PAID BY: J & A TRADING CO." in Miami. This may have prompted the trial judge.

The record before us is not sufficient to pass upon this portion of the controversy. The bill of lading shows that 498 boxes of meat, weighing 31,068¾ pounds were shipped. The stipulation shows that Al Hark diverted 246 boxes weighing 9,520 pounds. The remaining 252 boxes, containing 21,548 pounds were delivered to Broward.

We have no hesitancy in declaring that Refrigerated, by misdelivery of the diverted meat, breached its contract of carriage and forfeited its right to receive compensation to that extent. Superficially it would appear that Refrigerated would be entitled to recover for the carriage of that portion of the meat ultimately delivered to Broward. However, we make no holding in the latter regard; we merely recognize the considerations involved.

On remand, the trial judge will reconsider the counter-claim and enter such judgment as the facts may indicate and justice may require.

Affirmed in part and remanded.

COOPER, C.J., and FONES, BROCK and HARBISON, JJ., concur.

Notes

1. Why did the court apply section 89 of the FBLA rather than section 7–403 of the UCC? Does it make any difference?

2. Does the result really depend in part on the statute or would it have been enough merely for the court to have invoked the language of the straight bill of lading?

3. In Rountree v. Lydick-Barmann, 150 S.W.2d 173 (Tex.Civ.App. 1941), the seller was Lydick-Barmann, the buyer Crone Co., and the carrier Rountree. The carrier issued to Lydick-Barmann a bill which was captioned: "Uniform Motor Carrier Straight Bill of Lading—Original—Not Negotiable—Domestic." The bill also acknowledged receipt of the goods from seller (Lydick-Barmann) at its address in Fort Worth, Texas "Con-

signed to Lydick-Barmann Company, destination 616 Street, Louisiana City, Little Rock, Ark. State. Notify Crone Company." Seller had no office or agent at the street address in Little Rock given in the bill of lading. The carrier delivered to Crone Company and seller was never paid. Held, for seller, Lydick-Barmann. "Notify Crone Co. was not equivalent to 'Consigned to Crone Co.' When the carrier learned that it could not deliver to Lydick-Barmann at the address given, it should have sought instructions from Lydick-Barmann."

4. In *Refrigerated Transport Co.*, the bill of lading was non-negotiable which is by far the most common case. But a not uncommon transaction is one in which a seller in a foreign country ships goods to the U.S. pursuant to an agreement whereby the carrier issues a negotiable bill of lading to the seller who then sends it and a draft to a bank in the U.S. who acts as collecting agent on behalf of the seller by taking payment from the buyer and endorsing the bill to the buyer who then presents it to the carrier and receives the goods. Such an arrangement breaks down if the carrier delivers the goods to the buyer without insisting on the bill of lading. This is what happened in Koreska v. United Cargo Corp., 23 A.D.2d 37, 258 N.Y.S.2d 432 (1965) and the carrier was held liable to the seller (who did not receive payment from the buyer). The carrier may have a defense in such a case, however, as when the carrier can show that the buyer already had acquired the bill of lading from the collecting agent (without payment) so that the carrier's wrong was not the cause of the loss. Such a defense prevailed in The Pere Marquette Ry. v. J.F. French & Co., 254 U.S. 538, 41 S.Ct. 195, 65 L.Ed. 391 (1921). Still other defenses may be available in such cases. The carrier may be able to show that the seller or the seller's agent waived the requirement of picking up the bill of lading from the buyer. Or the carrier may be able to show that the seller ratified the misdelivery by accepting a partial payment from the buyer subsequently.

5. Sometimes the unpaid seller will find that the collecting agency (often a bank) will be liable. Such a case is Bunge v. First Nat'l Bank, 118 F.2d 427 (3d Cir.1941) where the bank became liable to the seller for accepting a bad check and handing over the bill of lading duly endorsed to the buyer. The court said the bank became liable "when it received something other than money in payment."

Note: Terminology

The carrier's so-called "absolute liability" for misdelivery can be extracted from the text of sections 88 and 89 of the FBLA, 7–403 of the Code, and the contract of carriage of the parties. But it does not clarify analysis to say that the liability is absolute. After all, the contract between shipper and carrier calls on the carrier to deliver to a given party, and when the carrier fails to do this, a breach of contract occurs. The liability of a carrier for misdelivery is no more and no less absolute than the liability of any party for breach of contract. Ordinarily, it is no defense for the party who breaks his contract to respond that what he did under the circumstances was reasonable, or even that it was his very best effort.

Note: Substitutes for Surrender of "Order" Bills

When one uses a negotiable bill of lading he expects that the carrier will not surrender the goods until the original copy of the bill is presented to him. As we saw, the fine print at the top of such bill provides: "The surrender of this original ORDER BILL OF LADING properly indorsed shall be required before delivery of the property." UCC 7–502 makes plain the idea that this bill of lading embodies the rights to the goods; it specifies that one to whom a document of title has been duly negotiated acquires thereby "title to the document, title to the goods and the direct obligation of the issuer to hold or deliver the goods according to the terms of the document. * * *"

What happens when in the humdrum of real life the mailman fails to get the original of the order bill of lading to the bank and instead returns it with a stamp, "undeliverable," or when the bank loses the bill, or takes two or three days to process the bill and the goods have arrived in the meantime? Of course somebody is going to have to pay a charge to the railroad for holding the goods. And if the goods are melons or peaches or other perishable commodities, it would be intolerable and in no one's interest to have them rot on the siding while everyone hunted for the bill of lading. Shippers and carriers have worked out certain substitutes for surrender of the original bill. These provisions are described in § 3 of Rule 7 of the Uniform Freight Classification and they read as follows:

> **Substitute 1:** cash or its equivalent to the carrier equal to 125% of the invoice value of the property.

> **Substitute 2:** a specific bond of indemnity equal to double the invoice value.

> **Substitute 3:** a blanket bond of indemnity. This bond can be used repeatedly so long as the bill-of-lading is surrendered within five days of delivery of the freight. If the bill-of-lading does not become available within that time, Substitutes 1 or 2 must be substituted.

> **Substitute 4:** an open-end bond. (If an order-notify bill is lost the surety automatically assumes liability for the lading in perpetuity. The open-bond becomes an individual bond, without limit, on each car released.)

If the one for whom delivery is intended under the order bill of lading has not been able to procure the original of the order bill, he can offer any one of the four substitutes and thereby procure the goods. Of course the effect of the substitute is to provide the carrier with a fund out of which he can satisfy his liability for breaching his contract with the shipper.

One way to avoid the problem is this: The shipper can retain control of the goods by using a straight bill of lading if he names himself as the consignee. The following excerpt taken from a letter of the late Mr. J.L. Shissler, Jr., former General Traffic Manager of the Pillsbury Company, explains the Pillsbury Company's use of this method:

> "Under Section 4 of Rule 7 of the Uniform Freight Classification the rail carriers provide for shipments under straight bills-of-lading consigned to one party with provision for notification to a second party

with surrender of a written order prior to delivery. Under this system we would simply bill a car to ourselves with the carrier to advise the customer. The bill-of-lading carries the notation 'Do not surrender except upon receipt of written order from The Pillsbury Company.' A delivery order is prepared and accompanies the draft to the bank. When the customer accepts the draft, he receives the delivery order. This in turn he presents to the carrier's destination agent for release of the car.

"In the event the delivery order is lost or delayed the consignee can secure release of the car on the same four substitutes available under the order-notify bill.

"Perhaps, at this point I should point out the difference in the two methods. Under the order bill, once the shipment moves neither the shipper nor the receiver can release the car without surrender of the bill or use of one of the four substitutes. Under the straight-notify bill the receiver must either surrender the delivery order or use one of the four substitutes. The consignor, however, can release cars by simply notifying the carrier in writing that delivery can be made without surrender of the delivery order."

Observe that in the type of transaction Mr. Shissler describes, the buyer does not pay a sight draft; rather, he "accepts" a time draft as a condition of getting the goods. See UCC 3–410. This device affords seller less protection than does use of a sight draft, yet more protection than sale on open account. Do you see why?

SECTION 5. ASSERTION OF CLAIMS AGAINST SELLER, BUYER OR OWNER BY THIRD PARTIES (Herein of "negotiability")

Third parties (parties other than the seller, the buyer, and the bailee) sometimes assert claims to the goods at some stage of the transaction, and this can cause a breakdown. These parties include: (1) persons who claim to be creditors of the seller or buyer, (2) persons who claim to be purchasers from the seller or buyer, and (3) other persons claiming paramount title (e.g. an alleged prior owner).

Generally, the buyer will be best off in these cases if he has acquired title to the goods by taking (through due negotiation) negotiable documents covering them. Both Article Seven of the Code (UCC 7–104) and the Federal Bill of Lading Act distinguish between negotiable and non-negotiable documents. The relevant sections of the FBLA provide as follows:

82. Straight bill of lading

A bill in which it is stated that the goods are consigned or destined to a specified person is a straight bill. Aug. 29, 1916, c. 415, § 2, 39 Stat. 539.

83. Order bill of lading; negotiability

A bill in which it is stated that the goods are consigned or destined to the order of any person named in such bill is an order bill. Any provision in such a bill or in any notice, contract, rule, regulation, or tariff that it is nonnegotiable shall be null and void and shall not affect its negotiability within the meaning of this chapter unless upon its face and in writing agreed to by the shipper. Aug. 29, 1916, c. 415, § 3, 39 Stat. 539.

The most common type of transaction in which a buyer purchases a *negotiable* bill occurs when a contract between him and his seller calls for him to pay "cash against documents." (See section 2 of this chapter.) Today this type of transaction is not nearly as common in domestic trade as in import-export transactions. As we saw earlier, when a buyer agrees to pay "cash against documents," this ordinarily calls for him to pay a sight draft presented by the seller's agent in exchange for a negotiable bill of lading which entitles the buyer to procure the goods from the carrier and without which the carrier will not deliver them. The seller is not obligated to hand over the bill (and thus control over the goods) until the buyer pays the draft, and the buyer does not have to pay in advance but only simultaneously with acquiring the bill (the means to procure the goods from the carrier when they arrive).

What rights does a good faith purchaser of a negotiable document acquire? First, he generally gets the same rights against the bailee as the bailor had, including the right to have the bailee care for the goods and the right to have the bailee deliver in accordance with the purchaser's instructions. Thus, section 112 of the FBLA provides that the transferee gets "the direct obligation of the carrier to hold possession of the goods for him according to the terms of the bill as fully as if the carrier had contracted directly with him." Section 7–502(1) of Article Seven includes a similar provision. Second, a good faith purchaser of a negotiable bill of lading gets (under section 111 of the FBLA) "such title to the goods as the person negotiating the bill to him had or had ability to convey to a purchaser in good faith for value. * * *" Under section 7–502 of Article Seven, the purchaser gets (subject to UCC 7–503), "title to the document" and "title to the goods." Third, once the bailee issues a negotiable document covering the goods, whatever title to the goods that the document covers can generally be transferred only by appropriate transfer of the document. That is, appropriate transfer of the document is generally the exclusive method of moving title to the goods. Under Article Seven for a purchaser of a negotiable document to acquire rights under UCC 7–502, he must take by "due negotiation." The Article Seven requirements for due negotiation are set forth in UCC 7–501. Under the FBLA, for the purchaser to acquire the rights set forth in section 111, he must "give value therefor in good faith, without notice," and take by indorsement or delivery (as provided in sections 107 and 108).

Problem 10–1

Seller and buyer entered a contract for the purchase of 500 wooden rails. Seller got a negotiable bill of lading from the carrier while the rails were still in seller's yard to be loaded on nearby boxcars. Two days later buyer bought and paid for the bill and took the same by due negotiation. A day later, Ajax, a creditor of seller, levied on the rails while still in seller's yard. As between Ajax and buyer, who prevails? Cf., UCC 7–602, 7–501 and 7–502. See also FBLA section 103.

Problem 10–2

Construct an example in which the holder of a negotiable document received from the seller prevails under the Code over another purchaser of the same goods covered by the bill. Also be sure to note the exception in UCC 7–205.

Problem 10–3

Joe held a negotiable warehouse receipt in "order" form. Art stole the receipt and artfully forged it to John, a good faith purchaser. Joe claims the goods. John claims the goods. To whom must the bailee deliver under the Code? (And where does UCC 7–404 come into play?)

LINEBURGER BROS. v. HODGE

Supreme Court of Mississippi, 1951.
212 Miss. 204, 54 So.2d 268.

ALEXANDER, JUSTICE.

Separate bills were filed against the Federal Compress & Warehouse Company, a corporation, by E.S. Vancleve, J.R. Hodge, and E.A. Bates & Company, a partnership, each praying for a mandatory injunction against the defendant to compel delivery of cotton held by the defendant to them as purchasers and holders of the warehouse receipts covering the number of bales of cotton held respectively by each of the complainants, or in the alternative for the value of the cotton thereby represented. The total number of bales is twenty-four, Vancleve claiming nine, Hodge six, and E.A. Bates & Company nine.

It is adequately shown that all of the cotton was grown and ginned by Lineburger Brothers, B.C. Lineburger, J.G. Outlaw and F.A. Little, and stolen by one J.V. Carr from a gin where the cotton had been processed and tagged. This asportation occurred at night and was conducted with the aid of a truck driver who was not a regular employee of Carr. Early the next morning Carr carried the cotton to the defendant warehouse, and, after weighing, had the receipts issued in three fictitious names and delivered to him. Carr took the receipts to nearby towns and sold the cotton, so identified, to the three complainants in separate lots. The purchasers gave their separate checks to Carr who procured payment by endorsing them respectively in the names of the three fictitious persons. He then disappeared and has not since been located.

As stated, the three buyers filed their separate bills against the warehouse. The gin company was not made a party. Upon application of the planters or owners, they were allowed to intervene and claim the cotton. From a decree dismissing the petition of the intervenors, absolving the warehouse of negligence in the issuance of the receipts, and awarding title to the respective warehouse receipts to the purchasers with full rights to claim the cotton thereby represented, after paying storage charges to the warehouse, the planters, or owners, appeal. A cross-appeal is filed by the complainants which urges that in event of a reversal of the decree, they be awarded a decree against the warehouse for the value of the cotton.

We deal first with the cross-appeal. It is grounded chiefly upon the alleged negligence of the warehouse in issuing the receipts to Carr in the names given by him.

* * *

Regardless of the plausibility of the contention of the appellees, there was an issue of fact in the matter of negligence of the warehouse, and we find no basis for overturning the finding of the chancellor, whose acquittance of the warehouse must of necessity have been upon such absence of negligence.

We approach, then, the rights of the appellants, the planters and owners. As heretofore stated, they had given Carr no authority to take and haul away any of this cotton. Specific instructions, including the time and identity of cotton to be so hauled, were always given, and Carr knew this. It is immaterial whether the warehouse knew of this limitation upon Carr's authority. It is sufficient that this limitation was understood between Carr and appellants. Here there was no dispute, and it is without question that the taking by Carr, under all the circumstances, was larceny, and that the receipts were fraudulently obtained. The next morning Carr was seen and made two different and untrue statements as to where the receipts were. One of these reports was to one of the owners who had discovered that the cotton was missing and was seeking to locate the receipts. There was no one at the gin when the cotton was abstracted, except Carr, his driver, and Mrs. Carr and her small son. The manager of the gin was not present, and he later testified that he had instructions that Carr was not to haul the Lineburger cotton except upon specific instructions. We repeat that the gin is not a party here and the test of the right of the owners must depend on whether this cotton was under any circumstances entrusted to Carr by permission and knowledge of the owners.

We find that the cotton was not so entrusted to Carr, and since the cotton was in fact stolen and the receipts fraudulently obtained, the defense of apparent authority, although available to the warehouse, does not aid the claim of the purchasers of the receipts.

It was held in Unger v. Abbott, 92 Miss. 563, 46 So. 68, that the rule caveat emptor applies against the claim of an innocent purchaser of warehouse receipts who purchased them from the owner's servant who had been sent with cotton to a compress company with instructions to have it weighed and to bring the receipts back to the owner, but who, contrary to his authority and instructions, took the receipts in his own name and sold them.

If it be observed that this case was decided prior to our statutes upon Warehouse Receipts, Chap. 16, Vol. 4, Code 1942, attention is directed to Section 5051, which is as follows: "A negotiable receipt may be negotiated: * * *

> "(b) By any person to whom the possession or custody of the receipt has been entrusted by the owner, if, by the terms of the receipt, the warehouseman undertakes to deliver the goods to the order of the person to whom the possession or custody of the receipt has been entrusted, or if at the time of such entrusting the receipt is in such form that it may be negotiated by delivery."

We look next at Section 5052: "A person to whom a negotiable receipt has been duly negotiated acquires thereby:

> "(a) Such title to the goods as the person negotiating the receipt to him had or had ability to convey to a purchaser in good faith for value, and also such title to the goods as the depositor or person to whose order the goods were to be delivered by the terms of the receipt had or had ability to convey to a purchaser in good faith for value, and * * *."

Section 5058 is also in point. It is as follows: "The validity of the negotiation of a receipt is not impaired by the fact that such negotiation was a breach of duty on the part of the person making the negotiation, or by the fact that the owner of the receipt was induced by fraud, mistake, or duress to entrust the possession or custody of the receipt to such person, if the person to whom the receipt was negotiated, paid or a person to whom the receipt was subsequently negotiated, paid value therefor, without notice of the breach of duty, or fraud, or mistake or duress."

Appellees cite for support Weil Bros., Inc. v. Keenan, 180 Miss. 697, 178 So. 90. Here there was an interpleader suit filed by the warehouse. The testimony disclosed that the receipts had been entrusted to one Spencer by the owner, and were misappropriated by the former. After recognizing that one, especially a trespasser, can not convey a better title than he has, the Court found that the receipts had been entrusted to the thief and an innocent purchaser was protected. To the same effect is Lundy v. Greenville Bank & Tr. Co., 179 Miss. 282, 174 So. 802, and other cases cited by appellees. See also 56 Am.Jur.Warehouses, Sec. 62.

Our statutes do not go so far as those of some other states in protecting a bona fide purchaser of negotiable receipts in cases where the receipts had been stolen. See 56 Am.Jur., Warehouses, Sec. 53. Since such receipts were not negotiable at common law, their negotiability is to be measured by our statutes.

We hold, therefore, that neither the cotton nor the receipts had been entrusted to Carr by the owners and that the latter are not estopped to set up their claim to the cotton as against the several appellees who purchased the receipts.

* * *

The assertion wants no support that the statutes referred to were designed to insure the negotiability of warehouse receipts and to facilitate commerce in the market places where cotton is bought and sold. The innocent purchaser of a negotiable receipt is guaranteed an assurance without which the traffic could not be conducted. Yet, such assurance must take into account the older principle that an owner of cotton may not be divested of title by a trespasser or a thief. In order to strike a just balance between these two concepts the statutes were enacted. The buyer must still beware lest he is buying receipts which have been fraudulently obtained or cotton which has been stolen. We need not analyze the statutes to divine whether the owner, who has voluntarily clothed another with indicia of ownership or entrusted him with possession of receipts, is barred of recovery from an innocent purchaser by principles of estoppel or pursuant to the rule that where two innocent persons must suffer from a fraud, he who reposes confidence in the fraudulent agent must suffer. It is enough that the statute recognizes title in the innocent purchaser who has bought receipts from one to whom they have been entrusted by the owner.

Here, as in all such cases, one of two innocent persons must suffer the loss. The thief has stolen or fraudulently obtained property from someone. We hold that the unlawful act was committed against the owners and that the title to the cotton remains in them. As stated in Unger v. Abbott, supra, "(The appellees) are to be condoled with for their loss by this swindle; but their misfortune can not affect the right of (the appellants) to have (their) cotton. * * * 'Caveat emptor' applies." [92 Miss. 563, 46 So. 68.]

The cause will be reversed and decree awarded to the appellants for the cotton, and the Federal Compress & Warehouse Company is directed to hold the same to the order of appellants, but without storage charges thereon. The cross-appeal is thereby decided adversely.

Reversed and decree here for appellants.

Notes

1. Would this case have been decided the same way under UCC 7–501, 7–502, and 7–503? Explain. What if Carr had been the manager of the gin with power to store?

2. In re Jamestown Farmers Elevator Inc., 49 B.R. 661, 41 UCC Rep Serv. 578 (Bkrtcy.N.D.1985) posed a parallel problem. There, the goods were not stolen and then warehoused and passed to buyers. Rather, Bank

had a security interest in the goods, yet allowed debtor to warehouse them and procure a further loan from third party, giving the receipts as security. Held: third party prevails over bank under UCC 7–503.

SECTION 6. A PARTY TO THE SALE REPUDIATES, BECOMES INSOLVENT, OR THE LIKE

A party to the sale may repudiate or become insolvent while the goods (1) are in the hands of a carrier or other bailee and (2) a document of title covering the goods is outstanding. Suppose, for example, that while the goods are en route, the buyer repudiates or becomes insolvent. What may the seller do? May he "stop in transit" under UCC 2–705? May he divert? This depends on (1) the terms of the outstanding document and (2) the applicable statutory and case law. In any event, any new carriage or delivery instructions of the seller will be addressed to the carrier (or other bailee).

It is important to distinguish between the carrier's *right* (without fear of suit) to follow the instructions of a consignor or consignee and its *duty* to do so. In some cases a carrier must follow instructions; in others it may but need not. Likewise one should distinguish a shipper-seller's rights and powers vis-a-vis the carrier from those vis-a-vis his buyer-consignee. The shipper may have the power to halt shipment, but his act may constitute a breach of his sales contract. UCC 2–705(1) gives the seller a right to stop delivery in a case in which "he discovers the buyer to be insolvent" or in the case of the "delivery of carload, truckload, planeload or larger shipments of express or freight when the buyer repudiates or fails to make a payment due before delivery, or if for any other reason the seller has a right to withhold or reclaim the goods." Subsection (3) of UCC 2–705 specifies certain limits on this right to stop. For example, the carrier is not obliged to obey any order to stop a shipment under an order bill until the document has been surrendered.

UCC 7–303(1) gives the carrier the authority but not the obligation to divert a shipment on instructions from:

(a) the holder of a negotiable bill; or

(b) the consignor on a non-negotiable bill notwithstanding contrary instructions from the consignee; or

(c) the consignee on a non-negotiable bill in the absence of contrary instructions from the consignor, if the goods have arrived at the billed destination or if the consignee is in possession of the bill; or

(d) the consignee on a non-negotiable bill if he is entitled as against the consignor to dispose of them.

Note well that the quoted section of the UCC states the law of *intra-state* shipment. Unless the courts adopt it as the federal common law, one must still search for that common law in the federal cases interpreting the Federal Bills of Lading Act in interstate shipments. Because case law is scarce and because the Code represents the current thinking of people who deal with bills of lading, one can hope that the federal courts will adopt the Code rules as the federal common law under the Bills of Lading Act where that Act does not speak explicitly.

CLOCK v. MISSOURI–KANSAS–TEXAS RAILROAD CO. v. CRAWFORD

United States District Court, Eastern District of Missouri, 1976.
407 F.Supp. 448.

OPINION

NANGLE, DISTRICT JUDGE.

Plaintiff Gerald Clock brought this action to recover the cost of goods which were allegedly converted by defendant Missouri-Kansas-Texas Railroad Company. By amended complaint, plaintiff added Stanley L. Crawford as defendant. Plaintiff also alleges that defendant Railroad breached its obligation to deliver the goods. Prior to the filing of plaintiff's amended complaint, defendant Railroad filed a third-party complaint against Crawford, alleging that if the Railroad should be liable to plaintiff, third-party defendant would be liable to the Railroad to the extent of the liability to plaintiff. Crawford now being a defendant in this action, defendant Railroad's complaint is in fact a cross-claim and will be treated as such.

This case was tried before the Court without a jury. The Court having considered the pleadings, the testimony of the witnesses, the documents in evidence, and being otherwise fully advised in the premises, hereby makes the following findings of fact and conclusions of law as required by Rule 52, Federal Rules of Civil Procedure:

FINDINGS OF FACT

1. Plaintiff, Gerald Clock, is, and was at all times relevant herein, a citizen of the State of Indiana. Defendant, Missouri-Kansas-Texas Railroad Company ("Railroad") is a corporation incorporated under the laws of the State of Delaware, having its principal place of business in Texas. Defendant Stanley L. Crawford, is, and was at all times relevant herein, a citizen of the State of Oklahoma.

2. On January 14, 1975, Crawford sold two carloads of bulk ammonium nitrate fertilizer to Buford Cunningham and received two checks in payment therefor. On the same date, the goods were placed in the care and custody of defendant Railroad for shipment from Oklahoma to Eaton Agricultural Center in Indiana. Defendant Railroad issued bills of lading to cover the goods. The bills of lading were signed by Crawford. Both bills of lading specify on the top of each that they are

UNIFORM STRAIGHT BILL OF LADING

ORIGINAL—NOT NEGOTIABLE

3. At the time of sale, Crawford knew that Cunningham was going to sell the goods to a third party. Soon after the sale to Cunningham, Cunningham did sell the goods to plaintiff for $30,195.12. At the time of this sale, plaintiff had no knowledge of any infirmities in title, or right to possession, by Cunningham.

4. On January 23, 1975, the bank notified Crawford that there were insufficient funds in Cunningham's account to cover the checks. Accordingly, they were returned to Crawford.

5. The goods were still in transit at this point. Crawford instructed the Railroad to hold the railroad cars containing the goods until further instructions from him. Defendant Railroad complied.

6. On February 3, 1975, Crawford certified to defendant Railroad that he was the true owner of the goods and he issued a reconsignment order on the goods, instructing that they be sent to Farmers Union Coop, instead of Eaton Agricultural Center. Defendant Railroad complied with these instructions.

7. Plaintiff furnished replacement goods to Eaton Agricultural Center of a like quantity and value, and acquired the right, title and interest of Eaton Agricultural Center to the goods, by reason of an assignment by Eaton Agricultural Center executed on February 10, 1975.

CONCLUSIONS OF LAW

This Court has jurisdiction over the subject matter and of the parties. 28 U.S.C. § 1332.

The bills of lading involved herein are straight bills of lading. 49 U.S.C. §§ 82, 86. It is clear that "[a] straight bill can not be negotiated free from existing equities * * *". 49 U.S.C. § 109. While not negotiable, straight bills are transferable. The transferee stands in the shoes of the transferor, acquiring no additional rights over those held by the transferor. See *Arizona Feed v. Southern Pacific Transportation Co.*, 21 Ariz.App. 346, 519 P.2d 199 (1974); *Southern Pacific Co. v. Agencia Joffroy, S.A.*, 65 Ariz. 65, 174 P.2d 278 (1946); *Quality Shingle Co. v. Old Oregon Lumber & Shingle Co.*, 110 Wash. 60, 187 P. 705 (1920); § 400.7–104, R.S.Mo. (1969).

A carrier may deliver goods to "[a] person lawfully entitled to the possession of the goods" or to the consignee. 49 U.S.C. § 89. The question for determination therefore is whether Crawford was lawfully entitled to possession of the goods. While it is true that title passes to a buyer when the seller completes his performance under the contract, § 400.2–401, R.S.Mo. (1969), it is equally true that

where the buyer * * * fails to make a payment due * * * the aggrieved seller may

(a) withhold delivery of such goods;

(b) stop delivery by any bailee ∗ ∗ ∗;

∗ ∗ ∗

(d) resell and recover damages ∗ ∗ ∗

∗ ∗ ∗

(f) cancel. § 400.2–703, R.S.Mo. (1969).

It is the Court's conclusion, therefore, that upon the failure of the checks presented by Cunningham to Crawford, Crawford was "lawfully entitled to the possession of the goods". Plaintiff, as transferee of a straight bill of lading, can not have any greater rights than did Cunningham, and can not have the status of a bona fide purchaser for value. Since Crawford was entitled to possession of the goods, defendant Railroad can not be liable for delivering the goods in accordance with Crawford's instructions. 49 U.S.C. § 89, *Turner Lumber & Investment Co. v. Chicago, R.I. & P. Ry. Co.*, 223 Mo.App. 564, 16 S.W.2d 705 (1929).

The applicable provisions of the Commercial Code provide that

(1) Unless the bill of lading otherwise provides, the carrier may deliver the goods to a person or destination other than that stated in the bill or may otherwise dispose of the goods on instructions from

(b) the consignor on a nonnegotiable bill notwithstanding contrary instructions from the consignee ∗ ∗ ∗ § 400.7–303, R.S. Mo. (1969).

Under the facts established herein, Crawford was the consignor, as Crawford was "the person from whom the goods have been received for shipment". § 400.7–102(c), R.S.Mo. (1969). Since the bills of lading were nonnegotiable, and defendant Railroad delivered the goods pursuant to the instructions of the consignor, there can be no liability. See Comments, § 400.7–303 and § 400.7–504(3), R.S.Mo. (1969).

Under 49 U.S.C. § 112, the authority of the shipper to stop shipment in transit and redirect it is well established. See *Weyerhaeuser Timber Co. v. First National Bank of Portland*, 150 Or. 172, 38 P.2d 48 (1934); *Cashmere Fruit Growers' Union v. Great Northern Railway Co.*, 149 Wash. 319, 270 P. 1038 (1928), *cert. denied*, 279 U.S. 851, 49 S.Ct. 347, 73 L.Ed. 994; *Quality Shingle Co. v. Old Oregon Lumber & Shingle Co.*, *supra*. The same right is recognized in the Commercial Code. See §§ 400.2–703 and 400.2–705. Accordingly there can be no recovery by plaintiff against Crawford.

Plaintiff has claimed that both the Railroad and Crawford converted the shipments in question to their own use. Conversion has been defined as " ∗ ∗ ∗ an *unauthorized* assumption and exercise of the right of ownership over the personal property of another to the exclusion of the owners' right". *Carson Union May Stern Co. v. Pennsylvania Railroad Co.*, 421 S.W.2d 540 (Mo.App.1967) [emphasis in the original]. Having concluded that Crawford was lawfully entitled to possession of the goods, it is clear that recovery for conversion will not lie.

The cases cited by plaintiff are inapposite as they involve a bona fide purchaser for value. Under the authority of 49 U.S.C. § 81 *et seq.,* there can not be such status where one is a transferee under a straight bill of lading. *North American Van Lines, Inc. v. Heller,* 371 F.2d 629 (5th Cir.1967) is equally unavailing since the Court concludes that Crawford was lawfully entitled to possession.

Accordingly, judgment will be for defendants Railroad and Crawford. Since plaintiff will not recover any damages from defendant Railroad, judgment will be for defendant Crawford on the Railroad's cross-claim.

Problem 10–4

Seller ships under a straight bill of lading and names buyer (in the same state) as consignee. The shipment is a full truckload of leather. On the day the shipment leaves the seller's city, seller receives a "Dun & Bradstreet" on buyer which shows that buyer's fortunes have gone into precipitous decline and that he may have become insolvent.

1. If he instructs truck company not to deliver goods to buyer, will it comply? If it refuses, does he have a cause of action against it? (UCC 7–303, 2–705)

2. If carrier does stop shipment, will seller be in breach of his contract with buyer? (UCC 2–705, 2–609)

3. Would it change your answer if buyer had already received his copy of the bill of lading and had transferred his interest in it and the goods to a third party by an assignment of that bill and had given notice of such transfer to the carrier? (UCC 7–504)

4. Would it make any difference that the shipment was under a negotiable bill of lading and the bill had been negotiated to the third party? (UCC 7–502, 2–705)

5. In this problem does UCC 2–705 enlarge seller's rights against buyer, his control of the goods, neither, or both?

6. If the buyer had not become insolvent and was not otherwise in breach of the contract and if seller ordered the truck company to return the shipment to him, do you think the company would have complied? Would it have had any liability to buyer for doing so?

SECTION 7. BAILEE'S NON–RECEIPT, MISDESCRIPTION OR THE LIKE—EFFECTS ON BUYERS, SELLERS AND FINANCERS

For a variety of reasons the carrier or other bailee may issue documents covering goods that it did not receive, or misdescribe the goods it did receive. As a result buyers or *financers* of buyers (or of sellers for that matter) may rely on the documents to their detriment. The relevant Code sections are UCC 7–203 & 7–301. Relevant sections of the Federal Bill of Lading Act (49 U.S.C.A.) provide:

§ 100. Loading by carrier; counting packages, etc.; contents of bill

When goods are loaded by a carrier, such carrier shall count the packages of goods if package freight, and ascertain the kind and quantity if bulk freight, and such carrier shall not, in such cases, insert in the bill of lading or in any notice, receipt, contract, rule, regulation, or tariff, "Shipper's weight, load, and count," or other words of like purport, indicating that the goods were loaded by the shipper and the description of them made by him, or in case of bulk freight and freight not concealed by packages the description made by him. If so inserted contrary to the provisions of this section, said words shall be treated as null and void and as if not inserted therein.

§ 101. Loading by shipper; contents of bill; ascertainment of kind and quantity on request

When package freight or bulk freight is loaded by a shipper and the goods are described in a bill of lading merely by a statement of marks or labels upon them or upon packages containing them, or by a statement that the goods are said to be goods of a certain kind or quantity or in a certain condition, or it is stated in the bill of lading that packages are said to contain goods of a certain kind or quantity or in a certain condition, or that the contents or condition of the contents of packages are unknown, or words of like purport are contained in the bill of lading, such statements, if true, shall not make liable the carrier issuing the bill of lading, although the goods are not of the kind or quantity or in the condition which the marks or labels upon them indicate, or of the kind or quantity or in the condition they were said to be by the consignor. The carrier may also by inserting in the bill of lading the words "Shipper's weight, load, and count," or other words of like purport, indicate that the goods were loaded by the shipper and the description of them made by him; and if such statement be true, the carrier shall not be liable for damages caused by the improper loading or by the nonreceipt or by the misdescription of the goods described in the bill of lading: *Provided, however,* Where the shipper of bulk freight installs and maintains adequate facilities for weighing such freight, and the same are available to the carrier, then the carrier, upon written request of such shipper and when given a reasonable opportunity so to do, shall ascertain the kind and quantity of bulk freight within a reasonable time after such written request, and the carriers shall not in such cases insert in the bill of lading the words "Shipper's weight," or other words of like purport, and if so inserted contrary to the provisions of this section, said words shall be treated as null and void and as if not inserted therein.

§ 102. *Liability for nonreceipt or misdescription of goods*

If a bill of lading has been issued by a carrier or on his behalf by an agent or employee the scope of whose actual or apparent authority includes the receiving of goods and issuing bills of lading therefor for transportation in commerce among the several States and with foreign nations, the carrier shall be liable to (a) the owner of goods covered by a straight bill subject to existing right of stoppage in transitu or (b) the holder of an order bill, who has given value in good faith, relying upon the description therein of the goods, or upon the shipment being made upon the date therein shown, for damages caused by the nonreceipt by the carrier of all or part of the goods upon or prior to the date therein shown, or their failure to correspond with the description thereof in the bill at the time of its issue.

G.A.C. COMMERCIAL CORP. v. WILSON

United States District Court, Southern District of New York, 1967.
271 F.Supp. 242.

BRYAN, DISTRICT JUDGE.

Plaintiff G.A.C. Commercial Corporation (G.A.C.), a Delaware corporation, brings this action sounding in fraud against the five individual defendants and in negligence against a New York corporation, Norwood & St. Lawrence Railroad Co. (Norwood), a rail carrier in interstate commerce. Defendant Norwood now moves, pursuant to Rule 12(c), F.R.Civ.P., for judgment on the pleadings dismissing the fourth count of the complaint. Since matters outside the pleadings have been presented and considered the motion will be treated as one for summary judgment under Rule 56, F.R.Civ.P.

The gravamen of the action is spelled out in the first three counts of the complaint, laid solely against the individual defendants. It is alleged that on October 17, 1963, plaintiff G.A.C. entered into an accounts receivable financing agreement with St. Lawrence Pulp & Paper Corp. (St. Lawrence), a New York corporation. Under the terms of the agreement G.A.C. was to make advances to St. Lawrence, which agreed to "pledge, assign and transfer to G.A.C. all the [b]orrower's right, title and interest in and to accounts receivable * * * then owing" to St. Lawrence.

Pursuant to the agreement St. Lawrence forwarded copies of its invoices together with copies of bills of lading to G.A.C., which, upon receipt, advanced the monies to St. Lawrence at the agreed discount. Repayment of the debts due was guaranteed in writing by the defendant Wilson who was a corporate officer of St. Lawrence. G.A.C. ultimately advanced $356,883.57 under the financing agreement, no part of which has been repaid. St. Lawrence is now a bankrupt.

The first claim for relief seeks recovery of the entire amount from the individual guarantor Wilson. The second claim alleges that certain of the accounts receivable forwarded to plaintiff were false and fraudulent, and that in reliance upon these accounts G.A.C. advanced the sum of $254,173.42 which has not been repaid. The individual defendants, who, with the exception of Lalvani, are described as officers and/or directors of St. Lawrence, are charged with knowledge that these accounts were false and fraudulent. The third claim simply adds a conspiracy allegation against the individual defendants describing a scheme to "defraud and deceive the plaintiff" by forwarding false and fraudulent accounts receivable.

This motion is addressed to the fourth claim for relief laid solely against Norwood. That claim alleges that the fraudulent accounts receivable described were "upon the form of bill of lading" of defendant Norwood "and were countersigned by its agent." Norwood is charged with negligence in failing to require any inspection of the quantity of goods shipped before verifying the bills of lading and in permitting a situation to occur in which the fraudulent and nonexistent accounts could be forwarded to G.A.C.

Norwood's answer alleges failure to state a claim on which relief can be granted and contributory negligence. By way of separate defense it denies any knowledge or information as to the falsity of the bills of lading or with respect to the financing agreement between St. Lawrence and G.A.C. The answer also alleges that the bills of lading involved are "uniform straight bill[s] of lading—not negotiable," as in fact they are, under Section 2 of the Federal Bills of Lading Act. 49 U.S.C.A. § 82.

The controversy here concerns 62 invoices and accompanying straight bills of lading forwarded to G.A.C. by St. Lawrence during 1964. Sixty of these bills concern interstate shipments of paper from St. Lawrence in Norfolk, New York, to Mohegan Converters in Hillside, New Jersey, and involve advances of $245,811.19. Each of the sixty interstate bills was on Norwood's bill of lading, and it is conceded for purposes of this motion, though denied in the answer, that the bills were signed by one of Norwood's agents.

The other two bills involve advances of $8,362.23 on two intrastate shipments from St. Lawrence to Norwood Converting, Inc. in Norfolk, New York, and to Board of Education Depository, Long Island City, New York, respectively. The bills of lading on these shipments were not on Norwood forms and were not signed by Norwood's agents. In fact there is no evidence that Norwood issued these bills or had anything to do with them.

The method by which the alleged fraudulent scheme was carried out appears for purposes of this motion to be as follows: the bankrupt St. Lawrence, as part of its facilities in Norfolk, New York, maintained a railroad siding connected with the lines of defendant carrier which had a freight office approximately ⅛th of a mile from the siding. St. Lawrence was permitted to load freight at its spur track in preparation for shipments on defendant's line. The railroad cars were sealed by St.

Lawrence with seals provided by the railroad. St. Lawrence also prepared the bills of lading on blanks furnished in quadruplicate by defendant Norwood. The bills thus prepared were then presented to Norwood's agent who signed the original and one copy without inspecting the contents of the cars. No notation such as "contents of packages unknown" or "shipper's weight, load and count" was written on the bills. The signed copies were returned to St. Lawrence and forwarded with the invoices to G.A.C. which made advances on the goods described, which, as it turned out, had not been shipped.

Since sixty of the bills of lading were issued by a common carrier for the transportation of goods in interstate commerce, the issues as to these bills are controlled by the provisions of the Federal Bills of Lading Act. 49 U.S.C.A. § 81. This statute stands as "a clear expression of the determination of Congress to take the whole subject matter of such bills of lading within its control." 2 Williston, Sales § 406a, at 535 (rev. ed. 1948); see Adams Express Co. v. Croninger, 226 U.S. 491, 33 S.Ct. 148, 57 L.Ed. 314 (1913). As such, it squarely bars the fourth claim asserted against defendant Norwood on the sixty bills representing interstate shipments.

Prior to the passage of the Federal Bills of Lading Act "the United States courts held that a carrier was not liable for the act of its agent in issuing a bill of lading for goods where no goods had in fact been received." Josephy v. Panhandle & S.F. Ry., 235 N.Y. 306, 310, 139 N.E. 277, 278 (1923); see, e.g., Clark v. Clyde S.S. Co., 148 F. 243 (S.D. N.Y.1906). The liability of carriers for acts of their agents was expanded, but not drastically, by the passage of the federal legislation which draws a sharp distinction between order bills of lading and straight bills where in fact the goods are never received for shipment by the carrier. Under § 22 of the Act, 49 U.S.C. § 102, "[i]f a bill of lading has been issued by a carrier or on his behalf by an agent or employee * * *, the carrier shall be liable to * * * the holder of an order bill, who has given value in good faith, relying upon the description therein of the goods, * * * for damages caused by the nonreceipt by the carrier of all or part of the goods upon or prior to the date therein shown." However, the liability of the carrier for nonreceipt extends only to "the owner of goods covered by a straight bill," [1] provided, of course, he also gives value in good faith in reliance upon the description

---

1. Section 22 of the Act, 49 U.S.C. § 102, in its complete form, reads as follows:

§ 102. Liability for nonreceipt or misdescription of goods

"If a bill of lading has been issued by a carrier or on his behalf by an agent or employee the scope of whose actual or apparent authority includes the receiving of goods and issuing bills of lading therefor for transportation in commerce among the several States and with foreign nations, the carrier shall be liable to (a) the owner of goods covered by a straight bill subject to existing right of stoppage in transitu or (b) the holder of an order bill, who has given value in good faith, relying upon the description therein of the goods, or upon the shipment being made upon the date therein shown, for damages caused by the nonreceipt by the carrier of all or part of the goods upon or prior to the date therein shown, or their failure to correspond with the description thereof in the bill at the time of its issue."

of goods contained in the bill. See Strohmeyer & Arpe Co. v. American Line S.S. Corp., 97 F.2d 360, 362 (2d Cir.1938).

It is clear that a party in the position of Norwood is not included within the narrow category of those liable on a straight bill under the federal legislation. In the first place there is no question that the straight bills of lading here involved are nonnegotiable. * * * As a consequence plaintiff G.A.C., as apparent transferee of these bills and invoices representing accounts receivable under the agreement with St. Lawrence, upon notification to the carrier of the transfer,[2] could only "become the direct obligee of whatever obligations the carrier owed to the transferor of the bill immediately before the notification." 49 U.S. C.A. § 112; see id. § 109. Norwood obviously owed St. Lawrence nothing because no goods in fact were received. There was therefore no outstanding obligation to G.A.C. * * *

By no stretch of the imagination does G.A.C. qualify as an "owner of goods covered by a straight bill" who can sue the carrier under § 22 of the Federal Bills of Lading Act, 49 U.S.C.A. § 102, for representing that goods in fact had been received. The reason for this is that it is completely illusory to attempt to assign an "owner" to non-existent goods. R. Braucher, Documents of Title 23 (1958); 2 S. Williston, Sales § 419a, at 576–77 (rev. ed. 1948). While the consignee is generally deemed to have title to goods shipped under a straight bill of lading, see George F. Hinrichs, Inc. v. Standard Trust & Sav. Bank, 279 F. 382, 386 (2d Cir.1922), even he cannot sue the carrier for representing in a straight bill that non-existent goods had in fact been received. Martin Jessee Motors v. Reading Co., 87 F.Supp. 318 (E.D.Pa.), aff'd, 181 F.2d 766 (3d Cir.1950). The rationale applied in Martin Jessee Motors—that the consignee can prevail against the carrier "only by proving its title to specific property," 181 F.2d at 767—applies a fortiori to bar the claim of G.A.C. Plaintiff's interest in the "aggregate face value of the accounts receivable pledged as security" [3] under no conceivable reading of the statute can be deemed an "[ownership] of goods covered by a straight bill." G.A.C. is not one of the favored few who can recover under the Federal Bills of Lading Act. * * *

Plaintiff G.A.C. fares no better with respect to the two bills of lading representing intrastate shipments in New York. Of decisive importance, of course, are the facts that these shipments were not on Norwood forms and were not signed by Norwood's agents. Even if they were, the carrier would escape liability. Although the awkward term "owner" in 49 U.S.C.A. § 102 has been replaced by the word "consignee" in the Uniform Commercial Code § 7–301 and the Uniform Bills of Lading Act § 23, each of which would govern the issues of liability on one of the bills of lading representing an intrastate shipment,[4] the

2. The defendant Norwood apparently first received notice from G.A.C. by letter dated February 16, 1965. See Def.Ex.B.

3. Accounts Receivable Agreement Between St. Lawrence and G.A.C., Oct. 17, 1963, ¶ 3.

4. One of the bills is dated September 24, 1964; the other is dated September 28,

change is immaterial for purposes of this case. Plaintiff, perhaps an assignee, transferee or pledgee of the non-negotiable bills, though it claims not to be, is certainly not a "consignee," which is the only party protected. 2 Anderson, Uniform Commercial Code 261 n. 9 (1961); see R. Braucher, Documents of Title 23–24 (1958). Contrast U.C.C. § 7–203. Thus, as with the sixty interstate bills, G.A.C. cannot successfully sue on the two intrastate bills.

G.A.C. cannot avoid the results dictated by the statute by casting its claim for relief in terms of common law negligence. G.A.C. was sent sixty straight interstate bills of lading by St. Lawrence. The alleged negligence consists of Norwood's permitting a situation to develop in which St. Lawrence could make untrue representations that goods had in fact been shipped under the straight bills. G.A.C. claims that it relied to its detriment upon certain statements contained in the bills. The action is based on the bills not on Norwood's negligence. * * * A holding to the contrary would permit any party to circumvent the restrictions of the Federal Bills of Lading Act through the insertion of a talismanic characterization of its claim as one for "negligence." It is quite plain, however, that the declaration in 49 U.S.C.A. § 81—"bills of lading issued by any common carrier for the transportation of goods" between the states "shall be governed by this chapter"—must be taken to preclude alternative and supplementary liability under state law. * * * The substance of the rule cannot be avoided by the form of the complaint.

* * *

It is true that the result dictated by the federal legislation may lead to some inequities. A straight bill under the Federal Bills of Lading Act is obviously not a good security risk. Casenote, 63 Harv.L. Rev. 1439, 1440 (1950). The fraud of the shipper by failing to deliver goods to the carrier can result, as it did here, in misleading statements on the bills of lading, which operate to the detriment of banks and other commercial financers making advances on the basis of the bills. See Olivier Straw Goods Corp. v. Osaka Shosen Kaisha, 27 F.2d 129, 134 (2d Cir.1928) (A. Hand, J.). Moreover, the carrier can readily prevent such a situation from arising by inserting "in the bill of lading the words, 'Shipper's weight, load, and count,' or other words of like purport" to "indicate that the goods were loaded by the shipper and the description of them made by him." 49 U.S.C.A. § 101.

But the overriding policy considerations in the Act look the other way on the issue of liability. First, "[t]here is nothing in the statute to indicate that the mere omission of the words 'Shipper's weight, load, and count' in and of itself makes the carrier liable for damages to goods improperly loaded. The omission of the statutory words merely serves to shift upon the carrier the burden of proving that the goods were improperly loaded by the shipper, and that the damage ensued from

1964. In New York the Uniform Commercial Code superseded the Uniform Bills of Lading Act on September 27, 1964.

that cause." Modern Tool Corp. v. Pennsylvania R. Co., 100 F.Supp. 595, 596–597 (D.N.J.1951); see U.C.C. § 7–301(4). According to the allegations the true culprits in this case were the shipper and its agents; there is no reason to saddle defendant Norwood with liability simply because it did not insert the "Shipper's weight, load, and count" language in the bills. In addition, practicality demands loading arrangements such as those here, where the shipper places his goods aboard and seals the railroad car which the carrier has provided. Section 21 of the Act, 49 U.S.C.A. § 101, anticipates that shippers are expected to do much of the counting and loading on their own sidings or spur tracks. The rapid flow of commerce might well be hindered if the carrier in every instance were charged with ascertaining whether in fact there were goods behind every one of its straight bills.

Moreover, denying security value to a straight bill of lading does not work a hardship upon banks and other commercial institutions. G.A.C., as a knowledgeable lender, is fully aware of the risks inherent in straight bills, and could well have required order bills to protect itself. See Chicago & Northwestern Ry. v. Stevens Nat'l Bank, 75 F.2d 398 (8th Cir.1935). It nevertheless chose to rely upon straight bills to lend money to the now bankrupt St. Lawrence at a profitable rate of interest. Wiser now, G.A.C. seeks to shift its loss to Norwood, an undoubtedly solvent defendant. The Federal Bills of Lading Act protects against this type of hindsight by requiring the lender to accept this kind of security subject to the defenses between the carrier and the shipper.

The motion of defendant Norwood for judgment on the pleadings treated as a motion for summary judgment is granted.

It is so ordered.

Notes

Seller delivered 61 bales of an inferior cotton known as "grabbots" to Carrier for shipment to Buyer. Carriers agent, knowing it to be false, issued a negotiable bill of lading to the Seller's order which described the goods as "61 bales of cotton." In the trade, this description meant "merchantable lint cotton," not "grabbots," an inferior grade. As was customary, Seller indorsed the bill of lading to Buyer, drew a draft on buyer for the purchase price, $3,965, and sent the documents through banking channels to the Buyer. Buyer paid the draft before the goods arrived. After delivery, the goods were stored in a warehouse and, later, destroyed by fire. Buyer sued Carrier for the difference between the amount of the draft paid and the value of the "grabbots", some $2,953, on the theory that the Carrier failed to use ordinary care in issuing the bill of lading. *Held,* for Buyer. The goods were misdescribed and Carrier's agent had notice of this and that the buyer might rely in good faith on that description in paying the sight draft. It was negligence for Carrier to issue the bill of lading without an appropriate qualification under these circumstances. Chicago, R.I. & P.R. Co. v. Cleveland, 61 Okl. 64, 160 P. 328 (1916).

SECTION 8. SALE OF GOODS LOCATED IN A WAREHOUSE— AN ADDENDUM

Sellers not uncommonly sell goods already stored in a warehouse. Since goods in a warehouse are not in motion and are not necessarily the subject of an executory sale transaction, the problems of control over goods in the hands of warehousemen are not as severe as those encountered with goods in the hands of the carrier. UCC 7–403(1) tells us that unless the bailee establishes one of the several defenses there described, the warehouseman is obliged to deliver the goods to "a person entitled under the document." A "person entitled" is defined by subsection (4) as follows: "[The] holder in the case of a negotiable document, or the person to whom delivery is to be made by the terms of or pursuant to written instructions under a non-negotiable document." Moreover UCC 7–403(3) instructs "the bailee [to] cancel the document or conspicuously note the partial delivery thereon or be liable to any person to whom the document is duly negotiated."

Thus the holder of a negotiable document and at least the first possessor-bailor on a non-negotiable document control the goods. The upshot of these rules is that the warehouseman with any sense will demand to see a negotiable warehouse receipt and make a notation on it before he will make any delivery under that warehouse receipt. However he will honor delivery orders signed by the person whom he believes to be the owner of a non-negotiable document without demanding the production of that document. One can easily see the potential for fraud if the owner of a non-negotiable warehouse receipt transfers it to one party and thereafter issues a delivery order to a second party. Presumably each of these acts constitutes "written instructions under a non-negotiable document." In this connection consider the following problem:

Problem 10–5

Repeunzel has 10,000 cans of beans. He puts them in a warehouse and receives a non-negotiable warehouse receipt. On December 1 he transfers his interest in the non-negotiable warehouse receipt together with possession of that receipt to Cicero. On December 3 he signs a non-negotiable delivery order instructing the warehouseman to deliver all of the beans to Leroy. On December 5 Leroy presents his delivery order and takes the beans. On December 10 Cicero comes to you for advice about his rights against the warehouseman. What are his rights? You may assume that everyone except for Repeunzel gave value and acted in good faith. See UCC 7–403, 7–503, 7–504, 7–402, 7–404.

Part Five

THE RECEIPT-INSPECTION STAGE

Chapter Eleven

THE BUYER'S RIGHTS TO INSPECT, TO REJECT, OR TO REVOKE ACCEPTANCE OF THE GOODS

SECTION 1. IMPORTANCE TO BUYER OF DISCOVERING NON-CONFORMITY PRIOR TO ACCEPTANCE OR PAYMENT

It is at the "receipt-inspection" stage that the buyer typically has his first opportunity to determine whether the seller's performance conforms to the contract. The seller's failure to perform may take a variety of forms, including breach of delivery obligations (UCC 2–301, 2–307, 2–308, 2–507(1), 2–503, 2–504 & 2–505), failure to perform on time (UCC 2–309), delivery of less than the contract quantity, and, perhaps most important in the usual transaction, non-compliance with contract requirements as to quality of goods sold (UCC 2–313, 314 & 315). Many non-conformities will be readily discoverable ("patent"); others will be harder to discover ("latent"). For non-conformity discovered at the receipt-inspection stage, the buyer *may*, depending upon the circumstances, have a choice between (1) such "goods-oriented" remedies as "rejection" (UCC 2–601) and revocation of acceptance (UCC 2–608), and (2) "damages-oriented" remedies (UCC 2–713 and 2–714). And the buyer may be able, in the circumstances, to combine these remedies, e.g., throw the goods back at the seller and also seek damages. See UCC 2–711(1).

383

Why might it be important for the buyer to discover non-conformity and reject the goods prior to accepting or paying for them? We will consider sales on credit first, for they are more usual. Although such a buyer need not worry about being out the price before he finds a defect, he may wish to avoid costly unloading and storage of bulky goods. And he should be concerned to identify any non-conformity at least in advance of "acceptance" (UCC 2–606). Absent this, acceptance imposes a duty on the buyer to pay, UCC 2–607(1), and buyers do not want to pay for significantly non-conforming goods. Moreover, acceptance precludes *rejection* of the goods. UCC 2–607(2) and 2–601. But it is true that this does necessarily mean the buyer will be unable rightfully to throw the goods back at the seller. Even after acceptance, should the non-conformity then be discovered, the buyer may be able to revoke his acceptance under UCC 2–608. But we will see that it is harder to throw goods back at a seller under UCC 2–608 than it is under UCC 2–601. Finally, the burden of establishing breach with regard to accepted goods is on the buyer. UCC 2–607(4). Thus it remains true that so far as goods-oriented remedies are concerned the buyer will be best off if he discovers non-conformity prior to acceptance and rejects. But if the buyer either discovers a defect and rejects or later revokes acceptance, the buyer will in both instances escape the bargain (which may in itself be highly advantageous), and also shift any resulting loss due to depreciation back on the seller.

SECTION 2. BUYER'S RIGHT TO "INSPECT" BEFORE ACCEPTANCE OR PAYMENT—GENERAL RULES AND EXCEPTIONS

The general rule is that the buyer has a right to inspect the goods before payment or acceptance, and this is true even in deals in which the seller discharges his delivery obligations at the point of shipment, e.g. "F.O.B. point of origin." UCC 2–513 and 2–310. Note, too, that this rule applies to cash on the barrelhead deals.

What of exceptions? First of all, the buyer can, of course, by contract, agree in so many words to give up the right to inspect prior to acceptance or payment. Second (and this frequently confuses students) the buyer can give up the right of prior inspection before payment by agreeing to a *mode* of payment inconsistent with such a right. For examples see UCC 2–513(3)(a) and (b). For exceptions to this exception, see the "except" clause in UCC 2–513(3)(b) and 2–512(1)(a). Note, too, that payment in a deal calling for payment before inspection does not constitute acceptance. UCC 2–512(2).

A. The General Right to Inspect

Problem 11–1 skip

Suppose that student A, who was on the law review and actually attended class, agreed to sell his notes from the course on Commercial Transactions to student B for $100. The agreement was made on January

20 and A was to deliver the notes on February 1 at the law school. On February 1, A and B met to complete the exchange. A had placed the notes in a green canvas bag. Displaying the bag, A said to B: "Here are the notes. May I please have the $100." B refused to pay until he had a chance to inspect the contents of the bag. A refused either to untie the string around or relinquish possession of the bag. When the impasse could not be broken, A stated to B that the "deal was off." Later that afternoon A sold the notes to student C for $150. What is the legal position of A and B under the UCC?

Do you agree with the following analysis?

The basic question is whether B had a duty to accept and pay for the notes at the time when A cancelled the contract. UCC 2–301. At first blush, this seems to turn on whether A has tendered delivery of the goods. If tender has been made, A is entitled to "acceptance of the goods and to payment according to the contract" under UCC 2–507(1) and a tender of payment by B is a condition to A's "duty to tender and complete any delivery." UCC 2–511(1). If the contract requires A to tender delivery at a particular place, i.e., the law school, the tender must meet the standards of UCC 2–503(1). Has it done so here? The answer is that no matter how closely A's conduct matches the language of UCC 2–503(1), B's duty to tender payment or be in breach of the contract has not yet arisen. On the facts of this case, B "has a right before payment or acceptance to inspect" the goods. UCC 2–513(1). By refusing to grant this "right," A has "impaired" his tender of delivery. UCC 2–503, comment 2. Cf. UCC 2–311(3). At the very least, B is excused from any contractual duty to pay the price. See Consolidated Boiler Corp. v. Bogue Electric Co., 141 N.J. Equity 550, 561–64, 58 A.2d 759, 766–68 (1948). In addition, A's unjustified cancellation is a repudiation which entitles B to the appropriate remedies specified in UCC 2–711.

B. Inspection in Documentary Deals

Documentary sales were studied in Chapter Ten. Here we *focus* on their possible impact on the buyer's inspection rights.

Problem 11–2

Maple Woods, Inc., a manufacturer, agreed to sell 10 dining room sets to Rosen's Furniture, a retail business located 1,000 miles away in the city of Baker.

(1) If the contract said nothing of mode of payment or inspection, but Maple Woods, worried about Rosen's credit, shipped the goods "under reservation" by procuring a non-negotiable bill of lading naming itself as consignee, UCC 2–505(1)(b), would this be a breach of contract? Would it "alter" Rosen's right to inspect? UCC 2–310(b) and 2–513(1) and (3). What if Maple Woods shipped C.O.D.? Would the carrier allow inspection before payment? Are there two contracts here: one between Maple Woods and the carrier, and one between Maple Woods and Rosen's?

(2) If the contract called for Rosen's to pay against a sight draft with bill of lading (negotiable) attached, would Rosen's be entitled to inspect before payment? Would it make any difference that the goods happened to arrive in Baker ahead of the documents? UCC 2–513 and Comment 5.

(3) If the documents were in due form but the goods had been destroyed by fire while in the carrier's possession and Rosen's knew this, could it dishonor the sight draft without breaching the contract?

In Chapter Ten we saw that the seller realizes several advantages via use of the "sight draft with negotiable bill of lading" technique. Can he retain any of these and still allow inspection before payment? Buyers can bargain to have seller stamp the bill of lading, even a negotiable one "inspection allowed." Here the carrier would still retain control on behalf of the shipper-seller. Another way the buyer might try to protect himself is via so-called "third-party inspection", which is the subject of the next case.

BARTLETT & CO., GRAIN v. MERCHANTS CO.

United States Court of Appeals, Fifth Circuit, 1963.
323 F.2d 501, 7 A.L.R.3d 541.

WISDOM, CIRCUIT JUDGE.

This action is for breach of contract. The subject of the contract is a barge load of corn which, according to official inspection certificates, was one grade when shipped and two very different grades when it reached its destination. As we see it, the case turns on the construction of a contract which contains two apparently inconsistent provisions. The overall issue is whether the loss should fall on the purchaser or the seller. The district court decided in favor of the buyer. We reverse and remand.

The Merchants Company, and buyer and appellee, is a Mississippi corporation. As the Vicksburg Terminal Division, it is in the business of buying and selling grains. As the Valley Mills Division it manufactures feeds. Bartlett and Company, the seller and appellant, is a Missouri Corporation which maintains grain storage facilities in six mid-western states, including terminal elevators on the Missouri River at Nebraska City, Nebraska. Its general offices are in Kansas City, Missouri.

Merchants contracted through a broker to purchase from Bartlett four barge loads of No. 2 yellow corn. The terms and conditions of sale are found in three documents: (1) a confirmation order from Bartlett to Valley Mills (Merchants); (2) a confirmation order from the broker to both parties; and (3) a confirmation of purchase from Valley Mills (Merchants), signed "accepted" by B.O. Cottier, Bartlett's official secretary in charge of merchandising. The contract called for four barges of No. 2 yellow corn at 5¼ cents under the Chicago July option, F.O.B. the buyer's barges, "*If seller elects to load at Nebraska City 'In Barge' Official Weights & Grades to Govern.*" Merchant's confirmation order, accepted by Bartlett's representative, contained the following clause: "Mark bills of lading 'inspection allowed'. If draft is paid at sight, *we do not waive our right to reject shipment in event quality proves to be below contract grade.*"

Bartlett loaded four double-skin barges, furnished by the buyer, at Nebraska City, Nebraska, on June 19, 1959. The grain in only one of these barges, ABL–2519, is involved in this dispute. That barge was examined at Nebraska City by a federally licensed grain inspector, who, on the date the loading was completed, certified that the barge contained No. 2 yellow corn. Meanwhile, since Merchants had sold four barges of No. 2 yellow corn to O.J. Walls in Guntersville, Alabama, Merchants routed the barges to Guntersville and applied the grain in barge ABL–2519 on the Walls contract. While the barge was in transit from Nebraska City to Guntersville, Merchants paid Bartlett for the grain by draft with the bill of lading attached.

The grain arrived in Guntersville on July 7, Walls first discovered it to be partly "overheating and musty" on July 13. He refused to accept it, since it was below contract grade, and he called for a federal appeal grade inspection. At this inspection, on July 16, 1959, it was certified that approximately 17,000 bushels of the corn in barge ABL–2519 were No. 1 yellow corn and approximately 15,000 bushels were sample grade yellow corn. Walls agreed to handle the barge for Merchants's account and accordingly unloaded, trucked, dried, turned, stored, and again trucked the grain. For these services he charged $7,164.61 and deducted that amount from Merchants's invoice. Both parties to this action agree that these charges were excessive, but Merchants contends that no one else was available to perform the services.

Merchants then sued Bartlett, seeking $7,164.61 for breach of contract and $5,000 in punitive damages. The suit was originally brought in a Mississippi state court as an attachment in chancery (a quasi-in rem action) by attaching Bartlett's deposits in a Mississippi bank. The suit was removed to the United States District Court for the Southern District of Mississippi where it was tried before the court without a jury. The district court found that the grain inspection certificate of June 19, 1959, at Nebraska City "was erroneous and inaccurate"; that it was "not fair * * * and failed to reveal the true condition in this barge on the date of shipment."

The district court found that an inescapable inference from the evidence * * * [is] that barge was loaded in Nebraska City with an excessive amount of molded wheat which contaminated the cargo and accounted for the unsalable condition at Guntersville." The court held that Merchants was not bound by the certificate's recitals, because of the clause in Merchants's purchase confirmation, accepted by Bartlett, giving the buyer the right to reject shipment in the event that the quality proved to be below contract grade. The court awarded damages in the amount of $6,500 with six per cent interest from July 3, 1959, against the funds in the hands of the resident bank. The suit was dismissed as to Bartlett personally for lack of in personam jurisdiction. The court declined to award punitive damages, since the court found no evidence of gross negligence, willfulness, or oppressiveness on the part of the seller.

On appeal, Bartlett makes two major contentions. First, Bartlett contends that there is no evidence the grain in barge ABL–2519 was other than No. 2 yellow corn when it left Nebraska City in the buyer's barge. Second, the official grade certificate at origin should have been conclusive under the terms of the sale agreement, in the absence of gross neglect or willful wrongdoing.

[The Court determined that the law of Missouri governed.]

* * *

I. THE BUYER'S RIGHT TO INSPECT

A buyer dealing with a distant vendor and purchasing goods of a specified quality without first seeing them has a right to inspect them upon receipt. * * * And, in the absence of any contractual provision to the contrary, the buyer may reject an F.O.B. shipment at destination. * * * But the parties may agree instead to abide by the judgment of another, and that judgment, if honestly exercised, is binding on the buyer. * * * The buyer cannot thereafter substitute his own inspection for that conducted by the third party.

* * *

Such an inspection is held to have a conclusive effect even if there is no express provision in the contract that it shall be final. * * *

The contract in question here provides that " 'in barge' official weights & grades" are to govern—if the shipment is made from Nebraska City. But—if the shipment is made from Omaha, although "official in 'in barge' grades" still govern, "*destination official weights*" are to govern. Thus, the contract is drawn to distinguish between an inspection where the grain is loaded and an inspection at its destination. An inspection at the destination is to determine the *weight,* if the grain is loaded at Omaha. That is the only circumstance in which a destination inspection is to control. The terms of the contract therefore required that the transaction be governed by the origin *grades and weights,* since the grain was shipped from Nebraska City.

As we noted, where an inspection by a third party is stipulated, it supersedes the buyer's right to inspect. Merchants, however, seeks to avoid this result by urging that the clause in its printed form contract, which was accepted by Bartlett's agent, gave it the right to inspect at destination and to reject the shipment if the *quality* proved to be below the specified grade at the destination. This interpretation of the contract would nullify the provision for inspection at origin. The obvious purpose of that inspection at origin was to establish a certain, reliable, and objective standard at a fixed place and time to give the transaction certainty. It would serve little use to have this inspection if the buyer were free to accept or reject the shipment after its arrival on the basis of its own inspection at destination. To the extent then that the *printed* clause in the contract may be interpreted to allow Merchants the right, for which it contends, to reject on the basis of its own destination inspection, it is inconsistent with the *typewritten* clause providing for one official inspection at origin. In such case the typed portions prevail. * * *

The contract before us, however, may be construed so as to reconcile the two clauses and thus satisfy the very sensible canon of construction requiring that effect be given to all terms of the contract. The typed clause provides that official grades are to govern, whereas the printed clause, upon which Merchants relies, reserves to it the "right to reject shipment *in event* quality proves to be below contract grade." (Emphasis supplied.) This gives Merchants the right to reject, *if* the quality does not satisfy the contractual requirements; it does not give Merchants the right to determine *whether* the quality measures up to the standard specified. Thus Merchants could reject the grain, if the grade given it by the Nebraska City inspector proved to be lower than that specified in the contract, but the reservation clause does not give it the power to ascertain the grade independently of the origin inspection. Furthermore, this reserved right to reject is expressly conditioned on the draft being paid at sight. Since it is possible that the draft would be paid before receipt of the inspection certificate, this is a reasonable provision. It simply avoids any question that payment of the sight draft might be deemed a waiver of the right to reject the shipment. See Ryder & Brown Co. v. E. Lissberger Co., 1938, 300 Mass. 438, 15 N.E.2d 441, 118 A.L.R. 521, 525–526, in which the court assumed that the right to reject is lost when the title passes to the buyer on payment of a sight draft.

The testimony of Merchants's agent shows that in the customary dealings in the trade lower prices are fixed on condition that there is no right to reject on the basis of a destination inspection when the grain is inspected at origin. Mr. Harriss, Merchants's manager, agreed that Mr. Walls, who received the shipment in Alabama and bought on the same terms as Merchants, had no right to inspect the shipment at Guntersville. Moreover, the broker testified that his confirmation order showed the entire arrangement between the two parties; that it contained no right to reject. We hold, therefore, that Merchants did not have any right to reject the shipment destination on the basis of inspection at destination. * * *

[The Court reversed the Judgment of the district court and remanded the case for the trial court to ascertain whether there existed fraud, bad faith, or gross mistake amounting to fraud which would warrant setting the inspection certificate aside.]

Notes

1. Considering the legal effect of third-party inspection, what commercial interests of either seller or buyer are protected by establishing such procedures and insuring their finality? Is UCC 2–515 relevant to this problem?

2. If the buyer has paid before inspecting the goods and, after discovering a non-conformity when the goods arrive, brings suit to recover the price and damages for breach of warranty, who has the burden of proving the condition of the goods at the time loaded on the barges, the buyer-plaintiff or the seller-defendant? Suppose the goods have been totally destroyed in transit without the fault of the buyer, who thereafter claims that they did not conform at the time of tender by the seller. Under the UCC, the critical time is at "tender of delivery." UCC 2–725(2), 2–503(2), 2–504, 2–509(1), and UCC 2–510(1). While UCC 2–607(4) provides that the "burden is on the buyer to establish any breach with respect to the goods accepted," there is no specific allocation for other situations. Under the Uniform Sales Act, the principal antecedent of Article Two, the burden was placed upon the party seeking affirmative relief here, the buyer. Glanzer v. J.K. Armsby Co., 100 Misc. 476, 165 N.Y.S. 1006 (S.Ct.1917). This result has been criticized in cases where the goods have been lost in transit: "In the situation where the goods are completely destroyed while in transit, the seller alone will know the facts about conformity. Where the seller delivers the goods which do not conform to the contract and the buyer has not impliedly approved them by acceptance, the seller by virtue of experience in fulfilling the terms of the contract will be better able to sustain the burden of proof in an action for non-delivery. But where the buyer has refused to accept the goods and has sold them justifiably on behalf of the seller, the facts on conformity are then peculiarly within the knowledge of the buyer." Note, 20 U.Chi.L.Rev. 125, 130 (1952). Do you agree? Should the concern over proper burden of proof allocation be influenced by the feasibility and availability of third-party inspection at the point of shipment as with many agricultural commodities? See S–Creek Ranch, Inc. v. Monier & Co., 509 P.2d 777 (Wyo.1973) (buyer must prove goods defective at time risk of loss was to pass).

C. Inspection in Overseas Transactions

This chapter has focused upon the relationship between the buyer's "right" of inspection and his "duty" to accept the goods and pay the contract price. In non-credit domestic transactions under the UCC where a shipment is under an f.o.b. term, the buyer has no right to inspect before payment unless otherwise agreed where the contract calls for payment against documents of title. UCC 2–513(3). The reverse is true in overseas sales where greater shipping distances delay even more the seller's ability to receive payment. Accordingly, the usual practice, reflected in the cases and the Revised American Foreign Trade Definitions of 1941, is that unless otherwise agreed the buyer must pay against documents of title even though the goods are still in the middle of the ocean. See E. Clemens Horst Co. v. Biddel Bros., (1912) A.C. 18. While the buyer must wait until the goods arrive to inspect, he can discount the documents of title or use them as collateral to obtain a loan if the delay puts him under a financial strain. This approach is reflected in the UCC when shipment, whether domestic or overseas, is on a C.I.F. or C & F basis. The UCC seems to rely upon use of the shipping term C.I.F. or C & F to establish the seller's right to payment and does not clearly state whether the usual practice would apply in an overseas sale under a different shipping term. See UCC 2–320(4) and 2–321(3). The Final Act of the United Nations Conference on Contracts for the International Sale of Goods, approved in Vienna in 1980, provides that the buyer is "not bound to pay the price until he has had an opportunity to examine the goods, unless procedures for delivery or payment agreed upon by the parties are inconsistent with his having such an opportunity." Article 58(3). But Article 58(2) states that if the contract involves "carriage of the goods, the seller may dispatch the goods on terms whereby the goods, or documents controlling their disposition, will not be handed over to the buyer except against payment of the price." These and other issues are well treated in J. Honnold, Uniform Law for International Sales 333–39 (1982). The United States Senate ratified the United Nations Convention on Contracts for the International Sale of Goods on December 11, 1986. The treaty becomes effective on January 1, 1988.

A common practice in international sales, however, is for the seller to obtain payment contemporaneously with shipment of the goods. This is accomplished through a letter of credit. In essence, the buyer (customer) obtains from a bank (issuer) a promise for the benefit of the seller (beneficiary) that it will honor a draft drawn on it upon presentation of required documents and compliance with other terms in the letter of credit, which has been sent to the seller. See UCC 5–102(1)(a) and 5–103(1). This is a "documentary" credit which is normally irrevocable. See UCC 5–106(2). Thus, the issuing bank on behalf of the buyer agrees to pay the price against documents presented by the seller shortly after those documents have been issued by the carrier, and usually at the place where the goods have been shipped. While this device does not preclude the buyer's right of inspection when the goods arrive, UCC 5–114(1) provides that the issuing bank cannot dishonor the seller's demand which complies with the credit even though the goods or the documents do not conform with the underlying contract for sale. Compare UCC 2–512. An important case testing the scope of inspection in a transaction using a letter of credit is Banco Espanol de Credito v. State Street Bank & T. Co., 385 F.2d 230 (1st Cir.1967).

SECTION 3. BUYER'S RIGHT TO REJECT THE GOODS

A. Introduction: Rejection Under Pre-Code Law

If a promisor's tendered performance conforms in every way to the contract, the buyer must accept and pay for it or break the contract. UCC 2–507(1). Conversely, if the promisor repudiates the contract or fails to tender any performance at all, the promisee is excused from rendering any return performance and, since the promisor's breach is material, may cancel the contract and pursue appropriate remedies. But suppose that the promisor tenders some but not all of the promised performance and then fails to complete the job. Under what circumstances can the promisee seize upon the defective performance as a ground for avoiding any contractual duty to pay for work actually done?

In construction and personal service contracts where, in the absence of agreement to the contrary, the duty to pay is "constructively" conditioned upon completion of all or part of the work, it is usually said that the constructive condition is satisfied by "substantial" performance. See Patterson, *Constructive Conditions in Contracts,* 42 Colum.L. Rev. 903 (1942). Stated another way, if the promisor's defective performance is not material, the promisee must pay for the work at the contract price, adjusted for any damages caused by the breach. Who can forget Judge Cardozo's "sermon" in the classic case of Jacob & Youngs v. Kent, 230 N.Y. 239, 129 N.E. 889 (1921): "The transgressor whose default is unintentional and trivial may hope for mercy if he will offer atonement for his wrong." Since the promisor has rendered an expensive performance which, in many cases, has conferred benefits upon the promisee and is extremely difficult to return, the substantial performance doctrine blunts the rigors of constructive conditions by limiting the promisee's ability to avoid liability under the contract. According to Restatement, Contracts § 275 (1932) and Restatement (Second) of Contracts § 241, whether the promisee can treat the non-performance as material will depend upon several factors: the extent to which the injured party will obtain the substantial benefits which he could reasonably have anticipated; the extent to which the injured party may be adequately compensated in damages for lack of complete performance; the greater or less hardship on the party failing to perform in terminating the contract; the willful, negligent, or innocent behavior of the party failing to perform, and the greater or less uncertainty that the party failing to perform will perform the remainder of the contract. In short, the question is whether the non-performance substantially impairs the value of the bargain to the promisee. If more than substantial performance is desired, the services of an architect or third party expert can be employed. His refusal to issue a certificate or give approval until the specifications are met expressly conditions the promisee's duty to pay and is final and conclusive unless fraudulent or made in bad faith. See Restatement (Second) of Contracts § 227, Ill. No. 5.

In contracts for the sale of goods, however, pre-code law generally held that the doctrine of "substantial" performance is not applicable. See J.W. Anderson & Co., Inc. v. Tomlinson Chair Mfg. Co., Inc., 206 N.C. 42, 172 S.E. 538 (1934); Note, 33 Colum.L.Rev. 1021 (1933). This position can be justified on the following grounds. When a buyer rejects a defective tender by a seller, he does not retain any of the goods without payment. Even though the seller has invested time and expense in obtaining the goods and preparing the tender, upon rejection he still has the goods and may dispose of them elsewhere. Since the element of unjust enrichment present in construction and various other contracts is absent in such a sale of goods case, it makes some sense to put the responsibility for making a perfect tender upon the seller rather than getting involved in a complicated evaluation of objective and subjective factors which underlie the substantial performance doctrine. At the very least if the seller has in fact made a defective tender and the buyer's dissatisfaction is honest and genuine, there seems to be less reason for invoking the doctrine of substantial performance to limit the power to reject.

This justification was reflected, to a large degree, in the Uniform Sales Act, especially where the seller had breached a warranty of quality, USA §§ 12 & 69(1), or had tendered less than the quantity called for by the contract, USA § 44. See Prescott & Co. v. Powles & Co., 113 Wash. 177, 193 P. 680 (1920) (general rule is that the delivery of goods under an executory contract must be of the exact quantity ordered). However, more concern for the interests of the seller was expressed where the non-conformity merely involved delay or the manner of shipment or delivery. See 2 Williston, Sales §§ 452a–453e (rev. ed. 1948). Cf. Continental Grain Co. v. Simpson Feed Co., Inc., 102 F.Supp. 354 (E.D.Ark.1951), affirmed 199 F.2d 284 (8th Cir.1952). This concern was heightened when the delay or defect caused no measurable damage and the facts strongly suggested that the buyer had seized upon the non-conformity as a reason to avoid an unprofitable bargain or to take advantage of a price break. See LeRoy Dyal Co. v. Allen, 161 F.2d 152, 153–56 (4th Cir.1947) (rejection improper under both the common law and the Perishable Agricultural Commodities Act). As a result, there was some criticism of the so-called "perfect tender" rule under pre-Code law. Honnold, *Buyer's Right of Rejection*, 97 U.Pa.L.Rev. 457 (1949). We will now see that the Code cuts back the perfect tender rule rather dramatically.

B. Scope of Rejection Right Under the Code

Suppose a buyer, in the exercise of his inspection right, discovers some defect in the seller's tender of delivery—a defect in quality or quantity, delay, an improper tender or documents not in due form. Assume further that this defect is relatively insignificant. May the buyer reject the goods, thus avoiding the contract, or must he accept them with an appropriate adjustment in the contract price? As we have seen, this is an important question. If rejection is effective the goods remain at the seller's risk, UCC 2–510(1), and the buyer may pursue appropriate remedies under UCC 2–711 as if no tender had been made. If rejection would be ineffective and acceptance required, title and risk of loss would upon acceptance pass to the buyer who must pay for the goods at the contract rate, subject to any adjustment for the nonconformity. UCC 2–607(1), 2–714, 2–717. If the buyer improperly rejects, the seller may pursue appropriate remedies under UCC 2–703. See UCC 2–301, 2–602(3).

UCC 2–601 provides that unless the breach is of an installment contract or there is agreement to the contrary, "if the goods or the tender of delivery fail in any respect to conform to the contract, the buyer may (a) reject the whole; or (b) accept the whole; or (c) accept any commercial unit or units and reject the rest." Thus the Code in 2–601 appears to adopt a "perfect tender" rule regardless of the nature of the defect or its impact upon the buyer, subject only to agreement, special rules for installment contracts, UCC 2–612(3) and the buyer's option to accept part or all of the goods. See Moulton Cavity & Mold, Inc. v. Lyn-Flex Indus., Inc., 396 A.2d 1024 (Me.1979) (trial court erred in charge that UCC 2–601 was satisfied by "substantial performance"). And it is true that the Permanent Editorial Board of the UCC declined to follow a recommendation that the buyer's right to reject be limited to cases of material breach. The Board's reasons were that the buyer should not be required to guess at his peril whether a breach is material and that proof of materiality would sometimes require disclosure of the buyer's private affairs, such as trade secrets and processes. Without more, it might seem that the only other limit upon the rejection remedy is the possibility that a buyer will not discover the non-conformity until after acceptance. In that event, the buyer can revoke his acceptance only if the non-conformity of the lot or unit "substantially impairs its value to him." UCC 2–608(1). But we will now introduce other important limits.

Problem 11–3

The Case of the Lady Dove Tomatoes

Sodfill, Inc., is a grower of vegetables and Blurtaste Co. is a manufacturer of catsup. On April 1, the parties entered into a written contract for the sale of 1,000 bushels of Lady Dove tomatoes at $4.50 per bushel, to be shipped f.o.b. point of shipment on or before July 15 and delivered to Blurtaste in "green" condition, a term having definite meaning in the trade. The goods were to be delivered in a single lot and payment was to be made 30 days after the goods were received. Nothing was said in the agreement about rejection. Assuming that there is no evidence regarding the impact upon the value of the bargain, could Blurtaste properly reject all of the goods in the following circumstances:

1. a timely tender of 990 bushels of "green" Lady Doves;

2. a timely tender of 1,000 bushels of tomatoes, 10 of which did not contain "green" Lady Doves;

3. a tender of 1,000 bushels of "green" Lady Doves which were shipped on July 16;

4. a tender of 1,000 bushels of "green" Lady Doves which were shipped on July 14 but, because of an erroneous delivery instruction by Sodfill, did not arrive until 3 days after the normal time for shipment had expired (see UCC 2–504 & 2–614).

5. Could Blurtaste accept 500 bushels of good tomatoes and reject 500 bushels of bad without incurring liability for the whole? See UCC 2–601, 2–105(6).

6. Suppose Sodfill agreed to ship 500 bushels by July 15 and the balance by August 1, payment to be made by September 1. Could the buyer reject if the first tender was: 10 bushels short; 1% off on quality; shipped 1 day late? See UCC 2–612.

7. If you represented Sodfill, what sort of clause would you draft to limit or eliminate the buyer's rejection right under UCC 2–601? How could you insure that it became part of the contract?

1. Good Faith as a Limit on the Right to Reject

Suppose in the case of Sodfill v. Blurtaste the seller is able to establish that the real reason for the buyer's rejection is a drop in the market price of tomatoes to $3.00 per bushel. If the buyer assigns as a reason for rejection an insubstantial breach by the seller, has he violated the obligation of good faith imposed by UCC 1–203 on the "performance or enforcement" of "every contract or duty within this Act?" It has been suggested that a buyer will "often try to escape from a performance quite within the business understanding of the contract, though not quite the legal, if he finds either that he can purchase the very same goods at a cheaper price on the open market or that his resale market has all but disappeared." The desire to avoid losses or to make greater profits "overcomes the possible desire to be a 'squareshooter' and to shoulder his part of that risk of price fluctuation which any present contract for future delivery carries, both for the seller and for the buyer." Eno, *Price Movement and Unstated Objections to the Defective Performance of Sales Contracts*, 44 Yale L.J. 782, 801 (1935). According to Judge Learned Hand, in this setting "such words as * * * 'good faith' appear to us to obscure the issue. The promisor may in fact be satisfied with the performance, but not with the bargain, in which case, of course, he must pay. * * *" Thompson-Starrett Co. v. La Belle Iron Works, 17 F.2d 536, 541 (2d Cir.1927). But is the conclusion one which a court should reach under the UCC? If so, does this cut down the Code's "perfect tender" rule in 2–601?

NEUMILLER FARMS, INC. v. CORNETT

Supreme Court of Alabama, 1979.
368 So.2d 272.

SHORES, JUSTICE.

Jonah D. Cornett and Ralph Moore, Sellers, were potato farmers in DeKalb County, Alabama. Neumiller Farms, Inc., Buyer, was a corporation engaged in brokering potatoes from the growers to the makers of potato chips. The controversy concerns Buyer's rejection of nine loads of potatoes out of a contract calling for twelve loads. A jury returned a verdict of $17,500 for Sellers based on a breach of contract. Buyer appealed. We affirm.

From the evidence, the jury could have found the following:

On March 3, 1976, the parties signed a written contract whereby Sellers agreed to deliver twelve loads of chipping potatoes to Buyer during July and August, 1976, and Buyer agreed to pay $4.25 per hundredweight. The contract required that the potatoes be United States Grade No. 1 and "chipt [sic] to buyer satisfaction." As the term was used in this contract, a load of potatoes contains 430 hundredweight and is valued at $1,827.50.

Sellers' potato crop yielded twenty to twenty-four loads of potatoes and Buyer accepted three of these loads without objection. At that time, the market price of chipping potatoes was $4.25 per hundredweight. Shortly thereafter, the market price declined to $2.00 per hundredweight.

When Sellers tendered additional loads of potatoes, Buyer refused acceptance, saying the potatoes would not "chip" satisfactorily. Sellers responded by having samples of their crop tested by an expert from the Cooperative Extension Service of Jackson County, Alabama, who reported that the potatoes were suitable in all respects. After receiving a letter demanding performance of the contract, Buyer agreed to "try one more load." Sellers then tendered a load of potatoes which had been purchased from another grower, Roy Hartline. Although Buyer's agent had recently purchased potatoes from Hartline at $2.00 per hundredweight, he claimed dissatisfaction with potatoes from the same fields when tendered by Sellers at $4.25 per hundredweight. Apparently the jury believed this testimony outweighed statements by Buyer's agents that Sellers' potatoes were diseased and unfit for "chipping."

Subsequently, Sellers offered to purchase the remaining nine loads of potatoes from other growers in order to fulfill their contract. Buyer's agent refused this offer, saying " * * * 'I'm not going to accept any more of your potatoes. If you load any more I'll see that they're turned down.' * * * 'I can buy potatoes all day for $2.00.' " No further efforts were made by Sellers to perform the contract.

At the time of Buyer's final refusal, Sellers had between seventeen and twenty-one loads of potatoes unharvested in their fields. Approximately four loads were sold in Chattanooga, Tennessee; Atlanta, Georgia; and local markets in DeKalb County. Sellers' efforts to sell their potato crop to other buyers were hampered by poor market conditions. Considering all of the evidence, the jury could properly have found that Sellers' efforts to sell the potatoes, after Buyer's final refusal to accept delivery, were reasonable and made in good faith.

This case presents three questions: 1) Was Buyer's refusal to accept delivery of Sellers' potatoes a breach of contract? 2) If so, what was the proper measure of Sellers' damages? and 3) Was the $17,500 jury verdict within the amount recoverable by Sellers under the proper measure of damages?

§ 7–2–703, Code of Alabama 1975 (UCC), specifies an aggrieved seller may recover for a breach of contract "Where the buyer *wrongfully* rejects * * * goods * * *" (Emphasis added.) We must determine whether there was evidence from which the jury could find that the Buyer acted wrongfully in rejecting delivery of Sellers' potatoes.

A buyer may reject delivery of goods if either the goods or the tender of delivery fails to conform to the contract. § 7–2–601, Code of Alabama 1975. In the instant case, Buyer did not claim the tender was inadequate. Rather, Buyer asserted the potatoes failed to conform to the requirements of the contract; i.e., the potatoes would not chip to buyer satisfaction.

The law requires such a claim of dissatisfaction to be made in good faith, rather than in an effort to escape a bad bargain. Shelton v. Shelton, 238 Ala. 489, 192 So. 55 (1939); Jones v. Lanier, 198 Ala. 363, 73 So. 535 (1916); Electric Lighting Co. v. Elder Bros., 115 Ala. 138, 21 So. 983 (1896).

Buyer, in the instant case, is a broker who deals in farm products as part of its occupation and, therefore, is a "merchant" with respect to its dealings in such goods. § 7–2–104, Code of Alabama 1975. In testing the good faith of a merchant, § 7–2–103, Code of Alabama 1975, requires " * * * honesty in fact and the observance of reasonable commercial standards of fair dealing in the trade." A claim of dissatisfaction by a merchant-buyer of fungible goods must be evaluated using an objective standard to determine whether the claim is made in good faith. Because there was evidence that the potatoes would "chip" satisfactorily, the jury was not required to accept Buyer's subjective claim to the contrary. A rejection of goods based on a claim of dissatisfaction, which is not made in good faith, is ineffectual and constitutes a breach of contract for which damages are recoverable.

We next consider the proper measure of damages under the UCC. * * * [The court held that the jury verdict on damages was compatible with UCC 2–708(2) and that the judgment should be affirmed.]

* * *

Questions

1. Did the court need to invoke an obligation of good faith or could the court simply have relied on UCC 2–601 and UCC 2–313? What was the relevant contract language?

2. How does the Code define and delineate obligations of good faith?

2. The Seller's Right to Cure as a Limit on the Right to Reject

UCC 2–508, in two circumstances, permits the seller to cure a defective tender and thus avoid the buyer's rejection remedy under 2–601. The first circumstance, stated in UCC 2–508(1), is fairly straightforward. If "the time for performance has not yet expired" and the buyer has rejected a non-conforming tender, the seller, "may seasonably notify the buyer of his intention to cure and may then within the contract time make a conforming delivery." Note that if the conditions of UCC 2–508(1) are met, the seller has the right to cure whether the buyer likes it or not. However, the buyer may not compel the seller to cure under any circumstances. If the buyer wants a defect corrected by the seller, his basic recourse is a negotiated agreement. Otherwise, he must reject and cover under UCC 2–712. One scholar has argued that UCC 2–508 should be repealed because it imposes inefficient legal restraints upon post-breach bargaining. Schwartz, *Cure and Revocation for Quality Defects: The Utility of Bargains,* 16 Bost.Coll.Indus. & Com.L.Rev. 543 (1975).

There are some notable variations on this theme. Many manufacturers of complex, expensive goods seek, with the help of retailers, to make a single warranty that the goods are "free from defects in material and workmanship" and to limit the remedy for breach of that warranty to "repair or replacement" of defects. If these efforts are successful, the buyer must permit the seller to cure and may not reject the goods under UCC 2–601 or revoke acceptance under UCC 2–608. See UCC 2–719.

The second circumstance, found in UCC 2–508(2), is undoubtedly explained by the fact that many defective tenders are quite within the business understanding of the contract though not quite the legal. Here, the seller ought to have a chance to cure even though the time for performance has expired. But when does a seller have "reasonable grounds" to believe that his non-conforming tender will be acceptable to the seller?

T.W. OIL, INC. v. CONSOLIDATED EDISON CO. OF NEW YORK, INC.

Court of Appeals of New York, 1982.
57 N.Y.2d 574, 457 N.Y.S.2d 458, 443 N.E.2d 932.

OPINION OF THE COURT

FUCHSBERG, JUDGE.

In the first case to wend its way through our appellate courts on this question, we are asked, in the main, to decide whether a seller who, acting in good faith and without knowledge of any defect, tenders nonconforming goods to a buyer who properly rejects them, may avail itself of the cure provision of subdivision (2) of section 2–508 of the Uniform Commercial Code. We hold that, if seasonable notice be given, such a seller may offer to cure the defect within a reasonable period beyond the time when the contract was to be performed so long as it has acted in good faith and with a reasonable expectation that the original goods would be acceptable to the buyer.

The factual background against which we decide this appeal is based on either undisputed proof or express findings at Trial Term. In January, 1974, midst the fuel shortage produced by the oil embargo, the plaintiff (then known as Joc Oil USA, Inc.) purchased a cargo of fuel oil whose sulfur content was represented to it as no greater than 1%. While the oil was still at sea en route to the United States in the tanker *M T Khamsin,* plaintiff received a certificate from the foreign refinery at which it had been processed informing it that the sulfur content in fact was .52%. Thereafter, on January 24, the plaintiff entered into a written contract with the defendant (Con Ed) for the sale of this oil. The agreement was for delivery to take place between January 24 and January 30, payment being subject to a named independent testing agency's confirmation of quality and quantity. The contract, following a trade custom to round off specifications of sulfur content at, for instance, 1%, .5% or .3%, described that of the *Khamsin* oil as .5%.[1] In the course of the negotiations, the plaintiff learned that Con Ed was then authorized to buy and burn oil with a sulfur content of up to 1% and would even mix oils containing more and less to maintain that figure.

When the vessel arrived, on January 25, its cargo was discharged into Con Ed storage tanks in Bayonne, New Jersey.[2] In due course, the independent testing people reported a sulfur content of .92%. On this basis, acting within a time frame whose reasonableness is not in question, on February 14 Con Ed rejected the shipment. Prompt negotiations to adjust the price failed; by February 20, plaintiff had offered a price reduction roughly responsive to the difference in sulfur reading, but Con Ed, though it could use the oil, rejected this proposition out of hand. It was insistent on paying no more than the latest prevailing price, which, in the volatile market that then existed, was some 25% below the level which prevailed when it agreed to buy the oil.

The very next day, February 21, plaintiff offered to cure the defect with a substitute shipment of conforming oil scheduled to arrive on the *S.S. Appollonian Victory* on February 28. Nevertheless, on February 22, the very day after the cure was proffered, Con Ed, adamant in its intention to avail itself of the intervening drop in prices, summarily rejected this proposal too. The two cargos were subsequently sold to third parties at the best price obtainable, first that of the *Appollonian* and, sometime later, after extraction from the tanks had been accomplished, that of the *Khamsin*.[3]

There ensued this action for breach of contract,[4] which, after a somewhat unconventional trial course, resulted in a nonjury decision for the plaintiff in the sum of $1,385,512.83, essentially the difference between the original contract price of $3,360,667.14 and the amount received by the plaintiff by way of resale of the *Khamsin* oil at what the court found as a matter of fact was a negotiated price which, under

---

1. Confirmatorily, Con Ed's brief describes .92% oil as "nominally" 1% oil.

2. The tanks already contained some other oil, but Con Ed appears to have had no concern over the admixture of the differing sulfur contents. In any event, the efficacy of the independent testing required by the contract was not impaired by the commingling.

3. Most of the *Khamsin* oil was drained from the tanks and sold at $10.75 per barrel. The balance was retained by Con Ed

in its mixed form at $10.45 per barrel. The original price in January had been $17.875 per barrel.

4. The plaintiff originally also sought an affirmative injunction to compel Con Ed to accept the *Khamsin* shipment or, alternatively, the *Appollonian* substitute. However, when a preliminary injunction was denied on the ground that the plaintiff had an adequate remedy at law, it amended its complaint to pursue the latter remedy alone.

all the circumstances,[5] was reasonably procured in the open market. To arrive at this result, the Trial Judge, while ruling against other liability theories advanced by the plaintiff, which, in particular, included one charging the defendant with having failed to act in good faith in the negotiations for a price adjustment on the *Khamsin* oil (Uniform Commercial Code, § 1–203), decided as a matter of law that subdivision (2) of section 2–508 of the Uniform Commercial Code was available to the plaintiff even if it had no prior knowledge of the nonconformity. Finding that in fact plaintiff had no such belief at the time of the delivery, that what turned out to be a .92% sulfur content was "within the range of contemplation of reasonable acceptability" to Con. Ed., and that seasonable notice of an intention to cure was given, the court went on to hold that plaintiff's "reasonable and timely offer to cure" was improperly rejected (*sub nom. Joc Oil USA v. Consolidated Edison Co. of N.Y.*, 107 Misc.2d 376, 390, 434 N.Y.S.2d 623 [Shanley N. Egeth, J.]). The Appellate Division, 84 A.D.2d 970, 447 N.Y.S.2d 572, having unanimously affirmed the judgment entered on this decision, the case is now here by our leave (CPLR 5602, subd. [a], par. 1, cl. [i]).

In support of its quest for reversal, the defendant now asserts that the trial court erred (a) in ruling that the verdict on a special question submitted for determination by a jury was irrelevant to the decision of this case, (b) in failing to interpret subdivision (2) of section 2–508 of the Uniform Commercial Code to limit the availability of the right to cure after date of performance to cases in which the seller knowingly made a nonconforming tender and (c) in calculating damages on the basis of the resale of the nonconforming cargo rather than of the substitute offered to replace it. For the reasons which follow, we find all three unacceptable.

* * *

II

We turn then to the central issue on this appeal: Fairly interpreted, did subdivision (2) of section 2–508 of the Uniform Commercial Code require Con Ed to accept the substitute shipment plaintiff tendered? In approaching this question, we, of course, must remember that a seller's right to cure a defective tender, as allowed by both subdivisions of section 2–508, was intended to act as a meaningful limitation on the absolutism of the old perfect tender rule, under which, no leeway being allowed for any imperfections, there was, as one court put it, just "no room * * * for the doctrine of substantial performance" of commercial obligations (*Mitsubishi Goshi Kaisha v. Aron & Co.*, 16 F.2d 185, 186 [Learned Hand, J.]; see Note, Uniform Commercial Code, § 2–508; Seller's Right to Cure Non-Conforming Goods, 6 Rutgers—Camden L.J. 387–388).

5. These circumstances included the fact that the preliminary injunction was not denied until April so that, by the time the *Khamsin* oil was sold in May, almost three months had gone by since its rejection.

In contrast, to meet the realities of the more impersonal business world of our day, the code, to avoid sharp dealing, expressly provides for the liberal construction of its remedial provisions (§ 1–102) so that "good faith" and the "observance of reasonable commercial standards of fair dealing" be the rule rather than the exception in trade (see § 2–103, subd. [1], par. [b]), "good faith" being defined as "honesty in fact in the conduct or transaction concerned" (Uniform Commercial Code, § 1–201, subd. [19]). As to section 2–508 in particular, the code's Official Comment advises that its mission is to safeguard the seller "against surprise as a result of sudden technicality on the buyer's part" (Uniform Commercial Code, § 2–106, Comment 2; see, also, Peters, Remedies for Breach of Contracts Relating to the Sale of Goods under the Uniform Commercial Code: A Roadmap for Article Two, 73 Yale L.J. 199, 210; 51 N.Y.Jur., Sales, § 101, p. 41).

Section 2–508 may be conveniently divided between provisions for cure offered when "the time for performance has not yet expired" (subd. [1]), a precode concept in this State (*Lowinson v. Newman,* 201 App.Div. 266, 194 N.Y.S. 253), and ones which, by newly introducing the possibility of a seller obtaining "a further reasonable time to substitute a conforming tender" (subd. [2]), also permit cure beyond the date set for performance. In its entirety the section reads as follows:

"(1) Where any tender or delivery by the seller is rejected because non-conforming and the time for performance has not yet expired, the seller may seasonably notify the buyer of his intention to cure and may then within the contract time make a conforming delivery.

"(2) Where the buyer rejects a non-conforming tender which the seller had reasonable grounds to believe would be acceptable with or without money allowance the seller may if he seasonably notifies the buyer have a further reasonable time to substitute a conforming tender."

Since we here confront circumstances in which the conforming tender came after the time of performance, we focus on subdivision (2). On its face, taking its conditions in the order in which they appear, for the statute to apply (1) a buyer must have rejected a nonconforming tender, (2) the seller must have had reasonable grounds to believe this tender would be acceptable (with or without money allowance), and (3) the seller must have "seasonably" notified the buyer of the intention to substitute a conforming tender within a reasonable time.[7]

In the present case, none of these presented a problem. The first one was easily met for it is unquestioned that, at .92%, the sulfur content of the *Khamsin* oil did not conform to the .5% specified in the

---

7. Essentially a factual matter, "seasonable" is defined in subdivision (3) of section 1–204 of the Uniform Commercial Code as "at or within the time agreed or if no time is agreed at or within a reasonable time". At least equally factual in character, a "reasonable time" is left to depend on the "nature, purpose and circumstances" of any action which is to be taken (Uniform Commercial Code, § 1–204, subd. [2]).

contract and that it was rejected by Con Ed. The second, the reasonableness of the seller's belief that the original tender would be acceptable, was supported not only by unimpeached proof that the contract's .5% and the refinery certificate's .52% were trade equivalents, but by testimony that, by the time the contract was made, the plaintiff knew Con Ed burned fuel with a content of up to 1%, so that, with appropriate price adjustment, the *Khamsin* oil would have suited its needs even if, at delivery, it was, to the plaintiff's surprise, to test out at .92%. Further, the matter seems to have been put beyond dispute by the defendant's readiness to take the oil at the reduced market price on February 20. Surely, on such a record, the trial court cannot be faulted for having found as a fact that the second condition too had been established.

As to the third, the conforming state of the *Appollonian* oil is undisputed, the offer to tender it took place on February 21, only a day after Con Ed finally had rejected the *Khamsin* delivery and the *Appollonian* substitute then already was en route to the United States, where it was expected in a week and did arrive on March 4, only four days later than expected. Especially since Con Ed pleaded no prejudice (unless the drop in prices could be so regarded), it is almost impossible, given the flexibility of the Uniform Commercial Code definitions of "seasonable" and "reasonable" (n. 7, *supra*), to quarrel with the finding that the remaining requirements of the statute also had been met.

Thus lacking the support of the statute's literal language, the defendant nonetheless would have us limit its application to cases in which a seller *knowingly* makes a nonconforming tender which it has reason to believe the buyer will accept. For this proposition, it relies almost entirely on a critique in Nordstrom, Law of Sales (§ 105), which rationalizes that, since a seller who believes its tender is conforming would have no reason to think in terms of a reduction in the price of the goods, to allow such a seller to cure after the time for performance had passed would make the statutory reference to a money allowance redundant.[8] Nordstrom, interestingly enough, finds it useful to buttress this position by the somewhat dire prediction, though backed by no empirical or other confirmation, that, unless the right to cure is confined to those whose nonconforming tenders are knowing ones, the incentive of sellers to timely deliver will be undermined. To this it also adds the somewhat moralistic note that a seller who is mistaken as to

---

8. The premise for such an argument, which ignores the policy of the code to prevent buyers from using insubstantial remediable or price adjustable defects to free themselves from unprofitable bargains (Hawkland, Sales and Bulk Sales Under the Uniform Commercial Code, pp. 120–122), is that the words "with or without money allowance" apply only to sellers who believe their goods will be acceptable with such an allowance and not to sellers who believe their goods will be acceptable without such an allowance. But, since the words are part of a phrase which speaks of an otherwise unqualified belief that the goods will be acceptable, unless one strains for an opposite interpretation, we find insufficient reason to doubt that it intends to include both those who find a need to offer an allowance and those who do not.

the quality of its goods does not merit additional time (Nordstrom, *loc. cit.*). Curiously, recognizing that the few decisions extant on this subject have adopted a position opposed to the one for which it contends, Con Ed seeks to treat these as exceptions rather than exemplars of the rule (e.g., *Wilson v. Scampoli,* 228 A.2d 848 (D.C.App.) [goods obtained by seller from their manufacturer in original carton resold unopened to purchaser; seller held within statute though it had no reason to believe the goods defective]; *Appleton State Bank v. Lee,* 33 Wis.2d 690, 148 N.W.2d 1 [seller mistakenly delivered sewing machine of wrong brand but otherwise identical to one sold; held that seller, though it did not know of its mistake, had a right to cure by substitution]).[9]

That the principle for which these cases stand goes far beyond their particular facts cannot be gainsaid. These holdings demonstrate that, in dealing with the application of subdivision (2) of section 2–508, courts have been concerned with the reasonableness of the seller's belief that the goods would be acceptable rather than with the seller's pretender knowledge or lack of knowledge of the defect (*Wilson v. Scampoli, supra;* compare *Zabriskie Chevrolet v. Smith,* 99 N.J.Super. 441, 240 A.2d 195).

It also is no surprise then that the aforementioned decisional history is a reflection of the mainstream of scholarly commentary on the subject (e.g., 1955 Report of N.Y.Law Rev.Comm., p. 484; White & Summers, Uniform Commercial Code [2d ed.], § 8–4, p. 322; 2 Anderson, Uniform Commercial code [2d ed.], § 2–508:7; Hogan, The Highways and Some of the Byways in the Sales and Bulk Sales Articles of the Uniform Commercial Code, 48 Cornell L.Q. 1, 12–13; Note, Uniform Commercial Code, § 2–508: Seller's Right to Cure Non-Conforming Goods, 6 Rutgers—Camden L.J. 387, 399; Note, Commercial Law—The Effect of the Seller's Right to Cure on the Buyer's Remedy of Rescission, 28 Ark.L.Rev. 297, 302–303).

White and Summers, for instance, put it well, and bluntly. Stressing that the code intended cure to be "a remedy which should be carefully cultivated and developed by the courts" because it "offers the possibility of conforming the law to reasonable expectations and of thwarting the chiseler who seeks to escape from a bad bargain" (*op. cit.,* at pp. 322–324), the authors conclude, as do we, that a seller should have recourse to the relief afforded by subdivision (2) of section 2–508 of the Uniform Commercial Code as long as it can establish that it had reasonable grounds, tested objectively, for its belief that the goods would be accepted (*ibid.,* at p. 321). It goes without saying that the test of reasonableness, in this context, must encompass the concepts of "good faith" and "commercial standards of fair dealing" which perme-

---

9. The only New York case to deal with this section involved a seller who knowingly tendered a "newer and improved version of the model that was actually ordered" on the contract delivery date. The court held he had reasonable grounds to believe the buyer would accept the newer model (*Bartus v. Riccardi,* 55 Misc.2d 3, 284 N.Y.S.2d 222 [Utica City Ct., Hymes, J.]).

ate the code (Uniform Commercial Code, § 1–201, subd. [19]; §§ 1–203, 2–103, subd. [1], par. [b]).[10]

As to the damages issue raised by the defendant, we affirm without reaching the merits. At no stage of the proceedings before the trial court did the defendant object to the plaintiff's proposed method for their calculation, and this though the plaintiff gave ample notice of that proposal by means of a preliminary statement and pretrial memorandum filed with the court. So complete was defendant's acquiescence in the theory thus advanced that the plaintiff was permitted to introduce its proof of the *Khamsin* resale alone, and without opposition. Furthermore, in consensually submitting the four jointly framed advisory questions that went to the jury, the language of one of them, which was damages-related, indicates that both parties were acting on the assumption that the *Khamsin* oil was the one with which the court was to be concerned. And, even after the decision at nisi prius revealed that the Judge had acted on such an assumption, so far as the record shows, no motion was ever made to correct it.

It has long been the law that agreement on a theory of damages at trial, even if only implied, must control on appeal (see *Martin v. City of Cohoes,* 37 N.Y.2d 162, 165–166, 371 N.Y.S.2d 687, 332 N.E.2d 867, *supra; Hartshorn v. Chaddock,* 135 N.Y. 116, 123, 31 N.E. 997; 10 Carmody-Wait 2d, N.Y.Prac., § 70:419, p. 690).

For all these reasons, the order of the Appellate Division should be affirmed, with costs.

COOKE, C.J., and JASEN, GABRIELLI, JONES, WACHTLER and MEYER, JJ., concur.

Order affirmed.

ZABRISKIE CHEVROLET, INC. v. SMITH

New Jersey Superior Court, Law Division, 1968.
99 N.J.Super. 441, 240 A.2d 195.

[Defendant purchased a new car from plaintiff, giving a check in full payment. One day later, defendant's wife took delivery of the car. Before she negotiated the 2½ miles home, the car developed transmission trouble and there was no question but that the transmission was defective upon delivery. Defendant stopped payment on the check and informed plaintiff that the sale was cancelled. Plaintiff picked up the

---

10. Except indirectly, on this appeal we do not deal with the equally important protections the code affords buyers. It is as to buyers as well as sellers that the code, to the extent that it displaces traditional principles of law and equity (§ 1–103), seeks to discourage unfair or hypertechnical business conduct bespeaking a dog-eat-dog rather than a live-and-let-live approach to the marketplace (e.g., §§ 2–314, 2–315, 2–513, 2–601, 2–608).

Overall, the aim is to encourage parties to amicably resolve their own problems (*Ramirez v. Autosport,* 88 N.J. 277, 285, 440 A.2d 1345; compare Restatement, Contracts 2d, Introductory Note to chapter 10, p. 194 ["the wisest course is ordinarily for the parties to attempt to resolve their differences by negotiations, including clarification of expectations [and] cure of past defaults"]).

car and replaced the transmission. Defendant refused to take the repaired car and commenced negotiations for a new car. However, these negotiations foundered when defendant insisted that the cancellation was effective and plaintiff, denying this, insisted that no credit on a new deal could be given. Plaintiff sued defendant on the check. The court first held that the car was substantially defective upon delivery and that plaintiff's effort to disclaim the implied warranty of merchantability was invalid under UCC 2–316(2). The court next held that defendant did not accept the goods because there was no reasonable opportunity to inspect, UCC 2–606(1)(b) and, even so, the facts supported a revocation of acceptance under UCC 2–608(1)].

* * *

There having been no acceptance, the next issue presented is whether defendant properly rejected under the Code. That he cancelled the sale and rejected the vehicle almost concomitantly with the discovery of the failure of his bargain is clear from the evidence. N.J.S. 12A 2–601, N.J.S.A. delineates the buyer's rights following nonconforming delivery and reads as follows:

> "Subject to the provisions of this Chapter on breach in installment contracts (12A:2–612) and unless otherwise agreed under the sections on contractual limitations of remedy (12A:2–712 and 2–719), if the goods or the tender of delivery *fail in any respect to conform* to the contract, the buyer may

> "(a) reject the whole; * * *" (Italics added)

Section 12A:2–602 indicates that one can reject after taking possession. Possession, therefore, does not mean acceptance and the corresponding loss of the right of rejection; nor does the fact that buyer has a security interest along with possession eliminate the right to reject.

> "(1) Rejection of goods must be within a reasonable time after their delivery or tender. It is ineffective unless the buyer seasonably notifies the seller.

> "(2) Subject to the provisions of the two following sections on rejected goods (12A:2–603 and 2–604).

> "(a) after rejection any exercise of ownership by the buyer with respect to any commercial unit is wrongful as against the seller; and.

> "(b) if the buyer has before rejection taken *physical possession* of goods in which he does not have a *security* interest under the provisions of this Chapter (subsection (3) of 12A:2–711), he is under a duty after rejection to hold them with reasonable care at the seller's disposition for a time sufficient to permit the seller to remove them; but

> "(c) the buyer has no further obligations with regard to goods rightfully rejected." (Italics added)

N.J.S. 12A:2–106, N.J.S.A. defines conforming goods as follows:

"(2) Goods or conduct including any part of a performance are "conforming" or conform to the contract when they are in accordance with the obligations under the contract."

The Uniform Commercial Code Comment to that section states:

"2. Subsection (2): It is in general intended to continue the policy of requiring *exact performance* by the seller of his obligations as a condition to his right to require acceptance. However, the seller is in part safeguarded against surprise as a result of sudden technicality on the buyer's part by the provisions of Section 2–508 on seller's cure of improper tender or delivery. Moreover usage of trade frequently permits commercial leeways in performance and the language of the agreement itself must be read in the light of such custom or usage and also, prior course of dealing, and in a long term contract, the course of performance."

There was no evidence at the trial concerning any "custom or usage," although plaintiff in its brief argued that it is the usage of the automobile trade that a buyer accept a new automobile, although containing defects of manufacture, if such defects can be and are seasonably cured by the seller. Perhaps this represents prevailing views in the automobile industry which have, over the years, served to blanket injustices and inequities committed upon buyers who demurred in the light of the unequal positions of strength between the parties. The spirit of the Henningsen opinion, supra, contemplated these conditions which cried out for correction. In the present case we are not dealing with a situation such as was present in Adams v. Tramontin Motor Sales, 42 N.J.Super. 313, 126 A.2d 358 (App.Div.1956). In that case, brought for breach of implied warranty of merchantability, the court held that minor defects, such as adjustment of the motor, tightening of loose elements, fixing of locks and dome light, and a correction of rumbling noise, were not remarkable defects, and therefore there was no breach. Here the breach was substantial. The new car was practically inoperable and endowed with a defective transmission. This was a "remarkable defect" and justified rejection by the buyer.

Lastly, plaintiff urges that under the Code, N.J.S. 12A:2–508, N.J.S.A. it had a right to cure the nonconforming delivery. N.J.S. 12A:2–508, N.J.S.A. states:

"(1) Where any tender or delivery by the seller is rejected because non-conforming, and the *time for performance has not yet expired,* the seller may seasonably notify the buyer of his intention to cure and may then within the contract time make a conforming delivery.

"(2) Where the buyer rejects a non-conforming tender which the *seller had reasonable grounds to believe would be acceptable* with or without money allowance the seller may if he seasonably notifies the buyer have a further reasonable time to substitute a conforming tender." (Italics added)

The New Jersey Study Comment to 12A:2–508 reads:

"3. Subsection 2–508(2) has been applauded as a rule aimed at ending 'forced breaches.' See, Hawkland, Sales and Bulk Sales Under the Uniform Commercial Code, 120–122 (1958). * * * *

"Section 2–508 prevents the buyer from forcing the seller to breach by making a surprise rejection of the goods because of some minor non-conformity at a time at which the seller cannot cure the deficiency within the time for performance."

The Uniform Commercial Code Comment to 12A:2–508 reads:

"2. Subsection (2) seeks to avoid injustice to the seller by reason of a surprise rejection by the buyer. However, the seller is not protected unless he had 'reasonable grounds to believe' that the tender would be acceptable."

It is clear that in the instant case there was no "forced breach" on the part of the buyer, for he almost immediately began to negotiate for another automobile. The inquiry is as to what is intended by "cure," as used in the Code. This statute makes no attempt to define or specify what a "cure" shall consist of. It would appear, then, that each case must be controlled by its own facts. The "cure" intended under the cited section of the Code does not, in the court's opinion, contemplate the tender of a new vehicle with a substituted transmission, not from the factory and of unknown lineage from another vehicle in plaintiff's possession. It was not the intention of the Legislature that the right to "cure" is a limitless one to be controlled only by the will of the seller. A "cure" which endeavors by substitution to tender a chattel not within the agreement or contemplation of the parties is invalid.

/ Cure has limits

For a majority of people the purchase of a new car is a major investment, rationalized by the peace of mind that flows from its dependability and safety. Once their faith is shaken, the vehicle loses not only its real value in their eyes, but becomes an instrument whose integrity is substantially impaired and whose operation is fraught with apprehension. The attempted cure in the present case was ineffective.

Perhaps the only effective cure would be a new auto. (w/ good transmission!)

Accordingly, and pursuant to N.J.S. 12A:2–711, N.J.S.A., judgment is rendered on the main case in favor of defendant. On the counter-claim judgment is rendered in favor of defendant and against plaintiff in the sum of $124, being the amount of the deposit, there being no further proof of damages.

Defendant shall, as part of this judgment, execute for plaintiff, on demand, such documents as are necessary to again vest title to the vehicle in plaintiff.

McKENZIE v. ALLA–OHIO COALS, INC.

United States District Court, District of Columbia, 1979.
29 UCC Rep.Serv. 852, affirmed 610 F.2d 1000.

GASCH, DISTRICT JUDGE. This diversity action for breach of contract is before the court on cross-motions for summary judgment. Plaintiff contends that he is entitled to judgment in his favor because defendant wrongfully rejected coal shipped to it by plaintiff pursuant to their agreement. Plaintiff argues that the only remedy available to defendant was a reduction in the price of the coal, as set forth in a penalty clause contained in the purchase order. Defendant replies that the penalty clause was not the exclusive remedy, and that its timely rejection of the coal was fully justified. Plaintiff brought this action seeking recovery of approximately $7,000 as the difference between what defendant should have paid and what plaintiff received on resale. Plaintiff also seeks approximately $40,000 for the cost of demurrage and transporting the coal. Defendant counterclaimed for $800 in costs for inspecting the coal, and for compensatory and punitive damages for plaintiff's alleged misrepresentations made by plaintiff about delay and the quality of the coal.

BACKGROUND

Defendant Alla-Ohio is a coal broker who agreed to buy coal from plaintiff to resell to certain of its customers. The agreement resulted from oral negotiations over the telephone in June, 1977. During these negotiations, there was no discussion of possible penalties to be applied against deviations in the quality of the coal. On July 5, 1977, defendant sent to plaintiff a purchase order confirming the prior agreement, and specifying the order of 3,000 net tons of coal at an agreed price of $34.00 per net ton F.O.B. car. The letter-purchase order included the specification that the ash content of the coal not exceed 7.5%. The letter also stated: "Should the ash content exceed 7.5% dry, a penalty of $.80 per 1% of ash in excess of 7.5% shall be assessed, fractions in proportion." The letter also stipulated other specifications, including a Free Swelling Index (FSI) of "7 Min."

On or about July 21, 1977, plaintiff shipped 43 railroad cars containing approximately 3,000 tons of coal to Hampton Roads, Virginia for defendant. Plaintiff received defendant's July 5 letter-purchase order on July 25, 1977. The next day, plaintiff sent a reply to defendant, informing defendant that the purchase order did not conform to the oral understanding. Plaintiff also objected to the ash and FSI specifications, claiming 8% and 6, respectively, to be the correct standards. Plaintiff further objected to the penalty provisions, saying, "I consider this order to be incorrect and that all specifications on the coal should be on an as received basis." On July 28, 1977, defendant responded by asserting that the purchase order of July 5 was an accurate embodiment of the oral agreement. Defendant also noted that preliminary test results showed that the ash content of the coal was at least 13.5% and ranged upward. Plaintiff did not respond to the July 28 letter.

On August 15, 1977, defendant rejected the 43 railroad cars of coal, after completing tests of 42 of the cars. Plaintiff demanded that delivery be accepted but defendant refused. Subsequently, plaintiff found a buyer for the coal at a price of $26.74 per ton. The price defendant would have paid pursuant to the penalty clause in the purchase order would have been $29.20 per ton, according to plaintiff's calculation.

This case turns primarily on the issue of whether the penalty clause set out in the purchase order of July 5 was the exclusive remedy for defendant, or whether defendant was entitled to reject coal that did not conform to the specifications. There are, however, other matters which also must be untangled before resolution of the case may be achieved. Therefore, the court will undertake to examine the contentions of the parties roughly in chronological order.

I. The Contract and Its Terms

* * *

Under these circumstances, the court concludes that the contract between the parties contained penalty terms for excess ash content.

II. Limitation of Remedies

Plaintiff argues that the penalty clause was defendant's exclusive remedy in the event that the coal did not conform to the requirements of the contract, and that the parties did not intend to permit the "radical" remedy of rejection. * * * In the absence of an express indication in the writings of the parties, or a course of conduct clearly establishing use of only one kind of remedy, the court cannot conclude that the presumption that remedies be cumulative is overcome.

In addition, the UCC has codified the "perfect tender" rule of the common law,[2] and provides that goods not sold in installments may be rejected if they "fail in any respect to conform to the contract." UCC § 2–601. There is substantial authority, however, that the perfect tender rule has been greatly diminished, and that, where a buyer has suffered no damage, he should not be allowed to reject goods because of an insubstantial nonconformity. See J. White and R. Summers, supra § 8–3 at 256–57, and cases cited therein. Assuming this approach to be the correct one, in this case the nonconformity was substantial. The July 5 purchase order specified that the ash content of the coal was not to exceed 7.5%. The coal delivered to defendant had ash content of at least 13.5% and up to 16%.[3] Moreover, the UCC provides that if the

---

2. See Priest, Breach and Remedy for the Tender of Nonconforming Goods under the Uniform Commercial Code: An Economic Approach, 91 Harv.L.Rev. 960 (1978). Although plaintiff has suggested a novel economic analysis in conformance with the scholarly article cited above, the court declines plaintiff's invitation to undertake that approach on the facts presented.

3. See Letter from Ms. Ursula Mosby to Eugene McKenzie, July 28, 1977.

nonconformity will impair the value of the goods to the buyer because of the buyer's particular circumstances, he is entitled to reject the goods even though the seller had no advance knowledge of the circumstances. UCC § 2–608.[4] The coal ordered by defendant here was intended for use as metallugical coal. Metallurgical coal must be high quality coal and may have ash content no greater than 8%, or, for marginal grade metallurgical coal, no greater than 12%. See Defendant's Supplemental Memorandum at 9 n. 4. On the basis of the foregoing facts, the court concludes that the coal tendered by plaintiff did not conform substantially to the requirements of the contract. On that basis, defendant was entitled to reject the nonconforming coal.[5]

A troublesome question, however, is the potential capacity for the seller to cure a nonconforming performance. Under UCC § 2–508, a seller may cure after the time for performance has passed if (1) he had reasonable grounds to believe that a nonconforming tender would be acceptable, (2) he seasonably notifies the buyer of his intention to cure, and (3) he cures within a further reasonable time. Addressing these considerations, the court notes that it is unlikely that a reasonable seller in plaintiff's position would be ignorant of such drastic variances in the quality of the coal. Similarly, no evidence of trade custom in the record indicates that coal with such high ash content would be suitable for use as metallurgical coal, the purpose for which it was purchased. Therefore, the court finds that plaintiff did not have reasonable grounds for believing that a nonconforming tender would be acceptable. Furthermore, although there is evidence that plaintiff offered to take a reduced price for the coal, such attempted cure by price allowance is not one of the methods of cure approved by the UCC. See UCC § 2–508, Comment 4. Under all of these circumstances, then, plaintiff could make no effective cure short of tendering conforming coal. There was never any offer to do so, and defendant was justified in rejecting the high ash coal.

In sum, the contract between plaintiff and defendant did not limit the parties to accepting a price reduction for coal that did not meet the specifications for ash content that were imposed. The coal actually tendered deviated so substantially from the coal promised that defendant was entitled, after inspection, to reject the whole. UCC § 2–601. Furthermore, defendant is entitled to recover damages incurred in inspecting the coal. UCC § 2–715(1) provides in part that, "Incidental damages resulting from the seller's breach include expenses reasonably incurred in inspection * * * of goods rightfully rejected * * *" Defendant has by affidavit established that its inspection costs amount to $495.70.

* * * *

---

4. Although UCC § 2–608 governs revocations after acceptance of goods, and not rejection before acceptance, the analysis applicable to both §§ 2–608 and 2–601 is the same. See J. White and R. Summers, supra § 8–3, at 260.

5. A buyer is permitted a reasonable opportunity to inspect goods tendered under a contract, see UCC § 2–606, and may reject nonconforming goods within a reasonable time after inspection reveals the nonconformity, and the buyer must seasonably notify the seller of rejection. UCC § 2–602. Defendant in this case has complied with the above requirements.

Accordingly, in view of the foregoing, the court will deny plaintiff's motion for summary judgment, grant defendant's motion for summary judgment on plaintiff's claim, grant defendant's motion for summary judgment on the first count of its counterclaim, and will dismiss without prejudice the second count of defendant's counterclaim.

[Some footnotes omitted.]

C. Procedural Requirements of Effective Rejection

Suppose, upon inspection, the buyer finds a non-conformity which would justify rejection of the goods under UCC 2–601. What conditions must be met before the buyer can make an effective rejection? Section 2–602(1) provides that "rejection of goods must be within a reasonable time after their delivery and tender" and that the rejection is "ineffective unless the buyer seasonably notifies the seller." Compare UCC 2–607(3)(a). If the buyer has had a reasonable option under UCC 2–602(1), and fails to act, he has accepted the goods. Section 2–606(1)(b). A second set of problems concerns the content of the notice the buyer is to give the seller. Need it state all, part or none of the defects ascertainable by reasonable inspection as a condition to relying upon them to justify rejection? The UCC answer is provided in UCC 2–605(1). The pre-Code cases are collected and analyzed in Eno, *Price Movement and Unstated Objections to the Defective Performance of Sales Contracts*, 44 Yale L.J. 782 (1935).

Problem 11–4

Suppose that the seller tenders goods at the time specified in the contract. Upon inspection, the buyer finds what he considers to be two defects. Accordingly, he promptly notifies the seller that he is rejecting the goods, thus satisfying UCC 2–602(1). However, his notice of rejection specified only one defect and this later turns out to be an insufficient ground for rejection. The unstated objection, while present in fact, could have been cured by the seller under UCC 2–508(2). Shortly after the notice is received by the seller, the goods are destroyed while in the possession of the buyer but without his fault or negligence. May the seller recover the price of the destroyed goods from the buyer? See UCC 2–602, 2–605, 2–606, and 2–607(1). In Bead Chain Manufacturing Co. v. Saxton Products, Inc., 183 Conn. 266, 439 A.2d 314 (1981) the Supreme Court of Connecticut, Ellen Peters J, remarked that the "consequences of an ineffective rejection is that the buyer is held to have accepted the goods, and thereafter becomes liable for their purchase price." 439 A.2d at 318, n. 2.

INTERVALE STEEL CORP. v. BORG & BECK DIV., BORG–WARNER

United States District Court, Eastern District, Michigan, 1984.
578 F.Supp. 1081.

PRATT, DISTRICT JUDGE. This case involves the application of the Uniform Commercial Code, adopted by Michigan, M.C.L.A. § 440.1101 et seq., to the sale of steel by plaintiff to the defendant. The plaintiff, Intervale Steel Corporation (Intervale) is the successor to Barry Steel Corporation (Barry) and sold 22 coils of steel to the defendant Borg &

Beck (Borg), a division of Borg-Warner Corporation. The latter has refused to remit the purchase price and this suit ensued.

I. FACTS

Barry had sold steel to Borg for over 15 years. During most if not all of that period, the defendant's sales representative on the Borg account was Peter Adzema, a metallurgist who was also associated with Barry's quality control department. Adzema visited the Borg plant frequently and was fully aware of Borg's manufacturing processes and procedures. More particularly, Adzema testified he was familiar with Borg's practice regarding the partial fabrication of the parts in question here and the storage of the partially completed parts until customers placed an order, after which the parts would be completed. He was also aware that Borg did not conduct microscopic examinations of ordered steel and did not cut sample pieces from ordered steel and run those samples completely through the fabrication process.

Borg is engaged in the manufacturing or fabrication of parts and components for the automotive industry. In August, 1980, it ordered 98,195 pounds of high carbon cold rolled steel for use in the fabrication of the "Belleville Spring," a component of automobile clutch assemblies. The purchase order set forth the specifications for this steel, which were of critical importance due to the demanding requirements of the "Belleville Spring" and its function in clutch assemblies. The acceptance by plaintiff of the purchase order, of course, resulted in the plaintiff's grant of express and implied warranties of merchantability and fitness for the purpose intended.

Barry obtained the steel originally from Jones and Laughlin Steel in coils. Barry then unrolled the coils, treated the steel, rerolled the coils and on August 26 and 28 of 1980 delivered 22 coils to defendant at the agreed upon price.

Borg, in accordance with its usual practice, checked the steel for dimensional accuracy and chemical content. In August or early September, 1980, Borg began its fabrication process by stamping out "blanks" from strips of the coils and deburring (smoothing) the pieces. It then stored these blanks prior to any further processing pending the receipt of orders from its automotive customers. In late September, Borg removed the pieces from storage and resumed its fabrication process which involved forming by presses, heat treatment, "wheelabrating" (similar to sandblasting), "stroking" (a stress-removal process) and "load-testing" (a quality control measure). During the course of these latter steps, however, it was observed that the springs were cracking and evidencing other failures. Notice was immediately given to Barry and Borg halted production and began extensive testing of the steel. Borg tested for several weeks and communicated to Barry regularly with regard to the testing. Eventually, it was determined that the steel was indeed defective and that the cause was associated with the fact that, contrary to the specifications of that type of steel, it had been annealed [3] once, rather than twice.

Barry admitted the steel was defective and not fit for its intended use and conceded the same at trial. Upon discovering that the entire order had been stamped, after providing for some samples for its own testing and demonstrative purposes, Barry authorized Borg to scrap the steel.

The evidence also established that Borg did not conduct metallurgical or microscopic examinations of Barry steel and that Barry was aware of this. It was further established that it is not an industry practice to do so. Moreover, it was also established that "samples" of coil steel are not run through the complete fabrication process due to the high cost of, for example, unrolling the coil, taking samples from representative parts of the coil and tying up the production line for testing purposes.

Intervale, as a successor to Barry, then instituted this suit for $41,612.47, that figure representing the invoice price less credit for the scrap value realized by Borg. It is the position of plaintiff that Borg accepted the steel, is not entitled to revoke that acceptance and is precluded from maintaining an action or asserting the defense of breach of warranty.

II. Acceptance and Revocation

Borg argued that it did not "accept" the goods and should not be held obligated to pay the purchase price of the contract. See M.C.L.A. § 440.2607(1). Borg reasoned that it properly rejected the goods as required under §§ 2–601, 2–602 and 2–606. According to defendant, although it blanked out all the steel, it could reject the steel because defendant acted reasonably and rejected the goods as soon as the breach of warranty could be discovered. Borg supports this position by citing several cases which have found effective rejections by buyers despite their changing or using the goods. It is true that Borg acted reasonably, nonetheless, under the circumstances Borg's action can only be viewed to constitute acceptance of the steel.

First, under the Uniform Commercial Code, Borg's rejection after the steel was entirely stamped out was not effective.[7] Borg did not attempt to reject the steel until after it had received shipment, blanked all the steel, and stored the partially completed parts for over a month. In total, Borg retained the steel for over three months before it notified plaintiff of the problems with the steel. The determination of whether goods have been accepted is governed by § 2–606. That section states:

3. Annealization is the process of heating and slow cooling in order to toughen the steel and reduce brittleness.

7. A rejection of goods which is wrongful under the Code is deemed ineffective and the items are viewed as accepted. E.g. Blue Sky Forest Products, Inc. v. New Hampshire Doors Co., 663 P.2d 813, 36 UCC Rep. 1179 (Or.App.1983).

§2-606:

"(1) Acceptance of goods occurs when the buyer

"(a) after a reasonable opportunity to inspect the goods signifies to the seller that the goods are conforming or that he will take or retain them in spite of their non-conformity; or

"(b) fails to make an effective rejection (sub-section (1) of Section 2–602), but such acceptance does not occur until the buyer has had a reasonable opportunity to inspect them; or

"(c) does any act inconsistent with the seller's ownership; but if such act is wrongful as against the seller it is an acceptance only if ratified by him.

"(2) Acceptance of a part of any commercial unit is acceptance of that entire unit."

M.C.L.A. § 440.2606. Subsection (1)(b) appears to most appropriately apply in the instant case [8] and would require that Borg's rejection must be both seasonably given and within a reasonable time pursuant to § 2–602.[9]

Borg clearly did not reject the steel within a reasonable time. Not only is three months an over-long period to retain the goods before rejecting them, but Borg's stamping out of all the steel certainly makes its rejection untimely and ineffective. The Code requires that rejection will occur when the goods are tendered and inspected or after the buyer has had a reasonable time for inspection.[12] Timely rejection ensures the goods can be easily restored to the seller so that he can either make them conforming and tender them back to the buyer or simply sell the goods to another. In this way damages will be mitigated and commer-

---

8. Plaintiff argues that § 2–606(1)(c) applies to the instant case so that Borg's stamping out of the steel is an act inconsistent with the seller's ownership and means acceptance has occurred. A proper reading of § 2–606 suggests that subsection (1)(c) should only apply when the buyer acts with knowledge of the defect. Once the buyer discovers the defect and acts inconsistently with the seller's rights, then (1)(c) will deem the buyer to have accepted the goods. See M.C.L.A. § 440.2606, comments 3 and 4. In J. White & R. Summers, Uniform Commercial Code § 8–2, at 298–99 (2d Ed 1980) the authors correctly state:

"We would argue that acts done in ignorance of the defects which buyer could not have discovered are never covered by 2–606(1)(c). The use of the goods and passage of time might constitute an acceptance under 2–606(1)(a) or 2–606(1)(b). But if any use (and all use is theoretically inconsistent with seller's ownership) constitutes an inconsistent act as that term is used in 2–606(1)(c), then there will always be acceptance the minute the buyer uses the goods notwith-

standing the fact he had not yet had a 'reasonable opportunity to inspect' under 2–606(1)(a) and still has a 'reasonable time' to reject under 2–602 (and therefore has not accepted under 2–606(1)(b)). The only reading of 2–606(1)(c) which is consistent with the Code policy and which leaves elbow room for the other provisions of 2–606 is to find that use of goods in ignorance of the defective nature of the goods is not 'inconsistent' under 2–606(1)(c)."

(Emphasis supplied.) It should be noted that "any use" language of subsection (1)(c) requires this interpretation in order for the other subsections to have meaning. This does not mean a buyer's use, particularly substantial use, could not deem goods as accepted under (1)(a) or (b).

9. M.C.L.A. § 440.2602(1) states:

"Rejection of goods must be within a reasonable time after their delivery or tender. It is ineffective unless the buyer seasonably notifies the seller."

12. See generally J. White & R. Summers, supra, note 8, § 8–2, at 296–318.

[Margin handwritten notes:]

π says (1)(c) applies— but only if buyer knows of defect →

Court says (1)(b) applies!

cial loss curtailed. Rejection is generally not effective after the goods have been manufactured into parts.

Defendant might argue that it did not have "a reasonable opportunity to inspect" the goods as subsection (1)(b) requires, since the defect could not have been reasonably discovered until the steel was processed into parts. This argument is likewise unavailing. The "reasonable opportunity to inspect" provision is to ensure that a buyer's silence, without more, does not automatically impute acceptance until he has had adequate time [14] to inspect the goods. It does not imply that goods which have been drastically changed and used by the buyer can later be rejected and not viewed as accepted, despite the presence of a latent defect. Buyers who receive nonconforming goods with defects that are not easily detected are provided adequate remedies under the Code even though they have accepted the goods.[15] They do not lose the right to recover damages for the seller's breach of warranty by simply having accepted the goods.

This conclusion that Borg's attempt to reject is ineffective is further supported by the relationship the Code establishes between rejection and revocation. The Code provides two methods by which a buyer may act upon nonconforming goods: he may reject them before ever accepting the goods or he may revoke the goods once he has accepted them. The pertinent Code section governing revocation provides:

"(1) The buyer may revoke his acceptance of a lot or commercial unit whose nonconformity substantially impairs its value to him if he has accepted it

"(a) on the reasonable assumption that its nonconformity would be cured and it has not been seasonably cured; or

"(b) without discovery of such nonconformity if his acceptance was reasonably induced either by the difficulty of discovery before acceptance or by the seller's assurances.

"(2) Revocation of acceptance must occur within a reasonable time after the buyer discovers or should have discovered the ground for it and before any substantial change in condition of the goods which is not caused by their own defects. It is not effective until the buyer notifies the seller of it.

"(3) A buyer who so revokes has the same rights and duties with regard to the goods involved as if he had rejected them."

M.C.L.A. § 440.2608. As the Code suggests, a buyer may more readily reject goods than revoke acceptance since the standard for rejection is more relaxed. A buyer is presented with greater obstacles in order

---

14. The standard for "adequate" or "reasonable" time is dependent upon the particular circumstances of each case. MCLA § 440.1204(2) ("What is a reasonable time for taking any action depends on the nature, purpose and circumstances of such action.")

15. Section 2–714 provides that a buyer who accepts nonconforming goods can get damages basically for the reduction in value of the goods due to the nonconformity and any incidental or consequential damages the buyer incurs.

properly to revoke acceptance. For instance, a buyer may reject goods for relatively minor defects. He may not, however, revoke his acceptance unless the "nonconformity substantially impairs" the value of the goods. The difference in standards reflects the degree of prejudice the seller is exposed to in regard to the goods. A buyer's acceptance of the goods will most likely make the seller's ability to cure the nonconformity or resell the goods much more difficult.

Defendant could not avail itself of revocation because a "substantial change in the condition of the goods" was caused by Borg (the steel was stamped into parts) and "not caused by [the goods'] own defect." M.C.L.A. § 440.2608(2). Therefore, it would be a misapplication of the Code to allow defendant's rejection to be effective when it would not be permitted to revoke its acceptance.

Second, the cases defendant cites in support of its argument that it rightfully rejected the steel are not applicable. In each of those cases the contract expressly provided that rejection could occur even after the buyer had changed or used the material. Of course, parties to a contract are free to determine in their agreement when effective rejection can occur. The instant contract, however, cannot be viewed as modifying the Code provisions in regard to the time of rejection and acceptance. It is true that Adzema, Barry's sales representative who was a metallurgist and associated with Barry's quality control department, was familiar with Borg's fabrication schedule—that Borg did not sample test or examine microscopically the steel, and that it stamped, deburred and stored the steel pending customer orders. It is further true that despite his awareness of those procedures he did not object to them, nor suggest any alternatives or modifications. Yet, it is difficult to conclude that Adzema's knowledge of Borg's procedures can be said to imply that the parties' agreement modified the Code to allow Borg to reject the steel even after it had been stamped into parts. Although defendants do not make this contention, Borg could have more reasonably argued that the § 2–608(2) requirement that revocation is not effective if a substantial change in the condition of the goods had occurred was somehow modified by the parties' agreement. But it would be equally difficult to determine that the instant contract intended that modification of the Code also. Thus, Borg's rejection after the steel had been stamped out must be seen as ineffective. Moreover, Borg was likewise not permitted to revoke its acceptance once it had processed all the steel into parts. Defendant is thereby deemed to have accepted and retained the goods.

II. DEFENDANT'S RIGHT TO SET OFF DAMAGES FROM ITS OBLIGATION TO PAY PURCHASE PRICE

Since defendant accepted the goods under § 2–607(2) defendant became obligated for the purchase price of the steel minus the scrap value of the material which was already turned over to the plaintiff. However, since Borg notified Barry Steel of the breach within a reasonable time, defendant may withhold payment of the purchase price to the extent that it has suffered damages from the seller's breach. See M.C.L.A. § 440.2717.

* * *

In conclusion, defendant is entitled to set off the amount of the purchase price it owes plaintiff with its damages, which is the difference between the scrap value of the steel and the contract price of the material. Thus, plaintiff is not entitled to the $41,612.47 for which it brought this action.

[Some footnotes omitted.]

D. Buyer's Duties Regarding Rejected Goods

BORGES v. MAGIC VALLEY FOODS, INC.

Supreme Court of Idaho, 1980.
101 Idaho 494, 616 P.2d 273.

SHEPARD, J. This is an appeal from a judgment following a jury verdict which awarded plaintiffs-respondents Borges and G & B Land and Cattle Company $12,832.00 for potatoes received by defendant-appellant Magic West pursuant to a contract with respondents. We affirm.

In 1975, respondents grew and harvested approximately 45,000 c.w.t. of potatoes, which were stored in a cellar near Buhl, Idaho. Magic West inspected those potatoes and, although their inspection indicated that some contained a "hollow heart" defect, Magic West agreed to purchase them for $3.80 per c.w.t. "Hollow heart" indicates a vacant space in the middle of the potato. The purchase contract provided that "if internal problems develop making these potatoes unfit for fresh pack shipping, this contract becomes null and void." It was agreed that the cost of transporting the potatoes from the storage cellar to the processing plant would be borne by Magic West. Examination of the potatoes by State inspectors would occur at the plant to determine that the number of potatoes affected by the hollow heart defect did not exceed the limit prescribed for shipping under the fresh pack grade.

The potatoes were transported to the processing plant, where more than 30,000 c.w.t. were processed and shipped under the fresh pack grade. In March, 1976, State inspectors declared the remaining 4,838.77 c.w.t. of potatoes unfit for the fresh pack grade because of the increased incidence of hollow heart condition.[1] On March 31, 1976, the parties met to discuss the problem of the remaining potatoes and it was apparently agreed that Magic West should attempt to blend them with other potatoes of a higher grade in the hope that such a blend would meet fresh pack grade standards. That experiment failed and Magic West, without notifying the respondents, processed the remaining

1. There were also potatoes still in storage which Magic West never paid for due to the hollow heart problems. There is no dispute with regard to those potatoes. Respondents eventually sold them for $3.00 per c.w.t. to be used as french fries. There were also 702 c.w.t. of defective potatoes in transit to the plant on March 31, 1977. The respondents agreed to accept $1.25 per c.w.t. for those potatoes from Magic West.

4,838.77 c.w.t. of potatoes into flakes and sold them for $1.25 per c.w.t. The evidence in the record disclosed that the remaining potatoes could not be removed from the processing plant without destroying at least one-third of the potatoes.

Respondents demanded the contract price of $3.80 per c.w.t. for the potatoes sold as flakes. Magic West refused, and instead offered to pay $1.25 per c.w.t. This action resulted. The jury returned a general verdict to the respondents of $12,832.00 and the trial court also awarded $6,975.00 as and for attorney fees and costs to the respondents.[2]

Magic West's basic contention is that the 4,838.77 c.w.t. of potatoes were clearly defective and that they were never accepted. It is claimed that when Magic West processed the potatoes into flakes and sold them for $1.25 per c.w.t., they were only following respondents' instructions.

The potatoes in the instant case were clearly movable at the time they were identified in the contract, I.C. § 28–2–105, and, hence, were "goods" within the purview of the Idaho Uniform Commercial Code, I.C. §§ 28–2–101 to –2–725, and the dispute is governed by the provisions of the Uniform Commercial Code.

It is clear and undisputed that Magic West had the responsibility of transporting the potatoes from the storage cellar to the processing plant and that State inspection would occur at the plant. It is also clear that the 4,838.77 c.w.t. of potatoes, unable to make the fresh pack grade, did not conform to the contract and gave Magic West the right of rejection. IC § 28–2–601(a). Also, it is not disputed that when Magic West determined that the potatoes would not meet fresh pack grade, Magic West so notified the respondents and met with them to determine what disposition should be made of the potatoes. The record is unclear as to precisely what was decided at that March 31, 1976 meeting, but respondents apparently approved of Magic West's proposal to blend the defective potatoes with those with higher quality in an attempt to meet the fresh pack grade. However, it is clear that no agreement on price was reached at that meeting.

A buyer must pay the contract rate for any goods accepted. I.C. § 28–2–607(1). Generally, a buyer is deemed to have accepted defective goods when, knowing of the defect, he resells the goods without notifying the seller. See White & Summers, Uniform Commercial Code, § 8–2 (2d ed. 1980); 67 Am Jur2d Sales (1973). A buyer accepts goods whenever he does any act inconsistent with the seller's ownership. I.C. § 28–2–606(1)(c). Respondents assert that Magic West's processing of

---

2. Both parties agreed that the jury had apparently awarded respondents the full contract price of $3.80 per c.w.t. for the potatoes in dispute. If no deductions were made, a jury award of $3.80 per c.w.t. would have resulted in a jury verdict of $18,387.32 [$3.80 × 4838.77]. Obviously, some deductions were made although they are not apparent from the record and were not explained or challenged by counsel. For purposes of this appeal, we assume, as counsel do, that the jury awarded $3.80 per c.w.t. for the potatoes in dispute.

the remaining potatoes into flakes and the subsequent sale constituted acts inconsistent with the respondents' ownership.

Magic West argues, however, that their processing of the potatoes into flakes and their subsequent sale did not constitute an acceptance, but rather was a permissible resale under the provisions of either I.C. § 28–2–603(1) or I.C. § 28–2–604. I.C. § 28–2–603(1) provides:

> "Subject to any security interest in the buyer * * *, when the seller has no agent or place of business at the market of rejection a merchant buyer is under a duty after rejection of goods in his possession or control to follow any reasonable instructions received from the seller with respect to the goods and in the absence of such instructions to make reasonable efforts to sell them for the seller's account if they are perishable or threaten to decline in value speedily."

Court determined there were other instructions

I.C. § 28–2–604 provides:

> "Subject to the provisions of the immediately preceding section on perishables if the seller gives no instructions within a reasonable time after notification of rejection the buyer may store the rejected goods for the seller's account or reship them to him or resell them for the seller's account with reimbursement as provided in the preceding section. Such action is not acceptance or conversion."

We note that both I.C. § 28–2–603(1) and I.C. § 28–2–604 were given in their entirety as instructions to the jury. We find it unclear from the record whether the respondents had agents or a place of business at the "market of rejection." Also, the duty to resell under I.C. § 28–2–603(1) is triggered by an absence of instructions from a seller. Here, given the state of the record and its lack of clarity and the conflicting evidence, the jury could have reasonably found that the respondents did instruct Magic West to attempt to blend the potatoes, but did not instruct them to process the potatoes into flakes. While I.C. § 28–2–604 allows a buyer an option to resell rejected goods if the seller gives no instructions within a reasonable time after the notification of rejection, the jury could have reasonably found that respondents' instructions were only to blend the potatoes in hope of accomplishing fresh pack grade and that Magic West's processing of the potatoes into flakes and subsequent resale thereof was a precipitate action taken before the lapse of a reasonable time within which respondents could give further instructions.

In addition, even if a reasonable time had elapsed, thus permitting Magic West to resell the potatoes, the jury properly could have concluded that processing of the potatoes by Magic West was an acceptance rather than a resale. There was no evidence presented either of an attempt to resell the potatoes in the bins to an independent third party, or of the value of the potatoes in the bins, less damage caused by removal, should it have been effected. Absent any evidence that the $1.25 per c.w.t. offered by Magic West was the highest value obtainable for the potatoes, Magic West's use of the potatoes in the ordinary course of its own business (presumably for profit) was an act inconsistent with the seller's ownership, and constituted an acceptance of the goods. I.C. § 28–2–606(1)(c).

The jury was adequately and correctly instructed regarding the provisions of I.C. § 28–2–603(1) and I.C. § 28–2–604, which constituted Magic West's theory of its duty or option of resale because of an absence of instructions from respondents. The jury was at liberty to reject Magic West's theory of defense based on substantial, albeit conflicting, evidence that Magic West's resale of the potatoes after processing them into flakes constituted an acceptance and Magic West was hence liable for the full contract price.

We have examined appellants' remaining assignments of error and find them to be without merit.

Affirmed. Costs to respondents.

DONALDSON, C.J., BAKES, MCFADDEN and BISTLINE, JJ., concur.

Problem 11–5

Suppose in the Sodfill-Blurtaste problem, above, that the bill of lading had permitted inspection and that Blurtaste had discovered the defect in 1, above, while inspecting goods still in the possession of the carrier. Blurtaste did not take possession and promptly notified Sodfill of his decision to reject as required by UCC 2–602. Assume, further, that (1) the weather was quite hot, putting a strain on the refrigeration unit in the railroad car, (2) the tomato market had started a steady decline due to a bumper crop and (3) Sodfill had no local agent at the place of destination. Does Blurtaste have any obligation to Sodfill with regard to the rejected goods? If so, what would you advise Blurtaste to do? See UCC 2–602(2), 2–603 and 2–604.

Note: Perishable Agricultural Commodities

Under section 2(2) of the Perishable Agricultural Commodities Act, 7 U.S.C.A. § 499b, as amended, it is unlawful in interstate transactions "for any dealer to reject or fail to deliver in accordance with the terms of the contract without reasonable cause any perishable agricultural commodity bought or sold or contracted to be bought or sold in interstate * * * commerce by such dealer." The Act was "intended to prevent produce from becoming distress merchandise and to protect sellers who often were at great distance from the buyer." L. Gillarde & Co. v. Joseph Martinelli & Co., 168 F.2d 276, amended 169 F.2d 60, 61 (1st Cir.1948), cert. denied 335 U.S. 885. Remedies include reparation orders for aggrieved shippers and suspension or revocation of licenses. See Chidsey v. Geurin, 443 F.2d 584 (6th Cir.1971). The Secretary has defined "reject without reasonable cause" to include "refusing or failing without legal justification to accept produce within a reasonable time" and "advising the seller, shipper, or his agent that produce, complying with the contract, will not be accepted." 7 C.F.R. § 46.2(bb) (1986). Reasonable time for rejection is defined with reference to the type of produce and the method of shipment. 7 C.F.R. § 46.2(cc) (1986). A number of commonly used trade terms are crisply defined and, to the extent used by the parties, both preempt state law definitions, e.g., UCC 2–319, and define rights and duties. For example, "rolling acceptance final" means that the buyer "has no recourse against the seller because of any change in condition of the produce in transit" but if the shipment is not rejected the buyer has recourse in damages against the seller for any material breach. 7 C.F.R. § 46.43(t) (1986). The thrust of the definitions is to restrict or prohibit the rejection remedy, especially where the reason for rejection affects the condition or quality of the goods. See Schuman Co. v. Nelson, 219 F.2d 627 (3d Cir.1955) (under earlier regulations, "rolling acceptance final" does not preclude rejection for breach not relating to quality or condition of goods). Since buyers subject to the Act often pay against documents or under a letter of credit arrangement, the need for adequate inspection of the produce at the point of shipment is acute. Federal inspection is available and, in some cases, required under the Act. See 7 U.S.C.A. § 499n; 7 C.F.R. §§ 46.39 & 46.40 (1986); Cove Valley Packers, Inc. v. Pilgrim Fruit Co., 297 F.Supp. 200 (D.Mass.1969).

Note: "Avoidance" of the Contract in International Sales

Professor John Honnold has observed that one of the "thorniest problems" in the law of sales is "when will the breach by one party free the other party of his obligation to perform?" J. Honnold, Uniform Law for International Sales 65 (1982). This problem has special significance in international sales "because of the cost of transporting goods to a distant buyer and the difficulty of disposing of rejected goods." Ibid.

The 1980 United Nations Convention on Contracts for the International Sale of Goods, which the United States Senate ratified on Dec. 11, 1986 and which becomes effective on Jan. 1, 1988, deals with problems created by the seller's delay in performance or delivery of non-conforming documents or goods in the following manner.

Let us consider only the case of non-conforming goods or documents. Suppose the seller has tendered goods or documents which fail to conform to the contract. The buyer discovers the non-conformity after "examination" of the goods or documents, Article 38, and preserves his rights by giving "notice to the seller specifying the nature of the lack of conformity within a reasonable time after he has discovered it or ought to have discovered it." Article 39(1). What are these "rights"?

First, the buyer may recover damages for breach of contract. Article 74.

Second, the buyer may, in carefully defined situations, compel the seller either to deliver "substitute goods," if the breach is "fundamental," or to "remedy the lack of conformity by repair" if reasonable under all of the circumstances. Article 46. If this remedy is successful, the buyer will owe the price, subject to adjustment for any losses caused by the breach.

Third, the buyer may attempt to "avoid" the contract ("cancel" in UCC parlance)—a remedy that substitutes for "rejection" of the goods. "Avoidance" of the contract requires the buyer to: (a) establish that the non-conformity amounted to a "fundamental" breach, Article 49(1), and (b) give notice to the buyer of the attempt to avoid within a reasonable time after he "knew or ought to have known of the breach." Article 49(2)(b). See Article 26. A breach is "fundamental if it results in such detriment to the other party as substantially to deprive him of what he is entitled to expect under the contract, unless the party in breach did not foresee and a reasonable person of the same kind in the same circumstances would not have foreseen such a result."

Fourth, the "right" to avoid the contract for a fundamental breach, however, is limited by the seller's right to "cure" the defect by replacing or repairing the defective goods, Articles 37 (cure until date of delivery) and 48 (cure after delivery) or conforming the documents. Article 34. See Honnold at 184–85. Thus, if the buyer discovered a "fundamental" breach after delivery, the seller could prevent an "avoidance" of the contract by remedying "at his own expense any failure to perform his obligations, if he can do so without unreasonable delay and without causing the buyer unreasonable inconvenience. * * *" Article 48(1).

Enough has been said to indicate that the 1980 Convention has rejected a "perfect tender" rule for rules that require "fundamental" breach and maximize the seller's opportunity to cure. In short, the 1980 Convention seeks to preserve the contract and to foster adjustments, while protecting the buyer's right to damages for losses caused during the "cure" period. At the same time, one can see that the Convention's solution will not be simple to understand and administer and this problem is complicated by a sometimes murky drafting history. See Speidel, Book Review, 5 Nw.J.Int'l. Law & Bus. 432 (1983). Nevertheless, we believe Professor Honnold's book sheds considerable light on the 1980 Convention and recommend it as the perfect place to start. If your interest is piqued, go next to Rosett, *Critical Reflections on the United Nations Convention on Contracts for the International Sale of Goods,* 45 Ohio S.L.J. 305 (1984).

For now, you may wish to review the UCC's approach to the problem of "rejection" and "cancellation" and compare it with the 1980 Convention.

SECTION 4. NATURE AND CONSEQUENCES OF ACCEPTANCE

So far, we have focused upon the buyer's right to inspect and the remedy of rejection when defects in the seller's tender of delivery are actually discovered. Through both inspection and rejection the buyer seeks to avoid accepting defective goods. Now we will be concerned with three additional but related questions. First, exactly when does a buyer accept tendered goods? The critical section here is UCC 2–606. Second, what is the legal effect of an acceptance? This is particularly important when the goods accepted are actually non-conforming. See UCC 2–510(1) and UCC 2–607. Third, when may the buyer "revoke" his acceptance under UCC 2–608 and what is the effect of a proper revocation of acceptance? Regardless of how the acceptance occurs, a buyer with defective goods on his hands will be in a different and, perhaps, more difficult remedial posture than if the remedy of rejection had properly been invoked. Because the complexity of many goods and the casualness of most inspections naturally contribute to a high incidence of acceptance, a thorough appreciation of this "posture" by the commercial lawyer is required.

PLATEQ CORP. OF NORTH HAVEN v. MACHLETT LABORATORIES, INC.

Supreme Court of Connecticut, 1983.
189 Conn. 433, 456 A.2d 786.

Before SPEZIALE, C.J., and PETERS, ARTHUR H. HEALEY, PARSKEY and GRILLO, JJ.

PETERS, JUDGE.

In this action by a seller of specially manufactured goods to recover their purchase price from a commercial buyer, the principal issue is whether the buyer accepted the goods before it attempted to cancel the contract of sale. The plaintiff, Plateq Corporation of North Haven, sued the defendant, The Machlett Laboratories, Inc., to recover damages, measured by the contract price and incidental damages, arising out of the defendant's allegedly wrongful cancellation of a written contract for the manufacture and sale of two leadcovered steel tanks and appurtenant stands. The defendant denied liability and counterclaimed for damages. After a full hearing, the trial court found for the plaintiff both on its complaint and on the defendant's counterclaim. The defendant has appealed.

The trial court, in its memorandum of decision, found the following facts. On July 9, 1976, the defendant ordered from the plaintiff two leadcovered steel tanks to be constructed by the plaintiff according to specifications supplied by the defendant. The parties understood that the tanks were designed for the special purpose of testing x-ray tubes and were required to be radiation-proof within certain federal standards. Accordingly, the contract provided that the tanks would be tested for radiation leaks after their installation on the defendant's premises. The plaintiff undertook to correct, at its own cost, any deficiencies that this post-installation test might uncover.[1] The plaintiff had not previously constructed such tanks, nor had the defendant previously designed tanks for this purpose. The contract was amended on August 9, 1976, to add construction of two metal stands to hold the tanks. All the goods were to be delivered to the defendant at the plaintiff's place of business.[2]

Although the plaintiff encountered difficulties both in performing according to the contract specifications and in completing performance within the time required, the defendant did no more than call these

---

1. The contract incorporated precise specifications in the form of detailed drawings. The drawings for the tank and the tank cover contained specific manufacturing instructions as well as provision 6: "Tank with cover will be tested for radia-

tion leaks after installation. Any deficiencies must be corrected by the vendor."

2. The purchase order sent by the defendant to the plaintiff stipulated that the goods were to be shipped "F.O.B. Origin."

deficiencies to the plaintiff's attention during various inspections in September and early October, 1976. By October 11, 1976, performance was belatedly but substantially completed. On that date, Albert Yannello, the defendant's engineer, noted some remaining deficiencies which the plaintiff promised to remedy by the next day, so that the goods would then be ready for delivery. Yannello gave no indication to the plaintiff that this arrangement was in any way unsatisfactory to the defendant. Not only did Yannello communicate general acquiescence in the plaintiff's proposed tender but he specifically led the plaintiff to believe that the defendant's truck would pick up the tanks and the stands within a day or two. Instead of sending its truck, the defendant sent a notice of total cancellation which the plaintiff received on October 14, 1976. That notice failed to particularize the grounds upon which cancellation was based.[3]

On this factual basis, the trial court, having concluded that the transaction was a contract for the sale of goods falling within the Uniform Commercial Code, General Statutes §§ 42a–2–101 et seq., considered whether the defendant had accepted the goods. The court determined that the defendant had accepted the tanks, primarily by signifying its willingness to take them despite their nonconformities, in accordance with General Statutes § 42a–2–606(1)(a), and secondarily by failing to make an effective rejection, in accordance with General Statutes § 42a–2–606(1)(b). Once the tanks had been accepted, the defendant could rightfully revoke its acceptance under General Statutes § 42a–2–608 only by showing substantial impairment of their value to the defendant. In part because the defendant's conduct had foreclosed any post-installation inspection, the court concluded that such impairment had not been proved. Since the tanks were not readily resaleable on the open market, the plaintiff was entitled, upon the defendant's wrongful revocation of acceptance, to recover their contract price, minus salvage value, plus interest. General Statutes §§ 42a–2–703; 42a–2–709(1)(b). Accordingly, the trial court awarded the plaintiff damages in the amount of $14,837.92.

In its appeal, the defendant raises four principal claims of error. It maintains that the trial court erred: (1) in invoking the "cure" section, General Statutes § 42a–2–508, when there had been no tender by the plaintiff seller; (2) in concluding, in accordance with the acceptance section, General Statutes § 42a–2–606(1), that the defendant had "signified" to the plaintiff its willingness to take the contract goods; (3) in misconstruing the defendant's statutory and contractual rights of inspection; and (4) in refusing to find that the defendant's letter of cancellation was occasioned by the plaintiff's breach. We find no error.

---

3. The defendant sent the plaintiff a telegram stating: "This order is hereby terminated for your breach, in that you have continuously failed to perform according to your commitment in spite of additional time given you to cure your delinquency. We will hold you liable for all damages incured [sic] by Machlett including excess cost of reprocurement."

Upon analysis, all of the defendant's claims of error are variations upon one central theme. The defendant claims that on October 11, when its engineer Yannello conducted the last examination on the plaintiff's premises, the tanks were so incomplete and unsatisfactory that the defendant was rightfully entitled to conclude that the plaintiff would never make a conforming tender. From this scenario, the defendant argues that it was justified in cancelling the contract of sale. It denies that the seller's conduct was sufficient to warrant a finding of tender, or its own conduct sufficient to warrant a finding of acceptance. The difficulty with this argument is that it is inconsistent with the underlying facts found by the trial court. Although the testimony was in dispute, there was evidence of record to support the trial court's findings to the contrary. The defendant cannot sustain its burden of establishing that a trial court's findings of fact are clearly erroneous; Practice Book § 3060D; *Pandolphe's Auto Parts, Inc. v. Manchester,* 181 Conn. 217, 221–22, 435 A.2d 24 (1980); by the mere recitation in its brief of conflicting testimony entirely unsupported by reference to pages of the transcript. Practice Book § 3060F(b). There is simply no fit between the defendant's claims and the trial court's finding that, by October 11, 1976, performance was in substantial compliance with the terms of the contract. The trial court further found that on that day the defendant was notified that the goods would be ready for tender the following day and that the defendant responded to this notification by promising to send its truck to pick up the tanks in accordance with the contract.

On the trial court's finding of facts, it was warranted in concluding, on two independent grounds, that the defendant had accepted the goods it had ordered from the plaintiff. Under the provisions of the Uniform Commercial Code, General Statutes § 42a–2–606(1) "[a]cceptance of goods occurs when the buyer (a) after a reasonable opportunity to inspect the goods signifies to the seller * * * that he will take * * * them in spite of their nonconformity; or (b) fails to make an effective rejection." [10]

In concluding that the defendant had "signified" to the plaintiff its willingness to "take" the tanks despite possible remaining minor defects, the trial court necessarily found that the defendant had had a reasonable opportunity to inspect the goods. The defendant does not maintain that its engineer, or the other inspectors on previous visits, had inadequate access to the tanks, or inadequate experience to conduct a reasonable examination. It recognizes that inspection of goods when the buyer undertakes to pick up the goods is ordinarily at the seller's place of tender. See General Statutes §§ 42a–2–503, 42a–2–507, 42a–2–513; see also White & Summers, Uniform Commercial Code § 3–5 (2d Ed.1980). The defendant argues, however, that its contract, in provid-

---

10. General Statutes § 42a–2–606(1)(c) provides a third ground, the exercise of dominion, for finding acceptance but that ground was not considered by the trial court, presumably because it has no apparent factual relevance to the circumstances of this case. * * *

ing for inspection for radiation leaks after installation of the tanks at its premises, necessarily postponed its inspection rights to that time. The trial court considered this argument and rejected it, and so do we. It was reasonable, in the context of this contract for the special manufacture of goods with which neither party had had prior experience, to limit this clause to adjustments to take place after tender and acceptance. After acceptance, a buyer may still, in appropriate cases, revoke its acceptance, General Statutes § 42a–2–608, or recover damages for breach of warranty, General Statutes § 42a–2–714. The trial court reasonably concluded that a post-installation test was intended to safeguard these rights of the defendant as well as to afford the plaintiff a final opportunity to make needed adjustments. The court was therefore justified in concluding that there had been an acceptance within § 42a–2–606(1)(a). A buyer may be found to have accepted goods despite their known nonconformity and despite the absence of actual delivery to the buyer * * *.

The trial court's alternate ground for concluding that the tanks had been accepted was the defendant's failure to make an effective rejection. Pursuant to General Statutes § 42a–2–606(1)(b), an acceptance occurs when, after a reasonable opportunity to inspect, a buyer has failed to make "an effective rejection as provided by subsection (1) of section 42a–2–602." The latter subsection, in turn, makes a rejection "ineffective unless the buyer seasonably notifies the seller." General Statutes § 42a–2–605(1)(a) goes on to provide that a buyer is precluded from relying, as a basis for rejection, upon unparticularized defects in his notice of rejection, if the defects were such that, with seasonable notice, the seller could have cured by making a substituted, conforming tender. The defendant does not question the trial court's determination that its telegram of cancellation failed to comply with the requirement of particularization contained in § 42a–2–605(1). Instead, the defendant argues that the plaintiff was not entitled to an opportunity to cure, under General Statutes § 42a–2–508, because the plaintiff had never made a tender of the tanks. That argument founders, however, on the trial court's finding that the seller was ready to make a tender on the day following the last inspection by the defendant's engineer and would have done so but for its receipt of the defendant's telegram of cancellation. The trial court furthermore found that the defendant's unparticularized telegram of cancellation wrongfully interfered with the plaintiff's contractual right to cure any remaining post-installation defects. In these circumstances, the telegram of cancellation constituted both a wrongful and an ineffective rejection on the part of the defendant. See *Uchitel v. F.R. Tripler & Co.*, 107 Misc.2d 310, 434 N.Y.S.2d 77, 81–82 (Supreme Court 1980); White & Summers, supra, § 8–3, p. 315.

Once the conclusion is reached that the defendant accepted the tanks, its further rights of cancellation under the contract are limited by the governing provisions of the Uniform Commercial Code. "The buyer's acceptance of goods, despite their alleged nonconformity, is a watershed. After acceptance, the buyer must pay for the goods at the contract rate; General Statutes § 42a–2–607(1); and bears the burden of establishing their nonconformity. General Statutes § 42a–2–607(4)." *Stelco Industries, Inc. v. Cohen,* 182 Conn. 561, 563–64, 438 A.2d 759 (1980). After acceptance, the buyer may only avoid liability for the contract price by invoking the provision which permits revocation of acceptance. That provision, General Statutes § 42a–2–608(1), requires proof that the "nonconformity [of the goods] substantially impairs [their] value to him." * * * On this question which is an issue of fact; * * * the trial court again found against the defendant. Since the defendant has provided no basis for any argument that the trial court was clearly erroneous in finding that the defendant had not met its burden of proof to show that the goods were substantially nonconforming, we can find no error in the conclusion that the defendant's cancellation constituted an unauthorized and hence wrongful revocation of acceptance.

Finally, the defendant in its brief, although not in its statement of the issues presented, challenges the trial court's conclusion about the remedial consequences of its earlier determinations. Although the trial court might have found the plaintiff entitled to recover the contract price because of the defendant's acceptance of the goods; General Statutes §§ 42a–2–703(e) and 42a–2–709(1)(a); the court chose instead to rely on General Statutes § 42a–2–709(1)(b), which permits a price action for contract goods that cannot, after reasonable effort, be resold at a reasonable price.[19] Since the contract goods in this case were concededly specially manufactured for the defendant, the defendant cannot and does not contest the trial court's finding that any effort to resell them on the open market would have been unavailing. In the light of this finding, the defendant can only reiterate its argument, which we have already rejected, that the primary default was that of the plaintiff rather than that of the defendant. The trial court's conclusion to the contrary supports both its award to the plaintiff and its denial of the defendant's counterclaim.

There is no error.

In this opinion the other Judges concurred.

[Footnotes in which court quoted from statute omitted.]

19. * * * It should be noted that § 42a–2–709(1)(b) is not premised on a buyer's acceptance. Instead, it requires a showing that the goods were, before the buyer's cancellation, "identified to the contract." In the circumstances of this case, that precondition was presumably met by their special manufacture and by the defendant's acquiescence in their imminent tender. See White & Summers, Uniform Commercial Code, § 7–5 (2d Ed.1980). The defendant has not, on this appeal, argued the absence of identification.

It should further be noted that § 42a–2–709(1)(b), because it is not premised on acceptance, would have afforded the seller the right to recover the contract price even if the trial court had found the conduct of the buyer to be a wrongful rejection (because of the failure to give the seller an opportunity to cure) rather than a wrongful revocation of acceptance.

Notes

1. In Zabriskie Chevrolet, Inc. v. Smith, parts of which are reprinted supra at p. 404, the court had this to say about whether the defendant accepted a new car with a defective transmission:

"It is clear that a buyer does not accept goods until he has had a 'reasonable opportunity to inspect.' Defendant sought to purchase a new car. He assumed what every new car buyer has a right to assume and, indeed, has been led to assume by the high powered advertising techniques of the auto industry—that his new car, with the exception of very minor adjustments, would be mechanically new and factory-furnished, operate perfectly, and be free of substantial defects. The vehicle delivered to defendant did not measure up to these representations. Plaintiff contends that defendant had 'reasonable opportunity to inspect' by the privilege to take the car for a typical 'spin around the block' before signing the purchase order. If by this contention plaintiff equates a spin around the block with 'reasonable opportunity to inspect,' the contention is illusory and unrealistic. To the layman, the complicated mechanisms of today's automobiles are a complete mystery. To have the automobile inspected by someone with sufficient expertise to disassemble the vehicle in order to discover latent defects before the contract is signed, is assuredly impossible and highly impractical. Cf. Massari v. Accurate Bushing Co., 8 N.J. 299, 313, 85 A.2d 260. Consequently, the first few miles of driving become even more significant to the excited new car buyer. This is the buyer's first reasonable opportunity to enjoy his new vehicle to see if it conforms to what it was represented to be and whether he is getting what he bargained for. How long the buyer may drive the new car under the guise of inspection of new goods is not an issue in the present case. It is clear that defendant discovered the nonconformity within $7/10$ of a mile and minutes after leaving plaintiff's showroom. Certainly this was well within the ambit of 'reasonable opportunity to inspect.' That the vehicle was grievously defective when it left plaintiff's possession is a compelling conclusion, as is the conclusion that in a legal sense defendant never accepted the vehicle.

"Nor could the dealer under such circumstances require acceptance. Cf. Code Comment 2 (subsection 2) to N.J.S. 12A:2–106, N.J.S.A.:

'It is in general intended to continue the policy of requiring exact performance by the seller of his obligations as a condition to his right to require acceptance. * * *' "

2. Of the many cases involving UCC 2–606, the bulk involve the question whether the buyer, after having a reasonable opportunity to inspect the goods, has failed to "make an effective rejection," UCC 2–606(1)(b), that is, has failed to reject the goods within "a reasonable time after their delivery of tender." UCC 2–602(1). Like words or conduct indicating that the buyer will take the goods, silence for an unreasonable time induces the seller to believe that there is no problem with the tender of delivery. Whether an acceptance by failing to reject has occurred may turn on several factors, e.g., the nature of the defect (latent or patent), agreement on the time in which notice must be given, express warranties or assur-

ances that problems will be corrected by the buyer, effort or lack of it by the buyer to test or inspect the goods, use of the goods by the buyer after the defect was or should have been discovered, special conditions indicating that prompt action is required, and so forth. In most cases, the difficulty will be in applying the legal principles to complicated or controverted facts. More may be at stake than simply losing the right to reject. At some point an unreasonable delay in rejecting may foreclose either a subsequent revocation of acceptance, UCC 2–608(2), or any remedy for the non-conformity, UCC 2–607(3)(a).

3. Under UCC 2–607(2), as well as its predecessor, Uniform Sales Act § 49, the fact of acceptance does not automatically preclude further remedies even though the buyer had a reasonable opportunity to inspect and the defect was "patent." This is an apparent concession to the assumption that the normal buyer's inspection will be less than adequate to deal with the complexities of defective tenders or products. In short, the buyer will not be deprived of any remedy simply because he should have discovered the particular defect complained of. But if acceptance "precludes rejection of the goods accepted," UCC 2–607(2), and the "buyer must pay at the contract rate for any goods accepted," UCC 2–607(1), what remedies remain for the buyer? The choice is between "revoking" the acceptance under UCC 2–608 or seeking damages "for breach in regard to accepted goods" under UCC 2–714. If revocation of acceptance is available and pursued, the buyer "has the same rights and duties with regard to the goods involved as if he had rejected them." UCC 2–608(3). He may, if the breach goes to the entire contract, cancel, recover so much of the price as has been paid and "cover" under UCC 2–712 or recover damages under UCC 2–713. UCC 2–711(1). If UCC 2–608 is not invoked or unavailable, the buyer must pay the contract price reduced by the amount of damages caused by the breach, UCC 2–717, and measured under UCC 2–714 and UCC 2–715.

The distinction between "latent" and "patent" defects, however, does appear in the UCC. UCC 2–607(3)(a) provides that where a tender has been accepted "the buyer must within a reasonable time after he discovers or should have discovered any breach notify the seller of breach or be barred from any remedy." As we shall see, this provision has generated controversy where defects in accepted goods cause damage to person or property. In commercial cases, however, the purpose of notification would seem to be to inform the seller "that the transaction is claimed to involve a breach, and thus [open] the way for normal settlement through negotiation." UCC 2–607, comment 4. Unlike the detail required by UCC 2–605 when goods are rejected, the content of notification under UCC 2–607(3) "need merely be sufficient to let the seller know that the transaction is still troublesome and must be watched." Comment 4. Consider the following problem.

Problem 11–6

The "Red Carpet" Treatment

On October 19, Dr. Miron, a physician who owned some race horses, attended an auction without his trainer. He observed a race horse named "Red Carpet" as he was led into the ring for sale. During a lull in the bidding, the auctioneer recited Red Carpet's "track record" and warranted him to be "sound." Thereafter, bidding picked up and Dr. Miron was the high bidder at $32,000. He took immediate possession and transported Red Carpet by van to his barn at a racetrack some 50 miles away. The next morning, Dr. Miron's trainer inspected Red Carpet and found him to be lame. The left hind leg was swollen and sensitive. X-rays later revealed a broken splint bone. Before noon on October 20, Dr. Miron notified the seller that the horse was not sound as warranted and demanded that the horse be taken back. Seller refused and insisted that the full price be paid.

1. You have been retained to represent Dr. Miron. After some probing, you have accumulated the following evidence:

(a) X-rays showing a broken splint bone in the left hind leg;

(b) Expert testimony that a broken splint bone renders a race horse unsound and, because the symptoms appear quickly, can be discovered by an inspection;

(c) Dr. Miron's affidavit that he was an inexperienced horse buyer, that he attended the auction without a trainer, that he did not examine the horse before the sale and that he did not inspect the horse's legs before transporting him to the barn;

(d) The testimony of other persons who attended the sale that they had examined Red Carpet before the auction and found no symptoms of a broken splint bone;

(e) Testimony of Dr. Miron's trainer that the problem was found and notice given within 24 hours of the sale. However, no blood tests were taken to determine whether the horse had been drugged at the time of sale.

The Seller has agreed to take the horse back if Dr. Miron will pay $20,000. Otherwise, he will sue for the full price under UCC 2–709(1). What would you advise the good doctor to do?

2. Suppose that Dr. Miron could establish that Red Carpet was not sound when the hammer fell. The seller, however, argued that Dr. Miron had accepted the horse and that either revocation of acceptance was barred under UCC 2–608(2) or that the buyer was barred from any remedy under UCC 2–607(3). How would you respond?

3. Suppose that Dr. Miron conceded that he had accepted a lame horse and attempted to revoke that acceptance under UCC 2–608(2). Who has the burden of proof in this situation? Compare UCC 2–607(4). See also, Keck v. Wacker, 413 F.Supp. 1377 (E.D.Ky.1976), another horse case, holding that where an acceptance was revoked the burden was on the seller to show that the horse conformed to the contract. Does this make sense? See UCC 2–515.

[For horse lovers, the case upon which this problem is based is Miron v. Yonkers Raceway, Inc., 400 F.2d 112 (2d Cir.1968).]

SECTION 5. SCOPE OF BUYER'S RIGHT TO REVOKE ACCEPTANCE

One of the consequences of accepting goods is that the buyer loses the rejection remedy provided in UCC 2–601. UCC 2–607(2). He is not necessarily "stuck" with the goods, however, since UCC 2–608 provides a controlled opportunity to "revoke" the acceptance and states that a "buyer who so revokes has the same rights and duties with regard to the goods involved as if he had rejected them." UCC 2–608(3). There is a temptation to equate "revocation of acceptance" with the remedy of rescission given by section 69 of the Uniform Sales Act for breach of warranty with regard to accepted goods. This temptation should be resisted. An effective revocation of acceptance neutralizes the effect of acceptance and enables the buyer to cancel the contract and pursue other available remedies under UCC 2–711. See Welken v. Conley, 252 N.W.2d 311 (N.D.1977). The buyer, however, may wish to keep the contract intact and negotiate for the repair or replacement of the goods involved. In any event, if an effective revocation occurs the remedies available to the buyer are broader and more flexible than under the USA. This is not to say that UCC 2–608 is easy to work with—it is loaded with "weasel" words which must be particularized in each case. Yet the commercial lawyer should spend some time with this section since the frustrated buyer who is unable to get satisfaction from the seller will be likely to seek advice about what to do with non-conforming goods which have been accepted, are still in his possession and may have been paid for in whole or in part.

Note, for example, the conditions attached to the "revocation of acceptance" remedy.

First, what is the effect of accepting the goods under UCC 2–606 without discovering the non-conformity? Or, suppose the buyer knew of the non-conformity and still accepted the goods? In either case, the buyer is protected if the seller made assurances that known defects would be cured or that there were no defects. UCC 2–608(1)(a) & (b). In the former case, the ancient distinction between latent and patent defects seems to be preserved: a buyer is not foreclosed from revocation where the acceptance of non-conforming goods "was reasonably induced * * * by the difficulty of discovery before acceptance. * * *" UCC 2–608(1)(b).

Second, the non-conformity, to justify revocation, must "substantially impair" the value "to him" of the goods accepted. UCC 2–608(1). What does this mean? An emerging view is that the court must make an objective determination that the value of the goods has been substantially impaired but that the determination must be made from the perspective of the particular buyer. Thus, even though leaks and dry rot in a sloop could have been repaired, the defect occurred in a vital part of the boat and "severely undermined" the buyer's confidence in its integrity as a sailing vessel. Its value was "substantially impaired."

Third, revocation of acceptance "must occur within a reasonable time after the buyer discovers or should have discovered the ground for it * * *" UCC 2–608(2). What is prompt action and what is an unreasonable delay are questions of fact.

Fourth, the revocation of acceptance, even if otherwise proper, must occur "before any substantial change in condition of the goods which is not caused by their own defects." This puts a premium on quick action where perishable commodities are involved. It also limits the scope of revocation where the goods were components or other items to be used or consumed in a manufacturing process.

Finally, the revocation is "not effective until the buyer notifies the seller of it." UCC 2–608(2). Is it enough for the buyer to pick up the telephone and say to the seller: "That last delivery was a disaster. We're getting out of this deal?" Apparently not. In Solar Kinetics Corp. v. Joseph T. Ryerson & Son, Inc., 488 F.Supp. 1237 (D.Conn.1980), the court held that the notice, to be adequate, must inform the seller that the buyer has revoked, which goods are involved and the nature of the defect. Cf. UCC 2–607(3).

ATLAN INDUSTRIES, INC. v. O.E.M., INC.

United States District Court, Western District of Oklahoma, 1983.
555 F.Supp. 184.

MEMORANDUM AND ORDER

SAFFELS, DISTRICT JUDGE, Sitting by Designation.

This case involves a complaint for the price of goods sold by plaintiff to defendant. Defendant denies liability for the price of the goods, and contends that the goods contained a latent defect which caused them to be unacceptable and out of conformity with the specifications in the sales contract between plaintiff and defendant.

Plaintiff is a prime supplier of reground plastic and wide specification machinery in the plastics industry. The goods in dispute between defendant and plaintiff are nine hundred thirty-five pounds (935 lbs.) of "Noryl-R-Beige FN 215" at eighty-five cents (85¢) per pound, as described in plaintiff's invoice No. 16886; nine thousand nine hundred fifty pounds (9,950 lbs.) of "Noryl-R-Grey FN 215" at eighty-five cents (85¢) per pound, as described on plaintiff's invoice No. 17114; and seventeen thousand two hundred ninety-five pounds (17,295 lbs.) of "Noryl-R-Grey FN 215" at eighty-five cents (85¢) per pound, as described on plaintiff's invoice No. 17449.

FN 215 is a high density, very hard plastic used primarily in the computer industry for making computer cabinets. There are two types of FN 215 on the market. "Virgin" FN 215 is plastic material which has never been molded and is manufactured only by General Electric. FN 215 "regrind" is plastic which has been molded once or more in its life, has been scrapped and has been ground for use again in a molding process. Defendant is a company which molds plastic into various parts and sells them to the computer industry. Defendant was under contract to a computer company, Magnetic Peripherals, Inc. (hereinafter MPI), to mold a number of computer cabinet parts from FN 215. Plaintiff agreed to supply defendant with raw FN 215 for this molding job. Plaintiff did not know the end use of the FN 215 it was supplying to defendant, and the name of the user was kept secret.

After agreeing to supply defendant with FN 215, plaintiff contacted a supplier about a supply of reground FN 215. Plaintiff tested the FN 215 for contamination and foreign matter, and forwarded a 935–pound sample of the FN 215 to defendant for testing.

In the plastics industry, it is a common practice for a supplier of raw plastic to forward a sample to the molder for testing. The purpose of the test is to see if the plastic material will mold well. No injection molder has facilities to do any other test. The reason for testing regrind material is that some regrind is badly contaminated with metal, which clogs the injection molding equipment and requires the molding machine to be shut down and cleaned. "Regrind" is plastic which has been molded once, and then is ground into pellets to be re-used. The regrinding process sometimes leaves small pieces of metal and metal chips in the plastic.

FN 215 is an expensive plastic which is specially compounded for use in office machines and computers. FN 215 is heat sensitive, but is able to withstand temperatures of at least two hundred five degrees (205°). Because the material is generally used in office machines and computers, it is almost always painted after molding to improve its cosmetic appearance. Defendant does not paint the parts it molds; they forward them to the ultimate user, who paints them.

The particular shipments involved in this lawsuit were molded by defendant and forwarded to their ultimate user, MPI. MPI painted the parts and heated them in an infrared oven to dry the paint. The parts molded from FN 215 "regrind" supplied by plaintiff warped when exposed to the temperature of the infrared heat ovens. The computer parts were warping when exposed to temperatures of between one hundred thirty degrees (130°) and one hundred seventy degrees (170°). Noryl FN 215 will not warp at this temperature range. Defendant molded the entire shipment of Noryl FN 215 into computer parts and tendered them to MPI before the problem surfaced. MPI immediately rejected the goods as defective and non-conforming because of the warping problem. Defendant immediately notified plaintiff that MPI had rejected the goods because of warpage, and that the material supplied by plaintiff was defective and non-conforming.

Defendant was instructed by plaintiff sometime in March, 1982, to return the material to plaintiff. Subsequently, all but four thousand pounds (4,000 lbs.) of the material supplied by plaintiff was returned to plaintiff by defendant in substantially the same condition. Plaintiff was unable to furnish Noryl FN 215 from another source. Due to plaintiff's inability to furnish conforming FN 215, defendant purchased forty thousand pounds (40,000 lbs.) of FN 215 from General Electric at forty-two cents (42¢) per pound higher than plaintiff's price. Defendant invested eighty (80) hours of labor at Ten Dollars ($10) per hour to inspect and regrind the non-conforming FN 215 back to its original state to return to plaintiff. The material was reground because it would therefore be cheaper to ship and easier for plaintiff to resell. In addition, plaintiff agreed that it would be better to regrind the material.

This lawsuit is governed by Article 2 of the Uniform Commercial Code. The court finds that there was a contract for sale of goods between plaintiff and defendant. Plaintiff agreed to sell to defendant a known quantity of Noryl FN 215. It is undisputed that Noryl FN 215 does not warp at one hundred fifty degrees (150°), and it is undisputed that parts made from the Noryl FN 215 supplied by plaintiff did warp when exposed to temperatures of one hundred fifty degrees (150°). Therefore, we find that the goods tendered by plaintiff failed to conform to the contract. Pursuant to Okla.Stat. 12A, § 2–601, if goods fail in any respect to conform to a contract, the buyer may reject all of them or accept all of them.

Acceptance of goods occurs when the buyer, after a reasonable opportunity to inspect them, signifies to the seller that the goods are conforming or that he will take them despite their non-conformity, or where the buyer fails to make an effective rejection, or does any act inconsistent with the seller's ownership. Okla.Stat. 12A, § 2–606(1). A buyer is deemed to have accepted goods when, without making any effort to reject them, he receives the goods, processes them, and sells the finished product to a third-person. *A & G Construction Co., Inc. v. Reid Brothers Logging Co., Inc.*, 547 P.2d 1207 (Alaska 1976). Such actions on the part of the buyer are clearly inconsistent with ownership by the seller. Anderson, *Uniform Commercial Code*, § 2–606:31 (1971). The court finds defendant accepted the goods.

A buyer must pay at the contract rate for any goods he has accepted. Okla.Stat. 12A, § 2–607(1). However, a buyer may revoke his acceptance of goods whose non-conformity substantially impairs their value to him if he has accepted those goods without discovery of the non-conformity where his acceptance was reasonably induced by the difficulty of discovery before acceptance. Okla.Stat. 12A, § 2–608(1)(b). As a condition precedent to revoking acceptance, the buyer must show that the goods are both non-conforming and that the non-conformance substantially impairs the value of the goods to the buyer.

Goods are "conforming" when they are in accordance with the obligations under the contract. Okla.Stat. 12A, § 2–106(2). The Noryl FN 215 in issue in this case was not conforming because it would not tolerate the temperature that Noryl FN 215 is specifically able to tolerate.

The test for whether the non-conformity substantially impairs the value of the goods to the buyer is whether the non-conformity is such as will in fact cause a substantial impairment of the value to the buyer even though the seller had no advance knowledge as to the buyer's particular circumstances. Okla.Stat. 12A, § 2–608, Official Code Comment 2. The court finds that the non-conformity substantially impaired the value of the Noryl FN 215 to the buyer, plaintiff Atlan. FN 215 is primarily used to make computer cabinets and to house office machines. The plastic, when molded, is a dull, off-white or a dull, grey color. It is virtually always painted a more pleasant color before it is sold to its ultimate user. Noryl FN 215 does not have any other reasonable use. The Noryl FN 215 in question, when painted, could not withstand the temperatures in a drying oven. Therefore, the parts could not be painted and dried in the ordinary manner. If the parts could not be painted, they could not be used in the computer and office machinery industry. They were, therefore, substantially without value to the ultimate user and to the molder who had manufactured them. Therefore, the value of this particular Noryl FN 215 was substantially impaired because it did not conform to the characteristics inherent in normal Noryl FN 215.

If the buyer did not know of the non-conformity when he accepted the goods, he must show his acceptance was reasonably induced by the difficulty of discovering the non-conformity before acceptance. The undisputed testimony revealed that in the plastics industry it is common for a molder to test samples only to see whether or not they will mold well. The Noryl FN 215 in question was so tested and did mold well. Plaintiff contends that the defendant was under an additional duty to forward samples he had molded to his customer, MPI, to see whether or not the molded samples would conform to MPI's specifications. While this might be a reasonable provision to place in a contract for sale between plaintiff and defendant, the court finds that the law does not require the buyer to perform any more tests than are common in the industry. Okla.Stat. 12A, § 1–205(2).

Revocation of acceptance must occur within a reasonable time after the buyer discovers the non-conformity. There is no claim in this case that defendant unreasonably delayed notifying plaintiff of the non-conformity, and the court finds that plaintiff was notified within a reasonable time after defendant discovered the warping problem.

A buyer who revokes acceptance has the same rights with regard to the goods involved as if he had rejected them. Okla.Stat. 12A, § 2–608(3). "Rights" includes remedies. Okla.Stat. 12A, § 1–201(36). A buyer who has rightfully rejected goods has no further obligation in regard to those goods, including an obligation to pay their purchase price. Okla.Stat. 12A, § 2–602(2)(c). Therefore, the court finds against plaintiff on his complaint for the purchase price of the Noryl FN 215 involved in this lawsuit, and now turns to the question of defendant's remedies for rejection of non-conforming goods.

* * * *

It is by the court therefore ordered that plaintiff take nothing of defendant on plaintiff's complaint. It is further ordered that judgment be entered in favor of defendant and against plaintiff on defendant's counterclaim in the sum of Sixty-Four Thousand Fourteen and $^{47}/_{100}$

Dollars ($64,014.47). It is further ordered that costs are assessed against plaintiff.

JOHANNSEN v. MINNESOTA VALLEY FORD TRACTOR CO.

Supreme Court of Minnesota, 1981.
304 N.W.2d 654.

Considered and decided by the court en banc without oral argument.

OPINION

PETERSON, JUSTICE.

The defendants, Ford Motor Co. and Minnesota Valley Ford (dealer), appeal from the judgment entered in favor of the plaintiff, Harvey Johannsen, the buyer of a defective tractor manufactured by Ford and sold to him by the dealer. After a trial in which the jury found that Johannsen had effectively revoked his acceptance of a Ford Model 9700 tractor (9700), the district court entered judgment for the plaintiff in the amount of the purchase price of the tractor less an offset for use and depreciation. Defendants appeal from the order denying post-trial motions for judgment notwithstanding the verdict or a new trial and also appeal from the judgment. We affirm.

The plaintiff revoked his acceptance of the 9700 tractor pursuant to Minn.Stat. § 336.2–608(1)(b) (1980) after he experienced mechanical problems that substantially interfered with its intended use on his 330–acre farm. On July 13, 1977, plaintiff, together with his wife, went to the premises of the dealer to pick up his 1974 Ford Model 9600 tractor (9600), which had been taken to the dealer for repairs. Johannsen had experienced a number of problems with the fourth gear and hydraulic system of his 9600. The tractor had jumped out of fourth gear on a number of occasions while Johannsen was plowing. Johannsen expressed his concern to Brian Gaard, one of the dealer's employees, that the 9600 would again jump out of gear.

Gaard told Johannsen that the transmission of the new 1977 Ford Model 9700 had been redesigned to avoid the transmission defects of the 9600 and that he could solve his tractor transmission problems by purchasing a new 9700 for $26,000. Gaard did not tell Johannsen that Ford had sent a letter to its tractor dealers in May of that year detailing transmission defects in the 9700. Dealers were informed that some 9700's jumped out of fourth and/or eighth gear. They were instructed to check all 9700's in stock for the defect and to sell defective tractors only if they would lose a sale. Johannsen purchased a 9700 from the dealer and traded in his 9600.

The dealer delivered the tractor to Johannsen's farm in late July. The tractor jumped out of fourth gear upon its first use, and at about the same time the frost plugs blew out of the engine, causing a loss of all of the coolant. The dealer sent a repairman to plaintiff's farm on that day who told Johannsen to see the dealer about the transmission defect. On August 3, 1977, the tractor developed a fuel restriction problem and a hydraulic leak, which made it difficult to lower the implements into the soil. The dealer informed Johannsen that it could not fix the hydraulic defect until replacement parts became available in April, 1978. Johannsen told every serviceman who called at his farm that he wanted to return the tractor.

On September 19, 1977, Johannsen, by his attorney, formally notified the dealer in writing of his revocation of acceptance due to transmission, hydraulic and fuel line defects, and he directed the dealer to pick up the tractor immediately.

Johannsen continued to use the tractor after the written revocation and called the dealer on September 28 because the tractor continued to exhibit the same problems. The dealer made service calls on September 28, October 2, and October 9 in response to Johannsen's complaints. Ray Chaik, an employee of the dealer, told Johannsen that he could finish his fall work and bring the tractor in for winter servicing. Johannsen used the tractor for a total of 120 hours but was able to plow or disk only 150 acres of his farm with it. Approximately 90 of those hours were put on the tractor after the revocation letter of September 19. Johannsen put the tractor in storage in late October, 1977.

The defendants contend that the plaintiff did not effectively revoke his acceptance of the 9700 tractor because (1) he did not allow the defendants to attempt to cure the defects, (2) the defects did not substantially impair the value of the tractor, (3) the plaintiff did not revoke his acceptance of the tractor seasonably, and (4) the plaintiff continued to use the tractor after revocation of acceptance.

1. The defendants, although acknowledging that the seller's right to cure pursuant to Minn.Stat. § 336.2–508(2) (1980) is expressly limited by the language of the statute to cases in which the buyer rejects a nonconforming tender, argue that the right to cure should be incorporated into Minn.Stat. § 336.2–608(3) (1980) governing revocation of acceptance.[4] It is our view that any right to cure should be limited to cases in which the defects are minor, and we hold that the seller has no right to cure defects which substantially impair the good's value.

2. We reject defendants' contention that the jury's finding that the defects substantially impaired the value of the tractor to plaintiff is not supported by the evidence. In *Durfee v. Rod Baxter Imports, Inc.,* 262 N.W.2d 349, 353–54 (Minn.1977), we set forth guidelines to establish the substantial impairment requirement of Minn.Stat. § 336.2–608(1):

> [T]wo respected commentators suggest that the test ultimately rests on a commonsense perception of substantial impairment, akin to

---

4. Commentators are divided on the issue of whether the seller has a right to cure after the buyer revokes his acceptance. *See e.g.,* J. White & R. Summers, *Uniform Commercial Code,* 293 (1980) (no right to cure); *contra* 3 S. Williston, Williston on Sales 119 (Supp.1980).

the determination of a material breach under traditional contract law. White & Summers, Uniform Commercial Code, § 8–3, p. 257. The cases that involve revocation of acceptance of defective new automobiles are amenable to classification by this practical criterion. Minor defects not substantially interfering with the automobile's operation or with the comfort and security it affords passengers do not constitute grounds for revocation. On the other hand, if the defect substantially interferes with operation of the vehicle or a purpose for which it was purchased, a court may find grounds for revocation. Indeed, substantial impairment has been found even where the defect is curable, if it shakes the faith of the purchaser in the automobile.

Substantial evidence supports the jury's finding that the transmission and hydraulic defects substantially impaired the value of the tractor to plaintiff. He specifically purchased the 9700 to avoid problems with the essential fourth gear which he had experienced with the 9600. As a result of the defects, he was only able to use the tractor on 150 acres of his 330–acre farm. Plaintiff testified that due to the defect it took him two weeks to plow 50 acres of sweet corn ground, a task that should have taken less than 4 hours to complete. Under these circumstances, the jury's finding is supported by the evidence.

3. We likewise reject defendants' contention that plaintiff did not revoke his acceptance within a reasonable time after discovering the defect. The issue of what constitutes a reasonable time within the context of revocation of acceptance is a jury question that depends on the facts and circumstances of the case. We hold that the jury's finding that plaintiff's revocation was timely is supported by the evidence because it could have reasonably concluded that plaintiff gave notice within a reasonable time after discovering through his use of the tractor that it would not adequately perform the tasks for which it was purchased.

4. Defendants additionally contend that plaintiff's use of the tractor after he gave written notice of revocation of acceptance constitutes a second acceptance. Although the revoking buyer's continued use of defective goods may be wrongful under some circumstances,[5] we think that there can be no blanket rule which prohibits such a buyer from continuing to use the goods. A blanket rule prohibiting a revoking buyer from continuing to use the goods would contravene the code's rule of reasonableness and its underlying purpose of modernizing commercial transactions. We agree with those jurisdictions that have so held. See Minsel v. El Rancho Mobile Home Center, Inc., 32 Mich. App. 10, 188 N.W.2d 9 (1971). Fablok Mills, Inc. v. Cocker Machinery &

5. Minn.Stat. § 336.2–602(2)(a) (1980) provides that any exercise of ownership by a rejecting buyer is wrongful as against the seller. Defendants contend that because section 336–2–608(3) imposes upon revoking buyers the same rights and duties as if they had rejected the goods, that a revoking buyer's continued use of goods is always wrongful.

Foundry Co., 125 N.J.Super. 251, 310 A.2d 491 (Super.Ct.App.Div.1973), *cert. denied,* 64 N.J. 317; 315 A.2d 405 (1973).

The reasonableness of the buyer's use of a defective good after revocation is a question of fact for the jury that is to be based on the facts and circumstances of each case. Several factors that the jury may consider include the seller's instructions to the buyer after revocation of acceptance; the degree of economic and other hardship that the buyer would suffer if he discontinued using the defective good; the reasonableness of the buyer's use after revocation as a method of mitigating damages; the degree of prejudice to the seller; and whether the seller acted in bad faith.

We hold, limited to the facts and circumstances of this case, that the jury could find that plaintiff's continued use of the 9700 tractor was reasonable and did not constitute a waiver of his revocation of acceptance. The defects in the 9700 tractor were major. Employees of the dealer knew that Johannsen specifically purchased the 9700 to avoid the transmission defect in the 9600, knew of the possibility of the identical defect in the 9700, and yet they led Johannsen to believe that buying the 9700 would solve all of his tractor transmission problems. In addition, evidence in the record tends to show that Johannsen used the tractor only to perform necessary tasks.

We note that the trial court, based upon expert testimony, allowed the defendants a setoff for use and depreciation of the tractor. Allowing the seller to recover for the revoking buyer's use of the tractor best serves the equitable principle incorporated into the code through Minn.Stat. § 336.1–103 (1980)[6] that a party seeking rescission of a contract must return or offer to return that which he had received under it in order to restore the parties to the positions that they occupied prior to the transaction. *See Village of Wells v. Layne-Minnesota Co.,* 240 Minn. 132, 138, 60 N.W.2d 621, 625 (1953).

5. Defendants contend that the trial court improperly excluded for lack of foundation a warranty which limited a buyer's remedies to repair or replacement. Defendants asserted that plaintiff had been given a copy of Ford's standard warranty, but they were unable to produce an executed copy of the warranty. Plaintiff denied that he had executed any such warranty. We conclude that the trial court did not err in the exclusion of the alleged warranty.

The instructions given to the jury by the trial court are in conformity with the law as we have stated it. Defendants' other claims of error on evidentiary matters do not require discussion.

Affirmed.

6. Minn.Stat. § 336.1–103 (1978) provides: "Unless displaced by the particular provisions of this Act, the principles of law and equity, including the law merchant and the law relative to capacity to contract, principal and agent, estoppel, fraud, misrepresentation, duress, coercion, mistake, bankruptcy, or other validating or invalidating cause shall supplement its provisions."

Problem 11–7

On April 19, 1976, defendant Clarence Miller ordered a 1976 Dodge Royal Monaco station wagon from plaintiff Colonial Dodge which included a heavy-duty trailer package with extra wide tires.

On May 28, 1976, defendant picked up the wagon, drove it a short distance where he met his wife, and exchanged it for her car. Defendant drove that car to work while his wife returned home with the new station wagon. Shortly after arriving home, Mrs. Miller noticed that their new wagon did not have a spare tire. The following morning defendant notified plaintiff that he insisted on having the tire he ordered immediately, but when told there was no spare tire then available, he informed the salesman for plaintiff that he would stop payment on the two checks that were tendered as the purchase price, and that the vehicle could be picked up from in front of his home. Defendant parked the car in front of his home where it remained until the temporary ten-day registration sticker had expired, whereupon the car was towed by the St. Clair police to a St. Clair dealership. Plaintiff had applied for license plates, registration, and title in defendant's name. Defendant refused the license plates when they were delivered to him.

According to plaintiff's witness, the spare tire was not included in the delivery of the vehicle due to a nation-wide shortage caused by a labor strike. Some months later, defendant was notified his tire was available.

Plaintiff sued defendant for the purchase price of the car. On January 13, 1981, the trial court entered a judgment for plaintiff finding that defendant wrongfully revoked acceptance of the vehicle. The Court of Appeals decided that defendant never accepted the vehicle. On rehearing, the Court of Appeals, noting the trial court found the parties had agreed that there was a valid acceptance, affirmed the trial court's holding there was not a substantial impairment in value sufficient to authorize defendant to revoke acceptance of the automobile.

How should this case be resolved on appeal to the Supreme Court?

In the real case –
△ did a lot of traveling at odd hours.
No market to go out and buy spares due to strike.
(These facts might make this substantial impairment)

Chapter Twelve

SELLER'S BREACH OF WARRANTY AS TO THE QUALITY OF GOODS SOLD

SECTION 1. INTRODUCTION

A. *Warranty Theory: Some History*

Disputes over the quality of goods sold frequently end up in court. The buyer's claim is that the goods, because of a condition existing at the time of tender, failed to conform to his expectations regarding basic attributes or suitability. The seller's response may be that the buyer assumed the risk. More particularly, the argument is that since neither party knew of the condition at the time of delivery, i.e., both were equally ignorant, and the buyer could have discovered the condition by inspection or otherwise, there is no sound reason, absent fraud, deceit or mutual mistake, why the seller should bear the risk. Thus, the stage is set, the seller will contend, for application of the doctrine of caveat emptor, the "universal structural characteristic of the law of sales." Rabel, *The Nature of Warranty of Quality*, 24 Tulane L.Rev. 273 (1970). See Hamilton, *The Ancient Maxim of Caveat Emptor*, 49 Yale L.J. 1133 (1931).

One "sound" reason for protecting the buyer's expectations is found in the law of warranty. Warranty is a representational theory of liability. It depends upon the answers to two key questions: (1) What did the seller affirm, represent or promise, expressly or impliedly, about the quality of the goods sold to the buyer; and (2) Was the buyer justified in incorporating the representations into his expectations of quality? The first question poses primarily a question of fact. The second question is primarily a question of law. Clearly, not everything a seller says about the goods will become part of the contract for sale. To the extent that representations of quality become part of the agreement, however, they constitute a standard of quality—a warranty—to which the goods must conform at the time of delivery.

The Anglo-American history of warranty reveals, in commercial transactions at least,* a slow but steady erosion of the doctrine of caveat emptor. The following account, taken from the sources cited below, touches the doctrinal tip of a much larger social iceberg. Hillinger, *The Merchant of Section 2–314: Who Needs Him?*, 34 Hastings L.Rev. 747, 788–807 (1983); Titus, *Restatement (Second) of Torts Section 402A and the Uniform Commercial Code*, 22 Stan.L.Rev. 713, 728–344 (1970); Prosser, *The Implied Warranty of Merchantable Quality*, 27 Minn.L.Rev. 117 (1943); Llewellyn, *On Warranty of Quality and Society, I*, 36 Colum.L.Rev. 699, 716–31 (1936); Hamilton, *The Ancient Maxim Caveat Emptor*, 40 Yale L.J. 1133, 1163–78 (1931); Williston, *Representation and Warranty in Sales*, 27 Harv.L.Rev. 1 (1913); McClain, *Implied Warranties in Sales*, 7 Harv.L.Rev. 213 (1903).

Warranty disputes involving claims for economic loss first arose between sellers and buyers of goods who were in privity of contract. In the early 17th Century, however, they were asserted in tort as an action on the Case. The buyer had to establish the elements of deceit, i.e., that the seller made an express representation about the nature of the goods knowing it to be false.

By 1790, the action of Deceit, with its requirements of scienter by the representor and reliance by the representee, had developed into a separate writ or action. At about the same time, the English courts first permitted an express warranty claim to be brought in assumpsit, the action in which most contract claims were pursued.

By 1802, it was decided that scienter was not a requirement in Assumpsit for breach of an express warranty, but other limiting formalities, i.e., the representation must be an express term of the contract and intended by the seller to be a warranty, still remained. This early interaction between representations of quality made in exchange transactions and the tort forms of action led Dean Prosser to conclude that warranty was a "freak hybrid born of the illicit intercourse of tort and contract." Prosser, *The Assault Upon the Citadel (Strict Liability to the Consumer)*, 69 Yale L.J. 1099, 1126–27 (1960). The New York Court of Appeals, in a personal injury case, concluded: "Accordingly, for some 400 years the action rested not on an enforcible (sic) promise but on a wrong or tort. In the historical development of the law of warranty, however, as so often happens in law and life in general, accident was evidently confused with essence: from the fact that the cases which

---

* There are, in fact, three legal worlds of product liability. The first, with which these Chapters are concerned, concerns disputes over quality between commercial parties where only economic loss is involved. These disputes are governed, in the main, by Article 2. The second involves disputes between individuals and commercial sellers over "defective" products which have caused personal injuries. These disputes are governed by the law of torts, primarily the law of strict products liability. See Section 402A of the Restatement, Second, of Torts. The third involves disputes between individual consumers and commercial sellers over quality where economic loss and, perhaps, property damage has occurred. These are governed in part by Article 2 and in part by a patchwork of federal and supplemental state consumer protection laws. See Rice, *Product Quality Laws and the Economics of Federalism*, 65 B.U.L.Rev. 1 (1985).

arose involved contractual relationships and represented enforcible (sic) promises, the courts seem to have concluded that the contract was the essence of the action. * * * The occasion for the warranty was constituted a necessary condition of it." Randy Knitwear, Inc. v. American Cyanamid Co., 11 N.Y.2d 5, 226 N.Y.S.2d 363, 181 N.E.2d 399, 401 n. 2 (1962).

During the 19th Century, warranty theory developed into the tripartite form which we know today, an express warranty, an implied warranty of fitness for particular purpose and an implied warranty of merchantability (fitness for "ordinary" purposes). The implied warranties emerged, inferentially, at the point where the seller's express representations about or description of the goods failed to cover the exact issue in dispute. All three were captured, in the late 19th Century, by the British Sale of Goods Act and, later, in the American Uniform Sales Act. They appear as Sections 2–313, 2–314 and 2–315 of the Uniform Commercial Code. We will return to examine each and all in more detail.

Before looking at warranty theory under the UCC, a few general questions should be kept in mind.

First, warranties, arising as they do from contracts for sale, have been treated as terms of the contract. Two consequences flow from this treatment: (1) A breach of warranty is a breach of contract, entitling the seller to recover direct and consequential economic loss measured by the expectation interest; (2) Privity of contract has usually been required between the seller and buyer, especially where the buyer claims only economic loss. Are these consequences inevitable? For example, should a plaintiff injured in person by a defective product be permitted to recover under a warranty theory? Or, should a buyer who suffers only economic loss caused by an unmerchantable product manufactured by a remote seller be permitted to recover on a warranty theory without privity of contract?

Second, the tort of misrepresentation has developed apart from warranty theory. In general, the misrepresentation must be material and negligently made. In addition, the plaintiff must justifiably rely upon it and is limited, in many cases, to the recovery of out-of-pocket economic loss. But when the misrepresentation concerns goods sold, there is an obvious overlap with the theory of express warranty. Which should prevail in these cases, express warranties under the UCC or tort theory?

Third, in the last 25 years a special body of law has developed to protect individual consumers who purchase goods for personal, family or household purposes and suffer economic loss. Uneven though this development has been, it reflects a conclusion that there is usually an imbalance of capacity between the individual and the enterprise and that this imbalance creates a risk of exploitation in bargaining or unprovable fraud by the enterprise. The legal response includes the federal Magnuson-Moss Warranty Act and state legislation, such as the "lemon" laws. Is this development justified? If so, how much government regulation is necessary to correct the imbalance, whether it be in bargaining power, information or capacity for choice, and should that regulation be included in the UCC?

Fourth, defective and dangerous products manufactured by sellers frequently cause damage to the person or property of purchasers and other foreseeable users or consumers. Since the great case of *McPherson v. Buick Motor Company*, decided in 1920, injured parties have been able, privity or not, to sue the manufacturer in negligence. Since the 1960s, with the promulgation of Section 402A of the Restatement, Second, Torts, injured parties have been permitted to sue under the theory of strict products liability. Although negligence theory has not been preempted, it has been eclipsed by strict liability.

Given these developments in the law of products liability, to what extent does the UCC preempt tort law where the seller has breached a warranty and the buyer has suffered personal injuries or property loss? Should the buyer with both a claim in warranty and a claim in strict tort be able to choose which to pursue? And what about products that cause only economic loss or cause damage only to the goods sold? Should these claims be limited to warranty theory under the UCC or may they also be pursued under negligence or strict tort theory? What difference does it make? In the materials to follow, we will try to provide some answers to these questions.

B. Warranties Under the Code: An Introduction

According to Comment 4 to UCC 2–313, the basic purpose of warranty law is to determine "what it is that the seller has in essence agreed to sell." As you are now fully aware, agreement means the "bargain in fact as found in their language or by implication from other circumstances." UCC 1–201(3). Thus, whether the buyer's understanding of quality is consistent with the agreement may depend, among other things, upon the description, what the seller has said, common uses in the trade, the price paid and the extent to which the buyer has communicated particular needs to the seller. Interestingly enough, the more detailed the agreement on quality and the allocation of risks, the less room there is for legitimate dispute over conformity of the goods to the contract and the less likely it is that the warranty label will be applied to the controversy.

The UCC draftsmen, however, have selected an approach which yields warranties of different kinds, including express warranties, UCC 2–313, implied warranties of merchantability, UCC 2–314, and implied warranties of fitness for particular purpose, UCC 2–315—a tripartite approach. (The implied warranty of title, UCC 2–312, will be treated later.) In so doing, the draftsmen rejected the unitary approach suggested by the theory of contract and, at the same time, preserved the close tie between warranty and the contract. The initial question, therefore, will be whether the Code's tripartite approach to the problem supports any breach of warranty claim at all. The answer to this question will also be affected by the possible application of exclusionary rules, i.e., disclaimers or rules of interpretation, which neutralize facts which otherwise would support a warranty claim. See UCC 2–316, 2–317 & 2–202. These rules proceed on the assumption that what is rooted in contract can, under controlled circumstances, be taken away or altered by contract.

A second question is when did the buyer discover the alleged breach of warranty? This has immense practical importance. If the defect is discovered before acceptance, the remedy of rejection, UCC 2–601 through 2–605, and the remedial options in UCC 2–711(1) are available. The remedial problems become more complicated after acceptance, and the degree of complication is closely related to how soon thereafter the defect was discovered. The risks of delay are pinpointed in UCC 2–725(2), 2–608(2) and 2–607(3)(a). Other problems flowing from acceptance have to do with revoking acceptance, UCC 2–608(1), burden of proof, UCC 2–607(4), uncertainty in the measure of "direct" damage, UCC 2–714(2), and the increased risk that consequential damages will be involved. UCC 2–715(2). As a general rule, the earlier the breach is discovered and the quicker remedial options are exercised, the better off the buyer will be.

Another question is the extent to which the seller has validly altered by contract the normal remedies available to the buyer upon breach of warranty. Relevant Code sections include UCC 2–316, 2–718, 2–719 & 2–302. A final question is, of course, whether a warranty made by the seller has in fact been breached.

The problem and case that follow introduce the relevant Code warranty sections.

Problem 12–1

The Case of the Hot Casserole

Sam Sweeney owns and operates a supermarket which specializes in produce from many lands. The produce is displayed in open bins at one end of the store under a large sign which reads "Foods from Many Lands." Above each bin is space for a written description of the produce and a price. On the morning of March 5, Sam received a shipment of pepper beans from Africa. The dried beans, which closely resembled lima beans, were extremely hot to the taste. The beans were displayed in an empty bin but, because of the press of other matters, Sam did not describe the goods or fix a price at that time. Sam did not sell dried lima beans at this store, but they could be purchased at other stores for between $.20 and $.25 per pound. On the morning of March 6, Mrs. Banks, a new resident in the area, entered Sam's store for the first time. She wanted to purchase lima beans for a special casserole to be served that evening at a dinner party for her husband's new boss. Mrs. Banks did not notice the "Foods from Many Lands" sign. After walking around the produce bins, she found what seemed to be plain old garden variety lima beans. She asked a salesman the price and was told "$.23 a pound." Pointing to the unmarked bin, she stated, "I will take two pounds of those." The beans were weighed, put into a sack and paid for. Later that afternoon, Mrs. Banks prepared her special casserole which was served to her guests without the true nature of the beans being discovered. The casserole, of course, was somewhat difficult to eat and the dinner party, while interesting, was something less than a success. The next morning, a furious Mrs. Banks consults her attorney.

1. Does she have any legal recourse against Sam? What advice would you give?

2. Suppose that one of Mrs. Banks' guests had become violently ill after eating the beans. Would the guest have a warranty claim against Sam? See UCC 2–318.

3. At what point would Sam, who had knowledge superior to Mrs. Banks, be impressed with a duty to caution or warn about the special nature of the beans? See Addis v. Bernardin, Inc., 226 Kan. 241, 597 P.2d 250 (1979) (seller knew goods sold would not suit buyer's purposes).

HOBSON CONST. CO., INC. v. HAJOCA CORP.

Court of Appeals of North Carolina, 1976.
28 N.C.App. 684, 222 S.E.2d 709.

Plaintiff [Hobson] brought this action against defendant [Hajoca] for damages resulting from defective equipment purchased from Hajoca. It was alleged that the defects amounted to a breach of warranties. Hajoca denied that the equipment was defective and denied liability.

The case was tried without a jury and plaintiff's evidence tended to establish the following:

Triple Community Water Corporation [Water Corp.], located in Drexel, North Carolina, retained the services of Register & Cummings, Engineers, to prepare plans and specifications for a water treatment and conditioning plant. Hobson entered into a contract with the Water Corporation to construct the plant in accordance with the plans and specifications of the engineers.

The plant was to be built primarily for the purpose of filtering iron and manganese from the water supply. The engineers' specifications provided that "filter equipment shall be similar and equal to Diamond Model Three (3) DMG 84–45 as manufactured by Oshkosh Filter and Softener Company." Further specifications provided that the "plate shall contain a sufficient number of corrosion resistant segmented plastic distributors with stainless steel bolts to provide uniform distribution." It was established that Oshkosh was the only company that manufactured the segmented plastic distributors.

Hobson purchased from Hajoca three Diamond Model Three (3) DMG 84–45 filter tanks which were manufactured by Oshkosh. One of Hajoca's representatives stated to Hobson's president that the filter tanks being sold "should remove the iron and manganese from the water."

Near the bottom of each filter tank was a steel plate with fifty-two threaded holes with nipples screwed into them. A segmented plastic distributor head was attached to each nipple. The distributor heads were plastic with small holes through which the filtered water could pass.

The steel plate and distributor heads were covered with silica sand, and above the silica sand was a layer of "green sand." Raw water flowed into the tank at the top, chemicals were added, and the water was supposed to react with the chemicals and green sand in such a way that the iron and manganese would stick to the particles of green sand leaving the finished water to flow through the silica sand and distributor heads and on out the bottom of the tank.

Difficulties developed after the filter tanks were installed in April of 1971. The finished water contained silica sand and green sand, and not enough iron and manganese was removed to comply with government requirements. There were also other serious difficulties and problems. The distributor heads either ruptured or disintegrated and the silica sand and green sand that remained in the tanks became mixed together.

In December of 1971 plaintiff took out the distributor heads, nipples, silica sand and green sand, and bored 88 new holes into the steel plate. The 52 plastic distributor heads and nipples were replaced with 140 stainless steel ones manufactured by a different company. The water treatment plant worked very well thereafter and produced good water.

The president of Hobson testified that he believed the difficulties with the filter tanks were caused by an insufficient number of distributor heads for the amount of water passing through the tanks, and that the distributor heads broke under the excessive water pressure.

At the conclusion of plaintiff's evidence the trial court granted defendant's motion for involuntary dismissal under Rule 41(b) of the N.C. Rules of Civil Procedure. The court made findings of fact and conclusions of law and held that there was no breach by defendant of any express or implied warranty. Plaintiff appealed to this court.

ARNOLD, JUDGE.

* * *

Plaintiff maintains that the filter tanks were defective and in breach of the implied warranty of merchantability. We find no evidence that the tanks were unmerchantable. Plaintiff asserts that the distributor heads were not "fit for the ordinary purposes for which such goods are used" as required by G.S. 25–2–314(2). The evidence, however, merely establishes that the distributor heads were not fit for use under excessive water pressure as contained by the Water Corp.'s system, which was not the ordinary purpose for which the goods were sold.

In regards to any implied warranty of fitness for a particular purpose the court made the following conclusion: "The plaintiff has failed to present evidence of any implied warranty by Hajoca of the fitness of the system to perform its intended purpose, upon which plaintiff relied." That conclusion is supported by the court's finding that under its contract with the Water Corp. plaintiff was required by the specifications, prepared by the engineers, to use the equipment specified as the 3 Model DMG 84-4 [sic] [84-45] Diamond filter units manufactured by Oshkosh, and that plaintiff purchased "in reliance upon the specifications, and pursuant to its contract, and not in reliance upon any warranty, affirmation, or representation, express or implied, by Hajoca as to the merchantability or the fitness of the system for its intended use." There is no warranty of fitness for a particular purpose unless "the buyer is relying on the seller's skill or judgment to select or furnish suitable goods." G.S. 25-2-315.

G.S. 25-2-313 contains the requirements for express warranties. Any affirmation of fact or promise made by the seller concerning the goods sold is an express warranty if it "becomes part of the basis of the bargain." There was no express warranty in the present case in view of the following finding of fact made by the court: "The statements of Hajoca's manager to plaintiff to the effect that the apparatus 'should' be able to remove iron and manganese from the water did not amount to an affirmation of fact effecting [sic] the bargain between plaintiff and Hajoca."

Plaintiff further argues that notwithstanding any other statements made by Hajoca an express warranty arose from the fact that the tanks were described as "iron removal filters." This argument has no merit. There is no evidence that the tanks were not "iron removal filters." They simply failed to sufficiently filter the water under the system as it was designed by the Water Corp., and from the evidence the defect was in the plans and specifications of the engineers, and not the filter tanks.

The judgment appealed from is affirmed.

Affirmed.

Parker and Hedrick, JJ., concur.

Notes

In *Hobson*, the plaintiff lost on all three warranties. What additional facts would have supported a victory on all three claims?

SECTION 2. NON-COMPLIANCE WITH EXPRESS WARRANTIES

A. Liability for Statements Constituting "Core" Descriptions or as to Basic Attributes

Exactly what is an express warranty? Let us first consider what it was (or seemed to have been) before the Code.

CHANDELOR v. LOPUS

Exch. Chamber, 1625.
79 Eng. Rep. 3, Cro.Jac. 4.

Action upon the case. Whereas the defendant being a goldsmith, and having skill in jewels and precious stones, had a stone which he affirmed to Lopus to be a bezar-stone, and sold it to him for one hundred pounds; *ubi revera* it was not a bezar-stone: the defendant pleaded not guilty, and verdict was given and judgment entered for the plaintiff in the King's Bench.

But error was thereof brought in the Exchequer Chamber; because the declaration contains not matter sufficient to charge the defendant, viz. that he warranted it to be a bezar-stone, or that he knew that it was not a bezar-stone; for it may be, he himself was ignorant whether it were a bezar-stone or not.

And all the Justices and Barons (except Anderson) held, that for this cause it was error: for the bare affirmation that it was a bezar-stone, without warranting it to be so, is no cause of action: and although he knew it to be no bezar-stone it is not material; for every one in selling his wares will affirm that his wares are good, or the horse which he sells is sound; yet if he does not warrant them to be so, it is no cause of action, and the warranty ought to be made at the same time of the sale; as F.N.B. 94, c and 98, b; 5 Hen. 7, pl. 41; 9 Hen. 6, pl. 53; 12 Hen. 4, pl. 1, 42 Ass. 8; 7 Hen. 4, pl. 15. Wherefore, forasmuch as no warranty is alleged, they held the declaration to be ill.

ANDERSON to the contrary; for the deceit in selling it for a bezar, whereas it was not so, is cause of action.

But, notwithstanding, it was adjudged to be no cause, and the judgment reversed.

GILMORE, PRODUCTS LIABILITY: A COMMENTARY, 38 U.Chi. L.Rev. 103, 107–08 (1970).

"In connection with the point that most cases—perhaps all cases—are sensibly, or even 'correctly,' decided as of their own time and place, I will indulge myself in a brief digression on a landmark of the common law ∗ ∗ ∗—a case called Chandelor v. Lopus, which was decided by the Exchequer Chamber in 1625. A goldsmith had sold for £100 a stone which he affirmed to be a bezoar. The stone turned out not to be a bezoar. The disappointed buyer, who had presumably paid the price for a true bezoar, brought an action to recover damages for, as we should say, breach of warranty. Judgment for the goldsmith-seller: he had merely 'affirmed' that the stone was a bezoar without 'warranting' it to be one—wherefore the buyer's action did not lie. For several hundred years the case has been cited, with approval or with scorn, as illustrative of the extremely narrow scope of liability which seventeenth century law placed on sellers for the quality of the goods they sold.

"The report of the case does not bother to explain what a bezoar was—presumably everybody knew what a bezoar was, just as we all know what a diamond is. It occurred to me one day, in thinking about the case, that I for one had no idea what a bezoar might be. The new Oxford Dictionary proved to be illuminating. A bezoar (or 'bezar') was, descriptively, 'a calculus or concretion found in the stomachs of some animals, chiefly ruminants, formed of concentric layers of animal matter deposited round some foreign substance, which serves as a nucleus.' That explains everything except why a bezoar would have been worth £100 in the early 17th century. The true value of a bezoar, it appears, lay in its magic or, as we should say, medicinal properties: application of the bezoar to a diseased part of the body cured the disease. 'Everything that frees the body of any ailment,' it was said, 'is called the Bezoar of that ailment.' And the East India Company had reported in 1618 that: 'On the island of Borneo, diamonds, bezoar stones and gold might be obtained.'

"Now that we know more about bezoars than we did, we may begin to wonder whether our initial reaction to the holding in Chandelor v. Lopus was, historically, correct—or even relevant to the case. It was generally known that there were true, or magic, bezoars. It must also have been a matter of common knowledge that it was extremely difficult, if not impossible, to tell a true bezoar from a false one. And no doubt the attitude of the user counted for something: if I believed in my bezoar it might indeed preserve me from the plague while the same stone in the hands of a skeptical rationalist would be worthless. Under such circumstances a court might hesitate to impose liability on a seller who had merely said that, to the best of his knowledge, he believed (or affirmed) the stone to be a bezoar, but did not warrant it. It may be that the 17th century concept of liability was not as narrow as we have supposed it to be. This digression, at all events, goes to the point that law cases—and rules of law—are really not abstract propositions, although we like to phrase them, and talk about them, as if they were. The cases and the rules—and indeed the codifying statutes—are merely particular responses to particular states of fact (assumed to be true whether or not they are). The law is, and I dare say always will be, *ad hoc* and *ad hominem* to a fault."

[Footnotes omitted.]

SEIXAS v. WOODS

Supreme Court of New York, 1804.
2 Caines 48, 2 Am.Dec. 215.

Action on the case for selling peachum wood for brazilletto; the former being almost worthless, the latter of considerable value. The defendant received the wood from a house in New Providence, whose agent he was, and the invoice described it as brazilletto. He advertised it as such, had shown the invoice to the plaintiff, and had the bill made out for brazilletto. But it was not pretended that he knew that it was peachum, nor did the plaintiff suspect it to be such, as it was delivered from the vessel, and picked out from other wood by a person on behalf of the plaintiff. In fact, either party was ignorant that the wood was other than brazilletto, nor was any fraud imputed. On discovery of the real quality of the wood, it was tendered back to the defendant, and a return of the purchase money demanded. On his refusal, he having remitted the proceeds to his principal, the present action was brought, and a verdict was given for the plaintiffs, subject to the opinion of the court.

KENT, J.

* * *

In the case of Chandelor v. Lopus, Cro.Jac. 4, it was determined in the exchequer by all the judges except one, that for selling a jewel which as affirmed to be a bezoar stone when it was not, no action lay, unless the defendant knew it was not a bezoar stone or had warranted it to be one. This appears to be a case in point and decisive. * * * The mentioning the wood as brazilletto wood in the bill of parcels and in the advertisement some days previous to the sale, did not amount to a warranty to the plaintiffs. To make an affirmation at the time of the sale a warranty, it must appear by evidence to be so intended; Buller, J., 3 T.R. 57; Carth. 90; Salk. 210; and not to have been a mere matter of judgment and opinion, and of which the defendant had no particular knowledge. Here it is admitted the defendant was equally ignorant with the plaintiffs, and could have had no such intention. * * *

* * *

Notes

1. Did the New York court appropriately rely on *Chandelor v. Lopus?* Or, did the court "confuse accident with essence in an earlier court's decision and thereby stunt the law's growth?"

2. Suppose the seller and buyer are of relatively equal capacity and are equally ignorant about the nature of the goods sold. If the seller affirms or describes the goods (things) as a "bezoar stone" or as "brazilleto," how does one determine whether the seller has made a warranty or merely a statement purporting to be an opinion? For what they are worth, here are a few alternative tests. Which do you prefer?

A. The affirmation must be in writing and use the word "warrant" or "guarantee." This test was rejected in UCC 2–313(2).

B. The seller must intend the affirmation to be a warranty, i.e., state a "fact which is or should be within his own knowledge * * *, intending that the buyer should act on it. * * *" Denning, L.J. in Oscar Chess, Ltd. v. Williams, 1 All Eng.Rep. 325, 328–29 (C.A.1957). See Stoljar, *Conditions, Warranties and Descriptions of Quality in Sale of Goods,* Part I, 15 Mod.L.Rev. 425, 428–29 (1952).

The intention requirement was part of the pre-Code American law of warranty: "Though to constitute a warranty requires no particular form of words, the naked averment of a fact is neither a warranty itself nor evidence of it. In connection with other circumstances, it certainly may be taken into consideration; but the jury must be satisfied, from the whole that the vendor actually, and not constructively, consented to be bound for the truth of his representation." Gibson, C.J. in McFarland v. Newman, 9 Watts 55, 34 Am.Dec. 497 (Pa.1839). Accord: *Seixas v. Woods,* supra (warranty must appear from evidence to be intended); McNeir v. Greer-Hale Chinchilla Ranch, 194 Va. 623, 74 S.E.2d 165 (1953) (representations constituted warranty if seller intended that they should be relied upon and they were in fact relied upon by buyer as an inducement to purchase). But under UCC 2–313(2), the buyer need not have a "specific intention to make a warranty."

C. Regardless of the seller's actual intention, did the affirmation lead a reasonable buyer to believe that such statements had been made to induce the bargain and to make the purchase in reliance on them? See Section 12, Uniform Sales Act; Hansen v. Firestone Tire & Rubber Co., 276 F.2d 254, 257 (6th Cir.1960); Williston, Sales 206 (rev. ed. 1948). But see UCC 2–313(1)(a), where the affirmation or promise must become "part of the basis of the bargain."

D. None of the foregoing tests are appropriate. The question is whether the buyer is entitled to believe what the seller says about the goods. The answer will depend, in each case, upon the presence of certain factors which, in a proper combination, will induce the court to allow the case to reach the jury. These factors include but are not limited to:

a. The seller's statement was plain and unambiguous.

b. The seller's statement concerned a matter of objective importance to the buyer.

c. The attribute or quality involved was not something the buyer could easily ascertain on his own.

d. The seller was more of an expert in the matter than the buyer.

e. The buyer was not making up his own mind to buy entirely without regard to the seller's statements.

f. Nothing in the facts indicated that the seller should not be taken seriously.

g. The seller did not himself say things to the buyer that should have put him "on his guard" so to speak.

h. The remedy that the buyer sought was especially appropriate and would not be unduly harsh on the seller.

i. The price tends to support the buyer's claim.

Problem 12–2

The Case of the Unmarked Vitriol

Saldo is a dealer in dry chemicals, selling at wholesale to a variety of buyers. Saldo purchased 2,000 pounds of a copper sulphate described as "blue vitriol" from the Copco Mfgr. Co. The goods arrived in 20 barrels. The barrels were unmarked but the invoice described the goods as "vitriol." The barrels were offered for sale at a quarterly wholesale auction. One of the barrels was opened for prospective buyers to examine. It contained a bluish crystalline substance which one of the prospective buyers thought "looked strange." The purchasing agent of Barston Chemicals, Inc., a dealer which frequently sold at retail, also inspected the barrel. He stated to the auctioneer that while the substance looked like blue vitriol, it could be "green" vitriol, a less valuable chemical. Upon consultation with Saldo, the auctioneer announced that "the next sale will be a 20–barrel lot of blue vitriol in sound order." After spirited bidding, Barston Chemicals was high bidder at $.15 per pound. The price was paid and the goods were removed to the Barston warehouse, where they were immediately resold to a third party at $.18 per pound. The next day, however, it was discovered that the substance in the open barrel had turned green. Chemical analysis revealed that the substance was in fact "green" vitriol in sound order, worth about $.10 per pound at wholesale and $.13 per pound at retail. All of the other barrels contained "green" vitriol. In order to distinguish "green" from "blue" vitriol, either a chemical analysis must be done or the "green" vitriol allowed to stand in the open air for 10 or more hours. Barston promptly notified Saldo of the situation, revoked its acceptance, and demanded the return of the purchase price paid and damages for breach of warranty. The Barston purchasing agent stated that he was "not sure" what was in the barrel when he first examined it but after the auctioneer announced the sale, bid on the assumption that it was blue vitriol. Saldo claims that its officers honestly believed that the barrels contained blue vitriol, but that no warranty was intended and that Barston, as a professional chemical dealer, assumed the risk that the substance was green vitriol.

1. Did the seller make an express warranty in this case? If so, was it by affirmation or promise, description or sample? See UCC 2–313(1).

2. Suppose that the seller had stated that the goods were "vitriol" yet the buyer had assumed they were "blue" vitriol. What result? Compare UCC 2–313(1)(b) with UCC 2–314(2)(a). Does the description "vitriol" simply identify the goods or does it reveal basic attributes or quality? See Ziegel, *The Seller's Liability for Defective Goods at Common Law,* 12 McGill L.J. 183, 186–87 (1966).

SESSA v. RIEGLE

United States District Court, Eastern District of Pennsylvania, 1977.
427 F.Supp. 760, affirmed without opinion, 568 F.2d 770 (3d Cir.1978).

[Sessa purchased from Riegle a standard bred race horse named Tarport Conaway for $25,000. Before the sale, Sessa's friend Maloney examined the horse and reported that he "liked him." Also, Riegle, in a telephone conversation with Sessa, stated among other things that Sessa would like the horse and that he was a "good one" and "sound." The sale was then completed and, after problems in transportation were resolved, the horse was delivered some days later. Shortly thereafter the horse went lame in his hind legs due to a thrombosis which stopped the flow of blood through the arteries. The experts were unable to identify the cause of the thrombosis and the testimony did not establish that the condition was present before Riegle shipped the horse by carrier. Although the condition improved and Tarport Conaway was able to race, Sessa sued for damages under UCC 2–714(2) to be measured in part by the costs incurred in treating the condition.

The case was tried without a jury and the court, after making findings of fact, issued the following opinion.]

HANNUM, DISTRICT JUDGE.

* * *

II. EXPRESS WARRANTIES

On March 10, 1973, the day of the sale of Tarport Conaway, Sessa and Riegle had a telephone conversation during which the horse was discussed in general terms. Arrangements were made for transportation, and Riegle gave Sessa some instructions for driving Tarport Conaway based on Riegle's experience with him. Sessa contends that certain statements made by Riegle during that conversation constitute express warranties on which Riegle is liable in this action. The most important of these is Riegle's alleged statement that, "the horse is sound," or words to that effect.

In deciding whether statements by a seller constitute express warranties, the court must look to UCC § 2–313 which presents three fundamental issues. First, the court must determine whether the seller's statement constitutes an "affirmation of fact or promise" or "description of the goods" under § 2–313(1)(a) or (b) or whether it is rather "merely the seller's opinion or commendation of the goods" under § 2–313(2). Second, assuming the court finds the language used susceptible to creation of a warranty, it must then be determined whether the statement was "part of the basis of the bargain." If it was, an express warranty exists and, as the third issue, the court must determine whether the warranty was breached.

With respect to the first issue, the court finds that in the circumstances of this case, words to the effect that "The horse is sound" spoken during the telephone conversation between Sessa and Riegle constitute an opinion or commendation rather than express warranty. This determination is a question for the trier of fact. Gillette Dairy, Inc. v. Hydrotex Industries, Inc., 440 F.2d 969 (8th Cir.1971); Brunner v. Jensen, 215 Kan. 416, 524 P.2d 1175 (1974). There is nothing talismanic or thaumaturgic about the use of the word "sound." Whether use of that language constitutes warranty, or mere opinion or commendation depends on the circumstances of the sale and the type of goods sold. While § 2–313 makes it clear that no specific words need be used and no specific intent need be present, not every statement by a seller is an express warranty.

Several older Pennsylvania cases dealing with horse sales show that similar statements as to soundness are not always similarly treated under warranty law. In Wilkinson v. Stettler, 46 Pa.Super. 407 (1911), the statement that a horse "was solid and sound and would work any place" was held not to constitute an express warranty. This result was followed in Walker v. Kirk, 72 Pa.Super. 534 (1919) which considered the statement, "This mare is sound and all right and a good worker double." Walker was decided after the passage of § 12 of the Uniform Sales Act, the precursor of U.C.C. § 2–313 and thus presumably rests on the standard there established. The Official Comments to U.C.C. § 2–313 indicate that no changes in the law of warranties under Uniform Sales Act § 12 were intended.

Case precedent agrees with UCC

However, in Flood v. Yeager, 52 Pa.Super. 637 (1912) an express warranty was found where the plaintiff informed the defendant that, "he did not know anything at all about a horse and that he did not want * * * the defendant to make a mean deal with him; whereupon the defendant said that the horse was solid and sound; that he would guarantee him to be solid and sound" 52 Pa.Super. at 638. While all three of these cases are premised partly on the now displaced rule that specific intent to warrant is a necessary concomitant of an express warranty, they do show that statements of the same tenor receive varying treatment depending on the surrounding circumstances.

The results in these cases are all consistent with custom among horse traders as alluded to by Gene Riegle. He testified that it is "not a common thing" to guarantee a horse, that he has never guaranteed a horse unless he had an "understanding" with the buyer and that he did not guarantee Tarport Conaway. In other words, because horses are fragile creatures, susceptible to myriad maladies, detectable and undetectable, only where there is an "understanding" that an ignorant buyer, is relying totally on a knowledgeable seller not "to make a mean deal," are statements as to soundness taken to be anything more than the seller's opinion or commendation.

Also common in the "trade"

The facts suggest no special "understanding" between Sessa and Riegle. Sessa was a knowledgeable buyer, having been involved with standardbreds for some years. Also, Sessa sent Maloney, an even more knowledgeable horseman, as his agent to inspect the horse.

Also mitigating against the finding of express warranty is the nature of the conversation between Sessa and Riegle. It seemed largely collateral to the sale rather than an essential part of it. Although Sessa testified that Riegle's "personal guarantee" given during the conversation was the quintessence of the sale, the credible evidence suggests otherwise. While on the telephone, Riegle made statements to the effect that "the horse is a good one" and "you will like him." These bland statements are obviously opinion or commendation, and the statement, "The horse is sound," falling within their penumbra takes on their character as such.

Even so— probably wasn't part of the "bargain"

Under all the facts and circumstances of this case, it is clear to the court that Riegle's statements were not of such a character as to give rise to express warranties under § 2–313(1) but were opinion or commendation under § 2–313(2).

Even assuming that Riegle's statements could be express warranties, it is not at all clear that they were "part of the basis of the bargain," the second requisite of § 2–313. This is essentially a reliance requirement and is inextricably intertwined with the initial determination as to whether given language may constitute an express warranty since affirmations, promises and descriptions tend to become part of the basis of the bargain. It was the intention of the drafters of the U.C.C. not to require a strong showing of reliance. In fact, they envisioned that all statements of the seller became part of the basis of the bargain unless clear affirmative proof is shown to the contrary. See Official Comments 3 and 8 to U.C.C. § 2–313, 12A P.S. § 2–313.

It is Sessa's contention that his conversation with Riegle was the principal factor inducing him to enter the bargain. He would have the court believe that Maloney was merely a messenger to deliver the check. The evidence shows, however, that Sessa was relying primarily on Maloney to advise him in connection with the sale. Maloney testified that he had talked to Sessa about the horse on several occasions and expressed the opinion that he was convinced "beyond the shadow of a doubt" that he was a good buy. With respect to his authority to buy the horse he testified

> "Well, Mr. Sessa said he had enough confidence and faith in me and my integrity and honesty that I, what I did say about the horse, I was representing the horse as he is or as he was, and that if the horse, in my estimation, was that type of a horse and at that given price, the fixed price of $25,000 he would buy the horse."

When, at the airport, Maloney protested that he did not want to accept full responsibility to go to Ohio alone, Sessa told him " * * * I take your word. I—I trust your judgment and I trust your—your honesty, that if this horse is right, everything will be all right." In Ohio, Maloney examined the horse, jogged him and reported to Sessa over the telephone that he "liked him."

The court believes that Maloney's opinion was the principal, if not the only, factor which motivated Sessa to purchase the horse. The conversation with Riegle played a negligible role in his decision.

* * *

[The court concluded that even if an express warranty had been made, Sessa had accepted the horse and had failed to prove by a preponderance of the evidence that the horse was not sound at the time of tender.]

[Footnotes omitted.]

KEITH v. BUCHANAN

Court of Appeals of California, Second District, 1985.
173 Cal.App.3d 13, 220 Cal.Rptr. 392.

OCHOA, ASSOCIATE JUSTICE.

This breach of warranty case is before this court after the trial court granted defendants' motion for judgment at the close of plaintiff's case during the trial proceedings. We hold that an express warranty under section 2313 of the California Uniform Commercial Code was created in this matter, and that actual reliance on the seller's factual representation need not be shown by the buyer. The representation is presumed to be part of the basis of the bargain, and the burden is on the seller to prove that the representation was not a consideration inducing the bargain. We affirm all other aspects of the trial court's judgment but reverse in regard to its finding that no express warranty was created and remand for further proceedings consistent with this opinion.

[handwritten margin note: Actual reliance on the seller's factual representation need not be shown by the buyer. The representation is presumed to be part of the basis of the bargain & the burden is on the seller to prove that buyer's representation was not consider.]

STATEMENT OF FACTS

Plaintiff, Brian Keith, purchased a sailboat from defendants in November 1978 for a total purchase price of $75,610. Even though plaintiff belonged to the Waikiki Yacht Club, had attended a sailing school, had joined the Coast Guard Auxiliary, and had sailed on many yachts in order to ascertain his preferences, he had not previously owned a yacht. He attended a boat show in Long Beach during October 1978 and looked at a number of boats, speaking to sales representatives and obtaining advertising literature. In the literature, the sailboat which is the subject of this action, called an "Island Trader 41," was described as a seaworthy vessel. In one sales brochure, this vessel is described as "a picture of sure-footed seaworthiness." In another, it is called "a carefully well-equipped, and very seaworthy live-aboard vessel." Plaintiff testified he relied on representations in the sales brochures in regard to the purchase. Plaintiff and a sales representative also discussed plaintiff's desire for a boat which was ocean-going and would cruise long distances.

Plaintiff asked his friend, Buddy Ebsen, who was involved in a boat building, enterprise, to inspect the boat. Mr. Ebsen and one of his associates, both of whom had extensive experience with sailboats, observed the boat and advised plaintiff that the vessel would suit his stated needs. A deposit was paid on the boat, a purchase contract was entered into, and optional accessories for the boat were ordered. After delivery of the vessel, a dispute arose in regard to its seaworthiness.

Plaintiff filed the instant lawsuit alleging causes of action in breach of express warranty and breach of implied warranty. The trial court granted defendants' Code of Civil Procedure section 631.8 motion for judgment at the close of plaintiff's case. The court found that no express warranty was established by the evidence because none of the defendants had undertaken in writing to preserve or maintain the utility or performance of the vessel, nor to provide compensation for any failure in utility or performance. It found that the written statements produced at trial were opinions or commendations of the vessel. The court further found that no implied warranty of fitness was created because the plaintiff did not rely on the skill and judgment of defendants to select and furnish a suitable vessel, but had rather relied on his own experts in selecting the vessel.

DISCUSSION

I. Express Warranty

California Uniform Commercial Code section 2313 provides, inter alia, that express warranties are created by (1) any affirmation of fact or promise made by the seller to the buyer which relates to the goods and becomes part of the basis of the bargain, and (2) any description of the goods which is made part of the basis of the bargain. Formal words such as "warranty" or "guarantee" are not required to make a warranty, but the seller's affirmation of the value of the goods or an expression of opinion or commendation of the goods does not create an express warranty.

* * *

California Uniform Commercial Code section 2313, regarding express warranties, was enacted in 1963 and consists of the official text of Uniform Commercial Code section 2–313 without change. In deciding whether a statement made by a seller constitutes an express warranty under this provision, the court must deal with three fundamental issues. First, the court must determine whether the seller's statement constitutes an "affirmation of fact or promise" or "description of the goods" under California Uniform Commercial Code section 2313, subdivision (1)(a) or (b) or whether it is rather "merely the seller's opinion or commendation of the goods" under section 2313, subdivision (2). Second, assuming the court finds the language used susceptible to creation of a warranty, it must then be determined whether the statement was "part of the basis of the bargain." Third, the court must determine whether the warranty was breached. (See *Sessa v. Riegle* (E.D.Pa.1977) 427 F.Supp. 760, 765.)

A warranty relates to the title, character, quality, identity, or condition of the goods. The purpose of the law of warranty is to determine what it is that the seller has in essence agreed to sell. (*A.A. Baxter Corp. v. Colt Industries, Inc.* (1970) 10 Cal.App.3d 144, 153, 88 Cal.Rptr. 842.) "Express warranties are chisels in the hands of buyers and sellers. With these tools, the parties to a sale sculpt a monument representing the goods. Having selected a stone, the buyer and seller may leave it almost bare, allowing considerable play in the qualities that fit its contours. Or the parties may chisel away inexactitudes until a well-defined shape emerges. The seller is bound to deliver, and the buyer to accept, goods that match the sculpted form. [Fn. omitted.]" (*Special Project: Article Two Warranties in Commercial Transactions, Express Warranties—Section 2–313* (1978–79) 64 Cornell L.Rev. 30 (hereafter cited as *Warranties in Commercial Transactions*) at pp. 43–44.)

A. Affirmation of Fact, Promise or Description Versus Statement of Opinion, Commendation or Value

"The determination as to whether a particular statement is an expression of opinion or an affirmation of fact is often difficult, and frequently is dependent upon the facts and circumstances existing at the time the statement is made." (*Willson v. Municipal Bond Co.* (1936) 7 Cal.2d 144, 150, 59 P.2d 974.) Recent decisions have evidenced a trend toward narrowing the scope of representations which are considered opinion, sometimes referred to as "puffing" or "sales talk," resulting in an expansion of the liability that flows from broad statements of manufacturers or retailers as to the quality of their products. Courts have liberally construed affirmations of quality made by sellers in favor of injured consumers. (*Hauter v. Zogarts* (1975) 14 Cal.3d 104, 112, 120 Cal.Rptr. 681, 534 P.2d 377; see also 55 Cal.Jur.3d, Sales, § 74, p. 580.) It has even been suggested "that in an age of consumerism all seller's statements, except the most blatant sales pitch, may give rise to an express warranty." (1 Alderman and Dole, A Transactional Guide to the Uniform Commercial Code (2d ed. 1983) p. 89.)

Courts in other states have struggled in efforts to create a formula for distinguishing between affirmations of fact, promises, or descriptions of goods on the one hand, and value, opinion, or commendation statements on the other. The code comment indicates that the basic question is: "What statements of the seller have in the circumstances and in objective judgment become part of the basis of the bargain?" The commentators indicated that the language of subsection (2) of the code section was included because "common experience discloses that some statements or predictions cannot fairly be viewed as entering into the bargain." (See U.Com.Code com. 8 to Cal.U.Com.Code, § 2313, West's Ann.Com.Code (1964) p. 250.)

Statements made by a seller during the course of negotiation over a contract are presumptively affirmations of fact unless it can be demonstrated that the buyer could only have reasonably considered the statement as a statement of the seller's opinion. Commentators have noted several factors which tend to indicate an opinion statement. These are (1) a lack of specificity in the statement made, (2) a statement that is made in an equivocal manner, or (3) a statement which reveals that the goods are experimental in nature. (See *Warranties in Commercial Transactions, supra,* at pp. 61–65.)

It is clear that statements made by a manufacturer or retailer in an advertising brochure which is disseminated to the consuming public in order to induce sales can create express warranties. * * * In the instant case, the vessel purchased was described in sales brochures as "a picture of sure-footed seaworthiness" and "a carefully well-equipped and very seaworthy vessel." The seller's representative was aware that appellant was looking for a vessel sufficient for long distance ocean-going cruises. The statements in the brochure are specific and unequivocal in asserting that the vessel is seaworthy. Nothing in the negotiation indicates that the vessel is experimental in nature. In fact, one sales brochure assures prospective buyers that production of the vessel was commenced "after years of careful testing." The representations regarding seaworthiness made in sales brochures regarding the

Island Trader 41 were affirmations of fact relating to the quality or condition of the vessel.

B. "Part of the Basis of the Bargain" Test

Under former provisions of law, a purchaser was required to prove that he or she acted in reliance upon representations made by the seller. (*Grinnell v. Charles Pfizer & Co.* (1969) 274 Cal.App.2d 424, 440, 79 Cal.Rptr. 369.) California Uniform Commercial Code section 2313 indicates only that the seller's statements must become "part of the basis of the bargain." According to official comment 3 to this Uniform Commercial Code provision, "no particular reliance * * * need be shown in order to weave [the seller's affirmations of fact] into the fabric of the agreement. Rather, any fact which is to take such affirmations, once made, out of the agreement requires clear affirmative proof." (See U.Com.Code com. 3 to Cal.U.Com.Code, § 2313, West's Ann.Com. Code (1964) p. 249.)

The California Supreme Court, in discussing the continued viability of the reliance factor, noted that commentators have disagreed in regard to the impact of this development. Some have indicated that it shifts the burden of proving non-reliance to the seller, and others have indicated that the code eliminates the concept of reliance altogether. (*Hauter v. Zogarts, supra,* 14 Cal.3d at pp. 115–116, 120 Cal.Rptr. 681, 534 P.2d 377.) The court did not resolve this issue, but noted that decisions of other states prior to that time had "ignored the significance of the new standard and have held that consumer reliance still is a vital ingredient for recovery based on express warranty." (*Id.,* at p. 116, fn. 13, 120 Cal.Rptr. 681, 534 P.2d 377; see also *Fogo v. Cutter Laboratories, Inc.* (1977) 68 Cal.App.3d 744, 760, 137 Cal.Rptr. 417.)

The shift in language clearly changes the degree to which it must be shown that the seller's representation affected the buyer's decision to enter into the agreement. A buyer need not show that he would not have entered into the agreement absent the warranty or even that it was a dominant factor inducing the agreement. A warranty statement is deemed to be part of the basis of the bargain and to have been relied upon as one of the inducements for the purchase of the product. In other words, the buyer's demonstration of reliance on an express warranty is "not a prerequisite for breach of warranty, as long as the express warranty involved became part of the bargain. See White & Summers, Uniform Commercial Code (2d ed. 1980) § 9–4. If, however, the resulting bargain does not rest at all on the representations of the seller, those representations cannot be considered as becoming any part of the 'basis of the bargain.' * * *" (*Allied Fidelity Ins. Co. v. Pico* (Nev.S.Ct.1983) 656 P.2d 849, 850.)

The official Uniform Commercial Code comment in regard to section 2–313 "indicates that in actual practice affirmations of fact made by the seller about the goods during a bargain are regarded as part of the description of those goods; hence no particular reliance on such statements need be shown in order to weave them into the fabric of the agreement." (*Young & Cooper, Inc. v. Vestring* (1974) 214 Kan. 311, 521 P.2d 281, 291; *Brunner v. Jensen* (1974) 215 Kan. 416, 524 P.2d 1175, 1185.) It is clear from the new language of this code section that the concept of reliance has been purposefully abandoned. * * *

The change of the language in section 2313 of the California Uniform Commercial Code modifies both the degree of reliance and the burden of proof in express warranties under the code. The representation need only be part of the basis of the bargain, or merely a factor or consideration inducing the buyer to enter into the bargain. A warranty statement made by a seller is presumptively part of the basis of the bargain, and the burden is on the seller to prove that the resulting bargain does not rest at all on the representation.

The buyer's actual knowledge of the true condition of the goods prior to the making of the contract may make it plain that the seller's statement was not relied upon as one of the inducements for the purchase, but the burden is on the seller to demonstrate such knowledge on the part of the buyer. Where the buyer inspects the goods before purchase, he may be deemed to have waived the seller's express warranties. But, an examination or inspection by the buyer of the goods does not necessarily discharge the seller from an express warranty if the defect was not actually discovered and waived. * * *

Appellant's inspection of the boat by his own experts does not constitute a waiver of the express warranty of seaworthiness. Prior to the making of the contract, appellant had experienced boat builders observe the boat, but there was no testing of the vessel in the water.[3] Such a warranty (seaworthiness) necessarily relates to the time when the vessel has been put to sea (*Werner v. Montana* (1977) 117 N.H. 721, 378 A.2d 1130, 1134–35) and has been shown to be reasonably fit and adequate in materials, construction, and equipment for its intended purposes (*Daly v. General Motors Corp.* (1978) 20 Cal.3d 725, 739, 144 Cal.Rptr. 380, 575 P.2d 1162; *Vittone v. American President Lines* (1964) 228 Cal.App.2d 689, 693–694, 39 Cal.Rptr. 758).

In this case, appellant was aware of the representations regarding seaworthiness by the seller prior to contracting. He also had expressed to the seller's representative his desire for a long distance ocean-going vessel. Although he had other experts inspect the vessel, the inspection was limited and would not have indicated whether or not the

3. Evidence was presented of examination or inspection of the boat after the making of the contract of sale and prior to delivery and acceptance of the vessel. Such an inspection would be irrelevant to any issue of express warranty. Although it deals with implied warranties as opposed to express warranties, the Uniform Commercial Code comment 8 to section 2–316 (Cal.U.Com.Code, § 2316) is instructive: "Under paragraph (b) of subdivision (3) warranties may be excluded or modified by the circumstances where the buyer examines the goods or a sample or model of them *before entering into the contract.* 'Examination' as used in this paragraph is not synonymous with inspection before acceptance or at any other time after the contract has been made. It goes rather to the nature of the responsibility assumed by the seller at the time of the making of the contract." (See U.Com.Code com. 8 to Cal. U.Com.Code, § 2316, West's Ann.Com.Code (1964) p. 308, emphasis added.)

vessel was seaworthy. It is clear that the seller has not overcome the presumption that the representations regarding seaworthiness were part of the basis of this bargain.

IMPLIED WARRANTY *? * *

[The court upheld the trial court's conclusion that the seller did not make and breach an implied warranty of fitness for particular purpose under UCC 2–315: The buyer did not rely on the seller's skill and judgment in selecting a suitable boat.]

[Some footnotes omitted.]

Notes

1. The court in *Keith* cites with approval the three step "basis of the bargain" test employed in *Sessa* but then reaches the opposite result. Can the cases be reconciled? Should Buddy Ebsen be fired as an expert on seaworthiness?

2. Is the "basis of the bargain" test, in essence, the same as a "reliance" test? The answer in *Sessa* is yes: Basis of the bargain is "essentially a reliance requirement and is inextricably intertwined with the initial determination as to whether given language may constitute an express warranty since affirmations, promises and descriptions tend to become a part of the basis of the bargain." Duesenberg and King agree: "(F)or all practical purposes it is suggested that no great change was wrought by the Code. Whether one speaks of reliance or basis of the bargain, little difference exists between the two. * * * What is really crucial is whether the statement was made as an affirmation of fact, the goods did not live up to the statement, and the defect was not so apparent that the buyer could not be held to have discovered it for himself." Sales and Bulk Transfers 6.01, n. 2 (1980).

3. How do we know initially whether a statement is an affirmation of fact or an opinion? In Royal Business Machines, Inc. v. Lorraine Corp., 633 F.2d 34, 41 (7th Cir.1980), the court stated: "(T)he decisive test for whether a given representation is a warranty or merely an expression of the seller's opinion is whether the seller asserts a fact of which the buyer is ignorant or merely states an opinion or judgment on a matter of which the seller has no special knowledge and on which the buyer may be expected also to have an opinion and to exercise his judgment." Accord: Royal Typewriter Co. v. Xerographic Supplies Corp., 719 F.2d 1092 (11th Cir.1983).

B. Liability for Statements as to "Special Suitability"

Suppose the buyer wants to buy a racehorse that runs well on a slow track, or an office copier with low maintenance costs or a computer system that will process some rather complicated financial data. In short, the buyer has particular or special needs to be satisfied. Compare UCC 2–315.

It is, of course, quite possible that a properly informed seller will make an express warranty that the goods are fit or suitable for the buyer's particular purposes. Northern States Power Co. v. ITT Meyer Industries, 777 F.2d 405 (8th Cir.1985) (seller's technical specifications became part of basis of buyer's bargain). But, as the next case indicates, establishing such an express warranty may be more difficult than when the seller's statements go to core description or basic attributes.

AXION CORP. v. G.D.C. LEASING CORP.

Supreme Judicial Court of Massachusetts, 1971.
359 Mass. 474, 269 N.E.2d 664.

BRAUCHER, JUSTICE.

These cases arise out of the sale of three valve testing machines. The three machines were delivered and two of them were paid for. The seller brings two actions of contract for failure to pay for the third machine, and the buyer brings an action of contract or tort against the seller for damages for breach of express and implied warranties. The cases were consolidated for trial by jury. At the close of the evidence the judge denied the buyer's motions for directed verdicts in the two cases brought by the seller, and allowed the seller's motions for directed verdicts in all three cases. The cases are here on the buyer's exceptions to these actions.

The following facts are substantially undisputed except as indicated. Negotiations began in late 1963, and included a good deal of correspondence. The buyer's purchase order, "To Design and build" the first machine for $7,500, is dated January 9, 1964. The machine was delivered the following May and was paid for in June, 1964. There were many problems with it, and the parties and the buyer's parent company, Watts Regulator Company (Watts), worked together to solve them. In August, 1964, the seller by letter to the buyer listed twenty-eight "revisions in the next two valve setters to be built." The buyer ordered the second and third machines in October, 1964, for a total price of $14,950; they were delivered in December, 1964, and one of them was paid for in March, 1965. At the time of the second order, the first machine was sent back, modified to conform to the new design, then shipped back to the buyer and put into service.

Development and testing continued. In July, 1965, the buyer by letter told the seller it "would like to negotiate a price [for the third machine] which would take into account the amount of money and time that we have had to expend trying to perfect these devices." In August, 1965, the buyer told the seller that the third machine was useless and that the buyer would not pay for it unless it would meet a "plus or minus five per cent" specification. The seller then agreed to take back the third machine at the buyer's expense and to work on it. In January, 1966, representatives of the buyer went to the seller's plant to conduct a series of tests. The parties do not agree on the meaning of the specification or on what the tests showed. In February, 1966, the buyer notified the seller that it was reserving its rights for recovery of its losses and expenses, and that the third machine was unacceptable and would not be paid for.

*   *   *

Express warranties. Since the buyer has accepted the goods and has not revoked the acceptance, the seller may recover the unpaid portion of the price. UCC § 2–709(1)(a). But if the goods were nonconforming, the buyer may have an offsetting claim for damages. § 2–714. The buyer claims that there were breaches of express warranties, of an implied warranty of merchantability, and of an implied warranty of fitness for a particular purpose. The burden is on the buyer to establish such breaches. § 2–607(4).

The buyer claims express warranties made in the seller's preliminary correspondence. On October 12, 1963, the seller wrote: "About the valve adjustment, we would shoot for a mean of 125 psi [pounds per square inch] and hit it more closely than an operator can. * * * With the air pressure sensing there is bound to be a gain in accuracy * * *. Probably a better statement is that the tolerance will be better than it is by the present method." Again, on October 19, 1963, the seller wrote: "With few reservations the automatic valve setter would be a turnkey operation. * * * We would set up the unit at your plant, check it out, train the people stated, and make whatever changes are then indicated to meet the specifications. * * * Failing to meet performance specifications under these guidelines you could ship back the unit with no charge other than freight to New Fairfield."

The buyer now asserts that these letters created express warranties by "affirmation of fact" and "promise," UCC § 2–313(1)(a), that the machine would be a turnkey device and would be more accurate than the hand method. We think they savor more of prediction than of promise. The former general manager of the buyer understood a "turn-key device" to be "one which operates 100 per cent from the day you receive it," as distinguished from a prototype needing further development; he considered the first machine a "semi-experimental" prototype. The order for the first machine, dated January 9, 1964, was to design and build the machine "substantially as per" an attached inter-office letter of the buyer; that letter described the "automatic pressure setting procedure," referred to items which were "suggested," and closed with the following: "It is probable that some tolerances on this will have to be established but deviations from our basic specification can be determined when the machine is checked out." There was no "turnkey" warranty, and no warranty that the machine would be more accurate than the hand method.

The buyer also claims a breach of a warranty that the machine would set valves "entirely within the ± 5% range," quoting from the seller's letter of January 6, 1966. There was testimony that the buyer followed such a standard and that it was one of the specifications discussed between the parties and referred to in the letter of October 19, 1963. But the standard was not referred to in either of the purchase orders and was never written down with any precision until after the meeting in August, 1965.

At that meeting the parties seem to have thought they had reached an oral agreement on the five per cent specification, to be used in reëvaluating the third machine after the seller had reworked it, but their subsequent correspondence disclosed two conflicting versions: the seller's version called for the machine "to set within the prescribed 5% range 90% of the valves presented for setting"; the buyer's version allowed the machine to reject no more than ten per cent of the valves capable of being set, but required *all* of the valves set to be within the five per cent range. The seller's letter of January 6, 1966, pointed out the discrepancy, said it believed "that our equipment will satisfy also the new criterion, but subject to these conditions." One of the conditions was that the buyer "define the quantity of valves which may be incorrectly set and passed. * * * We are confident that * * * the machine will set valves entirely within the ± 5% range. Recognizing, however, the possibilities of mechanical aberration and therefore of 'strays,' we recommend as the standard that no more than 2% of the valves set by our machine as being within the ± 5% range may be rejected on the water test."

The buyer's representatives reported on January 12, 1966, that in tests made on January 10, 1966, the machine rejected twenty-four out of 452 valves (5.3%), set twenty-four more than five per cent too high (5.3%), and set eighteen more than five per cent too low (3.98%), a total of forty-two set out of tolerance range (9.3%). There was other testimony that all the valves in the test were set within the five per cent tolerance, and if the seller had agreed to the buyer's version of the five per cent specification, there would have been a question of fact whether the machine met the test. But there was no evidence that the seller agreed to the buyer's version, or that the buyer agreed either to the seller's original version or to its January 6, 1966, recommendation. In these circumstances, it cannot be said that the buyer carried its burden of establishing that its version of the five per cent specification became "part of the basis of the bargain" within UCC § 2–313(1)(a).

* * *

Exceptions overruled. [Footnotes omitted.]

Notes

1. In *Axion*, is it fair to say that the buyer tried and failed to establish that the seller made an express warranty that the goods were fit for buyer's particular purposes? Compare UCC 2–315. In Uganski v. Little Giant Crane & Shovel, Inc., 35 Mich.App. 88, 192 N.W.2d 580 (1971), the court concluded that the manufacturer of a crane—the only one of its kind—especially designed to meet a particular need of the buyer made and breached an express warranty that the crane would be suitable for that need.

2. S, a manufacturer, sold a number of office copying machines to B. The machines were to be leased to B's customers. S represented to B that the machines had a useful life of 10 years and that the "maintenance factor" was ½ cent per copy produced. B sued for damages, claiming, inter

alia, that the machines did not conform to the representations. Held, even though the machines were fit for "ordinary" purposes, i.e., they were merchantable, see UCC 2–314(1), the seller may have made and breached an express warranty of special suitability. Royal Typewriter Co. v. Xerographic Supplies Corp., 719 F.2d 1092, 1101–02 (11th Cir.1983). The court stated: "Such an express warranty regarding maintenance costs would be tantamount to a guarantee by Royal that no matter what XSC's wage costs and other expenses might reach during the life of the machine, XSC would spend ½ cent per copy for maintenance. To state the nature of such a statement illustrates the difficulty of its proof. Nevertheless, a guarantee is actionable under (UCC 2–313). * * * As unrealistic as such a guarantee may appear, Royal may have made such an express warranty regarding maintenance costs."

In an earlier case between the same seller and a different buyer, the transaction involved a series of copier sales "between the same parties over approximately an 18–month period and concerned two different machines." The court noted that the knowledge and reliance of the parties "may be expected to change in light of their experience during that time." The court concluded: "Therefore, as to each purchase, Booher's expanding knowledge of the capacities of the copying machines would have to be considered in deciding whether Royal's representations were part of the basis of the bargain. The same representations that could have constituted an express warranty early in the series of transactions might not have qualified as an express warranty in a later transaction if the buyer had acquired independent knowledge as to the fact asserted." Royal Business Machines, Inc. v. Lorraine Corp., 633 F.2d 34, 44 (7th Cir.1980).

DOWNIE v. ABEX CORP.

United States Court of Appeals, Tenth Circuit, 1984.
741 F.2d 1235.

[Plaintiffs, the Downies, sued for personal injuries suffered when an airplane passenger loading bridge (Jetway) manufactured by defendant, Abex, collapsed. The defendant filed a third-party complaint against General Motors, the manufacturer of ball-screw assembly which, allegedly, caused the Jetway to fail. The jury found that GM had made and breached a post-sale express warranty that the ball-screw assembly would not fail. The trial court, however, granted GM's motion for judgment n.o.v. on the express warranty claim. Upon appeal, the ruling of the trial court was reversed and the case remanded.]

* * *

II

A

Abex contends that the trial court erred in granting GM's motion for judgment n.o.v. on the express warranty issue. A trial judge may grant a motion for judgment notwithstanding the verdict only if "the facts and inferences point so strongly and overwhelmingly in favor of one party that the Court believes that reasonable men could not arrive at a contrary verdict." *Boeing Co. v. Shipman*, 411 F.2d 365, 374 (5th Cir.1969). Further, in considering a motion for judgment n.o.v. the trial judge must consider all the evidence and reasonable inferences therefrom in the light most favorable to the party against whom the motion is directed. *Wilkins v. Hogan*, 425 F.2d 1022, 1024 (10th Cir. 1970). Section 2–313 of the Uniform Commercial Code governs express warranties. It provides:

"(1) Express warranties by the seller are created as follows:

(a) Any affirmation of fact or promise made by the seller to the buyer which relates to the goods and becomes part of the basis of the bargain creates an express warranty that the goods shall conform to the affirmation or promise.

(b) Any description of the goods which is made part of the basis of the bargain creates an express warranty that the goods shall conform to the description."

Thus, we must determine whether a rational jury could have concluded that GM made an affirmation of fact or promise concerning the failed ball-screw assembly, and, if so, whether it could find that affirmation of fact or promise became part of the basis of the bargain.

B

The original GM warranty was limited to defects in materials and workmanship and specifically excluded all other express or implied warranties. However, the evidence would permit a reasonable jury to find that on at least three occasions GM represented to Abex that its ball-screw assembly was fail-safe and would prevent a free-fall of the Jetway even if the bearings fell out of the assembly.

First, there was the following testimony concerning an exchange that took place on March 30, 1977, when GM employees John Martuch and Lowell Smith made a sales maintenance call on the Jetway manufacturing facilities in Ogden, Utah:

"Q. (by Abex's counsel) And at that time did either you or Mr. Smith state to Russ Williams and Bob Saunders that if the balls were lost and the deflectors were in place, that there would be interference and there would be no free-fall?

A. (by Mr. Martuch) That is correct.

Q. And there was discussion about that being a fail-safe feature; isn't that correct?

A. That is correct.

Q. And in that discussion neither you nor Mr. Smith limited that statement to the 3–inch ball screw?

A. We were talking about specifically a 3–inch ball screw.

Q. But no one said 3–inch, did they?

A. They didn't have to. There was a print on the table that we were using as a reference that was a 3–inch ball screw.

Q. But no one said, 'We want to make perfectly certain that we're only talking about that drawing'?

A. We were talking about that assembly.

Q. But you never pointed that out, did you?

The Court: Gentlemen, Let's not talk two at one time. She's got to take everything here.

Q. (by Abex's counsel): You never specifically said that, though, did you?

A. Not that I remember."

R. X, 106–07.

Second, Martuch sent a letter to Abex dated April 7, 1977, which referred specifically to life/load charts for "the 3 inch and 4 inch BCD units you use." Pl.Ex. 8. The letter included ten copies of a document describing the design and operation of the patented yolk deflector system. The document stated, "If all balls should be lost from a ball nut equipped with deflectors, these yolk-type units will then cause the ball not to function as a threaded nut. This is a true fail safe feature." Pl.Ex. 7.

Third, GM invited Kenneth Noall and Russell Williams of Abex's Jetway division to Saginaw, Michigan, in May 1977 to observe a test of the fail-safe features of the ball-screw assembly. The test impressed Williams and he asked for and received the test sample. Noall remarked that the fail-safe feature was "worth its weight in gold to our customers." R. IX, 109.

GM argues that all discussions and representations regarding the safety of the ball-screw assemblies were limited to the three-inch assembly, and that the evidence unequivocally establishes that no one from Abex specifically recalled the use of the words "fail-safe" either during the conversations in Ogden or the testing in Saginaw. However, regardless of whether anyone specifically used the words "fail-safe," the literature on the ball-screw assemblies described the yolk deflector mechanism as a "fail safe feature" and did not distinguish between three- and four-inch assemblies. Pl.Ex. 7.[2] In 1977 the three- and four-

2. The full text of Plaintiff's Exhibit 7 is as follows:

"*Design Considerations for Maximum Reliability* (con't)

Deflection Yokes vs Pickup Fingers—There are currently two generally used methods of deflecting the bearing balls from the active circuit to the return tube—yoke deflectors and pickup fingers. The yoke deflectors are a patented innovation of Saginaw designed to provide the utmost reliability. Pickup fingers are simple extensions of the return tube guide and normally provide long trouble free service. However, obstructions in the ball groove, such as ice, and the force of skidding balls can break the finger off. If the outer finger of any circuit is broken, the balls in that circuit could be lost. Breakage of inner fingers result in balls being trapped between circuits and the failure of adjacent circuits can occur. The deflection yoke is a solid insert between circuits and outboard of the outer circuits. They are rugged enough to

inch ball-screw assemblies were the only assemblies with yolk deflectors that Abex used in its passenger loading bridges. GM knew that Abex used three- and four-inch assemblies to elevate the bridge. More important, GM, in an internal memorandum, acknowledged Abex's keen interest in the safety features of both the three- and four-inch assemblies. Lowell Smith, in a consumer contact report, stated, "I was requested by Bob Saunders of Jetway to supply a written communication to verify the deflectors in the 3" or 4" BCD ball screws will support the 10 ^{6}" load rating with the balls removed from the ball nut." Pl.Ex. 13. Kenneth Noall testified that he understood that the load compression test in Saginaw applied to all ball-screw assemblies equipped with yolk deflectors, R. IX, 105–06, and Russell Williams declared that GM never stated that its tests or representations were limited only to the three-inch assemblies. *Id.* at 230–31.

GM contends that even if GM salesmen and Abex engineers used the word "fail-safe," the use constituted mere puffing rather than any affirmation of fact or promise giving rise to an express warranty. The line between puffing and warranting is often difficult to draw, but the more specific the statement the more likely it constitutes a warranty. J. White & R. Summers, *Uniform Commercial Code* 329 (1980). On the basis of the evidence in the record and resolving all facts and inferences in the light most favorable to Abex, we conclude that a rational jury could have found that GM made affirmations of fact or promises that both the three- and four-inch ball-screw assemblies equipped with yolk deflectors were fail-safe.

C

We next must determine whether a rational jury could have found that GM's affirmations of fact or promises became part of the basis of the bargain for the sale of the ball-screw assemblies. UCC § 2–313 clearly contemplates that warranties made after the sale may become a basis of the bargain. Official Comment 7 to § 2–313 provides:

> "The precise time when words of description or affirmation are made ∗ ∗ ∗ is not material. The sole question is whether the language ∗ ∗ ∗ [is] fairly to be regarded as a part of the contract. If language is used after the closing of the deal (as when the buyer when taking delivery asks and receives an additional assurance), the warranty becomes a modification, and need not be supported by consideration if it is otherwise reasonable and in order."

In *Bigelow v. Agway, Inc.,* 506 F.2d 551 (2d Cir.1974), the court considered whether a salesman's oral statements constituted a valid post-sale warranty modification. In *Bigelow* a farmer sued the manufacturer and distributor of a chemical used to treat hay before baling. Although

chip away ice in the ball groove. They also fill the space between circuits, thus eliminating the possibility of balls being trapped between circuits. If all balls should be lost from a ball nut equipped with deflectors, these yoke-type units will then cause the ball nut to function as a threaded nut. This is a true fail safe feature."

most farmers will not bale hay with a moisture level higher than twenty to twenty-five percent, apparently the plaintiff was told that the chemical would safely permit the baling of hay with a higher moisture level. Two months after the sale and use of the chemical, defendant's salesman guaranteed that hay treated with the chemical was safe to bale even though it contained a moisture level of thirty-two to thirty-four percent. The farmer baled the hay, and the level of moisture resulted in a fire that destroyed his entire crop. Rejecting defendant's argument that the salesman's representation was not a basis of the bargain, the Second Circuit noted,

> "Although defendants might conceivably contend that since [the salesman's] representations postdated the delivery of the [treatment] * * * and therefore could not be the 'basis of the bargain' as required for recovery * * *, it is undisputed that the [salesman's] visit * * * was to promote the sale of the product. Thus, they might constitute an actionable modification of the warranty."

Id. at 555 n. 6. Similarly, in the case at bar a rational jury could have found that GM's post-sale representations about the safety of ball-screw assemblies with yolk deflectors were designed to promote future sales. This is especially true since GM sent Abex brochures discussing the safety features for distribution to Abex's customers.

GM argues, citing *Durbano Metals, Inc. v. A & K Railroad Materials, Inc.,* 574 P.2d 1159 (Utah 1978); *Terry v. Moore,* 448 P.2d 601 (Wyo. 1968); and *Speed Fastners Inc. v. Newsom,* 382 F.2d 395 (10th Cir.1967), that Abex must prove reliance on the express warranty in order to establish that the warranty was part of the basis of the bargain. Official Comment 3 to UCC § 2–313 states, "in actual practice affirmations of fact made by the seller * * * are regarded as part of the description of those goods; hence no particular reliance on such statements need be shown in order to weave them into the fabric of the agreement * * *." We need not decide whether an express warranty may exist without reliance, *see* J. White & R. Summers, *Uniform Commercial Code* 333 (1980) ("Possibly for lack of any other meaningful standard, courts must employ the test of whether buyer relied on the affirmation of fact or promise * * * "), because Abex presented sufficient evidence for a rational jury to find that Abex did rely on GM's express warranty. Robert Saunders, Director of Research and Development and Technical Marketing for Abex, testified that he was not concerned about making safety modifications on Abex's existing stock of ball-screw assemblies because of GM's representations:

> "Q. (by Abex's counsel) Did you feel it was necessary to either alter your existing stock or the ball screws out in the field with runout threads?
>
> A. (by Mr. Saunders) No.
>
> Q. Why not?

A. Because the design that we had, either the thread runout or—the washer was somewhat less critical because of the existence of the deflector yokes.

Q. All right. In other words, you weren't so concerned about the safety features because of the representations about the yoke deflectors?

A. That's correct."

R. IX, 42.

GM contends that Abex cannot recover for breach of express warranty because there was no mutual agreement to modify the limited written warranty as required by § 2–313. In *Cargill, Inc. v. Stafford,* 553 F.2d 1222, 1225 (10th Cir.1977), we noted that the UCC contains an objective test of mutuality of assent as "manifested by the conduct of the parties." On the basis of the evidence presented in this case, we hold that after resolving all factual inferences in favor of Abex, a rational jury could have found that both parties recognized and assented to a warranty on the absolute safety of ball-screw assemblies equipped with yolk deflectors.

III

GM contends that its breach of the express warranty did not proximately cause Abex damage because the collapse of the Jetway had nothing to do with the failure of the yolk deflectors. However, since Abex presented evidence that the screw free-fell through the nut and that GM warranted that the yolk deflectors would engage the nut, we must resolve any doubts in favor of Abex.

Reversed and remanded for further proceedings consistent with this opinion.

[Some footnotes omitted.]

SECTION 3. NON–COMPLIANCE WITH IMPLIED WARRANTIES

A. Introduction

The line between an express warranty and the implied warranties of merchantability, UCC 2–314, and fitness for particular purpose, UCC 2–315, can be very fine. The common ground, of course, is the contract description of the goods. Depending on the facts, the description can create an express warranty, UCC 2–313(1)(b), provide a standard to measure merchantability, UCC 2–314(1)(a), and describe goods which meet the buyer's particular purposes. See UCC 2–315. In fact, the "sale by description" is thought to be the transaction from which implied warranty theory evolved. See, e.g., Gardiner v. Gray, 4 Camb. 144, 171 Eng.Rep. 46 (1815); Prosser, *The Implied Warranty of Merchantable Quality,* 27 Minn.L.Rev. 117, 139–45 (1943); Williston, *Representation and Warranty in Sales—Heilbut v. Buckleton,* 27 Harv.L.Rev. 1, 13 (1913).

But if neither the description of the goods nor the seller's other affirmations or promises cover the buyer's particular expectations of quality, how, if at all, is the gap in the agreement to be filled? See UCC 2–314 & 2–315? Implied warranties are clearly terms of the agreement. Are they implied in fact or imposed by law? If the latter, what justifications support the imposition?

We will consider these questions in this Section.

Problem 12–3   *NOT FOR CLASS DISCUSSION*

Read UCC 2–314 and 2–315. Make up an abstract list of the basic types of facts a plaintiff would *not* have to prove to show breach of an implied warranty of merchantability but would have to prove to show breach of an implied warranty of fitness for a particular purpose.

B. Merchantability

UCC 2–314(1) provides that "a warranty that the goods shall be merchantable is implied in a contract for their sale if the seller is a merchant with respect to goods of that kind." Subsection (2) provides standards to measure merchantability and Subsection (3) provides that "other implied warranties may arise from course of dealing or usage of trade." But the implied warranty of merchantability may be "excluded or modified" by agreement, the content of which is regulated by UCC 2–316(2).

AGOOS KID CO., INC. v. BLUMENTHAL IMPORT CORP.

Supreme Judicial Court of Massachusetts, 1933.
282 Mass. 1, 184 N.E. 279.

[Blumenthal Import Corporation contracted to sell to Agoos Kid Company four thousand dozen "Bagdad goat skins dry salted." Payment was to be: "Net cash or domestic letter of credit against documents"; Agoos paid without inspecting the skins. Serious defects in the skins showed up for which Agoos sued Blumenthal. Plaintiff got judgment and Blumenthal appealed.]

CROSBY, J.

* * *

Upon the question whether there was an implied warranty of merchantable quality under [Uniform Sales Act 15(2)] the following facts were found: The goods described in the contracts known in the trade as "Bagdad goat skins dry salted" are a well known article of commerce. The defendant maintains an organization in various places in Asia Minor and India for the purpose of collecting dry salted skins for shipment to the United States and at the time of the collection of the skins in question it had a representative in Bagdad. At times such representatives buy from local collectors and butchers skins which have been cured by the dry salting process. This process is efficient in preserving the texture of the skins only when an attempt is not made to dry them too quickly by the hot rays of the sun, which is likely to result in a rotting of the inside of the skin, where it cannot be detected by ocular or manual inspection or in any other practicable way until the skins are put into the process of being made into leather. With reasonable precaution in the care and selection of the skins in the Orient, a certain number of improperly cured and rotted skins is likely to be found in a large lot. Both parties were aware of this fact. In the trade it is considered that a lot is normal if it does not appear that more than one and one half per cent, or at the most three per cent, are improperly cured and therefore worthless. "Certainly a lot containing more than three per cent of rotted skins is abnormal." It was found that so far as defects appeared the defendant was ignorant of their condition, and the same was true of the plaintiff until the defects were shown in the plaintiff's tannery. Beginning with the first pack of skins of the first shipment the plaintiff, on January 14, 1931, began the process of manufacturing them into leather, and at different times thereafter all the other packs were put through the process, and many of them showed that more than three per cent were rotten. The entire first shipment was finally put through the process, and it was found that "the defects in the first shipment were very material and important and extended to nearly half the skins contained in it." Upon the foregoing findings which were warranted by the evidence, the further finding was warranted that the goods delivered by the first shipment were not of merchantable quality.

The contracts in question were for a sale of goods by description and there was an implied warranty that they would correspond with the description. G.L. c. 106, § 16. "The goods are merchantable when they are of the general kind which they are described or supposed to be when bought." Williston on Sales (2d Ed.) § 243. "Where goods of a character commonly known in trade are ordered by description, and there is no inspection, there is an implied warranty that those furnished will be such as are merchantable under the descriptive term used by the parties. The purchaser is entitled to get what he ordered." Leavitt v. Fiberloid Co., 196 Mass. 440, 451, 82 N.E. 682, 687, 15 L.R.A., N.S., 855, and cases cited. See, also, Randall v. Newson, 2 Q.B.D. 102; Bristol Tramways, &c. Carriage Co., Ltd. v. Fiat Motors, Ltd., [1910] 2 K.B. 831, 841; Nichol v. Godts, 10 Ex. 191. The plaintiff did not contract to buy seven thousand dozen goat skins, one half of which were to be rotten and worthless. It agreed to buy that number of skins dry salted, and there was an implied warranty that, with the exception of not more than three per cent thereof, they should be of merchantable quality. Keown & McEvoy, Inc. v. Verlin, 253 Mass. 374, 377, 149 N.E. 115, 41 A.L.R. 1319, Whitty Manuf. Co. v. Clark, 278 Mass. 370, 180 N.E. 315. Although it was found that a lot of dry salted goat skins is deemed of merchantable quality and reasonably fit for the purpose of making it into leather if the defect here existing is limited to not more than three per cent of the lot, it was found that the first shipment was not merchantable throughout "within this definition, and was not reasonably fit throughout within this definition for the purpose of being made into leather." * * * [The court reversed because the trial court had excluded defendant's evidence of a custom in the trade to notify the seller of defective skins before starting to process them.]

Notes

1. In a seminal article, written in 1943, William Prosser, later a principal architect of strict tort liability, suggested three overlapping justifications for the implied warranty of merchantability. The first was that the seller had made a "misrepresentation of fact" upon which the buyer had relied. For Prosser, this was "obviously" a tort theory. The second was that the warranty "has in fact been agreed upon by the parties as an unexpressed term of the contract for sale." The warranty was inferred from language, conduct, circumstances and was "pure" contract. The third was that the warranty was "imposed by law" as a matter of policy. The loss from "defective" goods should be placed upon the seller "because he is best able to bear it and distribute it to the public, and because it is considered that the buyer is entitled to protection at the seller's expense." For the third justification, Prosser had in mind cases where defective food caused personal injuries to buyers and consumers. See Prosser, The Implied Warranty of Merchantable Quality, 27 Minn.L.Rev. 117, 122 (1943). Do you agree with Prosser's classifications?

2. Which justification(s) supports the result in *Agoos Kid Co.*? Can you add to the list?

VALLEY IRON & STEEL CO. v. THORIN

Supreme Court of Oregon, 1977.
278 Or. 103, 562 P.2d 1212.

LENT, J.

Plaintiff brought an action in assumpsit for the reasonable value of goods sold and delivered to the defendant. Defendant pleaded affirmative defenses, alleging breaches of the implied warranties of merchantability and fitness for particular purpose. ORS 72.3140; 72.3150. Following a trial to the court, judgment was entered in favor of plaintiff. Defendant appeals, claiming that the court erred in failing to find breaches of the implied warranties and improperly fixed the amount of damages.

Because of the trial court's general finding in favor of plaintiff, we review the evidence in the light most favorable to its contentions.

Plaintiff is a corporation engaged in the manufacture of cast iron products. In 1974 defendant was establishing a retail store to sell equipment and supplies for tree-planting contractors and workers. In September of that year, defendant's agent, Steven Gibbs, met with Roger Herring, Manager of Valley Iron & Steel. Mr. Gibbs inquired if plaintiff could manufacture castings of hoedad collars. A hoedad is a forestry tool used for planting seedling trees. The collar of a hoedad secures the metal blade to a wooden handle.

Mr. Gibbs showed plaintiff a sample collar casting made by Western Fire Equipment and asked if plaintiff could duplicate the casting. The sample collar was shown with a handle, and Mr. Gibbs explained that the tool was an impact tool used for planting trees and that occasionally rocks are struck during the planting process. Plaintiff's witness, Mr. Herring, testified:

"* * * Mr. Gibbs came in, spoke to me, told me that he needed this particular type of casting, briefly described its intended use, asked me if we could make them.

"I indicated we could. It was a very brief discussion in regards to the type of material we were going to use, and I indicated that because there was potential chance of hitting rock in this * * * operation * * * that it would have to be made out of somewhat of a durable material."

Mr. Herring suggested that the castings be made of durable iron. The parties agreed upon a price, and after defendant obtained a core box and pattern from the model collar, manufacturing commenced. The collars were delivered to defendant in early October, 1974.

Problems developed with the finished product. Defendant's customers complained that the castings were breaking. Eventually defendant returned up to 80% of the castings to the plaintiff. Another foundry later made satisfactory castings from the same core box and pattern but from mild steel instead of cast iron.

At the conclusion of the trial, the court made the following findings:

"I am not going to make any specific findings—just some general findings—but I will say that my general findings are based upon two findings, I suppose. One is that Mr. Gibbs' directions to Mr. Herring in this case were not sufficient in the sense that the court believes that he knew enough about what he was doing when he went out there to give directions, and the court does not feel that Mr. Herring did anything that was legally wrong and then didn't comply with what he said he was going to do.

"In other words, the court believes that the one at fault was Mr. Gibbs in this particular case. 'Fault' may not be exactly the correct word, but that it was the legal duty of Mr. Gibbs to do more than he did, rather than Mr. Herring doing more than he did.

"So, the court—then, the general finding is that I am finding for the plaintiff."

Defendant contends on appeal that the court erred in failing to find the existence of an implied warranty of merchantability under ORS 72.3140 and an implied warranty of fitness for a particular purpose under ORS 72.3150. ORS 72.3140 provides that:

"72.3140. Implied warranty: merchantability; usage of trade. (1) Unless excluded or modified as provided in ORS 72.3160, a warranty that the goods shall be merchantable is implied in a contract for their sale if the seller is a merchant with respect to goods of that kind * * *

"(2) Goods to be merchantable must be at least such as:

* * *

"(c) Are fit for the ordinary purposes for which such goods are used; * * *"

In denying defendant any recovery under this theory, the trial court must have concluded either that plaintiff was not a "merchant with respect to goods of that kind" or that the goods were "fit for the ordinary purposes for which such goods are used." It is undisputed that the products were "goods"[1] and that there was a "contract for their sale." Any implied warranty which existed was not excluded or modified under ORS 72.3160.[2]

"Merchant" is defined by ORS 72.1040 as "a person who deals in goods of the kind or otherwise by his occupation holds himself out as having knowledge or skill peculiar to the practices or goods involved in the transaction * * *." While the evidence shows that plaintiff was unfamiliar with hoedads and had not previously manufactured hoedad collars, plaintiff did hold itself out, by operating a foundry, as having skill in the "practice" of casting iron and presumably in the selection of materials to be used in manufacturing castings. Inasmuch as this transaction involved the selection of the type of metal appropriate for hoedad collars, plaintiff was a merchant.[3]

Likewise, plaintiff, for purposes of ORS 72.3140, was a merchant "with respect to goods of that kind"; i.e., castings. Whether this provision is interpreted broadly (in this case to mean castings) or narrowly (to mean hoedad collars) would depend upon the facts of the case. Only merchants, under the Code, warrant merchantability; and this is so because of their expertise or familiarity with the processes or products involved in the transaction. This skill or knowledge is presumed from previous similar transactions. Plaintiff has in the past assisted buyers in choosing particular types of metals to fulfill various tasks in its manufacture of castings.[4] Where the alleged unfitness

---

1. "Specially manufactured goods" are included within the definition of "goods" in ORS 72.1050.

2. We do not conclude that plaintiff, by promising to make the castings out of "durable iron" or saying that it was not performing engineering services, effectively modified or excluded any implied warranties as to the ingredients used in manufacturing the castings under ORS 72.3160. Such language does not "in common understanding call the buyer's attention to the exclusion of warranties and make plain that there is no implied warranty." ORS 72.3160(3)(a).

3. In Blockhead, Inc. v. Plastic Forming Company, Inc., 402 F.Supp. at 1017

(D.Conn.1975) the court held that: "The term 'practices' indicates that one may be a merchant of goods by virtue of his involvement in the process by which those goods are produced as well as by sale of the finished goods from inventory." (402 F.Supp. at 1025.)

4. Mr. Herring testified that he tried to imply to buyers that no guarantee was made as to the selection of the appropriate material for casting but that any lack of guarantee was not discussed with Mr. Gibbs. In special order situations like the present case, it was customary with plaintiff to use the "best efforts at foundry" as to the choice of the proper alloy.

under ORS 72.3140 arises from this type of choice, plaintiff should be held to the stricter standard imposed on merchants.[5]

The remaining issue is whether the collars were "fit for the ordinary purposes for which such goods are used." The ordinary purpose of custom-made castings depends upon their designated use. Without such a tag the uses would vary so much that any function could be isolated as "ordinary."

Were they fit?

The trial court felt that plaintiff was unaware of the intended use. However, the testimony of Mr. Herring shows the contrary. Plaintiff knew that the castings were to join the handle and blade in tree-planting impact tools which occasionally would strike rock. Since the castings were not fit for this purpose, the warranty was breached.

P did know the intended use

Similarly, plaintiff breached the warranty of fitness for a particular purpose. ORS 72.3150 provides:

2-315

"Implied warranty: fitness for particular purpose. Where the seller at the time of contracting has reason to know any particular purpose for which the goods are required and that the buyer is relying on the seller's skill or judgment to select or furnish suitable goods, there is unless excluded or modified under ORS 72.3160 an implied warranty that the goods shall be fit for such purpose."

Official Comment 1 to this section states that:

"Under this section the buyer need not bring home to the seller actual knowledge of the particular purpose for which the goods are intended or of his reliance on the seller's skill and judgment, if the circumstances are such that the seller has reason to realize the purpose intended or that the reliance exists. The buyer, of course, must actually be relying on the seller." *Must be actual reliance*

In this case, the undisputed evidence shows that the buyer made known the intended purpose and that the choice of metal to be used was left to the discretion of the seller. From this the seller had "reason to know" that buyer was relying on its judgment. It is also plain that the buyer did so rely. It follows that the warranty existed and evidence existed that it was breached.[6]

Seller had reason to know that buyer was in fact relying on its judgment.

The trial court rested its decision upon the "fault" of the defendant in failing to provide additional information on the intended use of the

---

5. Thus in cases where the seller possesses no degree of discretion so as to warrant his or her expertise; e.g., where the product is manufactured strictly in accordance with buyer specifications, there may be no implied warranties. See Official Comments to the U.C.C., § 2–316, Comment 9; School Supply Service Co. v. J.H. Keeney & Co., 410 F.2d 481, 483 (5th Cir. 1969); Rust Engineering Co. v. Lawrence Pumps, Inc., 401 F.Supp. 328, 333 (D.Mass. 1975).

6. Where goods are specially manufactured goods the ordinary purpose of such goods may be equivalent to their particular purpose for purposes of the warranty enumerated in ORS 72.3150. See, generally, Filler v. Rayex Corp., 435 F.2d 336 (7th Cir. 1970); Tennessee Carolina Transp., Inc. v. Strick Corp., 283 N.C. 423, 196 S.E.2d 711 (1973). Contra, Blockhead, Inc. v. Plastic Forming Company, Inc., supra n. 3.

Official Comment 2 to the Code states: "A contract may of course include both a warranty of merchantability and one of fitness for a particular purpose."

castings. "Fault," as such, is irrelevant when dealing with implied warranties. State ex rel. Western Seed v. Campbell, 250 Or. 262, 266, 442 P.2d 215 (1967). It is true that the existence of a warranty of fitness for a particular purpose depends in part upon the comparative knowledge and skill of the parties. Blockhead, Inc. v. Plastic Forming Company, Inc., 402 F.Supp. 1017, 1024 (D.Conn.1975). Here, however, defendant made known his general requirements and the purpose for which the goods were to be used. We fail to see what more the defendant could have disclosed. Where, as here, the needs of a buyer are disclosed and the seller has reason to know of the buyer's reliance, it is incumbent upon the seller to further inquire as to the buyer's wants before representing that the goods can be provided. Lewis v. Mobil Oil Corp., 438 F.2d 500 (8th Cir.1971). See also, Northern Plumbing Supply, Inc. v. Gates, 196 N.W.2d 70 (N.D.1972).

In this case the trial court found that the reasonable value of each casting was $3.75. She estimated the value of the goods returned to be $27.42. Implicit in this finding is the conclusion that 457 of the 571 pieces were returned to the seller.[7] Because we conclude that defendant rightfully revoked acceptance under ORS 72.6080(1)(b), inasmuch as the goods were unfit, defendant has no further obligation as to the returned goods. ORS 72.6020(2)(c). The defendant, however, is obligated to pay for the remaining 114 castings which it accepted. Accordingly, under our powers as enumerated in the Oregon Constitution, Am Art VII § 3, plaintiff's judgment is reduced to $427.50 (the value of 114 pieces at $3.75 per unit).

Affirmed as modified.

Notes

1. Why should the implied warranty of merchantability be limited to sellers who are merchants "with respect to goods of that kind?" UCC 2–314(1). As the court in *Thorin* recognizes, the merchant requirement for UCC 2–314(1) is narrower than the definition of "merchant" in UCC 2–104(1). Compare UCC 2–201(2) & 2–207(2). How can a seller who had never made or sold a hoedad collar be a merchant "with respect to goods of that kind?" See Fred J. Moore, Inc. v. Schinmann, 40 Wash.App. 705, 700 P.2d 754 (1985) (farmer who made "isolated" sale not a dealer in goods of that kind); Smith v. Stewart, 233 Kan. 904, 667 P.2d 358 (1983) (seller of used yacht does not make an implied warranty of merchantability).

2. Who is a merchant for purposes of UCC 2–314(1) is a mixed question of law and fact that depends upon the circumstances of each case. Ferragamo v. Massachusetts Bay Transportation Authority, 395 Mass. 581, 481 N.E.2d 477 (1985) (upheld jury verdict that MBTA is merchant with respect to sporadic sale of old trolley cars). The question whether a farmer

---

7. Testimony at the trial by Mr. Herring was that the individual castings weighed around two pounds apiece and that the scrap value was three cents per pound. If each piece was worth six cents as scrap, an offset of $27.42 equates to 457 returned castings. This is consistent with Mr. Herring's testimony that 60–8 of the castings were returned, as 457 is 80% of the 571 units sold.

who sells livestock or raises crops grown on his own land is a merchant is frequently litigated with diverse results. In Dotts v. Bennett, 382 N.W.2d 85 (Iowa 1986), however, the court rejected the argument that a farmer who sells only a crop grown annually (hay) was not, as a matter of law, a merchant. The jury verdict that the farmer was a merchant with respect to hay was supported by the following factors: "He had been a lifetime farmer; he had 100 to 150 acres in hay in 1981; he has sold about twenty percent of his hay for fifteen years; he has advertised hay for sale; at one time he sold a large quantity of hay to parties in southern Missouri; he has done some custom hay farming; he considers himself a knowledgeable hay farmer; and he has had continuing education in farming. * * * " 382 N.W.2d at 89. A related case is Vince v. Broome, 443 So.2d 23 (Miss.1983) (farmer held to be merchant with regard to cattle sold, four judges dissenting).

3. Cattle and other livestock are frequently sold at auction. Suppose the farmer-owner is not a merchant under UCC 2–314(1) but the auctioneer clearly is: He regularly deals in goods of that kind. Does the auctioneer make an implied warranty of merchantability? In Powers v. Coffeyville Livestock Sales Co., Inc., 665 F.2d 311 (10th Cir.1981), the answer was no if the auctioneer had revealed the identity of its principal. Disclosure prevented the auctioneer from being a seller at common law and the court incorporated the common law rule through UCC 1–103 to supplement the definition of seller in UCC 2–103(1)(d), which was ambiguous on the point.

DELANO GROWERS' COOPERATIVE WINERY v. SUPREME WINE CO., INC.

Supreme Judicial Court of Massachusetts, 1985.
393 Mass. 666, 473 N.E.2d 1066.

Before HENNESSEY, C.J., and LIACOS, NOLAN, LYNCH and O'CONNOR, JJ.

NOLAN, JUSTICE.

The plaintiff, Delano Growers' Cooperative Winery (Delano), appeals from a final judgment dismissing its complaint and awarding $160,634, with interest, to the defendant, Supreme Wine Co., Inc. (Supreme), on its counterclaim. Supreme appeals from that portion of the judgment which granted Delano an "offset" of $25,823.25 to Supreme's damages under the counterclaim. For the reasons stated below, we affirm the judgment. *[handwritten: Judgment Affirmed]*

Delano filed a complaint in Suffolk County Superior Court seeking $25,823.25 for wine sold and delivered. Supreme admitted receipt of the wine and filed a counterclaim for breach of contract alleging that earlier shipments of wine for which payment had been made and all of the wine for which no payment had been made had spoiled due to the presence of lactobacillus trichodes (Fresno mold). As a defense, Supreme asserted that it did not owe Delano $25,823.25 because the wine was not merchantable. Supreme also sought incidental and consequential damages alleging that the "sick wine" destroyed its reputation and market thereby forcing the company into liquidation.[1]

* * *

The facts as found by the master and accepted by the judge may be summarized as follows. Supreme operated a wine bottling plant in Boston from 1935 to November, 1978. It purchased finished wine, ready for bottling and consumption, from California, selling it to retailers after bottling under Supreme's label.

In 1968, Supreme began buying sweet wine from Delano, a California winery. By the spring of 1973, Supreme was purchasing all its sweet wine from Delano. Delano shipped this wine to Supreme's bottling plant in Boston in tank cars. When the wine arrived, Supreme took samples from each compartment of the tank cars. The samples were labeled, dated, sealed, and kept in Supreme's safe. Supreme then pumped the wine into redwood vats in its building. The wine was pumped through a filter into storage tanks from which it was later filtered into bottles for delivery.

Facts

Until April or May, 1973, Supreme did not experience any difficulty with Delano wine. Supreme then began receiving widespread returns of certain sweet wine from its customers. The wine was producing sediment, was cloudy, and contained a cottony or hairy substance. Supreme could identify the defective sweet wine as Delano wine because it purchased all its sweet wine from Delano. Supreme also *knew it was Delano* matched the returned defective wine with the samples taken from the Delano wine on delivery. This identification was corroborated somewhat by shipment records, the dates of bottling and the color to which the Delano wine was blended.

Supreme made oral reports and complaints about the problem to Delano. It also sent Delano samples from the Delano shipment. When the help promised by Harold Roland, Delano's manager, did not materi-

---

1. Supreme purchased all of its sweet wine and some of its nonsweet wine from Delano. Fresno mold only damaged the sweet wine. Supreme's customers began returning defective Delano wine prior to the shipment for which Delano claims in its complaint that it is owed $25,823.25 (the unpaid shipment). Supreme paid for all prior shipments. Supreme's customers continued to return defective Delano wine after Supreme received and bottled the wine in the unpaid shipment. One-half of the unpaid shipment consisted of sweet wine. The record does not indicate what portion of the unpaid shipment or total shipments consisted of damaged wine. However, we need not resolve this question to affirm the judgment in this case. Supreme proved that 8,000 cases of wine were defective. Supreme normally sold this wine to its retail customers for $13 per case. This per case price included the amount Supreme paid Delano for the wine, Supreme's other costs, and its profits. The judge calculated damages by multiplying the number of cases proved as damaged (8,000) by the per case price ($13). The resultant amount includes all of Supreme's cost for wine including the amount remaining unpaid on the last shipment. The judge then deducted the amount that Supreme had not paid for wine ($25,823.25) and made other adjustments as discussed below. This prevents overcompensating Supreme because the per case price ($13) included Supreme's cost for the wine as if it were actually paid. The $25,823.25 represents a portion of this cost that was not paid. This calculation also factors out any need to determine the amount of undamaged wine Supreme received as damages are based solely on the actual amount of defective wine.

Supreme proved that 8,000 cases of wine were defective

alize, Supreme purchased wine from another California grower in June, July, and August, 1973. Supreme bottled and sold that wine and received no complaints or returns on it. Roland, with renewed promises of assistance, induced Supreme to recommence purchasing from Delano in September, 1973.

Delano made four shipments of sweet wine to Supreme between September 28 and December 20, 1973. Each shipment invoice stated that payment was due forty-five days from the invoice date. Supreme paid all but the last invoice, which was in the amount of $25,823.25. It withheld payment for that amount as customers continued to return defective wine which was identified as Delano wine. When oral reports and complaints evoked no tangible help, Vito Bracciale, assistant to Supreme's president, wrote to Roland on April 9, 1974. This letter requested assistance and explained Supreme's crisis caused by the defective wine. The letter also indicated the high number of returns caused by this defective wine.

In response to this letter, Delano sent James Lunt, an assistant winemaker, to Supreme's bottling plant. His microscopic examination of the defective wine and a microscopic examination by Delano's chemist in California showed that the wine contained Fresno mold. Lunt had earlier observed the mold in the samples returned to Delano by Supreme. These were samples from the tank cars taken on arrival at Supreme and samples from wine returned by Supreme's customers.

[handwritten: Fresno mold observed in the samples too]

While Lunt was at Supreme, customers returned a number of cases of Delano wine containing Fresno mold. After examining these returns, Lunt told Supreme to pasteurize, refilter, rebottle, and resell the defective wine. Supreme followed Lunt's directions and reprocessed 8,000 cases of spoiled wine (5,000 cases returned from customers and 3,000 cases still on hand). During this process, 1,000 cases were lost through breakage, spillage, and shrinkage. Supreme sold the remaining cases of reprocessed wine at a reduced rate.

[handwritten: X]

[handwritten: Supreme resold the wine!]

* * *

2. *Delano's breach of the implied warranty of merchantability.* This sale of wine by Delano is governed by the Uniform Commercial Code, G.L. c. 106. Delano impliedly warranted that the goods were of merchantable quality. G.L. c. 106, § 2–314. See *Regina Grape Prods. Co. v. Supreme Wine Co.*, 357 Mass. 631, 635, 260 N.E.2d 219 (1970). This warranty required the wine to "pass without objection in the trade under the contract description" and be reasonably suited for ordinary uses for which goods of that kind are sold. G.L. c. 106, § 2–314(2)(a). See *Vincent v. Nicholas E. Tsiknas Co.*, 337 Mass. 726, 729, 151 N.E.2d 263 (1958); *Gilbert & Bennett Mfg. Co. v. Westinghouse Elec. Corp.*, 445 F.Supp. 537, 548 (D.Mass.1977).

[handwritten left margin: Sale of Wine is UCC gov'd]

[handwritten right margin: Delano breached the implied Warranty!]

[handwritten right margin: Clearly the Wine was bad]

The contract in this case required Delano to deliver "finished wine" to Supreme. Delano contends that, when it delivered wine that appeared good and which could be bottled, its obligation was satisfied. In support, Delano argues that all California sweet wine contained Fresno mold. Therefore, the presence of Fresno mold could not cause a wine to be unmerchantable. Furthermore, Delano states that an alleged trade usage required Supreme to add sulfur dioxide to the wine to inhibit further growth of these bacteria. Delano's arguments fail to persuade us.

[margin note: Should this have been more persuasive?]

Delano argues that uncontroverted testimony indicated that all California sweet wine contained Fresno mold. The judge acknowledged this testimony. However, the judge found that Supreme never experienced any trouble with bacteria until the 1973 problem with Delano wine. The sweet wine which Supreme bought from other California growers in 1973 did not present any bacterial problems. None of this wine was returned with Fresno mold. Furthermore, the judge found that the bacterial problem could have been prevented and controlled by Delano. Although Fresno mold may have been present in all California sweet wine, there is no indication that it was allowed to go unchecked and thereby destroy the merchantability of finished wine. Supreme's prior experience with Delano and its experience with other California sweet wine in 1973 indicate that the mold could be controlled. The presence of Fresno mold, as it was in the Delano wines, caused those wines to be unmarketable.

[margin note: Course of dealing between the parties controls interpretation on usage of trade]

Delano argues that Supreme's failure to follow minimum industry standards prevents it from recovering for the unmerchantable wine. The judge specifically ruled that Delano had failed to meet its burden of establishing such standards as a usage of trade applicable to Supreme. Even if Delano had met its burden, its argument would fail. A course of dealing between parties controls the interpretation of usage of trade. G.L. c. 106, § 1–205(4). In this case, Supreme consistently followed the same procedure in processing Delano wine since 1968. This clearly established a course of dealing between Delano and Supreme. Any usage of trade followed in areas outside of Massachusetts cannot control this long-standing course of dealing between the parties.

[margin note: Supreme had the burden of proof – it did prove breach of the Merchantibility]

Once Supreme initially accepted Delano wine it had the burden of establishing that there was a breach of the warranty of merchantability. *Axion Corp. v. G.D.C. Leasing Corp.*, 359 Mass. 474, 479, 269 N.E.2d 664 (1971). Supreme has met that burden. Supreme identified all the returned wine as Delano wine. Delano's chemist also found traces of Fresno mold in the samples "from the compartments of the tank cars in which Delano wine arrived in Boston and wine from the bottles returned by customers." The wine in its returned state was neither merchantable nor fit for bottling or consumption. Only through extensive reprocessing could Supreme mitigate the loss from this wine. The course of dealing between the parties supports the conclusion that the finished wine shipped by Delano normally was ready for bottling and drinking. Although the Delano sweet wine could be bottled shortly thereafter, it could not be drunk.

[margin note: Finished wine means ready for bottling And Drinking]

Delano was required to anticipate the environment in which it was reasonable for its product to be used. *Back v. Wickes Corp.*, 375 Mass.

633, 640–641, 378 N.E.2d 964 (1978). It was reasonably foreseeable that the unchecked presence of Fresno mold would substantially impair the value of the wine. That result occurred. The Delano wine could not pass in the trade as finished wine without objection, was not fit for the ordinary purposes for which finished wine was used, and therefore, was unmerchantable. See G.L. c. 106, § 2–314.

* * *

Notes

1. The buyer, to prevail, must establish that the goods were unmerchantable at the time the seller tendered delivery. See UCC 2–725(2). In *Delano Growers'*, to which standards of merchantability in UCC 2–314(2) did the wine fail to conform? How did the buyer avoid the possible conclusion that there was a normal amount of Fresno mold in the wine at delivery but that it got "out of hand" while the wine was being processed by the buyer?

[handwritten margin note: Samples taken at time of delivery also had mold.]

2. In most disputes over merchantability, the key factual question is whether goods sold under a contract description were "fit for the ordinary purposes for which such goods are used." UCC 2–314(2)(c). The trier of fact must know whether the product "conformed to the standard performance of like products used in the trade * * * (and this determination) depends upon testimony of persons familiar with industry standards and local practices and is a question of fact." Pisano v. American Leasing Co., 146 Cal.App.3d 194, 194 Cal.Rptr. 77, 80 (1983). Without any evidence of relevant trade standards or uses, the merchantability claim may fail. Royal Business Machines, Inc. v. Lorraine Corp., 633 F.2d 34 (7th Cir.1980). Similarly, if, because of the newness or complexity of the product, no average or usual standards for determining performance or quality can be determined, the "ordinary purposes" standard will not help the buyer. See, e.g., Price Brothers Co. v. Philadelphia Gear Corp., 649 F.2d 416 (6th Cir.1981).

Problem 12–4 *Omit*

Fisher's, a retail book store, has an extensive inventory in specialized categories, such as law, business, psychology and investments. A new investment book by Barry Greene, entitled "How to go Short in A Bear Market," was published by Big Red Company and heavily advertised in the trade journals as the "key" to success in selling short in the stock market and selling "Puts" in the option markets. Fisher's purchased 300 copies for resale and the books sold well. Mr. N.O. Vice, an inexperienced investor, purchased a copy of the book for $20 and, following Greene's advice, committed $25,000 of his funds over a three month period. He lost $15,000 of that investment before covering his shorts. About the same time, a scathing review of Greene's book by Malcolm P. Barron appeared in the Wall Street Journal. Barron stated that the advice was seriously flawed and should not be taken seriously. Other experts agreed and sales of the book dropped precipitously. Angered, N.O. Vice retains you as counsel to consider whether a law suit against either Fisher's or Big Red could be maintained on a warranty theory. Greene, who went long while others were going short, is now "long gone." What is your advice? Cf. Cardozo v. True, 342 So.2d 1053 (Fla.App.1977).

INTERNATIONAL PETROLEUM SERVICES, INC. v. S & N WELL SERVICE, INC.

Supreme Court of Kansas, 1982.
230 Kan. 452, 639 P.2d 29.

FROMME, JUSTICE:

International Petroleum Services, Inc., plaintiff, brought this action to recover for materials and repairs to three units of oil well servicing equipment. Two of these units had been sold previously by plaintiff to S & N Well Service, Inc., defendant herein. The third unit, which was repaired by plaintiff, was leased by defendant from another individual. Defendant filed an answer and a cross-petition. In the cross-petition defendant claimed breach of implied warranties arising from the sales of the equipment and asked for both ordinary and consequential damages. In addition, defendant sought disallowance of certain amounts claimed by plaintiff because plaintiff's charges were said to be unreasonable.

The case was tried to the court and judgment was entered on the petition in favor of plaintiff and against the defendant in the amount of $17,385.83. On defendant's cross-petition, defendant was given judgment against the plaintiff for $1,042.69. A judgment for the net amount of $16,343.14 was entered in favor of plaintiff and against the defendant. The defendant appealed and the Court of Appeals affirmed, 637 P.2d 496, under Rule No. 7.042(b) and (d) (228 Kan. lii, liii). The case is now before this court on an order granting defendant's Petition for Review.

There are two principal questions to be answered in this appeal. The first is whether the implied warranties mentioned in K.S.A. 84–2–314 and 84–2–315 apply to the sale of used goods. The second question is whether consequential damages resulting from a seller's breach of warranty are recoverable, and, if so, under what circumstances.

The uniform commercial code sections on implied warranties arising from the sale of goods cover merchantability, found in K.S.A. 84–2–314, and fitness for a particular purpose, found in K.S.A. 84–2–315. These sections are as follows:

* * *

Considering the above provisions of 84–2–314 it would be inaccurate to say the code defines merchantability. What this statute does is set minimum standards of merchantability. The statutory language is that "[g]oods to be merchantable must be at *least* such as * * *." Emphasis supplied. Thus more may be required by the parties' agreement, course of dealing, or usage of trade, but the minimum standards assure a buyer that if the goods received do not conform at least to normal commercial expectations, the buyer will have a cause of action by which he or she can secure compensation for losses suffered. Even though the seller may be careful not to make a single assertion of fact or promise about the goods, the ordinary buyer in a normal commercial transaction has a right to expect that the goods which are purchased will not turn out to be completely worthless. The purchaser cannot be expected to purchase goods offered by a merchant for sale and use and then find the goods are suitable only for the junk pile. On the other hand, a buyer who has purchased goods without obtaining an express warranty as to their quality and condition cannot reasonably expect that those goods will be the finest of all possible goods of that kind. Protection of the buyer under the uniform commercial code lies between these two extremes. If an item is used or is second hand, surely less can be expected in the way of quality than if the item is purchased new. See Nordstrom, Law of Sales § 76, pp. 232–238 (1970); and White-Summers, Uniform Commercial Code § 9–6, pp. 343–355 (second edition 1980) for further discussion of this subject.

In addition, we note that for a sale to give rise to the implied warranty *of merchantability* the seller must be a merchant.

*   *   *

All parties to this action agree that the plaintiff, International Petroleum Services, Inc., does manufacture and deal in well servicing equipment of the kind sold to defendant. We conclude that plaintiff was a merchant within the statutory definition when it sold the two units to the defendant.

In passing we note under K.S.A. 84–2–315, relating to the implied warranty of fitness for a particular purpose, there is no requirement that the seller be a merchant. However, the seller at the time of contracting must have reason to know the goods are being purchased for a particular purpose, and the seller must know further that the buyer is relying on the skill and judgment of the seller to select or furnish suitable goods. In such case an implied warranty that the goods shall be fit for such purpose may arise. Further discussion on the subject will follow later.

After examining the uniform commercial code—sales, we find no provision excluding the sale of used goods from the provisions of the code. K.S.A. 84–2–102 merely states that Article 2 on sales applies "to transactions in goods." K.S.A. 84–2–105(1) states:

> " 'Goods' means all things (including specially manufactured goods) which are movable at the time of identification to the contract for sale other than the money in which the price is to be paid, investment securities (article 8) and things in action."

The commentators generally have agreed that the implied warranties recognized by K.S.A. 84–2–314 and 84–2–315 apply to sales of both new and used goods. Note, *Sales: Extension of Implied Warranty of Merchantability to Used Goods,* 46 Mo.L.Rev. 249, 250 (1981); Stasney, *UCC Implied Warranty of Merchantability and Used Goods,* 26 Baylor L.Rev. 630, 637 (1974); Hunt, *Implied Warranties of Quality on Used Motor Vehicles in Texas,* 9 St. Mary's L.J. 308, 315 (1977); *Article Two*

Warranties in Commercial Transactions, 64 Cornell L.Rev. 30, 85 (1978). Texas seems to be the only state which has steadfastly refused to recognize implied warranties in the sale of used goods. The old adage "let the buyer beware" applies to the sale of used goods in Texas.

In *Atlas Industries, Inc. v. National Cash Register Co.,* 216 Kan. 213, 531 P.2d 41 (1975), this court recognized an implied warranty in the sale of a used accounting machine, without discussion as to applicability of these warranties to used goods. The parties in that case did not question whether the uniform commercial code—sales covered sales of used equipment.

We note the following statement which appears in the comments following K.S.A. 84–2–314:

> "3. A specific designation of goods by the buyer does not exclude the seller's obligation that they be fit for the general purposes appropriate to such goods. *A contract for the sale of second-hand goods, however, involves only such obligation as is appropriate to such goods for that is their contract description."* Comment 3. Emphasis supplied.

This comment by the drafters of the statute strongly indicates an intent to include sales of both new and used goods within the statutory provisions.

A few of the decisions from other states which have recognized an implied warranty of merchantability in the sale of used goods are: *Brown v. Hall,* 221 So.2d 454, 457 (Fla.Dist.Ct.App.1969); *Georgia Timberlands, Inc. v. Southern Airway Company,* 125 Ga.App. 404, 405, 188 S.E.2d 108 (1972); *Overland Bond and Inv. Corp. v. Howard,* 9 Ill. App.3d 348, 352, 292 N.E.2d 168 (1972); *Tracy v. Vinton Motors, Inc.,* 130 Vt. 512, 515, 296 A.2d 269 (1972).

We hold that the implied warranties recognized in K.S.A. 84–2–314 and 84–2–315 may arise from sales of both new and used goods.

* * *

It should be noted that the extent of the obligation of a merchant who sells used goods depends on the circumstances of the transaction. In the case of a sale by auction of used restaurant equipment it was held no implied warranty of merchantability attached. See *Regan Purchase & Sales v. Primavera,* 68 Misc.2d 858, 860, 328 N.Y.S.2d 490 (1972), wherein it is stated:

> "The specific question here is whether a breach of warranty is made out by evidence that used restaurant equipment bought at an auction did not function upon delivery, in the absence of any competent evidence establishing the character of the defect. The standard formulated in the Official Comment clearly requires careful attention to the realities of the individual transaction.

> "What we are concerned with here are two pieces of restaurant equipment—a dishwasher and an ice-maker—undoubtedly larger and more complex than similar equipment intended for home use—

both of which had undergone the heavy wear and tear normal in the operation of a restaurant. The possibility that individual components might be worn out or otherwise defective, requiring replacement or repair, is surely implicit in such a transaction.

"Where such pieces of equipment are purchased for continued commercial use at a significant discount from new equipment of the same kind, more is surely required to establish a breach of the warranty than the bare circumstance that they did not operate upon delivery."

Courts have recognized that any number of things can foul the operation of complex machinery, and in the case of used goods, not all of these problems amount to a breach of the warranty of merchantability. The buyer's knowledge that the goods are used, the extent of their prior use, and whether the goods are significantly discounted may help determine what standards of quality should apply to the transaction.

With the foregoing background we turn now to the specific facts of this case. S & N Well Service, Inc. began business in February, 1977. The president of the corporation, Mr. Smith, had been in this type of business since 1970 and had operated eleven oil well servicing rigs before he started the present company.

In February, 1977, Mr. Smith purchased from plaintiff one of the units now in question. It is referred to as a single drum Franks Unit. He was advised and understood the unit was used. The unit was equipped with a diesel engine, and plaintiff informed the purchaser that the engine had been checked out and approved by Detroit Diesel, a company specializing in the sale and servicing of diesel engines. However, no express warranty was given on the unit and no disclaimer was mentioned or declared by the seller. This particular machine had been built by plaintiff from components of several other used oil well servicing rigs. These had been purchased previously by plaintiff and the components from those machines were assembled in plaintiff's shop to make up Unit No. 1. The working parts such as the draw works and engine were used. Only a few of the components such as the cab and fenders were new. Defendant was advised of these facts. We find nothing in the record as to the price paid for the second-hand unit as compared to the price of a new unit.

Problems developed with Unit No. 1 after it had been used only two days. The fourth gear kept slipping out. A rebuilt differential unit was installed by plaintiff. The oil line to the air compressor was not connected properly when sold and the motor threw a connecting rod. The unit was returned to plaintiff. A new connecting rod was installed and the oil line was properly connected. No charges were made for these repairs. Thereafter, the unit worked fine for 90 days, at which time the engine began to misfire and the heat gauge indicated overheating. Close examination disclosed a head gasket was blown. It was then discovered the engine head was cracked and the pistons were cupped out. In effect, the engine was worn out and needed to be completely rebuilt. The machine was returned to the plaintiff.

The engine was then pulled and rebuilt by Diesel Equipment Company of Wichita. For the rebuilding of the engine and the work in pulling and reinstalling the engine plaintiff submitted a bill on invoice No. 9945 for $6,765.01. After defendant complained of the amount of these charges, the bill was reduced to $4,932.27. The defendant was apparently satisfied with this adjustment for a time but did not make payment. Plaintiff sued for the reduced amount.

Now we turn to the second unit purchased from plaintiff in March, 1977. This will be referred to as Unit No. 2. It was a Cardwell K-200 double drum unit. Before purchasing the unit Mr. Smith, acting for the defendant company, asked that the rig be modified from a dual axle to a single axle unit. The single axle left on the machine was too light and within the first few days of use the front axle bent. The rig was hauled in for repairs and the plaintiff company repaired the machine by exchanging the bent axle for a heavy duty axle. There was testimony by an officer of plaintiff company that they would have known the first single axle was too light if they had "ran the figures through right." In order to accommodate the new heavy axle, it was necessary to add larger rims and tires. The original invoice No. 9944 submitted for these charges totaled $3,982.07. The defendant company complained of the charges and again the bill was reduced, this time to $1,042.69 which equaled the cost of the rims and tires. Plaintiff sued for this amount. The trial court disallowed the amount finding there was a breach of warranty which required plaintiff as seller to make these repairs in order to return the value of the machine to the value it would have had at the time of sale if it had been as warranted.

As to Unit No. 1, the Franks Unit, the trial court considered the fact that this was a sale of used or second-hand goods. The unit was a highly complex machine known to be subject to heavy and sustained wear while in operation. It was made up of component parts of used machines of which neither party had knowledge concerning the extent of their use.

In Comment 7 appearing below K.S.A. 84-2-314, the authors of the UCC point out that in cases of doubt as to what quality is intended, the price at which a merchant closes a sale contract is an excellent index of the nature and scope of his obligation under the section. There was no evidence introduced in this case, however, as to the extent of the discount in the price of this used machinery. It is, therefore, nearly impossible to decide what standards of quality should apply to the transaction. We do know that the plaintiff merchant corrected the initial defects in the rig at its own expense. Plaintiff installed a rebuilt differential unit to repair the fourth gear, it connected the oil line to the air compressor, and it put in a new connecting rod in the engine. Thereafter, the unit worked fine for approximately 90 days before the diesel engine had to be rebuilt.

Under these facts and circumstances, we cannot say the trial court was in error in not allowing further damages for breach of the implied warranty of merchantability on Unit No. 1 (Franks Unit). The unit did operate satisfactorily for 90 days after the initial adjustments and repairs were made without charge. The machine was fit for the ordinary purposes for which such goods are generally used, and even after the diesel engine wore out it still could be and was rebuilt. This oil well servicing equipment was then put back in service. By way of analogy we note that used automobiles generally carry no more than a thirty day guarantee. The plaintiff merchant in the present case made no untrue promises or affirmations as to the condition of this machinery. The trial court found that the plaintiff had the diesel engine checked over by Detroit Diesel and that company had approved the engine as being in working condition.

We now consider Unit No. 2, the Cardwell Unit. As previously pointed out, this machine when sold to defendant was a used or second-hand unit. At the request of defendant it was modified by plaintiff company from a dual axle to a single axle unit. Within the first few days after it was put in use, it became inoperable because of a bent single axle. There was testimony that the plaintiff-merchant knew or should have known the machine could not operate on this single axle. It was not strong enough to support the machine. It appears that the unit was not fit for the ordinary purposes for which the machine was to be used since it became inoperable in the first few days of use.

Using the guidelines previously discussed, we agree with the trial court that plaintiff breached an implied warranty when it sold this used oil well servicing unit in such a condition. It knew or should have known the single axle was not strong enough to accommodate the machine after it was changed from a dual axle to a single axle unit. Therefore, the trial court properly allowed defendant to recover the $1,042.69 required to make it operable.

Note: *The Relevance of Price in Disputes Over Merchantability*

In *International Petroleum,* the court stated that "whether the goods are significantly discounted may help determine what standards of quality should apply to the transactions." See also, Testo v. Russ Dunmire Oldsmobile, Inc., 16 Wash.App. 39, 554 P.2d 349 (1976); UCC 2–314, Comment 7 (price at which a merchant is willing to sell an item is an "excellent index of the quality warranted and the nature and scope of his obligation"). Put differently, the price charged in context, especially where used goods are involved, will provide some assistance in determining the level of quality the buyer can reasonably expect.

This development is a retreat from Lord Mansfield's celebrated dictum in Stuart v. Wilkins, 99 Eng.Rep. 15, 19 (K.B.1778) that a "sound price" does not warrant a "sound product" but stops short of the conclusion that the price so perfectly communicates product risks that the buyer gets what he paid for. See Geistfeld, *The Price-Quality Relationship Revisited,* 16 J.Consumer Aff. 334 (1984) (factors other than quality of goods affect price and market dispersal).

In light of this, how would you resolve the following problem?

Problem 12–5 Omit

B, a farmer, purchased a used 1980 Dodge Rambler from S, a dealer, for $5,000. The four-wheel drive vehicle had been driven 80,000 "tough" miles without any serious mechanical problems. Although refusing to make any express warranties, the seller made no attempt to disclaim or exclude warranties at the time of sale.

Thirty days and 10,000 miles later, the engine failed due to a condition existing at the time of sale. B had the engine replaced for $2,500 and sued S for breach of the implied warranty of merchantability. At the trial, B established that the $5,000 purchase price was at the low end of the "blue book" range for 1980 Dodge Ramblers. B's expert testified that a 1980 Dodge Rambler with the particular condition of B's would have a fair market value of $750. On cross-examination, the expert conceded that the particular vehicle would "pass without objection in the trade under the contract description." B introduced no additional evidence. S moved for a directed verdict. What result?

C. Fitness for Particular Purpose

VAN WYK v. NORDEN LABORATORIES, INC.

Supreme Court of Iowa, 1984.
345 N.W.2d 81.

LARSON, JUSTICE.

A large number of cattle owned by the plaintiffs became sick shortly after injection of a vaccine produced by the defendant Norden Laboratories, Inc. and this suit followed. While several theories of liability were asserted by the plaintiffs, the court submitted only one: the implied warranty of fitness for a particular purpose (Iowa Code section 554.2315). The defendant appeals from a judgment for the plaintiffs, arguing that the court erred in submitting this theory under the facts of the case. It contends the implied warranty of fitness did not fit, so to speak. The plaintiffs cross-appeal, complaining that it was error to exclude certain expert evidence and to refuse submission of their alternative theories of strict liability and implied warranty of merchantability. We reverse on both appeals and remand.

In the fall of 1978, three groups of the plaintiffs' cattle, totaling about 750, were treated with a live-virus vaccine, manufactured by the defendant and called Resbo–3, serial 54. Some of the cattle had been raised by the plaintiffs, and some had been shipped in. Some were treated on the farm and some in a sale barn. The cattle were given other treatments such as worming, castration, and dehorning, simultaneously with the series 54 vaccine, but not all of them received the same combination of treatments. Yet, the incidence of bovine viral diarrhea (BVD) appeared, to a large extent, in all three herds. (BVD is one of the illnesses which the series 54 vaccine was designed to prevent.) Within a week of their injection, most of the cattle were sick. Almost 50 died. Plaintiffs' veterinarian witnesses testified that the sickness had been caused by the vaccine. They testified that before and after this incident they had used serial 54 vaccine without similar problems and that while it is reasonable to expect a few cattle to have an adverse reaction, they had never seen anything like the extent of sickness in this case. In view of this common denominator among the separate herds of cattle—their treatment with series 54 vaccine—a strong circumstantial case is claimed by the plaintiffs that the illness was in fact caused, or at least exacerbated by, the vaccine. No direct evidence of a defect was produced, however.

I. The Implied Warranty of Fitness

The only theory of liability submitted by the court was breach of implied warranty of fitness for a particular purpose, Iowa Code § 554.2315 (Uniform Commercial Code § 2–315). That section provides:

> Where the seller at the time of contracting has reason to know any particular purpose for which the goods are required and that the buyer is relying on the seller's skill or judgment to select or furnish suitable goods, there is unless excluded or modified under the next section an implied warranty that the goods shall be fit for such purpose.

The implied warranty of fitness for a particular purpose under section 554.2315 is perhaps better understood when viewed with the implied warranty of merchantability, or fitness for ordinary purposes. Iowa Code section 554.2314 sets out the latter:

* * *

The official comment to the Uniform Commercial Code illustrates the difference between "ordinary" and "particular" purposes under the respective warranties:

> A "particular purpose" differs from the ordinary purpose for which the goods are used in that it envisages a specific use by the buyer which is peculiar to the nature of his business whereas the ordinary purposes for which goods are used are those envisaged in the concept of merchantability and go to uses which are customarily made of the goods in question. For example, shoes are generally used for the purpose of walking upon ordinary ground, but a seller may know that a particular pair was selected to be used for climbing mountains.

U.C.C. § 2–315, Comment 2, 1 U.L.A. 483 (1976).

The warranty of merchantability, Iowa Code § 554.2314, is based on a purchaser's reasonable expectation that goods purchased from a "merchant with respect to goods of that kind" will be free of significant defects and will perform in the way goods of that kind should perform. It presupposes no special relationship of trust or reliance between the seller and buyer. In contrast, the warranty of fitness for a particular purpose, Iowa Code § 554.2315, is based on a special reliance by the buyer on the seller to provide goods that will perform a specific use envisaged and communicated by the buyer. Thus, any recovery under warranty for a specific purpose is predicated on a showing that (1) the seller had reason to know of the buyer's particular purpose; (2) the seller had reason to know the buyer was relying on the seller's skill or judgment to furnish suitable goods; and (3) the buyer in fact relied on the seller's skill or judgment to furnish suitable goods. *Semler v. Knowling,* 325 N.W.2d 395, 399 (Iowa 1982); J. White and R. Summers, *Handbook of the Law Under the Uniform Commercial Code* § 9–9 at 358 (2d Ed.1980). *See also Farm Bureau Mutual Insurance Co. v. Sandbulte,* 302 N.W.2d 104, 111 (Iowa 1981).

The warranty of fitness under section 554.2315 is said to turn on the "bargain-related" facts as to what the seller had reason to know about the buyer's purpose for the goods and about his reliance on the seller's skill or judgment in selecting them. *Jacobson v. Benson Motors, Inc.,* 216 N.W.2d 396, 404 (Iowa 1974). In this case the vaccine was not purchased by the veterinarians to treat these particular cattle but to keep in stock for their general veterinary practice. The plaintiffs, as owners of the cattle, and the defendant, had no direct dealing with regard to the vaccine. The decision as to what vaccine to use was made by the buyers' veterinarians, not by the defendant. There was no evidence that the seller had reason to know of any purpose for the plaintiffs' use of the vaccine, other than its ordinary use, or that the buyer was relying on the seller's skill and judgment in providing it. The implied warranty of fitness for a particular purpose would appear, therefore, to be inapplicable by its terms. *See* Iowa Code § 554.2315; *Semler v. Knowling,* 325 N.W.2d at 399; *Jacobson v. Benson Motors, Inc.,* 216 N.W.2d at 404.

The plaintiffs argue, however, that if the buyer's particular purpose is the same as its general use, a warranty of fitness arises, especially when the product has a specific and limited use. In that case, the other elements of the fitness warranty, i.e., the knowledge of the buyer's purpose, knowledge of the buyer's reliance, and the buyer's actual reliance, are apparently to be presumed. The plaintiffs cite only one case, *Tennessee Carolina Transportation Inc. v. Strick Corp.,* 283 N.C. 423, 196 S.E.2d 711 (1973), in support of this theory. That case involved the sale of truck trailers which proved to be faulty. There the court held that because the buyer's "specific use" was the same as the "general use" to which trailers are usually put, hauling cargo, the warranty of fitness would apply. It rejected the general rule that a "particular" use must be a use not normally expected to be made of the goods, a rule recognized by our cases, e.g., *Madison Silos v. Wassom,* 215 N.W.2d 494, 499–500 (Iowa 1974); *Peters v. Lyons,* 168 N.W.2d 759, 763 (Iowa 1969), and by the Uniform Commercial Code. *See* U.C.C. § 2–315, Comment 2, 1 U.L.A. 483 (1976).

Cases such as *Tennessee Carolina,* moreover, have been criticized as enlarging the fitness warranty beyond the intent of the drafters of the Uniform Commercial Code. *See* J. White and R. Summers, *supra,* § 9–9 at 357, n. 122.

In this case, written material furnished with the vaccine stated that "[f]or reducing the economic loss associated with these viruses, vaccination of healthy animals is recommended before or upon entering the feedlot or dairy herd. Vaccination of stressed animals should be delayed." Use of the vaccine on healthy, unstressed cattle, in accordance with these instructions, is the "ordinary" use for warranty purposes, according to the defendant, and the plaintiffs' evidence was aimed at showing a use in compliance with the instructions, in other words, an "ordinary" use. While there was contradicting evidence presented by the defendant that the cattle were stressed and perhaps not healthy at the time they were vaccinated, there is no claim by the plaintiffs that this deviation from ordinary use is itself a "particular" use. They merely claim that their use here is an ordinary use which we should consider as a particular use for warranty purposes. For the reasons to be discussed, we decline to do so.

Obviously, in some cases a buyer's particular purpose will be the same as the ordinary purpose for which a product is furnished. In that case, both types of implied warranty may arise. *See Jacobson v. Benson Motors, Inc.,* 216 N.W.2d 396, 404 (Iowa 1974) (sale of motor vehicle); *Madison Silos v. Wassom,* 215 N.W.2d 494, 499–500 (Iowa 1974) (stave silo); 1 R. Anderson, *Uniform Commercial Code,* § 2–314:60 (1970); Iowa Code § 554.2315, official comment 2. It is quite another matter, however, to impose an implied warranty of fitness solely on the basis of this identity of purpose. A particular purpose of the buyer is only one of the elements of that warranty; it still turns on what the seller had reason to know—both as to the buyer's particular purpose and as to the buyer's reliance on the seller's skill and judgment. *Jacobson,* 216 N.W.2d at 404. There are no bargain-related facts in this case to support a finding of these elements and we will not assume their existence merely on the basis of the limited-use nature of cattle vaccine. We will not assume, as the plaintiffs suggest, that the seller had reason to know of the buyers' particular purpose, and their reliance on the skill and judgment of the seller, merely because cattle vaccine is only usable for one purpose. As the record shows in this case, the vaccine may still be used in different ways, some anticipated by the seller and some not. (The defendant claims it was used in a manner proscribed by the written material accompanying the vaccine.)

The plaintiffs have an alternative theory: They claim that the seller had actual reason to know of the particular purpose for the vaccine and to know of the buyers' reliance on the skill and judgment of the seller so as to come within the literal requirements of the implied warranty of fitness. They rely on evidence that sales representatives of the defendant made regular calls on Dr. Hauser, that they discussed the vaccine, and that "[i]t is reasonable to infer from this fact that the representative was familiar with the vaccination procedures of Dr. Hauser and with the use he made of the vaccine." There is no evidence that the representative had reason to know the proposed use of the vaccine on these specific cattle, or even that it was to be used in circumstances similar to these, that is when other treatments such as worming, castration, and dehorning would accompany the vaccination, or that there would be a possibility the cattle could already be incubating the disease. Any conclusion that the defendant was put on notice of the plaintiffs' particular use is simply too speculative.

It was error to submit the theory of warranty of fitness for a particular purpose.

* * *

COMMENT, MANUFACTURER'S RESPONSIBILITY FOR DEFECTIVE PRODUCTS, 54 Calif.L.Rev. 1681, 1691, n. 48 (1966).

"Communication between buyer, seller, and manufacturer play no small role in determining whether or not a product is being supplied which will meet the particular economic needs of the commercial consumer. For example, in a typical * * * situation of the purchase of a heavy-duty diesel truck, most manufacturers offer dozens of different combinations of vehicle wheelbase, engines, transmissions, axles, suspension systems, air brakes, fifth wheel devices, and other component parts, all of which play a vital role in determining the capacity of a truck to meet various hauling requirements of the purchaser. Normally, the experienced trucker comes to the dealer with a good idea of the purpose for which he will use the truck, and often, based on his previous experience with similar vehicles in similar applications, with a fairly specific notion of the type of major component parts he will require. Dealer and customer go over in detail these needs, correlating them with the particular options which the manufacturer offers, and in effect arrive at some preliminary conclusions about the 'design' of the particular vehicle. Even at this stage the manufacturer may be involved, since a phone call to the factory by the dealer may answer a question like: 'Will an X diesel engine, coupled with a Y transmission and a Z rear axle enable our customer to achieve a road speed of S miles per hour under normal conditions?' Beyond this, the manufacturer becomes involved in the selection process when he receives the sales order from the dealer and submits it for review to his engineering department; the engineers may suggest several changes to be incorporated. Ultimately, the customer receives a heavy-duty truck which is reasonably tailored to his specific needs.

"Another method of merchandising commonly used in the trucking industry is for a manufacturer to build a certain number of what are called 'stock' trucks, which are then sold or consigned to the dealer. These are built with no particular customer in mind, or perhaps it should be said with the average customer in mind; these are analogous to an automobile dealer's 'showroom' models in that they incorporate most of the standard, *i.e.,* most popular, combinations of running gear. While not tailored to the specific needs of the customer, they of course do have the advantage of being available for immediate delivery. Normally, when a dealer recognizes that a customer's needs can be reasonably satisfied with a 'stock' truck, he will attempt to locate one within the dealer network which will serve the purpose, perhaps with a modification of a few component parts. Here, too, the manufacturer may become involved in the selling process through conferences concerning the ability of a particular 'stock' truck to meet the customer's needs.

"Thus the customer plays an important role in the selection process which is altogether different than that of the average new-car buyer who 'selects' such items as whitewall tires, radio, and heater. The component parts of a truck chosen by buyer, dealer, and/or manufacturer play an important role in determining whether or not the vehicle will be 'fit for a particular purpose,' * * * and the customer's communication of these economic needs is vital. While no spectacular case can be made out for the use of sales law where a manufacturer sells a truck which is so defective as to be virtually unsuited for any purpose, the requirement that the buyer's needs be communicated to the manufacturer before an implied warranty of fitness for a particular purpose would arise * * * would certainly tend to serve the useful purpose of enabling a court to determine whether or not the product was 'defective' in relation to the reasonable expectations of the buyer."

LEWIS v. MOBIL OIL CORP.

United States Court of Appeals, Eighth Circuit, 1971.
438 F.2d 500.

GIBSON, CIRCUIT JUDGE.

In this diversity case the defendant appeals from a judgment entered on a jury verdict in favor of the plaintiff in the amount of $89,250 for damages alleged to be caused by use of defendant's oil.

Plaintiff Lewis has been doing business as a sawmill operator in Cove, Arkansas, since 1956. In 1963, in order to meet competition, Lewis decided to convert his power equipment to hydraulic equipment. He purchased a hydraulic system in May 1963, from a competitor who was installing a new system. The used system was in good operating condition at the time Lewis purchased it. It was stored at his plant until November 1964, while a new mill building was being built, at which time it was installed. Following the installation, Lewis requested from Frank Rowe, a local Mobil oil dealer, the proper hydraulic fluid to operate his machinery. The prior owner of the hydraulic system had used Pacemaker oil supplied by Cities Service, but plaintiff had been a customer of Mobil's for many years and desired to continue with Mobil. Rowe said he didn't know what the proper lubricant for Lewis' machinery was, but would find out. The only information given to Rowe by Lewis was that the machinery was operated by a gear-type pump;

Rowe did not request any further information. He apparently contacted a Mobil representative for a recommendation, though this is not
entirely clear, and sold plaintiff a product known as Ambrex 810. This
is a straight mineral oil with no chemical additives.

Within a few days after operation of the new equipment commenced, plaintiff began experiencing difficulty with its operation. The
oil changed color, foamed over, and got hot. The oil was changed a
number of times, with no improvement. By late April 1965, approximately six months after operations with the equipment had begun, the
system broke down, and a complete new system was installed. The
cause of the breakdown was undetermined, but apparently by this time
there was some suspicion of the oil being used. Plaintiff Lewis requested Rowe to be sure he was supplying the right kind of oil. Ambrex 810
continued to be supplied.

From April 1965 until April 1967, plaintiff continued to have
trouble with the system, principally with the pumps which supplied the
pressure. Six new pumps were required during this period, as they
continually broke down. During this period, the kind of pump used
was a Commercial pump which was specified by the designer of the
hydraulic system. The filtration of oil for this pump was by means of a
metal strainer, which was cleaned daily by the plaintiff in accordance
with the instruction given with the equipment.

In April 1967, the plaintiff changed the brand of pump from a
Commercial to a Tyrone pump. The Tyrone pump, instead of using the
metal strainer filtration alone, used a disposable filter element in
addition. Ambrex 810 oil was also recommended by Mobil and used
with this pump, which completely broke down three weeks later. At
this point, plaintiff was visited for the first time by a representative of
Mobil Oil Corporation, as well as a representative of the Tyrone pump
manufacturer.

On the occasion of this visit, May 9, 1967, plaintiff's system was
completely flushed and cleaned, a new Tyrone pump installed, and on
the pump manufacturer's and Mobil's representative's recommendation, a new oil was used which contained certain chemical additives,
principally a "defoamant." Following these changes, plaintiff's system
worked satisfactorily up until the time of trial, some two and one-half
years later.

Briefly stated, plaintiff's theory of his case is that Mobil supplied
him with an oil which was warranted fit for use in his hydraulic
system, that the oil was not suitable for such use because it did not
contain certain additives, and that it was the improper oil which caused
the mechanical breakdowns, with consequent loss to his business. The
defendant contends that there was no warranty of fitness, that the
breakdowns were caused not by the oil but by improper filtration, and
that in any event there can be no recovery of loss of profits in this case.

I. The Existence of Warranties

Defendant maintains that there was no warranty of fitness in this case, that at most there was only a warranty of merchantability and that there was no proof of breach of this warranty, since there was no proof that Ambrex 810 is unfit for use in hydraulic systems generally. We find it unnecessary to consider whether the warranty of merchantability was breached, although there is some proof in the record to that effect, since we conclude that there was a warranty of fitness.

Plaintiff Lewis testified that he had been a longtime customer of Mobil Oil, and that his only source of contact with the company was through Frank Rowe, Mobil's local dealer, with whom he did almost all his business. It was common knowledge in the community that Lewis was converting his sawmill operation into a hydraulic system. Rowe knew this, and in fact had visited his mill on business matters several times during the course of the changeover. When operations with the new machinery were about to commence, Lewis asked Rowe to get him the proper hydraulic fluid. Rowe asked him what kind of a system he had, and Lewis replied it was a Commercial-pump type. This was all the information asked or given. Neither Lewis nor Rowe knew what the oil requirements for the system were, and Rowe, knew that Lewis knew nothing more specific about his requirements. Lewis also testified that after he began having trouble with his operations, while there were several possible sources of the difficulty the oil was one suspected source, and he several times asked Rowe to be sure he was furnishing him with the right kind.

Rowe's testimony for the most part confirmed Lewis'. It may be noted here that Mobil does not contest Rowe's authority to represent it in this transaction, and therefore whatever warranties may be implied because of the dealings between Rowe and Lewis are attributable to Mobil. Rowe admitted knowing Lewis was converting to a hydraulic system and that Lewis asked him to supply the fluid. He testified that he did not know what should be used and relayed the request to a superior in the Mobil organization, who recommended Ambrex 810. This is what was supplied.

When the first Tyrone pump was installed in April 1967, Rowe referred the request for a proper oil recommendation to Ted Klock, a Mobil engineer. Klock recommended Ambrex 810. When this pump failed a few weeks later, Klock visited the Lewis plant to inspect the equipment. The system was flushed out completely and the oil was changed to DTE–23 and Del Vac Special containing several additives. After this, no further trouble was experienced.

This evidence adequately establishes an implied warranty of fitness. Arkansas has adopted the Uniform Commercial Code's provision for an implied warranty of fitness:

"Where the seller at the time of contracting has reason to know any particular purpose for which the goods are required and that the buyer is relying on the seller's skill or judgment to select or furnish suitable goods, there is unless excluded or modified under the next section an implied warranty that the goods shall be fit for such purpose." 7C Ark.Stat.Ann. § 85–2–315 (1961).

Under this provision of the Code, there are two requirements for an implied warranty of fitness: (1) that the seller have "reason to know" of the use for which the goods are purchased, and (2) that the buyer relies on the seller's expertise in supplying the proper product. Both of these requirements are amply met by the proof in this case. Lewis' testimony, as confirmed by that of Rowe and Klock, shows that the oil was purchased specifically for his hydraulic system, not for just a hydraulic system in general, and that Mobil certainly knew of this specific purpose. It is also clear that Lewis was relying on Mobil to supply him with the proper oil for the system, since at the time of his purchases, he made clear that he didn't know what kind was necessary.

Mobil contends that there was no warranty of fitness for use in his particular system because he didn't specify that he needed an oil with additives, and alternatively that he didn't give them enough information for them to determine that an additive oil was required. However, it seems that the circumstances of this case come directly within that situation described in the first comment to this provision of the Uniform Commercial Code:

"1. Whether or not this warranty arises in any individual case is basically a question of fact to be determined by the circumstances of the contracting. Under this section the buyer need not bring home to the seller *actual knowledge of the particular purpose* for which the goods are intended or of his reliance on the seller's skill and judgment, if the circumstances are such that the seller has reason to realize the purpose intended or that the reliance exists." 7C Ark.Stat.Ann. § 85–2–315, Comment 1 (1961) (emphasis added).

Here Lewis made it clear that the oil was purchased for his system, that he didn't know what oil should be used, and that he was relying on Mobil to supply the proper product. If any further information was needed, it was incumbent upon Mobil to get it before making its recommendation. That it could have easily gotten the necessary information is evidenced by the fact that after plaintiff's continuing complaints, Mobil's engineer visited the plant, and, upon inspection, changed the recommendation that had previously been made.

Additionally, Mobil contends that even if there were an implied warranty of fitness, it does not cover the circumstances of this case because of the abnormal features which the plaintiff's system contained, namely an inadequate filtration system and a capacity to entrain excessive air. There are several answers to this contention. First of all, the contention goes essentially to the question of causation—i.e., whether the damage was caused by a breach of warranty or by some other cause—and not to the existence of a warranty of fitness in the first place. Secondly, assuming that certain peculiarities in the plaintiff's system did exist, the whole point of an implied warranty of fitness is that a product be suitable for a specific purpose, and that a seller should not supply a product which is not so suited. Thirdly, there is no evidence in the record that the plaintiff's system was unique or abnormal in these respects. It operated satisfactorily under the prior owner, and the new system has operated satisfactorily after it was adequately cleaned and an additive type oil used.

* * * Thus, Mobil's defense that there was no warranty of fitness because of an "abnormal use" of the oil is not appropriate here.

[The court next held that there was adequate evidence to sustain the jury's verdict that the plaintiff's damage was caused by the breach of warranty and not by variations in the plaintiff's system or inadequate maintenance.]

* * *

Notes

1. Was UCC 2–315 the proper warranty provision for application in *Lewis*? Put another way, could the court have reached the same result under an express warranty or an implied warranty of merchantability?

2. Suppose Mr. Lewis had asked Mr. Rowe to provide him with literature describing "oil that I might use in my new commercial hydraulic equipment." If Rowe had furnished literature describing oil with and oil without chemical additives and Mr. Rowe had thereafter ordered Ambrex 810, would the subsequent sale be with an implied warranty of fitness for particular purpose? To test your judgment, see Axion Corp. v. G.D.C. Leasing Corp., 359 Mass. 474, 269 N.E.2d 664 (1971) (reprinted at p. 463, supra).

3. Assuming that Mr. Lewis relied upon Mobil's skill and judgment, suppose Mobil had established that Ambrex 810 would work satisfactorily in some "commercial pump" hydraulic systems but not work in the particular system owned by Mr. Lewis. Assume further that Mr. Lewis was using his system for ordinary purposes. Should this affect the result in the case?

Chapter Thirteen

WARRANTY LITIGATION: BUYER'S PROOF, SELLER'S DEFENSES

SECTION 1. INTRODUCTION

To recover damages for a claimed breach of warranty, the buyer must plead and prove that: (1) the seller made some warranty, express or implied, (2) the warranty was breached, see UCC 2–607(4), and (3) the breach "caused" the damages sought. Compare UCC 2–715(2)(b). Since failure to satisfy any of these three requirements is fatal to the claim, it is important for the buyer's attorney to master the strategies for proof.

In addition, the buyer has a number of possible defenses to the claim.

First, a buyer who has accepted the goods may fail to give the notice required by UCC 2–607(3)(a). If so, the claim is barred.

Second, the seller may claim, by way of an affirmative defense, that the buyer misused the goods or failed to follow directions for use. Similarly, the seller may argue that the buyer should have discovered the non-conformity before use or assumed the risk by using goods with a known non-conformity. If so, the buyer's claim may be barred or, at the very least, the damages reduced.

Third, the seller may assert that the suit is time barred under the statute of limitations, UCC 2–725. This defense has posed some complicated questions for the courts.

Fourth, the seller may argue that the warranty claim is inappropriate and should be dismissed. Suppose there is no privity of contract and the buyer, bypassing the retailer, sues the product manufacturer for breach of warranty. Is lack of privity a defense? Or suppose that there is privity of contract between the parties but the UCC statute of limitations has run on the warranty claim. Can the buyer "escape" the UCC statute of limitations by invoking a tort theory, such as strict liability or negligence?

Note: Warranty as a Theory of Strict but Limited Liability

Why is a seller strictly liable for breach of warranty? According to Professor William Bishop, in Bishop, *The Contract-Tort Boundary and the Economics of Insurance*, 12 J.Legal Stud. 241 (1983), the reason is that warranties, when regarded as information provided by the seller to the buyer, are a form of insurance in a setting where there is imperfect information. At the time of contracting, the seller is in the best position, cost considered, to determine the true condition of the goods or to assess their suitability for use. To use the jargon, the seller is the "least-cost-information-provider." When the seller, without a disclaimer, provides information about the goods to the seller in the form of representations, including the price charged, the buyer should be able to hold the seller strictly liable for accuracy, provided that the scope of liability is limited. The warranty, therefore, is guaranteed but limited information for which the buyer has paid. (Bishop argues that "strict duties with known, limited liabilities are the preferred, albeit second best alternative to perfect information." Id. at 246.)

What limitations should be imposed upon this form of strict liability? Two such limitations, derived from insurance, are the need to avoid adverse selection and moral hazard.

Adverse selection refers to the probability that the worst risks in a given population will be the most likely to obtain insurance. The insurer, here the seller, must obtain information about the riskiness of the insured. Otherwise, the insurer may insure a "selection of the population whose average risk is adversely different from the general population." Id. at 245. According to Bishop, this limitation provides the buyer with an incentive to convey information to the seller when the value of the information to the seller is greater than the cost to the buyer of transmitting it.

This limitation works in at least two ways under the Code: (1) the seller's warranty does not reach a buyer's particular purposes for the goods unless "at the time of contracting" the seller "has reason to know of any particular purpose for which the goods are required," UCC 2–315, a limitation which we covered in Chapter 19, Section 3(B), and (2) the seller is not liable for any consequential "loss resulting from general or particular requirements and needs" of which, at the time of contracting, he had no "reason to know." UCC 2–715(2)(a). This problem is treated in Chapter Fourteen.

Moral hazard involves the risk that a buyer will fail, either before or after the loss occurred, to take reasonable action to avoid or to minimize the loss. Even though the risk is "average" or communicated to the seller, the buyer may fail to take precautions whose cost to him is less than their value to the insurer. Economic theory and contract law in general suggest that the buyer should bear those losses which he could have avoided by a reasonable expenditure of time and effort.

As you read the materials in this Chapter and Chapter Fourteen, make a list of the limitations upon warranty liability associated with either adverse selection or moral hazard.

Does Bishop's analysis offer a persuasive explanation of the nature of warranty? Is it a useful analogy to insurance?

SECTION 2. THE EFFECT OF PLAINTIFF'S FAILURE TO GIVE NOTICE REQUIRED BY UCC 2–607(3)

Access to various buyer's remedies is hedged by notice requirements. Thus, an attempt at rejection is "ineffective unless the buyer seasonably notifies the seller," UCC 2–602(1), and a revocation of acceptance is "not effective until the buyer notifies the seller of it." UCC 2–608(2). Similarly, where a tender has been accepted and acceptance has not been revoked under UCC 2–608, the "buyer must within a reasonable time after he discovers or should have discovered any breach notify the seller of breach or be barred from any remedy; * * *" UCC 2–607(3)(a). Note that UCC 2–607(3)(a) says "barred" from any remedy, not that the buyer is simply shunted to a less desirable remedy. Also, the buyer may be "barred" even though the nonconformity was not actually discovered.

A number of continuing questions surround the judicial interpretation of UCC 2–607(3)(a):

(1) What purposes are served by notice in commercial cases?

(2) When "should" the buyer have discovered the breach?

(3) When does a "reasonable time" expire?

(4) At what point does the buyer "notify" the seller?

(5) What should the form and content of the notice be?

Regardless of how these questions are answered from case to case, two things are clear: (1) The buyer must, at the very least, plead and prove that adequate notice was given to state a cause of action for breach of warranty, and (2) The notice condition does not apply to actions grounded in strict products liability, i.e., where a defective product has caused damage to person or property. See Restatement, Torts 402A, Comment m.

Problem 13–1

Bristow, the holder of a McDonalds franchise, contracted with Stiko, Inc. a manufacturer, for 17 dozen pans expressly designed for the preparation of Big Mac sandwiches. A December 1 shipment date was agreed. On November 28, Stiko telephoned Bristow to say that they were having "a bit of trouble" and that the pans "could not be delivered until late January." Bristow replied that timely delivery was important and if the pans were not shipped by December 1, "we will consider that you have breached the contract." The pans were shipped on January 17. Bristow accepted the pans and there was no further communication until Stiko sued for the contract price in May. Bristow claimed an offset from the contract price based upon damages for late delivery. The trial court, relying on UCC 2–607(3), denied the offset and entered judgment for the contract price. In his memorandum opinion, the trial judge held that UCC 2–607(3) required notice after acceptance. Here none was given. Further, even if the answer were treated as a notice, "the delay was unreasonable as a matter of law."

What arguments will you make on appeal?

STANDARD ALLIANCE IND. v. BLACK CLAWSON CO.

United States Court of Appeals, Sixth Circuit, 1978.
587 F.2d 813.

[Defendant sold Plaintiff a 175 ton "horizontal automatic radial forging facility", known as the "green monster." After extensive negotiations where Plaintiff persuaded Defendant to manufacture the machine to meet Plaintiff's special needs, Defendant made a series of express performance warranties and agreed to repair or replace defective parts for one year after acceptance. Implied warranties were disclaimed and consequential damages were excluded in the agreement. There were problems with the machine from the start. For five months, Defendant, with Plaintiff's assistance, attempted to remedy the difficulties. Defendant then ceased working on the machine. Thereafter, efforts by Plaintiff, under new ownership, to resolve the problems were unsuccessful and the machine was dismantled and sold for scrap. Just over eleven months after Defendant ceased efforts to repair the machine, Plaintiff brought suit on various warranty theories, claiming damages in excess of $525,000. After trial, the trial court submitted two questions to the jury: 1) did Defendant breach the negotiated performance warranties; and 2) did Defendant breach the express warranty to repair and replace defective parts? The jury found for Plaintiff on both questions. On appeal, Defendant argued that the claim based upon breach of performance warranties was barred by the statute of limitations. Defendant also argued that the claim based upon breach of the warranty to repair and replace was barred because Plaintiff failed to give notice as required by UCC 2–607(3).]

KEITH, CIRCUIT JUDGE.

* * *

B. NOTICE AND COUNT II

Standard Alliance's claim against Black Clawson is not ended by our decision on Count I. In Count II, Standard Alliance alleges a cause of action for breach of the express warranty to repair or replace defective parts. This cause of action, which is virtually identical to Count I, was not barred by the statute of limitations. Thus, even if Standard Alliance sued too late on its claim that the machine was defective, it did sue on time on its claim that Black Clawson failed to repair the machine.

Black Clawson concedes that suit on Count II was timely filed, but strongly argues that it had no knowledge that anything was wrong with the machine after it quit work on it and that plaintiff's failure to report the machine's defects barred the suit.

To recapitulate: The machine was installed in October of 1967, and plaintiff's employees attempted to make it operable. A letter was sent to Black Clawson on December 27, 1967, fully outlining the machine's defects. Black Clawson responded by sending a team of employees to try to fix the machine. These employees were at Standard Alliance's plant for over five months. On June 21, 1968, Black Clawson's repairmen left Standard Alliance's plant, never to return. Plaintiff claims that this action constituted knowing abandonment of the unrepaired machine. Black Clawson claims that it thought that the machine was satisfactorily repaired and that it knew nothing about any further problems.

The controlling statute is UCC § 2–607(3)(a) which provides:

"The buyer must within a reasonable time after he discovers or should have discovered any breach notify the seller of breach or be barred from any remedy."

Whether proper notice was given is a question of fact. * * *

Moreover, inasmuch as § 2–607 operates as a condition precedent to any recovery, the burden of proof is on the plaintiff to show that notice was given within a reasonable time. * * *

The district judge submitted the notice issue to the jury, which found for the plaintiff. The question presented here is whether the district judge erred when he refused to overrule the jury's decision and enter judgment N.O.V. for the defendant.

The standard which defendant must meet is a stiff one. To grant a directed verdict or J.N.O.V., the evidence must be "such that there can be but one reasonable conclusion as to the proper verdict." Wolfel v. Sanborn, 555 F.2d 583, 593 (6th Cir.1977). Ohio's standard is the same. Ohio R.Civ.Pro. 50(A). See O'Day v. Webb, 29 Ohio St.2d 215, 280 N.E.2d 896 (1972). If the evidence is clear, however, a court can rule as a matter of law that a party failed to give proper notice. * * *

The notice requirement of § 2–607 is explained by Official Comment 4:

"The time of notification is to be determined by applying commercial standards to a merchant buyer. 'A reasonable time' for notification from a retail consumer is to be judged by different standards so that in his case it will be extended, for the rule of requiring notification is designated to defeat commercial bad faith, not to deprive a good faith consumer of his remedy.

"The content of the notification need merely be sufficient to let the seller know that the transaction is still troublesome and must be watched. There is no reason to require that the notification which saves the buyer's rights under this section must include a clear statement of all the objections that will be relied on by the buyer, as under the section covering statements of defect upon rejection (Section 2–605). Nor is there reason for requiring the notification to be a claim for damages or of any threatened litigation or other resort to a remedy. The notification which saves the buyer's rights under this Article need only be such as informs the seller that the transaction is claimed to involve a breach, and thus opens the way for normal settlement through negotiation."

Some courts and commentators have taken the liberal view that almost any kind of notice of dissatisfaction is sufficient. "Quite clearly the drafters [of the UCC] intended a loose test; a scribbled note on a bit of toilet paper will do." J. White & R. Summers Uniform Commercial Code 347 (1972). See e.g., Lewis v. Mobil Oil Corp., 438 F.2d 500, 509 (8th Cir.1971); Metro Investment Corp. v. Portland Rd. Lumber Yard, Inc., 263 Or. 76, 501 P.2d 312 (1972). Other courts have required more than minimal notice where both parties were merchants engaged in on-going transactions. Eastern Air Lines, Inc. v. McDonnell Douglas Corp., 532 F.2d 957, 970–980 (1976); Kopper Glo Fuel, Inc. v. Island Lake Coal Co., 436 F.Supp. 91, 95–97 (E.D.Tenn.1977). * * *

There is no dispute that Standard Alliance gave timely notice that the machine was not in compliance with the performance warranties and that Black Clawson then spent over five months trying to fix the machine. The dispute concerns whether defendant was properly notified that the repairs were inadequate.

Black Clawson's argument can be conveniently subdivided into two subparts. First, it contends that it understood the machine to be operating properly on June 21, 1968, and that it had no knowledge that the machine was defective after that date. Second, it contends that it had no notice that Standard Alliance considered it to be in breach of the warranty to repair or replace defective parts.

The jury's implicit finding that Black Clawson had knowledge that the machine was defective and improperly repaired is supportable by the evidence. Black Clawson Vice-President Romagano did testify that he thought that the machine was repaired on July 21, 1968, and that he had no idea anything was wrong afterward. The jury, however, could have disbelieved this testimony, relying on a June 24, 1968, memo written by Mr. Romagano which reveals that the machine suffered repeated failures on both June 20, 1968, and June 21, 1968. In addition, the jury could have credited letters written in June, July and August of 1968 from Mr. Romagano to a Black Clawson subcontractor, Reliance Electric Co., complaining about the failings of the machine's electric drive, a critical component. Finally, the jury could have believed expert testimony that the machine was so poorly designed that it could not be made to operate in synchronization nor be repaired to meet any of the express warranties. If so, the jury could have reasonably inferred that defendant was aware that its attempts to repair were an utter failure. Thus, there exists evidence to support a jury finding that Black Clawson had knowledge that it was in breach of the repair or replace warranty.[1]

The critical issue is whether Black Clawson had notice that it was considered to be in breach. Black Clawson emphatically argues that there is no evidence at all that it received notice of breach after it quit repair work on June 21, 1968. Standard Alliance directs us to none, and our independent examination of the record reveals none. Incredible as it may seem, Black Clawson quit repair work on June 21, 1968 and was never told anything was wrong until May 29, 1969, when suit was filed.[2]

Standard Alliance argues that it fully informed Black Clawson of the machine's defects at the beginning and that Black Clawson abandoned the machine knowing that it was defective and unrepaired. Under these circumstances, the question presented is whether it was necessary to give additional notice of the failure of repair efforts.

We think that notice should have been given. Section 2–607 expressly requires notice of "any" breach. Comment 4 says that notice "need only be such as informs the seller that the transaction is claimed to involve a breach." The express language of the statute and the official comment mandate notice regardless whether either or both parties had actual knowledge of breach. * * *

1. The evidence is not one-sided, however. The record indicates that the machine would operate, but was subject to breakdowns and produced a poor product. Repair efforts at times achieved temporary success or offered the hope of success. For example, in a July 15, 1968 internal memorandum, Standard Alliance's Harold Challman indicated that with two weeks of certain indicated repairs, the machine would be ready to make a production run. There thus exists some basis for Black Clawson's subjective belief that the machine was in compliance with the page twelve warranties. Internal Black Clawson memoranda, notably an October 3, 1968 memo from Vice-President Romagano to President Landegger support this belief.

This confusion further underscores the need to give clear notice; especially in a commercial setting where two companies have interacted at different levels, from President to maintenance worker.

2. Black Clawson pressed this issue at trial. Standard Alliance's President Erwin Schulze admitted that no written notice was sent; he did not know whether oral notice was given. Executive Vice-President William G. Shaw, who at the time was head of Standard Alliance's forging division, knew of no communication between the parties concerning the machine's defects after June 21, 1968. Roy

W. Clansky, a Standard Alliance Vice-Chairman of the Board intimately involved in the machine's purchase, testified that Black Clawson never failed to respond when called. He did not recall ever getting in touch with his counterpart at Black Clawson to complain about the machine after January 4, 1968. Russell E. Reum, Standard Alliance's purchasing agent, knew of no notice to Black Clawson indicating dissatisfaction with repair efforts after January of 1968. Black Clawson Executive Alfred Romagano testified that Black Clawson never heard a complaint about the machine after June of 1968.

The evidence in the record concerning the circumstances of Black Clawson's termination of repair efforts on June 21, 1968, shows an amicable parting after months of mutual cooperation. Contacts between the parties after June 21, 1968, were minimal and most had nothing to do with the machine's defects. Standard Alliance invited Black Clawson to a trade association tour of its plant in September, 1968, and discussed settling "backcharge" claims for repairs. In addition, two brief service calls were made. Although the record as to the service calls and backcharge negotiations is sketchy, * * * there is no evidence that the issue of breach of warranty was ever raised directly, and Standard Alliance does not argue that it was.

We also note that this same result would take place under § 2–607's predecessor, section 49 of the Uniform Sales Act.[3] Judge Learned Hand's oft-quoted words applying section 49 are equally applicable here:

> "The plaintiff replies that the buyer is not required to give notice of what the seller already knows, but this confuses two quite different things. The notice 'of the breach' required is not of the facts, which the seller presumably knows quite as well as, if not better than, the buyer, but of buyer's claim that they constitute a breach. The purpose of the notice is to advise the seller that he must meet a claim for damages, as to which, rightly or wrongly, the law requires that he shall have early warning."

American Mfg. Co. v. United States Shipping Board E.F. Corp., 7 F.2d 565, 566 (2d Cir.1925), cited with approval in Columbia Axle Co. v. American Automobile Ins. Co., 63 F.2d 206 (6th Cir.1933).

An examination of the policy reasons which underlie 2–607 further support our view. Notice of breach serves two distinct purposes. First, express notice opens the way for settlement through negotiation between the parties. Comment Four, supra; Eckstein v. Cummins, 41 Ohio App.2d 1, 321 N.E.2d 897, 901 (1974). Second, proper notice minimizes the possibility of prejudice to the seller by giving him "ample opportunity to cure the defect, inspect the goods, investigate the claim or do whatever may be necessary to properly defend himself or minimize his damages while the facts are fresh in the minds of the parties." Note, Notice of Breach and the Uniform Commercial Code, 25 U.Fla.L. Rev. 520, 522 (1973). * * * Compare 3 Williston on Sales (4th Ed.), § 22–11 and White & Summers, supra at 344 which identify three policy reasons behind the notice requirement: 1) To enable the seller to make adjustments or replacement or to suggest opportunities for cure; 2) To enable the seller to prepare for negotiation or litigation; and 3) To give the seller peace of mind from stale claims. See Steel & Wire Corp. v. Thyssen, Inc., 20 U.C.C.Rep. 892 (E.D.Mich.1976). See also Mattos, Inc. v. Hash, 279 Md. 371, 368 A.2d 993, 996 (1977) (protection against stale claims is the purpose of the statute of limitations, not the purpose of section 2–607(3)).

We do not know whether this lengthy, acrimonious lawsuit could have been settled beforehand. We do know that Standard Alliance's failure to give notice precluded the possibility of compromise.

More important, the record contains evidence suggesting the kind of prejudice which § 2–607's notice requirement seeks to avoid. After Standard Alliance sold its Forgings Division to "the Wiener Group" on

---

3. Section 49 provided:

"In the absence of express or implied agreement of the parties, acceptance of the goods by the buyer shall not discharge the seller from liability in damages or other legal remedy for breach of any promise or warranty in the contract to sell or the sale. But, if, after acceptance of the goods, the buyer fails to give notice to the seller of the breach of any promise or warranty within a reasonable time after the buyer knows, or ought to know of such breach, the seller shall not be liable therefor."

September 30, 1968, Wiener attempted to put the machine into operation. When that failed, the machine lay dormant. On May 28, 1969, the day before suit was filed, Standard Alliance, in cooperation with Wiener, started the machine and filmed its malfunctions. On July 14, 1969, a scant six weeks after suit was filed, Wiener began to dismantle the machine. Although Black Clawson was informed of the machine's sale, it never inspected the machine after terminating repair efforts on June 21, 1968, nor was it aware that the machine was to be destroyed.

Standard Alliance contends that the destruction of the machine by a third party was proper and that Black Clawson was remiss in not seeking to inspect the machine during the six-week period after suit was filed, but before the machine was destroyed. This ignores the realities of the litigation process. Six weeks is an insignificant period of time in a case such as this which has dragged on for over nine years. In addition, it was pure chance that the machine was destroyed when it was; Wiener could have taken the machine apart whenever it wanted. Had Black Clawson gotten even minimal notice that it was being held in breach, it might very well have sought inspection and perhaps even made its own film of the machine.

Measuring the impact of potential prejudice here is, of course, difficult since Black Clawson was unable to have its own experts examine the machine. Standard Alliance emphasizes that Black Clawson designed and built the machine and worked on it for over five months. As the machine's creator, it arguably did not need to inspect it. Also, the evidence that the machine was defective was overwhelming. On the other hand, preparing for litigation is a sui generis task. Black Clawson may have been able to put on a spirited defense, especially as to damages, had it gotten early notice and followed up by inspecting the machine. Whatever the degree of prejudice to Black Clawson, UCC § 2–607's notice requirement is designed to forestall the very difficulties which developed here. While we see no justification for the strong language in defendant's brief charging a conspiracy to hide the facts and destroy the machine, we think that this case demonstrates the wisdom of section 2–607's requirement of prompt notice.

Black Clawson also raises independent objections to the film and the circumstances of the machine's destruction, arguing that it should have had specific advance notice of both the film's production and of the machine's demolition. We need not decide these issues. We do note, however, that this court has never sanctioned the sporting theory of justice. Adherents of the theory among the bar are reminded that a law suit is a serious matter; there is no room for games of hide and seek. Neither the federal rules nor statutory law can anticipate every twist and turn which can take place in litigation. "Legal" moves by ingenious litigants will not be countenanced where injustice would result.

These events further demonstrate the merit in those cases which hold merchants to higher standards of good faith than consumers. * * * Black Clawson and Standard Alliance worked together at all times. Black Clawson responded promptly when informed that the machine was not working properly; commercial good faith mandated that it be told that repair efforts had failed and that it was being held in breach. A new car buyer can be excused for failing, in ignorance and exasperation, to notify a car dealer of an obvious breach after persistent repair efforts have ended in failure. A merchant like Standard Alliance cannot be so excused, it should have met section 2–607's non-rigorous notice requirements.

Standard Alliance points to two cases, Ernst v. General Motors Corp., 482 F.2d 1047 (5th Cir.1973), appeal following remand, 537 F.2d 105 (5th Cir.1976), and Metro Invest. Corp. v. Portland Rd. Lumber Yard, Inc., 263 Or. 76, 501 P.2d 312 (1972), for the proposition that proper notice, once given, is sufficient for all related breaches. Standard Alliance's position is that since it concededly gave proper notice that the machine was defective on December 27, 1967, it did not have to give notice later on that repair efforts to cure the defects had failed.

We reject this argument. In Ernst, supra, the court merely concluded that a letter complaining of delays in the start-up of a construction project could be reasonably construed to encompass problems caused by severe winter working conditions which would not have occurred but for the delay. Also, the court did not think that once initial complaint about delay was made, that additional notice of delay had to be given on a regular basis. In Metro Invest. Corp., supra, the buyer gave prompt notice of a defect. The parties met and agreed to wait and see if the defect improved. The Oregon Supreme Court found that the initial notice was sufficient, even though no complaint was made for two years thereafter.

In the instant case, the two warranties are distinct and notice serves different functions for each. When the machine was found to be in breach of the page twelve performance warranties, notice was necessary so that Black Clawson could come in and try to fix the machine. When repair efforts failed, and Black Clawson was allegedly in breach of its warranty to repair or replace defective parts, notice would alert Black Clawson that Standard Alliance thought that repairs were defective and that perhaps litigation was contemplated. At this point, the parties could have discussed settlement, and Black Clawson could have sought evidentiary support for its position that the machine was indeed repaired. Black Clawson was alerted that the machine was defective, but not alerted that its repair efforts were defective. We cannot allow notice of one breach to be carried over to create notice of a subsequent related, but distinct, breach.

We realize that our holding bars what is apparently a meritorious claim. Standard Alliance's inexplicable failure to give any notice whatsoever that Black Clawson was in breach of its repair/replace warranty is fatal; underlying standards of commercial good faith, codified in UCC § 2–607, mandate this result.

Our ruling makes it unnecessary to consider the numerous other issues raised concerning the liability or the damages trial.

* * *

[Some footnotes omitted.   Others renumbered.]

Notes

1.   UCC 2–607(3)(a) states that the buyer must "notify the seller of breach or be barred from any remedy."   In Comment 4, however, there is an apparent conflict: Is the notice sufficient if it "merely" lets the seller know that the "transaction is still troublesome and must be watched" or must the notice inform the seller that the "transaction is claimed to involve a breach * * *?"   The latter interpretation, embraced by *Standard Alliance,* would require notice of the buyer's conclusion both that the goods failed to conform to the warranties and that the non-conformity was considered to be a breach.

If, as White and Summers suggest at p. 421, the principal reason for requiring notice "is to enable the seller to make adjustments or replacements or to suggest opportunities for cure to the end of minimizing the buyer's loss and reducing the seller's own liability to the buyer," is such a strict notice requirement necessary?   In Paulson v. Olson Implement Co., Inc., 107 Wis.2d 510, 319 N.W.2d 855 (1982), the court held that a seller who had received a timely notice of nonconformity and was unable to effect a cure was not entitled to a further notice from the buyer before the law suit was filed.   Compare K & M Joint Venture v. Smith International, Inc., 669 F.2d 1106 (6th Cir.1982), in which the court held that the buyer's claims was barred because of its failure to give the seller any indication that it was claiming a breach of warranty or that it considered the seller to be liable to it.

2.   What amendment to UCC 2–607(3)(a) would you recommend to resolve this issue?   Would it be sufficient simply to substitute the word "nonconformity" for breach?

Problem 13–2

Your client entered into a contract to purchase a specified quantity of yarn.   The expected quality was spelled out in some detail.   As part of the contract, client agreed to the following clauses in the sales contract:

"2.   No claims relating to excessive moisture content, short weight, count variations, twist, quality or shade shall be allowed *if made after weaving, knitting, or processing,* or more than 10 days after receipt of shipment.   * * * The buyer shall within 10 days of the receipt of the merchandise by himself or agent examine the merchandise for any and all defects."

"4.   This instrument constitutes the entire agreement between the parties, superseding all previous communications, oral or written, and no changes, amendments or additions hereto will be recognized unless in writing signed by both seller and buyer or buyer's agent. It is expressly agreed that no representations or warranties, express or implied, have been or are made by the seller except as stated herein, and the seller makes no warranty, express or implied, as to the fitness for buyer's purposes of yarn purchased hereunder, seller's obligations, except as expressly stated herein, being limited to the *delivery of good merchantable yarn of the description stated herein.*"

The yarn was tendered on March 1 and, after an inspection, accepted by client on March 2. Thereafter the yarn was cut and knitted into sweaters and the finished product was washed. During the washing, which took place on March 15 and 16, it was discovered that the color of the yarn had "shaded," that is, there was a variation in color from piece to piece and within the pieces. This was clearly a defect that made the yarn unmerchantable and could not have been discovered by a reasonable inspection. Client promptly gave notice to the seller of the defect. Since revocation of acceptance was not possible (do you see why?), client asserted a claim for damages under UCC 2–714(2) and 2–715(2). Seller, pointing to the contract, denied any liability.

Client comes to you for advice. Is the clause enforceable? See UCC 1–204, 2–302 & 2–719. After you have completed your analysis, you may wish to compare it with Wilson Trading Corp. v. David Ferguson, Ltd., 23 N.Y.2d 398, 297 N.Y.S.2d 108, 244 N.E.2d 685 (1968).

SECTION 3. PROOF OF BREACH: EFFECT OF LACK OF CAUSATION AND PLAINTIFF'S CONTRIBUTORY BEHAVIOR

In Chapter Twelve, the primary issue was whether the seller had made a warranty, express or implied, to the buyer. Here we are concerned about what the buyer must prove to establish a breach of that warranty and that the breach caused the loss complained of. The answers turn, in part, upon the type of warranty made and the quantum and quality of proof required to get the case to the jury. In addition, the seller must be alert to possible misuse of the goods by the buyer and other conduct suggesting contributory "fault" or assumption of risk. These issues frequently arise in commercial litigation. See, e.g., Phelan and Falhof, *Proving a Defect in a Commercial Products Liability Case*, 24 Trial Law.Guide 10 (1980).

According to Mr. Phelan, an experienced Chicago trial attorney, the plaintiff maximizes the chances of proving both breach and causation when the facts and inferences from the following sources are cumulated:

1. The allegedly non-conforming product;

2. The circumstances surrounding the "accident;"

3. The life history of the product;

4. Relevant trade usages and practices with regard to products of the same description; and

5.   Conduct by the buyer in inspecting, maintaining and using the product, both before and after the "accident."

CHATFIELD v. SHERWIN–WILLIAMS CO.

Supreme Court of Minnesota, 1978.
266 N.W.2d 171.

PER CURIAM.

In this action to recover damages allegedly resulting from breaches of warranty in the sale of red barn paint, the jury found by a special verdict that defendant paint manufacturer breached an express warranty that the paint was "good barn paint" and the implied warranties of merchantability and fitness for a particular purpose. It also found that the breaches were a direct cause of plaintiff's damages; that plaintiff was negligent and his negligence was a direct cause of his consequential damages; that 85 percent of the fault causing such consequential damages was attributable to defendant and 15 percent to plaintiff; and that plaintiff sustained general damages of $1,116 and consequential damages of $13,357. The court ordered judgment for plaintiff for $14,473, the total amount assessed by the jury. Defendant appeals, challenging the sufficiency of the evidence to establish breaches of the warranties and that such breaches were a proximate cause of plaintiff's damages. Defendant also contends that plaintiff is precluded from recovery of damages because he did not follow defendant's directions in using its product. Our review satisfies us that the issues raised were properly submitted to the jury and that the judgment appealed from should be affirmed.

In the winter of 1974, plaintiff, an experienced professional painter of farm buildings, purchased 330 gallons of "Commonwealth Ranch Red" paint from defendant for $4.65 per gallon. Before making the purchase plaintiff asked Wendell Swenson, manager of defendant's Wilmar store, if it would be good paint and if he would have any trouble with it. Swenson told plaintiff that people had used this paint on barns for many years and that it was "tried and true." He added, "Besides, this is Sherwin-Williams, you know. It couldn't have a bad name and be that big." Plaintiff then purchased the paint, used 240 gallons on barns and other buildings at 11 farms, and sold the rest to his father who is also a professional painter.

The label on the paint cans plaintiff purchased contained the following directions:

"New Wood and Extremely Weathered Surfaces:

Add 1 to 2 quarts of raw linseed oil per gallon to the *first coat*. Brush it well into surface. When spraying follow immediately with thorough brushing to work paint into pores. Second coat should be brushed on at package consistency or thinned with up to a pint of S–W exolvent or turpentine per gallon for spraying."

Plaintiff admitted that he never added as much as 1 to 2 quarts of linseed oil and said that when he used that much the paint wrinkled. He said that when painting dry areas, he added as much linseed oil as he thought necessary, depending on the condition of the wood. He thought a ratio of 20 percent was usually correct. He said that under the eaves and along the upper two-thirds of the buildings the wood is often in better condition than the wood below, the lower 5 or 6 feet of a barn usually requiring linseed oil. Plaintiff did not apply the paint with a brush, claiming that his spraying equipment made the paint penetrate into the surfaces far more thoroughly than brushing could.

Several customers testified that plaintiff spray-painted their buildings with Commonwealth Ranch Red during the summer of 1975. The buildings varied in age (from a barn built in 1906 to one built in 1965) and in their need for paint. The customers said they were well satisfied with plaintiff's work in preparing the surfaces and painting the buildings. Within 1 to 4 months after the jobs were completed, however, the owners noticed that the color was fading on their buildings. Witnesses said the surfaces looked chalky, the color continued to bleach, and the paint was chipping and could be rubbed off. Plaintiff testified that the buildings which his father had painted with the 90 gallons he had obtained from plaintiff also faded. After receiving complaints from his customers, plaintiff in turn made complaints to defendant which were ignored for several months. Finally, in April 1975, defendant sent George Linmark, a chemist employed by defendant, to investigate the matter. Linmark looked at the buildings plaintiff had painted on two farms and told him, plaintiff testified, that the wood had been well prepared and the paint well applied. Plaintiff testified that Linmark could not explain why the fading had occurred. Subsequently, plaintiff received a letter saying that defendant had decided to do nothing about the paint because the fading "was to be expected with that quality of paint."

Plaintiff admitted on cross-examination that he had read the instructions on the paint cans and had not added as much linseed oil as they directed. When plaintiff rested, defendant moved for a directed verdict on the ground that plaintiff's evidence showed no negligence on its part and showed that plaintiff had been negligent in using his judgment instead of the manufacturer's. The court denied the motion.

Defendant then called Linmark, a chemist with experience in formulating Sherwin-Williams paint, as an expert witness. He said that the 330 gallons of paint which plaintiff had bought was from a 3,000–gallon batch and that defendant had received no complaints about the rest of the batch. Although defendant stores a sample from each batch it manufactures, it did not test any sample from the batch which was the source of plaintiff's paint to see if it would fade, apparently because it was not clear at first which batch had been the source of plaintiff's purchase.

Linmark testified that paint has two essential ingredients, pigments and vehicles or binders. In Commonwealth Ranch Red, the pigment which gives the color is iron oxide, comprising 14 percent of the pigment, and most of the rest of the pigment is calcium carbonate, which by itself is a white powder but is colorless when added to the paint. The vehicle or binder holds the pigment and causes the paint to adhere to the surface of a building. The binder in defendant's paint consisted of tall oil alkyd resin, blown fish oil, mineral spirits, and raw linseed oil. In Linmark's opinion the fading was caused by insufficient reinforcement of the paint with more linseed oil. He said that on weathered surfaces some of the binder in the paint soaks into the wood or old paint if the new paint being applied is not reinforced with linseed oil, and that when the remaining binder is eroded by the ultraviolet rays of the sun, the pigment stands loose. Thus, he said, the calcium carbonate in Commonwealth Ranch Red became visible, giving the paint the appearance of fading.

Linmark also testified that paint wrinkles if applied too thickly and that linseed oil in any quantity does not cause wrinkling. He admitted telling plaintiff in April 1975 that he had done a good job and that in Linmark's opinion there was "a fade problem." He looked at only two of the sets of buildings plaintiff had painted and admitted that he did not know whether plaintiff had added enough linseed oil in the various jobs. He also said that the paint plaintiff purchased was "the bottom of the line."

In rebuttal, plaintiff's father, Robert Chatfield, testified that he used some of the 90 gallons he had acquired from plaintiff and that he too received complaints of fading. He added 1 quart of linseed oil to 5 gallons of paint while painting a barn for a customer and found that the paint became too thin and would run. He said he applied some of the paint to part of his own buildings without using any linseed oil and they also faded. He purchased other Commonwealth Ranch Red from defendant's Wilmar store himself and applied it to his buildings without adding linseed oil. He said the areas to which he had applied this paint did not fade.

In submitting the case to the jury, the trial court refused to charge that defendant was not liable if plaintiff's use of the product was abnormal or not in accordance with adequate instructions. He instructed the jury that in determining whether plaintiff was negligent they could consider whether he used the paint in accordance with defendant's directions and submitted questions in response to which, as stated, the jury found plaintiff negligent and attributed 15 percent of the fault causing his consequential damage to that negligence.

1. Although apparently not contesting the existence of the warranties on which plaintiff brought suit, defendant argues that its motions for a directed verdict and for judgment notwithstanding the verdict should have been granted because plaintiff did not adduce sufficient proof that the paint faded prematurely because of an inher-

ent defect and thus did not establish any breach of the warranties. It also argues that plaintiff did not prove that any breach of warranty proximately caused his damages, as is essential to recovery. Heil v. Standard Chemical Mfg. Co., 301 Minn. 315, 323, 223 N.W.2d 37, 41 (1974). Defendant's contentions require an examination of plaintiff's evidence in the light most favorable to the verdict.

At the time defendant moved for a directed verdict, plaintiff had presented testimony that he had done a good workmanlike job, testimony which permitted the jury to infer that poor workmanship did not cause the fading. Plaintiff's proof also showed that some areas he had painted did not need linseed oil and that the paint had faded quite uniformly within 1 to 4 months after application, both in areas where he had used linseed oil and in areas where he had not. He admitted that he never added as much linseed oil as defendant's directions advised he should use with "extremely weathered" surfaces but said he added it in a ratio of 20 percent when he thought it was needed. He further testified that defendant informed him that fading was to be expected with a paint of the quality of Commonwealth Ranch Red. This evidence, although it does not directly establish the cause of the fading, furnishes substantial support for the inference that the paint faded because of an inherent defect.

Defendant urges, however, that plaintiff was required to have the paint analyzed and to present expert testimony about the existence and nature of any alleged defect. Although the importance of expert testimony in products liability actions has been emphasized in several cases, this court has said that there is no hard-and-fast rule requiring plaintiff to introduce such testimony. Peterson v. Crown Zellerbach Corp., 296 Minn. 438, 209 N.W.2d 922 (1973). In several earlier breach-of-warranty cases, chemical analysis of the product was not required to establish the breach of warranty. * * *

In Nelson v. Wilkins Dodge, Inc., Minn., 256 N.W.2d 472, 476 (1977), an action for breach of implied warranties in the sale of a pickup, the court held that a defective condition can be proved by circumstantial evidence, saying:

"Plaintiffs assert that there can be no question that proximate cause has been demonstrated with respect to the paint bubbles, the inverted taillight covers, and the loosened windshield-wiper blade and arm and shift lever. Defendant suggests that the paint bubbles and the loosened windshield wiper, horn bracket, and shift lever just as probably resulted from the continuous and hard use to which plaintiffs put the pickup as from any defect inherent in the vehicle when plaintiffs purchased it. Although liability for breach of warranty attaches only when a defect existing in the goods causes a breakdown in quality, * * * generally no specific defect need be alleged, and a defective condition can be proved by circumstantial evidence * * * No direct evidence was introduced as to the causes of the conditions in question. It is reasonable to suppose, however, that vehicles that are fit for ordinary purposes probably do not display these defects this early, even if they are driven a great deal within a short period of time. Thus, the causes of the faulty paint, windshield wiper, horn bracket, and shift lever were questions that should have been decided by the jury. A fortiori, the cause of the inverted taillight covers was a jury question."

Other courts have also held that circumstantial evidence may be sufficient to show the causal relation between the use of a warranted product and the injury which followed its use. See, 77 C.J.S. Sales, § 367. Thus, in Yormack v. Farmers Co-op. Assn. of N.J., 11 N.J.Super. 416, 78 A.2d 421 (1950), in an action for breach of a statutory implied warranty of quality and fitness in the sale of an insecticide (carbolineum) for use about chicken roosts, the court said (11 N.J.Super. 423, 78 A.2d 424):

"We recognize the absence of any evidence which definitely informed the jury of the particular ingredient or constituent of the carbolineum which would in reasonable probability gravely injure and kill the chickens. Proof of unfitness does not necessarily require that degree of exactness and precision. * * *

"Furthermore it was not necessary for the plaintiff to prove by direct evidence the causal relation between the use of the carbolineum and the injurious result; it could be established by circumstantial evidence."

We conclude that although plaintiff's proof of causation was not direct, if his evidence is viewed in the light most favorable to the verdict, the jury could infer from the fact that the fading was quite uniform that the presence or absence of linseed oil had no effect on the fading. Defendant admitted that there was a "fade problem" and fading within so short a time was to be expected with Commonwealth Ranch Red. From this it could be inferred that it was not "good barn paint," not of merchantable quality, and not suitable for the purpose for which plaintiff bought it. Thus, defendant's motions for a directed verdict and for judgment notwithstanding the verdict were properly denied.

2. Defendant also argues that, assuming the warranties involved here were breached, plaintiff is precluded from recovery of damages because he used the paint contrary to the directions and such "misuse" was beyond the scope of the warranties. Although defendant cites several cases in support of this claim—Chisholm v. J.R. Simplot Co., 94 Idaho 682, 495 P.2d 1113 (1972); Elanco Products Co. v. Akin-Tunnell, 516 S.W.2d 726 (Tex.Civ.App.1974); Iverson Paints, Inc. v. Wirth Corp., 94 Idaho 43, 480 P.2d 889 (1971); Brown v. General Motors Corp., 355 F.2d 814 (4 Cir.1966)—all are distinguishable from this case. In the Chisholm case, watering the fields within a specified time was essential to activate the weed killer which was alleged to have been defective, and the importance of following that direction should have been obvious to plaintiffs. In Iverson also, the directions for using the machine were very precise, and they were almost completely ignored—neither of

which is the fact here. In the Elanco case the manufacturer had stressed the necessity of following directions and had disclaimed any affirmations made about the product unless the directions were followed. The court accordingly treated compliance with the directions as a condition precedent to the existence of the express warranty sued on. Here no comparable stress was laid on the importance of the directions, and they certainly were not specific and precise as to quantity. In Brown, plaintiff did not establish that there had been a breach of warranty, and that his use of a tractor by starting it when it was in gear was abnormal and unpredictable. Plaintiff used the paint here for its intended purpose.

We conclude that the trial court correctly instructed the jury that it could consider whether plaintiff complied with defendant's directions in determining whether he was negligent and whether his negligence was a cause of his consequential damages.

We also find little merit in defendant's argument that, if there was a defect in the paint, plaintiff failed to mitigate his damages by continuing to use the paint after he found it wrinkled when combined with the prescribed amount of linseed oil. Plaintiff did not know the paint would fade because, as he thought, defendant's directions called for too much linseed oil. Defendant's argument also assumes that plaintiff was at all times required to add linseed oil, a conclusion not compelled by the evidence. In any event, the court properly instructed the jury on plaintiff's duty to mitigate damages after learning of the breaches of warranty.

Defendant urges, finally, that the trial court improperly awarded plaintiff all of the consequential damages assessed by the jury and argues that these damages should have been reduced by 15 percent to reflect the proportion of fault which the jury attributed to plaintiff's negligence. Whether a comparative-fault principle should be applied in breach-of-warranty actions has not been determined in this state. Wenner v. Gulf Oil Corp., Minn., 264 N.W.2d 374, filed February 17, 1978. Although reducing a party's consequential damages by an amount reflecting the extent to which his own conduct caused them appears to be equitable, appropriate under Minn.St. 336.2–715(2)(b), and compatible with our approach in a recent products liability action based on strict liability, Busch v. Busch Const. Co., Minn., 262 N.W.2d 377 (1977), we decline to consider this issue since it was not presented to the trial court and has been raised for the first time on appeal. International Union of Operating Eng. v. City of Mpls., 305 Minn. 364, 233 N.W.2d 748 (1975).

Affirmed.

Notes

1. No sample was offered from the batch of paint purchased and applied to the barns. How did the buyer survive the seller's motion for directed verdict? In American Fertilizer Specialists v. Wood, 635 P.2d 592,

595–96 (Okl.1981), the court, in affirming the trial court's decision for the buyer, stated: "Facts may be proved by circumstantial, as well as by positive or direct evidence, and it is not necessary that the proof rise to that degree of certainty which will exclude every other reasonable conclusion than the one arrived at by the trier of facts. It is only required that it appear more probable that the defendant's poor grass crop was the result of the failure of the fertilizer sold by plaintiff to defendant to nourish and enrich defendant's grass lands than any other possible cause."

2. The buyer, in *Chatfield,* concededly failed to follow the seller's printed directions for use. Why didn't the buyer's failure constitute either a use of the product that was not ordinary, thereby undercutting the claim that an implied warranty of merchantability was breached, or a misuse of a product otherwise fit for ordinary purposes, thereby establishing that breach of warranty did not cause the loss? (In Hutchinson Utilities Commission v. Curtiss-Wright Corp., 775 F.2d 231 (8th Cir.1985), the Eighth Circuit, relying on *Chatfield,* held that an agreed inspection schedule was not a condition precedent to the buyer's claim and that a defect in the goods rather than the failure to inspect was the "proximate" cause of the loss.)

3. Assuming that the plaintiff in *Chatfield* was, to some degree, at "fault" in mixing the paint, what effect should that have on the issues of liability and remedy? Consider these possibilities:

(a) The warranty, although made, was not breached;

(b) Although the warranty was made and breached, the plaintiff's "fault" barred it from recovery;

(c) The plaintiff's "fault", whether misuse or failure to discover, is no per se bar, but it may be considered in determining whether the breach caused the loss complained of; and

(d) The plaintiff's "fault" may be used to reduce damages otherwise proximately caused by the breach.

Which, if any, of these possibilities did *Chatfield* employ?

4. The Minnesota Comparative Negligence Statute, Minn.Stat.Ann. § 604.01(1) (Supp.1987), provides that contributory fault is no bar in an action to "recover damages for fault resulting in death or injury to person or property, if the contributory fault was not greater than the fault of the person against whom recovery is sought, but any damages allowed shall be diminished in proportion to the amount of fault attributable to the person recovering." In 1978, the statute was amended to define "fault" to include "breach of warranty, unreasonable assumption of risk not constituting an express consent, misuse of a product and unreasonable failure to avoid an injury or to mitigate damages." § 604.01(1a). The Supreme Court of Minnesota has since held that, in an action to recover for personal injuries and economic loss allegedly caused by a breach of warranty, it was proper to use the plaintiff's "fault" to reduce consequential damages but not direct damages caused by the breach. Peterson v. Bendix Home Systems, Inc., 318 N.W.2d 50 (Minn.1982). Should these later developments change the outcome in *Chatfield?*

Problem 13–3

The courts and legislatures, in applying concepts of comparative fault to product liability suits, have stopped short of cases where only economic loss is involved: The plaintiff, when suing on a warranty theory, must claim damages to person or property before any "fault" comparison will be made. An example is Fiske v. MacGregor Div. of Brunswick, 464 A.2d 719 (R.I.1983). The issues are discussed in Leff & Pinto, *Comparative Negligence in Strict Products Liability: The Courts Render the Final Judgment,* 89 Dick.L.Rev. 915 (1985); Sobelsohn, *Comparing Fault,* 60 Ind.L.J. 413 (1985); Note, *Use of the Comparative Negligence Doctrine in Warranty Actions,* 45 Ohio St. U.L.J. 763 (1984).

As we shall see in Section 5, infra, Article 2 of the UCC is the exclusive source of law in warranty disputes where only economic loss is involved. How does Article 2 deal with problems of the buyer's fault? With this question in mind, re-read Article 2, Parts Six and Seven. Make a list of the "penalties," if any, that the buyer must pay for failure to take reasonable steps to discover the non-conformity or otherwise to avoid the loss.

SECTION 4. THE STATUTE OF LIMITATIONS

Read UCC 2–725 and work the following problem.

Problem 13–4

On May 1, 1982, Seller and Buyer, a grain dealer, entered a written contract for the sale of three prefabricated metal grain bins, each 30 feet tall, for a total price of $50,000. The bins were to be shipped to Buyer FOB Point of Destination and Seller agreed to erect and install them at Buyer's place of business. The contract provided, inter alia, that "the above described bins will, if properly installed, withstand winds up to 90 MPH."

The bins were shipped on June 1, 1982 and arrived on June 5, 1982. The buyer removed the disassembled parts from the carrier and notified the Seller, who completed the installation by July 1, 1982. On June 15, 1986, a severe storm with winds up to 80 MPH hit the area where Buyer did business. Two of the bins were toppled by the wind, resulting in damage to the bins and the stored grain. An expert will testify that the internal support seams had gradually and imperceptibly deteriorated since installation.

Buyer's attorney has asked you, his associate, whether the statute of limitations has run.

STANDARD ALLIANCE INDUS., INC. v. BLACK CLAWSON CO.

United States Court of Appeals, Sixth Circuit, 1978.
587 F.2d 813.

[The facts and the court's opinion on the notice issue are reprinted, supra at p. 503.]

*   *   *

A. The Statute of Limitations and Count I

Chronology is important to a precise understanding of the issues. The machine was delivered and assembled at Standard Alliance's plant in the fall of 1967. The machine proved defective, and Standard Alliance wrote Black Clawson on December 27, 1967, delineating exactly what was wrong with the machine and requesting that Black Clawson fix it. Black Clawson worked on the machine until June 21, 1968, when it abandoned repair efforts. This suit was filed on May 29, 1969.

The original contract contained a one-year limitations period; * the minimum allowable under UCC § 2–725(1). UCC § 2–725(1) also provides that the limitations period begins to run when the cause of action accrues. UCC § 2–725(2) explains that a cause of action accrues when a breach occurs. A breach of warranty is deemed to occur upon tender of delivery "except that where a warranty explicitly extends to future performance of the goods and discovery of the breach must await the time of such performance the cause of action accrues when the breach is or should have been discovered." UCC § 2–725(2). Black Clawson argues that the machine was tendered in the fall of 1967 and that, even granting that the warranty extends to future performance, the cause of action under Count I accrued no later than December 27, 1967, when Standard Alliance wrote its letter claiming that the machine was defective. Standard Alliance makes numerous arguments in reply. Primarily, we must consider the question of when breach occurred. This involves analysis of two separate issues: when tender of delivery was made; whether the warranty extended to future performance. In addition, we must consider various estoppel and policy arguments.

Standard Alliance first contends, with some support in the record, that novel machines like the one here often have long "shakedown" periods before they can be made to function properly. The import of its argument is that "tender" of a defective machine should not be deemed to take place until the machine is made to run properly. Since the machine in the instant case did not function properly when initially installed in October of 1967, Standard Alliance argues, tender of delivery was never really made until June 21, 1968, when Black Clawson halted its efforts to get the machine going. Thus, even assuming that the warranty did not extend to future performance, the earliest a breach could have occurred and a cause of action accrued, on Standard Alliance's theory, was June 21, 1968.

This argument is plausible, but withers upon proper examination of the Uniform Commercial Code. UCC § 2–503(1) defines "tender of delivery" as requiring " * * * that the seller put and hold conforming goods at the buyer's disposition * * * " Comment 1 to UCC § 2–503

---

* Based upon information provided by counsel, the editors of the Callaghan Uniform Commercial Code Reporting Service state that the exact language of the "limi-tation" clause was as follows: "Any action or arbitration proceeding for breach of this agreement must be brought within one year after the cause of action has accrued."

explains that at times "tender" means "due tender" meaning " * * * an offer coupled with a present ability to fulfill all the conditions resting on the tendering party [which must be] followed by actual performance if the other party shows himself ready to proceed." "At other times [tender] is used to refer to an offer of goods or documents under a contract as if in fulfillment of its conditions even though there is a defect when measured against the contract obligation." Id. We think that "tender" as used in UCC § 2–725(2) is the latter and not the former. A contrary interpretation would extend the statute of limitations indefinitely into the future since a defect at the time of delivery would prevent proper "due tender" from taking place until it was corrected. Under section 2–725, a cause of action accrues upon initial installation of the product regardless whether it functions properly or not so long as the warranty does not extend to future performance. See Val Decker Packing Co. v. Corn Products Sales Co., 411 F.2d 850 (6th Cir.1969).

Secondly, Standard Alliance argues that the page twelve warranties ** did extend to future performance under section 2–725(2), and that the statute of limitations thus ran from the date of discovery of the defect. It particularly points to the phrase, "Black Clawson warrants that the subject machinery *will* perform the following mechanical functions." Plaintiff's argument proves too much. Since all contracts contain future promises, words of futurity such as "will" are common. When the contract at issue here was signed, the machine was not yet built; the word "will" was necessarily used. The proper question is whether the statute of limitations is meant to run from the day of delivery or from the day when a defect is found sometime in the future.

Most courts have been very harsh in determining whether a warranty explicitly extends to future performance. Emphasizing the word "explicitly," they have ruled that there must be specific reference to a future time in the warranty. As a result of this harsh construc-

---

** The negotiated performance or "page twelve warranties" provided:

"The following express warranties, which relate to mechanical function only become an adjunct to our contract clause # 1 page 11 and supersede all references to warranties that may be contained in the description of the machine pages 2–7, either expressed or implied.

"Black Clawson warrants that the subject machinery will perform the following mechanical functions:

"1. Press will deliver 1000 ton ram capacity at 150 strokes per minute @ ¼" from bottom dead center.

"2. Press will have a maximum speed of 250 strokes per minute—with a range of 10 to 250 SPM.

"3. Rams at bottom of stroke will have a parallelism of within .005".

"4. Peel and press will trace template within plus or minus .015".

"5. Feed adjustments will have a range up to 0.375" per second.

"6. Peel rotation will have a range of 5 to 100 RPM and will be designed to lock at the 90° positions.

"7. Peel traverse speed will have a range of 1 ft/minute to 45 ft/minute, and will be designed to lock in position.

"8. The mechanical functions can be programmed to operate in automatic sequence in the specified capacities and accuracies or may be operator interrupted and/or commanded as required.

"The quality and quantity of production is not the responsibility of the seller."

tion, most express warranties cannot meet the test and no implied warranties can since, by their very nature, they never "explicitly extend to future performance." * * *

Two rare examples where express warranties were found to explicitly extend to future performance are Rempe v. General Electric Co., 28 Conn.Super. 160, 254 A.2d 577 (1969) (product was to "work properly for a lifetime") and Mittasch v. Seal Lock Burial Vault, Inc., 42 A.D.2d 573, 344 N.Y.S.2d 101 (1973) (warranty that vault "will give satisfactory service at all times").

It is clear that a buyer and a seller can freely negotiate to extend liability into the future; that is why specific allowance was made for warranties "explicitly" extending to future performance. * * * In the absence of explicit agreement, however, UCC § 2–725(2) reflecting the drafters' intention to establish a reasonable period of time, four years,[16] beyond which business persons need not worry about stale warranty claims is applicable. This policy consideration underlying § 2–725 makes it acceptable to bar implied warranty claims brought more than a specified number of years after the sale; otherwise merchants could be forever liable for breach of warranty on any goods which they sold. * * * Similarly, an express warranty which makes no reference at all to any future date should not be allowed to extend past the limitations period. Thus, where a manufacturer warrants that a welder will meet certain performance warranties, but makes no mention of how long the warranties are meant to last; the statute of limitations begins to run at delivery. * * *

Where, however, an express warranty is made which extends for a specific period of time, i.e. one year, the policy reasons behind strict application of the limitations period do not apply. If a seller expressly warrants a product for a specified number of years, it is clear that, by this action alone, he is explicitly warranting the future performance of the goods for that period of time. As J. White & R. Summers Uniform Commercial Code 342 (1972), points out, if an automobile is warranted to last for twenty-four thousand miles or four years, the warranty should extend to future performance. If the car fails within the warranty period, the limitations period should begin to run from the day the defect is or should have been discovered.

In the case at bar, Black Clawson expressly warranted the machine for a period of one year. Thus, we hold that the warranties explicitly extended to future performance for a period of one year. Therefore, under § 2–725(2) the cause of action accrued when Standard Alliance discovered or should have discovered that the machine was defective, so long as the defect arose within the warranty period.[17]

16. We are aware that some states have adopted a limitations period greater than four years, e.g. Wis.Stat. § 402.725 (6 years); Okla.Stat. tit. 12A § 2–725 (5 years). Ohio, however, follows the majority of the states in establishing a four year period. Ohio Rev.Code § 1302.98 [UCC § 2–725]. The parties agree that Ohio law governs this diversity action.

17. Centennial Ins. Co. v. General Electric Co., [253 N.W.2d 696] and Voth v.

Unfortunately, this holding does not assist the plaintiff. Under the contractual limitations period, Standard Alliance had one year from the date of discovery of defect to bring suit. Standard Alliance reported the machine's problems to Black Clawson by letter on December 27, 1967. At least as of this date, Standard Alliance had discovered the breach. Since suit was not brought until over a year later, on May 29, 1969, this action is barred by section 2–725(2). See Gemini Typographers v. Mergenthaler Lino Co., 48 A.D.2d 637, 368 N.Y.S.2d 210 (1975).

Plaintiff thirdly argues that Black Clawson should be estopped from asserting the statute of limitations as a defense because it promised to repair the defects and spent over five months attempting to do so. In effect, plaintiff contends that it reasonably relied on the repair efforts, to its detriment. Decisions in other jurisdictions are split.

* * *

We must determine what the Ohio courts would do if confronted with this issue. Although we have been unable to find direct case authority, an examination of the statute is illuminative. UCC § 2–725(4), as promulgated by the drafters of the Uniform Commercial Code, states:

> "This section does not alter *the law* on tolling of the statute of limitations nor does it apply to causes of action which have accrued before this Act becomes effective." (Emphasis added)

Ohio's version of UCC § 2–725(4) is codified at Ohio Rev.Code § 1302.98(d). That section provides:

> "This section does not alter *sections 2305.15 and 2305.16 of the [Ohio] Revised Code* on tolling of the statute of limitations nor does it apply to causes of action which have accrued before this Act becomes effective." (Emphasis added)

Thus, when the Ohio legislature adopted the Uniform Commercial Code, it substituted "sections 2305.15 and 2305.16 of the [Ohio] Revised Code" for "the law" in the text of UCC § 2–725(4). This significant change in the UCC's wording requires that we limit our analysis to the two Ohio statutes cited.

An examination of these statutes reveals that the limitation period is tolled if a defendant has removed himself from the state, Ohio Rev. Code § 2305.15, or if a plaintiff has suffered from some type of disability. Ohio Rev.Code § 2305.16. Neither is applicable here.

It is, of course, quite possible that the Ohio courts would apply the doctrine of equitable estoppel in a case where an innocent purchaser

Chrysler Motor Corp., [545 P.2d 371], indicated that contractual provisions to repair or replace defective parts for a period of one year were not warranties extending into the future for one year, but remedies to be invoked should something go wrong. We see no conceptual distinction between saying that a product is warranted for one year against defects, the remedy limited to repair or replacement and saying that should a breach be discovered within one year, the seller will repair or replace defective parts. Both are warranties explicitly extending to future performance. We recognize that there may be differences between remedies and warranties, * * * but we do not believe that these distinctions make a difference here.

has relied to his detriment on a seller's promises to repair. "The principle that ' * * * no man may take advantage of his own wrong' prevents a defendant whose actions have induced a plaintiff to delay filing a suit until after the running of the limitation period from asserting the statute of limitations as a defense to the action." Ott v. Midland-Ross Corp., 523 F.2d 1367, 1370 (6th Cir.1975). See Markese v. Ellis, 11 Ohio App.2d 160, 229 N.E.2d 70 (1967). Here, however, we have two corporate behemoths, well able to look out for themselves, and no evidence that one lulled the other into not suing on time. * * *

Standard Alliance's two remaining arguments, unsupported by any authority, merit only brief mention. Standard Alliance argues that this court should toll the running of the limitations period or otherwise find timely filing because the limitations period was contractually reduced from four years to one year. It would also find significant that approximately one-half the one-year limitations period was spent in attempted repairs.

The one-year limitations period is specifically allowed by UCC § 2–725(1). We see nothing unfair about this provision in a negotiated contract between two parties of equal bargaining power. Similarly, we find no prejudice to plaintiff resulted from the lengthy repair time. Standard Alliance still had time to file suit on the original breach of warranty claim even after termination of the repair efforts; it also had a cause of action under Count II for failure to fulfill the repair or replacement warranty.[20]

* * *

[Some footnotes omitted.]

Notes

1. In Dowling v. Southwestern Porcelain, Inc., 237 Kan. 536, 701 P.2d 954 (1985), the court held that where the buyer contracted to purchase a completed silo to be installed by the seller, the statute of limitations began to run when the installation was completed, not when the component parts were delivered.

2. Seller, in furnishing spandrel and visions panels for a building, represented that the goods would be free from defects in material and workmanship for a "period of twenty years." The exclusive remedy for breach was limited to replacement of defective panels. The panels, which were delivered between 1974 and 1976, were defective. The buyer sued for damages in 1981 and the district court granted the seller's motion to dismiss based upon the statute of limitations: The court held that seller had only made replacement commitments, not warranties explicitly extending to future performance. *Held,* reversed. The warranties, by explic-

---

20. Our disposition of Count I on limitations grounds makes it unnecessary to consider the interesting question whether notice of breach had to be given a second time, after repairs failed. Since the repair or replacement warranty is also a remedy to be invoked if the machine did not meet its performance warranties, there is certainly room to argue that UCC § 2–607(3) requires notice that the repair or replacement remedy has failed "of its essential purpose" under UCC § 2–719(2).

itly stating a time beyond delivery when the condition would exist, extended the warranty to "future" performance of the goods, with a limitation of the remedy to replacement in the event of a breach. The buyer filed suit within 4 years of the time the breach was or "should have been discovered." R.W. Murray Co. v. Shatterproof Glass Corp., 697 F.2d 818 (8th Cir. 1983).

3. Suppose that S, upon delivery on November 1, 1980, explicitly stated that "this warranty shall last for three years." B "should have" discovered a nonconformity on November 1, 1986 and actually discovered the defect on July 1, 1987. B sued S on October 30, 1987. S moved to dismiss on grounds that B failed to give notice under UCC 2–607(3)(a) before filing suit. What result?

4. For samples of literature highly critical of UCC 2–725, see Williams, *The Statute of Limitations, Prospective Warranties, and Problems of Interpretation in Article 2 of the UCC,* 52 G.W.L.Rev. 67 (1983); Note, *UCC Section 2–725: A Statute Uncertain in Application and Effect,* 46 Ohio St. U.L.Rev. 755 (1985).

Problem 13–5

B contracted to purchase factory equipment from S on June 1, 1984. S warranted that the goods were free from defects in material and workmanship for the period of one year after installation and agreed to repair or replace defective parts or work. The equipment was delivered and installed on July 1, 1984. On June 1, 1985, B notified S that the machine had stopped working. S, on June 5, arrived at B's plant and attempted to "cure" the problem. After three weeks of effort, the equipment still did not work. S left the premises on June 26, 1985 insisting that he would repair the machine. "Don't worry," he said. In August, 1985, B notified S that the cure had not worked and that he considered S in breach. Again, S assured B that a cure would be forthcoming. S never returned to the plant and B removed the equipment from the floor and put it in storage. In July, 1989, B consults you, his attorney, about the matter. Has the statute of limitations run on B's claim for breach of warranty?

SECTION 5. THE LIMITATIONS OF WARRANTY THEORY

To summarize, warranty is a theory of strict but limited liability. Warranties arise when the seller makes representations, express or implied, about the quality of goods sold upon which a buyer is entitled to depend. Disputes involving warranties are resolved within Article 2 of the UCC, which has a set of limitations and policies associated primarily with exchange transactions, i.e., contracts for the sale of goods. In addition to limitations associated with concerns about adverse selection and moral hazard, which have been noted, Article 2 also permits the parties by agreement to disclaim or limit warranties and limit remedies for breach, issues which will be treated in Chapter Fourteen.

A number of recurring problems, however, have tested the nature of warranty theory and, perforce, the limitations of Article 2. We will identify some of them here, and follow with a decision where the issues are put to the test.

First, should warranty theory be extended to transactions where personal or professional services predominate and the transfer of goods is incidental? The usual answer is no, unless the defendant has expressly promised or represented that the services, when performed, will achieve a specific result. Without an express commitment to achieve a particular result, the performance of the services is judged under tort standards—negligence—rather than implied warranty. See, e.g., Milau Associates v. North Ave. Development, 42 N.Y.2d 482, 398 N.Y.S.2d 882, 368 N.E.2d 1247 (1977); Greenfield, *Consumer Protection in Service Transactions—Implied Warranties and Strict Liability in Tort,* 1974 Utah L.Rev. 661. (Query whether there is much difference between a tort duty to perform services with reasonable care and an implied warranty that the services will be "reasonably fit" for ordinary purposes.)

Second, suppose a seller sells unmerchantable goods which cause damage to the person or property of a buyer. Suppose, further, that the buyer would be foreclosed from recovery by one or more limitations upon warranty liability found in the Code, e.g., failure to give notice of the breach, lack of contractual privity, an enforceable disclaimer or expiration of the statute of limitations. Does Article 2 preempt the dispute or may the buyer also pursue the claim in strict products liability or negligence, where tort rather than contract limitations apply?

Despite the fact that Article 2 explicitly covers personal injury and property damage claims, see UCC 2–715(2)(b), 2–719(3) and 2–318, Alternatives A and B, the usual answer to the question is no: Neither the drafters of Article 2 nor the state legislatures which enacted it intended to preempt the developing theory of strict liability under Section 402A of the Restatement, Second of Torts. See Phipps v. General Motors Corp., 278 Md. 337, 363 A.2d 955 (1976); Murray, *Products Liability vs. Warranty Claims: Untangling the Web,* 3 J.Law & Commerce 269 (1983); Wade, *Tort Liability for Products Causing Physical Injury and Article 2 of the U.C.C.,* 48 Mo.L.Rev. 1 (1983). For contrary opinions, see Cline v. Prowler Industries of Maryland, 418 A.2d 968 (Del.Super.1980); Shanker, *A Reexamination of Prosser's Products Liability Cross Word Game: The Strict or Stricter Liability of Commercial Code Sales Warranty,* 29 Case Wes.Res.L.Rev. 550 (1979) (Article 2 applies to physical damage claims). The upshot is that a plaintiff who is injured in person or property by a defective product may escape Article 2 for the more favorable law of Tort, if he so elects.

Third, suppose a commercial buyer in privity with the seller suffers damage to property or pure economic loss from a breach of warranty. No personal injuries are involved. May the buyer "escape" from Article 2 into tort by invoking either strict products or negligence theory? To put the matter concretely, suppose that the statute of limitations has run under UCC 2–725(1) but has not run in tort. As *Spring Motors,* infra, reveals, the judicial answer is clear where pure economic loss is involved—UCC 2–725 controls—but is uncertain where damage to personal property has occurred.

Fourth, suppose a commercial buyer has suffered pure economic loss caused by an unmerchantable product but is not in privity of contract with the manufacturer. If the buyer cannot escape the UCC into tort, lack of privity is no defense and warranty theory must be pursued. May the manufacturer, who is a seller, defend on the ground that there was no privity of contract? See the next case.

Finally, suppose the buyer is a consumer, i.e., a person who purchased the goods for personal, family or household purposes, who has suffered only economic loss. How, if at all, should the answers to the third and fourth questions, above, differ? Should the "ordinary" consumer with less overall capacity than the professional seller be entitled to greater protection than a commercial buyer and, if so, what and why? See, e.g., Rice, *Product Quality Laws and the Economics of Federalism,* 65 B.U.L.Rev. 1 (1985); Vogel, *Squeezing Consumers: Lemon Laws, Consumer Warranties, and a Proposal for Reform,* 1985 Ariz. St.L.Rev. 589, and Chapter Fourteen, Section 5.

SPRING MOTORS DISTRIBUTORS, INC. v. FORD MOTOR COMPANY

Supreme Court of New Jersey, 1985.
98 N.J. 555, 489 A.2d 660.

The opinion of the Court was delivered by

POLLOCK, J.

The fundamental issue on this appeal concerns the rights of a commercial buyer to recover for economic loss caused by the purchase of defective goods. More specifically, the question is whether the buyer should be restricted to its cause of action under the Uniform Commercial Code (hereinafter U.C.C. or the Code) or should be allowed to pursue a cause of action predicated on principles of negligence and strict liability. The difference is important because the buyer in the present case instituted its action beyond the four-year period provided by the U.C.C., *N.J.S.A.* 12A:2–725, but within the six-year period applicable to tort actions, *N.J.S.A.* 2A:14–1.

The defendants are a motor vehicle manufacturer, its dealer, and a supplier of transmissions. The gravamen of the complaint is that defects in the transmissions, which were installed in commercial trucks, caused the buyer to sustain a loss in the benefit of its bargain and consequential damages. Specifically, the buyer sought recovery for repair, towing, and replacement parts, as well as for lost profits and a decrease in the value of the trucks.

The trial court perceived the matter as sounding in contract and found that the plaintiff had not instituted its action within the four-year period provided by the U.C.C. *N.J.S.A.* 12A:2–725. In an unreported decision, the court granted summary judgment for defendants. The Appellate Division reversed on the ground that the action was more appropriately characterized as one in strict liability in tort, not contract, and that the six-year period of limitations applicable for tort actions had not expired. 191 *N.J.Super.* 22, 465 *A.2d* 530 (1983). We granted defendants' petition for certification. 95 *N.J.* 208, 470 *A.2d* 427 (1983).

We hold that a commercial buyer seeking damages for economic loss resulting from the purchase of defective goods may recover from an immediate seller and a remote supplier in a distributive chain for breach of warranty under the U.C.C., but not in strict liability or negligence. We hold also that the buyer need not establish privity with the remote supplier to maintain an action for breach of express or implied warranties. Accordingly, the four-year period of limitations provided by the Code, *N.J.S.A.* 12A:2–275, not the six-year general statute of limitations, *N.J.S.A.* 2A:14–1, determines the time within which an action must be commenced against the immediate seller and remote supplier.

I

Because this matter is presented on defendants' motion for summary judgment, we accept as true plaintiff's version of the facts, according that version the benefit of all favorable inferences. *Pierce v. Ortho Pharmaceutical Corp.,* 84 *N.J.* 58, 61, 417 *A.2d* 505 (1980). Plaintiff, Spring Motors Distributors, Inc. (Spring Motors), which is in the business of selling and leasing trucks, operates a fleet of 300 vehicles. Spring Motors agreed to purchase from defendant Turnpike Ford Truck Sales, Inc. (Turnpike) 14 model LN8000 trucks made by defendant Ford Motor Company (Ford) at a purchase price of $265,029.80. Turnpike is a Ford dealer, and throughout these proceedings the two defendants have been treated as a single entity.

In the agreement, Spring Motors specified that the trucks should be equipped with model 390V transmissions made by Clark Equipment Company (Clark), a supplier to Ford. Spring Motors specified Clark transmissions because of "excellent service and parts availability on past models" and because of Clark's advertisements and brochures.

At the time of the sale to Spring Motors, Ford issued a form warranty with each truck to

> repair or replace any of the following parts that are found to be defective in factory material or workmanship under normal use in the United States or Canada on the following basis: * * * any part during the first 12 months or 12,000 miles of operations, whichever is earlier * * * transmission case and all internal transmission parts (including auxiliary transmission) * * * after 12,000 miles and during the first 12 months or 50,000 miles of operation, whichever is earlier, for a charge of 50% of the dealer's

regular warranty charge to Ford for parts and labor. * * * For series 850 and higher trucks, any part of the * * * transmission * * * for the first 12 months or 100,000 miles of operation, whichever is earlier * * *.

The warranty also stated: "To the extent allowed by law, this WARRANTY IS IN PLACE OF all other warranties, express or implied, including ANY IMPLIED WARRANTY OF MERCHANTABILITY OR FITNESS." Furthermore, the Ford warranty expressly stated: "Under this warranty, repair or replacement of parts is the only remedy, and loss of use of the vehicle, loss of time, inconvenience, commercial loss or consequential damages are not covered."

The warranty that Clark extended to Ford provided: "WARRANTY. Clark Equipment Company ('Clark') warrants to Buyer that each new Clark axle, transmission, torque converter and drive train product, and components thereof, shall be free from defects and material and workmanship under normal use and maintenance" for 12 months or 12,000 miles for on-highway vehicles used on highways or 2,000 miles for off-highway equipment. At Clark's option, the warranty could be limited to repairs or replacements. The warranty also stated: "THIS WARRANTY IS IN LIEU OF ALL OTHER WARRANTIES (EXCEPT OF TITLE), EXPRESSED OR IMPLIED, AND THERE IS NO IMPLIED WARRANTY OF MERCHANTABILITY OR OF FITNESS FOR A PARTICULAR PURPOSE. IN NO EVENT SHALL CLARK BE LIABLE FOR INCIDENTAL, CONSEQUENTIAL OR SPECIAL DAMAGES."

Spring Motors took delivery of the trucks in November 1976, and leased them to Economic Laboratories, Inc. (Economic), which used the trucks in cities and on highways for their intended purpose of hauling. Spring Motors, which serviced the trucks during the period of the lease, began experiencing problems with the performance of the Clark transmissions as early as February 1977. The problems persisted, and Spring Motors communicated directly with Clark, writing in October 1977 that it had "had nothing but trouble" with the transmissions. Later correspondence, dated January 26, 1978, confirmed that Clark analyzed the transmissions and found that "the failure in these gear boxes was a result of improper angle degree in the way certain gears were cut," resulting "in additional strain on the actual gear and the mating gear and related shafts." Still later, Spring Motors pointed out that the transmission failures had cost it "several thousand dollars in out of pocket expenses plus many additional thousands of dollars in lost revenues, customer ill will, replacement equipment, etc."

Clark provided Spring Motors with replacement parts, but the transmission failures continued. On July 11, 1978, Spring Motors wrote to Clark that in the absence of a satisfactory response by August 1, it would remove and replace the Clark transmissions and "take whatever action is necessary to hold you financially responsible." Thereafter, on November 1, 1979, Spring Motors and Economic terminated the truck lease and, as part of a settlement, Economic purchased the trucks for $247,580.97. Four years and one month after the delivery of the trucks, on December 23, 1980, Spring Motors instituted this action.

In the complaint, which contained three counts, Spring Motors sought judgment against all defendants for consequential damages: the expenses of towing, repairs, and replacement of parts; lost profits; and decrease in market value of the trucks. The first count asserted that the defendants breached certain express and implied warranties; the second count claimed a violation of the Magnuson-Moss Act, 15 *U.S.C.* § 2301 to –2312, a claim that Spring Motors no longer pursues; and the third count sought recovery in strict liability and negligence.

The trial court found that a lack of privity barred the action between Spring Motors and Clark and that the four-year period of limitations under the U.C.C., *N.J.S.A.* 12A:2–725, barred any action against Ford and Turnpike. The Court further found the six-year statute of limitations, *N.J.S.A.* 2A:14–1, pertaining to tort actions for property damage, inapplicable. Consequently, the trial court dismissed the complaint as to all defendants.

The Appellate Division affirmed the dismissal of the breach of warranty claim in the first count, but reversed the dismissal of the tort claims, without discussing the negligence aspect of the third count. That court concluded that Spring Motors, as a commercial buyer, could maintain its strict-liability claim against all defendants. 191 *N.J. Super.* at 41, 465 *A.*2d 530. The court also determined that the six-year limitation period provided by *N.J.S.A.* 2A:14–1 applied and that plaintiff's action was, therefore, timely. *Id.* at 44, 465 *A.*2d 530.

We granted petitions for certification by Ford, Turnpike, and Clark to review that part of the Appellate Division judgment that reversed the dismissal of the tort claims. Spring Motors did not file a cross-petition seeking review of the dismissal of the warranty claims, and that issue is not before us.

II

If the legal relationships among the parties are governed by the U.C.C., then plaintiff's action, which was instituted more than four years after the delivery of the trucks, is time-barred. Hence, one question is whether the Code provides the exclusive remedies available to Spring Motors. In answering that question, we turn to the structure and purpose of the Code, which constitutes a comprehensive system for determining the rights and duties of buyers and sellers with respect to contracts for the sale of goods. *Ramirez v. Autosport,* 88 *N.J.* 277, 285–90, 440 *A.*2d 1345 (1982). Its underlying purpose is to clarify and make uniform throughout the United States the law governing commercial transactions. *N.J.S.A.* 12A:1–102.

The Code provides for express warranties regarding the quality of goods, *N.J.S.A.* 12A:2–313, as well as implied warranties of merchantability, *N.J.S.A.* 12A:2–314, and of fitness for a particular purpose, *N.J.S.A.* 12A:2–315. As is subsequently discussed in greater detail, a seller's warranty, whether express or implied, extends to members of the buyer's family or his household guests, who are viewed as third-party beneficiaries, and a seller may not exclude or limit the extension of those warranties to such persons. *N.J.S.A.* 12A:2–318.

Subject to requirements of good faith, diligence, and reasonableness, parties may vary the terms of the Code. *N.J.S.A.* 12A:1–102. A seller may exclude or modify its liability on warranties, and if in writing, the exclusion or modification must be "conspicuous." *N.J.S.A.* 12A:2–316. Furthermore, a buyer and seller may agree to limit the buyer's remedy to the repair and replacement of parts. *N.J.S.A.* 12A:2–719(1)(a). Similarly, the parties may agree to limit or exclude consequential damages, "unless the limitation or exclusion is unconscionable." *N.J.S.A.* 12A:2–719(3). Although a limitation of consequential damages for personal injuries in the case of consumer goods is *prima facie* unconscionable, a limitation of damages for a commercial loss is not. *Id.*

When a seller delivers goods that are not as warranted, the buyer's measure of damage is the difference between the value of the defective goods and the value they would have had if they had been as warranted. *N.J.S.A.* 12A:2–714. In a proper case, a buyer may also recover incidental damages, which include reasonable expenses incidental to the breach, *N.J.S.A.* 12A:2–715; consequential damages, including losses resulting from the buyer's particular needs of which the seller had knowledge, *id.* at (2)(a); and property damage, *id.* at (2)(b).

Economic loss can take the form of either direct or consequential damages. A direct economic loss includes the loss of the benefit of the bargain, *i.e.*, the difference between the value of the product as represented and its value in its defective condition. Consequential economic loss includes such indirect losses as lost profits. J. White & R. Summers, *Handbook of the Law Under the Uniform Commercial Code* §§ 11–4 to 11–6 at 405–10 (2d ed. 1980) [hereinafter cited as White & Summers]; Note, "Economic Loss in Products Liability Jurisprudence," 66 *Colum.L.Rev.* 917, 918 (1966); Note, "Manufacturer's Liability to Remote Purchasers for 'Economic Loss' Damages—Tort or Contract?," 114 *U.Pa.L.Rev.* 539, 542 (1966). Because it presents a claim for economic loss, which is not normally recoverable in a tort action, rather than a claim for physical harm, this case probes the boundary between strict liability and the U.C.C. The delineation of that boundary requires a brief summary of the history and nature of strict liability.

One year before the adoption of the U.C.C. in New Jersey, this Court delivered its landmark opinion in *Henningsen v. Bloomfield Motors, Inc.,* 32 *N.J.* 358, 161 *A.*2d 69 (1960). *Henningsen* involved a defective automobile that crashed and caused property damage to the car and personal injuries to the driver, who was the owner's wife. The Court affirmed a judgment in favor of the plaintiffs on the theory of breach of implied warranty of fitness. Justice Francis wrote in now familiar language: "[U]nder modern marketing conditions, when a manufacturer puts a new automobile in the stream of trade and promotes its purchase by the public, an implied warranty that it is reasonably suitable for use as such accompanies it into the hands of the ultimate purchaser." 32 *N.J.* at 384, 161 *A.2d* 69. By extending a warranty of safety to consumers of all products, not just those intended for human consumption, *Henningsen* removed the notion of privity of contract from all cases involving the sale of defective goods that cause physical injury.

Prosser describes the effect of the *Henningsen* holding as "the most rapid and altogether spectacular overturn of an established rule in the entire history of the law of torts." W. Prosser & W. Page Keeton, *Handbook of the Law of Torts* § 97 at 690 (5th ed. 1984) [hereinafter cited as Prosser & Keeton]. Courts throughout the country followed the lead of New Jersey, *id.,* and the American Law Institute (ALI) included a new section, 402A, captioned "Special Liability of Seller of Product for Physical Harm to User or Consumer," in the *Restatement (Second) of Torts.* The comment to section 402A disavows that the section is governed by the warranty provisions of the U.C.C. or by U.C.C. limitations on the scope and content of the warranties.

Underlying the *Henningsen* decision was the Court's recognition that consumers were in an unequal bargaining position with respect to automobile manufacturers and dealers, who required them to sign standard contracts. *Henningsen, supra,* 32 *N.J.* at 389–404, 161 *A.2d* 69. One of the main purposes of strict liability, as declared in *Henningsen,* is the allocation of the risk and distribution of the loss to the better risk-bearer. *Id.* at 379, 161 *A.2d* 69; *Suter v. San Angelo Foundry & Mach. Co.,* 81 *N.J.* 150, 173, 406 *A.2d* 140 (1979). Generally, the manufacturer, who is better able to eliminate defects from its product and who can spread the cost of the risk among all of its customers, is the better risk-bearer. *Restatement, supra,* § 402A comment c. By contrast, the individual consumer is poorly situated to bear the entire risk of loss from injuries caused by a defective product. Through allocation of the risk of loss to the manufacturer, strict liability achieves its objective of protecting the consumer who, because of unequal bargaining power, cannot protect him or herself.

The year after the *Henningsen* decision, 1961, the Legislature adopted the U.C.C., effective January 1, 1963. *L.*1961, *c.* 120. Then in 1965 this Court decided *Santor v. A. & M. Karagheusian, Inc.,* 44 *N.J.* 52, 207 *A.2d* 305, which, like *Henningsen,* involved facts that occurred before the adoption of the U.C.C. In *Santor,* a carpet manufacturer sold a defective carpet to a consumer through its wholly-owned distributor. The Court found that the consumer could recover against the manufacturer, although there was no privity between the parties and the action was for an economic loss.

The action was couched in terms of a breach of implied warranty of merchantability, *id.* at 63, 207 *A.2d* 305, but the Court acknowledged that the action could be described better as one in strict liability. *Id.* at 63–67, 207 *A.2d* 305.   In *Santor,* Justice Francis made clear that neither mass advertising by the manufacturer nor personal injuries to the consumer was essential to the invocation of strict liability. *Id.* at 65, 207 *A.2d* 305.   Echoing his words in *Henningsen,* he stated that the purpose of a strict-liability action was to shift the risk of loss so that it was borne by "the makers of the products who put them in the channels of trade, rather than by the injured or damaged persons who ordinarily are powerless to protect themselves." *Id.*   Like the plaintiff in *Henningsen,* the plaintiff in *Santor* was an individual consumer. Furthermore, the action was for a direct economic loss, and the Court limited recovery to the lost benefit of the bargain, *i.e.,* "the difference between the price paid by the plaintiff and the actual market value of the defective carpeting at the time when plaintiff knew or should have known it was defective ∗ ∗ ∗." *Id.* at 68–69, 207 *A.2d* 305.

∗ ∗ ∗

[The court discussed other New Jersey decisions which held that the tort rather than the UCC statute of limitations governed where a defective product caused damage to person or property.]

As the preceding cases demonstrate, the U.C.C. rules pertaining to the sale of goods overlap the doctrine of strict liability for placing a defective product in the stream of commerce.   One reason for the overlap is that strict liability, in this regard, evolved from implied warranties of fitness and merchantability under the U.C.C. and its predecessor, the Uniform Sales Act.   Those warranties originated as a matter of social policy to compensate consumers who sustained personal injuries from defective food.   Prosser & Keeton, *supra,* § 97 at 690. Neither the ALI, which published the *Restatement (Second) of Torts,* nor the permanent editorial board of the U.C.C., which operates as a joint project of the ALI ∗ ∗ ∗ and the Commissioners on Uniform State Laws, has undertaken to resolve the overlap between strict liability as declared in section 402A and the breach of warranty provisions under the U.C.C.   112 *N.J.L.J.* 700 (1983).

From the perspective of the injured party, strict liability generally provides a more congenial environment than contract principles, which may prevent recovery because of a lack of privity with the manufacturer.   In addition to privity, the Code retains two other requirements that may pose considerable obstacles to a buyer.   The first requirement is that of notice to a seller of a breach of warranty, *N.J.S.A.* 12A:2–607(3); the second arises from the seller's ability to limit or disclaim liability to an innocent purchaser. *N.J.S.A.* 12A:2–316.   A buyer who does not deal directly with a manufacturer cannot negotiate over the terms of a disclaimer and might find it impossible to give the manufacturer notice of the breach of warranty following an injury.   Prosser & Keeton, *supra,* § 97 at 691–92.   Strict liability, on the other hand, circumvents the technical requirements of the U.C.C. with respect to privity, notice, and limitation of damages.   Avoiding those requirements is particularly important for persons outside the distributive chain who sustain physical damage caused by a defective product.

By comparison, the U.C.C. emphasizes the simplification of the law governing commercial transactions and the expansion of commercial practices through agreement. *N.J.S.A.* 12A:1–102. Underlying the U.C.C. policy is the principle that parties should be free to make contracts of their choice, including contracts disclaiming liability for breach of warranty. Once they reach such an agreement, society has an interest in seeing that the agreement is fulfilled. Consequently, the U.C.C. is the more appropriate vehicle for resolving commercial disputes arising out of business transactions between persons in a distributive chain.

The problem is ascertaining where on the spectrum to place a cause of action brought by a commercial entity, or even a consumer, for purely economic loss. One gains perspective by reviewing the decisions of this Court and those of the Supreme Court of California.

As explained earlier, this Court's decision in *Henningsen* was couched in warranty terms. In *Greenman v. Yuba Power Prods., Inc.,* 59 *Cal.*2d 57, 27 *Cal.Rptr.* 697, 701, 377 *P.*2d 897, 901 (1962), which involved personal injuries sustained by a husband from a defective power saw purchased by his wife, the California court drew on *Henningsen,* but declared that the cause of action could be more appropriately denominated as strict liability in tort.

The cross-pollination between the two jurisdictions continued through our *Santor* decision, which relied on *Greenman.* Five months later, however, when the California court was confronted with an individual's claim for economic loss resulting from the purchase of a defective truck, that court rejected *Santor* and held that the consumer could not recover in strict liability for economic loss. *Seely v. White Motor Co.,* 63 *Cal.*2d 9, 45 *Cal.Rptr.* 17, 403 *P.*2d 145 (1965).

In *Seely,* an individual owner-driver purchased a truck for use in his heavy duty hauling business. From the time the purchaser took possession, the truck bounced violently, but the dealer was unable to correct the defect. Thereafter, a brake failure caused the truck to overturn. The truck sustained property damage, and Seely, who stopped making payments after the accident, sued the dealer and the manufacturer for lost profits and the money paid on the purchase price of the truck.

Chief Justice Traynor, writing for the majority of the court, affirmed a judgment for Seely. The absence of privity did not preclude judgment against the manufacturer for the breach of an express warranty that the truck was "free from defects in material and workmanship under normal use and service * * *." *Seely, supra,* 63 *Cal.*2d at 13, 45 *Cal.Rptr.* at 20, 403 *P.*2d at 148. After reaching that result, the court rejected plaintiff's alternative contention of strict liability. The court ruled that in the absence of personal injuries or property damage strict liability was inapplicable. Although the truck had been damaged, the court sustained a finding of the trial court that defendant had not created the defect that caused the damage.

While rejecting plaintiff's right to recover in strict liability, Chief Justice Traynor observed that the law of sales has been carefully articulated to govern economic relationships between suppliers and consumers. He stated further that strict liability was not intended to undermine the warranty provisions of the U.C.C., but "to govern the distinct problem of physical injuries." *Seely, supra,* 63 *Cal.*2d at 15, 45 *Cal.Rptr.* at 21, 403 *P.*2d at 149.

In a concurring and dissenting opinion, Justice Peters embraced *Santor,* and stated that an individual consumer should be allowed to recover in strict liability for economic damages such as those sustained by Seely. *Seely, supra,* 63 *Cal.*2d at 20–22, 45 *Cal.Rptr.* at 25–27, 403 *P.*2d at 153–55. According to Justice Peters, the roles played by the parties and the nature of the transaction, not the nature of the damage, were important. *Id.* He also distinguished transactions involving consumers from those "*within* the world of commerce, where parties generally bargain on a somewhat equal plane and may be presumed to be familiar with the legal problems involved when defective goods are purchased." *Seely, supra,* 63 *Cal.*2d at 27, 45 *Cal.Rptr.* at 29, 403 *P.*2d at 157 (emphasis in original).

* * *

[The court reviewed decisions from other states and the views of commentators, the substantial majority of which favored the result in *Seely* rather than that in *Santor.*]

In the present case, which involves an action between commercial parties, we need not reconsider the *Santor* rule that an ultimate consumer may recover in strict liability for direct economic loss. To determine whether a commercial buyer may recover economic loss, however, we must reconsider the policies underlying the doctrine of strict liability and those underlying the U.C.C. Those policy considerations include, among others, the relative bargaining power of the parties and the allocation of the loss to the better risk-bearer in a modern marketing system. As a general rule, the rights and duties of a buyer and seller are determined by the law of sales, which throughout this century has been expressed first in the Uniform Sales Act and more recently in the U.C.C. As indicated, however, strict liability evolved as a judicial response to inadequacies in sales law with respect to consumers who sustained physical injuries from defective goods made or distributed by remote parties in the marketing chain.

The considerations that give rise to strict liability do not obtain between commercial parties with comparable bargaining power. *Iowa Elec. Light & Power Co. v. Allis-Chalmers Mfg. Co., supra,* 360 *F.Supp.* at 32 (stating doctrine of strict liability loses all meaning when plaintiff is a large company suing for commercial loss). Furthermore, perfect parity is not necessary to a determination that parties have substantially equal bargaining positions. *Cf. Moreira Constr. Co., Inc. v. More-*

trench Corp., 97 *N.J.Super.* 391, 394–95, 235 *A.*2d 211 (App.Div.1967), *aff'd o.b.*, 51 *N.J.* 405, 241 *A.*2d 236 (1968) (refusing to apply rule of *Santor* to suit between corporations even though plaintiff was a small company and defendant was the world's largest well point company). Suffice it to state that Spring Motors had sufficient bargaining power to persuade Ford to install Clark transmissions in the trucks that were the subject of the contract.

Insofar as risk allocation and distribution are concerned, Spring Motors is at least as well situated as the defendants to assess the impact of economic loss. Indeed, a commercial buyer, such as Spring Motors, may be better situated than the manufacturer to factor into its price the risk of economic loss caused by the purchase of a defective product. *See* Note, "Economic Loss in Products Liability Jurisprudence," *supra*, 66 *Colum.L.Rev.* at 952–58.

Presumably the price paid by Spring Motors for the trucks reflected the fact that Ford was liable for repair or replacement of parts only. By seeking to impose the risk of loss on Ford, Spring Motors seeks, in effect, to obtain a better bargain than it made. In such a context, the imposition of the risk of loss on the manufacturer might lead to price increases for all of its customers, including individual consumers. *Id.* at 956–57. As between commercial parties, then, the allocation of risks in accordance with their agreement better serves the public interest than an allocation achieved as a matter of policy without reference to that agreement.

Delineation of the boundary between strict liability and the U.C.C. requires appreciation not only of the policy considerations underlying both sets of principles, but also of the role of the Legislature as a coordinate branch of government. By enacting the U.C.C., the Legislature adopted a carefully-conceived system of rights and remedies to govern commercial transactions. Allowing Spring Motors to recover from Ford under tort principles would dislocate major provisions of the Code. For example, application of tort principles would obviate the statutory requirement that a buyer give notice of a breach of warranty, *N.J.S.A.* 12A:2–607, and would deprive the seller of the ability to exclude or limit its liability, *N.J.S.A.* 12A:2–316. In sum, the U.C.C. represents a comprehensive statutory scheme that satisfies the needs of the world of commerce, and courts should pause before extending judicial doctrines that might dislocate the legislative structure.

By allowing this case to proceed under strict liability principles, the Appellate Division erred, * * * it relied too heavily on *Santor*, which did not consider the effect of the U.C.C. on a commercial transaction.

* * *

For the preceding reasons, we hold that a commercial buyer seeking damages for economic loss only should proceed under the U.C.C. against parties in the chain of distribution. Hence, we reverse that part of the judgment of the Appellate Division that permitted Spring

Motors to maintain against the defendants an action in strict liability for economic loss.

III

What we have said about Spring Motors' strict liability claim applies substantially to its negligence claim. Underlying that conclusion is the principle that a seller's duty of care generally stops short of creating a right in a commercial buyer to recover a purely economic loss. Thus viewed, the definition of the seller's duty reflects a policy choice that economic losses inflicted by a seller of goods are better resolved under principles of contract law. In that context, economic interests traditionally have not been entitled to protection against mere negligence.

* * *

Although the nature of the damage may be a useful point of distinction, it also signals more subtle differences in the roles that tort and contract play in our legal system. The differences include judicial evaluation of the status, relationship, and expectations of the parties; the ability of the parties to protect themselves against the risk of loss either by contractual provision or by insurance, and the manner in which the loss occurred. *See Pennsylvania Glass Sand Corp. v. Caterpillar Tractor Co.*, 652 *F.*2d 1165, 1173 (3rd Cir.1981) (allowing recovery for damage to defective machinery resulting from fire caused by defect). This evaluation reflects, among other things, policy choices about the relative roles of contracts and tort law as sources of legal obligations. As among commercial parties in a direct chain of distribution, contract law, expressed here through the U.C.C., provides the more appropriate system for adjudicating disputes arising from frustrated economic expectations.

* * *

It follows from our determination that Spring Motors should be restricted to its U.C.C. remedies as against Ford and Turnpike Ford that the appropriate statute of limitations is the four-year time bar contained in *N.J.S.A.* 12A:2–725. More than four years elapsed between the date of the delivery of the trucks and the institution of this action against Ford and Turnpike Ford. Consequently, Spring Motors' suit against them is time-barred.

We also conclude that Spring Motors should be restricted to its U.C.C. remedies against Clark, which are time-barred because of the expiration of the four-year period of limitations provided by the Code. The trial court dismissed Spring Motors' warranty claim against Clark not because of late filing, but because of lack of privity, and the Appellate Division affirmed the dismissal of the warranty claim. 191 *N.J.Super.* at 48, 465 *A.*2d 530. Spring Motors did not cross-petition for certification on that issue and has not pursued it before us. Nonetheless, as we subsequently explain, we conclude that the better rule is to restrict parties that are part of a single distributive chain to the U.C.C.

in a suit for economic loss arising out of a commercial transaction. Prosser & Keeton, *supra,* § 101 at 708.

We conclude that the absence of privity between a remote supplier and an ultimate purchaser should not preclude the extension to the purchaser of the supplier's warranties made to the manufacturer. We reach that conclusion notwithstanding our recognition that the Code generally applies to parties in privity, *Herbstman v. Eastman Kodak Co.,* 68 *N.J.* 1, 9–10, 342 *A.*2d 181 (1975); *Heavner v. Uniroyal, Inc., supra,* 63 *N.J.* at 150, 305 *A.*2d 412, and that no privity exists between Spring Motors and Clark.

Privity, the relationship between two contracting parties, developed as a means of limiting relief on warranties. At this late date, little purpose would be served by a lengthy discussion of the erosion of privity as a defense in modern products liability law. * * *

More recently, strict liability in New Jersey has evolved as a means of permitting a consumer to recover for physical damage and direct economic loss against a remote seller, notwithstanding the absence of privity. Insofar as indirect economic losses arising out of a commercial transaction between business entities are concerned, we believe that the U.C.C., not tort law, provides the more appropriate analytical framework. By recognizing the supervening role of the U.C.C. in that context, we come closer to fulfilling the expectations of the parties and the intent of the Legislature. The intended effect of our decision is to satisfy the combined, if occasionally contending, goals of simplifying the law pertaining to business transactions and providing a system of compensation that responds to the needs of the commercial world.

Fundamental to our decision is the role of privity in modern business law, a role that is often described in terms of vertical and horizontal relationships. A vertical relationship describes one that exists between parties in a distributive chain, *i.e.,* between a manufacturer, wholesaler, retailer, and ultimate buyer. A buyer within this chain that did not buy goods directly from the named defendant would be a "vertical non-privity plaintiff" as to that defendant. 2 Hawkland, *supra,* § 2–318:01 at 419; White & Summers, *supra,* § 11–2 at 399. Here, Spring Motors, which purchased the trucks from Ford, is in vertical privity with the Ford defendants, but not with Clark. Thus, Spring Motors is a vertical non-privity plaintiff as to Clark.

"Horizontal non-privity," on the other hand, describes the relationship between the retailer and someone, other than the buyer, who has used or consumed the goods. For example, in an action against a retailer, a "horizontal non-privity plaintiff" would refer to the buyer's spouse or child, but not to the buyer. White & Summers, *supra,* § 11–2 at 399.

In drafting the U.C.C., the Commissioners on Uniform State Laws acknowledged the decline of horizontal privity as a defense to an action for personal injuries caused by the purchase of defective goods. Consequently, section 318, adopted in New Jersey as *N.J.S.A.* 12A:2–318 and now identified as "Alternative A," extends warranties horizontally to "any natural person who is in the family or household of [the] buyer or who is a guest in his home if it is reasonable to expect that such person may use, consume, or be affected by the goods and who is injured in person by breach of the warranty." With respect to vertical privity, the drafters specifically state that the section is "neutral and is not intended to enlarge or restrict the developing case law on whether the seller's warranties, given to his buyer who resells, extend to other persons in the distributive chain." Official Comment 3, § 2–318.

Courts in some states that have adopted Alternative A, however, have abolished the requirement of horizontal privity and allowed "any person," natural or legal, to sue a party in the distributive chain for breach of warranty. *See, e.g., Salvador v. Atlantic Steel Boiler Co.,* 457 *Pa.* 24, 26, 319 *A.2d* 903, 904 (1974) (lack of horizontal privity may no longer bar the plaintiff from recovering for personal injuries under breach of warranty); *JKT Co., Inc. v. Hardwick,* 274 *S.C.* 413, 416, 265 *S.E.2d* 510, 512 (1980) (no valid reason exists for distinguishing between consumer plaintiffs and corporate plaintiffs on the issue of horizontal privity).

In other states, legislatures have refused to adopt Alternative A. California was the first to criticize the section as "a step backward" and to omit the section from its version of the Code. Permanent Editorial Board note, following Official Comment to section 2–318. Still other states developed variants of section 318. In 1966, to stem the proliferation of non-uniform provisions, the members of the Permanent Editorial Board of the U.C.C. recommended Alternatives B and C. *Id.;* 3 Anderson, *Uniform Commercial Code UCC,* § 2–318:2 at 400 (3rd ed. 1983) [hereinafter cited as Anderson]. Respectively, these alternatives provide that:

ALTERNATIVE B

A seller's warranty whether express or implied extends to any natural person who may reasonably be expected to use, consume or be affected by the goods and who is injured in person by breach of the warranty. A seller may not exclude or limit the operation of this section.

ALTERNATIVE C

A seller's warranty whether express or implied extends to any person who may reasonably be expected to use, consume or be affected by the goods and who is injured by breach of the warranty. A seller may not exclude or limit the operation of this section with respect to injury of the person of an individual to whom the warranty extends.

Alternatives B and C go beyond Alternative A in eroding the privity defense. Alternative C, for example, allows "any person" on the horizontal level, including a corporation, to sue for breach of warranty. *Cf. N.J.S.A.* 12A:1–201(30) (defining person as an individual or an organization) and *N.J.S.A.* 12A:1–201(28) (defining organization as including a corporation). Some treatises declare that Alternative C eliminates the requirement of vertical privity, 2 Hawkland, *supra,* § 2–318:04 at 430; Anderson, *supra,* § 2–318:31 at 417, but another text disagrees, White & Summers, *supra,* §§ 11–5 to –6 at 406–10.

The Permanent Editorial Board's comment on Alternative C states that the section reflects "the trend of more recent decisions as indicated by Restatement of Torts 2d § 402A * * *, extending the rule beyond personal injuries." As previously indicated, in most jurisdictions section 402A precludes claims for economic loss. In New Jersey, however, a consumer may recover direct economic loss in a strict liability action against a remote supplier. *Santor v. A & M Karagheusian, Inc., supra,* 44 *N.J.* 52, 207 *A.2d* 305. Because the Code provides the more appropriate framework for resolving disputes between commercial entities, we eschew permitting recovery by a business entity for economic loss under principles of strict liability. Nonetheless, it is consistent with the principles underlying *Santor* and with the intent of the Code's drafters to recognize a claim under the U.C.C. for economic loss in a breach of warranty action without regard to vertical privity.

Furthermore, a plaintiff in a suit for breach of warranty against a remote seller, like a plaintiff in a strict liability action, need not establish privity with or negligence by the defendant. To this extent, our recognition of a warranty action for economic loss by a commercial buyer parallels our recognition in *Santor* of a similar claim by a consumer. One significant difference, of course, is that the plaintiff in a warranty action need not establish the existence of a defect; the failure of the goods to perform as warranted is sufficient. By bringing the action within the ambit of the Code, we believe we come closer to fulfilling the expectations of the parties and the intention of the Legislature that the Code should govern commercial transactions.

* * *

Eliminating the requirement of vertical privity is particularly appropriate in the present action where Spring Motors read advertisements published by Clark, specifically requested Clark transmissions, expected the transmissions to be incorporated into trucks to be manufactured by Ford, contracted with Ford only, and now seeks to recover its economic loss. Given the nature of the transaction and the expectations of the parties, the absence of a direct contractual relationship should not preclude Spring Motors from asserting a cause of action for breach of express warranty against Clark. Because the Code, not principles of tort law, governs the relationship between Spring Motors and Clark, the appropriate period of limitations is that provided by the Code. As previously indicated, the expiration of this period bars Spring Motors' claim against Clark.

Because any action by Spring Motors against Clark is time-barred, we need not determine the outer limits of a suit by an ultimate purchaser against a remote supplier for economic loss. Therefore, we reserve determination on the effectiveness of a remote manufacturer's disclaimer or limitation on express and implied warranties to an ultimate purchaser that did not have the opportunity to negotiate over the terms of the agreement. *N.J.S.A.* 12A:2–316: *N.J.S.A.* 12A:2–719. White & Summers, *supra,* § 11–6 at 409 (the extent to which a remote seller may disclaim warranties is an unresolved issue). We note, however, that in certain circumstances a buyer may recover incidental and consequential damages. *N.J.S.A.* 12A:2–715. We also leave unreviewed the Code requirement that a purchaser notify the seller about the defective condition of the product. *N.J.S.A.* 12A:2–607(3). Similarly, we do not resolve whether a warranty of fitness for a particular purpose, unlike an implied warranty of merchantability, extends only to parties in privity with the seller. *See Pawelec v. Digitcom, Inc.,* 192 *N.J.Super.* 474, 477–78, 471 *A.2d* 60 (App.Div.1984) (holding that implied warranty of fitness for a particular purpose, unlike implied warranty of merchantability, requires privity). For our purposes, it is sufficient to acknowledge that a commercial buyer in a distributive chain may maintain an action under the U.C.C. for purely economic loss arising out of a breach of warranty by a remote supplier.

Accordingly, we reverse the judgment of the Appellate Division and reinstate the dismissal of the complaint as to all defendants.

*   *   *

[Justice Handler concurred in the result. He concluded that the Court's ruling on privity was, in essence, dictum because of the interaction between Clark and Spring Motors, both before and after the purchase. In short, the privity ruling was attenuated. In addition, he expressed reservations about whether Spring Motors, a commercial buyer, needed the extra protection, when it was capable of bargaining with the dealer or Ford. Although an imbalance in capacity between even commercial parties might justify a direct suit against the manufacturer, no such imbalance was evident in this case.]

Problem 13–6

Suppose, in *Spring Motors,* that the transmissions manufactured by Clark were unmerchantable, UCC 2–314(2). Furthermore, assume that Spring Motors had purchased the trucks from Ford without knowing whose transmissions would be used and, after the problems arose, Ford not Clark made all efforts to "cure." Finally, assume that Spring Motors suffered substantial direct and consequential economic loss caused by the transmissions.

1. Under the reasoning in Spring Motors, can Spring Motors sue Clark under a warranty theory for economic losses caused by the unmerchantable transmissions? Why?

2. If the privity defense is no bar, which if any of Article 2's limitations upon warranty claims should apply to Spring Motors?

Problem 13–7

B, a commercial fisherman, owns a fishing vessel powered by two diesel engines. B needs extra power to reach distant fishing grounds and to operate gear designed for dragging the bottom. S, a dealer, recently sold and installed a new diesel engine in the boat. The engine was manufactured by M but B dealt only with S, who knew B's particular needs, and relied upon S to obtain a suitable engine. In the contract for sale, however, S limited its liability for any breach of warranty to repair and replacement of defective parts and excluded any liability for consequential damages. Assume that this limitation is effective between S and B. M, in turn, had limited its liability to S in a similar manner.

Shortly thereafter, when B was on the fishing grounds some 60 miles from port, a loud "crack" was heard and smoke poured from the new engine. The engine was quickly shut down and, although the smoke stopped, the engine would not start. When B returned to port, limping under one engine, S discovered that a defective part, manufactured by C, had disintegrated within, and had caused substantial damage to, the engine. Furthermore, B learned that he had missed a "truly remarkable" run on King Crabs at the spot where the engine malfunctioned.

S informed B that the entire engine should be replaced and that this form of "cure" was beyond the scope of the limited warranty.

1. Assess the strength of B's warranty claims, if any, against M and C.

2. Would B have a tort claim against either or both? What difference would it make?

Chapter Fourteen

BUYER'S REMEDIES FOR BREACH OF WARRANTY FOR ACCEPTED GOODS UNDER THE CODE AND PER AGREEMENT (HEREIN, TOO, OF DISCLAIMERS)

SECTION 1. INTRODUCTION

First, some words in summary. If the commercial buyer can establish that a warranty was made and breached, the timing of that discovery will be critical to the available remedy choices. If the breach was discovered before acceptance, then rejection may be a proper remedy. UCC 2–601. If the breach was discovered after acceptance and the buyer acts fast, a revocation of acceptance may be proper under UCC 2–608. In both cases, the goods are "thrown back" at the seller. Unless the seller has a right to cure under UCC 2–508 or under the contract, the seller is basically responsible for disposing of the goods and the buyer may shoot for the remedies contained in UCC 2–711.

But our buyer may never reach this position, either because he wants to accept the goods despite their defects, or because he is unable to reject or revoke acceptance, or because the breach may have rendered the goods worthless. What then? Again, if the buyer has given proper notice under UCC 2–607(3), initiated suit before the statute of limitations expires, UCC 2–725, and established that a warranty was made to him and breached, the remedies for breach with regard to accepted goods are available. See UCC 2–714 & 2–715.

In this Chapter, we will, first, explore the scope of protection under these sections. Next we will consider the extent to which the seller can, by agreement with the buyer, disclaim warranties under UCC 2–316 and alter remedies and exclude consequential damages under UCC 2–719.

SECTION 2. THE DIRECT DAMAGE FORMULA: UCC 2–714

UCC 2–714, entitled "Buyer's Damages for Breach in Regard to Accepted Goods," is a functional counterpart of UCC 2–712 and UCC 2–

713. All three sections attempt to preserve the benefit of the buyer's bargain with the seller. See UCC 1–106(1). Under UCC 2–714, however, the buyer still has the goods and is liable for their price, UCC 2–607(1), & 2–719(1)(a), subject to the power, upon notice to the seller, to "deduct all or any part of the damages resulting from any breach of the contract from any part of the price still due under the same contract." UCC 2–717. Furthermore, UCC 2–714 is somewhat open-ended and difficult to apply with precision. For example:

1. UCC 2–714(2) provides the measure of damages for breach of warranty. To what disputes does UCC 2–714(1) apply? How does one determine what losses resulted "in the ordinary course of events from the seller's breach as determined by any manner which is reasonable?"

2. In UCC 2–714(2), how does the buyer prove the "difference at the time and place of acceptance between the value of goods accepted and the value they would have had if they had been as warranted?"

3. In UCC 2–714(2), what "special circumstances" show proximate damages of a different amount?

4. How is the line between "direct" damages under UCC 2–714(2) and "incidental and consequential damages" under UCC 2–715 to be drawn?

Problem 14–1   4/6

1. Sunshine Cannery contracted on May 1 to purchase 10,000 bushels of # 1 grade tomatoes for $10 a bushel from Seller, a grower. The market price at that time was $8 a bushel. On August 10, the time for delivery, Seller tendered 10,000 bushels of # 2 grade tomatoes. Caught at the end of the canning season, Sunshine accepted the goods. The market value of the tomatoes accepted was $7 per bushel. The market value of # 1 grade tomatoes was $9 per bushel. Seller claims the contract price of $100,000. What damages may Sunshine deduct under UCC 2–714(2)?

2. Assume, above, that at the time of acceptance # 1 tomatoes had risen in value to $12 per bushel and # 2 tomatoes were worth $9 per bushel. What damages?

3. Suppose, in (1) above, the Seller tendered and Sunshine accepted what passed in the trade as # 1 tomatoes. Upon unpacking, however, the entire lot was found to be decayed and suffering from the notorious Law School Rot. Sunshine salvaged the lot for $1,000 and replaced it from another grower for $13 per bushel. What damages? Should Sunshine recover the difference between the replacement cost and the salvage value?

SOO LINE RAILROAD CO. v. FRUEHAUF CORP.

United States Court of Appeals, Eighth Circuit, 1977.
547 F.2d 1365.

[Fruehauf agreed to manufacture, sell and deliver 500 railroad hopper cars to Soo Line for the approximate price of $9,750,000. After delivery, Soo Line discovered cracks in the structure and weld of many cars. Fruehauf refused to repair, claiming it had no responsibility for the alleged defects, and Soo implemented its own program of repair at a total cost of $506,862.78. Soo Line brought suit on the theories of breach of warranty and negligence. The jury found for Soo Line on the warranty theory and the trial court ruled as a matter of law that certain contract provisions were ineffective to limit Fruehauf's liability. The jury, in a special verdict, awarded Soo Line $975,970 "for the difference between the value of the cars as accepted and their value if built to conform to the contract specifications" and additional amounts for consequential and incidental damages. The verdict on the "difference in value" issue reflected that Soo Line's repairs "did not fully restore the cars to totally acceptable operating condition." Fruehauf appealed. The trial court's judgment was affirmed.]

STEPHENSON, CIRCUIT JUDGE.

* * *

III.

The third issue in this appeal is whether the district court erred in allowing the testimony of T.R. Klingel, an expert witness who testified with respect to the diminution in value of the railroad cars resulting from their structural collapse. In general, Klingel expressed the opinion that the market value of the railcars as actually constructed was approximately $1,000,000 or $2,000 per car less than the value of the cars had they been built in accordance with the contract.

Klingel, who is executive vice president of Soo Line, testified initially that the market value of the railcars had they been constructed according to the contract would have approximated their purchase price of $19,500 per car. He further expressed the opinion, over Magor's objection, that the fair market value of the cars as actually constructed was at the most $17,500 per car. Klingel's opinion, as to the diminution in fair market value of the railcars, basically derived from his viewpoint that a hypothetical buyer of the cars would be confronted with immediate and substantial expenditures for repair and continuation of financing costs without any concomitant receipt of revenue while the railcars were out of service being repaired, and even after the repairs the buyer would possess rebuilt and patched cars worth less than those properly constructed.

Appellant contends that the trial court erred in allowing Klingel's testimony on damages. In Magor's view, Klingel was not qualified to provide expert opinion on the necessity and cost of repair because he allegedly did not possess sufficient practical or technical knowledge. Magor asserts additionally that Klingel's prediction of future maintenance costs was speculatively improper without proof that such damages are reasonably certain to occur. Finally, Magor claims that Klingel's reliance on financing costs as a basis for damages erroneously resulted in a duplicate consequential damage award for revenue lost while the railcars were being repaired.

The trial court's determination that Klingel possessed adequate qualifications, pursuant to Fed.R.Evid. 702, to testify with respect to the diminished market value of the railcars was not an abuse of discretion or clear error of law. * * * Fed.R.Evid. 702 is not limited to experts in the strictest sense of the word but also encompasses a large group called "skilled" witnesses, such as owners, bankers, and landowners testifying on the value of property. * * *

Klingel's responsibilities as Soo Line's executive vice president included overseeing the operations of all trains and the maintenance of all rolling stock and fixed property. He also was charged with determination of the market value of the railroad's rolling stock. Klingel was directly familiar with the railcars manufactured by Magor, and he collaborated closely with Soo Line's mechanical department and H.D. Hollis concerning the problematic conditions in the Magor-constructed railcars. In some instances, Klingel conducted personal inspections of the railcars. Klingel's knowledge was such that his opinion on valuation most likely assisted the trier of fact in arriving at the truth. * * *

In reviewing the substance of Klingel's testimony on valuation, the measure of damages and the limits of relevancy are set by the substantive law of Minnesota. See Johnson v. Serra, 521 F.2d 1289, 1294 (8th Cir.1975). Under Minnesota law, the measure of damages applicable to breach of contract is the difference between the actual value of the cars at the time of acceptance and the value they would have had if they had been as warranted. Minn.Stat.Ann. § 336.2–714(2). * * * The buyer is not limited to repair costs when repair does not completely restore the goods to the value which they would have had if built in conformity with the contract; remaining diminution in value may also be recovered. * * *

Taking into consideration the structural and welding defects existing in the cars manufactured for Soo Line by Magor, Klingel expressed the opinion that the reasonable market value per car was $17,500 at the most. Klingel further opined that he would probably discount the purchase price of the cars by an additional $1,000 or $2,000, which would result in a fair market value of approximately $15,500 per car.

In formulating the diminution in fair market value of the cars, Klingel properly placed reliance on the necessity for present and future repairs and the fact that even a rebuilt patched railcar would be worth less than a correctly constructed one. * * * The record reflects that approximately $1,000 per car in immediate repair costs was expended by Soo Line and that, even after implementation of the repairs, Soo Line had experienced continued maintenance costs beyond those expended for cars other than those manufactured by Magor.

Klingel also stated that a hypothetical buyer of the railcars would discount the purchase price because the buyer's financing costs would continue while the cars were out of service being repaired with no ability to generate revenue. Klingel testified that approximately $200,000 and $400 per car in interest payments would be lost without concomitant benefit during repairs. This statement, of course, may not be considered as evidence of diminution in value of the Soo Line railcars. Cost of financing is not an element of reduced market value pursuant to Minn.Stat.Ann. § 336.2–714. Nonetheless, we reject appellant's contention that this aspect of Klingel's testimony rendered inadmissible his overall opinion on the diminution in market value of the railcars. An objection that an expert's opinion is based on elements of damage not lawfully recoverable generally relates to the weight rather than the admissibility of the testimony. * * *

In addition, the trial court carefully instructed the jury with respect to this element of damages. It stated in part as follows:

"The measure of damages is, generally speaking, the difference between the fair market value of the cars as accepted by Soo Line, and the fair market value they would have had if they had not been deficient in the particulars in which you found them deficient. This is called the difference or diminution in value approach.

* * *

"If you find that the repair of the cars restored the cars to substantially the same condition as they would have been in if properly manufactured, the difference or diminution value is the same as the reasonable cost of repairing the cars.

"So, if the repair costs actually restored them then the repair cost would equal the diminution in value. However, if you find that the repair of the cars did not restore them to substantially the same condition as they would have been if properly manufactured, then the difference or diminution in value is the reasonable cost of repair, plus the difference between the fair market value of the covered hopper cars if they had been manufactured without faults or defects, and the fair market value of the repairs.

"The total figure, however, cannot exceed the difference between the fair market value as accepted, and the fair market value in the defective condition you find.

" * * * [The court then gave an illustration.]

"Therefore, if you find that the repairs of the cars placed the cars in a better condition than they would have been at the time of acceptance if they had been properly manufactured, then the difference or diminution in value recoverable by plaintiffs is the difference between the fair market value of the covered hopper cars as accepted by Soo Line and the fair market value they would have had if Magor had manufactured them properly. So, Soo Line in this situation would not be able to recover the full amount spent for repairs.

"In the course of the charge and the special verdict you will find use of the word value. Value is described as the highest price in terms of money for which a product would have sold on the open market, the seller having a reasonable time within which to sell and being willing to sell but not forced to do so; the buyer being ready, willing and able to buy, but not forced to do so, and a full opportunity to inspect the property in question and to determine its condition, suitability for use, and all things about the property that would naturally and reasonably affect its market value."

Moreover, there is sufficient evidence in the record upon which the jury could have relied in awarding $975,970 or $1,951.94 per car, approximately 10% of their original cost, for diminution in market value of the cars. It cannot be said that the verdict constituted a shocking result. * * *

For similar reasons, we reject appellant's assertion that Klingel's reference to "future maintenance costs" was unduly speculative and erroneous. Klingel merely expressed an opinion on the present value of the railcars at the time of acceptance in light of known risks associated with existing defects. Soo Line had already experienced increased maintenance costs with Magor cars previously repaired. Klingel's testimony overall had sufficient probative value to outweigh the danger that it would lead the jury to assess damages on an improper basis. * * * Magor had adequate opportunity to cross-examine and refute Klingel's testimony on valuation. * * * Under these circumstances, we conclude that the trial court did not commit an abuse of discretion in the admission of Klingel's testimony concerning the diminution in market value of the railroad cars resulting from their structural failure.

* * *

[Footnotes omitted]

CHATLOS SYSTEMS, INC. v. NATIONAL CASH REGISTER CORP.

United States Court of Appeals, Third Circuit, 1982.
479 F.Supp. 738 (D.N.J.1979), *affirmed in part, remanded in part*, 635 F.2d 1081 (3d Cir.1980), *decision of District Court on remand affirmed*, 670 F.2d 1304 (3d Cir.1982), *motion for rehearing denied*, 33 U.C.C.Rep.Serv. 935.

[In July 1974, National Cash Register Corporation (NCR) sold Chatlos Systems, Inc. (Chatlos) an NCR 399/656 disc computer system (NCR 399). The base price of $46,020 included the computer (hardware) for $40,165 and the software, consisting of 6 computer programs, for $5,855. In addition, Chatlos's paid NCR $5,621 for a service agreement and agreed to finance the purchase through a lease from a third party to whom Chatlos sold the system. Chatlos's total cost, including finance charges, for the system was $75,783.

NCR expressly warranted that the six computer programs, e.g., accounts receivable, payroll, order entry, inventory deletion, state income tax and cash receipts, would meet Chatlos's particular business needs. For breach of warranty, however, NCR limited its obligation to the repair or replacement of defective parts or workmanship and excluded any liability for consequential damages.

The hardware was delivered in December, 1974. Despite the presence of a programmer, sent by NCR, and continuing efforts to "cure" by NCR, only two of the programs, payroll and state taxes, functioned properly. The hardware furnished would not operate the other programs to satisfy Chatlos's needs. For example, the system could not delete selected information on a disc without deleting all of the information stored. Efforts to "cure" were discontinued in September, 1976.

Chatlos sued NCR for damages resulting from a breach of warranty. The district court awarded Chatlos damages of $57,153 under UCC 2–714(2), the difference between the value of the system as warranted, $75,783, and the value of the system delivered, $18,630. In addition, the district court awarded consequential and incidental damages of $63,560 under UCC 2–715, for a total recovery of $120,711.

On remand, the district court, on the basis of the previous record made in the case, fixed the fair market value of the NCR 399 as warranted at the time of acceptance at $207,826.50. It reached that figure by valuing a hypothetical system, i.e., the hardware that should have been supplied, at $131,250 and the software that would have functioned as warranted at $76,575.50, for a total of $207,826.50. The court then determined that the present value of the computer hardware, which Chatlos retained, was $6,000. Putting no value on the accepted payroll program, the court deducted the $6,000 and arrived at an award of $201,826.50 plus prejudgment interest of 8 percent. NCR appealed again to the Court of Appeals.]

PER CURIAM.

[The court stated that the question was whether the district court erred in its determination of damages under UCC 2–714(2), which provides: "The measure of damages for breach of warranty is the difference at the time and place of acceptance between the value of the goods accepted and the value they would have had if they had been as warranted, unless special circumstances show proximate damages of a different amount."]

* * *

Waiving the opportunity to submit additional evidence as to value on the remand which we directed, appellant chose to rely on the record of the original trial and submitted no expert testimony on the market value of a computer which would have performed the functions NCR had warranted. Notwithstanding our previous holding that contract price was not necessarily the same as market value, 635 F.2d at 1088, appellant faults the district judge for rejecting its contention that the contract price for the NCR 399/656 was the only competent record evidence of the value of the system as warranted. The district court relied instead on the testimony of plaintiff-appellee's expert, Dick

Brandon, who, without estimating the value of an NCR model 399/656, presented his estimate of the value of a computer system that would perform all of the functions that the NCR 399/656 had been warranted to perform. Brandon did not limit his estimate to equipment of any one manufacturer; he testified regarding manufacturers who could have made systems that would perform the functions that appellant had warranted the NCR 399/656 could perform. He acknowledged that the systems about which he testified were not in the same price range as the NCR 399/656. Appellant likens this testimony to substituting a Rolls Royce for a Ford, and concludes that the district court's recomputed damage award was therefore clearly contrary to the evidence of fair market value—which in NCR's view is the contract price itself.

Appellee did not order, nor was it promised, merely a specific NCR computer model, but an NCR computer system with specified capabilities. The correct measure of damages, under N.J.Stat.Ann. § 12A:2-714(2), is the difference between the fair market value of the goods accepted and the value they would have had if they had been as warranted. Award of that sum is not confined to instances where there has been an increase in value between date of ordering and date of delivery. It may also include the benefit of a contract price which, for whatever reason quoted, was particularly favorable for the customer. Evidence of the contract price may be relevant to the fair market value, but it is not controlling. Mulvaney v. Tri State Truck & Auto Body, Inc., 70 Wis.2d 760, 767, 235 N.W.2d 460, 465 (1975). Appellant limited its fair market value analysis to the contract price of the computer model it actually delivered.[3] Appellee developed evidence of the worth of a computer with the capabilities promised by NCR, and the trial court properly credited the evidence.[4]

Appellee was aided, moreover, by the testimony of Frank Hicks, NCR's programmer, who said that he told his company's officials that

3. At oral argument, counsel for appellant responded to questions from the bench, as follows:

Judge Rosenn: "Your position also is that you agree, number one, that the fair market value is the measure of damages here."

Counsel for Appellant: "Yes, sir."

Judge Rosenn: "The fair market value you say, in the absence of other evidence to the contrary that is relevant, is the contract price. That is the evidence of fair market value."

Counsel: "That's right."

Judge Rosenn: "Now seeing that had the expert or had the plaintiff been able to establish testimony that there were other machines on the market that were similar to your machine—"

Counsel: "Yes."

Judge Rosenn: "That the fair market value of those was $50,000, that would have been relevant evidence but it had to be the same machine—same type machine."

Counsel: "Well, I would say that the measure of damages as indicated by the statute requires the same machine—'the goods'—in an operable position."

4. We find the following analogy, rather than the Rolls Royce-Ford analogy submitted by appellant, to be on point:

Judge Weis: "If you start thinking about a piece of equipment that is warranted to lift a thousand pounds and it will only lift 500 pounds, then the cost of something that will lift a thousand pounds gives you more of an idea and that may be—"

Counsel for Appellee: "That may be a better analogy, yes."

Judge Weis: "Yes."

the "current software was not sufficient in order to deliver the program that the customer [Chatlos] required. They would have to be rewritten or a different system would have to be given to the customer." Appendix to Brief for Appellee at 2.68. Hicks recommended that Chatlos be given an NCR 8200 but was told, "that will not be done." Id. at 2.69. Gerald Greenstein, another NCR witness, admitted that the 8200 series was two levels above the 399 in sophistication and price. Id. at 14.30. This testimony supported Brandon's statement that the price of the hardware needed to perform Chatlos' requirements would be in the $100,000 to $150,000 range.

Essentially, then, the trial judge was confronted with the conflicting value estimates submitted by the parties. Chatlos' expert's estimates were corroborated to some extent by NCR's supporters. NCR, on the other hand, chose to rely on contract price. Credibility determinations had to be made by the district judge. Although we might have come to a different conclusion on the value of the equipment as warranted had we been sitting as trial judges, we are not free to make our own credibility and factual findings. We may reverse the district court only if its factual determinations were clearly erroneous. Krasnov v. Dinan, 465 F.2d 1298 (3d Cir.1972).[5]

Upon reviewing the evidence of record, therefore, we conclude that the computation of damages for breach of warranty was not clearly erroneous. We hold also that the district court acted within its discretion in awarding pre-judgment interest, Chatlos Systems, Inc. v. National Cash Register Corp., 635 F.2d at 1088.

The judgment of the district court will be affirmed.

ROSENN, CIRCUIT JUDGE, dissenting. The primary question in this appeal involves the application of Article 2 of the Uniform Commercial Code as adopted by New Jersey in N.J.S.A. 12A:2–101 et seq. (1962) to the measure of damages for breach of warranty in the sale of a computer system. I respectfully dissent because I believe there is no probative evidence to support the district court's award of damages for the breach of warranty in a sum amounting to almost five times the purchase price of the goods. The measure of damages also has been misapplied and this could have a significant effect in the marketplace, especially for the unique and burgeoning computer industry.

* * *

Chatlos contends before this court, as it had before the district court on remand, that under its benefit of the bargain theory the fair market value of the goods as warranted was several times the purchase price of $46,020. As the purchaser, Chatlos had the burden of proving the extent of the loss. Council Brothers, Inc. v. Ray Burner Co., 473 F.2d 400, 408 (5th Cir.1973). In remanding to the district court for a

---

5. The dissent essentially is based on disagreement with the estimates provided by Chatlos' expert, Brandon. The record reveals that he was well qualified; the weight to be given his testimony is the responsibility of the factfinder, not an appellate court.

reassessment of the damages, we did not reject the contract price for the goods sold as the proper valuation of the computer as warranted. We merely corrected the district court's misconception that the language of the New Jersey statute precluded consideration of fair market value. We held that "value" in § 2–714(2) must mean fair market value at the time and place of acceptance. We pointed out:

> "*It may be assumed that in many cases* fair market value and contract price are the same, and therefore, if a party wishes to show a difference between the two he should produce evidence to that effect."

Chatlos Systems, Inc. v. National Cash Register Corp., 635 F.2d 1081, 1088 (3d Cir.1980) (emphasis added) on remand, No. 77–2548 (D NJ. filed Mar. 12, 1981). Thus, the sole issue before us now is whether the district court erred in fixing the fair market value of the computer system as warranted at the time of acceptance in August 1975 at $207,826.50.

II.

A.

I believe that the district court committed legal error. The majority conclude that the standard of review of the district court's determination of the fair market value of the goods for the purpose of awarding damages is whether the trial judge's determination of market value is clearly erroneous. I disagree. Had the court merely miscalculated the amount of damages, I might agree with the majority's standard, for then our concern would be with basic facts. Here, however, no evidence was introduced as to the market value of the specific goods purchased and accepted had the system conformed to the warranty. Thus, the matter before us is one of legal error, and our standard of review is plenary. But even under the standard applied by the majority, the district court should be reversed because its determination of the market value is not supported by probative evidence.

There are a number of major flaws in the plaintiff's attempt to prove damages in excess of the contract price. I commence with an analysis of plaintiff's basic theory. Chatlos presented its case under a theory that although, as a sophisticated purchaser, it bargained for several months before arriving at a decision on the computer system it required and the price of $46,020, it is entitled, because of the breach of warranty, to damages predicated on a considerably more expensive system. Stated another way, even if it bargained for a cheap system, i.e., one whose low cost reflects its inferior quality, because that system did not perform as bargained for, it is now entitled to damages measured by the value of a system which, although capable of performing the identical functions as the NCR 399, is of far superior quality and accordingly more expensive.

The statutory measure of damages for breach of warranty specifically provides that the measure is the difference at the time and place of acceptance between the value "of the goods accepted" and the "value they would have had if they had been as warranted." The focus of the statute is upon "the goods accepted"—not other hypothetical goods which may perform equivalent functions. "Moreover, the value to be considered is the reasonable market value of the *goods delivered,* not the value of the goods to a particular purchaser or for a particular purpose." KLPR–TV, Inc. v. Visual Electronics Corp., 465 F.2d 1382, 1387 (8th Cir.1972) (emphasis added). The court, however, arrived at value on the basis of a hypothetical construction of a system as of December 1978 by the plaintiff's expert, Brandon. The court reached its value by working backward from Brandon's figures, adjusting for inflation.

In presenting its case Chatlos developed its expert testimony as though it were seeking "cover" damages—the cost for the replacement of the computer system under § 2–712 of the statute. First, "cover" damages are obviously inappropriate here because both the district court and this court in its earlier decision held that the measure of damages is governed by section 2–714(2). Furthermore, Chatlos did not "cover" in this case and, although there was testimony that it would use an IBM Series 1 mini-computer to perform the NCR 399 functions, the president of Chatlos personally testified that the IBM "wasn't purchased with intent to replace the 399 system at the time of purchase." Second, Chatlos gave no evidence as to the cost of the IBM Series 1 computer system. However, under the applicable section of the statute, § 2–714, the measure of damages is specifically confined to "the difference between the value of the *goods accepted* and the value they would have had if they had been as warranted" and does not include "the difference between the cost of *cover* and the contract price" as provided by § 2–712.

Although NCR warranted performance, the failure of its equipment to perform, absent any evidence of the value of any NCR 399 system on which to base fair market value, does not permit a market value based on systems wholly unrelated to the goods sold. Yet, instead of addressing the fair market value of the NCR 399 had it been as warranted, Brandon addressed the fair market value of another system that he concocted by drawing on elements from other major computer systems manufactured by companies such as IBM, Burroughs, and Honeywell, which he considered would perform "functions identical to those contracted for" by Chatlos. He conceded that the systems were "[p]erhaps not within the same range of dollars that the bargain was involved with" and he did not identify specific packages of software. Brandon had no difficulty in arriving at the fair market value of the inoperable NCR equipment but instead of fixing a value on the system had it been operable attempted to fashion a hypothetical system on which he placed a value. The district court, in turn, erroneously adopted that value as the fair market value for an operable NCR 399 system. NCR rightly contends that the "comparable" systems on which Brandon drew were substitute goods of greater technological power and capability and not acceptable in determining damages for breach of warranty under § 2–714. Furthermore, Brandon's hypothetical system did not exist and its valuation was largely speculation.

* * *

III.

The purpose of the N.J.S.A. 12A:2–714 is to put the buyer in the same position he would have been in if there had been no breach. See Uniform Commercial Code § 1–106(1). The remedies for a breach of warranty were intended to compensate the buyer for his loss; they were not intended to give the purchaser a windfall or treasure trove. The buyer may not receive more than it bargained for; it may not obtain the value of a superior computer system which it did not purchase even though such a system can perform all of the functions the inferior system was designed to serve. Thus, in Meyers v. Antone, 227 A.2d 56 (D.C.App.1967), the court held that where the buyers contracted for a properly functioning used oil heating system which proved defective, they were free to substitute a gas system (which they did), change over to forced air heating, or even experiment with a solar heating plant. "They could not, however, recover the cost of such systems. They contracted for a used oil system that would function properly, and can neither receive more than they bargained for nor be put in a better position than they would have been had the contract been fully performed." Id. at 59 (citations omitted).

This court, in directing consideration of fair market value as the starting point in deciding damages noted Chatlos' contention that exclusive use of contract price deprives the dissatisfied buyer of the "benefit of his bargain." We accepted the concept of "benefit of the bargain" and explicated our understanding of the concept as follows:

"If the value of the goods rises between the time the contract is executed and the time of acceptance, the buyer should not lose the advantage of a favorable contract price because of the seller's breach of warranty. Conversely, if the value drops, the seller is entitled to the resulting lower computation."

Chatlos, supra, 635 F.2d at 1088. Ironically, this example of benefit of the bargain is actually based on contract price. If on the date of acceptance the fair market value of the goods has risen or declined from the contract price, the variation must be taken into account in awarding damages. But here plaintiff's market value figures, accepted by the district court on remand, have no connection whatsoever with the contract price.

Although it may be that the "benefit of the bargain" concept is applicable to situations involving other than periodic fluctuations in market prices, the cases cited by Chatlos stand only for the premise that the proved market value of the goods in question must be accepted.

* * *

Even if we were to accept plaintiff's theory that the value of other systems may be used to establish the value of the specific computer system purchased, the cases cited by Chatlos to support its theory are distinguishable.   *   *   *

Because Brandon's testimony does not support Chatlos' grossly extravagant claim of the fair market value of the NCR 399 at the time of its acceptance, the only evidence of the market value at the time is the price negotiated by the parties for the NCR computer system as warranted.

> There are many cases in which the goods will be irreparable or not replaceable and therefore the costs of repair or replacement can not serve as a yardstick of the buyer's damages.   *   *   * When fair market value cannot be easily determined * * * the purchase price may turn out to be strong evidence of the value of the goods as warranted.

J. White & R. Summers, Uniform Commercial Code § 10–2, at 380 (2d ed. 1980) (footnotes omitted).

*   *   *

Thus, where there is no proof that market value of the goods differs from the contract price, the contract price will govern, * * * and in this case that amounts to $46,020. Chatlos has retained the system hardware and the district court fixed its present value in the open market at $6,000. The court properly deducted this sum from the damages awarded.

*   *   *

VI.

On this record, therefore, the damages to which plaintiff is entitled are $46,020 less $6,000, the fair market value at time of trial of the retained hardware, and less $1,000, the fair market value of the payroll program, or the net sum of $39,020.

Accordingly, I would reverse the judgment of the district court and direct it to enter judgment for the plaintiff in the sum of $39,020 with interest from the date of entry of the initial judgment at the rate allowed by state law. [some footnotes omitted.]

HILL v. BASF WYANDOTTE CORP.

Supreme Court of South Carolina, 1984.
280 S.C. 174, 311 S.E.2d 734.

LITTLEJOHN, JUSTICE:

This case comes before us as a certified question from the United States District Court, District of South Carolina, pursuant to Supreme Court Rule 46.

The question presented is as follows:

> Given the distinction between (1) actual or direct and (2) consequential damages as set forth in §§ 36–2–714 and 36–2–715 of

the South Carolina Code of Laws, 1976, as amended, what is the measure of actual damages in a herbicide failure case where there is a valid limitation of consequential, special or indirect damages?

This is a breach of warranty case involving an alleged herbicide failure which caused crop damage.

Plaintiff Hill (Farmer) purchased a quantity of the herbicide, Basalin, from a retail distributor. Basalin is manufactured by defendant BASF Wyandotte Corporation (BWC).

Among other things, to each can of Basalin there were attached the following statements:

1) "BWC" warrants that this product conforms to the chemical description on the label and is reasonably fit for the purpose referred to in the Directions for Use subject to the inherent risks referred to above.

2) In no case shall "BWC" or the Seller be liable for consequential, special or indirect damages resulting from the use or handling of this product, and

3) Read "CONDITIONS OF SALE AND WARRANTY" before buying or using. If terms are not acceptable, return product at once, unopened.

Farmer alleges that he used Basalin on approximately 1,450 acres of soybeans and another herbicide, Treflan, on approximately 200 acres. He further alleges that although there was a severe drought that year, the Treflan treated crops were significantly better than the Basalin crops both in quality and yield per acre.

Farmer initially brought suit in United States District Court on oral and written warranties for damages. A jury awarded him $207,725.00. BWC appealed and the Fourth Circuit Court of Appeals reversed and remanded the case, holding that only the written warranties on the labels of the product apply and that the limitation of remedies quoted above is valid. *Hill v. BASF Wyandotte Corp.*, 696 F.2d 287 (4th Cir.1982).

In footnote 6 the court stated:

We express no opinion as to whether under subsections (1) and (2) of § 36–2–714 and on the evidence that may be adduced on retrial the appropriate measure of damages would be the purchase price of the herbicide or some other measure.

This question was certified to us by the trial court after remand.

Ordinarily, *S.C.Code Ann.* § 36–2–714(2) (1976) is controlling as the measure of damages in a breach of warranty case. This section provides:

(2) The measure of damages for breach of warranty is the difference at the time and place of acceptance between the value of the goods accepted and the value they would have had if they had

been as warranted, *unless special circumstances show proximate damages of a different amount.* (Emphasis added.)

We find that the formula in this subsection is inapplicable to a herbicide failure case. This formula is most appropriate where the nonconforming good can be repaired or replaced and value (both as warranted and as accepted) can be defined with certainty.

A herbicide failure is a latent defect in the product. There is no reasonable way a farmer can determine in advance whether a herbicide will perform as warranted. Discovery of the problem must await the development of the crop at which time it is usually too late to correct.

The value of a herbicide as warranted is difficult to define. Price and value are not equivalents. From the farmer's perspective, the value of the herbicide is a healthy crop at maturity. In the manufacturer's viewpoint, the value is its selling price.

The value as accepted is equally uncertain and difficult to define. There is no market for such goods and thus no market price. If anything, it has a negative value.

In our view, the inability of a court to ascertain with certainty the value of goods both as warranted and as accepted creates a special circumstance within the meaning of § 36–2–714(2). It is this special circumstance which removes cases of this type from the § 36–2–714(2) measure of damages into subsection (1).

Subsection (1) provides:

(1) Where the buyer has accepted goods and given notification (subsection (3) of § 36–2–607) he may recover as damages for any nonconformity of tender the loss resulting in the ordinary course of events from the seller's breach as determined in any manner which is reasonable.

Official Comment 2 to § 36–2–714 indicates that subsection (1) is applicable in breach of warranty cases.

It has consistently been held by this Court that the measure of actual damages, in cases similar to this, is the value the crop would have had if the product had conformed to the warranty less the value of the crop actually produced, less the expense of preparing for market the portion of the probable crop prevented from maturing. *See, McCown Clark Co. v. Muldrow,* 116 S.C. 54, 106 S.E. 771 (1929); *Amerson v. F.C.X. Co–Op Service,* 227 S.C. 520, 88 S.E.2d 605 (1955); *W.R. Grace and Co. v. LaMunion,* 245 S.C. 1, 138 S.E.2d 337 (1964) and *Simmons v. Ciba–Geigy Corp.,* 279 S.C. 26, 302 S.E.2d 17 (1983). *See also, Klein v. Asgrow Seed Co.,* 246 Cal.App.2d 87, 54 Cal.Rptr. 609, 620 (1966). We hold this formula to be appropriate in the present case.

BWC has argued that this formula includes lost profits and that lost profits are a consequential damage barred by the limitation of remedies on the cans of Basalin. We disagree.

In *W.R. Grace and Co., supra,* it was noted that the ". . . destruction or loss of a mature crop, which has a realizable value in excess of the cost of harvesting, processing and marketing, results in a monetary loss to the owner, regardless of whether the farming operation would, otherwise, have been profitable."

If the measure of damages we have adopted includes an element of lost profits, such inclusion is merely coincidental as the measure covers the direct loss resulting in the ordinary course of events from the alleged breach of the warranty. *See,* § 36–2–714(1).

The foregoing is the order of this Court.

LEWIS, C.J., and NESS, GREGORY and HARWELL, JJ., concur.

Notes

1. In Martin v. Joseph Harris Co., Inc., 767 F.2d 296 (6th Cir.1985), the plaintiffs purchased and planted cabbage seed infected with "black leg" fungus from the defendant. When the condition was discovered, plaintiffs took action to minimize the damage but still lost a "large portion" of their cabbage crop. Because of the high demand for cabbage, caused by the "black leg" epidemic, plaintiffs were able to sell the smaller cabbage crop at a profit equal to or higher than in previous years. Defendant argued that there is "no breach of the implied warranty of merchantability where there is no economic loss." Although "black leg" was damaging the plaintiffs' cabbage, the "law of supply and demand was making them * * * whole."

The court of appeals affirmed the district court's conclusion that the defendant's attempt to disclaim warranties and exclude liability for consequential damages was unconscionable. The court also affirmed the district court's decision to uphold a jury verdict of $52,000 for the plaintiffs.

"(W)e are persuaded by the district court's finding that the defendant's sale of diseased seed to these two plaintiffs did not create the increased market price. Similarly, we note that [they] purchased some healthy seed from other companies and some other farmers produced completely healthy crops. To further complicate the problem, there was evidence to the effect that the black leg epidemic was partially caused by the sale of diseased seed by other merchants and, thus, the rise in the market price of cabbage did not result entirely from Harris Seed's breach. Therefore, following the dictates of U.C.C. 1–106(1). * * * in order to put Martin and Rick in the same position as many of their neighboring farmers who purchased healthy seed, we hold that the proper measure of damages as applied by the district court is the difference in value between the cabbage crops actually raised by these plaintiffs and the cabbage crops that they would have raised if their seed had not been diseased." [767 F.2d at 302–03.]

2. In *Chatlos* the court enforced the clause excluding liability for consequential damages and awarded the buyer rather extravagant "direct" damages under UCC 2–714(2). In *Hill,* the court enforced the clause excluding liability for consequential damages and awarded the buyer the net value of the lost crop as "direct" damages under UCC 2–714(1). In

Martin, the court invalidated the clause excluding liability for consequential damages and awarded damages for the net value of the lost crop, citing UCC 1–106(1) but not UCC 2–714 or 2–715. Assuming that the excluder clauses were not enforceable in all three cases, how should the damages claimed be classified, as "direct" or "consequential?"

SECTION 3. INCIDENTAL AND CONSEQUENTIAL DAMAGES: UCC 2–715

Commercial buyers purchase goods for use, perhaps to resell to customers or to consume in the business. If accepted goods fail to conform to warranties made, the buyer's planned use of the goods may be impaired. Put differently, a result of the breach may be that the buyer is deprived of the use of the goods during the time when they are being repaired or replaced.

Damages resulting from loss of use are called consequential damages and are recoverable under UCC 2–714(3) & 2–715(2). They may be recovered without proof of either "special circumstances" or a "tacit agreement" of the seller to assume them, see R.I. Lampus Co. v. Neville Cement Products Corp., 474 Pa. 199, 378 A.2d 288 (1977), if four conditions are satisfied:

(1) The loss results "from general or particular requirements and needs of which the seller at the time of contracting had reason to know," UCC 2–715(2)(a). Compare UCC 2–315 and the *Chatlos* case.

(2) The buyer has mitigated damages, i.e., the loss "could not reasonably be prevented by cover or otherwise," UCC 2–715(2)(a). The burden is on the seller to prove that the buyer failed to mitigate. Cates v. Morgan Portable Building Corp., 780 F.2d 683 (7th Cir.1985). But see International Petrol. Serv., Inc. v. S & N Well Serv., 230 Kan. 452, 639 P.2d 29, 38 (1982) (burden of proving mitigation on buyer).

(3) The breach was the substantial cause in fact of the loss. Compare UCC 2–715(2)(b). Overstreet v. Norden Laboratories, Inc., 669 F.2d 1286 (6th Cir.1982) (no proof that allegedly defective vaccine caused mares to abort foals).

(4) The type and amount of loss is proved by the buyer with reasonable certainty. Horizons, Inc. v. Avco Corp., 714 F.2d 862 (8th Cir.1983).

The conditions are easy to state. Applying them is another matter.

NEZPERCE STORAGE CO. v. ZENNER

Supreme Court of Idaho, 1983.
105 Idaho 464, 670 P.2d 871.

[In March, 1976, Zenner, a wheat farmer, sold Nezperce 2,000 bushels of "spring" wheat. Nezperce resold a portion of the wheat to eight farmers. Six weeks after planting, it became obvious that some of the wheat was not maturing and that the seed had been a mixture of spring and winter wheat. Since winter wheat requires several weeks of freezing weather to mature, the farmers suffered a crop failure. Nezperce settled the farmer's claims for $84,000 and brought suit against Zenner for indemnification.

Zenner, who grew both winter and spring wheat, had harvested his crop in August, 1975 and, according to his testimony, stored it in different bins over the winter. The Winter of 1975–76 was severe and much of the winter wheat planted in the previous fall was killed. A shortage of spring wheat developed, of which Zenner was aware at the time of the sale to Nezperce. Zenner also knew that Nezperce was purchasing his wheat to meet the shortage of spring wheat in the Camas Prairie area.

Nezperce cleaned and bagged the wheat without mixing it with another variety. Nezperce performed a successful "germination" to determine if the seed would grow but did not conduct other tests, i.e., a "grow out" test or an electrofloresis test, to determine if the seed was in fact spring wheat. The evidence was conflicting as to whether either test was available or practical.

The jury returned a verdict that Zenner had made and breached an express warranty and that Nezperce should recover the amount of the settlement made with the farmers.]

* * *

Although many of the allegations of the Nezperce complaint and the Zenners' counterclaim were disputed at trial, the essential arguments upon this appeal are the Zenners' assertions of error relating to the findings of the jury that Joseph Zenner was aware of the shortage of spring wheat seed in the Camas Prairie area and that he knew or had reason to know that Nezperce was purchasing his wheat for processing into spring wheat seed for resale to its customers; that the award of consequential damages was improper and that Nezperce did not reasonably mitigate its damages by testing the seed.

The propriety of awarding consequential damages in the instant case is governed by I.C. § 28–2–715(2)(a), which provides in pertinent part:

"(2) Consequential damages resulting from the seller's breach include

(a) Any loss resulting from general or particular requirements and needs of which the seller at the time of contracting had reason to know and which could not reasonably be prevented by cover or otherwise. * * *"

Clearly, Nezperce sustained a "loss" in reimbursing its customers for the damages they suffered by purchasing and planting seed which was not spring wheat. In a breach of warranty action, indemnification for this kind of a loss is proper when a seller such as Nezperce receives a warranty from a supplier such as Zenner and passes that warranty on to customers. * * *

As stated in *Clark v. International Harvester Co.,* 99 Idaho 326, 346, 581 P.2d 784, 804 (1978), "there are certain limitations on the right to recover consequential damages under § 28–2–715(2)(a). First, the losses must have resulted from needs which the seller knew or had reason to know at the time of contracting." Here the special interrogatories returned by the jury indicate that Zenner was aware of the shortage of spring wheat seed in the Camas Prairie area and that Zenner had reason to realize that "Nezperce Storage Company's purpose in purchasing MP–1 wheat was to meet an apparent shortage of spring wheat seed on the Camas Prairie," and that Zenner had reason to know that Nezperce was buying the wheat from Zenner to process it into spring wheat seed for resale. Those findings are supported by substantial, albeit conflicting, evidence, and therefore they will not be disturbed on appeal. I.R.C.P. 52(a); *Ellis v. Northwest Fruit & Produce,* 103 Idaho 821, 654 P.2d 914 (1982); *Jolley v. Clay,* 103 Idaho 171, 646 P.2d 413 (1982); *Rueth v. State,* 103 Idaho 74, 644 P.2d 1333 (1982). Hence, the foreseeability requirement of I.C. § 28–2–715(2)(a) has been satisfied.

The propriety of an award of consequential damages must also satisfy the second condition of I.C. § 28–2–715(2)(a), *i.e.,* that they could not have been *reasonably* prevented by cover or otherwise. As to this condition, the Court in *Clark v. International Harvester Co.,* 99 Idaho 326, 347, 581 P.2d 784, 805 (1978), held that "the plaintiffs were only required to take reasonable efforts to mitigate their damages, [citation] and the burden of proving that the damages could have been minimized was on the defendants". In *S.J. Groves & Sons Co. v. Warner Co.,* 576 F.2d 524, 528 (3rd Cir.1978), it was held that, in an action to recover consequential damages under the same UCC provision, "[t]he requirement of * * * mitigation of damages is not an absolute, unyielding one, but is subject to the circumstances," and "[t]he test for plaintiff's efforts [to mitigate damages] is reasonableness * * *." *Id.,* at n. 5. In the instant case the Zenners presented testimony attempting to convince the jury that Nezperce could have mitigated or avoided its consequential damages by subjecting the seed to tests to determine seed variety prior to the time it resold the seed to its customers. As indicated in *West v. Whitney-Fidalgo Seafoods, Inc.,* 628 P.2d 10 (Alaska 1981), and *AES Technology Systems, Inc. v. Coherent Radiation,* 583 F.2d 933 (7th Cir.1978), the question of whether Nezperce acted properly to mitigate its damages is a factual matter to be determined by the trier of the fact. Here the jury specifically found:

> "it [was] reasonable for plaintiff Nezperce Storage to sell the seed it manufactured from the Zenner wheat to its customers without doing any more than the facts show it did do to determine whether or not such seed was actually of a spring wheat variety."

That finding is supported by substantial, albeit conflicting, testimony and will not be disturbed on appeal. I.R.C.P. 52(a); *Ellis v. Northwest Fruit & Produce, supra; Jolley v. Clay, supra; Rueth v. State, supra.*

The Zenners argue that the finding of the jury should be disregarded because the jury was not properly instructed as to what a "reasonable man" would have done in that the court failed to give Zenners' submitted instructions regarding negligence per se. We disagree and find no error in the refusal of the trial court to give Zenners' requested instructions. In the instant case we need not decide whether negligence per se can ever be used to limit a party's consequential damages under I.C. § 28–2–715(2)(a). While a court may adopt the requirements of a legislative enactment as the standard of conduct of a reasonable man, *Brizendine v. Nampa Meridian Irrigation Dist.,* 97 Idaho 580, 548 P.2d 80 (1976), that doctrine is ordinarily applied in negligence actions where a plaintiff has suffered injury by a defendant who was in violation of a statute or ordinance. However,

> "In order for the violation of a statute to be pertinent in a particular case, the statute must be * * * designed to protect (1) the class of persons in which the plaintiff is included (2) against the type of harm which has in fact occurred as a result of its violation." *Kinney v. Smith,* 95 Idaho 328, 331, 508 P.2d 1234, 1237 (1973); *Anderson v. Blackfoot Livestock Commission Co.,* 85 Idaho 64, 375 P.2d 704 (1962); *Curoe v. Spokane Etc. R.R. Co.,* 32 Idaho 643, 186 P. 1101 (1920); *W. PROSSER, LAW OF TORTS* § 36 (4th ed. 1971).

The statute at issue, I.C. § 22–417(3), imposes penalties upon one who sells seeds which are incorrectly labeled when the person selling the seed "has failed to obtain an invoice or growers declaration giving kind, or kind and variety * * * and to take such other precautions as may be necessary to insure the identity to be that stated." We deem it clear and obvious that, in the instant case, the statute was designed to protect the following class of persons: those customers who purchased the seed from Nezperce. Cases construing similar seed laws, *e.g., Agr. Services Ass'n, Inc. v. Ferry-Morse Seed Co., Inc.,* 551 F.2d 1057 (6th Cir. 1977), and *Klein v. Asgrow Seed Co.,* 246 Cal.App.2d 87, 54 Cal.Rptr. 609 (1966), have so held. Equally clearly, the statute was not designed to provide protection to the Zenners, who can best be described as suppliers of mislabeled seed. Hence, we deem the statute and the doctrine of negligence per se in the instant case irrelevant. *See also S.J. Groves & Sons Co. v. Warner, supra,* which states:

> "Where both the plaintiff and the defendant have had equal opportunity to reduce the damages by the same act and it is equally reasonable to expect the defendant to minimize damages, the defendant is in no position to contend that the plaintiff failed to mitigate. Nor will the award be reduced on account of damages the defendant could have avoided as easily as the plaintiff." At page 530; *See also Shea—S & M Ball v. Massman—Kiewit—Early,* 606 F.2d 1245 (D.C.Cir.1979).

* * *

The judgment of the district court is affirmed. Costs to respondents. No attorney fees allowed.

Notes

1. Suppose Zenner warranted the wheat to be spring wheat, knew that Nezperce intended to resell it to his customers but was unaware of the shortage of spring wheat seed in the Camas Prairie area. Should that alter the result in this case?

2. Suppose that Zenner sold and delivered grain described as "spring wheat" to Nezperce in the Fall of 1975 at $5.00 per bushel. Nezperce immediately resold 50% to customers for April, 1976 delivery at $6.00 per bushel. All of the Zenner wheat was stored together. In March, after the big chill, the price of spring wheat had risen to $20. Nezperce resold the balance to customers for $22 per bushel. Nezperce then had an electroforesis test performed on a sample of Zenner wheat and discovered that it was mixed substantially with winter wheat. Nezperce promptly purchased replacement spring wheat in the open market for $22 per bushel, which was delivered to customers, and sold the Zenner wheat for $5 per bushel. What damages should Nezperce recover for Zenner's breach of warranty?

3. How does the Code treat expenditures made by the buyer after the breach is discovered? If they are made to repair or replace the nonconforming goods, they may be recoverable as "direct" damages under UCC 2–714(2): Repair or replacement costs are frequently used to measure the value of the goods as warranted. In addition to *Soo Line,* see Vista St. Clair, Inc. v. Landry's Commercial Furnishings, Inc., 57 Or.App. 254, 643 P.2d 1378 (1982). If they are made to avoid losses or to pursue permissible remedies, they may be "incidental" damages under UCC 2–715(1). Or, they may be "consequential" damages under UCC 2–715(2)(a). How is the line to be drawn between incidental and consequential damages? The question is important, for incidental damages need not satisfy all the conditions for the recovery of consequential damages and will not be covered by clauses in the contract purporting to exclude the seller's liability for consequential damages. See, e.g., Reynolds Metals Co. v. Westinghouse Elec. Corp., 758 F.2d 1073 (5th Cir.1985).

4. The buyer's claim for consequential damages caused by the seller's delay or nondelivery is treated in Chapter Eight, Section 6.

LEWIS v. MOBIL OIL CORP.

United States Court of Appeals, Eighth Circuit, 1971.
438 F.2d 500.

[The facts and the decision on the warranty issue in this case are reprinted in Section 3(c) of Chapter 19. We now turn to the damages issues.]

* * *

III. DAMAGES

The question with which we are here confronted is what damages are recoverable by the plaintiff for the defendant's breach of warranty. The applicable statutes are §§ 2–714(2), (3) and 2–715 of the Uniform

Commercial Code, 7C Ark.Stats.Ann. §§ 85–2–714(2), (3), 85–2–715 (1961), which provide in pertinent part: [The court quoted UCC 2–714(2) and (3) and UCC 2–715.]

* * *

In the instant case the ordinary measure of damages for breach of warranty is not applicable, since the plaintiff-buyer did not pay a price exceeding the value of the goods delivered. Rather, since the breach was of an implied warranty of fitness for a particular purpose, the "special circumstances" exception is applicable here. The proximate damages in this case consisted of the plaintiff's incidental and consequential damages which may be recoverable. The incidental damages consist of the excessive amounts of oil used in the system and the costs incurred in the repair and replacement of mechanical parts damaged by the oil's failing to function properly. There is no controversy between the parties as to the allowability of these damages. There are two major points of controversy on damages: (1) for what period of time are damages recoverable and (2) whether loss of profits during the time plaintiff was unable to operate at full capacity are recoverable.

[The court first rejected plaintiff's "unique" theory that damages should be recoverable for the period of time after the correct oil was used and the system was operating satisfactorily. Plaintiff had argued that the drain on his financial resources during the period of difficulty had restricted his ability to operate at 100% capacity later on. In the view of the court, the cause of this condition was inadequate capitalization not breach of warranty and the proper remedy was a bank loan at the time not damages in subsequent litigation.]

* * *

A more troublesome question is whether the plaintiff should be allowed to recover damages for the full two and one-half year period during which he was using Ambrex 810. Under § 2–715(2)(a) of the Uniform Commercial Code, only those losses are recoverable "which could not reasonably be prevented by cover or otherwise." 7C Ark.Stat. Ann. § 85–2–715 (1961). The "cover" provision of the Uniform Commercial Code, § 2–712, is not applicable here, since that section applies to the buyer's remedies upon failure of the seller to deliver goods or upon the rightful rejection of goods known to be defective. Hence the question here is whether the plaintiff's damage could otherwise have been reasonably prevented. The applicable doctrine is stated by Professor Williston:

"* * * [D]amages which the plaintiff might have avoided with reasonable effort without undue risk, expense, or humiliation are either not caused by the defendant's wrong or need not have been, and, therefore, are not to be charged against him.

"The principle has wide application and frequently involves the establishment of a standard of reasonable conduct.

* * *

"Where inferior goods have been furnished under a contract, the buyer cannot recover greater consequential damages caused by using them when he knew of their unfitness, than would have been caused by another possible course, although the seller had sold the goods for that purpose. And the principle is general that there can be no recovery for consequences that reasonably could have been avoided." 11 S. Williston, Contracts § 1353 (Jaeger, 3d ed. 1968) (footnotes omitted). * * *

Defendant's argument on this issue is not precise, but the gist of its complaint is that the plaintiff used Ambrex 810 for a period of two and one-half years, during which time there was at least some suspicion that the oil was not functioning properly, and that plaintiff should have taken steps to solve his problems sooner than he did. It is unclear to us whether or not the defendant is contending that the plaintiff used Ambrex 810 with actual knowledge of its unfitness, so as to preclude at least in part his recovery of damages caused by its use. If such is the claim, it is clearly refuted by the evidence. Neither plaintiff nor the Mobil dealer who sold him Ambrex 810 knew the chemical composition of the oil nor what the exact requirements of plaintiff's equipment were. Plaintiff was relying on Mobil to provide him with the proper oil and it was not discovered during that time that the oil was improper. Indeed, plaintiff changed the brand of pump he was using because of the possibility that the problem was mechanical. It was not until a Mobil engineer visited the mill and changed the type of oil recommended that it was discovered that an improper oil had been supplied.

Neither does the defendant precisely phrase its argument in terms of a failure to give timely notice under Ark.Stat.Ann. § 85–2–607, although it relies on an Arkansas case under this section, Ingle v. Marked Tree Equipment Co., 244 Ark. 1166, 428 S.W.2d 286 (1968). However, it seems that under the circumstances of this case, the reasonable notice required by this section was given by the plaintiff. * * *

* * *

Here there is not the slightest suggestion of bad faith on the part of the plaintiff. Furthermore the evidence shows that soon after using Ambrex 810, plaintiff notified the Mobil dealer, Rowe, that he wasn't sure if a proper oil was being supplied, and was constantly in touch with Rowe about his problems thereafter. Mobil certainly had notice that the "transaction [was] still troublesome and must be watched." Defendant continued to supply Ambrex 810. Therefore we cannot conclude that any damages must be barred under this section. See Boeing Airplane Co. v. O'Malley, 329 F.2d 585, 593–596 (8th Cir.1964). The trial judge properly instructed the jury that the plaintiff must have notified the defendant within a reasonable time after he should have discovered the breach, and we cannot say that the jury's verdict was erroneous in this respect.

The only way in which it would have been possible for plaintiff's damages to have been minimized in this case would have been for him to have brought in an independent expert to assess the cause of his trouble. While such a course might have been desirable, and would probably have saved both plaintiff and defendant considerable expense, we cannot say that failure to do so requires a reduction of damages allowable under § 2–715 of the Uniform Commercial Code as a matter of law. This is essentially a question of the plaintiff's duty to use diligence to minimize his damages, which is ordinarily a question of fact for the jury. The trial judge properly instructed the jury that plaintiff had the duty to use diligence to minimize his damages, that defendant was not liable for any damages which resulted from plaintiff's failure to minimize his damages, and that diligence meant the care of a reasonably careful person under the circumstances of the case. The jury's verdict reflects its finding that the plaintiff had acted reasonably in these circumstances, and again we cannot say that it lacks evidentiary support.

Plaintiff was in continuous contact with both the manufacturer of his equipment and with the defendant in an effort to ascertain the cause of his problems. Various remedies were tried and failed until the oil problem was ultimately identified. Throughout this period, defendant continued to supply plaintiff with Ambrex 810, knowing both of his reliance on it to supply the proper oil and his difficulties in operation. Thus we do not think that defendant can rely on plaintiff's failure to obtain an independent opinion to absolve it of liability for its breach of warranty. "The duty to mitigate damages is not an unlimited one * * *." Steele v. J.I. Case Company, 197 Kan. 554, 419 P.2d 902, 911 (1966). We conclude that defendant should be liable for all of plaintiff's damages during the period he was using Ambrex 810.

The final question to be determined is whether under Arkansas law, loss of profits may be recovered as consequential damages for breach of warranty. Defendant relies on a series of Arkansas cases which stand for the proposition that loss of profits cannot be recovered unless the circumstances of the transaction are such as to make it reasonable to assume that the defendant knew he was to be held responsible for such damages and agreed to such liability. See Hawkins v. Delta Spindle of Blytheville, Inc., 245 Ark. 830, 434 S.W.2d 825 (1968); Lamkins v. International Harvester Co., 207 Ark. 637, 182 S.W.2d 203 (1944); Hooks Smelting Co. v. Planters' Compress Co., 72 Ark. 275, 79 S.W. 1052 (1904). The problem with this argument is that all of these cases are non-Code cases which rely on a rule which is expressly rejected by the Uniform Commercial Code Official Commentary to § 2–715:

> "2. * * * The 'tacit agreement' test for the recovery of consequential damages is rejected. * * *

> "3. * * * It is not necessary that there be a conscious acceptance of an insurer's liability on the seller's part, nor is his

obligation for consequential damages limited to cases in which he fails to use due effort in good faith.

"Particular needs of the buyer must generally be made known to the seller while general needs must rarely be made known to charge the seller with knowledge.

"Any seller who does not wish to take the risk of consequential damages has available the section on contractual limitation of remedy." 7C Ark.Stat.Ann. § 85–2–715, Comments 2 and 3 (1961).

The question essentially is whether lost profits are damages which the seller had reason to know of at the time the contract was made. With respect to breach of warranty, lost profits are held to be foreseeable if they are proximately caused by and are the natural result of the breach. 5 A. Corbin, Contracts § 1012 (1964); Seely v. White Motor Co., 63 Cal.2d 9, 45 Cal.Rptr. 17, 403 P.2d 145, 148–149 (1965). Cf. Superwood Corp. v. Larson-Stang, Inc., 311 F.2d 735 (8th Cir.1963). Where a seller provides goods to a manufacturing enterprise with knowledge that they are to be used in the manufacturing process, it is reasonable to assume that he should know that defective goods will cause a disruption of production, and loss of profits is a natural consequence of such disruption. Hence, loss of profits should be recoverable under those circumstances. Here, the defendant seller knew that the oil it was supplying to plaintiff was to be used in the operation of the sawmill. It also knew that a defective oil would cause the sawmill equipment to operate improperly. It is a natural consequence of the failure of the equipment to function that production would be curtailed and loss of profits would follow. See 5 A. Corbin, Contracts § 1013, p. 92 (1964). We think these damages are the proximate result of the breach and should be recoverable.

Most jurisdictions which have considered the question of the recoverability of lost profits under the Uniform Commercial Code for a breach of warranty in circumstances similar to those in the instant case seem to have allowed them. * * *

We think Arkansas would follow this rule. * * *

* * *

Defendant also contends there was no proper proof of lost profits in this case, and that the damages were purely speculative. We do not agree. While it is true that the damages were excessive in this case because they were allowed for an improper time period, we do not think that the method utilized was unreasonable under the circumstances of this case. First of all, the plaintiff offered considerable evidence that there was a substantial market for his lumber which he was not able to supply. Evidence was offered of a number of customers who testified they would have bought more of his lumber had it been available. A substantial part of plaintiff's business was done as an exclusive supplier of timbers to a bridge building company. Plaintiff was the only sawmill operator who would furnish these timbers with the close tolerances demanded; he was unable to supply all of that customer's needs.

In addition to this market evidence, there is evidence of the profits made by his business both before and after using Ambrex 810. These were substantial, even in the later period when he was unable to operate at full capacity. During the period he was using Ambrex 810 they were significantly less, due to the lost production and added expenses. Past profits of an established business may be utilized to prove loss of profits as an element of damages. 5 A. Corbin, Contracts § 1023 (1964); 11 S. Williston, Contracts § 1346A (Jaeger, 3d ed. 1968). And under the circumstances of this case, we think the jury was entitled to take account of the profits earned by plaintiff once the business was operating successfully after the breach of warranty. While the lost profits could not be proved with absolute certainty of course, we think a reasonable approximation can be made from the evidence in this case.

To summarize our decision in this case, having reviewed the evidence as a whole and the instructions of the able trial judge, we conclude that there was a warranty of fitness for a particular purpose in this case, that the warranty was breached, and that the defendant was liable for the damages caused by this breach, including loss of profits during the time plaintiff was using Ambrex 810. Defendant is not liable for any loss of profits which may have occurred after plaintiff quit using Ambrex 810. The jury's verdict was in the single amount of $89,250. We are unable to determine from the record what would be a proper amount to award for direct damages plus loss of profits for the appropriate time period. Therefore, the judgment must be reversed and remanded for a new trial on the issue of damages.

On Petitions for Rehearing

The petitions for rehearing of both the appellant and the appellee raise questions as to the issue of damages for loss of profits which merit some further comment. At the outset, we would note that the record and the arguments are not entirely clear as to how this element of damages was submitted in this particular case. While we adhere to our opinion that loss of profits is a proper element of damages in a case of this sort, these damages must of course be proved with a certain degree of specificity. For the purposes of this memorandum we will discuss the damages in this case in round figures approximating those in the record.

Plaintiff's profit records show that for the four years prior to his shift to new equipment and using Ambrex 810, he made a total profit of $32,000. In 1961, his profit was $19,000, in 1962, $7,000, in 1963, $8,000, and in 1964, the year in which he was converting his equipment, he had a loss of $2,000. This works out to an annual rate of profits in the pre-Ambrex period of $8,000, and we are not saying that any particular period of time prior to the period the damage was sustained should be used as the basis for calculation. It appears obvious that the immediate prior year's profit has more relevancy to the issue of what profits might be anticipated in the following years than do the more remote years' profits. Likewise, on the other end of the calculation the immediate succeeding year's profit after the use of Ambrex was discontinued would be of greater relevancy than the succeeding years. But even eliminating the year of conversion, this is an annual rate of $11,000. During the period he was using Ambrex 810, approximately 30 months, he made a total of $12,000, for an annual rate of $4,800. In the post-Ambrex period, a period of 24 months, he made a total of $41,000, for an annual rate of approximately $20,500.

The jury verdict in this case was for $89,250, of which approximately $9250 may be attributed to direct damages, leaving $80,000 as the recovery for loss of profits. As we will shortly demonstrate, such a recovery, if it is interpreted as being limited to loss of profits for only the period in which Ambrex 810 was being used, bears no reasonable relationship to the proof in the record of plaintiff's capacity for making profits, with or without Ambrex 810. We were thus confronted with the problem of determining what the basis of this recovery was. We were led by certain arguments made in plaintiff's brief to the conclusion that this recovery represented a loss of profits during the period Ambrex 810 was used, plus a loss of profits for the period of time after Ambrex 810 was used because of his inability to operate at full capacity. We held that such later profits could not be recovered. Plaintiff now contends that the loss of profits recovery did not extend to the later period and was confined to the period in which he was using Ambrex 810. We accept this interpretation of the damage award and find this award is excessive.

If the $80,000 loss of profits is confined to the 30–month period during which Ambrex 810 was used, to this figure must be added the $12,000 in profits which he actually made. This works out to an annual rate of profits of approximately $37,000. There simply is no proof in the record that plaintiff has ever approached such a profit record. Plaintiff argues that his post-Ambrex profit rate, during which he was operating at 50–60 per cent capacity must be inflated to a 100 per cent capacity rate in order to determine his profit rate during the time he was using Ambrex 810. We cannot agree that such a method of determining loss of profits is acceptable, for this accomplishes much the same result as that we disapproved in our original interpretation of the damage award—i.e., it penalizes the defendant Mobil Oil Company for the plaintiff's capital structure and bears no reasonable relationship to actual damages caused by the use of Ambrex 810.

We further wish to emphasize the fact that nothing said in our prior opinion should be taken to mean that the profit rate made in the post-Ambrex period is the sole measure of damages in the period of the use of Ambrex 810. In view of the immediate proximity in time of these two periods, the significant increase in profits in the post-Ambrex period is highly suggestive of the fact that additional profits could have been made in the period Ambrex was used, and may be used as a guide as to what those profits should have been, at least as to their outer limit. However, there is also proof in the record that the market conditions of the plaintiff's business were not entirely similar, particularly in the fact that the selling price for lumber was fluctuating.

Plaintiff's recovery for a loss of profits must take into account these different market conditions, his actual production capacity, his type of operation, its efficiency and any and all other relevant factors that would have a bearing upon and that would influence the amount of profits during the period that profits are recoverable as well as the years used for comparative purposes. See Frank Sullivan Company v. Midwest Sheet Metal Works, 335 F.2d 33, 41 (8th Cir.1964).

Other questions raised in the petitions for rehearing have been considered and rejected as being without merit. The judgment must still be reversed and remanded for a new trial on the issue of damages.

Both petitions for rehearing are denied.

DELANO GROWER'S CO–OP. v. SUPREME WINE CO.

Supreme Judicial Court of Massachusetts, 1985.
393 Mass. 666, 473 N.E.2d 1066.

[The court's decision on the liability issue is printed supra in Chapter Twelve, § 3.]

* * *

6. *Calculation of damages for lost good will.* Delano argues that there is no basis in the record for the conclusion that it caused injury to Supreme's business reputation. The master found that the primary reason for Supreme's decline in sales after 1973 was the defective Delano wine. This finding was prima facie evidence of the causal connection between Delano's acts and the damage to Supreme's business reputation. At trial, Delano presented the testimony of several former Supreme customers to rebut the evidence of a causal connection. Supreme presented testimony of its former officers to support the evidence that Delano caused the injury to Supreme's business reputation. This record is hardly one, as Delano argues, that is totally devoid of any basis for finding a causal connection between Delano's acts and Supreme's damages. Rather, it exhibits an instance where the judge was required to weigh the credibility of the evidence before him and to determine whether a causal connection existed. The judge's finding that Supreme had proved a causal connection between its loss of business reputation and Delano's breach is not clearly erroneous.

Delano contends that the record contains scant evidence supporting a valuation of Supreme's good will. However, it did not produce any direct evidence at trial before the judge which rebutted Supreme's evidence of the good will value. At trial, Supreme presented the testimony of an expert in business appraising. This expert had over eight years' experience as a business broker engaged in buying and selling businesses in and around Boston. In this connection he was required to appraise a business's value, including the value of its good will. The judge's acceptance of the expert testimony implies that he found this expert sufficiently qualified to render an opinion. *Commonwealth v. Boyd*, 367 Mass. 169, 183, 326 N.E.2d 320 (1975). A finding that this expert possessed sufficient knowledge, skill, and experience to render an opinion was neither an abuse of discretion nor erroneous as matter of law. *Id.* See P.J. Liacos, Massachusetts Evidence 112 (5th ed. 1981).

The expert valued the business at $593,700, including assets and good will. The assets were valued at $237,092. This valuation was based on the business records introduced in evidence and certain other facts. This was a sufficient basis for his opinion. *Uberto v. Kaufman*, 348 Mass. 171, 173, 202 N.E.2d 822 (1964). Supreme's president and its treasurer testified that Supreme's value was $500,000.

The judge found that Supreme's loss of good will attributable to Delano's breach was $100,000. He based this on the evidence in the record and an examination of valuation methods. He rejected Supreme's theories supporting its valuation as lacking factual grounding. In determining the value of Supreme's good will, the judge was not bound by the expert testimony. P.J. Liacos, *supra* at 117, citing *Dodge v. Sawyer*, 288 Mass. 402, 408, 193 N.E. 15 (1934).

Delano argues that the trial judge relied on extraneous materials, not admitted at trial, in determining good will. Specifically, he discussed certain statistics from Business Week, indicating an increased consumption of wine and a growth in the wine industry. This reference occurred in a lengthy discussion of various methods used in valuing good will. This same discussion specifically refers to evidence introduced at trial which sufficiently supported a valuation of the lost good will. There is no clear indication to what degree, if any, the discussion of the extraneous material influenced the good will valuation. The judge found sufficient grounds to reduce the value from that given by Supreme. Where there was sufficient evidence to warrant a valuation of lost good will and the causal connection of that loss, we will not upset this finding. It was not clearly erroneous and was based on the judge's weighing the credibility of the evidence before him. The weight given this evidence was then used in accepted formulations of good will to determine the damage. We do not require that such damages be proved with mathematical certainty. *Productora e Importadora de Papel, S.A. de C.V. v. Fleming*, 376 Mass. 826, 840, 383 N.E.2d 1129 (1978). The judge did not err in calculating the damages for good will.

Neither party has addressed the issue whether lost good will is a proper consequential damage under G.L. c. 106, § 2–715. This court has stated that prospective profits are recoverable in the appropriate case. *Matsushita Elec. Corp. of America v. Sonus Corp.*, 362 Mass. 246,

264, 284 N.E.2d 880 (1972). In examining whether good will is also recoverable, we note that Pennsylvania, in disallowing such recovery, based its decision on the interpretation of its prior law, which did not allow recovery for good will. *Harry Rubin & Sons v. Consolidated Pipe Co. of America,* 396 Pa. 506, 153 A.2d 472 (1959). Other cases in which recovery for good will has been denied are based on the speculative nature of damages in the particular case or on a failure of proof. 96 A.L.R.3d § 18[b], at 396 (1979). Cf. 96 A.L.R.3d § 18[a], at 395 (1979) (loss of good will held recoverable). Under our law as it was before the enactment of the Uniform Commercial Code, "[l]oss of good will [was] recognized as an element of damages flowing from the use of unfit material received from one who warranted it to be fit." *Royal Paper Box Co. v. Munro & Church Co.,* 284 Mass. 446, 452, 188 N.E. 223 (1933) (interpreting G.L. [Ter.Ed.] c. 106, § 17[1]). Where a seller of goods reasonably knows that substantially impaired goods provided for resale could affect continued operations and established good will, the buyer's loss of good will caused by the seller's breach is properly recoverable as consequential damages unless the loss could have been prevented by cover or otherwise. G.L. c. 106, § 2–715(2)(a). This is not a harsh result as the seller may contractually limit this remedy. Uniform Commercial Code § 2–715, comment 3 1A U.L.A. 446 (1976). In this case, Supreme's loss of good will was found to be a direct consequence of Delano's breach. Once sufficiently ascertained, the award of damages for lost good will was properly allowed.

* * *

[Footnotes omitted.]

SECTION 4. SELLER'S DISCLAIMER OF WARRANTY AND CONTRACTUAL MODIFICATION OF REMEDIES FOR BREACH

MARTIN v. JOSEPH HARRIS CO., INC. 4/6

United States Court of Appeals, Sixth Circuit, 1985.
767 F.2d 296.

MILBURN, CIRCUIT JUDGE.

The defendant, Joseph Harris Co., Inc., brings this appeal following the district court's granting the plaintiffs' motion for a judgment not withstanding the verdict and a second trial in plaintiffs' action for damages as a result of defective seeds. Because we hold that the district court was correct in holding that, under the facts of this case, the disclaimer of warranty and limitation of remedy clause used by the defendant was unconscionable under Michigan law, and because we further hold that the district court properly held that the implied warranty of merchantability was breached as a matter of law, we affirm.

I.

Plaintiffs Duane Martin and Robert Rick ("Martin and Rick") were commercial farmers in Michigan. In August of 1972, Martin and Rick placed independent orders for cabbage seed with the defendant, Joseph Harris Co., Inc. ("Harris Seed"), a national producer and distributor of seed. Plaintiffs had been customers of Harris Seed for several years and, as in earlier transactions, the order form supplied by Harris Seed included a clause disclaiming the implied warranty of merchantability and limiting buyers' remedies to the purchase price of the seed.[1] A similar clause was also used by Harris Seed's competitors for the same purpose. Neither of the plaintiffs read the clause nor did the salesman make any attempt either to point it out or to explain its purpose.

Three to four months after placing their orders, plaintiffs received Harris Seed's 1973 Commercial Vegetable Growers Catalog. Included in the lower right-hand corner of one page of the catalog was a notification that Harris Seed would no longer "hot water" treat cabbage seed. Hot water treatment had successfully been used since 1947 to eradicate a fungus known as *phoma lingam* or "black leg," a seed borne disease that causes affected plants to rot before maturing.[2]

Plaintiffs planted their cabbage crop in April and May of 1973, using, among other seed, that supplied by Harris Seed. In mid-July, Harris Seed notified plaintiffs that the seed lot used to fill plaintiffs' order was infected with black leg. Although plaintiffs attempted to minimize the effect of the disease, large portions of their cabbage crops were destroyed. However, in marketing their smaller than usual crop, both plaintiffs made a profit equal to or higher than previous years. This unusual profit margin was due to the rise in market price for cabbage in 1973, which in turn was affected in part by the fact that the 1973 black leg epidemic reduced the amount of available cabbage.

On August 5, 1975, plaintiffs brought this action. After a hearing on the enforceability of the disclaimer of warranty and limitation of liability clause, the district court ruled that the clause was unconscionable and, therefore, unenforceable. A jury was impaneled to try plaintiffs' legal liability theories of negligence and breach of implied

1. The disclaimer of warranties and exclusion of remedies clause, which was printed in the order form, seed catalogs and on the seed packages, appeared as follows:

NOTICE TO BUYER: Joseph Harris Company, Inc. warrants that seeds and plants it sells conform to the label descriptions as required by Federal and State seed laws. IT MAKES NO OTHER WARRANTIES, EXPRESS OR IMPLIED, OF MERCHANTABILITY, FITNESS FOR PURPOSE, OR OTHERWISE, AND IN ANY EVENT ITS LIABILITY FOR BREACH OF ANY WARRANTY OR CONTRACT WITH RESPECT TO SUCH SEEDS OR PLANTS IS LIMITED TO THE PURCHASE PRICE OF SUCH SEEDS OR PLANTS.

No question has been raised as to whether this clause complies with the requirements of Mich.Comp.Laws Ann. § 440.2316 (U.C.C. § 2–316).

2. According to testimony at trial, the only black leg epidemic between 1947 and 1973 was in 1966, and was traced to cabbage seed imported from Australia. The 1947 and the 1973 black leg was traced to State of Washington produced cabbage seed.

warranty. Following a six-day trial the jury returned a verdict against plaintiffs on both theories; however, the district court granted the plaintiffs' motion for a j.n.o.v. on the implied warranty issue. A second jury impaneled to hear the issue of damages returned verdicts in favor of Martin in the amount of Thirty-six Thousand ($36,000.00) Dollars and in favor of Rick in the amount of Sixteen Thousand ($16,000.00) Dollars.

II.

Our review of the district court's rulings in this diversity case is controlled by the State of Michigan's version of the Uniform Commercial Code, Mich.Comp.Laws Ann. § 440.1101 *et seq.* As we have often stated, "[w]hen this court is reviewing a district judge's interpretation of state law, we give 'considerable weight' to the interpretation of the judge." *Bagwell v. Canal Insurance Co.,* 663 F.2d 710, 712 (6th Cir. 1981). Accordingly, "if a federal district judge has reached a permissible conclusion upon a question of local law, the Court of Appeals should not reverse even though it may think the law should be otherwise." *Insurance Co. of North America v. Federated Mutual Insurance Co.,* 518 F.2d 101, 106 n. 3 (6th Cir.1975) (quoting *Rudd-Melikian, Inc. v. Merritt,* 282 F.2d 924, 929 (6th Cir.1960)).

A.

The first issue raised by Harris Seed is whether the district court erred in holding the disclaimer and limitation clause unconscionable under U.C.C. § 2–302. The question of the unconscionability of a contract clause is one of law for the court to decide in light of "its commercial setting, purpose and effect." U.C.C. § 2–302. Since the Code does not define unconscionability, the district court reviewed case law to aid it in its resolution of this question.

A threshhold problem in this context is whether under Michigan law warranty disclaimers which comply with U.C.C. § 2–316 are limited by U.C.C. § 2–302. In holding Harris Seed's disclaimer clause unconscionable under the facts of this case, the district court implicitly held that U.C.C. § 2–302 is a limitation on U.C.C. § 2–316. Harris Seed argues that by enacting § 2–316 the Michigan Legislature "unequivocally [authorized the] exclusion or modification of the implied warranty of merchantability by disclaimer." We have been presented with no Michigan cases resolving this issue; however, a number of arguments support the district court's conclusion that § 2–316 is not insulated from review under § 2–302. First, § 2–302 provides that "any clause" of a contract may be found unconscionable. Similarly, "section 2–316 does not state expressly that all disclaimers meeting its requirements are immune from general policing provisions like section 2–302. * * *" J. White & R. Summers, *Handbook of the Law Under the Uniform Commercial Code,* § 12–11, at 476 (2d Ed.1980). Had the drafters of the Uniform Commercial Code or the Michigan Legislature chosen to limit the application of § 2–302, language expressly so stating could easily have been included. Furthermore, as pointed out by Professors White and Summers:

> Comment 1 [to § 2–302] lists and describes ten cases which are presumably intended to illustrate the underlying basis of the section: In seven of those cases disclaimers of warranty were denied full effect. It is difficult to reconcile the intent on the part of the draftsman to immunize disclaimers from the effect of 2–302 with the fact that they used cases in which courts struck down disclaimers to illustrate the concept of unconscionability.

Id. (footnotes omitted). Therefore, because this issue is unsettled under Michigan law and according the district court's conclusion "considerable weight," we hold that the district court correctly relied upon § 2–302 as a limitation on § 2–316.

We next turn to a more troublesome subissue; viz., whether within the special facts of this case the disclaimer and exclusionary clause was unconscionable under Michigan law. As has often been stated, commercial contracts will rarely be found unconscionable, *see, e.g., A & M Produce Co. v. FMC Corp.,* 135 Cal.App.3d 473, 186 Cal.Rptr. 114 (1982), *Stanley A. Klopp, Inc. v. John Deere Co.,* 510 F.Supp. 807, 810 (E.D.Pa. 1981), *aff'd,* 676 F.2d 688 (3rd Cir.1982),[4] because in the commercial setting the relationship is between business parties and is not so one-sided as to give one party the bargaining power to impose unconscionable terms on the other party.

In making its determination of unconscionability, the district court relied upon *Allen v. Michigan Bell Telephone,* 18 Mich.App. 632, 171 N.W.2d 689 (1969).[5] In *Allen* an insurance agent contracted with Michigan Bell Telephone Company to place advertisements in the classified telephone directory. When the advertisements were not included, he brought an action for damages. To defend the action,

---

4. It is unclear whether the contract at issue is a commercial contract. As noted by the district court, some courts have held farmers and ranchers are not merchants. *See, e.g., Fear Ranches, Inc. v. Berry,* 470 F.2d 905 (10th Cir.1972); *Cook Grains, Inc. v. Fallis,* 239 Ark. 962, 395 S.W.2d 555 (1965). Other courts have taken the opposite position and held farmers are merchants. *See, e.g., Campbell v. Yokel,* 20 Ill. App.2d 702, 313 N.E.2d 628 (1974); *Nelson v. Union Equity Co-Operative Exchange,* 548 S.W.2d 352 (Tex.1977). Although these cases deal with the definition of "merchant" in § 2–104 for purposes of application to § 2–201(2) (the "between merchants" exception to the statute of frauds), the inquiry is relevant here for purposes of determining whether the transaction at issue occurred in a true "commercial setting," where unconscionability is rarely found. However, since we hold that, even if considered a "commercial setting," the

clause at issue was unconscionable under the facts of this case, we do not reach the issue.

5. Although it may be, as Harris Seed argues, that the criticisms of *Allen* by courts, *see, e.g., Robinson Insurance & Real Estate, Inc. v. Southwestern Bell,* 366 F.Supp. 307 (W.D.Ark.1973), and commentators, *see* J. White & R. Summers, *Handbook of the Law Under the Uniform Commercial Code,* § 4–9, at 172 (2d Ed.1980) are well founded, the Michigan Appellate Court's holding is nevertheless an appropriate guide to our inquiry in the present case. *Cf. Simpson v. Jefferson Standard Life Insurance Co.,* 465 F.2d 1320, 1323 (6th Cir.1972) ("[d]ecisions of intermediate state courts must be followed by the federal courts unless there is reason to believe they would not be followed by the state's highest court.").

Michigan Bell Telephone Company relied on a limitation of remedies clause which, if upheld, would have limited the plaintiff's recovery to the contract price. In refusing to uphold the limitation, the Michigan court stated "the principle of freedom to contract does not carry a license to insert any provision in an agreement which a party deems advantageous." *Id.* at 691–92. Rather, the court stated that:

> [i]mplicit in the principle of freedom of contract is the concept that at the time of contracting each party has a realistic alternative to acceptance of the terms offered. Where goods and services can only be obtained from one source (or several sources on non-competitive terms) the choices of one who desires to purchase are limited to acceptance of the terms offered or doing without. Depending on the nature of the goods or services and the purchaser's needs, doing without may or may not be a realistic alternative. Where it is not, one who successfully exacts agreement to an unreasonable term cannot insist on the court's enforcing it on the ground that it was "freely" entered into, when it was not. * * *

> There are then two inquiries in a case such as this: (1) what is the relative bargaining power of the parties, their relative economic strength, the alternative sources of supply, in a word, what are their options?: (2) is the challenged term substantively reasonable?

Id. at 692.

With reference to the test announced in *Allen,* Harris Seed argues that the relative bargaining power of the parties is not a proper consideration under § 2–302. This is an issue on which courts and commentators have taken varying approaches. *Compare, e.g., Phillips Machinery Co. v. LeBlond, Inc.,* 494 F.Supp. 318 (N.D.Okla.1980) (no requirement of equality of bargaining power, but rather must be some element of deception or substantive unfairness) *and Majors v. Kalo Laboratories, Inc.,* 407 F.Supp. 20, 23 (M.D.Ala.1975) ("[T]he Official Comment to § 2–302 suggests that [consideration of bargaining power] would be inappropriate.") *with Kerr-McGee Corp. v. Northern Utilities, Inc.,* 673 F.2d 323, 329 (10th Cir.1982) (relative considerations include whether "there was a gross inequality of bargaining power.") *and* J. White & R. Summers, *supra,* § 12–11, at 477 ("[o]ne can argue that when a seller has such a strong bargaining position that he can impose a perfectly drafted disclaimer, which operates to deprive the buyer of virtually all protection that a law would otherwise provide, and he refuses to bargain at all concerning its scope, then that clause has become 'oppressive' and so 'one-sided' as to be unconscionable."). We agree with the district court that relative bargaining power is an appropriate consideration in determining unconscionability under the Michigan Uniform Commercial Code.

Other closely related factors suggested by the Michigan court in *Allen* for determining the presence of procedural unconscionability are the relative economic strength of the parties and the alternative sources of supply. With reference to the relative economic strength of the parties, we note that Harris Seed is a large national producer and distributor of seed, dealing here with independent, relatively small farmers. As to alternative sources of supply, the farmers were faced with a situation where all seed distributors placed disclaimers and exclusionary clauses in their contracts. Thus, this presents a situation where "goods [could] only be obtained from * * * several sources on non-competitive terms * * * and doing without [was] not a realistic alternative." *Allen, supra,* 171 N.W.2d at 692.

Another pertinent factor considered by the district court in its unconscionability finding was that Harris Seed's salesman did not make Martin and Rick, who were uncounseled laymen, aware of the fact that the clauses in question altered significant statutory rights. Such a disclosure is an important consideration under Michigan law. *Mallory v. Conida Warehouses, Inc.,* 134 Mich.App. 28, 350 N.W.2d 825, 827 (1984); *cf. Johnson v. Mobil Oil Corp.,* 415 F.Supp. 264, 269 (E.D. Mich.1976) ("[b]efore a contracting party with * * * immense bargaining power * * * may limit its liability vis-a-vis an uncounseled layman * * * it has an affirmative duty to obtain the voluntary knowing assent of the other party.").

Furthermore, although the terms of the 1972 sale appeared to be the same as in previous years (unknown to Martin and Rick), Harris Seed decided to discontinue the hot water treatment of its cabbage seed, a standard practice for the previous twenty-six years. This decision by Harris Seed was one which had far-reaching consequences to the purchasers of its cabbage seed. As noted above, hot water treatment had been successful in preventing black leg in Washington State produced cabbage seed since 1947, and although Martin and Rick were unaware of the potential effects of black leg, or indeed even what black leg was, Harris Seed had considerable expertise in such matters.

Another important consideration is the fact that the presence of black leg in cabbage seed creates a *latent* defect. Although in many cases the fact that a latent defect is present seems to be dispositive, see *Majors v. Kalo Laboratories, Inc.,* 407 F.Supp. 20 (M.D.Ala.1975); *Corneli Seed Company v. Ferguson,* 64 So.2d 162 (Fla.1953), we note only that it is important to the disposition of this case.

Significantly, in the present case not only was the defect latent, but it was also one which was within the control of Harris Seed to prevent. Even if Martin and Rick had been apprised of and understood the significance of Harris Seed's decision to discontinue hot water treatment, they would have been unable to detect the presence of the disease in the seed until their crop had developed into young plants. If Harris Seed were permitted to rely on the disclaimer and limitation clause to avoid liability under the facts of this case, the farmers who had no notice of, ability to detect, or control over the presence of the black leg could lose their livelihood. On the other hand, Harris Seed which had the knowledge, expertise and means to prevent the disease would only lose a few hundred dollars. Given the unique facts of this case, and giving "considerable weight" to the district court's decision that Michigan law would not permit the disclaimer and limitation clause to be enforced under such circumstances, we affirm the district court's finding of unconscionability.

*   *   *

[Some footnotes omitted.]

Notes

1. Did the seller's disclaimer satisfy the requirements of UCC 2–316(2)? How would you describe those requirements?

2. How could the seller have avoided the result in this case?

3. Note that the disclaimer was printed on the order form supplied by the seller. In seed cases, the courts have been even more hostile to disclaimers printed on the package or bag of seeds and not seen by the buyer until after the contract is formed, if at all. See, e.g., Gold Kist, Inc. v. Citizens & Southern National Bank of South Carolina, 286 S.C. 272, 333 S.E.2d 67 (1985) (disclaimer not part of agreement).

4. The United States and many states have enacted laws to protect the purchasers of seeds from falsely labeled products. The laws are backed by criminal sanctions. See 7 U.S.C.A. § 1551 (1985). These seed statutes, however, do not preempt Article 2 of the UCC. Thus, even if the seller complies with the statutory labeling requirements, it may still be liable for breach of warranty under the UCC. See, e.g., Hanson v. Funk Seeds International, 373 N.W.2d 30 (S.D.1985).

Problem 14–2

B, an experienced commercial fisherman, purchased a new diesel engine for his fishing boat from S. The engine was installed by S. Over the next 4 months, however, a number of mechanical problems arose, including the emission of excessive quantities of heavy black smoke. S was unable to correct them and the engine was removed from the boat. Experts will testify that it was unmerchantable.

At the time of contracting, B had signed a purchase order prepared by S. The face of the purchase order contained a number of terms and conditions. In the center of the face, this statement appeared: BOTH THIS ORDER AND ITS ACCEPTANCE ARE SUBJECT TO TERMS AND CONDITIONS STATED IN THIS ORDER. On the reverse side of the order at the top of the page, the following words appeared: TERMS AND CONDITIONS. Under that caption were eleven numbered paragraphs, one of which contained a disclaimer in the following form: THE SELLER HEREBY DISCLAIMS AND EXCLUDES ALL IMPLIED WARRANTIES, INCLUDING THE IMPLIED WARRANTY OF MERCHANTABILITY. B did not nor was he asked to read anything on the back of the purchase order. B received a fully executed copy of the order by mail before the engine was installed.

B sued S for damages resulting from breach of an implied warranty of merchantability. S defended on the ground that the warranty had been effectively disclaimed under UCC 2–316(2). What result?

Problem 14–3

S, a boat dealer, advertised a 42 foot Pearson sailing sloop for sale. The boat was manufactured in 1960 and had a wooden hull. B, an experienced sailor, had never owned a sloop with a wooden hull. Without the assistance of a third party, B examined the boat carefully and could find nothing wrong. She questioned S who, at various times stated: "This beauty was her owner's pride and joy. It's in great shape;" "The boat is sound. It rides the waves like a dream;" "The wood is solid throughout. We will replace any dry rot free of charge."

B agreed to purchase the sloop for $50,000. At the time of contracting, B signed a writing prepared by S which on the front provided, in part, as follows: "WARRANTIES. Buyer is buying the goods AS IS WHERE IS and no representations or statements have been made by seller except as herein stated, so that no warranty, express or implied, arises apart from this writing."

B took delivery of the boat, paid the price and went for a long, wet sail. The boat appeared to leak at the stern. An expert was hired to inspect the area and found extensive dry rot, which had clearly been there at the time of the sale. The estimated cost to repair the boat was $15,000.

B claimed damages for breach of warranty, measured by the cost to repair. S argued that all warranties, express or implied, had been disclaimed, citing UCC 2–316(1) & 2–202, UCC 2–316(3)(a) and UCC 2–316(3)(b). Is S correct?

SINGER CO. v. E.I. du PONT de NEMOURS & CO.

United States Court of Appeals, Eighth Circuit, 1978.
579 F.2d 433.

[Plaintiff, a manufacturer of airconditioners and furnaces, acquired an electrodeposition paint system to paint the metal or ware in the products. Under this system, pre-treated ware is conveyed through an electrically charged paint tank and coated with paint in an electroplating process. Defendant agreed to provide paint for the 22,000 gallon tank. From the beginning, Plaintiff had trouble with the paint. Ware emerging from this system was blotched and streaked and had to be repainted. Defendant, which had supervised the installation of the system, tried unsuccessfully for over six months to correct the problem. Ultimately, the Defendant's paint was removed from the tank and replaced with another brand. Plaintiff sued for damages. The key question was the cause of the defective painting. Plaintiff, arguing that the paint was at fault, claimed that Defendant had breached an express warranty and an implied warranty of fitness for particular purpose. Defendant argued that the paint conformed to any express warranty and that no implied warranties were made. Over Defendant's objection, the trial court instructed the jury on the implied warranty issue but not on express warranty. The jury returned a verdict for Plaintiff in the amount of $108,367. Defendant appealed.]

Verdict for π

HANSON, SENIOR DISTRICT JUDGE.

* * *

No dispute that UCC properly governs

While disagreeing on whether the trial court should have instructed as to an implied warranty of fitness for a particular purpose, the parties are properly in accord that the Illinois adoption of the Uniform Commercial Code governs the disposition of this case. * * * There is also no dispute that the "all tests" provision of the contract, which specified such set standards as color and texture that the paint was to satisfy upon pretreated laboratory test panels, was an express warranty pursuant to § 2–313(1)(b) of the U.C.C. But Singer claims that the contract further preserved an implied warranty of fitness, a warranty that pursuant to Section 2–315 assured plaintiff the paint supplied would satisfactorily cover its substrate. A paragraph in the contract provided:

Also no dispute that the "all tests" provision was an express warranty pursuant to (1)(b)

> "None of the provisions or remedies herein are in lieu of any claims for damages Buyer may have at law or equity under the Uniform Commercial Code or otherwise, for the breach of any contracts or warranties with Buyer, which rights are specifically reserved by Buyer."

Du Pont contends that parties who have an express warranty regarding a contracted for item cannot also have an implied warranty of fitness for that same item. The warranty of fitness for a specific purpose is alleged to have been limited by expressly defining it in a set of specifications, and Du Pont claims that to find otherwise would permit Singer to escape the parties' true contractual bargain.

Pertinent sections of the U.C.C., and the comments pursuant thereto, lend inferential support to Singer's position that the implied warranty of fitness was cumulative to and not excluded by the express warranty. Section 2–316(2), with regard to the exclusion or modification of such warranties, states:

> "* * * [T]o exclude or modify any implied warranty of fitness the exclusion must be by a writing *and conspicuous*." (Emphasis added.)

Comment 9 to that section provides in part:

> "The situation in which *the buyer gives* precise and complete *specifications to the seller* is not explicitly covered in this section, but this is a frequent circumstance by which the *implied warranties may be excluded*. The warranty of fitness for a particular purpose would not normally arise since in such a situation there is usually *no reliance on the seller by the buyer*." (Emphasis added.)

Seller provided the paint specs & remained in control of the task

See also U.C.C. § 2–315, comment 2. Because the evidence in this case fully indicates that it was not the buyer but the seller who in fact recommended and supplied the paint specifications, and remained in

Therefore Court below also correct to look at implied warranty & not express warranty.

BUT - since purported exclusions were not "conspicuous"

control of the paint tank, it would appear that the trial court did not err in its determination that an implied warranty of fitness was at issue. This is especially so in view of the purported exclusion of this warranty, which could be scarcely termed "conspicuous."

A reading of the U.C.C. to suggest that an express warranty and an implied warranty of fitness are not necessarily mutually exclusive, as Singer has argued, receives support from Code authority.

> "The fact that a warranty of fitness for a particular purpose does or does not exist has no bearing on any other warranty or theory of product liability. Conversely, the fact that there may be some other basis for liability of the defendant does not preclude the existence of a warranty for a particular purpose. *Thus the fact that there is a warranty of conformity to sample [an express warranty] does not preclude the existence of a warranty for a particular purpose.*" (Emphasis added.) Anderson, Uniform Commercial Code § 2–315:5 (1970).

See also White and Summers, Uniform Commercial Code § 12–7 (1972); 67 Am.Jr.2d Sales § 501 (1973). Relevant case law, in the balance, further indicates that an express warranty would not control under the circumstances of this case.

Cases can be found prior to the adoption of the U.C.C. to support Du Pont's argument of mutual exclusiveness. This court, without specific adoption of the position, recognized in Hercules Powder Co. v. Rich, 3 F.2d 12 (8th Cir.1924) that there was law to the effect that an implied warranty of fitness could not prevail in the presence of an express warranty on the same item or subject.

> "An express warranty excludes an implied warranty relating to the same subject or of the same general nature, on the theory that no warranty should be implied where the parties with relation to the very same subject have expressed by words the warranty by which they will be bound." Id. at 18.

There was also case law to the contrary. * * * But while there may have once been a split of authority, we fail to find since the general adoption of the above-quoted sections of the U.C.C. any case holding directly in favor of Du Pont's mutual exclusivity agreement. * * * In fact unless the exclusion of the implied warranty of fitness is specifically and conspicuously excluded, courts, often relying upon § 2–317, have found that such implied and express warranties can be cumulative and co-exist within the same agreement. Multivision Northwest, Inc. v. Jerrold Electronics Corp., 356 F.Supp. 207 (N.D.Ga. 1972); Murray v. Kleen Leen, Inc., 41 Ill.App.3d 436, 354 N.E.2d 415 (1976); Water Works & Industrial Supply Co. v. Wilburn, 437 S.W.2d 951 (Ky.1969).

Du Pont, in arguing the law upon appeal, relies principally upon two types of cases that have arisen under the U.C.C.: those in which there has been a showing that the buyer, in possession or control of the item, failed to follow the express warranty specifications; and those where an enforceable disclaimer of an implied warranty has been established. With respect to the first type of case, it is clear that the trial court did not confront a situation where a buyer in possession or control of an item failed to follow seller's specifications used the item in a manner for which it was not intended, lost that for which he had contracted, and then erroneously claimed a breach of an implied warranty for fitness. * * * Here, Du Pont, as the seller, was in control of the disputed item. No one denied that Du Pont was throughout this time in control of Singer's paint tank, directing its operation and determining its contents.

(2.) The disclaimer cases are likewise inapplicable. Even without a paragraph in the contract reserving all further warranties under the U.C.C., Du Pont would have difficulty in arguing that an express warranty of the paint effected a disclaimer of any further warranty. It is clear from these cases that disclaimers under the Code are not favored and are limited whenever possible. Admiral Oasis Hotel Corp. v. Home Gas Industries, Inc., 68 Ill.App.2d 297, 216 N.E.2d 282 (1965); Dobias v. Western Farmers Association, 6 Wash.App. 194, 491 P.2d 1346 (1971); Annot., 73 A.L.R.3d 248 (1976).

Du Pont also argues in general that to permit Singer to assert an implied warranty of fitness would be to allow utilization of the U.C.C. in avoidance of the parties' true bargain. The true bargain, though, is less than apparent from the face of the contract. This was not a situation where a buyer ordered according to specifications and then claimed an implied warranty of fitness when the product failed to measure up to expectations. In this instance, the buyer approached the seller describing the results desired and the seller professed to be able to supply it, thereby inducing a reliance that created the possibility of an implied warranty of fitness. Notwithstanding the express warranty contained within the specifications particularly defining and describing the item to be supplied, there may have been a further warranty that an item with those specifications would accomplish certain results or be adequate for the specified purpose. That is, the accomplishment of the purpose might be viewed as the essence of the contractual undertaking, and not the mere furnishing of the specified item. Nothing within this contract, or in writings or statements subsequent to it, indicate whether the end of the agreement was the specified item or the use for which the item was intended. Cf. Construction Aggregates, supra.

Du Pont simply failed to negotiate a contract that clearly delineated and limited allocation of risk. This case would never have arisen had defendant, as a party to and a scrivener of the contract, either inserted a specific disclaimer or demanded that the warranty savings clause be deleted.

Having left the contract ambiguous, the question as to whether use rather than supply of the product was intended to be of the essence, as well as questions regarding buyer's reliance and seller's knowledge of that reliance, are for jury determination. * * *

* * *

The judgment appealed from is affirmed.   [Footnotes omitted.]

Problem 14–4

B, a baker, planned to expand its capacity by 30%. Accordingly, on March 1, it ordered a custom made oven from S, a manufacturer, to be delivered not later than September 1. B informed S of its planned expansion and stated that "time was of the essence:" B had developed a new bread for hotels and restaurants and wanted to be in production for the Fall convention season. S and B negotiated over how to deal with the risk of delay in delivery.

1. After discussing B's current profit margin and the probabilities that an expansion would be profitable, S agreed, in a clause labeled LIQUIDATED DAMAGES, to pay B $500 for every day of a non-excusable delay in delivery. S did not deliver the oven until October 1. B claimed liquidated damages in the amount of $30,000. S, however, can establish that the convention business during September was very slow and that, at best, B would have made only $2,500 in net profits if the oven had been delivered on time. Is the agreed damage clause enforceable under UCC 2–718?

2. Suppose that the clause was labeled LIMITATION OF DAMAGES S agreed to pay "not more than $500 for each day of unexcused delay." The oven was delivered on October 1. B is prepared to establish that the convention market boomed during September and that the delay in delivery deprived it of at least $2,500 in net profits per day. B claims that the limitation clause was unreasonable. Is B correct. See UCC 2–718 & 2–719.

CAYUGA HARVESTER, INC. v. ALLIS–CHALMERS CORP.

Supreme Court of New York, Appellate Division, 1983.
95 A.D.2d 5, 465 N.Y.S.2d 606.

HANCOCK, JUSTICE:

Under the Uniform Commercial Code, the parties to a sale may, within certain limitations, allocate the risks of their bargain by limiting the remedy of the buyer (Uniform Commercial Code, § 2–719, subd. 1, par. a). When, however, a limited remedy such as an exclusive repair and replacement warranty fails of its essential purpose, the buyer is relieved of its restrictions and may resort to other remedies as provided in section 2–719 (subd. 2). The Code also permits the parties to agree to exclude consequential damages unless the exclusion is unconscionable (Uniform Commercial Code, § 2–719, subd. 3). Here the contract in issue contains both an exclusive repair and replacement warranty and an exclusion of consequential damages; plaintiff claiming that the limited remedy failed of its essential purpose seeks to recover consequential as well as other damages for breach of warranty. A major question arises from plaintiff's contention that proof of the failure of the limited repair and replacement warranty would free it not only from the restrictions of that clause but also from the clause excluding consequential damages.

The action arises out of the sale of an N–7 harvesting machine manufactured by defendant Allis-Chalmers Corporation ("Allis"). Plaintiff, the operator of an extensive corn-growing business in Cato, New York, purchased the machine for $142,213 from defendant R.C. Church & Sons, Inc. ("Church"), a farm machinery dealer, under a written purchase order containing a limited repair and replacement warranty and an exclusion of consequential damages. The balance of the purchase price, after a down payment of $36,989.80, was financed through defendant Allis-Chalmers Credit Corporation ("Allis Credit"). Plaintiff alleges that the machine did not operate or function properly and that it suffered numerous failures and breakdowns preventing it from making a timely and effective harvest of its 1981 corn crop.

The issues considered concerning various sections of the Uniform Commercial Code are as follows:

I. A. whether the limited repair and replacement warranty failed of its essential purpose (§ 2–719, subd. 2);

B. if so, whether, despite the failure, the consequential damages exclusion remains in effect; and

C. whether the clause excluding consequential damages is unconscionable (§§ 2–719, subd. 3; 2–302, subds. 1, 2).

* * *

I

We consider first the grant of summary judgment dismissing the first two causes of action against Allis alleging breaches of express warranties. In the purchase order under the "Allis-Chalmers New Farm Equipment Warranty", Allis gave an express warranty limited to the repair or replacement of defective parts in the following provisions which we quote in part:

WHAT IS WARRANTED

Allis-Chalmers Corporation ("Company") warrants new farm equipment sold by it to be merchantable and free of defects in workmanship and material at the time of shipment from the Company's factory. THERE ARE NO WARRANTIES WHICH EXTEND BEYOND THOSE EXPRESSLY STATED HEREIN. The warranty is made to the original purchaser or lessee from an authorized Allis-Chalmers Dealer of each item of new Allis-Chalmers farm equipment.

1. *Equipment Warranty.* Parts which are defective in workmanship and material as delivered will be repaired or replaced as follows:

* * *

(There follow several paragraphs detailing the terms and conditions of Allis' obligation to make repairs and replacements and the periods during which the warranty is effective.)

I. Remedies Exclusive

THE COMPANY'S LIABILITY, WHETHER IN CONTRACT OR IN TORT, ARISING OUT OF WARRANTIES, REPRESENTATIONS, INSTRUCTIONS, OR DEFECTS FROM ANY CAUSE SHALL BE LIMITED EXCLUSIVELY TO REPAIRING OR REPLACING PARTS UNDER THE CONDITIONS AS AFORESAID, AND IN NO EVENT WILL THE COMPANY BE LIABLE FOR CONSE-QUENTIAL DAMAGES, INCLUDING BUT NOT LIMITED TO LOSS OF CROPS, LOSS OF PROFITS, RENTAL OR SUBSTITUTE EQUIPMENT, OR OTHER COMMERCIAL LOSS.

Clause purports to limit liability for any Consequential dmgs.

In granting Allis' motions Special Term held that the provision excluding consequential damages in Paragraph "I", above, was, as a matter of law, not unconscionable under Uniform Commercial Code (§§ 2–719, subd. 3; 2–302, subd. 1) and that it acted as a total bar to plaintiff's express warranty claims. The court did not find it necessary to reach the issues before us concerning the alleged failure of the essential purpose of the repair and replacement warranty under the Uniform Commercial Code (§ 2–719, subd. 2) and the effect of that failure on the exclusion of consequential damages.

At Special Term they held that not so a matter of law unconscionable

A

Ordinarily, whether circumstances have caused a "limited remedy to fail of its essential purpose" (Uniform Commercial Code, § 2–719, subd. 2) is a question of fact for the jury and one necessarily to be resolved upon proof of the circumstances occurring after the contract is formed (see *Johnson v. John Deere Co.*, 306 N.W.2d 231, 237, 238 [S.D.1981]). It should be noted that in order to establish a failure of a limited remedy under section 2–719 (subd. 2) it is not necessary to show that the warrantor's conduct in failing to effect repairs was wilfully dilatory or even negligent. Rather, the section is to apply "whenever an exclusive remedy, which may have appeared fair and reasonable at the inception of the contract, as a result of later circumstances operates to deprive a party of a substantial benefit of the bargain" (*Clark v. International Harvester Co.*, 99 Idaho 326, 340, 581 P.2d 784; see Uniform Commercial Code, § 2–719, Official Comment 1; White & Summers, Handbook of the Law under the Uniform Commercial Code, [2d ed.], § 12–10). The damage to the buyer is the same whether the seller diligently but unsuccessfully attempts to honor his promise or acts negligently or in bad faith (see *Beal v. General Motors Corp.*, 354 F.Supp. 423, 427 [D.C. Del., 1973]). Moreover, a "delay in supplying the remedy can just as effectively deny the purchaser the product he expected as can the total inability to repair. In both instances the buyer loses the substantial benefit of his purchase" (*Chatlos Systems, Inc. v. National Cash Register Corp.*, 635 F.2d 1081, 1085 [CCA 3d, 1980]). Thus, if it is found at trial that plaintiff, because of defendant

May prevail even though no bad faith.

Allis' failure to repair or replace parts within a reasonable time, has been deprived of a substantial benefit of its bargain, it may prevail even though, as is the case here, there is no claim of bad faith or wilfully dilatory conduct and the record demonstrates that defendant made extensive efforts to comply.

The precise question here is whether plaintiff has made a prima facie showing that the limited remedy failed of its essential purpose. On our review of the record we hold that plaintiff has made such a showing and that Special Term was in error in granting summary judgment dismissing the first two causes of action against Allis in their entirety (C.P.L.R. 3212, subd. b). Mr. Sheckler, plaintiff's president, states in an affidavit "that the N–7 combine purchased by plaintiff suffered over 100 mechanical failures and over 100 parts replacements resulting in over 640 actual hours of machine down-time. Because of the inoperability of the N–7 combine a full eight months were required for plaintiff to complete the process of driving the combine over all the acres of corn." Annexed to plaintiff's affidavits are a detailed log of the numerous machine failures and a lengthy list of warranty claims totaling many thousands of dollars submitted by Church to Allis covering work performed and parts supplied from the delivery of the machine in July of 1981 through February, 1982.

It is settled that a finding that a limited warranty has failed of its essential purpose frees the buyer to pursue his remedies under other provisions of the Uniform Commercial Code as if the clause did not exist (see *S.M. Wilson & Co. v. Smith Intern., Inc.*, 587 F.2d 1363 [CCA 9th, 1978]; *County Asphalt, Inc. v. Lewis Welding & Engineering Corp.*, 323 F.Supp. 1300, 1309 [S.D.N.Y.1970], affd. 444 F.2d 372 [CCA 2d, 1971], cert. den. 404 U.S. 939, 92 S.Ct. 272, 30 L.Ed.2d 252; *Johnson v. John Deere Co.*, 306 N.W.2d 231, 236 [S.D.1981], supra). Plaintiff would, therefore, not be precluded by the exclusive remedy clause from recovering under the usual measure of damages in warranty cases; i.e., "the difference at the time and place of acceptance between the value of the goods accepted and the value they would have had if they had been as warranted" (Uniform Commercial Code, § 2–714, subd. 2) (see *American Elec. Power Co., Inc. v. Westinghouse Elec. Corp.*, 418 F.Supp. 435, 457, 458 [S.D.N.Y.1976]; *County Asphalt, Inc. v. Lewis Welding & Engineering Corp.*, supra, p. 1309; *Johnson v. John Deere Co.*, supra, p. 236).

Order for Summary Judgment should be Reversed.

The order granting summary judgment to defendant Allis should be reversed to the extent that it dismisses the first and second causes of action in their entirety.

B

Does the Consequential damage exclusion fail?

We come next to the legal question whether the consequential damage exclusion in Paragraph "I" would survive a finding that the limited repair and replacement warranty in that paragraph had failed of its essential purpose. We have found no controlling authority on the

No Authority here

point in this state, and the numerous decisions in federal courts and the courts of other states are in conflict.

As we view it, the problem requires a two-step analysis: first, construing Paragraph "I" in its context as one clause in a contract concerning a substantial commercial transaction in order to ascertain the allocation of the risks as intended by the parties; and, second, determining whether that agreed-upon allocation of the risks leaves "at least a fair quantum of remedy for breach of the obligations or duties outlined in the contract" (McKinney's Cons.Laws of N.Y., Book 62½, Part 1, Uniform Commercial Code, § 2–719, Official Comment 1, p. 691). Paragraph "I" states:

> THE COMPANY'S LIABILITY, WHETHER IN CONTRACT OR IN TORT, ARISING OUT OF WARRANTIES, REPRESENTATIONS, INSTRUCTIONS, OR DEFECTS FROM ANY CAUSE SHALL BE LIMITED EXCLUSIVELY TO REPAIRING OR REPLACING PARTS UNDER THE CONDITIONS AS AFORESAID, AND IN NO EVENT WILL THE COMPANY BE LIABLE FOR CONSEQUENTIAL DAMAGES, INCLUDING BUT NOT LIMITED TO LOSS OF CROPS, LOSS OF PROFITS, RENTAL OR SUBSTITUTE EQUIPMENT, OR OTHER COMMERCIAL LOSS.

Preliminarily, it may be helpful to set forth two factors which are material to our analysis and, we think, significant: (1) this is not a case involving bad faith or wilfully dilatory conduct on the part of the defendant (compare, e.g., *Jones & McKnight Corp. v. Birdsboro Corp.*, 320 F.Supp. 39, 43 [D.C. Ill., 1970]; *Adams v. J.I. Case Co.*, 125 Ill.App. 2d 388, 402, 261 N.E.2d 1: and (2) plaintiff, if it should succeed in proving that the limited warranty has failed, would, regardless of a contrary ruling on the survivability of the consequential damages exclusion, be permitted to recover damages allowed by Uniform Commercial Code (§ 2–714, subd. 2) (see subpart A, supra).

Plaintiff argues that the promise of defendant to repair and replace defective parts in the first part of Paragraph "I" and the clause exempting defendant from the assessment of consequential damages in the second part are mutually dependent, i.e., that a failure on the part of defendant to perform its obligations under the first, as a matter of law, deprives it of its exemption under the second part and frees plaintiff from its limitations. Defendant, on the other hand, maintains that the two provisions are unrelated and independent.

In our view defendant has the better of the argument. Certainly, no wording in Paragraph "I", itself, indicates that the provisions are interrelated or that the failure of defendant to perform under the repair and replacement warranty deprives it of the protection of the consequential damages exclusion. The purposes of the two clauses are totally discrete: that of the first is to restrict defendant's obligations under the transaction to repairing or replacing defective parts while that of the second is to rule out a specific type of damage. Each clause stands on its own and may be given effect without regard to the other. Thus, the plain meaning of Paragraph "I" appears to favor defendant.

Nor, given the larger context of Paragraph "I" as one term in a transaction involving the sale of an expensive piece of farm machinery to a large commercial grower, would it be reasonable to give it a different construction. Adopting plaintiff's interpretation, defendant's failure to repair and replace defective parts would, despite its good-faith efforts to fulfill its obligations, subject it to a lawsuit for consequential damages and loss of profits which, in view of the size of plaintiff's operation, could result in a recovery many times the value of the N–7 combine. It defies reason to suppose that defendant could have intended to assume such risks. The contrary construction urged by defendant entails a more plausible allocation of the risks and one that the parties could reasonably have had in mind: i.e., that a failure of the repair and replacement warranty, despite defendant's good faith efforts to comply, would permit plaintiff to recover the ordinary breach of warranty damages (Uniform Commercial Code, § 2–714, subd. 2) but not loss of profits or other consequential damages.

We find nothing in the Uniform Commercial Code that rules out defendant's construction. On the contrary, under Uniform Commercial Code (§ 2–719) the "parties are left free to shape their remedies to their particular requirements and reasonable agreements limiting or modifying remedies are to be given effect" (McKinney's Cons.Laws of N.Y., Book 62½, Part 1, Uniform Commercial Code, § 2–719, Official Comment 1, p. 691), provided that the remedy limitations are not unconscionable and that "there be at least a fair quantum of remedy for breach of the obligations or duties outlined in the contract" (McKinney's Cons. Laws of N.Y., Book 62½, Part 1, Uniform Commercial Code, § 2–719, Official Comment 1, p. 691). Moreover, Uniform Commercial Code (§ 2–719, subd. 3) provides specifically that consequential damages "may be limited or excluded unless the limitation or exclusion is unconscionable." In a similar vein, the Official Comment 3 to section 2–719 states: "Subsection (3) recognizes the validity of clauses limiting or excluding consequential damages but makes it clear that they may not operate in an unconscionable manner. Actually such terms are merely an allocation of unknown or undeterminable risks. The seller in all cases is free to disclaim warranties in the manner provided in Section 2–316" (McKinney's Cons.Laws of N.Y., Book 62½, Part 1, Uniform Commercial Code, § 2–719, Official Comment 3, p. 691). In sum, plaintiff has offered no good reason why the consequential damage exclusion clause should not be given effect in these circumstances, where the failure of the repair and replacement warranty is not due to bad faith or willfully dilatory conduct. That the clause be given effect here would be an allocation of the risks which leaves the buyer a fair quantum of remedy as required by the Code and one that the parties to this commercial contract could reasonably have intended. We conclude, therefore, that if plaintiff succeeds in establishing that the repair and replacement warranty failed of its essential purpose (Uniform

Commercial Code, § 2–719, subd. 2), the exclusion of consequential damages provided by Paragraph "I" remains in effect.

As stated, the decisions are in conflict but the proper rule, we think, is that set forth in *Chatlos Systems, Inc. v. National Cash Register Corp.*, 635 F.2d 1081, 1086 [CCA 3d, 1980], supra: "The limited remedy of repair and a consequential damages exclusion are two discrete ways of attempting to limit recovery for breach of warranty. (Citations omitted.) The Code, moreover, tests each by a different standard. The former survives unless it fails of its essential purpose, while the latter is valid unless it is unconscionable. We therefore see no reason to hold, as a general proposition, that the failure of the limited remedy provided in the contract, without more, invalidates a wholly distinct term in the agreement excluding consequential damages."

* * *

The leading cases cited as supporting the opposite view are *Jones & McKnight Corp. v. Birdsboro Corp.*, 320 F.Supp. 39 [DC Ill., 1970], supra, and *Adams v. J.I. Case Co.*, 125 Ill.App.2d 388, 261 N.E.2d 1, supra (see also *Koehring Co. v. A.P.I., Inc.*, 369 F.Supp. 882 [DC Mich., 1974]; *Beal v. General Motors Corp.*, 354 F.Supp. 423 [DC Del., 1973], supra; *Clark v. International Harvester Co.*, 99 Idaho 326, 581 P.2d 784, supra; *Ehlers v. Chrysler Motor Corp.*, 88 S.D. 612, 226 N.W.2d 157; *Goddard v. General Motors Corp.*, 60 Ohio St.2d 41, 396 N.E.2d 761; *Murray v. Holiday Rambler, Inc.*, 83 Wis.2d 406, 265 N.W.2d 513).

On analysis, however, neither *Jones & McKnight* nor *Adams* is inconsistent with our holding. Each case involves outright repudiation of the repair and replacement warranty or conduct by the seller that was wilfully dilatory. Thus, in *Jones & McKnight* the court held that the buyer was entitled to assume that the seller "would not be unreasonable or wilfully dilatory in making good their warranty in the event of defects in the machinery and equipment" and refused to allow the defendant "to shelter itself behind one segment of the warranty when it has allegedly repudiated and ignored its very limited obligations under another segment of the same warranty" (*Jones & McKnight Corp. v. Birdsboro Corp.*, supra, p. 43). Similarly, in *Adams* the court, in holding that the repair and replacement warranty and the consequential damages exclusion were "not separable" held that "plaintiff could not have made [its] bargain and purchase with knowledge that defendant [ ] would be unreasonable, or, * * * wilfully dilatory or careless and negligent in making good [its] warranty in the event of its breach" (*Adams v. J.I. Case Co.*, supra, 125 Ill.App.2d at p. 402, 261 N.E.2d 1).

We need not decide whether we would follow *Jones & McKnight* and *Adams* if plaintiff could contend, as did the buyers in those cases, that in agreeing to the consequential damages exclusion it never contemplated that defendant would not make good-faith efforts to effect repairs. That issue is not before us.

While not all of the cases following the *Jones & McKnight* and *Adams* rule involve bad faith or wilful repudiation of the repair and replacement warranty, several arise from non-commercial sales where the purchaser was an individual consumer (see, e.g., *Clark v. International Harvester Co.,* supra; *Ehlers v. Chrysler Motor Corp.,* supra; *Goddard v. General Motors Corp.,* supra; *Murray v. Holiday Rambler, Inc.,* supra). Moreover, in *Clark v. International Harvester Co.* (supra), which entailed a purchase of a tractor by an individual custom farmer, the court points to a factor not present in the case at bar, i.e., that there "was a significant disparity in bargaining power between the parties in this case" (*Clark v. International Harvester Co.,* supra, 99 Idaho at p. 343, 581 P.2d 784).

[margin note: π Cannot recover Consequential damages, but Can be entitled to §2-714 damages]

Although we hold that plaintiff may not recover consequential damages, it will, if successful at trial, be entitled to other damages (Uniform Commercial Code, § 2–714, subd. 2). The order granting summary judgment should, therefore, be modified to a grant of partial summary judgment dismissing only those elements of the first two causes of action against Allis which seek consequential damages.

* * *

Finally, we analyze plaintiff's contentions that Paragraph "I" is unconscionable under sections 2–719 (subd. 3) and 2–302 (subds. 1, 2) of the Code. A determination as to the conscionability of a contract relates to the circumstances existing at the time of its formation (Uniform Commercial Code, § 2–302, subd. 1). As a practical matter, however, the determination is inevitably made after a dispute has arisen. Thus, the agreement must be tested as to conscionability as it is applied to the particular breach which has occurred. Here, there is no claim of bad faith or that the failure to repair was wilfully dilatory, and we have held that the parties did not intend in Paragraph "I" that defendant's good faith but unsuccessful efforts to repair would negate the consequential damages exclusion. We have also held that such an agreed upon allocation of the risks does not offend the Code requirement that there be at least a fair quantum of remedy for breach of defendant's obligations. We must now decide whether this agreed upon allocation of the risks is unconscionable.

* * *

[margin note: Not Unconscionable]

On this record, in view of the nature of plaintiff's business as a large commercial grower, the size of the transaction involved, the fact that plaintiff had available other sources for purchasing similar equipment, the experience of its president and his familiarity with similar damage exclusion clauses, we agree with Special Term that plaintiff was not put in a bargaining position where it lacked a meaningful choice; nor was the agreement allocating the risk of crop loss and other consequential damages to the plaintiff, provided that good faith efforts be made to fulfill the repair warranty, unreasonably favorable to the defendant (see *Matter of State of New York v. Avco Fin. Serv. of N.Y.,* 50 N.Y.2d 383, 429 N.Y.S.2d 181, 406 N.E.2d 1075, supra).

The significant facts germane to the conscionability issue were essentially undisputed and we hold that Special Term correctly determined, as a legal question, that Paragraph "I" was not unconscionable and properly did so on the affidavits and other documents before it without the aid of a hearing (see Uniform Commercial Code, § 2–302).

* * *

[Footnotes omitted.]

Notes

1. *Cayuga Harvester* involved a fairly typical risk allocation package with four parts: (1) A limited warranty, i.e., that the goods were "merchantable and free of defects in material and workmanship at the time of shipment. * * *; (2) A disclaimer of all other warranties, express or implied plus a "merger" clause; (3) An agreed, exclusive limited remedy for breach, i.e., the "repair or replacement" of parts which are "defective in workmanship and material as delivered" within a stated period of time; and (4) An exclusion in any event of liability for consequential damages for liability, "whether in contract or tort, arising out of any warranties made." These packages vary from industry to industry, but the thrust is essentially the same. See Transamerica Oil Corp. v. Lynes, Inc., 723 F.2d 758 (10th Cir.1983), where the court concluded that a similar limitation was so "pervasive" in the trade that the parties must have contracted with reference to it.

The problem arises when, after a defect is discovered, the seller is unable or unwilling to repair it within the stated time.

> This rosy picture of the limited repair warranty, however, rests upon at least three assumptions: that the warrantor will diligently make repairs, that such repairs will indeed 'cure' the defects, and that consequential loss in the interim will be negligible. So long as these assumptions hold true, the limited remedy appears to operate fairly and * * * will usually withstand contentions of 'unconscionability.' But when one of these assumptions proves false in a particular case, the purchaser may find that the substantial benefit of the bargain has been lost.

Eddy, *On the "Essential" Purposes of Limited Remedies: The Metaphysics of U.C.C. Section 2–719(2)*, 65 Calif.L.Rev. 28, 63 (1977).

When a disappointed buyer attacks the limited remedy, the cases tend to agree on the questions which must be answered and that the answers may vary from case to case. Here is a brief sample.

1. Was the limited remedy "expressly agreed to be exclusive"? UCC 2–719(1)(b). If not, resort to it by the buyer is optional. See, e.g., Leininger v. Sola, 314 N.W.2d 39 (N.D.1981). If so, it is "the sole remedy."

2. Did the "circumstances cause an exclusive or limited remedy to fail of its essential purpose. * * *?" UCC 2–719(2). If not, it is enforceable. If so, "remedy may be had as provided in this Act." The most common "circumstances" are the seller's failure to "cure" the defect within the time stated or a reasonable time. As Judge Aspen put it: A limited remedy of repair and replacement fails of its essential purposes when it is inadequate

to provide the buyer with goods which conform to the contract within a reasonable time. * * * It is irrelevant to this standard whether the seller's failure to correct the defect is willful or not." Custom Automated Machinery v. Penda Corp., 537 F.Supp. 77 (N.D.Ill.1982). See also, Rudd Construction Equipment Co., Inc. v. Clark Equipment Co., 735 F.2d 974 (6th Cir.1984) (limited remedy fails essential purpose when defect causes fire which destroyed goods before seller had opportunity to cure).

3. If the limited remedy of repair or replacement failed its essential purpose, what is the effect on the total risk allocation package? More particularly, if the failure enables the buyer to pursue normal remedies for "direct" damages under UCC 2–714, what about the clause excluding consequential damages?

There are three closely related sub-questions. First, did the parties intend the exclusion clause to be an integral part of the risk allocation package? If so, the failure of one part spells the doom of the entire package, with the result that the buyer can pursue consequential damages under UCC 2–715(2). See Waters v. Massey-Ferguson, Inc., 775 F.2d 587 (4th Cir.1985); Milgard Tempering, Inc. v. Selas Corp. of America, 761 F.2d 553 (9th Cir.1985) (whether clause is separable a question of intent). If the exclusion clause was intended to be separate from the risk allocation, was the clause conscionable at the time the contract was made? UCC 2–719(3) & 2–302. See S.M. Wilson & Co. v. Smith Int'l, Inc., 587 F.2d 1363 (9th Cir. 1978). If so, consequential damages are not available. Third, if the exclusion clause was separate and conscionable at the time of contracting, was the seller's failure to "cure" so arbitrary or in such bad faith that it would be unfair to deprive the buyer of the substantial benefit of its bargain? A few courts have, on appropriate facts, taken this position. See, e.g., Fiorito Bros., Inc. v. Fruehauf Corp., 747 F.2d 1309 (9th Cir.1984); Caterpillar Tractor Co. v. Waterson, 13 Ark.App. 77, 679 S.W.2d 814 (1984).

Where does *Cayuga Harvester* fit in this range of possibilities?

Note: Contracting out of Tort Liability

In *Cayuga Harvester,* the seller attempted to exclude or "contract out" of "liability * * * in tort, arising out of warranties, representations, instructions, or defects from any cause," at least to the extent consequential damages were involved. What is the effect of these provisions?

If a defect in the product caused personal injuries, strict products liability would apply and the clause would be unenforceable (against public policy) against the plaintiff. See Note, *Enforcing Waivers in Products Liability,* 69 Va.L.Rev. 1111 (1983).

Between commercial parties ("extraordinary" consumers) where only economic loss is involved, the seller is, in most states, not liable in either strict products liability or negligence. In short, the buyer can pursue a warranty but not a tort theory. Review *Spring Motors,* supra at 527. Thus, the disclaimer would be tested under the Code, not in tort.

But suppose a defect in the product caused both economic loss and damage to the property sold, e.g., a defective part caused extensive damage to a turbine sold to the buyer but to no other property. Does warranty or tort theory apply and, if the latter, is the exclusion clause enforceable outside of the Code?

In this borderland between contract and tort where commercial parties are involved and property damage is confined to the goods sold, many courts have concluded that strict tort liability applies if the nature of the defect, the risk created and the manner in which the accident occurred raised an issue of product safety. The emphasis is upon the nature of the risk created to person and property, not upon the type of damage actually caused.

On the tort side of the line, the UCC does not apply. Nevertheless, commercial parties can agree to exculpate the seller from tort liability or from consequential damages if high standards insuring the quality of bargaining have been met. Thus, in Salt River Project Agr. v. Westinghouse Electric Co., 143 Ariz. 368, 694 P.2d 198 (1984), a turbine case, the court upheld an exculpation clause where the parties dealt in a commercial setting from positions of relatively equal bargaining strength, bargained over the specifications of the product and negotiated concerning the risk of loss from defects in the product. See McNichols, *Who Says That Strict Tort Disclaimers Can Never Be Effective? The Courts Disagree,* 28 Okl.L.Rev. 494 (1975).

SECTION 5. CONSUMER BUYERS, PRODUCT WARRANTIES AND ECONOMIC LOSS

An individual purchases a car, or a stereo or furniture or even a mobile home from a dealer for personal, family or household purposes. In short, they are consumer goods. See UCC 9–109(1). A common assumption is that consumer buyers, as a class, have less capacity than the professional seller to protect themselves in the bargain. They are at a disadvantage in assessing risk, evaluating quality, obtaining adequate information, bargaining over contract provisions and pursuing remedies if problems arise. They are "ordinary" consumers who are more susceptible to exploitation or unprovable fraud by the seller than a commercial or "extraordinary" buyer. (The distinction between "ordinary" and "extraordinary" consumers was advanced by Justice Peters, dissenting in Seely v. White Motor Co., 69 Cal.2d 9, 403 P.2d 145 (1965), to draw the line between warranty and tort in products liability cases. According to Peters, the test should depend upon the "relative roles played by the parties to the purchase contract and the nature of the transaction" rather than the type of loss caused and ask whether, at the time of contracting, the goods were sold to a commercial party or to an "ordinary consumer who is usually unable to protect himself * * *" or a commercial buyer who possessed "more bargaining power than does the usual individual who purchases * * * on the retail level." 403 P.2d at 152–58.)

The conclusion from this, is sometimes disputed, see, e.g., Schwartz & Wilde, *Imperfect Information in Markets for Contract Terms: The Examples of Warranties and Security Interests,* 69 Va.L.Rev. 1387 (1983); compare Kronman, *Paternalism and the Law of Contracts,* 92

Yale L.J. 763, 766–74 (1983) (assessing risk of unprovable fraud by seller), is that consumers need more legal protection than commercial buyers.

When the losses are solely economic, the consumer buyer's legal protection from breach of warranty by the seller is, without more, governed by the UCC. Additional, albeit uneven, protection is provided by the Magnuson-Moss Warranty Act on the federal level and, in some states, consumer protection legislation, including the so-called "lemon" laws.

In this Section, we will see how the consumer buyer of a "big ticket" item, a new car, might fare under this mix of federal and state law against the risk allocation package discussed in Section 4, supra. For general background and more detail, we recommend, Rice, *Product Quality Laws and the Economics of Federalism,* 65 B.U.L.Rev. 1 (1985). See also, Braucher, *An Informal Resolution Model of Consumer Product Warranty Law,* 1985 Wis.L.Rev. 1405; Vogel, *Squeezing Consumers: Lemon Laws, Consumer Warranties, and a Proposal for Reform,* 1985 Ariz.St.L.J. 589; Coffinberger & Samuels, *Legislative Responses to the Plight of New Car Purchasers,* 18 U.C.C.L.J. 168 (1985); Miller & Kanter, *Litigation under Magnuson-Moss,* 13 U.C.C.L.J. 10 (1980).

VENTURA v. FORD MOTOR CORP.

Superior Court of New Jersey, Appellate Division, 1981.
180 N.J.Super. 45, 433 A.2d 801.

[Marino Auto sold Ventura a new 1978 Ford. The car was substantially impaired due to persistent and continual stalling and hesitation. Ventura sued both Marino Auto and Ford, the manufacturer, for damages and Marino Auto cross-claimed against Ford for indemnification. At the conclusion of the non-jury trial, the trial judge concluded that Ford had breached a warranty to Ventura, made through Marino Auto, but that Ventura had not proven damages against Ford. Ventura, however, could recover attorney's fees in the amount of $5,165 from Ford under the Magnuson-Moss Warranty Act, 15 U.S.C.A. § 2310(d)(2). In addition, despite an attempt by the dealer to disclaim all warranties, express or implied, Ventura could revoke its acceptance against and recover the purchase price less an allowance for use, a total of $6,745.59, from Marino Auto. Finally, the trial court entered a judgment in favor of Marino Auto against Ford for $2,910.59 and rejected Ventura's claims for interest, punitive damages and treble damages.

On appeal, the judgment was affirmed. The court assumed that Marino Auto's disclaimer of the implied warranty of merchantability was valid under the UCC, and concluded that the judgment was supported by the Magnuson-Moss Warranty Act.]

* * *

The Magnuson-Moss Warranty-Federal Trade Commission Improvement Act, *supra*, was adopted on January 4, 1975, 88 *Stat.* 2183. Its purpose was to make "warranties on consumer products more readily understandable and enforceable." Note, 7 *Rutgers-Camden L.J.* 379 (1976). The act enhances the consumer's position by allowing recovery under a warranty without regard to privity of contract between the consumer and warrantor, by prohibiting the disclaimer of implied warranties in a written warranty, and by enlarging the remedies available to a consumer for breach of warranty, including the award of attorneys' fees. *Id.* The requirement of privity of contract between the consumer and the warrantor has been removed by assuring consumers a remedy against all warrantors of the product.[3] A consumer is defined in 15 *U.S.C.A.* § 2301(3) as follows:

> (3) The term 'consumer' means a buyer (other than for purposes of resale) of any consumer product, any person to whom such product is transferred during the duration of an implied or written warranty (or service contract) applicable to the product, and any other person who is entitled by the terms of such warranty (or service contract) or under applicable State law to enforce against the warrantor (or service contract) the obligations of the warranty (or service contract).

A "supplier" is defined as any person engaged in the business of making a consumer product directly or indirectly available to consumers, § 2301(4), and a "warrantor" includes any supplier or other person who gives or offers to give a written warranty or who is obligated under an implied warranty. § 2301(5). The term "written warranty" is defined in § 2301(6) to include:

> (A) any written affirmation of fact or written promise made in connection with the sale of a consumer product by a supplier to a buyer which relates to the nature of the material or workmanship and affirms or promises that such material or workmanship is defect free or will meet a specified level of performance over a specified period of time, or

> (B) any undertaking in writing in connection with the sale by a supplier of a consumer product to refund, repair, replace or take other remedial action with respect to such product in the event that such product fails to meet the specifications set forth in the undertaking.

The Magnuson-Moss Warranty Act provides for two types of written warranties on consumer products, those described as "full" warranties and those described as "limited" warranties. 15 *U.S.C.A.* § 2303. The nature of the "full" warranty is prescribed by § 2304. It expressly provides in subsection (a)(4) that a consumer must be given the election

---

3. In Miller and Kanter, "Litigation Under Magnuson-Moss: New Opportunities in Private Actions," 13 *U.C.C.L.J.* 10, 21–22 (1980), the authors discuss the broad definition of a consumer and state that "an assumption is now created that no privity restriction exists."

to receive a refund or replacement without charge of a product or part which is defective or malfunctions after a reasonable number of attempts by the warrantor to correct such condition. For the breach of any warranty, express or implied, or of a service contract (defined in 15 *U.S.C.A.* § 2301(8)), consumers are given the right to sue for damages and "other legal and equitable relief" afforded under state or federal law, 15 *U.S.C.A.* § 2310(d); 15 *U.S.C.A.* § 2311(b)(1).

Appellant Ford contends that the trial judge improperly invoked § 2304 of the act as a basis for allowing "rescission" in the case since the warranty given by Ford was a limited warranty and not a full warranty. 15 *U.S.C.A.* § 2303(a)(2) provides that all warranties that do not meet federal minimum standards for warranty contained in § 2304 shall be conspicuously designated a "limited warranty." "Limited" warranties protect consumers by prohibiting disclaimers of implied warranties, § 2308, but are otherwise not described in the act. Note, *supra,* 7 *Rutgers-Camden L.J.* at 381. Clearly, Ford's warranty, which is quoted later in this opinion, was a limited warranty.

15 *U.S.C.A.* § 2308 provides as follows:

(a) No supplier may disclaim or modify (except as provided in subsection (b) of this section) any implied warranty to a consumer with respect to such consumer product if (1) such supplier makes any written warranty to the consumer with respect to such consumer product, or (2) at the time of sale, or within 90 days thereafter, such supplier enters into a service contract with the consumer which applies to such consumer product.

(b) For purposes of this chapter (other than section 2304(a)(2) of this title), implied warranties may be limited in duration to the duration of a written warranty of reasonable duration, if such limitation is conscionable and is set forth in clear and unmistakable language and prominently displayed on the face of the warranty.

(c) A disclaimer, modification, or limitation made in violation of this section shall be ineffective for purposes of this chapter and State law.

We will first consider the application of this act to the dealer, Marino Auto. As quoted above, paragraph 7 of the purchase order-contract provides that there are no warranties, express or implied, made by the selling dealer or manufacturer except, in the case of a new motor vehicle, "the warranty expressly given to the purchaser upon delivery of such motor vehicle. * * *" This section also provides: "The selling dealer also agrees to promptly perform and fulfill all terms and conditions of the owner service policy." Ford contended in the trial court that Marino Auto had "a duty" to properly diagnose and make repairs, that such duty was "fixed both by the express warranty * * * which they passed on * * * and by the terms of [paragraph 7 of the contract with plaintiff]" by which Marino Auto expressly undertook "to perform its obligations under the owner service policy." See

15 *U.S.C.A.* § 2310(f); 16 *C.F.R.* § 700.4 (1980). The provision in paragraph 7 in these circumstances is a "written warranty" within the meaning of § 2301(6)(B) since it constitutes an undertaking in connection with the sale to take "remedial action with respect to such product in the event that such product fails to meet the specifications set forth in the undertaking. * * *" In our view the specifications of the undertaking include, at the least, the provisions of the limited warranty furnished by Ford, namely:

LIMITED WARRANTY (12 MONTHS OR 12,000 MILES/19,312 KILOMETRES) 1978 NEW CAR AND LIGHT TRUCK

Ford warrants for its 1978 model cars and light trucks that the Selling Dealer will repair or replace free any parts, except tires, found under normal use in the U.S. or Canada to be defective in factory materials or workmanship within the earlier of 12 months or 12,000 miles/19,312 km from either first use or retail delivery. All we require is that you properly operate and maintain your vehicle and that you return for warranty service to your Selling Dealer or any Ford or Lincoln-Mercury Dealer if you are traveling, have moved a long distance or need emergency repairs. Warranty repairs will be made with Ford Authorized Service or Remanufactured Parts.

THERE IS NO OTHER EXPRESS WARRANTY ON THIS VEHICLE.[4]

The record does not contain a written description of the "owner service policy" which the dealer agreed to perform. Nevertheless, since Ford is the appellant here, we take its contentions at trial and documents in the record to establish the dealer's obligation to Ford and to plaintiff to make the warranty repairs on behalf of Ford (subject to the right of reimbursement or other terms that may be contained in their agreement). For the purpose of this appeal we are satisfied that the dealer's undertaking in paragraph 7 constitutes a written warranty within the meaning of 15 *U.S.C.A.* § 2301(6)(B). Accordingly, having furnished a written warranty to the consumer, the dealer as a supplier may not "disclaim or modify [except to limit in duration] any implied warranty to a consumer. * * *" The result of this analysis is to invalidate the attempted disclaimer by the dealer of the implied war-

---

4. The warranty also provided:

TO THE EXTENT ALLOWED BY LAW:

1. ANY IMPLIED WARRANTY OF MERCHANTABILITY OR FITNESS IS LIMITED TO THE 12 MONTH OR 12,000–MILE/19,312–KM DURATION OF THIS WRITTEN WARRANTY.

2. NEITHER FORD NOR THE SELLING DEALER SHALL HAVE ANY RESPONSIBILITY FOR LOSS OF USE OF THE VEHICLE, LOSS OF TIME, IN-CONVENIENCE, COMMERCIAL LOSS OR CONSEQUENTIAL DAMAGES.

Some states do not allow limitations on how long an implied warranty lasts or the exclusion or limitation of incidental or consequential damages, so the above limitations may not apply to you.

This warranty gives you specific legal rights, and you also may have other rights which vary from state to state.

ranties of merchantability and fitness.[5] Being bound by those implied warranties arising under state law, *N.J.S.A.* 12A:2–314 and 315, Marino Auto was liable to plaintiff for the breach thereof as found by the trial judge, and plaintiff could timely revoke his acceptance of the automobile and claim a refund of his purchase price. *N.J.S.A.* 12A:2–608 and *N.J.S.A.* 12A:2–711. *Zabriskie Chevrolet, Inc. v. Smith,* 99 *N.J.Super.* 441, 240 *A.*2d 195 (Law Div.1968). In this connection we note that the trial judge found that plaintiff's attempted revocation of acceptance was made in timely fashion, and that finding has adequate support in the evidence.

As the trial judge noted, 15 *U.S.C.A.* § 2310(d)(1) provides that a consumer who is damaged by the failure of a warrantor to comply with any obligation under the act, or under a written warranty or implied warranty or service contract, may bring suit "for damages and other legal and equitable relief. ＊ ＊ ＊" Although the remedy of refund of the purchase price is expressly provided by the Magnuson-Moss Warranty Act for breach of a full warranty, granting this remedy under state law for breach of a limited warranty is not barred by or inconsistent with the act. 15 *U.S.C.A.* § 2311(b)(1) provides that nothing in the act restricts "any right or remedy of any consumer under State law or other Federal law." See also 15 *U.S.C.A.* § 2311(c)(2). Thus, for breach of the implied warranty of merchantability, plaintiff was entitled to revoke acceptance against Marino Auto, and a judgment for the purchase price less an allowance for the use of the vehicle was properly entered against Marino Auto. *N.J.S.A.* 12A:2–608 and 711. *Cf.* 15 *U.S.C.A.* § 2301(12) which defines "refund" as the return of the purchase price "less reasonable depreciation based on actual use where permitted" by regulations.

Plaintiff also could have recovered damages against Ford for Ford's breach of its written limited warranty. Marino Auto was Ford's representative for the purpose of making repairs to plaintiff's vehicle under the warranty. *See Henningsen v. Bloomfield Motors, Inc.,* supra, 32 *N.J.* at 374, 161 *A.*2d 69; *cf. Conte v. Dwan Lincoln-Mercury, Inc.,* 172 *Conn.* 112, 122–126, 374 *A.*2d 144, 149–150 (Sup.Ct.Err.1976). The limited warranty expressly required the purchaser to return the vehicle "for warranty service" to the dealer or to any Ford or Lincoln-Mercury dealer if the purchaser is traveling or has moved a long distance or needs emergency repairs. Ford contends that it put purchasers on notice that they should advise Ford's district office if they have problems with their cars that a dealer is unable to fix. The record contains a document listing "frequently asked warranty questions" which states:

> The Dealership where you purchased your vehicle has the responsibility for performing warranty repairs; therefore, take your vehicle to that Dealership. ＊ ＊ ＊ If you encounter a service problem,

---

5. The same holding would apply if the undertaking by Marino Auto to perform the "owner service policy" is construed as a "service contract." 15 *U.S.C.A.* § 2308(a), *supra.*

refer to the service assistance section of your Owner's Guide for suggested action.

We do not read these provisions as requiring notice to Ford as a condition of relief against Ford when Ford's dealer has failed after numerous attempts to correct defects under warranty.

Normally, the measure of damages for a breach of warranty is the difference between the price paid by the purchaser and the market value of the defective product. *Santor v. A & M Karagheusian, Inc., supra,* 44 *N.J.* at 63, 68–69, 207 *A.2d* 305; *see Herbstman v. Eastman Kodak Co., supra,* 68 *N.J.* at 11, 342 *A.2d* 181. However, as Judge Conford said in his concurring opinion in *Herbstman, supra,* 68 *N.J.* at 15–16, 342 *A.2d* 181, under principles of strict liability in tort a purchaser may be entitled to rescind the transaction and receive the return of the purchase price from the manufacturer without privity if the defect causes substantial impairment of value of the product. The strict liability in tort doctrine as developed in this state in the *Santor case, supra,* eliminated the need for privity of contract between the purchaser and the manufacturer as a condition for the purchaser's claim for his loss of bargain caused by a defect in the product. As noted above, the Magnuson-Moss Warranty Act accomplished the same result.

One question posed by this case is whether recovery of the purchase price from the manufacturer was available to plaintiff for breach of the manufacturer's warranty. If the warranty were a full warranty plaintiff would have been entitled to a refund of the purchase price under the Magnuson-Moss Warranty Act. Since Ford's warranty was a limited warranty we must look to state law to determine plaintiff's right to damages or other legal and equitable relief. 15 *U.S.C.A.* § 2310(d)(1). Once privity is removed as an obstacle to relief we see no reason why a purchaser cannot also elect the equitable remedy of returning the goods to the manufacturer who is a warrantor and claiming a refund of the purchase price less an allowance for use of the product. *See Seely v. White Motor Co.,* 63 *Cal.2d* 9, 45 *Cal.Rptr.* 17, 20, 403 *P.2d* 145, 148 (Sup.Ct.1965); *Durfee v. Rod Baxter Imports, Inc., supra,* 262 *N.W.2d* at 357–358, where the Minnesota Supreme Court held as a matter of state law that lack of privity does not bar a purchaser of a foreign car from revoking acceptance and recovering the purchase price from the distributor of such cars as distinguished from the local dealer. The decision was made without regard to the Magnuson-Moss Warranty Act.

We are dealing with the breach of an express contractual obligation. Nothing prevents us from granting an adequate remedy under state law for that breach of contract, including rescission when appropriate. Under state law the right to revoke acceptance for defects substantially impairing the value of the product (*N.J.S.A.* 12A:2–608) and to receive a refund of the purchase price (*N.J.S.A.* 12A:2–711) are rights available to a buyer against a seller in privity. Where the manufacturer gives a warranty to induce the sale it is consistent to allow the same type of remedy as against that manufacturer. *See Durfee v. Rod Baxter Imports, Inc., supra; cf. Seely v. White Motor Co., supra.* Only the privity concept, which is frequently viewed as a relic these days, *Koperski v. Husker Dodge, Inc.,* 208 *Neb.* 29, 45, 302 *N.W.*2d 655, 664 (Sup.Ct.1981); *see Kinlaw v. Long Mfg. N.C., Inc.,* 298 *N.C.* 494, 259 *S.E.*2d 552 (Sup.Ct.1979), has interfered with a rescission-type remedy against the manufacturer of goods not purchased directly from the manufacturer. If we focus on the fact that the warranty creates a direct contractual obligation to the buyer, the reason for allowing the same remedy that is available against a direct seller becomes clear. Although the manufacturer intended to limit the remedy to the repair and replacement of defective parts, the failure of that remedy, *see N.J. S.A.* 12A:2–719(2); *Goddard v. General Motors Corp.,* 60 *Ohio St.*2d 41, 396 *N.E.*2d 761 (Sup.Ct.1979); *Seely v. White Motor Co., supra,* and the consequent breach of the implied warranty of merchantability which accompanied the limited warranty by virtue of the Magnuson-Moss Warranty Act, make a rescission-type remedy appropriate when revocation of acceptance is justified. *Durfee v. Rod Baxter Imports, Inc., supra,* 262 *N.W.*2d at 357.

Lastly, we consider Ford's contention that a counsel fee was improperly granted to plaintiff since no judgment was entered in favor of plaintiff against Ford and Ford contends it was not given adequate notice of the defects in the car. 15 *U.S.C.A.* § 2310(d)(2) provides that a consumer who "prevails in any action brought [in any court] under paragraph (1) of this subsection * * * may be allowed by the court to recover as part of the judgment * * * expenses (including attorney's fees based on the actual time expended). * * *" This section is subject to the provisions contained in § 2310(e). Subsection (e) provides that, with certain exceptions, no action based upon breach of a written or implied warranty or service contract may be prosecuted unless a person obligated under the warranty or service contract "is afforded a reasonable opportunity to cure such failure to comply." Here that opportunity was given to Ford's designated representative to whom the purchaser was required to bring the car. A direct employee of Ford, Bednarz, also met with plaintiff or his wife and was made aware of some difficulty with the car. We are not certain of the extent of Ford's knowledge of those difficulties. However, in our view the opportunities given to Marino Auto to repair the vehicle satisfied the requirements of 15 *U.S.C.A.* § 2310(e) in this case.

As noted, Ford also contends that a counsel fee could not be awarded against Ford because plaintiff did not recover a judgment against Ford. The Magnuson-Moss Warranty Act permits a prevailing consumer to recover attorney's fees "as part of the judgment." The trial judge found that Ford had breached its warranty and that the car's value was substantially impaired. He entered no damage judgment against Ford. However, in the absence of proof of actual damages, plaintiff was entitled to a judgment against Ford for nominal damages. *Ruane Dev. Corp. v. Cullere*, 134 *N.J.Super.* 245, 252, 339 A.2d 229 (App.Div.1975); *Ench v. Bluestein*, 52 *N.J.Super.* 169, 173–174, 145 A.2d 44 (App.Div.1958); *Winkler v. Hartford Accident and Indem. Co.*, 66 *N.J.Super.* 22, 29, 168 A.2d 418 (App.Div.), certif. den. 34 *N.J.* 581, 170 A.2d 544 (1961); *Packard Englewood Motors, Inc. v. Packard Motor Car Co.*, 215 *F.*2d 503, 510 (3 Cir.1954). Ford was not prejudiced by the failure of the trial judge to enter a judgment for nominal damages to which the award of attorney's fees could be attached. *See Nobility Homes, Inc. v. Ballentine*, 386 *So.*2d 727, 730–731 (Sup.Ct.Ala. 1980). The award of counsel fees fulfills the intent of the Magnuson-Moss Warranty Act. Without such an award consumers frequently would be unable to vindicate warranty rights accorded by law.

As to the amount of counsel fees allowed by the trial judge, we find no abuse of discretion. The allowance was for actual time spent at an hourly rate of $75. Consideration could properly be given to the fact that plaintiff's attorney undertook this claim on a contingency basis with a relatively small retainer. *DR* 2–106(A)(8). The normal breach of warranty case ought not require four separate appearances before the trial court. To some extent this was not in the control of plaintiff's attorney, and plaintiff might have obtained all the relief required against Ford on the first day of trial. But it did not work out that way. In other cases it may be possible to stipulate damages and simplify the issues, thus limiting the cost of this type of litigation for consumers and suppliers alike. But the issues raised in this case were novel in this State, and no one can be faulted for the difficulty and time consumed in this litigation.

We have stated that in an appropriate case a consumer could recover the purchase price from a manufacturer for breach of a limited warranty causing a substantial impairment of the value of the product. The application of the Magnuson-Moss Warranty Act is one distinction between this case and *Herbstman v. Eastman Kodak Co.*, *supra*, 68 *N.J.* at 9–12, n. 1, 342 A.2d 181. However, we need not determine whether plaintiff had the right to such relief in this case. Ordinarily, a purchaser seeking such relief after unsuccessful repairs should be required to give timely notice to the manufacturer of revocation of acceptance of defective goods and of his demand for a refund of the purchase price. *See Durfee v. Rod Baxter Imports, Inc.*, *supra*, 262 *N.W.*2d at 353. Plaintiff's complaint alleges that such notice and demand were given to Ford in this case, but no finding was made by the trial judge on plaintiff's claim against Ford. Having determined that plaintiff was entitled to a judgment for nominal damages and counsel fees against Ford, and that judgments against Marino Auto and for indemnification by Ford were properly entered, it makes no difference in this case whether plaintiff was also entitled to a refund of his purchase price from Ford.

The result in this case differs from that reached in *Edelstein v. Toyota Motors Distributors*, *supra*. However, the differences in the cases, the absence there of proof of any warranty from defendants, and the apparent failure of the purchaser to rely on the Magnuson-Moss Warranty Act make it unnecessary for us to comment on that holding.

Affirmed.

Notes

Here are some questions about the *Ventura* case.

1. The court assumes that the Dealer had effectively disclaimed all warranties under the Code. How does the Magnuson-Moss Warranty Act support the court's conclusion that, nevertheless, the dealer breached an implied warranty of merchantability?

Note that the dealer failed to "cure" the problem and that the buyer's remedy included revocation of acceptance, UCC 2–608(1), and a refund of the price, UCC 2–711(1), adjusted for the value of buyer's use after the revocation. Consequential damages were not claimed. Compare Bogner v. General Motors Corp., 117 Misc.2d 929, 459 N.Y.S.2d 679 (N.Y.Civ.Ct.1982) (although consequential damages excluded, court awards damages for emotional distress). See also, Ramirez v. Autosport, 88 N.J. 277, 440 A.2d 1345 (1982) (buyer properly rejects camper-van for defects, cancels contract and recovers price); Jacobs v. Rosemount Dodge-Winnebago South, 310 N.W.2d 71 (Minn.1981) (limited remedy fails essential purpose, buyer permitted to revoke acceptance and recover consequential damages).

2. Suppose that the dealer made no "written warranty," see 15 U.S. C.A. § 2301(6), and effectively disclaimed all warranties under UCC 2–316. Would the buyer have any claims against the dealer under either the Magnuson-Moss Act or the UCC?

A few states have passed special consumer legislation to deal with perceived shortcomings in the Code. See, for example, Section 2–316A of the Massachusetts UCC, enacted in 1973:

2–316A. Limitation of Exclusion or Modification of Warranties

The provisions of section 2–316 shall not apply to sales of consumer goods, services or both. Any language, oral or written, used by a seller or manufacturer of consumer goods and services, which attempts to exclude or modify any implied warranties of merchantability and fitness for a particular purpose or to exclude or modify the consumer's remedies for breach of those warranties, shall be unenforceable.

Any language, oral or written, used by a manufacturer of consumer goods, which attempts to limit or modify a consumer's remedies for breach of such manufacturer's express warranties, shall be unenforceable, unless such manufacturer maintains facilities within the commonwealth sufficient to provide reasonable and expeditious performance of the warranty obligations.

The provisions of this section may not be disclaimed or waived by agreement.

3. The manufacturer, Ford Motor Company, made a written, "limited" warranty to Ventura. The express warranty was breached and the

dealer failed to "cure." What was the maximum protection, liability and remedy, to which Ventura was entitled against Ford under the Magnuson-Moss Act? Read the entire statute, please. Why was Ventura's recovery limited to the recovery of attorney's fees?

4. Suppose that Ford (or the Dealer) had made a written, "full" warranty to Ventura. To what additional protection would Ventura be entitled? See, particularly, 15 U.S.C.A. § 2304(a). How does this differ from protection available under the UCC when a limited remedy "fails" its essential purpose?

As a matter of practice, few manufacturers or sellers are willing to make "full" written warranties, and there is no penalty imposed for that omission under *Magnuson-Moss.*

Problem 14–5

Assume the same facts as in Ventura v. Ford Motor Company. Assume, also, that the state where the dispute arose had enacted a "New-Car Buyer Protection Act," based upon that enacted in Illinois. Ill.Rev.Stat. Ch. 121½, Par. 1201–08.

What protection does this "Lemon Law" add to that available under the Magnuson-Moss Warranty Act?

How does the "Lemon Law" mesh with the applicable provisions of the UCC?

NEW–CAR BUYER PROTECTION ACT

1201. Short title

§ 1. This Act shall be known and may be cited as the New-Car Buyer Protection Act.

1202. Definitions

§ 2. For the purposes of this Act, the following words have the meanings ascribed to them in this Section.

(a) "Consumer" means an individual who purchases a new car from the seller for the purposes of transporting himself and others, as well as their personal property, for primarily personal, household or family purposes.

(b) "Express warranty" has the same meaning, for the purposes of this Act, as it has for the purposes of the Uniform Commercial Code.

(c) "New car" means a passenger car, as defined in Section 1–157 of The Illinois Vehicle Code, which does not qualify under the definition of a used motor vehicle, as set forth in Section 1–216 of that Code. The term does not include motor homes, mini motor homes or van campers, as defined in Section 1–145.01 of The Illinois Vehicle Code.

(d) "Nonconformity" refers to a new car's failure to conform to all express warranties applicable to such car, which failure substantially impairs the use, market value or safety of that car.

(e) "Seller" means the manufacturer of a new car, that manufacturer's agent or distributor or that manufacturer's authorized dealer.

(f) "Statutory warranty period" means the period of one year or 12,000 miles, whichever occurs first after the date of the delivery of a new car to the consumer who purchased it.

1203. Failure of new car to conform to express warranties—Remedies—Presumption—Allowance for consumer use—Suspension of warranty period

§ 3.   (a) If after a reasonable number of attempts the seller is unable to conform the new car to any of its applicable express warranties, the manufacturer shall either provide the consumer with a new car of like model line, if available, or otherwise a comparable motor vehicle as a replacement, or accept the return of the car from the consumer and refund to the consumer the full purchase price of the new car, including all collateral charges, less a reasonable allowance for consumer use of the car.

(b) A presumption that a reasonable number of attempts have been undertaken to conform a new car to its express warranties shall arise where, within the statutory warranty period,

(1) the same nonconformity has been subject to repair by the seller, its agents or authorized dealers during the statutory warranty period, 4 or more times, and such nonconformity continues to exist; or

(2) the car has been out of service by reason of repair of nonconformities for a total of 30 or more business days during the statutory warranty period.

(c) A reasonable allowance for consumer use of a car is that amount directly attributable to the wear and tear incurred by the new car as a result of its having been used prior to the first report of a nonconformity to the seller, and during any subsequent period in which it is not out of service by reason of repair.

(d) The fact that a new car's failure to conform to an express warranty is the result of abuse, neglect or unauthorized modifications or alterations is an affirmative defense to claims brought under this Act.

(e) The statutory warranty period of a new car shall be suspended for any period of time during which repair services are not available to the consumer because of a war, invasion or strike, or a fire, flood or other natural disaster.

(f) Refunds made pursuant to this Act shall be made to the consumer, and lien holder if any exists, as their respective interests appear.

(g) For the purposes of this Act, a manufacturer sells a new car to a consumer when he provides that consumer with a replacement car pursuant to subsection (a).

(h) In no event shall the presumption herein provided apply against a manufacturer, his agent, distributor or dealer unless the manufacturer has received prior direct written notification from or on behalf of the consumer, and has an opportunity to correct the alleged defect.

1204. Informal settlement procedure—Notice

§ 4. (a) The provisions of subsection (a) of Section 3 shall not apply unless the consumer has first resorted to an informal settlement procedure applicable to disputes to which that subsection would apply where

(1) The manufacturer of the new car has established such a procedure;

(2) The procedure conforms:

(i) substantially with the provisions of Title 16, Code of Federal Regulation, Part 703, as from time to time amended, and

(ii) to the requirements of subsection (c); and

(3) The consumer has received from the seller adequate written notice of the existence of the procedure.

Adequate written notice includes but is not limited to the incorporation of the informal dispute settlement procedure into the terms of the written warranty to which the car does not conform.

(b) If the consumer is dissatisfied with the decision reached in an informal dispute settlement procedure or the results of such a decision, he may bring a civil action to enforce his rights under subsection (a) of Section 3. The decision reached in the informal dispute settlement procedure is admissible in such a civil action. The period of limitations for a civil action to enforce a consumer's rights or remedies under subsection (a) of Section 3 shall be extended for a period equal to the number of days the subject matter of the civil action was pending in the informal dispute settlement procedure.

(c) A disclosure of the decision in an informal dispute settlement procedure shall include notice to the consumer of the provisions of subsection (b).

1205. Application of Uniform Commercial Code

§ 5. Persons electing to proceed and settle under this Act shall be barred from a separate cause of action under Chapter Five.

1206. Limitations

§ 6. Any action brought under this Act shall be commenced within eighteen months following the date of original delivery of the motor vehicle to the consumer.

1207. Seller to provide statement of consumer's rights

§ 7. The seller who sells a new car to a consumer, shall, upon delivery of that car to the consumer, provide the consumer with a written statement clearly and conspicuously setting forth in full detail the consumer's rights under subsection (a) of Section 3, and the presumptions created by subsection (b) of that Section.

———

VOGEL, SQUEEZING CONSUMERS: LEMON LAWS, CONSUMER WARRANTIES, AND A PROPOSAL FOR REFORM, 1985 Ariz.St. L.J. 589, 615, 644–47.

* * *

Acting on consumer complaints, legislatures in 37 states have passed lemon laws to help car owners. Although the laws vary in many important respects, they still have a number of features in common. First, the lemon laws apply only to new cars and generally only to cars purchased for noncommercial purposes. Second, the laws require the manufacturer to conform the vehicle to the terms of the warranty upon receiving notice of the problem from the consumer. If the manufacturer is unable to correct the defect within a stated period of time or after a certain number of attempts, the lemon laws allow purchasers to return defective cars and to receive either a refund of the purchase price or a replacement vehicle. However, the refund or replacement remedy may not be available to a consumer unless he or she gives the manufacturer notice that efforts to repair the car have failed. Finally, a number of lemon laws also restrict the resale of returned vehicles to other purchasers.

* * *

As has been seen, the lemon laws by themselves do not provide consumers with an effective remedy. In many respects, they simply restate the present law. In other respects they are more restrictive than alternative legal remedies. Consequently, if a consumer has a warranty problem, it may be necessary to bring an action under the UCC, the Magnuson-Moss Warranty Act, and the lemon law. Generally, the lemon laws allow for this. With the exception of Arizona, Florida, Illinois, New Mexico, North Dakota, and Tennessee,* all the lemon laws contain a provision which states that the lemon law does not limit rights or remedies under other law.**

* ARIZ.REV.STAT.ANN. § 44–1261 to –1265 (Supp. 1984–85); FLA.STAT.ANN. § 681.10–.108 (West Supp.1985); 1985 N.D.Sess.Laws 1378, § (6); TENN.CODE ANN. § 55–24–108 (Supp.1984). The Tennessee lemon law specifically forecloses any action under another law if the consumer chooses to sue under the lemon law. Given the deficiencies of the lemon law, this provision is highly undesirable. In Tennessee, a consumer might fare better ignoring the lemon law and suing under the U.C.C. The Illinois and New Mexico lemon laws specifically bar any action under the U.C.C. if the consumer sues under the lemon law. ILL.ANN.STAT. ch. 121, ¶ 1205 § 5 (Smith-Hurd 1984–85); 1985 N.M.Laws 126, § 5.

** ALASKA STAT. ch. 101, § 45.45.340 (Supp.1984); COLO.REV.STAT. § 42–12–105 (1984); CONN.GEN.STAT.ANN. § 42–179(h) (West Supp.1985); DEL.CODE ANN. tit. 6 § 5008 (Supp.1984); 1985 Kan.Sess.Laws 118, § 2; LA.REV.STAT.ANN. § 51:1946 (West Supp.1985); ME.REV.STAT.ANN. tit. 10, § 1162(1) (Supp.1984–85); MD.COM.LAW CODE ANN. § 14–1501(b) (Supp.1984); MASS.

GEN.LAWS ANN. ch. 90, § 7N½ (5) (West Supp.1985); MINN.STAT.ANN. § 325F.655(8) (West Supp.1985); MO.ANN.STAT. § 407.579 (Vernon Supp.1985); MONT.CODE ANN. § 61–4–506 (1983) and 1985 Mont.Laws 295; NEB.REV.STAT. § 60–2708 (1984); NEV. REV.STAT. § 598.786 (1983); N.H.REV.STAT. ANN. § 357–D:7 (1984); N.J.STAT.ANN. § 56:12–27 (West Supp.1985); N.Y.GEN. BUS.LAW § 198–a(f) (Consol.Supp. 1984–85); OR.REV.STAT. § 646.375 (1983); PA.STAT. ANN. tit. 73, § 1962 (Purdon 1985); R.I.GEN.LAWS § 31–5.2–6 (Supp.1984); TEX. REV.CIV.STAT.ANN. art. 4413(36), § 6.07(f) (Vernon Supp.1985); 1985 Utah Laws 29, §§ 13–21–6(3); VT.STAT.ANN. tit. 9, § 4178 (Supp.1984); VA.CODE § 59.1–207.13(F) (Supp.1984); WASH.REV.CODE ANN. § 19.118.070 (Supp.1984); W.VA.CODE § 46A–6A–9 (Supp.1984); WIS.STAT.ANN. § 218.015(5) (West 1984–85); WYO.STAT. § 40–17–101(e) (Supp.1985). The Mississippi law does not specifically state whether other remedies are allowed. 1985 Miss. Laws 224, §§ 1–9.

If lawmakers wish to provide increased protection to purchasers of automobiles, there are certain modifications which would make the lemon laws more effective: (1) clear rules or standards; (2) presumptions which ease the burden of proof, (3) a minimum of technicalities; and (4) a choice between a refund and other damages or a replacement vehicle. They could also publicize consumers' rights under the improved laws.

For consumers and manufacturers to know their rights under the lemon laws, the laws must contain clear rules or standards specifying when the consumer may return the defective car and seek a refund or a replacement vehicle. The lemon laws make strides in this direction by spelling out the number of repair attempts and the number of days a car must be in the shop for repair before the consumer can invoke the refund and replacement provision. However, the standard is often stricter than that governing failure of essential purpose under the UCC. Consumers need a clear rule that does not grant an unreasonable amount of time to repair the car. There is little reason to require that the consumer give the manufacturer more than one repair attempt or one week in the shop. The consumer should not have to suffer through numerous trips to the dealer or long delays in repair.

Specification of a time for repair can significantly ease the burden of the consumer. The easier it is for the consumer to prove that he or she is entitled to the remedies under the lemon laws, the more likely that the consumer will seek redress and reach an equitable agreement with the manufacturer. A short, but reasonable, statutory period should suffice. If the consumer is able to show that the defect was not repaired within the period (perhaps a week), the presumption would apply. The manufacturer would then have the burden of establishing that more time was necessary and reasonable under the circumstances.

The typical lemon law contains other provisions which are unclear. For example, the laws do not define what constitutes substantial impairment of value, safety, or use. As a result, consumers will often not know what they are entitled to, even if the lemon law applies. These terms can be defined and clarified, as has been done in some cases interpreting UCC section 2–608. Specific provision should be made for taking account of the consumer's individual circumstances, as well as of clusters or groups of defects that substantially impair the value of the car.

Having clear rules and presumptions that ease the burden of proof will not mean much if other technical requirements deprive a consumer of the ability to use the lemon law. The notice requirements are especially troublesome. Consumers rarely know about notice requirements and often fail to comply with them. The only notice requirement the lemon laws should contain is the requirement that the consumer notify the dealer of the problem with the car. As was mentioned, the manufacturer will find out about the problem when the dealer seeks reimbursement for the warranty work. The manufacturer should have the responsibility of seeing to it that the dealer supplies it with this information promptly.

Once the consumer establishes that the car was not or could not be fixed, the lemon laws should provide that the consumer can choose between a refund or a replacement vehicle. If the consumer opts for a replacement vehicle, the manufacturer should be required to supply one of equal value. If the consumer chooses a refund, the lemon law should allow the recovery of the purchase price, collateral charges, and incidental and consequential damages when appropriate. If the manufacturer is allowed an offset for use, it should only cover use before the defects occurred and the manufacturer should have the burden of establishing its right to any offset and its amount.

All such changes will have little effect, however, if consumers do not fully understand them. The usual approach to informing consumers is to require the dealers and the manufacturers to supply a written statement which explains consumers' rights under the lemon law. The experience with the Magnuson-Moss Warranty Act indicates that this approach is ineffective. Consequently, legislators should consider using the broadcast media and newspapers to present information concerning consumer remedies. Public service ads on radio and television could greatly increase awareness of consumer warranty rights. Certainly, there is enough talent and knowledge available to structure such a campaign and the expense of conducting it is not likely to be much more than that of printing forms. A number of state and federal consumer protection agencies already conduct such campaigns, and there is no reason why similar efforts cannot be mounted to inform consumers of their rights under automobile lemon laws.

Part Six

DISPUTES AMONG CREDITORS OVER POSSESSION OF GOODS SOLD

Chapter Fifteen

RIGHTS OF OWNERS, SELLERS OR BUYERS TO GOODS NOT IN THEIR POSSESSION: CLAIMS OF THIRD PARTIES

SECTION 1. INTRODUCTION

When a person has good title to chattels, our legal system affords him extensive protection against a wide range of claims by third persons to the goods. A sale is a transaction whereby title is passed "from the seller to the buyer for a price * * *." UCC 2–106(1). In an effort to clarify when title passes in a contract for sale, Article 2 prescribes the conditions which must exist before any interest in goods can pass, UCC 2–105(1), makes a careful distinction between present and future sales, UCC 2–106(1), and provides an intricate set of rules to assist in transactions where the parties have not otherwise explicitly agreed. UCC 2–401. To this extent, Article 2 closely follows the Uniform Sales Act.

Here, however, the resemblance ends. UCC 2–401 provides that "each provision of this Article with regard to the rights, obligations and remedies of the seller, the buyer, purchasers or other third parties applies irrespective of title to the goods except where the provision refers to such title." See also UCC 9–202, where the same policy is announced for secured transactions. As stated in the comment to UCC 2–101, the "purpose is to avoid making practical issues between practical men turn on the location of an intangible something, the passing of which no man can prove by evidence and to substitute for such abstractions proof of words and actions of a tangible character." Two such practical issues are risk of loss and the seller's action for the price. Under the USA they turned on which party had title to the goods. Under the UCC they are determined by such considerations as whether the seller has completed his tender of delivery, UCC 2–509, or whether the buyer has accepted the goods, UCC 2–709(1).

It is clear that the rules about title contained in UCC 2–401 may be relevant in resolving controversies beyond the scope of Article 2, e.g., the right of the buyer's creditors to levy on goods still in the seller's possession, the coverage of an insurance policy, the applicability of a state sales tax or the criminal responsibility of a person accused of larceny. However, when the transaction is within the scope of Article 2, title becomes relevant only when the applicable provisions specifically refer to title. Such specific reference is made in UCC 2–403 and UCC 2–312. The range of problems emanating from these sections and their frequent overlap with Article 9 and the special difficulties posed by "bulk" sales will be the subject of this Chapter.

Under UCC 2 title is only relevant when specifically mentioned (ie in 2-403 + 2-312)

SECTION 2. RIGHTS OF BUYERS IN GOODS SOLD

A. *Claims of "True" Owners*

Problem 15–1

Abbie, a widow, owned a 10–carat diamond valued at $60,000. Boscoe, a thief, stole the diamond from Abbie's wall safe and sold it to Casper, a diamond merchant, for $55,000. Casper honestly believed that Boscoe was the true owner. Casper then sold the diamond to Dimwit, a buyer in the ordinary course of business, for $60,000. May Abbie replevy the diamond from Dimwit? See UCC 2–403. Assume that the common law gives Casper only "void title," not "voidable title." Justice v. Fabey, 541 F.Supp. 1019 (E.D.Pa.1982) (yes).

Problem 15–2

Suppose that Abbie delivered the diamond to Casper for the purpose of having the clasp on the necklace in which the stone was set repaired. Casper, with intent to defraud, removed the stone from the necklace and sold it to Dimwit, a buyer in the ordinary course of business. May Abbie replevy the diamond from Dimwit? See UCC 2–403(2), (3), and UCC 1–201(9). Cf. Carlsen v. Rivera, 382 So.2d 825 (Fla.App.1980) (no).

Problem 15–3

Suppose that Abbie owned several diamonds and was in the habit of lending the stones to her society friends for use on important occasions. She charged a good fee for this service and was, of course, fully insured against loss. Abbie leased the stone worth $60,000 to Bessie to be worn at the Muckraker's Ball. Bessie, who was short of cash, sold the diamond to

Casper for $55,000. Casper, who had purchased in good faith, sold the stone to Dimwit, a buyer in the ordinary course of business, for $65,000. May Abbie (or her insurance company claiming by subrogation) replevy the necklace from Dimwit? See UCC 2–403(1), (2). Assume that the common law only gives Bessie, as a lessee, void title.

How should the court deal with the argument made by Dimwit that Bessie in fact had a voidable title under UCC 2–403 because she took in a transaction of "purchase" as that term is defined in UCC 2–403 and 1–201? (Dimwit's argument was rejected in similar circumstances by the Indiana Court of Appeals in McDonald's Chevrolet, Inc. v. Johnson, 176 Ind.App. 399, 376 N.E.2d 106 (1978)).

Problem 15–4

While vacationing in Miami Beach, Abbie was approached by a middle-aged man who asked if the lovely diamond necklace was for sale. He said that his name was Boscoe and offered to pay $90,000. Abbie, who was a bit short of cash, agreed to sell but then balked when Boscoe started to write a check. She wanted cash. Boscoe assured her that he was solvent and stated that he was Mr. Fred C. Boscoe of Grosse Pointe. Abbie excused herself from the room and confirmed by a telephone call to a friend in Detroit that Mr. Fred C. Boscoe owned a large home in Grosse Pointe and was a vice-president of a well-known automobile manufacturer. Abbie returned to the room and informed the man that she would accept a check for the stone. Boscoe then drew a counter check on a Detroit bank and delivered it to Abbie in exchange for the necklace. The check, of course, bounced and Abbie then discovered that her purchaser had no account at that bank and was not Mr. Fred C. Boscoe of Grosse Pointe. Further, before disappearing, the "rogue" had sold the diamond for $91,000 to Dimwit, who purchased the stone in good faith. May Abbie replevy the stone from Dimwit? See UCC 2–403(1)(a).

Problem 15–5

In Problem 15–4 would it make any difference if the transaction and the exchange of check for necklace had been completed by mail?

Problem 15–6

Suppose, in Problem 15–2, above, that Casper and Dimwit had entered into a contract for the sale of the stone, delivery and payment to take place in 10 days. Is Abbie's interest cut off at this point or must payment and delivery first take place? Suppose there has been payment but not delivery? Delivery but no payment? Part payment? See UCC 2–403. Compare UCC 1–201(44).

INMI–ETTI v. ALUISI

Court of Appeals of Maryland, 1985.
63 Md.App. 293, 492 A.2d 917.

[Appellant, a resident of Nigeria, ordered a new Honda Prelude while visiting her sister in the United States. Butler, an acquaintance of her family, offered to assist. Appellant returned to Nigeria, leaving cash with the sister to complete the purchase. The sale was completed and a certificate of title was issued in appellant's name. The car, however, was delivered to Butler, who removed it from the sister without permission. The sister had an arrest warrant issued, but it was later quashed. Butler, claiming that appellant was an absconding debtor, then brought suit against her and filed an application for an attachment on the Honda. When appellant did not answer, Butler was granted a summary judgment. Thereafter, appellee, a deputy sheriff, executed the writ of attachment on the Honda but left it in Butler's possession.

Butler, representing that he was the owner, then contracted to sell the Honda to Pohanka, a dealer, for $7,200. Pohanka paid Butler $2,000 and agreed to pay the balance when Butler obtained a certificate of title. After executing a false affidavit in his application for a certificate of title, Butler was issued a certificate in his own name by the Motor Vehicle Administration. Butler then returned to Pohanka and exchanged the certificate for the balance of the contract price.

Appellant, upon returning to the United States, had Butler's summary judgment set aside. In addition, she sued Butler and Pohanka for conversion and appellee for negligent attachment. In the lower court, appellant obtained a default judgment against Butler. The court, however, granted a summary judgment to Pohanka and appellee. On appeal, the summary judgment in favor of appellee was sustained but the summary judgment in favor of Pohanka was reversed.]

* * *

I.

In order for the appellant to establish her right to summary judgment against Pohanka, we must be convinced that the record before the lower court contained undisputed facts and inferences properly deducible therefrom, demonstrating that Pohanka committed a conversion of the appellant's vehicle as a matter of law. Former Md. Rule 610 (new Md.Rule 2–501). In *Interstate Ins. Co. v. Logan,* 205 Md. 583, 588–89, 109 A.2d 904 (1959), the Court of Appeals summarized the law of conversion:

> [F]orcible dispossession of personal property is not essential to constitute a conversion. A "conversion" is any distinct act of ownership or dominion exerted by one person over the personal property of another in denial of his right or inconsistent with it. *Merchants' National Bank of Baltimore v. Williams,* 110 Md. 334, 72 A. 1114 [(1909)]; Martin v. W.W. Lanahan & Co., 133 Md. 525, 105 A. 777 [(1919)].

* * * In the instant case it is undisputed that Pohanka exerted acts of use or ownership over the automobile in question by selling it on February 1, 1982. Nevertheless, our analysis cannot end here. We explain.

At common law the maxim was: "He who hath not cannot give (nemo dat qui non habet)." Black's Law Dictionary 935 (5th ed. 1979). Although at times the Uniform Commercial Code may seem to the reader as unintelligible as the Latin phrases which preceded it, we find in § 2–403 of the Code a definite modification of the above maxim. That section states: * * *.

Md.Code (1975), § 2–403 of the Commercial Law Article. *See generally* Hawkland UCC Series § 2–403:01 *et seq.* for an enlightening history of the origins of § 2–403.

In short, the answer to the appellant's claim against Pohanka depends on whether Butler had "void" or "voidable" title at the time of the purported sale to Pohanka. If Butler had voidable title, then he had the power to vest good title in Pohanka.[1] If, on the other hand, Butler possessed void title (i.e., no title at all), then Pohanka received no title and is liable in trover for the conversion of the appellant's automobile. Preliminarily, we note that there was no evidence that Butler was a "merchant who deals in goods of that kind" (i.e. automobiles). Md.Code, *supra,* §§ 2–403(2) and 2–104(1). Therefore the entrustment provisions of § 2–403(2)–(3) do not apply.

It has been observed that:

> Under 2–403, voidable title is to be distinguished from void title. A thief, for example, "gets" only void title and without more cannot pass any title to a good faith purchaser. "Voidable title" is a murky concept. The Code does not define the phrase. The comments do not even discuss it. Subsections (1)(a)–(d) of 2–403 clarify the law as to particular transactions which were "troublesome under prior law." Beyond these, we must look to non-Code state law.

J. White & R. Summers, Handbook of the Law Under the Uniform Commercial Code § 3–11 (2d ed. 1980) (footnote omitted). White and Summers further explain that: subsection (a) of § 2–403(1) deals with cases where the purchaser *impersonates* someone else; subsection (b) deals with "rubber checks"; subsection (c) deals with "*cash sales*";[2] and subsection (d) deals with cases of *forged checks* and other acts fraudulent to the seller. *Id.* None of these subsections apply to the facts of the present case and we, therefore, must turn to "non-Code state law" to determine whether Butler had voidable title.

Hawkland, *supra,* § 403:04, suggests that "voidable title" may only be obtained when the owner of the goods makes a voluntary transfer of the goods. He reaches that conclusion from the Code definitions of the words "delivery" and "purchase" and summarizes:

---

1. Inasmuch as we decide this case on the basis of a motion for summary judgment, and the evidence regarding Pohanka's good faith purchaser for value status is disputed, we must assume here that Pohanka was entitled to that status.

2. See *First National Bank of Ariz. v. Carbajal,* 132 Ariz. 263, 645 P.2d 778, 781–82 (1982).

Section 2–403(1)(d) does not create a voidable title in the situation where the goods are wrongfully taken, as contrasted with delivered voluntarily because of the concepts of "delivery" and "purchaser" which are necessary preconditions. "Delivery" is defined by section 1–201(14) "with respect to instruments, documents of title, chattel paper or securities" to mean "voluntary transfer of possession." By analogy, it should be held that goods are not delivered for purposes of section 2–403 unless they are voluntarily transferred. Additionally, section 2–403(1)(d) is limited by the requirement that the goods "have been delivered under a transaction of purchase." "Purchase" is defined by section 1–201(32) to include only voluntary transactions. A thief who wrongfully takes goods is not a purchaser within the meaning of this definition, but a swindler who fraudulently induces the victim to voluntarily deliver them is a purchaser for this purpose. This distinction, reminiscent of the distinction between larceny and larceny by trick made by the common law, is a basic one for the understanding of the meaning of section 2–403(1)(d).

Hawkland later states that the above language applies generally to § 2–403(1) and not merely to subsection (1)(d). *See* Hawkland, *supra,* § 2–403:05. The following cases and, indeed, (a) through (d) of § 2–403(1) seem to support Hawkland's theory that only a voluntary transfer by the owner can vest "voidable title" in a "person."

* * *

Without attempting to specify all the situations which could give rise to a voidable title under § 2–403 of the Uniform Commercial Code, we refer to the above authorities to support our conclusion that voidable title under the Code can only arise from a voluntary transfer or delivery of the goods by the owner. If the goods are stolen or otherwise obtained against the will of the owner, only void title can result.

Under the undisputed facts of the present case Butler possessed void title when Pohanka dealt with him. Although the record simply is not sufficient for us to decide whether Butler actually stole the appellant's vehicle, it is undisputed that the appellant at no time made a voluntary transfer to Butler. Thus, Pohanka obtained no title, and its sale of the vehicle constituted a conversion of the appellant's property. We believe the above analysis sufficient to impose liability upon Pohanka. We will nevertheless answer certain of Pohanka's collateral arguments.

We reject any notion that Butler obtained voidable title to the vehicle as a result of the attachment on original process carried out pursuant to former Maryland District Rules G40–60.

* * *

The only way Butler could have obtained title in the vehicle through those attachment proceedings was if he had purchased it at a judicial sale. That clearly never occurred.

Implicit in all that we have said so far is the fact that Butler did not obtain title (voidable or otherwise) merely from the fact that he was able to convince the Motor Vehicle Administration to issue a certificate of title for the automobile to him. Although "[a] certificate of title issued by the Administration is prima facie evidence of the facts appearing on it," Md.Code (1977, 1984 Repl.Vol.), § 13–107 of the Transportation Article, the erroneous issuance of such a certificate cannot divest the title of the true owner of the automobile. *Metropolitan Auto Sales v. Koneski,* 252 Md. 145, 249 A.2d 141 (1969); *Huettner v. Sav. Bank of Balto.,* 242 Md. 477, 219 A.2d 559 (1966); *Lawrence v. Graham,* 29 Md.App. 422, 349 A.2d 271 (1975).

Likewise, we find unpersuasive Pohanka's argument that since Butler had possession of the automobile and a duly issued certificate of title in his name, Pohanka should be protected as a "good faith purchaser for value" under § 2–403 of the Commercial Law Article, *supra.* Such status under that section of the Uniform Commercial Code is relevant in situations where the seller (transferor) is possessed of voidable title. It does not apply to the situation presented by the instant case where the seller had no title at all. * * *

Finally, whether Pohanka converted the vehicle with innocent intent is immaterial. The Restatement (Second) of Torts § 229 (1979) provides:

> One who receives possession of a chattel from another with the intent to acquire for himself or for a third person a proprietary interest in the chattel which the other has not the power to transfer is subject to liability for conversion to a third person then entitled to the immediate possession of the chattel.

Comment e. to § 299 explains:

> Under the rule stated in this Section, one receiving a chattel from a third person with intent to acquire a proprietary interest in it is liable without a demand for its return by the person entitled to possession, *although he takes possession of the chattel without knowledge or reason to know that the third person has no power to transfer the proprietary interest.* The mere receipt of the possession of the goods under such circumstances is a conversion.

(Emphasis added).

Accordingly, we shall reverse the summary judgment in favor of Pohanka and enter judgment in favor of the appellant against Pohanka for $8,200, an amount representing the agreed fair market value of the appellant's automobile at the time of its conversion, plus interest at 10 percent per annum from February 1, 1982, the date when Pohanka sold the automobile. Md.Rule 1075. * * *

Note: Certificates of Title and the BFP of Motor Vehicles

Almost all states have statutes which require motor vehicles to be "titled." Suppose that Owner, whose certificate of title is in the possession of a secured party, entrusts the motor vehicle to a car dealer for repairs. Suppose, further, that the dealer, without Owner's or secured party's consent, puts the car on the lot and sells it to Cal in the ordinary course of business. Cal pays cash and takes delivery of the car only, without knowledge of Owner's title or the outstanding security interest. Assume owner pays off secured party and seeks return of the car from Cal, certificate of title in hand. May owner replevy the car from Cal, or is Cal entitled to a duly endorsed certificate?

Under the Code the answer would appear to be no: UCC 2–402(3) does not apply. UCC 2–403(2) protects Cal and title has passed under UCC 2–401. But the critical question, then, is whether the particular certificate of title act involved preempts 2–403(2) and, in effect, conditions passage of title upon delivery of the certificate. In some states it does, e.g., Messer v. Averill, 28 Mich.App. 62, 183 N.W.2d 802 (1970) but in most states it doesn't, e.g., Godfrey v. Gilsdorf, 86 Nev. 714, 476 P.2d 3 (1970); Martin v. Nager, 192 N.J.Super. 189, 469 A.2d 519 (1983). Even where the Code controls, however, a buyer may have some responsibility for inquiring after the required certificate. See Mattek v. Malofsky, 42 Wis.2d 16, 165 N.W.2d 406 (1969) (merchant buyer from dealer to whom titled car had been entrusted is "unreasonable as a matter of law" in not obtaining the required certificate); Reliance Insurance Co. v. Market Motors, Inc., 498 A.2d 571 (D.C.App.1985); Ellsworth v. Worthey, 612 S.W.2d 396 (Mo.App. 1981).

Assume Owner does not pay off secured party and it is secured party who seeks return of the car from Cal. Similarly, while UCC 9–307(1) may protect the buyer against the perfected security interest, this result is subject to any specific rule of priority contained in a preemptive certificate of title act. Compare Williams v. Western Surety Co., 6 Wash.App. 300, 492 P.2d 596 (1972) (buyer wins under Code) with Security Pacific Nat'l Bank v. Goodman, 24 Cal.App.3d 131, 100 Cal.Rptr. 763 (1972) (buyer loses under California statute.)

These issues are well treated in Kunz, *Motor Vehicle Ownership Disputes Involving Certificate of Title Acts and Article Two of the U.C.C.*, 39 Bus.Law. 1599 (1984).

JOHNSON & JOHNSON PROD. v. DAL INTERN. TRADING

United States Court of Appeals, Third Circuit, 1986.
798 F.2d 100.

OPINION OF THE COURT

STAPLETON, CIRCUIT JUDGE.

This is an appeal from a preliminary injunction restraining appellants from selling, distributing, or otherwise disposing of certain products manufactured by appellees and in appellants' possession. Because we conclude that the district court committed an error of law and that the present record will not support a resolution of the legally relevant issue in appellees' favor, we will vacate the preliminary injunction.

I.

Appellants are Quality King Manufacturing, Inc. and Quality King Distributors, Inc., both New York corporations ("Quality King"). Quality King is an independent distributor of national brand health and beauty aids. Its customers include large wholesalers and retail chains. Quality King participates in the so-called "gray market," where imported products are sold in the United States outside the manufacturer's distribution system, often contrary to the wishes of the manufacturer.

Appellees are Johnson & Johnson Products, Inc. ("J & J"), a New Jersey corporation, Johnson & Johnson, Ltd. ("J & J Ltd."), a corporation organized under the laws of Great Britain, and Johnson & Johnson Baby Products Company, a New Jersey corporation. Appellees are all operating subsidiaries of Johnson & Johnson, Inc., a New Jersey corporation.

Appellees claimed in the district court that J & J Ltd., which has its place of business in Great Britain, was fraudulently induced to sell 80,000 dozen toothbrushes and certain baby products to Dal International Trading Company, an instrumentality of the Polish People's Republic (hereinafter "Dal"). The alleged fraud consisted of an oral misrepresentation by Dal in February of 1985 that it intended to distribute the products in Poland only. But for this fraudulent assurance, say appellees, J & J Ltd. would not have entered the transaction.

In March of 1985, Dal ordered the products from J & J Ltd. No written contract was entered. However, J & J Ltd. did execute, in April of 1985, a written contract related to the Dal transaction with Wendexim Trading Company, Ltd., a British firm. The reason for the inclusion of Wendexim in the Dal transaction was the weakness of Polish currency, which necessitated an intermediate barter trade. This intermediate step involved an agreement under which Dal shipped a quantity of wood to Wendexim in return for Wendexim's transmittal of the payment for the wood to J & J Ltd., in satisfaction of Dal's obligation to pay J & J Ltd. for the toothbrushes and baby products.

At the end of June, 1985, J & J Ltd. delivered the toothbrushes to Dal at a J & J Ltd. factory in West Germany. The baby products were shipped from Great Britain at the beginning of June, 1985. Subsequently, J & J Ltd. learned that some or all of these goods had been diverted from their intended destination of Poland and were en route to the United States.

J & J Ltd. investigators followed the goods to the United States, where they came into the possession of Quality King. The goods were packaged in cartons, some of which bore J & J Ltd. shipping labels. The production codes on these labels corresponded to those of the products designated for Dal.

The route by which the J & J Ltd. products came into Quality King's hands was not fully documented below. In early 1985, a British firm called Cubro Trading Company, Ltd. somehow learned of the availability of the J & J Ltd. products and passed this information to Morris Greenfield, the proprietor of Tereza Merchandise Corporation in New York. Greenfield was not interested in the products but advised Glenn Nussdorf, the vice president of Quality King, of the availability of the goods. Nussdorf prepared a purchase order for 75,000 dozen toothbrushes in February of 1985, about the time when Dal and J & J Ltd. were negotiating the sale of 80,000 dozen toothbrushes. Later, Nussdorf added baby products to this purchase order.

Nussdorf had never done business with Cubro before this transaction, so he used Greenfield as an intermediary. The details of the transaction are unclear due to discrepancies in the record as to the disbursements made by Quality King. What is clear is that Quality King purchased and received the goods.

Before the goods arrived at Quality King's warehouse, the J & J Ltd. shipping labels had been stripped from most of the shipping cartons. Greenfield and Nussdorf testified that this was a common gray market practice designed to obscure the identity of supply sources. The protection of these sources is important to gray market middlemen, Nussdorf and Greenfield testified, because if the sources became known, the middlemen would be bypassed in subsequent transactions.

The J & J Ltd. products were priced by it for the Polish market at a level lower than the wholesale price in the United States for Johnson & Johnson products, and even lower than the wholesale price normally offered in Great Britain by J & J Ltd. By purchasing these products in Europe, Quality King was thus in a position to distribute them in the United States at prices below those being charged by J & J.

II.

The district court granted the preliminary injunction after concluding that appellees were likely to prevail on the merits, that appellees would suffer irreparable harm if the injunction were not granted, that an injunction would not harm any other interested person, and that an injunction would not be contrary to the public interest. * * *

The court predicted that appellees would prevail on the merits because it found that Quality King was not a good faith purchaser under Section 2–403(1) of the Uniform Commercial Code (UCC). Under this provision of the UCC, a seller with voidable title, such as that acquired by common law fraud, can transfer good title to a subsequent good faith purchaser. For merchants like Quality King, the UCC defines good faith as "honesty in fact and the observance of reasonable commercial standards of fair dealing in the trade." UCC § 2–103(1)(b). If the subsequent purchaser lacks good faith, however, he acquires only the seller's voidable title and may be required to surrender the goods to the defrauded party.

While the district court concluded that Quality King had no actual knowledge of the alleged fraud, it found that the gray market transaction was conducted under "suspicious circumstances" that "cried out for inquiry." District Court Opinion at 23–24. In the district court's view, Quality King, as a result, should have made inquiries that would have uncovered the voidable title. In the absence of such inquiries, the court concluded, Quality King could not be said to have been "honest in fact."

The most suspicious circumstance noted by the court was the fact that "the entire trade in which Quality King is engaged is conducted in a manner designed to insulate a purchaser of goods from knowledge of potential illegality." District Court Opinion at 22. That is, the gray market trade practice of purposely obscuring the chain of title suggested to the court a silent conspiracy to avoid the consequences of bad faith purchase by preventing the transmission of actual knowledge of fraud in prior transactions. This practice was illustrated by the fact that the J & J Ltd. shipping labels had been stripped prior to arrival at Quality King's warehouse.

An additional suspicious circumstance, in the district court's view, was the fact that Nussdorf used Greenfield as an intermediary, thereby indicating Nussdorf's mistrust of Cubro. Finally, the price of the goods was so low that "Quality King must have known that * * * [J & J Ltd. would not have knowingly sold] * * * its products in Europe for resale in the United States." District Court Opinion at 24.

III.

The district court was undoubtedly justified in concluding that Quality King had reason to suspect that appellees would not approve of a sale of the toothbrushes and baby products to a U.S. distributor. Further, we believe the district court, having reached this conclusion, could appropriately infer that Quality King, in the minds of its officers and agents, subjectively suspected that appellees would not approve of its purchase of these goods. We believe the legally relevant question, however, is whether Quality King knew that the goods had been obtained from J & J Ltd. by fraud, or suspected as much and closed its eyes to the truth. This is a far different question involving an inquiry as to whether Quality King knew or had some reason to know that Dal orally represented to J & J Ltd. that it would distribute only in Poland and that this representation was made at a time when Dal had an affirmative intent to do otherwise.[2] The district court did not address this legally relevant question, and we believe the present record will not support an affirmative answer to it.

While the district court relied heavily on what it understood to be the nature of the gray goods market, there was very little evidence

2. It is important to note that the title of a purchaser from Dal would not have been voidable if all Dal had done was resell the goods in violation of a contract clause prohibiting resale outside Poland. If, at the time of contracting with J & J Ltd., Dal had intended to restrict the distribution of goods to Poland and only later decided to distribute the goods elsewhere, no fraudulent inducement to contract would have existed. J & J Ltd. would then have had a cause of action against Dal for breach of contract but subsequent purchasers from Dal would obtain good title. UCC § 2–403(1).

before it concerning that market and *no* evidence before it on the legitimacy of the means by which goods normally get into the gray goods market. The only substantial testimony concerning the workings of that market was the testimony given by Messrs. Nussbaum and Greenfield. Their testimony indicated only that the gray market exists because prices are often lower overseas than in the United States, and that gray market sellers are reluctant to reveal their supply sources for fear of being bypassed in subsequent transactions. This testimony provided a plausible explanation about why there is a gray goods market and why merchants in that market do not generally inquire about the intermediate sources in the distribution chain. However, it does not provide a basis for an inference that all those involved in importing less expensive gray goods know or suspect that there is a defect in the title of the goods which they purchase. Nor does the fact that Quality King was cautious in its dealings with Cubro, its immediate supplier, add enough to win the day for appellees.

Rather than address the legally relevant question of whether Quality King subjectively knew or suspected that there was a flaw in the title of one of its predecessors, the district court found that the circumstances called for inquiry and that, if Quality King had investigated, it would have learned that it was acquiring a voidable title. It is not as clear to us as to the district court that inquiry in this case would have uncovered the fraud. We consider that unimportant, however, because we believe the court committed an error of law when it held that Quality King had a duty to inquire and charged it with the knowledge that an investigation would have arguably disclosed.

The purpose of the good faith purchaser doctrine, codified in Sections 2–403 and 2–102 of the UCC, is to promote commerce by reducing transaction costs; it allows people safely to engage in the purchase and sale of goods without conducting a costly investigation of the conduct and rights of all previous possessors in the chain of distribution. Gilmore, The Commercial Doctrine of Good Faith Purchase, 63 YALE L.J. 1057, 1057 (1954) (The good faith purchaser " * * * is protected * * * to the end that commercial transactions may be engaged in without elaborate investigation of property rights and in reliance on the possession of property by one who offers it for sale * * * "; Farnsworth, Good Faith Performance and Commercial Reasonableness under the Uniform Commercial Code, 30 U.CHI.L.REV. 666, 671 (1963) ("Authority happens to favor the subjective test [of good faith purchase] in order to promote the circulation of goods and commercial paper."); Hawkland, Curing an Improper Tender of Title to Chattels: Past, Present and Commercial Code, 46 MINN.L.REV. 697, 721 (1962); 3 ANDERSON ON THE UNIFORM COMMERCIAL CODE 569–570 (3d ed. 1983). The imposition on a purchaser of a duty to investigate is thus fundamentally at odds with the rationale underlying these two sections of the UCC. Accordingly, in the absence of clear and controlling precedent so requiring, we are unwilling to sanction the imposition of such a duty on one in the position of Quality King.

As the district court recognized, we are required to apply the law of New Jersey, the forum state. *Erie R.R. Co. v. Tompkins,* 304 U.S. 64, 58 S.Ct. 817, 82 L.Ed. 1188 (1938). Neither the district court nor the appellees have referred us to any New Jersey case which suggests that its Supreme Court would impose a duty of inquiry upon a purchaser of goods under the circumstances of this case and we believe the New Jersey case law suggests the contrary.

The only case relied on by the appellees is a New York case, *Porter v. Wertz,* 68 A.D.2d 141, 416 N.Y.S.2d 254, 259 (1979), *aff'd on other grounds,* 53 N.Y.2d 696, 439 N.Y.S.2d 105, 421 N.E.2d 500 (1981). In *Porter,* a painting was entrusted to an art merchant who asked Peter Wertz, a delicatessen employee, to find a buyer for the painting. Wertz sold it to an art gallery that was unaware of the circumstances by which Wertz had come into possession of the painting. The lower court ruled that the gallery was not protected by UCC Section 2–403 because Wertz was not an art merchant selling the painting in the ordinary course of business. In addition, the court held that even if Wertz had been an art merchant, the gallery would not have been protected by the good faith purchaser provision of Section 2–403 because of its failure to inquire as to Wertz' source. The New York Court of Appeals affirmed on the first ground and withheld opinion on the second. *Porter,* 439 N.Y.S.2d at 107, 421 N.E.2d at 502. Whether or not a duty of inquiry exists in New York in these circumstances is accordingly unclear.

* * *

[The Court, based upon *Breslin v. New Jersey Investors, Inc.,* 70 N.J. 466, 361 A.2d 1 (1976), predicted that New Jersey would "not impose on Quality King a duty to inquire." Rather, "whether Quality King was honest in fact is to be 'determined by looking to the mind of [Quality King]' and not to 'what the state of mind of a prudent man should have been' as a result of inquiry."]

We also note that by adopting the subjective, "pure heart and * * * empty head" standard of *Lawson v. Weston,* 170 Eng.Rep. 640 (K.B.1801), the New Jersey Supreme Court would be aligning itself with the prevailing view of the good faith purchaser concept. *See Goodman v. Simonds,* 61 U.S. (20 How.) 343, 15 L.Ed. 934 (1857) (adopting subjective standard of *Lawson*); Braucher, The Legislative History of the Uniform Commercial Code, 58 COLUM.L.REV. 798, 812 (1958) ("honesty in fact" standard is subjective); Farnsworth, 30 U.CHI.L.REV. at 671.

As we have previously noted, the district court did not make, and the record will not support, a finding that Quality King suspected that fraud had been committed by a predecessor in interest. Accordingly, we may assume for present purposes that New Jersey would exclude from the good faith purchase category one who, though without actual knowledge, subjectively suspects that the title is flawed and proceeds with the purchase despite his or her suspicions. A purchaser may not be certain of the existence of a flaw and still have knowledge of sufficient facts to keep him from being fairly characterized as having been "honest in fact." Excluding such a person from the good faith purchaser category is not the same, however, as judging a purchaser by the facts he or she might have obtained through an investigation of all prior transfers of the goods. By adopting the latter approach, the district court in this case imposed a burden on commerce which we believe the UCC did not intend that it should bear.

We hold, therefore, that the district court erred in concluding on this record that Quality King had a duty to inquire into the chain of title of the gray market goods.[4] Since the only inference supported by the record is that Quality King had neither knowledge nor suspicion of a fraud by Dal, appellees did not demonstrate a likelihood of ultimate success and Quality King was improperly enjoined *pendente lite*.

IV.

For the foregoing reasons, we will vacate the preliminary injunction.

[Some footnotes omitted.]

B. Claims of Secured Parties and Other Lien Holders

IN RE GARY AIRCRAFT CORP.

United States Court of Appeals, Fifth Circuit, 1982.
681 F.2d 365.

WISDOM, CIRCUIT JUDGE:

I.

This dispute over the ownership of one airplane and of the proceeds of the sale of another requires us to determine the reach of the Federal Aviation Act and its impact on state law. We also explore the protection accorded buyers against secured creditors by state law.

In December 1971, Gary Aircraft Corporation ("Gary"), the plaintiff-appellee, entered into a letter of understanding stating its intention to purchase four airplanes from Frederick B. Ayer & Associates, Inc. ("Ayer"), a dealer in aircraft. Two of these airplanes are the subject of the controversy here. Gary did not complete the purchase, but Arthur Stewart, its president, carried out the transaction in his individual capacity, purchasing the first plane in controversy here, N8222H, on December 22, 1971 for $5,000, and the second, N8221H, on January 4,

---

4. At oral argument, appellees suggested that the district court's decision may have rested in part on that portion of the definition of good faith that refers to an objective standard: "the observance of reasonable commercial standards of fair dealing in the trade." UCC § 2–103(1)(b). While the court spoke at length about practices in the gray goods market, it did not find that it was the practice in that market to investigate the chain of title. Indeed, the evidence suggested that this was not normally done. When a party relies upon trade practice in a situation of this kind, it bears the burden of producing admissible evidence of that practice. *Brattleboro Auto Sales v. Subaru*, 633 F.2d 649, 651 (2d Cir.1980). Since appellees tendered no evidence of trade practice, this portion of the definition of good faith does not aid them.

1972, also for $5,000. On the date of each sale, the airplane purchased was subject to a security interest held by General Dynamics Corporation ("General Dynamics"), the defendant-appellant. General Dynamics held its interest under a security agreement executed by Ayer on February 20, 1969. Under that agreement, Ayer was authorized to sell the collateral, unless it was in default on its obligations to General Dynamics. In case of default, Ayer could not sell without the written consent of General Dynamics. General Dynamics recorded its security agreement with the Federal Aviation Administration on March 3, 1969. On the dates of the sales to Stewart, Ayer was in default.

Crawford, the vice-president of Gary, requested a title search from the Aircraft Owners and Pilots Association on January 4, 1972. The AOPA reported the results on January 5, 1972. On August 3, 1972, approximately seven months after the sale, Stewart recorded his bill of sale with the FAA. Over the next four years, Crawford communicated periodically with Ayer, requesting that Ayer take action to secure the release of General Dynamic's security interest.

In March 1974, Stewart sold one of the group of four planes to Gary for $13,275. He transferred the two planes at issue here to Gary on November 7, 1975, apparently without consideration. Gary executed a mortgage on the aircraft in favor of the Victoria Bank and Trust Company, the third party defendant. The Victoria Bank recorded its interest with the FAA. On May 28, 1976, General Dynamics informed Gary that it had learned that the aircraft were registered in Gary's name and that General Dynamics was asserting a security interest in the property.

On October 28, 1976, Gary initiated Chapter XI proceedings under the Bankruptcy Act. It brought this action in the bankruptcy court, seeking to sell Airplane N8222H free and clear of liens. Upon the agreement of all interested parties, the court permitted the sale of the airplane, and the proceeds were deposited with the court. The second airplane remains in the possession of Gary.

The bankruptcy court, affirmed by the district court, held that Gary was entitled to the proceeds of the sale of Airplane N8222H and to the possession of Airplane N8221H, free of any interest asserted by General Dynamics. General Dynamics appeals, presenting three theories. First, it contends that the Federal Aviation Act grants it priority because it recorded its security interest with the Federal Aviation Administration before Stewart purchased the aircraft. Second, even if the FAA does not govern the priority question but instead remits it to Texas law, which protects a buyer in the ordinary course of business against the perfected security interest of his seller's creditor, General Dynamics argues that Stewart could not take free of its interest because, according to General Dynamics, Stewart could not qualify as a buyer in the ordinary course of business. Finally, General Dynamics contends that, even if Stewart did qualify as a buyer in the ordinary course, he could not transfer his status to Gary, and Gary did not qualify in its own right so, in Gary's hands, the aircraft are subject to the interest of General Dynamics. Concluding that the FAA does not govern priorities in interests in aircraft, that Stewart, as a buyer in the ordinary course of business, took free of General Dynamic's interest, and that Gary takes the title of its transferor, we affirm.

* * *

III.

Under the Uniform Commercial Code, enacted as the Texas Business and Commerce Code, a buyer in the ordinary course of business is one who, in good faith and without knowledge that the sale to him is in violation of the ownership rights or security interest of a third party, buys from a person in the business of selling goods of that kind. Tex. Bus. & Com.Code Ann. § 1.201(9) (Vernon Supp.1982). Such a buyer takes free of a security interest created by his seller, even if that interest is perfected and even if the buyer knows of its existence. *Id.,* § 9.307(a).

Since Gary claims its title through Stewart, it cannot hold the aircraft and the proceeds free of General Dynamic's lien unless Stewart held the aircraft free of the lien, as a buyer in the ordinary course of business under section 9.307(a). General Dynamics offers three arguments that it contends require reversal of the holding that Stewart qualified as a buyer in the ordinary course of business.

First, General Dynamics contends that the bankruptcy court misapplied the burden of proof. The burden on this issue does rest with the party claiming the status of a buyer in the ordinary course of business, as General Dynamics urges. *See International Harvester Co. v. Glendenning,* Tex.Civ.App.—Dallas 1974, 505 S.W.2d 320, 324. Nonetheless, General Dynamics cannot prevail on this argument, for we agree with the district court that an examination of the entire opinion of the bankruptcy court shows that it did not misapply the burden of proof. * * *

Second, General Dynamics contends that, even if the bankruptcy judge acted properly in his assignment of the burden of proof, the holding must be reversed because the bankruptcy court considered Stewart's knowledge on December 22, 1971 and January 4, 1972, the dates of purchase, rather than on August 3, 1972, the date of recordation. The district court found some merit in General Dynamic's argument that Stewart's knowledge was to be evaluated as of August 3 but declined to choose between the dates of purchase and the date of recordation, holding that use of the date of purchase would be harmless error because Stewart did not know of the default by Ayer even on August 3. General Dynamics argues to us that the district court's disposition of this issue was improper because August 3 was the relevant time, but the bankruptcy court had made no finding on the state of Stewart's knowledge in August. We disagree with General Dynamics on both grounds.

We conclude that the dates of purchase were the relevant dates. The rule of § 9.307(a) is designed to protect the innocent buyer against prior security interests in retail goods because he cannot be expected to discover those interests, while the secured party may generally be assumed to have authorized the sale of inventory by a retailer. *See generally, e.g.,* J. White & R. Summers, Uniform Commercial Code § 25–14 at 1070 (2d ed. 1980). But this "protection" leaves the buyer vulnerable if he cannot be certain of it until he records. Were that the rule, a buyer who discovered a violated security agreement after purchasing but before recording could have given consideration, in good faith and without knowledge, and taken possession of the goods but he would take a position subordinate to that of the secured lender. Measuring knowledge at the time of sale or earlier, however, prevents any gap in protection, for a potential buyer who discovers a violated security interest at the time of purchase can always decide not to buy.[13]

In the alternative, we conclude that the bankruptcy judge did find that in August Stewart was without knowledge of any violation of the security agreement between Ayer and General Dynamics. His opinion stated that Stewart was unaware of the lien until after the time of purchase, "and *even then* the mortgage appeared to authorize Ayer to sell free of any lien. * * * Stewart became *and remained* a buyer in ordinary course of business." Bankruptcy Court Op. at 6 (emphasis added).

Third, General Dynamics challenges the correctness of the holding that Stewart bought in good faith and without knowledge that the sale to him was in violation of the rights of General Dynamics. Our holding above was based on alternative grounds—that the dates of purchase are the dates on which Stewart's knowledge is relevant and that the bankruptcy court found that Stewart acted in good faith and had no knowledge on the date of recordation. In keeping with that alternative holding, we will consider Stewart's knowledge and good faith on both dates, although General Dynamics's argument deals mainly with the date of recordation.

13. We find additional support for our conclusion that the dates of purchase are the relevant dates in the limited nature of the current controversy over when the protection of the buyer in the ordinary course attaches. Although there is some debate as to whether one who qualifies as a buyer in the ordinary course prevails over the secured lender if the lender attempts to foreclose before the buyer takes possession of the goods, no one seems to question that, from the time of delivery, the buyer prevails. *See* T. Quinn, UCC Commentary and Law Digest ¶ 3–307[A][8] (1978); Note, *When Does a Buyer Become a Buyer in Ordinary Course?* UCC §§ 1–201(9), 9–307(1): A Test and a Proposal, 60 Neb.L. Rev. 848, 875 (1981); compare, *e.g., Jones v. One Fifty Foot Gulfstar Motor Sailing Yacht,* 5 Cir.1980, 625 F.2d 44, 47 n. 4 (dictum) (the date of contract marks the beginning of protection, at least where the buyer has made partial payment) *with Martin Marietta Corp. v. New Jersey Nat'l Bank,* 3 Cir.1979, 612 F.2d 745, 749 (assuming, without deciding, that the date of identification of the goods to the contract marks the beginning of protection) *and with Chrysler Corp. v. Adamatic, Inc.,* 1973, 59 Wis.2d 219, 208 N.W.2d 97, 106–07 (the passage of title marks the beginning of protection). Although one might argue that the buyer's qualification should be determined as of a date earlier than that on which the protection takes effect, surely the qualification should not be determined as of a *later* date.

The holding that Stewart had no knowledge that the sale violated the security agreement between Ayer and General Dynamics is not clearly erroneous. There is nothing in the record to show any knowledge on the dates of purchase, for the results of the title search did not arrive until January 5, 1972, the day after the second purchase. Once those results arrived, there is nothing to indicate that Stewart saw the security agreement before August 3, 1972, and, even if he did, that agreement appeared to authorize the sale. The record supports the conclusion that Stewart first learned of the default by Ayer from General Dynamics's letter of May 28, 1976. We cannot re-evaluate Stewart's credibility in denying knowledge; that was a question for the trial judge.

General Dynamics also contends that Stewart did not act in good faith, suggesting that he knowingly bought the planes for less than their value and that, though he was experienced in the sale of aircraft, did not undertake a title search before purchasing.[16] To show that Stewart purchased below market value, General Dynamics relies on the gain on the later sale of one of the planes and on the use of a higher value in the 1975 mortgage agreement between Gary and its bank. Stewart apparently made no profit on the sale of the group of planes, and, indeed, his profit on a sale four years down the line is but weak evidence that he originally paid less than fair value for the planes and even weaker evidence that he was aware that this was a bargain too good to be true. Similarly, the use of a higher value in a mortgage agreement consummated three years later is weak evidence of the 1972 market value.

Stewart's failure to undertake a title search presents a question only slightly more troublesome. The Texas courts have repeatedly stated that the test of good faith is not negligence or diligence and that it is immaterial that the buyer was aware of facts that would put a reasonably prudent person on inquiry. To lose his status as a buyer in

---

16. General Dynamics also notes a number of other facts that it views as evidence of Stewart's bad faith: (1) Stewart purchased the planes in his individual capacity, (2) he waited seven months to record his title, (3) he gave two planes to Gary and sold another one to Gary at a large gain, (4) in August 1976, Stewart and Gary obtained an indemnification agreement from Ayer, and (5) Gary's files contained a rough draft of a letter, never sent, that misrepresented the date on which Gary learned of the lien. The first three facts are obviously completely irrelevant to the question of Stewart's good faith. The indemnification agreement, obtained some four and a half years after the purchase, shows little about Stewart's good faith on that date or on the date of recordation; if anything, it tends to establish that he acted in good faith because he saw no need for such an agreement at those times. Finally, we are unmoved by General Dynamics's arguments that the rough draft of the letter establishes bad faith. First, the letter was clearly labelled a draft and was never sent, so, at most, it could establish that Stewart thought about acting in bad faith and decided not to do so. Second, the letter was drafted in 1976, long after Stewart's good or bad faith ceased to be relevant. Third, examination of the letter indicates that the author was uncertain of the date of the discovery of the liens, placed it shortly after Gary's sale of one of the planes and only later filled in that date, suggesting that there was no purposeful misrepresentation of the date of the discovery. Finally, the record does not establish that Stewart drafted the letter, and he denied having done so.

the ordinary course, the buyer must have actual knowledge of facts or circumstances that amount to bad faith. * * *. Thus, although a reasonably prudent person with Stewart's experience might have conducted a title search with the FAA before purchasing, Stewart's failure to do so does not, without more, establish that he acted in bad faith. * * *. Nor did Stewart have actual knowledge of any circumstances that would put him in bad faith. We decline to overrule the holding that Stewart acted in good faith.

IV.

General Dynamics next argues that, even if Stewart qualifies as a buyer in the ordinary course of business, Gary cannot take good title for one of two reasons—first, the security interest was not created by Gary's seller and, second, Gary gave no consideration for the planes. Neither argument has merit.

The first argument is based on the limitation in section 9.307(a): a buyer in the ordinary course of business takes free of a security interest only if it was created by his seller. *See, e.g., National Shawmut Bank v. Jones,* 1967, 108 N.H. 386, 236 A.2d 484. General Dynamics, noting that the security interest it asserts was not created by Stewart (Gary's seller) but by Ayer, contends that Gary cannot be protected against that interest. This argument misses the mark, for Gary does not claim under section 9.307(a). On the contrary, its position is that Stewart took good title under section 9.307(a), and Gary, as Stewart's transferee, took whatever title Stewart had, under section 2.403(a), the "shelter" provision. It is therefore of no consequence that Gary's seller did not create the security interest. General Dynamics attempts to rebut this reasoning by relying on language in *National Shawmut Bank* stating that section 2–403 of the Uniform Commercial Code cannot provide an escape from the limitations of section 9–307. In *National Shawmut Bank* an individual sold a car, subject to a security interest, to a dealer, who then sold it to a buyer in the ordinary course of business. Since the security interest was not created by his seller, the last buyer in the chain could not take free and clear of the interest under section 9–307 of the UCC. Section 2.403(a) provides that a purchaser of goods acquires all title that his transferor had or had power to transfer, and that a seller with voidable title can transfer good title. If, under that provision, a retailer who bought subject to a security interest was one with voidable title and had the power to transfer good title, the "created by his seller" limitation of section 9.307(a) would be without any effect, so the *National Shawmut Bank* court held that section 2.403(a) does not provide an escape to section 9.307(a). That rule has been approved by the commentators, *see* J. White & R. Summers, Uniform Commercial Code § 25–15 (2d ed. 1980), and we do not question it. But the rule is that section 2.403(a) is not available to save one who buys when the seller's title is subject to a security interest but who does not qualify under section 9.307(a). It certainly does not mean that section 2.403(a) is not available to subsequent transferees from a successful section 9.307(a) buyer, as General Dynamics urges. *See* Skilton, *Buyer in the Ordinary Course of Business under Article 9 of the Uniform Commercial Code,* 1974 Wis.L.Rev. 1, 76 (viewing the point as "obvious"). If General Dynamics were correct, section 9.307(a) would be of scant benefit to the "protected" buyer in the ordinary course, for good title means little if one cannot transfer it. We hold that the lien of General Dynamics was extinguished upon the sale by Ayer to Stewart under section 9.307(a), and the subsequent sale to Gary could not resurrect it.

Finally, General Dynamics contends that Gary cannot take good title under section 2.403(a) because it furnished no consideration, receiving the aircraft as a gift. We disagree. Section 2.403(a) applies to a "purchaser" of goods, and section 1.201 defines a "purchaser" as one who takes by "sale, discount, negotiation, mortgage, pledge, lien, issue or reissue, *gift* or any other voluntary transaction". § 1.201(32), (33) (emphasis added). The language could not be clearer. When the draftsmen of the Code wished to require consideration, they used the terms "buyer", "seller", and "sale", defined in sections 2.106(a) and 2.103(a)(1) to require consideration, instead of "purchaser", "transferor", and "purchase". *See, e.g.,* §§ 2.313, 2.314, 2.315. We cannot imagine applying any rule other than that a donee takes the title that his donor had.

V.

We hold that the FAA does not preempt the provisions of the Texas Business and Commerce Code relating to the priority of interests in aircraft. Therefore, Stewart, as a buyer in the ordinary course of business, took the aircraft free and clear of the lien of General Dynamics. And Gary, as the transferee of Stewart, also took free and clear of the lien. Consequently, Gary is entitled to the possession of the remaining airplane and the proceeds of the airplane that was sold. The case is affirmed.

[Some footnotes omitted.]

EXECUTIVE FINANCIAL SERVICES, INC. v. PAGEL

Supreme Court of Kansas, 1986.
238 Kan. 809, 715 P.2d 381.

[Executive Financial Services (EFS) purchased three tractors from Tri-County Farm Equipment Company (Tri-County), a John Deere dealership. EFS then leased the tractors to Mohr-Loyd Leasing, a partnership between the owners of Tri-County. The "lease" was a financing transaction, subject to Article 9, and EFS perfected its security interest in the tractors by filing. EFS neither took possession of the tractors nor segregated them from other tractors held for sale by Tri-County.

Tri-County sold tractor # 1 to Thompson Implement Company, a merchant engaged in the business of selling farm equipment. Thompson, in turn, sold the tractor to Pagel, a buyer in the ordinary course of business. Pagel granted John Deere a purchase money security interest in the tractor, which Deere perfected by filing a financing statement. Tractor # 2 was sold by Thompson to Allen, who also granted Deere a purchase money security interest which Deere perfected by filing. Tractor # 3 was sold by Thompson to Morse. Deere took a purchase money security interest in the tractor but, because it was not perfected on time, it was subject to a preexisting security interest of PCA on Morse's equipment and machinery.

When Mohr-Loyd defaulted on the leases, EFS brought suit, inter alia, to recover the tractors from Pagel, Allen and Morse. The lower courts granted the defendants a summary judgment on the ground that they took free of EFS's security interest under UCC 2–403(2). The cases were consolidated on appeal and the judgments were affirmed. The Supreme Court first held that the transaction between EFS and Mohr-Loyd Leasing was "essentially a financing transaction whereby EFS acquired a security interest in the three tractors.]

* * *

Having so determined, we turn to the issue of whether the buyers of the tractors took free of EFS's security interest pursuant to K.S.A. 84–9–307(1), which provides:

> "A buyer in ordinary course of business * * * other than a person buying farm products from a person engaged in farming operations takes free of a security interest *created by his seller* even though the security interest is perfected and even though the buyer knows of its existence." (Emphasis added.)

Under this section, if Allen, Riverview Farms, Thompson and Pagel were "buyers in ordinary course of business" they would take free of any security interest created "by the seller," which is Tri-County. However, K.S.A. 84–9–307(1) is inapplicable to the facts in this case because Mohr-Loyd created the security interest in question—not Tri-County. A buyer in ordinary course can only take free of a security interest created "by his seller." Since the seller of the tractors, Tri-County, did not create the security interest, the buyers cannot take free of that interest under 84–9–307(1).

We next consider whether, as a matter of law, EFS entrusted the three tractors to Tri-County and, under K.S.A. 84–2–403(2), thereby lost any interest it had in them.

The entrustment doctrine is codified at K.S.A. 84–2–403(2):

> "Any entrusting of possession of goods to a merchant who deals in goods of that kind gives him power to transfer all rights of the entruster to a buyer in ordinary course of business."

"Entrusting" is defined in K.S.A. 84–2–403(3):

> " 'Entrusting' includes any delivery and any acquiescence in retention of possession regardless of any condition expressed between the parties to the delivery or acquiescence and regardless of whether the

procurement of the entrusting or the possessor's disposition of the goods have been such as to be larcenous under the criminal law."

Since this statute has not been considered by the court in an analogous fact situation, some general background regarding its purpose and effect is helpful.

The Kansas Comment 1983 to K.S.A. 84–2–403 briefly describes the purpose of the provisions in question:

> "Subsections (2) and (3) extend prior law in protecting buyers in ordinary course of business from hidden entrusting arrangements with merchant-sellers who deal in goods of the kind. Under these subsections, an owner who entrusts goods to a merchant who deals in goods of the kind may lose his rights as against a buyer in ordinary course of business. Under prior law, such good faith purchasers were protected only under the doctrines of estoppel and the like."

At common law, the mere entrustment of goods to a merchant who dealt in goods of a kind did not estop the owner from recovering them from a bona fide purchaser for value. This common law rule has been reversed by UCC § 2–403(2), which provides that any entrusting of possession of goods to a merchant who deals in goods of that kind accords the merchant power to transfer all the entruster's rights to a buyer in ordinary course of business. Hawkland, UCC Series § 2–403:07, p. 611 (1984).

The entrustment doctrine operates on the assumption that both the entruster and the buyer have been equally harmed by the dishonesty of the merchant-dealer, and resolves the issue in favor of the buyer. This result is explained in Hawkland, UCC Series § 2–403:07, as follows:

> "In a broad sense, § 2–402(2) exemplifies one effort to 'modernize the law governing commercial transactions' in keeping with the underlying philosophy of the UCC. Accordingly, when a housewife takes her vacuum cleaner for repairs to a merchant who also is in the business of selling vacuum cleaners new and old, the sale by him to a buyer in the ordinary course of business passes a good title to the latter. In this case, the equities of the housewife and the buyer may be said to be equal. The housewife may not have been prudent in entrusting her goods to the dishonest dealer, but, by the same token, the buyer may not have been prudent in buying from him. On the assumption that both the entruster and buyer have been equally victimized by the dishonesty of the merchant-dealer, § 2–403(2) resolves the issue so as to free the marketplace, rather than protect the original owner's property rights. The rule, however, is an absolute one and does not depend in its operation on any balancing of equities or notions of comparative negligence." p. 612.

Entrusting typically falls into one of four fact patterns. These patterns are illustrated in White and Summers, Uniform Commercial Code § 3–11, p. 143 (2d ed. 1980):

> "First, Ernie Entruster turns his car over to Dave Dealer so that Dave can sell it for Ernie. A buyer in ordinary course takes free of Ernie's

ownership rights. Second, a wholesaler gives Dealer the goods 'on consignment' or under a 'floor planning' agreement. A buyer in ordinary course from Dealer is not bound by any 'title retention' agreement between Dealer and the wholesaler as to passage of title. Third, George leaves goods to be repaired with Dealer who resells them to a buyer in ordinary course. Finally, Edgar buys goods from Dealer but leaves the goods in Dealer's hands. A buyer in ordinary course cuts off Edgar's interest."

The last example is similar to the fact pattern in the present case. EFS purchased three tractors from Tri-County, but left the tractors on Tri-County's lot. Tri-County later resold the tractors to third parties in ordinary course of business. The situation is made more complicated, however, by the fact that prior to the resale by Tri-County, EFS leased the tractors to Mohr-Loyd Leasing, which operated from the same business premises as Tri-County. Furthermore, EFS obtained a security interest in the tractors from Mohr-Loyd Leasing.

Prior to applying K.S.A. 84–2–403(2) to the facts of the instant case, we must consider its potential conflict with our previous application of 84–9–307(1).

Appellant contends that if a buyer does not qualify for the preferred treatment of K.S.A. 84–9–307(1) because the competing security interest is not created by the seller, the buyer cannot then argue it took free of the security interest under the entrustment theory of 84–2–403(2). This argument has received support among some courts and commentators.

White and Summers argue that priority disputes between secured creditors and subsequent purchasers must be governed exclusively by Article 9 and that a subsequent purchaser who is disappointed under 84–9–307 cannot fall back on 84–2–403 and argue that it renders him superior to a prior security interest. They point to the language of 84–9–306(2) which states:

"Except where *this article* otherwise provides, a security interest continues in collateral notwithstanding sale, exchange or other disposition thereof unless the disposition was authorized by the secured party in the security agreement or otherwise. ＊ ＊ ＊" (Emphasis added.)

See White and Summers, Uniform Commercial Code § 25–15, pp. 1073–74 (2d ed. 1980).

There is also authority, however, for applying the entrustment theory where a buyer is unable to prevail under 84–9–307(1). In his treatise, The Law of Secured Transactions Under the Uniform Commercial Code ¶ 3.4[3] (1985 Cum.Supp. No. 3), Professor Barkley Clark recognizes that an entrustment theory may be applicable, even when 84–9–307(1) is not applicable:

"But even if the buyer in ordinary course loses his protection under § 9–307(1) because the security interest was created further up the line, he may be able to prevail on a different theory. This is what happened in In re Woods, where the buyer discovered that a bank had a perfected security interest in the collateral created by a previous owner. The court determined that the ultimate buyer could prevail on an *entrustment* theory under §§ 2–403(2) and 2–403(3). Those subsections provide that a person who 'entrusts' the possession of goods to a dealer loses title to a buyer in ordinary course from the dealer. In the usual case, the outright owner entrusts the goods to the dealer for repair. In this case, it was the bank with its prior perfected security interest which did the entrusting. Certainly there is nothing in the language of § 2–403 that would limit that provision to outright owners as entrusters. The Woods case makes the important point that a prior secured party may do sufficient 'entrusting' so that its security interest is lost, even though the security interest was not created by the dealer to which the goods were entrusted. The court in Woods suggested yet another theory to protect the ordinary course buyer: Insofar as the prior secured party permitted the collateral to be delivered to the dealer, it authorized the sale free of its security interest under § 9–306(2). Finally, under either alternative theory, the ultimate buyer was protected even though it knew of the bank's prior perfected security interest; the court correctly concluded that, in order for the secured party to prevail, it would have to show that the ordinary course buyer knew that the sale was in violation of the prior security interest."

The facts here, as in In re Woods, 25 B.R. 924 (Bkrtcy.Tenn.1982), are distinguishable from the usual case. Typically, the entruster and the holder of the security interest are separate entities with the security holder not involved in the entrustment. In such a case the security interest would continue in the goods because under K.S.A. 84–2–403(2) only the "rights of the entruster" would be transferred. Here, however, the security holder is the entruster and its rights as such are transferred to the buyer.

For K.S.A. 84–2–403(2) to be applicable, three steps are required: (1) An entrustment of goods to (2) a merchant who deals in goods of that kind followed by a sale by such merchant to (3) a buyer in ordinary course of business.

Neither party argues Tri-County is not a "merchant who deals in goods of that kind," but they disagree as to whether EFS entrusted the tractors to Tri-County and whether one of the transferees was a buyer in the ordinary course of business.

The first question for our consideration is whether EFS entrusted the goods to Tri-County. As noted earlier, "entrusting" is defined at K.S.A. 84–2–403(3) and includes "any delivery and any acquiescence in retention of possession."

In support of their theory of entrustment, appellees point out that although EFS purchased the tractors from Tri-County, it did not take possession of them. Nor did EFS segregate the tractors from Tri-County's other inventory, identify the tractors in any way as EFS's property, or otherwise manifest any sign of ownership which would be evidence to a subsequent purchaser. Appellees contend that by its lack of action, EFS acquiesced in Tri-County's retention of possession of the tractors.

On the other hand, EFS argues that the mere fact that EFS did not take possession of the tractors does not justify the conclusion that EFS acquiesced in the retention of possession of the tractors by Tri-County. EFS contends that once it leased the tractors to Mohr-Loyd Leasing with the understanding and representation by Mohr-Loyd that the tractors would be leased out to farmers, it became impossible for EFS to acquiesce in the retention of possession of the tractors by Tri-County.

The reason possession was left with the merchant-seller is immaterial under the Code. 3 Anderson, Uniform Commercial Code § 2–403:42, pp. 592–93. The entrustment definition specifically provides that an entrustment can occur "regardless of any condition expressed between the parties to the delivery or acquiescence. . . ." K.S.A. 84–2–403(3).

Thus, the key factor here is EFS's knowledge that the tractors would remain in the Tri-County lot. The fact that EFS expected Mohr-Loyd to eventually lease the tractors to farmers is immaterial. We conclude the tractors were entrusted to Tri-County by EFS.

EFS next contends that even if an entrustment occurred, the Johnson County District Court improperly applied K.S.A. 84–2–403(2) to the transaction involving Riverview Farms because Riverview Farms was not a buyer in ordinary course of business. There is no dispute that Allen and Thompson Implement were buyers in ordinary course of business.

K.S.A. 84–1–201(9) defines "buyer in ordinary course of business":

> " 'Buyer in ordinary course of business' means a person who in good faith and without knowledge that the sale to him is in violation of the ownership rights or security interest of a third party in the goods buys in ordinary course from a person in the business of selling goods of that kind. * * * 'Buying' may be for cash or by exchange of other property or on secured or unsecured credit and includes receiving goods or documents of title under a preexisting contract for sale but does not include a transfer in bulk or as security [for] or in total or partial satisfaction of a money debt."

"Good faith" is defined at K.S.A. 84–1–201(19); " 'Good faith' means honesty in fact in the conduct or transaction concerned."

First, EFS argues the model No. 8640 tractor was not acquired by Riverview Farms for cash or other valid consideration. Rather, EFS contends the tractor was acquired by utilizing $30,000 of credit owed to Riverview Farms by Tri-County. This contention is based on the fact that in March of 1982, Riverview Farms received two checks from Tri-County totalling nearly $30,000. Ted Morse, one of the partners in Riverview Farms, was unable to explain why the checks were given to Riverview Farms. A few months later in August 1982, Riverview

Farms delivered a model No. 8630 tractor to Tri-County to be sold by Tri-County.

Appellees argue Riverview Farms acquired the model No. 8640 tractor in an even exchange for the No. 8630 tractor. They concede Tri-County initially offered to sell the No. 8640 tractor to Riverview Farms for a trade-in of the No. 8630 tractor plus $10,000. Later, however, Tri-County agreed to accept the No. 8630 tractor in an even exchange for the No. 8640 tractor. Appellees explained the $30,000 payment to Riverview Farms as credit received when Tri-County sold a No. 7020 tractor and disc which Riverview Farms had traded to Tri-County.

K.S.A. 84–1–201(9) specifically provides that a transfer in total or partial satisfaction of a money debt does not give the purchaser the status of a "buyer in ordinary course." Thus, if Riverview Farms acquired the No. 8640 tractor as the result of a credit obtained initially for the model No. 8630 tractor and the extinguishment of a money debt, it did not have "buyer in ordinary course" status. However, if Riverview Farms acquired the No. 8640 tractor in an even exchange for the No. 8630, it did have buyer in ordinary course status since 84–1–201(9) includes an exchange within the definition of "buying."

The Johnson County District Court made specific findings that Riverview Farms had no actual notice that Mohr-Loyd Leasing existed, that Mohr-Loyd leased the No. 8640 tractor from EFS, or that EFS claimed any interest in the tractor. We conclude the facts justify the district court's ruling that Riverview Farms, like Thompson, Pagel and Allen, was a buyer in ordinary course of business.

We hold all three tractors were entrusted to Tri-County, a merchant who deals in tractors, by EFS and then sold to Allen, Thompson Implement and Riverview Farms in ordinary course of business.

A final issue presented by this appeal is whether EFS may be estopped from claiming any interest in the tractors. We need not discuss this issue since the case is resolved by our application of the entrustment provisions of K.S.A. 84–2–403(2) and (3).

The judgments of the trial courts are affirmed.

Notes

The *Pagel* case, by using UCC 2–403(2), expands the protection of a buyer in ordinary course of business beyond that granted by UCC 9–307(1). Is this result sound? How does the court deal with UCC 2–403(4), which states that the "rights of other purchasers of goods ∗ ∗ ∗ are governed by the Articles on Secured Transactions (Article 9) ∗ ∗ ∗"?

Note: Rights of Buyer When Goods in Seller's Possession

In a contest with a secured party with a perfected security interest, at what point does a buyer become a "buyer in the ordinary course of business?" Assuming that the conditions in UCC 1–201(37) are satisfied, including the giving of value, there are three possibilities.

First, the status is not achieved until the goods are delivered by the seller. This was a requirement under the Uniform Trust Receipts Act and it has some support in UCC 9–301(1)(c), where the buyer is other than in the ordinary course, and in the case law. See, e.g., Chrysler Corp. v. Adamatic, Inc., 59 Wis.2d 219, 208 N.W.2d 97 (1973), where the court stated that the "status" of a buyer in ordinary course must be determined "as of the time he actually took possession of the goods." Section 9–307(1), however, does not require that possession be transferred.

Second, the status is achieved when the buyer obtains title to the goods even though possession has not been transferred. Obtaining title before delivery requires that the goods be both existing and identified to the contract, see UCC 2–105(2) & 2–501(1), and that the parties agree that title shall pass before delivery. See UCC 2–401(1). Thus, where a buyer made progress payments to a seller who was manufacturing goods for the buyer and the parties agreed that title to all parts and components and to the goods in process should pass to the buyer when the seller acquired them, Kinetics Technology International Corp. v. Fourth National Bank of Tulsa, 705 F.2d 396 (10th Cir.1983), held that the status was achieved when title passed to the buyer under the agreement. Accord: Puget Sound Nat. Bank v. Honeywell, Inc., 40 Wash.App. 313, 698 P.2d 584, 587 (1985).

Third, the status is achieved when the goods are identified to the contract under UCC 2–501(1), even though neither title nor possession have passed. Support for this position can be found in Martin Marietta Corp. v. New Jersey National Bank, 612 F.2d 745 (3d Cir.1979), and Big Knob Vol. Fire Co. v. Lowe & Moyer Garage, 338 Pa.Super. 257, 487 A.2d 953, 956–58 (1985). Thus, the "special property interest" obtained by identification is sufficient to confirm the status of BIOCB and to support an action by the buyer to replevy the goods or to obtain specific performance. See UCC 2–716. See also Tanbro Fabrics Corp. v. Deering Milliken, Inc., 39 N.Y.2d 632, 385 N.Y.S.2d 260, 350 N.E.2d 590 (1976), where the court apparently held that a buyer with at least as "special property" interest became a BIOCB even though the secured party of his seller had possession of the goods.

If, in each of these cases, the buyer has advanced all or part of the contract price to the seller, which approach makes the most sense? Clearly, if the status of BIOCB depends upon the transfer of possession to the buyer, the presumed problems associated with "ostensible ownership" are resolved. The buyer will not be asserting a property interest of which no public notice has been given to reclaim goods in the seller's possession. Compare Note, *"Bailment for Processing:" Article Nine Security Interest or Title Retention Contract*, 61 Ore.L.Rev. 441 (1982), written by the son of one of your co-authors. But will the buyer's interest be adequately protected before delivery?

The answer is yes if the buyer could create and perfect an Article 9 purchase money security interest in the goods being manufactured by the seller and obtain priority over any existing perfected security interests in the collateral. See UCC 9–107 & 9–312(3). This step, however, is easier to recommend than to implement. In short, there are several practical pitfalls in the path of the "financing buyer" which interfere with the use of Article 9. A full exploration of this step should be postponed until you study the materials on Secured Transactions and, more particularly, Chapter 7. See, generally, Jackson & Kronman, *A Plea for the Financing Buyer,* 85 Yale L.J. 1 (1975) (buyer may be unable to insure that funds advanced to seller are used in fact to obtain materials and components for completed goods).

SECTION 3. SELLER'S WARRANTY OF TITLE

In Section 2, a primary question was when does the buyer of goods get "good" title from a seller whose title is defective or nonexistent? Another was when does the buyer "take free" from a perfected security interest? These questions are often litigated when the "true" owner or secured party asserts claims to goods in the possession of the buyer. If "true" owner wins, the buyer will be deprived of the goods and, of course, the benefit of his bargain. Does the buyer have any recourse against his seller? If so, what remedies are available? If "true" owner loses, the buyer may keep the goods. However, he has been put through the stress and expense of a law suit and may have been temporarily deprived of possession. Does he have any recourse against his seller? In short, we are here concerned with whether the seller has made and breached a warranty of title under UCC 2–312 and what the buyer must and may do to achieve adequate redress.

SUMNER v. FEL–AIR, INC.

Supreme Court of Alaska, 1984.
680 P.2d 1109.

OPINION

RABINOWITZ, JUSTICE.

This appeal arises from a dispute over the sale of a Piper Navajo airplane by William Sumner, an Anchorage commercial aircraft dealer, to Fel-Air, Inc., a Barrow air taxi operator. In March 1976, Sumner and Fel-Air orally agreed to the basic terms of the sale, including the purchase price of $105,000.00. Sumner was to receive a Piper Aztec aircraft valued at $30,000 as a downpayment on the Navajo. Fel-Air was to remit the $75,000 balance of the purchase price in monthly installments of $2,000. Interest on the unpaid balance was to accrue at a rate of 12%. These terms were confirmed in a March 31, 1976, letter from Fel-Air's general manager to Sumner.

The Navajo was delivered to Fel-Air in April 1976. Sumner received the Aztec as a downpayment in accordance with the parties' agreement. The Navajo began to experience mechanical difficulties and was taken to Seattle Flight Service for repairs in the early summer of 1976. Two months later, after paying a repair bill of $20,000, Fel-Air regained use of the airplane.

Fel-Air sent the Navajo back to Seattle for repairs in October 1976. Two months later, while the plane was still in the custody of Seattle Flight Service, the president of Century Aircraft, Inc. informed Fel-Air that title to the Navajo was held by Century rather than by Sumner. Century's president had also told Seattle Flight Service that Century owned the aircraft. Sumner's interest in the Navajo was that of a lessee with an option to purchase. After the discovery that Century was the record owner of the Navajo, Seattle Flight Service filed a mechanic's lien against the Navajo for unpaid repair bills.

Fel-Air asserted that it telephoned Sumner in December 1976 and requested either a conditional sales contract or bill of sale which would provide the Federal Aviation Administration with a record of Fel-Air's authority to operate the Navajo, or a full refund of payments made to date on the Navajo, including return of the Aztec. Fel-Air contended that Sumner assured it that the contract would be prepared within three days. Sumner testified that he did not remember such a conversation.

In May of 1977, Fel-Air ceased making monthly payments on the Navajo. On May 10, 1978, Sumner sent a telegram to Fel-Air demanding satisfaction of the lien Seattle Flight Service had filed and payment of monthly installments then due. Fel-Air did not respond. Sumner discharged the $8,000 lien himself and had the plane flown back to Anchorage.

Sumner arranged to have the Navajo's documents of title held in escrow to assure Fel-Air that it would receive title upon payment of the balance of the purchase price and upon compensation of Sumner for payments made to satisfy the Seattle Flight Service lien. On August 3, 1977, the escrow arrangement was completed. The balance then due on the aircraft, including the payment made to discharge the mechanic's lien, was $64,936.47.

Fel-Air subsequently filed suit against Sumner, alleging Sumner had breached implied warranties of merchantability and title and that he was liable to Fel-Air for fraud and misrepresentation. Sumner denied these claims and alleged that Fel-Air had abandoned the Navajo, requested that consideration paid by Fel-Air be deemed an offset for rent owed to Sumner for use of the Navajo, and filed a counterclaim for the $8,000 he had paid to discharge the lien.

The case was tried to the superior court sitting without a jury. The court rejected Fel-Air's claims for breach of the warranty of merchantability and negligent and intentional misrepresentation. However, it concluded that Sumner had breached a warranty of title to the aircraft and awarded Fel-Air $51,166.82 in damages. This sum represented the value of the Aztec used as a downpayment ($30,000), and $21,700 in monthly payments made by Fel-Air to Sumner, less the $533.18 expense of transporting the plane back to Alaska saved by Fel-Air as a result of the breach. Pre-judgment interest accruing at 8% per annum from February 1, 1977, to May 1, 1980, was also awarded, and totaled $13,300.16. Judgment against Sumner was entered for $64,466.98. Fel-Air was also awarded costs and attorney's fees. This appeal followed.

BREACH OF WARRANTY OF TITLE

Title 45 of the Alaska Statutes adopts Article 2 of the Uniform Commercial Code as the applicable law of sales in Alaska. Under A.S. 45.02.312, an implied warranty of title accompanies the sale of goods in Alaska. It may expressly be disclaimed. A focal point of the parties' dispute is whether Sumner excluded or modified by specific language the warranty of title. Sumner does not claim that he had good title to the Navajo, but rather alleges that he informed Fel-Air that he leased, but did not own, the Navajo. Fel-Air denies that it was so informed.

The superior court specifically found that Sumner did not inform Fel-Air prior to the sale that he had neither title to the Navajo nor the right to sell it, and that the circumstances surrounding the transaction did not give Fel-Air any reason to know that Sumner did not claim title to the plane in himself. The court concluded that Sumner had therefore breached the warranty of title imposed by A.S. 45.02.312.

Sumner concedes that the superior court's conclusion that there was no express or implied disclaimer of the A.S. 45.02.312 warranty was a finding of fact which may be reversed only if clearly erroneous. Alaska R.Civ.P. 52(a); *Uchitel Co. v. Telephone Co.*, 646 P.2d 229, 233 (Alaska 1982); *Strack v. Miller*, 645 P.2d 184, 186 (Alaska 1982). In the case at bar, the superior court's factual finding was based upon an assessment of the credibility of conflicting testimonial evidence. We have observed that "[i]t is the trial court's function, and not that of a reviewing court, to judge the credibility of the witnesses and to weigh conflicting evidence. This is especially true where the trial court's decision depends largely upon oral testimony." *Penn v. Ivey*, 615 P.2d 1, 3 (Alaska 1980) (citations omitted). Thus, particular deference must be accorded to the superior court's finding that Sumner did not disclaim the A.S. 45.02.312 warranty of title. After review of the entire record before us, and guided by these principles of appellate review, we conclude that the superior court's finding that an implied warranty of title accompanied the sale of the Navajo must be upheld. The question now becomes whether or not Sumner breached that warranty.[8]

Since Sumner did not have good title to the plane when he purported to convey it to Fel-Air, the answer to this question may seem obvious. Yet both parties agree that Century "entrusted" the plane to

---

8. Sumner argues that Fel-Air should be held to have had "constructive notice" of Century's interest prior to consummation of the sale, since pertinent documents of title to the Navajo were on file at the Federal Aviation Administration (FAA) at that time. This argument is without merit. It is clear from the wording of A.S. 45.02.312 that only actual knowledge on the part of the buyer of the seller's lack of title, or of circumstances which would reasonably lead the buyer to reach such a conclusion, can defeat the statutory warranty. The official commentary to § 2–312 of the U.C.C. specifically states that "[t]he 'knowledge' referred to in subsection 1(b) is actual knowledge as distinct from notice." § 2–312 comment 1, 1 U.L.A. 303 (1976).

Sumner within the meaning of A.S. 45.02.403. Under the UCC a merchant to whom goods have been entrusted may give a buyer a better title than the merchant himself possessed. To quote A.S. 45.02.403(b):

> An entrusting of possession of goods to a merchant who deals in goods of that kind gives him power to transfer all rights of the entruster to a buyer in ordinary course of business.

Because Sumner had possession of the Navajo and was a dealer in airplanes, he had the power to transfer all of Century's rights, including its good title to the airplane. Given the facts as the parties have presented them, Fel-Air could have defeated any attempt by Century to regain possession of the Navajo.

It does not follow from the fact that the parties now agree that Fel-Air's title was good that Sumner did not breach the implied warranty of title. This question has divided the commentators. Compare 1 Anderson, Uniform Commercial Code § 2–312:36 (3d ed. 1982) (warranty not breached) with 1 Alderman, A Transactional Guide to the Uniform Commercial Code § 1.53–52 (2d ed. 1983) (warranty breached, seller should have chance to cure). Alderman emphasizes the full text of UCC 2–312(a)(1), which provides:

> (a) Subject to (b) of this section there is in a contract for sale a warranty by the seller that
>
> (1) the title conveyed shall be good, *and its transfer rightful.*

A.S. 45.02.312(a) and (a)(1) (emphasis added). As Alderman states, the entrustee's "wrongfulness (lack of right) in making the conveyance * * * is unquestionable, for the transfer of title [is] not made pursuant to any 'right'". Alderman, *supra,* at 266–67. Here Sumner's lease-purchase arrangement with Century did not authorize him to transfer title to Fel-Air. The transfer he made to Fel-Air was wrongful, and thus we conclude that the warranty UCC 2–312(a)(1) establishes was breached.

Wright v. Vickaryous, 611 P.2d 20 (Alaska 1980), supports this conclusion. *Wright* suggests that a court attempting to determine whether or not a warranty of title was breached must consider the facts as they appeared to the buyer at the time title was called into question. If a reasonable buyer would conclude that "marketable title" had not been conveyed to him, the seller—assuming that he does not save the transaction by showing that the facts are not what the buyer believes them to be—has breached the warranty of title. A "substantial shadow" on title is enough to justify the buyer's refusal to proceed with his contractual performance.[10] Similarly in the instant case the revelation

---

10. In *Wright* various third parties had taken security interests in the seller's cattle. All of them orally consented to the sale, thus releasing their security interests pursuant to UCC 9–306(2). However, the liens remained on the books, the buyer discovered them, and delivery of the cattle was refused, the seller all this time failing to point out that the security interests had been released. We held that this circumstance put a "substantial shadow" on the title and justified refusing to proceed with

of Century's interest in the Piper Navajo cast such a shadow on the transaction between Sumner and Fel-Air.

To dispel a similar shadow, the buyer in *Wright* would have had to call all the people he believed to be lienholders; had he done so, he would have discovered that their liens had been released. To dispel the shadow of Century Aircraft, Fel-Air would have had to become an expert on the UCC and would then have had to determine that Sumner had not stolen or borrowed the Navajo from Century, that Sumner was indeed a "merchant who deals in [airplanes]" as the UCC defines "merchant," and that Fel-Air itself qualified as a "buyer in ordinary course of business." The parties' present agreement on these matters does not mean that these things were obvious at the time the transaction between Sumner and Fel-Air began to break down. Even if we decided to ignore A.S. 45.02.312's intimation that a "wrongful" transfer of title breaches the warranty which that section contains, we would be loath to conclude that a breach did not occur in this case. The superior court correctly decided that Sumner breached the implied warranty of title.

* * *

For the foregoing reasons, the judgment of the superior court is affirmed.

[Some footnotes omitted.]

Note: Fifty Ways to Breach the 2–312 Warranty of Title

Paradoxically, the warranty of title was broken in Sumner v. Fel-Air, although the buyer actually got good title. Is the result supported by any specific language in UCC 2–312? Is such a result justified?

A breach of warranty of title has been held to occur when the seller of a motor vehicle fails to provide his purchaser with adequate proof of ownership because of the reasonable doubts which faulty documentation (number on title certificate did not correspond with number on frame of vehicle) raises as to the validity of the title the buyer acquires. Jefferson v. Jones, 286 Md. 544, 408 A.2d 1036 (1979). Here, because of the faulty documentation, the vehicle was seized by the police and the buyer had to incur legal expenses to resolve the matter favorably, expenses he then successfully sought from the seller.

Beyond full adverse ownership claims, various "clouds" have been held to breach the title warranty. Elias v. Dobrowolski, 120 N.H. 212, 412 A.2d 1035 (1980) (valid filed security interest of which buyer had no actual knowledge); Wright v. Vickaryous, 611 P.2d 20 (Alaska 1980) (security interests the prior discharge of which had not been communicated to buyer who then rejected the cattle); National Crane Corp. v. Ohio Steel Tube Co., 213 Neb. 782, 332 N.W.2d 39 (1983) (tax liens); Catlin Aviation Co. v. Equilease Corp., 626 P.2d 857 (Okl.1981) (repairman's lien); Jeanneret v.

the sales contract. *Wright* explicitly recognized that the buyer could successfully have defended himself against any former lienholder's lawsuit, but reasoned that the risk of such a lawsuit was enough to excuse the buyer's refusal to accept delivery.

Vichey, 693 F.2d 259 (2d Cir.1982) (regulations of foreign country applicable to export of paintings could constitute cloud if not complied with).

Not just any assertion of a claim by a third party will breach the warranty of title. Unfounded claims that are also not colorable will not. C.F. Sales, Inc. v. Amfert, Inc., 344 N.W.2d 543 (Iowa 1983).

Also, whenever the buyer has reason to know that the seller does not claim title to himself or that he is purporting to sell only such right or title as he or a third person may have, there is no warranty of title. UCC 2–312(2). For example, where a buyer of a used car received from the seller a certificate of title listing another person as the seller, the jury could have found that the buyer had such "reason to know." Spoon v. Herndon, 167 Ga.App. 794, 307 S.E.2d 693 (1983). But under 2–312(2), a warranty of title or the like can be "excluded or modified only by specific language." Rockdale Cable T.V. Co. v. Spadora, 97 Ill.App.3d 754, 53 Ill.Dec. 171, 423 N.E.2d 555 (1981) (language in bill of sale purporting to transfer "all Seller's right, title, and interest, of every kind and nature, in and to" held insufficiently specific).

UNIVERSAL C.I.T. CREDIT CORP. v. STATE FARM MUT. AUTO. INS. CO.

Court of Appeals of Missouri, 1973.
493 S.W.2d 385.

WASSERSTROM, JUDGE.

This four-party litigation poses the always difficult question of which one of several innocent parties should bear the loss of stolen goods. The specific factual context in which that question arises here is undisputed.

Kansas City Automobile Auction Company is engaged in a business of conducting sales at auction on behalf of automobile dealers having surplus automobiles. The bidders who attend these weekly auctions are also automobile dealers. On September 24, 1969, one of these auctions was conducted by Auction Company, and the Dodge automobile that is the subject of present controversy was sold to Jack Banning Ford Sales, Inc.

Thereafter, Banning resold this Dodge automobile to Donald L. Sensenich. This purchase was financed by Universal C.I.T. Credit Corporation. The credit transaction was in the form of a security agreement signed by Banning and Sensenich, which was then assigned by Banning to C.I.T. Sensenich also procured collision insurance covering the automobile, with a loss payable clause to C.I.T.

Subsequently, the Dodge automobile in question was demolished in a highway accident. In connection with the investigation accompanying the wreck, it was discovered that the automobile had been stolen prior to the time that it came into the hands of Auction Company, and that therefore, the auction sale on September 24, 1969, did not convey good title.

Upon acquiring the information concerning this insufficiency of title, Sensenich terminated any further payment to C.I.T., and he promptly gave notice to Banning of revocation of his acceptance of the automobile. Banning in turn gave notice to Auction Company and requested that Auction Company satisfy the demands of Sensenich. Auction Company denied liability.

Faced with this impasse, C.I.T. filed suit against Sensenich in Count I on the security agreement, and against the insurance company in Count II on the insurance policy. A settlement (accomplished in some manner not disclosed by the transcript on appeal) was made with the insurance company, and Count II of the C.I.T. petition was dismissed before trial.

Sensenich filed answer to Count I of the C.I.T. petition, and also filed a third-party petition bringing in Banning as a third-party defendant. Sensenich's third-party petition against Banning alleged generally the suit against him by C.I.T. and claimed indemnity from fourth-party petition against Auction Company alleging a right to reimbursement under an implied warranty of title from Auction Company to Banning.

The case was tried without a jury, and the trial court entered judgment for C.I.T. against Sensenich for the balance due under the security agreement, after giving credit for the insurance recovery, and also allowed attorney's fees in favor of C.I.T. of 15% as provided in the security agreement, the total so allowed to C.I.T. being $2,207.78. Judgment was also entered in favor of Sensenich against Banning in the sum of $2,998.50. The exact manner of computation of the latter figure is not disclosed by the abbreviated record filed on this appeal, but Sensenich states in his briefs, and his after-trial motion and the court's ruling thereon support the inference, that the sum awarded to Sensenich did not include any allowance for attorney's fee to him, either in resisting the C.I.T. suit or in pressing the third-party claim against Banning.

The judgment further awarded Banning the sum of $3,523.50 against Auction Company. While the abbreviated transcript on appeal does not show how this figure was computed, the parties in their briefs are in agreement that the award to Banning consisted of the judgment against him in favor of Sensenich plus an allowance of $525.00 as an attorney's fee to Banning in defending against the Sensenich claim. * * * The record indicates that Banning has gone out of business.

Auction Company, on its appeal, presents these points: (1) that there is no legal basis for liability against it, for the reason that an auctioneer acts solely as an agent and cannot be held to have given any implied warranty; and (2) that if it is liable at all, its liability must be confined to the value of the automobile at the time of the auction sale, which was the price paid by Banning of $2,415.00.

The points upon which Sensenich relies on his appeal are: (1) that he should have been awarded attorney's fees both in resisting the C.I.T.

claim and also for prosecuting his third-party claim against Banning; and (2) that all judgments should have been as net damages directly against Auction Company for each of the three claimants.

* * *

II

Auction Company's principal argument on this appeal is that as an auctioneer it was a mere agent, and that any implied warranties were those of its principal who was the dealer who had delivered the car for sale at auction. This question has as its starting point the Uniform Commercial Code, § 400.2–312 V.A.M.S., which now codifies the law of implied warranty of title in connection with the sale of chattels. This section provides that there shall be a warranty that the title conveyed is good, except under "circumstances which give the buyer reason to know that the person selling does not claim title in himself * * *"

* * *

[T]he correct recourse for purposes of interpretation must be to the common law of this State, in accordance with the provision of § 400.1–103. * * *

Under the common law of this state, as well as under the law generally, an auctioneer is liable as a seller and is held to the burdens of an implied warranty of title, unless the auctioneer discloses the name of his principal at the time of sale. This principle is stated succinctly in the early case of Schell v. Stephens, 50 Mo. 375, l. c. 379, as follows;

"The mere fact that defendants were acting as auctioneers is not of itself notice that they were not selling their own goods, and they must be deemed to have been vendors, and responsible as such for title, unless they disclosed at the time the name of the princi-pal."

The same rule has been followed consistently since. * * *

Auction Company argues that it should not be held as a seller, because of some evidence in the record emphasized by it to the effect that Banning should have known that the Dodge automobile in ques-tion was being sold by Auction Company merely in its capacity as an auctioneer. That argument proceeds on a mistaken view of the law. As stated in the Schell case quoted above, the mere fact that a defendant is acting as an auctioneer is not in itself sufficient notice to provide immunity from liability. The requirement is that auctioneer disclose the name of its principal, and the record in this case is abundantly clear that this was not done. It is conceded that on the copy of the sales receipt delivered to Banning, the name of Auction Company's principal was purposely blocked out. The evidence by Auction Company itself was that this practice was intentional in order to prevent the buying dealer from "going around" the Auction Compa-ny. It was also conceded by Clemmons, Auction Company's general manager, that a bidder was not advised and could not ascertain the name of the selling dealer until after the sale had already been consummated. Under these admitted facts, Auction Company must be held to the obligation of an implied warranty to Banning. Moreover, there is sufficient evidence in the record to support a finding that Banning did not know either actually or constructively whether Auction Company was selling as agent or principal; and under these circumstances, it must be deemed that the trial court did so find. Rule 73.01(b), V.A.M.R.

III

Auction Company's alternative argument is that if liable at all, its liability cannot exceed the value of the automobile, measured by the amount received by it from Banning. In making this argument, Auction Company is relying basically on the general measure of damages for breach of warranty as set forth in § 400.2–714 V.A.M.S.; and it denies that this case comes within the concept of "consequential damages" which is recognized by § 400.2–714(3).

The extent to which consequential damages will be allowed is provided in § 400.2–715(2)(a), where that term is defined as including "any loss resulting from general or particular requirements and needs of which the seller at the time of contracting had reason to know * * *" This statutory definition of allowable consequential damages is essentially the same as the rule at common law. Under the common law, the courts of this State prior to the Uniform Commercial Code in an unbroken line of cases have held that a buyer may collect as consequential damages his expenses including attorney's fees in defending title after having given notice to his seller that a third party is claiming adversely. * * *

This result is especially compelled under the circumstances of this case. Under the evidence here, Auction Company should have known and must have realized that Banning would have loss beyond the wholesale value of the car paid by him, should it turn out that the title to the car was defective. By Auction Company's own argument, it knows that all bidders who attend its auction sales are automobile dealers. Obviously, those dealers are buying automobiles for resale; and also obviously, those dealers will be warranting title in turn to their vendees. Thus, if the title received by the auction bidder, in this case Banning, turned out to be bad, then the bidder-purchaser would stand to lose a good deal more than the bare original auction purchase price. For this reason, it must be concluded that the potential loss within the contemplation of the parties included costs which might be incurred in defending suits by subvendees, as well as lost profit of the resale and incidental expense.

In support of its contention that judgment will not lie against it for the attorney's fees paid by Banning in defense of the Sensenich claim, Auction Company cites 46 Am.Jur., Sales, § 755, p. 884, where it is stated: "* * * it has been held that the measure of damages against the original seller cannot be increased by reason of liability subsequently incurred by the buyer on account of independent warranties of the same property to later purchasers." In support of that statement, the text cites Smith v. Williams, 117 Ga. 782, 45 S.E. 394. An opposite result was reached in Thurston v. Spratt, 52 Me. 202. The Smith case is also out of harmony with the philosophy of the Missouri decisions on this point cited above. No significant distinction can be perceived for present purposes whether the claim made against the buyer is by a subvendee or someone completely outside the chain of transactions initiated by Auction Company. Moreover, the Smith case is readily distinguishable from the present case on the ground that the case at bar involves a sale to a dealer who the seller was bound to know would make a resale of the goods in the ordinary course of his business, whereas there is nothing in the Smith opinion to indicate that this was true in that case.

It follows that there was no error in including in Banning's judgment an allowance for attorney's fee incurred in defense of the Sensenich claim.

* * *

V

Sensenich's next claim of error is stated by him as follows: "The court erred in failing to enter judgment under impleader practice as net damages for each other party (plus all costs on Count 1) against fourth-party defendant". * * * To the extent that Sensenich is attempting to make complaint on behalf of Banning in this regard, no such complaint lies because Banning did get a judgment direct against Auction Company. Therefore, our consideration of this assignment reduces itself to the narrow question of whether Sensenich is entitled to a direct judgment against Auction Company. In this connection, it must be noted that Sensenich did not make Auction Company a party to his third-party petition, he did not attempt to state any cause of action against Auction Company, and he did not pray any relief against Auction Company. More fundamentally, however, he had no right of action against Auction Company as a matter of substantive law.

The law on this subject is that a warranty of title on personal property runs only to the immediate buyer and does not extend to subvendees. For this purpose, a warranty of title does not run with the chattel in the manner that a covenant for title runs with land. As stated in Crocker v. Barron, Mo.App., 234 S.W. 1032, l. c. 1033, a case involving suit for breach of warranty of title on personal property: "Warranties of Chattels are available only between parties to the contract, and not in favor of third parties." The law generally is similarly stated in 77 C.J.S. Sales § 352, p. 1259, as follows: "A subvendee has no right of action for breach of warranty to the original purchaser or against one who sold the goods to the person from whom the purchaser bought."

It is true that the requirement of privity in suits on some warranties has been greatly relaxed in recent years. However, that relaxation has occurred for the most part in cases of personal injury where there exists some element of tort. * * * This case does not come within the rationale of the cases which have, in selected situations, permitted recovery on warranties (usually relating to quality or fitness) without the necessity of privity of contract.

* * *

All motions filed in this court now pending are overruled. The appeal by Banning is dismissed. The judgment of the trial court is affirmed.

All concur. *Judgment Affirmed*

Notes

1. Why did the court "credit" Sensenich with the proceeds of the insurance policy? Instead, why not subrogate the insurance company to the claims of C.I.T. against Sensenich?

2. Does the holding on privity and the fact that Banning has gone out of business mean that Sensenich will have no recovery?

.3. If you were the judge how would you deal with the following argument: Since the true owner has not appeared to assert his interest, the warranty of title issues are essentially irrelevant to this law suit. Sensenich is in exactly the same circumstance as he would have been in had he had good title and destroyed the car. The Auction Company should have to make payment neither to Banning nor to Sensenich because the title it conveyed proved to be good at least for the useful life of this car. Thus even though the warranty of good title was breached, no damage was ever suffered by anybody as a result of that. How do you respond to such an argument if you represent Sensenich or Banning?

MENZEL v. LIST

New York Court of Appeals, 1969.
24 N.Y.2d 91, 298 N.Y.S.2d 979, 246 N.E.2d 742.

BURKE, JUDGE.

In 1932 Mrs. Erna Menzel and her husband purchased a painting by Marc Chagall at an auction in Brussels, Belgium, for 3,800 Belgian francs (then equivalent to about $150). When the Germans invaded Belgium in 1940, the Menzels fled and left their possessions, including the Chagall painting, in their apartment. They returned six years later and found that the painting had been removed by the German authorities and that a receipt for the painting had been left. The location of the painting between the time of its removal by the Germans in 1941 and 1955 is unknown. In 1955 Klaus Perls and his wife, the proprietors of a New York art gallery, purchased the Chagall from a Parisian art gallery for $2,800. The Perls knew nothing of the painting's previous history and made no inquiry concerning it, being content to rely on the reputability of the Paris gallery as to authenticity and title. In October, 1955 the Perls sold the painting to Albert List for $4,000. However, in 1962, Mrs. Menzel noticed a reproduction of the Chagall in an art book accompanied by a statement that the painting was in Albert List's possession. She thereupon demanded the painting from him but he refused to surrender it to her.

Mrs. Menzel then instituted a replevin action against Mr. List and he, in turn, impleaded the Perls, alleging in his third-party complaint that they were liable to him for breach of an implied warranty of title. At the trial, expert testimony was introduced to establish the painting's fair market value at the time of trial. The only evidence of its value at the time it was purchased by List was the price which he paid to the Perls. The trial court charged the jury that, if it found for Mrs. Menzel against List, it was also to "assess the value of said painting at such an amount as you believe from the testimony represents its present value." The jury returned a verdict for Mrs. Menzel and she entered a judgment directing the return of the painting to her or, in the alternative, that List pay to her the value of the painting, which the jury found to be $22,500. (List has, in fact, returned the painting to Mrs. Menzel.) In addition, the jury found for List as against the Perls, on his third-party complaint, in the amount of $22,500, the painting's present value, plus the costs of the Menzel action incurred by List. 49 Misc.2d 300, 267 N.Y.S.2d 804.

The Perls appealed to the Appellate Division, First Department, from that judgment and the judgment was unanimously modified, on the law, by reducing the amount awarded to List to $4,000 (the purchase price he had paid for the painting), with interest from the date of the purchase. In a memorandum, the Appellate Division held that the third-party action was for breach of an implied warranty of *quiet* possession and, accordingly, held that the Statute of Limitations had not run on List's claim since his possession was not disturbed until the judgment for Mrs. Menzel. 28 A.D.2d 516, 279 N.Y.S.2d 608. In addition, the court held that the "applicable measure of damages was the price List paid for the painting at the time of purchase, together with interest", citing three New York cases (Staats v. Executors of Ten Eyck, 3 Caines 111, 113; Armstrong v. Percy, 5 Wend. 535; Case v. Hall & Van Elten, 24 Wend. 102).

List filed a notice of appeal as of right from the unanimous modification insofar as it reduced the amount of his judgment to $4,000, with interest from the date of purchase. The Perls filed a notice of cross appeal from so much of the Appellate Division's order as failed to dismiss the third-party complaint, denied costs and disbursements and fixed the date from which interest was to run on List's judgment. The Perls have now abandoned the cross appeal as to the failure to dismiss the third-party complaint and the denial of costs and disbursements, leaving only the issue as to the date from which interest should run.

List's appeal and the Perls' cross appeal present only questions of law for resolution, the facts having been found by the jury and affirmed by the Appellate Division (its modification was on the law as to the proper measure of damages and the running of interest). The issue on

Issue

the main appeal is simply what is or should be the proper measure of damages for the breach of an implied warranty of title (or quiet possession) in the sale of personal property. The cases cited by the Appellate Division do not hold that the measure of damages is the purchase price plus interest. The *Staats* case (*supra*) was an action for breach of a real property covenant in which there was dicta to the effect that the rule was the same for personal property. The dicta was compromised one year later by the same jurist (Chief Justice KENT who wrote the opinion in *Staats* in Blasdale v. Babcock, 1 Johns. 517 [1806], where it was held that the buyer was entitled to recover in damages the amount which he had been compelled to pay to the true owner, the actual value of the chattel. In Armstrong v. Percy, 5 Wend. 535, *supra* the buyer recovered the purchase price but only because the chattel, a horse, was found to have depreciated in value below the price paid. In Case v. Hall & Van Elten, 24 Wend. 102, *supra*, there is contained a statement which is pure dicta to the effect that warranty damages are the purchase price (the action was in contract for goods sold and delivered). The parties have cited no New York case which squarely meets the issue and it is, therefore, concluded that, contrary to the counter assertions of the parties, neither "purchase plus interest" (Perls) nor "value at date of dispossession" (List) is presently the law of this State. In fact, there is a marked absence of case law on the issue. One legislative source has described this paucity of case law with the understatement that "[t]he implied warranty of title under the Uniform Sales Act [N.Y. Personal Property Law, Consol.Laws, c. 41, § 94] has seldom been invoked." (1955 Report of N.Y.Law Rev.Comm., Vol. 1, p. 387, n. 68, citing Pinney v. Geraghty, 209 App.Div. 630, 205 N.Y.S. 645, a case dealing with the effect of the vendor's ignoring a vouching-in notice.) Furthermore, the case law in other jurisdictions in this country provides no consistent approach, much less "rule", on this issue and it is difficult even to add up jurisdictions to pinpoint a "majority" and a "minority". One attempt to collect and organize the law in this country on this issue concludes that there are at least four distinct "rules" for measuring the damages flowing from the breach of a personal property warranty of title (1) purchase price plus interest; (2) "value", without specification as to the time at which value is to be determined; (3) value at the time of dispossession; and (4) value at the time of the sale (Ann., Breach of Warranty of Title—Damages, 13 A.L.R.2d 1369). Interestingly enough, the annotator was able to find New York cases each of which used language which would apparently suggest that a different one of these four "rules" was *the* rule. (Ann., *supra*, p. 1380.) In the face of such unsettled and unconvincing "precedent", the issue is one which is open to resolution as a question which is actually one of first impression.

4 different rules:

At the time of the sale to List and at the commencement of the *Menzel* replevin action, there was in effect the New York counterpart to section 13 of the Uniform Sales Act (N.Y.Personal Property Law, § 94

[PPL]) which provided that "In a contract to sell or a sale, unless contrary intention appears, there is

1.   An implied warranty on the part of the seller that * * * he has a right to sell the goods * * *

2.   An implied warranty that the buyer shall have and enjoy quiet possession of the goods as against any lawful claims existing at the time of the sale".

In addition, section 150 of the PPL provided for remedies for breach of warranty and subdivision 6 provided: "The measure of damages for breach of warranty is the loss directly and naturally resulting, in the ordinary course of events, from the breach of warranty." Subdivision 7 applies, by its terms, only to a breach of warranty of quality and is, therefore, not controlling on the question of damages for breach of warranty of title and quiet enjoyment. (3 Williston, Sales [rev.ed.], § 615, n. 9.) Thus, the Perls' reliance on this subdivision is misplaced. The Perls contend that the only loss directly and naturally resulting, in the ordinary course of events, from their breach was List's loss of the purchase price. List, however, contends that that loss is the present market value of the painting, the value which he would have been able to obtain if the Perls had conveyed good title. The Perls support their position by reference to the damages recoverable for breach of warranty of quiet possession as to real property. However, this analogy has been severely criticized by a leading authority in these terms: "This rule [limiting damages to the purchase price plus interest] virtually confines the buyer to rescission and restitution, a remedy to which the injured buyer is undoubtedly entitled if he so elects, but it is a violation of general principles of contracts to deny him in an action on the contract such damages *as will put him in as good a position as he would have occupied had the contract been kept*." (11 Williston, Contracts [3d ed.], § 1395A, p. 484 [emphasis added].) Clearly, List can only be put in the same position he would have occupied if the contract had been kept by the Perls if he recovers the value of the painting at the time when, by the judgment in the main action, he was required to surrender the painting to Mrs. Menzel or pay her the present value of the painting. Had the warranty been fulfilled, i.e., had title been as warranted by the Perls, List would still have possession of a painting currently worth $22,500 and he could have realized that price at an auction or private sale. If List recovers only the purchase price plus interest, the effect is to *put* him in the same position he would have occupied *if the sale had never been made*. Manifestly, an injured buyer is not compensated when he recovers only so much as placed him in *status quo ante* since such a recovery implicitly denies that he had suffered any damage. This rationale has been applied in Massachusetts in a case construing a statute identical in language to section 150 (subd. 6) of the PPL where the buyer was held entitled to the value "which [he] lost by not receiving a title to it as warranted. * * * His loss cannot be measured by the [price] that he paid for the machine.

He is entitled to the benefit of his bargain" (Spillane v. Corey, 323 Mass. 673, 675, 84 N.E.2d 5 [1949]; see, also, Pillgrene v. James J. Paulman, Inc., 6 Terry 225, 226, 45 Del. 225–226, 71 A.2d 59 [1950] ["The purpose of compensatory damages is to place the buyer in as good condition as he would have occupied had the title been good."]). This measure of damages reflects what the buyer has actually lost and it awards to him only the loss which has directly and naturally resulted, in the ordinary course of events, from the seller's breach of warranty.

An objection raised by the Perls to this measure of damages is that it exposes the innocent seller to potentially ruinous liability where the article sold has substantially appreciated in value. However, this "potential ruin" is not beyond the control of the seller since he can take steps to ascertain the status of title so as to satisfy himself that he himself is getting good title. (Mr. Perls testified that to question a reputable dealer as to his title would be an "insult." Perhaps, but the sensitivity of the art dealer cannot serve to deprive the injured buyer of compensation for a breach which could have been avoided had the insult been risked.) Should such an inquiry produce no reasonably reliable information as to the status of title, it is not requiring too much to expect that, as a reasonable businessman, the dealer would himself either refuse to buy or, having bought, inform his vendee of the uncertain status of title. Furthermore, under section 94 of the PPL, the seller could modify or exclude the warranties since they arise only "unless contrary intention appears". Had the Perls taken the trouble to inquire as to title, they could have sold to List subject to any existing lawful claims unknown to them at the time of the sale. Accordingly, the "prospects of ruin" forecast as flowing from the rule are not quite as ominous as the argument would indicate. Accordingly, the order of the Appellate Division should be reversed as to the measure of damages and the judgment awarding List the value of the painting at the time of trial of the *Menzel* action should be reinstated.

On the cross appeal by the Perls, the issue is as to the time from which interest should run on the judgment in favor of List against the Perls. The Appellate Division indicated that interest should be recovered from the date of purchase in October, 1955, but it did so only in conjunction with its determination that the measure of damages should be the purchase price paid by List on that date. Manifestly, the present-value measure of damages has no necessary connection with the date of purchase and is, in fact, inconsistent with the running of interest from the date of purchase since List's possession was not disturbed until the judgment directing delivery of the painting to Mrs. Menzel, or, in the alternative, paying her the present value of the painting. Accordingly, List was not damaged until that time and there is no basis upon which to predicate the inclusion of interest from the date of purchase. Accordingly, on the cross appeal, the order of the Appellate Division, insofar as it directed that interest should run from the date of purchase, should be reversed and interest directed to be included from the date on which Mrs. Menzel's judgment was entered, May 10, 1966.

SCILEPPI, BERGAN, BREITEL and JASEN, JJ., concur.

FULD, C.J., and KEATING, J., taking no part.

Order reversed, with costs to third-party plaintiff-appellant-respondent, and case remitted to Supreme Court, New York County, for further proceedings in accordance with the opinion herein.

Notes

1. Would the court reach the same result under UCC 2–312? Is this result sound?

2. Would you, as purchaser of the painting, be able to collect from the dealer reasonable attorney fees for defending against the replevin action and asserting the breach of warranty claim as consequential damages under UCC 2–715(2)? See De La Hoya v. Slim's Gun Shop, 80 Cal.App.3d Supp. 6, 146 Cal.Rptr. 68 (1978); Universal C.I.T. Credit Corp. v. State Farm Mut. Auto. Ins. Co., 493 S.W.2d 385 (Mo.App.1973) (attorney fees incurred in defending against claims are recoverable damages).

Problem 15–7

1. On October 1, Domino Truck Sales, Inc. sold and delivered to Paul's Lines, Inc., a second-hand diesel tractor for $5,000. Paul made a down payment consisting of $1,500 cash and a truck valued at $1,000 and agreed to pay the balance in equal monthly installments commencing on December 1. Domino created and perfected by filing a security interest in the tractor. Paul operated two tractor-trailer rigs (the new purchase was a replacement) out of the town where Domino did business. Over the past five years, Paul's lines has averaged an annual net profit of $75,000 doing 45% of its business in the State of New York.

On October 15, Paul discovered that there was an unpaid fuel tax lien in the amount of $2,000 against the tractor in the State of New York. A New York permit for operation could not be obtained until the lien was paid. He promptly advised the president of Domino who expressed surprise and promised to have it removed. By November 25, nothing had been done. Paul again visited Domino and stated that the truck could not be profitably operated without access to New York and that he would not make any monthly payments until the lien was removed. Domino's president repeated his promise to remove the lien but, on December 10, after Paul had failed to make his first payment, repossessed the tractor. It is now December 15. The New York lien has not been removed and Paul has already lost more than two months of profits that could have been earned by operating in that state. Domino still has the tractor but, in an effort to resell, has received a $4,500 offer from a trucker which does no business in New York.

Assuming that Paul could block the resale and recover the tractor if Domino's repossession was improper, what are the rights of the parties under the UCC? Consider both the questions posed by UCC 2–312 and the remedies available to Paul.

2. Suppose that Domino Truck Sales was unable to pass good title to Paul and that one year after the truck had been delivered the "true" owner had it replevied. The evidence will show that the value of the truck at the time of delivery was $7,500, Paul had spent $2,000 in repairs, the value of the use to Paul over the year was $4,800 and that the truck was worth $5,000 on the date of replevin. Paul claims damages in the amount of $7,500, the difference in value between the truck received and the truck as warranted. UCC 2–714(2). Is this correct? How much should Paul recover against Domino for breach of warranty?

SECTION 4. RIGHTS OF SELLER VERSUS CLAIMS OF THIRD PARTIES TO GOODS IN POSSESSION OF BUYER

A. Introduction

In Section 2, we considered the extent to which a good faith buyer of goods for value can obtain better title than his seller or take free from a perfected security interest in the goods created by his seller or another secured party. In Section 5, infra, we will examine how the Bulk Sales Law, Article 6, gives unsecured creditors of the seller power to avoid certain presumptively fraudulent transfers to a buyer. These problems can implicate Articles 2, 6 and 9 of the UCC. In addition, the possibility of a breach of the warranty of title, treated in Section 3, hangs over the entire proceedings.

In this Section, we will treat a more focused variation of the same problem. Suppose a seller has delivered possession of goods sold to the buyer. Suppose, further, that credit has been extended in both transactions. To what extent can the seller recover possession of the goods from the buyer without perfecting a security interest under Article 9? In what circumstances can possession be reclaimed without the conclusion that the parties intended to create a security interest which should have been perfected under Article 9? See UCC 9–102(1).

These problems extend beyond the parties to the transaction. They involve third parties as well—secured parties who have perfected a security interest under Article 9, purchasers from the party in possession, and lien creditors. They also raise issues similar to those posed when possession is sought by bailors, lessors under a "true" lease, and consignors—parties who are not sellers and buyers but whose property interest in the goods frequently resembles a security interest. These problems have been treated extensively in Chapter Seven. See, generally, Baird & Jackson, *Possession and Ownership: An Examination of the Scope of Article 9*, 35 Stan.L.Rev. 175 (1983).

Transactional hair splitting aside, there is a common theme: Whenever a seller asserts a property interest to recover possession of goods who has defaulted in payment, someone, frequently a trustee in bankruptcy, will contend that the interest is, in fact, a security interest that should have been perfected under Article 9. The questions, therefore, involve a proper characterization of the interest, the scope of Article 9, see UCC 1–201(37), 9–102(1), and the extent to which the party seeking possession should, in planning the transaction, create and perfect a security interest under Article 9.

B. Possession Retained

In a contract for sale, it is clear that if the goods are existing and indentified, the buyer will obtain, at least, a special property interest and, at most, title. In short, the buyer could be the owner of the goods before they are delivered.

It is also clear that, as between the parties, the seller may withhold delivery of the goods if the buyer has become insolvent, UCC 2–702(1), or otherwise breached the contract, UCC 2–703, even though the time for delivery has arrived. By retaining possession, the seller has, in effect, a security interest arising under Article 2. See UCC 9–113. If the dispute cannot be resolved by agreement, the seller can resort to remedies for breach of contract under UCC 2–703, including resale of the goods under UCC 2–706. Resale is a method of enforcing this possessory security interest arising under Article 2, but, unlike the enforcement of security interests arising under Article 9, the seller has no obligation to account to the buyer for any surplus. Compare UCC 9–504(2) with UCC 2–706(6).

Assuming that possession is retained, the seller's rights in the goods should also be effective against creditors of and purchasers from the buyer. Or should they? Consider the following problem.

Problem 15–8

S agreed to manufacture factory equipment according to B's specifications for $100,000. Under the agreement, title was to pass to B when conforming goods were identified to the contract. In addition, B agreed to pay $50,000 upon delivery and to give S a promissory note, due six months after delivery, for the balance. S completed and identified conforming goods to the contract on July 1. On August 1, the date for delivery, S tendered delivery but B failed to pay the $50,000 due. Shortly thereafter, S was beset with the following claims by third parties who had dealt with B:

1. Bank, who had a perfected security interest in B's equipment, existing and after-acquired. Bank argued that B had "rights in the collateral" on July 1, the security interest attached on that date, see UCC 9–203(1), and that it was perfected with priority over S, citing UCC 9–312(5).

2. Lien creditor, whose judgment against B was executed by levy on July 15.

3. Buyer, who paid B $90,000 for the goods, to be delivered later, on July 20.

Which, if any, of these parties should prevail over S, the party in possession of the goods? See UCC 2–403, 2–702, 2–703, 9–113, 9–301(1) & 9–312(5).

Problem 15–9

In Problem 15–8, above, suppose that S had shipped a carload of goods to B "FOB the point of shipment." This meant that both title, UCC 2–401(1), and risk of loss, UCC 2–509(1)(a), passed to B even though the goods were still in the possession of the carrier. Suppose, further, that the carrier issued a non-negotiable bill of lading, naming B as the person entitled to the goods. Suppose, finally, that B repudiated the contract while the goods were in transit. If S were able to stop delivery of the goods against the carrier under UCC 2–705, would this be effective against the third parties asserting claims to the goods? (See In re Hillcrest Foods, Inc., 40 B.R. 360 (Bkrtcy.Me.1984), where the court held that UCC 9–113 was effective until the buyer obtained lawful possession of the goods from the carrier. The seller had shipped FOB point of shipment and obtained a negotiable bill of lading. When the carrier delivered the goods to the buyer without surrender of the indorsed bill, the buyer did not obtain lawful possession.)

IN RE BLACK & WHITE CATTLE CO.

United States Court of Appeals, Ninth Circuit, 1986.
783 F.2d 1454.

BEEZER, CIRCUIT JUDGE:

This appeal involves the rights of a financing buyer of cattle under California law and the Bankruptcy Code. Granada Cattle Services, Inc., Granada Management Corp., (formerly Premier Angus, Inc.), Granada Corp., and Integrated Cattle Systems IV (collectively "Granada"), appeal a partial summary judgment, granted by the bankruptcy court and affirmed by the district court, in favor of appellee Black & White Cattle Co. ("B & W"). The bankruptcy court held Granada has no interest in certain cattle held by B & W, the debtor and debtor in possession, pursuant to a cattle feeding agreement between the parties. We affirm in part and reverse in part.

FACTS

B & W is a California limited partnership, currently in Chapter 11 bankruptcy proceedings, which operated a calf raising facility and a feed lot facility at two separate California locations. Granada is composed of various Texas corporations and partnerships in the business of buying feeder cattle for their customers, causing them to be fed and raised by third parties until they reach slaughter weight, and then selling them for beef.

In February 1981 Granada and B & W began negotiating a "Cattle Feeding Agreement" (the "Agreement"), which was finally executed on July 17. The Agreement provided that B & W would purchase approximately 6,000 day-old calves "on behalf of" or "for the account of"

Granada's customers, which are referred to collectively throughout the Agreement as the "Owner," and that "Owner" would retain title to any cattle that it "placed on the facilities." B & W was obligated to reimburse "Owner" for certain losses suffered from the death of "Owner's animals." The Agreement also provided that the cattle could be commingled with other cattle in the calf yard and feed lot facilities "[a]fter the cattle have been properly tagged and identified. * * *" The Agreement was to last for three years.

Between May 15 and June 16, 1981, while the Agreement was being negotiated, B & W acquired numerous calves from its regular suppliers. Among the undifferentiated, commingled calves acquired at that time were 1,204 that B & W later identified as those covered by the Agreement (and the subject of this action). Granada contends, and the bankruptcy court found, that the 1,204 calves were purchased by B & W pursuant to an oral agreement entered into with Granada on May 14. Granada reimbursed B & W for the cost of the 1,204 calves and paid B & W's various monthly charges for caring for the animals, as required by the Agreement.

Although the Agreement was executed on July 17, it had an effective date of May 15 to cover the "Cattle on hand."

After July 17, B & W continued to care for the calves at its calf yard until they were delivered to the feed lot as each reached the desired weight. The deliveries occurred between August 13 and October 15, 1981. Upon reaching the feed lot, B & W for the first time identified the 1,204 cattle as those covered by the Agreement by placing the animals in a separate pen and by giving each an identifying ear tag. The cattle were branded with a brand registered to one of B & W's general partners.

On April 23, 1982, some months after the last of the cattle were delivered to the feed lot, B & W filed a Chapter 11 bankruptcy petition. B & W subsequently filed an adversary proceeding as debtor and debtor in possession in the Bankruptcy Court for the Central District of California seeking, among other things, an order declaring invalid Granada's claimed interest in the 1,204 head of cattle still on B & W's feed lot.[1]

The bankruptcy court granted partial summary judgment in favor of B & W. The court invalidated Granada's claim of ownership on the ground that Granada did not comply with California Civil Code § 3440.[2] The court reasoned that § 3440 requires actual delivery to and posses-

1. Although the Agreement contemplated the purchase of 6,000 head of cattle, when B & W fell into financial difficulties, Granada instructed B & W not to acquire additional cattle pursuant to the Agreement. Therefore, only the 1,204 head of cattle initially acquired are now at issue.

2. At the time this action was filed, § 3440 provided in relevant part:

Conclusive presumption of fraud. Every transfer of personal property and every lien on personal property made by a person having at the time the possession or control of the property, and not accompanied by an immediate delivery followed by an actual and continued change of possession of the things transferred, is conclusively presumed fraudulent and void as against the transferor's creditors while he

sion by a buyer to avoid a conclusive presumption of fraud against the seller's creditors. The district court summarily affirmed the bankruptcy court's action. Granada appeals.

ANALYSIS

C. Effect of Cal.Civ.Code § 3440

The Agreement that B & W purchase calves "on behalf of" or "for the account of" Granada was signed on July 17 and made retroactive to the day the first animal was purchased. Granada contends that under the terms of the Agreement the cattle were acquired by B & W as agents for Granada, that Granada had title to the cattle at all times and B & W never had title, and that there was therefore no transfer to be set aside by the operation of § 3440. This argument is without merit.

B & W bought the newborn calves directly from suppliers in its own name. B & W spent its own funds and paid suppliers with checks drawn on B & W's account. B & W took possession of the calves and branded them with a brand registered to a general partner of B & W. B & W agreed to and in fact did bear the risk of loss of the newborn calves. At the time of purchase, moreover, the calves were not identified to B & W's contract with Granada. In short, B & W possessed sufficient indicia of ownership to be called the owner of the calves. Although contracting parties may agree to transfer or divest title retroactively, it would be stretching the fiction to say that B & W never had title. The very purpose of § 3440 demands this conclusion; to allow parties to defeat § 3440 by characterizing their relationship as an agency agreement would emasculate § 3440. The July 17 contract, therefore, constituted a transfer of title.[3]

Granada contends that although it did not have actual possession of the cattle, the tagging and segregation of the animals at the feed yard constituted constructive possession sufficient to satisfy the statute. The only facts relevant to this issue are undisputed, namely, that the cattle were at all times in B & W's actual possession, that after they arrived at the feed lot they were segregated from the other animals and given ear tags identifying them as Granada animals, and that they bore a brand registered to a B & W general partner.

remains in possession and the successors in interest of those creditors, and as against any person on whom the transferor's estate devolves in trust for the benefit of others than the transferor and as against purchasers or encumbrancers in good faith subsequent to the transfer.

* * *

Subdivision (2) of § 2402 of the Commercial Code is not restricted by the provisions of this section.

The several recent amendments to § 3440 are not relevant to this appeal.

3. For other cases utilizing this indicia of ownership approach in dealing with problems of ostensible ownership, see generally, *In re Medomak Canning Co.,* 25 U.C.C.Rep. 437 (Bankr.D.Me.1977) (bailment versus sale), *aff'd,* 588 F.2d 818 (1st Cir.1978); *In re Sitkin Smelting & Refining Inc.,* 639 F.2d 1213 (5th Cir.1981) (same); *see also* D. Baird & T. Jackson, *Security Interests in Personal Property* 1–114 (1984).

Constructive or symbolic delivery "is not altogether forbidden, since not all species of property are subject to the same kind of possession. But symbolic or constructive delivery is insufficient when the nature of the property and the situation of the parties render it practicable to make actual physical delivery." * * * The only question is whether, under California law, cattle are the type of property that the statute requires to be actually physically delivered.

If delivery is practicable, segregation and labeling will not satisfy the delivery and possession requirements. * * * On the other hand, where the property is "not property of which manual possession could be taken," labeling has been held to satisfy a similar Washington statute. * * * Although no case has decided directly whether penned cattle are too bulky to make actual delivery impracticable, or whether they may be constructively delivered by tagging or segregation, every case in which penned cattle have been sold but not physically delivered has held the sale void. * * * These cases, along with the prior transfer of the same animals from the calf yard to the feed lot, and the generally ambulatory nature of the healthy living animals, strongly imply that physical delivery of cattle in general and these animals in particular was entirely practicable, with the result that constructive delivery will not satisfy the requirements of § 3440.

Therefore, no genuine issue of material fact regarding the delivery and possession of the animals existed, and the bankruptcy judge correctly ruled that the tagging and segregation of the cattle did not satisfy the statutory possession and delivery requirements.[7]

D.   Effect of Cal.Comm.Code § 2402(2)

The foregoing analysis, however, does not end our inquiry into the operation of § 3440. The last paragraph of Cal.Civ.Code § 3440 provides that "[s]ubdivision (2) of Section 2402 of the Commercial Code is not restricted by the provisions of this section." Section 2402(2) provides:

> (2) A creditor of the seller may treat a sale or an identification of goods to a contract for sale as void if as against him a retention of possession by the seller is fraudulent under any rule of law of the state where the goods are situated, except that retention of possession in good faith and current course of trade by a merchant-seller for a commercially reasonable time after a sale or identification is not fraudulent.

The official code comment to § 2402 clarifies its purpose:

> Purposes of Changes and New Matter: To avoid confusion on ordinary issues between current sellers and buyers and issues in the field of preference and hinderance by making it clear that:

---

7. A financing buyer may now protect its interest through the filing of a financing statement prior to the date of the intended transfer. *See* Cal.Civ.Code § 3440.1(h)(1); Cal.Comm.Code § 9401.

* * * 2. The retention of possession of the goods by a merchant seller for a commercially reasonable time after a sale or identification in current course is exempted from attack as fraudulent.

The effect of § 2402(2) on the operation of § 3440 is to eliminate the conclusive presumption of fraud where all the requirements are met. *See Gardner v. Sullivan & Crowe Equipment Co.*, 17 Cal.App.3d 592, 597, 94 Cal.Rptr. 893, 895 (1971).

The bankruptcy court's primary objection to the application of § 2402(2) in the instant case was that B & W's retention of possession of the cattle after the transfer was not for a commercially reasonable time. The court reasoned that

> section [2402(2)] basically restates the rule of § 3440. The rationale of this rule likewise parallels that of § 3440. It seeks to protect creditors against a debtor who gives a deceptive appearance of ownership by retaining possession after title has passed to a third party. Unlike § 3440, this section provides a very limited exception where goods are retained for a commercially reasonable period of time.

The bankruptcy court's reasoning essentially reads the statutory exception out of existence. The legislative history of §§ 3440 and 2402 requires greater respect for the effect of § 2402.

Prior to 1963, California Civil Code §§ 1746 and 3440 governed the rights of buyers of undelivered goods and creditors of sellers.[8] In 1963, the California Legislature expanded the rights of buyers by adopting § 2402(2) along with the remainder of the Uniform Commercial Code. The California Code Comments state that "[s]ubdivision (2) is similar to former Civil Code § 1746 (creditor's rights against sold goods in seller's possession), except that under the Commercial Code there is no fraud if in good faith a merchant-seller retains possession for a reasonable time after the sale in the course of trade." Cal.Comm.Code § 2402 (West 1964). The Legislature expressly repealed § 1746. 1963 Cal.Stat. c. 819, p. 1997, § 2, effective January 1, 1965. The expansion of buyers' rights, therefore, altered the existing law. Section 3440, however, temporarily remained unchanged.

The Legislature recognized the potential conflict between § 3440 and the newly adopted § 2402(2). In 1967, the Legislature amended § 3440 by adding the language that stated that § 3440 would not restrict § 2402(2). 1967 Cal.Stat. c. 799, p. 2200, § 1; *see* California Committee on Continuing Education of the Bar, Review of Selected 1967 Code Legislation 48 (1967). This language limits § 3440, not § 2402(2). To the extent that § 2402(2) provides a buyer of goods with

---

8. Section 1746 provided:

CREDITOR'S RIGHTS AGAINST SOLD GOODS IN SELLER'S POSSESSION. Where a person having sold goods continues in possession of the goods, or of negotiable documents of title to the goods, and such retention of possession is fraudulent in fact or is deemed fraudulent under any rule of law, a creditor or creditors of the seller may treat the sale as void.

Cal.Civ.Code § 1746, *repealed,* 1963 Cal. Stat. c. 819, p. 1997, § 2, effective January 1, 1965.

greater rights than does § 3440, such a result is the direct product of a deliberate legislative decision. Contrary to the bankruptcy court's conclusion, § 2402(2) is not equivalent to § 3440; section 2402(2) is a significant departure from prior law. This expansion of buyers' rights is consistent with the broad purpose of the Commercial Code to accommodate commercial practices. *See* Cal.Comm.Code § 1102(2)(b).

Recognition of a buyer's rights under § 2402(2) does not render § 3440 nugatory. Section 3440 applies when § 2402(2) does not. *See Gardner v. Sullivan & Crowe Equipment Co.,* 17 Cal.App.3d at 596, 94 Cal.Rptr. at 895. Section 2402(2) only applies when the seller is a merchant, and he retains possession in good faith, in the current course of trade, and for a commercially reasonable time. If any of these conditions are absent, § 2402(2) will not apply and § 3440 will govern.

The bankruptcy court concluded that B & W's actions were not reasonable because Granada was never to obtain actual possession of the cattle. The court's emphasis on delivery to Granada is misplaced. Commercial contracts frequently require delivery of goods to someone other than the immediate buyer. The proper focus is on the time of retention of possession by the seller, not on the identity of the person to whom the goods are to be delivered. Cal.Comm.Code § 2402(2).

The court also expressed concern regarding the indefiniteness of the time of retention of possession by B & W. The agreement between B & W and Granada provided that B & W would deliver the cattle to Granada's customers when the cattle reached slaughter weight. Although this provision did not specify a particular date of delivery, it did specify a definite and identifiable condition precedent to B & W's duty to deliver the cattle. *See e.g., Houghland v. Rothblum Packing Co.,* 99 Cal.App. 631, 279 P. 159 (1929) (contract requiring seller to deliver sheep "after fattening" held enforceable on grounds that industry practice indicated that delivery was within reasonable time). The time of delivery, therefore, was definite.

The evidence offered by Granada in opposition to the motion for summary judgment indicated that Granada and B & W had valid business reasons for delaying delivery. B & W's primary obligation was to raise and feed the cattle for distribution to California customers of Granada. Although delivery to Granada in Texas was possible, such a course of action would have defeated Granada's purpose for hiring a California feed lot operator. Moreover, Granada offered affidavit testimony indicating that such feeding arrangements are common in the cattle industry. This evidence created a genuine issue of material fact regarding the commercial reasonableness of the time of retention of possession of the cattle. Summary judgment, therefore, was improper on this issue.[9]

* * *

9. The bankruptcy court also noted that since B & W had never before entered into a similar agreement, the retention of possession was not in B & W's current course of trade. The bankruptcy court construed "current course of trade" too narrowly. The uncontested evidence establishing that B & W is in the business of buying, raising, and selling cattle. This is exactly what the agreement with Granada entailed. The fact that B & W's relationship with Granada differed somewhat from B & W's previ-

CONCLUSION

The bankruptcy court's determination that B & W transfered title to Granada without sufficient change of possession to satisfy Cal.Civ. Code § 3440 is affirmed. The court's determination that Cal.Comm. Code § 2402(2) and the corresponding exception to Cal.Civ.Code § 3440 did not apply is reversed and remanded for resolution of factual disputes. * * *

On remand, the court shall consider the customs and practices of the cattle industry to determine whether B & W's retention of possession was commercially reasonable.

If the court on remand determines that B & W's retention of possession was not commercially reasonable within the meaning of Cal. Comm.Code § 2402(2), then Granada shall be entitled to an award of $432,058.02 plus such interest as the court finds appropriate. Granada is entitled to costs incurred for this appeal.

Affirmed in part, reversed in part and remanded.

C. Possession Delivered to Buyer

1. Credit Sales

A seller who delivers possession of goods sold to the buyer on credit may create and perfect a security interest in those goods under Article 9. This would be a "purchase money" security interest, see UCC 9–107, which might have priority over pre-existing security interests if the conditions of UCC 9–312(3) & (4) were met. If the buyer defaulted, i.e., failed to pay the price when due, the seller, as a secured party, could enforce the security interest by repossessing the goods, UCC 9–501(1) & 9–503, selling them in a commercially reasonable manner, UCC 9–504(3), and applying the proceeds to the obligation, UCC 9–504(1).

What about claims of third parties to the goods? Our secured party-seller: (1) would clearly have priority over a subsequent lien creditor, UCC 9–301(1)(b); (2) could have priority over an existing secured party with a perfected security interest in after-acquired property, UCC 9–312(3) & (4); and (3) might lose the security interest to a buyer in the ordinary course of business from B, UCC 9–307(1), but would retain a security interest in the proceeds of the sale. In short, playing the Article 9 game is the route to maximum protection in this situation.

ous practice does not mean that the retention of possession was outside of B & W's current course of trade.

B & W also argues that since § 2402(1) only applies to unsecured creditors with statutory rights not possessed by Granada (i.e., rights under Cal.Comm.Code §§ 2502 & 2716), Granada also has no rights under § 2402(2), which B & W characterizes as an exception to § 2402(1). Section 2402(2) specifically refers to "creditors," however, which the legislature has expressly defined to include "a general creditor, a secured creditor, a lien creditor and * * * a trustee in bankruptcy. * * *" Cal.Comm. Code § 1201(12) (West 1970). The legislature should be presumed to have understood the terms it used in both subsections and expressly defined elsewhere. Section 2402(2) is therefore applicable here if all its requirements are met.

If, however, the seller delivers the goods and retains title until the price is paid, the effect is to create a security interest in the goods which is subject to Article 9. See UCC 9–102(1) & 1–201(37). Unless that security interest is perfected under Article 9 by filing or otherwise, it is vulnerable to creditors of and purchasers from the buyer. The reasons for this become clear when you read UCC 9–301(1).

What happens if the seller delivers the goods in a credit transaction without playing the Article 9 game? Consider the following problem, drawn from In re Samuels & Co., 526 F.2d 1238 (5th Cir.1976), cert. denied *sub nom.,* 429 U.S. 834, 97 S.Ct. 99, 50 L.Ed.2d 99 (1976).

Problem 15–10

Farmer raises cattle for beef. When the cattle are ready, Farmer sells them to Bravo, a meat processor. Bravo agrees to pay the price within 30 days after delivery. On March 1, Farmer delivered 50 head of cattle to Bravo for $35,000. Unknown to Farmer, Bravo was insolvent at that time. UCC 1–201(33).

1. Assume that no third parties are involved. If Farmer discovers the insolvency on March 8, what can he do to reclaim the cattle from Bravo. See UCC 2–702(2). Suppose the cattle have been processed and sold but the proceeds of that sale can be identified. Can Farmer reclaim the proceeds under UCC 2–702(2). Compare UCC 9–306. (The cases disagree. An affirmative answer was given in United States v. West Side Bank, 732 F.2d 1258, 1263 (5th Cir.1984), reprinted in Chapter seven, supra, where the court stated that to "hold otherwise would in many instances render the statutory remedy a nullity.")

2. Suppose that Farmer, on March 8, made an oral demand on Bravo for the cattle, which had not yet been slaughtered. On March 6, however, Eric, a creditor, had obtained a judicial lien on all of Bravo's personal property. Can Farmer reclaim the cattle from Bravo free from Eric's lien? See UCC 2–702(3). Note that the '72 version of UCC 2–702(3) does not mention lien creditors. What does one do next? See UCC 1–103.

3. Suppose that Farmer made an oral demand on March 8. On March 6, however, Bravo had filed a voluntary case in bankruptcy. Could Farmer reclaim the cattle against the trustee? The answer is no. Do you see why? Read UCC 9–301(3) and Sections 544(a) and 546 of the Bankruptcy Code.

4. How would Farmer, who made an oral demand on March 8, fare against a buyer from Bravo who, on March 6, had paid the price and satisfied the conditions of ordinary course of business, UCC 1–201(9), but had not taken possession from Bravo on March 8? See UCC 2–702(3).

5. The last (but not least) variation. Suppose that First Bank had created and perfected an Article 9 security interest in Bravo's "inventory, existing and after-acquired," on February 1. The effect of this is that when Bravo obtains "rights" in the cattle (upon delivery by Farmer), First Bank's security interest attaches to and becomes perfected in the cattle. Assuming that First Bank is unaware of Farmer's claim but has made no new advances between March 1 and March 8, could Farmer effectively reclaim

against First Bank? Most courts have held no. Do you see why? See UCC 1–201(32).

Note: The Reclaiming Credit Seller in Bankruptcy

Section 546(c) of the Bankruptcy Code provides that the avoidance powers of the trustee in Sections 544(a), 545, 547 and 549 are "subject to any statutory or common law right of a seller of goods that has sold goods to the debtor, in the ordinary course of such seller's business, to reclaim such goods if the debtor has received such goods while insolvent, but—(1) such a seller may not reclaim any such goods unless such seller demands in writing reclamation of such goods before ten days after receipt of such goods by the debtor * * *." This provision has been criticized as unduly restrictive, in that it (1) narrows the scope of reclamation available under UCC 2–702(2) and (2) is the exclusive avenue of relief for the reclaiming seller under the Bankruptcy Code. See Mann & Phillips, *Section 546(c) of the Bankruptcy Reform Act: An Imperfect Resolution of the Conflict Between the Reclaiming Seller and the Bankruptcy Trustee*, 54 Am.Bankr.L.J. 239 (1980). In short, unless the reclaiming seller satisfies both UCC 2–702(2) and Section 546(c), the reclamation claim will fail against the trustee. Even then, it may still be subject to the claim of a "floating lienor" who qualifies as a good faith "purchaser" under UCC 2–403. See, e.g., Lavonia Manufacturing Co. v. Emery Corp., 52 B.R. 944 (E.D.Pa.1985). See also, McDonnell, *The Floating Lienor as Good Faith Purchaser*, 50 S.Cal.L.Rev. 429 (1977), who explores the equities of that result.

2. Cash Sales

HOLIDAY RAMBLER CORP. v. FIRST NATIONAL BANK & TRUST CO. OF GREAT BEND, KANSAS

United States Court of Appeals, Tenth Circuit, 1983.
723 F.2d 1449.

SEYMOUR, CIRCUIT JUDGE.

Holiday Rambler Corporation, a manufacturer of recreational vehicles, brought this diversity action against the First National Bank and Trust Company of Great Bend, Kansas. It alleged that First National had wrongfully diverted funds owed to Holiday Rambler by one of its dealers, Kansas Kamper Center, Inc. The district court granted summary judgment for First National, from which Holiday Rambler now appeals. We affirm.

I.

BACKGROUND

When reviewing a district court's summary judgment, we consider the record in the light most favorable to the party opposing the motion * * * and all ambiguities and disagreements must be resolved in its favor * * *. Viewed in this way, the record reveals the following.

Kansas Kamper engaged in the retail sales and service of recreational vehicles and mobile homes. In June 1978, when John R. Morris purchased control of Kansas Kamper, Holiday Rambler conducted a thorough investigation to determine the dealership's credit-worthiness under the new ownership. As a result of that investigation, Holiday Rambler concluded that the dealership's financial condition was "poor." Nevertheless, Holiday Rambler decided to continue to sell campers to Kansas Kamper on a cash-on-delivery (c.o.d.) basis, even though the manufacturer could have insisted upon the economically-safer "floor-plan" basis.[2] Holiday Rambler further elected to accept as payment Kansas Kamper's company checks rather than insisting upon cash, certified check, or bank money order.

In February and March of 1979, Holiday Rambler delivered four campers to Kansas Kamper, accepting in payment four uncertified company checks drawn on the dealer's checking account at First National. Shortly after each sale, Kansas Kamper went to First National to obtain loans, using the campers as collateral. The bank credited Kansas Kamper's checking account with amounts equal to 90 per cent of the camper's invoice price, in exchange for notes and security agreements covering each of the campers. When Holiday Rambler presented its Kansas Kamper checks for payment, however, the Kansas Kamper account had insufficient funds and the checks were dishonored. Between the time of the loans to Kansas Kamper and Holiday Rambler's presentment of its checks for payment, Kansas Kamper had issued checks to the bank at its request to pay some outstanding obligations that Kansas Kamper owed to the bank, leaving insufficient funds to cover Holiday Rambler's checks.

Rather than immediately attempting to reclaim the campers, or taking steps to perfect its security interests in the vehicles, Holiday Rambler instead chose to rely on representations by Morris that the checks would be made good. The manufacturer ran the checks through the bank a second time, and again the checks were dishonored. In May 1979, Kansas Kamper filed for bankruptcy, by which time it had sold three of the campers to customers in the ordinary course of business.

---

2. There is a considerable difference between a c.o.d. and a "floor plan" method of payment. The difference was explained by Holiday Rambler's Vice President of Dealer Finance:

"In a c.o.d. dealership, the dealership issues a check directly to Holiday Rambler Corporation or our agent in payment of that unit, at which point the m.s.o.'s [manufacturer's statements of origin] are passed to the dealership upon our receipt of that, in the form of a check or cash, certified funds, et cetera.

"In the case of a floor plan, we contact—approximately one week prior to production we contact the lender, secure an approval from the lender to pay for that unit through the floor plan funds that have been extended to the dealership to reserve x number of dollars for that unit. The certificate of origin and the original invoice copy is sent directly to the lender on the day of invoicing after the unit has been completed. The lender then issues a check to Holiday Rambler Corporation in payment of that unit. They then perfect their own security documents with the dealer, depending on the arrangement with the dealership, whether that be individual trust receipts, et cetera. That is the bank's business."

Rec., vol. VII. at 35–36.

It used the proceeds from those sales to cancel the notes and security agreements previously executed with the bank. The fourth camper remained in Kansas Kamper's possession at the time of its bankruptcy petition; it was later sold at the bankruptcy court's direction. To date, Holiday Rambler remains unpaid for the four vehicles.

Holiday Rambler brought this action against First National for damages equal to the value of the four dishonored checks, plus incidentals. The issues before the court in the summary judgment proceedings were whether under Article Two of the Kansas Uniform Commercial Code Holiday Rambler maintained a right to reclaim the campers as a cash seller with priority over any interest held by First National, and whether First National's security interests were invalid because they were created fraudulently.

The district court concluded as a matter of law that the bank had valid, perfected security interests in the campers that took priority over Holiday Rambler's asserted claim to the vehicles. The court then rejected plaintiff's remaining fraud claim, concluding that First National had collected a legitimate debt from Kansas Kamper which depleted Kansas Kamper's account to the point that it could not pay Holiday Rambler.

On appeal, Holiday Rambler cites as error the district court's determination that the company had lost its right to reclaim, and the court's resolution of the fraud claim. It also contends that it had a breach of contract claim against First National that should have been addressed.

II.

CASH SELLER'S RIGHT TO RECLAIM GOODS

Holiday Rambler asserts the district court erred in determining that the company had lost its right to reclaim the campers. In a sale of goods, the buyer's right to retain or dispose of goods is conditional upon the seller's right of reclamation. *See* Kansas Comment 1983 to Kan. U.C.C.Ann. § 84-2-507 (Ensley 1983). As long as Holiday Rambler retained a right to reclaim the vehicles, Kansas Kamper could not give First National enforceable security interests because a security interest cannot attach or become enforceable until the debtor has rights in the collateral. Kan.U.C.C.Ann. § 84-9-203(1)(c).

When a seller discovers that a buyer has received goods on credit while insolvent, the seller may reclaim the goods upon demand made within ten days after the buyer's receipt of the goods. Kan.U.C.C.Ann. § 84-2-702. Although the Code has no specific provision for cash sellers, Kan.U.C.C.Ann. §§ 84-2-507(2), Official Comment 3 to 84-2-507, and 84-2-511(3), when read together, provide a right to reclaim for sellers who accept checks that are subsequently dishonored. *See* Kansas Comment 1983 to § 84-2-507; *see also, e.g., Szabo v. Vinton Motors, Inc.,* 630 F.2d 1, 3 (1st Cir.1980); *In re Helms Veneer Corp.,* 287 F.Supp. 840 (W.D.Va.1968).

Thus, section 84–2–507(2) states:

"Where payment is due and demanded on the delivery to the buyer of goods * * *, his right as against the seller to retain or dispose of them is conditional upon his making the payment due."

Section 84–2–511(3) states that "payment by check is conditional and is defeated as between the parties by dishonor of the check on due presentment." Taken together, these sections provide that a seller of goods who receives in payment a check that is subsequently dishonored has a right to reclaim the goods from the buyer. As long as the seller retains this right to reclaim, the buyer's right to title in the goods is subject to it. However, a seller does not retain its right to reclaim indefinitely. Official Comment 3 to § 84–2–507 provides:

"Subsection (2) deals with the effect of a conditional delivery by the seller and in such a situation makes the buyer's 'right as against the seller' conditional upon payment * * *. *Should the seller after making such a conditional delivery fail to follow up his rights, the condition is waived.* The provision of this Article for a ten-day limit within which the seller may reclaim goods delivered on credit to an insolvent buyer is also applicable here." (emphasis supplied.)

If a seller fails to "follow up his rights," he loses his right to reclaim. The sale to the buyer is then no longer conditional, and the buyer can sell or give a security interest in the goods to a subsequent purchaser free of any retained right in the seller to reclaim them. The question in this case is whether Holiday Rambler failed to follow up its rights.

It is undisputed that Holiday Rambler made no effort to repossess the four vehicles for two to three months after delivery. However, Holiday Rambler argues that, under Kansas law, "whether a cash seller of merchandise [has] waived his rights as a cash seller [is] a factual question to be resolved by a jury." Brief of Appellant at 14. First National, on the other hand, argues that a cash seller's right to reclaim is waived as a matter of law if not exercised within ten days of delivery. Cases can be found in various jurisdictions to support both positions. *Compare Szabo,* 630 F.2d at 3; *Helms,* 287 F.Supp. at 846; *Stowers v. Mahon (In re Samuels),* 526 F.2d 1238, 1245 (5th Cir.), *cert. denied,* 429 U.S. 834, 97 S.Ct. 98, 50 L.Ed.2d 99 (1976), *with Burk v. Emmick,* 637 F.2d 1172, 1176 (8th Cir.1980). In determining the applicable law in this diversity case, however, we are bound to follow what we determine to be the law of Kansas.

Holiday Rambler relies heavily on an old Kansas Supreme Court case, *People's State Bank v. Brown,* 80 Kan. 520, 103 P. 102 (1909). *Brown* held that whether a seller has waived his right to reclaim is determined by whether he acted "within a reasonable time" to recover possession of the property. *Id.,* 103 P. at 104. Holiday Rambler further argues that the subsequent adoption of the Uniform Commercial Code in Kansas did not affect the holding in *Brown,* relying primarily upon the fact that the Kansas Comment following § 84–2–511 at one time cited *Brown* with approval. *See* Kan.U.C.C.Ann. § 84–2–511, Kansas Comment (Weeks 1965). Whatever view of the law the Kansas Legislature may have had at the time of those comments, that view apparently has changed. The Kansas Comment 1983 to § 84–2–511 no longer cites *Brown,* but rather refers the reader to its 1983 comments to § 84–2–507 for the law respecting a cash seller's right of reclamation. In this latter comment, the Kansas Legislature declares:

> "Subsection (2) [§ 84–2–507(2)] makes clear that the buyer's rights as against the seller are conditional upon payment. Many courts have fashioned a seller's right of reclamation in bad check cases out of this subsection by reading it together with 84–2–511(3). Most such courts have imposed a 10–day limitation on this right, borrowing from 84–2–702. Official UCC Comment 3 to this section supports this. For illustrative cases, see *In re Helms Veneer Corp.,* 287 F.Supp. 840 (W.D.Va.1968); *Szabo v. Vinton Motors, Inc.,* 630 F.2d 1 (1st Cir.1980)."

Kan.U.C.C.Ann. § 84–2–507, Kansas Comment 1983.

It is thus apparent that Kansas has adopted the ten-day limitation on a cash seller's right to reclaim. We need not decide whether the ten-day period begins to run from the date of delivery or from the day a seller first receives notice that his check has been dishonored, for in this case Holiday Rambler failed to repossess within either period. Holiday Rambler therefore waived its right to reclaim and Kansas Kamper acquired full rights in the goods. Consequently, First National's security interest in the goods must prevail unless there is merit to Holiday Rambler's claim that the security interest was fraudulently obtained.

III.

FRAUD

We agree with the district court that the facts alleged by Holiday Rambler do not constitute fraud under Kansas law. First, no fraudulent representation is alleged to have been made by First National. Second, even though a line of cases exists in Kansas that seems to recognize the possibility of actual fraud even absent an express representation, * * * the acts by First National in this case do not amount to fraud under the theory of those cases. The cases look to all the surrounding facts and circumstances to see if there exists some "artifice, trick [or] design," * * * or "an act of deception or cunning intentionally and effectively used to cheat a person of his rights." * * *.

> "A general rule supported by many cases is that a person engaged in a business transaction with another can commit a legal fraud only by * * * such * * * conduct or artifice * * * as will *mislead the other party or throw him off his guard and thus cause him to omit inquiry or examination which he would otherwise make.*"

37 Am.Jur.2d *Fraud and Deceit,* § 224 (1968) (emphasis supplied).

Holiday Rambler has not alleged that, by act, artifice, trick, or any other fraudulent device, First National induced Holiday Rambler to accept uncertified checks from Kansas Kamper as payment for its campers. Holiday Rambler does not claim that First National caused its failure to exercise its right to reclaim or to perfect its security interests in the campers after it learned its checks had been dishonored. Indeed, Holiday Rambler's fraud allegations amount to nothing more than the assertion that the bank loaned money, reserved a security interest, and accepted Kansas Kamper checks to offset existing debts, *when it knew* the goods upon which the security interests were based had not yet been paid for.

Holiday Rambler cites no authority for the proposition that mere knowledge that goods are unpaid for invalidates an otherwise legitimate security interest. The Code does not inquire into such knowledge on the part of a secured party. See Kan.U.C.C.Ann. § 84–9–203, 84–9–312(5), and Kansas Comment 1983 to 84–9–312, subsection (5) ("The first-to-file-or-perfect rule is based upon the 'pure race' concept: knowledge is irrelevant"). Rather, if properly employed, the Code protects unpaid sellers in a variety of other ways. *See, e.g.,* Kan.U.C.C.Ann. §§ 84–2–507, 84–2–702, 84–9–113, 84–9–201, 84–9–203, 84–9–301, 84–9–302, 84–9–312, 84–9–401, 84–9–501. Holiday Rambler simply failed to avail itself of the protections provided by the Code and by commonly-known commercial practice. Accordingly, we affirm the district court on this issue.

* * *

[Some footnotes omitted.]

Notes

1. Assuming that Holiday Rambler exercised its reclamation right in a timely manner, upon what theory is it entitled to regain possession from the buyer free of the Bank's claimed security interest? Would the same theory apply if a lien creditor had intervened or the buyer had resold the goods before the reclamation right was exercised? Compare Iola State Bank v. Bolan, 235 Kan. 175, 679 P.2d 720 (1984), where the court concluded that the "cash" sale doctrine under which a cash buyer did not receive and could not pass an interest in the goods until payment in full was "abolished by adoption of the UCC." The court held, however, that the "floating lienor," claiming as a purchaser, had not acted in good faith.

2. If a "cash" seller was entitled to reclaim against a lien creditor of the buyer under state law, would that reclamation right hold up against a trustee in bankruptcy? Consider the following argument:

MANN & PHILLIPS, THE RECLAIMING CASH SELLER AND THE BANKRUPTCY CODE 39 S.W.L.J. 603, 651-53 (1985).

A. SUMMARY OF OUR POSITION

Although the textual discussion of the matter was equivocal, we believe that UCC section 2-507(2) should apply solely to those cash sales not involving payment by check or draft, and UCC section 2-511(3) should be the lone provision governing check or draft cases. Regardless of which section is applicable, the right to reclaim when payment is not made or the check or draft is dishonored should be regarded as inherent to the section in question and as in no way dependent on UCC section 2-702(2). Moreover, UCC section 2-702(2)'s ten-day demand requirement should have no application to cash sale cases in general, and to bad check cases in particular. Due presentment of the check and a demand for reclamation, however, must be made within a reasonable time after notice of dishonor.

UCC section 2-403 should govern all priority questions involving the competing rights of the UCC cash seller and third parties. UCC section 2-403(1) resolves the previous uncertainty surrounding the conflict between the cash seller and the good faith purchaser by subordinating the former to the latter. Since most article 9 secured parties qualify as good faith purchasers for value, UCC section 2-403(1) also enables these parties to defeat the reclaiming cash seller. Section 2-403, however, enables the cash seller to defeat the lien creditor circuitously by compelling reference to UCC section 1-103, which authorizes the use of pre-UCC state law. Under pre-UCC priority rules the cash seller triumphed over the lien creditor.

When the buyer goes into bankruptcy, the reclaiming cash seller should usually be able to prevail in a clash with the trustee. Section 546(c) of the Bankruptcy Code should have no application in such situations. Although judicial interpretations of the section and the section's legislative history provide some support for a contrary position, they are decidedly outweighed by the section's express language, which clearly and unambiguously excludes the cash seller. As a result, a trustee wishing to defeat the cash seller's reclamation petition must utilize other bankruptcy provisions. The two weapons in the trustee's arsenal best suited for this task, sections 544(a) and 547 of the Bankruptcy Code, are unlikely to prove sufficient. The trustee's success under Bankruptcy Code section 544(a) depends upon whether a hypothetical ideal lien creditor assuming that status on the date of bankruptcy can defeat a reclaiming cash seller. Since the reclaiming cash seller will defeat a lien creditor, the cash seller will also defeat a trustee utilizing Bankruptcy Code section 544(a). For a number of reasons articulated above, the reclaiming cash seller should also overcome a trustee asserting that the reclamation is preferential under Bankruptcy Code section 547. To summarize, a seller who complies with either UCC section 2-507(2) or section 2-511(3) should be able to reclaim from the buyer, lien creditors of the buyer, and the buyer's trustee. Good faith purchasers from the buyer and article 9 secured parties, however, generally have rights in the goods superior to those of the reclaiming cash seller.

This interpretation of the cash seller's reclamation rights is in marked contrast to the results that should obtain when a credit seller attempts to reclaim goods sold to the buyer. Unlike the unpaid cash seller, an unsecured credit seller is ordinarily unable to reclaim the goods upon the buyer's failure to pay. Instead, such a seller is limited to such damages as the UCC makes available. Only when the specific conditions of UCC section 2–702(2) are met can the credit seller reclaim. These conditions impose procedural limitations on the exercise of the credit sale reclamation right that are more restrictive than those we believe should apply to the cash seller. The credit seller may reclaim only if the buyer is insolvent and, in most cases, only if demand has been made within ten days after the receipt of the goods. The cash sale reclamation right, on the other hand, is clearly not premised on the buyer's insolvency, and the ten-day demand limitation should not apply in the cash sale context. In addition, the UCC seems to give the reclaiming cash seller more remedial options than the reclaiming credit seller. UCC section 2–702(3) provides that the seller's reclamation of the goods excludes all other remedies. In contrast, neither UCC section 2–507(2) nor section 2–511(3) contains such a limitation. In a proper case, accordingly, the cash seller may be able to reclaim and still recover various types of damages from the buyer. Recovery of such damages is foreclosed to the credit seller who successfully reclaims the goods under UCC section 2–702.

The reclaiming cash seller should also fare better against third parties than his credit sale counterpart. Here the main difference between the two sellers occurs in the bankruptcy context. Under UCC sections 2–403(1) and 2–702(3) both the cash and credit sellers will be subordinate to a good faith purchaser for value. For that reason, both sellers should also lose to a party with a security interest in the goods. Despite the tremendous confusion on this question, however, both the cash and credit sellers should defeat a lien creditor's competing interest in the goods. In bankruptcy the UCC section 2–702 seller's fate is exclusively controlled by Bankruptcy Code section 546(c), while the cash seller's prospects are determined under other Bankruptcy Code provisions. Because Bankruptcy Code section 546(c)'s ten-day written demand limitation will often pose a major obstacle to reclamation and because no ten-day limitation should apply in most cash sale cases, the credit seller should fare less well in bankruptcy than his cash sale counterpart.

[Footnotes omitted] "Copyright, 1985, by Southern Methodist University. Reprinted with permission from Southwestern Law Journal."

3. Consignments

From the foregoing, it is clear that a seller who delivers goods to a buyer on credit will encounter resistance from creditors of and purchasers from the buyer when it seeks, upon non-payment, to regain possession. Unless the seller has perfected a security interest in the goods, the resistance may escalate to a victory for those third parties. The lesson here is plain: When ownership interests, however described, are separated from possession or control of the goods, the need to give public notice to neutralize the perils of ostensible ownership, i.e., the "secret lien," increases.

Another transaction where this need for public notice is evident is the consignment. Here an owner of goods delivers them to an agent or "factor," who is usually a merchant with regard to goods of that kind, with power to sell them to third parties. The owner retains title and fixes the price and conditions of sale. If the goods are sold, the factor delivers possession to the buyer and the title passes directly from the owner. The factor, after taking a commission, accounts to the owner for the price. If the goods are not sold, they are returned by the factor to the owner, usually without obligation. In the interim between delivery and sale, most consignment agreements permit the owner to recover the goods and obligate the factor to return them on request.

A number of questions shroud this transaction with uncertainty.

1. When is the transaction a "true" consignment and when is it a "consignment intended for security?" See UCC 1–201(37)? A leading case stated that the "easiest way to determine the intention of the parties is to concentrate on the function of the consignment." The court continued:

> (C)onsignments are used in two ways: (1) As a security consignment where the goods go to the merchant who is unwilling to risk finding a market for the goods so the "title" remains in the consignor; and (2) as a price-fixing device. Number (1) is clearly a secured transaction with the reservation of title to goods acting as collateral. Number (2) is designed only to insure resale maintenance and has nothing to do with security.

Columbia International Corp. v. Kempler, 46 Wis.2d 550, 562–63, 175 N.W.2d 465, 470–71 (1970). But see Hawkland, *The Proposed Amendments to Article 9 of the UCC: Consignments and Equipment Leases*, 77 Com.L.J. 108, 109 (1972), who suggests that the distinction between true and false consignments was "never clearly articulated or defined by the common law courts" and this "led to uncertain results and made consignment planning hazardous." (For example, suppose that the function of the transaction was to control resale prices and to require the consignee to pay for all or part of the price, even though there was no sale of the goods.) See also Harrington, *The Law of Consignments: Anti-Trust and Commercial Pitfalls*, 34 Bus.Law. 431, 446 (1979), who claims that "any widespread consignment program aimed at resale price maintenance must be viewed as suspect, particularly if there are any elements of coercion of distributors." In short, the characterization process is uncertain and the anti-trust problem lurks in the background.

2. Even if the transaction is a "true" consignment and not within the scope of Article 9, UCC 1–201(37) provides that "a consignment is in any event subject to the provisions on consignment sales (Section 2–326)." At a minimum, UCC 2–326(3) appears to deal with a transaction that is a "true" consignment and not a "sale or return." See UCC 2–326(2) & 2–327(2). See also, General Electric Co. v. Pettingell Supply Co., 347 Mass. 631, 199 N.E.2d 326 (1964), holding that UCC 2–326(3) applies to a transaction which establishes only a principal-agent relationship.

Read UCC 2–326(3) carefully. Note that if three conditions are satisfied, i.e., (1) the goods are "delivered to a person for sale," (2) the person "maintains a place of business at which he deals in goods of the kind involved"; and (3) the person does business "under a name other than the name of the person making delivery," then with respect to the creditors of the person doing business, the "goods are deemed to be on sale or return." In short, the goods are subject to the claims of the consignee's creditors while in the consignee's possession. See UCC 2–326(2).

How is the consignor to deal with this problem of ostensible ownership? Work the following problems.

Problem 15–11

1. Under a "true" consignment, Consignor intends to deliver goods (textbooks) to a Consignee who operates a university bookstore under its own name. Consignor discovers that a secured party has perfected a security interest in Consignee's "inventory, existing and after-acquired." There is no applicable law "providing for a consignor's interest * * * to be evidenced by a sign," UCC 2–326(3)(a), and there is no certain basis for establishing that Consignee is "generally known by his creditors to be substantially engaged in selling the goods of others." UCC 2–326(3)(b). How can Consignor avoid Secured Party's security interest? See UCC 9–408, & 9–114. Compare UCC 9–312(3). If Consignor files under UCC 9–408 and complies with UCC 9–114, what is the effect against Secured Party? What about a lien creditor? What about a purchaser of the goods from Consignee? See UCC 2–403.

2. Suppose that Consignee did not maintain a place of business where he dealt with textbooks. Rather, Consignee entered into contracts with retail outlets under which Consignee would insure that textbooks were delivered in exchange for a commission on sales. Under the contract with Consignor, the books were delivered directly to the retail outlets: Consignee never had possession or control. Consignee, however, would remit the price for books sold and insure that unsold books were returned. Is this transaction subject to UCC 2–326(3)? In re Mincow Bag Co., 29 A.D.2d 400, 401, 288 N.Y.S.2d 364, 366 (1968), affirmed mem. 24 N.Y.2d 776, 300 N.Y.S.2d 115, 248 N.E.2d 26 (1969) held, over a dissent, that it was not: "The unwary could not have been led into becoming creditors * * * based on any ostensible ownership of the merchandise." But this transaction is neither fish (a consignment covered by UCC 2–326(3)) nor fowl (a sale or

return covered by UCC 2–326(2)). Can (should) Consignor make a UCC 9–408, 9–114 filing anyway?

3. Suppose the transaction was a "sale or return" rather than a consignment. How does the seller protect itself against the buyer's creditors? Should it create and perfect a security interest under Article 9 or can it simply comply with UCC 2–326(3)? See American National Bank of Denver v. First National Bank of Glenwood Springs, 28 Colo.App. 486, 476 P.2d 304 (1970), holding that the exceptions in UCC 2–326(3) did not apply to a "sale or return" and the goods were subject to the buyer's creditors. But see Simmons First National Bank v. Wells, 279 Ark. 204, 650 S.W.2d 236 (1983), holding that UCC 2–326(3) may apply to a bailment as well as a consignment.

SECTION 5. ARTICLE 6, THE BULK SALE: ANOTHER LIMITATION ON THE DOCTRINE OF BONA FIDE PURCHASE

Suppose that Sam owns and uses various types of personal property in his business—equipment, fixtures, inventory and intangibles. Sam is in reasonably good financial health. There are no judgment liens outstanding. Sam, however, owes Cal, an unsecured creditor, $50,000, and owes $75,000 to Bank, who has perfected a security interest under Article 9 in Sam's "inventory, existing and after-acquired."

From Cal's perspective, there is a continuing risk that Sam might sell some or all of the assets that would, in the case of a financial disaster, be marshalled to pay the claims of Cal and other unsecured creditors. Where inventory is concerned, Cal is subject to Bank's security interest in any event, whether Bank claims the security interest in inventory or the identifiable proceeds of sales in the ordinary course of business. Where other assets are involved, Cal has no interest in either the assets or the proceeds from any sale unless Sam has practiced some form of fraud. Thus, if Sam made a fraudulent transfer, i.e., a sale while insolvent where no "fair consideration" was received, Cal could avoid the transfer and recover the assets for the estate.

But suppose that Sam received "fair" consideration for a sale of inventory or equipment and did not inform Cal or other unsecured creditors before or after the sale. If financial disaster then strikes or Sam dissipates the proceeds, does Cal have any legal grounds to complain? If so, when and against whom?

Article 6, the Bulk Sales Law, provides some protection to Cal when Sam makes a "bulk" transfer of inventory or a transfer of a "substantial part" of the equipment if made "in connection with a bulk transfer of inventory." UCC 6–102. The operative provision is UCC 6–105 which reads, in part, as follows: " * * * Any bulk transfer subject to this article * * * is ineffective against any creditor of the transferor unless at least ten days before he takes possession of the goods or pays for them, whichever happens first, the transferee gives notice of the transfer in the manner and to the persons hereafter provided." Put differently, unless the notice conditions are satisfied, Cal would have a claim, established by a judicial lien, to the assets in the hands of B, even though the transaction between Sam and B was enforceable between them and otherwise passed good title.

Cal, therefore, is given protection against what the drafter's concluded was "two common forms of commercial fraud, namely: (a) The merchant, owing debts, who sells out his stock in trade to a friend for less than it is worth, pays his creditors less than he owes them, and hopes to come back into the business through the back door some time in the future," and (b) The merchant, owing debts, who sells out his stock in trade to any one for any price, pockets the proceeds, and disappears leaving his creditors unpaid." Comment 2, UCC 6–101.

But what, exactly, is a bulk sale? What enterprises are subject to Article 6? What transfers are "excepted" from the Act? Read UCC 6–102 & 103 and the following case.

OUACHITA ELECTRIC COOPERATIVE CORP. v. EVANS–ST. CLAIR

Court of Appeals of Arkansas, 1984.
12 Ark.App. 171, 672 S.W.2d 660.

CORBIN, JUDGE.

Appellant, Ouachita Electric Cooperative Corporation, sued for the collection of past due electric bills in the amount of $37,676.80 for electricity furnished to St. Clair Rubber Company of Arkansas. Appellant sought to charge appellee, Evans-St. Clair, Inc., the purchaser of certain assets of St. Clair Rubber Company of Arkansas, with this responsibility. Appellant alleged below and here on appeal that the transfer of assets violated the Bulk Sales Act of Arkansas, Ark.Stat. Ann. §§ 85–6–101–109 (Add.1961), and that the transfer was a fraudulent conveyance. The chancellor found to the contrary on both issues, but awarded judgment to appellant in the amount of $37,676.80 against St. Clair Rubber Company of Arkansas. We affirm.

On August 3, 1982, St. Clair Rubber Company of Arkansas ("St. Clair"), St. Clair Rubber Company located in Michigan ("St. Clair-Michigan"), National Acceptance Company of America ("NAC") and Evans-St. Clair, Inc. ("Evans-St. Clair") entered into an agreement whereby St. Clair and St. Clair-Michigan would transfer certain machinery, equipment, tools and other property they owned to Evans-St. Clair. In return for the transfer, Evans-St. Clair paid NAC $200,000.00 in cash and signed a promissory note to NAC in the sum of $500,000.00. NAC had previously made loans to St. Clair and St. Clair-Michigan totaling $2,244,524.21 and had a blanket perfected security interest in all the assets transferred to Evans-St. Clair which was cross-collateralized so that the assets of both St. Clair companies secured the full indebtedness. NAC agreed not to sue St. Clair, St. Clair-Michigan, or Mr. S.S. Livingstone, the prior owner and seller of St. Clair, if Evans-St.

Clair defaulted on the $500,000.00 promissory note, and further agreed to release any and all security interest which it had in the remaining assets of St. Clair, St. Clair-Michigan and Mr. Livingstone upon payment of $1,544,524.21, a net reduction of indebtedness by $700,000.00.

No inventory was transferred as part of the asset purchase. Evans-St. Clair did receive an option to purchase the inventory at a price equal to 50% of the St. Clair companies' book value, subject to the right of these companies to sell the inventory to anyone else at any time as part of the transaction. If Evans-St. Clair had not purchased the inventory at the end of one year, the St. Clair companies had the right to demand that Evans-St. Clair purchase the inventory still on hand at its wholesale fair market value. At the date of trial, approximately ⅓ of the inventory had been used on an as-needed basis by Evans-St. Clair. The remaining ⅔'s of the inventory was still located at the Evans-St. Clair plant in East Camden and was identifiable as the St. Clair companies' property. The value paid for the assets purchased was arrived at by Evans-St. Clair in reliance upon appraisals furnished by an appraisal company which had a good reputation and had been relied upon in the past by Evans Industries, the parent company of Evans-St. Clair. The representations of the St. Clair companies' owner, Mr. S.S. Livingstone, were also relied upon in arriving at the amount of consideration to be paid. The machinery and equipment located in Michigan were appraised at a forced liquidation value of $167,787.00; the machinery and equipment in Arkansas were appraised at a forced liquidation value of $497,731.00, with $56,925.00 to be subtracted for the toxological boot equipment which was deleted from the transfer; and the real estate in Michigan conveyed was valued at approximately $100,000.00, based upon a three-year old appraisal. Evans-St. Clair negotiated for these assets as a whole package, and not as separate purchases. The allocation of purchase prices set forth in the Bills of Sale was made at the request of NAC, for its own internal accounting purposes.

Appellant contends that the transfer was in violation of the Bulk Sales Act. Ark.Stat.Ann. § 85–6–102 (Add.1961), defines bulk transfers as follows:

(1) A 'bulk transfer' is any transfer in bulk and not in the ordinary course of the transferor's business of a major part of the materials, supplies, merchandise or other inventory (Section 9–109 [§ 85–9–109]) of an enterprise subject to this Article [chapter].

(2) A transfer of a substantial part of the equipment (Section 9–109 [§ 85–9–109]) of such an enterprise is a bulk transfer if it is made in connection with a bulk transfer of inventory, but not otherwise.

(3) The enterprises subject to this Article [chapter] are all those whose principal business is the sale of merchandise from stock, including those who manufacture what they sell.

(4) Except as limited by the following section all bulk transfers of goods located within this state are subject to this Article [chapter].

Appellant Ouachita Electric Cooperative Corporation argues that a bulk transfer between appellees took place since a major part of the materials, supplies, merchandise and other inventory was sold as well as a substantial part of the equipment as evidenced by the Bill of Sale. Appellant also contends that the fact that title to the inventory did not pass immediately should not be decisive in a determination of a bulk transfer. Finally, appellant argues that although a transfer to a lien creditor in lieu of foreclosure would be within the provisions set out above, the facts in the instant case do not establish a transfer to NAC. We do not agree.

The provisions of the Bulk Sales Act are primarily for the protection of creditors of the seller and compliance with the Act is not compulsory, insofar as the seller is concerned, unless compliance is required by the buyer. *Herrick v. Robinson*, 267 Ark. 576, 595 S.W.2d 637 (1980). We believe the evidence clearly supports the chancellor's finding that the transaction between appellees was not in violation of the Act. The trial court in the case at bar based its finding on the following evidence: (1) no inventory was transferred by the August 3, 1982, agreement; (2) on the day of trial, approximately ⅔'s of all the inventory on hand as of the August 3, 1982, agreement to transfer had not been purchased by appellee; (3) the ⅓ of the inventory which had been used was purchased by appellee on a daily basis, when needed in its industrial process, but not in bulk; and (4) the transfer was in settlement of a valid security interest, and did not harm the position of any unsecured creditors.

Ark.Stat.Ann. § 85–6–103(3) (Supp.1983), provides in part: "The following transfers are not subject to this Article [chapter]: transfers in settlement of realization of a lien or other security interest." NAC had a perfected security interest in all the assets purchased from St. Clair and St. Clair-Michigan, and the assets of both of the companies stood as collateral for an indebtedness which was undisputedly far in excess of their value. Evans-St. Clair paid $700,000.00 to NAC, and the St. Clair companies transferred the assets to Evans-St. Clair. NAC reduced these companies' obligation to it by $700,000.00, and agreed not to sue or look to the St. Clair companies for payment in the event that Evans-St. Clair defaulted on the $500,000.00 note. The transfer was clearly in satisfaction of NAC's security interest. Appellant in its brief cites *Starman v. John Wolfe, Inc.*, 490 S.W.2d 377 (Mo.App.1973), for the proposition that in order to come within the § 85–6–103(3) exception, the transfer should be made to the holder of the security interest and not to a transferee for the benefit of the security interest holder. We agree with appellee that *Starman, supra*, cannot be properly interpreted for such a broad proposition, since in that case the consideration paid for the transfer was not used entirely to pay the superior lien held by the secured creditor, but rather was used to pay in part other parties for the benefit of the transferor, resulting in a preference to some creditors. Furthermore, in *Starman, supra*, there was no evidence in the record to support the proposition that the alleged secured creditor even had a security interest in the property transferred.

In *American Metal Finishers, Inc. v. Palleschi,* 55 App.Div.2d 499, 391 N.Y.S.2d 170, 20 U.C.C.Rept.Ser. 1283 (1977), the plaintiff complained that the transfer would not qualify under U.C.C. § 6–103(3) because the property transfer was made to a third person who assumed the indebtedness of the transferor with a secured creditor who held a security interest in the property transferred. The New York court disagreed, stating as follows:

> The chief rationale of the Bulk Transfers article is the avoidance of the "major bulk sales risk" of "[t]he merchant, owing debts, who sells out his stock in trade * * *, pockets the proceeds, and disappears leaving his creditors unpaid" (citations omitted). But where the transfer is in settlement of a lien or security interest, there are no cash proceeds with which the seller could abscond. Thus, where the consideration is settlement of an indebtedness with no receipt of cash proceeds, the protective purposes of the Bulk Transfers article do not apply.

> We see no reason to read subdivision (3) of § 6–103 of the Uniform Commercial Code so restrictively as to add a requirement that the transferee must be the holder of the security interest, thus ruling out transfer to one who in good faith takes over the position of the security holder. The interposition of such new party is not that of an officious volunteer; it serves a socially beneficial purpose of avoidance of foreclosure with its concomitant hardships to creditors, employees and the commercial community.

Similarly, we cannot say appellant in the instant case was prejudiced by the transaction. If St. Clair had closed its doors, NAC could have replevied the collateral and sold it in satisfaction of its security interest. If appellant had levied upon the collateral, any proceeds from a sale would have been subject to the prior security interest of NAC, which secured an indebtedness of $2,244,524.21. St. Clair could have transferred the property directly to NAC without any conceivable violation of the Bulk Sales Act.

The Bulk Sales Act of Arkansas does not purport to regulate agreements to sell inventory in the future. Here we have an option to purchase agreement for the sale of inventory in the future which is not a transfer of inventory and, therefore, is not subject to the Bulk Sales Act, since Ark.Stat.Ann. § 85–6–102(1) (Add.1961), by its terms applies only to "transfers in bulk." The Bulk Sales Act does not purport to regulate agreements for the sale of inventory as opposed to actual transfers of inventory because until the inventory is actually sold, title to it remains in the seller and is at all times subject to being levied upon by the seller's creditor. An agreement to sell the inventory gives the purchaser no property interest in the inventory, but is merely an executory contractual right. Accordingly, we find no merit to this contention.

Appellant also contends that the trial court erred in finding that the transfer was not a fraudulent conveyance pursuant to Ark.Stat. Ann. § 68–1302 (Repl.1979). This statute provides as follows:

> Every conveyance or assignment, in writing or otherwise, of any estate or interest in lands, or in goods and chattels, or things in action, or of any rents issuing therefrom, and every charge upon lands, goods or things in action, or upon the rents and profits thereof, and every bond, suit, judgment, decree or execution, made or contrived with the intent to hinder, delay or defraud creditors or other persons of their lawful actions, damages, forfeitures, debts or demands, as against creditors and purchasers prior and subsequent, shall be void.

Fraud is never presumed, but must be affirmatively proved, and the burden of proving fraud is upon the party who alleges it and relies on it. *Rees v. Craighead Inv. Co., Inc.,* 251 Ark. 336, 472 S.W.2d 92 (1971). In a suit to set aside a fraudulent conveyance, the allegation of fraud must be shown by a preponderance of the evidence. *Killian v. Hayes,* 251 Ark. 121, 470 S.W.2d 939 (1971). It has also been held that while fraud may be established by circumstantial evidence, the circumstances must be so strong and well connected as to clearly show fraud. *Stringer v. Georgia State Savings Assoc. of Savannah,* 218 Ark. 683, 238 S.W.2d 629 (1951). Badges or indicia of fraudulent conveyances include insolvency or indebtedness of the transferor, inadequate or fictitious consideration, retention by the debtor of property, the pendency or threat of litigation, secrecy or concealment, and the fact that disputed transactions were conducted in a manner differing from usual business practices. *Harris v. Shaw,* 224 Ark. 150, 272 S.W.2d 53 (1954).

In the case at bar we cannot say that the finding of the chancellor that the transfer was not fraudulent is against the preponderance of the evidence. The assets transferred were the subject of a perfected security interest in favor of NAC which secured an indebtedness of $2,244,524.21 of St. Clair and St. Clair-Michigan. The assets purchased were negotiated as an entire package and not as separate parcels. While the Bill of Sale for the Arkansas assets showed approximately $440,000.00 of assets being transferred at a stated purchase price of $225,000.00, the Michigan Bill of Sale showed assets having a liquidation value of only $167,787.00 and real property having a value of only $100,000.00 which was purchased from St. Clair-Michigan at a price of $475,000.00. All of the assets of both St. Clair companies were pledged to secure the $2,244,524.21 indebtedness to NAC. The allocation of the monies as reflected on the Bills of Sale was at the suggestion of and for the internal accounting purposes of NAC. Furthermore, appellant offered no evidence at trial which would contradict the appraised values of the property transferred.

The $700,000.00 was paid to the lienholder, NAC, in the form of $200,000.00 cash and a $500,000.00 promissory note. It was not paid to St. Clair. Consideration flowed to St. Clair in that NAC agreed not to look to St. Clair for payment in the event that Evans-St. Clair defaulted under the terms of the $500,000.00 promissory note, and further agreed to release the assets of St. Clair upon payment of $1,544,524.21, which constituted a reduction in St. Clair's liability to NAC by $700,000.00. A conveyance by a debtor to a third party of mortgaged property is supported by adequate consideration if the third party grantee agrees to pay the debts owed by the grantor and which are secured by the property. *First State Bank of Corning v. Gilchrist,* 190 Ark. 356, 79 S.W.2d 281 (1935).

In *Sieb's Hatcheries v. Lindley,* 111 F.Supp. 705 (W.D.Ark.1953), the district court quoted from a prior Arkansas decision as follows:

> The creditor who seeks to set aside a conveyance as fraudulent must show that his debtor has disposed of property that might otherwise have been subjected to the satisfaction of his debt.

Here, the record is barren of any evidence which would demonstrate that the lien of NAC was not perfected, or that the value of the assets transferred exceeded the amount secured by the assets.

The transfer would not have been fraudulent unless an inadequate consideration was established. The preference of one creditor over another does not in itself make the transfer to the preferred creditor void or voidable as a fraudulent conveyance. *Nicklaus v. Peoples Bank & Trust Co., Russellville, Ark.,* 258 F.Supp. 482 (E.D.Ark.1965), *aff'd,* 369 F.2d 683 (8th Cir.1966). The consideration in this case was clearly adequate. Appellant presented no evidence which would indicate that a greater price could have been obtained. In determining fraudulent intent on the part of the parties to a transaction, mere inadequacy of price for consideration is insufficient; it is only when the inadequacy of price is so gross that it shocks the conscience, and furnishes satisfactory and decisive evidence of fraud, that it will be sufficient proof that the purchase is not *bona fide.* *Fluke v. Sharum,* 118 Ark. 229, 176 S.W. 684 (1915). We find no merit to this point. In conclusion, we cannot say that the chancellor's findings were clearly erroneous (clearly against the preponderance of the evidence), A.R.C.P. Rule 52(a), and we affirm.

Affirmed.

CRACRAFT and GLAZE, JJ., agree.

Notes (with answers!)

1. Was the seller, St. Clair Rubber Company, an "enterprise" subject to Article 6? UCC 6–103(3). (Yes.) Suppose S was a lessor rather than a seller of inventory? (No, if "sale" is read literally.) Suppose the total value of the assets sold was $1,000? (There is no *de minimis* limitation.)

2. If St. Clair Rubber sold "a substantial part" of its equipment not in the ordinary course of business, why wasn't the sale a bulk transfer? (Because no inventory was transferred.) Is Article 6 clear enough about when a transfer occurs in a contract to sell inventory? (No.) When a

transfer is "not in the ordinary course of the transferor's business?" When a transfer is a "major part" or a "substantial part" of the assets involved?

3. S, a restaurant, owned equipment valued at $200,000. S also owed unsecured creditors $300,000. Without notice to the creditors, S sold the equipment to B for $190,000, closed the restaurant, gave what was left of its food inventory to charity and left with the cash for the Bahamas. Is this a bulk transfer? (Not under 6–102 in the uniform text, but yes in at least 16 states which have amended the statute).

4. Suppose S, an enterprise within UCC 6–103(3) and heavily laden with unsecured creditors, was advised that the Bulk Sales Act would not apply if it sold all or substantially all of its corporate stock to B, rather than inventory or equipment. Is that advice correct? (Yes.) Should it be? (Not according to Rapson, U.C.C. Article 6: Should it Be Revised or "Deep-Sixed"?, 38 Bus.Law. 1753 (1983) infra p. 956.)

5. True or False: If a present transfer of inventory was "in settlement or realization of a lien or other security interests," 6–103(3), it is unnecessary to consider whether either the seller or the transfer were within the scope of Article 6. (True.)

Problem 15–12

S, a sole proprietorship, owned and operated a used book store in leased premises. The average monthly value of the inventory was $100,000 and the equipment was valued at $15,000. S had several unsecured creditors with claims totalling $20,000. There were no secured creditors or judgment lien creditors. The book store grossed around $200,000 per year.

S, who was ready to retire, reached an agreement to sell all of the inventory and equipment and to assign the lease to B for $125,000 cash. B, who intended to operate the bookstore under a new name, did not wish to assume S's business debts. The agreed price, therefore, was reached on the assumption that S would pay all business creditors.

Assume that the transfer of inventory and equipment is a "bulk" sale under UCC 6–102 by an "enterprise" subject to Article 6. B needs advice on the following questions.

A. Could the transfer be excepted from Article 6 under UCC 6–103? (Subsections 6 and 7 are obvious possibilities.)

B. Assuming that UCC 6–106 has not been enacted in our jurisdiction and the sale is not at auction, UCC 6–108, what must B do to comply with Article 6? See UCC 6–104, 6–105, 6–107 & 6–109. Suppose there are creditors of which B is unaware at the time of transfer?

C. Still assuming that UCC 6–106 does not apply, what happens in the following situation: Notice is not given in time to one creditor with a $1,000 claim who was entitled to it. Other unsecured creditors, with claims totalling $14,000, were given notice. Within 6 months of the transfer, see UCC 6–111, the entire inventory "turned over." Assuming that the creditor brings a timely action, which of the following assertions are correct:

1. All of the unsecured creditors may pursue claims even though only one did not receive notice;

2. Claims may be asserted against books sold by B to its customers;

3. B is liable as a converter of assets in which creditors had an enforceable claim;

4. B is personally liable for the amount of the debt;

5. The creditors entitled to notice may pursue claims against the identifiable proceeds of sale, including books purchased with those proceeds.

D. Suppose the state has enacted UCC 6–106. (16 states have). How, if at all, would UCC 6–106 change the scope of B's obligation and the answers to C, above?

RAPSON, U.C.C. ARTICLE 6: SHOULD IT BE REVISED OR "DEEP–SIXED"? 38 The Business Lawyer 1753, 1762–66 (1983).

This leads us to the next question: If the special classification of coverage of Article 6 is no longer justifiable, should the statute be expanded to cover all businesses, or would it make commercial sense to scrap the entire statute? Article 6, in its present form and under the proposed revision, imposes substantial burdens on bulk purchasers in order to protect sellers' creditors. On balance, does the imposition of that burden serve a commercially useful purpose?

WHAT ARE THE CREDITORS' REMEDIES IF THE PARTIES COMPLY WITH ARTICLE 6?

Assume that seller and buyer have contracted for an all-cash sale (with no down payment) of a business that is clearly covered by Article 6; that the jurisdiction has not enacted section 6–106; that the seller has the secret undisclosed intention of pocketing the proceeds and disappearing without paying his creditors; that seller and buyer fully comply with all the requirements of the present Article 6, with seller furnishing a complete and accurate sworn list of all his creditors; and that, pursuant to section 6–105, "at least 10 days before" the buyer either "takes possession of the goods or pays for them" he "gives notice of the transfer in the manner" provided by section 6–107.[48] Assume further that absent extraordinary circumstances, a creditor cannot acquire a lien against the business assets until he obtains a judgment against the seller; and that (as is usually the case) the jurisdiction's rules of civil procedure require that the creditor first institute a lawsuit and that the seller has twenty days to answer following service of process.[49]

------

48. U.C.C. section 6–107(3) 1978 requires that the notice "be delivered personally or sent by registered or certified mail. * * * "

49. If the closing of the sale was scheduled for a Monday, a notice mailed by certified mail on the second preceding Thursday would be "ten days before" and timely. Thus, a creditor receiving notice on the following Monday would have no more than five business (or court) days to take action. *See* Hawkland, *Remedies of Bulk Transfer Creditors Where There Has Been Compliance with Article 6*, 74 Com. L.J. 257, 258 (1969).

What are the rights and remedies of an unsecured creditor who receives notice of that bulk transfer? Specifically, (1) Does the buyer have any further duties to that creditor? and (2) Does the fact that a bulk sale is about to take place entitle the creditor to any kind of extraordinary relief against the closing of the sale or the assets themselves, such as an injunction, attachment, or the like?

The answer clearly seems to be no to both questions. As stated by the Maryland Court of Appeals: "The sanction for noncompliance, established by the Bulk Transfer Act, is that the transfer is ineffective against the seller's creditors who may levy, attach or garnish the goods transferred to a buyer. § 6–104 and § 6–105; see § 6–111, Official Comment 2. Where there is compliance, however, that sanction is unavailable." [50] According to Chancellor Hawkland: "It is generally held that the liquidation of one's inventory is not, of itself, proof of an intent to defraud creditors. * * * " [51] The conclusion is inescapable. In a jurisdiction that has not enacted section 6–106, if the parties comply with Article 6, the notice given to the creditor affords him little or no practical remedies, absent grounds for extraordinary relief.

If the jurisdiction has enacted section 6–106, the conclusion is quite different. The creditor has significant protection. The buyer must apply the purchase price to the debts owed to the creditors, and, if there is not enough money to go around, then the sales proceeds must be applied pro rata. If the buyer breaches this duty he may end up having to pay twice.[52] Clearly, section 6–106 gives very meaningful protection to the creditors, but only by imposing very substantial burdens upon the purchaser.[53]

Is this logical? The avowed purpose of a bulk sale statute is to protect creditors of businesses against the risk that sellers of those businesses will pocket the proceeds and disappear, leaving the creditors unpaid.[54] Yet, the majority of jurisdictions, by rejecting section 6–106, have a toothless statute that does not effectively serve that purpose when the parties comply.

Why have most jurisdictions rejected section 6–106 [55] and the opportunity to put teeth into the statute? The answer may well lie in a

50. FICO Inc. v. Ghingher, 287 Md. 150, 411 A.2d 430 (1980) (emphasis added).

51. Hawkland, *supra* note 49, at 258.

52. If noncompliance with U.C.C. section 6–106 results in the buyer becoming personally liable for the debt * * * and the debt is not otherwise satisfied, that would be the result. If the seller goes into bankruptcy, that is also the result. * * *.

53. Suppose the seller takes back a purchase money negotiable note as part of the payment of the purchase price and then discounts it with a party qualifying as a holder in due course (U.C.C. § 3–302)? Whom does the bulk purchaser pay when

the note becomes due? The holder in due course or the seller's creditors? The answer may be that he has to pay both. The solution is to make the note nonnegotiable.

54. Official Comment 2(b) to U.C.C. § 6–101 (1978).

55. Section 6–106 is presented in the Official Text as an optional provision "bracketed to indicate division of opinion as to whether or not it is a wise provision. * * * " Section 6–106 reflects the pre-U.C.C. minority "Pennsylvania rule." It may be that such bracketing deterred adoption. If section 6–106 (or any other provision) is the better rule, brackets should not be used.

sense of discomfort with the means by which Article 6 attempts to protect the seller's creditors, especially section 6–106.

The rationale of Article 6 is that the creditors should be protected by imposing substantial burdens and sanctions upon *buyers* of business-es, even though they may have acted in good faith and paid top dollar for the purchase. Is that really fair? Does it make sense to place burdens upon a *buyer* in order to protect creditors of the seller who have taken the risk of extending unsecured credit? Can we support a value judgment that the purchaser should bear the risk that a seller will not pay his creditors? If not, as has happened in most jurisdic-tions,[56] section 6–106 will be rejected and the purchaser will have no duty to apply the purchase proceeds to the payment of the seller's debts. Compliance with Article 6 will be achieved by notifying the creditors, but the purpose of Article 6 will be frustrated because the creditors will not have practical remedies.

Do the Consequences of Noncompliance With Article 6 Make Commercial Sense?

By contrast, if the bulk purchaser fails to notify the creditors the sanctions for noncompliance are drastic. The sale is "ineffective" as to the seller's creditors,[57] which means that the creditors can enforce their claims by resorting to the purchased assets, even though the purchaser has paid the purchase price in full.[58]

The consequences of failing to comply with Article 6 *may* be more severe in a jurisdiction which has section 6–106. The authorities are divided whether noncompliance with section 6–106 merely furnishes an additional ground for rendering the transaction ineffective against the seller's creditors, or whether it also results in the buyer being personal-ly liable for the seller's debts.[59]

The proposed revision deals directly with the question. First, it wisely introduces the concept of "omitted" creditor [60] and makes it clear that noncompliance makes the sale ineffective only as to an omitted creditor, and not as to all the creditors including those who receive notice—a theoretical possibility under present Article 6. Second, it would add new sections 6–104(4) and 6–106(5) to provide that the bulk purchaser is not personally liable unless he thereafter

---

56. * * *.

57. U.C.C. §§ 6–104(1) and 6–105 (1978).

58. As stated in Official Comment 2 to U.C.C. § 6–104 (1978): "Any such creditor or creditors may therefore disregard the transfer and levy on the goods as still belonging to the transferor, or a receiver representing them can take them by what-ever procedure the local law provides."

59. * * *.

60. U.C.C. section 6–104(1) would be amended to define an "omitted" creditor as follows:

An "omitted" creditor is a creditor (Sec-tion 6–109) who has not been notified of the bulk transfer as provided by sections 6–105 and 6–107 or who has not had the protection provided by this section [or sec-tion 6–106], but a creditor is not omitted after the full payment of his claim has been tendered to him by the transferor or transferee.

transfers the property to a purchaser for value in good faith and without notice of any noncompliance * * * in which case the transferee shall be personally liable to the creditors (Section 6–109) in an amount measured by the fair market value of the property at the time it was subsequently transferred to the said purchaser.[61]

Thus, the sanction for noncompliance would be identical in all jurisdictions whether or not they had enacted section 6–106. This proposal is questionable. It would remove the compulsion of immediate personal liability for noncompliance with section 6–106. Consequently, it would make the alternative of complete noncompliance with Article 6 more attractive because the parties incur no additional risk by not paying the creditors pursuant to section 6–106. If the buyer is not going to apply the purchase price to the creditors' claims, there is no point in notifying them and stirring them up—and the sanction is no worse.

Logically, if we are to retain Article 6, there is little point in doing so without requiring compliance with section 6–106 and making the bulk purchasers personally liable for noncompliance. Otherwise, the statute is a time-consuming, expensive burden having minimal practical benefits.

The proposed revision would significantly increase the burdens and risks of bulk purchasers. Section 6–104(3) would be amended to place an objective duty of care on the bulk purchaser to make reasonable inquiries concerning the completeness and accuracy of the creditors' list:

> (3) Responsibility for the completeness and accuracy of the list of creditors rests on the transferor, and the transfer is not rendered ineffective by errors or omissions therein unless the fact of such errors or omissions is known or disclosed to or reasonably discoverable by the transferee. Such fact is known to or disclosed to or reasonably discoverable by the transferee if, prior to the giving of notice provided in Section 6–105, it is revealed by the transferor's regular bookkeeping records, its existence is known or in any way made known to the transferee, or it would be discovered by his reasonable inquiry concerning the transferor's creditors.

This revision is designed to reject the controversial decision of the New York Court of Appeals in *Adrian Tabin Corp. v. Climax Boutiques, Inc.*[62] permitting the bulk purchaser to rely upon an "affidavit of no creditors" furnished by the seller of an ongoing business. Under the revision, the purchaser would be required to "make reasonable inquir-

---

61. In essence, the buyer would become "liable for damages as a converter when he conveys the property to a bona fide purchaser and cuts off the creditors' rights to reach that property." Final Report, *Justifications for Changes in § 6–106*, par. 2.

Inasmuch as the property is usually inventory held for sale, that is a likely result.

62. Adrian Tabin Corp. v. Climax Boutiques, Inc., 34 N.Y.2d 210, 356 N.Y.S.2d 606, 313 N.E.2d 66 (1974).

ies concerning the transferor's creditors and examine the books of the transferor." [63]

The change would adopt the pre-Code New York rule [64] and apply to any creditor's list, not just affidavits of no creditors. If one believes that the substantial burdens imposed on purchasers by Article 6 are a justifiable means of protecting sellers' creditors, the revision makes sense because it is consistent with the objective of furnishing meaningful protection to the creditors. However, the added burden and risk may be highly objectionable to purchasers of businesses. One of the motivations for a buyer to enter into an asset sale, as distinguished from a stock sale, is that the buyer does not want to be concerned with the seller's creditors.[65] This would no longer be the case under revised section 6–104(3).

The decision to retain Article 6 requires a value judgment that a commercially useful purpose is served by allocating to the bulk purchaser the risk that the seller will not pay his creditors. *If* such a judgment is sound, the protection afforded creditors should be made meaningful by adopting this revision to section 6–104(3) and by requiring enactment of section 6–106. "Copyright 1983 by the American Bar Association. All rights reserved. Reprinted with the permission of the American Bar Association and its section of Corporation, Banking and Business Law.

IN RE McBEE

United States Court of Appeals, Fifth Circuit, 1983.
714 F.2d 1316.

[Colley owned a Gun Shop. In January, 1979, National Bank created and perfected a security interest in Colley's "inventory, existing

---

63. Final Report, *Justifications for Changes in § 6–104,* par. 2.

64. *See* Adrian Tabin Corp. v. Climax Boutiques, Inc., 34 N.Y.2d at 213, 356 N.Y.S.2d at 608, 313 N.E.2d at 67, (1974).

65. This is no longer possible in acquisitions of manufacturing businesses in jurisdictions adopting the "product line" approach to successor corporation liability for injuries caused by defective products. As enunciated by the New Jersey Supreme Court in Ramirez v. Amsted Indus., Inc., 86 N.J. 332, 431 A.2d 811 (1981):

[W]e hold that where one corporation acquires all or substantially all the manufacturing assets of another corporation, even if exclusively for cash, and undertakes essentially the same manufacturing operation as the selling corporation, the purchasing corporation is strictly liable for injuries caused by defects in units of the same product line, even if previously manufactured and distributed by

the selling corporation or its predecessor. The social policies underlying strict products liability in New Jersey are best served by extending strict liability to a successor corporation that acquires the business assets and continues to manufacture essentially the same line of products as its predecessor, particularly where the successor corporation benefits from trading its product line on the name of the predecessor and takes advantage from its accumulated good will, business reputation and established customers.

Id. at 358, 431 A.2d at 825. *Accord* Cyr v. B. Offen & Co., Inc., 501 F.2d 1145 (1st Cir. 1974); Turner v. Bituminous Casualty Co., 397 Mich. 406, 244 N.W.2d 873 (1976); Ray v. Alad Corp., 19 Cal.3d 22, 136 Cal.Rptr. 574, 560 P.2d 3 (1977); Dawejko v. Jorgensen Steel Co., 290 Pa.Super. 15, 434 A.2d 106 (1981).

and after acquired." In April, 1980, Wholesale Supply sold Colley goods on credit and created and perfected a security interest in "inventory" and everything else in sight. Colley, on May 5, 1980, made a "bulk" transfer to McBee, who agreed to comply with the Texas version of Article 6, but did not. Texas had enacted UCC 6–106. Thereafter, on July 16, 1980, Republic Bank created and perfected a security interest in McBee's inventory, existing and after acquired. McBee filed a petition in bankruptcy on October 22, 1980. The inventory remaining at the time of bankruptcy was auctioned by the trustee, producing some $40,000 in proceeds, and all three secured parties asserted security interests in it.

The Court of Appeals reversed the bankruptcy court's decision that National Bank had an unperfected security interest and, after concluding that the bulk transfer was not "effective" under the Texas version of Article 6, determined priorities as follows: (1) National Bank had priority over Wholesale Supply to the extent of the value of the inventory at the time of the bulk sale, not at the time of bankruptcy; (2) Wholesale Supply had priority in the remainder of that value; and (3) Republic Bank's priority was limited to the "excess value, if any, of the sale proceeds over the value of the inventory which existed when the business was transferred and which was transferred in bulk.]

* * *

2. PRIORITIES

The general rule, of course, is that priorities of perfected security claims are determined in the order of filing. *See* Tex.Bus. & Comm. Code Ann. § 9.312(e) (Vernon 1968 & Supp.1982–1983). *See generally* J. White & R. Summers, *Uniform Commercial Code* 1036–42 (2d ed. 1980). Having found National Bank's interest perfected, the order of priority in accordance with the "first to file" rule is clear: first, National Bank, followed by Wholesale Supply, and then Republic Bank. This determination of general priorities, however, does not end our inquiry.

The collateral at issue here is the gun shop inventory held by *McBee* at the time of bankruptcy. Republic Bank, the last creditor in time to file, clearly held a security interest in *McBee*'s inventory. On the other hand, National Bank and Wholesale Supply, the initial creditors to file, held a security interest in the inventory, including "after-acquired property," of the gun shop when owned by *Colley*. This intervening bulk sale of the gun shop and its inventory from Colley to McBee raises the question of whether, and to what extent, the transferor's creditors, National Bank and Wholesale Supply, retain priority over the transferee's subsequent creditor, here Republic Bank. This question must be analyzed in light of the fact that the bulk sale from Colley to McBee was not made in accordance with the requirements of Article 6 of the U.C.C., dealing with bulk sales.

Article 6 of the U.C.C. defines, in general terms, the rights, liabilities and responsibilities of the parties to a bulk sale. As adopted in Texas, Section 6.105 requires that the transferee give notice to the transferor's creditors, in accordance with Section 6.107, *before* the bulk transfer is made. This before-the-fact notice provision affords the transferor's creditors an opportunity to act before the sale to protect their security interests. Another protection, afforded by Section 6.106,[13] is a requirement upon the transferee to see that the relevant part of the proceeds of the sale finds its way into the hands of the transferor's creditors. Texas is among the minority of jurisdictions which has adopted this optional provision, providing further remedial concern for a transferor's creditors in a bulk sale.[14]

The provisions of Article 6, if complied with, also protect the transferee and his future creditors. Secured creditors of the transferor cannot assert any claims against the transferee or his property after a complying bulk transfer; the transferee will not "pay twice" for property thus freed from prior security interests. Similarly, the transferee obtains clear title to the transferred assets and may obtain credit on the unencumbered property. The transferee's creditors also need not be concerned with the possibility that prior creditors, in the chain of title, will assert previously perfected interests in the transferee's property.

If the provisions of Article 6 are not complied with, Sections 6.104 and 6.105 state that the transfer is "ineffective" against the transferor's creditors. Tex.Bus. & Comm.Code Ann. §§ 6.104, 6.105 (Vernon 1968). The term "ineffective" is nowhere explicitly defined in the Code, nor by Texas case law. In the immediate case, it is conceded that the transfer from Colley to McBee did not comply with Article 6, despite the fact that McBee had covenanted to comply with the bulk transfer provisions. The bankruptcy court examined the policies underlying Articles 6 and 9, as well as other specific provisions in both articles, and concluded that the term "ineffective" meant that the creditor's original interest and rights are unaffected by the transfer, and continue in the collateral as they would have if the collateral were still owned by the transferor. The court thus concluded that Colley's perfected creditors retained their interest in the collateral, despite the transfer, and retained priority over transferee McBee's non-purchase money credi-

---

13. This section provides:

§ 6.106. Application of the Proceeds

In addition to the requirements of the two preceding sections:

(1) Upon every bulk transfer subject to this chapter for which new consideration becomes payable except those made by sale at auction it is the duty of the transferee to assure that such consideration is applied so far as necessary to pay those debts of the transferor which are either shown on the list furnished by the transferor (Section 6.104) or filed in writing in the place stated in the notice (Section 6.107) within thirty days after the mailing of such notice. This duty of the transferee runs to all the holders of such debts, and may be enforced by any of them for the benefit of all.

(2) If any of said debts are in dispute the necessary sum may be withheld from distribution until the dispute is settled or adjudicated.

(3) If the consideration payable is not enough to pay all of the said debts in full distribution shall be made pro rata.

14. White and Summers found that in 1980 eighteen states, including Texas, had enacted this provision. *See* J. White & R. Summers, *Uniform Commercial Code* 758 & n. 12 (2d ed. 1980).

tors. We agree that these pre-transfer interests retain priority to the extent of the value of the inventory-collateral transferred in the non-complying bulk sale.

In the absence of a bulk sales law, creditors generally would lose all security interest in collateral once transferred to a new owner; the secured creditor's recourse would lie against the debtor-transferor, including an interest in any proceeds received by the transferor from the bulk sale. In many cases, this would leave the secured creditor without any effective remedy. The value received upon transfer might be far less than that of the transferred collateral, or by the time the creditor learned of the transfer little, if any, of the sales proceeds might be recoverable from the debtor-transferor.

Article 6 of the U.C.C., as adopted by Texas, changes the relative position of the parties affected by a bulk sale. "The Bulk Transfers Act and related predecessors were enacted for the protection of creditors who sell goods and merchandise to others on credit for inventory and resale." *Anderson & Clayton Co. v. Earnest,* 610 S.W.2d 846, 848 (Tex. Civ.App.—Amarillo 1980). As summarized above, Article 6 places certain requirements upon the parties to the bulk sale. These requirements serve to notify the transferor's creditors of the intended sale, thus permitting the creditors to protect their security interests *before* the transfer. They also protect the transferee and his subsequent creditors by bringing to light and terminating all prior security claims to the transferred property.

Had Article 6 been complied with, transferor-Colley's secured creditors—National Bank and Wholesale Supply—would have retained no interest in the gun shop in McBee's hands. There is no evidence, however, of any attempt at compliance, although McBee had contracted to do so in her sale agreement with Colley. As a result, Colley's secured creditors were left without the benefit of Article 6's remedial provisions, most notably those requiring notice to the transferor's creditors. Furthermore, these creditors, National Bank and Wholesale Supply, were unable to avail themselves of the additional remedial provision, Section 6–106, adopted in a minority of jurisdictions including Texas, which requires a transferee to see that the relevant part of the proceeds of the sale finds its way into the hands of the transferor's creditors.

The Code provides that this total noncompliance makes the transfer "ineffective" as to the transferor's creditors. Given the remedial purpose behind Article 6, particularly as adopted in Texas, it is clear that by "ineffective" the Code drafters intended that the pre-transfer security interests survive the transfer, despite the fact that the collateral is no longer owned by the debtor. Republic Bank argues that this result is untenable, particularly with regard to new property purchased by the transferee and never owned by the transferor. At first glance, this argument is appealing: how can a debtor-transferor give his secured creditors an interest in property he no longer owns and, more significantly, in post-transfer property acquired by the transferee which the transferor never owned?

Upon analysis, however, the facial logical persuasiveness and the equitable underpinning of this argument disappears. The transferor gives his creditors a security interest in *his* property which may, as in the immediate case, cover "after-acquired property." It is Article 6, which provides as a "sanction for non-compliance" that the transfer is ineffective against creditors of the transferor. Tex.Bus. & Comm.Code Ann. § 6.106 official comment 2 (Vernon 1968). If this result were not reached, the remedial purposes behind Article 6 would be severely, if not wholly, undercut. The entire Article could be ignored with impunity; the remedial notice provisions, which serve to awaken unknowing creditors to press their claims before transfer, would be avoided. Clearly, a transferee cannot complain if, by his non-compliance, the transferor's creditors' claims attach to his property as they had prior to sale.

The immediate case proves the importance of the statutory requirement. Transferee McBee cannot complain. She was aware of National Bank's interest in the inventory and after-acquired property of the gun shop, yet she breached her specific covenant to comply with Article 6 in her sale agreement with Colley. Nor can the transferee's creditors be heard to complain of the protections afforded the transferor's creditors. The transferee's creditors should inquire as to a debtor's source of title where circumstances warrant. *See* Tex.Bus. & Comm.Code Ann. § 9.402(g) official comment 8 (Vernon Supp.1982–1983). Where, as in the immediate case, a bulk transfer has recently taken place, a subsequent creditor can and should inquire as to whether the transfer complied with Article 6. We find that the underlying policies of the Code are best supported by an interpretation which favors the unknowing prior creditor over the subsequent potential creditor. It is more equitable to place the burden on the potential subsequent creditor to check Article 6 compliance upon application for credit than to require constant vigilance of a prior creditor who, in the absence of notification, may rightfully assume that no bulk transfer cutting off his security interest has occurred.

We find further support for our conclusion in the statutory pattern. The transferor's creditor is not saved harmless forever in a non-complying bulk transfer. Article 6 limits the period in which a transferor's creditor may assert a security interest to six months after the non-complying bulk transfer, unless there has been concealment of the transfer. Tex.Bus. & Comm.Code Ann. § 6.111 (Vernon 1968). This limitations period evidences a policy that at some point a diligent creditor should realize that a transfer has occurred absent concealment of that fact and despite his lack of notice. If the prior creditor does not exercise such diligence, his security interest in the transferred property is lost. This time limitation was met in this case by National and Wholesale Supply. The time limitation supports our conclusion that Article 6 is a reasonable and balanced provision in preserving the security interests of the transferor's creditors effective against the transferee.

* * *

Republic Bank argues that Section 6.110 protects its interest from those of the transferor's creditors. Section 6.110 provides that:

> When the title of a transferee to property is subject to a defect by reason of his noncompliance with the requirements of this chapter, then:
>
> (1) a purchaser of any of such property from such transferee who pays no value or who takes with notice of such noncompliance takes subject to such defect, but
>
> (2) a purchaser for value in good faith and without such notice takes free of such defect.

Tex.Bus. & Comm.Code Ann. § 6.110 (Vernon 1968). Republic Bank reasons that: (1) there is no finding or evidence that it had notice of McBee's failure to comply with Article 6; (2) the term "purchaser" includes a secured party such as Republic Bank under U.C.C. §§ 1.201(32), (33); and therefore (3) its interest is held free of any prior security interests by operation of Section 6.110(2).

This argument is not persuasive. While it is true under the Code that the general term "purchaser" may include a secured party, we find it clear that the term as used in Section 6.110 was not intended to include secured creditors.

As we find, *supra*, Article 6 clearly contemplates that transferors' creditors retain their security interest in the transferred collateral in the event of total noncompliance. This contemplated result would be frustrated were an extensive reading given to the term "purchaser" in Section 6.110 to cover subsequent creditors. Further we doubt whether a subsequent creditor could assert a claim that it took its interest "without notice." If a prior security interest is perfected, the burden is on the subsequent creditor to search for that claim. His failure to receive actual notice cannot be held as a defense to the priority of the prior perfected lien. Since Article 6 clearly provides that after a non-complying bulk transfer the transferor creditors' security interests remain effective, such interests may not be cut off by a broad reading of Section 6.110 at odds with the specific purpose behind Article 6.

* * *

[Some footnotes omitted.]

Notes

1. *McBee* holds that a perfected security interest survives a bulk transfer that did not comply with Article 6 and has priority over a perfected security interest which attached after the bulk sale, to the extent of the value of the inventory at the time of the transfer. What does the court, say, in dictum, about these questions: (A) Does an unperfected security interest continue in assets after a bulk transfer that fails to

comply with Article 6?, and (B) Does a perfected security interest continue with priority in assets after a bulk transfer where the buyer complied with Article 6?

2. Does what *McBee* says about these questions appear to be sound? Professor Harris, in an illuminating article which deals with these questions and more, argues that Articles 9 and 6 deal with related but different kinds of fraud. Article 9 requires public notice by filing or possession to overcome the assumption that creditors of the debtor in possession will be mislead. The failure to perfect means that the "secret lien" will be subordinated to lien creditors and other secured parties but not to unsecured creditors. Article 6 requires notice to certain creditors to give them an opportunity for protection in the "bulk" sale. Failure to give notice means, at a minimum, that the creditors could obtain a judicial lien on the goods sold to and now owned by B. Against this background, Harris concludes, inter alia, that *McBee* was incorrect to the extent that it attempted to employ Article 6 to alter property rights and priorities determined under Article 9: He suggests that Article 6 should be amended to specify that its protection of good faith purchasers "addresses only the right of aggrieved creditors to reach goods transferred in a noncomplying bulk sale and does not affect property rights that are regulated elsewhere." Harris, *The Interaction of Articles 6 and 9 of the Uniform Commercial Code: A Study in Conveyancing, Priorities, and Code Interpretation,* 39 Vand.L.Rev. 179, 247 (1986).

3. The current version of Article 6 has been criticized. For a sampling of these criticisms and some proposals for reform, see the Rapson extract, supra, and the articles in 38 The Business Lawyer 1397, 1729–1794.

Chapter Sixteen
LETTER OF CREDIT

SECTION 1. INTRODUCTION

To most students the letter of credit will be a completely foreign item. In the United States the use of such letters originated in foreign trade, and they still find their most frequent use there. In the last two decades they have been used much more frequently in domestic transactions, both trade and non-trade.

A. *Traditional Letters of Credit*

To understand the names of the players in this drama and their general responsibilities consider a case in which a Danish seller is going to sell goods to a Newark, New Jersey buyer. If the parties have dealt with one another over a long period of time, the seller might be willing to ship to the buyer on open credit and to rely upon the buyer's willingness and ability to make payment upon receipt of the goods. If the seller has not dealt with the buyer, he would be foolish to make such an arrangement without doing extensive investigation about the buyer's creditworthiness and reliability. Conversely, the buyer could prepay for the goods, but then he would be taking the entire risk of default. He would be forced to pay without any assurance that the goods had been manufactured, much less manufactured correctly. The letter of credit represents an intermediate position between the two suggested. In such a setting the Newark buyer might procure a letter of credit from his bank; that letter would promise (i.e., put the bank's credit behind the agreement) to pay the purchase price to the seller upon presentation of certain documents. Usually these documents would consist at least of an invoice and bills of lading that showed shipment. They may also include an inspection certificate or a certificate of insurance or other documents.

Note that the American bank officer will make payment at his or her desk. The officer will look at the documents presented and only at those documents. The condition of the goods—that they are marred and scarred, defective or out of style—will be not just irrelevant, but unknown, to the bank officer. In this setting the bank is labeled the "issuer," the American buyer is the "customer," and the Danish seller is the "beneficiary." The bank should look at the transaction as though it were a loan to its "customer," i.e., the person with whom it deals in Newark. If it is unwilling to make that loan, it probably should not write the letter of credit. The bank is essentially relying upon its customer in this transaction, and it will likely have no knowledge of the seller or of the seller's capabilities. The seller, on the other hand, is relying upon the bank. It assumes, correctly, that the bank is less likely to go bankrupt than is a random buyer, that the bank is less likely to withhold some or all of the payment on a trumped up ground and, if the bank is a large international bank, the bank's reputation may itself be known to the Danish seller.

By entering into a letter of credit transaction, how have the parties altered the risks and responsibilities that would otherwise be present in a conventional sales transaction? First, and most obvious, the transaction has, in effect, substituted the credit of the American bank for the credit of its customer. If the customer goes into bankruptcy, that will be no defense to the bank's payment. The risk of the customer's bankruptcy has thus been shifted from the seller (in a credit transaction) to the buyer's bank. Secondly, the debt obligation of the buyer has likely become more liquid. Assume, for example, that shipment is to occur 90 days after the agreement is signed. If the obligation to pay is backed by a letter of credit by a well-known American bank, it is likely that the Danish seller will be able to borrow against that obligation much more readily than if it were simply peddling the obligation of the Newark buyer.

Third, the transaction has shifted the litigation cost and probably shifted the forum in any subsequent dispute. If the buyer later claims that the goods were defective, the buyer will now be made into a plaintiff instead of a defendant because of the letter of credit transaction. This is because the bank will have paid the Danish seller and the burden will be upon the American buyer to find the seller and bring suit against him. If the buyer had not paid, he could simply set off and thus force the seller to come to him. Usually this means not only that the American buyer will be the plaintiff, but also that he will have to go to Denmark to sue. With the expansion of the long-arm statutes and such, and with the more expansive view of doing business, it will now be more likely than formerly that the American buyer could get jurisdiction in the American court over the Danish seller, but that will not invariably be true. So the third and fourth functions of the letter of credit are to shift the burden of bringing suit and in many cases to shift the forum from the hometown of one party to the hometown of the other.

Finally, the letter of credit reduces costs by comparison with other insurance and security devices such as bonds and surety agreements. That is so because the bank presumably already knows its "customer" and need not do an extensive credit search to determine whether to issue the letter of credit. It can call upon its pre-existing knowledge to decide that it will issue a letter and that knowledge, gained from other transactions, will enable it to make an accurate estimation of the credit risk.

Problem 16–1

Examine the document set out below. It is a letter of credit. By referring to it answer the questions that follow.

No. G.C. 58954 irrevocable $97,460.00

THE FIRST NATIONAL BANK OF CHICAGO
CHICAGO 90, ILLINOIS

November 29, 1979

Associated Steel Corporation,
176 West Adams Street
Chicago, Illinois
or Assigns   This letter of credit is
Assignable and divisi-
ble

GENTLEMEN:

WE HEREBY AUTHORIZE YOU TO DRAW AT _____ SIGHT ON _____ FOR ANY SUM OR SUMS NOT EXCEEDING IN ALL Ninety Seven Thousand Four Hundred Sixty U.S. Dollars FOR ACCOUNT OF Decker Steel Co., Grand Rapids, Michigan.

Drafts are to be accompanied by the following documents:

Commercial invoices showing approximately 500 tons prime Thomas quality 36 inch by coil hot rolled steel.

Railroad or truck clean bill of lading issued to order of shipper blank endorsed notify Decker Steel Company, 1620 Turner Avenue, N.W., Grand Rapids 4, Michigan, and showing shipment from New York, New York to Grand Rapids, Michigan.

This credit will remain in force until February 29, 1980 and drafts must be negotiated on or before that date.

WE HEREBY AGREE WITH DRAWERS, ENDORSERS AND BONA FIDE HOLDERS OF DRAFTS NEGOTIATED UNDER AND IN COMPLIANCE WITH THE TERMS OF THIS CREDIT THAT THE SAME SHALL BE DULY HONORED UPON PRESENTATION AT THE COUNTER OF The First National Bank of Chicago. EACH AMOUNT DRAWN MUST BE ENDORSED ON THE REVERSE HEREOF BY THE NEGOTIATING BANK.

INSURANCE _____

DRAFTS UNDER THIS CREDIT MUST BEAR UPON THEIR FACE THE WORDS:

''DRAWN UNDER THE FIRST NATIONAL
BANK OF CHICAGO''

CREDIT NO. G.C. <u>58954</u> DATED <u>November 19, 1979</u>

RESPECTFULLY YOURS,

THE FIRST NATIONAL BANK OF
CHICAGO

Assistant Vice President

Assistant Cashier

Questions

1. Who is the customer, who the beneficiary, and who the issuer?

2. Assume that Associated Steel and First National Bank of Chicago decided to cancel the letter of credit:

    a. After it had been mailed but before it had been delivered to Associated Steel.

    b. After it had been delivered to Associated Steel but before Associated had taken any action in reliance upon it.

Could they do so?

3. The letter specifically states that it is assignable. In view of the statement in UCC 5–116(3), how does the fact that this document is "assignable" give the beneficiary greater rights that he would have even if it were not assignable?

B. Standby Letter of Credit

In the past twenty years a pattern of transactions quite unrelated to international trade or, indeed, to the sale of goods of any sort, has grown up in the United States. This is the issuance of "standby" letters of credit. To the dismay of federal regulators and to the concern of accountants, much of this growth has occurred off the balance sheet, and sometimes, one suspects, without careful consideration of the exposure that a large body of standby letters of credit presents to the issuer of those credits. First, what is a standby letter of credit? Basically, it is one in which the issuer promises to make payment to a beneficiary on the occurrence of a default by the customer other than a default in the shipment of goods. For example, a bank might issue a letter of credit to an owner that promises to make payment to the owner in the event that a builder defaults in constructing a home or a building. A bank might grant a letter of credit to a football player (beneficiary) to secure the payment of a multi-year salary by a shaky football team in a new league. It is even conceivable that a letter of credit could be issued on behalf of a seller, as customer, to a buyer to agree to pay the buyer a certain amount of money in case the seller did not deliver goods.

In general the same rules of law apply to the liabilities under standby letters of credit as under those for the sale of goods. One might wish to distinguish the two, first, because standbys present somewhat different risks to the issuer than do traditional letters of credit and, secondly, because they present somewhat different practical issues in connection with the obligations of payment and responsibilities for performance by the beneficiary and the issuer.

If the buyer fails to pay for the goods in our Denmark/Newark transaction, the bank at least will have a security interest (assuming it has executed the proper documents; see UCC 9–304) in the goods and will be able to recoup some of its loss by resale of those goods. In a traditional case, therefore, its exposure is somewhat limited. Compare that with the traditional standby case in which it promises to pay a city $500,000 upon certification that the curb and gutter contractor has defaulted. If the curb and gutter contractor is now in bankruptcy, the payment of the $500,000 to the municipality may be a dead loss for the bank. Thus, the bank's exposure tends to be larger because of the absence of any obvious security growing out of the transaction in the standby case.

Even more significant, in your editor's view, is a distinction in the obligation which the bank secures between the two different kinds of letters. In the traditional letter of credit the bank is making a bet upon its customer's ability to pay money. That is grist for a banker's mill: determining whether a customer can pay money. In a standby case, a bank is making a bet on its customer's ability and willingness to do something that may be much more complex—to build gutters, to drill a well, to construct a development of houses, etc. Here one suspects some bankers are over their heads and are less likely to make an accurate prediction than in the former case. For all of those reasons the federal bank regulators cluck nervously, but ineffectually, as they watch their chicks write a larger and larger volume of standby letters of credits.

C. Documents

What then are the documents that compose the usual letter of credit transaction and what are the basic legal liabilities? In the usual transaction there will be at least three separate documents. First there will be the underlying contract between the beneficiary and the customer. This is the contract of sale between the Danish seller and the Newark buyer; in a standby case it is the contract for the construction of the curbs and gutters by the local contractor and the municipality. Second is the letter of credit itself. As one will see from the letter quoted below, it is addressed to the beneficiary and signed by the issuer. A wise lawyer will call it a letter of credit, not a contract, not a guarantee, not a bond. The third contract is between the issuer and the customer. Examination of this contract shows the guts of the letter of credit transaction, namely, a potential loan to the customer. In it the customer will promise to pay the bank (usually before the bank has to pay the beneficiary), it will grant the bank a security interest to secure any payments that must be made under the letter, and it will make still other promises to the bank. Many bank officers and their lawyers have rued the day when they issued a letter of credit without first having secured the customer's signature on the contract, or having secured that signature on a contract without all of the proper terms.

How does one characterize the legal relation established by the execution of these various documents? The characterizations that come to mind and the analogies that one most easily draws are all flawed in important ways. The bank is not really a guarantor. Nor is its obligation on the letter of credit exclusively a contractual one. Moreover, strictly speaking, the "beneficiary" is not really a beneficiary of the underlying agreement between the bank and the customer. Finally, the bank's issuance of the money to the beneficiary might be regarded as a loan to the customer, but most would not so characterize it. Perhaps the writing of the letter itself should be regarded as a commitment to make a loan to the customer, not so?

NOM DE LA BANQUE ÉMETTRICE - NAME OF ISSUING BANK
Issuing Bank Limited International Division
23, High Street
London S.W. 25
 	
Lieu et date d'émission - Place and date of issue
London
           13 October 1984
	Irrevocable documentary credit
	Crédit documentaire irrévocable Number - Numero
	                         16358
	
	Date and place of expiry - Date et lieu de validité 30 November 1984
	at counters of advising bank

Applicant - Donneur d'ordre

Joan's Boutique
14 Charlotte Street
London W.C.36

Beneficiary - Bénéficiaire

The Eastern Trading Company
29, London Road
Hong Kong

Advising Bank - Banque notificatrice   Ref or - No Réf.

Bank "X"
35 Kings Road North
Hong Kong

Amount - Montant HK$ 10,000 (Hong Kong Dollars ten thousand)

Credit available with - Crédit utilisable chez

[ ] by sight payment / par paiement à vue   [X] by acceptance / par acceptation   [ ] by negotiation / par negociation

[ ] by deferred payment at / par paiement différé à

against the documents detailed herein
contre les documents précisés ci-après

Partial shipments / Expéditions partielles	Transhipment / Transbordement
allowed / autorisées [X] not allowed / non autorisées	allowed / autorisées [X] not allowed / non autorisées

Shipment/dispatch/taking in charge from/at
Embarquement/expédition/prise en charge de/a   Hong Kong

for transportation to
a destination de   Heathrow Airport, London

[X] and beneficiary's draft at   90 days sight
et la traite du bénéficiaire au
on Bank "X", 35 Kings Road North, Hong Kong
sur

SIGNED INVOICE IN THREE COPIES certifying that the goods are in accordance with Joan's Boutique Order Number 35 dated 14.8.1984.

AIR CONSIGNMENT NOTE evidencing goods dispatched to Joan's Boutique, 14 Charlotte Street, London W.C. 36 marked "Freight Paid".

PACKING LIST IN TRIPLICATE

We are informed that insurance is being arranged by our principals.

covering Ladies Dresses
C and F Heathrow Airport, London

Documents to be presented within
Documents à présenter dans les   [7]   days after the date of issuance of the transport documents but within the validity of the credit
jours après la date d'émission du ou des documents de transport mais dans la période de validité du crédit

We hereby issue the Documentary Credit in your favour. It is subject to the Uniform Customs and Practice for Documentary Credits 1983 Revision, International Chamber of Commerce, Paris, France, Publication No. 400, and engages us in accordance with the terms thereof. The number and the date of the credit and the name of our bank must be quoted on all drafts required. The credit is available by negotiation, each presentation must be noted on the reverse of this advice by the bank where the credit is available.

Nous émettons par la présente ce crédit documentaire en votre faveur. Il est soumis aux Règles et Usances Uniformes relatives aux Crédits Documentaires (Révision 1983, Publication No. 400 de la Chambre de Commerce Internationale, Paris, France) et nous engage selon leurs termes. Le numéro et la date du crédit ainsi que le nom de notre banque devront être mentionnés sur toute traite requise. Si le crédit est utilisable par négociation chaque présentation devra être inscrite au verso de cet avis par la banque où le crédit est utilisable.

Issuing Bank Limited International Division
23, High Street
London S.W. 25

This document consists of
Ce document consiste en   [1]   signed page(s)
page(s) signée(s)

Notes

1. Would the bank pay on the following draft?

Pay to the order of <u>Eastern Trading Company $10,000 H.K.</u>

<u>—Ten thousand dollars Hong Kong—</u>

To: Issuing Bank Ltd.
      25 High Street
      London S.W. 25

                              a.R. Rogers
                              Eastern Trading Co.

[E1124]

---

2. What if the invoices presented appeared to have a stamp on the signature line or a printed inscription? Should the bank pay against those?

3. If the letter of credit set out above were changed to a standby letter of credit, what would the conditions of performance say?

INVOICE	FACTURE FACTURA	RECHNUNG FACTUUR		Sheet No. 1

Seller (Name, Address, VAT Reg.No.)
Clearchem PLC
Riverside Works, Warren Road
Banbury
Oxfordshire
United Kingdom

Invoice No. & Date (Tax Point)	Seller's Reference
RT 67244 8 Nov 84	SPEX/548/789/DEM

Buyer's Reference	Other Reference
Order ARB-548771	

Consignee
General Trading Company Limited
Suite 18/88, Eastern House
3487 Soleiman Jamshid Mojdeh
Riyadh
Saudi Arabia

Buyer (if not Consignee)

Country of Origin of Goods	Country of Destination
UK (EEC)	Saudi Arabia

Import licence 892E-44319

Terms of Delivery and Payment
CIF Jeddah
Confirmed Irrevocable Letter of
Credit payable at sight
Payment should be made through:
British Bank Limited
88 Waterloo Place, London SW1
Account no. 120 7532 68

Vessel/Aircraft etc.	Port of Loading
Orient Adventurer	Liverpool

Port of Discharge
Jeddah

Marks and Numbers and Container No.
G.T.C.
ARB-548771
Riyadh
via Jeddah
1-80

Number and Kind of Packages / Description of Goods	TT Code No.	Total Gross Wt (Kg)	Total Cube (m³)
1 x 20ft Container Chemical products in drums		kg 2141.8	20.620

Total Net Wt(Kg)
2000.0

Item/pkges	Gross/Net/Cube	Description	Quantity	Unit Price	Selling Price
1)	816.8 750.0 7.620	Product D101/5877 Hydrofluoric Acid Solution 50% w/w	30 drums	17.26 /25kg	517.80
2)	1325.0 1250.0 13.000	Product D100/6755 Antimony Trichloride	50 drums	20.47 /25kg	1023.50
					———— 1541.30
		Freight Insurance			180.55 39.70

We hereby guarantee that this is a true and correct invoice and that the goods referred to are of the origin, manufacture and production of the United Kingdom.

Invoice Total	
GBP £	1761.55

Name of signatory
AC Smith, Director

Place and Date of Issue
Banbury   8 NOV 1984

Signature
AC Smith

© SITPRO 1984 V3

Notes

Assume that the letter of credit described the commodity as 816.8 Product D101/5857; 750.0 Hydrofluoric Acid; 7.620 Solution 50% w/w.

1. Under which of the following descriptions would you reject the invoice as improper if you were an employee of the issuing bank?

    a. "816.8 Product D101/5877."

    b. Description as set out in the invoice printed above, but listing 29 or alternatively 32 drums.

    c. "750.0 Hydrofluoric Acid."

2. What if the invoice was not that of Clearchem, but an invoice with a proper description of Ambercamp, a related company also located in Banbury? See UPC Article 41.

3. Assume that the invoice contained the precise description, but that an insurance certification was included that described the product merely as "Approximately 30 drums, more or less, hydrofluoric acid."

4. What if the invoice or bill of lading came to the bank not through the mail but by a computer connection from the carrier or shipper, between the sender's computer and bank, which when properly stimulated printed out the above invoice? Would such a document be acceptable? See Article 22. How would you authenticate a document in such case?

D. Sources of Law

There are two significant sources of law in addition to the cases. The first is Article 5 of the Uniform Commercial Code. As section 5–102 will disclose, that Article covers not just documentary credits issued by a bank, but also credits issued by nonbanks. Subsection (3) contains a curious disclaimer:

> This Article deals with some but not all of the rules and concepts of letters of credit as such rules or concepts have developed prior to this act or may hereafter develop. The fact that this Article states a rule does not by itself require, imply or negate application of the same or a converse rule to a situation not provided for or to a person not specified by this Article.

At the conclusion of this chapter the student should have some familiarity with each of the seventeen sections in Article 5.

The second important source of non-case law is a document entitled the Uniform Customs and Practices for Documentary Credits. This is a document issued by the International Chamber of Commerce and, by agreement, it governs a large share of all letters of credit written in international transactions. A current copy is set out beginning at p. 778. A comparison of Article 5 with the rules in the Uniform Customs and Practices shows that they are by no means identical, but it would be mistake to believe that they contain significantly different rules of law; they do not. The basic rules are the same under either. Because of long experience and because it is devoted explicitly to the international trade arena, the Uniform Customs and Practices will have many detailed provisions that deal explicitly with the sale of goods. For example, Article 14 contains a series of specific rules on the kinds of documents that are appropriate, the kinds of descriptions that are necessary, etc. These rules can be determinative in a case governed by the UCP; they can be persuasive in one governed by the Uniform Commercial Code. At the behest of its banks, New York added the following non-uniform amendment to 5–102. In New York 5–102(4) reads as follows:

> Unless otherwise agreed, this Article 5 does not apply to a letter of credit or a credit if by its terms or by agreement, course of dealing or usage of trade such letter of credit or credit is subject in whole or in part to the Uniform Customs and Practice for Commercial Documentary Credits fixed by the 13th or by any subsequent Congress of the International Chamber of Commerce.

In an earlier version of this book we accused Henry Harfield, then a partner in Sherman and Sterling, and America's preeminent expert on letters of credit, of leading the New York lawyers in an attack on the UCC out of a neurotic attachment to the Uniform Customs and Practices. Mr. Harfield responded to that charge as follows:

"Dear Professor White:

> "∗ ∗ ∗ As regards the matter discussed and the material referred to in the second paragraph of your letter, I gladly waive any rights I may have and am content that this letter constitutes my release of any liability you may have to me for defamation. On the other hand, you will understand that I cannot and do not undertake to indemnify you against liability to others arising out of the inaccuracy of your statements. The New York Bar was far from uniform in its reaction to the Uniform Commercial Code in general and to Article 5 in particular. I can well imagine that those outstanding members of the Bar who supported the Code with apostolic zeal (and there are many of them) might feel justifiably aggrieved at their unwarranted inclusion with a group of intellectual muckers. At the other end of the spectrum, there is good ground for umbrage by those outstanding members of the New York Bar (and there are many of them) who then were and still are persuaded that the Code is the most mischievous piece of contrivance since the Communist Manifesto. Each of these groups may regard as actionable, your proposed assertion that I was their leader.

> "That statement is simply not supported by the record. The facts are that the New York Bar was divided, perhaps even fragmented, and the proceedings before the Law Revision Commission resembled a Donnybrook rather than a knightly tournament. There was a significant group who supported Article 5 in all its aspects and they had their leaders who were devout and dedicated men. There was a group which regarded Article 5, in every aspect,

as anathema and they had their leaders who were devout and dedicated men; but I was not a leader of either group. My recollection is that my approach was singular, objective, statesman-like, and always reasonable. For this I deserve no credit; it is just my nature. * * *"

"Faithfully yours,

"Henry Harfield."

Because of the provision in the New York law and because a large share of all international letters of credit are written in New York by New York banks, many letter of credit transactions in the United States will not be governed by the Uniform Commercial Code, but by the UCP. It is important, therefore, that the student know the UCP, not just as a basis for analogy in Code cases, but as the governing law in many transactions.

Almost all of the cases, an incredibly complex array, arise out of a single problem. Nearly all ask the question: Was the bank which was presented with certain documents required to pay? The basic rule is that if there is compliance with the documentary requirements of the letter, the bank must pay, even though there is a breach of the underlying contract, even though its own customer has gone bankrupt, even though the world is about to come to an end. However, beginning with the *Sztejn* case, infra 742, the courts and now the Uniform Commercial Code have recognized at least one exception to the bank's obligation to pay on presentation of complying documents, the so-called fraud exception. Many of the cases that now come to the court call upon it to draw the line between fraud on the one hand (where payment is excused) and cases of mere breach of the underlying contract (where payment is not excused).

Many other cases deal in tedious detail with the form of documents that are necessary to comply with the credits. When the bank wishes not to pay, it will of course examine the documents microscopically and will seize on any small detail as a basis for its refusal to pay and as an excuse. Usually the defect in the documents is not the true reason the bank has chosen not to pay. It probably has chosen not to pay because its customer has asked it not to pay, because its customer has gone bankrupt, or because, for some other reason, it believes it or its customer will not be reimbursed. Each time the bank is freed from payment by a court, a little chip is taken out of the solid rock of letter of credit law and practice. Each time the courts grant an injunction against payment, in the words of Henry Harfield: "I fear that the sacred cow of equity may trample the tender vines of letter of credit law." Harfield, *Code, Custom, and Conscience in Letter of Credit Law,* 4 UCC L.J. 7, 11 (1971). Thus, many of the cases are bitterly fought wars over words with nary a mention of the true motivation of the bank and of the other party.

A final set of cases involves the right of a bank who has paid to be repaid out of the assets of its customer, to be subrogated to its customer's or beneficiary's rights or otherwise to protect itself by taking and selling the underlying assets.

SECTION 2.   THE ISSUER'S DUTY TO PAY, UCC 5–109, 5–114, THE BASIC RULE

The issuer's duty to its customer is to examine the documents presented and to refuse to pay if the documents are not correct. That duty is set out under UCC 5–109. The issuer's duty to the beneficiary, on the other hand, is the duty to honor on proper presentation and that duty is specified as follows in UCC 5–114(1):

> An issuer must honor a draft or demand for payment which complies with the terms of the relevant credit regardless of whether the goods or documents conform to the underlying contract for sale or other contract between the customer and the beneficiary. The issuer is not excused from honor of such a draft or demand by reason of an additional general term that all documents must be satisfactory to the issuer, but an issuer may require that specified documents must be satisfactory to it.

In the next section we will concern ourselves with exceptions to the duty to honor based upon fraud in the underlying transaction. Those are covered by UCC 5–114(2). To understand UCC 5–114(1) and the cases in this section, imagine a letter of credit department in a large bank. Here are many clerical workers, sophisticated clerical workers, but clerical workers nevertheless. On the one hand they have a stack of letters of credit that call for certain kinds of bills of lading, invoices, insurance certificates, certificates of inspection, certifications of default, etc. The letters have dates of expiration and call for specific kinds of drafts signed by particular persons. The bank officers sitting with these documents look from one to the other and ultimately decide whether the conditions have been met.

The job is the same on the bitterest winter day as it is at the height of summer. It is uninfluenced by the destruction of the goods in the most violent storm of the century, by the bankruptcy of the buyer or the seller, or, theoretically, by any other set of events going on outside the room where our hypothetical bank officers are sitting. The issue is plain and simple in every instance: do these documents meet the conditions of this letter?

Sometimes even that is not an easy question to answer. We will see in the cases that follow that reasonable people could differ and reasonable judges have differed about the exact standards that should be applied in determining whether or not the conditions have been met. Moreover, there will be cases in which the true party in interest, the customer, wants to waive certain conditions of the letter, and others in which the bank's behavior may estop it from claiming that the conditions were not met. Finally there are mysterious provisions in the

Code on indemnity (5–113) and on the warranties to be given by the beneficiary (5–111) that may influence the bank's responsibility in ways that are not too clear. Nor should one assume that the job of this bank employee is easy at times when the bank's best customer has spoken to the president of the bank who in turn has spoken to the bank officer, and when all of them would rather not see the customer's $500,000 go out in payment, for example, to an Iranian national company never to be seen again. The question then becomes very difficult: to whom does the bank owe its allegiance—to its best customer or to this abstract image of the letter of credit and to its sanctity and utility? More often than a cynic might expect, the sanctity of the letter of credit prevails over the customer's wishes.

BANCO ESPANOL de CREDITO v. STATE STREET BANK AND TRUST CO.

United States Circuit Court, Third Circuit, 1967.
385 F.2d 230, cert. denied 390 U.S. 1013, 88 S.Ct. 1263, 20 L.Ed.2d 163 (1968),
appeal after remand 409 F.2d 711 (1969).

Before ALDRICH, CHIEF JUDGE, McENTEE and COFFIN, CIRCUIT JUDGES.

COFFIN, CIRCUIT JUDGE. This suit began as a claim by appellant, a Spanish bank (Banco Espanol), against appellee, a domestic bank (State Street), for the latter's allegedly wrongful refusal to accept and pay two drafts drawn upon it pursuant to two irrevocable commercial letters of credit. Each letter was issued by State Street at the behest of its customer, Robert Lawrence, Inc. (Lawrence), a Boston clothing concern. Banco Espanol was designated the advising bank and two Spanish suppliers (Alcides and Longuer) were named as beneficiaries. The cases were consolidated for trial in the district court sitting without a jury and, following judgment for State Street, appellant took these appeals.

The issue is whether State Street, whose letters of credit, as amended, called for the presentation of an inspection certificate by a named firm stipulating "that the goods are in conformity with the order", was justified in refusing to honor the drafts of Banco Espanol on the ground that the inspection certificate did not meet the terms of the letters of credit.

The transaction was initiated by Lawrence to finance the purchase of raincoats, beach jackets, knit shirts, and cardigans from Alcides and Longuer. Based upon preliminary arrangements apparently worked out by an intermediary, of which more later, Lawrence obtained two irrevocable letters of credit from State Street. One letter covered Lawrence orders Nos. 101, 102, and 103 for beach jackets, outer coats and cotton garments in the revised final amount of $105,630, and the other covered Lawrence order No. 100 for wool knit shirts and cardigans in the revised final amount of $13,320. Both letters constituted Banco Espanol the correspondent bank, and required signed invoices, customs invoices, inspection certificates, and full sets of clean on board ocean bills of lading dated not later than March 31, 1963.

At the time of issuance of the letters of credit, State Street called to the attention of its customer, Lawrence, that the requirement of an inspection certificate without a named inspector left a hazardous gap in the documents. Lawrence replied that the letters would be later amended to include the name of an inspection agent.

The next three and one half months were significantly devoted to continuing efforts to resolve this problem. On November 22, 1962 one of the Spanish manufacturers (Alcides) wrote Lawrence's representative that it agreed with the idea of naming an inspection agent and suggested that Lawrence put forward a name. Lawrence's man replied shortly that since he would be in Barcelona near the time of delivery, he would be the inspector. Accordingly, State Street sought to amend the letters in January. Foreseeably, this was not acceptable to the beneficiary as Lawrence learned in early February. Lawrence then wrote State Street (notwithstanding the hiatus in the letters of credit which State Street had noted) that it should not make payment unless inspection certificates were signed by a party acceptable to it. It further agreed to indemnify State Street for any damages resulting from carrying out these instructions, coupling this with a threat to refuse reimbursement if payment were made.

After a meeting between Lawrence and State Street, the object of which was to decide what to do about the inspection issue, a representative of Lawrence went to Spain. This trip resulted in an amendment to the letters of credit, cabled to Alcides on March 1, 1963, which required the inspection certificate to be issued by Supervigilancia Sociedad General de Control S.A. (Supervigilancia) certifying that "the goods are in conformity with the order". While it is not clear on whose initiative this firm was selected, it was apparently well regarded by the State Street official who had been closely associated with this transaction.

Identification of the underlying orders to which the letters of credit referred is not an easy task. In the first place, the record before us contains no document purporting to be an order for the shirts and cardigans (No. 100—the Longuer order). As to the Alcides order, we face two sets of somewhat inconsistent documents, both of which Lawrence sent to the manufacturer: two unnumbered papers dated November 5 and 6, 1962, labelled "order placed by Cavendish Co."— apparently an intermediary for Lawrence; and three papers dated November 13, 1962, labelled "stock sheet", and bearing numbers 101, 102, and 103. Though the earlier set is the only one bearing the label "order" there is evidence both external and internal that it was superseded by the latter: a reference in a letter from Lawrence's representative that he had to create orders to match the numbers in the letter of credit; a reference in another letter to asterisks in the orders—which are found only in the "stock sheets", not in the "orders"; additional documentary requirements in the "stock sheets", not found in the "orders"; and a major change in half the sizes specified in one "order", from "small" to "medium". We cite such minutiae because of the difficulty of interpretation created by Lawrence and because of the assertion of appellee's counsel at trial that the inspecting agency could not determine what the orders were. Leaving aside consideration of what might be the legal effect of a buyer-created impossibility of clear identification of orders where a letter of credit required a certificate of conformity to order, we simply observe here that close scrutiny of the two sets of papers reveals that the "stock sheets" supplanted the earlier "orders".

In any event the most important notation found on the "stock sheets"—and not on the "orders"—was "Coats [and jackets] to be as sample inspected in Spain. Letter of credit to be cashed by presentation of bill of lading and signature of superintendent or local inspection (buyers preference) (will confirm)."

The amendment to the letters of credit—appointing Supervigilancia the inspecting agent—was accepted by the major manufacturer involved—Alcides (and presumably Longuer)—on March 12, 1963 on which date both manufacturers requested Supervigilancia to begin inspection. State Street notified Lawrence on March 13.

Then began a barrage of cabled messages from Lawrence to both Supervigilancia and the manufacturers, which was to endure for two weeks. On March 13 Supervigilancia was asked, without explanation, to delay inspection until further instructions from Lawrence. On March 14, it was told that Lawrence had cabled the manufacturers to postpone shipment to permit Supervigilancia to inspect according to samples "they air mailing you directly". On the same day another cable was sent to Supervigilancia saying that Lawrence was airmailing "our approved samples per order and instructions". On the next day Supervigilancia was told to obtain three complete sets of samples properly marked from each concern, send two to Lawrence, and await instructions. On March 18 this message was repeated.

After these two conflicting sets of instructions, Supervigilancia, on March 23, cabled Lawrence, saying in effect that it was going ahead, acting "according your own indications on credits and orders". To this Lawrence replied on March 25 that Supervigilancia should "withhold certificate until after arrival and inspection of goods by your New York correspondent * * *." This, if we read it aright, is a third position taken by Lawrence. At this point in time the latest date for completion of the bills of lading was five days away, March 31, with no alternative shipping date available within that period.

Supervigilancia, on March 26, executed its two certificates of inspection. It divided each certificate into two parts. The first part tended to the matter at hand saying that (1) it had carried out its inspection

"* * * basing ourselves on the details shown in the orders or Stocksheets Nos. [100], 101, 102 and 103 * * * and in the samples that were handed to us by the Requirer [Alcides and Longuer], that corresponded, according to his sayings ratified in presence of a Public Notary, to the samples seen and approved by the Delegate of Firm ROBERT LAWRENCE INC., during his stay in Barcelona, and with [sic] are mentioned in the notes appearing in orders Stocksheets Nos. [100], 101, 102 and 103, where there is a note reading:

'COATS or JACKETS [Germents (sic)] TO BE AS SAMPLE INSPECTED IN SPAIN' ";

that (2) the letters of credit required it to certify "THAT THE GOODS ARE IN CONFORMITY WITH THE ORDER"; that (3) a ten per cent random sample had been taken; and that (4) the "whole * * * [was] found conforming to the conditions estipulated [sic] on the Order-Stocksheets."

The second part of each certificate contained a chronological account of the cabled messages we have summarized, followed by this language: "Requirer * * * is formally requiring us for delivering this certificate what we are doing today under reserves, not as far as the goods are concerned, which correspond to the samples seen and produced referred to at the beginning of this certificate, but to the existing difference between both interested parties as per the quoted cables."

All documents were presented to Banco Espanol, which honored them and made payment or the equivalent on March 28 and 29. On April 3 State Street cabled its refusal to accept the drafts on it "because accompanying inspection certificates nonconforming with terms of credits which require certificates certifying goods are in conformity with the orders". A later letter amplified its position by specifying that the certificates merely indicated conformity to samples alleged by the seller to "correspond" to other samples allegedly approved by the buyer and that the certificates were issued "under reserves".

The district court sustained this position, referring to the requirement that documents strictly conform to letter of credit provisions, and pointing out that each certificate failed in three respects: (1) that it merely certified that the goods conformed to "conditions"—which left it unclear if the conformity was to the whole of the order or only part; (2) that there was a doubt whether the "order-stock-sheet" was different from the order; and (3) that the certificate was confined to samples handed to the inspecting agency by a representative of the manufacturer. The court concluded that " * * * this was not the unqualified certificate required by the letter of credit and defendant bank was justified in its refusal to accept it."

We do not agree. Since, in our view, the third alleged defect noted by the court presents the most difficult problem, we shall deal with it first.

We note, at the outset, that an issuing bank's duty to honor a demand for payment is, to some extent, determined by statute. The

Uniform Commercial Code, M.G.L.A. (Mass.) c. 106 § 5–114(1) (1958), provides, in relevant part, that "An issuer must honor a draft or demand for payment which complies with the terms of the relevant credit regardless of whether the goods or documents conform to the underlying contract for sale or other contract between the customer and the beneficiary."[1] This Code provision, however, simply codifies long-standing decisional law and does not assist us here in determining whether the inspection certificate submitted by Supervigilancia complied with the terms of the credit.

We take as a starting point the substantial body of case law which establishes and supports the general rule that documents submitted incident to a letter of credit are to be strictly construed. This is because international financial transactions rest upon the accuracy of documents rather than on the condition of the goods they represent. But we note some leaven in the loaf of strict construction. Not only does *haec verba* not control absolutely, see, e.g., O'Meara v. National Park Bank, 239 N.Y. 386, 146 N.E. 636, 39 A.L.R. 747 (1925), but some courts now cast their eyes on a wider scene than a single document. We are mindful, also, of the admonition of several legal scholars that the integrity of international transactions (i.e., rigid adherence to material matters) must somehow strike a balance with the requirement of their fluidity (i.e., a reasonable flexibility as to ancillary matters) if the objective of increased dealings to the mutual satisfaction of all interested parties is to be enhanced. See, e.g., Mentschicoff, How to Handle Letters of Credit, 19 Bus.Lawyer 107, 111 (1963). Finally, we recognize that this is not a litigation about the nomenclature of goods. Consequently, we are not measurably helped by such cases as those cited in the margin which turn on discrepancies between the actual terms of invoices or bills of lading and requirements of a letter of credit.

What we face here is a matter of procedure which can, in the first instance, be structured by the purchasing party. How may a buyer in the international market place be assured before payment that his purchase as delivered is of the quality agreed upon by the parties? As buyers become more concerned about quality, this issue is likely to become more important. That there are so few cases or comments addressed to the issue of reasonable precautions to assure quality is indicative of the relatively novel status of the problem, at least so far as courts have dealt with it. We are mindful of the testimony in this case that an official of appellee, a busy bank, engaged in passing upon the issuance of 1,500 to 2,000 letters of credit a year for several decades, has encountered in this case his first experience with a letter of credit calling for a certificate of conformity to the order.

1. The district court noted that

"Both parties appear to agree that the case is governed by the Uniform Commercial Code as enacted in Massachusetts. Plaintiff [appellant] also relies upon the Uniform Customs and Practice for Docu- mentary Credits issued by the Internation- al Chamber of Commerce, particularly Ar- ticle 8 thereof. This, however, in substance states only what is contained in the Uniform Commercial Code."

What are the realities of such a requirement on the part of the buyer? It is not enough that he receive the quantity of goods he ordered, nor that he receive goods capable of standard measure or grade. He must also, in such a case as this, receive them cut, tailored, sewn according to a style he has in mind. He must therefore rely on a sample he has seen and liked. Being in a distant part of the globe, the buyer must usually elect one of two alternatives. He may be present during the inspection process to verify the sample or he may select, with his seller's acquiescence, a person or firm in whom he has confidence to represent him. Unless he elects to be present, he is acting on faith—faith that the representative is capable and honest, and faith that the representative has the right samples or criteria to serve as a standard. Even if he mails an approved sample direct to the representative, he must rely on the integrity of the mails.

This act of faith—or its converse, the risk that merchandise will not turn out as hoped—is that of the buyer. As one contemporary student has written,

> " * * * there is one risk against which protection is required and which is less easy to guard against. That is the risk that the goods shipped may not comply with the terms of the sales contract as to quality. This is a risk which normally the buyer will have to bear * * * but * * * [he] can guard against the risk by requiring in his letter of request to the bankers that, in addition to the usual shipping documents, the vendor shall deliver a certificate of quality showing the goods to be as specified in the contract, signed by some responsible person at the place of shipment. The only risk then left to the buyer is that the person nominated to give the certificate may fail in his duty. But an entire absence of risk would mean an absence of business." A.G. Davis, The Law Relating to Commercial Letters of Credit, 3d ed., London, Sir Isaac Pitman & Sons Ltd., 1963, p. 19.

Or, in the words of other scholars,

> "The requirement of such other documents, and particularly certificates of analysis, quality, weight, and the like, is a reasonable precaution for a prudent buyer to take, since he may in this way obtain some measure of assurance that the merchandise is as ordered * * *. The bank is under no obligation and bears no responsibility for the accuracy of any such representations and certificates. Nevertheless, through selection of a reputable third party, the buyer does have a degree of assurance that the merchandise is as represented." Ward and Harfield, Bank Credits and Acceptances, 4th ed., Ronald Press, 1958, p. 45.

These observations go to the heart of this case. For the buyer here—Lawrence—was striving to assure the delivery of quality goods. To be sure, it deliberately postponed the problem when it caused the letters of credit to be issued without resolving the question of the inspecting agent. Then it naively sought to have the sellers accept one of its own representatives. It had long since sewn the seeds of dispute by sending to the sellers both "stock sheets" which were really orders and "orders" which were merely preliminary papers. When it finally reached agreement with the seller as to an inspecting agency, it neglected to specify precisely how it would conduct the inspection operation, leaving only the bland instruction that the goods must conform to orders. And, so far as the inspecting agency was concerned, the orders merely referred to samples that might very well have been inspected in Spain at some past time.

Consequently when faced on the eve of the shipping deadline both with a barrage of contradictory telegrams from the buyer and with samples which the sellers under oath stated "corresponded" with samples approved earlier by the buyer's representative in Barcelona, Supervigilancia had to act to the dissatisfaction of one of the parties to the basic contract. That it took the word, under oath, of the seller as to the appropriateness of the sample is no more than any inspector must ordinarily do. Unless the buyer is physically present (and Lawrence presumably could have arranged this during the frenetic two week period of cable traffic), the inspector must take someone's word that he is judging by the proper samples.

Even in the well known case of O'Meara v. National Park Bank, 239 N.Y. 386, 146 N.E. 636, 39 A.L.R. 747, (1925), a letter of credit calling for newsprint to "test 11/12–32 pounds" was held to be satisfied by an affidavit that annexed samples "stated [by the affiant] to be representative of the shipment" met the prescribed test. We fail to see how this is any more reliable than the affidavit of "correspondence" in the instant case.

In Basse & Selve v. Bank of Australasia, 90 L.T.R. (n.s.) 618 (K.B. 1904), the letter of credit covering a purchase of cobalt ore called for a certificate of analysis of a local chemist showing at least five per cent protoxide. The shipper (bent on delivering worthless ore) gave the chemist a packet of ore for analysis. The chemist furnished a certificate that the ore he examined contained the requisite amount of protoxide. But the negotiating bank refused to pay since there was nothing to indicate that the ore examined was that described in the bill of lading. The unscrupulous shipper then gave the chemist a packet of ore marked as was the bill of lading, "P.M. 2680 bags representing 100 tons". The chemist then referred in his certificate to "The sample of cobalt ore marked 'P.M. 2680 bags representing 100 tons' received from you * * *." The bank paid the shipper and prevailed in a suit against it by its customer to recover the sum so paid. The court said:

> "It is said that [the certificate] professes to show merely the test of the contents of a sample packet with a mark upon it, and does not purport to show a test of the bill of lading of 100 tons of ore. This, I think, is a fanciful objection. Large quantities of produce are necessarily tested by means of samples. Such samples are drawn either by the servants of the owner of the goods or (as it

seems) by the servants of the analyst, and if the samples are carefully and skilfully drawn they generally fairly represent the bulk. But in this case it would be no part of the bank's duty to see to the sampling or to ascertain that it was fairly done." 90 L.T.R. (n.s.) at 620.

So we say in this case that, while the sample may be just as misleading as the ore sample in Basse & Selve, the advising bank was equally justified in paying on the strength of the documents.

We see no significant difference in Supervigilancia being told by the manufacturers that the samples were those approved by the buyer and being told that they "corresponded" to such samples. Webster's Dictionary (3d Int'l ed.) gives such meanings of "correspond" as "in agreement", "conformity", "equivalent", "match", "equal". In the context and considering the language difficulty, we think these meanings apply more than the looser ones like "analogous", "parallel", or "similar". In effect, Lawrence in this case, by providing as a referent to the letter of credit requirement of conformity to orders merely the early cryptic description on the stock sheets ("Coats * * * to be as samples inspected in Spain"), procured no more reliable assurance of authenticity than the credit termination clause in Fair Pavilions, Inc. v. First Nat. City Bank, 24 A.D.2d 109, 264 N.Y.S.2d 255 (1965), which was to be triggered " * * * if our Travelers Letter of Credit Department receives * * * from an officer (or one describing himself therein as an officer) of [bank's customer] an affidavit that one or more * * * events * * * has occurred." 264 N.Y.S.2d at 256.

Moreover, if there be ambiguity surrounding the words "correspond" or "sample approved in Spain" we would, like the court in *Fair Pavilions,* " * * * take the words as strongly against the issuer as a reasonable reading will justify. * * *." Supra at 258.

To hold otherwise—that a buyer could frustrate an international transaction on the eve of fulfillment by a challenge to authenticity of sample—would make vulnerable many such arrangements where third parties are vested by buyers with inspection responsibilities but where, apart from their own competence and integrity, there is no iron-clad guarantee of the sample itself.

As for the argument that Supervigilancia's finding that the goods conform "to the conditions stipulated on the Order-Stock-sheets" is a meaningful variance from the terms of the letters of credit, we confess to semantic myopia. "The conditions" mean, as we read the certificates, all the conditions, hence the order itself. As for the dual use by the agency of the words "Order-Stock-sheets", we have already indicated both the nature and cause of the confusion and conclude that Supervigilancia acted solomonically in borrowing the substance of the stock sheets and the label of the "orders". We do not see how it could have done otherwise.

The remaining contention that "under reserves" has some mysterious meaning which infects the entire certificate is not borne out by the inapposite cases cited to us and is directly refuted by the limiting language immediately following—"not as far as the goods are concerned". Further reading of the document indicates clearly that the phrase was directed to the underlying dispute between buyer and seller, which could not be the concern of the advising bank.

We hold, therefore, that the inspection certificate in this case conformed in all significant respects to the requirements of the letter of credit.

Appellee has urged that, in the event we might reverse the district court's judgment, the case should be remanded for a new trial or at least further findings, since the district court did not find it necessary to reach additional defenses. Appellant urges otherwise. It is not clear to us which is correct. We reverse the judgment of the District Court and remand for such further proceedings, consistent with this opinion, as the court feels appropriate. We do say that these additional defenses were not argued before us, nor directly passed upon, but whether this is chargeable to appellee, so that judgment should be entered for appellant forthwith, we leave to the district judge before whom this case was originally heard. [Footnotes omitted.]

COURTAULDS NORTH AMERICA, INC. v. NORTH CAROLINA NATIONAL BANK

United States Court of Appeals, Fourth Circuit, 1975.
528 F.2d 802.

BRYAN, SENIOR CIRCUIT JUDGE. A letter of credit with the date of March 21, 1973 was issued by the North Carolina National Bank at the request of and for the account of its customer, Adastra Knitting Mills, Inc. It made available upon the drafts of Courtaulds North America, Inc. "up to" $135,000.00 (later increased by $135,000.00) at "60 days date" to cover Adastra's purchases of acrylic yarn from Courtaulds. The life of the credit was extended in June to allow the drafts to be "drawn and negotiated on or before August 15, 1973." Bank refused to honor a draft for $67,346.77 dated August 13, 1973 for yarn sold and delivered to Adastra. Courtaulds brought this action to recover this sum from Bank.

The defendant denied liability chiefly on the assertion that the draft did not agree with the letter's conditions, viz., that the draft be accompanied by a "Commercial invoice in triplicate stating [inter alia] that it covers * * * 100% acrylic yarn"; instead, the accompanying invoices stated that the goods were "Imported Acrylic Yarn."

Upon cross motions for summary judgment on affidavits and a stipulation of facts, the District Court held defendant Bank liable to Courtaulds for the amount of the draft, interest and costs. It concluded that the draft complied with the letter of credit when each invoice is read together with the packing lists stapled to it, for the lists stated on their faces: "Cartons marked:—100% Acrylic." After considering the insistent rigidity of the law and usage of bank credits and acceptances, we must differ with the District Judge and uphold Bank's position.

The letter of credit prescribed the terms of the drafts as follows:

"Drafts to be dated same as Bills of Lading. Draft(s) to be accompanied by:

"1. Commercial invoice in triplicate stating that it covers 100,000 lbs. 100% Acrylic Yarn, Package Dyed at $1.35 per lb., FOB Buyers Plant, Greensboro, North Carolina Land Duty Paid.

"2. Certificate stating goods will be delivered to buyers plant land duty paid.

"3. Inland Bill of Lading consigned to Adastra Knitting Mills, Inc. evidencing shipment from East Coast Port to Adastra Knitting Mills, Inc., Greensboro, North Carolina."

The shipment (the last) with which this case is concerned was made on or about August 8, 1973. On direction of Courtaulds bills of lading of that date were prepared for the consignment to Adastra from a bonded warehouse by motor carrier. The yarn was packaged in cartons and a packing list referring to its bill of lading accompanied each carton. After the yarn was delivered to the carrier, each bill of lading with the packing list was sent to Courtaulds. There invoices for the sales were made out, and the invoices and packing lists stapled together. At the same time, Courtaulds wrote up the certificate, credit memorandum and draft called for in the letter of credit. The draft was dated August 13, 1973 and drawn on Bank by Courtaulds payable to itself.

All of these documents—the draft, the invoices and the packing lists—were sent by Courtaulds to its correspondent in Mobile for presentation to Bank and collection of the draft which for the purpose had been endorsed to the correspondent.

This was the procedure pursued on each of the prior drafts and always the draft had been honored by Bank save in the present instance. Here the draft, endorsed to Bank, and the other papers were sent to Bank on August 14. Bank received them on Thursday, August 16. Upon processing, Bank found these discrepancies between the drafts with accompanying documents and the letter of credit: (1) that the invoice did not state "100% Acrylic Yarn" but described it as "Imported Acrylic Yarn," and (2) "Draft not drawn as per terms of [letter of credit], Date [August 13] not same as Bill of Lading [August 8] and not drawn 60 days after date" [but 60 days from Bill of Lading date 8/8/73]. Finding of fact 24. Since decision of this controversy is put on the first discrepancy we do not discuss the others.

On Monday, August 20, Bank called Adastra and asked if it would waive the discrepancies and thus allow Bank to honor the draft. In response, the president of Adastra informed Bank that it could not waive any discrepancies because a trustee in bankruptcy had been appointed for Adastra and Adastra could not do so alone. Upon word

(S., S. & W.) Sales ACB—25

of these circumstances, Courtaulds on August 27 sent amended invoices to Bank which were received by Bank on August 27. They referred to the consignment as "100% Acrylic Yarn", and thus would have conformed to the letter of credit had it not expired. On August 29 Bank wired Courtaulds that the draft remained unaccepted because of the expiration of the letter of credit on August 15. Consequently the draft with all the original documents was returned by Bank.

During the life of the letter of credit some drafts had not been of even dates with the bills of lading, and among the large number of invoices transmitted during this period, several did not describe the goods as "100% Acrylic Yarn." As to all of these deficiencies Bank called Adastra for and received approval before paying the drafts. Every draft save the one in suit was accepted.

Conclusion of Law

The factual outline related is not in dispute, and the issue becomes one of law. It is well phrased by the District Judge in his "Discussion" in this way:

> "The only issue presented by the facts of this case is whether the documents tendered by the beneficiary to the issuer were in conformity with the terms of the letter of credit."

The letter of credit provided:

> "Except as otherwise expressly stated herein, this credit is subject to the 'Uniform Customs and Practice for Documentary Credits (1962 revision), the International Chamber of Commerce, Brochure No. 222'." Finding of fact 6.

Of particular pertinence, with accents added, are these injunctions of the Uniform Customs:

> "Article 7.—Banks must examine all documents with reasonable care to ascertain that they *appear on their face* to be in accordance with the terms and conditions of the credit."

> "Article 8.—In documentary credit operations all parties concerned deal in documents and not in goods.

>   *   *   *

> "If, upon receipt of the documents, the issuing bank considers that they *appear on their face* not to be in accordance with the terms and conditions of the credit, that bank must determine, on the basis of the documents alone, whether to claim that payment, acceptance or negotiation was not effected in accordance with the terms and conditions of the credit."

>   *   *   *

> "Article 9.—Banks *   *   * do [not] assume any liability or responsibility *for the description*, *   *   * quality, *   *   * of the goods represented thereby *   *   *"

>   *   *   *

"The description of the goods in the commercial *invoice* must correspond with the description in the credit. *In the remaining documents the goods may be described in general terms.*"

Also to be looked to are the North Carolina statutes, because in a diversity action, the Federal courts apply the same law as would the courts of the State of adjudication. Here applied would be the Uniform Commercial Code—Letters of Credit, Chap. 25 G.S.N.C. Especially to be noticed are these sections:

"§ 25–5–109. Issuer's obligation to its customer.—

"(1) An issuer's obligation to its customer includes good faith and observance of any general banking usage but unless otherwise agreed does not include liability or responsibility

"(a) for performance of the underlying contract for sale or other transaction between the customer and the beneficiary; or

*   *   *

"(c) based on knowledge or lack of knowledge of any usage of any particular trade.

"(2) An issuer must examine documents with care so as to ascertain that on their face they appear to comply with the terms of the credit but unless otherwise agreed assumes no liability or responsibility for the genuineness, falsification or effect of any document which appears on such examination to be regular on its face."

In utilizing the rules of construction embodied in the letter of credit—the Uniform Customs and state statute—one must constantly recall that the drawee bank is not to be embroiled in disputes between the buyer and the seller, the beneficiary of the credit. The drawee is involved only with documents, not with merchandise. Its involvement is altogether separate and apart from the transaction between the buyer and seller; its duties and liability are governed exclusively by the terms of the letter, not the terms of the parties' contract with each other. Moreover, as the predominant authorities unequivocally declare, the beneficiary must meet the terms of the credit—and precisely—if it is to exact performance of the issuer. Failing such compliance there can be no recovery from the drawee. That is the specific failure of Courtaulds here.

Free of ineptness in wording the letter of credit dictated that each invoice express on its face that it covered 100% acrylic yarn. Nothing less is shown to be tolerated in the trade. No substitution and no equivalent, through interpretation or logic, will serve. Harfield, Bank Credits and Acceptances (5th Ed. 1974), at p. 73, commends and quotes aptly from an English case: "There is no room for documents which are almost the same, or which will do just as well." Equitable Trust Co. of N.Y. v. Dawson Partners, Ltd., 27 Lloyd's List Law Rpts. 49, 52 (1926). Although no pertinent North Carolina decision has been laid before us, in many cases elsewhere, especially in New York, we find the tenet of Harfield to be unshaken.

At trial Courtaulds prevailed on the contention that the invoices in actuality met the specifications of the letter of credit in that the packing lists attached to the invoices disclosed on their faces that the packages contained "cartons marked:—100% acrylic". On this premise it was urged that the lists were a part of the invoice since they were appended to it, and the invoices should be read as one with the lists, allowing the lists to detail the invoices. But this argument cannot be accepted. In this connection it is well to revert to the distinction made in Uniform Customs, supra, between the "invoice" and the "remaining documents", emphasizing that in the latter the description may be in general terms while in the invoice the goods must be described in conformity with the credit letter.

The District Judge's pat statement adeptly puts an end to this contention of Courtaulds:

> "In dealing with letters of credit, it is a custom and practice of the banking trade for a bank to only treat a document as an invoice which clearly is marked on its face as 'invoice'". Finding of fact 46.

This is not a pharisaical or doctrinaire persistence in the principle, but is altogether realistic in the environs of this case; it is plainly the fair and equitable measure. (The defect in description was not superficial but occurred in the statement of the *quality* of the yarn, not a frivolous concern.) The obligation of the drawee bank was graven in the credit. Indeed, there could be no departure from its words. Bank was not expected to scrutinize the collateral papers, such as the packing lists. Nor was it permitted to read into the instrument the contemplation or intention of the seller and buyer. Adherence to this rule was not only legally commanded, but it was factually ordered also, as will immediately appear.

Had Bank deviated from the stipulation of the letter and honored the draft, then at once it might have been confronted with the not improbable risk of the bankruptcy trustee's charge of liability for unwarrantably paying the draft moneys to the seller, Courtaulds, and refusal to reimburse Bank for the outlay. Contrarily, it might face a Courtaulds claim that since it had depended upon Bank's assurance of credit in shipping yarn to Adastra, Bank was responsible for the loss. In this situation Bank cannot be condemned for sticking to the letter of the letter.

Nor is this conclusion affected by the amended or substituted invoices which Courtaulds sent to Bank after the refusal of the draft. No precedent is cited to justify retroactive amendment of the invoices or extension of the credit beyond the August 15 expiry of the letter.

Finally, the trial court found that although in its prior practices Bank had pursued a strict-constructionist attitude, it had nevertheless on occasion honored drafts not within the verbatim terms of the credit letter. But it also found that in each of these instances Bank had first procured the authorization of Adastra to overlook the deficiencies. This truth is verified by the District Court in its Findings of Fact:

"42. It is a standard practice and procedure of the banking industry and trade for a bank to attempt to obtain a waiver of discrepancies from its customer in a letter of credit transaction. This custom and practice was followed by NCNB in connection with the draft and documents received from Courtaulds.

"43. Following this practice, NCNB had checked all previous discrepancies it discovered in Courtaulds' documents with its customer Adastra to see if Adastra would waive those discrepancies noted by NCNB. Except for the transaction in question, Adastra waived all discrepancies noted by NCNB.

"44. It is not normal or customary for NCNB, nor is it the custom and practice in the banking trade, for a bank to notify a beneficiary or the presenter of the documents that there were any deficiencies in the draft or documents if they are waived by the customer."

This endeavor had been fruitless on the last draft because of the inability of Adastra to give its consent. Obviously, the previous acceptances of truant invoices cannot be construed as a waiver in the present incident.

For these reasons, we must vacate the decision of the trial court, despite the evident close reasoning and research of the District Judge, Courtaulds North America, Inc. v. North Carolina N.B., 387 F.Supp. 92 (M.D.N.C. 1975). Entry of judgment in favor of the appellant Bank on its summary motion is necessary.

Reversed and remanded for final judgment.

Notes

1. The two cases set out above are commonly cited as being in conflict. Applying the Uniform Customs and Practices (appendix to this chapter) to the two of them, can their holdings be read as consistent?

2. Assuming that their holdings are inconsistent and that Judge Coffin is truly espousing a less strict standard of interpretation, who is right and what policies are at issue?

The doctrines of estoppel and waiver found in the common law and those of indemnity and warranties set out in Article 5 offer, in the words of Judge Coffin, some "leaven" for the loaf. On the one hand they accommodate the practical necessity of paying in certain circumstances against documents that are not adequate. On the other hand they give some room for a court's requiring or approving deviation from the strict standards.

MARINO INDUSTRIES CORP. v. CHASE
MANHATTAN BANK, N.A.

United States Court of Appeals, Second Circuit, 1982.
686 F.2d 112.

FRIEDMAN, CHIEF JUDGE, UNITED STATES COURT OF CLAIMS. This is an appeal from a judgment of the United States District Court for the Eastern District of New York entered upon the opinion of United States Magistrate John L. Caden dismissing, after trial, a suit seeking recovery under two letters of credit that the defendant, Chase Manhattan Bank ("Chase"), issued to the plaintiff, Marino Industries Corp. ("Marino"). The magistrate held that Chase justifiably refused to pay under the letters because Marino had not complied with the requirements in the letters for obtaining payment. We affirm in part, reverse in part, and remand for further proceedings.

I.

The dispute grew out of a contract under which Marino, a manufacturer of construction materials, agreed with Bautechnik GmbH, a German company, to ship material to a job site in Kassim, Saudi Arabia. At Bautechnik's request, the Berliner Bank in West Germany issued two similar irrevocable letters of credit in favor of Marino. Chase confirmed the letters. One letter was for $212,456.48, and the other was for $489,956.41. Both letters explicitly were subject to the Uniform Customs and Practice for Documentary Credits (1974 Revision), International Chamber of Commerce Publication No. 290, which, under New York laws, supersedes the Uniform Commercial Code. N.Y.U.C.C.L. § 5–102(4) (McKinney 1964).

Each letter was to be paid in two installments: 40 percent when the goods were shipped and 60 percent when they were received. The letters contained detailed requirements that Marino was required to follow to obtain payment. Marino shipped all the goods to Saudi Arabia. After Bautechnik went bankrupt in late November or early December 1980, Chase refused to pay three of Marino's drafts under the letters, on the ground that Marino had not complied with the requirements for payment.

The complaint, filed in the district court after the suit had been transferred from the New York State Supreme Court where it originally had been filed, contains two counts. Count I seeks recovery of $99,083.80 for Chase's refusal to pay the plaintiff's draft for that amount under the first letter of credit. Count II seeks $270,779.84 for Chase's refusal to make payments of $46,388.00 and $224,391.84 under the second letter. Both parties agreed to a trial before a United States Magistrate.

After trial, the magistrate dismissed the complaint. He held that with respect to each of the three payments Chase refused to make, Marino had not complied with the requirements for payment in the letter. The magistrate rendered a comprehensive opinion discussing in detail the various respects in which he found that Marino had not complied, and made findings of fact and conclusions of law. Marino has appealed from the judgment dismissing the complaint, and Chase has cross-appealed from the magistrate's resolution of one subsidiary issue against Chase.

*   *   *

III.

Chase refused to pay three different drafts on the two letters that Marino presented. Since each refusal was made for different reasons, we discuss each claim separately. In determining whether Chase's refusal to pay was justified, we are guided by and apply the general principles governing letters of credit just summarized.

A. THE $99,000 CLAIM

The first claim was for $99,083.80. It was made under the 60 percent portion of the first letter of credit, i.e., Marino sought payment from Chase after the goods had been received in Saudi Arabia.

To obtain payment Marino was required to submit a certificate that the goods had been inspected prior to shipment and a certificate that the goods had been received. The letters specified precisely what these certificates were required to state. As extended, the letter of credit expired on Monday, December 1, 1980. This meant that to obtain payment Marino was required to submit by that date certificates that conformed to the requirements in the letter.

1. Marino submitted the inspection certificates on October 15, 1980. On October 17, a Chase employee prepared a discrepancy sheet covering the certificates, which noted various respects in which they did not comply with the requirements in the letter. One of the defects noted was that the certificates did not include copies of the invoices for the shipped goods. The discrepancy sheet contains handwritten comments based upon phone conversations with Marino. The record does not show when these comments were written or which of the deficiencies Chase called to Marino's attention.

On December 2, 1980, the day after the letter had expired, Chase returned the inspection certificates to Marino because the bank was "not able to utilize" them. An accompanying memorandum stated that Chase had "contacted Miss Cinthya [apparently a Marino employee] on the phone several times." It requested Marino: "Please complete requirement of L/C and send documents to us complete." On December 8, Marino resubmitted the inspection certificates to Chase.

2. The letter of credit required the certificates of receipt to be "signed by [a] Midica [sic] [Mdica was the joint venture in Saudi Arabia] representative confirming the arrival of the material on job site Kassim." An amendment to the letter of credit provided that in lieu of a Mdica signature, the notarized signature of the freight forwarder, Zuest & Bachmeier Ag., would be accepted. Berliner Bank had sent to Chase

three signature samples of Mdica representatives acceptable to it. Chase never told Marino that only those three signatures would be acceptable or that other signatures would be acceptable if they identified the signer as a Mdica representative (as a Chase representative testified at trial).

On Wednesday, November 26, 1980, a Marino representative, Mr. DeWeil, delivered the certificates of receipt to Pacifico Bautista in Chase's Letter of Credit Department. According to the magistrate, "Mr. Bautista refused to accept the certificates of receipt because they did not contain an authorized signature. * * * In order to rectify the absence of an authorized signature, Mr. Bautista told Mr. DeWeil to have the certificates of receipt countersigned by an officer of the international freight forwarding company, Zust Bachmeier." Mr. DeWeil had the certificates countersigned about 5 p.m., that day, but because it was then too late to return them to the bank, he took the certificates to Marino's office on Long Island.

Mr. Pagano, Marino's vice president in charge of exporting, testified that on Monday, December 1 (the date on which the letter expired), he told Mr. Bautista on the telephone that he had six countersigned certificates of receipt and asked Mr. Bautista when he should bring them in. According to Mr. Pagano, Mr. Bautista "decided that I could send them the following day and hopefully that we would get paid as soon as possible." On cross-examination Mr. Pagano stated that the expiration date of the letter had not been mentioned. Mr. Pagano mailed the certificates of receipt the following day (December 2).

On December 8, Chase informed Marino that it would not make payment because proper certificates had not been timely presented. On December 10 and 12, Chase, with Marino's approval, cabled the Berliner Bank, stated that payment had not been made "due to late presentation" and asked, "May we pay [?]" Berliner Bank cabled back "Do not pay * * * as presented too late." Berliner Bank also rejected a third cabled request from Chase for permission to pay.

3. The magistrate held that Marino had not made a timely presentation of the necessary documents and that Chase had not waived the requirement of timely presentation. He apparently accepted Chase's evidence that bringing documents to the bank and taking them back to have them countersigned, as happened on November 26, "is not a presentation of documents." The magistrate stated that documentary evidence showed that "a full set of documents was not received by Chase until December 8, 1980—eight days after the expiration of the letter of credit on November 30, 1980" and that "[i]n the face of such documentary proof, it is unrealistic to give credence to plaintiff's assertion that there was a timely presentation of conforming documents."

In holding that Chase had not waived the timely presentation requirement, the magistrate pointed to Pagano's admission that neither in his telephone conversation of December 1, 1980, with Mr. Bautista nor in a subsequent meeting with Ms. Soula Stephanides of Chase, at which Marino contended Chase also had waived timely presentation, was it mentioned that the letter had expired. The magistrate further ruled that Chase's cabled requests to the Berliner Bank to make late payment were not waivers but merely were "a courtesy to plaintiff."

4. As we have noted, an important corollary of the strict compliance rule is that the letter of credit must specify precisely and clearly the requirements for payment and that ambiguities in the letter are to be resolved against the bank. Nothing in the letter in this case indicated that the requirement that the certificates of receipt be "signed by [a] Mdica representative" could be satisfied only if one of the three acceptable signatures that Berliner Bank had submitted to Chase was affixed. If that was a condition of payment, Chase was required so to inform Marino. Sun Bank, 609 F.2d at 833; 34 N.Y.Jur. Letters of Credit § 13 at 431 (1964). Similarly, if Chase would accept signatures of other Mdica representatives provided they were expressly identified as such, as Chase's representative testified at trial, Chase also was required to inform Marino of that condition of payment.

The magistrate did not determine whether the signature on the certificates was that of a Mdica representative. On the remand that we order, the magistrate should determine that fact. If the answer is affirmative, Marino made a timely presentation of the certificates of receipt (on November 26) that complied with the requirements in the letter.

Even if Marino had not made a timely presentation on November 26, there is the question whether Chase waived the time limit when, according to Mr. Pagano, Mr. Bautista, on December 1, 1980, authorized Mr. Pagano to submit the documents after that date. The fact that neither Pagano nor Bautista referred to the expiration date of the bill in that conversation is not necessarily dispositive of the question, although it is significant. The magistrate did not determine whether Mr. Bautista had authority to make such a commitment. It would seem, however, that Mr. Bautista had at least apparent authority to do so, upon which Marino's representative was justified in relying.

5. If Marino made a timely presentation of proper certificates of receipt or if Chase waived the time limit, Marino still was not entitled to payment unless it also timely presented certificates of inspection. As noted, Marino supplied those certificates to Chase on October 15, well in advance of the expiration date of the letter.

Chase's initial inspection of those certificates revealed what Chase believed to be various defects, including the failure to include with the certificates copies of the invoices for the goods. The record does not show, however, whether at that time Chase called these alleged deficiencies to Marino's attention. When Chase finally returned the invoices to Marino for correction on December 2, 1980, the letter had expired.

The letter of credit required Marino to submit

"[c]lean inspection certificate, 4 copies, issued by superintendent-company acting in conformity with the regulations of S.G.S. (Societe Generale de Surveillance) stating the full compliance of the quantities and qualities of the goods with the specifications, the commercial invoice and the instructions given by Dietrich Garski Bautechnik KG, Berlin."

This is somewhat ambiguous. It is unclear whether Marino was required to submit a single inspection certificate stating that the goods complied with the three conditions, or to submit separately the certificates, the invoices and the instructions. In light of the obvious purpose of the requirement to insure that the goods shipped were as ordered, the most reasonable reading of the provision is that Marino was required to submit a single certificate stating that the "quantities and qualities of the goods" complied with "[i] the specifications, [ii] the commercial invoices, and [iii] the instructions given by" Bautechnik (the purchaser). The magistrate did not determine whether the certificates Marino submitted complied with this requirement.

A further problem with respect to the certificates of inspection is presented by the fact that Chase waited a month-and-a-half before returning them to Marino for correction. Under article 8(d) of the Uniform Customs & Practice for Documentary Credits, Chase had "a reasonable time" within which to examine the documentation. See N.Y.U.C.C. § 5–112(1)(a) (giving banks three banking days). If Chase had returned the certificates promptly, Marino would have had ample time to correct any deficiencies. By not returning the certificates until after the letter had expired, Chase made it impossible for Marino to correct any deficiencies and still make timely presentation. Cf. Barclays Bank D.C.O. v. Mercantile National Bank, 481 F.2d 1224, 1236 (5th Cir. 1973), cert dismissed, 414 U.S. 1139 (1974) (when bank says documents conform, it cannot then deny conformity after expiration). There is a question, therefore, whether Chase is estopped from relying upon defects in the certificates of inspection as a justification for refusing payment.

6. We therefore conclude that we cannot affirm the magistrate's dismissal of the $99,000 claim. The portion of the judgment that dismissed that claim is reversed, and this portion of the case is remanded to the magistrate for further proceedings in accordance with this opinion.

*   *   *

CONCLUSION

The judgment of the United States District Court for the Eastern District of New York is affirmed in part and reversed in part, and the case is remanded to it for further proceedings before the magistrate on the $99,000 claim in accordance with this opinion.

Problem 16–2

Chase was the beneficiary of a letter of credit issued by Equibank in Pittsburgh. The letter provided that Chase (the "take out" lender on a construction contract) had a right to draw upon Equibank if the underlying debtor failed to complete the loan transaction. Equibank was the interim lender to the developer. The developer failed to carry out the construction on time and on April 30 Chase sent (1) a certification "that [developer] has defaulted and the default has not been cured" and (2) a demand for payment of $108,000.

The letter of credit expired on April 30, 1973. In the afternoon of April 30 a representative of Chase had a phone conversation with a representative of Equibank. The Chase employee stated that the Equibank employee agreed that the document could be forwarded through "domestic collections." Because such collections take several days, the demand did not arrive in Pittsburgh until late in the first week of May when it was rejected on the ground the letter of credit had expired on April 30.

1. Can Chase win on the ground of estoppel?

2. Can it win on the ground of waiver?

3. Would it matter that only three hours intervened between the expiration of the letter on April 30 and the phone conversation?

4. On behalf of Chase can you use UCC 2–209?

DIXON, IRMAOS & CIA v. CHASE MANHATTAN Bank

United States Court of Appeals, Second Circuit, 1944.
144 F.2d 759.

SWAN, CIRCUIT JUDGE.

This appeal raises interesting and important questions as to letters of credit covering C.I.F. shipments abroad. The plaintiff, an exporter of cotton in Sao Paulo, Brazil, contracted to sell cotton to a purchaser in Belgium. A Belgian bank requested the Chase Bank to issue in favor of the plaintiff two irrevocable letters of credit for $7,000 and $3,500 respectively to finance such sales. Chase Bank did so and mailed them to Sao Paulo, where they were received by the plaintiff on May 2, 1940. They bound Chase Bank to honor 90 day drafts drawn under the credits, if presented at its office on or before May 15, 1940 and accompanied by specified documents, including a "full set of bills of lading" evidencing shipment of a stated quantity and quality of cotton "C.I.F. Ghent/Antwerp." One of the letters of credit (both being the same in form) is set out in the margin.[1] The plaintiff duly shipped the

1. "The Chase National Bank of The City of New York

"April 8, 1940.

"Confirmed Irrevocable Straight Credit

"Dixon Irmaos and Cia Ltda.,

"Sao Paulo, Brazil

"Gentlemen:

"We are instructed by Banque de Bruxelles, S.A., Brussels, Belgium to advise you that they have opened their irrevocable credit in your favor for account of by order of Georgie Alost under their credit Number 40466 for a sum or sums not exceeding

cotton to its Belgian customer in two lots, receiving for each shipment two originals of the bills of lading. Instead of prepaying freight the plaintiff shipped the goods freight collect and deducted the freight charges from the invoice price. Through the Guaranty Trust Company of New York, the plaintiff's representative, drafts and documents were presented to Chase Bank on May 15, 1940, but only one of the set of two bills of lading was delivered. In lieu of the other, which was in the mail and not yet arrived in New York, an indemnity agreement or guaranty against loss resulting from its absence was tendered by the Guaranty Trust Company.[2] Chase Bank had no objection to the form of the guaranty or to the responsibility of the guarantor, but it refused the drafts on two grounds: (1) Absence of a full set of the bills of lading and (2) failure to prepay the freight. The plaintiff then brought the present action to recover the amount of its drafts, $5,587.15 under the larger letter of credit and $2,757.49 under the smaller. The case was tried without a jury. At the conclusion of the evidence each side moved for judgment. Decision being reserved, the district judge thereafter rendered an opinion and filed findings of fact and law. He gave judgment for the defendant on the ground that the tender of less than a full set of bills of lading did not comply with the terms of the letters of credit.

Assuming for the moment that a C.I.F. shipment does not require the shipper to prepay freight if the freight charges are credited against the invoice price, the Guaranty Trust Company's tender to Chase Bank

a total of About $7000.00 (Seven Thousand Dollars) U.S. Currency available by your drafts on us at 90 days sight, in duplicate to be accompanied by

"Commercial invoice in triplicate, or invoice copy

"Insurance certificate which must cover land and sea risks into the mills, and showing merchandise covered onboard the steamer named and/or other steamer or steamers

"Full set bills of lading. Port or custody bills of lading acceptable evidencing shipment of 22 tons Bresilian Sao Paulo Cotton type MINI shipped during April 1940, CIF Ghent/Antwerp

"All documents in name of La Georgie.

"All drafts so drawn must be marked 'Drawn under Chase National Bank Credit No. E71582'

"The above mentioned correspondent engages with you that all drafts drawn under and in compliance with the terms of this credit will be duly honored on delivery of documents as specified if presented at this office on or before May 15, 1940; we confirm the credit and thereby undertake that all drafts drawn and presented as above specified will be duly honored by us.

"Unless otherwise expressly stated, this credit is subject to the uniform customs and practice for commercial documentary credits fixed by the Seventh Congress of the International Chamber of Commerce and certain guiding provisions.

"Yours very truly,

"C.F.Wellman
Assistant Manager

"F.N. Powelson
Assistant Cashier"

2. The Guaranty Trust Company's indemnity agreement stated:

"In consideration of your accepting the above described draft, we hereby agree to hold you harmless from any and all consequences which might arise due to the following discrepancy:

"Only 1 copy presented out of a set of 2 bills of lading issued.

"It is understood that this guarantee will remain in force until such time as you may obtain a release from your clients.

"We shall thank you to take the necessary steps to obtain this release as soon as possible and inform us promptly when it has been obtained."

of drafts and documents fully met the requirements of the letters of credit, except for the fact that one original bill of lading out of each set of two was missing. The plaintiff contends that this fact did not defeat the adequacy of its tender because the evidence established the existence of a custom among New York banks issuing letters of credit to finance a shipment from outside the United States and calling for a "full set of bills of lading", to accept in lieu of a missing part of the set a guaranty by a responsible New York bank against any loss resulting from the absence of the missing part. On this subject the trial judge made the following findings of fact:

"12. The letters of guaranty of the Guaranty Trust Company tendered to the defendant are in the usual form of guaranties tendered by and accepted by leading New York Banks issuing commercial credits, when less than all bills of lading are presented under credits calling for a full set of bills of lading.

"12A. The Guaranty Trust Company was and is a prime and leading New York bank with sound financial standing.

"12B. The defendant raised no objection to the form of the guaranties tendered by the Guaranty Trust Company nor with the financial responsibility of the Guaranty Trust Company.

"13. On May 15, 1940, and for some time prior thereto, there existed a general and uniform custom among New York banks, exporters and importers to the effect that in lieu of a missing bill or missing bills of lading presented under credits calling for a full set of bills of lading, that the bank issuing the credits would accept in lieu of the missing bill or bills of lading, a guaranty of a leading New York bank, if it determined the guaranty to be satisfactory in form and if it was satisfied as to the responsibility of the bank issuing the guaranty. The bank issuing the credit was, however, free to exercise its own discretion and make its own determination as to whether it would accept a guaranty in lieu of a missing bill of lading."

We are not entirely clear as to the meaning of the final sentence of finding 13. If it means that the issuer of credit is free to reject the tendered guaranty if doubts are entertained regarding the guarantor's financial responsibility or the sufficiency of the form of the document, it is not inconsistent with the custom stated in the first sentence and may be disregarded; in these respects Chase Bank was satisfied with the guaranty tendered by Guaranty Trust Company. But if it means that even when so satisfied the bank issuing the credit may reject the tendered guaranty and refuse to accept the draft, it is inconsistent with the stated custom and is unsupported by the evidence. Numerous witnesses, experts in the fields of banking and of commerce, testified to the existence of the custom; not one testified to a single instance where a tender such as was here made had been rejected and the draft dishonored solely on the ground that the set of bills of lading was incomplete. Indeed, it is clear that the Chase Bank would in this very case have honored the drafts, had they been presented before the

German invasion of Belgium. One of its witnesses naively said that before May 15, 1940 it was the custom to accept such a guaranty as was tendered, but not on that date or thereafter—as though the determining moment were not at the latest when the plaintiff acted upon the letters of credit. In short, the existence of the custom was established beyond dispute.

It is true, as the defendant argues, that the law requires strict compliance with the terms of a letter of credit. International Banking Corp. v. Irving Nat. Bank, 2 Cir., 283 F. 103. It is likewise true that numerous cases, several of which are cited by the defendant, declare that evidence of a custom is not admissible to contradict the unambiguous terms of a written contract.

* * *

* * * But it is also well settled "that parties who contract on a subject-matter concerning which known usages prevail, incorporate such usages by implication into their agreements, if nothing is said to the contrary." Hostetter v. Park, 137 U.S. 30, 40, 11 S.Ct. 1, 4, 34 L.Ed. 568. * * *

Williston, Contracts, rev. ed. §§ 650, 652, 1081A. In our opinion the custom under consideration explains the meaning of the technical phrase "full set of bills of lading" and is incorporated by implication into the terms of the defendant's letters of credit. No authority on the precise point has come to our attention. The statement of Bankes, L.J. in Scott & Co., Ltd. v. Barclay's Bank, Ltd., [1923] 2 K.B. 1, 11, upon which the defendant relies, is inapposite because no custom such as the court found here was there proved or attempted to be proved. Finally, the defendant urges that the reference in the concluding paragraph of the letters of credit to the uniform customs and practice for commercial documentary credits fixed by the Seventh Congress of the International Chamber of Commerce excludes incorporation into the contracts of any other custom. We do not think so. Those customs do not deal with the meaning of a "full set of bills of lading." Hence the problem whether the New York custom gives meaning to those words is unaffected by the reference to those other customs. The reasonableness and utility of the local New York custom is obvious. It is absolutely essential to the expeditious doing of business in overseas transactions in these days when one part of the bill of lading goes by air and another by water. Unless an indemnity can be substituted for the delayed part, not only does quick clearance of such transactions become impossible but also the universal practice of issuing bills of ladings in sets and sending the different parts by separate mails loses much of its purpose. We conclude therefore that the defendant's first ground for dishonor of the drafts was not a valid reason.

The second ground for dishonor was that while the credits specified a C.I.F. shipment, the plaintiff deducted freight charges from the invoices and shipped the goods freight collect. On this subject the court made the following findings:

"15. The ordinary and accepted meaning of a C.I.F. contract is that the contract price includes the cost of the goods, the cost of insurance and the cost of freight to the point of destination. The term does not imply the time when or the place where the freight is to be paid and there was no uniform practice in New York on May 15, 1940 or prior thereto of prepaying freight to the point of destination under a C.I.F. shipment. The practice was that it was sometimes prepaid and sometimes deducted from the invoice.

"16. The 'American Foreign Trade Definitions' are incorporated by reference in the letters of credit and such definitions, including the definition of a C.I.F. contract, is a part of the credit. Under the definition of a C.I.F. contract as defined in 'American and Foreign Trade Definitions' there is no requirement that a shipper must prepay freight.

*   *   *

"18. The tender of documents showing a deduction of freight from the invoices was not a deviation from the requirement of defendant's credits calling for C.I.F. shipment."

We agree with this conclusion. In the case of a sight draft, it is wholly immaterial to the buyer whether freight is prepaid or credit given on the invoice price. In the case of a time draft, it is true that the buyer may be deprived of the credit period as to part of the purchase price, that is, so much of it as the freight amounts to. In the case at bar the freight was $1359.14. The measure of any possible loss to the buyer is the interest upon this sum for the period between arrival of the goods and the date the drafts would fall due and the possible inconvenience of being called upon for early payment in cash of this portion of the price. The bills of lading were endorsed "on board" on May 5th and, if we assume the voyage would take 30 days, the buyer would not be called upon for the freight until June 5th. The draft if accepted on May 15th would have been due 90 days later, that is, the buyer would have had to pay freight about 70 days earlier than he would otherwise have paid such sum. Interest at 6% would amount to about $17. On a transaction involving about $9,700 such a sum is insignificant. The law has not cut so fine. The point of possible inconvenience is taken care of by ancient usage. The seller has so long had the option of shipping either freight collect or freight prepaid that the cases recognize the option as part of the standard meaning of the term C.I.F., making no distinction between prepayment or shipping freight collect and crediting it on the invoice irrespective of whether the draft be time or sight. *   *   * As the court pointed out in finding 16 the American and Foreign Trade definitions provide that under a C.I.F. contract the seller must pay the freight but make no mention of prepayment. Furthermore, if the buyer sells the documents before arrival of the goods, as frequently happens in C.I.F. transactions, whether freight was prepaid will be wholly immaterial to him.

The judgment for the defendant is reversed and judgment directed in favor of the plaintiff.

Notes

1. What was the real reason Chase and its customer did not want to pay in this case?

2. Can you formulate a general rule that would tell you when custom may be used to repair an apparently defective presentation of documents and when custom would not achieve this?

FIRST ARLINGTON NATIONAL BANK v. STATHIS
Court of Appeals of Illinois, 1983.
115 Ill.App.3d 402, 71 Ill.Dec. 195, 450 N.E.2d 833.

SULLIVAN, J. This appeal is from the entry of summary judgment for Gus Stathis (defendant) in an action for declaratory judgment brought to determine the rights and obligations of the parties under a letter of credit issued by the plaintiff bank. Plaintiff contends that the trial court erred in ruling that (1) none of the exceptions contained in § 5–114(2) of the Uniform Commercial Code (the Code) (Ill.Rev.Stat. 1979, ch. 26, par. 5–114(2)) excused plaintiff's duty to honor the letter of credit; (2) defendant did not breach any warranties made by him pursuant to § 5–111(1) of the Code (Ill.Rev.Stat. 1979, ch. 26, par. 5–111(1)); (3) none of the other warranty sections of the Code were applicable to the transaction in question; and (4) defendant was entitled to prejudgment interest pursuant to § 2 of "An Act in relation to the rate of interest and other charges in connection with sales on credit and the lending of money" (the Interest Act) (Ill.Rev.Stat. 1979, ch. 74, par. 2) [1] from the date of his demand for payment. In his cross-appeal, defendant maintains that the trial court erred in limiting its award of prejudgment interest to 5%.

In a prior appeal in this case, First Arlington National Bank v. Stathis (1980), 90 Ill.App.3d 802, 413 N.E.2d 1288, we reversed the trial court's entry of summary judgment for plaintiff and remanded for further consideration of defendant's cross-motion for summary judgment. The facts of the transaction in question are set forth in detail in that opinion, and the parties presented no additional evidence after remand; therefore, we shall repeat only such facts as are relevant to the issues herein.

In 1973, defendant agreed to sell certain real estate to Ralph Edgar, Denis Rintz, and Phillip Grandinetti, Jr., and as partial consideration therefor received a promissory note dated March 30, 1973 (the March note), executed by the three purchasers and their wives in the principal amount of $575,000 with an interest rate of 8% on the outstanding principal. The debt was to be secured by a letter of credit

---

1. Now codified at Ill.Rev.Stat. 1981, ch.
17, par. 6402.

in the amount of $575,000 which was to be replaced each year at least 30 days before its expiration date. If the letter of credit was not renewed, or if the purchasers defaulted in the payment of either interest or principal, the balance due was immediately payable without notice.

Plaintiff issued the required letter of credit, to expire May 5, 1974, in exchange for a note executed by Rintz, Edgar, and Grandinetti in the principal amount of $575,000 at 10% interest, secured by certain property, and the pledge of collateral, i.e., a certificate of deposit in the amount of $187,000 owned by Grandinetti and real estate owned by Rintz and Edgar. The letter of credit guaranteed payment of $575,000 to defendant upon default of the March note, provided that his demand was accompanied by the March note, endorsed by him without recourse to the order of plaintiff; any documents securing the note; defendant's notarized statement that the note was due by reason of acceleration and a detailed statement of the nature of the default; defendant's notarized statement that demand had been made on the makers, and the demand was not complied with for a period of at least 10 days following the demand; and copies of the demand letters.

The makers defaulted on the first payment of interest, due on March 30, 1974, and failed to provide a timely renewal of the letter of credit. On April 23, 1974, Grandinetti, desirous of avoiding litigation concerning the interest due, entered into an agreement with defendant (the Grandinetti agreement). Pursuant thereto, Grandinetti executed a note for one-third of the first interest installment, due June 5, 1974, and a second note for the remaining two-thirds, payable on demand. Defendant agreed to attempt to collect the remaining two-thirds of the interest from the Edgars and Rintzes (Grandinetti's wife was not mentioned) and, if successful, cancel the second note.[2]

On April 25, 1974, defendant sought payment on the letter of credit and presented to plaintiff the documents required by the terms thereof. Plaintiff refused to pay, claiming that, among other defects, the March note did not comply with the letter of credit in that the Grandinetti agreement effectively released Grandinetti's wife from liability on the March note and, as a result, released the other comakers as well by application of § 3–606 of the Code. (Ill.Rev.Stat. 1979, ch. 26, par. 3–606.) It filed a complaint for declaratory judgment and, in granting plaintiff's motion for summary judgment therein and denying defendant's cross-motion, the trial court ruled that plaintiff was not required to honor the letter of credit as a result of the Grandinetti agreement. On appeal, we held that plaintiff could not look beyond the documents presented to the underlying agreement in determining whether to honor the letter of credit. (First Arlington National Bank v. Stathis (1980), 90 Ill.App.3d 802, 809, 413 N.E.2d 1288, 1295.) Since the documents presented complied on their face with the letter of credit (90

2. This unpaid interest was the subject matter of defendant's counterclaim against the Grandinettis, Edgars, and Rintzes, which is not before us in this appeal.

Ill.App.3d 802, 816, 413 N.E.2d 1288, 1299) and there was no fraud arising from the Grandinetti agreement which would justify dishonoring the letter of credit (90 Ill.App.3d 802, 811, 413 N.E.2d 1288, 1295), plaintiff was required to honor the demand pursuant to § 5–114 of the Code (Ill.Rev.Stat. 1979, ch. 26, par. 5–114), and we reversed the order granting summary judgment to plaintiff and denying it to defendant. However, because plaintiff had raised other arguments in opposition to defendant's motion for summary judgment which were not considered by the trial court in ruling thereon, we remanded the matter for further consideration.

On remand, the parties agreed that the only remaining issue with regard to defendant's motion for summary judgment was whether he breached any warranties on presentment of his draft for payment under the letter of credit. Plaintiff argued that the Grandinetti agreement, which allegedly released Grandinetti's comakers from liability on the March note, and defendant's failure to deliver to it the personal judgment notes executed by Grandinetti under the agreement, breached warranties made by defendant under §§ 5–111, 3–417, 4–207, 7–507, and 8–306 of the Code. (Ill.Rev.Stat. 1979, ch. 26, pars. 5–111, 3–417, 4–207, 7–507, 8–306.) The trial court concluded that our prior opinion barred any consideration of the Grandinetti agreement as grounds for dishonoring the letter of credit. However, it went on to rule that the only applicable warranty was § 5–111(1), and that defendant warranted thereunder merely that the tendered documents complied on their face with the terms of the letter of credit; that this warranty was not breached; and that, in any event, the Grandinetti agreement did not release any of the comakers, contrary to plaintiff's assertion. It further ruled that defendant was entitled to prejudgment interest from April 25, 1974, the date of his demand for payment, at the rate of 5%, "although a greater rate of interest would be more equitable in the present situation." These cross-appeals followed.

OPINION

Plaintiff first contends that the trial court erred in ruling that none of the exceptions to an issuer's duty to honor a demand which complies on its face with the terms of the letter of credit excused plaintiff's duty to honor. It relies on § 5–114(2)(b) of the Code (Ill.Rev.Stat. 1979, ch. 26, par. 5–114(2)(b)), which provides in relevant part:

> "(2) Unless otherwise agreed when documents appear on their face to comply with the terms of a credit but a required document does not in fact conform to the warranties made on negotiation or transfer of a document of title (Section 7–507) or of a security (Section 8–306) or is forged or fraudulent or there is fraud in the transaction
>
>   *   *   *
>
> "(b) * * * as against its customer, an issuer acting in good faith may honor the draft or demand for payment despite notification from the customer of fraud, forgery or other defect not apparent on the face

of the documents but a court of appropriate jurisdiction may enjoin such honor."

The trial court held that the warranties under §§ 7–507 and 8–306 (Ill.Rev.Stat. 1979, ch. 26, pars. 7–507, 8–306) are inapplicable to the transaction in question and that plaintiff could not relitigate the question of fraud in the transaction, which was decided adversely to it in our prior opinion. Plaintiff apparently concedes the inapplicability of §§ 7–507 and 8–306 but maintains that the trial court read § 5–114(2)(b) too restrictively, and that the intent of the drafters was clearly to include not only the warranties arising thereunder but also those arising under §§ 3–417 and 4–207 (Ill.Rev.Stat. 1979, ch. 26, pars. 3–417, 4–207). It further argues that because defendant did not disclose the Grandinetti agreement when making presentment, the fraud contemplated by § 5–114(2)(b) was present.

With regard to its first argument, plaintiff cites as its sole authority the official comment to the Code. (Ill.Ann.Stat., ch. 26, par. 5–114, Uniform Commercial Code Comment, at 600 (Smith-Hurd 1963).) However, a careful reading of that commentary in its entirety discloses no such intention to include warranties other than those specifically mentioned in the statute. Therefore, we must look to the general rules of statutory construction to determine the intention of the drafters. The statutory language itself is the best indicator of that intention

* * * In the instant case, the language used by the legislature is unambiguous and leaves no room for expansion by the interpretation. Two code sections are specifically set forth, and had the legislature wished to include others, it could have done so easily, as it did in § 5–111(1) of the Code (Ill.Rev.Stat. 1979, ch. 26, par. 5–111(1)). Moreover, even if we were to resort to rules of construction, the most pertinent in the instant situation is that the enumeration of certain exceptions in a statute implies the exclusion of all others. (People ex rel. Difanis v. Barr (1980), 83 Ill.2d 191, 414 N.E.2d 731.) Thus, express inclusion of §§ 7–507 and 8–306 here would imply that the legislature intended to exclude all other warranty provisions.

* * * Plaintiff next contends that the trial court erred in ruling that defendant did not breach any warranties made by him under § 5–111(1) of the Code (Ill.Rev.Stat. 1979, ch. 26, par. 5–111(1)). It argues that the trial court construed this warranty too narrowly in holding that defendant warranted thereunder merely that the documents submitted complied on their face with the terms of the credit. Plaintiff theorizes that this warranty provision also "protects both the issuer of a letter of credit and its customers from the harsh and limiting effects of the rule that an issuer must honor a demand for payment if the documents appear on their face to conform to the terms of the credit." Therefore, it posits, § 5–111(1) permits it to do what § 5–114 forbids; that is, look to the underlying contract between defendant and its customers in determining whether it has a duty to honor the letter of credit.

Section 5–111(1) provides in relevant part that " * * * the beneficiary by transferring or presenting a documentary draft or demand for payment warrants to all interested parties that the necessary conditions of the credit have been complied with * * *." (Ill.Rev.Stat. 1979, ch. 26, par. 5–111(1).) The parties have not cited, nor has our own research discovered, any cases delineating the scope of the phrase "the necessary conditions of the credit." Neither the Illinois nor the official commentary to the Code defines the phrase in question. The official comment states that "[t]he purpose of this section is to state the peculiar warranty of performance made by a beneficiary * * *." (Ill.Ann.Stat., ch. 26, par. 5–111, Uniform Commercial Code Comment, at 590 (Smith-Hurd 1963).) The Illinois comment appears to acknowledge an ambiguity in the phrase by stating that "[t]he term 'necessary conditions of credit' is not a defined one. It presumably includes the genuineness of the documents. Beyond that the cases are not clear." (Ill.Ann.Stat., ch. 26, par. 5–111, Illinois Code Comment, at 590 (Smith-Hurd 1963).) However, two recent decisions in other states imply that § 5–111(1) is at least coextensive with § 5–114.

In Werner v. A.L. Grootemaat & Sons (1977), 80 Wis.2d 513, 259 N.W.2d 310, the court stated, in dictum, that an issuer who wrongfully honors may have a remedy against the beneficiary under § 5–111(1). (80 Wis.2d 513, 524–25 n. 22, 259 N.W.2d 310, 315–16 n. 22.) Since an issuer wrongfully honors only when it pays on presentation of documents which do not conform on their face to the terms of the credit, a beneficiary warrants under § 5–111(1) that the documents do conform. Werner further indicates that a customer would have a breach of warranty action under § 5–111(1) if the issuer were to honor a letter of credit despite the existence of one of the exceptions set forth in § 5–114(2)(b), as it is permitted to do under that section without jeopardizing its right to reimbursement. (80 Wis.2d 513, 524, 259 N.W.2d 310, 315.) The latter interpretation is also evident, although unstated, in Boucher & Slack Contractors, Inc. v. McLean (La.App. 1980), 382 So.2d 1030, 1034, and supported by the official commentary to § 5–114, which states in relevant part:

> "When * * * no innocent third parties * * * are involved the issuer is no longer under a duty to honor; but * * * the issuer if he acts in good faith is given the privilege of honoring the draft as against its customer, that is to say, with a right of reimbursement against him. * * * In the event of honor, an action by the customer against the beneficiary will lie by virtue of either the underlying contract or Section 5–111(1) of this Article." Ill.Ann.Stat., ch. 26, par. 5–114, Uniform Commercial Code Comment, at 601 (Smith-Hurd 1963).

It appears, then, that the warranties of § 5–111(1) are at least as broad as the circumstances encompassed by § 5–114. Even this interpretation, however, is too narrow to justify denial of summary judgment for defendant, since we have already determined that the documents in question comply on their face with the terms of the letter of credit, and none of the exceptions set forth in § 5–114 are applicable to this transaction. For this reason plaintiff asserts, as noted above, that the warranties of § 5–111(1) are broader in scope and allow the court to go beyond the face of the documents and consider the facts and circumstances of the underlying contract between defendant and its customers. In effect, plaintiff asserts it is not enough that it is protected by its right of reimbursement under § 5–114(3) if it rightfully honors the letter of credit, and by the beneficiary's warranty under § 5–111(1) if it wrongfully honors. It would have us hold that under § 5–111(1) it may also take advantage of any defenses its customers might have to the underlying contract, even where those defenses fall short of the defenses contemplated by § 5–114(2)(b).

The obvious flaw in plaintiff's position is that, if adopted, it would convert the letter of credit into a contract of guaranty or suretyship, for it destroys the sole distinguishing feature between them. As our supreme court stated in Pastor v. National Republic Bank (1979), 76 Ill.2d 139, 147, 390 N.E.2d 894, 897:

> "Although the use of letters of credit is often referred to as being in the nature of a guaranty or a suretyship arrangement, it does not assume the legal significance of either. Under the letter of credit the issuer is bound in the first instance to pay the beneficiary. It is an individual undertaking of the issuer to pay the beneficiary, and the obligation is not subject to the various defenses available to a guaranty or a surety undertaking."

Thus, under a guaranty, the courts must look to the rights and obligations of the parties to the underlying contract in determining the rights and obligations of the guarantor, for a true guaranty is a secondary obligation (Republic National Bank v. Northwest National Bank (Tex. 1978), 578 S.W.2d 109, 114); whereas, a letter of credit is a primary obligation independent of the underlying transaction (Professional Modular Surface, Inc. v. Uniroyal, Inc. (1982), 108 Ill.App.3d 1046, 440 N.E.2d 117). Therefore, even an agreement among beneficiaries and customers releasing or cancelling the underlying obligation will not affect a beneficiary's right to demand payment on an irrevocable letter of credit. (See Housing Securities, Inc. v. Maine National Bank (Me. 1978), 391 A.2d 311.) If we were to accept plaintiff's argument, the stringent duty to honor contained in § 5–114(1) would be completely abrogated, destroying the basic purpose of a letter of credit "to eliminate the risk to the beneficiary that the customer will refuse or halt payment because of alleged deficiencies in the beneficiary's performance." O'Grady v. First Union National Bank (1978), 296 N.C. 212, 232, 250 S.E.2d 587, 600.

For these reasons, we believe that the basic warranties under § 5–111(1) are that the documents comply on their face with the terms of the letter of credit, and that none of the exceptions set forth in § 5–114(2)(b) are present. The warranty provisions do not authorize the issuer to assert defenses which its customer might have to the underlying contract. We need not determine under the facts before us whether other warranties are encompassed by the provision that "the necessary conditions of the credit have been complied with."

We turn next to defendant's assertion of error in the trial court's ruling that defendant did not breach any other warranties under the Code. Section 5–111(1) provides that the warranties contained therein are "in addition to any warranties arising under Articles 3, 4, 7 and 8." (Ill.Rev.Stat. 1979, ch. 26, par. 5–111(1).) Plaintiff contends that the warranties arising under §§ 3–417 and 4–207 (Ill.Rev.Stat. 1979, ch. 26, pars. 3–417, 4–207) relating to the presentment and transfer of negotiable instruments are applicable to the present situation because defendant was required to transfer the March note to it. It argues that defendant has breached thereunder his warranties that he has good title to the instrument, that the transfer is otherwise rightful, and that no defense of any party is good against him.

Initially, we note that the warranties made under §§ 3–417 and 4–207 are identical in their terms, except that § 3–417 is applicable to one who obtains payment or transfers an instrument and receives consideration therefor, while § 4–207 applies to customers and collecting banks that obtain payment or transfer for consideration. It is unclear to us why plaintiff persists in its argument that both are applicable here, since it admits that the warranties are the same. Nevertheless, it is our view that § 4–207 is obviously inapplicable to the present situation, since defendant is neither a collecting bank as defined in § 4–105(d) of the Code (Ill.Rev.Stat. 1979, ch. 26, par. 4–105(d)) nor a customer as defined in § 4–104(1)(e) (Ill.Rev.Stat. 1979, ch. 26, par. 4–104(1)(e)).

With regard to § 3–417, we note that it is applicable to "[a]ny person who transfers an instrument and receives consideration." (Ill.Rev.Stat. 1979, ch. 26, par. 3–417(2).) It is established that these warranties are not made by one who does not receive consideration. (Oak Park Currency Exchange, Inc. v. Maropoulos (1977), 48 Ill.App.3d 437, 363 N.E.2d 54.) Plaintiff posits that if it were to pay defendant's demand, he would receive consideration for the March note. However, plaintiff's obligation to pay is unrelated to the March note; it is obligated to pay under the letter of credit, and will pay on the draft presented as provided in the letter of credit. If § 3–417 has any application at all in this situation, it is to that draft, not to the underlying note, and plaintiff has not pointed to any warranties breached by defendant's presentment of the draft for payment.

Furthermore, it is our view that plaintiff is not injured in any way by the alleged inability to recover on the March note. Since we have determined that it must honor the letter of credit, plaintiff has a right of reimbursement reinforced by a secured note at 10% interest. Surely that means of recovery is preferable to an unsecured, defaulted note bearing 8% interest. In addition, even assuming arguendo that defendant made the warranty asserted under § 3–417, we do not believe that there are any defenses good against him. Plaintiff argues that defendant's alleged release of Mrs. Grandinetti from liability for the accrued interest released Mrs. Rintz and Mrs. Edgar from liability on the March note pursuant to § 3–606 of the Code. (Ill.Rev.Stat. 1979, ch. 26, par. 3–606.) However, that section provides in relevant part that "[t]he holder discharges any party to the instrument *to the extent that* * * * the holder * * * releases or agrees not to sue any person against whom the party has * * * a right of recourse * * *." (Emphasis added.) The phrase "to the extent that" indicates that a release may be pro tanto, and courts considering the phrase have so held, whether the release was the result of impairment of the right of recourse (Provident Bank v. Gast (1979), 57 Ohio St.2d 102, 386 N.E.2d 1357) or impairment of collateral (Farmers State Bank v. Cooper (1980), 227 Kan. 547, 608 P.2d 929). Thus, it appears that when the person against whom a right of recourse is held is partially discharged, others who are only secondarily liable are also discharged, but only to the extent that their rights have been impaired.

In the instant case, the alleged release of Mrs. Grandinetti arises from the omission of her name from the following paragraph of the Grandinetti agreement:

"4. That said judgment note for $32,515.11 is being executed and delivered by GRANDINETTI for the purpose of indemnifying STATHIS with regard to the aforesaid balance of interest due him and STATHIS hereby agrees as follows:

(a) That he shall pursue * * * RALPH EDGAR, JUDY EDGAR * * *, DENIS J. RINTZ and MARILYN RINTZ * * * for the collection of said balance of interest in the sum of $32,515.11 * * *."

Such a release, however, would only relieve Mrs. Grandinetti of liability for the $32,515.11 in interest. It follows that the other accommodation makers would be released only to the extent that their right of recourse against Mrs. Grandinetti is impaired; that is, on two-thirds of the first interest installment. Since the paragraph in question does not purport to release Mrs. Grandinetti from liability on the note, it could not release Mrs. Rintz or Mrs. Edgar thereon.

Plaintiff has made herein a number of assertions unsupported by pertinent citations to authority or argument as required by Supreme Court Rule 341(e)(7) (73 Ill.2d R. 341(e)(7)). First, in arguing that it was excused from honoring by virtue of defendant's breach of warranties under § 511(1), plaintiff maintained that defendant was obliged to transfer to it "the whole note," including the accrued interest which was the subject matter of the Grandinetti agreement. It cited four cases in support of its proposition that it, rather than defendant, was entitled to that interest—all of which were totally inapplicable and, if they had any value, supported defendant's position. Moreover, plaintiff failed to cite authority for its contention that the interest was unpaid when it received the March note, although defendant admittedly took two notes as payment of accrued interest *before* transferring the March note to plaintiff. Next, plaintiff states that defendant breached three warranties under § 3–417; i.e., that no defense was good against him, that he had good title to the March note, and that the transfer was otherwise rightful. Despite this assertion, plaintiff has neither cited authority nor presented arguments with regard to the latter two warranties. Finally, plaintiff makes the conclusory statement, unsupported by argument or citation, that the Grandinetti agreement, which concerned solely the payment of accrued interest, constituted an extension of time for payment of the March note. It argues that this alleged extension of time released the accommodation makers under § 3–606, thus breaching defendant's warranties under § 4–317, but apparently expects us to take the underlying premise on faith. It is unnecessary for us to address any of these arguments, since the first is disposed of by our determination that plaintiff may not look to the underlying agreement in deciding whether to honor the letter of credit, and the latter two are irrelevant since we have ruled that § 3–417 is inapplicable to the present transaction. However, even if those arguments were not so disposed of, we would be justified in deeming them waived (Department of Transportation v. Association of Franciscan Fathers (1981), 93 Ill.App.3d 1141, 418 N.E.2d 36) for, as one court aptly stated, "a reviewing court is entitled to have the issues clearly defined with pertinent authority cited and is not simply a depository in which the appealing party may dump the burden of argument and research" (Williamson v. Opsahl (1981), 92 Ill.App.3d 1087, 1089, 416 N.E.2d 783, 784).

*   *   *

For the foregoing reasons, the orders of the trial court are affirmed.

Affirmed.

WILSON, P.J., and LORENZ, J., concur. [Some footnotes omitted.]

Notes

1. The warranty provision in UCC 5–111 is infrequently cited. Surely the *Stathis* court is correct in concluding that it should not be read to incorporate the idea of compliance with the underlying contract; otherwise, it would completely override the principle that the underlying contract and the contract to pay are separate. Presumably it would give rise to a cause of action for breach of warranty in a case in which there was a forged indorsement. It might have an impact in other cases as well, but case law, at least, does not recognize any significant area for its operation.

2. Can you think of a case where it would clearly apply?

3. Consider its impact in the following situation: Beneficiary presents documents that fail to comply with the terms of the credit in some detail that would have permitted bank to refuse payment. Bank overlooks or ignores the detail and pays only to find that its customer has not reimbursed it and has in fact filed in Chapter 11 that very day. Bank sues Beneficiary for return of its payment citing 5–111.

Problem 16–3

Assume the Bank has asked you whether it must pay in each of the following cases:

1. Letter of credit calls for "clean bill of lading." The bills presented contain the notation "Shippers load and count." Does that make them not clean?

2. What of a bill of lading that says "Carrier not responsible for rust." See Articles 17 and 18 of the UCP.

3. A letter of credit issued to the beneficiary "Danish Furniture Company" calls for invoices specifying certain items. Ultimately a draft is presented together with invoices that correctly describe the goods, but the invoices are those of "Copenhagen Manufacturers," not of "Danish Furniture Company." Beneficiary asserts that the two companies are one and the same. Must Bank pay? (See UCC 5–116.)

Problem 16–4

National Builders agreed to sell two prefabricated houses to Mohammud Sofan, a resident of the Yemen Arab Republic. Sofan procured a letter of credit issued by the Yemen Bank for Reconstruction in favor of National Builders. Irving Bank in New York was the confirming bank and National Builders designated National Bank of Washington as its collecting bank. National Bank of Washington sent Irving all of the documents required, but there were several discrepancies, among them the fact that the bill of lading listing the party to be notified by the shipping company as "Mohammud Soran." Irving agreed to request authorization from the Yemen Bank to pay the letter of credit despite the discrepancy. No authorization was forthcoming, and Irving refused to pay. National Builders now sues Irving and argues among other things the following:

1. A mistake as to a single letter in a name is insignificant and forms no basis for dishonor.

2. National Bank's promise to indemnify if the name in fact caused confusion on delivery to Yemen and to hold it harmless for any damages suffered because of the presence of the letter "r" instead of "f" required it to honor.

3. Irving was estopped from claiming the discrepancy because it held the documents for several days before it notified National Bank of Washington of the deficiency.

4. In any event the case should not have been decided on summary judgment because there was a legitimate issue of fact on the question whether "Soran" properly identifies "Sofan."

Problem 16–5

1. Bank calls you in with the following problem. It appears that Bank issued a letter of credit on behalf of its customer, a football team in a newly formed professional league to the beneficiary, who was their star quarterback, Lance Bugalowski. At the time the bank issued a letter of

credit, it believed that the football team would make a go of it, and it issued the credit despite the fact that the team had no security. The team is now teetering on the verge of bankruptcy. It appears unlikely that the league will operate in the next year. Unfortunately the letter of credit obligation to Bugalowski is for $500,000 each of the next three years. The letter has an expiration date three years hence. It says neither that it is revocable or irrevocable. Is the letter revocable and, if so, can the bank revoke it and thus avoid its obligation to Bugalowski? Assume alternatively that the letter is governed by the Uniform Customs and Practices or by the Uniform Commercial Code.

2. Assume that one year has passed and that the football team has gone into bankruptcy and that Bugalowski is about to make a demand on the letter. From reading the local press you understand that Bugalowski has now signed a contract as the principal quarterback for a west coast NFL team and, according to the papers, will be earning in excess of $750,000 a year. Presumably that gain would be set off as mitigation against any damages that he could claim against the customer. Can the bank use that fact to escape any obligation to pay?

A youngster in your office has suggested the following: Any demand now would breach the warranties under UCC 5–111 because Bugalowski does not meet the conditions, namely, having a good claim against the club. Secondly, the youngster has suggested that the Bank simply refuse to pay, take an assignment of the club's rights against Bugalowski and assert them in a counterclaim when he sues the Bank. Will the trustee in bankruptcy of the Club agree to such an assignment, and if so, will it work? Finally, your colleague has suggested that the automatic stay under 362 as applied in the Club's bankruptcy will bar any suit against the Bank by Bugalowski. What do you suggest?

At this point the student would be wise to read the entire Uniform Customs and Practices. It is hardly useful to attempt to remember everything reported there, but it would be well to know the kinds of things that one might find there and to file away the UCP as a source of information on what terms and documents are acceptable and what ones are not. Note, for example, the rule in Article 34 that in many cases will permit a tolerance of plus or minus three percent. There too one finds a definition of the word "about" or "circa."

SECTION 3. ISSUER'S RIGHT TO DISHONOR BECAUSE OF FRAUD

Section 5–114(2) recognizes the bank's right to refuse to honor where a document is "forged or fraudulent or there is fraud in the transaction ＊ ＊ ＊". Note, however that UCC 5–114(2) permits an issuer acting in good faith to honor despite allegations of fraud, but the last clause in UCC 5–114(2)(b) suggests that "a court of appropriate jurisdiction may enjoin such honor." The extent to which UCC 5–114(2) and the cases decided under that rule cut back on the independence principle and authorize a bank to refuse payment has been a topic of continuing debate in the courts and in the scholarly literature.

First, how does one distinguish between "fraud" and mere breach of contract? As we will see, the case which spawned the subsection, Sztejn v. J. Henry Schroder Banking Corp., infra page 742, might have been characterized merely as a case of gross and intentional breach of contract.

The second issue present in UCC 5–114(2) is what standard the court is to apply in determining whether to enjoin payment—the question whether the bank that has not been enjoined may use UCC 5–114(2) to justify a refusal of payment.

Professor Dolan has argued persuasively for a narrow interpretation of UCC 5–114(2). Surely he is right in cautioning the courts against broad interpretation of that subsection. An expansive view of it could undermine the utility of the letter of credit and give every bank under pressure from a powerful customer a colorable excuse for refusal to pay. Also lurking in the subsection is the question, what kind of fraud and by whom? Must the fraud be committed by the beneficiary or is it enough that there be fraud in some transaction one step remote from the beneficiary? What, for example, of the case in which a general partner of an oil well drilling partnership defrauds the bank's customer but causes the letter of credit to be drawn with the general partner's bank as the beneficiary? In such case, the beneficiary bank might be completely innocent of the fraud.

The last decade has seen a great deal of stress applied to UCC 5–114(2) and the principles there expressed. This stress has arisen largely out of letters of credit written by American banks for American customers to Iranian beneficiaries. After the overthrow of the Shah and the rupture of relations between Iran and the United States, the various Iranian beneficiaries of the letters of credit called or threatened to call them. Of course the American customers feared that if payment were made and the money transmitted to Iran, the American customers would never have an opportunity to get a fair trial on their rights on the underlying contract. A customer might concede, for example, that the documents presented met the terms of the credit, but maintain that it had failed to perform the contract because of force majeure or because it was actively prevented from doing so by the Iranian officials who were now seeking payment under the letter. In such cases it is not easy to prove fraud, yet there was enormous political and economic pressure not to pay such letters. Not all of the American courts covered themselves with glory.

J. DOLAN, THE LAW OF LETTERS OF CREDIT: COMMERCIAL AND STANDBY CREDITS 7–45 TO 7–50.

[E] IRANIAN CASES

[i] Strict cases. The analysis of the *Intraworld* and *Dynamics* cases is helpful in explaining several decisions involving standby credit disputes that arose out of the U.S./Iranian political problems of 1979. It is the practice of economically strong buyers, especially government

buyers dealing with economically weaker sellers, to insist on performance guaranties when they enter into supply contracts. In the Iranian
cases, the American sellers induced Iranian banks to issue those guaranties by having a domestic bank issue a standby credit in favor of the
Iranian bank. Generally, the standby credit would call for the Iranian
bank's draft and a certificate to the effect that it had been required to
honor its guaranty. When the Iranian revolution interrupted commerce between the United States and Iran, sellers became anxious
about the standby credits. Political and diplomatic turmoil prevented
performance of the underlying agreements, and the Iranian political
and financial structure appeared to be in the hands of persons who did
not inspire the confidence that their counterparts in Amsterdam or
London inspire. The sellers resorted to the courts.

Some of the cases lent themselves to resolution on the grounds that
the account parties had not satisfied the equity prerequisites for injunctive relief. In *KMW International v. Chase Manhattan Bank, N.A.,* for
example, the account party sought an injunction alleging that the
Iranian buyer had breached the contract of sale and that any draw on
the credit would be fraudulent. There had been no draw, however, and
the court held that no injunction against payment should issue. The
plaintiff's claim for damages was too speculative and conjectural to
satisfy the rules of equity. The court did, however, order the issuer to
give the account party three days' notice before honoring any demand.
In *United Technologies Corp. v. Citibank, N.A.,* the account party
alleged that it had performed the contract of sale and that any demand
under the credit would be wrongful. The court denied the injunction,
holding that the account party had an adequate remedy at law in the
event a draft was fraudulent. In *American Bell International Inc. v.
Islamic Republic of Iran,* the account party claimed that the Iranian
buyer had breached the contract of sale, and alleged further that the
beneficiary's demand, which the issuer had received, was not timely.
The court refused to grant the injunction. In response to the account
party's argument that the demand was not timely, the court noted that
if, in fact, the issuer honored a late demand, the account party would
have an adequate remedy at law—a suit for money damages against the
issuer. In *Werner Lehara International, Inc. v. Harris Trust & Savings
Bank,* the court held that the plaintiff, who was seeking injunctive
relief before the beneficiary made any demand, did not satisfy the
equity prerequisites and had not made out a case of fraud.

It is perhaps also significant that in the *Werner Lehara, KMW,* and
American Bell cases the courts weighed against the account party the
fact that an injunction might affect the banking relationships of the
issuer adversely. It is clear that the issuers in these cases were
nervous about the effect the injunctions would have in general on the
reputation of credits issued by American banks and by the implicit
threat of retaliation from the Iranian government or Iranian banks. In
United Technologies, the court explicitly found such eventualities too
speculative to be considered.

The *Werner Lehara, KMW,* and *American Bell* cases reject firmly the account party's argument that the demands of the Iranian beneficiaries were or would be fraudulent. Those courts viewed the contests as contract disputes, the risks of which the account parties should have foreseen when they entered into the sales contract. The courts refused to let the account parties shift to the banks or to the letter-of-credit industry in general a contract risk that inheres in international sales, a risk of political upheaval. In *United Technologies,* the court did not consider it necessary to decide that issue.

The conclusion of these cases that there was no fraud in the transaction sufficient to invoke the rule of Section 5–114(2) is consistent with the general rule. It may be that the beneficiaries of the guaranties issued by the Iranian banks were guilty of fraud when those beneficiaries required the Iranian banks to pay under the guaranties. The plaintiff's allegations suggest as much. Fraud in that guaranty transaction is not fraud in the letter-of-credit transaction as the *Sztejn* rule requires. The certificates required in the *KMW* and the *American Bell* cases, moreover, did not invite the courts to look into that related contract as the *NMC* and *O'Grady* cases did. The Iranian certificates recited only that the beneficiary was called upon to pay under the letter of guaranty. These carefully drawn credits do not pierce the barrier that insulates the credit from the underlying transaction and do not force the court to look at that underlying transaction.

While a significant number of courts dealing with standby credits issued to Iranian beneficiaries granted notice injunctions requiring the issuer to delay honoring a credit for a short period of time, the more significant cases are those such as *KMW, American Bell,* and *United Technologies.* The latter demonstrate the obstacles facing an account party once the demand arrives. These cases show a marked willingness to enforce the equity prerequisites and a marked unwillingness to relax the strict fraud rule of *Sztejn* or to reallocate the commercial and political risks that these merchant sellers must now shoulder under letter-of-credit law.

[ii] Less strict cases. The adherence to the strict *Sztejn* rule was not unanimous. In *Itek Corp. v. First National Bank,* the defendant bank issued a standby credit to an Iranian bank which, in turn, issued a guarantee to the Iranian Ministry of War. The account party had agreed to sell optical equipment to the Iranian government, and the sales contract contained a force majeure clause permitting either party to cancel the contract before performance under it was complete. The U.S. Department of State revoked the account party's export license, and the account party notified Iran of its election to terminate the contract under the force majeure clause. Subsequently, the account party obtained a temporary restraining order against the issuer; and when the beneficiary presented a conforming demand under the credit, the court enjoined payment. The *Itek* court held that because the account party's suit against the Iranian government would be futile, irreparable injury was evident. With respect to the fraud question, the court held that Section 5–114(2) establishes an exception to the independence principle, but the court also held that it was not necessary to probe the question of whether the fraud would be in the credit transaction or in the underlying transaction. The *Itek* court found the fraud so "blatant" and "undisputed" that it issued the restraining order.

A similar disposition to find fraud was evident in *Touche Ross & Co. v. Manufacturers Hanover Trust Co.*, where the credit ran to the benefit of an Iranian bank that had issued a letter of guaranty to the Iranian Ministry of War. The underlying contract contained a force majeure clause and stipulated that upon invocation of the clause all letters of guaranty would terminate. The account party invoked the force majeure clause, and the court concluded, therefore, that there could be no legitimate call on the letter of credit. In short, the *Touche Ross* court resolved the underlying contract questions, concluded that the equities were with the account party, and issued the injunction.

The unlikelihood of recovery under the Iranian court system influenced the court in *Harris Corp. v. National Iranian Radio & Television*. In that case, the court rejected the argument that the account party was attempting to reallocate the risks. The court acknowledged that the purpose of the credit was to permit the Iranian buyer to recover its down payment, but the court refused to accept the view that the account party should bear the risk of a fraudulent demand. To the issuer's argument that the account party could have protected itself by negotiating different terms, the court responded vaguely that such an argument ignores "the realities of the drafting of commercial documents." The *Harris Corp.* case rejects the view that the letter of credit used in Middle Eastern transactions reflects the increased bargaining strength of the Middle Eastern buyer and is a device with a purpose of permitting the buyer to recover its down payment automatically. If the *Harris Corp.* case were accepted as the majority rule, such buyers could avoid its effect in a number of ways. They could refuse to accept credits issued by American banks (as Iranian buyers have apparently done), could refuse to make a down payment, or could insist that the down payment be held by the Middle Eastern bank that issues the guaranty letter. Although the account party in the *Harris Corp.* case might find solace in the result, it is doubtful that American sellers in general will be pleased by these attempts by strong buyers to avoid the *Harris Corp.* rule. [Footnotes omitted.]

SZTEJN v. J. HENRY SCHRODER BANKING CORP.

Supreme Court of New York, Special Term, 1941.
177 Misc. 719, 31 N.Y.S.2d 631.

SHIENTAG, JUSTICE.

This is a motion by the defendant, the Chartered Bank of India, Australia and China, (hereafter referred to as the Chartered Bank), made pursuant to Rule 106(5) of the Rules of Civil Practice to dismiss the supplemental complaint on the ground that it fails to state facts sufficient to constitute a cause of action against the moving defendant. The plaintiff brings this action to restrain the payment or presentment for payment of drafts under a letter of credit issued to secure the purchase price of certain merchandise, bought by the plaintiff and his coadventurer, one Schwarz, who is a party defendant in this action. The plaintiff also seeks a judgment declaring the letter of credit and drafts thereunder null and void. The complaint alleges that the documents accompanying the drafts are fraudulent in that they do not represent actual merchandise but instead cover boxes fraudulently filled with worthless material by the seller of the goods. The moving defendant urges that the complaint fails to state a cause of action against it because the Chartered Bank is only concerned with the documents and on their face these conform to the requirements of the letter of credit.

On January 7, 1941, the plaintiff and his coadventurer contracted to purchase a quantity of bristles from the defendant Transea Traders, Ltd. (hereafter referred to as Transea) a corporation having its place of business in Lucknow, India. In order to pay for the bristles, the plaintiff and Schwarz contracted with the defendant J. Henry Schroder Banking Corporation (hereafter referred to as Schroder), a domestic corporation, for the issuance of an irrevocable letter of credit to Transea which provided that drafts by the latter for a specified portion of the purchase price of the bristles would be paid by Schroder upon shipment of the described merchandise and presentation of an invoice and a bill of lading covering the shipment, made out to the order of Schroder.

The letter of credit was delivered to Transea by Schroder's correspondent bank in India, Transea placed fifty cases of material on board a steamship, procured a bill of lading from the steamship company and obtained the customary invoices. These documents describe the bristles called for by the letter of credit. However, the complaint alleges that in fact Transea filled the fifty crates with cowhair, other worthless material and rubbish with intent to simulate genuine merchandise and defraud the plaintiff and Schwarz. The complaint then alleges that Transea drew a draft under the letter of credit to the order of the Chartered Bank and delivered the draft and the fraudulent documents to the "Chartered Bank at Cawnpore, India, for collection for the account of said defendant Transea". The Chartered Bank has presented the draft along with the documents to Schroder for payment. The plaintiff prays for a judgment declaring the letter of credit and draft thereunder void and for injunctive relief to prevent the payment of the draft.

For the purposes of this motion, the allegations of the complaint must be deemed established and "every intendment and fair inference is in favor of the pleading" Madole v. Gavin, 215 App.Div. 299, at page

300, 213 N.Y.S. 529, at page 530; McClare v. Massachusetts Bonding & Ins. Co., 266 N.Y. 371, 373, 195 N.E. 15. Therefore, it must be assumed that Transea was engaged in a scheme to defraud the plaintiff and Schwarz, that the merchandise shipped by Transea is worthless rubbish and that the Chartered Bank is not an innocent holder of the draft for value but is merely attempting to procure payment of the draft for Transea's account.

It is well established that a letter of credit is independent of the primary contract of sale between the buyer and the seller. The issuing bank agrees to pay upon presentation of documents, not goods. This rule is necessary to preserve the efficiency of the letter of credit as an instrument for the financing of trade. One of the chief purposes of the letter of credit is to furnish the seller with a ready means of obtaining prompt payment for his merchandise. It would be a most unfortunate interference with business transactions if a bank before honoring drafts drawn upon it was obliged or even allowed to go behind the documents, at the request of the buyer and enter into controversies between the buyer and the seller regarding the quality of the merchandise shipped. If the buyer and the seller intended the bank to do this they could have so provided in the letter of credit itself, and in the absence of such a provision, the court will not demand or even permit the bank to delay paying drafts which are proper in form. O'Meara Co. v. National Park Bank of New York, 239 N.Y. 386, 146 N.E. 636, 39 A.L.R. 747. * * * Of course, the application of this doctrine presupposes that the documents accompanying the draft are genuine and conform in terms to the requirements of the letter of credit. Lamborn v. Lake Shore Banking & Trust Co., 196 App.Div. 504, 188 N.Y.S. 162; affirmed 231 N.Y. 616, 132 N.E. 911; Bank of Montreal v. Recknagel, 109 N.Y. 482, 17 N.E. 217; 38 Y.L.J. 111, 112.

However, I believe that a different situation is presented in the instant action. This is not a controversy between the buyer and seller concerning a mere breach of warranty regarding the quality of the merchandise; on the present motion, it must be assumed that the seller has intentionally failed to ship any goods ordered by the buyer. In such a situation, where the seller's fraud has been called to the bank's attention before the drafts and documents have been presented for payment, the principle of the independence of the bank's obligation under the letter of credit should not be extended to protect the unscrupulous seller. It is true that even though the documents are forged or fraudulent, if the issuing bank has already paid the draft before receiving notice of the seller's fraud, it will be protected if it exercised reasonable diligence before making such payment. * * * However, in the instant action Schroder has received notice of Transea's active fraud before it accepted or paid the draft. The Chartered Bank, which under the allegations of the complaint stands in no better position than Transea, should not be heard to complain because Schroder is not forced to pay the draft accompanied by documents covering a transaction which it has reason to believe is fraudulent.

Although our courts have used broad language to the effect that a letter of credit is independent of the primary contract between the buyer and seller, that language was used in cases concerning alleged breaches of warranty; no case has been brought to my attention on this point involving an intentional fraud on the part of the seller which was brought to the bank's notice with the request that it withhold payment of the draft on this account. The distinction between a breach of warranty and active fraud on the part of the seller is supported by authority and reason. As one court has stated: "Obviously, when the issuer of a letter of credit knows that a document, although correct in form, is, in point of fact, false or illegal, he cannot be called upon to recognize such a document as complying with the terms of a letter of credit." Old Colony Trust Co. v. Lawyers' Title & Trust Co., 2 Cir., 297 F. 152 at page 158, certiorari denied 265 U.S. 585, 44 S.Ct. 459, 68 L.Ed. 1192. * * *

No hardship will be caused by permitting the bank to refuse payment where fraud is claimed, where the merchandise is not merely inferior in quality but consists of worthless rubbish, where the draft and the accompanying documents are in the hands of one who stands in the same position as the fraudulent seller, where the bank has been given notice of the fraud before being presented with the drafts and documents for payment, and where the bank itself does not wish to pay pending an adjudication of the rights and obligations of the other parties. While the primary factor in the issuance of the letter of credit is the credit standing of the buyer, the security afforded by the merchandise is also taken into account. In fact, the letter of credit requires a bill of lading made out to the order of the bank and not the buyer. Although the bank is not interested in the exact detailed performance of the sales contract, it is vitally interested in assuring itself that there are some goods represented by the documents. * * *

On this motion only the complaint is before me and I am bound by its allegation that the Chartered Bank is not a holder in due course but is a mere agent for collection for the account of the seller charged with fraud. Therefore, the Chartered Bank's motion to dismiss the complaint must be denied. If it had appeared from the face of the complaint that the bank presenting the draft for payment was a holder in due course, its claim against the bank issuing the letter of credit would not be defeated even though the primary transaction was tainted with fraud. This I believe to be the better rule despite some authority to the contrary. See Old Colony Trust Co. v. Lawyers' Title & Trust Co., 2 Cir., 297 F. 152, certiorari denied 265 U.S. 585, 44 S.Ct. 459, 68 L.Ed. 1192; Thayer, Irrevocable Credits in International Commerce, 37 C.L.R. 1326, 1344; Campbell, Guaranties & The Suretyship Phases of Letters of Credit, 85 U. of Pa.L.R. 261, 272; but see Finkelstein, Legal Aspects of Commercial Letters of Credit, p. 248; O'Meara Co. v. National Park Bank of New York, 239 N.Y. 386, 401, 146 N.E. 636, 39 A.L.R. 747.

The plaintiff's further claim that the terms of the documents presented with the draft are at substantial variance with the requirements of the letter of credit does not seem to be supported by the documents themselves.

Accordingly, the defendant's motion to dismiss the supplemental complaint is denied.

Problem 16–6

At 1:00 on a lazy Friday afternoon as you are having your second martini at your favorite eating club, you are called to the phone and receive the following frantic message from your best client: He tells you that he has procured the issuance of a letter of credit naming his seller as the beneficiary, that he has it on excellent authority that his seller has sealed several freight cars and procured bills of lading stating that the goods are enclosed in those cars, when in fact they are not. He informs you that these documents are now in the hands of seller's bank in a distant city and will probably be presented for payment on Monday morning to the issuing bank in your city. The letter of credit calls for payment of $100,000 and your client is certain that he will have a difficult if not impossible time getting the money back from the seller once it gets into his hands. If the case is governed by the Uniform Commercial Code, what action will you take?

COLORADO NATIONAL BANK OF DENVER v. BOARD OF COUNTY COMMISSIONERS OF ROUTT COUNTY, COLO.

Supreme Court of Colorado, 1981.
634 P.2d 32.

HODGES, CHIEF JUSTICE.

We granted certiorari to review the court of appeals' decision affirming a district court's judgment holding the petitioner, the Colorado National Bank of Denver (the Bank), liable for the face amounts of three letters of credit it issued to secure the completion of road improvements by its customer, the Woodmoor Corporation (Woodmoor). * * * We reverse the judgment as to letters of credit No. 1156 and No. 1157, and affirm the judgment as to letter of credit No. 1168.

Woodmoor planned to develop a mountain recreation community in Routt County, Colorado (the County), to be known as Stagecoach. Early in 1973, Woodmoor obtained plat approval from the Routt County Board of County Commissioners (the Commissioners) for several Stagecoach subdivisions. Pursuant to section 30–28–137, C.R.S. 1973 (1977 Repl Vol 12), and county subdivision regulations, approval of three of these subdivision plats was conditioned upon Woodmoor's agreement to provide a bond or other undertaking to ensure the completion of roads in accordance with the subdivision design specifications. Accordingly, subdivision improvements agreements were executed between Woodmoor and the county.

At Woodmoor's request, the Bank issued three letters of credit to secure Woodmoor's obligations under the agreements. The first two letters of credit, No. 1156 and No. 1157, were issued January 23, 1973 in the respective amounts of $158,773 and $77,330 bearing expiry dates of December 31, 1975. The third letter of credit No. 1168 was issued March 7, 1973 in the amount of $113,732 bearing an expiry date of December 31, 1976. The face amounts of the letters of credit were identical to the estimated costs of the road and related improvements in the respective subdivision improvements agreements. The County was authorized by each letter of credit to draw directly on the Bank, for the account of Woodmoor, up to the face amount of each letter of credit. Each letter of credit required the County, in order to draw on the letters of credit, to submit fifteen-day sight drafts accompanied by:

> "A duly-signed statement by the Routt County Board of Commissioners that improvements have not been made in compliance with a Subdivision Improvements Agreement between Routt County and the Woodmoor Corporation dated [either January 9, 1973 or March 7, 1973] and covering the [respective subdivisions] at Stagecoach and that payment is therefore demanded hereunder."

Woodmoor never commenced construction of the roads and related improvements. On December 31, 1975, the expiry date of letters of credit No. 1156 and No. 1157, the County presented two demand drafts to the Bank for the face amounts of $158,773 and $77,330. The demand drafts were accompanied by a resolution of the Commissioners stating that Woodmoor had failed to comply with the terms of the subdivision improvements agreements and demanded payment of the face amounts of the letters of credit. On January 5, 1976, within three banking days of the demand,[1] the Bank dishonored the drafts. The Bank did not specifically object to the County's presentation of demand drafts rather than fifteen-day sight drafts as required by the letters of credit.

On December 22, 1976, the County presented the Bank with a demand draft on letter of credit No. 1168 which was accompanied by the required resolution of the Commissioners. The Bank dishonored this draft because of the County's nonconforming demand, viz., that a demand draft was submitted rather than a fifteen-day sight draft. On December 29, 1976, the County presented a fifteen-day sight draft to the Bank. This draft was not accompanied by the resolution of the Commissioners. On December 31, 1976, the Bank dishonored this draft.

The County sued to recover the face amounts of the three letters of credit plus interest from the dates of the demands. The Bank answered the County's complaints alleging several affirmative defenses. The fundamental premise of the Bank's defenses was the assertion that the County would receive a windfall since it had not expended or commit-

---

1. Under § 4–5–112(1)(a), C.R.S. 1973, a bank called upon to honor drafts under a letter of credit may defer until the close of the third banking day following receipt of the documents.

ted to spend any funds to complete the road improvements specified in the subdivision improvements agreements.

The County filed a motion in limine seeking a determination by the trial court to exclude evidence concerning matters beyond the four corners of the letters of credit and the demands made on the letters of credit. The Bank replied by filing a cross-motion in limine seeking a ruling that it would not be precluded at trial from offering evidence outside the four corners of the letters of credit. The trial court, after extensive briefing by the parties and a hearing, granted the County's motion to limit the admissibility of evidence to the letters of credit, documents and drafts presented thereunder, the demands on the letters of credit, and the Bank's refusals to honor the County's demands for payment.

The remaining issues were whether the County's demands conformed to the letters of credit or, if not, whether the Bank had waived nonconforming demands, and whether interest ought to be awarded. The parties agreed on a stipulated set of facts concerning these remaining issues. The Bank did, however, make an offer of proof as to the rejected affirmative defenses. The Bank would have attempted to prove that the subdivisions in question remained raw, undeveloped mountain property for which there was no viable market and that the County had neither constructed, made commitments to construct, nor planned to construct the roads or other improvements described in the subdivision improvements agreements secured by the letters of credit. These allegations were disputed by the County.

The trial court entered judgment against the Bank for the face amounts of the letters of credit plus accrued interest at the statutory rate from the date of the County's demands. Costs were awarded in favor of the County. The Bank's motion for new trial was denied, and the Bank appealed.

The court of appeals affirmed the judgment of the trial court ruling that standby letters of credit are governed by article 5 of the Uniform Commercial Code, section 4–5–101 et seq. C.R.S. 1973, and that an issuer must honor a draft or demand for payment which complies with the terms of the relevant credit regardless of whether the goods or documents conform to the underlying contract. The court of appeals affirmed the trial court's refusal to consider any evidence regarding the County's alleged windfall. The court of appeals also held that any defects in the form of the County's demands were waived by the Bank.

I.

We first address the question whether the trial court properly limited the evidence to be presented at trial to the letters of credit, the demands by the County, and the Bank's replies to the demands. The Bank has continually asserted during each stage of this action that it ought to be permitted to show that the County will receive a windfall if the County is permitted to recover against the letters of credit. The

Bank requested an opportunity to prove that the County will utilize the funds it would receive in a manner other than that specified in the road improvements agreements. Fundamentally, the Bank seeks to litigate the question of the completion of the purpose of the underlying performance agreements between Woodmoor and the County. This the Bank cannot do.

An overview of the history and law concerning letters of credit is useful in the consideration of this issue. The letter of credit arose to facilitate international commercial transactions involving the sale of goods. * * * Today the commercial utility of the letter of credit in both international and domestic sale of goods transactions is unquestioned and closely guarded. * * * Harfield, The Increasing Domestic Use of the Letter of Credit, 4 U.C.C.L.J. 251 (1972); Verkuil, Bank Solvency and Guaranty Letters of Credit, 25 Stan.L.Rev. 716 (1973). In recent years, the use of the letter of credit has expanded to include guaranteeing or securing a bank's customer's promised performance to a third party in a variety of situations. * * * This use is referred to as a standby letter of credit. Article five of the Uniform Commercial Code governs both traditional commercial letters of credit and standby letters of credit. * * *

Three contractual relationships exist in a letter of credit transaction. * * * Justice, Letters of Credit: Expectations and Frustrations, 94 Banking L.J. 424 (1977); Verkuil, Bank Solvency and Guaranty Letters of Credit, supra. Underlying the letter of credit transaction is the contract between the bank's customer and the beneficiary of the letter of credit, which consists of the business agreement between these parties. Then there is the contractual arrangement between the bank and its customer whereby the bank agrees to issue the letter of credit, and the customer agrees to repay the bank for the amounts paid under the letter of credit. See also § 4–5–114(3), C.R.S. 1973. Finally, there is the contractual relationship between the bank and the beneficiary of the letter of credit created by the letter of credit itself. The bank agrees to honor the beneficiary's drafts or demands for payment which conform to the terms of the letter of credit. See generally §§ 4–5–103(1)(a) and 4–5–114(1), C.R.S. 1973; White and Summers, Uniform Commercial Code § 18–6 (2d ed 1980).

It is fundamental that the letter of credit is separate and independent from the underlying business transaction between the bank's customer and the beneficiary of the letter of credit. * * * Arnold & Bransilver, The Standby Letter of Credit—The Controversy Continues, 10 U.C.C.L.J. 272 (1978); * * * "The letter of credit is essentially a contract between the issuer and the beneficiary and is recognized by [article 5 of the Uniform Commercial Code] as independent of the underlying contract between the customer and the beneficiary. * * * In view of this independent nature of the letter of credit engagement the issuer is under a duty to honor the drafts for payment which in fact conform with the terms of the credit without reference to their compliance with the terms of the underlying contract." Section 4–5–114, Official Comment 1, C.R.S. 1973.

The independence of the letter of credit from the underlying contract has been called the key to the commercial vitality of the letter of credit. * * * The bank must honor drafts or demands for payment under the letter of credit when the documents required by the letter of credit appear on their face to comply with the terms of the credit. Section 4–5–114(2), C.R.S. 1973. An exception to the bank's obligation to honor an apparently conforming draft or demand for payment, see Foreign Venture Ltd. Partnership v. Chemical Bank, 59 App.Div.2d 352, 399 N.Y.S.2d 114 (1977), is when a required document is, inter alia, forged or fraudulent, or there is fraud in the transaction. Section 4–5–114(2). The application of this narrow exception is discussed in detail later in this opinion.

As mentioned above, letters of credit have recently come to be used to secure a bank's customer's performance to a third party. When a letter of credit is used to secure a bank's customer's promised performance to a third party, in whatever capacity that might be, the letter of credit is referred to as a "guaranty letter of credit," see East Bank of Colorado Springs v. Dovenmuehle, supra; Verkuil, Bank Solvency and Guaranty Letters of Credit, supra, or a "standby letter of credit," Arnold & Bransilver, The Standby Letter of Credit—The Controversy Continues, supra, 12 CFR § 7.1160 (1980). Standby letters of credit are closely akin to a suretyship or guaranty contract. The bank promises to pay when there is a default on an obligation by the bank's customer. "If for any reason performance is not made, or is made defectively, the bank is liable without regard to the underlying rights of the contracting parties." Verkuil, Bank Solvency and Guaranty Letters of Credit, supra at 723.

While banks cannot, as a general rule, act as a surety or guarantor of another party's agreed performance, see generally Lord, The No-Guaranty Rule and the Standby Letter of Credit Controversy, 96 Banking L.J. 46 (1979), the legality of standby letters of credit has been uniformly recognized. * * * What distinguishes a standby letter of credit from a suretyship or guaranty contract is that the bank's liability rests upon the letter of credit contract rather than upon the underlying performance contract between the bank customer and the beneficiary of the letter of credit. * * *

The utilization by banks of standby letters of credit is now widespread, although some commentators suggest that bankers may not appreciate the legal obligations imposed by the standby letter of credit. Where the bank issues a standby letter of credit, the bank naturally expects that the credit will not be drawn on in the normal course of events, i.e., if the customer of the bank fulfills its agreed-upon performance, then the credit will not be drawn upon. This expectation of the bank must be compared to the bank's expectation with respect to a traditional letter of credit issued as a means of financing a sale of goods. In the latter situation, the bank expects that the credit will always be drawn upon. * * * It has been suggested that bankers may be lax in considering the credit of a customer with respect to issuing a standby letter of credit to secure the integrity of its customer to complete an agreed-upon performance since it could be easily assumed by the bank that demand for payment would never be made. * * * One solution suggested by many commentators is that the issuing bank treat a standby letter of credit like an unsecured loan. National Banks issuing standby letters of credit are subject to the lending limits of 12 U.S.C. § 84 (1976).

We now turn to a discussion of the present case, and why the Bank cannot introduce evidence beyond that directly relating to its contract with the County. As discussed above, the letters of credit, and the Bank's obligations thereunder, are separate and independent from the underlying subdivision improvements agreements between Woodmoor and the County. The fact that the letters of credit issued by the Bank are standby letters of credit does not alter this general rule. The Bank is bound by its own contracts with the County.

Each of the letters of credit prepared and issued by the Bank in this case sets forth specifically the condition for payment, i.e., that Woodmoor failed to make the improvements in conformance with the respective subdivision improvements agreements. Had the Bank desired additional conditions for payment, such as the actual completion of the road improvements prior to payment under the letters of credit, it could have incorporated such a condition in the letters of credit. * * * To demand payment under the letters of credit, the County was only required to submit a "duly-signed statement by the [Commissioners] that improvements have not been made in compliance with [the] Subdivision Improvements Agreement[s]. * * * "

The Bank cannot litigate the performance of the underlying performance contracts. "[P]erformance of the underlying contract is irrelevant to the Bank's obligations under the letter of credit." West Virginia Housing Development Fund v. Sroka, supra at 1114 (W.D.Pa. 1976). * * * Likewise, the question of whether the beneficiary of the letter of credit has suffered any damage by the failure of the bank's customer to perform as agreed is of no concern. Mid-States Mortgage Corp. v. National Bank of Southfield, 77 Mich.App. 651, 259 N.W.2d 175 (1977). Further, a bank cannot challenge the utilization of funds paid under a letter of credit. * * *

The Bank argues that it is entitled to dishonor the County's drafts under § 4–5–114(2), C.R.S. 1973. This section provides: [quoting]

Under this section, the issuer of a letter of credit may in good faith honor a draft or demand for payment notwithstanding notice from its customer that documents are forged, or fraudulent, or there is fraud in the transaction. The issuer may, however, be enjoined from honoring such drafts or demands for payment. Impliedly, the issuer may also refuse to honor such drafts or demands for payment when it has been notified by its customer of these defects. Section 4–5–114, Official Comment 2, C.R.S. 1973. * * *

In this case, the Bank has not argued, nor can it reasonably assert, that the documents presented by the County are forged or fraudulent. The Bank has not challenged the authenticity of the drafts and demands for payment by the County or the truthfulness of the statements that the requirements of the underlying subdivision improvements agreements have not been fulfilled. The Bank does assert, however, that there has been fraud in the transaction on the basis that the funds the County would receive would be utilized by the County other than to pay for the completion of the road improvements.

Fundamentally, "fraud in the transaction," as referred to in § 4–5–114(2), must stem from conduct by the beneficiary of the letter of credit as against the customer of the bank. See generally White and Summers, Uniform Commercial Code § 18–6 (2d ed. 1980). It must be of such an egregious nature as to vitiate the entire underlying transaction so that the legitimate purposes of the independence of the bank's obligation would no longer be served. * * * "[I]t is generally thought to include an element of intentional misrepresentation in order to profit from another. * * *" West Virginia Housing Development Fund v. Sroka, supra. This fraud is manifested in the documents themselves, and the statements therein, presented under the letter of credit. * * * One court has gone so far as to say that only some defect in these documents would justify a bank's dishonor. O'Grady v. First Union National Bank of North Carolina, 296 N.C. 212, 250 S.E.2d 587 (1978).

In this case, the Bank has not asserted that there is fraud in the transaction between Woodmoor and the County, nor can it reasonably make such an argument. No facts have been pled to establish fraud which vitiated the entire agreement between the County and Woodmoor. No fraud has been asserted by the Bank's offer of proof which would entitle it to dishonor the County's drafts and demands for payment. * * *

Thus, the trial court properly granted the County's motion in limine excluding all evidence beyond the four corners of the letters of credit, the demands thereunder, and the Bank's replies.

* * *

[Some footnotes omitted.]

Notes

1. If the allegations of the bank are correct, the risk against which the letters of credit were issued, namely that there would be a subdivision built, but that the subdividers would not provide the roads, will never arise. If, in such a case, the bank must pay the money and the county can keep the money, the law is "a ass," not so?

2. Had you advised the bank, how would you have drafted the letter to avoid the problem? (One of your editors is advised that the president of

the bank typed out the letter on his very own typewriter without assistance of counsel.)

3. If the promise behind the developer's agreement to provide roads had been a conventional surety bond, how would that have changed the legal obligations?

CROMWELL v. COMMERCE & ENERGY BANK

Supreme Court of Louisiana, 1985.
464 So.2d 721.

DIXON, CHIEF JUSTICE. The plaintiffs in these consolidated cases seek reversal of the Court of Appeal decision in which the court found that plaintiffs were not entitled to enjoin the defendant banks from paying on standby letters of credit issued by the banks. We affirm the court of appeal decision insofar as it denies injunctive relief.

FACTS

The plaintiffs in these five consolidated actions consist of the twenty-eight investors who purchased limited partnership interests in Combined Investments, Limited (C.I., Ltd.), a Louisiana limited partnership. C.I., Ltd. was formed by Combined Equities, Incorporated (C.E., Inc.), a company engaged in the syndication and management of investment partnerships. C.E., Inc. was the general partner of C.I., Ltd.

As security for their capital contribution in C.I., Ltd., the limited partners were required to execute letters of credit in favor of C.I., Ltd. The letters of credit were issued by fourteen Louisiana banks. The issuing banks were sued by the plaintiffs in order to prevent the beneficiary from drawing on the letters of credit. The primary basis of plaintiffs' claim was alleged fraudulent activities on the part of C.E., Inc. and C.I., Ltd.

The final beneficiary of the letters of credit was European American Bank (EAB). EAB became the beneficiary under the letters of credit as security for a ten million dollar line of credit established in favor of C.I., Ltd. EAB intervened in these cases in order to assert its right to draw on the letters of credit.

In addition to EAB, several other parties intervened in these cases to assert their interests. C.E., Inc. and C.I., Ltd. intervened in order to refute the plaintiffs' claim that they defrauded the plaintiff-investors.

*   *   *

The formation of C.I., Ltd. began on June 1, 1981, when C.E., Inc. commenced offering partnership units in C.I., Ltd. C.E., Inc. had been in the business of syndicating partnerships since its formation in 1976. C.E., Inc. and its affiliated companies derived their income from fees charged for a variety of managerial and financial services provided to limited partnerships.

Prior to the creation of C.I., Ltd., the C.E., Inc. staff prepared a Private Placement Memorandum (PPM), a two hundred twenty page document which detailed the proposed structure of C.I., Ltd. and listed the terms of the partnership offering. All of the limited partners received a copy of the PPM prior to their investment in C.I., Ltd. The PPM included financial information and historical data concerning the general partner (C.E., Inc.) as well as a series of closing documents which were to be completed by each investor.

The closing documents were comprised of a series of forms to be completed by the investors. One of the purposes of the closing documents of the PPM was to require each investor to appoint an experienced investment advisor ("offeree representative") to review the PPM and advise him concerning the risks of the offering. The investors were each required to provide detailed information regarding their personal finances. Each investor was required to warrant that he was financially able to bear the risks of an investment in C.I., Ltd.

According to the PPM, the partnership's primary objectives were to acquire, transfer and invest in real estate in order to generate cash flow and to obtain long term capital gains. It was also the intention of C.I., Ltd. to secure significant tax advantages for the limited partners. These tax savings were to be obtained by passing through many of C.I., Ltd.'s losses onto the limited partners.

The PPM also indicated that C.I., Ltd. was a "blind pool" offering, since at the time of the offering the partnership did not own any property nor did it intend to acquire any specific property. The risks of such an offering were described in the PPM:

"RISK OF UNSPECIFIED INVESTMENTS

"The proceeds of this Offering are intended to be invested in Properties which have not yet been selected. There can be no assurance as to if or when the proceeds from the Offering will be fully invested. Pending investment of Limited Partners' capital contributions, the General Partner is not required to invest Partnership funds in any particular manner and during such period investors will not have the opportunity to earn any return on such contributions. Persons who purchase Units will not have an opportunity to evaluate for themselves the specific Properties in which funds of the Partnership will be invested or the terms of any such investments and, accordingly, the Limited Partners must depend solely upon the General Partner with respect to the selection of investments. * * *" PPM, p 27.

Originally the syndication of C.I., Ltd. was intended solely to be accomplished through the sale of up to one hundred limited partnership interests. The purchase price of each unit was $250,000. In order to pay this sum, each limited partner was required to contribute $20,000 in cash, a two year, non-interest bearing demand note for $30,000, and a demand note for $200,000. Each investor was also required to obtain a $200,000 standby letter of credit, securing the $200,000 note.

The highly leveraged terms of the capital contribution allowed the limited partners to obtain significant tax advantages. The federal tax laws allow limited partnerships to pass through losses to their limited partners, based on the amount of the partner's money "at risk." Under the C.I., Ltd. proposal, each partner had $250,000 at risk in spite of the fact that his initial cash investment was only $20,000. During 1981 the partnership passed along a $76,000 tax loss to each investment unit.

Thirty-nine units in C.I., Ltd. were sold and the partnership officially came into existence on September 23, 1981. By the end of November, 1981 all plaintiffs except one had purchased interests; the last purchase was April 13, 1982.

In accordance with the terms of the capital contribution, each plaintiff secured a $200,000 letter of credit from his bank. The letters of credit were all issued in accordance with a form included in the closing package of the PPM. That form provided:

'' (LETTERHEAD OF BANK)

ADDRESS

(Date)

Irrevocable Letter of Credit

Combined Investments, Ltd., a
Louisiana Limited Partnership
5551 Corporate Boulevard
Suite 3-A
Baton Rouge, Louisiana

Dear Sirs:

We hereby open our Irrevocable Letter of Credit in your favor for the account of (Name of Investor) (Address of Investor), for a sum or sums not exceeding in the aggregate the sum of Two Hundred Thousand and No/100 ($200,000.00) Dollars, available by your drafts drawn on (Bank), (Address of Bank), at sight to be accompanied by:

An Affidavit signed by an officer of the holder of this Letter of Credit certifying that a default exists under

(i) any loan of Combined Investments, Ltd., a Louisiana Limited Partnership, due such holder, or

(ii) any indebtedness of (Name of Investor) due such holder,

which this Letter of Credit may secure.

Drafts must be drawn and negotiated on or before July 1, 1982, on which date this Letter of Credit expires. This Letter may be drafted against in full without being accompanied by the Affidavit referred to above from June 1, 1982 until July 1, 1982 if this Letter of Credit is not renewed by June 1, 1982 for a period of one year expiring July 1, 1983 in the face amount of $200,000 and in a form acceptable to the Beneficiary, its transferees or assigns.

The right to draw under this Letter of Credit is, by the holder hereof, absolutely irrevocable and unconditional (except as set forth herein) and is transferable and/or assignable in whole or in part.

Each draft must be marked 'Drawn under (<u>Bank</u>), (<u>Address of Bank</u>), Letter of Credit Number _____, Dated _____, 19_, and the amount of each draft so drawn endorsed by the negotiating bank. The final draft drawn under this Letter of Credit must be accompanied by this Letter of Credit. This credit is subject to the Uniform Customs and Practice for Documentary Credits, 1974 Revision, fixed by the International Chamber of Commerce Brochure No. 290.

We hereby agree with Drawers, Endorsers and Bona Fide Holders of Drafts drawn under and in compliance with the Credit that the same shall be duly honored upon presentation to the Drawee Bank as specified above.

Sincerely,

(NAME OF BANK)

By: _____

By: _____

(NOTE: NEED SIGNATURES OF TWO (2) BANK OFFICERS)'' PPM Closing Documents, Form 3-A.

The limited partners' letters of credit were intended to be used to secure bank financing for C.I., Ltd. The original letter of credit named C.I., Ltd. as beneficiary. In order to secure financing, the letters of credit were to be transferred to lending banks.

After its formation in September, 1981, C.I., Ltd., acting through its general partner, negotiated loans from Mercantile National Bank of Dallas and First National Bank of Lafayette. The Mercantile loan was for 5.4 million dollars and the First National loan was for 2.4 million dollars. In order to secure the loans, the letters of credit were transferred to the banks along with security interests in the demand notes. As further security for the financing, C.E., Inc. and two of its principal officers, Robert Jackson and E. Hardy Swyers, guaranteed payment of the loans.

The proceeds of the Mercantile and First National loans were used primarily to invest in other limited partnerships which were related to C.E., Inc. These affiliated partnerships generally owned real estate interests such as condominiums, hotels and apartments. Some of these investments were in the form of loans to the other limited partnerships.

C.I., Ltd.'s first contact with EAB took place in September, 1981. Representatives of EAB and C.E., Inc. met to discuss the establishment of a line of credit which would replace the Mercantile and First

National loans. Through the consolidation of the prior loans with EAB, C.E., Inc. hoped to obtain a lower interest rate on its outstanding debt.

Subsequent meetings and discussions led to EAB's approval of a 10 million dollar line of credit for C.I., Ltd. The loan agreement was signed on March 15, 1982. Prior to the approval of the line of credit, EAB conducted an investigation into the credit worthiness of C.I., Ltd. and lengthy negotiations took place between EAB and C.I., Ltd.

EAB's primary representative throughout the negotiation process was Dennis Devito, the assistant vice president in charge of partnership lending. Devito first learned of C.E., Inc. on September 2, 1981 when he was contacted by Alan Jacobs, a New York attorney who was representing C.E., Inc. As a result of his discussions with Jacobs, Devito requested that C.E., Inc. forward the PPM of C.I., Ltd. to the bank.

On September 16, 1981 a meeting took place between representatives of EAB and C.I., Ltd. at the offices of EAB in New York. Devito, Jerold Frier, EAB's vice president, and Harvey Horowitz, a member of the partnership lending division, represented EAB at the meeting. C.E., Inc. was represented at the meeting by Alan Jacobs, E. Hardy Swyers, vice chairman of the board, and Gil Guidry, bank financing manager. The structure of C.I., Ltd. and the possibility of a 20 million dollar credit facility were discussed at the meeting. Subsequent to that meeting, Devito prepared a preliminary loan memorandum and went ahead with the loan approval process.

On September 22, 1981 Devito and Alan Churchill, EAB's vice president of real estate advisory services, made a day long trip to C.E., Inc. headquarters in Baton Rouge. The purpose of the meeting was for Devito and Churchill to familiarize themselves with the operation of C.E., Inc. and to meet its officers. Churchill went along on the trip because of his experience with real estate loans. A file memo written by Devito, which was introduced at trial, indicates that Churchill was satisfied with the operation of C.E., Inc.

Subsequent to the initial meetings, C.I., Ltd. sent a variety of financial data and other information concerning C.I., Ltd. and C.E., Inc. to EAB. One of the documents received by EAB was a portfolio of C.E., Inc., dated September, 1981, which gave specific details concerning the management of C.E., Inc. and its investments. Audited financial statements of C.E., Inc. for the fiscal year ending March 31, 1981 were also sent to EAB.

The bank conducted a credit reference check of C.E., Inc. by contacting five banks and three certified public accountants that had done business with C.E., Inc. The banks, except for Capital Bank & Trust Company, Baton Rouge, indicated that their relationship with C.E., Inc. was very satisfactory. Capital Bank indicated that it had increased its line of credit with C.E., Inc. due to cash flow problems. The accountants contacted by EAB recommended C.E., Inc. as a client.

After reviewing the information furnished by C.I., Ltd. and the credit references, an "internal offering memorandum" was prepared by Devito. This memorandum consisted of a loan proposal for a 10 million dollar credit facility to be secured by letters of credit of the limited partners of C.I., Ltd. The memorandum also included an inhouse appraisal of C.I., Ltd. and its general partner. The final paragraph of the memo set forth a recommendation in favor of approval of the C.I., Ltd. loan. This recommendation was primarily based upon the fact that the loan was to be secured by irrevocable letters of credit naming the bank as beneficiary.

The inter-office memo was approved by the bank on October 30, 1981. The bank's approval of the loan on that date was followed by several months of delay before the actual signing of the loan agreement on March 15, 1982. During that interval, EAB and C.I., Ltd. negotiated with regard to the language of the final loan agreement.

On December 10, 1981 EAB sent a proposed loan agreement to C.E., Inc. for review. On December 11, Robert Jackson, the chairman of C.E., Inc. and Glenn Bodin, the senior vice president of C.E., Inc., had dinner with Churchill and Devito to discuss the terms of the loan agreement.

On December 17, 1981 Churchill sent out an internal memo to Devito which stated that: "As of 2:30 today, no commitment of any kind should be made to Combined Equities prior to my review and approval." Churchill circulated the memo after hearing from a confidential source that C.E., Inc. was slow in its payment of a loan. Devito subsequently met with Churchill and on December 18 Churchill released his hold on the commitment to C.I., Ltd.

In response to Churchill's concerns, Devito contacted Capital Bank in Baton Rouge on December 19 to inquire about the credit worthiness of C.E., Inc. Keith Miller, the vice president of Capital Bank, indicated to Devito that the bank's overall relationship with C.E., Inc. was satisfactory but that C.E., Inc. was experiencing some cash flow difficulties. Miller indicated that these problems were the result of the fast growth of C.E., Inc., the delayed closing of real estate syndications and the fact that the cash of C.E., Inc. was not consolidated at a single bank. He also stated that C.E., Inc. was attempting to address these problems.

On January 25, 1982 EAB received a set of financial statements for C.E., Inc. and its subsidiaries. The most recent statements were for the year ending March 31, 1981. Those statements revealed that C.E., Inc. owned assets of $5,904,708 and that it sustained a net loss of $990,913. Devito attributed this loss to the seasonal nature of the real estate syndication business. He also testified that the March 31, 1981 statements of C.E., Inc. were just one set of many financial statements relied on in approving the credit facility.

EAB sent an amended draft of the loan agreement to C.E., Inc. on February 26, 1982. This amended version incorporated several changes which had been requested by C.E., Inc.

The loan agreement was finally signed on March 15, 1982 in New Orleans. Dwayne Broussard, C.E., Inc.'s legal counsel, and Gil Guidry were present at the signing on behalf of C.I., Ltd. Devito signed on behalf of EAB. Immediately prior to the signing of the agreement, four changes to the loan agreement were "penciled" in at the request of the C.E., Inc. representatives. The plaintiffs attach significance to a change made with regard to the guarantees of Robert Jackson and C.E., Inc. Prior to the change, the last sentence of § 2.06 provided: "The bank will only call on the Guarantees after having drawn under the Letters of Credit." The following phrase was added to that sentence at the time of the signing: "and only upon the failure or inability of the issuing bank to make payment under the terms of the Letters of Credit."

Following the consummation of the loan, the limited partners were contacted by C.I., Ltd. and advised to have new letters of credit issued naming EAB as beneficiary. This reissuance was accomplished by having new letters of credit issued in favor of C.I. Ltd. and then transferring those letters of credit to EAB. EAB contacted Mercantile National Bank of Dallas and First National Bank of Lafayette regarding payment of the prior loans. Those banks were instructed to cancel the letters of credit which they held. Upon the receipt of the new letters of credit, EAB paid off the Mercantile and First National loans with the proceeds of the new credit facility.

EAB placed C.I., Ltd. in default in September, 1982. On November 24, EAB drew drafts on the issuing banks for payment under the letters of credit. The plaintiffs sought and obtained a temporary restraining order which enjoined the issuing banks from honoring the drafts by EAB. A hearing was subsequently held after which the trial judge granted a preliminary injunction preventing honor of the drafts. The court held that the plaintiffs were entitled to injunctive relief under R.S. 10:5–114(2) since there was "fraud in the transaction."

The trial court based its holding of fraud on the acts of C.E., Inc. while acting as the general partner of C.I., Ltd. The court found that C.E., Inc. had disregarded the provisions of the PPM in making investments for C.I., Ltd. Also, the court found that C.E., Inc. did not fulfill its representation in the PPM that it would provide up to 5 million dollars in the event of negative cash flow for C.I., Ltd.

The court found that EAB had knowledge of these facts constituting fraud and therefore knew or should have known of the fraud being perpetrated on the investors. Therefore, the court found that EAB made the loan in bad faith. For these reasons, EAB was prohibited from drafting under the letters of credit.

The Court of Appeal reversed, holding that no fraud occurred within the intendment of R.S. 10:5–114(2). Therefore, injunctive relief was denied. The court found that the trial court erroneously concluded that EAB committed a fraud. The court did not decide whether C.E., Inc. had acted fraudulently since under its interpretation of R.S. 10:5–

114, such fraud would not have been grounds for an injunction against the issuing banks.

The plaintiffs sought writs from this court to have the trial court judgment reinstated. They claim that the Court of Appeal erroneously overturned the factual findings of the trial court, misconstrued the meaning of "fraud in the transaction" and erroneously accorded EAB rights greater than those of C.I., Ltd.

ISSUES

In order to determine whether the issuing banks may be enjoined from paying under the letters of credit, the following issues must be decided:

1.   What is the meaning of "fraud in the transaction," in R.S. 10:5–114(2), as applied to standby letters of credit which are used to secure bank financing?

2.   Whether such fraud occurred in this case, entitling plaintiffs to the injunctive relief provided for in R.S. 10:5–114(2)(b)?

The right to enforce payment of drafts issued under a letter of credit is governed by R.S. 10:5–114, which provides: [quoting]

* * *

FRAUD IN THE TRANSACTION

The primary issue in this case is the interpretation of "fraud in the transaction" in R.S. 10:5–114. Under that provision, the issuing banks must honor EAB's drafts unless the documents presented by EAB were " * * * forged or fraudulent or there is fraud in the transaction." R.S. 10:5–114(2). The plaintiffs do not dispute the validity of the documents submitted by EAB. Therefore, the only issue is whether there was "fraud in the transaction." If such fraud is found to exist, a court is empowered, under R.S. 10:5–114(2)(b), to enjoin the issuing banks from honoring drafts under the credit.

There is more than one "transaction" involved when letters of credit are issued. The first is the contract between the customer and the issuing bank, present in all cases; the conventional case involves a sale and delivery of goods; the standby case involves a contract or performance, or a loan by the beneficiary bank to a borrower, secured by the customer's letter of credit. If the credit secures a loan by the beneficiary bank, that loan is the underlying transaction.

The plaintiffs maintain that "transaction" should be interpreted in its broadest sense. It is their position that by not qualifying "transaction," the drafters intended it to be given by a very general and expansive interpretation. More specifically, they claim that "if a fraud is practiced that would ultimately cause a loss to the customer, injunction will lie against honor regardless of who perpetrated the fraud."

Furthermore, they contend that "transaction" must be understood to include the underlying transaction between the limited partners and C.I., Ltd. Plaintiffs maintain that by not giving transaction a general meaning, lending banks would be permitted to "launder fraud," thereby damaging the integrity of the judicial system.

The intervenors advocate a restrictive interpretation of "transaction." They claim that an injunction may be properly issued only when fraudulent documents are issued, or when the beneficiary commits active fraud against the investors who obtained the letters of credit.

The UCC was adopted in Louisiana in an effort to harmonize the commercial law of Louisiana with that of the other states.[4] We should, therefore, examine the jurisprudence of other states interpreting R.S. 10:5–114(2).[5]

The most frequently cited case on the "fraud in the transaction" exception to UCC § 5–114(2) is Sztejn v. Henry Schroder Banking Corp., 177 Misc. 719, 31 N.Y.S.2d 631 (Sup.Ct.N.Y. 1941). Although Sztejn arose before the drafting of the UCC, most commentators and courts agree that Sztejn was the impetus for the fraud exception.

* * *

In spite of its decision in favor of the plaintiff, the court was careful to leave the independence principle intact:

> "It is well established that a letter of credit is independent of the primary contract of sale between the buyer and the seller. The issuing bank agrees to pay upon presentation of documents, not goods. This rule is necessary to preserve the efficiency of the letter of credit as an instrument for the financing of trade. One of the chief purposes of the letter of credit is to furnish the seller with a ready means of obtaining prompt payment for his merchandise. It would be a most unfortunate interference with business transactions if a bank before honoring drafts drawn upon it was obliged or even allowed to go behind the documents, at the request of the buyer and enter into controversies between the buyer and the seller regarding the quality of the merchandise shipped. If the buyer and the seller intended the bank to do this they could have so provided in the letter of credit itself, and in the absence of such a provision, the court will not demand or even permit the bank to delay paying drafts which are proper in form. * * * Of course, the application of this doctrine presupposes that the documents accompanying the draft are genuine and conform in terms to the requirements of the letter of credit. * * * " (Citations omitted). 31 N.Y.S.2d at 633–34.

The Sztejn court, in determining whether the customer could stop the issuing bank from honoring the draft, determined that the underlying transaction was fraudulent and that the Chartered Bank (presenting the draft for payment on behalf of Transea) was in no better position than the fraudulent Transea.

4. R.S. 10:1–102(2)(c).

5. R.S. 10:5–114 varies in two respects from the uniform version of 5–114. However, the differences are minor and have no bearing on the issues in this case.

In R.S. 10:5–114(1), "for sale or other contract" was omitted as being unnecessary. In R.S. 10:5–114(2), a reference to UCC Articles 7 and 8 was omitted.

Sztejn was a commercial letter of credit case which involved active fraud on the part of the beneficiary. The bank (Chartered) that presented the draft for payment was merely the correspondent for the issuing bank, not a holder in due course, but an agent of the seller-beneficiary charged with fraud. The court refused to allow a seller-beneficiary to profit from its own fraudulent conduct.

The Sztejn holding was applied to standby letters of credit in Shaffer v. Brooklyn Park Garden Apartments, 311 Minn. 452, 250 N.W.2d 172 (1977). In Shaffer, two purchasers of units in a limited partnership had letters of credit issued in favor of the limited partnership as part of their capital contribution. The letters of credit provided they could be drawn on only after presentment of a promissory note and a certification by the partnership that the investors had failed "to meet payment of authorized loans which are payable." 250 N.W.2d at 175. The letters of credit were subsequently transferred to Wayzata Bank & Trust Company as security for loans to the partnership.

The partnership experienced financial difficulty and Wayzata Bank & Trust Company attempted to draw on the letters of credit. In compliance with the letter of credit, Wayzata presented notes and certifications by the partnership that the investors had failed "to meet payment of authorized loans which are payable."

The investors sued to enjoin Wayzata from drawing on the letters of credit, claiming that the certifications were false. The court found that an injunction was proper because *plaintiffs sought the injunction on the basis of fraud in the documentation.* The court reasoned that:

> " * * * [W]here injunctive relief is sought, the fraud alleged must be in respect to the documents presented and not as to the underlying transaction. The allegations of fraud made by [the plaintiff-investors] is appropriate for injunctive relief since it concerns the certifications by [the partnership] presented by Wayzata." 250 N.W.2d at 180.

Another standby letter of credit situation was faced in O'Grady v. First Union National Bank, 250 S.E.2d 587 (N.C. 1978). In that case, the attachment of a letter of credit to a note it purported to secure, but which had been substituted for the original note and which omitted the signature of one endorser was interpreted by the court as a case involving "fraudulent documentation" which would give rise to injunctive relief. Plaintiffs before us interpret the case as involving fraud "in the underlying transaction."

* * *

Finally, in Cappaert Enterprises v. Citizens and Southern International Bank of New Orleans, 486 F.Supp. 819 (E.D.La. 1980), plaintiff, Cappaert Enterprises, sued to enjoin a Kuwait bank from collecting under a letter of credit which was issued to secure a loan. The letter of credit was obtained by a joint venture comprised of Cappaert and United Fisheries of Kuwait. A dispute developed between Cappaert and United concerning performance of the joint venture agreement.

Cappaert sued to enjoin the Kuwait bank from drawing on the letter of credit, claiming that United had committed a fraud against it.

The district court concluded that Cappaert's claim of "fraud in the transaction" was without merit. The court relied heavily on the principle of independence between the letter of credit and the underlying transaction. According to the court:

> "The accuracy of Cappaert's allegation that United Fisheries acted fraudulently in its role as a joint venturer is immaterial to the resolution of this issue, for impropriety in the underlying agreement is irrelevant to an interpretation of the letter of credit. * * *" 486 F.Supp. at 826.

As illustrated in the foregoing cases the independence principle is a strong influence in the decision of cases throughout the country. Adherence to that basic principle is necessary in order to protect the commercial utility of letters of credit.

Nevertheless, the jurisprudence and literature recognize and illustrate the need to extend the meaning of "fraud in the transaction" at least a step beyond fraudulent documentation. The strongest reason for such an extended interpretation is to deny rewarding fraudulent conduct by letter of credit beneficiaries. One author writes:

> "Notwithstanding dictum to the contrary in some of the cases, *the holding of the court in NMC Enterprises, Inc. v. Columbia Broadcasting System, Inc. that fraud in the underlying transaction is sufficient to justify relief is the better rule.* Since the issuer's obligation on a letter of credit is generally completely independent of the underlying transaction, the customer who obtains a letter of credit assumes the risk that payment may be made when the beneficiary has not properly performed the underlying contract. Moreover, the beneficiary may have required the letter of credit in part to assure that a dispute regarding performance of the underlying contract would not delay payment. By obtaining a letter of credit, however, the customer should not be required to assume the risk of making payment to a beneficiary who has engaged in fraudulent conduct in the underlying transaction. Furthermore, a rule that precludes injunctive relief where the fraud is in the underlying transaction will compensate the beneficiary for wrongful acts in situations where the customer will not have an effective legal remedy for the fraudulent conduct and thus tend to encourage fraud, a policy that should be avoided. As the court said in Dynamics Corp. of America v. Citizens & Southern Nat. Bank, there is as much public interest in discouraging fraud as in encouraging the use of letters of credit.
>
>   "*While fraud in the underlying transaction should be sufficient to justify injunctive relief, mere failure to properly perform the underlying contract does not constitute fraud.* * * *" (Emphasis added). Hawkland & Holland, UCC Series § 5–114.09 (Art 5).

In the case before us, the "underlying transaction" is the loan transaction between EAB and C.I., Ltd. If the beneficiary EAB was guilty of fraud with respect to the plaintiffs (investors/customers), it should not be permitted to profit from that fraud.

If the banks want an instrument which will be paid without question upon demand, with no recourse by parties upon whom responsibility lies, other means are available.

Our holding is consistent with the cases cited by the parties as well as those found by our research. In all of the cases where letters of credit have been enjoined, the courts have found that either the documents were defective or the beneficiary was guilty of fraud. For example, in Sztejn, the customer sought to enjoin the payment of a draft, presented by the agent of the fraudulent beneficiary, at a time after the issuing bank had notice of the fraudulent shipment by the beneficiary.

Under the foregoing interpretation of "fraud in the transaction," it must now be decided whether such fraud occurred in this case. In accordance with our interpretation of R.S. 10:5–114(2), our analysis will be limited to the loan transaction and the conduct and knowledge of the beneficiary, EAB.

There is more than one measure of "fraud" in the various jurisdictions in the United States.

Cases and writers have called Sztejn an example of "egregious" fraud, and some have required "egregious" fraud in the transaction before according relief to the customer. (KMW International v. Chase Manhattan Bank, 27 UCC Rep. 203, 606 F.2d 10 (C.A.2 1979); Colorado National Bank of Denver v. Board of County Commissioners of Routt County, supra).

Cases and authorities have distinguished "egregious" fraud from "intentional" fraud, and have advocated "intentional" fraud as the better standard to afford injunctive relief to the customer. Hawkland & Holland UCC Series § 5–114:09 (Art 5).

Civil Code provisions defining fraud and the rights of the fraud victim establish standards for commercial transactions in Louisiana and would seem to require the same results reached in most of the fraud cases involving letters of credit.

"Fraud is a misrepresentation or a suppression of the truth made with the intention either to obtain an unjust advantage for one party or to cause a loss or inconvenience to the other. Fraud may also result from silence or inaction." C.C. 1953.

"Fraud does not vitiate consent when the party against whom the fraud was directed could have ascertained the truth without difficulty, inconvenience, or special skill.

"The exception does not apply when a relation of confidence has reasonably induced a party to rely on the other's assertions or representations." C.C. 1954.

"Error induced by fraud need not concern the cause of the obligation to vitiate consent, but it must concern a circumstance that has substantially influenced that consent." C.C. 1955.

"Fraud committed by a third person vitiates the consent of a contracting party if the other party knew or should have known of the fraud." C.C. 1956.

"Fraud need only be proved by a preponderance of the evidence and may be established by circumstantial evidence." C.C. 1957.

"The party against whom rescission is granted because of fraud is liable for damages and attorney fees." C.C. 1958.

Plaintiffs maintain that EAB obtained knowledge of fraudulent practices in its investigation of C.E., Inc. and C.I., Ltd. The trial court agreed with plaintiffs and found that the entire letter of credit transaction was permeated with fraud; the court also found that EAB had notice of the fraud. Such findings, if supported by the evidence, would warrant injunctive relief under our interpretation of R.S. 10:5–114.

The trial court relied on several factual findings in reaching its determination that "fraud in the transaction" occurred. The first finding relied on by the trial court was that the principals of C.E., Inc. made oral representations to the plaintiffs that C.I., Ltd. was going to invest directly in real estate. Contrary to these representations, C.I., Ltd. invested primarily in other partnerships. These representations have no relevance to the conduct of EAB since they were not written and it was not shown that EAB knew about them.

Secondly, the trial court found that EAB had knowledge of cash flow problems at C.E., Inc. This finding is supported by the testimony of Devito and the December 17, 1981 memo which placed the loan on hold. In spite of this knowledge, it is undisputed that EAB had received a significant number of positive recommendations concerning C.E., Inc.'s ability to pay its debts. It cannot be said that EAB's knowledge that a cash flow problem had existed constitutes fraud.

According to the trial court, the PPM misrepresented that C.E., Inc. could fund five million dollars of capital to C.I., Ltd. The PPM stated that C.E., Inc. would " * * * fund no more than $5,000,000 of working capital and/or negative cash flow * * *" (PPM, p 24). The plaintiffs argue that the trial court found that EAB knew that C.E., Inc. could not fulfill its funding commitment. They claim that this knowledge constituted fraud.

In addition to the above statement in the PPM regarding a capital commitment, the PPM also specifically described the risk of C.E., Inc. becoming unable to make funds available to C.I., Ltd. This risk is described on page 33 of the PPM as follows:

"There can be no assurance that the General Partner [C.E., Inc.] shall have funds available to it or shall be able to make funds available to the Partnership [C.I., Ltd.] in either case sufficient in amount to satisfy the obligations of the Partnership."

At best, C.E., Inc.'s funding commitment was equivocal. Therefore, EAB did not obtain knowledge of fraud as a result of its review of the funding provisions in the PPM.

According to the trial court, EAB learned from the first supplement to the PPM that C.I., Ltd. had made investments which did not fall within the primary investment objectives stated in the PPM. The PPM stated that C.I., Ltd. intended to invest "primarily" in "existing Properties, such as apartment buildings and complexes, hotels, motels, office buildings and complexes and similar income producing properties." (PPM, p 18). The PPM qualified the above representation in the following terms:

> "It should be noted that although the Partnership currently intends to invest primarily in real property, the Partnership Agreement does not restrict the Partnership in any way from acquiring or investing in any other type of property or investment." (PPM, p 18).

The supplement to the PPM stated that C.I., Ltd. had made eight investments. The largest investment was the purchase of the Bourbon Orleans Hotel in New Orleans for $12,867,300. The majority of the remaining investments consisted of interests purchased in other partnerships. Contrary to the findings of the trial court, EAB cannot be held to have known that these investments were inconsistent with the representations stated in the PPM. The largest of these investments, the Bourbon Orleans Hotel, fell squarely within the primary investment objectives of the PPM. With regard to the other investments, the PPM clearly stated that no guarantees could be given regarding the types of investments to be made by C.I., Ltd.

The trial court attached significance to the fact that the March, 1981 audit of C.E., Inc. was "qualified" due to the existence of outstanding payables and receivables with its affiliated partnerships. The audit report contained the qualification since the scope of the audit did not extend to the affiliated partnerships. Such a qualification, standing alone, is not evidence of fraud on the part of EAB. Devito testified at trial that most syndicators would not have even provided audited financial statements.

The trial court found that since EAB knew that the proceeds of the EAB loan were to be used to pay off prior partnership loans, EAB had notice of an impropriety. The acknowledged reason for obtaining the EAB financing was to replace the Mercantile and FNB loans with lower interest financing. This purpose was legitimate and it was disclosed to the investors.[7] Therefore, EAB's knowledge of the proposed use of the

---

7. The investors received letters from C.E., Inc. which stated that:

"In order to obtain substantial savings for Combined Investments, Ltd., the general partner has decided to take advantage of an opportunity to transfer to another bank the loan to which your Letter of Credit is now pledged as collateral. Transfer of this loan (now held by Mercantile National Bank at Dallas) to European American Bank and Trust of New York will enable the partnership to decrease the interest rate on this loan by one and one-half (1½%) percent, and therefore to acquire an annual savings of interest in the approxi-

proceeds was perfectly consistent with the interests of the plaintiff-investors.

*   *   *

Based on our foregoing analysis of the facts relied on by the trial court, we find that there was no evidence of fraud or knowledge of fraud on the part of EAB. Therefore, the "fraud in the transaction" exception of R.S. 10:5–114(2)(b) is not applicable to this case. The trial court's contrary holding was erroneous. Therefore, the Court of Appeal decision reversing the trial court in this respect must be affirmed.

OTHER DEFENSES

We now address plaintiffs' contention that EAB is subject to all of the defenses which could be asserted against C.I., Ltd., since EAB was a mere assignee of the letters of credit from C.I., Ltd. The trial court rejected this argument and found that EAB was entitled to the protected status accorded by the independence principle. We find that EAB was a beneficiary under the letters of credit in its own right and therefore it was not subject to defenses assertable against prior beneficiaries under different letters of credit.

At the time of the EAB loan, the investors were asked to have new letters of credit issued. The investors knew that the letters of credit were to be used to secure bank financing and that EAB would have the right to draw on the credit in case of default. As the new letters of credit were issued, the issuing banks simultaneously wrote EAB acknowledging that " *   *   * European American Bank & Trust shall be deemed for all purposes to be the beneficiary of the Letter of Credit."

*   *   *

[Some footnotes omitted.]

Notes

1. Three cheers for the Louisiana Supreme Court. The customers will ultimately get exactly what they deserve in this case, not so? The moral of the story might be as follows: when a sophisticated investor spends a lot of money to buy a tax deduction, even a hometown court won't bend the law to protect his interests.

2. This case shows a quintessential standby letter of credit. The letter has nothing to do with goods; it serves purely as a guarantee of the investors' promises to pay. With the decline in oil and gas prices and with the failure of a number of banks that had made substantial loans to drillers and others in the oil field (Penn Square in Oklahoma City is the best example) many such letters of credit have been called and many courts have faced the question how to define "fraud in the transaction" in such cases. Invariably in such cases the investors have argued that they (the limited partners) were defrauded by the general partner and that this in turn is enough to upset the letter of credit under UCC 5–114. The Louisiana court rejects that argument and is correct in doing so, not so?

mate amount of $115,692." (Letter to the Anderson and Savoy Partnership).

What form of interaction by the beneficiary bank with the underlying partnership would be necessary for a court to find the bank involved in the fraud and thus subject to the defense? For example, in the Penn Square case investors alleged that Penn Square (the beneficiary of the letters from other banks) was itself deeply involved with many of the general partners and had first-hand knowledge that the value of their oil and gas prospects were overstated. Based on such allegations, some courts enjoined payment on those letters.

3. If the court had concluded that there was fraud in the underlying transaction, could EAB have argued successfully under UCC 5–114(2)(a) that it was the "holder of the draft or demand which has taken the draft or demand under the credit and under circumstances which would make it a holder in due course"? If not, could the transaction have been arranged to give it that protection? It is unclear whether the court is addressing that issue at the end of the opinion, but it seems to be talking more generally about the independence issue.

SECTION 4. RIGHTS AGAINST THE GOODS, THE CUSTOM-ER, AND OTHERS

At the outset we suggested that the bank should regard a letter of credit as tantamount to a loan to its customer and should realize at minimum that it is extending a line of credit to the customer that may be drawn upon. Recognizing that fact, the bank typically will require the customer to execute a document of the kind set out below. Note that the security agreement gives the bank the right to demand payment before it has to pay the money itself. It gives the bank a security interest in the assets that are subject to the credit and in some cases in other assets. Note that UCC 5–114(3) gives the bank a statutory right of "immediate reimbursement," and to be put "in available funds" no later than the day before maturity. Note that UCC 9–304(5) is specifically designed to give a bank a 21 day perfected security interest in goods or documents that are the subject of a letter of credit transaction.

COMMERCIAL LETTER OF CREDIT APPLICATION AND SECURITY AGREEMENT

(APPLICANT: RETAIN INSIDE COPY FOR YOUR FILES.)

To: **NATIONAL BANK OF DETROIT**
International Division
Detroit, Michigan 48232

L/C No.

Date

Please issue an irrevocable Letter of Credit as set forth below and forward to Beneficiary or your correspondent by

☐ Airmail   ☐ Airmail, with short preliminary cable advice   ☐ Full Cable, for delivery to the beneficiary.

For Bank use ONLY unless you designate advising bank	FOR ACCOUNT OF (APPLICANT)
IN FAVOR OF (BENEFICIARY)	AMOUNT
	Drafts must be presented for negotiation or presented to drawee on or before (Expiry Date)

☐ TRANSFERRABLE AND THIRD PARTY SHIPPER ALLOWED

Available by drafts at ☐ Sight   ☐ _____ Days' After _____ drawn, at your option, on you or your correspondent for _____ % of the Invoice value.

When accompanied by the following documents as checked:

☐ COMMERCIAL INVOICE in _____ copies covering: *(Specify Commodity, omitting details as to Grade, Quality, and the like)*

Terms ☐ C & F
      ☐ CIF }   Port/Country _____   ☐ Other _____
      ☐ FOB }   *(Please specify)*

☐ SPECIAL U. S. CUSTOMS INVOICE

☐ CERTIFICATE OF ORIGIN

☐ PACKING LIST

☐ INSURANCE POLICY OR CERTIFICATE covering: *(State risks required)* _____

☐ Insurance effected by ourselves. We agree to keep insured until transaction completed.

☐ SHIPPING DOCUMENTS (Full set required if more than one original has been issued)
☐ On Board Ocean Bills of Lading consigned to the order of National Bank of Detroit
☐ Original signed Air Waybill   CONSIGNED TO: _____
☐ Original signed Truck Blading } _____
☐ Other: _____ } _____

"Notify" Party: _____

Shipment From:	Latest Shipping Date	Partial Shipments	☐ Permitted	☐ Prohibited
To:		Transshipments	☐ Permitted	☐ Prohibited
		Freight	☐ Collect	☐ Prepaid

☐ OTHER DOCUMENTS: _____

☐ SPECIAL INSTRUCTIONS
☒ You may instruct negotiating bank to forward all documents in a single airmailing.
☐ All banking charges outside of the U.S. are for the beneficiaries account.
☐ Other _____

ALL DOCUMENTS MUST BE PRESENTED TO NEGOTIATING OR PAYING BANK WITHIN _____ DAYS AFTER THE DATE OF ISSUANCE OF SHIPPING DOCUMENTS BUT WITHIN VALIDITY OF LETTER OF CREDIT.

Any questions concerning this application should be referred to:

_____

Phone: (_____) _____

ALL PAYMENTS HEREUNDER TO BE CHARGED TO OUR NBD ACCOUNT NO. _____

NBD 7329 9/80

This Application is made pursuant to Letter of Credit Security Agreement Terms and Conditions which appear as part of this form and apply to this Application and the credit issued pursuant hereto, receipt of which Terms and Conditions is hereby acknowledged.

_____
Applicant Signature/Title   [E1226]

COMMERCIAL LETTER OF CREDIT—REIMBUR.S.EMENT AND SECURITY AGREEMENT TERMS AND CONDITIONS

To: National Bank of Detroit
       International Division
       Detroit, Michigan 48232

1. OBLIGATION OF BANK TO ISSUE CREDITS

Except for a contrary provision in the application for Letter of Credit ("Credit"), the terms and conditions herein set forth shall apply to issuance of the Credit, provided, until issuance of said Credit, you shall be under no obligation to issue the same.

2. OBLIGATION TO PAY

(a) DRAFTS OR ACCEPTANCES

As to drafts or acceptances drawn or purporting to be drawn under the Credit, we agree: (i) in the case of each sight draft, to reimburse you at your office, on demand, the amount paid on such drafts, or, if so demanded by you, to pay to you at your office in advance the amount required to pay such draft; and (ii) in case of each acceptance, to pay to you, at your office, the amount thereof, on demand, but in no event later than maturity, or, in case the acceptance is not payable at your office, then in time to reach the place of payment at maturity. As to drafts or acceptances which are payable in other than U.S. Currency to pay or reimburse you, on demand, in U.S. Currency the equivalent of the amount paid, or estimated by you to be paid, at your current rate of exchange as of the date of payment or at the date of transmission by you for cable transfers to the place of payment where and in the currency in which draft or acceptance is payable, or if there is no such rate at said time, then at such rate as you may fix.

(b) As to documents presented for payment at sight pursuant to the credit, without drafts, we agree our obligation thereunder shall be the same as though sight drafts had been presented or accompanied such documents.

(c) COMMISSIONS, CHARGES, EXPENSES, FEES AND INTEREST

We agree to pay you on demand such commission based on the amount of the credit as is your then current scheduled charges for the particular credit and all charges and expenses paid or incurred by you including, without limitation, FDIC Assessments and the cost of maintenance of required reserves, if any (including expenses of collection or of exercise of your rights hereunder as to security or otherwise and legal fees) and interest on the amount of any payment made by you under the credit and not reimbursed by us as herein provided (plus interest on commissions, charges and expenses not so reimbursed) at the rate of 3% per annum more than the prime rate announced by you as the prime rate for your commercial loans then in effect (which prime rate may not necessarily be the lowest rate charged by you to any of your customers), but not an amount greater than is allowable under the laws of the State of Michigan.

(d) ADVICE FROM CORRESPONDENTS

Telegraphic or other notice from your correspondent or agents of payment, acceptance, or other action under the Credit shall be presumptive evidence of our liability hereunder to reimburse you.

3. ADMINISTRATION OF CREDIT

(a) "UNIFORM CUSTOMS AND PRACTICES FOR DOCUMENTARY CREDITS"

The "Uniform Customs and Practice for Documentary Credits, 1983 revision, ICC Publication N° 400" of the International Chamber of Commerce (copy of which is available from you at our request) shall govern the rights and liabilities of you and us hereunder to the same effect as if stated word for word herein, and the Credit issued hereunder shall be subject to, and be governed by, the provisions of said uniform customs and practices unless the context of this agreement shall be contrary thereto, or in addition thereto, in which event any contrary or additional obligation or liability of us hereunder shall be as stated herein and your rights, obligation or liability as stated herein shall each govern notwithstanding the provisions of said uniform customs and practices which shall be thereby deemed to be superseded and not applicable to the extent of such contrary or additional provisions of this agreement, but not otherwise.

(b) REGULATIONS AND FOREIGN LAW * * *

(c) RELEASE OF PROPERTY OR DOCUMENTS

If you deliver to us, or upon our order, any of the property, documents or instruments relative to the Credit, or held by you as security hereunder, prior to payment in full of all our obligations secured hereby, we will deliver to you trust receipts thereof, or other security agreements and statements of trust receipt financing, or other financing statements, complying with applicable law and in such form as you may request, and pay all necessary filing fees, it being understood that any such delivery is made in reliance upon this Agreement and that your rights specified herein shall be an addition to your rights under any such applicable law, trust receipt or security agreement. Upon any transfer, sale, delivery or surrender or endorsement of any document or instrument at any time held by you, or for your account by any of your correspondents, relative to the Credit, on trust receipt or otherwise, we will indemnify and hold you and any such correspondents harmless from and against each and every claim, demand, action or suit asserted by reason thereof.

(d) STEAMSHIP GUARANTY—AIR RELEASE * * *

(e) LICENSES—INSURANCE * * *

(f) RESPONSIBILITIES OF YOU AND AGENTS

The users of the Credit shall be deemed our agents and we assume all risks of their acts and omissions. Neither you nor your correspondents shall be responsible: for the description, quantity, weight, quality, condition, packing, delivery, value or existence of the property purporting to be represented by documents; for any difference in character, quality, quantity, condition or value of the property from that expressed in documents; for the form, sufficiency, accuracy, genuineness, falsification or legal effect of any documents, even if such documents should in fact prove to be in any or all respects invalid, insufficient, fraudulent or forged; for the time, place, manner or order in which shipment is made; for partial or incomplete shipment, or failure or omissions to ship any or all of the property referred to in the Credit; for the character, adequacy, validity, or genuineness of any insurance; for the solvency or responsibility of any insurer, or for any other risk connected with insurance; for any deviation from instructions, delay, default or fraud by the shipper or anyone else in connection with the property or the shipping thereof; for the solvency, responsibility or relationship to the property of any party issuing any documents in connection with the property; for delay in arrival or failure to arrive of either the property or any of the documents relating thereto; for delay in giving or failure to give notice of arrival or any other notice; for any breach of contract between the shippers or vendors and ourselves or any of us; for failure of any draft to bear any reference or adequate reference to the Credit, or failure of documents to accompany any draft at negotiation, or failure of any person to note the amount of any draft on the reverse of the Credit, or to surrender or take up the Credit or to send forward documents apart from drafts as required by the terms of the Credit, each of which provisions, if contained in the Credit itself, it is agreed may be waived by you; or for errors, omissions, interruptions or delays in transmission or delivery of any messages, by mail, cable, telegraph, wireless, or otherwise, whether or not they be in cipher; nor shall you be responsible for any errors, neglect, or default of any of your correspondents; and none of the above shall affect, impair, or prevent the vesting of any of your rights or powers hereunder. In furtherance and extension, and not in limitation of, the specific provisions hereinbefore set forth, we agree that any action taken by you or by any correspondent of yours under or in connection with the Credit or the relative drafts, documents or property, if taken in good faith, shall be binding on us and shall not put you or your correspondents under any resulting liability to us; and we make like agreement as to any inaction or omission, unless in breach of good faith. We agree that any objection to action taken by you or any correspondent shall be deemed ratified by us unless within 10 days after receipt of such documents or acquisitions of knowledge thereof objection and notice to you is made by us.

    (g) COPIES OF DOCUMENTS * * *

    (h) DRAFT LESS THAN CREDIT AMOUNT * * *

4. SECURITY INTERESTS

As security for the prompt payment of all our obligations and liabilities hereunder, and in addition to any other security given to you by separate agreement, you are hereby granted a continuing security interest in and, the right to possession and disposition of, all property shipped, stored or dealt with in connection with the Credit, or the drafts drawn thereunder, and to all drafts, documents or instruments or contracts (including shipping documents or warehouse receipts or policies or certificates of insurance) or inventory or accounts or chattel paper or contract rights or general intangibles, arising from or in connection with this Credit, regardless of whether such property or documents or instruments, or other security herein described, are in your actual or constructive possession, or in transit to you, your agents, or correspondents, and the proceeds thereof, and we hereby further grant you a right of set-off upon all deposits and credits with you until our obligations or liabilities to you have been paid and discharged. We agree that this Agreement may be filed as a financing statement or that we will execute such financing statements or other documents or writings as shall be necessary, in your judgment, to perfect or maintain your security interest, as aforesaid, and to pay all costs of filing. We also agree you may execute on our behalf such financing statement and we do irrevocably appoint you as our attorney in fact for such purpose. You shall have all rights and remedies of a secured party under the Uniform Commercial Code of Michigan and you shall give us five (5) days prior written notice to the time and place of any sale upon exercise of your right to sale, public or private, before or after maturity, unless such security is perishable or threatens to decline speedily in value or is of a type customarily sold on a recognized market. You may discount, settle, compromise or extend any obligation, constituting such security, and sue thereon in your name. You shall not be liable for failure to collect or demand payment of, or protest or give notice of, or nonpayment of, any obligations, included in such security or part thereof, or for any delay, nor shall you be under any obligation to take any action in respect of such security, including any obligation to file, record or maintain or establish the validity, priority, or enforceability of your rights in or to the security. Any property or documents representing security hereunder may be held by you in your name or your nominee's name, all without notice and whether a Default exists, or not. Proceeds of sale or transfer of the security shall be applied, in order, to expenses of retaking, holding, preparing for sale, and the reasonable attorney fees and legal expenses incurred or paid by you, and then, to our obligation hereunder until paid in full.

5. DEFAULT

We shall be in Default under this agreement upon occurrence of any one of the following:

(a) Failure to perform or observe any of the terms and conditions hereof; or

(b) Failure to pay, when due, whether upon your demand or otherwise, any amounts due hereunder; or

(c) Any warranty, representation or statement made to or furnished you is untrue in any material respect; or

(d) The loss, theft, destruction, sale or encumbrance of any part or all of the security for this agreement; or

(e) The death, incapacity, insolvency, dissolution, termination of existence, suspension of business or if a receiver is appointed for any part of our property, or if we make an assignment for the benefit of creditors, or upon the commencement of bankruptcy or insolvency proceedings by or against us, or upon the issuance or service of any levy, lien, writ of attachment or garnishment or execution or similar process against us, or any of our property; or

(f) Failure to pay, when due, any tax; or

(g) If, in your sole opinion, our financial responsibility is impaired; or

(h) Any event occurs which results or could result in the acceleration of the maturity of any of our indebtedness to you or to others under any note, agreement or undertaking, in which event you shall have the right to take possession of the security given herein, set-off against same, or the rights of a secured creditor, with or without process of law, and foreclose, sell or otherwise liquidate the security both as herein provided and as provided in the Uniform Commercial Code of the State of Michigan.

6. MODIFICATION OF CREDIT

All extensions, including extensions of maturity or time for presentation of drafts, acceptances or documents, or renewals of the credit or increase or other modification of the terms hereof, or a temporary advance or acceptance or loan in connection with the credit, with or without further documentation or notice or agreement, shall continue to be governed by this agreement.

7. WAIVER

No delay on your part in the exercise of any of your rights or remedies shall operate as a waiver, nor shall any single or partial waiver, or any right or remedy preclude any other further exercise thereof, or the exercise of any other right or remedy, and no waiver or indulgence by you of any default shall be effective unless in writing and signed by you, nor shall a waiver on any one occasion be construed as a bar, or waiver of, any such right on any future occasion.

8. GOVERNING LAW * * *

9. BINDING EFFECT * * *

10. CONSTRUCTION * * *

11. PARTICIPANT * * *

12. DAMAGES

Your liability, if any, for your negligence, acts of omission or otherwise shall be limited to direct actual damages, but without liability for general, punitive or special damages or other consequential damages resulting therefrom.

Revised 1/8/86 (Commercial)

Problem 16–7

Answer the following questions with respect to the Reimbursement and Security Agreement set out above.

1. Assume that Bank knew that drafts for $500,000 would be presented under the letter on Tuesday. Would it have a right to demand payment by the customer of $500,000 on Monday? If the customer refused to pay, what rights would the Bank have under the Reimbursement and Security Agreement?

2. Assume that Bank made payment and now seeks reimbursement under the $500,000 letter of credit and that customer argues that the invoices were not in proper form because the description was not exactly the same as the description on the letter of credit. How will the Agreement affect that dispute between the Bank and its customer? (See (3)(f).)

3. If the customer fails to pay, the Bank has possession of the invoices and bills of lading. Does it have a perfected security interest? If it cannot liquidate the security within a short period of time, how can it maintain perfection of that security interest if the customer refuses to sign a financing statement? (See (4).)

4. What if the Bank extended the time for the beneficiary to present drafts under the letter by one day and the customer then complained that the Bank had violated their agreement? Does the agreement give the Bank the right to issue such waivers and extensions on behalf of customer?

To what extent can the Bank be subrogated to, and otherwise enjoy, rights of Beneficiary? The case that follows deals with that question.

IN RE ECONOMIC ENTERPRISES, INC.
United States Bankruptcy Court, District Connecticut, 1984.
44 B.R. 230.

ALAN H.W. SHIFF, BANKRUPTCY JUDGE. Merchants Bank & Trust Co. (MBT) brings this motion in two counts. First, for relief from the automatic stay under Code § 362(a) in order to commence foreclosure proceedings against property of Galaxy Associates (Galaxy), a debtor under Chapter 11, and second, to participate "pari passu" with the first mortgagee, Citytrust Company (Citytrust). The parties have agreed that this proceeding should be limited to second count. Accordingly, this Memorandum and Order will be confined to the so-called pari passu issue as it relates to the two above captioned Chapter 11 cases.

BACKGROUND

Economic Enterprises, Inc. (Economic), a land developer, now a Chapter 11 debtor and former owner of the Galaxy property, requested that Citytrust finance the construction of condominium units on premises at Fairview Avenue, in Norwalk, Connecticut. Citytrust conditioned approval of the construction mortgage loan on several terms, including Economic's acquisition of an irrevocable letter of credit on terms satisfactory to Citytrust.

On or about December 23, 1981, MBT issued an irrevocable letter of credit to Economic as "customer" and Citytrust as "beneficiary."[1] On the same day, Economic executed a promissory note and construction mortgage deed in favor of Citytrust.

Subsequently, the condition for payment of the letter of credit, i.e. default by Economic on the note to Citytrust, occurred and Citytrust demanded payment from MBT. It is undisputed that MBT paid the full value of the letter of credit to Citytrust.

MBT now contends that because it paid the full value of the letter of credit, it should be subrogated to the first mortgage rights of Citytrust to the extent of the $400,000.00 it paid to Citytrust.[2]

DISCUSSION

The law of the State of Connecticut, which adopts Article 5 of the Uniform Commercial Code, is clear that an issuer of a letter of credit may not look to the underlying contract between its customer and the beneficiary of the letter of credit in connection with its duty to honor the letter of credit. New York Life Insurance Co. v. Hartford National Bank & Trust Co., 173 Conn. 492 (1977); see Conn.Gen.Stat.Ann. §§ 421–5–109, 42a–5–114, and Official Comments thereto.

1. See Conn.Gen.Stat.Ann. § 42a–5–103 for definitions.

2. MBT used the term "pari passu." While pari passu contemplates that credi-tors share in assets on an equal basis, MBT specifically requests that it be entitled to share ratably in the first mortgage to the extent of $400,000.

MBT argues that the prohibition against utilizing the underlying contract as a defense to payment does not prevent a court of equity from allowing an issuer to be subrogated to the rights of a beneficiary after payment to a beneficiary. The only authority MBT presents in support of that argument is an article written by a member of the Oregon bar, which cites no judicial authority for that proposition. Moreover, the author comments upon the precautions an issuer might take at the time a letter of credit is issued if the issuer intends to assert a right of subrogation.

> "Insofar as issuers do not want to rely on the subrogation argument, however, they might want to consider altering the documents required of the beneficiary of a standby letter of credit to include an explicit assignment of the beneficiary's security interest in the customer's assets[, a]lthough courts would not be absolutely bound to recognize this assignment."

The beneficiary here, Citytrust, did not agree to an assignment of part of its first mortgage. Indeed it insisted upon an irrevocable letter of credit, not a mere guaranty, as a condition to the granting of a construction mortgage loan.

MBT further contends, by way of analogy, that the Official Comment to UCC § 5–109 supports its argument. That comment provides in pertinent part:

> "The customer will normally have direct recourse against the beneficiary if performance fails, whereas the issuer will have such recourse only by assignment of or in a proper case subrogation to the rights of the customer."

This court does not agree with the logic of MBT's analogy. Simply because MBT might "in a proper case" be subrogated to the rights of Economic (customer), it does not follow that it should be subrogated to the rights of Citytrust (beneficiary). An issuer may not invade the underlying contract after payment on a letter of credit when the customer has no cause of action against the beneficiary. To allow an issuer an equitable right of subrogation under these circumstances would violate the spirit and intent of the law developing under Article 5 which, as noted, prohibits an issuer from interfering with the underlying contract unless explicit language in the letter of credit so provides.

In Data General Corp. v. Citizens National Bank, 502 F.Supp. 776, 788 (D.Conn. 1980), the court explained:

> "[A]n issuing bank's duty to a beneficiary is unrelated to the relationship between the bank and its customer. If a bank issues a letter of credit without first securing funds from its customer, * * * the beneficiary should not be prejudiced by the bank's deliberate inaction or inadvertence."

*   *   *

[T]he equities in this case favor the legal result. While Citytrust has the sole security of a first mortgage on the property now owned by

Galaxy, MBT has security which includes the personal guaranty of three persons and mortgages on three unrelated properties as well as a second mortgage on the Galaxy property.

ORDER

For the foregoing reasons, Merchants Bank & Trust Company is not entitled to be subrogated to the rights of Citytrust or to otherwise interfere with Citytrust's rights under its first mortgage on the Galaxy property.

It is so ordered.

[Some footnotes omitted.]

Notes

1. What policy reasons do you see for or against the court's outcome in this case?

2. If you represented the issuing bank and sought to avoid this problem, how could you do it?

3. If creditor's obligation had been secured by a conventional guarantee instead of a letter of credit, presumably the guarantor would have been subrogated to the creditor's claim against the debtor. Can you justify the distinction between that case and the case involving the letter of credit?

How in general can the bank protect itself from the kind of exposure it faced in the *Economic Enterprises* case and in the *Routt County* case when the bank is issuing a classic standby letter and when by hypothesis there will be little or no security arising out of the underlying transaction if it is called upon to pay?

THE UNIFORM CUSTOMS AND PRACTICES FOR DOCUMENTARY CREDITS

As an instrument for conducting business, often on an international level, documentary credits had to have standard definitions and terminology to be fully effective. Principles had to be formulated which were to be applicable to international law and set up in the form of brief concise rules for common usage and practice. These would have to suit all users without causing hindrance or restraint.

The ICC carried out a number of projects in this connection as part of its general activities. Based on a brochure published in 1924 by Union syndicale des banques francaises and reversing rules formulated at ICC Congresses in 1933 and 1951, the results appeared in 1962 as "Brochure No. 222".

Further work, done by the ICC Commission on Banking Technique and Practice, under the chairmanship of Mr. B.S. Wheble, led to a revised version in 1974. This became "Publication No. 290" under the title "Uniform Customs and Practice for Documentary Credits" to which banks in some 156 countries have already adhered.

The latest up-dating is the 1983 Revision (Publication No. 400). It became effective from 1st October, 1984.

It has received the following "blessing" of UNCITRAL.

The United Nations Commission on International Trade Law

Expressing its appreciation to the International Chamber of Commerce for having transmitted to it the revised text of "Uniform Customs and Practice for Documentary Credits", which was approved by the Commission on Banking Technique and Practice of the ICC and adopted by the Council of the ICC on 21 June 1983;

Congratulating the ICC on having made a further contribution to the facilitation of international trade by bringing up to date its rules on documentary credit practice to allow for developments in transport technology and changes in commercial practices;

Having regard to the fact that, in revising the 1974 text of "Uniform Customs and Practice for Documentary Credits", the ICC has taken into account the observations made by Governments and banking and trade institutions of countries not represented within it and transmitted to it through the Commission;

Noting that "Uniform Customs and Practice for Documentary Credits" constitutes a valuable contribution to the facilitation of international trade;

Commends the use of the 1983 revision, as from 1 October 1984, in transactions involving the establishment of a documentary credit.

A. General Provisions and Definitions

Article 1

These articles apply to all documentary credits, including, to the extent to which they may be applicable, standby letters of credit, and are binding on all parties thereto unless otherwise expressly agreed. They shall be incorporated into each documentary credit by wording in the credit indicating that such credit is issued subject to Uniform Customs and Practice for Documentary Credits, 1983 revision, ICC Publication No. 400.

Article 2

For the purposes of these articles, the expressions "documentary credit(s)" and "standby letter(s) of credit" used herein (hereinafter referred to as "credit(s)"), mean any arrangement, however named or described, whereby a bank (the issuing bank), acting at the request and on the instructions of a customer (the applicant for the credit),

i   is to make a payment to or to the order of a third party (the beneficiary), or is to pay or accept bills of exchange (drafts) drawn by the beneficiary, or

ii authorizes another bank to effect such payment, or to pay, accept or negotiate such bills of exchange (drafts), against stipulated documents, provided that the terms and conditions of the credit are complied with.

ARTICLE 3

Credits, by their nature, are separate transactions from the sales or other contract(s) on which they may be based and banks are in no way concerned with or bound by such contract(s), even if any reference whatsoever to such contract(s) is included in the credit.

ARTICLE 4

In credit operations all parties concerned deal in documents, and not in goods, services and/or other performances to which the documents may relate.

ARTICLE 5

Instructions for the issuance of credits, the credits themselves, instructions for any amendments thereto and the amendments themselves must be complete and precise.

In order to guard against confusion and misunderstanding, banks should discourage any attempt to include excessive detail in the credit or in any amendment thereto.

ARTICLE 6

A beneficiary can in no case avail himself of the contractual relationships existing between the banks or between the applicant for the credit and the issuing bank.

B. FORM AND NOTIFICATION OF CREDITS

ARTICLE 7

a. Credits may be either

i revocable, or

ii irrevocable.

b. All credits, therefore, should clearly indicate whether they are revocable or irrevocable.

c. In the absence of such indication the credit shall be deemed to be revocable.

ARTICLE 8

A credit may be advised to a beneficiary through another bank (the advising bank) without engagement on the part of the advising bank, but that bank shall take reasonable care to check the apparent authenticity of the credit which it advises.

ARTICLE 9

a. A revocable credit may be amended or cancelled by the issuing bank at any moment and without prior notice to the beneficiary.

b. However, the issuing bank is bound to:

i reimburse a branch or bank with which a revocable credit has been made available for sight payment, acceptance or negotiation, for any payment, acceptance or negotiation made by such branch or bank prior to receipt by it of notice of amendment or cancellation, against documents which appear on their face to be in accordance with the terms and conditions of the credit.

ii reimburse a branch or bank with which a revocable credit has been made available for deferred payment, if such branch or bank has, prior to receipt by it of notice of amendment or cancellation, taken up documents which appear on their face to be in accordance with the terms and conditions of the credit.

ARTICLE 10

a. An irrevocable credit constitutes a definite undertaking of the issuing bank, provided that the stipulated documents are presented and that the terms and conditions of the credit are complied with:

i if the credit provides for sight payment—to pay, or that payment will be made;

ii if the credit provides for deferred payment—to pay, or that payment will be made, on the date(s) determinable in accordance with the stipulations of the credit;

iii if the credit provides for acceptance—to accept drafts drawn by the beneficiary if the credit stipulates that they are to be drawn on the issuing bank, or to be responsible for their acceptance and payment at maturity if the credit stipulates that they are to be drawn on the applicant for the credit or any other drawee stipulated in the credit;

iv if the credit provides for negotiation—to pay without recourse to drawers and/or bona fide holders, draft(s) drawn by the beneficiary, at sight or at a tenor, on the applicant for the credit or on any other drawee stipulated in the credit other than the issuing bank itself, or to provide for negotiation by another bank and to pay, as above, if such negotiation is not effected.

b. When an issuing bank authorizes or requests another bank to confirm its irrevocable credit and the latter has added its confirmation, such confirmation constitutes a definite undertaking of such bank (the confirming bank), in addition to that of the issuing bank, provided that the stipulated documents are presented and that the terms and conditions of the credit are complied with:

i if the credit provides for sight payment—to pay, or that payment will be made;

ii if the credit provides for deferred payment—to pay, or that payment will be made, on the date(s) determinable in accordance with the stipulations of the credit;

iii if the credit provides for acceptance—to accept drafts drawn by the beneficiary if the credit stipulates that they are to be drawn on the confirming bank, or to be responsible for their acceptance and payment at maturity if the credit stipulates that they are to be drawn on the applicant for the credit or any other drawee stipulated in the credit;

iv if the credit provides for negotiation—to negotiate without recourse to drawers and/or bona fide holders, draft(s) drawn by the beneficiary, at sight or at a tenor, on the issuing bank or on the applicant for the credit or on any other drawee stipulated in the credit other than the confirming bank itself.

c. If a bank is authorized or requested by the issuing bank to add its confirmation to a credit but is not prepared to do so, it must so inform the issuing bank without delay. Unless the issuing bank specifies otherwise in its confirmation authorization or request, the advising bank will advise the credit to the beneficiary without adding its confirmation.

d. Such undertakings can neither be amended nor cancelled without the agreement of the issuing bank, the confirming bank (if any), and the beneficiary. Partial acceptance of amendments contained in one and the same advice of amendment is not effective without the agreement of all the above named parties.

ARTICLE 11

a. All credits must clearly indicate whether they are available by sight payment, by deferred payment, by acceptance or by negotiation.

b. All credits must nominate the bank (nominated bank) which is authorized to pay (paying bank), or to accept drafts (accepting bank), or to negotiate (negotiating bank), unless the credit allows negotiation by any bank (negotiating bank).

c. Unless the nominated bank is the issuing bank or the confirming bank, its nomination by the issuing bank does not constitute any undertaking by the nominated bank to pay, to accept, or to negotiate.

d. By nominating a bank other than itself, or by allowing for negotiation by any bank, or by authorizing or requesting a bank to add its confirmation, the issuing bank authorizes such bank to pay, accept or negotiate, as the case may be, against documents which appear on their face to be in accordance with the terms and conditions of the credit, and undertakes to reimburse such bank in accordance with the provisions of these articles.

ARTICLE 12

a. When an issuing bank instructs a bank (advising bank) by any teletransmission to advise a credit or an amendment to a credit, and intends the mail confirmation to be the operative credit instrument, or the operative amendment, the teletransmission must state "full details to follow" (or words of similar effect), or that the mail confirmation will be the operative credit instrument or the operative amendment. The issuing bank must forward the operative credit instrument or the operative amendment to such advising bank without delay.

b. The teletransmission will be deemed to be the operative credit instrument or the operative amendment, and no mail confirmation should be sent, unless the teletransmission states "full details to follow" (or words of similar effect), or states that the mail confirmation is to be the operative credit instrument or the operative amendment.

c. A teletransmission intended by the issuing bank to be the operative credit instrument should clearly indicate that the credit is issued subject to Uniform Customs and Practice for Documentary Credits, 1983 revision, ICC Publication No. 400.

d. If a bank uses the services of another bank or banks (the advising bank) to have the credit advised to the beneficiary, it must also use the services of the same bank(s) for advising any amendments.

e. Banks shall be responsible for any consequences arising from their failure to follow the procedures set out in the preceding paragraphs.

ARTICLE 13

When a bank is instructed to issue, confirm or advise a credit similar in terms to one previously issued, confirmed or advised (similar credit) and the previous credit has been the subject of amendment(s), it shall be understood that the similar credit will not include any such amendment(s) unless the instructions specify clearly the amendment(s) which is/are to apply to the similar credit. Banks should discourage instructions to issue, confirm or advise a credit in this manner.

ARTICLE 14

If incomplete or unclear instructions are received to issue, confirm, advise or amend a credit, the bank requested to act on such instructions may give preliminary notification to the beneficiary for information only and without responsibility. The credit will be issued, confirmed, advised or amended only when the necessary information has been received and if the bank is then prepared to act on the instructions. Banks should provide the necessary information without delay.

C. LIABILITIES AND RESPONSIBILITIES

ARTICLE 15

Banks must examine all documents with reasonable care to ascertain that they appear on their face to be in accordance with the terms and conditions of the credit. Documents which appear on their face to be inconsistent with one another will be considered as not appearing on their face to be in accordance with the terms and conditions of the credit.

ARTICLE 16

a. If a bank so authorized effects payment, or incurs a deferred payment undertaking, or accepts, or negotiates against documents which appear on their face to be in accordance with the terms and conditions of a credit, the party giving such authority shall be bound to reimburse the bank which has effected payment, or incurred a deferred payment undertaking, or has accepted, or negotiated, and to take up the documents.

b. If, upon receipt of the documents, the issuing bank considers that they appear on their face not to be in accordance with the terms and conditions of the credit, it must determine, on the basis of the documents alone, whether to take up such documents, or to refuse them and claim that they appear on their face not to be in accordance with the terms and conditions of the credit.

c. The issuing bank shall have a reasonable time in which to examine the documents and to determine as above whether to take up or to refuse the documents.

d. If the issuing bank decides to refuse the documents, it must give notice to that effect without delay by telecommunication or, if that is not possible, by other expeditious means, to the bank from which it received the documents (the remitting bank), or to the beneficiary, if it received the documents directly from him. Such notice must state the discrepancies in respect of which the issuing bank refuses the documents and must also state whether it is holding the documents at the disposal of, or is returning them to, the presentor (remitting bank or the beneficiary, as the case may be). The issuing bank shall then be entitled to claim from the remitting bank refund of any reimbursement which may have been made to that bank.

e. If the issuing bank fails to act in accordance with the provisions of paragraphs (c) and (d) of this article and/or fails to hold the documents at the disposal of, or to return them to, the presentor, the issuing bank shall be precluded from claiming that the documents are not in accordance with the terms and conditions of the credit.

f. If the remitting bank draws the attention of the issuing bank to any discrepancies in the documents or advises the issuing bank that it has paid, incurred a deferred payment undertaking, accepted or negoti- ated under reserve or against an indemnity in respect of such discrep- ancies, the issuing bank shall not be thereby relieved from any of its obligations under any provision of this article. Such reserve or indem- nity concerns only the relations between the remitting bank and the party towards whom the reserve was made, or from whom, or on whose behalf, the indemnity was obtained.

ARTICLE 17

Banks assume no liability or responsibility for the form, sufficien- cy, accuracy, genuineness, falsification or legal effect of any documents, or for the general and/or particular conditions stipulated in the docu- ments or superimposed thereon; nor do they assume any liability or responsibility for the description, quantity, weight, quality, condition, packing, delivery, value or existence of the goods represented by any documents, or for the good faith or acts and/or omissions, solvency, performance or standing of the consignor, the carriers, or the insurers of the goods, or any other person whomsoever.

ARTICLE 18

Banks assume no liability or responsibility for the consequences arising out of delay and/or loss in transit of any messages, letters or documents, or for delay, mutilation or other errors arising in the transmission of any telecommunication. Banks assume no liability or responsibility for errors in translation or interpretation of technical terms, and reserve the right to transmit credit terms without translating them.

ARTICLE 19

Banks assume no liability or responsibility for consequences arising out of the interruption of their business by Acts of God, riots, civil commotions, insurrections, wars or any other causes beyond their control, or by any strikes or lockouts. Unless specifically authorized, banks will not, upon resumption of their business, incur a deferred payment undertaking, or effect payment, acceptance or negotiation under credits which expired during such interruption of their business.

ARTICLE 20

a. Banks utilising the services of another bank or other banks for the purpose of giving effect to the instructions of the applicant for the credit do so for the account and at the risk of such applicant.

b. Banks assume no liability or responsibility should the instructions they transmit not be carried out, even if they have themselves taken the initiative in the choice of such other bank(s).

c. The applicant for the credit shall be bound by and liable to indemnify the banks against all obligations and responsibilities imposed by foreign laws and usages.

ARTICLE 21

a. If an issuing bank intends that the reimbursement to which a paying, accepting or negotiating bank is entitled shall be obtained by such bank claiming on another branch or office of the issuing bank or on a third bank (all hereinafter referred to as the reimbursing bank) it shall provide such reimbursing bank in good time with the proper instructions or authorization to honour such reimbursement claims and without making it a condition that the bank entitled to claim reimbursement must certify compliance with the terms and conditions of the credit to the reimbursing bank.

b. An issuing bank will not be relieved from any of its obligations to provide reimbursement itself if and when reimbursement is not effected by the reimbursing bank.

c. The issuing bank will be responsible to the paying, accepting or negotiating bank for any loss of interest if reimbursement is not provided on first demand made to the reimbursing bank, or as otherwise specified in the credit, or mutually agreed, as the case may be.

D. DOCUMENTS

ARTICLE 22

a. All instructions for the issuance of credits and the credits themselves and, where applicable, all instructions for amendments thereto and the amendments themselves, must state precisely the document(s) against which payment, acceptance or negotiation is to be made.

b. Terms such as "first class", "well known", "qualified", "independent", "official", and the like shall not be used to describe the issuers of any documents to be presented under a credit. If such terms are incorporated in the credit terms, banks will accept the relative documents as presented, provided that they appear on their face to be in accordance with the other terms and conditions of the credit.

c. Unless otherwise stipulated in the credit, banks will accept as originals documents produced or appearing to have been produced:

i by reprographic systems;

ii by, or as the result of, automated or computerized systems;

iii as carbon copies,

if marked as originals, always provided that, where necessary, such documents appear to have been authenticated.

ARTICLE 23

When documents other than transport documents, insurance documents and commercial invoices are called for, the credit should stipulate by whom such documents are to be issued and their wording or data content. If the credit does not so stipulate, banks will accept such documents as presented, provided that their data content makes it possible to relate the goods and/or services referred to therein to those referred to in the commercial invoice(s) presented, or to those referred to in the credit if the credit does not stipulate presentation of a commercial invoice.

ARTICLE 24

Unless otherwise stipulated in the credit, banks will accept a document bearing a date of issuance prior to that of the credit, subject to such document being presented within the time limits set out in the credit and in these articles.

D.1. TRANSPORT DOCUMENTS (DOCUMENTS INDICATING LOADING ON BOARD OR DISPATCH OR TAKING IN CHARGE)

ARTICLE 25

Unless a credit calling for a transport document stipulates as such document a marine bill of lading (ocean bill of lading or a bill of lading covering carriage by sea), or a post receipt or certificate of posting:

a. banks will, unless otherwise stipulated in the credit, accept a transport document which:

i appears on its face to have been issued by a named carrier, or his agent, and

ii indicates dispatch or taking in charge of the goods, or loading on board, as the case may be, and

iii consists of the full set of originals issued to the consignor if issued in more than one original, and

iv meets all other stipulations of the credit.

b. Subject to the above, and unless otherwise stipulated in the credit, banks will not reject a transport document which:

i bears a title such as "Combined transport bill of lading", "Combined transport document", "Combined transport bill of lading or port-to-port bill of lading", or a title or a combination of titles of similar intent and effect, and/or

ii indicates some or all of the conditions of carriage by reference to a source or document other than the transport document itself (short form/blank back transport document), and/or

iii indicates a place of taking in charge different from the port of loading and/or a place of final destination different from the port of discharge, and/or

iv relates to cargoes such as those in containers or on pallets, and the like, and/or

v contains the indication "intended", or similar qualification, in relation to the vessel or other means of transport, and/or the port of loading and/or the port of discharge.

c. Unless otherwise stipulated in the credit in the case of carriage by sea or by more than one mode of transport but including carriage by sea, banks will reject a transport document which:

i indicates that it is subject to a charter party, and/or

ii indicates that the carrying vessel is propelled by sail only.

d. Unless otherwise stipulated in the credit, banks will reject a transport document issued by a freight forwarder unless it is the FIATA Combined Transport Bill of Lading approved by the International Chamber of Commerce or otherwise indicates that it is issued by a freight forwarder acting as a carrier or agent of a named carrier.

ARTICLE 26

If a credit calling for a transport document stipulates as such document a marine bill of lading:

a. banks will, unless otherwise stipulated in the credit, accept a document which:

i appears on its face to have been issued by a named carrier, or his agent, and

ii indicates that the goods have been loaded on board or shipped on a named vessel, and

iii consists of the full set of originals issued to the consignor if issued in more than one original, and

iv meets all other stipulations of the credit.

b. Subject to the above, and unless otherwise stipulated in the credit, banks will not reject a document which:

i bears a title such as "Combined transport bill of lading", "Combined transport document", "Combined transport bill of lading or port-to-port bill of lading", or a title or a combination of titles of similar intent and effect, and/or

ii indicates some or all of the conditions of carriage by reference to a source or document other than the transport document itself (short form/blank back transport document), and/or

iii indicates a place of taking in charge different from the port of loading, and/or a place of final destination different from the port of discharge, and/or

iv relates to cargoes such as those in containers or on pallets, and the like.

c. Unless otherwise stipulated in the credit, banks will reject a document which:

i indicates that it is subject to a charter party, and/or

ii indicates that the carrying vessel is propelled by sail only, and/or

iii contains the indication "intended", or similar qualification in relation to

• the vessel and/or the port of loading—unless such document bears an on board notation in accordance with article 27(b) and also indicates the actual port of loading, and/or

• the port of discharge—unless the place of final destination indicated on the document is other than the port of discharge, and/or

iv is issued by a freight forwarder, unless it indicates that it is issued by such freight forwarder acting as a carrier, or as the agent of a named carrier.

ARTICLE 27

a. Unless a credit specifically calls for an on board transport document, or unless inconsistent with other stipulation(s) in the credit, or with article 26, banks will accept a transport document which indicates that the goods have been taken in charge or received for shipment.

b. Loading on board or shipment on a vessel may be evidenced either by a transport document bearing wording indicating loading on board a named vessel or shipment on a named vessel, or, in the case of a transport document stating "received for shipment", by means of a notation of loading on board on the transport document signed or initialled and dated by the carrier or his agent, and the date of this notation shall be regarded as the date of loading on board the named vessel or shipment on the named vessel.

ARTICLE 28

a. In the case of carriage by sea or by more than one mode of transport but including carriage by sea, banks will refuse a transport document stating that the goods are or will be loaded on deck, unless specifically authorized in the credit.

b. Banks will not refuse a transport document which contains a provision that the goods may be carried on deck, provided it does not specifically state that they are or will be loaded on deck.

ARTICLE 29

a. For the purpose of this article transhipment means a transfer and reloading during the course of carriage from the port of loading or place of dispatch or taking in charge to the port of discharge or place of destination either from one conveyance or vessel to another conveyance or vessel within the same mode of transport or from one mode of transport to another mode of transport.

b. Unless transhipment is prohibited by the terms of the credit, banks will accept transport documents which indicate that the goods will be transhipped, provided the entire carriage is covered by one and the same transport document.

c. Even if transhipment is prohibited by the terms of the credit, banks will accept transport documents which:

i incorporate printed clauses stating that the carrier has the right to tranship, or

ii state or indicate that transhipment will or may take place, when the credit stipulates a combined transport document, or indicates carriage from a place of taking in charge to a place of final destination by different modes of transport including a carriage by sea, provided that the entire carriage is covered by one and the same transport document, or

iii state or indicate that the goods are in a container(s), trailer(s), "LASH" barge(s), and the like and will be carried from the place of taking in charge to the place of final destination in the same container(s), trailer(s), "LASH" barge(s), and the like under one and the same transport document, or

iv state or indicate the place of receipt and/or of final destination as "C.F.S." (container freight station) or "C.Y." (container yard) at, or associated with, the port of loading and/or the port of destination.

ARTICLE 30

If the credit stipulates dispatch of goods by post and calls for a post receipt or certificate of posting, banks will accept such post receipt or certificate of posting if it appears to have been stamped or otherwise authenticated and dated in the place from which the credit stipulates the goods are to be dispatched.

ARTICLE 31

a. Unless otherwise stipulated in the credit, or inconsistent with any of the documents presented under the credit, banks will accept transport documents stating that freight or transportation charges (hereinafter referred to as "freight") have still to be paid.

b. If a credit stipulates that the transport document has to indicate that freight has been paid or prepaid, banks will accept a transport document on which words clearly indicating payment or prepayment of freight appear by stamp or otherwise, or on which payment of freight is indicated by other means.

c. The words "freight prepayable" or "freight to be prepaid" or words of similar effect, if appearing on transport documents, will not be accepted as constituting evidence of the payment of freight.

d. Banks will accept transport documents bearing reference by stamp or otherwise to costs additional to the freight charges, such as costs of, or disbursements incurred in connection with, loading, unloading or similar operations, unless the conditions of the credit specifically prohibit such reference.

ARTICLE 32

Unless otherwise stipulated in the credit, banks will accept transport documents which bear a clause on the face thereof such as "shippers load and count" or "said by shipper to contain" or words of similar effect.

ARTICLE 33

Unless otherwise stipulated in the credit, banks will accept transport documents indicating as the consignor of the goods a party other than the beneficiary of the credit.

ARTICLE 34

a. A clean transport document is one which bears no superimposed clause or notation which expressly declares a defective condition of the goods and/or the packaging.

b. Banks will refuse transport documents bearing such clauses or notations unless the credit expressly stipulates the clauses or notations which may be accepted.

c. Banks will regard a requirement in a credit for a transport document to bear the clause "clean on board" as complied with if such transport document meets the requirements of this article and of article 27(b).

D2. INSURANCE DOCUMENTS

ARTICLE 35

a. Insurance documents must be as stipulated in the credit, and must be issued and/or signed by insurance companies or underwriters, or their agents.

b. Cover notes issued by brokers will not be accepted, unless specifically authorised by the credit.

ARTICLE 36

Unless otherwise stipulated in the credit, or unless it appears from the insurance document(s) that the cover is effective at the latest from the date of loading on board or dispatch or taking in charge of the goods, banks will refuse insurance documents presented which bear a date later than the date of loading on board or dispatch or taking in charge of the goods as indicated by the transport document(s).

ARTICLE 37

a. Unless otherwise stipulated in the credit, the insurance document must be expressed in the same currency as the credit.

b. Unless otherwise stipulated in the credit, the minimum amount for which the insurance document must indicate the insurance cover to have been effected is the CIF (cost insurance and freight * * * "named port of destination") or CIP (freight/carriage and insurance paid to "named point of destination") value of the goods, as the case may be, plus 10%. However, if banks cannot determine the CIF or CIP value, as the case may be, from the documents on their face, they will accept as such minimum amount the amount for which payment, acceptance or negotiation is requested under the credit, or the amount of the commercial invoice, whichever is the greater.

ARTICLE 38

a. Credits should stipulate the type of insurance required and, if any, the additional risks which are to be covered. Imprecise terms such as "usual risks" or "customary risks" should not be used; if they are used, banks will accept insurance documents as presented, without responsibility for any risks not being covered.

b. Failing specific stipulations in the credit, banks will accept insurance documents as presented, without responsibility for any risks not being covered.

ARTICLE 39

Where a credit stipulates "insurance against all risks", banks will accept an insurance document which contains any "all risks" notation or clause, whether or not bearing the heading "all risks", even if indicating that certain risks are excluded, without responsibility for any risk(s) not being covered.

ARTICLE 40

Banks will accept an insurance document which indicates that the cover is subject to a franchise or an excess (deductible), unless it is specifically stipulated in the credit that the insurance must be issued irrespective of percentage.

D3. COMMERCIAL INVOICE

ARTICLE 41

a. Unless otherwise stipulated in the credit, commercial invoices must be made out in the name of the applicant for the credit.

b. Unless otherwise stipulated in the credit, banks may refuse commercial invoices issued for amounts in excess of the amount permitted by the credit. Nevertheless, if a bank authorised to pay, incur a deferred payment undertaking, accept, or negotiate under a credit accepts such invoices, its decision will be binding upon all parties, provided such bank has not paid, incurred a deferred payment undertaking, accepted or effected negotiation for an amount in excess of that permitted by the credit.

c. The description of the goods in the commercial invoice must correspond with the description in the credit. In all other documents, the goods may be described in general terms not inconsistent with the description of the goods in the credit.

D4. OTHER DOCUMENTS

ARTICLE 42

If a credit calls for an attestation or certification of weight in the case of transport other than by sea, banks will accept a weight stamp or declaration of weight which appears to have been superimposed on the transport document by the carrier or his agent unless the credit specifically stipulates that the attestation or certification of weight must be by means of a separate document.

E. MISCELLANEOUS PROVISIONS

QUANTITY AND AMOUNT

ARTICLE 43

a. The words "about", "circa" or similar expressions used in connection with the amount of the credit or the quantity or the unit price stated in the credit are to be construed as allowing a difference not to exceed 10% more or 10% less than the amount or the quantity or the unit price to which they refer.

b. Unless a credit stipulates that the quantity of the goods specified must not be exceeded or reduced, a tolerance of 5% more or 5% less will be permissible, even if partial shipments are not permitted, always provided that the amount of the drawings does not exceed the amount of the credit. This tolerance does not apply when the credit stipulates the quantity in terms of a stated number of packing units or individual items.

PARTIAL DRAWINGS AND/OR SHIPMENTS

ARTICLE 44

a. Partial drawings and/or shipments are allowed, unless the credit stipulates otherwise.

b. Shipments by sea, or by more than one mode of transport but including carriage by sea, made on the same vessel and for the same voyage, will not be regarded as partial shipments, even if the transport documents indicating loading on board bear different dates of issuance and/or indicate different ports of loading on board.

c. Shipments made by post will not be regarded as partial shipments if the post receipts or certificates of posting appear to have been stamped or otherwise authenticated in the place from which the credit stipulates the goods are to be dispatched, and on the same date.

d. Shipments made by modes of transport other than those referred to in paragraphs (b) and (c) of this article will not be regarded as partial shipments, provided the transport documents are issued by one and the same carrier or his agent and indicate the same date of issuance, the same place of dispatch or taking in charge of the goods and the same destination.

DRAWINGS AND/OR SHIPMENTS BY INSTALMENTS

ARTICLE 45

If drawings and/or shipments by instalments within given periods are stipulated in the credit and any instalment is not drawn and/or shipped within the period allowed for that instalment, the credit ceases to be available for that and any subsequent instalments, unless otherwise stipulated in the credit.

EXPIRY DATE AND PRESENTATION

ARTICLE 46

a. All credits must stipulate an expiry date for presentation of documents for payment, acceptance or negotiation.

b. Except as provided in Article 48(a), documents must be presented on or before such expiry date.

c. If an issuing bank states that the credit is to be available "for one month", "for six months" or the like, but does not specify the date from which the time is to run, the date of issuance of the credit by the issuing bank will be deemed to be the first day from which such time is to run. Banks should discourage indication of the expiry date of the credit in this manner.

ARTICLE 47

a. In addition to stipulating an expiry date for presentation of documents, every credit which calls for a transport document(s) should also stipulate a specified period of time after the date of issuance of the transport document(s) during which presentation of documents for payment, acceptance or negotiation must be made. If no such period of time is stipulated, banks will refuse documents presented to them later than 21 days after the date of issuance of the transport document(s). In every case, however, documents must be presented not later than the expiry date of the credit.

b. For the purpose of these articles, the date of issuance of a transport document(s) will be deemed to be:

i in the case of a transport document evidencing dispatch, or taking in charge, or receipt of goods for shipment by a mode of transport other than by air—the date of issuance indicated on the transport document or the date of the reception stamp thereon whichever is the later.

ii in the case of a transport document evidencing carriage by air—the date of issuance indicated on the transport document or, if the credit stipulates that the transport document shall indicate an actual flight date, the actual flight date as indicated on the transport document.

iii in the case of a transport document evidencing loading on board a named vessel—the date of issuance of the transport document or, in the case of an on board notation in accordance with article 27(b), the date of such notation.

iv in cases to which Article 44(b) applies, the date determined as above of the latest transport document issued.

ARTICLE 48

a. If the expiry date of the credit and/or the last day of the period of time after the date of issuance of the transport document(s) for presentation of documents stipulated by the credit or applicable by virtue of Article 47 falls on a day on which the bank to which presentation has to be made is closed for reasons other than those referred to in Article 19, the stipulated expiry date and/or the last day of the period of time after the date of issuance of the transport document(s) for presentation of documents, as the case may be, shall be extended to the first following business day on which such bank is open.

b. The latest date for loading on board, or dispatch, or taking in charge shall not be extended by reason of the extension of the expiry date and/or the period of time after the date of issuance of the transport document(s) for presentation of document(s) in accordance with this article. If no such latest date for shipment is stipulated in the credit or amendments thereto, banks will reject transport documents indicating a date of issuance later than the expiry date stipulated in the credit or amendments thereto.

c. The bank to which presentation is made on such first following business day must add to the documents its certificate that the documents were presented within the time limits extended in accordance with Article 48(a) of the Uniform Customs and Practice for Documentary Credits, 1983 revision, ICC Publication No. 400.

ARTICLE 49

Banks are under no obligation to accept presentation of documents outside their banking hours.

LOADING ON BOARD, DISPATCH AND TAKING IN CHARGE (SHIPMENT)

ARTICLE 50

a. Unless otherwise stipulated in the credit, the expression "shipment" used in stipulating an earliest and/or a latest shipment date will be understood to include the expressions "loading on board", "dispatch" and "taking in charge".

b. The date of issuance of the transport document determined in accordance with Article 47(b) will be taken to be the date of shipment.

c. Expressions such as "prompt", "immediately", "as soon as possible", and the like should not be used. If they are used, banks will interpret them as a stipulation that shipment is to be made within thirty days from the date of issuance of the credit by the issuing bank.

d. If the expression "on or about" and similar expressions are used, banks will interpret them as a stipulation that shipment is to be made during the period from five days before to five days after the specified date, both end days included.

DATE TERMS

ARTICLE 51

The words "to", "until", "till", "from", and words of similar import applying to any date term in the credit will be understood to include the date mentioned. The word "after" will be understood to exclude the date mentioned.

ARTICLE 52

The terms "first half", "second half" of a month shall be construed respectively as from the 1st to the 15th, and the 16th to the last day of each month, inclusive.

ARTICLE 53

The terms "beginning", "middle", or "end" of a month shall be construed respectively as from the 1st to the 10th, the 11th to the 20th, and the 21st to the last day of each month, inclusive.

F. TRANSFER

ARTICLE 54

a. A transferable credit is a credit under which the beneficiary has the right to request the bank called upon to effect payment or acceptance or any bank entitled to effect negotiation to make the credit available in whole or in part to one or more other parties (second beneficiaries).

b. A credit can be transferred only if it is expressly designated as "transferable" by the issuing bank. Terms such as "divisible", "fractionnable", "assignable", and "transmissible" add nothing to the meaning of the term "transferable" and shall not be used.

c. The bank requested to effect the transfer (transferring bank), whether it has confirmed the credit or not, shall be under no obligation to effect such transfer except to the extent and in the manner expressly consented to by such bank.

d. Bank charges in respect of transfers are payable by the first beneficiary unless otherwise specified. The transferring bank shall be under no obligation to effect the transfer until such charges are paid.

e. A transferable credit can be transferred once only. Fractions of a transferable credit (not exceeding in the aggregate the amount of the credit) can be transferred separately, provided partial shipments are not prohibited, and the aggregate of such transfers will be considered as constituting only one transfer of the credit. The credit can be transferred only on the terms and conditions specified in the original credit, with the exception of the amount of the credit, of any unit prices stated therein, of the period of validity, of the last date for presentation of documents in accordance with Article 47 and the period for shipment, any or all of which may be reduced or curtailed, or the percentage for which insurance cover must be effected, which may be increased in such a way as to provide the amount of cover stipulated in the original credit, or these articles. Additionally, the name of the first beneficiary can be substituted for that of the applicant for the credit, but if the name of the applicant for the credit is specifically required by the original credit to appear in any document other than the invoice, such requirement must be fulfilled.

f. The first beneficiary has the right to substitute his own invoices (and drafts if the credit stipulates that drafts are to be drawn on the applicant for the credit) in exchange for those of the second beneficiary, for amounts not in excess of the original amount stipulated in the credit and for the original unit prices if stipulated in the credit, and upon such substitution of invoices (and drafts) the first beneficiary can draw under the credit for the difference, if any, between his invoices and the second beneficiary's invoices. When a credit has been transferred and the first beneficiary is to supply his own invoices (and drafts) in exchange for the second beneficiary's invoices (and drafts) but fails to do so on first demand, the paying, accepting or negotiating bank has the right to deliver to the issuing bank the documents received under the credit, including the second beneficiary's invoices (and drafts) without further responsibility to the first beneficiary.

g. Unless otherwise stipulated in the credit, the first beneficiary of a transferable credit may request that the credit be transferred to a second beneficiary in the same country, or in another country. Further, unless otherwise stipulated in the credit, the first beneficiary shall have the right to request that payment or negotiation be effected to the second beneficiary at the place to which the credit has been transferred, up to and including the expiry date of the original credit, and without prejudice to the first beneficiary's right subsequently to substitute his own invoices and drafts (if any) for those of the second beneficiary and to claim any difference due to him.

ASSIGNMENT OF PROCEEDS

ARTICLE 55

The fact that a credit is not stated to be transferable shall not affect the beneficiary's right to assign any proceeds to which he may be, or may become, entitled under such credit, in accordance with the provisions of the applicable law.

*

Index

VALUE
Determination of market value, 281–286

WAIVER
In letter of credit transaction, 717–722
To excuse performance, 227–228, 244–245

WAREHOUSE RECEIPTS
Generally, 341
Law governing, 353
Rights of good faith purchaser in, 364–370
Risk of loss, 314–319

WAREHOUSEMAN
Delivery of goods against documents, 382
Duty of care, 319

WARRANTY, 757–805
See also Express Warranty; Implied Warranty of Fitness; Implied Warranty of Merchantability
Between commercial buyers, 527–542
Consumer context, 593–608
Contributory behavior, 511–518
Direct damages for breach after acceptance, 543–608
History, 441–445, 449–450
Importance of notice of breach, 501–511
Litigation, 500–542
Of title, 636–640
Proof of breach by buyer, 500, 511–542
Provisions under Article 2, pp. 23–24
Requirements necessary to qualify, 445–448
Service sector, 526

†